D1603962

THE ENGLISH PHILOSOPHERS
FROM BACON TO MILL

THE ENGLISH PHILOSOPHERS
FROM BACON TO MILL

EDITED, WITH AN INTRODUCTION,

BY EDWIN A. BURTT

THE MODERN LIBRARY

NEW YORK

THE MODERN LIBRARY
is published by RANDOM HOUSE, INC.
New York, New York
Manufactured in the United States of America

PREFACE

THE ANTHOLOGY of British philosophers here published includes the most important works of all the thinkers of recognized eminence in the field from the time of Francis Bacon to that of John Stuart Mill. These works are reprinted without omissions save in the case of Hobbes' *Leviathan,* Locke's *Essay Concerning Human Understanding,* and Bentham's *Principles of Morals and Legislation;* even with these, more material is contained than has usually been provided in the previously available volumes of selections from these men. The first part of this statement needs a slight modification in regard to Bacon's *Novum Organum,* where a portion of the concluding list of "prerogative instances" is omitted. The standard editions have been used; in Locke's case additions made by the author after the first edition of the *Essay* have been indicated by square brackets. The punctuation adopted by the authors has been retained, while the spelling and capitalization have been modernized.

I wish to acknowledge a special indebtedness to Professor Gail Kennedy of Amherst College for helpful suggestions as to the selections to be included.

Ithaca, N. Y.   E. A. BURTT
June, 1939

CONTENTS

INTRODUCTION

by EDWIN A. BURTT

PHILOSOPHY has something in common with the naïve reflections in which unsophisticated people engage, and with the abstract and exact inquiries of science; there are also important differences between philosophy and each of these modes of thinking. But the similarities and dissimilarities naturally vary greatly according as we pursue one or the other of these two lines of comparison. An excellent way of apprehending what essentially distinguishes philosophy is to embark briefly on such a comparative study.

Persons untrained in habits of logical discrimination frequently ask questions expressing curiosity not about this or that particular object but about some very comprehensive or speculative problem. Such wonderment is especially evident in the questions naturally asked by children when they reach the age at which a generalized interest is possible. Few parents, I suppose, have avoided the challenge to satisfy a youthful desire to know who made the world, what our habitat was before we were born, or why it is wrong not to submit to the restrictions which established custom places upon childish impulse. And although even unsophisticated maturity comes to smile upon some such queries, it continues to ask the others, and adds to them equally general puzzles which only a very precocious child would entertain. Whether our waking experience may not after all be nothing but a dream is one of these additions; how a good God can permit evil in his world is another.

Now the fundamental feature in common between philosophy and the uncritical reflections of common life lies just in the fact that both raise such comprehensive and ultimate questions. Philosophers, as philosophers, are not concerned with the detailed adjustments of means to ends which nine-tenths of the time constitute the matter of everyday thinking, nor with the satisfactions of curiosity about specific puzzling occurrences which almost fill the remaining tenth. It is their business to deal with the themes of vast and general scope, on which common sense also occasionally theorizes, or problems involving peculiar difficulties that no established technique is quite able to meet. But when philosophers ask these questions they ask them in a different way—a way which betrays the acceptance of a kind of intellectual responsiblity which the

man in the street has not assumed. He has not assumed this responsibility because he is unconscious of its absence, and has not learned that
wise discrimination in attacking these questions is necessary if the
quest is to escape futility, a discrimination only achieved through severe
logical training.

Thus, instead of inquiring "Who made the world?" the philosopher
will be more likely to ask: "How did the present order of events come
to be what it is?" Why the difference? Well, the reason for his dissatisfaction with the former of these two questions is twofold. In the first
place, he detects a serious ambiguity in the word "world," which an
untrained mind may fail to note but which renders the question entirely
hopeless until it is removed. We often mean by "world" the entire complex of entities and events, including those which have occurred in the
past or will occur in the future as well as those spread out before us in
the present. Now, if this is what the question means, it is obviously
inconsistent with itself and cannot possibly be answered. For the world
as thus defined contains within itself all beings who have ever made anything as well as everything that has ever been made; it cannot therefore
permissibly be treated as an object of the verb "made." We cannot
logically inquire into the origin of the world at all in this sense of the
term. On the other hand if we mean some partial selection from the
comprehensive totality just mentioned, what selection do we intend? No
particular part is clearly indicated by the word, and the question remains quite indeterminate until it has been decided what part is meant.
Many people would doubtless mean that portion of the universe which
we call "physical," but it cannot be assumed that all must do so.

In the second place, the philosopher observes the presence, in the
question "Who made the world?" of certain assumptions which he
knows are so debatable that others who have seriously reflected about
the matter will have no patience with him if he takes them for granted
without systematic justification. Even though he replace, then, the word
"world" by "the world of matter" or "the present order of events," he
will be conscious of the possibility that it may not have been "made"
at all, but came to be what it is through some essentially different process. This is the case even if he be a theist in his philosophy and therefore,
as far as his own thinking is concerned, regards the word "made" as
appropriately used in this connection. For since he is aware that some
of his readers will presumably not be theists, he realizes that it is incumbent on him to formulate the question in such a way as not to imply
in advance any disputed answer to it; the considerations that support
his theism may appropriately be introduced only after the question has
been stated, and not by the form of the question itself. Otherwise many

persons will toss his book aside without even considering what he has to say.

This instance will serve as an illustration of what is meant by the intellectual responsibility accepted by a philosopher that is usually not consciously assumed by the man without logical training. They share in common an interest in certain big and appealing problems; but the philosopher has learned to discriminate between questions that may not pertinently be asked and the more or less similar ones that may properly be raised, as well as between ways of formulating queries that prejudge the answer in an unfortunate manner and ways that are essentially impartial. Since the aims of intellectual discourse forbid the posing of meaningless problems, and confusing a question with its subsequently awaited answer, philosophy's contribution here is in large part to clarify unsophisticated discussion by showing how its perplexities should be expressed; it need hardly be added, perhaps, that similar discriminative acumen in its prosecution of their solutions is also displayed.

In the assumption of such intellectual responsibility lies the main common feature which unites philosophy with science. The details of approved scientific method vary greatly between different branches of science, and even some of the more general aspects of exact inquiry depend sufficiently on the distinctive nature of science so that we are not surprised at their absence in philosophical investigations. But every serious intellectual endeavor must needs respect certain general rules of procedure which the undisciplined mind is apt to violate on occasion; the whole history of reflective toil has been required to teach their necessity in the guidance of man's mind whenever he embarks upon any pursuit of dependable truth. These rules are precisely those which the phrase "intellectual responsibility" is intended to embrace and imply; they are exhibited in science as fully as in philosophy. Insistence on clarity in the meaning of our terms, on consistency in the affirmations made by the use of these terms, and on humble respect for all discoverable facts that are relevant to the problems we are attempting to solve —these are three of the most fundamental rules which must be applied wherever genuine intellectual responsibility is accepted. Both the scientist and the philosopher are aware of this necessity while the man in the street is usually not.

The major difference between science and philosophy lies in the circumstance that the former disavows the task of dealing with the kind of question that is of common concern to philosophy and unsophisticated speculation. The scientist, as such, refuses to take the entire universe as his province. He confines his researches to limited fields where the applicability of accepted methods of analysis, measurement, and explanation appears to be assured. At times he proffers rather general theories, purporting to account for large masses of fact, but these theories never claim to embrace everything without exception, and they are normally such as established procedures of verification are essentially competent to test. When a theory transcends such limited generality, or when it must devise its own method of verification, we have left the realm of science for that of philosophy. It is a consequence of this latter restriction that the scientist, as such, disclaims responsibility even for quite specific problems whose form of statement implies entities or conditions with which his techniques are powerless to deal. The question mentioned above regarding the principles which rightfully govern our moral conduct will illustrate this limitation. The anthropologist is prepared to tell us, so far as available facts justify any conclusions, what restrictions on human conduct have in fact obtained in this, that, or the other community at such and such a time, but if he is asked what restrictions *ought* to obtain he will plead, in his capacity as scientist, at least, that the word "ought" implies something that his scientific procedures are powerless to handle—a normative standard quite irreducible to any observed facts. Yet the question seems to be not only pertinently raised but very important, deserving the most careful and logically responsible discussion attainable. Lest the breach thus left open be abandoned entirely to the uncritical judgments of common sense and the often dogmatic, piously prejudiced pronouncements of theologians, philosophers jump into it with the quest for such wise and disciplined evaluations as a cautious, relatively impartial survey of the dependable goods of human experience can at any time muster.

What, then, is philosophy? It is essentially the persistent effort to transcend the limitations of science while respecting the fundamental standards of intellectual attainment upon which science has come to insist. It is a queer hybrid in the realm of reflective inquiry, produced through the fertilization of the spontaneous speculations of common sense about ultimate things by the responsible discipline of scientific logic. The philosopher is a child in his open-eyed wonderment at the world; a man of mature research in the critical and rigorous fashion in which that wonderment is satisfied.

But the history of philosophy, in the West, at any rate, indicates that this quest can be pursued under the influence of either of two major alternative convictions. These convictions concern the relation between knowledge and life. Philosophy purports to attain a generalized knowledge; but what are the scope and significance of the wisdom it achieves? Is philosophic understanding coextensive with the whole of man's life and experience, and is it the supreme accomplishment of which life at its best and fullest is capable? Or does life essentially transcend knowledge, being a larger and more significant whole in relation to whose ends our philosophic apprehensions should be viewed as subordinate though still very valuable means?

Throughout the development of philosophy in ancient times a national difference may be detected in this regard between the Greeks and the Romans. The most influential Greek thinkers took for granted the first of these viewpoints. For them there was nothing in life that essentially transcends the competence of reason; for them, moreover, rational contemplation of the ultimate truth of things was the highest attainment in human experience, the self-justifying good toward which all the varied practical activities of life must be regarded merely as contributory values. Life exists for the sake of the comprehensive insight that philosophy can achieve; not insight for the sake of life. The Romans, on the other hand, with their remarkable genius for administration and their consuming interest in practical affairs, took, in general, the alternative viewpoint. They cared little for metaphysics; the kind of speculation which seemed to them most pertinent was moral and social philosophy, seeking clarification of the significant goods and commanding duties of life and providing the practical knowledge necessary to their fuller realization. For them the supreme faculty in man was not reason, but a dutiful will—a will disciplined by reason into respect for order, but still ultimately focused upon the themes of practical endeavor rather than the absorptions of metaphysical contemplation. The high-water mark of Greek speculation was Platonic and Aristotelian ontology; of Roman thought, the moral, political, and legal theories of Stoicism.

Now the same difference prominently reappears in modern philosophy, although not, of course, in precisely the same form. French philosophy, to be sure, is too variegated to be classified in these terms; it exhibits a persistent metaphysical interest while practical concerns also are never forgotten; a tendency to approach philosophy through sociological considerations has been its most distinctive feature, especially during the last century. But German and English philosophy continue, though in a novel way, the speculative feud of the Greeks and Romans. German thinkers have tended to adopt the same fundamental viewpoint regarding the relation between knowledge and life as the Greeks; the merely practical and utilitarian is for them a disparaged realm. One who allows himself to be captivated by its appeal is thereby forfeiting something of the rational dignity that rightfully pertains to man. The supreme task of mind is to apprehend absolute and ultimate truth, which transcends the limitations of phenomenal experience and the inevitable disappointments of practical endeavor. Man exists to know, not merely to do. There are many exceptions, of course, but this has been the dominant quality of German philosophy from the time of Leibniz to the present. And even the exceptions are often not unqualifiedly such. Kant, for example, made moral practice supreme over metaphysical cognition, but he also made an absolute and rational principle or law of practice supreme over practice; reason for him is never instrumental to anything other than itself.

In this exaltation of rational insight into ultimates the German philosophers exhibit few of the detailed characteristics of the Greek mind; once we descend from this basic common feature, differences are far more prominent than similarities. The fresh pioneering curiosity, forthright simplicity, and eager artistry of the Greek classics is replaced by a ponderous, professorial passion for system. We move in an atmosphere of patient, conscientious manipulation of scholarly distinctions and unifications, often lapsing into dull and lifeless pedantry. That these differences should coexist with a common view of the nature and task of philosophy is a rather surprising circumstance, yet it remains true that for German as well as Greek, man lives to think and to realize the fullness of reason; he does not just think to live.

English philosophy shares the practical temper of the Romans. Again there are many exceptions, and again the manner in which this practical temper displays itself is very different; in particular, it must be said that while Rome produced few really first-rate philosophers in comparison with Greece, Great Britain has shown itself quite equal in philosophic competence to the nations across the Channel. The most important differences, of course, arise from the different distinctive genius of the English people, together with the changed historical and cultural situation which their developing philosophy has been called upon to face. Britishers express more generally and uncompromisingly than other peoples the modern European emphasis on individualism and personal freedom. Forswearing as rather unsportsmanlike the privilege of exploiting each other beyond what the rules of fair play would permit, they find compensation in a more conscious and aggressive effort at the control of physical nature than other races have displayed, at least until the latter learned the trick from them.

But a practical interest, directed into appropriate channels by these circumstances, has been pervasive and fundamental in English philosophy. Life, for the typical English thinker, essentially outreaches knowledge and is far more inclusive. The assumption that the human mind can comprehend the whole of things and rest secure in the contemplation of ultimate truth strikes him as not only preposterous in the nature of the case, but grievously lacking in the humility appropriate to man's finite station and limited capacities. Mind—*our* mind, the only mind we can exercise—is simply not equal to the totality of the universe. Its knowledge is always partial and tentative, condemned to an indefinite process of irregular growth in its exploration of the mysteries that surround it. Moreover, there is something intrinsically opaque to reason about the very existence of individual objects and the occurrence of particular events—all that understanding can really do is to describe the regular connections that experimentally obtain between these irrational and arbitrary entities. Reason cannot swallow its objects wholesale and digest their very substance; it can only trace their practically significant relations. Finally, and most important of all, life, for the influential and representative British philosophers, is more valuable than knowledge. Its supreme and self-justifying end is not metaphysical insight, nor even a balanced and well-rounded wisdom concerning man and his world, but happiness. And what is happiness? In the eyes of these thinkers, it is a state in which all the varied delights of which human nature is capable, including the distinctive pleasures of the intellect along with others, constitute a harmonious whole of enduring contentment, pain being reduced to a minimum and the intenser but more fickle joys subordinated to those which promise constancy and display expansive power. The pleasures of knowledge belong among these more dependable joys but do not exhaust them, and they are not, therefore, of themselves, the final human good to which everything else may be properly treated as means. The rest of life does not exist for the sake of knowledge; rather, knowledge exists for the sake of a happy life. Its relation to life as a whole is both that of a significant part and a major instrument. Its role is to clarify the supreme good by critical analysis, to point out the methods suitable to its richer and wider attainment, and to contribute its own distinctive satisfactions to that integrated complex of contentments which the word "happiness" denotes.

Thus oriented, English philosophy has naturally been somewhat chary of metaphysical speculations in the traditional sense of a science or theory of reality as a whole. Its metaphysics typically reduces to epistemology, and an epistemology written from an obviously practical standpoint. British philosophers found it necessary to attack the problem of knowledge, not primarily as a theoretical matter involved in a systematic investigation of reality, but as a means of justifying their concentration upon practical concerns by showing the futility of any endeavor to apprehend ultimate truth. Man's knowledge, suited to his place and station, is severely limited in its scope and legitimate pretensions; it is sufficient to guide us toward the fulfillment of duty and the attainment of happiness, but not toward a final comprehension of the vast environment in which our quest for happiness is set. On the positive side, the English thinkers found an outlet for their philosophic interests in two main directions. On the one hand, they were profoundly concerned to provide an adequate methodology for the natural sciences which were developing so rapidly during the period in which these philosophers lived. And the methodology they offered, taking for granted a fundamentally practical interpretation of scientific method, was for this reason empirical in its foundation as contasted with the rationalism of prevailing continental philosophies of science. For them, explanation of an event, whatever else it might be, must render possible successful prediction and control of similar events in the future; now the difference between successful and unsuccessful prediction cannot be tested by rational deduction but only by experience of the predicted occurrence when it takes place. Hence the final criteria of true explanation from this standpoint are empirical. It is not enough that our ideas about an event be clear and deductively consistent with whatever premises seem most reasonable. Only when our direct perceptual commerce with it, in the most cautious and searching exercise of eye, ear, and touch, fully approves, may we pronounce an idea true. On the other hand, British philosophers were eager to establish on secure foundations a sound moral and social philosophy, and to indicate its main implications for a theory of politics, of economic processes, of education, and of law. They wished to illumine the legitimate ends of human conduct in the light of analyses of appropriate means for their realization, and they participated actively in reform movements which aimed to establish these ends in quite concrete ways. This aspect of English philosophy culminated in the moral theory known as utilitarianism, which, partially anticipated by many earlier thinkers, came to clear, systematic expression in the work of Bentham and the Mills.

It should be noted again that in these summary characterizations we are speaking of a dominant trend to which there are naturally many exceptions. In fact, toward the end of the nineteenth century, under the powerful influence of the German philosopher Hegel, the exceptions seemed to have become the rule, and since then there has been no decisive indication of a return to the earlier pattern of English thought. But in this volume our concern is with English philosophy in the three centuries that are now past; it is happily not our duty to attempt the more difficult task of assessing its trends in the present or its promise for the future.

At the beginning of the period which the present anthology covers, this distinctive genius of English thought gained most vigorous expression in the context provided by the struggle of what we now call modern science to gain an appropriate method. Francis Bacon's main contribution to philosophy is an attempt to meet this need. He offered a comprehensive program for the complete renovation and redirection of scientific knowledge, and the part of this program which has proved of enduring significance is the system of "helps" for the senses and the understanding which Bacon insisted are essential if the mind is not to run astray in its quest for truth. These helps were devised with an eye to the correction of what this philosopher conceived to be the fundamental defects of previous scientific thought—its readiness to leap from a few observations of fact to the most general principles of nature, from which more specific laws were derived by deduction, and its failure to see clearly and prosecute steadily the true goal of science. Bacon met the first defect by offering a detailed theory of induction, not all of whose underlying assumptions have stood the test of subsequent criticism, but whose specific canons of experimental procedure have become a part of the enduring structure of successful science. These canons express Bacon's insight into the necessity of going to the empirical facts in a much more humble and persistently teachable mood than had been explicitly required by previous theories of method, and with definite safeguards against the tendencies to error that experience shows to be characteristic of the human intellect. He met the second defect by maintaining that the proper end of scientific inquiry is to extend the empire of man over nature, to "endow human life with new discoveries and powers." Recognition of this end is important, he contended, because it is not something external to the course of investigation but determines the latter's very essence—the "form" or law by which a bit of nature is to be inductively explained is the same as that dynamic pattern of processes by which it is dependably produced. Subsequent science has exemplified this conception in its experimental procedures.

During the middle and the latter part of the seventeenth century British philosophy was challenged to clarify the principles of political organization. This was the turbulent period of the civil wars, the Cromwellian régime, the Restoration, and the "Glorious Revolution" of 1688. To Thomas Hobbes the prime source of this intolerable confusion lay in the competition of political control over the "ghostly" authority claimed by the Roman and Presbyterian clergy; the only solution of the evil lay in recognizing an absolute and undivided sovereignty in the established government of the state. But this theory of sovereignty was no isolated affair, possessing independent validity; in Hobbes' mind it was an integral part of a vast system of truth embracing physical nature and man as an individual as well as political society, all derived from certain basic principles of body and motion. And these principles are selected in accordance with the same practical aim that Bacon had so persuasively championed. "Science is the knowledge of consequences, and dependence of one fact upon another: by which, out of that we can presently do, we know how to do something else when we will, or the like, another time;

because when we see how anything comes about, upon what causes, and by what manner; when the like causes come into our power, we see how to make it produce the like effects." [1] John Locke, however, coming half a century later, and deeply committed in his sympathies to the successful parliamentarian party, was convinced that the political structure approved by Hobbes was no civil government at all. Possession of absolute authority leaves those who wield it in the "state of nature" rather than that of law and justice in relation to their fellow-citizens. Ultimate authority, therefore, can only lie in the people as a whole, and the only form of government which can appropriately express this principle is that which leaves the executive and "federative" functions subordinate to a legislative assembly composed of elected representatives of the people. Locke was a firm believer in freedom and tolerance—freedom for the individual to live his own life and maintain certain rights (especially property rights) against the power of his government, and tolerance in both politics and religion for all who are not themselves, on principle, intolerant.

But Locke's work as a political theorist was only part of his significant philosophical achievement. He also wrote his famous *Essay Concerning Human Understanding*. The great enemy of tolerance, he saw, was the tendency of men to be dogmatic in their beliefs, and this dogmatism, in turn, rested on the assumption that the knowledge to which those beliefs pretend is absolutely certain. But, as a matter of fact, we are apt to be most dogmatic about just those persuasions which are least able to make good any claim of self-evidence or demonstrability. Locke noted that this situation was particularly obvious in matters religious. He was sure himself that the being of a God and the Christhood of Jesus could be certainly proved, but not at all the sectarian doctrines, fanatical adherence to which led men to abandon the spirit of brotherhood and violate the freedom of their fellows in the most ruthless ways. It seemed to him that he might undermine this dogmatic intolerance by inquiring systematically into "the original, certainty, and extent of human knowledge, together with the grounds and degrees of belief, opinion, and assent. . . . If by this inquiry into the nature of the understanding, I can discover the powers thereof, how far they reach, to what things they are in any degree proportionate, and where they fail us, I suppose it may be of use to prevail with the busy mind of man to be more cautious in meddling with things exceeding its comprehension. . . . We should not then, perhaps, be so forward, out of an affectation of an universal knowledge, to raise questions, and perplex ourselves and others with disputes, about things to which our understandings are not suited." And the extent to which Locke shared the practical attitude toward knowledge

[1] *Leviathan*, Part I, Ch. V.

characteristic of British philosophy is quickly revealed in the sequel. "It is of great use to the sailor to know the length of his line, though he cannot with it fathom all the depths of the ocean; it is well he knows that it is long enough to reach the bottom at such places as are necessary to direct his voyage, and caution him against running upon shoals that may ruin him. Our business here is not to know all things, but those which concern our conduct." [2]

In carrying out this inquiry Locke met a number of unanticipated difficulties, one of which set the major problem with which his greatest successors in modern philosophy were compelled to deal. The French thinker Descartes, who lived a generation earlier than Locke, had maintained an extreme dualism in his ontology, sundering mind from physical nature so completely that there remained no direct contact between the two; even our perceptions of a physical object became purely mental events, originally caused by, but in existence quite detached from, the objects which we apprehend through their aid. Locke (agreeing in this with most of his contemporaries) took for granted in his analysis this dualistic ontology, but when he came to analyze knowledge on the basis thus assumed he realized that a serious objection might well be raised. How justify the supposition that knowledge reaches beyond our own ideas? What, on these terms, can give warrant that there exist, in addition to our perceptions and concepts, physical things to which these mental affairs in any respect correspond? Locke comforts us with the assurance that doubt is unnecessary on such a vital matter, but he does so by appealing to principles that derive no support whatever from the main body of conclusions established in the *Essay*. His successors Berkeley and Hume insisted on greater consistency in dealing with this problem. Berkeley, being of a pious and aggressive temper, seized upon the opportunity thus offered boldly to deny the existence of anything beyond minds and their ideas; the chief support of atheism and scepticism, he thought, was the current philosophic and scientific belief in a world of physical matter independent of mind and moving in accordance with its own mechanical laws. What we call an external physical body is simply a collection of perceptions maintained in existence and given their dependable order by the mind of God. But is it not as difficult, on Locke's dualistic premises, to prove the existence of God's mind, or even our own, as to prove the existence of a physical world? Hume saw that this was the case—at least if we add the further premise, likewise accepted by Locke and Berkeley, that our perceptions and ideas are independent of each other in their occurrence, being connected merely by rather indeterminate and quite feeble principles of association. If we propose to be consistent with these doctrines, it was obvious to Hume that

[2] Introduction to the *Essay*, Secs. 2, 4, 6.

all we could possibly know is the cluster of our own present perceptions; matter, God, and mind (as a real entity imposing a necessary unity on past, present, and future experience) become alike unknowable. We are lost in a scepticism which can only be temporarily and partially remedied by turning away from rational analysis to practical interests, and submitting to the control of instinctive tendencies incapable of intellectual justification.

Despite this sceptical outcome, however, Hume marks the culmination of the major trends which had been most evident in British philosophy prior to his day. He was as profoundly concerned to establish a constructive philosophy of science as to reach a consistent theory of the competence of knowledge. But the latter naturally imposed rigid limits on the former; there can be no knowledge of an external world, or of mind, hence the only positive task of science is to describe the sequence of human perceptions through the aid of such loose-knit principles of association as emperical inquiry may disclose. This gives him none the less what he calls a science of human nature, which takes account of all the canons of valid induction emphasized by Bacon and Newton, and which appears to Hume the ultimate science on whose principles all our persuasions on whatever subject depend.

After Hume, the main themes of epistemological speculation passed to the continent, where Kant and his successors exploited them in directions essentially foreign to the English bent of mind. British philosophy was thus left free to turn systematic and fairly unfettered attention to the inquiry which its distinctive genius had all along intimated as most fundamental. If everything else in knowledge and life is relative to practical human ends, is it not the basic task of philosophy to indicate what the supreme end is—pointing out its locus in existence, and its concrete implications for detailed problems in morals, government, economics, and law? This task had not been neglected by earlier thinkers but it had not been carried out with a self-conscious unity of method, resting on typically English principles. Hobbes, to be sure, had supplied a unified method but it was ultimately mechanistic rather than empirical; Bacon and Locke were characteristically English in championing empiricism but their controlling ends—the empire of man over nature and tolerance in human affairs—were given no systematic justification. This state of affairs is remedied in the philosophy that appears in the work of Bentham and the two Mills. The method here is (so far as concerns its intent, at least) consistently empirical, and the principles established are harmonious with the practical temper of the English mind—its basic assumption that the goods of reason and knowledge are but part of and instrumental to a larger whole of values in which human life finds its appropriate goal. The historical context in which this trend of speculation develops is, however, somewhat different from that contemplated by any earlier philosopher, and the detailed results are naturally affected by this circumstance; the context is that of the Industrial Revolution with its wholly ramifying social consequences, and the urge toward democratization of English society and politics.

Jeremy Bentham set aside the theological and rationalistic beliefs with regard to morals which had confused the thinking of his empiricist predecessors[3] when they attacked the ultimate problems of moral theory, and enthroned as the sole standard of human right and wrong what is directly disclosed as good and evil in immediate experience—namely, pleasure in the one case, pain in the other. Now since their goodness or badness is so obvious imperically that it cannot be gainsaid, pleasure and pain are psychologically coercive, as well as ethically authoritative; we inevitably seek to preserve and reinstate pleasure, to terminate and avoid pain. What need of moral theory, then? On this basis will we not always do what we ought to do? No, for pleasures often bring painful consequences; pain sometimes pleasurable ones; we cannot, therefore, simply identify pleasure and pain as natural motive and as ethical standard. When they operate in the former capacity we mean these experiences as directly felt or clearly anticipated; when in the latter role we mean such a long-run balance of pleasures over pains—happiness, in a single word—as the most adequate foresight of the future and the wisest control of present conduct in the light of it might hope to attain. Here is the need of moral theory: to lay down the general principles necessary to guide men in the attainment of such foresight and the exercise of such control. Moreover, people differ greatly in their capacity to follow such guidance while at the same time—such is Bentham's democratic assumption— they are equal in their right to hapiness; a "lot" of pleasure or pain is just as good or bad when experienced by one man as when experienced by any other. Thus arises the need of political, legal, educational, and economic analysis: to show how, given the present intellectual and social inequalities of men and the motives to personal pleasure which inevitably rule them, the richest attainment of enduring happiness and its most democratic apportionment in the community of mankind may be secured.

Bentham himself contributed toward this program keen statements of the basic moral principles presupposed in this approach and of their applications in the reformation of law. James Mill wrote the psychological theory needed to ground these analyses, and supplied applications in a number of other fields, notably government, education, and economics, His son, John Stuart Mill, rendered this "utilitarianism," as the school of philosophy under consideration was called, more sensitive, urbane, and appealing, at some cost to its inner consistency. And he gave ex-

---

[3] Hume is a notable exception.

pression, in clearer form than any of his predecessors had done, to the individualism which their emphasis on freedom and toleration in human conduct really implied.

With Mill, the distinctive epoch in British philosophy contemplated by our anthology came to at least a temporary close. After him, new points of view and new problems arise reflecting the emergence of evolutionary science, the influx of post-Kantian German philosophies, and the development of new techniques in logic and the methodology of science. These developments provide in large measure the context in which contemporary philosophical discussion in Great Britain must be understood.

BIBLIOGRAPHY

General: W. R. Sorley, *A History of English Philosophy* (1921); B. Willey, *The Seventeenth Century Background* (1934); H. J. Laski, *Political Thought in England: From Locke to Bentham* (1920); Leslie Stephen, *History of English Thought in the Eighteenth Century*, 2 vols. (1876); Leslie Stephen, *The English Utilitarians*, 3 vols. (1900); R. Metz, *A Hundred Years of British Philosophy* (English trans. by Harvey, Jessop, and Stuart, 1938).

On Bacon: J. M. Robertson, *The Philosophical Works of Francis Bacon* (1905); T. Fowler, *Bacon* (1881); R. W. Church, *Bacon* (1884); C. D. Broad, *The Philosophy of Francis Bacon* (1926); M. Sturt, *Francis Bacon, A Biography* (1932).

On Hobbes: G. C. Robertson, *Hobbes* (1886); Leslie Stephen, *Hobbes* (1904); John Laird, *Hobbes* (1934); F. Tönnies, *Hobbes, Leben und Lehre* (2nd ed., 1912).

On Locke: H. R. Fox-Bourne, *Life of John Locke* (1876); A. C. Fraser, *Prolegomena* to his edition of Locke's *Essay* (1894); J. Gibson, *Locke's Theory of Knowledge and Its Historical Relations* (1917); S. P. Lamprecht, *The Moral and Political Philosophy of John Locke* (1918); R. Aaron, *John Locke* (1937).

On Berkeley: A. C. Fraser, *Life and Letters of George Berkeley* (1871); *Berkeley* (1881); G. Dawes Hicks, *Berkeley* (1932); A. A. Luce, *Berkeley and Malebranche* (1934); R. Metz, *George Berkeley, Leben und Lehre* (1925); J. Wild, *George Berkeley, A Study of His Life and Philosophy* (1936).

On Hume: J. H. Burton, *Life and Correspondence of David Hume* (1846); T. H. Green, *Introductions* to the Green and Grose editions of certain of Hume's works (1874-5); T. H. Huxley, *Hume* (1879); C. W. Hendel, Jr., *Studies in the Philosophy of David Hume* (1925); R. W. Church, *Hume's Theory of the Understanding* (1935); J. Laird, *Hume's Philosophy of Human Nature* (1932); J. Y. T. Greig, *David Hume* (1931).

On Bentham: John Bowring, *Life of Bentham* in Vol. X of his edition of Bentham's works (1838-43); C. M. Atkinson, *Jeremy Bentham, His Life and Work* (1905); J. S. Mill, *Bentham* (in *Dissertations and Discussions*, Vol. I, 1859); E. Halévy, *The Growth of Philosophic Radicalism* (1928).

On James Mill: A. Bain, *James Mill, A Biography* (1882); G. S. Bower, *Hartley and James Mill* (1881).

On John Stuart Mill: J. S. Mill, *Autobiography,* (Coss edition, 1924); A. Bain, *J. S. Mill: A Criticism* (1882); W. L. Courtenay, *The Metaphysics of J. S. Mill* (1879); C. Douglas, *J. S. Mill: A Study of His Philosophy* (1895); G. Morlan, *America's Heritage from John Stuart Mill* (1936).

The standard edition of Bacon's works is that of Spedding, Ellis, and Heath (1861-74); of Hobbes, that of Sir William Molesworth (1839-45); of Locke, the eleventh edition of his works, published in 1812; of Berkeley, that of A. C. Fraser (1871); of Bentham, that of Sir John Bowring (1838-43). There are at present no editions of corresponding completeness in the case of the other philosophers here represented.

For fuller bibliographies of the period covered, consult Sorley's *History of English Philosophy* above cited.

FRANCIS BACON

FRANCIS BACON

FRANCIS BACON (1561-1626) was the youngest son of Sir Nicholas Bacon, Lord Keeper of the Great Seal. He was educated at Trinity College, Cambridge, where he acquired the distaste for barren scholastic studies that later led him to search for a new method in the sciences. In 1576 he was sent to France, in the suite of the English ambassador, as part of his education for a political career. When the sudden death of his father destroyed his prospects of easy and rapid preferment at Elizabeth's court, he entered the law as a career suited to his talents, was called to the bar, and, in 1584, took a seat in Parliament. Bacon immediately became a leading member of the Commons, but his enemies at court long prevented him from obtaining any office. He never received an important appointment from Elizabeth. With the accession of James, however, Bacon's rise was rapid. In the years 1607-1618 he successively became Solicitor-General, Attorney-General, Privy-Councillor, Lord Keeper, and Lord Chancellor. He was made Baron Verulam in 1618 and, three years later, created Viscount St. Albans.

But his professional and business life was not in his eyes particularly important. Amid all the business and distraction of a crowded legal and parliamentary career, he kept at work upon a grandiose scheme, formed while he was still young, for a *Great Instauration,* or total renovation of the sciences. In 1605 he published the *Advancement of Learning,* a classification and critical survey of all the existing sciences, and in 1620 his greatest work, the *Novum Organum,* an exposition of the new experimental method.

Bacon had now realized his cherished ambitions. He held one of the highest offices in the realm, and he had published the first two parts of his great intellectual undertaking. Then suddenly he fell, in disgrace, from his great eminence. In the struggles between James and the Parliament over the royal grants of monopolies Bacon had defended the King's prerogative. His enemies in Parliament accused him of bribery and corruption in the exercise of his judicial office. Bacon made full submission at the trial, but it was not shown that his acceptance of gifts from suitors (a common practice of the time) had in any way influenced his decisions.

Disgraced and exiled from the court, Bacon devoted his last years to writing and experimentation. He composed a *History of Henry VII,* an enlarged Latin version of the *Advancement of Learning,* and wrote a number of smaller treatises designed partially to complete the later parts of his *Great Instauration.*

The introductory portions of the *Great Instauration* are reprinted herewith, followed by the *Novum Organum.* They are given entire, except for a part of the lengthy list of "Prerogative Instances" with which *the Novum Organum* concludes.

THE GREAT INSTAURATION

Prooemium

FRANCIS OF VERULAM

REASONED THUS WITH HIMSELF,
AND JUDGED IT TO BE FOR THE INTEREST OF THE PRESENT AND FUTURE
GENERATIONS THAT THEY SHOULD BE MADE ACQUAINTED
WITH HIS THOUGHTS

BEING convinced that the human intellect makes its own difficulties, not using the true helps which are at man's disposal soberly and judiciously; whence follows manifold ignorance of things, and by reason of that ignorance mischiefs innumerable; he thought all trial should be made, whether that commerce between the mind of man and the nature of things, which is more precious than anything on earth, or at least than anything that is of the earth, might by any means be restored to its perfect and original condition, or if that may not be, yet reduced to a better condition than that in which it now is. Now that the errors which have hitherto prevailed, and which will prevail forever, should (if the mind be left to go its own way), either by the natural force of the understanding or by help of the aids and instruments of logic, one by one correct themselves, was a thing not to be hoped for: because the primary notions of things which the mind readily and passively imbibes, stores up, and accumulates (and it is from them that all the rest flow) are false, confused, and overhastily abstracted from the facts; nor are the secondary and subsequent notions less arbitrary and inconstant: whence it follows that the entire fabric of human reason which we employ in the inquisition of nature, is badly put together and built up, and like some magnificent structure without any foundation. For while men are occupied in admiring and applauding the false powers of the mind, they pass by and throw away those true powers, which, if it be supplied with the proper aids and can itself be content to wait upon nature instead of vainly affecting to overrule her, are within its reach. There was but one course left, therefore,—to try the whole thing anew upon a better plan, and to commence a total reconstruction of sciences, arts, and all human knowledge, raised upon the proper foundations. And this, though in the project and undertaking it may seem a thing infinite and beyond the powers of man, yet when it comes to be dealt with it will be found sound and sober, more so than what has been done hitherto. For of this there is some issue; whereas in what is now done in the matter of science there is only a whirling round about, and perpetual agitation, ending where it began. And although he was well aware how solitary an enterprise it is, and how hard a thing to win faith and credit for; nevertheless he was resolved not to abandon either it or himself, nor to be deterred from trying and entering upon that one path which is alone open to the human mind. For better it is to make a beginning of that which may lead to something, than to engage in a perpetual struggle and pursuit in courses which have no exit. And certainly the two ways of contemplation are much like those two ways of action, so much celebrated, in this—that the one, arduous and difficult in the beginning, leads out at last into the open country; while the other, seeming at first sight easy and free from obstruction, leads to pathless and precipitous places.

Moreover, because he knew not how long it might be before these things would occur to anyone else, judging especially from this, that he has found no man hitherto who has applied his mind to the like, he resolved to publish at once so much as he has been able to complete. The cause of which haste was not ambition for himself, but solicitude for the work; that in case of his death there might remain some outline and project of that which he had conceived, and some evidence likewise of his honest mind and inclination towards the benefit of the human race. Certain it is that all other ambition whatsoever seemed poor in his eyes compared with the work which he had in hand; seeing that the matter at issue is either nothing, or a thing so great that it may well be content with its own merit, without seeking other recompense.

Preface

That the state of knowledge is not prosperous nor greatly advancing; and that a way must be opened for the human understanding entirely different from any hitherto known, and other helps provided, in order that the mind may exercise over the nature of things the authority which properly belongs to it.

IT SEEMS to me that men do not rightly understand either their store or their strength, but overrate the one and underrate the other. Hence it follows, that either from an extravagant estimate of the value of the arts which they possess, they seek no further; or else from too mean an estimate of their own powers, they spend their strength in small matters and never put it fairly to the trial in those which go to the main. These are as the pillars of fate set in the path of knowledge; for men have neither desire nor hope to encourage them to penetrate further. And since opinion of store is one of the chief causes of want, and satisfaction with the present induces neglect of provision for the future, it becomes a thing not only useful, but absolutely necessary, that the excess of honor and admiration with which our existing stock of inventions is regarded be in the very entrance and threshold of the work, and that frankly and without circumlocution, stripped off, and men be duly warned not to exaggerate or make too much of them. For let a man look carefully into all that variety of books with which the arts and sciences abound, he will find everywhere endless repetitions of the same thing, varying in the method of treatment, but not new in substance, insomuch that the whole stock, numerous as it appears at first view, proves on examination to be but scanty. And for its value and utility it must be plainly avowed that that wisdom which we have derived principally from the Greeks is but like the boyhood of knowledge, and has the characteristic property of boys: it can talk, but it cannot generate; for it is fruitful of controversies but barren of works. So that the state of learning as it now is appears to be represented to the life in the old fable of Scylla, who had the head and face of a virgin, but her womb was hung round with barking monsters, from which she could not be delivered. For in like manner the sciences to which we are accustomed have certain general positions which are specious and flattering; but as soon as they come to particulars, which are as the parts of generation, when they should produce fruit and works, then arise contentions and barking disputations, which are the end of the matter and all the issue they can yield. Observe also, that if sciences of this kind had any life in them, that could never have come to pass which has been the case now for many ages—that they stand almost at a stay, without receiving any augmentations worthy of the human race; insomuch that many times not only what was asserted once is asserted still, but what was a question once is a question still, and instead of being resolved by discussion is only fixed and fed; and all the tradition and succession of schools is still a succession of masters and scholars, not of inventors and those who bring to further perfection the things invented. In the mechanical arts we do not find it so: they, on the contrary, as having in them some breath of life, are continually growing and becoming more perfect. As originally invented they are commonly rude, clumsy, and shapeless; afterwards they acquire new powers and more commodious arrangements and constructions; in so far that men shall

sooner leave the study and pursuit of them and turn to something else,
than they arrive at the ultimate perfection of which they are capable.
Philosophy and the intellectual sciences, on the contrary, stand like
statues, worshiped and celebrated, but not moved or advanced. Nay,
they sometimes flourish most in the hands of the first author, and afterwards degenerate. For when men have once made over their judgments
to others' keeping, and (like those senators whom they called *Pedarii*)
have agreed to support some one person's opinion, from that time they
make no enlargement of the sciences themselves, but fall to the servile
office of embellishing certain individual authors and increasing their
retinue. And let it not be said that the sciences have been growing gradually till they have at last reached their full stature, and so (their course
being completed) have settled in the works of a few writers; and that
there being now no room for the invention of better, all that remains is to
embellish and cultivate those things which have been invented already.
Would it were so! But the truth is that this appropriating of the sciences
has its origin in nothing better than the confidence of a few persons and
the sloth and indolence of the rest. For after the sciences had been in
several parts perhaps cultivated and handled diligently, there has risen
up some man of bold disposition, and famous for methods and short
ways which people like, who has in appearance reduced them to an art,
while he has in fact only spoiled all that the others had done. And yet this
is what posterity like, because it makes the work short and easy, and
saves further inquiry, of which they are weary and impatient. And if anyone take this general acquiescence and consent for an argument of weight,
as being the judgment of Time, let me tell him that the reasoning on
which he relies is most fallacious and weak. For, first, we are far from
knowing all that in the matter of sciences and arts has in various ages
and places been brought to light and published; much less, all that has
been by private persons secretly attempted and stirred; so neither the
births nor the miscarriages of Time are entered in our records. Nor, secondly, is the consent itself and the time it has continued a consideration
of much worth. For however various are the forms of civil polities, there
is but one form of polity in the sciences; and that always has been and
always will be popular. Now the doctrines which find most favor with the
populace are those which are either contentious and pugnacious, or
specious and empty; such, I say, as either entangle assent or tickle it.
And therefore no doubt the greatest wits in each successive age have been
forced out of their own course; men of capacity and intellect above the
vulgar having been fain, for reputation's sake, to bow to the judgment of
the time and the multitude; and thus if any contemplations of a higher
order took light anywhere, they were presently blown out by the winds
of vulgar opinions. So that Time is like a river, which has brought down

to us things light and puffed up, while those which are weighty and solid
have sunk. Nay, those very authors who have usurped a kind of dictator-
ship in the sciences and taken upon them to lay down the law with such
confidence, yet when from time to time they come to themselves again,
they fall to complaints of the subtlety of nature, the hiding-places of
truth, the obscurity of things, the entanglement of causes, the weakness of
the human mind; wherein nevertheless they show themselves never the
more modest, seeing that they will rather lay the blame upon the common
condition of men and nature than upon themselves. And then whatever
any art fails to attain, they ever set it down upon the authority of that
art itself as impossible of attainment; and how can art be found guilty
when it is judge in its own cause? So it is but a device for exempting
ignorance from ignominy. Now for those things which are delivered and
received, this is their condition: barren of works, full of questions; in
point of enlargement slow and languid; carrying a show of perfection
in the whole, but in the parts ill filled up; in selection popular, and unsatisfactory even to those who propound them; and therefore fenced
round and set forth with sundry artifices. And if there be any who have
determined to make trial for themselves, and put their own strength to
the work of advancing the boundaries of the sciences, yet have they not
ventured to cast themselves completely loose from received opinions or
to seek their knowledge at the fountain; but they think they have done
some great thing if they do but add and introduce into the existing sum
of science something of their own; prudently considering with themselves
that by making the addition they can assert their liberty, while they retain the credit of modesty by assenting to the rest. But these mediocrities
and middle ways so much praised, in deferring to opinions and customs,
turn to the great detriment of the sciences. For it is hardly possible at
once to admire an author and to go beyond him; knowledge being as
water, which will not rise above the level from which it fell. Men of this
kind, therefore, amend some things, but advance little; and improve the
condition of knowledge, but do not extend its range. Some, indeed, there
have been who have gone more boldly to work, and taking it all for an
open matter and giving their genius full play, have made a passage for
themselves and their own opinions by pulling down and demolishing
former ones; and yet all their stir has but little advanced the matter;
since their aim has been not to extend philosophy and the arts in substance and value, but only to change doctrines and transfer the kingdom
of opinions to themselves; whereby little has indeed been gained, for
though the error be the opposite of the other, the causes of erring are the
same in both. And if there have been any who, not binding themselves
either to other men's opinions or to their own, but loving liberty, have
desired to engage others along with themselves in search, these, though

honest in intention, have been weak in endeavor. For they have been content to follow probable reasons, and are carried round in a whirl of arguments, and in the promiscuous liberty of search have relaxed the severity of inquiry. There is none who has dwelt upon experience and the facts of nature as long as is necessary. Some there are indeed who have committed themselves to the waves of experience, and almost turned mechanics; yet these again have in their very experiments pursued a kind of wandering inquiry, without any regular system of operations. And besides they have mostly proposed to themselves certain petty tasks, taking it for a great matter to work out some single discovery;—a course of proceeding at once poor in aim and unskillful in design. For no man can rightly and successfully investigate the nature of anything in the thing itself; let him vary his experiments as laboriously as he will, he never comes to a resting place, but still finds something to seek beyond. And there is another thing to be remembered: namely, that all industry in experimenting has begun with proposing to itself certain definite works to be accomplished, and has pursued them with premature and unseasonable eagerness; it has sought, I say, experiments of Fruit, not experiments of Light; not imitating the divine procedure, which in its first day's work created light only and assigned to it one entire day; on which day it produced no material work, but proceeded to that on the days following. As for those who have given the first place to Logic, supposing that the surest helps to the sciences were to be found in that, they have indeed most truly and excellently perceived that the human intellect left to its own course is not to be trusted; but then the remedy is altogether too weak for the disease, nor is it without evil in itself. For the Logic which is received, though it be very properly applied to civil business and to those arts which rest in discourse and opinion, is not nearly subtle enough to deal with nature; and in offering at what it cannot master, has done more to establish and perpetuate error than to open the way to truth.

Upon the whole therefore, it seems that men have not been happy hitherto either in the trust which they have placed in others or in their own industry with regard to the sciences; especially as neither the demonstrations nor the experiments as yet known are much to be relied upon. But the universe to the eye of the human understanding is framed like a labyrinth; presenting as it does on every side so many ambiguities of way, such deceitful resemblances of objects and signs, natures so irregular in their lines, and so knotted and entangled. And then the way is still to be made by the uncertain light of the sense, sometimes shining out, sometimes clouded over, through the woods of experience and particulars; while those who offer themselves for guides are (as was said) themselves also puzzled, and increase the number of errors and wanderers. In circumstances so difficult, neither the natural force of man's judgment nor even any accidental felicity offers any chance of success. No excellence of wit, no repetition of chance experiments, can overcome such difficulties as these. Our steps must be guided by a clue, and the whole way from the very first perception of the senses must be laid out upon a sure plan. Not that I would be understood to mean that nothing whatever has been done in so many ages by so great labors. We have no reason to be ashamed of the discoveries which have been made, and no doubt the ancients proved themselves in everything that turns on wit and abstract meditation, wonderful men. But as in former ages when men sailed only by observation of the stars, they could indeed coast along the shores of the old continent or cross a few small and mediterranean seas; but before the ocean could be traversed and the new world discovered, the use of the mariner's needle, as a more faithful and certain guide, had to be found out: in like manner the discoveries which have been hitherto made in the arts and sciences are such as might be made by practice, meditation, observation, argumentation—for they lay near to the senses, and immediately beneath common notions; but before we can reach the remoter and more hidden parts of nature, it is necessary that a more perfect use and application of the human mind and intellect be introduced.

For my own part at least, in obedience to the everlasting love of truth, I have committed myself to the uncertainties and difficulties and solitudes of the ways, and relying on the divine assistance have upheld my mind both against the shocks and embattled ranks of opinion, and against my own private and inward hesitations and scruples, and against the fogs and clouds of nature, and the phantoms flitting about on every side; in the hope of providing at last for the present and future generations guidance more faithful and secure. Wherein if I have made any progress, the way has been opened to me by no other means than the true and legitimate humiliation of the human spirit. For all those who before me have applied themselves to the invention of arts have but cast a glance or two upon facts and examples and experience, and straightway proceeded, as if invention were nothing more than an exercise of thought, to invoke their own spirits to give them oracles. I, on the contrary, dwelling purely and constantly among the facts of nature, withdraw my intellect from them no further than may suffice to let the images and rays of natural objects meet in a point, as they do in the sense of vision; whence it follows that the strength and excellency of the wit has but little to do in the matter. And the same humility which I use in inventing I employ likewise in teaching. For I do not endeavor either by triumphs of confutation, or pleadings of antiquity, or assumption of authority, or even by the veil of obscurity, to invest these inventions of

mine with any majesty; which might easily be done by one who sought
to give luster to his own name rather than light to other men's minds.
I have not sought (I say) nor do I seek either to force or ensnare men's
judgments; but I lead them to things themselves and the concordance
of things, that they may see for themselves what they have, what they
can dispute, what they can add and contribute to the common stock.
And for myself, if in anything I have been either too credulous or too
little awake and attentive, or if I have fallen off by the way and left the
inquiry incomplete, nevertheless I so present these things naked and
open, that my errors can be marked and set aside before the mass of
knowledge be further infected by them; and it will be easy also for others
to continue and carry on my labors. And by these means I suppose that
I have established for ever a true and lawful marriage between the empirical and the rational faculty, the unkind and ill-starred divorce and
separation of which has thrown into confusion all the affairs of the human
family.

Wherefore, seeing that these things do not depend upon myself, at
the outset of the work I most humbly and fervently pray to God the
Father, God the Son, and God the Holy Ghost, that remembering the
sorrows of mankind and the pilgrimage of this our life wherein we wear
out days few and evil, They will vouchsafe through my hands to endow
the human family with new mercies. This likewise I humbly pray, that
things human may not interfere with things divine, and that from the
opening of the ways of sense and the increase of natural light there may
arise in our minds no incredulity or darkness with regard to the divine
mysteries; but rather that the understanding being thereby purified and
purged of fancies and vanity, and yet not the less subject and entirely
submissive to the divine oracles, may give to faith that which is faith's.
Lastly, that knowledge being now discharged of that venom which the
serpent infused into it, and which makes the mind of man to swell, we
may not be wise above measure and sobriety, but cultivate truth in
charity.

And now having said my prayers, I turn to men; to whom I have certain salutary admonitions to offer and certain fair requests to make. My
first admonition (which was also my prayer) is that men confine the
sense within the limits of duty in respect of things divine: for the sense
is like the sun, which reveals the face of earth, but seals and shuts up
the face of heaven. My next, that in flying from this evil they fall not
into the opposite error, which they will surely do if they think that the
inquisition of nature is in any part interdicted or forbidden. For it was
not that pure and uncorrupted natural knowledge whereby Adam gave
names to the creatures according to their propriety, which gave occasion
to the fall. It was the ambitious and proud desire of moral knowledge to

judge of good and evil, to the end that man may revolt from God and give laws to himself, which was the form and manner of the temptation. Whereas of the sciences which regard nature, the divine philosopher declares that "it is the glory of God to conceal a thing, but it is the glory of the King to find a thing out." Even as though the divine nature took pleasure in the innocent and kindly sport of children playing a hide and seek, and vouchsafed of his kindness and goodness to admit the human spirit for his playfellow at that game. Lastly, I would address one general admonition to all: that they consider what are the true ends of knowledge, and that they seek it not either for pleasure of the mind, or for contention, or for superiority to others, or for profit, or fame, or power, or any of these inferior things; but for the benefit and use of life; and that they perfect and govern it in charity. For it was from lust of power that the angels fell, from lust of knowledge that man fell; but of charity there can be no excess, neither did angel or man ever come in danger by it.

The requests I have to make are these. Of myself I say nothing; but in behalf of the business which is in hand I entreat men to believe that it is not an opinion to be held, but a work to be done; and to be well assured that I am laboring to lay the foundation, not of any sect or doctrine, but of human utility and power. Next, I ask them to deal fairly by their own interests, and laying aside all emulations and prejudices in favor of this or that opinion, to join in consultation for the common good; and being now freed and guarded by the securities and helps which I offer from the errors and impediments of the way, to come forward themselves and take part in that which remains to be done. Moreover, to be of good hope, nor to imagine that this *Instauration* of mine is a thing infinite and beyond the power of man, when it is in fact the true end and termination of infinite error; and seeing also that it is by no means forgetful of the conditions of mortality and humanity (for it does not suppose that the work can be altogether completed within one generation, but provides for its being taken up by another); and finally that it seeks for the sciences not arrogantly in the little cells of human wit, but with reverence in the greater world. But it is the empty things that are vast: things solid are most contracted and lie in little room. And now I have only one favor more to ask (else injustice to me may perhaps imperil the business itself)—that men will consider well how far, upon that which I must needs assert (if I am to be consistent with myself), they are entitled to judge and decide upon these doctrines of mine; inasmuch as all that premature human reasoning which anticipates inquiry, and is abstracted from the facts rashly and sooner than is fit, is by me rejected (so far as the inquisition of nature is concerned) as a thing uncertain, confused, and ill built up; and I cannot be fairly asked to abide by the decision of a tribunal which is itself on its trial.

The Plan of the Work

The work is in six Parts:—

I. *The Divisions of the Sciences.*
II. *The New Organon; or, Directions concerning the Interpretation of Nature.*
III. *The Phenomena of the Universe; or, a Natural and Experimental History for the Foundation of Philosophy.*
IV. *The Ladder of the Intellect.*
V. *The Forerunners; or, Anticipations of the New Philosophy.*
VI. *The New Philosophy; or, Active Science.*

The Arguments of the Several Parts

IT BEING part of my design to set everything forth, as far as may be, plainly and perspicuously (for nakedness of the mind is still, as nakedness of the body once was, the companion of innocence and simplicity), let me first explain the order and plan of the work. I distribute it into six parts.

The first part exhibits a summary or general description of the knowledge which the human race at present possesses. For I thought it good to make some pause upon that which is received; that thereby the old may be more easily made perfect and the new more easily approached. And I hold the improvement of that which we have to be as much an object as the acquisition of more. Besides which it will make me the better listened to; for "He that is ignorant (says the proverb) receives not the words of knowledge, unless thou first tell him that which is in his own heart." We will therefore make a coasting voyage along the shores of the arts and sciences received; not without importing into them some useful things by the way.

In laying out the divisions of the sciences, however, I take into account not only things already invented and known, but likewise things omitted which ought to be there. For there are found in the intellectual, as in the terrestrial globe, waste regions as well as cultivated ones. It is no wonder, therefore, if I am sometimes obliged to depart from the ordinary divisions. For in adding to the total you necessarily alter the parts and sections; and the received divisions of the sciences are fitted only to the received sum of them as it stands now.

With regard to those things which I shall mark as omitted, I intend not merely to set down a simple title or a concise argument of that which is wanted. For as often as I have occasion to report anything as deficient, the nature of which is at all obscure, so that men may not perhaps easily understand what I mean or what the work is which I have in my head; I shall always (provided it be a matter of any worth) take care to subjoin either directions for the execution of such work, or else a portion of the work itself executed by myself as a sample of the whole: thus giving assistance in every case either by work or by counsel. For if it were for the sake of my own reputation only and other men's interests were not concerned in it, I would not have any man think that in such cases merely some light and vague notion has crossed my mind, and that the things which I desire and offer at are no better than wishes; when they are in fact things which men may certainly command if they will, and of which I have formed in my own mind a clear and detailed conception. For I do not propose merely to survey these regions in my mind, like an augur taking auspices, but to enter them like a general who means to take possession.—So much for the first part of the work.

Having thus coasted past the ancient arts, the next point is to equip the intellect for passing beyond. To the second part therefore belongs the doctrine concerning the better and more perfect use of human reason in the inquisition of things, and the true helps of the understanding; that thereby (as far as the condition of mortality and humanity allows) the intellect may be raised and exalted, and made capable of overcoming the difficulties and obscurities of nature. The art which I introduce with this view (which I call Interpretation of Nature) is a kind of logic; though the difference between it and the ordinary logic is great, indeed immense. For the ordinary logic professes to contrive and prepare helps and guards for the understanding, as mine does; and in this one point they agree. But mine differs from it in three points especially: viz., in the end aimed at, in the order of demonstration, and in the starting point of the inquiry.

For the end which this science of mine proposes is the invention not of arguments but of arts; not of things in accordance with principles, but of principles themselves; not of probable reasons, but of designations and directions for works. And as the intention is different, so accordingly is the effect: the effect of the one being to overcome an opponent in argument, of the other to command nature in action.

In accordance with this end is also the nature and order of the demonstrations. For in the ordinary logic almost all the work is spent about the syllogism. Of induction the logicians seem hardly to have taken any serious thought, but they pass it by with a slight notice, and hasten on to the formulae of disputation. I on the contrary, reject demonstration by syllogism, as acting too confusedly, and letting nature slip out of its hands. For although no one can doubt that things which agree in a middle term agree with one another (which is a proposition of mathematical certainty), yet it leaves an opening for deception; which is this. The syllogism consists of propositions; propositions of words; and words are the tokens and signs of notions. Now if the very notions of the mind (which are as the soul of words and the basis of the whole structure) be improperly and overhastily abstracted from facts, vague, not sufficiently definite, faulty in short in many ways, the whole edifice tumbles. I therefore reject the syllogism; and that not only as regards principles (for to principles the logicians themselves do not apply it) but also as regards middle propositions; which, though obtainable no doubt by the syllogism, are, when so obtained, barren of works, remote from practice, and altogether unavailable for the active department of the sciences. Although therefore I leave to the syllogism and these famous and boasted modes of demonstration their jurisdiction over popular arts and such as are matter of opinion (in which department I leave all as it is), yet in dealing with the nature of things I use induction throughout, and that in the minor propositions as well as the major. For I consider induction to be that form of demonstration which upholds the sense, and closes with nature, and comes to the very brink of operation, if it does not actually deal with it.

Hence it follows that the order of demonstration is likewise inverted. For hitherto the proceeding has been to fly at once from the sense and particulars, up to the most general propositions, as certain fixed poles for the argument to turn upon, and from these to derive the rest by middle terms: a short way, no doubt, but precipitate; and one which will never lead to nature, though it offers an easy and ready way to disputation. Now my plan is to proceed regularly and gradually from one axiom to another, so that the most general are not reached till the last; but then when you do come to them you find them to be not empty notions, but well defined, and such as nature would really recognize as her first principles, and such as lie at the heart and marrow of things.

But the greatest change I introduce is in the form itself of induction and the judgment made thereby. For the induction of which the logicians speak, which proceeds by simple enumeration, is a puerile thing; concludes at hazard; is always liable to be upset by contradictory instance; takes into account only what is known and ordinary; and leads to no result.

Now what the sciences stand in need of is a form of induction which shall analyze experience and take it to pieces, and by a due process of exclusion and rejection lead to an inevitable conclusion. And if that ordinary mode of judgment practiced by the logicians was so laborious, and found exercise for such great wits, how much more labor must we be prepared to bestow upon this other, which is extracted not merely out of the depths of the mind, but out of the very bowels of nature.

Nor is this all. For I also sink the foundations of the sciences deeper and firmer; and I begin the inquiry nearer the source than men have done heretofore; submitting to examination those things which the common logic takes on trust. For first, the logicians borrow the principles of each science from the science itself; secondly, they hold in reverence the first notions of the mind; and lastly, they receive as conclusive the immediate informations of the sense, when well disposed. Now upon the first point, I hold that true logic ought to enter the several provinces of science armed with a higher authority than belongs to the principles of those sciences themselves, and ought to call those putative principles to account until they are fully established. Then with regard to the first notions of the intellect: there is not one of the impressions taken by the intellect when left to go its own way, but I hold it for suspected, and no way established, until it has submitted to a new trial and a fresh judgment has been thereupon pronounced. And lastly, the information of the sense itself I sift and examine in many ways. For certain it is that the senses deceive; but then at the same time they supply the means of discovering their own errors; only the errors are here, the means of discovery are to seek.

The sense fails in two ways. Sometimes it gives no information, sometimes it gives false information. For first, there are very many things which escape the sense, even when best disposed and no way obstructed; by reason either of the subtlety of the whole body, or the minuteness of the parts, or distance of place, or slowness or else swiftness of motion, or familiarity of the object, or other causes. And again when the sense does apprehend a thing its apprehension is not much to be relied upon. For the testimony and information of the sense has reference always to man, not to the universe; and it is a great error to assert that the sense is the measure of things.

To meet these difficulties, I have sought on all sides diligently and faithfully to provide helps for the sense—substitutes to supply its failures, rectifications to correct its errors; and this I endeavor to accomplish not so much by instruments as by experiments. For the subtlety of experiments is far greater than that of the sense itself, even when assisted by exquisite instruments; such experiments, I mean, as are skillfully and artificially devised for the express purpose of determining the point in question. To the immediate and proper perception of the sense therefore I do not give much weight; but I contrive that the office of the sense shall be only to judge of the experiment, and that the experiment itself shall judge of the thing. And thus I conceive that I perform the office of a true priest of the sense (from which all knowledge in nature must be sought, unless men mean to go mad) and a not unskillful interpreter of its oracles: and that while others only profess to uphold and

cultivate the sense, I do so in fact. Such then are the provisions I make
for finding the genuine light of nature and kindling and bringing it to
bear. And they would be sufficient of themselves, if the human intellect
were even, and like a fair sheet of paper with no writing on it. But since
the minds of men are strangely possessed and beset, so that there is no
true and even surface left to reflect the genuine rays of things, it is necessary to seek a remedy for this also.

Now the idols, or phantoms, by which the mind is occupied are either
adventitious or innate. The adventitious come into the mind from without; namely, either from the doctrines and sects of philosophers, or
from perverse rules of demonstration. But the innate are inherent in the
very nature of the intellect, which is far more prone to error than the
sense is. For let men please themselves as they will in admiring and almost adoring the human mind, this is certain: that as an uneven mirror
distorts the rays of objects according to its own figure and section, so
the mind, when it receives impressions of objects through the sense,
cannot be trusted to report them truly, but in forming its notions mixes
up its own nature with the nature of things.

And as the first two kinds of idols are hard to eradicate, so idols of
this last kind cannot be eradicated at all. All that can be done is to
point them out, so that this insidious action of the mind may be marked
and reproved (else as fast as old errors are destroyed new ones will
spring up out of the ill complexion of the mind itself, and so we shall
have but a change of errors, and not a clearance); and to lay it down
once for all as a fixed and established maxim, that the intellect is not
qualified to judge except by means of induction, and induction in its
legitimate form. This doctrine then of the expurgation of the intellect to
qualify it for dealing with truth, is comprised in three refutations: the
refutation of the Philosophies, the refutation of the Demonstrations, and
the refutation of the Natural Human Reason. The explanation of which
things, and of the true relation between the nature of things and the
nature of the mind, is as the strewing and decoration of the bridal
chamber of the Mind and the Universe, the Divine Goodness assisting;
out of which marriage let us hope (and be this the prayer of the bridal
song) there may spring helps to man, and a line and race of inventions
that may in some degree subdue and overcome the necessities and miseries of humanity. This is the second part of the work.

But I design not only to indicate and mark out the ways, but also to
enter them. And therefore the third part of the work embraces the Phenomena of the Universe; that is to say, experience of every kind, and
such a natural history as may serve for a foundation to build philosophy
upon. For a good method of demonstration or form of interpreting na-

ture may keep the mind from going astray or stumbling, but it is not any excellence of method that can supply it with the material of knowledge. Those however who aspire not to guess and divine, but to discover and know; who propose not to devise mimic and fabulous worlds of their own, but to examine and dissect the nature of this very world itself; must go to facts themselves for everything. Nor can the place of this labor and search and world-wide perambulation be supplied by any genius or meditation or argumentation; no, not if all men's wits could meet in one. This therefore we must have, or the business must be forever abandoned. But up to this day such has been the condition of men in this matter, that it is no wonder if nature will not give herself into their hands.

For first, the information of the sense itself, sometimes failing, sometimes false; observation, careless, irregular, and led by chance; tradition, vain and fed on rumor; practice, slavishly bent upon its work; experiment, blind, stupid, vague, and prematurely broken off; lastly, natural history trivial and poor:—all these have contributed to supply the understanding with very bad materials for philosophy and the sciences.

Then an attempt is made to mend the matter by a preposterous subtlety and winnowing of argument. But this comes too late, the case being already past remedy; and is far from setting the business right or sifting away the errors. The only hope therefore of any greater increase or progress lies in a reconstruction of the sciences.

Of this reconstruction the foundation must be laid in natural history, and that of a new kind and gathered on a new principle. For it is in vain that you polish the mirror if there are no images to be reflected; and it is as necessary that the intellect should be supplied with fit matter to work upon, as with safeguards to guide its working. But my history differs from that in use (as my logic does) in many things,—in end and office, in mass and composition, in subtlety, in selection also and setting forth, with a view to the operations which are to follow.

For first, the object of the natural history which I propose is not so much to delight with variety of matter, or to help with present use of experiments, as to give light to the discovery of causes and supply a suckling philosophy with its first food. For though it be true that I am principally in pursuit of works and the active department of the sciences, yet I wait for harvest-time, and do not attempt to mow the moss or to reap the green corn. For I well know that axioms once rightly discovered will carry whole troops of works along with them; and produce them, not here and there one, but in clusters. And that unseasonable and puerile hurry to snatch by way of earnest at the first works which come within reach, I utterly condemn and reject, as an Atalanta's apple that hinders the race. Such then is the office of this natural history of mine.

Next, with regard to the mass and composition of it: I mean it to be a history not only of nature free and at large (when she is left to her own course and does her work her own way),—such as that of the heavenly bodies, meteors, earth and sea, minerals, plants, animals,—but much more of nature under constraint and vexed; that is to say, when by art and the hand of man she is forced out of her natural state, and squeezed and molded. Therefore I set down at length all experiments of the mechanical arts, of the operative part of the liberal arts, of the many crafts which have not yet grown into arts properly so called, so far as I have been able to examine them and as they conduce to the end in view. Nay (to say the plain truth) I do in fact (low and vulgar as men may think it) count more upon this part both for helps and safeguards than upon the other; seeing that the nature of things betrays itself more readily under the vexations of art than in its natural freedom.

Nor do I confine the history to bodies; but I have thought it my duty besides to make a separate history of such virtues as may be considered cardinal in nature. I mean those original passions or desires of matter which constitute the primary elements of nature such as dense and rare, hot and cold, solid and fluid, heavy and light, and several others.

Then again, to speak of subtlety: I seek out and get together a kind of experiment much subtler and simpler than those which occur accidentally. For I drag into light many things which no one who was not proceeding by a regular and certain way to the discovery of causes would have thought of inquiring after; being indeed in themselves of no great use: which shows that they were not sought for on their own account; but having just the same relation to things and works which the letters of the alphabet have to speech and words—which, though in themselves useless, are the elements of which all discourse is made up.

Further, in the selection of the relations and experiments I conceive I have been a more cautious purveyor than those who have hitherto dealt with natural history. For I admit nothing but on the faith of eyes, or at least of careful and severe examination; so that nothing is exaggerated for wonder's sake, but what I state is sound and without mixture of fables or vanity. All received or current falsehoods also (which by strange negligence have been allowed for many ages to prevail and become established) I proscribe and brand by name; that the sciences may be no more troubled with them. For it has been well observed that the fables and superstitions and follies which nurses instill into children do serious injury to their minds; and the same consideration makes me anxious, having the management of the childhood as it were of philosophy in its course of natural history, not to let it accustom itself in the

beginning to any vanity. Moreover, whenever I come to a new experiment of any subtlety (though it be in my own opinion certain and approved), I nevertheless subjoin a clear account of the manner in which
I made it; that men knowing exactly how each point was made out,
may see whether there be any error connected with it, and may arouse
themselves to devise proofs more trustworthy and exquisite, if such can
be found; and finally, I interpose everywhere admonitions and scruples
and cautions, with a religious care to eject, repress, and as it were ex-
orcise every kind of phantasm.

Lastly, knowing how much the sight of man's mind is distracted by
experience and history, and how hard it is at the first (especially for
minds either tender or preoccupied) to become familiar with nature, I
not unfrequently subjoin observations of my own, being as the first offers, inclinations, and as it were glances of history towards philosophy;
both by way of an assurance to men that they will not be kept for ever
tossing on the waves of experience, and also that when the time comes
for the intellect to begin its work, it may find everything the more ready.
By such a natural history then as I have described, I conceive that a
safe and convenient approach may be made to nature, and matter supplied of good quality and well prepared for the understanding to work
upon.

And now that we have surrounded the intellect with faithful helps
and guards, and got together with most careful selection a regular army
of divine works, it may seem that we have no more to do but to proceed
to philosophy itself. And yet in a matter so difficult and doubtful there
are still some things which it seems necessary to premise, partly for convenience of explanation, partly for present use.

Of these the first is to set forth examples of inquiry and invention
according to my method, exhibited by anticipation in some particular
subjects; choosing such subjects as are at once the most noble in themselves among those under inquiry, and most different one from another;
that there may be an example in every kind. I do not speak of those
examples which are joined to the several precepts and rules by way of
illustration (for of these I have given plenty in the second part of the
work); but I mean actual types and models, by which the entire process
of the mind and the whole fabric and order of invention from the beginning to the end, in certain subjects, and those various and remarkable, should be set as it were before the eyes. For I remember that in
the mathematics, it is easy to follow the demonstration when you have
a machine beside you, whereas without that help all appears involved
and more subtle than it really is. To examples of this kind,—being in

fact nothing more than an application of the second part in detail and at large,—the fourth part of the work is devoted.

The fifth part is for temporary use only, pending the completion of the rest; like interest payable from time to time until the principal be forthcoming. For I do not make so blindly for the end of my journey, as to neglect anything useful that may turn up by the way. And therefore I include in this fifth part such things as I have myself discovered, proved, or added,—not however according to the true rules and methods of interpretation, but by the ordinary use of the understanding in inquiring and discovering. For besides that I hope my speculations may in virtue of my continual conversancy with nature have a value beyond the pretensions of my wit; they will serve in the meantime for wayside inns, in which the mind may rest and refresh itself on its journey to more certain conclusions. Nevertheless I wish it to be understood in the meantime that they are conclusions by which (as not being discovered and proved by the true form of interpretation) I do not at all mean to bind myself. Nor need anyone be alarmed at such suspensions of judgment, in one who maintains not simply that nothing can be known, but only that nothing can be known except in a certain course and way; and yet establishes provisionally certain degrees of assurance, for use and relief until the mind shall arrive at a knowledge of causes in which it can rest. For even those schools of philosophy which held the absolute impossibility of knowing anything, were not inferior to those which took upon them to pronounce. But then they did not provide helps for the sense and understanding, as I have done, but simply took away all their authority: which is quite a different thing—almost the reverse.

The sixth part of my work (to which the rest is subservient and ministrant) discloses and sets forth that philosophy which by the legitimate, chaste, and severe course of inquiry which I have explained and provided is at length developed and established. The completion however of this last part is a thing both above my strength and beyond my hopes. I have made a beginning of the work—a beginning, as I hope, not unimportant:—the fortune of the human race will give the issue;—such an issue, it may be, as in the present condition of things and men's minds cannot easily be conceived or imagined. For the matter in hand is no mere felicity of speculation, but the real business and fortunes of the human race, and all power of operation. For man is but the servant and interpreter of nature: what he does and what he knows is only what he has observed of nature's order in fact or in thought; beyond this he knows nothing and can do nothing. For the chain of causes cannot by any force be loosed or broken, nor can nature be commanded except by being obeyed. And so those twin objects, *human knowledge* and *human power*, do really meet in one; and it is from ignorance of causes that operation fails.

And all depends on keeping the eye steadily fixed upon the facts of nature and so receiving their images simply as they are. For God forbid that we should give out a dream of our own imagination for a pattern of the world; rather may He graciously grant to us to write an apocalypse or true vision of the footsteps of the Creator imprinted on his creatures.

Therefore do Thou, O Father, who gavest the visible light as the first fruits of creation, and didst breathe into the face of man the intellectual light as the crown and consummation thereof, guard and protect this work, which coming from Thy goodness returneth to Thy glory. Thou when Thou turnedst to look upon the works which Thy hands had made, sawest that all was very good, and didst rest from Thy labors. But man, when he turned to look upon the work which his hands had made, saw that all was vanity and vexation of spirit, and could find no rest therein. Wherefore if we labor in Thy works with the sweat of our brows, Thou wilt make us partakers of Thy vision and Thy sabbath. Humbly we pray that this mind may be steadfast in us, and that through these our hands, and the hands of others to whom Thou shalt give the same spirit, Thou wilt vouchsafe to endow the human family with new mercies.

THE SECOND PART OF THE WORK,

THE NEW ORGANON;

TRUE DIRECTIONS

THE INTERPRETATION OF NATURE

Preface

THOSE who have taken upon them to lay down the law of nature as a thing already searched out and understood, whether they have spoken in simple assurance or professional affectation, have therein done philosophy and the sciences great injury. For as they have been successful in inducing belief, so they have been effective in quenching and stopping inquiry; and have done more harm by spoiling and putting an end to other men's efforts than good by their own. Those on the other hand who have taken a contrary course, and asserted that absolutely nothing can be known—whether it were from hatred of the ancient sophists, or from uncertainty and fluctuation of mind, or even from a kind of fulness of learning, that they fell upon this opinion,—have certainly advanced reasons for it that are not to be despised; but yet they have neither started from true principles nor rested in the just conclusion, zeal and affectation having carried them much too far. The more ancient of the Greeks (whose writings are lost) took up with better judgment a position between these two extremes,—between the presumption of pronouncing on everything, and the despair of comprehending anything; and though frequently and bitterly complaining of the difficulty of inquiry and the obscurity of things, and like impatient horses champing the bit, they did not the less follow up their object and engage with nature; thinking (it seems) that this very question—viz., whether or no anything can be known—was to be settled not by arguing, but by trying. And yet they too, trusting entirely to the force of their understanding, applied no rule, but made everything turn upon hard thinking and perpetual working and exercise of the mind.

Now my method, though hard to practice, is easy to explain; and it is this. I propose to establish progressive stages of certainty. The evidence of the sense, helped and guarded by a certain process of correction, I retain. But the mental operation which follows the act of sense I for the most part reject; and instead of it, I open and lay out a new and certain path for the mind to proceed in, starting directly from the simple sensuous perception. The necessity of this was felt no doubt by those who attributed so much importance to logic; showing thereby that they were in search of helps for the understanding, and had no confidence in the native and spontaneous process of the mind. But this remedy comes too late to do any good, when the mind is already, through the daily intercourse and conversation of life, occupied with unsound doctrines and beset on all sides by vain imaginations. And therefore that art of logic, coming (as I said) too late to the rescue, and no way able to set matters right again, has had the effect of fixing errors rather than disclosing truth. There remains but one course for the recovery of a sound and healthy condition,—namely, that the entire work of the understanding be commenced afresh, and the mind itself be from the very outset not left to take its own course, but guided at every step; and the business be done as if by machinery. Certainly if in things mechanical men had set to work with their naked hands, without help or force of instruments, just as in things intellectual they have set to work with little else then the naked forces of the understanding, very small would the matters have been which, even with their best efforts applied in conjunction, they could have attempted or accomplished. Now (to pause awhile upon this example and look in it as in a glass) let us suppose that some vast obelisk were (for the decoration of a triumph or some such magnificence) to be removed from its place, and that men should set to work upon it with their naked hands; would not any sober spectator think them mad? And if they should then send for more people, thinking that in that way they might manage it, would he not think them all the madder? And if they then proceeded to make a selection, putting away the weaker hands, and using only the strong and vigorous, would he not think them madder than ever? And if lastly, not content with this, they resolved to call in aid the art of athletics, and required all their men to come with hands, arms, and sinews well anointed and medicated according to the rules of art, would he not cry out that they were only taking pains to show a kind of method and discretion in their madness? Yet just so it is that men proceed in matters intellectual,—with just the same kind of mad effort and useless combination of forces,—when they hope great things either from the number and co-operation or from the excellency and acuteness of individual wits; yea, and when they endeavor by logic (which may be considered as a kind of athletic art) to strengthen the sinews of the understanding: and yet with all this study and endeavor it is apparent to any true judgment that they are but applying the naked intellect all the time; whereas in every great work to be done by the hand of man it is manifestly impossible, without instruments and machinery, either for the strength of each to be exerted or the strength of all to be united.

Upon these premises two things occur to me of which, that they may not be overlooked, I would have men reminded. First it falls out fortunately as I think for the allaying of contradictions and heart-burnings, that the honor and reverence due to the ancients remains untouched and undiminished; while I may carry out my designs and at the same time reap the fruit of my modesty. For if I should profess that I, going the same road as the ancients, have something better to produce, there must needs have been some comparison or rivalry between us (not to be avoided by any art of words) in respect of excellency or ability of wit; and though in this there would be nothing unlawful or new (for if there be anything misapprehended by them, or falsely laid down, why may not I, using a liberty common to all, take exception to it?), yet the contest, however just and allowable, would have been an unequal one perhaps, in respect of the measure of my own powers. As it is, however,— my object being to open a new way for the understanding, a way by them untried and unknown,—the case is altered; party zeal and emulation are at an end; and I appear merely as a guide to point out the road; an office of small authority, and depending more upon a kind of luck than upon any ability or excellency. And thus much relates to the persons only. The other point of which I would have men reminded relates to the matter itself.

Be it remembered then that I am far from wishing to interfere with the philosophy which now flourishes, or with any other philosophy more correct and complete than this which has been or may hereafter be propounded. For I do not object to the use of this received philosophy, or others like it, for supplying matter for disputations or ornaments for discourse,—for the professor's lecture and for the business of life. Nay more, I declare openly that for these uses the philosophy which I bring forward will not be much available. It does not lie in the way. It cannot be caught up in passage. It does not flatter the understanding by conformity with preconceived notions. Nor will it come down to the apprehension of the vulgar except by its utility and effects.

Let there be therefore (and may it be for the benefit of both) two streams and two dispensations of knowledge; and in like manner two tribes or kindreds of students in philosophy—tribes not hostile or alien to each other, but bound together by mutual services;—let there in short be one method for the cultivation, another for the invention, of knowledge.

And for those who prefer the former, either from hurry or from considerations of business or for want of mental power to take in and embrace the other (which must needs be most men's case), I wish that they may succeed to their desire in what they are about, and obtain what they are pursuing. But if any man there be who, not content to rest in and use the knowledge which has already been discovered, aspires to penetrate further; to overcome, not an adversary in argument, but nature in action; to seek, not pretty and probable conjectures, but certain and demonstrable knowledge;—I invite all such to join themselves, as true sons of knowledge, with me, that passing by the outer courts of nature, which numbers have trodden, we may find a way at length into her inner chambers. And to make my meaning clearer and to familiarize the thing by giving it a name, I have chosen to call one of these methods or ways *Anticipation of the Mind*, the other *Interpretation of Nature*.

Moreover I have one request to make. I have on my own part made it my care and study that the things which I shall propound should not only be true, but should also be presented to men's minds, how strangely soever preoccupied and obstructed, in a manner not harsh or unpleasant. It is but reasonable however (especially in so great a restoration of learning and knowledge) that I should claim of men one favor in return; which is this:—If anyone would form an opinion or judgment either out of his own observation, or out of the crowd of authorities, or out of the forms of demonstration (which have now acquired a sanction like that of judicial laws), concerning these speculations of mine, let him not hope that he can do it in passage or by the by; but let him examine the thing thoroughly; let him make some little trial for himself of the way which I describe and lay out; let him familiarize his thoughts with that subtlety of nature to which experience bears witness; let him correct by seasonable patience and due delay the depraved and deep-rooted habits of his mind; and when all this is done and he has begun to be his own master, let him (if he will) use his own judgment.

APHORISMS

THE INTERPRETATION OF NATURE

AND

THE KINGDOM OF MAN

APHORISM

i

MAN, being the servant and interpreter of nature, can do and understand so much and so much only as he has observed in fact or in thought of the course of nature: beyond this he neither knows anything nor can do anything.

ii

Neither the naked hand nor the understanding left to itself can effect much. It is by instruments and helps that the work is done, which are as much wanted for the understanding as for the hand. And as the instruments of the hand either give motion or guide it, so the instruments of the mind supply either suggestions for the understanding or cautions.

iii

Human knowledge and human power meet in one; for where the cause is not known the effect cannot be produced. Nature to be commanded must be obeyed; and that which in contemplation is as the cause is in operation as the rule.

iv

Towards the effecting of works, all that man can do is to put together or put asunder natural bodies. The rest is done by nature working within.

v

The study of nature with a view to works is engaged in by the mechanic, the mathematician, the physician, the alchemist, and the magician; but by all (as things now are) with slight endeavor and scanty success.

vi

It would be an unsound fancy and self-contradictory to expect that things which have never yet been done can be done except by means which have never yet been tried.

vii

The productions of the mind and hand seem very numerous in books and manufactures. But all this variety lies in an exquisite subtlety and derivations from a few things already known; not in the number of axioms.

viii

Moreover the works already known are due to chance and experiment rather than to sciences; for the sciences we now possess are merely systems for the nice ordering and setting forth of things already invented; not methods of invention or directions for new works.

ix

The cause and root of nearly all evils in the sciences is this—that while we falsely admire and extol the powers of the human mind we neglect to seek for its true helps.

x

The subtlety of nature is greater many times over than the subtlety of the senses and understanding; so that all those specious meditations, speculations, and glosses in which men indulge are quite from the purpose, only there is no one by to observe it.

xi

As the sciences which we now have do not help us in finding out new works, so neither does the logic which we now have help us in finding out new sciences.

xii

The logic now in use serves rather to fix and give stability to the errors which have their foundation in commonly received notions, than to help the search after truth. So it does more harm than good.

xiii

The syllogism is not applied to the first principles of sciences, and is applied in vain to intermediate axioms; being no match for the subtlety of nature. It commands assent therefore to the proposition, but does not take hold of the thing.

xiv

The syllogism consists of propositions, propositions consist of words, words are symbols of notions. Therefore if the notions themselves (which is the root of the matter) are confused and overhastily abstracted from the facts, there can be no firmness in the superstructure. Our only hope therefore lies in a true induction.

xv

There is no soundness in our notions whether logical or physical. Substance, Quality, Action, Passion, Essence itself, are not sound notions: much less are Heavy, Light, Dense, Rare, Moist, Dry, Generation, Corruption, Attraction, Repulsion, Element, Matter, Form, and the like; but all are fantastical and ill defined.

xvi

Our notions of less general species as Man, Dog, Dove, and of the immediate perceptions of the sense, as Hot, Cold, Black, White, do not materially mislead us; yet even these are sometimes confused by the flux and alteration of matter and the mixing of one thing with another. All the others which men have hitherto adopted are but wanderings, not being abstracted and formed from things by proper methods.

xvii

Nor is there less of willfulness and wandering in the construction of axioms than in the formations of notions; not excepting even those very principles which are obtained by common induction; but much more in the axioms and lower propositions educed by the syllogism.

xviii

The discoveries which have hitherto been made in the sciences are such as lie close to vulgar notions, scarcely beneath the surface. In order to penetrate into the inner and further recesses of nature, it is necessary that both notions and axioms be derived from things by a more sure and guarded way; and that a method of intellectual operation be introduced altogether better and more certain.

xix

There are and can be only two ways of searching into and discovering truth. The one flies from the senses and particulars to the most general axioms, and from these principles, the truth of which it takes for settled and immovable, proceeds to judgment and to the discovery of middle axioms. And this way is now in fashion. The other derives axioms from the senses and particulars, rising by a gradual and unbroken ascent, so that it arrives at the most general axioms last of all. This is the true way, but as yet untried.

xx

The understanding left to itself takes the same course (namely, the former) which it takes in accordance with logical order. For the mind longs to spring up to positions of higher generality, that it may find rest there; and so after a little while wearies of experiment. But this evil is increased by logic, because of the order and solemnity of its disputations.

xxi

The understanding left to itself, in a sober, patient, and grave mind, especially if it be not hindered by received doctrines, tries a little that other way, which is the right one, but with little progress; since the understanding, unless directed and assisted, is a thing unequal, and quite unfit to contend with the obscurity of things.

xxii

Both ways set out from the senses and particulars, and rest in the highest generalities; but the difference between them is infinite. For the one just glances at experiment and particulars in passing, the other dwells duly and orderly among them. The one, again, begins at once by establishing certain abstract and useless generalities, the other rises by gradual steps to that which is prior and better known in the order of nature.

xxiii

There is a great difference between the *Idols* of the human mind and the *Ideas* of the divine. That is to say, between certain empty dogmas, and the true signatures and marks set upon the works of creation as they are found in nature.

xxiv

It cannot be that axioms established by argumentation should avail for the discovery of new works; since the subtlety of nature is greater many times over than the subtlety of argument. But axioms duly and orderly formed from particulars easily discover the way to new particulars, and thus render sciences active.

xxv

The axioms now in use, having been suggested by a scanty and manipular experience and a few particulars of most general occurrence, are made for the most part just large enough to fit and take these in: and therefore it is no wonder if they do not lead to new particulars. And if some opposite instance, not observed or not known before, chance to come in the way, the axiom is rescued and preserved by some frivolous distinction; whereas the truer course would be to correct the axiom itself.

xxvi

The conclusions of human reason as ordinarily applied in matter of nature, I call for the sake of distinction *Anticipations of Nature* (as a thing rash or premature). That reason which is elicited from facts by a just and methodical process, I call *Interpretation of Nature.*

xxvii

Anticipations are a ground sufficiently firm for consent; for even if men went mad all after the same fashion, they might agree one with another well enough.

xxviii

For the winning of assent, indeed, anticipations are far more powerful than interpretations; because being collected from a few instances, and those for the most part of familiar occurrence, they straightway touch the understanding and fill the imagination; whereas interpretations on the other hand, being gathered here and there from very various and widely dispersed facts, cannot suddenly strike the understanding; and therefore they must needs, in respect of the opinions of the time, seem harsh and out of tune; much as the mysteries of faith do.

xxix

In sciences founded on opinions and dogmas, the use of anticipations and logic is good; for in them the object is to command assent to the proposition, not to master the thing.

xxx

Though all the wits of all the ages should meet together and combine and transmit their labors, yet will no great progress ever be made in science by means of anticipations; because radical errors in the first concoction of the mind are not to be cured by the excellence of functions and remedies subsequent.

xxxi

It is idle to expect any great advancement in science from the superinducing and engrafting of new things upon old. We must begin anew from the very foundations, unless we would revolve forever in a circle with mean and contemptible progress.

xxxii

The honor of the ancient authors, and indeed of all, remains untouched; since the comparison I challenge is not of wits or faculties, but of ways and methods, and the part I take upon myself is not that of a judge, but of a guide.

xxxiii

This must be plainly avowed: no judgment can be rightly formed either of my method or of the discoveries to which it leads, by means of anticipations (that is to say, of the reasoning which is now in use): since I cannot be called on to abide by the sentence of a tribunal which is itself on its trial.

xxxiv

Even to deliver and explain what I bring forward is no easy matter; for things in themselves new will yet be apprehended with reference to what is old.

xxxv

It was said by Borgia of the expedition of the French into Italy, that they came with chalk in their hands to mark out their lodgings, not with arms to force their way in. I in like manner would have my doctrine enter quietly into the minds that are fit and capable of receiving it; for confutations cannot be employed, when the difference is upon first principles and very notions and even upon forms of demonstration.

xxxvi

One method of delivery alone remains to us; which is simply this: we must lead men to the particulars themselves, and their series and order;

while men on their side must force themselves for awhile to lay their notions by and begin to familiarize themselves with facts.

xxxvii

The doctrine of those who have denied that certainty could be attained at all, has some agreement with my way of proceeding at the first
setting out; but they end in being infinitely separated and opposed. For
the holders of that doctrine assert simply that nothing can be known; I
also assert that not much can be known in nature by the way which is
now in use. But then they go on to destroy the authority of the senses
and understanding; whereas I proceed to devise and supply helps for
the same.

xxxviii

The idols and false notions which are now in possession of the human
understanding, and have taken deep root therein, not only so beset men's
minds that truth can hardly find entrance, but even after entrance obtained, they will again in the very instauration of the sciences meet and
trouble us, unless men being forewarned of the danger fortify themselves
as far as may be against their assaults.

xxxix

There are four classes of idols which beset men's minds. To these for
distinction's sake I have assigned names,—calling the first class *Idols of
the Tribe;* the second, *Idols of the Cave;* the third, *Idols of the Market-
place;* the fourth, *Idols of the Theater.*

xl

The formation of ideas and axioms by true induction is no doubt the
proper remedy to be applied for the keeping off and clearing away of
idols. To point them out, however, is of great use, for the doctrine of
idols is to the interpretation of nature what the doctrine of the refutation of sophisms is to common logic.

xli

The Idols of the Tribe have their foundation in human nature itself,
and in the tribe or race of men. For it is a false assertion that the sense
of man is the measure of things. On the contrary, all perceptions, as well
of the sense as of the mind, are according to the measure of the individual and not according to the measure of the universe. And the human
understanding is like a false mirror, which, receiving rays irregularly,
distorts and discolors the nature of things by mingling its own nature
with it.

xlii

The Idols of the Cave are the idols of the individual man. For every-one (besides the errors common to human nature in general) has a cave or den of his own, which refracts and discolors the light of nature; ow-ing either to his own proper and peculiar nature or to his education and conversation with others; or to the reading of books, and the au-thority of those whom he esteems and admires; or to the differences of impressions, accordingly as they take place in a mind preoccupied and predisposed or in a mind indifferent and settled; or the like. So that the spirit of man (according as it is meted out to different individuals) is in fact a thing variable and full of perturbation, and governed as it were by chance. Whence it was well observed by Heraclitus that men look for sciences in their own lesser worlds, and not in the greater or common world.

xliii

There are also idols formed by the intercourse and association of men with each other, which I call Idols of the Market-place, on account of the commerce and consort of men there. For it is by discourse that men associate; and words are imposed according to the apprehension of the vulgar. And therefore the ill and unfit choice of words wonderfully ob-structs the understanding. Nor do the definitions or explanations where-with in some things learned men are wont to guard and defend them-selves, by any means set the matter right. But words plainly force and overrule the understanding, and throw all into confusion, and lead men away into numberless empty controversies and idle fancies.

xliv

Lastly, there are idols which have immigrated into men's minds from the various dogmas of philosophies, and also from wrong laws of demon-stration. These I call Idols of the Theater; because in my judgment all the received systems are but so many stage-plays, representing worlds of their own creation after an unreal and scenic fashion. Nor is it only of the systems now in vogue, or only of the ancient sects and philosophies, that I speak: for many more plays of the same kind may yet be com-posed and in like artificial manner set forth; seeing that errors the most widely different have nevertheless causes for the most part alike. Nei-ther again do I mean this only of entire systems, but also of many prin-ciples and axioms in science, which by tradition, credulity, and negli-gence have come to be received.

But of these several kinds of idols I must speak more largely and ex-actly, that the understanding may be duly cautioned.

xlv

The human understanding is of its own nature prone to suppose the existence of more order and regularity in the world than it finds. And though there be many things in nature which are singular and unmatched, yet it devises for them parallels and conjugates and relatives which do not exist. Hence the fiction that all celestial bodies move in perfect circles; spirals and dragons being (except in name) utterly rejected. Hence too the element of fire with its orb is brought in, to make up the square with the other three which the sense perceives. Hence also the ratio of density of the so-called elements is arbitrarily fixed at ten to one. And so on of other dreams. And these fancies affect not dogmas only, but simple notions also.

xlvi

The human understanding when it has once adopted an opinion (either as being the received opinion or as being agreeable to itself) draws all things else to support and agree with it. And though there be a greater number and weight of instances to be found on the other side, yet these it either neglects and despises, or else by some distinction sets aside and rejects; in order that by this great and pernicious predetermination the authority of its former conclusions may remain inviolate. And therefore it was a good answer that was made by one who when they showed him hanging in a temple a picture of those who had paid their vows as having escaped shipwreck, and would have him say whether he did not now acknowledge the power of the gods,—"Aye," asked he again, "but where are they painted that were drowned after their vows?" And such is the way of all superstition, whether in astrology, dreams, omens, divine judgments, or the like; wherein men, having a delight in such vanities, mark the events where they are fulfilled, but where they fail, though this happen much oftener, neglect and pass them by. But with far more subtlety does this mischief insinuate itself into philosophy and the sciences; in which the first conclusion colors and brings into conformity with itself all that come after, though far sounder and better. Besides, independently of that delight and vanity which I have described, it is the peculiar and perpetual error of the human intellect to be more moved and excited by affirmatives than by negatives; whereas it ought properly to hold itself indifferently disposed towards both alike. Indeed in the establishment of any true axiom, the negative instance is the more forcible of the two.

xlvii

The human understanding is moved by those things most which strike and enter the mind simultaneously and suddenly, and so fill the imagina·

tion; and then it feigns and supposes all other things to be somehow, though it cannot see how, similar to those few things by which it is surrounded. But for that going to and fro to remote and heterogeneous instances, by which axioms are tried as in the fire, the intellect is altogether slow and unfit, unless it be forced thereto by severe laws and overruling authority.

xlviii

The human understanding is unquiet; it cannot stop or rest, and still presses onward, but in vain. Therefore it is that we cannot conceive of any end or limit to the world; but always as of necessity it occurs to us that there is something beyond. Neither again can it be conceived how eternity has flowed down to the present day: for that distinction which is commonly received of infinity in time past and in time to come can by no means hold; for it would thence follow that one infinity is greater than another, and that infinity is wasting away and tending to become finite. The like subtlety arises touching the infinite divisibility of lines, from the same inability of thought to stop. But this inability interferes more mischievously in the discovery of causes: for although the most general principles in nature ought to be held merely positive, as they are discovered, and cannot with truth be referred to a cause; nevertheless the human understanding being unable to rest still seeks something prior in the order of nature. And then it is that in struggling towards that which is further off it falls back upon that which is more nigh at hand,—namely, on final causes; which have relation clearly to the nature of man rather than to the nature of the universe, and from this source have strangely defiled philosophy. But he is no less an unskilled and shallow philosopher who seeks causes of that which is most general, than he who in things subordinate and subaltern omits to do so.

xlix

The human understanding is no dry light, but receives an infusion from the will and affections; whence proceed sciences which may be called "sciences as one would." For what a man had rather were true he more readily believes. Therefore he rejects difficult things from impatience of research; sober things, because they narrow hope; the deeper things of nature, from superstition; the light of experience, from arrogance and pride, lest his mind should seem to be occupied with things mean and transitory; things not commonly believed, out of deference to the opinion of the vulgar. Numberless in short are the ways, and sometimes imperceptible, in which the affections color and infect the understanding.

l

But by far the greatest hindrance and aberration of the human understanding proceeds from the dullness, incompetency, and deceptions of the senses; in that things which strike the sense outweigh things which do not immediately strike it, though they be more important. Hence it is that speculation commonly ceases where sight ceases, insomuch that of things invisible there is little or no observation. Hence all the working of the spirits inclosed in tangible bodies lies hid and unobserved of men. So also all the more subtle changes of form in the parts of coarser substances (which they commonly call alteration, though it is in truth local motion through exceedingly small spaces) is in like manner unobserved. And yet unless these two things just mentioned be searched out and brought to light, nothing great can be achieved in nature, as far as the production of works is concerned. So again the essential nature of our common air, and of all bodies less dense than air (which are very many), is almost unknown. For the sense by itself is a thing infirm and erring; neither can instruments for enlarging or sharpening the senses do much: but all the truer kind of interpretation of nature is effected by instances and experiments fit and apposite; wherein the sense decides touching the experiment only, and the experiment touching the point in nature and the thing itself.

li

The human understanding is of its own nature prone to abstractions and gives a substance and reality to things which are fleeting. But to resolve nature into abstractions is less to our purpose than to dissect her into parts; as did the school of Democritus, which went further into nature than the rest. Matter rather than forms should be the object of our attention, its configurations and changes of configuration, and simple action, and law of action or motion; for forms are figments of the human mind, unless you will call those laws of action forms.

lii

Such then are the idols which I call *Idols of the Tribe;* and which take their rise either from the homogeneity of the substance of the human spirit, or from its preoccupation, or from its narrowness, or from its restless motion, or from an infusion of the affections, or from the incompetency of the senses, or from the mode of impression.

liii

The *Idols of the Cave* take their rise in the peculiar constitution, mental or bodily, of each individual; and also in education, habit, and accident. Of this kind there is a great number and variety; but I will instance those the pointing out of which contains the most important caution, and which have most effect in disturbing the clearness of the understanding.

liv

Men become attached to certain particular sciences and speculations, either because they fancy themselves the authors and inventors thereof, or because they have bestowed the greatest pains upon them and become most habituated to them. But men of this kind, if they betake themselves to philosophy and contemplations of a general character, distort and color them in obedience to their former fancies; a thing especially to be noticed in Aristotle, who made his natural philosophy a mere bondservant to his logic, thereby rendering it contentious and well nigh useless. The race of chemists again out of a few experiments of the furnace have built up a fantastic philosophy, framed with reference to a few things; and Gilbert also, after he had employed himself most laboriously in the study and observation of the lodestone, proceeded at once to construct an entire system in accordance with his favorite subject.

lv

There is one principal and as it were radical distinction between different minds, in respect of philosophy and the sciences; which is this: that some minds are stronger and apter to mark the differences of things, others to mark their resemblances. The steady and acute mind can fix its contemplations and dwell and fasten on the subtlest distinctions; the lofty and discursive mind recognizes and puts together the finest and most general resemblances. Both kinds however easily err in excess, by catching the one at gradations the other at shadows.

lvi

There are found some minds given to an extreme admiration of antiquity, others to an extreme love and appetite for novelty; but few so duly tempered that they can hold the mean, neither carping at what has been well laid down by the ancients, nor despising what is well introduced by the moderns. This however turns to the great injury of the sciences and philosophy: since these affectations of antiquity and novelty are the humors of partisans rather than judgments; and truth is to be sought for not in the felicity of any age, which is an unstable thing, but in the light of nature and experience, which is eternal. These factions therefore must be abjured, and care must be taken that the intellect be not hurried by them into assent.

lvii

Contemplations of nature and of bodies in their simple form break up and distract the understanding, while contemplations of nature and bodies in their composition and configuration overpower and dissolve the understanding: a distinction well seen in the school of Leucippus and Democritus as compared with the other philosophies. For that school is so busied with the particles that it hardly attends to the structure; while the others are so lost in admiration of the structure that they do not penetrate to the simplicity of nature. These kinds of contemplation should therefore be alternated and taken by turns; that so the understanding may be rendered at once penetrating and comprehensive, and the inconveniences above mentioned, with the idols which proceed from them, may be avoided.

lviii

Let such then be our provision and contemplative prudence for keeping off and dislodging the Idols of the Cave, which grow for the most part either out of the predominance of a favorite subject, or out of an excessive tendency to compare or to distinguish, or out of partiality for particular ages, or out of the largeness or minuteness of the objects contemplated. And generally let every student of nature take this as a rule, —that whatever his mind seizes and dwells upon with peculiar satisfaction is to be held in suspicion, and that so much the more care is to be taken in dealing with such questions to keep the understanding even and clear.

lix

But the *Idols of the Market-place* are the most troublesome of all: idols which have crept into the understanding through the alliances of words and names. For men believe that their reason governs words; but it is also true that words react on the understanding; and this it is that has rendered philosophy and the sciences sophistical and inactive. Now words, being commonly framed and applied according to the capacity of the vulgar, follow those lines of division which are most obvious to the vulgar understanding. And whenever an understanding of greater acuteness or a more diligent observation would alter those lines to suit the true divisions of nature, words stand in the way and resist the change. Whence it comes to pass that the high and formal discussions of learned men end oftentimes in disputes about words and names; with which (according to the use and wisdom of the mathematicians) it would be more prudent to begin, and so by means of definitions reduce them to order. Yet even definitions cannot cure this evil in dealing with natural and material things; since the definitions themselves consist of words, and those words beget others; so that it is necessary to recur to individual instances, and those in due series and order; as I shall say presently when I come to the method and scheme for the formation of notions and axioms.

lx

The idols imposed by words on the understanding are of two kinds. They are either names of things which do not exist (for as there are things left unnamed through lack of observation, so likewise are there names which result from fantastic suppositions and to which nothing in reality corresponds), or they are names of things which exist, but yet confused and ill-defined, and hastily and irregularly derived from realities. Of the former kind are Fortune, the Prime Mover, Planetary Orbits, Elements of Fire, and like fictions which owe their origin to false and idle theories. And this class of idols is more easily expelled, because to get rid of them it is only necessary that all theories should be steadily rejected and dismissed as obsolete.

But the other class, which springs out of a faulty and unskillful abstraction, is intricate and deeply rooted. Let us take for example such a word as *humid*, and see how far the several things which the word is used to signify agree with each other; and we shall find the word *humid* to be nothing else than a mark loosely and confusedly applied to denote a variety of actions which will not bear to be reduced to any constant meaning. For it both signifies that which easily spreads itself round any other body; and that which in itself is indeterminate and cannot solidize; and that which readily yields in every direction; and that which easily divides and scatters itself; and that which easily unites and collects itself; and that which readily flows and is put in motion; and that which readily clings to another body and wets it; and that which is easily reduced to a liquid, or being solid easily melts. Accordingly when you come to apply the word,—if you take it in one sense, flame is humid; if in another, air is not humid; if in another, fine dust is humid; if in another, glass is humid. So that it is easy to see that the notion is taken by abstraction only from water and common and ordinary liquids, without any due verification.

There are however in words certain degrees of distortion and error. One of the least faulty kinds is that of names of substances, especially of lowest species and well-deduced (for the notion of *chalk* and of *mud* is good, of *earth* bad); a more faulty kind is that of actions, as *to generate, to corrupt, to alter;* the most faulty is of qualities (except such as are the immediate objects of the sense) as *heavy, light, rare, dense,* and the like. Yet in all these cases some notions are of necessity a little better than others, in proportion to the greater variety of subjects that fall within the range of the human sense.

lxi

But the *Idols of the Theater* are not innate, nor do they steal into the understanding secretly, but are plainly impressed and received into the mind from the play-books of philosophical systems and the perverted rules of demonstration. To attempt refutations in this case would be merely inconsistent with what I have already said: for since we agree neither upon principles nor upon demonstrations there is no place for argument. And this is so far well, inasmuch as it leaves the honor of the ancients untouched. For they are no wise disparaged—the question between them and me being only as to the way. For as the saying is, the lame man who keeps the right road outstrips the runner who takes a wrong one. Nay it is obvious that when a man runs the wrong way, the more active and swift he is the further he will go astray.

But the course I propose for the discovery of sciences is such as leaves but little to the acuteness and strength of wits, but places all wits and understandings nearly on a level. For as in the drawing of a straight line or a perfect circle, much depends on the steadiness and practice of the hand, if it be done by aim of hand only, but if with the aid of rule or compass, little or nothing; so is it exactly with my plan. But though particular confutations would be of no avail, yet touching the sects and general divisions of such systems I must say something; something also touching the external signs which show that they are unsound; and finally something touching the causes of such great infelicity and of such lasting and general agreement in error; that so the access to truth may be made less difficult, and the human understanding may the more willingly submit to its purgation and dismiss its idols.

lxii

Idols of the Theater, or of Systems, are many, and there can be and perhaps will be yet many more. For were it not that now for many ages men's minds have been busied with religion and theology; and were it not that civil governments, especially monarchies, have been averse to such novelties, even in matters speculative; so that men labor therein to the peril and harming of their fortunes,—not only unrewarded, but exposed also to contempt and envy: doubtless there would have arisen many other philosophical sects like to those which in great variety flourished once among the Greeks. For as on the phenomena of the heavens many hypotheses may be constructed, so likewise (and more also) many various dogmas may be set up and established on the phenomena of philosophy. And in the plays of this philosophical theater you may observe the same thing which is found in the theater of the poets, that stories invented for the stage are more compact and elegant, and more as one would wish them to be, than true stories out of history.

In general however there is taken for the material of philosophy either a great deal out of a few things, or a very little out of many things; so that on both sides philosophy is based on too narrow a foundation of experiment and natural history, and decides on the authority of too few cases. For the rational school of philosophers snatches from experience a variety of common instances, neither duly ascertained nor diligently examined and weighed, and leaves all the rest to meditation and agitation of wit.

There is also another class of philosophers, who having bestowed much diligent and careful labor on a few experiments, have thence made bold to educe and construct systems; wresting all other facts in a strange fashion to conformity therewith.

And there is yet a third class, consisting of those who out of faith and veneration mix their philosophy with theology and traditions; among whom the vanity of some has gone so far aside as to seek the origin of science among spirits and genii. So that this parent stock of errors— this false philosophy—is of three kinds; the *sophistical,* the *empirical,* and the *superstitious.*

lxiii

The most conspicuous example of the first class was Aristotle, who corrupted natural philosophy by his logic: fashioning the world out of categories; assigning to the human soul, the noblest of substances, a genus from words of the second intention; doing the business of density and rarity (which is to make bodies of greater or less dimensions, that is, occupy greater or less spaces), by the frigid distinction of act and power; asserting that single bodies have each a single and proper motion, and that if they participate in any other, then this results from an external cause; and imposing countless other arbitrary restrictions on the nature of things: being always more solicitous to provide an answer to the question and affirm something positive in words, than about the inner truth of things; a failing best shown when his philosophy is compared with other systems of note among the Greeks. For the *homœomera* of Anaxagoras; the atoms of Leucippus and Democritus; the Heaven and Earth of Parmenides; the Strife and Friendship of Empedocles; Heraclitus's doctrine how bodies are resolved into the indifferent nature of fire, and remolded into solids; have all of them some taste of the natural philosopher,—some savor of the nature of things, and experience, and bodies; whereas in the physics of Aristotle you hear hardly anything but the words of logic; which in his metaphysics also, under a more imposing name, and more forsooth as a realist than a nominalist, he has handled over again. Nor let any weight be given to the fact that in his books on animals, and his *Problems,* and other of his treatises, there is frequent dealing with experiments. For he had come to his conclusion before: he did not consult experience, as he should have done, in order to the framing of his decisions and axioms; but having first determined the question according to his will, he then resorts to experience, and bending her into conformity with his placets leads her about like a captive in a procession: so that even on this count he is more guilty than his modern followers, the schoolmen, who have abandoned experience altogether.

lxiv

But the empirical school of philosophy gives birth to dogmas more deformed and monstrous than the sophistical or rational school. For it has its foundations not in the light of common notions (which, though it be a faint and superficial light, is yet in a manner universal, and has reference to many things) but in the narrowness and darkness of a few experiments. To those therefore who are daily busied with these experiments, and have infected their imagination with them, such a philosophy seems probable and all but certain; to all men else incredible and vain. Of this there is a notable instance in the alchemists and their dogmas; though it is hardly to be found elsewhere in these times, except perhaps in the philosophy of Gilbert. Nevertheless with regard to philosophies of this kind there is one caution not to be omitted; for I foresee that if ever men are roused by my admonitions to betake themselves seriously to experiment and bid farewell to sophistical doctrines, then indeed through the premature hurry of the understanding to leap or fly to universals and principles of things, great danger may be apprehended from philosophies of this kind; against which evil we ought even now to prepare.

lxv

But the corruption of philosophy by superstition and an admixture of theology is far more widely spread, and does the greatest harm, whether to entire systems or to their parts. For the human understanding is obnoxious to the influence of the imagination no less than to the influence of common notions. For the contentious and sophistical kind of philosophy ensnares the understanding; but this kind, being fanciful and tumid and half poetical, misleads it more by flattery. For there is in man an ambition of the understanding, no less than of the will, especially in high and lofty spirits.

Of this kind we have among the Greeks a striking example in Pythagoras, though he united with it a coarser and more cumbrous superstition; another in Plato and his school, more dangerous and subtle. It shows itself likewise in parts of other philosophies, in the introduction of abstract forms and final causes and first causes, with the omission in most cases of causes intermediate, and the like. Upon this point the greatest caution should be used. For nothing is so mischievous as the apotheosis of error; and it is a very plague of the understanding for vanity to become the object of veneration. Yet in this vanity some of the moderns have with extreme levity indulged so far as to attempt to found a system of natural philosophy on the first chapters of Genesis, on the book of Job, and other parts of the sacred writings; seeking for the dead among the living: which also makes the inhibition and repression of it the more important, because from this unwholesome mixture of things human and divine there arises not only a fantastic philosophy but also an heretical religion. Very meet it is therefore that we be sober-minded, and give to faith that only which is faith's.

lxvi

So much then for the mischievous authorities of systems, which are founded either on common notions, or on a few experiments, or on superstition. It remains to speak of the faulty subject-matter of contemplations, especially in natural philosophy. Now the human understanding is infected by the sight of what takes place in the mechanical arts, in which the alteration of bodies proceeds chiefly by composition or separation, and so imagines that something similar goes on in the universal nature of things. From this source has flowed the fiction of elements, and of their concourse for the formation of natural bodies. Again, when man contemplates nature working freely, he meets with different species of things, of animals, of plants, of minerals; whence he readily passes into the opinion that there are in nature certain primary forms which nature intends to educe, and that the remaining variety proceeds from hindrances and aberrations of nature in the fulfillment of her work, or from the collision of different species and the transplanting of one into another. To the first of these speculations we owe our primary qualities of the elements; to the other our occult properties and specific virtues; and both of them belong to those empty *compendia* of thought wherein the mind rests, and whereby it is diverted from more solid pursuits. It is to better purpose that the physicians bestow their labor on the secondary qualities of matter, and the operations of attraction, repulsion, attenuation, conspissation, dilatation, astriction, dissipation, maturation, and the like; and were it not that by those two compendia which I have mentioned (elementary qualities, to wit, and specific virtues) they corrupted their correct observations in these other matters,—

either reducing them to first qualities and their subtle and incommensurable mixtures, or not following them out with greater and more diligent observation to third and fourth qualities, but breaking off the scrutiny prematurely,—they had made much greater progress. Nor are powers of this kind (I do not say the same, but similar) to be sought for only in the medicines of the human body, but also in the changes of all other bodies.

But it is a far greater evil that they make the quiescent principles, *wherefrom*, and not the moving principles, *whereby*, things are produced, the object of their contemplation and inquiry. For the former tend to discourse, the latter to works. Nor is there any value in those vulgar distinctions of motion which are observed in the received system of natural philosophy, as generation, corruption, augmentation, diminution, alteration, and local motion. What they mean no doubt is this: If a body, in other respects not changed, be moved from its place, this is *local motion;* if without change of place or essence, it be changed in quality, this is *alteration;* if by reason of the change the mass and quantity of the body do not remain the same, this is *augmentation* or *diminution;* if they be changed to such a degree that they change their very essence and substance and turn to something else, this is *generation* and *corruption.* But all this is merely popular, and does not at all go deep into nature; for these are only measures and limits, not kinds of motion. What they intimate is *how far*, not *by what means*, or *from what source.* For they do not suggest anything with regard either to the desires of bodies or to the development of their parts: it is only when that motion presents the thing grossly and palpably to the sense as different from what it was, that they begin to mark the division. Even when they wish to suggest something with regard to the causes of motion, and to establish a division with reference to them, they introduce with the greatest negligence a distinction between motion natural and violent; a distinction which is itself drawn entirely from a vulgar notion, since all violent motion is also in fact natural; the external efficient simply setting nature working otherwise than it was before. But if, leaving all this, anyone shall observe (for instance) that there is in bodies a desire of mutual contact, so as not to suffer the unity of nature to be quite separated or broken and a vacuum thus made; or if anyone say that there is in bodies a desire of resuming their natural dimensions or tension, so that if compressed within or extended beyond them, they immediately strive to recover themselves, and fall back to their old volume and extent; or if anyone say that there is in bodies a desire of congregating towards masses of kindred nature,—of dense bodies, for instance, towards the globe of the earth, of thin and rare bodies towards the compass of the sky; all these and the like are truly physical kinds of motion;—but those others are entirely logical and scholastic, as is abundantly manifest from this comparison.

Nor again is it a less evil, that in their philosophies and contemplations their labor is spent in investigating and handling the first principles of things and the highest generalities of nature; whereas utility and the means of working result entirely from things intermediate. Hence it is that men cease not from abstracting nature till they come to potential and uninformed matter, nor on the other hand from dissecting nature till they reach the atom; things which, even if true, can do but little for the welfare of mankind.

lxvii

A caution must also be given to the understanding against the intemperance which systems of philosophy manifest in giving or withholding assent; because intemperance of this kind seems to establish idols and in some sort to perpetuate them, leaving no way open to reach and dislodge them.

This excess is of two kinds: the first being manifest in those who are ready in deciding; and render sciences dogmatic and magisterial; the other in those who deny that we can know anything, and so introduce a wandering kind of inquiry that leads to nothing; of which kinds the former subdues, the latter weakens the understanding. For the philosophy of Aristotle, after having by hostile confutations destroyed all the rest (as the Ottomans serve their brothers), has laid down the law on all points: which done, he proceeds himself to raise new questions of his own suggestion, and dispose of them likewise; so that nothing may remain that is not certain and decided,—a practice which holds and is in use among his successors.

The school of Plato, on the other hand, introduced *Acatalepsia*, at first in jest and irony, and in disdain of the older sophists, Protagoras, Hippias, and the rest, who were of nothing else so much ashamed as of seeming to doubt about anything. But the New Academy made a dogma of it, and held it as a tenet. And though theirs is a fairer seeming way than arbitrary decisions; since they say that they by no means destroy all investigation, like Pyrrho and his Refrainers, but allow of some things to be followed as probable, though of none to be maintained as true; yet still when the human mind has once despaired of finding truth, its interest in all things grows fainter; and the result is that men turn aside to pleasant disputations and discourses and roam as it were from object to object, rather than keep on a course of severe inquisition. But, as I said at the beginning and am ever urging, the human senses and understanding, weak as they are, are not to be deprived of their authority, but to be supplied with helps.

lxviii

So much concerning the several classes of idols, and their equipage:
all of which must be renounced and put away with a fixed and solemn
determination, and the understanding thoroughly freed and cleansed;
the entrance into the kingdom of man, founded on the sciences, being
not much other than the entrance into the kingdom of heaven, whereinto none may enter except as a little child.

lxix

But vicious demonstrations are as the strongholds and defenses of
idols; and those we have in logic do little else than make the world the
bond-slave of human thought, and human thought the bond-slave of
words. Demonstrations truly are in effect the philosophies themselves
and the sciences. For such as *they* are, well or ill established, such are
the systems of philosophy and the contemplations which follow. Now in
the whole of the process which leads from the sense and objects to
axioms and conclusions, the demonstrations which we use are deceptive
and incompetent. This process consists of four parts, and has as many
faults. In the first place, the impressions of the sense itself are faulty;
for the sense both fails us and deceives us. But its shortcomings are to
be supplied, and its deceptions to be corrected. Secondly, notions are ill
drawn from the impressions of the senses, and are indefinite and confused, whereas they should be definite and distinctly bounded. Thirdly,
the induction is amiss which infers the principles of sciences by simple
enumeration, and does not, as it ought, employ exclusions and solutions
(or separations) of nature. Lastly, that method of discovery and proof
according to which the most general principles are first established, and
then intermediate axioms are tried and proved by them, is the parent of
error and the curse of all science. Of these things however, which now
I do but touch upon, I will speak more largely, when, having performed
these expiations and purgings of the mind, I come to set forth the true
way for the interpretation of nature.

lxx

But the best demonstration by far is experience, if it go not beyond
the actual experiment. For if it be transferred to other cases which are
deemed similar, unless such transfer be made by a just and orderly process, it is a fallacious thing. But the manner of making experiments which
men now use is blind and stupid. And therefore, wandering and straying
as they do with no settled course, and taking counsel only from things
as they fall out, they fetch a wide circuit and meet with many matters,
but make little progress; and sometimes are full of hope, sometimes are

distracted; and always find that there is something beyond to be sought. For it generally happens that men make their trials carelessly, and as it were in play; slightly varying experiments already known, and, if the thing does not answer, growing weary and abandoning the attempt. And even if they apply themselves to experiments more seriously and earnestly and laboriously, still they spend their labor in working out some one experiment, as Gilbert with the magnet, and the chemists with gold, —a course of proceeding not less unskillful in the design than small in the attempt. For no one successfully investigates the nature of a thing in the thing itself; the inquiry must be enlarged, so as to become more general.

And even when they seek to educe some science or theory from their experiments, they nevertheless almost always turn aside with overhasty and unseasonable eagerness to practice; not only for the sake of the uses and fruits of the practice, but from impatience to obtain in the shape of some new work an assurance for themselves that it is worth their while to go on; and also to show themselves off to the world, and so raise the credit of the business in which they are engaged. Thus, like Atalanta, they go aside to pick up the golden apple, but meanwhile they interrupt their course, and let the victory escape them. But in the true course of experience, and in carrying it on to the effecting of new works, the divine wisdom and order must be our pattern. Now God on the first day of creation created light only, giving to that work an entire day, in which no material substance was created. So must we likewise from experience of every kind first endeavor to discover true causes and axioms; and seek for experiments of Light, not for experiments of Fruit. For axioms rightly discovered and established supply practice with its instruments, not one by one, but in clusters, and draw after them trains and troops of works. Of the paths however of experience, which no less than the paths of judgment are impeded and beset, I will speak hereafter; here I have only mentioned ordinary experimental research as a bad kind of demonstration. But now the order of the matter in hand leads me to add something both as to those *signs* which I lately mentioned,—signs that the system of philosophy and contemplation in use are in a bad condition,—and also as to the *causes* of what seems at first so strange and incredible. For a knowledge of the signs prepares assent; an explanation of the causes removes the marvel: which two things will do much to render the extirpation of idols from the understanding more easy and gentle.

lxxi

The sciences which we possess come for the most part from the Greeks. For what has been added by Roman, Arabic, or later writers is

not much nor of much importance: and whatever it is, it is built on the
foundation of Greek discoveries. Now the wisdom of the Greeks was
professorial and much given to disputations; a kind of wisdom most
adverse to the inquisition of truth. Thus that name of Sophists, which
by those who would be thought philosophers was in contempt cast back
upon and so transferred to the ancient rhetoricians, Gorgias, Protag
oras, Hippias, Polus, does indeed suit the entire class, Plato, Aristotle,
Zeno, Epicurus, Theophrastus, and their successors Chrysippus, Car-
nades, and the rest. There was this difference only, that the former
class was wandering and mercenary, going about from town to town,
putting up their wisdom to sale, and taking a price for it; while the latter was more pompous and dignified, as composed of men who had fixed
abodes, and who opened schools and taught their philosophy without reward. Still both sorts, though in other respects unequal, were professorial; both turned the matter into disputations, and set up and battled
for philosophical sects and heresies; so that their doctrines were for the
most part (as Dionysius not unaptly rallied Plato) "the talk of idle old
men to ignorant youths." But the elder of the Greek philosophers,
Empedocles, Anaxagoras, Leucippus, Democritus, Parmenides, Heraclitus, Xenophanes, Philolaus, and the rest (I omit Pythagoras as a
mystic), did not, so far as we know, open schools; but more silently
and severely and simply,—that is, with less affectation and parade,—
betook themselves to the inquisition of truth. And therefore they were
in my judgment more successful; only that their works were in the
course of time obscured by those slighter persons who had more which
suits and pleases the capacity and tastes of the vulgar: time, like a
river, bringing down to us things which are light and puffed up, but
letting weighty matters sink. Still even they were not altogether free
from the failing of their nation; but leaned too much to the ambition
and vanity of founding a sect and catching popular applause. But the
inquisition of truth must be despaired of when it turns aside to trifles of
this kind. Nor should we omit that judgment, or rather divination, which
was given concerning the Greeks by the Egyptian priest,—that "they
were always boys, without antiquity of knowledge or knowledge of antiquity." Assuredly they have that which is characteristic of boys; they
are prompt to prattle, but cannot generate; for their wisdom abounds in
words but is barren of works. And therefore the signs which are taken
from the origin and birthplace of the received philosophy are not good.

lxxii

Nor does the character of the time and age yield much better signs
than the character of the country and nation. For at that period there
was but a narrow and meager knowledge either of time or place; which

is the worst thing that can be, especially for those who rest all on experience. For they had no history, worthy to be called history, that went back a thousand years; but only fables and rumors of antiquity. And of the regions and districts of the world they knew but a small portion; giving indiscriminately the name of Scythians to all in the North, of Celts to all in the West; knowing nothing of Africa beyond the hither side of Ethiopia, of Asia beyond the Ganges; much less were they acquainted with the provinces of the New World, even by hearsay or any well-founded rumor; nay, a multitude of climates and zones, wherein innumerable nations breathe and live, were pronounced by them to be uninhabitable; and the travels of Democritus, Plato, and Pythagoras, which were rather suburban excursions than distant journeys, were talked of as something great. In our times on the other hand both many parts of the New World and the limits on every side of the Old World are known, and our stock of experience has increased to an infinite amount. Wherefore if (like astrologers) we draw signs from the season of their nativity or birth, nothing great can be predicted of those systems of philosophy.

lxxiii

Of all signs there is none more certain or more noble than that taken from fruits. For fruits and works are as it were sponsors and sureties for the truth of philosophies. Now, from all these systems of the Greeks, and their ramifications through particular sciences there can hardly after the lapse of so many years be adduced a single experiment which tends to relieve and benefit the condition of man, and which can with truth be referred to the speculations and theories of philosophy. And Celsus ingenuously and wisely owns as much, when he tells us that the experimental part of medicine was first discovered, and that afterwards men philosophized about it, and hunted for and assigned causes; and not by an inverse process that philosophy and the knowledge of causes led to the discovery and development of the experimental part. And therefore it was not strange that among the Egyptians, who rewarded inventors with divine honors and sacred rites, there were more images of brutes than of men; inasmuch as brutes by their natural instinct have produced many discoveries, whereas men by discussion and the conclusions of reason have given birth to few or none.

Some little has indeed been produced by the industry of chemists; but it has been produced accidentally and in passing, or else by a kind of variation of experiments, such as mechanics use; and not by any art or theory; for the theory which they have devised rather confuses the experiments than aids them. They too who have busied themselves with natural magic, as they call it, have but few discoveries to show, and

those trifling and imposture-like. Wherefore, as in religion we are
warned to show our faith by works, so in philosophy by the same rule
the system should be judged of by its fruits, and pronounced frivolous if
it be barren; more especially if, in place of fruits of grape and olive, it
bear thorns and briars of dispute and contention.

lxxiv

Signs also are to be drawn from the increase and progress of systems
and sciences. For what is founded on nature grows and increases; while
what is founded on opinion varies but increases not. If therefore those
doctrines had not plainly been like a plant torn up from its roots, but
had remained attached to the womb of nature and continued to draw
nourishment from her, that could never have come to pass which we
have seen now for twice a thousand years; namely, that the sciences
stand where they did and remain almost in the same condition; receiving
no noticeable increase, but on the contrary, thriving most under their
first founder, and then declining. Whereas in the mechanical arts, which
are founded on nature and the light of experience, we see the contrary
happen, for these (as long as they are popular) are continually thriving
and growing, as having in them a breath of life; at first rude, then convenient, afterwards adorned, and at all times advancing.

lxxv

There is still another sign remaining (if sign it can be called, when it
is rather testimony, nay, of all testimony the most valid); I mean the
confession of the very authorities whom men now follow. For even they
who lay down the law on all things so confidently, do still in their more
sober moods fall to complaints of the subtlety of nature, the obscurity of
things, and the weakness of the human mind. Now if this were all they
did, some perhaps of a timid disposition might be deterred from further
search, while others of a more ardent and hopeful spirit might be whet-
ted and incited to go on farther. But not content to speak for themselves, whatever is beyond their own or their master's knowledge or
reach they set down as beyond the bounds of possibility, and pronounce,
as if on the authority of their art, that it cannot be known or done;
thus most presumptuously and invidiously turning the weakness of their
own discoveries into a calumny on nature herself, and the despair of the
rest of the world. Hence the school of the New Academy, which held
Acatalepsia as a tenet and doomed men to perpetual darkness. Hence
the opinion that forms or true differences of things (which are in fact
laws of pure act) are past finding out and beyond the reach of man.
Hence too those opinions in the department of action and operation; as
that the heat of the sun and of fire are quite different in kind,—lest men

should imagine that by the operations of fire anything like the works of nature can be educed and formed. Hence the notion that composition only is the work of man, and mixture of none but nature,—lest men should expect from art some power of generating or transforming natural bodies. By this sign, therefore, men will easily take warning not to mix up their fortunes and labors with dogmas not only despaired of but dedicated to despair.

lxxvi

Neither is this other sign to be omitted;—that formerly there existed among philosophers such great disagreement, and such diversities in the schools themselves; a fact which sufficiently shows that the road from the senses to the understanding was not skillfully laid out, when the same groundwork of philosophy (the nature of things to wit) was torn and split up into such vague and multifarious errors. And although in these times disagreements and diversities of opinion on first principles and entire systems are for the most part extinguished, still on parts of philosophy there remain innumerable questions and disputes, so that it plainly appears that neither in the systems themselves nor in the modes of demonstration is there anything certain or sound.

lxxvii

And as for the general opinion that in the philosophy of Aristotle at any rate there is great agreement; since after its publication the systems of older philosophers died away, while in the times which followed nothing better was found; so that it seems to have been so well laid and established as to have drawn both ages in its train; I answer in the first place, that the common notion of the falling off of the old systems upon the publication of Aristotle's works is a false one; for long afterwards, down even to the times of Cicero and subsequent ages, the works of the old philosophers still remained. But in the times which followed, when on the inundation of barbarians into the Roman empire human learning had suffered shipwreck, then the systems of Aristotle and Plato, like planks of lighter and less solid material, floated on the waves of time, and were preserved. Upon the point of consent also men are deceived, if the matter be looked into more keenly. For true consent is that which consists in the coincidence of free judgments, after due examination. But far the greater number of those who have assented to the philosophy of Aristotle have addicted themselves thereto from prejudgment and upon the authority of others; so that it is a following and going along together, rather than consent. But even if it had been a real and widespread consent, still so little ought consent to be deemed a sure and solid confirmation, that it is in fact a strong presumption the other way.

For the worst of all auguries is from consent in matters intellectual (divinity excepted, and politics where there is right of vote). For nothing pleases the many unless it strikes the imagination, or binds the understanding with the bands of common notions, as I have already said. We may very well transfer therefore from moral to intellectual matters, the saying of Phocion, that if the multitude assent and applaud men ought immediately to examine themselves as to what blunder or fault they may have committed. This sign therefore is one of the most unfavorable. And so much for this point; namely, that the signs of truth and soundness in the received systems and sciences are not good; whether they be drawn from their origin, or from their fruits, or from their progress, or from the confessions of their founders, or from general consent.

lxxviii

I now come to the *causes* of these errors, and of so long a continuance in them through so many ages; which are very many and very potent; —that all wonder how these considerations which I bring forward should have escaped men's notice till now, may cease; and the only wonder be, how now at last they should have entered into any man's head and become the subject of his thoughts; which truly I myself esteem as the result of some happy accident, rather than of any excellence of faculty in me; a birth of time rather than a birth of wit. Now, in the first place, those so many ages, if you weigh the case truly, shrink into a very small compass. For out of the five and twenty centuries over which the memory and learning of men extends, you can hardly pick out six that were fertile in sciences or favorable to their development. In times no less than in regions there are wastes and deserts. For only three revolutions and periods of learning can properly be reckoned; one among the Greeks, the second among the Romans, and the last among us, that is to say, the nations of Western Europe; and to each of these hardly two centuries can justly be assigned. The intervening ages of the world, in respect of any rich or flourishing growth of the sciences, were unprosperous. For neither the Arabians nor the schoolmen need be mentioned; who in the intermediate times rather crushed the sciences with a multitude of treatises, than increased their weight. And therefore the first cause of so meager a progress in the sciences is duly and orderly referred to the narrow limits of the time that has been favorable to them.

lxxix

In the second place there presents itself a cause of great weight in all ways; namely, that during those very ages in which the wits and learning of men have flourished most, or indeed flourished at all, the least part of their diligence was given to natural philosophy. Yet this very philosophy it is that ought to be esteemed the great mother of the sciences. For all arts and all sciences, if torn from this root, though they may be polished and shaped and made fit for use, yet they will hardly grow. Now it is well known that after the Christian religion was received and grew strong, by far the greater number of the best wits applied themselves to theology; that to this both the highest rewards were offered, and helps of all kinds most abundantly supplied; and that this devotion to theology chiefly occupied that third portion or epoch of time among us Europeans of the West; and the more so because about the same time both literature began to flourish and religious controversies to spring up. In the age before, on the other hand, during the continuance of the second period among the Romans, the meditations and labors of philosophers were principally employed and consumed on moral philosophy, which to the heathen was as theology to us. Moreover in those times the greatest wits applied themselves very generally to public affairs; the magnitude of the Roman empire requiring the services of a great number of persons. Again, the age in which natural philosophy was seen to flourish most among the Greeks, was but a brief particle of time; for in early ages the Seven Wise Men, as they were called (all except Thales) applied themselves to morals and politics; and in later times, when Socrates had drawn down philosophy from heaven to earth, moral philosophy became more fashionable than ever, and diverted the minds of men from the philosophy of nature.

Nay, the very period itself in which inquiries concerning nature flourished, was by controversies and the ambitious display of new opinions corrupted and made useless. Seeing therefore that during those three periods natural philosophy was in a great degree either neglected or hindered, it is no wonder if men made but small advance in that to which they were not attending.

lxxx

To this it may be added that natural philosophy, even among those who have attended to it, has scarcely ever possessed, especially in these later times, a disengaged and whole man (unless it were some monk studying in his cell, or some gentleman in his country house), but that it has been made merely a passage and bridge to something else. And so this great mother of the sciences has with strange indignity been degraded to the offices of a servant; having to attend on the business of medicine or mathematics, and likewise to wash and imbue youthful and unripe wits with a sort of first dye, in order that they may be the fitter to receive another afterwards. Meanwhile let no man look for much progress in the sciences—especially in the practical part of them—unless natural philosophy be carried on and applied to particular sciences, and

particular sciences be carried back again to natural philosophy. For
want of this, astronomy, optics, music, a number of mechanical arts,
medicine itself,—nay, what one might more wonder at, moral and political philosophy, and the logical sciences,—altogether lack profoundness,
and merely glide along the surface and variety of things; because after
these particular sciences have been once distributed and established,
they are no more nourished by natural philosophy; which might have
drawn out of the true contemplation of motions, rays, sounds, texture
and configuration of bodies, affections, and intellectual perceptions, the
means of imparting to them fresh strength and growth. And therefore it
is nothing strange if the sciences grow not, seeing they are parted from
their roots.

lxxxi

Again there is another great and powerful cause why the sciences have
made but little progress; which is this. It is not possible to run a course
aright when the goal itself has not been rightly placed. Now the true
and lawful goal of the sciences is none other than this: that human life
be endowed with new discoveries and powers. But of this the great majority have no feeling, but are merely hireling and professorial; except
when it occasionally happens that some workman of acuter wit and
covetous of honor applies himself to a new invention; which he mostly
does at the expense of his fortunes. But in general, so far are men from
proposing to themselves to augment the mass of arts and sciences, that
from the mass already at hand they neither take nor look for anything
more than what they may turn to use in their lectures, or to gain, or to
reputation, or to some similar advantage. And if any one out of all the
multitude court science with honest affection and for her own sake, yet
even with him the object will be found to be rather the variety of contemplations and doctrines than the severe and rigid search after truth.
And if by chance there be one who seeks after truth in earnest, yet even
he will propose to himself such a kind of truth as shall yield satisfaction
to the mind and understanding in rendering causes for things long since
discovered, and not the truth which shall lead to new assurance of works
and new light of axioms. If then the end of the sciences has not yet been
well placed, it is not strange that men have erred as to the means.

lxxxii

And as men have misplaced the end and goal of the sciences; so again,
even if they had placed it right, yet they have chosen a way to it which
is altogether erroneous and impassable. And an astonishing thing it is to
one who rightly considers the matter, that no mortal should have seriously applied himself to the opening and laying out of a road for the

human understanding direct from the sense, by a course of experiment orderly conducted and well built up; but that all has been left either to the mist of tradition, or the whirl and eddy of argument, or the fluctuations and mazes of chance and of vague and ill-digested experience. Now let any man soberly and diligently consider what the way is by which men have been accustomed to proceed in the investigation and discovery of things; and in the first place he will no doubt remark a method of discovery very simple and inartificial; which is the most ordinary method, and is no more than this. When a man addresses himself to discover something, he first seeks out and sets before him all that has been said about it by others; then he begins to meditate for himself; and so by much agitation and working of the wit solicits and as it were evokes his own spirit to give him oracles: which method has no foundation at all, but rests only upon opinions and is carried about with them.

Another may perhaps call in logic to discover it for him; but that has no relation to the matter except in name. For logical invention does not discover principles and chief axioms, of which arts are composed, but only such things as appear to be consistent with them. For if you grow more curious and importunate and busy, and question her of probations and invention of principles or primary axioms, her answer is well known: she refers you to the faith you are bound to give to the principles of each separate art.

There remains simple experience; which, if taken as it comes, is called accident; if sought for, experiment. But this kind of experience is no better than a broom without its band, as the saying is;—a mere groping, as of men in the dark, that feel all round them for the chance of finding their way; when they had much better wait for daylight, or light a candle, and then go. But the true method of experience on the contrary first lights the candle, and then by means of the candle shows the way; commencing as it does with experience duly ordered and digested, not bungling or erratic, and from it educing axioms, and from established axioms again new experiments; even as it was not without order and method that the divine word operated on the created mass. Let men therefore cease to wonder that the course of science is not yet wholly run, seeing that they have gone altogether astray; either leaving and abandoning experience entirely, or losing their way in it and wandering round and round as in a labyrinth; whereas a method rightly ordered leads by an unbroken route through the woods of experience to the open ground of axioms.

lxxxiii

This evil however has been strangely increased by an opinion or conceit, which though of long standing is vain and hurtful; namely, that the dignity of the human mind is impaired by long and close intercourse with experiments and particulars, subject to sense and bound in matter; especially as they are laborious to search, ignoble to meditate, harsh to deliver, illiberal to practice, infinite in number, and minute in subtlety. So that it has come at length to this, that the true way is not merely deserted, but shut out and stopped up; experience being, I do not say abandoned or badly managed, but rejected with disdain.

lxxxiv

Again, men have been kept back as by a kind of enchantment from progress in the sciences by reverence for antiquity, by the authority of men accounted great in philosophy, and then by general consent. Of the last I have spoken above.

As for antiquity, the opinion touching it which men entertain is quite a negligent one, and scarcely consonant with the word itself. For the old age of the world is to be accounted the true antiquity; and this is the attribute of our own times, not of that earlier age of the world in which the ancients lived; and which, though in respect of us it was the elder, yet in respect of the world it was the younger. And truly as we look for greater knowledge of human things and a riper judgment in the old man than in the young, because of his experience and of the number and variety of the things which he has seen and heard and thought of; so in like manner from our age, if it but knew its own strength and chose to essay and exert it, much more might fairly be expected than from the ancient times, inasmuch as it is a more advanced age of the world, and stored and stocked with infinite experiments and observations.

Nor must it go for nothing that by the distant voyages and travels which have become frequent in our times, many things in nature have been laid open and discovered which may let in new light upon philosophy. And surely it would be disgraceful if, while the regions of the material globe,—that is, of the earth, of the sea, and of the stars,—have been in our times laid widely open and revealed, the intellectual globe should remain shut up within the narrow limits of old discoveries.

And with regard to authority, it shows a feeble mind to grant so much to authors and yet deny time his rights, who is the author of authors, nay rather of all authority. For rightly is truth called the daughter of time, not of authority. It is no wonder therefore if those enchantments of antiquity and authority and consent have so bound up men's powers that they have been made impotent (like persons bewitched) to accompany with the nature of things.

lxxxv

Nor is it only the admiration of antiquity, authority, and consent, that has forced the industry of man to rest satisfied with the discoveries already made; but also an admiration for the works themselves of which the human race has long been in possession. For when a man looks at the variety and the beauty of the provision which the mechanical arts have brought together for men's use, he will certainly be more inclined to admire the wealth of man than to feel his wants: not considering that the original observations and operations of nature (which are the life and moving principle of all that variety) are not many nor deeply fetched, and that the rest is but patience, and the subtle and ruled motion of the hand and instruments;—as the making of clocks (for instance) is certainly a subtle and exact work: their wheels seem to imitate the celestial orbs, and their alternating and orderly motion, the pulse of animals: and yet all this depends on one or two axioms of nature.

Again, if you observe the refinement of the liberal arts, or even that which relates to the mechanical preparation of natural substances; and take notice of such things as the discovery in astronomy of the motions of the heavens, of harmony in music, of the letters of the alphabet (to this day not in use among the Chinese) in grammar: or again in things mechanical, the discovery of the works of Bacchus and Ceres—that is, of the arts of preparing wine and beer, and of making bread; the discovery once more of the delicacies of the table, of distillations and the like; and if you likewise bear in mind the long periods which it has taken to bring these things to their present degree of perfection (for they are all ancient except distillation), and again (as has been said of clocks) how little they owe to observations and axioms of nature, and how easily and obviously and as it were by casual suggestion they may have been discovered; you will easily cease from wondering, and on the contrary will pity the condition of mankind, seeing that in a course of so many ages there has been so great a dearth and barrenness of arts and inventions. And yet these very discoveries which we have just mentioned, are older than philosophy and intellectual arts. So that, if the truth must be spoken, when the rational and dogmatical sciences began the discovery of useful works came to an end.

And again, if a man turn from the workshop to the library, and wonder at the immense variety of books he sees there, let him but examine and diligently inspect their matter and contents, and his wonder will assuredly be turned the other way; for after observing their endless repetitions, and how men are ever saying and doing what has been said and done before, he will pass from admiration of the variety to astonishment at the poverty and scantiness of the subjects which till now have occupied and possessed the minds of men.

And if again he descend to the consideration of those arts which are

deemed curious rather than safe, and look more closely into the works of
the alchemists or the magicians, he will be in doubt perhaps whether he
ought rather to laugh over them or to weep. For the alchemist nurses
eternal hope, and when the thing fails, lays the blame upon some error
of his own; fearing either that he has not sufficiently understood the
words of his art or of his authors (whereupon he turns to tradition and
auricular whispers), or else that in his manipulations he has made some
slip of a scruple in weight or a moment in time (whereupon he repeats
his trials to infinity); and when meanwhile among the chances of experiment he lights upon some conclusions either in aspect new or for
utility not contemptible, he takes these for earnest of what is to come,
and feeds his mind upon them, and magnifies them to the most, and
supplies the rest in hope. Not but that alchemists have made a good
many discoveries, and presented men with useful inventions. But their
case may be well compared to the fable of the old man, who bequeathed
to his sons gold buried in a vineyard, pretending not to know the exact
spot; whereupon the sons applied themselves diligently to the digging of
the vineyard and though no gold was found there, yet the vintage by
that digging was made more plentiful.

Again the students of natural magic, who explain everything by sympathies and antipathies, have in their idle and most slothful conjectures
ascribed to substances wonderful virtues and operations; and if ever
they have produced works, they have been such as aim rather at admiration and novelty than at utility and fruit.

In superstitious magic on the other hand (if of this also we must
speak), it is especially to be observed that they are but subjects of a
certain and definite kind wherein the curious and superstitious arts, in
all nations and ages, and religions also, have worked or played. These
therefore we may pass. Meanwhile it is nowise strange if opinion of
plenty has been the cause of want.

lxxxvi

Further, this admiration of men for knowledges and arts,—an admiration in itself weak enough, and well-nigh childish,—has been increased
by the craft and artifices of those who have handled and transmitted
sciences. For they set them forth with such ambition and parade, and
bring them into the view of the world so fashioned and masked, as if
they were complete in all parts and finished. For if you look at the
method of them and the divisions, they seem to embrace and comprise
everything which can belong to the subject. And although these divisions are ill filled out and are but as empty cases, still to the common
mind they present the form and plan of a perfect science. But the first

and most ancient seekers after truth were wont, with better faith and better fortune too, to throw the knowledge which they gathered from the contemplation of things, and which they meant to store up for use, into aphorisms; that is, into short and scattered sentences, not linked together by an artificial method; and did not pretend or profess to embrace the entire art. But as the matter now is, it is nothing strange if men do not seek to advance in things delivered to them as long since perfect and complete.

lxxxvii

Moreover the ancient systems have received no slight accession of reputation and credit from the vanity and levity of those who have propounded new ones; especially in the active and practical department of natural philosophy. For there have not been wanting talkers and dreamers who, partly from credulity, partly in imposture, have loaded mankind with promises, offering and announcing the prolongation of life, the retardation of age, the alleviation of pain, the repairing of natural defects, the deceiving of the senses; arts of binding and inciting the affections, of illuminating and exalting the intellectual faculties, of transmuting substances, of strengthening and multiplying motions at will, of making impressions and alterations in the air, of bringing down and procuring celestial influences, arts of divining things future, and bringing things distant near, and revealing things secret; and many more. But with regard to these lavish promisers, this judgment would not be far amiss; that there is as much difference in philosophy between their vanities and true arts, as there is in history between the exploits of Julius Caesar or Alexander the Great, and the exploits of Amadis of Gaul or Arthur of Britain. For it is true that those illustrious generals really did greater things than these shadowy heroes are even feigned to have done; but they did them by means and ways of action not fabulous or monstrous. Yet surely it is not fair that the credit of true history should be lessened because it has sometimes been injured and wronged by fables. Meanwhile it is not to be wondered at, if a great prejudice is raised against new propositions, especially when works are also mentioned, because of those imposters who have attempted the like; since their excess of vanity, and the disgust it has bred, have their effect still in the destruction of all greatness of mind in enterprises of this kind.

lxxxviii

Far more however has knowledge suffered from littleness of spirit and the smallness and slightness of the tasks which human industry has proposed to itself. And what is worst of all, this very littleness of spirit comes with a certain air of arrogance and superiority.

For in the first place there is found in all arts one general device, which has now become familiar,—that the author lays the weakness of his art to the charge of nature: whatever his art cannot attain he sets down on the authority of the same art to be in nature impossible. And truly no art can be condemned if it be judge itself. Moreover the philosophy which is now in vogue embraces and cherishes certain tenets, the purpose of which (if it be diligently examined) is to persuade men that nothing difficult, nothing by which nature may be commanded and subdued, can be expected from art or human labor; as with respect to the doctrine that the heat of the sun and of fire differ in kind, and to that other concerning mixture, has been already observed. Which things, if they be noted accurately, tend wholly to the unfair circumscription of human power, and to a deliberate and factitious despair; which not only disturbs the auguries of hope, but also cuts the sinews and spur of industry, and throws away the chances of experience itself; and all for the sake of having their art thought perfect, and for the miserable vainglory of making it believed that whatever has not yet been discovered and comprehended can never be discovered or comprehended hereafter.

And even if a man apply himself fairly to facts, and endeavor to find out something new, yet he will confine his aim and intention to the investigation and working out of some one discovery and no more; such as the nature of the magnet, the ebb and flow of the sea, the system of the heavens, and things of this kind, which seem to be in some measure secret, and have hitherto been handled without much success. Whereas it is most unskillful to investigate the nature of any thing in the thing itself; seeing that the same nature which appears in some things to be latent and hidden is in others manifest and palpable; wherefore in the former it produces wonder, in the latter excites no attention; as we find it in the nature of consistency, which in wood or stone is not observed, but is passed over under the appellation of solidity, without further inquiry as to why separation or solution of continuity is avoided; while in the case of bubbles, which form themselves into certain pellicles, curiously shaped into hemispheres, so that the solution of continuity is avoided for a moment, it is thought a subtle matter. In fact what in some things is accounted a secret has in others a manifest and well-known nature, which will never be recognized as long as the experiments and thoughts of men are engaged on the former only.

But generally speaking, in mechanics old discoveries pass for new, if a man does but refine or embellish them, or unite several in one, or couple them better with their use, or make the work in greater or less volume than it was before, or the like.

Thus then it is no wonder if noble inventions and worthy of mankind have not been brought to light, when men have been contented and delighted with such trifling and puerile tasks, and have even fancied that in them they have been endeavoring after, if not accomplishing, some great matter.

lxxxix

Neither is it to be forgotten that in every age natural philosophy has had a troublesome adversary and hard to deal with; namely, superstition, and the blind and immoderate zeal of religion. For we see among the Greeks that those who first proposed to men's then uninitiated ears the natural causes for thunder and for storms, were thereupon found guilty of impiety. Nor was much more forbearance shown by some of the ancient fathers of the Christian church to those who on most convincing grounds (such as no one in his senses would now think of contradicting) maintained that the earth was round, and of consequence asserted the existence of the antipodes.

Moreover, as things now are, to discourse of nature is made harder and more perilous by the summaries and systems of the schoolmen; who having reduced theology into regular order as well as they were able, and fashioned it into the shape of an art, ended in incorporating the contentious and thorny philosophy of Aristotle, more than was fit, with the body of religion.

To the same result, though in a different way, tend the speculations of those who have taken upon them to deduce the truth of the Christian religion from the principles of philosophers, and to confirm it by their authority; pompously solemnizing this union of the sense and faith as a lawful marriage, and entertaining men's minds with a pleasing variety of matter, but all the while disparaging things divine by mingling them with things human. Now in such mixtures of theology with philosophy only the received doctrines of philosophy are included; while new ones, albeit changes for the better, are all but expelled and exterminated.

Lastly, you will find that by the simpleness of certain divines, access to any philosophy, however pure, is well nigh closed. Some are weakly afraid lest a deeper search into nature should transgress the permitted limits of sober-mindedness; wrongfully wresting and transferring what is said in holy writ against those who pry into sacred mysteries, to the hidden things of nature, which are barred by no prohibition. Others with more subtlety surmise and reflect that if second causes are unknown everything can more readily be referred to the divine hand and rod; a point in which they think religion greatly concerned; which is in fact nothing else but to seek to gratify God with a lie. Others fear from past example that movements and changes in philosophy will end in assaults on religion. And others again appear apprehensive that in the investigation of nature something may be found to subvert or at least shake the authority of religion, especially with the unlearned. But these two last fears seem to me to savor utterly of carnal wisdom; as if men in the recesses and secret thoughts of their hearts doubted and distrusted the strength of religion and the empire of faith over the sense, and therefore feared that the investigation of truth in nature might be dangerous to them. But if the matter be truly considered, natural philosophy is after the word of God at once the surest medicine against superstition, and the most approved nourishment for faith, and therefore she is rightly given to religion as her most faithful handmaid, since the one displays the will of God, the other his power. For he did not err who said "Ye err in that ye know not the Scriptures and the power of God," thus coupling and blending in an indissoluble bond information concerning his will and meditation concerning his power. Meanwhile it is not surprising if the growth of natural philosophy is checked, when religion, the thing which has most power over men's minds, has by the simpleness and incautious zeal of certain persons been drawn to take part against her.

XC

Again, in the customs and institutions of schools, academies, colleges, and similar bodies destined for the abode of learned men and the cultivation of learning, everything is found adverse to the progress of science. For the lectures and exercises there are so ordered, that to think or speculate on anything out of the common way can hardly occur to any man. And if one or two have the boldness to use any liberty of judgment, they must undertake the task all by themselves; they can have no advantage from the company of others. And if they can endure this also, they will find their industry and largeness of mind no slight hindrance to their fortune. For the studies of men in these places are confined and as it were imprisoned in the writings of certain authors, from whom if any man dissent he is straightway arraigned as a turbulent person and an innovator. But surely there is a great distinction between matters of state and the arts; for the danger from new motion and from new light is not the same. In matters of state a change even for the better is distrusted, because it unsettles what is established; these things resting on authority, consent, fame and opinion, not on demonstration. But arts and sciences should be like mines, where the noise of new works and further advances is heard on every side. But though the matter be so according to right reason, it is not so acted on in practice; and the points above mentioned in the administration and government of learning put a severe restraint upon the advancement of the sciences.

xci

Nay, even if that jealousy were to cease, still it is enough to check the growth of science, that efforts and labors in this field go unrewarded. For it does not rest with the same persons to cultivate sciences and to reward them. The growth of them comes from great wits; the prizes and rewards of them are in the hands of the people, or of great persons, who are but in very few cases even moderately learned. Moreover this kind of progress is not only unrewarded with prizes and substantial benefits; it has not even the advantage of popular applause. For it is a greater matter than the generality of men can take in, and is apt to be overwhelmed and extinguished by the gales of popular opinions. And it is nothing strange if a thing not held in honor does not prosper.

xcii

But by far the greatest obstacle to the progress of science and to the undertaking of new tasks and provinces therein, is found in this—that men despair and think things impossible. For wise and serious men are wont in these matters to be altogether distrustful; considering with themselves the obscurity of nature, the shortness of life, the deceitfulness of the senses, the weakness of the judgment, the difficulty of experiment and the like; and so supposing that in the revolution of time and of the ages of the world the sciences have their ebbs and flows; that at one season they grow and flourish, at another wither and decay, yet in such sort that when they have reached a certain point and condition they can advance no further. If therefore any one believes or promises more, they think this comes of an ungoverned and unripened mind, and that such attempts have prosperous beginnings, become difficult as they go on, and end in confusion. Now since these are thoughts which naturally present themselves to grave men and of great judgment, we must take good heed that we be not led away by our love for a most fair and excellent object to relax or diminish the severity of our judgment; we must observe diligently what encouragement dawns upon us and from what quarter; and, putting aside the lighter breeze of hope, we must thoroughly sift and examine those which promise greater steadiness and constancy. Nay, and we must take state-prudence too into our counsels, whose rule is to distrust, and to take the less favorable view of human affairs. I am now therefore to speak touching *hope;* especially as I am not a dealer in promises, and wish neither to force nor to ensnare men's judgments, but to lead them by the hand with their good will. And though the strongest means of inspiring hope will be to bring men to particulars; especially to particulars digested and arranged in my Tables of Discovery (the subject partly of the second, but much more of the

fourth part of my *Instauration*), since this is not merely the promise of
the thing but the thing itself: nevertheless that everything may be done
with gentleness, I will proceed with my plan of preparing men's minds;
of which preparation to give hope is no unimportant part. For without it
the rest tends rather to make men sad (by giving them a worse and
meaner opinion of things as they are than they now have, and making
them more fully to feel and know the unhappiness of their own condition) than to induce any alacrity or to whet their industry in making
trial. And therefore it is fit that I publish and set forth those conjectures
of mine which make hope in this matter reasonable: just as Columbus
did, before that wonderful voyage of his across the Atlantic, when he
gave the reasons for his conviction that new lands and continents might
be discovered besides those which were known before; which reasons,
though rejected at first, were afterwards made good by experience, and
were the causes and beginnings of great events.

xciii

The beginning is from God: for the business which is in hand, having
the character of good so strongly impressed upon it, appears manifestly
to proceed from God, who is the Author of Good, and the Father of
Lights. Now in divine operations even the smallest beginnings lead of a
certainty to their end. And as it was said of spiritual things, "The kingdom of God cometh not with observation," so is it in all the greater works
of Divine Providence; everything glides on smoothly and noiselessly,
and the work is fairly going on before men are aware that it has begun.
Nor should the prophecy of Daniel be forgotten, touching the last ages
of the world:—"Many shall go to and fro, and knowledge shall be
increased;" clearly intimating that the thorough passage of the world
(which now by so many distant voyages seems to be accomplished, or
in course of accomplishment), and the advancement of the sciences, are
destined by fate, that is, by Divine Providence, to meet in the same age.

xciv

Next comes a consideration of the greatest importance as an argument of hope; I mean that drawn from the errors of past time, and of
the ways hitherto trodden. For most excellent was the censure once
passed upon a government that had been unwisely administered. "That
which is the worst thing in reference to the past, ought to be regarded as
best for the future. For if you had done all that your duty demanded,
and yet your affairs were no better, you would not have even a hope left
you that further improvement is possible. But now, when your misfortunes are owing, not to the force of circumstances, but to your own

errors, you may hope that by dismissing or correcting these errors, a great change may be made for the better." In like manner, if during so long a course of years men had kept the true road for discovering and cultivating sciences, and had yet been unable to make further progress therein, bold doubtless and rash would be the opinion that further progress is possible. But if the road itself has been mistaken, and men's labor spent on unfit objects, it follows that the difficulty has its rise not in things themselves, which are not in our power, but in the human understanding, and the use and application thereof, which admits of remedy and medicine. It will be of great use therefore to set forth what these errors are; for as many impediments as there have been in times past from this cause, so many arguments are there of hope for the time to come. And although they have been partly touched before, I think fit here also, in plain and simple words, to represent them.

xcv

Those who have handled sciences have been either men of experiment or men of dogmas. The men of experiment are like the ant; they only collect and use: the reasoners resemble spiders, who make cobwebs out of their own substance. But the bee takes a middle course, it gathers its material from the flowers of the garden and of the field, but transforms and digests it by a power of its own. Not unlike this is the true business of philosophy: for it neither relies solely or chiefly on the powers of the mind, nor does it take the matter which it gathers from natural history and mechanical experiments and lay it up in the memory whole, as it finds it; but lays it up in the understanding altered and digested. Therefore from a closer and purer league between these two faculties, the experimental and the rational, (such as has never yet been made) much may be hoped.

xcvi

We have as yet no natural philosophy that is pure; all is tainted and corrupted: in Aristotle's school by logic; in Plato's by natural theology; in the second school of Platonists, such as Proclus and others, by mathematics, which ought only to give definiteness to natural philosophy, not to generate or give it birth. From a natural philosophy pure and unmixed, better things are to be expected.

xcvii

No one has yet been found so firm of mind and purpose as resolutely to compel himself to sweep away all theories and common notions, and

to apply the understanding, thus made fair and even, to a fresh examination of particulars. Thus it happens that human knowledge, as we have
it, is a mere medley and ill-digested mass, made up of much credulity
and much accident, and also of the childish notions which we at first
imbibed.

Now if anyone of ripe age, unimpaired senses, and well-purged mind,
apply himself anew to experience and particulars, better hopes may be
entertained of that man. In which point I promise to myself a like
fortune to that of Alexander the Great; and let no man tax me with
vanity till he have heard the end; for the thing which I mean tends to
the putting off of all vanity. For of Alexander and his deeds Aeschines
spake thus: "Assuredly we do not live the life of mortal men; but to
this end were we born, that in after ages wonders might be told of us;"
as if what Alexander had done seemed to him miraculous. But in the
next age Titus Livius took a better and a deeper view of the matter,
saying in effect, that Alexander "had done no more than take courage to
despise vain apprehensions." And a like judgment I suppose may be
passed on myself in future ages: that I did no great things, but simply
made less account of things that were accounted great. In the meanwhile,
as I have already said, there is no hope except in a new birth of science;
that is, in raising it regularly up from experience and building it afresh;
which no one (I think) will say has yet been done or thought of.

xcviii

Now for grounds of experience—since to experience we must come—
we have as yet had either none or very weak ones; no search has been
made to collect a store of particular observations sufficient either in
number, or in kind, or in certainty, to inform the understanding, or in
any way adequate. On the contrary, men of learning, but easy withal
and idle, have taken for the construction or for the confirmation of their
philosophy certain rumors and vague fames or airs of experience, and
allowed to these the weight of lawful evidence. And just as if some kingdom or state were to direct its counsels and affairs, not by letters and
reports from ambassadors and trustworthy messengers, but by the gossip
of the streets; such exactly is the system of management introduced into
philosophy with relation to experience. Nothing duly investigated, nothing verified, nothing counted, weighed, or measured, is to be found in
natural history: and what in observation is loose and vague, is in information deceptive and treacherous. And if anyone thinks that this is a
strange thing to say, and something like an unjust complaint, seeing that
Aristotle, himself so great a man, and supported by the wealth of so great
a king, has composed so accurate a history of animals; and that others

with greater diligence, though less pretense, have made many additions; while others, again, have compiled copious histories and descriptions of metals, plants, and fossils; it seems that he does not rightly apprehend what it is that we are now about. For a natural history which is composed for its own sake is not like one that is collected to supply the understand ing with information for the building up of philosophy. They differ in many ways, but especially in this; that the former contains the variety of natural species only, and not experiments of the mechanical arts. For even as in the business of life a man's disposition and the secret workings of his mind and affections are better discovered when he is in trouble than at other times; so likewise the secrets of nature reveal themselves more readily under the vexations of art than when they go their own way. Good hopes may therefore be conceived of natural philosophy, when natural history, which is the basis and foundation of it, has been drawn up on a better plan; but not till then.

xcix

Again, even in the great plenty of mechanical experiments, there is yet a great scarcity of those which are of most use for the information of the understanding. For the mechanic, not troubling himself with the investigation of truth, confines his attention to those things which bear upon his particular work, and will not either raise his mind or stretch out his hand for anything else. But then only will there be good ground of hope for the further advance of knowledge, when there shall be re- ceived and gathered together into natural history a variety of experi- ments, which are of no use in themselves, but simply serve to discover causes and axioms; which I call *experimenta lucifera,* experiments of *light,* to distinguish them from those which I call *fructifera,* experiments of *fruit.*

Now experiments of this kind have one admirable property and con- dition; they never miss or fail. For since they are applied, not for the purpose of producing any particular effect, but only of discovering the natural cause of some effect, they answer the end equally well which- ever way they turn out; for they settle the question.

c

But not only is a greater abundance of experiments to be sought for and procured, and that too of a different kind from those hitherto tried; an entirely different method, order, and process for carrying on and advancing experience must also be introduced. For experience, when it wanders in its own track, is, as I have already remarked, mere groping

in the dark, and confounds men rather than instructs them. But when it
shall proceed in accordance with a fixed law, in regular order, and without interruption, then may better things be hoped of knowledge.

ci

But even after such a store of natural history and experience as is
required for the work of the understanding, or of philosophy, shall be
ready at hand, still the understanding is by no means competent to deal
with it offhand and by memory alone; no more than if a man should
hope by force of memory to retain and make himself master of the
computation of an ephemeris. And yet hitherto more has been done in
matter of invention by thinking than by writing; and experience has
not yet learned her letters. Now no course of invention can be satisfactory unless it be carried on in writing. But when this is brought into
use, and experience has been taught to read and write, better things may
be hoped.

cii

Moreover, since there is so great a number and army of particulars,
and that army so scattered and dispersed as to distract and confound
the understanding, little is to be hoped for from the skirmishings and
slight attacks and desultory movements of the intellect, unless all the
particulars which pertain to the subject of inquiry shall, by means of
Tables of Discovery, apt, well arranged, and as it were animate, be drawn
up and marshaled; and the mind be set to work upon the helps duly
prepared and digested which these tables supply.

ciii

But after this store of particulars has been set out duly and in order
before our eyes, we are not to pass at once to the investigation and discovery of new particulars or works; or at any rate if we do so we must
not stop there. For although I do not deny that when all the experiments
of all the arts shall have been collected and digested, and brought within
one man's knowledge and judgment, the mere transferring of the experiments of one art to others may lead, by means of that experience
which I term *literate*, to the discovery of many new things of service
to the life and state of man; yet it is no great matter that can be hoped
from that: but from the new light of axioms, which having been educed
from those particulars by a certain method and rule, shall in their turn
point out the way again to new particulars, greater things may be looked
for. For our road does not lie on a level, but ascends and descends; first
ascending to axioms, then descending to works.

civ

The understanding must not however be allowed to jump and fly from particulars to remote axioms and of almost the highest generality (such as the first principles, as they are called, of arts and things), and taking stand upon them as truths that cannot be shaken, proceed to prove and frame the middle axioms by reference to them: which has been the practice hitherto; the understanding being not only carried that way by a natural impulse, but also by the use of syllogistic demonstration trained and inured to it. But then, and then only, may we hope well of the sciences, when in a just scale of ascent, and by successive steps not interrupted or broken, we rise from particulars to lesser axioms; and then to middle axioms, one above the other; and last of all to the most general. For the lowest axioms differ but slightly from bare experience, while the highest and most general (which we now have) are notional and abstract and without solidity. But the middle are the true and solid and living axioms, on which depend the affairs and fortunes of men; and above them again, last of all, those which are indeed the most general,—such I mean as are not abstract, but of which those intermediate axioms are really limitations.

The understanding must not therefore be supplied with wings, but rather hung with weights, to keep it from leaping and flying. Now this has never yet been done; when it is done, we may entertain better hopes of the sciences.

cv

In establishing axioms, another form of induction must be devised than has hitherto been employed; and it must be used for proving and discovering not first principles (as they are called) only, but also the lesser axioms, and the middle, and indeed all. For the induction which proceeds by simple enumeration is childish; its conclusions are precarious, and exposed to peril from a contradictory instance; and it generally decides on too small a number of facts, and on those only which are at hand. But the induction which is to be available for the discovery and demonstration of sciences and arts, must analyze nature by proper rejections and exclusions; and then, after a sufficient number of negatives, come to a conclusion on the affirmative instances: which has not yet been done or even attempted, save only by Plato, who does indeed employ this form of induction to a certain extent for the purpose of discussing definitions and ideas. But in order to furnish this induction or demonstration well and duly for its work, very many things are to be provided which no mortal has yet thought of; insomuch that greater labor will have to be spent in it than has hitherto been spent on the syllogism. And this induction must be used not only to discover axioms, but also in the formation of notions. And it is in this induction that our chief hope lies.

cvi

But in establishing axioms by this kind of induction, we must also examine and try whether the axiom so established be framed to the measure of those particulars only from which it is derived, or whether it be larger and wider. And if it be larger and wider, we must observe whether by indicating to us new particulars it confirm that wideness and largeness as by a collateral security: that we may not either stick fast in things already known, or loosely grasp at shadows and abstract forms; not at things solid and realized in matter. And when this process shall have come into use, then at last shall we see the dawn of a solid hope.

cvii

And here also should be remembered what was said above concerning the extending of the range of natural philosophy to take in the particular sciences, and the referring or bringing back of the particular sciences to natural philosophy; that the branches of knowledge may not be severed and cut off from the stem. For without this the hope of progress will not be so good.

cviii

So much then for the removing of despair and the raising of hope through the dismissal or rectification of the errors of past time. We must now see what else there is to ground hope upon. And this consideration occurs at once—that if many useful discoveries have been made by accident or upon occasion, when men were not seeking for them but were busy about other things; no one can doubt but that when they apply themselves to seek and make this their business, and that too by method and in order and not by desultory impulses, they will discover far more. For although it may happen once or twice that a man shall stumble on a thing by accident which, when taking great pains to search for it, he could not find; yet upon the whole it unquestionably falls out the other way. And therefore far better things, and more of them, and at shorter intervals, are to be expected from man's reason and industry and direction and fixed application, than from accident and animal instinct and the like, in which inventions have hitherto had their origin.

cix

Another argument of hope may be drawn from this—that some of the inventions already known are such as before they were discovered it could hardly have entered any man's head to think of; they would have been simply set aside as impossible. For in conjecturing what may be men set before them the example of what has been, and divine of the new with an imagination preoccupied and colored by the old; which way of forming opinions is very fallacious; for streams that are drawn from the springheads of nature do not always run in the old channels.

If, for instance, before the invention of ordnance, a man had described the thing by its effects, and said that there was a new invention, by means of which the strongest towers and walls could be shaken and thrown down at a great distance; men would doubtless have begun to think over all the ways of multiplying the force of catapults and mechanical engines by weights and wheels and such machinery for ramming and projecting: but the notion of a fiery blast suddenly and violently expanding and exploding would hardly have entered into any man's imagination or fancy; being a thing to which nothing immediately analogous had been seen, except perhaps in an earthquake or in lightning, which as *magnalia* or marvels of nature, and by man not imitable, would have been immediately rejected.

In the same way, if before the discovery of silk, anyone had said that there was a kind of thread discovered for the purposes of dress and furniture, which far surpassed the thread of linen or of wool in fineness and at the same time in strength, and also in beauty and softness; men would have begun immediately to think of some silky kind of vegetable, or of the finer hair of some animal, or of the feathers and down of birds; but of a web woven by a tiny worm, and that in such abundance, and renewing itself yearly, they would assuredly never have thought. Nay, if anyone had said anything about a worm, he would no doubt have been laughed at as dreaming of a new kind of cobwebs.

So again, if before the discovery of the magnet, any one had said that a certain instrument had been invented by means of which the quarters and points of the heavens could be taken and distinguished with exactness; men would have been carried by their imagination to a variety of conjectures concerning the more exquisite construction of astronomical instruments; but that anything could be discovered agreeing so well in its movements with the heavenly bodies, and yet not a heavenly body itself, but simply a substance of metal or stone, would have been judged altogether incredible. Yet these things and others like them lay for so many ages of the world concealed from men, nor was it by philosophy or the rational arts that they were found out at last, but by accident and occasion: being indeed, as I said, altogether different in kind and as remote as possible from anything that was known before; so that no preconceived notion could possibly have led to the discovery of them.

There is therefore much ground for hoping that there are still laid

up in the womb of nature many secrets of excellent use, having no
affinity or parallelism with anything that is now known, but lying entirely out of the beat of the imagination, which have not yet been found
out. They too no doubt will some time or other, in the course and revolution of many ages, come to light of themselves, just as the others did;
only by the method of which we are now treating they can be speedily
and suddenly and simultaneously presented and anticipated.

CX

But we have also discoveries to show of another kind, which prove
that noble inventions may be lying at our very feet, and yet mankind
may step over without seeing them. For however the discovery of gunpowder, of silk, of the magnet, of sugar, of paper, or the like, may seem
to depend on certain properties of things themselves and nature, there is
at any rate nothing in the art of printing which is not plain and obvious.
Nevertheless for want of observing that although it is more difficult to
arrange types of letters than to write letters by the motion of the hand,
there is yet this difference between the two, that types once arranged
serve for innumerable impressions, but letters written with the hand for
a single copy only; or perhaps again for want of observing that ink
can be so thickened as to color without running (particularly when the
letters face upwards and the impression is made from above)—for want,
I say, of observing these things, men went for so many ages without this
most beautiful discovery, which is of so much service in the propagation
of knowledge.

But such is the infelicity and unhappy disposition of the human mind
in this course of invention, that it first distrusts and then despises itself:
first will not believe that any such thing can be found out; and when
it is found out, cannot understand how the world should have missed it
so long. And this very thing may be justly taken as an argument of
hope; namely, that there is a great mass of inventions still remaining,
which not only by means of operations that are yet to be discovered,
but also through the transferring, comparing, and applying of those
already known, by the help of that learned experience of which I spoke,
may be deduced and brought to light.

cxi

There is another ground of hope that must not be omitted. Let men
but think over their infinite expenditure of understanding, time, and
means on matters and pursuits of far less use and value; whereof if but
a small part were directed to sound and solid studies, there is no difficulty that might not be overcome. This I thought good to add, because

I plainly confess that a collection of history natural and experimental, such as I conceive it and as it ought to be, is a great, I may say a royal work, and of much labor and expense.

cxii

Meantime, let no man be alarmed at the multitude of particulars, but let this rather encourage him to hope. For the particular phenomena of art and nature are but a handful to the inventions of the wit, when disjoined and separated from the evidence of things. Moreover this road has an issue in the open ground and not far off; the other has no issue at all, but endless entanglement. For men hitherto have made but short stay with experience, but passing her lightly by, have wasted an infinity of time on meditations and glosses of the wit. But if someone were by that could answer our questions and tell us in each case what the fact in nature is, the discovery of all causes and sciences would be but the work of a few years.

cxiii

Moreover I think that men may take some hope from my own example. And this I say not by way of boasting, but because it is useful to say it. If there be any that despond, let them look at me, that being of all men of my time the most busied in affairs of state, and a man of health not very strong (whereby much time is lost), and in this course altogether a pioneer, following in no man's track, nor sharing these counsels with anyone, have nevertheless by resolutely entering on the true road, and submitting my mind to *things*, advanced these matters, as I suppose, some little way. And then let them consider what may be expected (after the way has been thus indicated) from men abounding in leisure, and from association of labors, and from successions of ages: the rather because it is not a way over which only one man can pass at a time (as is the case with that of reasoning), but one in which the labors and industries of men (especially as regards the collecting of experience) may with the best effect be first distributed and then combined. For then only will men begin to know their strength, when instead of great numbers doing all the same things, one shall take charge of one thing and another of another.

cxiv

Lastly, even if the breath of hope which blows on us from that new continent were fainter than it is and harder to perceive; yet the trial (if we would not bear a spirit altogether abject) must by all means be made. For there is no comparison between that which we may lose by not trying and by not succeeding; since by not trying we throw away the chance of an immense good; by not succeeding we only incur the loss of a little human labor. But as it is, it appears to me from what has been said, and also from what has been left unsaid, that there is hope enough and to spare, not only to make a bold man try, but also to make a sober-minded and wise man believe.

cxv

Concerning the grounds then for putting away despair, which has been one of the most powerful causes of delay and hindrance to the progress of knowledge, I have now spoken. And this also concludes what I had to say touching the *signs* and *causes* of the errors, sluggishness, and ignorance which have prevailed; especially since the more subtle causes, which do not fall under popular judgment and observation, must be referred to what has been said on the idols of the human mind.

And here likewise should close that part of my *Instauration,* which is devoted to pulling down: which part is performed by three refutations; first, by the refutation of the *natural human reason,* left to itself; secondly, by the refutation of the *demonstrations;* and thirdly, by the refutation of the *theories,* or the received systems of philosophy and doctrine. And the refutation of these has been such, as alone it could be; that is to say, by signs and the evidence of causes; since no other kind of confutation was open to me, differing as I do from others both on first principles and on rules of demonstration.

It is time therefore to proceed to the art itself and rule of interpreting nature; still however there remains something to be premised. For whereas in this first book of aphorisms I proposed to prepare men's minds as well for understanding as for receiving what is to follow; now that I have purged and swept and leveled the floor of the mind, it remains that I place the mind in a good position and as it were in a favorable aspect towards what I have to lay before it. For in a new matter, it is not only the strong preoccupation of some old opinion that tends to create a prejudice, but also a false preconception or prefiguration of the new thing which is presented. I will endeavor therefore to impart sound and true opinions as to the things I propose, although they are to serve only for the time and by way of interest (so to speak), till the thing itself, which is the principal, be fully known.

cxvi

First, then, I must request men not to suppose that after the fashion of ancient Greeks, and of certain moderns, as Telesius, Patricius, Severinus, I wish to found a new sect in philosophy. For this is not what I am about; nor do I think that it matters much to the fortunes of men what abstract notions one may entertain concerning nature and the principles of things; and no doubt many old theories of this kind can be revived and many new ones introduced; just as many theories of the heavens may be supposed, which agree well enough with the phenomena and yet differ with each other.

But for my part I do not trouble myself with any such speculative and withal unprofitable matters. My purpose, on the contrary, is to try whether I cannot in very fact lay more firmly the foundations, and extend more widely the limits, of the power and greatness of man. And although on some special subjects and in an incomplete form I am in possession of results which I take to be far more true and more certain and withal more fruitful than those now received, (and these I have collected into the fifth part of my Instauration,) yet I have no entire or universal theory to propound. For it does not seem that the time is come for such an attempt. Neither can I hope to live to complete the sixth part of the Instauration (which is destined for the philosophy discovered by the legitimate interpretation of nature), but hold it enough if in the intermediate business I bear myself soberly and profitably, sowing in the meantime for future ages the seeds of a purer truth, and performing my part towards the commencement of the great undertaking.

cxvii

And as I do not seek to found a school, so neither do I hold out offers or promises of particular works. It may be thought indeed, that I who make such frequent mention of works and refer everything to that end, should produce some myself by way of earnest. But my course and method, as I have often clearly stated and would wish to state again, is this—not to extract works from works or experiments from experiments (as an empiric), but from works and experiments to extract causes and axioms, and again from those causes and axioms new works and experiments, as a legitimate interpreter of nature. And although in my tables of discovery (which compose the fourth part of the Instauration), and also in the examples of particulars (which I have adduced in the second part), and moreover in my observations on the history (which I have drawn out in the third part), any reader of even moderate sagacity and intelligence will everywhere observe indications and outlines of many noble works; still I candidly confess that the natural history which I now have, whether collected from books or from my own investigations, is neither sufficiently copious nor verified with sufficient accuracy to serve the purposes of legitimate interpretation.

Accordingly, if there be anyone more apt and better prepared for mechanical pursuits, and sagacious in hunting out works by the mere dealing with experiment, let him by all means use his industry to gather

from my history and tables many things by the way, and apply them to
the production of works, which may serve as interest until the principal
be forthcoming. But for myself, aiming as I do at greater things, I condemn all unseasonable and premature tarrying over such things as these;
being (as I often say) like Atalanta's balls. For I do not run off like a
child after golden apples, but stake all on the victory of art over nature
in the race; nor do I make haste to mow down the moss or the corn in
blade, but wait for the harvest in its due season.

cxviii

There will be found no doubt, when my history and tables of discovery
are read, some things in the experiments themselves that are not quite
certain, or perhaps that are quite false; which may make a man think
that the foundations and principles upon which my discoveries rest are
false and doubtful. But this is of no consequence; for such things must
needs happen at first. It is only like the occurrence in a written or printed
page of a letter or two mistaken or misplaced; which does not much
hinder the reader, because such errors are easily corrected by the sense.
So likewise may there occur in my natural history many experiments
which are mistaken and falsely set down, and yet they will presently
by the discovery of causes and axioms be easily expunged and rejected.
It is nevertheless true that if the mistakes in natural history and experiments are important, frequent, and continual, they cannot possibly be
corrected or amended by any felicity of wit or art. And therefore, if in
my natural history, which has been collected and tested with so much
diligence, severity, and I may say religious care, there still lurk at intervals certain falsities or errors in the particulars—what is to be said of
common natural history, which in comparison with mine is so negligent
and inexact? and what of the philosophy and sciences built on such a
sand (or rather quicksand)? Let no man therefore trouble himself for
this.

cxix

There will be met with also in my history and experiments many
things which are trivial and commonly known; many which are mean
and low; many, lastly, which are too subtle and merely speculative, and
that seem to be of no use; which kind of things may possibly avert and
alienate men's interest.

And first for those things which seem common; let men bear in mind
that hitherto they have been accustomed to do no more than refer and
adapt the causes of things which rarely happen to such as happen frequently; while of those which happen frequently they never ask the
cause, but take them as they are for granted. And therefore they do not

investigate the causes of weight, of the rotation of heavenly bodies, of heat, cold, light, hardness, softness, rarity, density, liquidity, solidity, animation, inanimation, similarity, dissimilarity, organization, and the like; but admitting these as self-evident and obvious, they dispute and decide on other things of less frequent and familiar occurrence.

But I, who am well aware that no judgment can be passed on uncommon or remarkable things, much less anything new brought to light, unless the causes of common things, and the causes of those causes, be first duly examined and found out, am of necessity compelled to admit the commonest things into my history. Nay, in my judgment philosophy has been hindered by nothing more than this—that things of familiar and frequent occurrence do not arrest and detain the thoughts of men, but are received in passing without any inquiry into their causes; insomuch that information concerning things which are not known is not oftener wanted than attention concerning things which are.

cxx

And for things that are mean or even filthy—things which (as Pliny says) must be introduced with an apology—such things, no less than the most splendid and costly, must be admitted into natural history. Nor is natural history polluted thereby; for the sun enters the sewer no less than the palace, yet takes no pollution. And for myself, I am not raising a capitol or pyramid to the pride of man, but laying a foundation in the human understanding for a holy temple after the model of the world. That model therefore I follow. For whatever deserves to exist deserves also to be known, for knowledge is the image of existence; and things mean and splendid exist alike. Moreover as from certain putrid substances—musk, for instance, and civet—the sweetest odors are sometimes generated, so too from mean and sordid instances there sometimes emanates excellent light and information. But enough and more than enough of this; such fastidiousness being merely childish and effeminate.

cxxi

But there is another objection which must be more carefully looked to: namely, that there are many things in this history which to common apprehension, or indeed to any understanding accustomed to the present system, will seem to be curiously and unprofitably subtle. Upon this point therefore above all I must say again what I have said already— that at first and for a time I am seeking for experiments of light, not for experiments of fruit; following therein, as I have often said, the example of the divine creation; which on the first day produced light only, and assigned to it alone one entire day, nor mixed up with it on that day any material work.

To suppose therefore that things like these are of no use is the same as to suppose that light is of no use, because it is not a thing solid or material. And the truth is that the knowledge of simple natures well examined and defined is as light; it gives entrance to all the secrets of nature's workshop, and virtually includes and draws after it whole bands and troops of works, and opens to us the sources of the noblest axioms; and yet in itself it is of no great use. So also the letters of the alphabet in themselves and apart have no use or meaning, yet they are the subject-matter for the composition and apparatus of all discourse. So again the seeds of things are of much latent virtue, and yet of no use except in their development. And the scattered rays of light itself, until they are made to converge, can impart none of their benefit.

But if objection be taken to speculative subtleties, what is to be said of the schoolmen, who have indulged in subtleties to such excess? in subtleties too that were spent on words, or at any rate on popular notions (which is much the same thing), not on facts or nature; and such as were useless not only in their origin but also in their consequences; and not like those I speak of, useless indeed for the present, but promising infinite utility hereafter. But let men be assured of this, that all subtlety of disputation and discourse, if not applied till after axioms are discovered, is out of season and preposterous; and that the true and proper or at any rate the chief time for subtlety is in weighing experience and in founding axioms thereon; for that other subtlety, though it grasps and snatches at nature, yet can never take hold of her. Certainly what is said of opportunity or fortune is most true of nature; she has a lock in front, but is bald behind.

Lastly, concerning the disdain to receive into natural history things either common, or mean, or over-subtle and in their original condition useless, the answer of the poor woman to the haughty prince, who had rejected her petition as an unworthy thing and beneath his dignity, may be taken for an oracle,—"Then leave off being king." For most certain it is that he who will not attend to things like these, as being too paltry and minute, can neither win the kingdom of nature nor govern it.

cxxii

It may be thought also a strange and a harsh thing that we should at once and with one blow set aside all sciences and all authors; and that too without calling in any of the ancients to our aid and support, but relying on our own strength.

And I know that if I had chosen to deal less sincerely, I might easily have found authority for my suggestions by referring them either to the old times before the Greeks (when natural science was perhaps more flourishing, though it made less noise, not having yet passed into the pipes and trumpets of the Greeks), or even, in part at least, to some of the Greeks themselves; and so gained for them both support and honor; as men of no family devise for themselves by the good help of genealogies the nobility of a descent from some ancient stock. But for my part, relying on the evidence and truth of things, I reject all forms of fiction and imposture; nor do I think that it matters any more to the business in hand, whether the discoveries that shall now be made were long ago known to the ancients, and have their settings and their risings according to the vicissitude of things and course of ages, than it matters to mankind whether the new world be that island of Atlantis with which the ancients were acquainted, or now discovered for the first time. For new discoveries must be sought from the light of nature, not fetched back out of the darkness of antiquity.

And as for the universality of the censure, certainly if the matter be truly considered, such a censure is not only more probable but more modest too, than a partial one would be. For if the errors had not been rooted in primary notions, there must have been some true discoveries to correct the false. But the errors being fundamental, and not so much of false judgment as of inattention and oversight, it is no wonder that men have not obtained what they have not tried for, nor reached a mark which they never set up, nor finished a course which they never entered on or kept.

And as for the presumption implied in it; certainly if a man undertakes by steadiness of hand and power of eye to describe a straighter line or more perfect circle than anyone else, he challenges a comparison of abilities; but if he only says that he with the help of a rule or a pair of compasses can draw a straighter line or a more perfect circle than anyone else can by eye and hand alone, he makes no great boast. And this remark, be it observed, applies not merely to this first and inceptive attempt of mine, but to all that shall take the work in hand hereafter. For my way of discovering sciences goes far to level men's wits, and leaves but little to individual excellence; because it performs everything by the surest rules and demonstrations. And therefore I attribute my part in all this, as I have often said, rather to good luck than to ability, and account it a birth of time rather than of wit. For certainly chance has something to do with men's thoughts, as well as with their works and deeds.

cxxiii

I may say then of myself that which one said in jest (since it marks the distinction so truly), "It cannot be that we should think alike, when

one drinks water and the other drinks wine." Now other men, as well in
ancient as in modern times, have in the matter of sciences drunk a
crude liquor like water, either flowing spontaneously from the understanding, or drawn up by logic, as by wheels from a well. Whereas I
pledge mankind in liquor strained from countless grapes, from grapes
ripe and fully seasoned, collected in clusters, and gathered, and then
squeezed in the press, and finally purified and clarified in the vat. And
therefore it is no wonder if they and I do not think alike.

cxxiv

Again, it will be thought, no doubt, that the goal and mark of knowledge which I myself set up (the very point which I object to in others)
is not the true or the best; for that the contemplation of truth is a
thing worthier and loftier than all utility and magnitude of works;
and that this long and anxious dwelling with experience and matter
and the fluctuations of individual things, drags down the mind to earth,
or rather sinks it to a very Tartarus of turmoil and confusion; removing
and withdrawing it from the serene tranquillity of abstract wisdom, a
condition far more heavenly. Now to this I readily assent; and indeed
this which they point at as so much to be preferred, is the very thing of
all others which I am about. For I am building in the human understanding a true model of the world, such as it is in fact, not such as a man's
own reason would have it to be; a thing which cannot be done without
a very diligent dissection and anatomy of the world. But I say that
those foolish and apish images of worlds which the fancies of men have
created in philosophical systems, must be utterly scattered to the
winds. Be it known then how vast a difference there is (as I said above)
between the idols of the human mind and the ideas of the divine. The
former are nothing more than arbitrary abstractions; the latter are the
creator's own stamp upon creation, impressed and defined in matter
by true and exquisite lines. Truth therefore and utility are here the very
same things: and works themselves are of greater value as pledges of
truth than as contributing to the comforts of life.

cxxv

It may be thought again that I am but doing what has been done
before; that the ancients themselves took the same course which I am
now taking; and that it is likely therefore that I too, after all this stir
and striving, shall come at last to some one of those systems which prevailed in ancient times. For the ancients too, it will be said, provided at
the outset of their speculations a great store and abundance of examples
and particulars, digested the same into notebooks under heads and
titles, from them completed their systems and arts, and afterwards, when

they understood the matter, published them to the world,—adding a few examples here and there for proof and illustration; but thought it superfluous and inconvenient to publish their notes and minutes and digests of particulars; and therefore did as builders do,—after the house was built they removed the scaffolding and ladders out of sight. And so no doubt they did. But this objection (or scruple rather) will be easily answered by anyone who has not quite forgotten what I have said above. For the form of inquiry and discovery that was in use among the ancients is by themselves professed, and appears on the very face of their writings. And that form was simply this. From a few examples and particulars (with the addition of common notions and perhaps of some portion of the received opinions which have been most popular) they flew at once to the most general conclusions, or first principles of science: taking the truth of these as fixed and immovable, they proceeded by means of intermediate propositions to educe and prove from them the inferior conclusions; and out of these they framed the art. After that, if any new particulars and examples repugnant to their dogmas were mooted and adduced, either they subtly molded them into their system by distinctions or explanations of their rules, or else coarsely got rid of them by exceptions; while to such particulars as were not repugnant they labored to assign causes in conformity with those their principles. But this was not the natural history and experience that was wanted; far from it; and besides, that flying off to the highest generalities ruined all.

cxxvi

It will also be thought that by forbidding men to pronounce and to set down principles as established until they have duly arrived through the intermediate steps at the highest generalities, I maintain a sort of suspension of the judgment, and bring it to what the Greeks call *Acatalepsia*,—a denial of the capacity of the mind to comprehend truth. But in reality that which I meditate and propound is not *Acatalepsia*, but *Eucatalepsia;* not denial of the capacity to understand, but provision for understanding truly; for I do not take away authority from the senses, but supply them with helps; I do not slight the understanding, but govern it. And better surely it is that we should know all we need to know, and yet think our knowledge imperfect, than that we should think our knowledge perfect, and yet not know anything we need to know.

cxxvii

It may also be asked (in the way of doubt rather than objection) whether I speak of natural philosophy only, or whether I mean that the other sciences, logic, ethics, and politics, should be carried on by this method. Now I certainly mean what I have said to be understood of them all; and as the common logic, which governs by the syllogism, extends not only to natural but to all sciences; so does mine also, which proceeds by induction, embrace everything. For I form a history and tables of discovery for anger, fear, shame, and the like; for matters political; and again for the mental operations of memory, composition and division, judgment and the rest; not less than for heat and cold, or light, or vegetation, or the like. But nevertheless since my method of interpretation, after the history has been prepared and duly arranged, regards not the working and discourse of the mind only (as the common logic does) but the nature of things also, I supply the mind with such rules and guidance that it may in every case apply itself aptly to the nature of things. And therefore I deliver many and diverse precepts in the doctrine of Interpretation, which in some measure modify the method of invention according to the quality and condition of the subject of the inquiry.

cxxviii

On one point not even a doubt ought to be entertained; namely, whether I desire to pull down and destroy the philosophy and arts and sciences which are at present in use. So far from that, I am most glad to see them used, cultivated, and honored. There is no reason why the arts which are now in fashion should not continue to supply matter for disputation and ornaments for discourse, to be employed for the convenience of professors and men of business; to be in short like current coin, which passes among men by consent. Nay I frankly declare that what I am introducing will be but little fitted for such purposes as these, since it cannot be brought down to common apprehension, save by effects and works only. But how sincere I am in my professions of affection and good will towards the received sciences, my published writings, especially the books on the Advancement of Learning, sufficiently show; and therefore I will not attempt to prove it further by words. Meanwhile I give constant and distinct warning that by the methods now in use neither can any great progress be made in the doctrines and contemplative part of sciences, nor can they be carried out to any magnitude of works.

cxxix

It remains for me to say a few words touching the excellency of the end in view. Had they been uttered earlier, they might have seemed like idle wishes; but now that hopes have been raised and unfair prejudices removed, they may perhaps have greater weight. Also, if I had finished all myself, and had no occasion to call in others to help and take part in the work, I should even now have abstained from such language, lest it might be taken as a proclamation of my own deserts. But since I want to quicken the industry and rouse and kindle the zeal of others, it is fitting that I put men in mind of some things.

In the first place then, the introduction of famous discoveries appears to hold by far the first place among human actions; and this was the judgment of the former ages. For to the authors of inventions they awarded divine honors; while to those who did good service in the state (such as founders of cities and empires, legislators, saviors of their country from long enduring evils, quellers of tyrannies, and the like) they decreed no higher honors than heroic. And certainly if a man rightly compare the two, he will find that this judgment of antiquity was just. For the benefits of discoveries may extend to the whole race of man, civil benefits only to particular places; the latter last not beyond a few ages, the former through all time. Moreover the reformation of a state in civil matters is seldom brought in without violence and confusion; but discoveries carry blessings with them, and confer benefits without causing harm or sorrow to any.

Again, discoveries are as it were new creations, and imitations of God's works; as well sang the poet:—

> To man's frail race great Athens long ago
> First gave the seed whence waving harvests grow,
> And *re-created* all our life below.

And it appears worthy of remark in Solomon, that though mighty in empire and in gold; in the magnificence of his works, his court, his household, and his fleet; in the luster of his name and the worship of mankind: yet he took none of these to glory in, but pronounced that "The glory of God is to conceal a thing; the glory of the king to search it out."

Again, let a man only consider what a difference there is between the life of men in the most civilized province of Europe, and in the wildest and most barbarous districts of New India; he will feel it be great enough to justify the saying that "man is a god to man," not only in regard of aid and benefit, but also by a comparison of condition. And this difference comes not from soil, not from climate, not from race, but from the arts.

Again, it is well to observe the force and virtue and consequences of discoveries; and these are to be seen nowhere more conspicuously than in those three which were unknown to the ancients, and of which the origin, though recent, is obscure and inglorious; namely, printing, gunpowder, and the magnet. For these three have changed the whole face and state of things throughout the world; the first in literature, the second in warfare, the third in navigation; whence have followed innumerable changes; insomuch that no empire, no sect, no star seems to have exerted greater power and influence in human affairs than these mechanical discoveries.

Further, it will not be amiss to distinguish the three kinds and as it were grades of ambition in mankind. The first is of those who desire to extend their own power in their native country; which kind is vulgar and degenerate. The second is of those who labor to extend the power of their country and its dominion among men. This certainly has more dignity, though not less covetousness. But if a man endeavor to estab-lish and extend the power and dominion of the human race itself over the universe, his ambition (if ambition it can be called) is without doubt both a more wholesome thing and a more noble than the other two. Now the empire of man over things depends wholly on the arts and sciences. For we cannot command nature except by obeying her.

Again, if men have thought so much of some one particular discovery as to regard him as more than man who has been able by some benefit to make the whole human race his debtor, how much higher a thing to dis-cover that by means of which all things else shall be discovered with ease! And yet (to speak the whole truth), as the uses of light are infinite, in enabling us to walk, to ply our arts, to read, to recognize one another; and nevertheless the very beholding of the light is itself a more excellent and a fairer thing than all the uses of it;—so assuredly the very contem-plation of things, as they are, without superstition or imposture, error or confusion, is in itself more worthy than all the fruit of inventions.

Lastly, if the debasement of arts and sciences to purposes of wicked-ness, luxury, and the like, be made a ground of objection, let no one be moved thereby. For the same may be said of all earthly goods; of wit, courage, strength, beauty, wealth, light itself, and the rest. Only let the human race recover the right over nature which belongs to it by divine bequest, and let power be given it; the exercise thereof will be governed by sound reason and true religion.

CXXX

And now it is time for me to propound the art itself of interpreting nature; in which, although I conceive that I have given true and most useful precepts, yet I do not say either that it is absolutely necessary (as if nothing could be done without it) or that it is perfect. For I am of opinion that if men had ready at hand a just history of nature and experience, and labored diligently thereon; and if they could bind them-selves to two rules,—the first, to lay aside received opinions and notions; and the second, to refrain the mind for a time from the highest generali-zations, and those next to them,—they would be able by the native and genuine force of the mind, without any other art, to fall into my form of interpretation. For interpretation is the true and natural work of the mind when freed from impediments. It is true however that by my precepts everything will be in more readiness, and much more sure.

Nor again do I mean to say that no improvement can be made upon these. On the contrary, I that regard the mind not only in its own faculties but in its connection with things, must needs hold that the art of discovery may advance as discoveries advance.

THE SECOND BOOK OF
APHORISMS
CONCERNING
THE INTERPRETATION OF NATURE
AND
THE KINGDOM OF MAN

APHORISM

i

ON A given body to generate and superinduce a new nature or new natures, is the work and aim of *human power*. Of a given nature to discover the form, or true specific difference, or nature-engendering nature, or source of emanation (for these are the terms which come nearest to a description of the thing), is the work and aim of *human knowledge*. Subordinate to these primary works are two others that are secondary and of inferior mark: to the former, the transformation of concrete bodies, so far as this is possible; to the latter, the discovery, in every case of generation and motion, of the latent process carried on from the manifest efficient and the manifest material to the form which is engendered; and in like manner the discovery of the latent configuration of bodies at rest and not in motion.

ii

In what an ill condition human knowledge is at the present time, is apparent even from the commonly received maxims. It is a correct position that "true knowledge is knowledge by causes." And causes again are not improperly distributed into four kinds: the material, the formal, the efficient, and the final. But of these the final cause rather corrupts than advances the sciences, except such as have to do with human action. The discovery of the formal is despaired of. The efficient and the material (as they are investigated and received, that is, as remote causes, without reference to the latent process leading to the form) are but slight and superficial, and contribute little, if anything, to true and active science. Nor have I forgotten that in a former passage I noted and corrected as an error of the human mind the opinion that forms give existence. For though in nature nothing really exists beside individual bodies, performing pure individual acts according to a fixed law, yet in philosophy this very law, and the investigation, discovery, and explanation of it, is the foundation as well of knowledge as of operation. And it is this law, with its clauses, that I mean when I speak of *forms;* a name which I the rather adopt because it has grown into use and become familiar.

iii

If a man be acquainted with the cause of any nature (as whiteness or heat) in certain subjects only, his knowledge is imperfect; and if he be able to superinduce an effect on certain substances only (of those susceptible of such effect), his power is in like manner imperfect. Now if a man's knowledge be confined to the efficient and material causes (which are unstable causes, and merely vehicles, or causes which convey the form in certain cases), he may arrive at new discoveries in reference to substances in some degree similar to one another, and selected beforehand; but he does not touch the deeper boundaries of things. But whosoever is acquainted with forms, embraces the unity of nature in substances the most unlike; and is able therefore to detect and bring to light things never yet done, and such as neither the vicissitudes of nature, nor industry in experimenting, nor accident itself, would ever have brought into act, and which would never have occurred to the thought of man. From the discovery of forms therefore results truth in speculation and freedom in operation.

iv

Although the roads to human power and to human knowledge lie close together, and are nearly the same, nevertheless on account of the pernicious and inveterate habit of dwelling on abstractions, it is safer to begin and raise the sciences from those foundations which have relation to practice, and to let the active part itself be as the seal which prints and determines the contemplative counterpart. We must therefore consider, if a man wanted to generate and superinduce any nature upon a given body, what kind of rule or direction or guidance he would most wish for, and express the same in the simplest and least abstruse language. For instance, if a man wishes to superinduce upon silver the yellow color of gold, or an increase of weight (observing the laws of matter), or transparency on an opaque stone, or tenacity on glass, or vegetation on some substance that is not vegetable,—we must consider, I say, what kind of rule or guidance he would most desire. And in the first place, he will undoubtedly wish to be directed to something which will not deceive him in the result, nor fail him in the trial. Secondly, he will wish for such a rule as shall not tie him down to certain means and particular modes of operation. For perhaps he may not have those means, nor be able conveniently to procure them. And if there be other means and other methods for producing the required nature (besides the one prescribed) these may perhaps be within his reach; and yet he shall be excluded by the narrowness of the rule, and get no good from them. Thirdly, he will desire something to be shown him which is not as difficult as the thing proposed to be done, but comes nearer to practice.

For a true and perfect rule of operation then the direction will be *that it be certain, free, and disposing or leading to action.* And this is the same thing with the discovery of the true form. For the form of a nature is such that, given the form, the nature infallibly follows. Therefore it is always present when the nature is present, and universally implies it, and is constantly inherent in it. Again, the form is such that if it be taken away, the nature infallibly vanishes. Therefore it is always absent when the nature is absent, and implies its absence, and inheres in nothing else. Lastly, the true form is such that it deduces the given nature from some source of being which is inherent in more natures, and which is better known in the natural order of things than the form itself. For a true and perfect axiom of knowledge then the direction and precept will be, *that another nature be discovered which is convertible with the given nature, and yet is a limitation of a more general nature, as of a true and real genus.* Now these two directions, the one active the other contemplative, are one and the same thing; and what in operation is most useful, that in knowledge is most true.

V

The rule or axiom for the transformation of bodies is of two kinds. The first regards a body as a troop or collection of simple natures. In gold, for example, the following properties meet. It is yellow in color; heavy up to a certain weight; malleable or ductile to a certain degree of extension; it is not volatile, and loses none of its substance by the action of fire; it turns into a liquid with a certain degree of fluidity; it is separated and dissolved by particular means; and so on for the other natures which meet in gold. This kind of axiom, therefore, deduces the thing from forms of simple natures. For he who knows the forms of yellow, weight, ductility, fixity, fluidity, solution, and so on, and the methods for superinducing them, and their gradations and modes, will make it his care to have them joined together in some body, whence may follow the transformation of that body into gold. And this kind of operation pertains to the first kind of action. For the principle of generating some one simple nature is the same as that of generating many; only that a man is more fettered and tied down in operation if more are required, by reason of the difficulty of combining into one so many natures, which do not readily meet except in the beaten and ordinary paths of nature. It must be said however that this mode of operation (which looks to simple natures though in a compound body) proceeds from what in nature is constant and eternal and universal, and opens broad roads to human power, such as (in the present state of things) human thought can scarcely comprehend or anticipate.

The second kind of axiom, which is concerned with the discovery of the Latent Process, proceeds not by simple natures, but by compound bodies, as they are found in nature in its ordinary course. As, for in- stance, when inquiry is made, from what beginnings, and by what method and by what process, gold or any other metal or stone is gener- ated, from its first menstrua and rudiments up to the perfect mineral; or in like manner by what process herbs are generated, from the first con- cretion of juices in the ground or from seeds up to the formed plant, with all the successive motions and diverse and continued efforts of nature. So also in the inquiry concerning the process of development in the gen- eration of animals, from coition to birth; and in like manner of other bodies.

It is not however only to the generations of bodies that this investiga- tion extends, but also to other motions and operations of nature. As, for instance, when inquiry is made concerning the whole course and con- tinued action of nutrition, from the first reception of the food to its complete assimilation; or again, concerning the voluntary motion of animals, from the first impression on the imagination and the continued efforts of the spirit up to the bendings and movements of the limbs; or concerning the motion of the tongue and lips and other instruments, and the changes through which it passes till it comes to the utterance of articulate sounds. For these inquiries also relate to natures concrete or combined into one structure, and have regard to what may be called particular and special habits of nature, not to her fundamental and universal laws which constitute Forms. And yet it must be confessed that this plan appears to be readier and to lie nearer at hand and to give more ground for hope than the primary one.

In like manner the operative which answers to this speculative part, starting from the ordinary incidents of nature, extends its operation to things immediately adjoining, or at least not far removed. But as for any profound and radical operations on nature, they depend entirely on the primary axioms. And in those things too where man has no means of operating, but only of knowing, as in the heavenly bodies (for these he cannot operate upon or change or transform), the investigation of the fact itself or truth of the thing, no less than the knowledge of the causes and consents, must come from those primary and catholic axioms con- cerning simple natures; such as the nature of spontaneous rotation, of attraction or magnetism, and of many others which are of a more general form than the heavenly bodies themselves. For let no one hope to decide the question whether it is the earth or heaven that really revolves in the diurnal motion, until he has first comprehended the nature of spontaneous rotation.

vi

But this Latent Process, of which I speak, is quite another thing than men, preoccupied as their minds now are, will easily conceive. For what I understand by it is not certain measures or signs or successive steps of process in bodies, which can be seen; but a process perfectly continuous, which for the most part escapes the sense.

For instance: in all generation and transformation of bodies, we must inquire what is lost and escapes; what remains, what is added; what is expanded, what contracted; what is united, what separated; what is continued, what cut off; what propels, what hinders; what predominates, what yields; and a variety of other particulars.

Again, not only in the generation or transformation of bodies are these points to be ascertained, but also in all other alterations and motions it should in like manner be inquired what goes before, what comes after; what is quicker, what more tardy; what produces, what governs motion; and like points; all which nevertheless in the present state of the sciences (the texture of which is as rude as possible and good for nothing) are unknown and unhandled. For seeing that every natural action depends on things infinitely small, or at least too small to strike the sense, no one can hope to govern or change nature until he has duly comprehended and observed them.

vii

In like manner the investigation and discovery of the Latent Configuration in bodies is a new thing, no less than the discovery of the Latent Process and of the Form. For as yet we are but lingering in the outer courts of nature, nor are we preparing ourselves a way into her inner chambers. Yet no one can endow a given body with a new nature, or successfully and aptly transmute it into a new body, unless he has attained a competent knowledge of the body so to be altered or transformed. Otherwise he will run into methods which, if not useless, are at any rate difficult and perverse and unsuitable to the nature of the body on which he is operating. It is clear therefore that to this also a way must be opened and laid out.

And it is true that upon the anatomy of organized bodies (as of man and animals) some pains have been well bestowed and with good effect; and a subtle thing it seems to be, and a good scrutiny of nature. Yet this kind of anatomy is subject to sight and sense, and has place only in organized bodies. And besides it is a thing obvious and easy, when compared with the true anatomy of the Latent Configuration in bodies which are thought to be of uniform structure: especially in things that have a specific character and their parts, as iron, stone; and again in parts of uniform structure in plants and animals, as the root, the leaf, the flower, flesh, blood, and bones. But even in this kind, human industry has not been altogether wanting; for this is the very thing aimed at in the separation of bodies of uniform structure by means of distillations and other modes of analysis,—that the complex structure of the compound may be made apparent by bringing together its several homogeneous parts. And this is of use too, and conduces to the object we are seeking; although too often fallacious in its results, because many natures which are in fact newly brought out and superinduced by fire and heat and other modes of solution are taken to be the effect of separation merely, and to have subsisted in the compound before. And after all, this is but a small part of the work of discovering the true configuration in the compound body; which configuration is a thing far more subtle and exact, and such as the operation of fire rather confounds than brings out and makes distinct.

Therefore a separation and solution of bodies must be effected, not by fire indeed, but by reasoning and true induction, with experiments to aid; and by a comparison with other bodies, and a reduction to simple natures and their forms, which meet and mix in the compound. In a word we must pass from Vulcan to Minerva, if we intend to bring to light the true textures and configurations of bodies; on which all the occult and, as they are called, specific properties and virtues in things depend; and from which too the rule of every powerful alteration and transformation is derived.

For example, we must inquire what amount of spirit there is in every body, what of tangible essence; and of the spirit, whether it be copious and turgid, or meager and scarce; whether it be fine or coarse, akin to air or to fire, brisk or sluggish, weak or strong, progressive or retrograde, interrupted or continuous, agreeing with external and surrounding objects or disagreeing, etc. In like manner we must inquire into the tangible essence (which admits of no fewer differences than the spirit),— into its coats, its fibers, its kinds of texture. Moreover the disposition of the spirit throughout the corporeal frame, with its pores, passages, veins and cells, and the rudiments or first essays of the organized body, fall under the same investigation. But on these inquiries also, and I may say on all the discovery of the Latent Configuration, a true and clear light is shed by the primary axioms, which entirely dispels all darkness and subtlety.

viii

Nor shall we thus be led to the doctrine of atoms, which implies the hypothesis of a vacuum and that of the unchangeableness of matter (both false assumptions); we shall be led only to real particles, such as really exist. Nor again is there any reason to be alarmed at the subtlety of the investigation, as if it could not be disentangled: on the contrary, the nearer it approaches to simple natures, the easier and plainer will everything become; the business being transferred from the complicated to the simple, from the incommensurable to the commensurable, from surds to rational quantities, from the infinite and vague to the finite and certain,—as in the case of the letters of the alphabet and the notes of music. And inquiries into nature have the best result when they begin with physics and end in mathematics. Again, let no one be afraid of high numbers or minute fractions. For in dealing with numbers it is as easy to set down or conceive a thousand as one, or the thousandth part of an integer as an integer itself.

ix

From the two kinds of axioms which have been spoken of, arises a just division of philosophy and the sciences; taking the received terms (which come nearest to express the thing) in a sense agreeable to my own views. Thus, let the investigation of forms, which are (in the eye of reason at least, and in their essential law) eternal and immutable, constitute *metaphysics;* and let the investigation of the Efficient Cause, and of Matter, and of the Latent Process, and the Latent Configuration (all of which have reference to the common and ordinary course of nature, not to her eternal and fundamental laws) constitute *physics.* And to these let there be subordinate two practical divisions: to physics, *mechanics;* to metaphysics, what (in a purer sense of the word) I call *magic,* on account of the broadness of the ways it moves in, and its greater command over nature.

x

Having thus set up the mark of knowledge, we must go on to precepts, and that in the most direct and obvious order. Now my directions for the interpretation of nature embrace two generic divisions: the one how to educe and form axioms from experience; the other how to deduce and derive new experiments from axioms. The former again is divided into three ministrations: a ministration to the sense, a ministration to the memory, and a ministration to the mind or reason.

For first of all we must prepare a *Natural and Experimental History,* sufficient and good; and this is the foundation of all; for we are not to imagine or suppose, but to discover, what nature does or may be made to do.

But natural and experimental history is so various and diffuse, that it confounds and distracts the understanding, unless it be ranged and presented to view in a suitable order. We must therefore form *Tables and Arrangements of Instances,* in such a method and order that the understanding may be able to deal with them.

And even when this is done, still the understanding, if left to itself and its own spontaneous movements, is incompetent and unfit to form axioms, unless it be directed and guarded. Therefore in the third place we must use *Induction,* true and legitimate induction, which is the very key of interpretation. But of this, which is the last, I must speak first, and then go back to the other ministrations.

xi

The investigation of Forms proceeds thus: a nature being given, we must first of all have a muster or presentation before the understanding of all known instances which agree in the same nature, though in substances the most unlike. And such collection must be made in the manner of a history, without premature speculation, or any great amount of subtlety. For example, let the investigation be into the Form of heat.

Instances Agreeing in the Nature of Heat.

1. The rays of the sun, especially in summer and at noon.
2. The rays of the sun reflected and condensed, as between mountains, or on walls, and most of all in burning-glasses and mirrors.
3. Fiery meteors.
4. Burning thunderbolts.
5. Eruptions of flame from the cavities of mountains.
6. All flame.
7. Ignited solids.
8. Natural warm-baths.
9. Liquids boiling or heated.
10. Hot vapors and fumes, and the air itself, which conceives the most powerful and glowing heat, if confined; as in reverbatory furnaces.
11. Certain seasons that are fine and cloudless by the constitution of the air itself, without regard to the time of year.
12. Air confined and underground in some caverns, especially in winter.
13. All villous substances, as wool, skins of animals, and down of birds, have heat.
14. All bodies, whether solid or liquid, whether dense or rare (as the air itself is), held for a time near the fire.

15. Sparks struck from flint and steel by strong percussion.

16. All bodies rubbed violently, as stone, wood, cloth, &c., insomuch that poles and axles of wheels sometimes catch fire; and the way they kindled fire in the West Indies was by attrition.

17. Green and moist vegetables confined and bruised together, as roses packed in baskets; insomuch that hay, if damp when stacked, often catches fire.

18. Quick lime sprinkled with water.

19. Iron, when first dissolved by strong waters in glass, and that without being put near the fire. And in like manner tin, &c., but not with equal intensity.

20. Animals, especially and at all times internally; though in insects the heat is not perceptible to the touch by reason of the smallness of their size.

21. Horse-dung and like excrements of animals when fresh.

22. Strong oil of sulphur and of vitriol has the effect of heat in burning linen.

23. Oil of marjoram and similar oils have the effect of heat in burning the bones of the teeth.

24. Strong and well rectified spirit of wine has the effect of heat; insomuch that the white of an egg being put into it hardens and whitens almost as if it were boiled; and bread thrown in becomes dry and crusted like toast.

25. Aromatic and hot herbs, as *dracunculus, nasturtium vetus,* &c., although not warm to the hand (either whole or in powder), yet to the tongue and palate, being a little masticated, they feel hot and burning.

26. Strong vinegar, and all acids, on all parts of the body where there is no epidermis, as the eye, tongue, or on any part when wounded and laid bare of the skin; produce a pain but little differing from that which is created by heat.

27. Even keen and intense cold produces a kind of sensation of burning;

Nec Borae penetrabile frigus adurit.[1]

28. Other instances.

This table I call the *Table of Essence and Presence.*

xii

Secondly, we must make a presentation to the understanding of instances in which the given nature is wanting; because the Form, as stated above, ought no less to be absent when the given nature is ab-

[1] Nor burns the sharp cold of the northern blast.

sent, than present when it is present. But to note all these would be endless.

The negatives should therefore be subjoined to the affirmatives, and the absence of the given nature inquired of in those subjects only that are most akin to the others in which it is present and forthcoming. This I call the *Table of Deviation, or of Absence in Proximity*.

Instances in Proximity where the Nature of Heat is Absent.

1. The rays of the moon and of stars and comets are not found to be hot to the touch; indeed the severest colds are observed to be at the full moons.

The larger fixed stars however, when passed or approached by the sun, are supposed to increase and give intensity to the heat of the sun; as is the case when the sun is in the sign Leo, and in the Dog-days.

2. The rays of the sun in what is called the middle region of the air do not give heat; for which there is commonly assigned not a bad reason, viz. that that region is neither near enough to the body of the sun from which the rays emanate, nor to the earth from which they are reflected. And this appears from the fact that on the tops of mountains, unless they are very high, there is perpetual snow. On the other hand it has been observed that on the peak of Teneriffe, and among the Andes of Peru, the very tops of the mountains are free from snow; which lies only somewhat lower down. Moreover the air itself at the very top is found to be by no means cold, but only rare and keen; insomuch that on the Andes it pricks and hurts the eyes by its excessive keenness, and also irritates the mouth of the stomach, producing vomiting. And it was observed by the ancients that on the top of Olympus the rarity of the air was such that those who ascended it had to carry sponges with them dipped in vinegar and water, and to apply them from time to time to their mouth and nose, the air being from its rarity not sufficient to support respiration; and it was further stated that on this summit the air was so serene, and so free from rain and snow and wind, that letters traced by the finger in the ashes of the sacrifices on the altar of Jupiter remained there till the next year without being at all disturbed. And at this day travelers ascending to the top of the Peak of Teneriffe make the ascent by night and not by day; and soon after the rising of the sun are warned and urged by their guides to come down without delay, on account of the danger they run lest the animal spirits should swoon and be suffocated by the tenuity of the air.

3. The reflection of the rays of the sun in regions near the polar circles is found to be very weak and ineffective in producing heat; insomuch that the Dutch who wintered in Nova Zembla, and expected their ship to be freed from the obstructions of the mass of ice which hemmed

her in by the beginning of July, were disappointed of their expectation, and obliged to take to their boat. Thus the direct rays of the sun seem to have but little power, even on the level ground; nor have the reflex much, unless they are multiplied and combined; which is the case when the sun tends more to the perpendicular; for then the incident rays make acuter angles, so that the lines of the rays are nearer each other; whereas on the contrary, when the sun shines very obliquely, the angles are very obtuse, and thus the lines of rays are at a greater distance from each other. Meanwhile it should be observed that there may be many operations of the sun, and those too depending on the nature of heat, which are not proportioned to our touch; so that in respect of us their action does not go so far as to produce sensible warmth, but in respect of some other bodies they have the effect of heat.

4. Try the following experiment. Take a glass fashioned in a contrary manner to a common burning-glass, and placing it between your hand and the rays of the sun, observe whether it diminishes the heat of the sun, as a burning-glass increases and strengthens it. For it is evident in the case of optical rays that according as the glass is made thicker or thinner in the middle as compared with the sides, so do the objects seen through it appear more spread or more contracted. Observe therefore whether the same is the case with heat.

5. Let the experiment be carefully tried, whether by means of the most powerful and best constructed burning-glasses, the rays of the moon can be so caught and collected as to produce even the least degree of warmth. But should this degree of warmth prove too subtle and weak to be perceived and apprehended by the touch, recourse must be had to those glasses which indicate the state of the atmosphere in respect of heat and cold. Thus, let the rays of the moon fall through a burning-glass on the top of a glass of this kind, and then observe whether there ensues a sinking of the water through warmth.

6. Let a burning-glass also be tried with a heat that does not emit rays or light, as that of iron or stone heated but not ignited, boiling water, and the like; and observe whether there ensue an increase of the heat, as in the case of the sun's rays.

7. Let a burning-glass also be tried with common flame.

8. Comets (if we are to reckon these too among meteors) are not found to exert a constant or manifest effect in increasing the heat of the season, though it is observed that they are often followed by droughts. Moreover bright beams and pillars and openings in the heavens appear more frequently in winter than in summer time, and chiefly during the intensest cold, but always accompanied by dry weather. Lightning, however, and coruscations and thunder, seldom occur in the winter, but about the time of great heat. Falling stars, as they are called, are com-

monly supposed to consist rather of some bright and lighted viscous substance, than to be of any strong fiery nature. But on this point let further inquiry be made.

9. There are certain coruscations which give light but do not burn. And these always come without thunder.

10. Eructations and eruptions of flame are found no less in cold than in warm countries, as in Iceland and Greenland. In cold countries too the trees are in many cases more inflammable and more pitchy and resinous than in warm; as the fir, pine, and others. The situations however and the nature of the soil in which eruptions of this kind usually occur have not been carefully enough ascertained to enable us to subjoin a Negative to this Affirmative Instance.

11. All flame is in all cases more or less warm; nor is there any Negative to be subjoined. And yet they say that the *ignis fatuus* (as it is called), which sometimes even settles on a wall, has not much heat; perhaps as much as the flame of spirit in wine, which is mild and soft. But still milder must that flame be, which according to certain grave and trustworthy histories has been seen shining about the head and locks of boys and girls, without at all burning the hair, but softly playing round it. It is also most certain that about a horse, when sweating on the road, there is sometimes seen at night, and in clear weather, a sort of luminous appearance without any manifest heat. And it is a well-known fact, and looked upon as a sort of miracle, that a few years ago a girl's stomacher, on being slightly shaken or rubbed, emitted sparks; which was caused perhaps by some alum or salts used in the dye, that stood somewhat thick and formed a crust, and were broken by the friction. It is also most certain that all sugar, whether refined or raw, provided only it be somewhat hard, sparkles when broken or scraped with a knife in the dark. In like manner sea and salt water is sometimes found to sparkle by night when struck violently by oars. And in storms too at night time, the foam of the sea when violently agitated emits sparks, and this sparkling the Spaniards call *Sea Lung*. With regard to the heat of the flame which was called by ancient sailors Castor and Pollux, and by moderns St. Elmo's Fire, no sufficient investigation thereof has been made.

12. Every body ignited so as to turn to a fiery red, even if unaccompanied by flame, is always hot; neither is there any Negative to be subjoined to this Affirmative. But that which comes nearest seems to be rotten wood, which shines by night, and yet is not found to be hot; and the putrefying scales of fish, which also shine in the dark, and yet are not warm to the touch; nor again is the body of the glow-worm, or of the fly called *Luciola*, found to be warm to the touch.

13. In what situation and kind of soil warm baths usually spring, has not been sufficiently examined; and therefore no Negative is subjoined.

14. To warm liquids I subjoin the Negative Instance of liquid itself in its natural state. For we find no tangible liquid which is warm in its own nature and remains so constantly; but the warmth is an adventitious nature, superinduced only for the time being; so that the liquids which in power and operation are hottest, as spirit of wine, chemical oil of spices, oil of vitriol and sulphur, and the like, which burn after a while, are at first cold to the touch. The water of natural warm baths on the other hand, if received into a vessel and separated from its springs, cools just like water that has been heated on a fire. But it is true that oily substances are less cold to the touch than watery, oil being less cold than water, and silk than linen. But this belongs to the Table of Degrees of Cold.

15. In like manner to hot vapor I subjoin as a Negative the nature of vapor itself, such as we find it with us. For exhalations from oily substances, though easily inflammable, are yet not found to be warm, unless newly exhaled from the warm body.

16. In like manner I subjoin as a Negative to hot air the nature of air itself. For we do not find here any air that is warm, unless it has either been confined, or compressed, or manifestly warmed by the sun, fire, or some other warm substance.

17. I here subjoin the Negative of colder weather than is suitable to the season of the year, which we find occurs during east and north winds; just as we have weather of the opposite kind with the south and west winds. So a tendency to rain, especially in winter time, accompanies warm weather; while frost accompanies cold.

18. Here I subjoin the Negative of air confined in caverns during the summer. But the subject of air in confinement should by all means be more diligently examined. For in the first place it may well be matter of doubt what is the nature of air in itself with regard to heat and cold. For air manifestly receives warmth from the influence of the heavenly bodies, and cold perhaps from the exhalations of the earth; and again in the middle region of air, as it is called, from cold vapors and snow; so that no opinion can be formed as to the nature of air from the examination of air that is at large and exposed; but a truer judgment might be made by examining it when confined. It is however necessary for the air to be confined in a vessel of such material as will not itself communicate warmth or cold to the air by its own nature, nor readily admit the influence of the outer atmosphere. Let the experiment therefore be made in an earthen jar wrapped round with many folds of leather to protect it from the outward air, and let the vessel remain tightly closed for three or four days; then open the vessel and test the degree of heat or cold by applying either the hand or a graduated glass.

19. In like manner a doubt suggests itself whether the warmth in wool, skins, feathers, and the like, proceeds from a faint degree of heat inherent in them, as being excretions from animals; or from a certain fat and oiliness, which is of a nature akin to warmth; or simply, as surmised in the preceding article, from the confinement and separation of the air. For all air that is cut off from connection with the outer air seems to have some warmth. Try the experiment therefore with fibrous substances made of linen; not of wool, feathers, or silk, which are excretions from animals. It should also be observed that all powders (in which there is manifestly air enclosed) are less cold than the whole substances they are made from; as likewise I suppose that all froth (as that which contains air) is less cold than the liquor it comes from.

20. To this no Negative is subjoined. For there is nothing found among us either tangible or spirituous which does not contract warmth when put near fire. There is this difference however, that some substances contract warmth more quickly, as air, oil, and water; others more slowly, as stone and metal. But this belongs to the Table of Degrees.

21. To this Instance I subjoin no Negative, except that I would have it well observed that sparks are produced from flint and steel, or any other hard substance, only when certain minute particles are struck off from the substance of the stone or metal; and that the attrition of the air does not of itself ever produce sparks, as is commonly supposed. And the sparks themselves too, owing to the weight of the ignited body, tend rather downwards than upwards; and on going out become a tangible sooty substance.

22. There is no Negative, I think, to be subjoined to this Instance. For we find among us no tangible body which does not manifestly gain warmth by attrition; insomuch that the ancients fancied that the heavenly bodies had no other means or power of producing warmth than by the attrition of the air in their rapid and hurried revolution. But on this subject we must further inquire whether bodies discharged from engines, as balls from cannon, do not acquire some degrees of heat from the very percussion, so as to be found somewhat warm when they fall. Air in motion, however, rather chills than warms, as appears from wind, bellows, and blowing with the mouth contracted. But motion of this kind is not so rapid as to excite heat, and is the motion of a mass, and not of particles; so that it is no wonder if it does not generate heat.

23. On this Instance should be made more diligent inquiry. For herbs and vegetables when green and moist seem to contain some latent heat, though so slight that it is not perceptible to the touch when they are single; but only when they are collected and shut up together, so

that their spirits may not breathe out into the air, but may mutually cherish each other; whereupon there arises a palpable heat, and sometimes flame in suitable matter.

24. On this Instance too should be made more diligent inquiry. For quick lime sprinkled with water seems to contract heat, either by the concentration of heat before dispersed, as in the above-mentioned case of confined herbs, or because the igneous spirit is irritated and exasperated by the water, so as to cause a conflict and reaction. Which of these two is the real cause will more readily appear if oil be poured on instead of water; for oil will serve equally well with water to concentrate the enclosed spirit, but not to irritate it. We should also extend the experiment both by employing the ashes and rusts of different bodies, and by pouring in different liquids.

25. To this Instance is subjoined the Negative of other metals which are softer and more fusible. For gold-leaf dissolved by *aqua regia* gives no heat to the touch; no more does lead dissolved in *aqua fortis;* neither again does quicksilver (as I remember); but silver itself does, and copper too (as I remember); tin still more manifestly; and most of all iron and steel, which not only excite a strong heat in dissolution, but also a violent ebullition. It appears therefore that the heat is produced by conflict; the strong waters penetrating, digging into, and tearing asunder the parts of the substance, while the substance itself resists. But where the substances yield more easily, there is hardly any heat excited.

26. To the heat of animals no Negative is subjoined, except that of insects (as above-mentioned), on account of their small size. For in fishes, as compared with land animals, it is rather a low degree than an absence of heat that is noted. But in vegetables and plants there is no degree of heat perceptible to the touch, either in their exudations or in their pith when freshly exposed. In animals however is found a great diversity of heat, both in their parts (there being different degrees of heat about the heart, in the brain, and on the skin) and in their accidents, as violent exercise and fevers.

27. To this Instance it is hard to subjoin a Negative. Indeed the excrements of animals when no longer fresh have manifestly a potential heat, as is seen in the enriching of soil.

28. Liquids, whether waters or oils, which possess a great and intense acridity, act like heat in tearing asunder bodies, and burning them after some time; yet to the touch they are not hot at first. But their operation is relative and according to the porosity of the body to which they are applied. For *aqua regia* dissolves gold but not silver; *aqua fortis,* on the contrary, dissolves silver, but not gold; neither dissolves glass, and so on with others.

29. Let trial be made of spirit of wine on wood; and also on butter, wax, or pitch; and observe whether by its heat it in any degree melts them. For the twenty-fourth instance exhibits a power in it that resembles heat in producing incrustation. In like manner therefore try its power in producing liquefaction. Let trial also be made with a graduated or calendar glass, hollow at the top; pour into the hollow spirit of wine well rectified, cover it up that the spirit may better retain its heat, and observe whether by its heat it makes the water sink.

30. Spices and acrid herbs strike hot on the palate, and much hotter on the stomach. Observe therefore on what other substances they produce the effects of heat. Sailors tell us that when large parcels and masses of spices are, after being long kept close, suddenly opened, those who first stir and take them out run the risk of fever and inflammation. It can also be tried whether such spices and herbs when pounded would not dry bacon and meat hung over them, as smoke does.

31. There is an acridity or pungency both in cold things, as vinegar and oil of vitriol, and in hot, as oil of marjoram and the like. Both alike therefore cause pain in animate substances, and tear asunder and consume the parts in such as are inanimate. To this Instance again there is no Negative subjoined. Moreover we find no pain in animals, save with a certain sensation of heat.

32. There are many actions common both to heat and cold, though in a very different manner. For boys find that snow after a while seems to burn their hands; and cold preserves meat from putrefaction, no less than fire; and heat contracts bodies, which cold does also. But these and similar instances may more conveniently be referred to the inquiry concerning Cold.

xiii

Thirdly, we must make a presentation to the understanding of instances in which the nature under inquiry is found in different degrees, more or less; which must be done by making a comparison either of its increase and decrease in the same subject, or of its amount in different subjects, as compared one with another. For since the Form of a thing is the very thing itself, and the thing differs from the form no otherwise than as the apparent differs from the real, or the external from the internal, or the thing in reference to man from the thing in reference to the universe; it necessarily follows that no nature can be taken as the true form, unless it always decrease when the nature in question decreases, and in like manner always increase when the nature in question increases. This Table therefore I call the *Table of Degrees* or the *Table of Comparison.*

Table of Degrees or Comparison in Heat.

I will therefore first speak of those substances which contain no degree
at all of heat perceptible to the touch, but seem to have a certain potential heat only, or disposition and preparation for hotness. After that I
shall proceed to substances which are hot actually, and to the touch, and
to their intensities and degrees.

1. In solid and tangible bodies we find nothing which is in its nature
originally hot. For no stone, metal, sulphur, fossil, wood, water, or carcass of animal is found to be hot. And the hot water in baths seems to
be heated by external causes; whether it be by flame or subterraneous
fire, such as is thrown up from Aetna and many other mountains, or by
the conflict of bodies, as heat is caused in the dissolutions of iron and
tin. There is therefore no degree of heat palpable to the touch in animate substances; but they differ in degree of cold, wood not being
equally cold with metal. But this belongs to the Table of Degrees in
Cold.

2. As far however as potential heat and aptitude for flame is concerned, there are many inanimate substances found strongly disposed
thereto, as sulphur, naphtha, rock oil.

3. Substances once hot, as horse-dung from animal heat, and lime or
perhaps ashes and soot from fire, retain some latent remains of their
former heat. Hence certain distillations and resolutions of bodies are
made by burying them in horse-dung, and heat is excited in lime by
sprinkling it with water, as already mentioned.

4. In the vegetable creation we find no plant or part of plant (as gum
or pitch) which is warm to the human touch. But yet, as stated above,
green herbs gain warmth by being shut up; and to the internal touch, as
the palate or stomach, and even to external parts, after a little time, as
in plasters and ointments, some vegetables are perceptibly warm and
others cold.

5. In the parts of animals after death or separation from the body, we
find nothing warm to the human touch. Not even horse-dung, unless enclosed and buried, retains its heat. But yet all dung seems to have a potential heat, as is seen in the fattening of the land. In like manner carcasses of animals have some such latent and potential heat; insomuch
that in burying grounds, where burials take place daily, the earth collects a certain hidden heat, which consumes a body newly laid in it
much more speedily than pure earth. We are told too that in the East
there is discovered a fine soft texture, made of the down of birds, which
by an innate force dissolves and melts butter when lightly wrapped in
it.

6. Substances which fatten the soil, as dung of all kinds, chalk, sea-
sand, salt, and the like, have some disposition to heat.

7. All putrefaction contains in itself certain elements of a slight heat, though not so much as to be perceived by the touch. For not even those substances which on putrefaction turn to animalculae, as flesh, cheese, &c., feel warm to the touch; no more does rotten wood, which shines in the dark. Heat however in putrid substances sometimes betrays itself by foul and powerful odors.

8. The first degree of heat therefore among those substances which feel hot to the touch, seems to be the heat of animals, which has a pretty great extent in its degrees. For the lowest, as in insects, is hardly perceptible to the touch; but the highest scarce equals the sun's heat in the hottest countries and seasons, nor is it too great to be borne by the hand. It is said however of Constantius, and some others of a very dry constitution and habit of body, that in violent fevers they became so hot as somewhat to burn the hand that touched them.

9. Animals increase in heat by motion and exercise, wine, feasting, venus, burning fevers, and pain.

10. When attacked by intermittent fevers, animals are at first seized with cold and shivering, but soon after they become exceedingly hot, which is their condition from the first in burning and pestilential fevers.

11. Let further inquiry be made into the different degrees of heat in different animals, as in fishes, quadrupeds, serpents, birds; and also according to their species, as in the lion, the kite, the man; for in common opinion fish are the least hot internally, and birds the hottest; especially doves, hawks, and sparrows.

12. Let further inquiry be made into the different degrees of heat in the different parts and limbs of the same animal. For milk, blood, seed, eggs, are found to be hot only in a moderate degree, and less hot than the outer flesh of the animal when in motion or agitated. But what the degree of heat is in the brain, stomach, heart, &c. has not yet been in like manner inquired.

13. All animals in winter and cold weather are cold externally, but internally they are thought to be even hotter.

14. The heat of the heavenly bodies, even in the hottest countries, and at the hottest times of the year and day, is never sufficiently strong to set on fire or burn the driest wood or straw, or even tinder, unless strengthened by burning-glasses or mirrors. It is however able to extact vapor from moist substances.

15. By the tradition of astronomers some stars are hotter than others. Of planets, Mars is accounted the hottest after the sun; then comes Jupiter, and then Venus. Others, again, are set down as cold; the moon, for instance, and above all Saturn. Of fixed stars, Sirius is said to be the hottest, then Cor Leonis or Regulus, then Canicula, and so on.

16. The sun gives greater heat the nearer he approaches to the per-

pendicular or zenith; and this is probably true of the other planets also, according to the proportion of their heat. Jupiter, for instance, is hotter, probably, to us when under Cancer or Leo than under Capricorn or Aquarius.

17. We must also believe that the sun and other planets give more heat in perigee, from their proximity to the earth, than they do in apogee. But if it happens that in some region the sun is at the same time in perigee and near the perpendicular, his heat must of necessity be greater than in a region where he is also in perigee, but shining more obliquely. And therefore the altitude of the planets in their exaltation in different regions ought to be noted, with respect to perpendicularity or obliquity.

18. The sun and other planets are supposed to give greater heat when nearer to the larger fixed stars. Thus when the sun is in Leo he is nearer Cor Leonis, Cauda Leonis, Spica Virginis, Sirius and Canicula, then when he is in Cancer, in which sign however he is nearer to the perpendicular. And it must be supposed that those parts of the heavens shed the greatest heat (though it be not at all perceptible to the touch) which are the most adorned with stars, especially of a larger size.

19. Altogether, the heat of the heavenly bodies is increased in three ways; first, by perpendicularity; secondly, by proximity or perigee; thirdly, by the conjunction or combination of stars.

20. The heat of animals, and of the rays of the heavenly bodies also (as they reach us), is found to differ by a wide interval from flame, though of the mildest kind, and from all ignited bodies; and from liquids also, and air itself when highly heated by fire. For the flame of spirit of wine, though scattered and not condensed, is yet sufficient to set paper, straw, or linen on fire; which the heat of animals will never do, or of the sun without a burning-glass or mirror.

21. There are however many degrees of strength and weakness in the heat of flame and ignited bodies. But as they have never been diligently inquired into, we must pass them lightly over. It appears however that of all flame that of spirit of wine is the softest, unless perhaps *ignis fatuus* be softer, and the flames or sparklings arising from the sweat of animals. Next to this, as I suppose, comes flame from light and porous vegetable matter, as straw, reeds, and dried leaves; from which the flame from hairs or feathers does not much differ. Next perhaps comes flame from wood, especially such as contains but little rosin or pitch; with this distinction however, that the flame from small pieces of wood (such as are commonly tied up in fagots) is milder than the flame from trunks and roots of trees. And this you may try any day in furnaces for smelting iron, in which a fire made with fagots and boughs of trees is of no great use. After this I think comes flame from oil, tallow, wax, and such like fat and oily substances, which have no great acrimony. But the

most violent heat is found in pitch and rosin; and yet more in sulpher, camphor, naphtha, rock-oil, and salts (after the crude matter is discharged), and in their compounds, as gunpowder, Greek fire (commonly called wild fire), and its different kind, which have so stubborn a heat that they are not easily extinguished by water.

22. I think also that the flame which results from some imperfect metals is very strong and eager. But on these points let further inquiry be made.

23. The flame of powerful lightning seems to exceed in strength all the former; for it has even been known to melt wrought iron into drops; which those other flames cannot do.

24. In ignited bodies too there are different degrees of heat, though these again have not yet been diligently examined. The weakest heat of all, I think, is that from tinder, such as we use to kindle flame with; and in like manner that of touchwood or tow, which is used in firing cannon. After this comes ignited wood or coal, and also bricks and the like heated to ignition. But of all ignited substances, the hottest, as I take it, are ignited metals; as iron, copper, &c. But these require further investigation.

25. Some ignited bodies are found to be much hotter than some flames. Ignited iron, for instance, is much hotter and more consuming than flame of spirit of wine.

26. Of substances also which are not ignited but only heated by fire, as boiling water and air confined in furnaces, some are found to exceed in heat many flames and ignited substances.

27. Motion increases heat, as you may see in bellows, and by blowing; insomuch that the harder metals are not dissolved or melted by a dead or quiet fire, till it be made intense by blowing.

28. Let trial be made with burning-glasses, which (as I remember) act thus. If you place a burning-glass at the distance of (say) a span from a combustible body, it will not burn or consume it so easily as if it were first placed at the distance of (say) half a span, and then moved gradually and slowly to the distance of the whole span. And yet the cone and union of rays are the same; but the motion itself increases the operation of the heat.

29. Fires which break out during a strong wind are thought to make greater progress against than with it; because the flame recoils more violently when the wind gives way than it advances while the wind is driving it on.

30. Flame does not burst out, nor it is generated, uless some hollow space be allowed it to move and play in; except the explosive flame of gunpowder, and the like, where compression and imprisonment increase its fury.

31. An anvil grows very hot under the hammer, insomuch that if it were made of a thin plate it might, I suppose, with strong and continuous blows of the hammer, grow red like ignited iron. But let this be tried by experiment.

32. But in ignited substances which are porous, so as to give the fire room to move, if this motion be checked by strong compression, the fire is immediately extinguished. For instance, when tinder, or the burning wick of a candle or lamp, or even live charcoal or coal, is pressed down with an extinguisher, or with the foot, or any similar instrument, the operation of the fire instantly ceases.

33. Approximation to a hot body increases heat in proportion to the degree of approximation. And this is the case also with light; for the nearer an object is brought to the light, the more visible it becomes.

34. The union of different heats increases heat, unless the hot substances be mixed together. For a large fire and a small fire in the same room increase one another's heat; but warm water plunged into boiling water cools it.

35. The continued application of a hot body increases heat, because heat perpetually passing and emanating from it mingles with the previously existing heat, and so multiplies the heat. For a fire does not warm a room as well in half an hour as it does if continued through the whole hour. But this is not the case with light; for a lamp or candle gives no more light after it has been long lighted, than it did at first.

36. Irritation by surrounding cold increases heat, as you may see in fires during a sharp frost. And this I think is owing not merely to the confinement and contraction of the heat, which is a kind of union, but also to irritation. Thus when air or a stick is violently compressed or bent, it recoils not merely to the point it was forced from, but beyond it on the other side. Let trial therefore be carefully made by putting a stick or some such thing into flame, and observing whether it is not burnt more quickly at the sides than in the middle of the flame.

37. There are many degrees in susceptibility of heat. And first of all it is to be observed how slight and faint a heat changes and somewhat warms even those bodies which are least of all susceptible of heat. Even the heat of the hand communicates some heat to a ball of lead or any metal, if held in it a little while. So readily and so universally is heat transmitted and excited, the body remaining to all appearance unchanged.

38. Of all substances that we are acquainted with, the one which most readily receives and loses heat is air; as is best seen in calendar glasses [air thermoscopes], which are made thus. Take a glass with a hollow belly, a thin and oblong neck; turn it upside down and lower it, with the mouth downwards and the belly upwards, into another glass vessel

containing water; and let the mouth of the inserted vessel touch the bottom of the receiving vessel, and its neck lean slightly against the mouth of the other, so that it can stand. And that this may be done more conveniently, apply a little wax to the mouth of the receiving glass, but not so as to seal its mouth quite up; in order that the motion, of which we are going to speak, and which is very facile and delicate, may not be impeded by want of a supply of air.

The lowered glass, before being inserted into the other, must be heated before a fire in its upper part, that is its belly. Now when it is placed in the position I have described, the air which was dilated by the heat will, after a lapse of time sufficient to allow for the extinction of that adventitious heat, withdraw and contract itself to the same extension or dimension as that of the surrounding air at the time of the immersion of the glass; and will draw the water upwards to a corresponding height. To the side of the glass there should be affixed a strip of paper, narrow and oblong, and marked with as many degrees as you choose. You will then see, according as the day is warm or cold, that the air contracts under the action of cold, and expands under the action of heat; as will be seen by the water rising when the air contracts, and sinking when it dilates. But the air's sense of heat and cold is so subtle and exquisite as far to exceed the perception of the human touch, insomuch that a ray of sunshine, or the heat of the breath, much more the heat of one's hand placed on the top of the glass, will cause the water immediately to sink in a perceptible degree. And yet I think that animal spirits have a sense of heat and cold more exquisite still, were it not that it is impeded and deadened by the grossness of the body.

39. Next to air, I take those bodies to be most sensitive of heat which have been recently changed and compressed by cold, as snow and ice; for they begin to dissolve and melt with any gentle heat. Next to them, perhaps, comes quicksilver. After that follow greasy substances, as oil, butter, and the like; then comes wood; then water; and lastly stones and metals, which are slow to heat, especially in the inside. These, however, when once they have acquired heat retain it very long; insomuch that an ignited brick, stone, or piece of iron, when plunged into a basin of water, will remain for a quarter of an hour, or thereabouts, so hot that you cannot touch it.

40. The less the mass of a body, the sooner is it heated by the approach of a hot body; which shows that all heat of which we have experience is in some sort opposed to tangible matter.

41. Heat, as far as regards the sense and touch of man, is a thing various and relative; insomuch that tepid water feels hot if the hand be cold, but cold if the hand be hot.

xiv

How poor we are in history anyone may see from the foregoing tables; where I not only insert sometimes mere traditions and reports (though never without a note of doubtful credit and authority) in place of history proved and instances certain, but am also frequently forced to use the words "Let trial be made," or "Let it be further inquired."

xv

The work and office of these three tables I call the Presentation of Instances to the Understanding. Which presentation having been made, Induction itself must be set at work; for the problem is, upon a review of the instances, all and each, to find such a nature as is always present or absent with the given nature, and always increases and decreases with it; and which is, as I have said, a particular case of a more general nature. Now if the mind attempt this affirmatively from the first, as when left to itself it is always wont to do, the result will be fancies and guesses and notions ill defined and axioms that must be mended every day; unless like the schoolmen we have a mind to fight for what is false; though doubtless these will be better or worse according to the faculties and strength of the understanding which is at work. To God, truly, the Giver and Architect of Forms, and it may be to the angels and higher intelligences, it belongs to have an affirmative knowledge of Forms immediately, and from the first contemplation. But this assuredly is more than man can do, to whom it is granted only to proceed at first by negatives, and at last to end in affirmatives, after exclusion has been exhausted.

xvi

We must make therefore a complete solution and separation of nature, not indeed by fire, but by the mind, which is a kind of divine fire. The first work therefore of true induction (as far as regards the discovery of Forms) is the rejection or exclusion of the several natures which are not found in some instance where the given nature is present, or are found in some instance where the given nature is absent, or are found to increase in some instance when the given nature decreases, or to decrease when the given nature increases. Then indeed after the rejection and exclusion has been duly made, there will remain at the bottom, all light opinions vanishing into smoke, a Form affirmative, solid and true and well defined. This is quickly said; but the way to come at it is winding and intricate. I will endeavor however not to overlook any of the points which may help us towards it.

xvii

But when I assign so prominent a part to Forms, I cannot too often warn and admonish men against applying what I say to those forms to which their thoughts and contemplations have hitherto been accustomed.

For in the first place I do not at present speak of Compound Forms, which are, as I have remarked, combinations of simple natures according to the common course of the universe; as of the lion, eagle, rose, gold, and the like. It will be time to treat of these when we come to the Latent Processes and Latent Configurations, and the discovery of them, as they are found in what are called substances or natures concrete.

And even in the case of simple natures I would not be understood to speak of abstract Forms and Ideas, either not defined in matter at all, or ill defined. For when I speak of Forms, I mean nothing more than those laws and determinations of absolute actuality, which govern and constitute any simple nature, as heat, light, weight, in every kind of matter and subject that is susceptible of them. Thus the Form of heat or the Form of light is the same thing as the Law of heat or the Law of light. Nor indeed do I ever allow myself to be drawn away from things themselves and the operative part. And therefore when I say (for instance) in the investigation of the Form of heat, "Reject rarity," or "Rarity does not belong to the form of heat;" it is the same as if I said, "It is possible to superinduce heat on a dense body," or "It is possible to take away or keep out heat from a rare body."

But if anyone conceive that my Forms too are of a somewhat abstract nature, because they mix and combine things heterogeneous (for the heat of heavenly bodies and the heat of fire seem to be very heterogeneous; so do the fixed red of the rose or the like, and the apparent red in the rainbow, the opal, or the diamond; so again do the different kinds of death, death by drowning, by hanging, by stabbing, by apoplexy, by atrophy; and yet they agree severally in the nature of heat, redness, death); if anone, I say, be of this opinion, he may be assured that his mind is held in captivity by custom, by the gross appearance of things, and by men's opinions. For it is most certain that these things, however heterogeneous and alien from each other, agree in the Form or Law which governs heat, redness and death; and that the power of man cannot possibly be emancipated and freed from the common course of nature, and expanded and exalted to new efficients and new modes of operation, except by the revelation and discovery of Forms of this kind. And yet, when I have spoken of this union of nature, which is the point of most importance, I shall proceed to the divisions and veins of nature, as well the ordinary as those that are more inward and exact, and speak of them in their place.

xviii

I must now give an example of the Exclusion or Rejection of natures which by the Tables of Presentation are found not to belong to the Form of heat; observing in the meantime that not only each table suffices for the rejection of any nature, but even any one of the particular instances contained in any of the tables. For it is manifest from what has been said that any one contradictory instance overthrows a conjecture as to the Form. But nevertheless for clearness' sake and that the use of the tables may be more plainly shown, I sometimes double or multiply an exclusion.

An Example of Exclusion, or Rejection of Natures from the Form of Heat.

1. On account of the rays of the sun, reject the nature of the elements.

2. On account of common fire, and chiefly subterraneous fires (which are the most remote and most completely separate from the rays of heavenly bodies), reject the nature of heavenly bodies.

3. On account of the warmth acquired by all kinds of bodies (minerals, vegetables, skin of animals, water, oil, air, and the rest) by mere approach to a fire, or other hot body, reject the distinctive or more subtle texture of bodies.

4. On account of ignited iron and other metals, which communicate heat to other bodies and yet lose none of their weight or substance, reject the communication or admixture of the substance of another hot body.

5. On account of boiling water and air, and also on account of metals and other solids that receive heat but not to ignition or red heat, reject light or brightness.

6. On account of the rays of the moon and other heavenly bodies, with the exception of the sun, also reject light and brightness.

7. By a comparison of ignited iron and the flame of spirit of wine (of which ignited iron has more heat and less brightness, while the flame of spirit of wine has more brightness and less heat), also reject light and brightness.

8. On account of ignited gold and other metals, which are of the greatest density as a whole, reject rarity.

9. On account of air, which is found for the most part cold and yet remains rare, also reject rarity.

10. On account of ignited iron, which does not swell in bulk, but keeps within the same visible dimensions, reject local or expansive motion of the body as a whole.

11. On account of the dilation of air in calendar glasses and the like, wherein the air evidently moves locally and expansively and yet acquires no manifest increase of heat, also reject local or expansive motion of the body as a whole.

12. On account of the ease with which all bodies are heated, without any destruction or observable alteration, reject a destructive nature, or the violent communication of any new nature.

13. On account of the agreement and conformity of the similar effects which are wrought by heat and cold, reject motion of the body as a whole, whether expansive or contractive.

14. On account of heat being kindled by the attrition of bodies, reject a principial nature. By principial nature I mean that which exists in the nature of things positively, and not as the effect of any antecedent nature.

There are other natures beside these; for these tables are not perfect, but meant only for examples.

All and each of the above mentioned natures do *not* belong to the Form of heat. And from all of them man is freed in his operations on heat.

xix

In the process of Exclusion are laid the foundations of true Induction, which however is not completed till it arrives at an Affirmative. Nor is the Exclusive part itself at all complete, nor indeed can it possibly be so at first. For Exclusion is evidently the rejection of simple natures; and if we do not yet possess sound and true notions of simple natures, how can the process of Exclusion be made accurate? Now some of the above-mentioned notions (as that of the nature of the elements, of the nature of heavenly bodies, of rarity) are vague and ill-defined. I therefore, well knowing and nowise forgetting how great a work I am about (viz., that of rendering the human understanding a match for things and nature), do not rest satisfied with the precepts I have laid down; but proceed further to devise and supply more powerful aids for the use of the understanding; which I shall now subjoin. And assuredly in the Interpretation of Nature the mind should by all means be so prepared and disposed, that while it rests and finds footing in due stages and degrees of certainty, it may remember withal (especially at the beginning) that what it has before it depends in great measure upon what remains behind.

xx

And yet since truth will sooner come out from error than from confusion, I think it expedient that the understanding should have permission,

after the three Tables of First Presentation (such as I have exhibited)
have been made and weighed, to make an essay of the Interpretation of
Nature in the affirmative way; on the strength both of the instances
given in the tables, and of any others it may meet with elsewhere. Which
kind of essay I call the *indulgence of the understanding,* or the *commencement of interpretation,* or the *First Vintage.*

First Vintage concerning the Form of Heat

It is to be observed that the Form of a thing is to be found (as
plainly appears from what has been said) in each and all the instances,
in which the thing itself is to be found; otherwise it would not be the
Form. It follows therefore that there can be no contradictory instance.
At the same time the Form is found much more conspicuous and evident in some instances than in others; namely in those wherein the nature of the Form is less restrained and obstructed and kept within
bounds by other natures. Instances of this kind I call *Shining or Striking Instances.* Let us now therefore proceed to the First Vintage concerning the Form of Heat.

From a survey of the instances, all and each, the nature of which
Heat is a particular case appears to be Motion. This is displayed most
conspicuously in flame, which is always in motion, and in boiling or sim-
mering liquids, which also are in perpetual motion. It is also shown in
the excitement or increase of heat caused by motion, as in bellows and
blasts; on which see Tab. 3. Inst. 29.; and again in other kinds of motion, on which see Tab. 3. Inst. 28. and 31. Again it is shown in the extinction of fire and heat by any strong compression, which checks and
stops the motion; on which see Tab. 3. Inst. 30. and 32. It is shown
also by this, that all bodies are destroyed, or at any rate notably altered,
by all strong and vehement fire and heat; whence it is quite clear that
heat causes a tumult and confusion and violent motion in the internal
parts of a body, which perceptibly tends to its dissolution.

When I say of Motion that it is as the genus of which heat is a species, I would be understood to mean, not that heat generates motion or
that motion generates heat (though both are true in certain cases), but
that Heat itself, its essence and quiddity, is Motion and nothing else;
limited however by the specific differences which I will presently subjoin, as soon as I have added a few cautions for the sake of avoiding
ambiguity.

Sensible heat is a relative notion, and has relation to man, not to the
universe; and is correctly defined as merely the effect of heat on the
animal spirits. Moreover, in itself it is variable, since the same body, according as the senses are predisposed, induces a perception of cold as
well as of heat. This is clear from Inst. 41. Tab. 3.

Nor again must the communication of Heat, or its transitive nature, by means of which a body becomes hot when a hot body is applied to it, be confounded with the Form of Heat. For heat is one thing, heating another. Heat is produced by the motion of attrition without any preceding heat, an instance which excludes heating from the Form of Heat. And even when heat is produced by the approach of a hot body, this does not proceed from the Form of Heat, but depends entirely on a higher and more general nature, viz., on the nature of assimilation or self-multiplication, a subject which requires a separate inquiry.

Again, our notion of fire is popular, and of no use; being made up of the combination in any body of heat and brightness, as in common flame and bodies heated to redness.

Having thus removed all ambiguity, I come at length to the true specific differences which limit Motion and constitute it the Form of Heat.

The first difference then is this. Heat is an expansive motion, whereby a body strives to dilate and stretch itself to a larger sphere or dimension than it had previously occupied. This difference is most observable in flame, where the smoke or thick vapor manifestly dilates and expands itself into flame.

It is shown also in all boiling liquid, which manifestly swells, rises, and bubbles; and carries on the process of self-expansion, till it turns into a body far more extended and dilated than the liquid itself, namely, into vapor, smoke, or air.

It appears likewise in all wood and combustibles, from which there generally arises exudation and always evaporation.

It is shown also in the melting of metals, which, being of the compactest texture, do not readily swell and dilate; but yet their spirit being dilated in itself, and thereupon conceiving an appetite for further dilation, forces and agitates the grosser parts into a liquid state. And if the heat be greatly increased it dissolves and turns much of their substance to a volatile state.

It is shown also in iron or stones, which, though not melted or dissolved, are yet softened. This is the case also with sticks, which when slightly heated in hot ashes become flexible.

But this kind of motion is best seen in air, which continuously and manifestly dilates with a slight heat, as appears in Inst. 38. Tab. 3.

It is shown also in the opposite nature of cold. For cold contracts all bodies and makes them shrink; insomuch that in intense frosts nails fall out from walls, brazen vessels crack, and heated glass on being suddenly placed in the cold cracks and breaks. In like manner air is contracted by a slight chill, as in Inst. 38. Tab. 3. But on these points I shall speak more at length in the inquiry concerning Cold.

Nor is it surprising that heat and cold should exhibit many actions in common (for which see Inst. 32. Tab. 2.), when we find two of the following specific differences (of which I shall speak presently) suiting either nature; though in this specific difference (of which I am now speaking) their actions are diametrically opposite. For heat gives an expansive and dilating, cold a contractive and condensing motion.

The second difference is a modification of the former; namely, that heat is a motion expansive or towards the circumference, but with this condition, that the body has at the same time a motion upwards. For there is no doubt that there are many mixed motions. For instance, an arrow or dart turns as it goes forward, and goes forward as it turns. And in like manner the motion of heat is at once a motion of expansion and a motion upwards. This difference is shown by putting a pair of tongs or a poker in the fire. If you put it in perpendicularly and hold it by the top, it soon burns your hand; if at the side or from below, not nearly so soon.

It is also observable in distillations *per descensorium;* which men use for delicate flowers, that soon lose their scent. For human industry has discovered the plan of placing the fire not below but above, that it may burn the less. For not only flame tends upwards, but also all heat.

But let trial be made of this in the opposite nature of cold; viz. whether cold does not contract a body downwards, as heat dilates a body upwards. Take therefore two iron rods, or two glass tubes, exactly alike; warm them a little, and place a sponge steeped in cold water or snow at the bottom of the one, and the same at the top of the other. For I think that the extremities of the rod which has the snow at the top will cool sooner than the extremities of the other which has the snow at the bottom; just as the opposite is the case with heat.

The third specific difference is this; that heat is a motion of expansion, not uniformly of the whole body together, but in the smaller parts of it; and at the same time checked, repelled, and beaten back, so that the body acquires a motion alternative, perpetually quivering, striving and struggling, and irritated by repercussion, whence springs the fury of fire and heat.

This specific difference is most displayed in flame and boiling liquids, which are perpetually quivering and swelling in small portions, and again subsiding.

It is also shown in those bodies which are so compact that when heated or ignited they do not swell or expand in bulk; as ignited iron, in which the heat is very sharp.

It is shown also in this, that a fire burns most briskly in the coldest weather.

Again, it is shown in this, that when the air is extended in a calendar glass without impediment or repulsion,—that is to say, uniformly and equably,—there is no perceptible heat. Also when wind escapes from confinement, although it burst forth with the greatest violence, there is no very great heat perceptible; because the motion is of the whole, without a motion alternating in the particles. And with a view to this, let trial be made whether flame does not burn more sharply towards the sides in the middle of the flame.

It is also shown in this, that all burning acts on minute pores of the body burnt; so that burning undermines, penetrates, pricks, and stings the body like the points of an infinite number of needles. It is also an effect of this, that all strong waters (if suited to the body on which they are acting) act as fire does, in consequence of their corroding and pungent nature.

And this specific difference (of which I am now speaking) is common also to the nature of cold; for in cold the contractive motion is checked by a resisting tendency to expand, just as in heat the expansive motion is checked by a resisting tendency to contract. Thus, whether the particles of a body work inward or outward, the mode of action is the same, though the degree of strength be very different; because we have not here on the surface of the earth anything that is intensely cold. See Inst. 27. Tab. 9.

The fourth specific difference is a modification of the last; it is, that the preceding motion of stimulation or penetration must be somewhat rapid and not sluggish, and must proceed by particles, minute indeed, yet not the finest of all, but a degree larger.

This difference is shown by a comparison of the effects of fire with the effects of time or age. Age or time dries, consumes, undermines and reduces to ashes, no less than fire; indeed with an action far more subtle; but because such motion is very sluggish, and acts on particles very small, the heat is not perceived.

It is also shown by comparing the dissolution of iron and gold. Gold is dissolved without any heat being excited, while the dissolution of iron is accompanied by a violent heat, though it takes place in about the same time. The reason is that in gold the separating acid enters gently and works with subtlety, and the parts of the gold yield easily; whereas in iron the entrance is rough and with conflict, and the parts of the iron have greater obstinacy.

It is shown also to some degree in some gangrenes and mortifications, which do not excite great heat or pain on account of the subtle nature of putrefaction.

Let this then be the First Vintage or Commencement of Interpretation concerning the Form of Heat, made by way of indulgence to the understanding.

Now from this our First Vintage it follows that the Form or true definition of heat (heat, that is, in relation to the universe, not simply in relation to man) is in few words as follows: *Heat is a motion, expansive, restrained, and acting in its strife upon the smaller particles of bodies.* But the expansion is thus modified: *while it expands all ways, it has at the same time an inclination upwards.* And the struggle in the particles is modified also: *it is not sluggish, but hurried and with violence.*

Viewed with reference to operation it is the same thing. For the direction is this: *If in any natural body you can excite a dilating or expanding motion, and can so repress this motion and turn it back upon itself, that the dilation shall not proceed equably, but have its way in one part and be counteracted in another, you will undoubtedly generate heat;*— without taking into account whether the body be elementary (as it is called) or subject to celestial influence; whether it be luminous or opaque; rare or dense; locally expanded or confined within the bounds of its first dimension; verging to dissolution or remaining in its original state; animal, vegetable, or mineral, water, oil or air, or any other substance whatever susceptible of the above-mentioned motion. Sensible heat is the same thing; only it must be considered with reference to the sense. Let us now proceed to further aids.

xxi

The Tables of First Presentation and the Rejection or process of Exclusion being completed, and also the First Vintage being made thereupon, we are to proceed to the other helps of the understanding in the Interpretation of Nature and true and perfect Induction. In propounding which, I mean, when Tables are necessary, to proceed upon the Instances of Heat and Cold; but when a small number of examples will suffice, I shall proceed at large; so that the inquiry may be kept clear, and yet more room be left for the exposition of the system.

I propose to treat then in the first place of *Prerogative Instances;* secondly, of the *Supports of Induction;* thirdly, of the *Rectification of Induction;* fourthly, of *Varying the Investigation according to the nature of the Subject;* fifthly, of *Prerogative Natures* with respect to Investigation, or of what should be inquired first and what last; sixthly, of the *Limits of Investigation,* or a Synopsis of all Natures in the Universe; seventhly, of the *Application to Practice,* or of things in their relation to

Man; eighthly, of *Preparations for Investigation;* and lastly, of the *Ascending and Descending Scale of Axioms.*

xxii

Among Prerogative Instances I will place first *Solitary Instances.* Those are Solitary Instances which exhibit the nature under investigation in subjects which have nothing in common with other subjects except that nature; or, again, which do not exhibit the nature under investigation in subjects which resemble other subjects in every respect except in not having that nature. For it is clear that such instances make the way short, and accelerate and strengthen the process of exclusion; so that a few of them are as good as many.

For instance, if we are inquiring into the nature of Color, prisms, crystals, which show colors not only in themselves but externally on a wall, dews, &c., are Solitary Instances. For they have nothing in common with the colors fixed in flowers, colored stones, metals, woods, &c., except the color. From which we easily gather that color is nothing more than a modification of the image of light received upon the object, resulting in the former case from the different degrees of incidence, in the latter from the various textures and configurations of the body. These instances are Solitary in respect of resemblance.

Again, in the same investigation, the distinct veins of white and black in marble, and the variegation of color in flowers of the same species, are Solitary Instances. For the black and white streaks in marble, or the spots of pink and white in a pink, agree in everything almost except the color. From which we easily gather that color has little to do with the intrinsic nature of a body, but simply depends on the coarser and as it were mechanical arrangement of the parts. These instances are Solitary in respect of difference. Both kinds I call *Solitary Instances,* or *Ferine,* to borrow a term from astronomers.

xxiii

Among Prerogative Instances I will next place *Migratory Instances.* They are those in which the nature in question is in the process of being produced when it did not previously exist, or on the other hand of disappearing when it existed before. And therefore, in either transition, such instances are always twofold, or rather it is one instance in motion or passage, continued till it reaches the opposite state. Such instances not only accelerate and strengthen the exclusive process, but also drive the affirmative or Form itself into a narrow compass. For the Form of a thing must necessarily be something which in the course of this migration is communicated, or on the other hand which in the course of this migration is removed and destroyed. And though every exclusion promotes the affirmative, yet this is done more decidedly when it occurs in the same than in different subjects. And the betrayal of the form in a single instance leads the way (as is evident from all that has been said) to the discovery of it in all. And the simpler the Migration, the more must the instance be valued. Besides Migratory Instances are of great use with a view to operation; because in exhibiting the form in connection with that which causes it to be or not to be, they supply a clear direction for practice in some cases; whence the passage is easy to the cases that lie next. There is however in these instances a danger which requires caution; viz. lest they lead us to connect the Form too much with the efficient, and so possess the understanding, or at least touch it, with a false opinion concerning the Form, drawn from a view of the efficient. But the efficient is always understood to be merely the vehicle that carries the Form. This is a danger however easily remedied by the process of exclusion legitimately conducted.

I must now give an example of a Migratory Instance. Let the nature to be investigated be Whiteness; an instance migrating to production or existence is glass whole and pounded. Again, simple water and water agitated into froth. For glass and water in their simple state are transparent, not white; whereas pounded glass and water in froth are white, not transparent. We must therefore inquire what has happened to the glass or water from this Migration. For it is obvious that the Form of Whiteness is communicated and conveyed by that pounding of the glass and that agitation of the water. We find, however, that nothing has been added except the breaking up of the glass and water into small parts, and the introduction of air. But we have made no slight advance to the discovery of the Form of Whiteness when we know that two bodies, both transparent but in a greater or less degree (viz. air and water, or air and glass), do when mingled in small portions together exhibit whiteness, through the unequal refraction of the rays of light.

But an example must at the same time be given of the danger and caution to which I alluded. For at this point it might readily suggest itself to an understanding led astray by efficient causes of this kind, that air is always required for the Form of Whiteness, or that Whiteness is generated by transparent bodies only; notions entirely false, and refuted by numerous exclusions. Whereas it will be found that (setting air and the like aside) bodies entirely even in the particles which affect vision are transparent, bodies simply uneven are white; bodies uneven and in a compound yet regular texture are all colors except black; while bodies uneven and in a compound, irregular, and confused texture are black. Here then I have given an example of an Instance Migrating to production or existence in the proposed nature of Whiteness. An Instance Migrating to destruction in the same nature of Whiteness, is froth or snow in dissolution. For the water puts off Whiteness and puts on transparency, on returning to its integral state without air.

Nor must I by any means omit to mention that under Migratory Instances are to be included not only those which are passing towards production and destruction, but also those which are passing towards increase and decrease; since these also help to discover the Form, as is clear from the above definition of Form and the Table of Degrees. Thus paper, which is white when dry, but when wetted (that is, when air is excluded and water introduced) is less white and approaches nearer to the transparent, is analogous to the above given Instances.

xxiv

After Prerogative Instances I will put in the third place *Striking Instances,* of which I have made mention in the First Vintage concerning Heat, and which I also call *Shining Instances,* or *Instances Freed and Predominant.* They are those which exhibit the nature in question naked and standing by itself, and also in its exaltation or highest degree of power; as being disenthralled and freed from all impediments, or at any rate by virtue of its strength dominant over, suppressing and coercing them. For since every body contains in itself many forms of natures united together in a concrete state, the result is that they severally crush, depress, break, and enthrall one another, and thus the individual forms are obscured. But certain subjects are found wherein the required nature appears more in its vigor than in others, either through the absence of impediments or the predominance of its own virtue. And instances of this kind strikingly display the Form. At the same time in these instances also we must use caution, and check the hurry of the understanding. For whatever displays the Form too conspicuously, and seems to force it on the notice of the understanding, should be held suspect, and recourse be had to a rigid and careful exclusion.

To take an example; let the nature inquired into be Heat. A Striking Instance of the motion of expansion, which (as stated above) is the main element in the Form of Heat, is a calendar glass of air. For flame, though it manifestly exhibits expansion, still, as susceptible of momentary extinction, does not display the progress of expansion. Boiling water too, on account of the easy transition of water to vapor or air, does not so well exhibit the expansion of water in its own body. Again, ignited iron and like bodies are so far from displaying the progress of expansion, that in consequence of their spirit being crushed and broken by the coarse and compact particles which curb and subdue it, the expansion itself is not at all conspicuous to the senses. But a calendar glass strikingly displays expansion in air, at once conspicuous, progressive, permanent, and without transition.

To take another example; let the nature inquired into be Weight. A Striking Instance of weight is quicksilver. For it far surpasses in weight all substances but gold, and gold itself is not much heavier. But quicksilver is a better instance for indicating the Form of Weight than gold; because gold is solid and consistent, characteristics which seem related to density; whereas quicksilver is liquid and teeming with spirit, and yet is heavier by many degrees than the diamond and other bodies that are esteemed the most solid. From which it is obvious that the Form of Heaviness or Weight depends simply on quantity of matter and not on compactness of frame. . . .[2]

lii

So much then for the Dignities or Prerogatives of Instances. It must be remembered however that in this Organum of mine I am handling logic, not philosophy. But since my logic aims to teach and instruct the understanding, not that it may with the slender tendrils of the mind snatch at and lay hold of abstract notions (as the common logic does), but that it may in very truth dissect nature, and discover the virtues and actions of bodies, with their laws as determined in matter; so that this science flows not merely from the nature of the mind, but also from the nature of things; no wonder that it is everywhere sprinkled and illustrated with speculations and experiments in nature, as examples of the art I teach. It appears then from what has been said that there are twenty-seven Prerogative Instances; namely, Solitary Instances; Migratory Instances; Striking Instances; Clandestine Instances; Constitutive Instances; Conformable Instances; Singular Instances; Deviating Instances; Bordering Instances; Instances of Power; Instances of Companionship and of Enmity; Subjunctive Instances; Instances of Alliance; Instances of the Fingerpost; Instances of Divorce; Instances of the Door; Summoning Instances; Instances of the Road; Instances Supplementary; Dissecting Instances; Instances of the Rod; Instances of the Course; Doses of Nature; Instances of Strife; Intimating Instances; Polychrest Instances; Magical Instances. Now the use of these instances, wherein they excel common instances, is found either in the Informative part or in the Operative, or in both. As regards the Informative, they assist either the senses or the understanding: the senses, as the five Instances of the Lamp: the understanding, either by hastening the Exclusion of the Form, as Solitary Instances;—or by narrowing and indicating more nearly the Affirmative of the Form, as Instances Migratory, Striking, of Companionship, and Subjunctive;—or by exalting the understanding and leading it to genera and common natures, either immedi-

[2] The next twenty-seven instances are omitted—*Editor.*

ately, as Instances Clandestine, Singular, and of Alliance; or in the next degree, as Constitutive; or in the lowest, as Conformable;—or by setting the understanding right when led astray by habit, as Deviating Instances;—or by leading it to the Great Form or Fabric of the Universe, as Bordering Instances;—or by guarding it against false forms and causes, as Instances of the Fingerpost and of Divorce. In the Operative Part, they either point out, or measure, or facilitate practice. They point it out, by showing with what we should begin, that we may not go again over old ground, as Instances of Power; or to what we should aspire if means be given, as Intimating Instances. The four Mathematical Instances measure practice: Polychrest and Magical Instances facilitate it.

Again out of these twenty-seven instances there are some of which we must make a collection at once, as I said above, without waiting for the particular investigation of natures. Of this sort are Instances Conformable, Singular, Deviating, Bordering, of Power, of the Dose, Intimating, Polychrest, and Magical. For these either help and set right the understanding and senses, or furnish practice with her tools in a general way. The rest need not be inquired into till we come to make Tables of Presentation for the work of the Interpreter concerning some particular nature. For the instances marked and endowed with these Prerogatives are as a soul amid the common instances of Presentation, and as I said at first, a few of them do instead of many; and therefore in the formation of the Tables they must be investigated with all zeal, and set down therein. It was necessary to handle them beforehand because I shall have to speak of them in what follows. But now I must proceed to the supports and rectifications of Induction, and then to concretes, and Latent Processes, and Latent Configurations, and the rest, as set forth in order in the twenty-first Aphorism; that at length (like an honest and faithful guardian) I may hand over to men their fortunes, now their understanding is emancipated and come as it were of age; whence there cannot but follow an improvement in man's estate, and an enlargement of his power over nature. For man by the fall fell at the same time from his state of innocency and from his dominion over creation. Both of these losses however can even in this life be in some part repaired: the former by religion and faith, the latter by arts and sciences. For creation was not by the curse made altogether and for ever a rebel, but in virtue of that charter "In the sweat of thy face shalt thou eat bread," it is now by various labors (not certainly by disputations or idle magical ceremonies, but by various labors) at length and in some measure subdued to the supplying of man with bread; that is. to the uses of human life.

THOMAS HOBBES

LEVIATHAN

THOMAS HOBBES

THOMAS HOBBES (1588-1679) was the son of a poor and ignorant country vicar. Through the assistance of an uncle, a well-to-do tradesman, he was enabled to prepare for the University, and, when not quite fifteen, was sent up to Magdalen Hall, Oxford. Here Hobbes was put through the same scholastic drill that had been imposed on Bacon at Cambridge, and, in consequence, he too acquired a rooted dislike for the universities.

In 1608 Hobbes became tutor and companion to the son of Lord Cavendish. This association with the Cavendish family continued, with some intermissions, throughout the rest of his life. In 1610 Hobbes toured the Continent with his pupil, and on their return became his secretary. It was then Hobbes' ambition to become a classical scholar and man of letters. He became acquainted with such men as Bacon, Herbert of Cherbury, and Ben Jonson. Bacon's philosophy, however, seems to have had no influence upon his intellectual development. Hobbes did not become seriously interested in philosophy until around his fortieth year. At that time he first began the study of mathematics and of the new physical sciences. In 1634, on another trip abroad, he visited Galileo in Italy and became acquainted in Paris with the leading thinkers of that intellectual center.

Meanwhile he had also become deeply concerned about the political issues of the time. Perceiving that the quarrel between King and Parliament might well lead to a rebellion, he set himself to work out the political part of his philosophy in a treatise entitled *The Elements of Law*, which, though not printed at the time, circulated freely in manuscript form. In 1640, when it was clear that civil war impended, Hobbes fled to France. He remained on the Continent for eleven years, associating with the brilliant group of philosophers and scientists in Paris, and serving for a while as tutor to the Prince of Wales, later Charles II. During this period he published a political analysis intended as the third part of a complete philosophical system, the *De Cive*, and composed his greatest work *Leviathan*. In 1651 Hobbes made his submission to the Council of State and returned to England. In the same year the *Leviathan* was published. The first part of his projected system, *De Corpore*, was issued in 1655 and the second, *De Homine*, in 1658. Hobbes' great intellectual task was now finished. The remainder of his long life was chiefly spent in fruitless and interminable controversies aroused by his hetero-dox opinions.

There follow selections from the first and second parts of *Leviathan*, and from Chapter XLIII of the third part.

LEVIATHAN

OR

THE MATTER, FORM, AND POWER

OF A

COMMONWEALTH

ECCLESIASTICAL AND CIVIL

Introduction

NATURE, the art whereby God hath made and governs the world, is by the *art* of man, as in many other things, so in this also imitated, that it can make an artificial animal. For seeing life is but a motion of limbs, the beginning whereof is in some principal part within; why may we not say, that all *automata* (engines that move themselves by springs and wheels as doth a watch) have an artificial life? For what is the heart, but a spring; and the nerves, but so many strings, and the joints, but so many wheels, giving motion to the whole body, such as was intended by the artificer? Art goes yet further, imitating that rational and most excellent work of nature, *man*. For by art is created that great *Leviathan* called a *Commonwealth*, or *State*, in Latin *Civitas*, which is but an artificial man; though of greater stature and strength than the natural, for whose protection and defense it was intended; and in which the sovereignty is an artificial soul, as giving life and motion to the whole body; the magistrates, and other officers of judicature and execution, artificial joints; reward and punishment, by which fastened to the seat of the sovereignty every joint and member is moved to perform his duty, are the nerves, that do the same in the body natural; the wealth and riches of all the particular members, are the strength; *salus populi,* the people's safety, its business; counselors, by whom all things needful for it to know are suggested unto it, are the memory; equity and laws, an artificial reason and will; concord, health; sedition, sickness; and civil war, death. Lastly, the pacts and covenants, by which the parts of this body politic were at first made, set together, and united, resemble that *fiat,* or the *let us make man,* pronounced by God in the creation.

To describe the nature of this artificial man, I will consider:

First, the *matter* thereof, and the *artificer;* both which is *man.*

Secondly, *how,* and by what *covenants* it is made; what are the *rights* and just *power* or *authority* of a *sovereign;* and what it is that preserveth or dissolveth it.

Thirdly, what is a *Christian commonwealth.*

Lastly, what is the *kingdom of darkness.*

Concerning the first, there is a saying much usurped of late, that wisdom is acquired, not by reading of books, but of men. Consequently whereunto, those persons that for the most part can give no other proof of being wise, take great delight to show what they think they have read in men, by uncharitable censures of one another behind their backs. But there is another saying not of late understood, by which they might learn truly to read one another if they would take the pains: that is, *nosce teipsum,* Read thyself; which was not meant, as it is now used, to countenance either the barbarous state of men in power towards their inferiors, or to encourage men of low degree to a saucy behavior towards their betters; but to teach us that from the similitude of the thoughts and passions of one man to the thoughts and passions of another, whosoever looketh into himself, and considereth what he doth when he does think, opine, reason, hope, fear, etc. and upon what grounds; he shall thereby read and know what are the thoughts and passions of all other men upon the like occasions. I say the similitude of *passions,* which are the same in all men, desire, fear, hope, etc.; not the similitude of the *objects* of the passions, which are the things desired, feared, hoped, etc.: for these the constitution individual, and particular education, do so vary, and they are so easy to be kept from our knowledge, that the characters of man's heart, blotted and confounded as they are with dissembling, lying, counterfeiting, and erroneous doctrines, are legible only to him that searcheth hearts. And though by men's actions we do discover their design sometimes; yet to do it without comparing them with our own, and distinguishing all circumstances by which the case may come to be altered, is to decipher without a key, and be for the most part deceived, by too much trust or by too much diffidence, as he that reads is himself a good or evil man.

But let one man read another by his actions never so perfectly, it serves him only with his acquaintance, which are but few. He that is to govern a whole nation, must read in himself not this or that particular man, but mankind; which though it be hard to do, harder than to learn any language or science, yet when I shall have set down my own reading orderly and perspicuously, the pains left another will be only to consider if he also find not the same in himself. For this kind of doctrine admitteth no other demonstration.

PART I: OF MAN

CHAPTER I

OF SENSE

CONCERNING the thoughts of man, I will consider them first singly, and afterwards in train, or dependence upon one another. Singly, they are everyone a *representation* or *appearance*, of some quality or other accident of a body without us, which is commonly called an *object*. Which object worketh on the eyes, ears, and other parts of a man's body, and by diversity of working produceth diversity of appearances.

The original of them all is that which we call *sense*, for there is no conception in a man's mind which hath not at first, totally or by parts, been begotten upon the organs of sense. The rest are derived from that original.

To know the natural cause of sense is not very necessary to the business now in hand; and I have elsewhere written of the same at large. Nevertheless, to fill each part of my present method, I will briefly deliver the same in this place.

The cause of sense is the external body, or object, which presseth the organ proper to each sense, either immediately, as in the taste and touch; or mediately, as in seeing, hearing, and smelling; which pressure, by the mediation of the nerves, and other strings and membranes of the body, continued inwards to the brain and heart, causeth there a resistance, or counter-pressure, or endeavor of the heart to deliver itself, which endeavor, because outward, seemeth to be some matter without. And this seeming, or fancy, is that which men call *sense;* and consisteth, as to the eye, in a light, or color figured; to the ear, in a sound; to the nostril, in an odor; to the tongue and palate, in a savor; and to the rest of the body, in heat, cold, hardness, softness, and such other qualities as we discern by feeling. All which qualities, called *sensible,* are, in the object that causeth them, but so many several motions of the matter, by which it presseth our organs diversely. Neither in us that are pressed, are they anything else but divers motions; for motion produceth nothing but motion. But their appearance to us is fancy, the same waking that dreaming. And as pressing, rubbing, or striking the eye makes us fancy a light, and pressing the ear produceth a din, so do the bodies also we see or hear, produce the same by their strong though unobserved action. For if those colors and sounds were in the bodies, or objects that cause them, they could not be severed from them, as by glasses, and in echoes by reflection, we see they are; where we know the thing we see is in one place, the appearance in another. And though at some certain distance the real and very object seem invested with the fancy it begets in us, yet still the object is one thing, the image or fancy is another. So that sense, in all cases, is nothing else but original fancy, caused, as I have said, by the pressure, that is, by the motion, of external things upon our eyes, ears, and other organs thereunto ordained.

But the philosophy schools, through all the universities of Christendom, grounded upon certain texts of Aristotle, teach another doctrine, and say, for the cause of vision, that the thing seen, sendeth forth on every side a *visible species,* in English, a visible show, apparition, or aspect, or a being seen; the receiving whereof into the eye is seeing. And for the cause of hearing, that the thing heard sendeth forth an *audible species,* that is an audible aspect, or audible being seen; which entering at the ear maketh hearing. Nay, for the cause of understanding also, they say the thing understood sendeth forth an *intelligible species,* that is, an intelligible being seen; which, coming into the understanding, makes us understand. I say not this as disproving the use of universities; but because I am to speak hereafter of their office in a commonwealth, I must let you see on all occasions by the way, what things would be amended in them; amongst which the frequency of insignificant speech is one.

CHAPTER II

OF IMAGINATION

THAT when a thing lies still, unless somewhat else stir it, it will lie still for ever, is a truth that no man doubts of. But that when a thing is in motion, it will eternally be in motion, unless somewhat else stay it, though the reason be the same, namely, that nothing can change itself, is not so easily assented to. For men measure, not only other men, but all other things, by themselves; and because they find themselves subject, after motion, to pain and lassitude, think everything else grows weary of motion, and seeks repose of its own accord; little considering whether it be not some other motion, wherein that desire of rest they find in themselves consisteth. From hence it is that the schools say, heavy bodies fall downwards out of an appetite to rest, and to conserve their nature in that place which is most proper for them; ascribing appetite, and knowledge of what is good for their conservation, which is more than man has, to things inanimate, absurdly.

When a body is once in motion, it moveth, unless something else hinder it, eternally; and whatsoever hindereth it cannot in an instant, but, in time and by degrees, quite extinguish it; and as we see in the water, though the wind cease, the waves give not over rolling for a long time after: so also it happeneth in that motion which is made in the internal parts of a man, then, when he sees, dreams, etc. For after the object is removed, or the eye shut, we still retain an image of the thing seen, though more obscure than when we see it. And this is it, the Latins call *imagination,* from the image made in seeing; and apply the same, though improperly, to all the other senses. But the Greeks call it *fancy;* which signifies appearance, and is as proper to one sense, as to another. Imagination therefore is nothing but *decaying sense;* and is found in men, and many other living creatures, as well sleeping as waking.

The decay of sense in men waking, is not the decay of the motion made in sense; but an obscuring of it, in such manner as the light of the sun obscureth the light of the stars; which stars do no less exercise their virtue, by which they are visible, in the day than in the night. But because amongst many strokes which our eyes, ears, and other organs receive from external bodies, the predominant only is sensible; therefore, the light of the sun being predominant, we are not affected with the action of the stars. And any object being removed from our eyes, though the impression it made in us remain, yet other objects more present succeeding and working on us, the imagination of the past is obscured and made weak, as the voice of a man is in the noise of the day. From whence it followeth that the longer the time is, after the sight or sense of any object, the weaker is the imagination. For the continual change of man's body destroys in time the parts which in sense were moved; so that distance of time, and of place, hath one and the same effect in us. For as at a great distance of place, that which we look at appears dim, and without distinction of the smaller parts; and as voices grow weak, and inarticulate; so also, after great distance of time, our imagination of the past is weak; and we lose, for example, of cities we have seen, many particular streets, and of actions, many particular circumstances. This decaying sense, when we would express the thing itself, I mean fancy itself, we call *imagination,* as I said before; but when we would express the decay, and signify that the sense is fading, old, and past, it is called *memory.* So that imagination and memory are but one thing, which for divers considerations hath divers names.

Much memory, or memory of many things, is called *experience.*

Again, imagination being only of those things which have been formerly perceived by sense, either all at once or by parts at several times; the former, which is the imagining the whole object as it was presented to the sense, is *simple* imagination, as when one imagineth a man, or horse, which he hath seen before. The other is *compounded;* as when, from the sight of a man at one time and of a horse at another, we conceive in our mind a centaur. So when a man compoundeth the image of his own person with the image of the actions of another man, as when a man imagines himself a Hercules or an Alexander, which happeneth often to them that are much taken with reading of romances, it is a compound imagination, and properly but a fiction of the mind. There be also other imaginations that rise in men, though waking, from the great impression made in sense: as from gazing upon the sun, the impression leaves an image of the sun before our eyes a long time after; and from being long and vehemently attent upon geometrical figures, a man shall in the dark, though awake, have the images of lines and angles before his eyes; which kind of fancy hath no particular name, as being a thing that doth not commonly fall into men's discourse.

The imaginations of them that sleep are those we call *dreams.* And these also, as all other imaginations, have been before, either totally or by parcels, in the sense. And because in sense, the brain and nerves, which are the necessary organs of sense, are so benumbed in sleep, as not easily to be moved by the action of external objects, there can happen in sleep no imagination, and therefore no dream, but what proceeds from the agitation of the inward parts of man's body; which inward parts, for the connection they have with the brain and other organs when they be distempered, do keep the same in motion; whereby the imaginations there formerly made, appear as if a man were waking; saving that the organs of sense being now benumbed, so as there is no new object which can master and obscure them with a more vigorous impression, a dream must needs be more clear, in this silence of sense, than our waking thoughts. And hence it cometh to pass that it is a hard matter, and by many thought impossible, to distinguish exactly between sense and dreaming. For my part, when I consider that in dreams I do not often nor constantly think of the same persons, places, objects, and actions, that I do waking; nor remember so long a train of coherent thoughts, dreaming, as at other times; and because waking I often observe the absurdity of dreams, but never dream of the absurdities of my waking thoughts; I am well satisfied that, being awake, I know I dream not, though when I dream I think myself awake.

And seeing dreams are caused by the distemper of some of the inward parts of the body, divers distempers must needs cause different dreams. And hence it is that lying cold breedeth dreams of fear, and raiseth the thought and image of some fearful object, the motion from the brain to the inner parts and from the inner parts to the brain being reciprocal; and that as anger causeth heat in some parts of the body when we are awake, so when we sleep the overheating of the same parts causeth anger, and raiseth up in the brain the imagination of an enemy. In the same manner, as natural kindness, when we are awake, causeth desire, and desire maketh heat in certain other parts of the body; so also too much heat in those parts, while we sleep, raiseth in the brain the imagination of some kindness shown. In sum, our dreams are the reverse of our waking imaginations; the motion when we are awake beginning at one end, and when we dream at another.

The most difficult discerning of a man's dream from his waking thoughts is, then, when by some accident we observe not that we have slept: which is easy to happen to a man full of fearful thoughts, and whose conscience is much troubled; and that sleepeth, without the circumstances of going to bed or putting off his clothes, as one that noddeth in a chair. For he that taketh pains, and industriously lays himself to sleep, in case any uncouth and exhorbitant fancy come unto him, cannot easily think it other than a dream. We read of Marcus Brutus (one that had his life given him by Julius Caesar, and was also his favorite, and notwithstanding murdered him), how at Philippi, the night before he gave battle to Augustus Caesar, he saw a fearful apparition, which is commonly related by historians as a vision; but considering the circumstances, one may easily judge to have been but a short dream. For sitting in his tent, pensive and troubled with the horror of his rash act, it was not hard for him, slumbering in the cold, to dream of that which most affrighted him; which fear, as by degrees it made him wake, so also it must needs make the apparition by degrees to vanish; and having no assurance that he slept, he could have no cause to think it a dream, or anything but a vision. And this is no very rare accident; for even they that be perfectly awake, if they be timorous and superstitious, possessed with fearful tales, and alone in the dark, are subject to the like fancies, and believe they see spirits and dead men's ghosts walking in churchyards; whereas it is either their fancy only, or else the knavery of such persons as make use of such superstitious fear, to pass disguised in the night to places they would not be known to haunt.

From this ignorance of how to distinguish dreams, and other strong fancies, from vision and sense, did arise the greatest part of the religion of the Gentiles in time past, that worshiped satyrs, fawns, nymphs, and the like; and nowadays the opinion that rude people have of fairies, ghosts, and goblins, and of the power of witches. For, as for witches, I think not that their witchcraft is any real power; but yet that they are justly punished, for the false belief they have that they can do such mischief, joined with their purpose to do it if they can; their trade being nearer to a new religion than to a craft or science. And for fairies, and walking ghosts, the opinion of them has, I think, been on purpose either taught or not confuted, to keep in credit the use of exorcism, of crosses, of holy water, and other such inventions of ghostly men. Nevertheless, there is no doubt but God can make unnatural apparitions; but that He does it so often as men need to fear such things more than they fear the stay or change of the course of nature, which He also can stay and change, is no point of Christian faith. But evil men, under pretext that God can do anything, are so bold as to say anything when it serves their turn, though they think it untrue; it is the part of a wise man, to believe them no farther than right reason makes that which they say appear credible. If this superstitious fear of spirits were taken away, and with it, prognostics from dreams, false prophecies, and many other things depending thereon, by which crafty ambitious persons abuse the simple people, men would be much more fitted than they are for civil obedience.

And this ought to be the work of the schools; but they rather nourish such doctrine. For, not knowing what imagination or the senses are, what they receive, they teach: some saying that imaginations rise of themselves, and have no cause; others, that they rise most commonly from the will; and that good thoughts are blown (inspired) into a man by God, and evil thoughts by the Devil; or that good thoughts are poured (infused) into a man by God, and evil ones by the Devil. Some say the senses receive the species of things, and deliver them to the common sense; and the common sense delivers them over to the fancy, and the fancy to the memory, and the memory to the judgment, like handling of things from one to another with many words making nothing understood.

The imagination that is raised in man, or any other creature indued with the faculty of imagining, by words, or other voluntary signs, is that we generally call *understanding;* and is common to man and beast. For a dog by custom will understand the call, or the rating of his master; and so will many other beasts. That understanding which is peculiar to man, is the understanding not only his will, but his conceptions and thoughts, by the sequel and contexture of the names of things into affirmations, negations, and other forms of speech; and of this kind of understanding I shall speak hereafter.

CHAPTER III

OF THE CONSEQUENCE OR TRAIN OF IMAGINATIONS

BY *consequence,* or *train* of thoughts, I understand that succession of one thought to another, which is called, to distinguish it from discourse in words, *mental discourse.*

When a man thinketh on anything whatsoever, his next thought after is not altogether so casual as it seems to be. Not every thought to every thought succeeds indifferently. But as we have no imagination, whereof we have not formerly had sense, in whole or in parts; so we have no transition from one imagination to another, whereof we never had the like before in our senses. The reason whereof is this. All fancies are motions within us, relics of those made in the sense; and those motions that immediately succeeded one another in the sense, continue also together after sense: insomuch as the former coming again to take place, and be predominant, the latter followeth, by coherence of the matter moved, in such manner as water upon a plane table is drawn which way any one part of it is guided by the finger. But because in sense, to one and the same thing perceived, sometimes one thing, sometimes another succeedeth, it comes to pass in time that in the imagining of anything, there is no certainty what we shall imagine next; only this is certain, it shall be something that succeeded the same before, at one time or another.

This train of thoughts, or mental discourse, is of two sorts. The first is *unguided, without design,* and inconstant; wherein there is no passionate thought, to govern and direct those that follow, to itself, as the end and scope of some desire or other passion: in which case the thoughts are said to wander, and seem impertinent one to another, as in a dream. Such are commonly the thoughts of men that are not only without company, but also without care of anything; though even then their thoughts are as busy as at other times, but without harmony; as the sound which a lute out of tune would yield to any man, or in tune to one that could not play. And yet in this wild ranging of the mind, a man may ofttimes perceive the way of it, and the dependence of one thought upon another. For in a discourse of our present civil war, what could seem more impertinent than to ask, as one did, what was the value of a Roman penny? Yet the coherence to me was manifest enough. For the thought of the war introduced the thought of the delivering up the king to his enemies; the thought of that, brought in the thought of the delivering up of Christ; and that again the thought of the thirty pence which was the price of that treason; and thence easily followed that malicious question, and all this in a moment of time; for thought is quick.

The second is more constant; as being *regulated* by some desire, and design. For the impression made by such things as we desire, or fear, is strong, and permanent, or, if it cease for a time, of quick return: so strong it is sometimes as to hinder and break our sleep. From desire ariseth the thought of some means we have seen produce the like of that which we aim at; and from the thought of that, the thought of means to that mean; and so continually, till we come to some beginning within our own power. And because the end, by the greatness of the impression, comes often to mind, in case our thoughts begin to wander, they are quickly again reduced into the way: which observed by one of the seven wise men, made him give men this precept, which is now worn out, *Respice finem;* that is to say, in all your actions, look often upon what you would have, as the thing that directs all your thoughts in the way to attain it.

The train of regulated thoughts is of two kinds: one, when of an effect imagined we seek the causes, or means that produce it; and this is common to man and beast. The other is, when imagining anything whatsoever, we seek all the possible effects that can by it be produced; that is to say, we imagine what we can do with it when we have it. Of which I have not at any time seen any sign but in man only; for this is a curiosity hardly incident to the nature of any living creature that has no other passion but sensual, such as are hunger, thirst, lust, and anger. In sum, the discourse of the mind, when it is governed by design, is nothing but seeking, or the faculty of invention, which the Latins called *sagacitas,* and *solertia*—a hunting out of the causes of some effect, present or past, or of the effects of some present or past cause. Sometimes a man seeks what he hath lost; and from that place and time wherein he misses it, his mind runs back, from place to place and time to time, to find where and when he had it; that is to say, to find some certain, and limited time and place, in which to begin a method of seeking. Again, from thence, his thoughts run over the same places and times, to find what action or other occasion might make him lose it. This we call remembrance, or calling to mind; the Latins call it *reminiscentia,* as it were a re-conning of our former actions.

Sometimes a man knows a place determinate within the compass whereof he is to seek; and then his thoughts run over all the parts thereof, in the same manner as one would sweep a room to find a jewel, or as a spaniel ranges the field till he find a scent, or as a man should run over the alphabet to start a rhyme.

Sometimes a man desires to know the event of an action; and then he thinketh of some like action past, and the events thereof one after another; supposing like events will follow like actions. As he that foresees what will become of a criminal, re-cons what he has seen follow on the like crime before; having this order of thoughts, the crime, the officer, the prison, the judge, and the gallows. Which kind of thoughts, is called foresight, and prudence, or providence; and sometimes wisdom; though such conjecture, through the difficulty of observing all circumstances, be very fallacious. But this is certain; by how much one man has more experience of things past than another, by so much also he is more prudent, and his expectations the seldomer fail him. The present only has a being in nature; things past have a being in the memory only, but things to come have no being at all; the future being but a fiction of the mind, applying the sequels of actions passed, to the actions that are present; which with most certainty is done by him that has most experience, but not with certainty enough. And though it be called prudence when the event answereth our expectation, yet in its own nature it is but presumption. For the foresight of things to come, which is providence, belongs only to Him by Whose will they are to come. From Him only, and supernaturally, proceeds prophecy. The best prophet naturally is the best guesser; and the best guesser, he that is most versed and studied in the matters he guesses at: for he hath most signs to guess by.

A *sign* is the evident antecedent of the consequent; and contrarily, the consequent of the antecedent, when the like consequences have been observed before; and the oftener they have been observed, the less uncertain is the sign. And therefore he that has most experience in any kind of business, has most signs whereby to guess at the future time; and consequently is the most prudent; and so much more prudent than he that is new in that kind of business, as not to be equalled by any advantage of natural and extemporary wit: though perhaps many young men think the contrary.

Nevertheless it is not prudence that distinguisheth man from beast. There be beasts that at a year old observe more, and pursue that which is for their good more prudently, than a child can do at ten.

As prudence is a *presumption* of the *future*, contracted from the *experience* of time *past;* so there is a presumption of things past taken from other things, not future, but past also. For he that hath seen by what courses and degrees a flourishing state hath first come into civil war, and then to ruin; upon the sight of the ruins of any other state, will guess the like war and the like courses have been there also. But this conjecture has the same uncertainty almost with the conjecture of the future; both being grounded only upon experience.

There is no other act of man's mind, that I can remember, naturally planted in him, so as to need no other thing to the exercise of it, but to be born a man and live with the use of his five senses. Those other faculties, of which I shall speak by and by, and which seem proper to man only, are acquired and increased by study and industry; and of most men learned by instruction, and discipline; and proceed all from the invention of words, and speech. For besides sense, and thoughts, and the train of thoughts, the mind of man has no other motion; though by the help of speech, and method, the same faculties may be improved to such a height, as to distinguish men from all other living creatures.

Whatsoever we imagine is *finite*. Therefore there is no idea or conception of anything we call *infinite*. No man can have in his mind an image of infinite magnitude, nor conceive infinite swiftness, infinite time, or infinite force, or infinite power. When we say anything is infinite, we signify only that we are not able to conceive the ends, the bounds of the things named; having no conception of the thing, but of our own inability. And therefore the name of God is used, not to make us conceive Him, for He is incomprehensible; and His greatness and power are unconceivable; but that we may honor Him. Also because whatsoever, as I said before, we conceive, has been perceived first by sense, either all at once or by parts: a man can have no thought, representing anything, not subject to sense. No man therefore can conceive anything but he must conceive it in some place, and indued with some determinate magnitude, and which may be divided into parts; nor that anything is all in this place and all in another place at the same time; nor that two or more things can be in one and the same place at once: for none of these things ever have, nor can be incident to sense; but are absurd speeches, taken upon credit, without any signification at all, from deceived philosophers, and deceived or deceiving schoolmen.

CHAPTER IV

OF SPEECH

THE invention of *printing*, though ingenious, compared with the invention of *letters* is no great matter. But who was the first that found the use of letters, is not known. He that first brought them into Greece, men say was Cadmus, the son of Agenor, king of Phoenicia. A profitable invention for continuing the memory of time past, and the conjunction of mankind dispersed into so many and distant regions of the earth; and withal difficult, as proceeding from a watchful observation of the divers motions of the tongue, palate, lips, and other organs of speech; whereby to make as many differences of characters, to remember them. But the most noble and profitable invention of all other, was that of *speech*, consisting of *names* or *appellations,* and their connection; whereby men register their thoughts, recall them when they are past, and also declare them one to another for mutual utility and conversation; without which there had been amongst men neither commonwealth, nor society, nor contract, nor peace, no more than amongst lions, bears, and wolves. The first author of speech was God himself, that instructed Adam how to name such creatures as He presented to his sight; for the Scripture goeth no further in this matter. But this was sufficient to direct him to add more names, as the experience and use of the creatures should give him occasion; and to join them in such manner, by degrees, as to make himself understood; and so, by succession of time, so much language might be gotten as he had found use for; though not so copious as an orator or philosopher has need of: for I do not find anything in the Scripture out of which, directly or by consequence, can be gathered that Adam was taught the names of all figures, numbers, measures, colors, sounds, fancies, relations; much less the names of words and speech, as *general, special, affirmative, negative, interrogative, optative, infinitive,* all which are useful; and least of all, of *entity, intentionality, quiddity,* and other insignificant words of the school.

But all this language gotten and augmented by Adam and his posterity, was again lost at the Tower of Babel, when, by the hand of God, every man was stricken, for his rebellion, with an oblivion of his former language. And being hereby forced to disperse themselves into several parts of the world, it must needs be that the diversity of tongues that now is, proceeded by degrees from them, in such manner as need, the mother of all inventions, taught them; and in tract of time grew everywhere more copious.

The general use of speech is to transfer our mental discourse into verbal, or the train of our thoughts into a train of words; and that for two commodities, whereof one is the registering of the consequences of our thoughts; which, being apt to slip out of our memory and put us to a new labor, may again be recalled by such words as they were marked by. So that the first use of names is to serve for *marks,* or *notes* of remembrance. Another is, when many use the same words, to signify, by their connection and order, one to another, what they conceive, or think of each matter; and also what they desire, fear, or have any other passion for. And for this use they are called *signs.* Special uses of speech are these: first, to register what by cogitation we find to be the cause of anything, present or past, and what we find things present or past may produce or effect; which, in sum, is acquiring of arts. Secondly, to show to others that knowledge which we have attained; which is, to counsel and teach one another. Thirdly, to make known to others our wills and purposes, that we may have the mutual help of one another. Fourthly, to please and delight ourselves and others, by playing with our words, for pleasure or ornament, innocently.

To these uses, there are also four correspondent abuses. First, when men register their thoughts wrong, by the inconstancy of the signification of their words; by which they register for their conception, that which they never conceived, and so deceive themselves. Secondly, when they use words metaphorically; that is, in other sense than that they are ordained for; and thereby deceive others. Thirdly, by words, when they declare that to be their will which is not. Fourthly, when they use them to grieve one another; for seeing nature hath armed living creatures, some with teeth, some with horns, and some with hands, to grieve an enemy, it is but an abuse of speech, to grieve him with the tongue, unless it be one whom we are obliged to govern; and then it is not to grieve, but to correct and amend. . . .

Seeing then that truth consisteth in the right ordering of names in our affirmations, a man that seeketh precise truth had need to remember what every name he uses stands for, and to place it accordingly, or else he will find himself entangled in words, as a bird in lime twigs, the more he struggles the more belimed. And therefore in geometry, which is the only science that it hath pleased God hitherto to bestow on mankind, men begin at settling the significations of their words; which settling of significations they call *definitions,* and place them in the beginning of their reckoning.

By this it appears how necessary it is for any man that aspires to true knowledge, to examine the definitions of former authors; and either to correct them, where they are negligently set down, or to make them himself. For the errors of definitions multiply themselves according as the reckoning proceeds, and lead men into absurdities, which at last they see, but cannot avoid without reckoning anew from the beginning, in which lies the foundation of their errors. From whence it happens that they which trust to books do as they that cast up many little sums into a greater, without considering whether those little sums were rightly cast up or not; and at last finding the error visible, and not mistrusting their first grounds, know not which way to clear themselves, but spend time in fluttering over their books; as birds that entering by the chimney, and finding themselves enclosed in a chamber, flutter at the false light of a glass window, for want of wit to consider which way they came in. So that in the right definition of names lies the first use of speech, which is the acquisition of science; and in wrong, or no definitions, lies the first abuse, from which proceed all false and senseless tenets: which make those men that take their instruction from the authority of books, and not from their own meditation, to be as much below the condition of ignorant men as men endued with true science are above it. For between true science and erroneous doctrines, ignorance is in the middle. Natural sense and imagination are not subject to absurdity. Nature itself cannot err; and as men abound in copiousness of language, so they become more wise, or more mad, than ordinary. Nor is it possible without letters for any man to become either excellently wise, or, unless his memory be hurt by disease or ill constitution of organs, excellently foolish. For words are wise men's counters, they do but reckon by them; but they are the money of fools, that value them by the authority of an Aristotle, a Cicero, or a Thomas, or any other doctor whatsoever, if but a man. . . .

CHAPTER V

OF REASON AND SCIENCE

WHEN a man *reasoneth,* he does nothing else but conceive a sum total, from *addition* of parcels; or conceive a remainder, from *subtraction* of one sum from another; which, if it be done by words, is conceiving of the consequence of the names of all the parts, to the name of the whole; or from the names of the whole and one part, to the name of the other part. And though in some things, as in numbers, besides adding and subtracting, men name other operations, as multiplying and dividing, yet they are the same; for multiplication is but adding together of things equal; and division, but subtracting of one thing as often as we can. These operations are not incident to numbers only, but to all manner of things that can be added together and taken one out of another. For as arithmeticians teach to add and subtract in numbers; so the geometricians teach the same in lines, figures, solid and superficial, angles, proportions, times, degrees of swiftness, force, power, and the like; the logicians teach the same in consequences of words; adding together two names to make an affirmation, and two affirmations to make a syllogism, and many syllogisms to make a demonstration; and from the sum, or conclusion of a syllogism, they subtract one proposition to find the other. Writers of politics add together pactions to find men's duties; and lawyers, laws and facts, to find what is right and wrong in the actions of private men. In sum, in what matter soever there is place for addition and subtraction, there also is place for reason; and where these have no place, there reason has nothing at all to do.

Out of all which we may define, that is to say determine, what that is which is meant by this word *reason,* when we reckon it amongst the faculties of the mind. For reason, in this sense, is nothing but *reckoning,* that is adding and subtracting, of the consequences of general names agreed upon for the marking and signifying of our thoughts: **I** say *marking* them when we reckon by ourselves, and *signifying* when we demonstrate or approve our reckonings to other men.

And, as in arithmetic, unpracticed men must, and professors themselves may often, err, and cast up false; so also in any other subject of reasoning, the ablest, most attentive, and most practiced men may deceive themselves, and infer false conclusions; not but that reason itself is always right reason, as well as arithmetic is a certain and infallible art: but no one man's reason, nor the reason of any one number of men, makes the certainty; no more than an account is therefore well cast up because a great many men have unanimously approved it. And therefore, as when there is a controversy in an account, the parties must by their own accord set up, for right reason, the reason of some arbitrator or judge, to whose sentence they will both stand, or their controversy must either come to blows or be undecided, for want of a right reason constituted by nature; so it is also in all debates of what kind soever. And when men that think themselves wiser than all others, clamor and demand right reason for judge, yet seek no more but that things should be determined by no other men's reason but their own, it is as intolerable in the society of men, as it is in play after trump is turned, to use for trump on every occasion that suit whereof they have most in their hand. For they do nothing else that will have every of their passions, as it comes to bear sway in them, to be taken for right reason, and that in their own controversies; betraying their want of right reason, by the claim they lay to it.

The use and end of reason is not the finding of the sum and truth of one, or a few consequences, remote from the first definitions, and settled significations of names; but to begin at these, and proceed from one consequence to another. For there can be no certainty of the last conclusion, without a certainty of all those affirmations and negations on which it was grounded and inferred. As when a master of a family, in taking an account, casteth up the sums of all the bills of expense into one sum, and not regarding how each bill is summed up by those that give them in account, nor what it is he pays for; he advantages himself no more than if he allowed the account in gross, trusting to every of the accountants' skill and honesty: so also in reasoning of all other things, he that takes up conclusions on the trust of authors, and doth not fetch them from the first items in every reckoning, which are the significations of names settled by definitions, loses his labor, and does not know anything, but only believeth.

When a man reckons without the use of words, which may be done in particular things, as when upon the sight of any one thing, we conjecture what was likely to have preceded, or is likely to follow upon it;

if that which he thought likely to follow, follows not, or that which he thought likely to have preceded it, hath not preceded it, this is called *error;* to which even the most prudent men are subject. But when we reason in words of general signification, and fall upon a general inference which is false, though it be commonly called error, it is indeed an *absurdity,* or senseless speech. For error is but a deception, in presuming that somewhat is past or to come; of which, though it were not past, or not to come, yet there was no impossibility discoverable. But when we make a general assertion, unless it be a true one, the possibility of it is inconceivable. And words whereby we conceive nothing but the sound, are those we call absurd, insignificant, and nonsense. And therefore if a man should talk to me of a round quadrangle, or, accidents of bread in cheese, or immaterial substances, or of a free subject, a free will, or any *free,* but free from being hindered by opposition; I should not say he were in an error, but that his words were without meaning, that is to say, absurd.

I have said before, in the second chapter, that a man did excel all other animals in this faculty, that when he conceived anything whatsoever, he was apt to inquire the consequences of it, and what effects he could do with it. And now I add this other degree of the same excellence, that he can by words reduce the consequences he finds to general rules, called *theorems,* or *aphorisms;* that is, he can reason, or reckon, not only in number, but in all other things whereof one may be added unto, or subtracted from another.

But this privilege is allayed by another; and that is, by the privilege of absurdity, to which no living creature is subject but man only. And of men, those are of all most subject to it that profess philosophy. For it is most true that Cicero saith of them somewhere, that there can be nothing so absurd but may be found in the books of philosophers. And the reason is manifest. For there is not one of them that begins his ratiocination from the definitions, or explications of the names they are to use; which is a method that hath been used only in geometry, whose conclusions have thereby been made indisputable.

(i) The first cause of absurd conclusions I ascribe to the want of method, in that they begin not their ratiocination from definitions; that is, from settled significations of their words: as if they could cast account without knowing the value of the numeral words, one, two, and three.

And whereas all bodies enter into account upon divers considerations, which I have mentioned in the precedent chapter; these considerations being diversely named, divers absurdities proceed from the confusion, and unfit connection of their names into assertions. And therefore:

(ii) The second cause of absurd assertions, I ascribe to the giving of names of *bodies* to *accidents,* or of *accidents* to *bodies;* as they do that say, faith is 'infused,' or 'inspired'; when nothing can be poured, or breathed into anything, but body; and that, extension is body; that phantasms are spirits, etc.

(iii) The third I ascribe to the giving of the names of the *accidents of bodies without us,* to the *accidents of our own bodies;* as they do that say the color is in the body, the sound is in the air, etc.

(iv) The fourth, to the giving of the names of *bodies* to *names or speeches;* as they do that say that there be things universal; that a living creature is genus, or a general thing, etc.

(v) The fifth, to the giving of the names of *accidents* to *names and speeches;* as they do that say the nature of a thing is its definition, a man's command is his will, and the like.

(vi) The sixth, to the use of metaphors, tropes, and other rhetorical figures, instead of words proper. For though it be lawful to say, for example, in common speech, "the way goeth, or leadeth hither, or thither"; "the proverb says this or that," whereas ways cannot go, nor proverbs speak; yet in reckoning, and seeking of truth, such speeches are not to be admitted.

(vii) The seventh, to names that signify nothing, but are taken up and learned by rote from the schools, as 'hypostatical', 'transubstantiate', 'consubstantiate', 'eternal-now', and the like canting of schoolmen.

To him that can avoid these things it is not easy to fall into any absurdity, unless it be by the length of an account; wherein he may perhaps forget what went before. For all men by nature reason alike, and well, when they have good principles. For who is so stupid, as both to mistake in geometry, and also to persist in it when another detects his error to him?

By this it appears that reason is not, as sense and memory, born with us; nor gotten by experience only, as prudence is: but attained by industry; first in apt imposing of names; and secondly by getting a good and orderly method in proceeding from the elements, which are names, to assertions made by connection of one of them to another; and so to syllogisms, which are the connections of one assertion to another, till we come to a knowledge of all the consequences of names appertaining to the subject in hand; and that is it, men call *science.* And whereas sense and memory are but knowledge of fact, which is a thing past and irrevocable, science is the knowledge of consequences, and dependence of one fact upon another: by which, out of that we can presently do, we know how to do something else when we will, or the like another time; because when we see how anything comes about, upon what causes, and by what manner; when the like causes come into our power, we see how to make it produce the like effects.

Children therefore are not endued with reason at all, till they have attained the use of speech; but are called reasonable creatures, for the possibility apparent of having the use of reason in time to come. And the most part of men, though they have the use of reasoning a little way, as in numbering to some degree, yet it serves them to little use in common life; in which they govern themselves, some better, some worse, according to their differences of experience, quickness of memory, and inclinations to several ends; but especially according to good or evil fortune, and the errors of one another. For as for *science,* or certain rules of their actions, they are so far from it, they know not what it is. Geometry they have thought conjuring; but for other sciences, they who have not been taught the beginnings and some progress in them, that they may see how they be acquired and generated, are in this point like children, that having no thought of generation, are made believe by the women that their brothers and sisters are not born, but found in the garden.

But yet they that have no science, are in better and nobler condition, with their natural prudence, than men that by misreasoning, or by trusting them that reason wrong, fall upon false and absurd general rules. For ignorance of causes, and of rules, does not set men so far out of their way, as relying on false rules, and taking for causes of what they aspire to, those that are not so, but rather causes of the contrary.

To conclude, the light of human minds is perspicuous words, but by exact definitions first snuffed, and purged from ambiguity: reason is the *pace;* increase of science, the *way;* and the benefit of mankind, the *end.* And, on the contrary, metaphors, and senseless and ambiguous words, are like *ignes fatui;* and reasoning upon them is wandering amongst innumerable absurdities; and their end, contention and sedition, or contempt.

As much experience is *prudence,* so is much science *sapience.* For though we usually have one name of wisdom for them both, yet the Latins did always distinguish between *prudentia* and *sapientia,* ascribing the former to experience, the latter to science. But to make their difference appear more clearly, let us suppose one man endued with an excellent natural use and dexterity in handling his arms; and another to have added to that dexterity, an acquired science, of where he can offend, or be offended by his adversary, in every possible posture or guard: the ability of the former would be to the ability of the latter, as prudence to sapience; both useful, but the latter infallible. But they that trusting only to the authority of books, follow the blind blindly, are like him that, trusting to the false rules of a master of fence, ventures presumptuously upon an adversary, that either kills or disgraces him.

The signs of science are some, certain and infallible; some, uncertain.

Certain, when he that pretendeth the science of anything, can teach the same—that is to say, demonstrate the truth thereof perspicuously to another; uncertain, when only some particular events answer to his pretence, and upon many occasions prove so as he says they must. Signs of prudence are all uncertain; because to observe by experience, and remember all circumstances that may alter the success, is impossible, But in any business whereof a man has not infallible science to proceed by, to forsake his own natural judgment, and be guided by general sentences read in authors and subject to many exceptions, is a sign of folly, and generally scorned by the name of pedantry. And even of those men themselves that in councils of the commonwealth love to show their reading of politics and history, very few do it in their domestic affairs, where their particular interest is concerned; having prudence enough for their private affairs, but in public they study more the reputation of their own wit than the success of another's business.

CHAPTER VI

OF THE INTERIOR BEGINNINGS OF VOLUNTARY MOTIONS; COMMONLY CALLED THE PASSIONS; AND THE SPEECHES BY WHICH THEY ARE EXPRESSED

THERE be in animals, two sorts of *motions* peculiar to them: one called *vital*, begun in generation and continued without interruption through their whole life; such as are the course of the blood, the pulse, the breathing, the concoction, nutrition, excretion, etc., to which motions there needs no help of imagination: the other is *animal motion,* otherwise called *voluntary motion;* as to go, to speak, to move any of our limbs, in such manner as is first fancied in our minds. That sense is motion in the organs and interior parts of man's body, caused by the action of the things we see, hear, etc.; and that fancy is but the relics of the same motion, remaining after sense, has been already said in the first and second chapters. And because going, speaking, and the like voluntary motions, depend always upon a precedent thought of *whither, which way,* and *what;* it is evident that the imagination is the first internal beginning of all voluntary motion. And although unstudied men do not conceive any motion at all to be there, where the thing moved is invisible; or the space it is moved in is, for the shortness of it, insensible; yet that doth not hinder but that such motions are. For let a space be never so little, that which is moved over a greater space, whereof that little one is part, must first be moved over that. These small beginnings of motion, within the body of man, before they appear in walking, speaking, striking, and other visible actions, are commonly called *endeavor*.

This endeavor, when it is toward something which causes it, is called *appetite*, or *desire;* the latter being the general name, and the other oftentimes restrained to signify the desire of food, namely hunger and thirst. And when the endeavor is fromward something, it is generally called *aversion*. These words, appetite and aversion, we have from the Latins; and they both of them signify the motions, one of approaching, the other of retiring. So also do the Greek words for the same, which are ὁρμή and ἀφορμή. For nature itself does often press upon men those truths which afterwards, when they look for somewhat beyond nature, they stumble at. For the Schools find in mere appetite to go, or move, no actual motion at all; but because some motion they must acknowledge, they call it metaphorical motion; which is but an absurd speech, for though words may be called metaphorical, bodies and motions can not.

That which men desire, they are also said to *love;* and to *hate* those things for which they have aversion. So that desire and love are the same thing; save that by desire, we always signify the absence of the object; by love, most commonly the presence of the same. So also by aversion, we signify the absence; and by hate, the presence of the object.

Of appetites and aversions, some are born with men; as appetite of food, appetite of excretion, and exoneration, which may also and more properly be called aversions, from somewhat they feel in their bodies; and some other appetites, not many. The rest, which are appetites of particular things, proceed from experience, and trial of their effects upon themselves or other men. For of things we know not at all, or believe not to be, we can have no further desire than to taste and try. But aversion we have for things not only which we know have hurt us, but also that we do not know whether they will hurt us or not.

Those things which we neither desire nor hate, we are said to contemn; *contempt* being nothing else but an immobility or contumacy of the heart in resisting the action of certain things, and proceeding from the heart is already moved otherwise by other more potent objects, or from want of experience of them.

And because the constitution of a man's body is in continual mutation, it is impossible that all the same things should always cause in him the same appetites and aversions; much less can all men consent in the desire of almost any one and the same object.

But whatsoever is the object of any man's appetite or desire, that is it which he for his part calleth *good;* and the object of his hate and aversion, *evil;* and of his contempt, *vile* and *inconsiderable*. For these words of good, evil, and contemptible, are ever used with relation to the person that useth them: there being nothing simply and absolutely so; nor any common rule of good and evil to be taken from the nature of the objects themselves; but from the person of the man, where there is no commonwealth; or, in a commonwealth, from the person that representeth it; or from an arbitrator or judge, whom men disagreeing shall by consent set up, and make his sentence the rule thereof.

The Latin tongue has two words, whose significations approach to those of good and evil, but are not precisely the same; and those are *pulchrum* and *turpe*. Whereof the former signifies that which by some apparent signs promiseth good; and the latter, that which promiseth evil. But in our tongue we have not so general names to express them by. But for *pulchrum* we say in some things, *fair;* in others, *beautiful*, or *handsome*, or *gallant*, or *honorable*, or *comely*, or *amiable;* and for *turpe*, *foul, deformed, ugly, base, nauseous*, and the like, as the subject shall require: all which words, in their proper places, signify nothing else but the *mien*, or countenance, that promiseth good and evil. So that of good there be three kinds: good in the promise, that is *pulchrum;* good in effect, as the end desired, which is called *jucundum, delightful;* and good as the means, which is called *utile, profitable:* and as many of evil; for evil in promise, is that they call *turpe;* evil in effect, and end, is *molestum, unpleasant, troublesome;* and evil in the means, *inutile, unprofitable, hurtful.*

As, in sense, that which is really within us, is, as I have said before, only motion, caused by the action of external objects; but in appearance—to the sight, light and color; to the ear, sound; to the nostril, odor, etc.: so, when the action of the same object is continued from the eyes, ears, and other organs to the heart, the real effect there is nothing but motion, or endeavor; which consisteth in *appetite* or *aversion*, to or from the object moving. But the appearance, or sense, of that motion is that we either call *delight* or *trouble* of mind.

This motion, which is called appetite—and, for the apparence of it, delight, and pleasure—seemeth to be a corroboration of vital motion, and a help thereunto; and therefore such things as caused delight, were not improperly called *jucunda, a juvando*, from helping or fortifying; and the contrary, *molesta, offensive*, from hindering and troubling the motion vital.

Pleasure, therefore, or delight, is the apparence, or sense of good; and molestation, or displeasure, the apparance, or sense of evil. And consequently all appetite, desire, and love, is accompanied with some delight more or less; and all hatred and aversion, with more or less displeasure and offense.

. Of pleasures or delights, some arise from the sense of an object present; and those may be called *pleasure of sense;* the word sensual, as it is used by those only that condemn them, having no place till there be laws. Of this kind are all onerations and exonerations of the body; as also all that is pleasant, in the sight, hearing, smell, taste, or touch. Others arise from the expectation that proceeds from foresight of the end, or consequence of things; whether those things in the sense please or displease. And these are *pleasures of the mind* of him that draweth those consequences, and are generally called *joy.* In the like manner, displeasures are some in the sense, and called *pain;* others in the expectation of consequences, and are called *grief.*

These simple passions called appetite, desire, love, aversion, hate, joy, and grief, have their names for divers considerations diversified. As first, when they one succeed another, they are diversely called from the opinion men have of the likelihood of attaining what they desire. Secondly, from the object loved or hated. Thirdly, from the consideration of many of them together. Fourthly, from the alteration or succession itself.

For appetite, with an opinion of attaining, is called *hope.*

The same, without such opinion, *despair.*

Aversion, with opinion of *hurt* from the object, *fear.*

The same, with hope of avoiding that hurt by resistance, *courage.*

Sudden courage, *anger.*

Constant hope, *confidence* of ourselves.

Constant despair, *diffidence* of ourselves.

Anger for great hurt done to another, when we conceive the same to be done by injury, *indignation.*

Desire of good to another, *benevolence, good will, charity.* If to man generally, *good nature.*

Desire of riches, *covetousness:* a name used always in signification of blame; because men contending for them, are displeased with one another attaining them; though the desire in itself be to be blamed, or allowed, according to the means by which these riches are sought.

Desire of office, or precedence, *ambition:* a name used also in the worse sense, for the reason before mentioned.

Desire of things that conduce but a little to our ends, and fear of things that are of but little hindrance, *pusillanimity.*

Contempt of little helps and hindrances, *magnanimity.*

Magnanimity in danger of death or wounds, *valor, fortitude.*

Magnanimity in the use of riches, *liberality.*

Pusillanimity in the same, *wretchedness, miserableness,* or *parsimony;* as it is liked or disliked.

Love of persons for society, *kindness.*

Love of persons for pleasing the sense only, *natural lust.*

Love of the same, acquired from rumination, that is, imagination of pleasure past, *luxury.*

Love of one singularly, with desire to be singularly beloved, *the passion of love.* The same, with fear that the love is not mutual, *jealousy.*

Desire, by doing hurt to another, to make him condemn some fact of his own, *revengefulness.*

Desire to know why, and how, *curiosity;* such as is in no living creature but *man:* so that man is distinguished, not only by his reason, but also by this singular passion, from other animals; in whom the appetite of food, and other pleasures of sense, by predominance, take away the care of knowing causes; which is a lust of the mind, that by a perseverance of delight in the continual and indefatigable generation of knowledge, exceedeth the short vehemence of any carnal pleasure.

Fear of power invisible, feigned by the mind, or imagined from tales publicly allowed, *religion;* not allowed, *superstition.* And when the power imagined, is truly such as we imagine, *true religion.*

Fear without the apprehension of why, or what, *panic terror:* called so from the fables that make Pan the author of them; whereas, in truth, there is always in him that so feareth first, some apprehension of the cause, though the rest run away by example, everyone supposing his fellow to know why. And therefore this passion happens to none but in a throng, or multitude of people.

Joy, from apprehension of novelty, *admiration;* proper to man, because it excites the appetite of knowing the cause.

Joy arising from imagination of a man's own power and ability, is that exultation of the mind which is called *glorying:* which if grounded upon the experience of his own former actions, is the same with *confidence;* but if grounded on the flattery of others, or only supposed by himself for delight in the consequences of it, is called *vainglory:* which name is properly given; because a well grounded confidence begetteth attempt, whereas the supposing of power does not, and is therefore rightly called *vain.*

Grief, from opinion of want of power, is called *dejection* of mind.

The vain-glory which consisteth in the feigning or supposing of abilities in ourselves, which we know are not, is most incident to young men, and nourished by the histories, or fictions, of gallant persons; and is corrected oftentimes by age and employment.

Sudden glory is the passion which maketh those grimaces called *laughier;* and is caused either by some sudden act of their own, that pleaseth them; or by the apprehension of some deformed thing in another, by comparison whereof they suddenly applaud themselves. And it is incident most to them that are conscious of the fewest abilities in themselves; who are forced to keep themselves in their own favor by observing the imperfections of other men. And therefore much laughter at the defects of others is a sign of pusillanimity. For of great minds, one of the proper works is, to help and free others from scorn; and compare themselves only with the most able.

On the contrary, sudden dejection is the passion that causeth *weeping;* and is caused by such accidents as suddenly take away some vehement hope, or some prop of their power: and they are most subject to it that rely principally on helps external, such as are women and children. Therefore some weep for the loss of friends, others for their unkindness, others for the sudden stop made to their thoughts of revenge, by reconciliation. But in all cases, both laughter and weeping are sudden motions; custom taking them both away. For no man laughs at old jests, or weeps for an old calamity.

Grief for the discovery of some defect of ability, is *shame,* or the passion that discovereth itself in *blushing;* and consisteth in the apprehension of something dishonorable; and in young men, is a sign of the love of good reputation, and commendable; in old men it is a sign of the same, but because it comes too late, not commendable.

The contempt of good reputation is called *impudence.*

Grief for the calamity of another is *pity,* and ariseth from the imagination that the like calamity may befall himself; and therefore is called also *compassion,* and in the phrase of this present time a *fellow-feeling:* and therefore for calamity arriving from great wickedness, the best men have the least pity; and for the same calamity those hate pity that think themselves least obnoxious to the same.

Contempt or little sense of the calamity of others, is that which men call *cruelty;* proceeding from security of their own fortune. For that any man should take pleasure in other men's great harms, without other end of his own, I do not conceive it possible.

Grief for the success of a competitor in wealth, honor, or other good, if it be joined with endeavor to enforce our own abilities to equal or exceed him, is called *emulation:* but joined with endeavor to supplant or hinder a competitor, *envy.*

When in the mind of man appetites and aversions, hopes and fears, concerning one and the same thing, arise alternately; and divers good and evil consequences of the doing or omitting the thing propounded, come successively into our thoughts; so that sometimes we have an appetite to it, sometimes an aversion from it, sometimes hope to be able to do it, sometimes despair or fear to attempt it; the whole sum of desires, aversions, hopes, and fears, continued till the thing be either done or thought impossible, is that we call *deliberation.*

Therefore of things past there is no deliberation; because manifestly impossible to be changed: nor of things known to be impossible, or thought so; because men know, or think, such deliberation vain. But of things impossible which we think possible, we may deliberate; not knowing it is in vain. And it is called *de-liberation* because it is a putting an end to the *liberty* we had of doing, or omitting, according to our own appetite or aversion.

This alternate succession of appetites, aversions, hopes, and fears, is no less in other living creatures than in man; and therefore beasts also deliberate.

Every deliberation is then said to *end,* when that whereof they deliberate is either done or thought impossible; because till then we retain the liberty of doing or omitting, according to our appetite or aversion.

In deliberation, the last appetite or aversion immediately adhering to the action, or to the omission thereof, is that we call the *will,*—the act, not the faculty, of willing. And beasts that have deliberation, must necessarily also have will. The definition of the will given commonly by the Schools, that it is a *rational appetite,* is not good. For if it were, then could there be no voluntary act against reason. For a *voluntary act* is that which proceedeth from the will, and no other. But if instead of a rational appetite, we shall say an appetite resulting from a precedent deliberation, then the definition is the same that I have given here. *Will,* therefore, *is the last appetite in deliberating.* And though we say in common discourse, a man had a will once to do a thing, that nevertheless he forbore to do; yet that is properly but an inclination, which makes no action voluntary; because the action depends not of it, but of the last inclination or appetite. For if the intervenient appetites make any action voluntary, then by the same reason all intervenient aversions should make the same action involuntary; and so one and the same action should be both voluntary and involuntary.

By this it is manifest that not only actions that have their beginning from covetousness, ambition, lust, or other appetites to the thing propounded, but also those that have their beginning from aversion, or fear of those consequences that follow the omission, are *voluntary actions.*

The forms of speech by which the passions are expressed, are partly the same, and partly different from those, by which we express our thoughts. And first, generally all passions may be expressed *indicatively;* as *I love, I fear, I joy, I deliberate, I will, I command:* but some of them have particular expressions by themselves, which nevertheless are not affirmations, unless it be when they serve to make other inferences, besides that of the passion they proceed from. Deliberation is expressed *subjunctively;* which is a speech proper to signify suppositions, with their consequences; as, *if this be done, then this will follow;* and differs not from the language of reasoning, save that reasoning is in general words; but deliberation for the most part is of particulars. The language of desire, and aversion, is *imperative;* as *do this, forbear that;* which when the party is obliged to do, or forbear, is *command;* otherwise *prayer;* or else *counsel.* The language of vain-glory, of indignation, pity and revengefulness, *optative:* but of the desire to know, there is a pecul-iar expression, called *interrogative;* as, *what is it, when shall it, how is it done,* and *why so?* Other language of the passions I find none: for cursing, swearing, reviling, and the like, do not signify as speech; but as the actions of a tongue accustomed.

These forms of speech, I say, are expressions, or voluntary significa-tions of our passions: but certain signs they be not; because they may be used arbitrarily, whether they that use them, have such passions or not. The best signs of passions present, are either in the countenance, motions of the body, actions, and ends, or aims, which we otherwise know the man to have.

And because in deliberation, the appetites and aversions are raised by foresight of the good and evil consequences, and sequels of the action whereof we deliberate; the good or evil effect thereof dependeth on the foresight of a long chain of consequences, of which very seldom any man is able to see to the end. But for so far as a man seeth, if the good in those consequences be greater than the evil, the whole chain is that which writers call *apparent,* or *seeming good.* And contrarily, when the evil exceedeth the good, the whole is *apparent,* or *seeming evil:* so that he who hath by experience, or reason, the greatest and surest prospect of consquences, deliberates best himself; and is able when he will, to give the best counsel unto others.

Continual success in obtaining those things which a man from time to time desireth, that is to say, continual prospering, is that men call *felic-ity;* I mean the felicity of this life. For there is no such thing as per-petual tranquillity of mind, while we live here; because life itself is but motion, and can never be without desire, nor without fear, no more than without sense. What kind of felicity God hath ordained to them that de-voutly honor Him, a man shall no sooner know, than enjoy; being joys, that now are as incomprehensible, as the word of schoolmen *beatifical vision* is unintelligible.

The form of speech whereby men signify their opinion of the good-ness of anything is *praise.* That whereby they signify the power and greatness of anything, is *magnifying.* And that whereby they signify the opinion they have of a man's felicity, is by the Greeks called μακαρισμός, for which we have no name in our tongue. And thus much is sufficient for the present purpose, to have been said of the *passions.*

CHAPTER VII

OF THE ENDS, OR RESOLUTIONS OF DISCOURSE

OF all discourse governed by desire of knowledge, there is at last an *end,* either by attaining or by giving over. And in the chain of discourse, wheresoever it be interrupted, there is an end for that time.

If the discourse be merely mental, it consisteth of thoughts that the thing will be, and will not be; or that it has been, and has not been, alternately. So that wheresoever you break off the chain of the man's discourse, you leave him in a presumption of 'it will be', or 'it will not be'; or 'it has been', or 'has not been'. All which is *opinion.* And that which is alternate appetite, in deliberating concerning good and evil; the same is alternate opinion, in the inquiry of the truth of past and future. And as the last appetite in deliberation, is called the *will;* so the last opinion in search of the truth of past, and future, is called the *judgment,* or *resolute and final sentence* of him that discourseth. And as the whole chain of appetites alternate, in the question of good or bad, is called *deliberation;* so the whole chain of opinions alternate, in the question of true or false, is called *doubt.*

No discourse whatsoever can end in absolute knowledge of fact, past or to come. For, as for the knowledge of fact, it is originally, sense; and ever after, memory. And for the knowledge of consequence, which I have said before is called science, it is not absolute but conditional. No man can know by discourse that this or that is, has been, or will be; which is to know absolutely: but only, that if this be, that is; if this has been, that has been; if this shall be, that shall be: which is to know conditionally; and that not the consequence of one thing to another, but of one name of a thing, to another name of the same thing.

And therefore, when the discourse is put into speech, and begins with the definitions of words, and proceeds by connection of the same into general affirmations, and of these again into syllogisms; the end or last sum is called the conclusion; and the thought of the mind by it signified, is that conditional knowledge, or knowledge of the consequence of words, which is commonly called *science.* But if the first ground of such discourse be not definitions, or if the definitions be not rightly joined together into syllogisms, then the end or conclusion is again *opinion,* namely of the truth of somewhat said, though sometimes in absurd and senseless words, without possibility of being understood. When two or more men know of one and the same fact, they are said to be *conscious* of it one to another; which is as much as to know it together. And because such are fittest witnesses of the facts of one another, or of a third;

it was, and ever will be reputed a very evil act, for any man to speak against his *conscience,* or to corrupt or force another so to do: insomuch that the plea of conscience has been always hearkened unto very diligently in all times. Afterwards, men made use of the same word metaphorically, for the knowledge of their own secret facts and secret thoughts; and therefore it is rhetorically said that the conscience is a thousand witnesses. And last of all, men, vehemently in love with their own new opinions, though never so absurd, and obstinately bent to maintain them, gave those their opinions also that reverenced name of conscience, as if they would have it seem unlawful to change or speak against them; and so pretend to know they are true, when they know at most but that they think so.

When a man's discourse beginneth not at definitions, it beginneth either at some other contemplation of his own, and then it is still called opinion; or it beginneth at some saying of another, of whose ability to know the truth, and of whose honesty in not deceiving, he doubteth not; and then the discourse is not so much concerning the thing as the person; and the resolution is called *belief,* and *faith:* faith, *in* the man; belief, both *of* the man, and *of* the truth of what he says. So that in belief are two opinions: one of the saying of the man; the other of his virtue. To *have faith in,* or *trust to,* or *believe a man,* signify the same thing; namely, an opinion of the veracity of the man: but to *believe what is said,* signifieth only an opinion of the truth of the saying. But we are to observe that this phrase, 'I believe in'; as also the Latin, *credo in;* and the Greek, πιστεύω εἰς, are never used but in the writings of divines. Instead of them, in other writings are put, 'I believe him', 'I trust him', 'I have faith in him', 'I rely on him'; and in Latin *credo illi, fido illi;* and in Greek, πιστεύω αὐτῷ: and that this singularity of the ecclesiastic use of the word hath raised many disputes about the right object of the Christian faith.

But by *believing in,* as it is in the creed, is meant not trust in the person, but confession and acknowledgment of the doctrine. For not only Christians but all manner of men do so believe in God, as to hold all for truth they hear Him say, whether they understand it or not; which is all the faith and trust can possibly be had in any person whatsoever: but they do not all believe the doctrine of the creed.

From whence we may infer, that when we believe any saying, whatsoever it be, to be true, from arguments taken not from the thing itself, or from the principles of natural reason, but from the authority and good opinion we have of him that hath said it; then is the speaker, or person we believe in or trust in, and whose word we take, the object of our faith; and the honor done in believing, is done to him only. And consequently, when we believe that the Scriptures are the word of God, having no immediate revelation from God Himself, our belief, faith, and trust is in the Church; whose word we take, and acquiesce therein. And they that believe that which a prophet relates unto them in the name of God, to take the word of the prophet, do honor to him, and in him trust and believe, touching the truth of what he relateth, whether he be a true or a false prophet. And so it is also with all other history. For if I should not believe all that is written by historians, of the glorious acts of Alexander or Caesar, I do not think the ghost of Alexander or Caesar had any just cause to be offended; or anybody else but the historian. If Livy say the gods made once a cow speak, and we believe it not; we distrust not God therein, but Livy. So that it is evident, that whatsoever we believe, upon no other reason than what is drawn from authority of men only, and their writings; whether they be sent from God or not, is faith in men only. . . .[1]

CHAPTER XI

OF THE DIFFERENCE OF MANNERS

By *manners*, I mean not here, decency of behavior; as how one should salute another, or how a man should wash his mouth, or pick his teeth before company, and such other points of the *small morals;* but those qualities of mankind, that concern their living together in peace, and unity. To which end we are to consider, that the felicity of this life, consisteth not in the repose of a mind satisfied. For there is no such *finis ultimus,* utmost aim, nor *summum bonum,* greatest good, as is spoken of in the books of the old moral philosophers. Nor can a man any more live, whose desires are at an end, than he, whose senses and imaginations are at a stand. Felicity is a continual progress of the desire, from one object to another; the attaining of the former, being still but the way to the latter. The cause whereof is, that the object of man's desire, is not to enjoy once only, and for one instant of time; but to assure for ever, the way of his future desire. And therefore the voluntary actions, and inclinations of all men, tend, not only to the procuring, but also to the assuring of a contented life; and differ only in the way: which ariseth partly from the diversity of passions, in divers men; and partly from the difference of the knowledge, or opinion each one has of the causes, which produce the effect desired.

So that in the first place, I put for a general inclination of all man-

---

[1] Chapters VIII-X treat of the following topics: "Of the Virtues Commonly Called Intellectual, and Their Contrary Defects," "Of the Several Subjects of Knowledge," "Of Power, Worth, Dignity, Honor and Worthiness."—*Editor.*

kind, a perpetual and restless desire of power after power, that ceaseth only in death. And the cause of this, is not always that a man hopes for a more intensive delight, than he has already attained to; or that he cannot be content with a moderate power: but because he cannot assure the power and means to live well, which he hath present, without the acquisition of more. And from hence it is, that kings, whose power is greatest, turn their endeavors to the assuring it at home by laws, or abroad by wars: and when that is done, there succeedeth a new desire; in some, of fame from new conquest; in others, of ease and sensual pleasure; in others, of admiration, or being flattered for excellence in some art, or other ability of the mind. . . .[2]

CHAPTER XIII

OF THE NATURAL CONDITION OF MANKIND AS CONCERNING THEIR FELICITY, AND MISERY

NATURE hath made men so equal, in the faculties of the body and mind; as that, though there be found one man sometimes manifestly stronger in body or of quicker mind than another, yet when all is reckoned together, the difference between man and man is not so considerable, as that one man can thereupon claim to himself any benefit, to which another may not pretend as well as he. For as to the strength of the body, the weakest has strength enough to kill the strongest, either by secret machination, or by confederacy with others that are in the same danger with himself.

And as to the faculties of the mind—setting aside the arts grounded upon words, and especially that skill of proceeding upon general and infallible rules, called science; which very few have, and but in few things; as being not a native faculty, born with us; nor attained, as prudence, while we look after somewhat else—I find yet a greater equality amongst men, than that of strength. For prudence is but experience, which equal time equally bestows on all men, in those things they equally apply themselves unto. That which may perhaps make such equality incredible, is but a vain conceit of one's own wisdom, which almost all men think they have in a greater degree than the vulgar; that is, than all men but themselves, and a few others, whom by fame, or for concurring with themselves, they approve. For such is the nature of men, that howsoever they may acknowledge many others to be more witty, or more eloquent, or more learned, yet they will hardly believe there be many so wise as themselves; for they see their own wit at hand,

[2] Chapter XII treats "Of Religion."—*Editor.*

and other men's at a distance. But this proveth rather that men are in that point equal, than unequal. For there is not ordinarily a greater sign of the equal distribution of anything, than that every man is contented with his share.

From this equality of ability, ariseth equality of hope in the attaining of our ends. And therefore if any two men desire the same thing, which nevertheless they cannot both enjoy, they become enemies; and in the way to their end, which is principally their own conservation, and sometimes their delectation only, endeavor to destroy, or subdue one another. And from hence it comes to pass that where an invader hath no more to fear than another man's single power; if one plant, sow, build, or possess a convenient seat, others may probably be expected to come prepared with forces united, to dispossess and deprive him, not only of the fruit of his labor, but also of his life or liberty. And the invader again is in the like danger of another.

And from this diffidence of one another, there is no way for any man to secure himself so reasonable as anticipation; that is, by force or wiles to master the persons of all men he can, so long, till he see no other power great enough to endanger him: and this is no more than his own conservation requireth, and is generally allowed. Also because there be some, that taking pleasure in contemplating their own power in the acts of conquest, which they pursue farther than their security requires; if others, that otherwise would be glad to be at ease within modest bounds, should not by invasion increase their power, they would not be able long time, by standing only on their defense, to subsist. And by consequence, such augmentation of dominion over men being necessary to a man's conservation, it ought to be allowed him.

Again, men have no pleasure, but on the contrary a great deal of grief, in keeping company, where there is no power able to overawe them all. For every man looketh that his companion should value him at the same rate he sets upon himself; and upon all signs of contempt, or undervaluing, naturally endeavors, as far as he dares (which amongst them that have no common power to keep them in quiet, is far enough to make them destroy each other), to extort a greater value from his contemners by damage, and from others by the example.

So that in the nature of man, we find three principal causes of quarrel. First, competition; second, diffidence; thirdly, glory.

The first maketh men invade for gain; the second, for safety; and the third, for reputation. The first use violence to make themselves masters of other men's persons, wives, children, and cattle; the second, to defend them; the third, for trifles, as a word, a smile, a different opinion, and any other sign of undervalue, either direct in their persons, or by reflection in their kindred, their friends, their nation, their profession, or their name.

Hereby it is manifest that during the time men live without a common power to keep them all in awe, they are in that condition which is called war; and such a war as is of every man against every man. For *war* consisteth not in battle only, or the act of fighting, but in a tract of time wherein the will to contend by battle is sufficiently known, and therefore the notion of *time* is to be considered in the nature of war, as it is in the nature of weather. For as the nature of foul weather lieth not in a shower or two of rain, but in an inclination thereto of many days together; so the nature of war consisteth not in actual fighting, but in the known disposition thereto, during all the time there is no assurance to the contrary. All other time is *peace*.

Whatsoever therefore is consequent to a time of war, where every man is enemy to every man; the same is consequent to the time, wherein men live without other security than what their own strength and their own invention shall furnish them withal. In such condition there is no place for industry, because the fruit thereof is uncertain: and consequently no culture of the earth; no navigation, nor use of the commodities that may be imported by sea; no commodious building; no instruments of moving, and removing, such things as require much force; no knowledge of the face of the earth; no account of time; no arts; no letters; no society; and which is worst of all, continual fear, and danger of violent death; and the life of man, solitary, poor, nasty, brutish, and short.

It may seem strange to some man that has not well weighed these things, that nature should thus dissociate, and render men apt to invade and destroy one another; and he may therefore, not trusting to this inference, made from the passions, desire perhaps to have the same confirmed by experience. Let him therefore consider with himself, when taking a journey, he arms himself and seeks to go well accompanied; when going to sleep, he locks his doors; when even in his house he locks his chests; and this when he knows there be laws, and public officers, armed, to revenge all injuries shall be done him: what opinion he has of his fellow-subjects, when he rides armed; of his fellow-citizens, when he locks his doors; and of his children, and servants, when he locks his chests. Does he not there as much accuse mankind by his actions, as I do by my words? But neither of us accuse man's nature in it. The desires, and other passions of man, are in themselves no sin. No more are the actions that proceed from those passions, till they know a law that forbids them: which till laws be made they cannot know; nor can any law be made, till they have agreed upon the person that shall make it.

It may peradventure be thought, there was never such a time nor condition of war as this; and I believe it was never generally so, over all the world: but there are many places where they live so now. For the savage people in many places of America, except the government of small families, the concord whereof dependeth on natural lust, have no government at all; and live at this day in that brutish manner, as I said before. Howsoever, it may be perceived what manner of life there would be, where there were no common power to fear; by the manner of life which men that have formerly lived under a peaceful government, use to degenerate into in a civil war.

But though there had never been any time wherein particular men were in a condition of war one against another; yet in all times, kings, and persons of sovereign authority, because of their independency, are in continual jealousies, and in the state and posture of gladiators; having their weapons pointing, and their eyes fixed on one another; that is, their forts, garrisons, and guns upon the frontiers of their kingdoms; and continual spies upon their neighbors; which is a posture of war. But because they uphold thereby the industry of their subjects, there does not follow from it that misery which accompanies the liberty of particular men.

To this war of every man against every man, this also is consequent: *that nothing can be unjust.* The notions of right and wrong, justice and injustice, have there no place. Where there is no common power, there is no law; where no law, no injustice. Force and fraud are in war the two cardinal virtues. Justice and injustice are none of the faculties neither of the body nor mind. If they were, they might be in a man that were alone in the world, as well as his senses and passions. They are qualities that relate to men in society, not in solitude. It is consequent also to the same condition, that there be no propriety, no dominion, no *mine* and *thine* distinct; but only that to be every man's, that he can get; and for so long as he can keep it. And thus much for the ill condition which man by mere nature is actually placed in; though with a possibility to come out of it, consisting partly in the passions, partly in his reason.

The passions that incline men to peace are fear of death, desire of such things as are necessary to commodious living, and a hope by their industry to obtain them. And reason suggesteth convenient articles of peace, upon which men may be drawn to agreement. These articles are they which otherwise are called the Laws of Nature whereof I shall speak more particularly in the two following chapters.

CHAPTER XIV

THE FIRST AND SECOND NATURAL LAWS, AND OF CONTRACTS

THE right of nature, which writers commonly call *jus naturale*, is the liberty each man hath to use his own power, as he will himself, for the preservation of his own nature; that is to say, of his own life; and consequently, of doing anything, which in his own judgment and reason, he shall conceive to be the aptest means thereunto.

By *liberty*, is understood, according to the proper signification of the word, the absence of external impediments: which impediments, may oft take away part of a man's power to do what he would; but cannot hinder him from using the power left him, according as his judgment and reason shall dictate to him.

A *law of nature, lex naturalis,* is a precept or general rule, found out by reason, by which a man is forbidden to do that which is destructive of his life, or taketh away the means of preserving the same; and to omit that by which he thinketh it may be best preserved. For though they that speak of this subject, use to confound *jus* and *lex, right* and *law;* yet they ought to be distinguished: because *right* consisteth in liberty to do or to forbear, whereas *law* determineth and bindeth to one of them; so that law, and right differ as much as obligation and liberty; which in one and the same matter are inconsistent.

And because the condition of man, as hath been declared in the precedent chapter, is a condition of war of everyone against everyone; in which case everyone is governed by his own reason, and there is nothing he can make use of that may not be a help unto him in preserving his life against his enemies: it followeth, that in such a condition every man has a right to everything; even to one another's body. And therefore, as long as this natural right of every man to everything endureth, there can be no security to any man, how strong or wise soever he be, of living out the time which nature ordinarily alloweth men to live. And consequently it is a precept, or general rule of reason, *that every man ought to endeavor peace, as far as he has hope of obtaining it; and when he cannot obtain it, that he may seek and use all helps and advantages of war.* The first branch of which rule containeth the first and fundamental law of nature; which is, *to seek peace and follow it.* The second, the sum of the right of nature; which is, *by all means we can, to defend ourselves.*

From this fundamental law of nature, by which men are commanded to endeavor peace, is derived this second law: *that a man be willing, when others are so too, as far forth as for peace and defense of himself he shall think it necessary, to lay down this right to all things; and be contented with so much liberty against other men, as he would allow other men against himself.* For as long as every man holdeth this right, of doing anything he liketh, so long are all men in the condition of war. But if other men will not lay down their right, as well as he, then there is no reason for anyone to divest himself of his: for that were to expose himself to prey, which no man is bound to, rather than to dispose himself to peace. This is that law of the Gospel: *whatsoever you require that others should do to you, that do ye to them.* And that law of all men, *quod tibi fieri non vis, alteri ne feceris.*

To *lay down* a man's *right* to anything, is to *divest* himself of the *liberty*, of hindering another of the benefit of his own right to the same. For he that renounceth or passeth away his right, giveth not to any other man a right which he had not before; because there is nothing to which every man had not right by nature: but only standeth out of his way, that he may enjoy his own original right, without hindrance from him, not without hindrance from another. So that the effect which redoundeth to one man, by another man's defect of right, is but so much diminution of impediments to the use of his own right original.

Right is laid aside, either by simply renouncing it, or by transferring it to another. By *simply renouncing,* when he cares not to whom the benefit thereof redoundeth. By *transferring,* when he intendeth the benefit thereof to some certain person or persons. And when a man hath in either manner abandoned or granted away his right; then is he said to be *obliged,* or bound, not to hinder those to whom such right is granted or abandoned, from the benefit of it; and that he *ought,* and it is his *duty,* not to make void that voluntary act of his own; and that such hindrance is *injustice,* and *injury,* as being *sine jure;* the right being before renounced, or transferred. So that injury, or injustice in the controversies of the world, is somewhat like to that, which in the disputations of scholars is called *absurdity.* For as it is there called an absurdity to contradict what one maintained in the beginning; so in the world, it is called injustice, and injury, voluntarily to undo that which from the beginning he had voluntarily done. The way by which a man either simply renounceth, or transferreth his right, is a declaration, or signification, by some voluntary and sufficient sign or signs, that he doth so renounce or transfer, or hath so renounced or transferred the same, to him that accepteth it. And these signs are either words only, or actions only, or, as it happeneth most often, both words and actions. And the same are the *bonds,* by which men are bound and obliged—bonds that have their strength, not from their own nature, for nothing is more easily broken than a man's word, but from fear of some evil consequence upon the rupture.

Whensoever a man transferreth his right, or renounceth it; it is either in consideration of some right reciprocally transferred to himself, or for some other good he hopeth for thereby. For it is a voluntary act; and of the voluntary acts of every man, the object is some *good to himself*. And therefor there be some rights which no man can be understood by any words, or other signs, to have abandoned or transferred. As first a man cannot lay down the right of resisting them that assault him by force, to take away his life; because he cannot be understood to aim thereby, at any good to himself. The same may be said of wounds, and chains, and imprisonment: both because there is no benefit consequent to such patience, as there is to the patience of suffering another to be wounded or imprisoned; as also because a man cannot tell, when he seeth men proceed against him by violence, whether they intend his death or not. And lastly the motive, an end for which this renouncing and transferring of right is introduced, is nothing else but the security of a man's person, in his life, and in the means of so preserving life as not to be weary of it. And therefore if a man by words, or other signs, seem to despoil himself of the end for which those signs were intended, he is not to be understood as if he meant it, or that it was his will, but that he was ignorant of how such words and actions were to be interpreted.

The mutual transferring of right, is that which men call *contract*.

There is difference between transferring of right to the thing, and transferring, or tradition—that is delivery—of the thing itself. For the thing may be delivered together with the translation of the right, as in buying and selling with ready money, or exchange of goods, or lands; and it may be delivered sometime after.

Again, one of the contractors may deliver the thing contracted for on his part, and leave the other to perform his part at some determinate time after, and in the meantime be trusted; and then the contract on his part is called *pact,* or *covenant:* or both parts may contract now to perform hereafter; in which cases, he that is to perform in time to come, being trusted, his performance is called *keeping of promise,* or faith; and the failing of performance, if it be voluntary, *violation of faith.*

When the transferring of right is not mutual; but one of the parties transferreth, in hope to gain thereby friendship, or service from another, or from his friends; or in hope to gain the reputation of charity, or magnanimity; or to deliver his mind from the pain of compassion; or in hope of reward in heaven; this is not contract, but *gift, free-gift, grace:* which words signify one and the same thing.

Signs of contract, are either *express,* or *by inference.* Express, are words spoken with understanding of what they signify: and such words are either of the time *present,* or *past;* as, *I give, I grant, I have given,*

I have granted, I will that this be yours: or of the future; as, *I will give, will grant:* which words of the future are called *promise.*

Signs by inference are sometimes the consequence of words; sometimes the consequence of silence; sometimes the consequence of actions; sometimes the consequence of forbearing an action; and generally a sign by inference, of any contract, is whatsoever sufficiently argues the will of the contractor.

Words alone, if they be of the time to come, and contain a bare promise, are an insufficient sign of a free-gift, and therefore not obligatory. For if they be of the time to come, as *tomorrow I will give,* they are a sign I have not given yet, and consequently that my right is not transferred, but remaineth till I transfer it by some other act. But if the words be of the time present, or past, as, *I have given,* or, *do give to be delivered tomorrow,* then is my tomorrow's right given away today; and that by the virtue of the words, though there were no other argument of my will. And there is a great difference in the signification of these words, *volo hoc tuum esse cras,* and *cras dabo;* that is, between *I will that this be thine tomorrow,* and, *I will give it thee tomorrow:* for the word *I will,* in the former manner of speech, signifies an act of the will present; but in the latter, it signifies a promise of an act of the will to come: and therefore the former words, being of the present, transfer a future right; the latter, that be of the future, transfer nothing. But if there be other signs of the will to transfer a right, besides words; then, though the gift be free, yet may the right be understood to pass by words of the future: as if a man propound a prize to him that comes first to the end of a race, the gift is free; and though the words be of the future, yet the right passeth: for if he would not have his words so be understood, he should not have let them run.

In contracts, the right passeth, not only where the words are of the time present, or past, but also where they are of the future: because all contract is mutual translation, or change of right; and therefore he that promiseth only, because he hath already received the benefit for which he promiseth, is to be understood as if he intended the right should pass: for unless he had been content to have his words so understood, the other would not have performed his part first. And for that cause, in buying, and selling, and other acts of contract, a promise is equivalent to a covenant; and therefore obligatory.

He that performeth first in the case of a contract, is said to *merit* that which he is to receive by the performance of the other; and he hath it as *due.* Also when a prize is propounded to many, which is to be given to him only that winneth; or money is thrown amongst many, to be enjoyed by them that catch it; though this be a free gift; yet so to win, or so to catch. is to *merit,* and to have it as *due.* For the right is transferred in the propounding of the prize, and in throwing down the money; though it be not determined to whom, but by the event of the contention. But there is between these two sorts of merit, this difference, that in contract, I merit by virtue of my own power, and the contractor's need; but in this case of free gift, I am enabled to merit only by the benignity of the giver: in contract, I merit at the contractor's hand that he should depart with his right; in this case of gift, I merit not that the giver should part with his right; but that when he has parted with it, it should be mine, rather than another's. And this I think to be the meaning of that distinction of the Schools, between *meritum congrui*, and *meritum condigni*. For God Almighty, having promised Paradise to those men, hoodwinked with carnal desires, that can walk through this world according to the precepts, and limits prescribed by him; they say, he that shall so walk, shall merit Paradise *ex congruo*. But because no man can demand a right to it, by his own righteousness, or any other power in himself, but by the free grace of God only; they say, no man can merit Paradise *ex condigno*. This I say, I think is the meaning of that distinction; but because disputers do not agree upon the signification of their own terms of art, longer than it serves their turn; I will not affirm anything of their meaning: only this I say; when a gift is given indefinitely, as a prize to be contended for, he that winneth meriteth, and may claim the prize as due.

If a covenant be made, wherein neither of the parties perform presently, but trust one another; in the condition of mere nature, which is a condition of war of every man against every man, upon any reasonable suspicion, it is void: but if there be a common power set over them both, with right and force sufficient to compel performance, it is not void. For he that performeth first, has no assurance the other will perform after; because the bonds of words are too weak to bridle men's ambition, avarice, anger, and other passions, without the fear of some coercive power; which in the condition of mere nature, where all men are equal, and judges of the justness of their own fears, cannot possibly be supposed. And therefore he which performeth first, does but betray himself to his enemy; contrary to the right, he can never abandon, of defending his life, and means of living.

But in a civil estate, where there is a power set up to constrain those that would otherwise violate their faith, that fear is no more reasonable; and for that cause, he which by the covenant is to perform first, is obliged so to do. . . .

CHAPTER XV

OF OTHER LAWS OF NATURE

FROM that law of nature by which we are obliged to transfer to another such rights as, being retained, hinder the peace of mankind, there followeth a third; which is this, *that men perform their covenants made:* without which, covenants are in vain, and but empty words; and the right of all men to all things remaining, we are still in the condition of war.

And in this law of nature, consisteth the fountain and original of *justice.* For where no covenant hath preceded, there hath no right been transferred, and every man has right to everything; and consequently, no action can be unjust. But when a covenant is made, then to break it is *unjust* and the definition of *injustice* is no other than *the not performance of covenant.* And whatsoever is not unjust, is *just.*

But because covenants of mutual trust, where there is a fear of not performance on either part, as hath been said in the former chapter, are invalid; though the original of justice be the making of covenants; yet injustice actually there can be none, till the cause of such fear be taken away; which while men are in the natural condition of war, cannot be done. Therefore before the names of just and unjust can have place, there must be some coercive power, to compel men equally to the performance of their covenants, by the terror of some punishment greater than the benefit they expect by the breach of their covenant; and to make good that propriety which by mutual contract men acquire, in recompense of the universal right they abandon: and such power there is none before the erection of a commonwealth. And this is also to be gathered out of the ordinary definition of justice in the Schools; for they say, that *justice is the constant will of giving to every man his own.* And therefore where there is no *own,* that is no propriety, there is no injustice; and where is no coercive power erected, that is, where there is no commonwealth, there is no propriety; all men having right to all things: therefore where there is no commonwealth, there nothing is unjust. So that the nature of justice consisteth in keeping of valid covenants; but the validity of covenants begins not but with the constitution of a civil power sufficient to compel men to keep them, and then it is also that propriety begins. . . .

As justice dependeth on antecedent covenant, so does *gratitude* depend on antecedent grace—that is to say, antecedent free gift—and is the fourth law of nature; which may be conceived in this form, *that a man which receiveth benefit from another of mere grace, endeavor that he which giveth it, have no reasonable cause to repent him of his good will.* For no man giveth but with intention of good to himself; because gift is voluntary; and of all voluntary acts, the object is to every man his own good; of which if men see they shall be frustrated, there will be no beginning of benevolence or trust, nor consequently of mutual help, nor of reconciliation of one man to another; and therefore they are to remain still in the condition of *war;* which is contrary to the first and fundamental law of nature, which commandeth men to *seek peace.* The breach of this law is called *ingratitude,* and hath the same relation to grace that injustice hath to obligation by covenant.

A fifth law of nature is *complaisance;* that is to say, *that every man strive to accommodate himself to the rest.* For the understanding whereof, we may consider that there is in men's aptness to society, a diversity of nature, rising from their diversity of affections; not unlike to that we see in stones brought together for building of an edifice. For as that stone which, by the asperity and irregularity of figure, takes more room from others than itself fills, and for the hardness cannot be easily made plain, and thereby hindereth the building, is by the builders cast away as unprofitable and troublesome: so also, a man that by asperity of nature will strive to retain those things which to himself are superfluous and to others necessary, and for the stubbornness of his passions cannot be corrected, is to be left, or cast out of society, as cumbersome thereunto. For seeing every man, not only by right but also by necessity of nature, is supposed to endeavor all he can to obtain that which is necessary for his conservation; he that shall oppose himself against it, for things superfluous, is guilty of the war that thereupon is to follow; and therefore doth that which is contrary to the fundamental law of nature, which commandeth to seek peace. The observers of this law may be called *sociable;* the Latins call them *commodi;* the contrary, stubborn, insociable, froward, intractable.

A sixth law of nature is this, *that upon caution of the future time, a man ought to pardon the offenses past of them that repenting, desire it.* For *pardon* is nothing but granting of peace; which though granted to them that persevere in their hostility, be not peace, but fear; yet not granted to them that give caution of the future time, is sign of an aversion to peace; and therefore contrary to the law of nature.

A seventh is, *that in revenges*—that is, retribution of evil for evil—*men look not at the greatness of the evil past, but the greatness of the good to follow.* Whereby we are forbidden to inflict punishment with any other design than for correction of the offender or direction of others. For this law is consequent to the next before it, that commandeth pardon upon security of the future time. Besides, revenge without respect to the example, and profit to come, is a triumph or glorying in the hurt of another, tending to no end; for the end is always somewhat to come, and glorying to no end is vain-glory and contrary to reason, and to hurt without reason tendeth to the introduction of war; which is against the law of nature, and is commonly styled by the name of *cruelty*.

And because all signs of hatred or contempt provoke to fight, insomuch as most men choose rather to hazard their life than not to be revenged, we may in the eighth place, for a law of nature, set down this precept, *that no man by deed, word, countenance, or gesture, declare hatred or contempt of another.* The breach of which law is commonly called *contumely*.

The question who is the better man, has no place in the condition of mere nature; where, as has been shown before, all men are equal. The inequality that now is, has been introduced by the laws civil. I know that Aristotle in the first book of his *Politics,* for a foundation of his doctrine, maketh men by nature, some more worthy to command, meaning the wiser sort, such as he thought himself to be for his philosophy; others to serve, meaning those that had strong bodies, but were not philosophers as he: as if master and servant were not introduced by consent of men, but by difference of wit; which is not only against reason, but also against experience. For there are very few so foolish, that had not rather govern themselves than be governed by others; nor when the wise in their own conceit contend by force with them who distrust their own wisdom, do they always, or often, or almost at any time, get the victory. If nature therefore have made men equal, that equality is to be acknowledged; or if nature have made men unequal: yet because men that think themselves equal, will not enter into conditions of peace, but upon equal terms, such equality must be admitted. And therefore for the ninth law of nature, I put this, *that every man acknowledge another for his equal by nature.* The breach of this precept is *pride*.

On this law dependeth another, *that at the entrance into conditions of peace, no man require to reserve to himself any right which he is not content should be reserved to everyone of the rest.* As it is necessary for all men that seek peace, to lay down certain rights of nature; that is to say, not to have liberty to do all they list; so is it necessary for man's life, to retain some; as right to govern their own bodies; enjoy air, water, motion, ways to go from place to place; and all things else without which a man cannot live, or not live well. If in this case, at the making of peace, men require for themselves, that which they would not have to be granted to others, they do contrary to the precedent law, that commandeth the acknowledgment of natural equality, and therefore also against the law of nature. The observers of this law, are those we call *modest,* and the breakers *arrogant* men. The Greeks call the violation of this law πλεονεξία; that is, a desire of more than their share.

Also if a man be trusted to judge between man and man, it is a precept of the law of nature, *that he deal equally between them.* For without that, the controversies of men cannot be determined but by war. He therefore that is partial in judgment, doth what in him lies, to deter men from the use of judges and arbitrators, and consequently against the fundamental law of nature, is the cause of war.

The observance of this law, from the equal distribution to each man, of that which in reason belongeth to him, is called *equity,* and, as I have said before, distributive justice; the violation, *exception of persons,* προσωποληψία.

And from this followeth another law, *that such things as cannot be divided, be enjoyed in common, if it can be; and if the quantity of the thing permit, without stint; otherwise proportionably to the number of them that have right.* For otherwise the distribution is unequal, and contrary to equity.

But some things there be, that can neither be divided, nor enjoyed in common. Then, the law of nature, which prescribeth equity, requireth *that the entire right, or else, making the use alternate, the first possession, be determined by lot.* For equal distribution is of the law of nature, and other means of equal distribution cannot be imagined.

Of *lots* there be two sorts, *arbitrary* and *natural.* Arbitrary is that which is agreed on by the competitors; natural is either *primogeniture,* which the Greek calls κληρονομία, which signifies, given by lot; or *first seizure.*

And therefore those things which cannot be enjoyed in common, nor divided, ought to be adjudged to the first possessor; and in some cases to the first born, as acquired by lot.

It is also a law of nature, *that all men that mediate peace, be allowed safe conduct.* For the law that commandeth peace, as the *end,* commandeth intercession, as the *means;* and to intercession the means is safe conduct.

And because, though men be never so willing to observe these laws, there may nevertheless arise questions concerning a man's action; first, whether it were done, or not done; secondly, if done, whether against the law, or not against the law; the former whereof is called a question of *fact,* the latter a question of *right:* therefore unless the parties to the question covenant mutually to stand to the sentence of another, they are as far from peace as ever. This other to whose sentence they submit is called an *arbitrator.* And therefore it is of the law of nature, *that they that are at controversy, submit their right to the judgment of an arbitrator.*

And seeing every man is presumed to do all things in order to his own benefit, no man is a fit arbitrator in his own cause; and if he were never so fit, yet equity allowing to each party equal benefit, if one be admitted to be judge, the other is to be admitted also; and so the controversy, that is, the cause of war, remains, against the law of nature.

For the same reason no man in any cause ought to be received for arbitrator, to whom greater profit or honor or pleasure apparently ariseth out of the victory of one party than of the other: for he hath taken, though an unavoidable bribe, yet a bribe; and no man can be obliged to trust him. And thus also the controversy and the condition of war remaineth, contrary to the law of nature.

And in a controversy of *fact*, the judge being to give more credit to one than to the other, if there be no other arguments must give credit to a third, or to a third and fourth, or more: for else the question is undecided, and left to force, contrary to the law of nature.

These are the laws of nature, dictating peace, for a means of the conservation of men in multitudes; and which only concern the doctrine of civil society. There be other things tending to the destruction of particular men; as drunkenness, and all other parts of intemperance; which may therefore also be reckoned amongst those things which the law of nature hath forbidden; but are not necessary to be mentioned, nor are pertinent enough to this place.

And though this may seem too subtle a deduction of the laws of nature, to be taken notice of by all men; whereof the most part are too busy in getting food, and the rest too negligent to understand; yet to leave all men inexcusable, they have been contracted into one easy sum, intelligible even to the meanest capacity; and that is, *Do not that to another, which thou wouldst not have done to thyself;* which sheweth him that he has no more to do in learning the laws of nature, but, when weighing the actions of other men with his own, they seem too heavy, to put them into the other part of the balance, and his own into their place, that his own passions, and self-love, may add nothing to the weight; and then there is none of these laws of nature that will not appear unto him very reasonable.

The laws of nature oblige *in foro interno;* that is to say, they bind to a desire they should take place: but *in foro externo,* that is, to the putting them in act, not always. For he that should be modest, and tractable, and perform all he promises, in such time and place where no man else should do so, should but make himself a prey to others, and procure his own certain ruin, contrary to the ground of all laws of nature, which tend to nature's preservation. And again, he that having sufficient security that others shall observe the same laws towards him, observes them not himself, seeketh not peace but war, and consequently the destruction of his nature by violence.

And whatsoever laws bind *in foro interno,* may be broken, not only by a fact contrary to the law, but also by a fact according to it, in case a man think it contrary. For though his action in this case be according to the law, yet his purpose was against the law; which, where the obligation is *in foro interno,* is a breach.

The laws of nature are immutable and eternal; for injustice, ingratitude, arrogance, pride, iniquity, acception of persons, and the rest, can never be made lawful. For it can never be that war shall preserve life, and peace destroy it.

The same laws, because they oblige only to a desire, and endeavor, I mean an unfeigned and constant endeavor, are easy to be observed. For in that they require nothing but endeavor, he that endeavoreth their performance fulfilleth them, and he that fulfilleth the law is just.

And the science of them is the true and only moral philosophy. For moral philosophy is nothing else but the science of what is good and evil, in the conversation and society of mankind. *Good* and *evil* are names that signify our appetites and aversions; which in different tempers, customs, and doctrines of men, are different: and divers men differ not only in their judgment on the senses of what is pleasant and unpleasant to the taste, smell, hearing, touch, and sight; but also of what is conformable or disagreeable to reason, in the actions of common life. Nay, the same man, in divers times, differs from himself; and one time praiseth, that is, calleth good, what another time he dispraiseth, and calleth evil: from whence arise disputes, controversies, and at last war. And therefore so long as a man is in the condition of mere nature, which is a condition of war, his private appetite is the measure of good and evil: and consequently all men agree on this, that peace is good, and therefore also the way, or means of peace, which, as I have shewed before, are justice, gratitude, modesty, equity, mercy, and the rest of the laws of nature, are good; that is to say, *moral virtues;* and their contrary *vices,* evil. Now the science of virtue and vice is moral philosophy; and therefore the true doctrine of the laws of nature, is the true moral philosophy. But the writers of moral philosophy, though they acknowledge the same virtues and vices; yet not seeing wherein consisted their goodness, nor that they come to be praised as the means of peaceable, sociable, and comfortable living, place them in a mediocrity of passions: as if not the cause, but the degree of daring, made fortitude; or not the cause, but the quantity of a gift, made liberality.

These dictates of reason, men used to call by the name of laws, but improperly: for they are but conclusions, or theorems, concerning what conduceth to the conservation and defense of themselves; whereas law, properly, is the word of him that by right hath command over others. But yet if we consider the same theorems as delivered in the word of God, that by right commandeth all things, then are they properly called laws. . . .[3]

PART II: OF COMMONWEALTH

CHAPTER XVII

OF THE CAUSES, GENERATIONS, AND DEFINITION OF A COMMONWEALTH

THE final cause, end, or design of men who naturally love liberty and dominion over others, in the introduction of that restraint upon themselves in which we see them live in commonwealths, is the foresight of their own preservation, and of a more contented life thereby; that is to say, of getting themselves out from that miserable condition of war, which is necessarily consequent, as hath been shown in Chapter XIII, to the natural passions of men, when there is no visible power to keep them in awe, and tie them by fear of punishment to the performance of their covenants and observation of those laws of nature set down in the fourteenth and fifteenth chapters.

For the laws of nature, as justice, equity, modesty, mercy, and, in sum, *doing to others as we would be done to,* of themselves, without the terror of some power to cause them to be observed, are contrary to our natural passions, that carry us to partiality, pride, revenge, and the like. And covenants, without the sword, are but words, and of no strength to secure a man at all. Therefore notwithstanding the laws of nature, which everyone hath then kept, when he has the will to keep them when he can do it safely; if there be no power erected, or not great enough for our security, every man will, and may, lawfully rely on his own strength and art, for caution against all other men. And in all places where men have lived by small families, to rob and spoil one another has been a trade, and so far from being reputed against the law of nature, that the greater spoils they gained, the greater was their honor; and men observed no other laws therein but the laws of honor; that is, to abstain from cruelty, leaving to men their lives, and instruments of husbandry. And as small families did then; so now do cities and kingdoms, which are but greater families, for their own security enlarge their dominions,

[3] Chapter XVI is entitled "Of Persons, Authors, and Things Personated."—*Editor.*

upon all pretenses of danger and fear of invasion, or assistance that may be given to invaders, and endeavor as much as they can to subdue or weaken their neighbors, by open force and secret arts, for want of other caution, justly; and are remembered for it in after ages with honor.

Nor is it the joining together of a small number of men, that gives them this security; because in small numbers, small additions on the one side or the other make the advantage of strength so great, as is sufficient to carry the victory, and therefore gives encouragement to an invasion. The multitude sufficient to confide in for our security, is not determined by any certain number, but by comparison with the enemy we fear; and is then sufficient, when the odds of the enemy is not of so visible and conspicuous moment, to determine the event of war, as to move him to attempt.

And be there never so great a multitude, yet if their actions be directed according to their particular judgments and particular appetites, they can expect thereby no defense nor protection, neither against a common enemy nor against the injuries of one another. For being distracted in opinions concerning the best use and application of their strength, they do not help but hinder one another; and reduce their strength by mutual opposition to nothing: whereby they are easily, not only subdued by a very few that agree together; but also when there is no common enemy, they make war upon each other, for their particular interests. For if we could suppose a great multitude of men to consent in the observation of justice, and other laws of nature, without a common power to keep them all in awe, we might as well suppose all mankind to do the same; and then there neither would be, nor need to be any civil government or commonwealth at all, because there would be peace without subjection.

Nor is it enough for the security, which men desire should last all the time of their life, that they be governed and directed by one judgment for a limited time, as in one battle or one war. For though they obtain a victory by their unanimous endeavor against a foreign enemy; yet afterwards, when either they have no common enemy, or he that by one part is held for an enemy, is by another part held for a friend, they must needs by the difference of their interests dissolve, and fall again into a war amongst themselves.

It is true that certain living creatures, as bees and ants, live sociably one with another, which are therefore by Aristotle numbered amongst political creatures; and yet have no other direction than their particular judgments and appetites; nor speech, whereby one of them can signify to another what he thinks expedient for the common benefit: and therefore some man may perhaps desire to know why mankind cannot do the same. To which I answer:

First, that men are continually in competition for honor and dignity, which these creatures are not; and consequently amongst men there ariseth on that ground, envy and hatred, and finally war; but amongst these not so.

Secondly, that amongst these creatures, the common good differeth not from the private; and being by nature inclined to their private, they procure thereby the common benefit. But man, whose joy consisteth in comparing himself with other men, can relish nothing but what is eminent.

Thirdly, that these creatures, having not, as man, the use of reason, do not see, nor think they see, any fault in the administration of their common business; whereas amongst men, there are very many that think themselves wiser, and able to govern the public better, than the rest; and these strive to reform and innovate, one this way, another that way; and thereby bring it into distraction and civil war.

Fourthly, that these creatures, though they have some use of voice in making known to one another their desires and other affections; yet they want that art of words by which some men can represent to others, that which is good in the likeness of evil, and evil in the likeness of good, and augment or diminish the apparent greatness of good and evil; discontenting men and troubling their peace at their pleasure.

Fifthly, irrational creatures cannot distinguish between *injury* and *damage;* and therefore as long as they be at ease, they are not offended with their fellows: whereas man is then most troublesome when he is most at ease; for then it is that he loves to shew his wisdom, and control the actions of them that govern the commonwealth.

Lastly, the agreement of these creatures is natural; that of men is by covenant only, which is artificial: and therefore it is no wonder if there be somewhat else required, besides covenant, to make their agreement constant and lasting; which is a common power, to keep them in awe, and to direct their actions to the common benefit.

The only way to erect such a common power, as may be able to defend them from the invasion of foreigners and the injuries of one another, and thereby to secure them in such sort as that, by their own industry, and by the fruits of the earth, they may nourish themselves and live contentedly; is, to confer all their power and strength upon one man, or upon one assembly of men, that may reduce all their wills, by plurality of voices, unto one will: which is as much as to say, to appoint one man, or assembly of men, to bear their person; and everyone to own and acknowledge himself to be author of whatsoever he that so beareth their person, shall act or cause to be acted in those things which concern the common peace and safety; and therein to submit their wills, everyone to his will, and their judgments, to his judgment. This is more than consent, or concord; it is a real unity of them all, in one and the same person, made by covenant of every man with every man, in such manner as if every man should say to every man, *"I authorize and give up my right of governing myself to this man, or to this assembly of men, on this condition, that thou give up thy right to him, and authorize all his actions in like manner."* This done, the multitude so united in one person, is called a *commonwealth,* in Latin *civitas.* This is the generation of that great LEVIATHAN, or rather, to speak more reverently, of that *mortal god,* to which we owe under the *immortal God,* our peace and defense. For by this authority, given him by every particular man in the commonwealth, he hath the use of so much power and strength conferred on him, that by terror thereof he is enabled to perform the wills of them all, to peace at home and mutual aid against their enemies abroad. And in him consisteth the essence of the commonwealth; which, to define it, is *one person, of whose acts a great multitude, by mutual covenants one with another, have made themselves every one the author, to the end he may use the strength and means of them all, as he shall think expedient, for their peace and common defense.*

And he that carrieth this person, is called *sovereign,* and said to have sovereign power; and everyone besides, his *subject.*

The attaining to this sovereign power is by two ways. One, by natural force; as when a man maketh his children to submit themselves and their children to his government, as being able to destroy them if they refuse; or by war subdueth his enemies to his will, giving them their lives on that condition. The other, is when men agree amongst themselves to submit to some man, or assembly of men, voluntarily, on confidence to be protected by him against all others. This latter, may be called a political commonwealth, or commonwealth by *institution;* and the former, a commonwealth by *acquisition.* And first, I shall speak of a commonwealth by institution.

CHAPTER XVIII

OF THE RIGHTS OF SOVEREIGNS BY INSTITUTION

A COMMONWEALTH is said to be *instituted,* when a multitude of men do agree and covenant, everyone with everyone, that to whatsoever man, or assembly of men, shall be given by the major part the right to present the person of them all, that is to say, to be their *representative;* everyone, as well he that voted for it as he that voted against it, shall authorize all the actions and judgments of that man, or assembly of men, in the same manner as if they were his own, to the end to live peaceably amongst themselves and be protected against other men.

From this institution of a commonwealth are derived all the *rights* and *faculties* of him, or them, on whom sovereign power is conferred by the consent of the people assembled.

First, because they covenant, it is to be understood they are not obliged by former covenant to anything repugnant hereunto. And consequently they that have already instituted a commonwealth, being thereby bound by covenant to own the actions and judgments of one, cannot lawfully make a new covenant amongst themselves, to be obedient to any other, in anything whatsoever, without his permission. And therefore, they that are subject to a monarch, cannot without his leave cast off monarchy, and return to the confusion of a disunited multitude; nor transfer their person from him that beareth it, to another man, or other assembly of men: for they are bound, every man to every man, to own, and be reputed author of all, that he that already is their sovereign shall do and judge fit to be done; so that any one man dissenting, all the rest should break their covenant made to that man, which is injustice: and they have also every man given the sovereignty to him that beareth their person; and therefore if they depose him, they take from him that which is his own, and so again it is injustice. Besides, if he that attempteth to depose his sovereign, be killed or punished by him for such attempt, he is author of his own punishment, as being by the institution, author of all his sovereign shall do; and because it is injustice for a man to do anything for which he may be punished by his own authority, he is also upon that title, unjust. And whereas some men have pretended for their disobedience to their sovereign, a new covenant, made not with men but with God, this also is unjust: for there is no covenant with God, but by mediation of somebody that representeth God's person; which none doth but God's lieutenant, who hath the sovereignty under God. But this pretense of covenant with God, is so evident a lie, even in the pretenders' own consciences, that it is not only an act of an unjust, but also of a vile and unmanly disposition.

Secondly, because the right of bearing the person of them all, is given to him they make sovereign, by covenant only of one to another, and not of him to any of them; there can happen no breach of covenant on the part of the sovereign; and consequently none of his subjects, by any pretense of forfeiture, can be freed from his subjection. That he which is made sovereign maketh no covenant with his subjects beforehand, is manifest; because either he must make it with the whole multitude, as one party to the covenant, or he must make a several covenant with every man. With the whole, as one party, it is impossible, because as

yet they are not one person: and if he make so many several covenants
as there be men, those covenants after he hath the sovereignty are void;
because what act soever can be pretended by any one of them for
breach thereof, is the act both of himself and of all the rest, because
done in the person, and by the right of every one of them in particular.
Besides, if any one, or more of them, pretend a breach of the covenant
made by the sovereign at his institution; and others, as one other of his
subjects, or himself alone, pretend there was no such breach: there is in
this case, no judge to decide the controversy; it returns therefore to the
sword again; and every man recovereth the right of protecting himself
by his own strength, contrary to the design they had in the institution.
It is therefore in vain to grant sovereignty by way of precedent covenant. The opinion that any monarch receiveth his power by covenant,
that is to say, on condition, proceedeth from want of understanding this
easy truth, that covenants being but words and breath, have no force to
oblige, contain, constrain, or protect any man, but what it has from the
public sword; that is, from the untied hands of that man, or assembly
of men that hath the sovereignty, and whose actions are avouched by
them all, and performed by the strength of them all, in him united. But
when an assembly of men is made sovereign, then no man imagineth
any such covenant to have passed in the institution; for no man is so
dull as to say, for example, the people of Rome made a covenant with
the Romans, to hold the sovereignty on such or such conditions; which
not performed, the Romans might lawfully depose the Roman people.
That men see not the reason to be alike in a monarchy and in a popular government, proceedeth from the ambition of some that are kinder
to the government of an assembly, whereof they may hope to participate, than of monarchy, which they despair to enjoy.

Thirdly, because the major part hath by consenting voices declared a
sovereign, he that dissented must now consent with the rest; that is, be
contented to avow all the actions he shall do, or else justly be destroyed
by the rest. For if he voluntarily entered into the congregation of them
that were assembled, he sufficiently declared thereby his will, and therefore tacitly covenanted to stand to what the major part should ordain;
and therefore if he refuse to stand thereto, or make protestation against
any of their decrees, he does contrary to his covenant, and therefore unjustly. And whether he be of the congregation or not, and whether his
consent be asked or not, he must either submit to their decrees, or be
left in the condition of war he was in before; wherein he might without
injustice be destroyed by any man whatsoever.

Fourthly, because every subject is by this institution author of all the
actions and judgments of the sovereign instituted; it follows that whatsoever he doth, it can be no injury to any of his subjects, nor ought he

to be by any of them accused of injustice. For he that doth anything by authority from another, doth therein no injury to him by whose authority he acteth: but by this institution of a commonwealth, every particular man is author of all the sovereign doth: and consequently he that complaineth of injury from his sovereign, complaineth of that whereof he himself is author; and therefore ought not to accuse any man but himself; no nor himself of injury, because to do injury to one's self, is impossible. It is true that they that have sovereign power may commit iniquity, but not injustice, or injury, in the proper signification.

Fifthly, and consequently to that which was said last, no man that hath sovereign power can justly be put to death, or otherwise in any manner by his subjects punished. For seeing every subject is author of the actions of his sovereign, he punisheth another for the actions committed by himself.

And because the end of this institution, is the peace and defense of them all, and whosoever has right to the end has right to the means; it belongeth of right, to whatsoever man or assembly that hath the sovereignty, to be judge both of the means of peace and defense, and also of the hindrances and disturbances of the same; and to do whatsoever he shall think necessary to be done, both beforehand, for the preserving of peace and security, by prevention of discord at home and hostility from abroad, and, when peace and security are lost, for the recovery of the same. And therefore,

Sixthly, it is annexed to the sovereignty, to be judge of what opinions and doctrines are averse, and what conducing to peace; and consequently, on what occasions, how far, and what men are to be trusted withal, in speaking to multitudes of people; and who shall examine the doctrines of all books before they be published. For the actions of men proceed from their opinions; and in the well-governing of opinions consisteth the well-governing of men's actions, in order to their peace and concord. And though in matter of doctrine nothing ought to be regarded but the truth, yet this is not repugnant to regulating the same by peace. For doctrine repugnant to peace can no more be true, than peace and concord can be against the law of nature. It is true that in a commonwealth, where, by the negligence or unskillfulness of governors and teachers, false doctrines are by time generally received; the contrary truths may be generally offensive. Yet the most sudden and rough bursting in of a new truth that can be, does never break the peace, but only sometimes awake the war. For those men that are so remissly governed, that they dare take up arms to defend or introduce an opinion, are still in war; and their condition not peace, but only a cessation of arms for fear of one another; and they live, as it were, in the precincts of battle continually. It belongeth therefore to him that hath the sovereign power, to be judge, or constitute all judges of opinions and doctrines, as a thing necessary to peace; thereby to prevent discord and civil war.

Seventhly, is annexed to the sovereignty, the whole power of prescribing the rules, whereby every man may know what goods he may enjoy, and what actions he may do, without being molested by any of his fellow-subjects; and this is it men call *propriety*. For before constitution of sovereign power, as hath already been shown, all men had right to all things; which necessarily causeth war: and therefore this propriety, being necessary to peace, and depending on sovereign power, is the act of that power, in order to the public peace. These rules of propriety, or *meum* and *tuum*, and of good, evil, lawful, and unlawful in the actions of subjects, are the civil laws; that is to say, the laws of each commonwealth in particular: though the name of civil law be now restrained to the ancient civil laws of the city of Rome; which being the head of a great part of the world, her laws at that time were in these parts the civil law.

Eighthly, is annexed to the sovereignty, the right of judicature; that is to say, of hearing and deciding all controversies which may arise concerning law, either civil or natural, or concerning fact. For without the decision of controversies, there is no protection of one subject against the injuries of another: the laws concerning *meum* and *tuum* are in vain; and to every man remaineth, from the natural and necessary appetite of his own conservation, the right of protecting himself by his private strength, which is the condition of war, and contrary to the end for which every commonwealth is instituted.

Ninthly, is annexed to the sovereignty, the right of making war and peace with other nations and commonwealths; that is to say, of judging when it is for the public good, and how great forces are to be assembled, armed, and paid for that end; and to levy money upon the subjects, to defray the expenses thereof. For the power by which the people are to be defended, consisteth in their armies; and the strength of an army, in the union of their strength under one command: which command the sovereign instituted, therefore hath; because the command of the militia, without other institution, maketh him that hath it sovereign. And therefore whosoever is made general of an army, he that hath the sovereign power is always generalissimo.

Tenthly, is annexed to the sovereignty, the choosing of all counsellors, ministers, magistrates, and offices, both in peace and war. For seeing the sovereign is charged with the end, which is the common peace and defense, he is understood to have power to use such means as he shall think most fit for his discharge.

Eleventhly, to the sovereign is committed the power of rewarding with riches, or honor, and of punishing with corporal or pecuniary pun-

ishment, or with ignominy, every subject according to the law he hath
formerly made; or if there be no law made, according as he shall judge
most to conduce to the encouraging of men to serve the commonwealth,
or deterring of them from doing disservice to the same.

Lastly, considering what value men are naturally apt to set upon
themselves, what respect they look for from others, and how little they
value other men; from whence continually arise amongst them, emulation, quarrels, factions, and at last war, to the destroying of one another
and diminution of their strength against a common enemy: it is necessary that there be laws of honor, and a public rate of the worth of such
men as have deserved or are able to deserve well of the commonwealth;
and that there be force in the hands of some or other, to put those laws
in execution. But it hath already been shown, that not only the whole
militia, or forces of the commonwealth, but also the judicature of all
controversies, is annexed to the sovereignty. To the sovereign therefore
it belongeth also to give titles of honor; and to appoint what order of
place and dignity each man shall hold; and what signs of respect, in
public or private meetings, they shall give to one another.

These are the rights which make the essence of sovereignty, and which
are the marks whereby a man may discern in what man, or assembly of
men, the sovereign power is placed and resideth. For these are incommunicable and inseparable. The power to coin money, to dispose of the
estate and persons of infant heirs, to have pre-emption in markets, and
all other statute prerogatives, may be transferred by the sovereign; and
yet the power to protect his subjects be retained. But if he transfer the
militia, he retains the judicature in vain, for want of execution of the
laws; or if he grant away the power of raising money, the militia is in
vain; or if he give away the government of doctrines, men will be
frighted into rebellion with the fear of spirits. And so if we consider any
one of the said rights, we shall presently see that the holding of all the
rest will produce no effect in the conservation of peace and justice, the
end for which all commonwealths are instituted. And this division is it
whereof it is said, *a kingdom divided in itself cannot stand:* for unless
this division precede, division into opposite armies can never happen.
If there had not first been an opinion received of the greatest part of
England, that these powers were divided between the King and the
Lords and the House of Commons, the people had never been divided
and fallen into this civil war; first between those that disagreed in politics, and after between the dissenters about the liberty of religion:
which have so instructed men in this point of sovereign right; and there
be few now in England that do not see that these rights are inseparable,
and will be so generally acknowledged at the next return of peace; and

so continue till their miseries are forgotten; and no longer, except the vulgar be better taught than they have hitherto been.

And because they are essential and inseparable rights, it follows necessarily that in whatsoever words any of them seem to be granted away, yet if the sovereign power itself be not in direct terms renounced, and the name of sovereign no more given by the grantees to him that grants them, the grant is void: for when he has granted all he can, if we grant back the sovereignty, all is restored, as inseparably annexed thereunto.

This great authority being indivisible, and inseparably annexed to the sovereignty, there is little ground for the opinion of them that say of sovereign kings, though they be *singulis majores,* of greater power than every one of their subjects, yet they be *universis minores,* of less power than them all together. For if by 'all together' they mean not the collective body as one person, then 'all together' and 'every one' signify the same, and the speech is absurd. But if by 'all together' they understand them as one person, which person the sovereign bears, then the power of all together is the same with the sovereign's power, and so again the speech is absurd: which absurdity they see well enough when the sovereignty is in an assembly of the people, but in a monarch they see it not; and yet the power of sovereignty is the same in whomsoever it be placed.

And as the power, so also the honor of the sovereign, ought to be greater than that of any or all the subjects. For in the sovereignty is the fountain of honor. The dignities of lord, earl, duke, and prince are his creatures. As in the presence of the master, the servants are equal and without any honor at all; so are the subjects, in the presence of the sovereign. And though they shine some more, some less, when they are out of his sight; yet in his presence, they shine no more than the stars in the presence of the sun.

But a man may here object that the condition of subjects is very miserable, as being obnoxious to the lusts, and other irregular passions, of him or them that have so unlimited a power in their hands. And commonly they that live under a monarch, think it the fault of monarchy; and they that live under the government of democracy, or other sovereign assembly, attribute all the inconvenience to that form of commonwealth; whereas the power in all forms, if they be perfect enough to protect them, is the same: not considering that the state of man can never be without some incommodity or other; and that the greatest that in any form of government can possibly happen to the people in general, is scarce sensible, in respect to the miseries and horrible calamities that accompany a civil war, or that dissolute condition of masterless men, without subjection to laws and a coercive power to tie their hands from rapine and revenge: nor considering that the greatest pressure of sovereign governors, proceedeth not from any delight or profit they can expect in the damage or weakening of their subjects, in whose vigor consisteth their own strength and glory; but in the restiveness of themselves, that unwillingly contributing to their own defense, make it necessary for their governors to draw from them what they can in time of peace, that they may have means on any emergent occasion or sudden need, to resist or take advantage on their enemies. For all men are by nature provided of notable multiplying glasses, that is their passions and self-love, through which every little payment appeareth a great grievance; but are destitute of those prospective glasses, namely moral and civil science, to see afar off the miseries that hang over them, and cannot without such payment be avoided.

CHAPTER XIX

OF THE SEVERAL KINDS OF COMMONWEALTH BY INSTITUTION, AND OF SUCCESSION TO THE SOVEREIGN POWER

THE DIFFERENCE of commonwealths consisteth in the difference of the sovereign, or the person representative of all and every one of the multitude. And because the sovereignty is either in one man, or in an assembly of more than one; and into that assembly either every man hath right to enter, or not everyone, but certain men distinguished from the rest; it is manifest, there can be but three kinds of commonwealth. For the representative must needs be one man, or more; and if more, then it is the assembly of all, or but of a part. When the representative is one man, then is the commonwealth a *monarchy;* when an assembly of all that will come together, then it is a *democracy,* or popular commonwealth; when an assembly of a part only, then it is called an *aristocracy.* Other kind of commonwealth there can be none; for either one, or more, or all, must have the sovereign power, which I have shown to be indivisible, entire.

There be other names of government in the histories and books of policy; as *tyranny,* and *oligarchy;* but they are not the names of other forms of government, but of the same forms misliked. For they that are discontented under *monarchy,* call it *tyranny;* and they that are displeased with *aristocracy,* call it *oligarchy;* so also, they which find themselves grieved under a *democra*cy, call it *anarchy,* which signifies want of government; and yet I think no man believes, that want of government, is any new kind of government; nor by the same reason ought they to believe, that the government is of one kind, when they like it, and another, when they mislike it, or are oppressed by the governors.

It is manifest, that men who are in absolute liberty, may, if they please, give authority to one man, to represent them every one; as well as give such authority to any assembly of men whatsoever; and consequently may subject themselves, if they think good, to a monarch, as absolutely, as to any other representative. Therefore, where there is already erected a sovereign power, there can be no other representative of the same people, but only to certain particular ends, by the sovereign limited. For that were to erect two sovereigns; and every man to have his person represented by two actors, that by opposing one another, must needs divide that power, which, if men will live in peace, is indivisible; and thereby reduce the multitude into the condition of war, contrary to the end for which all sovereignty is instituted. And therefore as it is absurd, to think that a sovereign assembly, inviting the people of their dominion, to send up their deputies, with power to make known their advice, or desires, should therefore hold such deputies, rather than themselves, for the absolute representatives of the people; so it is absurd also, to think the same in a monarchy. And I know not how this so manifest a truth, should of late be so little observed; that in a monarchy, he that had the sovereignty from a descent of six hundred years, was alone called sovereign, had the title of Majesty from every one of his subjects, and was notwithstanding never considered as their representative; the name without contradiction passing for the title of those men, which at his command were sent up by the people to carry their petitions, and give him, if he permitted it, their advice. Which may serve as an admonition, for those that are the true, and absolute representative of a people, to instruct men in the nature of that office, and to take heed how they admit of any other general representation upon any occasion whatsoever, if they mean to discharge the trust committed to them.

The difference between these three kinds of commonwealth, consisteth not in the difference of power; but in the difference of convenience, or aptitude to produce the peace, and security of the people; for which end they were instituted. And to compare monarchy with the other two, we may observe; first, that whosoever beareth the person of the people, or is one of that assembly that bears it, beareth also his own natural person. And though he be careful in his politic person to procure the common interest; yet he is more, or no less careful to produce the private good of himself, his family, kindred and friends; and for the most part, if the public interest chance to cross the private, he prefers the private: for the passions of men, are commonly more potent than their reason. From whence it follows, that where the public and private interest are most closely united, there is the public most advanced. Now in monarchy, the private interest is the same with the public. The riches, power, and honor of a monarch arise only from the riches, strength, and reputation of his subjects. For no king can be rich, nor glorious, nor secure, whose subjects are either poor, or contemptible, or too weak through want or dissention, to maintain a way against their enemies: whereas in a democracy, or aristocracy, the public prosperity confers not so much to the private fortune of one that is corrupt, or ambitious, as doth many times a perfidious advice, a treacherous action, or a civil war.

Secondly, that a monarch receiveth counsel of whom, when, and where he pleaseth; and consequently may hear the opinion of men versed in the matter about which he deliberates, of what rank or quality soever, and as long before the time of action, and with as much secrecy, as he will. But when a sovereign assembly has need of counsel, none are admitted but such as have a right thereto from the beginning; which for the most part are of those who have been versed more in the acquisition of wealth than of knowledge; and are to give their advice in long discourses, which may, and do commonly excite men to action, but not govern them in it. For the *understanding* is by the flame of the passions never enlightened, but dazzled. Nor is there any place, or time, wherein an assembly can receive counsel with secrecy, because of their own multitude.

Thirdly, that the resolutions of a monarch are subject to no other inconstancy than that of human nature; but in assemblies, besides that of nature, there ariseth an inconstancy from the number. For the absence of a few, that would have the resolution once taken, continue firm, which may happen by security, negligence, or private impediments, or the diligent appearance of a few of the contrary opinion, undoes today, all that was concluded yesterday.

Fourthly, that a monarch cannot disagree with himself, out of envy, or interest; but an assembly may; and that to such a height, as may produce a civil war.

Fifthly, that in monarchy there is this inconvenience; that any subject, by the power of one man, for the enriching of a favorite or flatterer, may be deprived of all he possesseth; which I confess is a great and inevitable inconvenience. But the same may as well happen, where the sovereign power is in an assembly: for their power is the same; and they are as subject to evil counsel, and to be seduced by orators, as a monarch by flatterers; and becoming one another's flatterers, serve one another's coveteousness and ambition by turns. And whereas the favorites of monarchs are few, and they have none else to advance but their own kindred; the favorites of an assembly, are many; and the kindred much more numerous, than of any monarch. Besides, there is no favorite of a monarch, which cannot as well succor his friends, as hurt his enemies; but orators, that is to say, favorites of sovereign assemblies, though they have great power to hurt, have little to save. For to accuse, requires less eloquence, such is man's nature, than to excuse; and condemnation, than absolution more resembles justice.

Sixthly, that it is an inconvenience in monarchy, that the sovereignty may descend upon an infant, or one that cannot discern between good and evil; and consisteth in this, that the use of his power, must be in the hand of another man, or of some assembly of men, which are to govern by his right, and in his name; as curators, and protectors of his person, and authority. But to say there is inconvenience, in putting the use of the sovereign power, into the hand of a man, or an assembly of men; is to say that all government is more inconvenient, than confusion, and civil war. And therefore all the danger that can be pretended, must arise from the contention of those, that for an office of so great honor, and profit, may become competitors. To make it appear, that this inconvenience, proceedeth not from that form of government we call monarchy, we are to consider, that the precedent monarch hath appointed who shall have the tuition of his infant successor, either expressly by testament, or tacitly, by not controlling the custom in that case received; and then such inconvenience, if it happen, is to be attributed, not to the monarchy, but to the ambition, and injustice of the subjects; which in all kinds of government, where the people are not well instructed in their duty, and the rights of sovereignty, is the same. Or else the precedent monarch hath not at all taken order for such tuition; and then the law of nature hath provided this sufficient rule, that the tuition shall be in him, that hath by nature most interest in the preservation of the authority of the infant, and to whom least benefit can accrue by his death, or diminution. For seeing every man by nature seeketh his own benefit, and promotion; to put an infant into the power of those, that can promote themselves by his destruction, or damage, is not tuition, but treachery. So that sufficient provision being taken, against all just quarrel, about the government under a child, if any contention arise to the disturbance of the public peace, it is not to be attributed to the form of monarchy, but to the ambition of subjects, and ignorance of their duty. On the other side, there is no great commonwealth, the sovereignty whereof is in a great assembly, which is not, as to consultations of peace, and war, and making of laws, in the same condition, as if the government were in a child. For as a child wants the judgment to dissent from counsel given him, and is thereby necessitated to take the advice of them, or him, to whom he is committed; so an assembly wanteth the liberty, to dissent from the counsel of the major part, be it good, or bad. And as a child has need of a tutor, or protector, to preserve his person and authority; so also, in great commonwealths, the sovereign assembly, in all great dangers and troubles, have need of *custodes libertatis;* that is, of dictators, or protectors of their authority; which are as much as temporary monarchs, to whom, for a time, they may commit the entire exercise of their power; and have, at the end of that time, been oftener deprived thereof, than infant kings, by their protectors, regents, or any other tutors.

Though the kinds of sovereignty be, as I have now shown, but three; that is to say, monarchy, where one man has it; or democracy, where the general assembly of subjects hath it; or aristocracy, where it is in an assembly of certain persons nominated, or otherwise distinguished from the rest; yet he that shall consider the particular commonwealths that have been, and are in the world, will not perhaps easily reduce them to three, and may thereby be inclined to think there be other forms, arising from these mingled together. As for example, elective kingdoms; where kings have the sovereign power put into their hands for a time; or kingdoms, wherein the king hath a power limited; which governments, are nevertheless by most writers called monarchy. Likewise if a popular, or aristocratical commonwealth, subdue an enemy's country, and govern the same, by a president, procurator, or other magistrate; this may seem perhaps at first sight, to be a democratical, or aristocratical government. But it is not so. For elective kings, are not sovereigns, but ministers of the sovereign; not limited kings, sovereigns, but ministers of them that have the sovereign power; nor are those provinces which are in subjection to a democracy or aristocracy of another commonwealth, democratically or aristocratically governed, but monarchically.

And first, concerning an elective king, whose power is limited to his life, as it is in many places of Christendom at this day; or to certain years or months, as the dictator's power amongst the Romans; if he have right to appoint his successor, he is no more elective but hereditary. But if he have no power to elect his successor, then there is some other man, or assembly known, which after his decease may elect anew, or else the commonwealth dieth, and dissolveth with him, and returneth to the condition of war. If it be known who have the power to give the sovereignty after his death, it is known also that the sovereignty was in them before; for none have right to give that which they have not right to possess, and keep to themselves, if they think good. But if there be none that can give the sovereignty, after the decease of him that was first elected; then has he power, nay he is obliged by the law of nature, to provide, by establishing his successor, to keep those that had trusted him with the government, from relapsing into the miserable condition of civil war. And consequently he was, when elected, a sovereign absolute.

Secondly, that king whose power is limited, is not superior to him, or them that have the power to limit it; and he that is not superior, is not supreme; that is to say not sovereign. The sovereignty therefore was always in that assembly which had the right to limit him; and by consequence the government not monarchy, but either democracy, or aristocracy; as of old time in Sparta; where the kings had a privilege to lead their armies; but the sovereignty was in the Ephori.

Thirdly, whereas heretofore the Roman people governed the land of Judea, for example, by a president; yet was not Judea therefore a democracy; because they were not governed by any assembly, into the which, any of them, had right to enter; nor an aristocracy; because they were not governed by any assembly, into which, any man could enter by their election: but they were governed by one person, which, though as to the people of Rome, was an assembly of the people, or democracy; yet as to the people of Judea, which had no right at all of participating in the government, was a monarch. For though where the people are governed by an assembly, chosen by themselves out of their own number, the government is called a democracy, or aristocracy; yet when they are governed by an assembly, not of their own choosing, it is a monarchy; not of one man, over another man; but of one people, over another people.

Of all these forms of government, the matter being mortal, so that not only monarchs, but also whole assemblies die, it is necessary for the conservation of the peace of men, that as there was order taken for an artificial man, so there be order also taken, for an artificial eternity of life; without which, men that are governed by an assembly, should return into the condition of war in every age; and they that are governed by one man, as soon as their governor dieth. This artificial eternity, is that which men call the right of *succession*.

There is no perfect form of government, where the disposing of the succession is not in the present sovereign. For if it be in any other particular man, or private assembly, it is in a person subject, and may be assumed by the sovereign at his pleasure; and consequently the right is in himself. And if it be in no particular man, but left to a new choice; then is the commonwealth dissolved; and the right is in him that can get it; contrary to the intention of them that did institute the commonwealth, for their perpetual, and not temporary security.

In a democracy, the whole assembly cannot fail, unless the multitude that are to be governed fail. And therefore questions of the right of succession, have in that form of government no place at all.

In an aristocracy, when any of the assembly dieth, the election of another into his room belongeth to the assembly, as the sovereign, to whom belongeth the choosing of all counselors and officers. For that which the representative doth, as actor, every one of the subjects doth, as author. And though the sovereign assembly may give power to others, to elect new men, for supply of their court; yet it is still by their authority, that the election is made; and by the same it may, when the public shall require it, be recalled.

The greatest difficulty about the right of succession, is in monarchy: and the difficulty ariseth from this, that at first sight, it is not manifest who is to appoint the successor; nor many times, who it is whom he hath appointed. For in both these cases, there is required a more exact ratiocination, than every man is accustomed to use. As to the question, who shall appoint the successor, of a monarch that hath the sovereign authority; that is to say, who shall determine of the right of inheritance, (for elective kings and princes have not the sovereign power in propriety, but in use only), we are to consider, that either he that is in possession, has right to dispose of the succession, or else that right is again in the dissolved multitude. For the death of him that hath the sovereign power in propriety, leaves the multitude without any sovereign at all; that is, without any representative in whom they should be united, and be capable of doing any one action at all; and therefore they are incapable of election of any new monarch; every man having equal right to submit himself to such as he thinks best able to protect him; or if he can, protect himself by his own sword; which is a return to confusion, and to the condition of a war of every man against every man, contrary to the end for which monarchy had its first institution. Therefore it is manifest, that by the institution of monarchy, the disposing of the successor, is always left to the judgment and will of the present possessor.

And for the question, which may arise sometimes, who it is that the monarch in possession, hath designed to the succession and inheritance of his power; it is determined by his express words, and testament; or by other tacit signs sufficient.

By express words, or testament, when it is declared by him in his lifetime, *viva voce,* or by writing; as the first emperors of Rome declared who should be their heirs. For the word heir does not of itself imply the children, or nearest kindred of a man; but whomsoever a man shall any way declare, he would have to succeed him in his estate. If therefore a monarch declare expressly, that such a man shall be his heir, either by word or writing, then is that man immediately after the decease of his predecessor, invested in the right of being monarch.

But where testament, and express words are wanting, other natural signs of the will are to be followed; whereof the one is custom. And therefore where the custom is, that the next of kindred absolutely succeedeth, there also the next of kindred hath right to the succession; for that, if the will of him that was in possession had been otherwise, he might have declared the same in his lifetime. And likewise where the custom is, that the next of the male succeedeth, there also the right of succession is in the next of the kindred male, for the same reason. And so it is if the custom were to advance the female. For whatsoever custom a man may by a word control, and does not, it is a natural sign he would have that custom stand.

But where neither custom, nor testament hath preceded, there it is to be understood, first, that a monarch's will is, that the government remain monarchical; because he hath approved that government in himself. Secondly, that a child of his own, male, or female, be preferred before any other; because men are presumed to be more inclined by nature, to advance their own children, than the children of other man; and of their own, rather a male than a female; because men, are naturally fitter than women, for actions of labor and danger. Thirdly, where his own issue faileth, rather a brother than a stranger; and so still the nearer in blood, rather than the more remote; because it is always presumed that the nearer of kin, is the nearer in affection; and it is evident that a man receives always, by reflection, the most honor from the greatness of his nearest kindred.

But it be lawful for a monarch to dispose of the succession by words of contract, or testament, men may perhaps object a great inconvenience; for he may sell, or give his right of governing to a stranger; which, because strangers, that is, men not used to live under the same government, nor speaking the same language, do commonly undervalue one another, may turn to the oppression of his subjects; which is indeed a great inconvenience; but it proceedeth not necessarily from the subjection to a stranger's government, but from the unskillfulness of the governors, ignorant of the true rules of politics. And therefore the Romans when they had subdued many nations, to make their government digestible, were wont to take away that grievance, as much as they thought necessary, by giving sometimes to whole nations, and sometimes to principal men of every nation they conquered, not only the privileges, but also the name of Romans; and took many of them into the senate, and offices of charge, even in the Roman city. And this was it our most wise king, King James, aimed at, in endeavoring the union of his two realms of England and Scotland. Which if he could have obtained, had in all likelihood prevented the civil wars, which make both those kingdoms, at this present, miserable. It is not therefore any injury to the people, for a monarch to dispose of the succession by will; though by the fault of many princes, it hath been sometimes found inconvenient. Of the lawfulness of it, this also is an argument, that whatsoever inconvenience can arrive by giving a kingdom to a stranger, may arrive also by so marrying with strangers, as the right of succession may descend upon them; yet this by all men is accounted lawful.

CHAPTER XX

OF DOMINION PATERNAL, AND DESPOTICAL

A COMMONWEALTH *by acquisition,* is that, where the sovereign power is acquired by force; and it is acquired by force, when men singly, or many together by plurality of voices, for fear of death, or bonds, do authorize all the actions of that man, or assembly, that hath their lives and liberty in his power.

And this kind of dominion, or sovereignty, differeth from sovereignty by institution, only in this, that men who choose their sovereign, do it for fear of one another, and not of him whom they institute; but in this case, they subject themselves, to him they are afraid of. In both cases they do it for fear; which is to be noted by them, that hold all such covenants, as proceed from fear of death or violence, void; which if it were true, no man, in any kind of commonwealth, could be obliged to obedience. It is true, that in a commonwealth once instituted, or acquired, promises proceeding from fear of death or violence, are no covenants, nor obliging, when the thing promised is contrary to the laws; but the reason is not, because it was made upon fear, but because he that promiseth, hath no right in the thing promised. Also, when he may lawfully perform, and doth not, it is not the invalidity of the covenant, that absolveth him, but the sentence of the sovereign. Otherwise, whensoever a man lawfully promiseth, he unlawfully breaketh; but when the sovereign, who is the actor, acquitteth him, then he is acquitted by him that extorted the promise, as by the author of such absolution.

But the rights, and consequences of sovereignty, are the same in both. His power cannot, without his consent, be transferred to another; he cannot forfeit it; he cannot be accused by any of his subjects, of injury; he cannot be punished by them; he is judge of what is necessary for peace; and judge of doctrines; he is sole legislator; and supreme judge of controversies; and of the times, and occasions of war, and peace; to him it belongeth to choose magistrates, counsellors, commanders, and all other officers, and ministers; and to determine of rewards, and punishments, honor, and order. The reasons whereof, are the same which are alleged in the precedent chapter, for the same rights, and consequences of sovereignty by institution.

Dominion is acquired two ways; by generation, and by conquest. The right of dominion by generation, is that, which the parent hath over his children; and is called *paternal*. And is not so derived from the generation, as if therefore the parent had dominion over his child because he begat him; but from the child's consent, either express, or by other sufficient arguments declared. For as to the generation, God hath ordained to man a helper; and there be always two that are equally parents: the dominion therefore over the child, should belong equally to both; and he be equally subject to both, which is impossible; for no man can obey two masters. And whereas some have attributed the dominion to the man only, as being of the more excellent sex; they misreckon in it. For there is not always that difference of strength, or prudence between the man and the woman, as that the right can be determined without war. In commonwealths, this controversy is decided by the civil law; and for the most part, but not always, the sentence is in favor of the father; because for the most part commonwealths have been erected by the fathers, not by the mothers of families. But the question lieth now in the state of mere nature; where there are supposed no laws of matrimony; no laws for the education of children; but the law of nature, and the natural inclination of the sexes, one to another, and to their children. In this condition of mere nature, either the parents between themselves dispose of the dominion over the child by contract; or do not dispose thereof at all. If they dispose thereof, the right passeth according to the contract. We find in history that the Amazons contracted with the men of the neighboring countries, to whom they had recourse for issue, that the issue male should be sent back, but the female remain with themselves: so that the dominion of the females was in the mother.

If there be no contract, the dominion is in the mother. For in the condition of mere nature, where there are no matrimonial laws, it cannot be known who is the father, unless it be declared by the mother; and therefore the right of dominion over the child dependeth on her will, and is consequently hers. Again, seeing the infant is first in the power of the mother, so as she may either nourish, or expose it; if she nourish it, it oweth its life to the mother; and is therefore obliged to obey her, rather than any other; and by consequence the dominion over it is hers. But if she expose it, and another find and nourish it, the dominion is in him that nourisheth it. For it ought to obey him by whom it is preserved; because preservation of life being the end, for which one man becomes subject to another, every man is supposed to promise obedience, to him, in whose power it is to save, or destroy him.

If the mother be the father's subject, the child, is in the father's power; and if the father be the mother's subject, as when a sovereign queen marrieth one of her subjects, the child is subject to the mother; because the father also is her subject.

If a man and woman, monarchs of two several kingdoms, have a child, and contract concerning who shall have the dominion of him, the right of the dominion passeth by the contract. If they contract not, the dominion followeth the dominion of the place of his residence. For the sovereign of each country hath dominion over all that reside therein.

He that hath dominion over the child, hath dominion also over the children of the child; and over their children's children. For he that hath dominion over the person of a man, hath dominion over all that is his; without which, dominion were but a title, without the effect.

The right of succession to paternal dominion, proceedeth in the same manner, as doth the right of succession of monarchy; of which I have already sufficiently spoken in the precedent chapter.

Dominion acquired by conquest, or victory in war, is that which some writers call *despotical,* from Δεσπότης, which signifieth a *lord,* or *master;* and is the dominion of the master over his servant. And this dominion is then acquired to the victor, when the vanquished, to avoid the present stroke of death covenanteth either in express words, or by other sufficient signs of the will, that so long as his life, and the liberty of his body is allowed him, the victor shall have the use thereof, at his pleasure. And after such covenant made, the vanquished is a *servant,* and not before: for by the word *servant,* whether it be derived from *servire,* to serve, or from *servare,* to save, which I leave to grammarians to dispute, is not meant a captive, which is kept in prison, or bonds, till the owner of him that took him, or bought him of one that did, shall consider what to do with him: for such men, commonly called slaves, have no obligation at all; but may break their bonds, or the prison; and kill, or carry away captive their master, justly: but one, that, being taken, hath corporal liberty allowed him; and upon promise not to run away, nor to do violence to his master, is trusted by him.

It is not therefore the victory, that giveth the right of dominion over the vanquished, but his own covenant. Nor is he obliged because he is conquered; that is to say, beaten, and taken, or put to flight; but because he cometh in, and submitteth to the victor; nor is the victor obliged by an enemy's rendering himself, without promise of life, to spare him for this his yielding to discretion; which obliges not the victor longer, than in his own discretion he shall think fit.

And that which men do, when they demand, as it is now called, *quarter,* which the Greeks called Ζωγρία, *taking alive,* is to evade the present fury of the victor, by submission, and to compound for their life, with ransom, or service: and therefore he that hath quarter, hath not his life given, but deferred till farther deliberation; for it is not a yielding on condition of life, but to discretion. And then only is his life in security, and his service due, when the victor hath trusted him with his corporal liberty. For slaves that work in prisons; or fetters, do it not of duty, but to avoid the cruelty of their taskmasters.

The master of the servant, is master also of all he hath: and may exact the use thereof; that is to say, of his goods, of his labor, of his servants, and of his children, as often as he shall think fit. For he holdeth his life of his master, by the covenant of obedience; that is, of owning, and authorizing whatsoever the master shall do. And in case the master, if he refuse, kill him, or cast him into bonds, or otherwise punish him for his disobedience, he is himself the author of the same; and cannot accuse him of injury.

In sum, the rights and consequences of both *paternal* and *despotical* dominion, are the very same with those of a sovereign by institution; and for the same reasons; which reasons are set down in the precedent chapter. So that for a man that is monarch of divers nations, whereof he hath, in one, sovereignty by institution of the people assembled, and in another by conquest, that is by the submission of each particular, to avoid death or bonds; to demand of one nation more than of the other, from the title of conquest, as being a conquered nation, is an act of ignorance of the rights of sovereignty; for the sovereign is absolute over both alike; or else there is no sovereignty at all; and so every man may lawfully protect himself, if he can, with his own sword, which is the condition of war.

By this it appears; that a great family, if it be not part of some commonwealth, is of itself, as to the rights of sovereignty, a little monarchy; whether that family consist of a man and his children; or of a man and his servants: or of a man, and his children, and servants together; wherein the father or master is the sovereign. But yet a family is not properly a commonwealth; unless it be of that power by its own number, or by other opportunities, as not to be subdued without the hazard of war. For where a number of men are manifestly too weak to defend themselves united, everyone may use his own reason in time of danger, to save his own life, either by flight, or by submission to the enemy, as he shall think best; in the same manner as a very small company of soldiers, surprised by an army, may cast down their arms, and demand quarter, or run away, rather than be put to the sword. And thus much shall suffice, concerning what I find by speculation, and education, of sovereign rights, from the nature, need, and designs of men, in erecting of commonwealths, and putting themselves under monarchs, or assemblies, entrusted with power enough for their protection. . . .

CHAPTER XXI

OF THE LIBERTY OF SUBJECTS

LIBERTY, OR FREEDOM, signifieth, properly, the absence of opposition:
by opposition, I mean external impediments of motion; and may be
applied no less to irrational and inanimate creatures, than to rational.
For whatsoever is so tied, or environed, as it cannot move but within a
certain space, which space is determined by the opposition of some
external body, we say it hath not liberty to go further. And so of all
living creatures, whilst they are imprisoned or restrained, with walls or
chains, and of the water whilst it is kept in by banks or vessels, that
otherwise would spread itself into a larger space, we use to say, they
are not at liberty to move in such manner, as without those external
impediments they would. But when the impediment of motion is in the
constitution of the thing itself, we use not to say it wants the liberty,
but the *power* to move; as when a stone lieth still, or a man is fastened
to his bed by sickness.

And according to this proper and generally received meaning of the
word, *a 'freeman' is he that in those things which by his strength and
wit he is able to do, is not hindered to do what he has a will to.* But
when the words 'free' and 'liberty' are applied to anything but bodies,
they are abused; for that which is not subject to motion is not subject
to impediment: and therefore, when it is said, for example, the way is
free, no liberty of the way is signified, but of those that walk in it
without stop. And when we say a gift is free, there is not meant any
liberty of the gift, but of the giver, that was not bound by any law or
covenant to give it. So when we 'speak freely,' it is not the liberty of
voice or pronunciation, but of the man, whom no law hath obliged to
speak otherwise than he did. Lastly, from the use of the word *free-will,*
no liberty can be inferred of the will, desire, or inclination, but the
liberty of the man; which consisteth in this, that he finds no stop, in
doing what he has the will, desire, or inclination to do.

Fear and liberty are consistent; as when a man throweth his goods
into the sea for *fear* the ship should sink, he doth it nevertheless very
willingly, and may refuse to do it if he will; it is therefore the action of
one that was *free:* so a man sometimes pays his debt, only for fear of
imprisonment, which because nobody hindered him from detaining, was
the action of a man at *liberty.* And generally all actions which men do
in commonwealths, for fear of the law, are actions which the doers had
liberty to omit.

Liberty and necessity are consistent: as in the water, that hath not only *liberty,* but a *necessity* of descending by the channel; so likewise in the actions which men voluntarily do: which, because they proceed from their will, proceed from *liberty;* and yet, because every act of man's will, and every desire, and inclination proceedeth from some cause, and that from another cause, in a continual chain, whose first link is in the hand of God the first of all causes, proceed from *necessity.* So that to him that could see the connection of those causes, the neces-sity of all men's voluntary actions, would appear manifest. And there-fore God, that seeth and disposeth all things, seeth also that the liberty of man in doing what he will, is accompanied with the necessity of do-ing that which God will, and no more nor less. For though men may do many things which God does not command, nor is therefore author of them; yet they can have no passion nor appetite to anything of which appetite God's will is not the cause. And did not His will assure the *necessity* of man's will, and consequently of all that on man's will de-pendeth, the *liberty* of men would be a contradiction, and impediment to the omnipotence and liberty of God. And this shall suffice, as to the matter in hand, of that natural liberty, which only is properly called liberty.

But as men, for the attaining of peace and conservation of themselves thereby, have made an artificial man, which we call a commonwealth; so also have they made artificial chains, called *civil laws,* which they themselves, by mutual covenants, have fastened, at one end, to the lips of that man or assembly to whom they have given the sovereign power, and at the other end to their own ears. These bonds, in their own na-ture but weak, may nevertheless be made to hold, by the danger, though not by the difficulty, of breaking them.

In relation to these bonds only it is, that I am to speak now of the *liberty of subjects.* For seeing there is no commonwealth in the world wherein there be rules enough set down, for the regulating of all the actions and words of men; as being a thing impossible: it followeth necessarily that in all kinds of actions by the laws pretermitted, men have the liberty of doing what their own reasons shall suggest, for the most profitable to themselves. For if we take liberty in the proper sense for corporal liberty; that is to say, freedom from chains and prison; it were very absurd for men to clamor as they do, for the liberty they so manifestly enjoy. Again, if we take liberty for an exemption from laws, it is no less absurd for men to demand as they do, that liberty by which all other men may be masters of their lives. And yet, as absurd as it is, this is it they demand; not knowing that the laws are of no power to protect them, without a sword in the hands of a man, or men, to cause those laws to be put in execution. The liberty of a subject lieth there-fore only in those things which in regulating their actions, the sovereign hath pretermitted: such as is the liberty to buy, and sell, and otherwise contract with one another; to choose their own abode, their own diet, their own trade of life, and institute their children as they themselves think fit; and the like.

Nevertheless we are not to understand that by such liberty, the sovereign power of life and death is either abolished or limited. For it has been already shown that nothing the sovereign representative can do to a subject, on what pretense soever, can properly be called injustice, or injury; because every subject is author of every act the sovereign doth; so that he never wanteth right to anything, otherwise than as he himself is the subject of God, and bound thereby to observe the laws of nature. And therefore it may, and doth often happen in commonwealths, that a subject may be put to death, by the command of the sovereign power, and yet neither do the other wrong; as when Jephtha caused his daughter to be sacrificed: in which, and the like cases, he that so dieth, had liberty to do the action for which he is, nevertheless, without injury put to death. And the same holdeth also in a sovereign prince that putteth to death an innocent subject. For though the action be against the law of nature, as being contrary to equity, as was the killing of Uriah by David; yet it was not an injury to Uriah, but to God. Not to Uriah, because the right to do what he pleased was given him by Uriah himself; and yet to God, because David was God's subject, and prohibited all iniquity by the law of nature: which distinction, David himself, when he repented the fact, evidently confirmed, saying, "To Thee only have I sinned." In the same manner, the people of Athens, when they banished the most potent of their commonwealth for ten years, thought they committed no injustice; and yet they never questioned what crime he had done, but what hurt he would do: nay they commanded the banishment of they knew not whom; and every citizen bringing his oystershell into the market place, written with the name of him he desired should be banished, without actually accusing him, sometimes banished an Aristides, for his reputation of justice, and sometimes a scurrilous jester, as Hyperbolus, to make a jest of it. And yet a man cannot say the sovereign people of Athens wanted right to banish them, or an Athenian the liberty to jest, or to be just.

The liberty whereof there is so frequent and honorable mention in the histories and philosophy of the ancient Greeks and Romans, and in the writings and discourse of those that from them have received all their learning in the politics, is not the liberty of particular men, but the liberty of the commonwealth; which is the same with that which every man then should have, if there were no civil laws nor commonwealth at all. And the effects of it also be the same. For as amongst masterless men, there is perpetual war of every man against his neigh-

bor; no inheritance, to transmit to the son, nor to expect from the
father; no propriety of goods or lands; no security; but a full and absolute liberty in every particular man: so in states, and commonwealths
not dependent on one another, every commonwealth, not every man,
has an absolute liberty, to do what it shall judge—that is to say, what
that man, or assembly that representeth it, shall judge—most conducing to their benefit. But withal, they live in the condition of a perpetual
war, and upon the confines of battle, with their frontiers armed, and
cannons planted against their neighbors round about. The Athenians
and Romans were free; that is, free commonwealths: not that any particular men had the liberty to resist their own representative, but that
their representative had the liberty to resist or invade other people.
There is written on the turrets of the city of Lucca in great characters
at this day, the word *libertas;* yet no man can thence infer that a particular man has more liberty or immunity from the service of the commonwealth there than in Constantinople. Whether a commonwealth be
monarchical or popular, the freedom is still the same.

But it is an easy thing for men to be deceived by the specious name
of liberty; and, for want of judgment to distinguish, mistake that for
their private inheritance and birthright, which is the right of the public
only. And when the same error is confirmed by the authority of men
in reputation for their writings on this subject, it is no wonder if it produce sedition and change of government. In these western parts of the
world, we are made to receive our opinions concerning the institution
and rights of commonwealths from Aristotle, Cicero, and other men,
Greeks and Romans, that living under popular states, derived those
rights not from the principles of nature, but transcribed them into their
books out of the practice of their own commonwealths, which were popular; as the grammarians describe the rules of language out of the practice of the time, or the rules of poetry out of the poems of Homer and
Virgil. And because the Athenians were taught, to keep them from desire of changing their government, that they were freemen, and all that
lived under monarchy were slaves; therefore Aristotle puts it down in
his *Politics* (Lib. VI, Cap. ii), "In democracy, liberty is to be supposed; for it is commonly held that no man is free in any other government." And as Aristotle, so Cicero and other writers have grounded
their civil doctrine on the opinions of the Romans, who were taught to
hate monarchy, at first, by them that having deposed their sovereign,
shared amongst them the sovereignty of Rome; and afterwards by their
successors. And by reading of these Greek and Latin authors, men
from their childhood have gotten a habit, under a false show of liberty,
of favoring tumults, and of licentious controlling the actions of their
sovereigns, and again of controlling those controllers; with the effusion

of so much blood, as I think I may truly say, there was never anything so dearly bought as these western parts have bought the learning of the Greek and Latin tongues.

To come now to the particulars of the true liberty of a subject—that is to say, what are the things which, though commanded by the sovereign, he may nevertheless without injustice refuse to do,—we are to consider, what rights we pass away when we make a commonwealth; or, which is all one, what liberty we deny ourselves by owning all the actions, without exception, of the man, or assembly, we make our sovereign. For in the act of our *submission* consisteth both our *obligation* and our *liberty;* which must therefore be inferred by arguments taken from thence: there being no obligation on any man which ariseth not from some act of his own; for all men equally are by nature free. And because such arguments must either be drawn from the express words, "I authorize all his actions," or from the intention of him that submitteth himself to his power, which intention is to be understood by the end for which he so submitteth; the obligation, and liberty of the subject, is to be derived either from those words or others equivalent, or else from the end of the institution of sovereignty, namely, the peace of the subjects within themselves and their defense against a common enemy.

First therefore, seeing sovereignty by institution is by covenant of everyone to everyone; and sovereignty by acquisition, by covenants of the vanquished to the victor, or child to the parent; it is manifest that every subject has liberty in all those things, the right whereof cannot by covenant be transferred. I have shewn before, in the fourteenth chapter, that covenants not to defend a man's own body are void. Therefore:

If the sovereign command a man, though justly condemned, to kill, wound, or maim himself; or not to resist those that assault him; or to abstain from the use of food, air, medicine, or any other thing, without which he cannot live; yet hath that man the liberty to disobey.

If a man be interrogated by the sovereign, or his authority, concerning a crime done by himself, he is not bound, without assurance of pardon, to confess it; because no man, as I have shown in the same chapter, can be obliged by covenant to accuse himself.

Again, the consent of a subject to sovereign power is contained in these words, "I authorize, or take upon me, all his actions"; in which there is no restriction at all of his own former natural liberty: for by allowing him to kill me, I am not bound to kill myself when he commands me. It is one thing to say, "Kill me, or my fellow, if you please"; another thing to say, "I will kill myself, or my fellow." It followeth therefore, that:

No man is bound by the words themselves, either to kill himself or any other man; and consequently, that the obligation a man may sometimes have, upon the command of the sovereign to execute any dangerous or dishonorable office, dependeth not on the words of our submission, but on the intention, which is to be understood by the end thereof. When therefore our refusal to obey, frustrates the end for which the sovereignty was ordained, then there is no liberty to refuse; otherwise there is.

Upon this ground, a man that is commanded as a soldier to fight against the enemy, though his sovereign have right enough to punish his refusal with death, may nevertheless in many cases refuse, without injustice; as when he substituteth a sufficient soldier in his place: for in this case he deserteth not the service of the commonwealth. And there is allowance to be made for natural timorousness; not only to women, of whom no such dangerous duty is expected, but also to men of feminine courage. When armies fight, there is on one side, or both, a running away; yet when they do it not out of treachery, but fear, they are not esteemed to do it unjustly, but dishonorably. For the same reason, to avoid battle is not injustice, but cowardice. But he that enrolleth himself a soldier, or taketh imprest money, taketh away the excuse of a timorous nature; and is obliged not only to go to the battle, but also not run from it, without his captain's leave. And when the defense of the commonwealth requireth at once the help of all that are able to bear arms, everyone is obliged; because otherwise the institution of the commonwealth, which they have not the purpose or courage to preserve, was in vain.

To resist the sword of the commonwealth in defense of another man, guilty or innocent, no man hath liberty; because such liberty takes away from the sovereign the means of protecting us, and is therefore destructive of the very essence of government. But in case a great many men together have already resisted the sovereign power unjustly, or committed some capital crime, for which every one of them expecteth death, whether have they not the liberty then to join together, and assist and defend one another? Certainly they have; for they but defend their lives, which the guilty man may as well do as the innocent. There was indeed injustice in the first breach of their duty; their bearing of arms subsequent to it, though it be to maintain what they have done, is no new unjust act. And if it be only to defend their persons, it is not unjust at all. But the offer of pardon taketh from them, to whom it is offered, the plea of self-defense, and maketh their perseverance in assisting, or defending the rest, unlawful.

As for other liberties, they depend on the silence of the law. In cases where the sovereign has prescribed no rule, there the subject hath the liberty to do, or forbear, according to his own discretion. And therefore such liberty is in some places more, and in some less; and in some times more, in other times less, according as they that have the sovereignty shall think most convenient. As for example, there was a time when in England a man might enter into his own land, and dispossess such as wrongfully possessed it, by force. But in after times, that liberty of forcible entry was taken away, by a statute made, by the king, in parliament. And in some places of the world, men have the liberty of many wives; in other places such liberty is not allowed.

If a subject have a controversy with his sovereign, of debt, or of right of possession of lands or goods, or concerning any service required at his hands, or concerning any penalty, corporal, or pecuniary, grounded on a precedent law; he hath the same liberty to sue for his right as if it were against a subject, and before such judges as are appointed by the sovereign. For seeing the sovereign demandeth by force of a former law and not by virtue of his power, he declareth thereby, that he requireth no more than shall appear to be due by that law. The suit therefore is not contrary to the will of the sovereign; and consequently the subject hath the liberty to demand the hearing of his cause, and sentence, according to that law. But if he demand or take anything by pretense of his power, there lieth, in that case, no action of law; for all that is done by him in virtue of his power, is done by the authority of every subject, and consequently he that brings an action against the sovereign, brings it against himself.

If a monarch, or sovereign assembly, grant a liberty to all or any of his subjects, which grant standing, he is disabled to provide for their safety, the grant is void; unless he directly renounce, or transfer the sovereignty to another. For in that he might openly, if it had been his will, and in plain terms, have renounced or transferred it, and did not; it is to be understood it was not his will, but that the grant proceeded from ignorance of the repugnancy between such a liberty and the sovereign power; and therefore the sovereignty is still retained; and consequently all those powers, which are necessary to the exercising thereof; such as are the power of war, and peace, of judicature, of appointing officers, and councillors, of levying money, and the rest named in the eighteenth chapter.

The obligation of subjects to the sovereign, is understood to last as long, and no longer, than the power lasteth by which he is able to protect them. For the right men have by nature to protect themselves, when none else can protect them, can by no covenant be relinquished. The sovereignty is the soul of the commonwealth; which once departed from the body, the members do no more receive their motion from it. The end of obedience is protection; which, wheresoever a man seeth it, either in his own or in another's sword, nature applieth his obedience to it, and his endeavor to maintain it. And though sovereignty, in the intention of them that make it, be immortal; yet it is in its own nature, not only subject to violent death, by foreign war; but also through the ignorance, and passions of men, it hath in it, from the very institution, many seeds of a natural mortality, by intestine discord.

If a subject be taken prisoner in war, or his person or his means of life be within the guards of the enemy, and hath his life and corporal liberty given him on condition to be subject to the victor, he hath liberty to accept the condition; and having accepted it, is the subject of him that took him, because he had no other way to preserve himself. The case is the same, if he be detained on the same terms in a foreign country. But if a man be held in prison, or bonds, or is not trusted with the liberty of his body, he cannot be understood to be bound by covenant to subjection; and therefore may, if he can, make his escape by any means whatsoever.

If a monarch shall relinquish the sovereignty both for himself and his heirs, his subjects return to the absolute liberty of nature; because, though nature may declare who are his sons, and who are the nearest of his kin; yet it dependeth on his own will, as hath been said in the precedent chapter, who shall be his heir. If therefore he will have no heir, there is no sovereignty, nor subjection. The case is the same, if he die without known kindred, and without declaration of his heir. For then there can no heir be known, and consequently no subjection be due.

If the sovereign banish his subject; during the banishment, he is not subject. But he that is sent on a message, or hath leave to travel, is still subject; but it is by contract between sovereigns, not by virtue of the covenant of subjection. For whosoever entereth into another's dominion, is subject to all the laws thereof; unless he have a privilege of the amity of the sovereigns, or by special license.

If a monarch subdued by war, render himself subject to the victor; his subjects are delivered from their former obligation, and become obliged to the victor. If he be held prisoner, or have not the liberty of his own body, he is not understood to have given away the right of sovereignty; and therefore his subjects are obliged to yield obedience to the magistrates formerly placed, governing not in their own name, but in his. For, his right remaining, the question is only of the administration; that is to say, of the magistates and officers; which, if he have not means to name, he is supposed to approve those which he himself had formerly appointed. . . .[4]

[4] In Chapters XXII-XXVIII Hobbes discusses the various particular powers and functions of the sovereign.—*Editor.*

CHAPTER XXIX

OF THOSE THINGS THAT WEAKEN, OR TEND TO
THE DISSOLUTION OF A COMMONWEALTH

THOUGH NOTHING can be immortal, which mortals make; yet, if men had the use of reason they pretend to, their commonwealths might be secured, at least from perishing by internal diseases. For by the nature of their institution, they are designed to live, as long as mankind, or as the laws of nature, or as justice itself, which gives them life. Therefore when they come to be dissolved, not by external violence, but intestine disorder, the fault is not in men, as they are the *matter;* but as they are the *makers,* and orderers of them. For men, as they become at last weary of irregular jostling, and hewing one another, and desire with all their hearts, to conform themselves into one firm and lasting edifice; so for want, both of the art of making fit laws, to square their actions by, and also of humility, and patience, to suffer the rude and cumbersome points of their present greatness to be taken off, they cannot without the help of a very able architect, be compiled into any other than a crazy building, such as hardly lasting out their own time, must assuredly fall upon the heads of their posterity.

Amongst the *infirmities* therefore of a commonwealth, I will reckon in the first place, those that arise from an imperfect institution, and resemble the diseases of a natural body, which proceed from a defectuous procreation.

Of which, this is one, *that a man to obtain a kingdom, is sometimes content with less power, than to the peace, and defense of the commonwealth is necessarily required.* From whence it cometh to pass, that when the exercise of the power laid by, is for the public safety to be resumed, it hath the resemblance of an unjust act; which disposeth great numbers of men, when occasion is presented, to rebel; in the same manner as the bodies of children, gotten by diseased parents, are subject either to untimely death, or to purge the ill quality, derived from their vicious conception, by breaking out into oil and scabs. And when kings deny themselves some such necessary power, it is not always, though sometimes, out of ignorance of what is necessary to the office they undertake; but many times out of a hope to recover the same again at their pleasure. Wherein they reason not well; because such as will hold them to their promises, shall be maintained against them by foreign commonwealths; who in order to the good of their own subjects let slip few occasions to *weaken* the estate of their neighbors. So was Thomas Becket, archbishop of Canterbury, supported against Henry the Second, by the Pope; the subjection of ecclesiastics to the commonwealth, having been dispensed with by William the Conqueror at his reception, when he took an oath, not to infringe the liberty of the Church. And so were the barons, whose power was by William Rufus, to have their help in transferring the succession from his elder brother to himself, increased to a degree inconsistent with the sovereign power, maintained in their rebellion against King John, by the French.

Nor does this happen in monarchy only. For whereas the style of the ancient Roman commonwealth, was, *the senate and people of Rome;* neither senate, nor people pretended to the whole power; which first caused the seditions, of Tiberius Gracchus, Caius Gracchus, Lucius Saturninus, and others; and afterwards the wars between the senate and the people, under Marius and Sylla; and again under Pompey and Caesar, to the extinction of their democracy, and the setting up of monarchy.

The people of Athens bound themselves but from one only action; which was, that no man on pain of death should propound the renewing of the war for the island of Salamis; and yet thereby, if Solon had not caused to be given out he was mad, and afterwards in gesture and habit of a madman, and in verse, propounded it to the people that flocked about him, they had had an enemy perpetually in readiness, even at the gates of their city; such damage, or shifts, are all commonwealths forced to, that have their power never so little limited.

In the second place, I observe the *diseases* of a commonwealth, that proceed from the poison of seditious doctrines, whereof one is, *that every private man is judge of good and evil actions.* This is true in the condition of mere nature, where there are no civil laws; and also under civil government, in such cases as are not determined by the law. But otherwise, it is manifest, that the measure of good and evil actions, is the civil law; and the judge the legislator, who is always representative of the commonwealth. From this false doctrine, men are disposed to debate with themselves, and dispute the commands of the commonwealth; and afterwards to obey, or disobey them, as in their private judgments they shall think fit; whereby the commonwealth is distracted and *weakened.*

Another doctrine repugnant to civil society, is, that *whatsoever a man does against his conscience, is sin;* and it dependeth on the presumption of making himself judge of good and evil. For a man's conscience, and his judgment is the same thing, and as the judgment, so also the conscience may be erroneous. Therefore, though he that is subject to no civil law, sinneth in all he does against his conscience, because he has no other rule to follow but his own reason; yet it is not so with him that lives in a commonwealth; because the law is the public conscience, by which he hath already undertaken to be guided. Otherwise, in such diversity, as there is of private consciences, which are but private opinions, the commonwealth must needs be distracted, and no man dare to obey the sovereign power, further than it shall seem good in his own eyes.

It hath been also commonly taught, *that faith and sanctity, are not to be attained by study and reason, but by supernatural inspiration, or infusion.* Which granted, I see not why any man should render a reason of his faith; or why every Christian should not be also a prophet; or why any man should take the law of his country, rather than his own inspiration, for the rule of his action. And thus we fall again in the fault of taking upon us to judge of good and evil; or to make judges of it, such private men as pretend to be supernaturally inspired, to the dissolution of all civil government. Faith comes by hearing, and hearing by those accidents, which guide us into the presence of them that speak to us; which accidents are all contrived by God Almighty; and yet are not supernatural, but only, for the great number of them that concur to every effect, unobservable. Faith and sanctity, are indeed not very frequent; but yet they are not miracles, but brought to pass by education, discipline, correction, and other natural ways, by which God worketh them in his elect, at such times as he thinketh fit. And these three opinions, pernicious to peace and government, have in this part of the world, proceeded chiefly from the tongues, and pens of unlearned divines, who joining the words of Holy Scripture together, otherwise than is agreeable to reason, do what they can, to make men think, that sanctity and natural reason, cannot stand together.

A fourth opinion, repugnant to the nature of a commonwealth, is this, *that he that hath the sovereign power is subject to the civil laws.* It is true, that sovereigns are all subject to the laws of nature; because such laws be divine, and cannot by any man, or commonwealth be abrogated. But to those laws which the sovereign himself, that is, which the commonwealth maketh, he is not subject. For to be subject to laws, is to be subject to the commonwealth, that is to the sovereign representative, that is to himself; which is not subjection, but freedom from the laws. Which error, because it setteth the laws above the sovereign, setteth also a judge above him, and a power to punish him; which is to make a new sovereign; and again for the same reason a third, to punish the second; and so continually without end, to the confusion, and dissolution of the commonwealth.

A fifth doctrine that tendeth to the dissolution of a commonwealth, is, *that every private man has an absolute propriety in his goods; such, as excludeth the right of the sovereign.* Every man has indeed a propriety that excludes the right of every other subject; and he has it only from the sovereign power; without the protection whereof, every other man should have equal right to the same. But if the right of the sovereign also be excluded, he cannot perform the office they have put him into; which is, to defend them both from foreign enemies, and from the injuries of one another; and consequently there is no longer a commonwealth.

And if the propriety of subjects, exclude not the right of the sovereign representative to their goods; much less to their offices of judicature, or execution, in which they represent the sovereign himself.

There is a sixth doctrine, plainly, and directly against the essence of a commonwealth; and it is this, *that the sovereign power may be divided.* For what is it to divide the power of a commonwealth, but to dissolve it; for powers divided mutually destroy each other. And for these doctrines, men are chiefly beholding to some of those that, making profession of the laws, endeavor to make them depend upon their own learning, and not upon the legislative power.

And as false doctrine, so also oftentimes the example of different government in a neighboring nation, disposeth men to alteration of the form already settled. So the people of the Jews were stirred up to reject God, and to call upon the prophet Samuel, for a king after the manner of the nations: so also the lesser cities of Greece, were continually disturbed, with seditions of the aristocratical, and democratical factions; one part of almost every commonwealth, desiring to imitate the Lacedemonians; the other, the Athenians. And I doubt not, but many men have been contented to see the late troubles in England, out of an imitation of the Low Countries; supposing there needed no more to grow rich, than to change, as they had done, the form of their government. For the constitution of man's nature, is of itself subject to desire novelty. When therefore they are provoked to the same, by the neighborhood also of those that have been enriched by it, it is almost impossible for them, not to be content with those that solicit them to change; and love the first beginnings, though they be grieved with the continuance of disorder; like hot-bloods, that having gotten the itch, tear themselves with their own nails, till they can endure the smart no longer.

And as to rebellion in particular against monarchy; one of the most frequent causes of it, is the reading of the books of policy, and histories of the ancient Greeks, and Romans; from which, young men, and all others that are unprovided of the antidote of solid reason, receiving a strong, and delightful impression, of the great exploits of war, achieved by the conductors of their armies, receive withal a pleasing idea, of all they have done besides; and imagine their great prosperity, not to have proceeded from the emulation of particular men, but from the virtue of their popular form of government: not considering the frequent seditions, and civil wars, produced by the imperfection of their policy. From the reading, I say, of such books, men have undertaken to kill their kings, because the Greek and Latin writers, in their books, and discourses of policy, make it lawful, and laudable, for any man so to do; provided, before he do it, he call him tyrant. For they say not *regicide,* that is, killing a king, but *tyrannicide,* that is, killing of a tyrant is lawful. From the same books, they that live under a monarch conceive an opinion, that the subjects in a popular commonwealth enjoy liberty; but that in a monarchy they are all slaves. I say, they that live under a monarchy conceive such an opinion; not they that live under a popular government: for they find no such matter. In sum, I cannot imagine, how anything can be more prejudicial to a monarchy, than the allowing of such books to be publicly read, without present applying such correctives of discreet masters, as are fit to take away their venom: which venom I will not doubt to compare to the biting of a mad dog, which is a disease the physicians call *hydrophobia,* or *fear of water.* For as he that is so bitten, has a continual torment of thirst, and yet abhorreth water; and is in such an estate, as if the poison endeavored to convert him into a dog; so when a monarchy is once bitten to the quick, by those democratical writers, that continually snarl at that estate; it wanteth nothing more than a strong monarch, which nevertheless out of a certain *tyrannophobia,* or fear of being strongly governed, when they have him, they abhor.

As there have been doctors, that hold there be three souls in a man; so there be also that think there may be more souls, that is, more sovereigns, than one, in a commonwealth; and set up a *supremacy* against the *sovereignty; canons* against *laws;* and a *ghostly authority* against the *civil;* working on men's minds, with words and distinctions, that of themselves signify nothing, but betray by their obscurity; that there walketh, as some think, invisibly another kingdom, as it were a kingdom of fairies, in the dark. Now seeing it is manifest, that the civil power, and the power of the commonwealth is the same thing; and that supremacy, and the power of making canons, and granting faculties, implieth a commonwealth; it followeth, that where one is sovereign, another supreme; where one can make laws, and another make canons; there must needs be two commonwealths, of one and the same subjects; which is a kingdom divided in itself, and cannot stand. For notwithstanding the insignificant distinction of *temporal* and *ghostly,* they are still two kingdoms, and every subject is subject to two masters. For seeing the *ghostly* power challengeth the right to declare what is sin, it challengeth by consequence to declare what is law, sin being nothing but the transgression of the law; and again, the civil power challenging to declare what is law, every subject must obey two masters, who both will have their commands be observed as law; which is impossible. Or, if it be but one kingdom, either the *civil*, which is the power of the commonwealth, must be subordinate to the *ghostly*, and then there is no sovereignty but the *ghostly;* or the ghostly must be subordinate to the *temporal*, and then there is no *supremacy* but the *temporal*. When therefore these two powers oppose one another, the commonwealth cannot but be in great danger of civil war and dissolution. For the *civil* authority being more visible, and standing in the clearer light of natural reason, cannot choose but draw to it in all times a very considerable part of the people; and the *spiritual*, though it stand in the darkness of School distinctions, and hard words, yet because the fear of darkness and ghosts, is greater than other fears, cannot want a party sufficient to trouble, and sometimes to destroy a commonwealth. And this is a disease which not unfitly may be compared to the epilepsy, or falling sickness, which the Jews took to be one kind of possession by spirits, in the body natural. For as in this disease, there is an unnatural spirit, or wind in the head that obstructeth the roots of the nerves, and moving them violently, taketh away the motion which naturally they should have from the power of the soul in the brain, and thereby causeth violent, and irregular motions, which men call convulsions, in the parts; insomuch as he that is seized therewith, falleth down sometimes into the water, and sometimes into the fire, as a man deprived of his senses; so also in the body politic, when the spiritual power, moveth the members of a commonwealth, by the terror of punishments, and hope of rewards, which are the nerves of it, otherwise than by the civil power, which is the soul of the commonwealth, they ought to be moved; and by strange, and hard words suffocates their understanding, it must needs thereby distract the people, and either overwhelm the commonwealth with oppression, or cast it into the fire of a civil war.

Sometimes also in the merely civil government, there be more than one soul; as when the power of levying money, which is the nutritive faculty, has depended on a general assembly; the power of conduct and command, which is the motive faculty, on one man; and the power of making laws, which is the rational faculty, on the accidental consent, not only of those two, but also of a third; this endangereth the commonwealth, sometimes for want of consent to good laws: but most often for want of such nourishment, as is necessary to life, and motion. For although few perceive, that such government, is not government, but division of the commonwealth into three factions, and call it mixed monarchy; yet the truth is, that it is not one independent commonwealth, but three independent factions; nor one representative person, but three. In the kingdom of God, there may be three persons independent without breach of unity in God that reigneth; but where men

reign, that be subject to diversity of opinions, it cannot be so. And therefore if the king bear the person of the people, and the general assembly
bear also the person of the people, and another assembly bear the person
of a part of the people, they are not one person, nor one sovereign, but
three persons, and three sovereigns.

To what disease in the natural body of man, I may exactly compare
this irregularity of a commonwealth, I know not. But I have seen a man,
that had another man growing out of his side, with a head, arms, breast,
and stomach, of his own: if he had had another man growing out of his
other side, the comparison might then have been exact.

Hitherto I have named such diseases of a commonwealth, as are of the
greatest, and most present danger. There be other not so great; which
nevertheless are not unfit to be observed. As first, the difficulty of raising
money, for the necessary uses of the commonwealth; especially in the
approach of war. This difficulty ariseth from the opinion, that every
subject hath a propriety in his lands and goods, exclusive of the sovereign's right to the use of the same. From whence it cometh to pass, that
the sovereign power, which foreseeth the necessities and dangers of the
commonwealth, finding the passage of money to the public treasury
obstructed, by the tenacity of the people, whereas it ought to extend
itself, to encounter, and prevent such dangers in their beginnings, con-
tracteth itself as long as it can, and when it cannot longer, struggles with
the people by stratagems of law, to obtain little sums, which not sufficing,
he is fain at last violently to open the way for present supply, or perish;
and being put often to these extremities, at last reduceth the people
to their due temper; or else the commonwealth must perish. Insomuch
as we may compare this distemper very aptly to an ague; wherein, the
fleshy parts being congealed, or by venomous matter obstructed, the
veins which by their natural course empty themselves into the heart,
are not, as they ought to be, supplied from the arteries, whereby there
succeedeth at first a cold contraction, and trembling of the limbs; and
afterward a hot, and strong endeavor of the heart, to force a passage
for the blood; and before it can do that, contenteth itself with the small
refreshments of such things as cool for a time, till, if nature be strong
enough, it break at last the contumacy of the parts obstructed, and
dissipateth the venom into sweat; or, if nature be too weak, the patient
dieth.

Again, there is sometimes in a commonwealth, a disease, which re-
sembleth the pleurisy; and that is, when the treasure of the commonwealth, flowing out of its due course, is gathered together in too much
abundance, in one, or a few private men, by monopolies, or by farms of
the public revenues; in the same manner as the blood in a pleurisy,

getting into the membrane of the breast, breedeth there an inflammation, accompanied with a fever, and painful stitches.

Also, the popularity of a potent subject, unless the commonwealth
have very good caution of his fidelity, is a dangerous disease; because the
people, which should receive their motion from the authority of the
sovereign, by the flattery and by the reputation of an ambitious man are
drawn away from their obedience to the laws, to follow a man, of whose
virtues, and designs they have no knowledge. And this is commonly of
more danger in a popular government, than in a monarchy; because an
army is of so great force, and multitude, as it may easily be made believe,
they are the people. By this means it was, that Julius Caesar, who was
set up by the people against the senate, having won to himself the affections of his army, made himself master both of senate and people.
And this proceeding of popular, and ambitious men, is plain rebellion;
and may be resembled to the effects of witchcraft.

Another infirmity of a commonwealth, is the immoderate greatness
of a town, when it is able to furnish out of its own circuit, the number,
and expense of a great army: as also the great number of corporations;
which are as it were many lesser commonwealths in the bowels of a
greater, like worms in the entrails of a natural man. To which may be
added, the liberty of disputing against absolute power, by pretenders to
political prudence; which though bred for the most part in the lees of
the people, yet amimated by false doctrines, are perpetually meddling
with the fundamental laws, to the molestation of the commonwealth;
like the little worms, which physicians call *ascarides*.

We may further add, the insatiable appetite, or βουλιμία, of enlarging dominion; with the incurable *wounds* thereby many times received from the enemy, and the *wens,* of ununited conquests, which are
many times a burden, and with less danger lost, than kept; as also the
lethargy of ease, and *consumption* of riot and vain expense.

Lastly, when in a war, foreign or intestine, the enemies get a final
victory; so as, the forces of the commonwealth keeping the field no
longer, there is no further protection of subjects in their loyalty; then
is the commonwealth *dissolved,* and every man at liberty to protect himself by such courses as his own discretion shall suggest unto him. For the
sovereign is the public soul, giving life and motion to the commonwealth;
which expiring, the members are governed by it no more, than the carcass of a man, by his departed, though immortal, soul. For though the
right of a sovereign monarch cannot be extinguished by the act of another; yet the obligation of the members may. For he that wants protection, may seek it anywhere; and when he hath it, is obliged, without
fraudulent pretense of having submitted himself out of fear, to protect

his protection as long as he is able. But when the power of an assembly is once suppressed, the right of the same perisheth utterly; because the assembly itself is extinct; and consequently, there is no possibility for the sovereignty to reenter. . . .[5]

CHAPTER XXXI

OF THE KINGDOM OF GOD BY NATURE

THAT the condition of mere nature—that is to say, of absolute liberty, such as is theirs that neither are sovereigns nor subjects—is anarchy, and the condition of war; that the precepts by which men are guided to avoid that condition, are the laws of nature; that a commonwealth without sovereign power, is but a word without substance, and cannot stand; that subjects owe to sovereigns simple obedience, in all things wherein their obedience is not repugnant to the laws of God: I have sufficiently proved, in that which I have already written. There wants only, for the entire knowledge of civil duty, to know what are those laws of God. For without that, a man knows not, when he is commanded anything by the civil power, whether it be contrary to the law of God or not: and so, either by too much civil obedience, offends the Divine Majesty; or through fear of offending God, transgresses the commandments of the commonwealth. To avoid both these rocks, it is necessary to know what are the laws divine. And seeing the knowledge of all law dependeth on the knowledge of the sovereign power, I shall say something in that which followeth, of the *Kingdom of God.*

God is king, let the earth rejoice, saith the psalmist. (xcvii. 1). And again, (*Psalm* xcix. 1) *God is king, though the nations be angry; and he that sitteth on the cherubims, though the earth be moved.* Whether men will or not, they must be subject always to the divine power. By denying the existence, or providence of God, men may shake off their ease, but not their yoke. But to call this power of God, which extendeth itself not only to man, but also to beasts, and plants, and bodies inanimate, by the name of kingdom, is but a metaphorical use of the word. For he only is properly said to reign, that governs his subjects by his word, and by promise of rewards to those that obey it, and by threatening them with punishment that obey it not. Subjects therefore in the kingdom of God, are not bodies inanimate, nor creatures irrational; because they understand no precepts as his; nor atheists, nor they that believe not

---

[5] Chapter XXX is entitled "Of the Office of the Sovereign Representative."—*Editor.*

that God has any care of the actions of mankind; because they acknowledge no word for his, nor have hope of his rewards or fear of his threaten-
ings. They therefore that believe there is a God that governeth the
world, and hath given precepts, and propounded rewards, and punishments to mankind, are God's subjects; all the rest, are to be understood
as enemies.

To rule by words, requires that such words be manifestly made
known; for else they are no laws: for to the nature of laws belongeth
a sufficient, and clear promulgation, such as may take away the excuse
of ignorance; which in the laws of men is but of one only kind, and that
is, proclamation, or promulgation by the voice of man. But God declareth his laws three ways; by the dictates of *natural reason,* by *revelation,* and by the *voice* of some man, to whom by the operation of
miracles, he procureth credit with the rest. From hence there ariseth a
triple word of God, *rational, sensible,* and *prophetic:* to which corre-
spondeth a triple hearing; *right reason, sense supernatural,* and *faith.*
As for sense supernatural, which consisteth in revelation or inspiration,
there have not been any universal laws so given, because God speaketh
not in that manner but to particular persons, and to divers men divers
things.

From the difference between the other two kinds of God's word, *rational,* and *prophetic,* there may be attributed to God, a twofold kingdom, *natural,* and *prophetic:* natural, wherein he governeth as many
of mankind as acknowledge his providence, by the natural dictates of
right reason; and prophetic, wherein having chosen out one peculiar
nation, the Jews, for his subjects, he governed them, and none but them,
not only by natural reason, but by positive laws, which he gave them by
the mouths of his holy prophets. Of the natural kingdom of God I intend to speak in this chapter.

The right of nature, whereby God reigneth over men, and punisheth
those that break his laws, is to be derived, not from his creating them,
as if he required obedience as of gratitude for his benefits; but from his
irresistible power. I have formerly shown, how the sovereign right
ariseth from pact; to show how the same right may arise from nature,
requires no more, but to show in what case it is never taken away. Seeing all men by nature had right to all things, they had right every one
to reign over all the rest. But because this right could not be obtained
by force, it concerned the safety of everyone, laying by that right, to
set up men, with sovereign authority, by common consent, to rule and
defend them; whereas if there had been any man of power irresistible,
there had been no reason, why he should not by that power have ruled
and defended both himself, and them, according to his own discretion.
To those therefore whose power is irresistible, the dominion of all men

adhereth naturally by their excellence of power; and consequently it is from that power, that the kingdom over men, and the right of afflicting men at his pleasure, belongeth naturally to God Almighty; not as Creator, and gracious; but as omnipotent. And though punishment be due for sin only, because by that word is understood affliction for sin; yet the right of afflicting, is not always derived from men's sin, but from God's power.

This question, *why evil men often prosper, and good men suffer adversity,* has been much disputed by the ancients, and is the same with this of ours, *by what right God dispenseth the prosperities and adversities of this life;* and is of that difficulty, as it hath shaken the faith, not only of the vulgar, but of philosophers, and which is more, of the Saints, concerning the Divine Providence. *How good,* saith David, (Psalm lxxiii. 1, 2, 3) *is the God of Israel to those that are upright in heart; and yet my feet were almost gone, my treadings had well-nigh slipt; for I was grieved at the wicked, when I saw the ungodly in such prosperity.* And Job, how earnestly does he expostulate with God, for the many afflictions he suffered, notwithstanding his righteousness? This question in the case of Job, is decided by God himself, not by arguments derived from Job's sin, but his own power. For whereas the friends of Job drew their arguments from his affliction to his sin, and he defended himself by the conscience of his innocence, God himself taketh up the matter, and having justified the affliction by arguments drawn from his power, such as this, *(Job xxxviii. 4) Where wast thou, when I laid the foundations of the earth?* and the like, both approved Job's innocence, and reproved the erroneous doctrine of his friends. Conformable to this doctrine is the sentence of our Saviour, concerning the man that was born blind, in these words, *Neither hath this man sinned, nor his fathers; but that the works of God might be made manifest in him.* And though it be said, *that death entered into the world by sin* (by which is meant, that if Adam had never sinned, he had never died, that is, never suffered any separation of his soul from his body), it follows not thence, that God could not justly have afflicted him, though he had not sinned, as well as he afflicteth other living creatures, that cannot sin.

Having spoken of the right of God's sovereignty, as grounded only on nature; we are to consider next, what are the Divine laws, or dictates of natural reason; which laws concern either the natural duties of one man to another, or the honor naturally due to our Divine Sovereign. The first are the same laws of nature, of which I have spoken already in the fourteenth and fifteenth chapters of this treatise; namely, equity, justice, mercy, humility, and the rest of the moral virtues. It remaineth therefore that we consider, what precepts are dictated to men, by their natural reason only, without other word of God, touching the honor and worship of the Divine Majesty.

Honor consisteth in the inward thought, and opinion of the power, and goodness of another; and therefore to honor God, is to think as highly of his power and goodness, as is possible. And of that opinion, the external signs appearing in the words and actions of men, are called *worship;* which is one part of that which the Latins understand by the word *cultus.* For cultus signifieth properly, and constantly, that labor which a man bestows on anything, with a purpose to make benefit by it. Now those things whereof we make benefit, are either subject to us, and the profit they yield, followeth the labor we bestow upon them, as a natural effect; or they are not subject to us, but answer our labor according to their own wills. In the first sense the labor bestowed on the earth, is called *culture;* and the education of children, a *culture* of their minds. In the second sense, where men's wills are to be wrought to our purpose, not by force, but by complaisance, it signifieth as much as courting, that is, a winning of favor by good offices; as by praises, by acknowledging their power, and by whatsoever is pleasing to them from whom we look for any benefit. And this is properly *worship:* in which sense *publicola,* is understood for a worshiper of the people; and *cultus Dei,* for the worship of God.

From internal honor, consisting in the opinion of power and goodness, arise three passions; *love,* which hath reference to goodness; and *hope,* and *fear,* that relate to power: and three parts of external worship; *praise, magnifying,* and *blessing:* the subject of praise, being goodness; the subject of magnifying and blessing, being power, and the effect thereof felicity. Praise, and magnifying are signified both by words, and actions: by words, when we say a man is good, or great; by actions when we thank him for his bounty, and obey his power. The opinion of the happiness of another, can only be expressed by words.

There be some signs of honor, both in attributes and actions, that be naturally so; as amongst attributes, *good, just, liberal,* and the like; and amongst actions, *prayers, thanks,* and *obedience.* Others are so by institution, or custom of men; and in some times and places are honorable; in others, dishonorable; in others, indifferent: such as are the gestures in salutation, prayer, and thanksgiving, in different times and places, differently used. The former is *natural;* the latter *arbitrary* worship.

And of arbitrary worship, there be two differences: for sometimes it is a *commanded,* sometimes *voluntary* worship; commanded, when it is such as he requireth, who is worshiped; free, when it is such as the worshiper thinks fit. When it is commanded, not the words, or gesture, but the obedience is the worship. But when free, the worship consists in the opinion of the beholders: for if to them the words, or actions by which we intend honor, seem ridiculous, and tending to contumely, they are no worship, because no signs of honor; because a sign is not a sign to him that giveth it, but to him to whom it is made, that is, to the spectator.

Again, there is a *public* and a *private* worship. Public, is the worship that a commonwealth performeth as one person. Private, is that which a private person exhibiteth. Public, in respect to the whole commonwealth, is free; but in respect to particular men, it is not so. Private, is in secret free; but in the sight of the multitude, it is never without some restraint, either from the laws or from the opinion of men; which is contrary to the nature of liberty.

The end of worship amongst men, is power. For where a man seeth another worshiped, he supposeth him powerful, and is the readier to obey him; which makes his power greater. But God has no ends: the worship we do Him, proceeds from our duty, and is directed, according to our capacity, by those rules of honor that reason dictateth to be done by the weak to the more potent men, in hope of benefit, for fear of damage, or in thankfulness for good already received from them.

That we may know what worship of God is taught us by the light of nature, I will begin with His attributes. Where, first, it is manifest, we ought to attribute to Him *existence*. For no man can have the will to honor that which he thinks not to have any being.

Secondly, that those philosophers who said the world, or the soul of the world, was God, spake unworthily of Him, and denied His existence. For by God, is understood the cause of the world; and to say the world is God, is to say there is no cause of it, that is, no God.

Thirdly, to say the world was not created, but eternal, seeing that which is eternal has no cause, is to deny there is a God.

Fourthly, that they who, attributing, as they think, ease to God, take from Him the care of mankind; take from Him His honor: for it takes away men's love and fear of Him, which is the root of honor.

Fifthly, in those things that signify greatness and power, to say He is *finite* is not to honor Him: for it is not a sign of the will to honor God, to attribute to Him less than we can; and finite is less than we can; because to finite, it is easy to add more.

Therefore to attribute *figure* to Him, is not honor; for all figure is finite:

Nor to say we conceive, and imagine, or have an *idea* of Him, in our mind; for whatsoever we conceive is finite:

Nor to attribute to Him *parts*, or *totality;* which are the attributes only of things finite:

Nor to say He is in this or that *place;* for whatsoever is in place, is bounded, and finite:

Nor that He is *moved,* or *resteth;* for both these attributes ascribe to Him place:

Nor that there be more Gods than one; because it implies them all finite; for there cannot be more than one infinite:

Nor to ascribe to Him (unless metaphorically, meaning not the passion but the effect) passions that partake of grief, as repentance, anger, mercy; or of want, as appetite, hope, desire; or of any passive faculty; for passion is power limited by somewhat else.

And therefore when we ascribe to God a *will,* it is not to be understood, as that of man, for a rational appetite; but as the power by which He effecteth everything.

Likewise when we attribute to Him *sight,* and other acts of sense; as also *knowledge,* and *understanding;* which in us is nothing else but a tumult of the mind, raised by external things that press the organical parts of man's body: for there is no such thing in God; and being things that depend on natural causes, cannot be attributed to him.

He that will attribute to God nothing but what is warranted by natural reason, must either use such negative attributes, as *infinite, eternal, incomprehensible;* or superlatives, as *most high, most great,* and the like; or indefinite, as *good, just, holy, creator,* and in such sense as if he meant not to declare what He is (for that were to circumscribe Him within the limits of our fancy), but how much we admire Him, and how ready we would be to obey Him; which is a sign of humility, and of a will to honor Him as much as we can. For there is but one name to signify our conception of His nature, and that is, *I am:* and but one name of His relation to us, and that is, *God;* in which is contained Father, King, and Lord.

Concerning the actions of divine worship, it is a most general precept of reason, that they be signs of the intention to honor God; such as are, first, *prayers.* For not the carvers, when they made images, were thought to make them gods; but the people that *prayed* to them.

Secondly, *thanksgiving;* which differeth from prayer in divine worship, no otherwise, than that prayers precede, and thanks succeed the benefit; the end, both of the one and the other, being to acknowledge God, for author of all benefits, as well past, as future.

Thirdly, *gifts,* that is to say, *sacrifices* and *oblations,* if they be of the best, are signs of honor; for they are thanksgivings.

Fourthly, not to swear by any but God, is naturally a sign of honor:

for it is a confession that God only knoweth the heart; and that no man's wit or strength can protect a man against God's vengeance on the perjured.

Fifthly, it is a part of rational worship, to speak considerately of God; for it argues a fear of him, and fear is a confession of his power. Hence followeth, that the name of God is not to be used rashly, and to no purpose; for that is as much, as in vain: and by order of the commonwealths, to make judgments certain; or between commonwealths, to avoid war. And that disputing of God's nature is contrary to his honor; for it is supposed, that in this natural kingdom of God, there is no other way to know anything, but by natural reason, that is, from the principles of natural science; which are so far from teaching us anything of God's nature, as they cannot teach us our own nature, nor the nature of the smallest creature living. And therefore, when men out of the principles of natural reason, dispute of the attributes of God, they but dishonor him; for in the attributes which we give to God, we are not to consider the signification of philosophical truth; but the signification of pious intention, to do him the greatest honor we are able. From the want of which consideration, have proceeded the volumes of disputation about the nature of God, that tend not to his honor, but to the honor of our own wits and learning; and are nothing else but inconsiderate and vain abuses of his sacred name.

Sixthly, in *prayers, thanksgivings, offerings,* and *sacrifices,* it is a dictate of natural reason, that they be every one in his kind the best, and most significant of honor. As for example, that prayers and thanksgiving, be made in words and phrases, not sudden, nor light, nor plebeian; but beautiful, and well composed. For else we do not God as much honor as we can. And therefore the heathens did absurdly, to worship images for gods; but their doing it in verse, and with music, both of voice and instruments, was reasonable. Also that the beasts they offered in sacrifice, and the gifts they offered, and their actions in worshiping, were full of submission, and commemorative of benefits received, was according to reason, as proceeding from an intention to honor him.

Seventhly, reason directeth not only to worship God in secret; but also, and especially, in public, and in the sight of men. For without that, that which in honor is most acceptable, the procuring others to honor him, is lost.

Lastly, obedience to his laws, that is, in this case to the laws of nature, is the greatest worship of all. For as obedience is more acceptable to God than sacrifice; so also to set light by his commandments, is the greatest of all contumelies. And these are the laws of that divine worship, which natural reason dictateth to private men.

But seeing a commonwealth is but one person, it ought also to exhibit to God but one worship; which then it doth when it commandeth it to be exhibited by private men, publicly. And this is public worship; the property whereof is to be *uniform*: for those actions that are done differently by different men, cannot be said to be a public worship. And therefore, where many sorts of worship be allowed, proceeding from different religions of private men, it cannot be said there is any public worship, nor that the commonwealth is of any religion at all.

And because words, and consequently the attributes of God, have their signification by agreement and constitution of men, those attributes are to be held significative of honor, that men intend shall so be; and whatsoever may be done by the wills of particular men, where there is no law but reason, may be done by the will of the commonwealth, by laws civil. And because a commonwealth hath no will, nor makes no laws but those that are made by the will of him or them that have the sovereign power; it followeth that those attributes which the sovereign ordaineth, in the worship of God, for signs of honor, ought to be taken and used for such, by private men in their public worship.

But because not all actions are signs by constitution, but some are naturally signs of honor, others of contumely; these latter, which are those that men are ashamed to do in the sight of them they reverence, cannot be made by human power a part of Divine worship; nor the former, such as are decent, modest, humble behavior, ever be separated from it. But whereas there be an infinite number of actions and gestures of an indifferent nature; such of them as the commonwealth shall ordain to be publicly and universally in use, as signs of honor and part of God's worship, are to be taken and used for such by the subjects. And that which is said in the Scripture, "It is better to obey God than man," hath place in the kingdom of God by pact, and not by nature.

Having thus briefly spoken of the natural kingdom of God, and His natural laws, I will add only to this chapter a short declaration of His natural punishments. There is no action of man in this life, that is not the beginning of so long a chain of consequences, as no human providence is high enough to give a man a prospect to the end. And in this chain, there are linked together both pleasing and unpleasing events; in such manner, as he that will do anything for his pleasure, must engage himself to suffer all the pains annexed to it; and these pains are the natural punishments of those actions, which are the beginning of more harm than good. And hereby it comes to pass that intemperance is naturally punished with diseases; rashness, with mischances; injustice, with the violence of enemies; pride, with ruin; cowardice, with oppression; negligent government of princes, with rebellion; and rebellion, with slaughter. For seeing punishments are consequent to the breach of laws, natural punishments must be naturally consequent to the breach of the laws of nature; and therefore follow them as their natural, not arbitrary effects. And thus far concerning the constitution, nature, and right of sovereigns, and concerning the duty of subjects, derived from the principles of natural reason. And now, considering how different this doctrine is from the practice of the greatest part of the world, especially of these western parts that have received their moral learning from Rome and Athens, and how much depth of moral philosophy is required in them that have the administration of the sovereign power; I am at the point of believing this my labor as useless as the commonwealth of Plato. For he also is of opinion that it is impossible for the disorders of state, and change of governments by civil war, ever to be taken away, till sovereigns be philosophers. But when I consider again, that the science of natural justice is the only science necessary for sovereigns and their principal ministers; and that they need not be charged with the sciences mathematical, as by Plato they are, farther than by good laws to encourage men to the study of them; and that neither Plato, nor any other philosopher hitherto, hath put into order, and sufficiently or probably proved all the theorems of moral doctrine, that men may learn thereby both how to govern and how to obey; I recover some hope, that one time or other, this writing of mine may fall into the hands of a sovereign who will consider it himself (for it is short, and I think clear) without the help of any interested or envious interpreter; and by the exercise of entire sovereignty, in protecting the public teaching of it, convert this truth of speculation into the utility of practice. . . .[6]

PART III: OF A CHRISTIAN COMMONWEALTH

CHAPTER XLIII

OF WHAT IS NECESSARY FOR A MAN'S RECEPTION INTO THE KINGDOM OF HEAVEN

THE MOST frequent pretext of sedition, and civil war, in Christian commonwealths, hath a long time proceeded from a difficulty, not yet suf-

[6] Parts III and IV of *Leviathan*, entitled "Of a Christian Commonwealth" and "Of the Kingdom of Darkness," are an attack on the pretensions to authority over the civil power put forward in Hobbes' time by the Roman and the Presbyterian clergy. By arguments chiefly based on citations from the Scriptures Hobbes attempts to show that the Church is rightfully under the control of the state, and that, therefore, the sovereign has supreme power over the practices of his subjects in matters of religion. There are added here only selections from the concluding chapter of Part III, and a "Review and Conclusion" appended by Hobbes to Part IV of the *Leviathan*.

ficiently resolved, of obeying at once both God and man, then when their commandments are one contrary to the other. It is manifest enough, that when a man receiveth two contrary commands, and knows that one of them is God's, he ought to obey that, and not the other, though it be the command even of his lawful sovereign (whether a monarch, or a sovereign assembly), or the command of his father. The difficulty therefore consisteth in this, that men, when they are commanded in the name of God, know not in divers cases, whether the command be from God, or whether he that commandeth do but abuse God's name for some private ends of his own. For as there were in the Church of the Jews, many false prophets, that sought reputation with the people, by feigned dreams and visions; so there have been in all times in the Church of Christ, false teachers, that seek reputation with the people, by fantastical and false doctrines; and by such reputation (as is the nature of ambition) to govern them for their private benefit.

But this difficulty of obeying both God and the civil sovereign on earth, to those that can distinguish between what is *necessary,* and what is not *necessary for their reception into the kingdom of God,* is of no moment. For if the command of the civil sovereign be such, as that it may be obeyed without the forfeiture of life eternal; not to obey it is unjust; and the precept of the apostle takes place: *Servants obey your masters in all things;* and *Children obey your parents in all things;* and the precept of our Saviour, *The Scribes and Pharisees sit in Moses' chair; all therefore they shall say, that observe and do.* But if the command be such as cannot be obeyed, without being damned to eternal death; then it were madness to obey it, and the council of our Saviour takes place, (*Matth.* x. 28), *Fear not those that kill the body, but cannot kill the soul.* All men therefore that would avoid, both the punishments that are to be in this world inflicted, for disobedience to their earthly sovereign, and those that shall be inflicted in the world to come, for disobedience to God, have need be taught to distinguish well between what is, and what is not necessary to eternal salvation.

All that is necessary to salvation, is contained in two virtures, *faith in Christ,* and *obedience to laws.* The latter of these, if it were perfect, were enough to us. But because we are all guilty of disobedience to God's law, not only originally in Adam, but also actually by our own transgressions, there is required at our hands now, not only *obedience* for the rest of our time, but also a *remission of sins* for the time past; which remission is the reward of our faith in Christ. That nothing else is necessarily required to salvation, is manifest from this, that the kingdom of heaven is shut to none but to sinners; that is to say, to the disobedient, or transgressors of the law; nor to them, in case they repent, and believe all the articles of Christian faith necessary to salvation.

The obedience required at our hands by God, that accepteth in all our actions the will for the deed, is a serious endeavor to obey him; and is called also by all such names as signify that endeavor. And therefore obedience is sometimes called by the names of *charity* and *love,* because they imply a will to obey; and our Saviour himself maketh our love to God, and to one another, a fulfilling of the whole law: and sometimes by the name of *righteousness;* for righteousness is but the will to give to everyone his own; that is to say, the will to obey the laws: and sometimes by the name of *repentance;* because to repent, implieth a turning away from sin, which is the same with the return of the will to obedience. Whosoever therefore unfeignedly desireth to fulfill the commandments of God, or repenteth him truly of his transgressions, or that loveth God with all his heart, and his neighbor as himself, hath all the obedience necessary to his reception into the kingdom of God. For if God should require perfect innocence, there could no flesh be saved.

But what commandments are those that God hath given us? Are all those laws which were given to the Jews by the hand of Moses, the commandments of God? If they be, why are not Christians taught to obey them? If they be not, what others are so, besides the law of nature? For our Saviour Christ hath not given us new laws, but counsel to observe those we are subject to; that is to say, the laws of nature, and the laws of our several sovereigns: nor did he make any new law to the Jews in his Sermon on the Mount, but only expounded the law of Moses, to which they were subject before. The laws of God therefore are none but the laws of nature, whereof the principal is, that we should not violate our faith, that is, a commandment to obey our civil sovereigns, which we constituted over us by mutual pact one with another. And this law of God, that commandeth obedience to the law civil, commandeth by consequence obedience to all the precepts of the Bible; which, as I have proved in the precedent chapter, is there only law, where the civil sovereign hath made it so; and in other places, but counsel; which a man at his own peril may without injustice refuse to obey.

Knowing now what is the obedience necessary to salvation, and to whom it is due; we are to consider next concerning faith, whom, and why we believe; and what are the articles, or points necessary to be believed by them that shall be saved. And first, for the person whom we believe, because it is impossible to believe any person, before we know what he saith, it is necessary he be one that we have heard speak. The person, therefore, whom Abraham, Isaac, Jacob, Moses, and the prophets, believed, was God himself, that spake unto them supernaturally: and the person, whom the apostles and disciples that conversed with Christ believed, was our Saviour himself. But of them, to whom neither God the Father, nor our Saviour, ever spake, it cannot be said that the person whom they believed, was God. They believed the apostles, and after them the pastors and doctors of the Church, that recommended to their faith the history of the Old and New Testament: so that the faith of Christians ever since our Saviour's time, hath had for foundation, first, the reputation of their pastors, and afterward, the authority of those that made the Old and New Testament to be received for the rule of faith; which none could do but Christian sovereigns; who are therefore the supreme pastors, and the only persons whom Christians now hear speak from God; except such as God speaketh to in these days supernaturally. But because there be many false prophets *gone out into the world,* other men are to examine such spirits, as St. John adviseth us, (1st Epistle iv. 1) *whether they be of God, or not.* And therefore, seeing the examination of doctrines belongeth to the supreme pastor, the person, which all they that have no special revelation are to believe, is, in every commonwealth, the supreme pastor, that is to say, the civil sovereign.

The causes why men believe any Christian doctrine, are various. For faith is the gift of God; and he worketh it in each several man, by such ways as it seemeth good unto himself. The most ordinary immediate cause of our belief, concerning any point of Christian faith, is, that we believe the Bible to be the word of God. But why we believe the Bible to be the word of God, is much disputed, as all questions must needs be, that are not well stated. For they make not the question to be, *why we believe it,* but, *how we know it;* as if *believing* and *knowing* were all one. And thence while one side ground their knowledge upon the infallibility of the Church, and the other side, on the testimony of the private spirit, neither side concludeth what it pretends. For how shall a man know the infallibility of the Church, but by knowing first the infallibility of the Scripture? Or how shall a man know his own private spirit to be other than a belief, grounded upon the authority and arguments of his teachers, or upon a presumption of his own gifts? Besides, there is nothing in the Scripture, from which can be inferred the infallibility of the Church; much less, of any particular Church; and least of all, the infallibility of any particular man.

It is manifest therefore, that Christian men do not know, but only believe the Scripture to be the word of God; and that the means of making them believe, which God is pleased to afford men ordinarily, is according to the way of nature, that is to say, from their teachers. It is the doctrine of St. Paul concerning Christian faith in general (*Rom.* x. 17), *Faith cometh by hearing,* that is, by hearing our lawful pastors. He saith also (verses 14, 15, of the same chapter), *How shall they believe in him of whom they have not heard? and how shall they hear without a preacher? and how shall they preach, except they be sent?* Whereby it is evident, that the ordinary cause of believing that the Scriptures are the word of God, is the same with the cause of the believing of all other articles of our faith, namely, the hearing of those that are by the law allowed and appointed to teach us, as our parents in their houses, and our pastors in the churches. Which also is made more manifest by experience. For what other cause can there be assigned, why in Christian commonwealths all men either believe, or at least profess the Scripture to be the word of God, and in other commonwealths scarce any; but that in Christian commonwealths they are taught it from their infancy; and in other places they are taught otherwise?

But if teaching be the cause of faith, why do not all believe? It is certain therefore that faith is the gift of God, and he giveth it to whom he will. Nevertheless, because to them to whom he giveth it, he giveth it by the means of teachers, the immediate cause of faith is hearing. In a school, where many are taught, and some profit, others profit not, the cause of learning in them that profit, is the master; yet it cannot be thence inferred, that learning is not the gift of God. All good things proceed from God; yet cannot all that have them, say they are inspired; for that implies a gift supernatural, and the immediate hand of God; which he that pretends to, pretends to be a prophet, and is subject to the examination of the Church.

But whether men *know,* or *believe,* or *grant* the Scriptures to be the word of God; if out of such places of them, as are without obscurity, I shall show what articles of faith are necessary, and only necessary for salvation, those men must needs *know, believe,* or *grant* the same.

The *unum necessarium,* only article of faith, which the Scripture maketh simply necessary to salvation, is this, that *Jesus is the Christ.* By the name of *Christ* is understood the king, which God had before promised by the prophets of the Old Testament, to send into the world, to reign (over the Jews, and over such of other nations as should believe in him), under himself eternally; and to give them that eternal life, which was lost by the sin of Adam. . . .

Belief of this one article is sufficient faith to obtain remission of sins to the *penitent,* and consequently to bring them into the kingdom of heaven. . . .

Seeing then it is necessary that faith and obedience, implied in the word repentance, do both concur to our salvation; the question by which of the two we are justified, is impertinently disputed. Nevertheless, it will not be impertinent, to make manifest in what manner each of them contributes thereunto; and in what sense it is said, that we are to be justified by the one, and by the other. And first, if by righteousness be understood the justice of the works themselves, there is no man that can be saved; for there is none that hath not transgressed the law of God. And therefore when we are said to be justified by works, it is to be understood of the will, which God doth always accept for the work itself, as well in good, as in evil men. And in this sense only it is, that a man is called *just,* or *unjust;* and that his justice justifies him, that is, gives him the title, in God's acceptation, of *just;* and renders him capable of *living by his faith,* which before he was not. So that justice justifies in that sense, in which to *justify,* is the same as that to *denominate a man just;* and not in the signification of discharging the law; whereby the punishment of his sins should be unjust.

But a man is then also said to be justified, when his plea, though in itself insufficient, is accepted; as when we plead our will, our endeavor to fulfill the law, and repent us of our failings, and God accepteth it for the performance itself. And because God accepteth not the will for the deed, but only in the faithful; it is therefore faith that makes good our plea; and in this sense it is, that faith only justifies. So that *faith* and *obedience* are both necessary to salvation; yet in several senses each of them is said to justify.

Having thus shown what is necessary to salvation; it is not hard to reconcile our obedience to God, with our obedience to the civil sovereign; who is either Christian, or infidel. If he be a Christian, he alloweth the belief of this article, that *Jesus is the Christ;* and of all the articles that are contained in, or are by evident consequence deduced from it: which is all the faith necessary to salvation. And because he is a sovereign, he requireth obedience to all his own, that is, to all the civil laws; in which also are contained all the laws of nature, that is all the laws of God: for besides the laws of nature, and the laws of the Church, which are part of the civil law (for the Church that can make laws is the commonwealth), there be no other laws divine. Whosoever therefore obeyeth his Christian sovereign, is not thereby hindered, neither from believing, nor from obeying God. But suppose that a Christian king should from this foundation *Jesus is the Christ,* draw some false consequences, that is to say, make some superstructions of hay or stubble, and command the teaching of the same; yet seeing St. Paul says he shall be saved; much more shall he be saved, that teacheth them by his command; and much more yet, he that teaches not, but only believes his lawful teacher. And in case a subject be forbidden by the civil sovereign to profess some of those his opinions, upon what just ground can he disobey? Christian kings may err in deducing a consequence, but who shall judge? Shall a private man judge, when the question is of his own obedience? Or shall any man judge but he that is appointed thereto by the Church, that is, by the civil sovereign that representeth it? Or if the pope, or an apostle judge, may he not err in deducing of a consequence? Did not one of the two, St. Peter or St. Paul, err in a superstructure, when St. Paul withstood St. Peter to his face? There can therefore be no contradiction between the laws of God, and the laws of a Christian commonwealth.

And when the civil sovereign is an infidel, every one of his own subjects that resisteth him, sinneth against the laws of God (for such are the laws of nature), and rejecteth the counsel of the apostles, that admonisheth all Christians to obey their princes, and all children and servants to obey their parents and masters in all things. And for their *faith*, it is internal, and invisible; they have the license that Naaman had, and need not put themselves into danger for it. But if they do, they ought to expect their reward in heaven, and not complain of their lawful sovereign; much less make war upon him. For he that is not glad of any just occasion of martyrdom, has not the faith he professeth, but pretends it only, to set some color upon his own contumacy. But what infidel king is so unreasonable, as knowing he has a subject, that waiteth for the second coming of Christ, after the present world shall be burnt, and intendeth then to obey him (which is the intent of believing that Jesus is the Christ), and in the meantime thinketh himself bound to obey the laws of that infidel king (which all Christians are obliged in conscience to do), to put to death or to persecute such a subject?

And thus much shall suffice, concerning the kingdom of God, and policy ecclesiastical. Wherein I pretend not to advance any position of my own, but only to show what are the consequences that seem to me deducible from the principles of Christian politics (which are the Holy Scriptures), in confirmation of the power of civil sovereigns, and the duty of their subjects. And in the allegation of Scripture, I have endeavored to avoid such texts as are of obscure or controverted interpretation; and to allege none, but in such sense as is most plain, and agreeable to the harmony and scope of the whole Bible; which was written for the re-establishment of the kingdom of God in Christ. For it is not the bare words, but the scope of the writer, that giveth the true light, by which any writing is to be interpreted; and they that insist upon single texts, without considering the main design, can derive nothing from them clearly; but rather by casting atoms of Scripture, as dust before men's eyes, make everything more obscure than it is; an ordinary artifice of those that seek not the truth, but their own advantage. . . .

A REVIEW, AND CONCLUSION

FROM the contrariety of some of the natural faculties of the mind, one to another, as also of one passion to another, and from their reference to

conversation, there has been an argument taken, to infer an impossibility
that any one man should be sufficiently disposed to all sorts of civil
duty. The severity of judgment, they say, makes men censorious, and
unapt to pardon the errors and infirmities of other men: and on the
other side, celerity of fancy, makes the thoughts less steady than is necessary, to discern exactly between right and wrong. Again, in all deliberations, and in all pleadings, the faculty of solid reasoning is necessary:
for without it, the resolutions of men are rash, and their sentences unjust: and yet if there be not powerful eloquence, which procureth attention and consent, the effect of reason will be little. But these are contrary faculties; the former being grounded upon principles of truth; the
other upon the passions and interests of men, which are different, and
mutable.

And amongst the passions, *courage* (by which I mean the contempt
of wounds, and violent death) inclineth men to private revenges, and
sometimes to endeavor the unsettling of the public peace: and *timorousness,* many times disposeth to the desertion of the public defense. Both
these, they say, cannot stand together in the same person.

And to consider the contrariety of men's opinions, and manners, in
general, it is, they say, impossible to entertain a constant civil amity
with all those, with whom the business of the world constrains us to converse: which business consisteth almost in nothing else but a perpetual
contention for honor, riches, and authority.

To which I answer, that these are indeed great difficulties, but not im-
possibilities: for by education, and discipline, they may be, and are
sometimes reconciled. Judgment and fancy may have place in the same
man; but by turns; as the end which he aimeth at requireth. As the Israelites in Egypt, were sometimes fastened to their labor of making
bricks, and other times were ranging abroad to gather straw: so also
may the judgment sometimes be fixed upon one certain consideration,
and the fancy at another time wandering about the world. So also reason, and eloquence, though not perhaps in the natural sciences, yet, in
the moral, may stand very well together. For wheresoever there is place
for adorning and preferring of error, there is much more place for adorning and preferring of truth, if they have it to adorn. Nor is there any
repugnacy between fearing the laws, and not fearing a public enemy;
nor between abstaining from injury, and pardoning it in others. There is
therefore no such inconsistence of human nature, with civil duties, as
some think. I have known clearness of judgment, and largeness of fancy;
strength of reason, and graceful elocution; a courage for the war, and a
fear for the laws, and all eminently in one man; and that was my most
noble and honored friend, Mr. Sidney Godolphin; who hating no man,

nor hated of any, was unfortunately slain in the beginning of the late civil war, in the public quarrel, by an undiscerned and an undiscerning hand.

To the Laws of Nature, declared in Chapter XV, I would have this added, *that every man is bound by nature, as much as in him lieth, to protect in war the authority, by which he is himself protected in time of peace.* For he that pretendeth a right of nature to preserve his own body, cannot pretend a right of nature to destroy him, by whose strength he is preserved: it is a manifest contradiction of himself. And though this law may be drawn by consequence, from some of those that are there already mentioned; yet the times require to have it inculcated, and remembered.

And because I find by divers English books lately printed, that the civil wars have not yet sufficiently taught men in what point of time it is, that a subject becomes obliged to the conqueror; nor what is conquest; nor how it comes about, that it obliges men to obey his laws: therefore for further satisfaction of men therein, I say, the point of time, wherein a man becomes subject to a conqueror, is that point, wherein having liberty to submit to him, he consenteth, either by express words, or by other sufficient sign, to be his subject. When it is that a man hath the liberty to submit, I have showed before in the end of Chapter XXI; namely, that for him that hath no obligation to his former sovereign but that of an ordinary subject, it is then, when the means of his life are within the guards and garrisons of the enemy; for it is then, that he hath no longer protection from him, but is protected by the adverse party for his contribution. Seeing therefore such contribution is everywhere, as a thing inevitable, notwithstanding it be an assistance to the enemy, esteemed lawful; a total submission, which is but an assistance to the enemy, cannot be esteemed unlawful. Besides, if a man consider that they who submit, assist the enemy but with part of their estates, whereas they that refuse, assist him with the whole, there is no reason to call their submission, or composition, an assistance; but rather a detriment to the enemy. But if a man, besides the obligation of a subject, hath taken upon him a new obligation of a soldier, then he hath not the liberty to submit to a new power, as long as the old one keeps the field, and giveth him means of subsistence, either in his armies, or garrisons: for in this case, he cannot complain of want of protection, and means to live as a soldier. But when that also fails, a soldier also may seek his protection wheresoever he has most hope to have it; and may lawfully submit himself to his new master. And so much for the time when he may do it lawfully, if he will. If therefore he do it, he is undoubtedly bound to be a true subject: for a contract lawfully made, cannot lawfully be broken.

By this also a man may understand, when it is, that men may be said to be conquered; and in what the nature of conquest, and the right of a conqueror consisteth: for this submission in itself implieth them all. Conquest, is not the victory itself; but the acquisition, by victory, of a right over the persons of men. He therefore that is slain, is overcome, but not conquered: he that is taken, and put into prison, or chains, is not conquered, though overcome; for he is still an enemy, and may save himself if he can: but he that upon promise of obedience, hath his life and liberty allowed him, is then conquered, and a subject; and not before. The Romans used to say, that their general had *pacified* such a *province,* that is to say, in English, *conquered* it; and that the country was *pacified* by victory, when the people of it had promised *imperata facere,* that is *to do what the Roman people commanded them:* this was to be conquered. But this promise may be either express, or tacit: express, by promise: tacit, by other signs. As for example, a man that hath not been called to make such an express promise, because he is one whose power perhaps is not considerable; yet if he live under their protection openly, he is understood to submit himself to the government: but if he live there secretly, he is liable to anything that may be done to a spy, and enemy of the state. I say not, he does any injustice; for acts of open hostility bear not that name; but that he may be justly put to death. Likewise, if a man, when his country is conquered, be out of it, he is not conquered, nor subject: but if at his return, he submit to the government, he is bound to obey it. So that *conquest,* to define it, is the acquiring of the right of sovereignty by victory. Which right, is acquired in the people's submission, by which they contract with the victor, promising obedience, for life and liberty.

In Chapter XXIX, I have set down for one of the causes of the dissolution of commonwealths, their imperfect generation, consisting in the want of an absolute and arbitrary legislative power; for want whereof, the civil sovereign is fain to handle the sword of justice unconstantly, and as if it were too hot for him to hold. One reason whereof, which I have not there mentioned, is this, that they will all of them justify the war, by which their power was at first gotten, and whereon, as they think, their right dependeth, and not on the possession. As if, for example, the right of the kings of England did depend on the goodness of the cause of William the Conqueror, and upon their lineal, and directest descent from him; by which means, there would perhaps be no tie of the subjects' obedience to their sovereign at this day in all the world: wherein whilst they needlessly think to justify themselves, they justify all the successful rebellions that ambition shall at any time raise against them, and their successors. Therefore I put down for one of the most effectual seeds of the death of any state, that the conquerors require not only a submission of men's actions to them for the future, but also an approbation of all their actions past; when there is scarce a commonwealth in the world, whose beginnings can in conscience be justified.

And because the name of tyranny, signifieth nothing more, nor less, than the name of sovereignty, be it in one, or many men, saving that they that use the former word, are understood to be angry with them they call tyrants; I think the toleration of a professed hatred of tyranny, is a toleration of hatred to commonwealth in general, and another evil seed, not differing much from the former. For to the justification of the cause of a conqueror, the reproach of the cause of the conquered, is for the most part necessary: but neither of them is necessary for the obligation of the conquered. And thus much I have thought fit to say upon the review of the first and second part of this discourse.

In Chapter XXXV, I have sufficiently declared out of the Scripture, that in the commonwealth of the Jews, God himself was made the sovereign, by pact with the people; who were therefore called his *peculiar people,* to distinguish them from the rest of the world, over whom God reigned not by their consent, but by his own power: and that in this kingdom Moses was God's lieutenant on earth; and that it was he that told them what laws God appointed them to be ruled by. But I have omitted to set down who were the officers appointed to do execution; especially in capital punishments; not then thinking it a matter of so necessary consideration, as I find it since. We know that generally in all commonwealths, the execution of corporal punishments, was either put upon the guards, or other soldiers of the sovereign power; or given to those, in whom want of means, contempt of honor, and hardness of heart, concurred, to make them sue for such an office. But amongst the Israelites it was a positive law of God their sovereign, that he that was convicted of a capital crime, should be stoned to death by the people; and that the witnesses should cast the first stone, and after the witnesses, then the rest of the people. This was a law that designed who were to be the executioners; but not that anyone should throw a stone at him before conviction and sentence, where the congregation was judge. The witnesses were nevertheless to be heard before they proceeded to execution, unless the fact were committed in the presence of the congregation itself, or in sight of the lawful judges; for then there needed no other witnesses but the judges themselves. Nevertheless, this manner of proceeding being not thoroughly understood, hath given occasion to a dangerous opinion, that any man may kill another, in some cases, by a right of zeal; as if the executions done upon offenders in the kingdom of God in old time, proceeded not from the sovereign command, but from the authority of private zeal: which, if we consider the texts that seem to favor it, is quite contrary.

First, where the Levites fell upon the people, that had made and worshiped the Golden Calf, and slew three thousand of them; it was by the commandment of Moses, from the mouth of God; as is manifest (*Exod*. xxxii. 27). And when the son of a woman of Israel had blasphemed God, they that heard it, did not kill him, but brought him before Moses, who put him under custody, till God should give sentence against him; as appears (*Levit*. xxiv. 11, 12). Again, (*Numb*. xxv. 6, 7), when Phinehas killed Zimri and Cosbi, it was not by right of private zeal: their crime was committed in the sight of the assembly; there needed no witness; the law was known, and he the heir-apparent to the sovereignty; and, which is the principal point, the lawfulness of his act depended wholly upon a subsequent ratification by Moses, whereof he had no cause to doubt. And this presumption of a future ratification, is sometimes necessary to the safety of a commonwealth; as in a sudden rebellion, any man that can suppress it by his own power in the country where it begins, without express law or commission, may lawfully do it, and provide to have it ratified, or pardoned, whilst it is in doing, or after it is done. Also (*Numb*. xxxv. 30) it is expressly said, *Whosoever shall kill the murderer, shall kill him upon the word of witnesses:* but witnesses suppose a formal judicature, and consequently condemn that pretense of *jus zelotarum*. The law of Moses concerning him that enticeth to idolatry, that is to say, in the kingdom of God to a renouncing of his allegiance (*Deut*. xiii. 8, 9), forbids to conceal him, and commands the accuser to cause him to be put to death, and to cast the first stone at him; but not to kill him before he be condemned. And (*Deut*. xvii. 4, 5, 6, 7), the process against idolatry is exactly set down: for God there speaketh to the people, as judge, and commandeth them, when a man is accused of idolatry, to inquire diligently of the fact, and finding it true, then to stone him; but still the hand of the witness throweth the first stone. This is not private zeal, but public condemnation. In like manner when a father hath a rebellious son, the law is (*Deut*. xxi. 18-21), that he shall bring him before the judges of the town, and all the people of the town shall stone him. Lastly, by pretense of these laws it was, that St. Stephen was stoned, and not by pretense of private zeal: for before he was carried away to execution, he had pleaded his cause before the high-priest. There is nothing in all this, nor in any other part of the Bible, to countenance executions by private zeal; which being oftentimes but a conjunction of ignorance and passion, is against the justice and peace of a commonwealth.

In Chapter xxxvi, I have said, that it is not declared in what manner God spake supernaturally to Moses: nor that he spake not to him sometimes by dreams and visions, and by a supernatural voice, as to other prophets: for the manner how he spake unto him from the mercy-seat, is expressly set down (*Numbers* vii. 89) in these words, *From that time forward, when Moses entered into the Tabernacle of the congregation to speak with God, he heard a voice which spake unto him from over the mercy-seat, which is over the Ark of the testimony; from between the cherubims he spake unto him*. But it is not declared in what consisteth the pre-eminence of the manner of God's speaking to Moses, above that of his speaking to other prophets, as to Samuel, and to Abraham, to whom he also spake by a voice (that is, by vision), unless the difference consist in the clearness of the vision. For *face to face*, and *mouth to mouth*, cannot be literally understood of the infiniteness, and incomprehensibility of the Divine nature.

And as to the whole doctrine, I see not yet, but the principles of it are true and proper; and the ratiocination solid. For I ground the civil rights of sovereigns, and both the duty and liberty of subjects, upon the known natural inclinations of mankind, and upon the articles of the law of nature; of which no man, that pretends but reason enough to govern his private family, ought to be ignorant. And for the power ecclesiastical of the same sovereigns, I ground it on such texts, as are both evident in themselves, and consonant to the scope of the whole Scripture. And therefore am persuaded, that he that shall read it with a purpose only to be informed, shall be informed by it. But for those that by writing, or public discourse, or by their eminent actions, have already engaged themselves to the maintaining of contrary opinions, they will not be so easily satisfied. For in such cases, it is natural for men, at one and the same time, both to proceed in reading, and to lose their attention, in the search of objections to that they had read before. Of which in a time wherein the interests of men are changed, (seeing much of that doctrine, which serveth to the establishing of a new government, must needs be contrary to that which conduced to the dissolution of the old), there cannot choose but be very many.

In that part which treateth of a Christian commonwealth, there are some new doctrines, which, it may be, in a state where the contrary were already fully determined, were a fault for a subject without leave to divulge, as being an usurpation of the place of a teacher. But in this time, that men call not only for peace, but also for truth, to offer such doctrines as I think true, and that manifestly tend to peace and loyalty, to the consideration of those that are yet in deliberation, is no more, but to offer new wine, to be put into new casks, that both may be preserved together. And I suppose, that then, when novelty can breed no trouble nor disorder in a state, men are not generally so much inclined to the reverence of antiquity, as to prefer ancient errors, before new and well-proved truth.

There is nothing I distrust more than my elocution, which nevertheless I am confident, excepting the mischances of the press, is not obscure. That I have neglected the ornament of quoting ancient poets,
orators, and philosophers, contrary to the custom of late time, whether I
have done well or ill in it, proceedeth from my judgment, grounded on
many reasons. For first, all truth of doctrine dependeth either upon *reason,* or upon *Scripture;* both which give credit to many, but never receive it from any writer. Secondly, the matters in question are not of
fact, but of *right,* wherein there is no place for *witnesses.* There is scarce
any of those old writers, that contradicteth not sometimes both himself
and others; which makes their testimonies insufficient. Fourthly, such
opinions as are taken only upon credit of antiquity, are not intrinsically
the judgment of those that cite them, but words that pass, like gaping,
from mouth to mouth. Fifthly, it is many times with a fraudulent design that men stick their corrupt doctrine with the cloves of other men's
wit. Sixthly, I find not that the ancients they cite, took it for an ornament, to do the like with those that wrote before them. Seventhly, it is
an argument of indigestion, when Greek and Latin sentences unchewed
come up again, as they use to do, unchanged. Lastly, though I reverence
those men of ancient time, that either have written truth perspicuously,
or set us in a better way to find it out ourselves; yet to the antiquity itself I think nothing due. For if we will reverence the age, the present is
the oldest. If the antiquity of the writer, I am not sure, that generally
they to whom such honor is given, were more ancient when they wrote,
than I am that am writing. But if it be well considered, the praise of ancient authors, proceeds not from the reverence of the dead, but from the
competition, and mutual envy of the living.

To conclude, there is nothing in this whole discourse, nor in that I
writ before of the same subject in Latin, as far as I can perceive, contrary either to the Word of God, or to good manners; or to the disturbance of the public tranquillity. Therefore I think it may be profitably
printed, and more profitably taught in the Universities, in case they also
think so, to whom the judgment of the same belongeth. For seeing the
Universities are the fountains of civil and moral doctrine, from whence
the preachers, and the gentry, drawing such water as they find, use to
sprinkle the same (both from the pulpit and in their conversation), upon
the people, there ought certainly to be great care taken, to have it pure,
both from the venom of heathen politicians, and from the incantation of
deceiving spirits. And by that means the most men, knowing their duties, will be the less subject to serve the ambition of a few discontented
persons, in their purposes against the state; and be the less grieved with
the contributions necessary for their peace, and defense; and the gover-

nors themselves have the less cause, to maintain at the common charge any greater army, than is necessary to make good the public liberty, against the invasions and encroachments of foreign enemies.

And thus I have brought to an end my discourse of civil and ecclesiastical government, occasioned by the disorders of the present time, without partiality, without application, and without other design than to set before men's eyes the mutual relation between protection and obedience; of which the condition of human nature, and the laws divine, both natural and positive, require an inviolable observation. And though in the revolution of states, there can be no very good constellation for truths of this nature to be born under (as having an angry aspect from the dissolvers of an old government, and seeing but the backs of them that erect a new), yet I cannot think it will be condemned at this time, either by the public judge of doctrine, or by any that desires the continuance of public peace. And in this hope I return to my interrupted speculation of bodies natural; wherein, if God give me health to finish it, I hope the novelty will as much please, as in the doctrine of this artificial body it useth to offend. For such truth, as opposeth no man's profit, nor pleasure, is to all men welcome.

JOHN LOCKE

An Essay
Concerning Human Understanding

An Essay
Concerning the True Original,
Extent, and End of Civil Government

JOHN LOCKE

John Locke (1632-1704) was the son of a country attorney. He grew up amid the disorders of the Civil War and entered Christ Church, Oxford, in 1652, where he remained as student and fellow for many years. Locke, like Bacon and Hobbes before him, greatly disliked the scholastic fare offered at the universities. From the reading of Descartes, who exercised a profound influence upon his subsequent intellectual development, Locke acquired a strong interest in contemporary philosophical and scientific questions. These interests brought him into contact with distinguished scientists such as Boyle and Sydenham. In 1668 he was elected a fellow of the Royal Society. It was during this time also that Locke's views on politics and religion were formed. He came to the opinion that the only basis for a permanent settlement of the violent quarrels of the time was a Protestant monarchy checked and controlled by the parliament, and a broad and comprehensive church establishment which would embrace a majority of the dissenting sects.

In 1666 an accidental meeting with Lord Ashley, later the first Earl of Shaftesbury, led to a lifelong friendship and association which changed the whole course of Locke's career. He became Ashley's secretary and confidential advisor, and held a number of governmental posts while his patron was in office. But in 1675 Locke was forced, because of failing health, to leave his employment and reside for nearly four years in France, where he spent his time chiefly in study and writing. On his return to England, he once more entered Shaftesbury's service. Four years later Shaftesbury, who had espoused the cause of the pretender Monmouth, was forced to flee to Holland, where Locke, shortly after, followed him. Here he remained until the Glorious Revolution of 1688.

On his return to England Locke issued in rapid succession a number of works, the fruit of years of meditation. The chief of these were his three *Letters on Toleration,* the *Two Treatises of Government* and the *Essay Concerning Human Understanding.* All were immediately successful and exerted a vast influence. Taken together they expressed a point of view that was to dominate English thought through the greater part of the eighteenth century. Locke spent a serene old age in the country household at Oates of his intimate friends Sir Francis and Lady Masham. His last years were occupied in revising successive editions of the *Essay,* replying to his critics, and writing a number of other works on economic, philosophical, and religious topics.

The works published herewith comprise selections from the second and fourth books of the *Essay Concerning Human Understanding* and the second *Treatise of Government* entire.

AN ESSAY CONCERNING
HUMAN UNDERSTANDING

The Epistle to the Reader

READER:

I HERE put into thy hands what has been the diversion of some of my idle and heavy hours; if it has the good luck to prove so of any of thine, and thou hast but half so much pleasure in reading as I had in writing it, thou wilt as little think thy money, as I do my pains, ill bestowed. Mistake not this for a commendation of my work; nor conclude, because I was pleased with the doing of it, that therefore I am fondly taken with it now it is done. He that hawks at larks and sparrows, has no less sport, though a much less considerable quarry, than he that flies at nobler game: and he is little acquainted with the subject of this treatise, the Understanding, who does not know, that as it is the most elevated faculty of the soul, so it is employed with a greater and more constant delight than any of the other. Its searches after truth are a sort of hawking and hunting, wherein the very pursuit makes a great part of the pleasure. Every step the mind takes in its progress towards knowledge makes some discovery, which is not only new, but the best, too, for the time at least.

For the understanding, like the eye, judging of objects only by its own sight, cannot but be pleased with what it discovers, having less regret for what has escaped it, because it is unknown. Thus he who has raised himself above the alms-basket, and not content to live lazily on scraps of begged opinions, sets his own thoughts on work, to find and follow truth, will (whatever he lights on) not miss the hunter's satisfaction: every moment of his pursuit will reward his pains with some delight, and he will have reason to think his time not ill spent, even when he cannot much boast of any great acquisition.

This, reader, is the entertainment of those who let loose their own thoughts, and follow them in writing; which thou oughtest not to envy them, since they afford thee an opportunity of the like diversion, if thou wilt make use of thy own thoughts in reading. It is to them, if they are thy own, that I refer myself; but if they are taken upon trust from others, it is no great matter what they are, they not following truth, but some meaner consideration; and it is not worth while to be concerned what he says or thinks, who says or thinks only as he is directed by another. If thou judgest for thyself, I know thou wilt judge candidly; and then I shall not be harmed or offended, whatever be the censure. For, though it be certain that there is nothing in this treatise of the truth whereof I am not fully persuaded, yet I consider myself as liable to mistakes as I can think thee; and know that this book must stand or fall with thee, not by any opinion I have of it, but thy own. If thou findest little in it new or instructive to thee, thou art not to blame me for it. It was not meant for those that had already mastered this subject, and made a thorough acquaintance with their own understandings, but for my own information, and the satisfaction of a few friends, who acknowledged themselves not to have sufficiently considered it.

Were it fit to trouble thee with the history of this *Essay*, I should tell thee, that five or six friends, meeting at my chamber, and discoursing on a subject very remote from this, found themselves quickly at a stand by the difficulties that rose on every side. After we had awhile puzzled ourselves, without coming any nearer a resolution of those doubts which perplexed us, it came into my thoughts that we took a wrong course; and that, before we set ourselves upon inquiries of that nature, it was necessary to examine our own abilities, and see what *objects* our understandings were, or were not, fitted to deal with. This I proposed to the company, who all readily assented; and thereupon it was agreed that this should be our first inquiry. Some hasty and undigested thoughts, on a subject I had never before considered, which I set down against our next meeting, gave the first entrance into this Discourse, which, having been thus begun by chance, was continued by entreaty; written by incoherent parcels; and, after long intervals of neglect, resumed again, as my humor or occasions permitted; and at last, in a retirement, where an attendance on my health gave me leisure, it was brought into that order thou now seest it.

This discontinued way of writing may have occasioned, besides others, two contrary faults, viz., that too little and too much may be said in it. If thou findest anything wanting, I shall be glad that what I have writ gives thee any desire that I should have gone further: if it seems too much to thee, thou must blame the subject; for when I put pen to paper, I thought all I should have to say on this matter would have been contained in one sheet of paper; but the further I went, the larger prospect I had: new discoveries led me still on, and so it grew insensibly to the bulk it now appears in. I will not deny but possibly it might be reduced to a narrower compass than it is; and that some parts of it might be contracted; the way it has been writ in, by catches, and many long

intervals of interruption, being apt to cause some repetitions. But, to
confess the truth, I am now too lazy, or too busy, to make it shorter.

I am not ignorant how little I herein consult my own reputation when
I knowingly let it go with a fault so apt to disgust the most judicious,
who are always the nicest readers. But they who know sloth is apt to
content itself with any excuse, will pardon me if mine has prevailed on
me where I think I have a very good one. I will not, therefore, allege in
my defense that the same motion, having different respects, may be convenient or necessary to prove or illustrate several parts of the same discourse; and that so it has happened in many parts of this; but, waiving
that, I shall frankly avow that I have sometimes dwelt long upon the
same argument, and expressed it different ways, with a quite different
design. I pretend not to publish this *Essay* for the information of men of
large thoughts and quick apprehensions; to such masters of knowledge I
profess myself a scholar, and therefore warn them beforehand not to expect anything here but what, being spun out of my own coarse thoughts,
is fitted to men of my own size, to whom, perhaps, it will not be unacceptable that I have taken some pains to make plain and familiar to
their thoughts some truths, which established prejudice, or the abstractedness of the ideas themselves, might render difficult. Some objects had
need be turned on every side; and when the notion is new, as I confess
some of these are to me, or out of the ordinary road, as I suspect they
will appear to others, it is not one simple view of it that will gain it admittance into every understanding, or fix it there with a clear and lasting impression. There are few, I believe, who have not observed in themselves or others, that what in one way of proposing was very obscure,
another way of expressing it has made very clear and intelligible;
though afterward the mind found little difference in the phrases, and
wondered why one failed to be understood more than the other. But
everything does not hit alike upon every man's imagination. We have
our understandings no less different than our palates; and he that thinks
the same truth shall be equally relished by everyone in the same dress,
may as well hope to feast everyone with the same sort of cookery; the
meat may be the same, and the nourishment good, yet everyone not be
able to receive it with that seasoning; and it must be dressed another
way, if you will have it go down with some even of strong constitutions.
The truth is, those who advised me to publish it, advised me, for this
reason, to publish it as it is; and since I have been brought to let it go
abroad, I desire it should be understood by whoever gives himself the
pains to read it. I have so little affection to be in print, that if I were
not flattered this *Essay* might be of some use to others, as I think it has
been to me, I should have confined it to the view of some friends, who
gave the first occasion to it. My appearing therefore in print being on

purpose to be as useful as I may, I think it necessary to make what I have to say as easy and intelligible to all sorts of readers as I can. And I had much rather the speculative and quick-sighted should complain of my being in some parts tedious, than that anyone, not accustomed to abstract speculations, or prepossessed with different notions, should mistake or not comprehend my meaning.

It will possibly be censured as a great piece of vanity or insolence in me, to pretend to instruct this our knowing age, it amounting to little less when I own that I publish this *Essay* with hopes that it may be useful to others. But if it may be permitted to speak freely of those who, with a feigned modesty, condemn as useless what they themselves write, methinks it savors much more of vanity or insolence to publish a book for any other end; and he fails very much of that respect he owes the public, who prints, and consequently expects that men should read, that wherein he intends not they should meet with anything of use to themselves or others: and should nothing else be found allowable in this treatise, yet my design will not cease to be so; and the goodness of my intention ought to be some excuse for the worthlessness of my present. It is that chiefly which secures me from the fear of censure, which I expect not to escape more than better writers. Men's principles, notions, and relishes are so different, that it is hard to find a book which pleases or displeases all men. I acknowledge the age we live in is not the least knowing, and therefore not the most easy to be satisfied. If I have not the good luck to please, yet nobody ought to be offended with me. I plainly tell all my readers, except half a dozen, this treatise was not at first intended for them; and therefore they need not be at the trouble to be of that number. But yet if anyone thinks fit to be angry, and rail at it, he may do it securely; for I shall find some better way of spending my time than in such kind of conversation. I shall always have the satisfaction to have aimed sincerely at truth and usefulness, though in one of the meanest ways. The commonwealth of learning is not at this time without master-builders, whose mighty designs in advancing the sciences will leave lasting monuments to the admiration of posterity: but everyone must not hope to be a Boyle or a Sydenham; and in an age that produces such masters as the great Huygenius, and the incomparable Mr. Newton, with some other of that strain, it is ambition enough to be employed as an under-laborer in clearing the ground a little, and removing some of the rubbish that lies in the way to knowledge; which certainly had been very much more advanced in the world, if the endeavors of ingenious and industrious men had not been much cumbered with the learned but frivolous use of uncouth, affected, or unintelligible terms introduced into the sciences, and there made an art of, to that degree that philosophy, which is nothing but the true knowledge of things, was thought unfit or uncapable to be brought into well-bred company and polite conversation. Vague and insignificant forms of speech, and abuse of language, have so long passed for mysteries of science; and hard or misapplied words, with little or no meaning, have, by prescription, such a right to be mistaken for deep learning and height of speculation; that it will not be easy to persuade either those who speak or those who hear them, that they are but the covers of ignorance, and hindrance of true knowledge. To break in 'ipon the sanctuary of vanity and ignorance will be, I suppose, some service to human understanding: though so few are apt to think they deceive or are deceived in the use of words, or that the language of the sect they are of has any faults in it which ought to be examined or corrected, that I hope I shall be pardoned if I have in the third book dwelt long on this subject; and endeavored to make it so plain, that neither the inveterateness of the mischief, nor the prevalency of the fashion, shall be any excuse for those who will not take care about the meaning of their own words, and will not suffer the significancy of their expressions to be inquired into. . . .

[The booksellers preparing for the Fourth Edition[1] of my *Essay,* gave me notice of it, that I might, if I had leisure, make any additions or alterations I should think fit. Whereupon I thought it convenient to advertise the reader, that besides several corrections I had made here and there, there was one alteration which it was necessary to mention, because it ran through the whole book, and is of consequence to be rightly understood. What I thereupon said was this:—

Clear and *distinct ideas* are terms which, though familiar and frequent in men's mouths, I have reason to think everyone who uses does not perfectly understand. And possibly 'tis but here and there one who gives himself the trouble to consider them so far as to know what he himself or others precisely mean by them. I have therefore in most places chose to put *determinate* or *determined,* instead of *clear* and *distinct,* as more likely to direct men's thoughts to my meaning in this matter. By those denominations, I mean some object in the mind, and consequently determined, i.e. such as it is there seen and perceived to be. This, I think, may fitly be called a determinate or determined idea, when such as it is at any time objectively in the mind and so determined there, it is annexed, and without variation determined, to a name or articulate sound, which is to be steadily the sign of that very same object of the mind, or determinate idea.

To explain this a little more particularly. By *determinate,* when applied to a simple idea, I mean that simple appearance which the mind has in its view, or perceives in itself, when that idea is said to be in it;

---

[1] Passages in brackets indicate changes made by Locke in the second, third and fourth editions of the *Essay.—Editor.*

by *determined,* when applied to a complex idea, I mean such an one as consists of a determinate number of certain simple or less complex ideas, joined in such a proportion and situation as the mind has before its view, and sees in itself, when that idea is present in it, or should be present in it, when a man gives a name to it. I say *should* be, because it is not everyone, nor perhaps anyone, who is so careful of his language as to use no word till he views in his mind the precise determined idea which he resolves to make it the sign of. The want of this is the cause of no small obscurity and confusion in men's thoughts and discourses. . . .]

INTRODUCTION

1. *An inquiry into the understanding, pleasant and useful.*—Since it is the *understanding* that sets man above the rest of sensible beings, and gives him all the advantage and dominion which he has over them, it is certainly a subject, even for its nobleness, worth our labor to inquire into. The understanding, like the eye, whilst it makes us see and perceive all other things, takes no notice of itself; and it requires art and pains to set it at a distance, and make it its own object. But whatever be the difficulties that lie in the way of this inquiry, whatever it be that keeps us so much in the dark to ourselves, sure I am that all the light we can let in upon our own minds, all the acquaintance we can make with our own understandings, will not only be very pleasant, but bring us great advantage in directing our thoughts in the search of other things.

2. *Design.*—This, therefore, being my purpose, to inquire into the original, certainty, and extent of *human knowledge,* together with the grounds and degrees of *belief, opinion,* and *assent,* I shall not at present meddle with the physical consideration of the mind, or trouble myself to examine wherein its essence consists or by what motions of our spirits, or alteration of our bodies, we come to have any sensation by our organs, or any *ideas* in our understandings; and whether those ideas do, in their formation, any or all of them, depend on matter or not. These are speculations which, however curious and entertaining, I shall decline, as lying out of my way in the design I am now upon. It shall suffice to my present purpose, to consider the discerning faculties of a man, as they are employed about the objects which they have to do with. And I shall imagine I have not wholly misemployed myself in the thoughts I shall have on this occasion, if, in this historical, plain method, I can give any account of the ways whereby our understandings come to attain those notions of things we have, and can set down any measures of the certainty of our knowledge, or the grounds of those persuasions which are to be found amongst men, so various, different, and wholly contradictory; and yet asserted somewhere or other with such assurance and confidence, that he that shall take a view of the opinions of mankind, observe their opposition, and at the same time consider the fondness and devotion wherewith they are embraced, the resolution and eagerness wherewith they are maintained, may perhaps have reason to suspect that either there is no such thing as truth at all, or that mankind hath no sufficient means to attain a certain knowledge of it.

3. *Method.*—It is therefore worth while to search out the bounds between opinion and knowledge, and examine by what measures, in things whereof we have no certain knowledge, we ought to regulate our assent, and moderate our persuasions. In order whereunto, I shall pursue this following method:—

First, I shall inquire into the original of those *ideas*, notions, or whatever else you please to call them, which a man observes, and is conscious to himself he has in his mind; and the ways whereby the understanding comes to be furnished with them.

Secondly, I shall endeavor to show what *knowledge* the understanding hath by those ideas, and the certainty, evidence, and extent of it.

Thirdly, I shall make some inquiry into the nature and grounds of *faith* or *opinion;* whereby I mean, that assent which we give to any proposition as true, of whose truth yet we have no certain knowledge: and here we shall have occasion to examine the reasons and degrees of assent.

4. *Useful to know the extent of our comprehension.*—If by this inquiry into the nature of the understanding, I can discover the powers thereof, how far they reach, to what things they are in any degree proportionate, and where they fail us, I suppose it may be of use to prevail with the busy mind of man to be more cautious in meddling with things exceeding its comprehension, to stop when it is at the utmost extent of its tether, and to sit down in a quiet ignorance of those things which, upon examination, are found to be beyond the reach of our capacities. We should not then, perhaps, be so forward, out of an affectation of an universal knowledge, to raise questions, and perplex ourselves and others with disputes, about things to which our understandings are not suited, and of which we cannot frame in our minds any clear or distinct perceptions, or whereof (as it has, perhaps, too often happened) we have not any notions at all. If we can find out how far the understanding can extend its view, how far it has faculties to attain certainty, and in what cases it can only judge and guess, we may learn to content ourselves with what is attainable by us in this state.

5. *Our capacity suited to our state and concerns.*—For though the comprehension of our understandings comes exceeding short of the vast extent of things, yet we shall have cause enough to magnify the bountiful Author of our being for that proportion and degree of knowledge He has bestowed on us, so far above all the rest of the inhabitants of this our mansion. Men have reason to be well satisfied with what God hath thought fit for them, since He has given them, as St. Peter says, πάντα πρὸς ζωὴν καὶ εὐσέβειαν, whatsoever is necessary for the conveniences of life, and information of virtue; and has put within the reach of their discovery, the comfortable provision for this life and the way that leads

to a better. How short soever their knowledge may come of an universal or perfect comprehension of whatsoever is, it yet secures their great concernments that they have light enough to lead them to the knowledge of their Maker, and the sight of their own duties. Men may find matter sufficient to busy their heads and employ their hands with variety, delight, and satisfaction, if they will not boldly quarrel with their own constitution, and throw away the blessings their hands are filled with, because they are not big enough to grasp everything. We shall not have much reason to complain of the narrowness of our minds, if we will but employ them about what may be of use to us; for of that they are very capable: and it will be an unpardonable as well as childish peevishness, if we undervalue the advantages of our knowledge, and neglect to improve it to the ends for which it was given us, because there are some things that are set out of the reach of it. It will be no excuse to an idle and untoward servant, who would not attend his business by candlelight, to plead that he had not broad sunshine. The candle that is set up in us shines bright enough for all our purposes. The discoveries we can make with this ought to satisfy us; and we shall then use our understandings right, when we entertain all objects in that way and proportion that they are suited to our faculties, and upon those grounds they are capable of being proposed to us; and not peremptorily or intemperately require demonstration, and demand certainty, where probability only is to be had, and which is sufficient to govern all our concernments. If we will disbelieve everything because we cannot certainly know all things, we shall do much-what as wisely as he who would not use his legs, but sit still and perish because he had no wings to fly.

6. *Knowledge of our capacity a cure of scepticism and idleness.*— When we know our own strength, we shall the better know what to undertake with hopes of success; and when we have well surveyed the *powers* of our own minds, and made some estimate what we may expect from them, we shall not be inclined either to sit still, and not set our thoughts on work at all, in despair of knowing anything; nor, on the other side, question everything, and disclaim all knowledge, because some things are not to be understood. It is of great use to the sailor to know the length of his line, though he cannot with it fathom all the depths of the ocean; it is well he knows that it is long enough to reach the bottom at such places as are necessary to direct his voyage, and caution him against running upon shoals that may ruin him. Our business here is not to know all things, but those which concern our conduct. If we can find out those measures whereby a rational creature, put in that state which man is in in this world, may and ought to govern his opinions and actions depending thereon, we need not be troubled that some other things escape our knowledge.

7. *Occasion of this Essay.*—This was that which gave the first rise to this Essay concerning the Understanding. For I thought that the first step towards satisfying several inquiries the mind of man was very apt to run into, was, to take a survey of our own understandings, examine our own powers, and see to what things they were adapted. Till that was done, I suspected we began at the wrong end, and in vain sought for satisfaction in a quiet and sure possession of truths that most concerned us, whilst we let loose our thoughts into the vast ocean of being; as if all that boundless extent were the natural and undoubted possession of our understandings, wherein there was nothing exempt from its decisions, or that escaped its comprehension. Thus men, extending their inquiries beyond their capacities, and letting their thoughts wander into those depths where they can find no sure footing, it is no wonder that they raise questions and multiply disputes, which, never coming to any clear resolution, are proper only to continue and increase their doubts, and to confirm them at last in perfect scepticism. Whereas, were the capacities of our understandings well considered, the extent of our knowledge once discovered, and the horizon found which sets the bounds between the enlightened and dark parts of things—between what is and what is not comprehensible by us—men would, perhaps with less scruple, acquiesce in the avowed ignorance of the one, and employ their thoughts and discourse with more advantage and satisfaction in the other.

8. *What 'idea' stands for.*—Thus much I thought necessary to say concerning the occasion of this inquiry into human understanding. But, before I proceed on to what I have thought on this subject, I must here, in the entrance, beg pardon of my reader for the frequent use of the word 'idea' which he will find in the following treatise. It being that term which, I think, serves best to stand for whatsoever is the *object* of the understanding when a man thinks, I have used it to express whatever is meant by phantasm, notion, species, or whatever it is which the mind can be employed about in thinking; and I could not avoid frequently using it.

I presume it will be easily granted me, that there are such *ideas* in men's minds. Everyone is conscious of them in himself; and men's words and actions will satisfy him that they are in others.

Our first inquiry, then, shall be, how they come into the mind. . . .[2]

---

[2] In Book I of the *Essay*, entitled "Neither Principles Nor Ideas Are Innate," Locke seeks to refute the theory, which he believes to be commonly accepted in his time, "that there are in the understanding certain innate principles; . . . as it were stamped upon the mind of man; which the soul receives in its very first being, and brings into the world with it." The appeal to such principles he considers to be the root of dogmatism and the chief obstacle to the progress of knowledge.—*Editor.*

BOOK II: OF IDEAS

CHAPTER I

OF IDEAS IN GENERAL, AND THEIR ORIGINAL

1. *Idea is the object of thinking.*—Every man being conscious to himself that he thinks, and that which his mind is applied about whilst thinking being the ideas that are there, it is past doubt that men have in their mind several ideas, such as are those expressed by the words whiteness, hardness, sweetness, thinking, motion, man, elephant, army, drunkenness, and others: it is in the first place then to be inquired, How he comes by them? I know it is a received doctrine, that men have native ideas and original characters stamped upon their minds in their very first being. This opinion I have at large examined already; and, I suppose, what I have said in the foregoing book will be much more easily admitted, when I have shown whence the understanding may get all the ideas it has, and by what ways and degrees they may come into the mind; for which I shall appeal to everyone's own observation and experience.

2. *All ideas come from sensation or reflection.*—Let us then suppose the mind to be, as we say, white paper, void of all characters, without any ideas; how comes it to be furnished? Whence comes it by that vast store, which the busy and boundless fancy of man has painted on it with an almost endless variety? Whence has it all the materials of reason and knowledge? To this I answer, in one word, from experience. In that all our knowledge is founded, and from that it ultimately derives itself. Our observation, employed either about external sensible objects, or about the internal operations of our minds, perceived and reflected on by ourselves, is that which supplies our understandings with all the materials of thinking. These two are the fountains of knowledge, from whence all the ideas we have, or can naturally have, do spring.

3. *The object of sensation one source of ideas.*—First, our senses, conversant about particular sensible objects, do convey into the mind several distinct perceptions of things, according to those various ways wherein those objects do affect them; and thus we come by those ideas we have of yellow, white, heat, cold, soft, hard, bitter, sweet, and all those which we call sensible qualities; which when I say the senses convey into the mind, I mean, they from external objects convey into the

mind what produces there those perceptions. This great source of most of the ideas we have, depending wholly upon our senses, and derived by them to the understanding, I call *sensation.*

4. *The operations of our minds the other source of them.*—Secondly, the other fountain, from which experience furnisheth the understanding with ideas, is the perception of the operations of our own mind within us, as it is employed about the ideas it has got; which operations when the soul comes to reflect on and consider, do furnish the understanding with another set of ideas which could not be had from things without; and such are perception, thinking, doubting, believing, reasoning, knowing, willing, and all the different actings of our own minds; which we, being conscious of, and observing in ourselves, do from these receive into our understandings as distinct ideas, as we do from bodies affecting our senses. This source of ideas every man has wholly in himself; and though it be not sense as having nothing to do with external objects, yet it is very like it, and might properly enough be called *internal sense.* But as I call the other sensation, so I call this *reflection,* the ideas it affords being such only as the mind gets by reflecting on its own operations within itself. By reflection, then, in the following part of this discourse, I would be understood to mean that notice which the mind takes of its own operations, and the manner of them, by reason whereof there come to be ideas of these operations in the understanding. These two, I say, viz., external material things as the object of sensation, and the operations of our own minds within as the objects of reflection, are, to me, the only originals from whence all our ideas take their beginnings. The term *operations* here, I use in a large sense, as comprehending not barely the actions of the mind about its ideas, but some sort of passions arising sometimes from them, such as is the satisfaction or uneasiness arising from any thought.

5. *All our ideas are of the one or the other of these.*—The understanding seems to me not to have the least glimmering of any ideas which it doth not receive from one of these two. *External objects* furnish the mind with the ideas of sensible qualities, which are all those different perceptions they produce in us; and *the mind* furnishes the understanding with ideas of its own operations.

These, when we have taken a full survey of them, and their several modes, [combinations, and relations,] we shall find to contain all our whole stock of ideas; and that we have nothing in our minds which did not come in one of these two ways. Let anyone examine his own thoughts, and thoroughly search into his understanding, and then let him tell me, whether all the original ideas he has there, are any other than of the objects of his senses, or of the operations of his mind considered as objects of his reflection; and how great a mass of knowledge soever he imagines to be lodged there, he will, upon taking a strict view, see that he has not any idea in his mind but what one of these two have imprinted, though perhaps with infinite variety compounded and enlarged by the understanding, as we shall see hereafter.

6. *Observable in children.*—He that attentively considers the state of a child at his first coming into the world, will have little reason to think him stored with plenty of ideas that are to be the matter of his future knowledge. It is by degrees he comes to be furnished with them; and though the ideas of obvious and familiar qualities imprint themselves before the memory begins to keep a register of time or order, yet it is often so late before some unusual qualities come in the way, that there are few men that cannot recollect the beginning of their acquaintance with them: and, if it were worth while, no doubt a child might be so ordered as to have but a very few even of the ordinary ideas till he were grown up to a man. But all that are born into the world being surrounded with bodies that perpetually and diversely affect them, variety of ideas, whether care be taken about it or not, are imprinted on the minds of children. Light and colors are busy at hand everywhere when the eye is but open; sounds and some tangible qualities fail not to solicit their proper senses, and force an entrance to the mind; but yet I think it will be granted easily, that if a child were kept in a place where he never saw any other but black and white till he were a man, he would have no more ideas of scarlet or green than he that from his childhood never tasted an oyster or a pineapple has of those particular relishes.

7. *Men are differently furnished with these according to the different objects they converse with.*—Men then come to be furnished with fewer or more simple ideas from without, according as the objects they converse with afford greater or less variety; and from the operations of their minds within, according as they more or less reflect on them. For, though he that contemplates the operations of his mind cannot but have plain and clear ideas of them; yet, unless he turn his thoughts that way, and considers them attentively, he will no more have clear and distinct ideas of all the operations of his mind, and all that may be observed therein, than he will have all the particular ideas of any landscape, or of the parts and motions of a clock, who will not turn his eyes to it, and with attention heed all the parts of it. The picture or clock may be so placed, that they may come in his way every day; but yet he will have but a confused idea of all the parts they are made of, till he applies himself with attention to consider them each in particular.

8. *Ideas of reflection later, because they need attention.*—And hence we see the reason why it is pretty late before most children get ideas of the operations of their own minds; and some have not any very clear or perfect ideas of the greatest part of them all their lives: because, though

they pass there continually, yet like floating visions, they make not deep impressions enough to leave in the mind, clear, distinct, lasting ideas, till the understanding turns inwards upon itself, reflects on its own operations, and makes them the objects of its own contemplation. Children, when they come first into it, are surrounded with a world of new things, which, by a constant solicitation of their senses, draw the mind constantly to them, forward to take notice of new, and apt to be delighted with the variety of changing objects. Thus the first years are usually employed and diverted in looking abroad. Men's business in them is to acquaint themselves with what is to be found without; and so, growing up in a constant attention to outward sensations, seldom make any considerable reflection on what passes within them till they come to be of riper years; and some scarce ever at all.

9. *The soul begins to have ideas when it begins to perceive.*—To ask, at what time a man has first any ideas, is to ask when he begins to perceive; *having ideas,* and *perception,* being the same thing. I know it is an opinion, that the soul always thinks; and that it has the actual perception of ideas in itself constantly, as long as it exists; and that actual thinking is as inseparable from the soul, as actual extension is from the body: which if true, to inquire after the beginning of a man's ideas is the same as to inquire after the beginning of his soul. For by this account, soul and its ideas, as body and its extension, will begin to exist both at the same time.

10. *The soul thinks not always; for this wants proofs.*—But whether the soul be supposed to exist antecedent to, or coeval with, or some time after, the first rudiments or organization, or the beginnings of life in the body, I leave to be disputed by those who have better thought of that matter. I confess myself to have one of those dull souls that doth not perceive itself always to contemplate ideas; nor can conceive it any more necessary for the soul always to think, than for the body always to move; the perception of ideas being, as I conceive, to the soul, what motion is to the body: not its essence, but one of its operations; and, therefore, though thinking be supposed never so much the proper action of the soul, yet it is not necessary to suppose that it should be always thinking, always in action. That, perhaps, is the privilege of the infinite Author and Preserver of all things, "who never slumbers nor sleeps;" but it is not competent to any finite being, at least not to the soul of man. We know certainly, by experience, that we sometimes think; and thence draw this infallible consequence—that there is something in us that has a power to think. But whether that substance perpetually thinks, or no, we can be no farther assured than experience informs us. For to say that actual thinking is essential to the soul, and inseparable from it, is to beg what is in question, and not to prove it by reason; which is nec-

essary to be done, if it be not a self-evident proposition. But whether this—that "the soul always thinks," be a self-evident proposition, that everybody assents to on first hearing, I appeal to mankind. [It is doubted whether I thought all last night, or no; the question being about a matter of fact, it is begging it to bring as a proof for it an hypothesis which is the very thing in dispute; by which way one may prove anything; and it is but supposing that all watches, whilst the balance beats, think, and it is sufficiently proved, and past doubt, that my watch thought all last night. But he that would not deceive himself ought to build his hypothesis on matter of fact, and make it out by sensible experience, and not presume on matter of fact because of his hypothesis; that is, because he supposes it to be so; which way of proving amounts to this,—that I must necessarily think all last night, because another supposes I always think, though I myself cannot perceive that I always do so.

But men in love with their opinions may not only suppose what is in question, but allege wrong matter of fact. How else could anyone make it an inference of mine, that a thing is not, because we are not sensible of it in our sleep? I do not say, there is no soul in a man because he is not sensible of it in his sleep; but I do say, he cannot think at any time, waking or sleeping, without being sensible of it. Our being sensible of it is not necessary to anything but to our thoughts; and to them it is, and to them it will always be, necessary, till we can think without being conscious of it.]

11. *It is not always conscious of it.*—I grant that the soul in a waking man is never without thought, because it is the condition of being awake; but whether sleeping without dreaming be not an affection of the whole man, mind as well as body, may be worth a waking man's consideration; it being hard to conceive that anything should think and not be conscious of it. If the soul doth think in a sleeping man without being conscious of it, I ask, whether, during such thinking, it has any pleasure or pain, or be capable of happiness or misery? I am sure the man is not, no more than the bed or earth he lies on. For to be happy or miserable without being conscious of it, seems to me utterly inconsistent and impossible. Or if it be possible that the soul can, whilst the body is sleeping, have its thinking, enjoyments, and concerns, its pleasure or pain, apart, which the man is not conscious of, nor partakes in, it is certain that Socrates asleep and Socrates awake is not the same person; but his soul when he sleeps, and Socrates the man, consisting of body and soul, when he is waking, are two persons; since waking Socrates has no knowledge of, or concernment for that happiness or misery of his soul, which it enjoys alone by itself whilst he sleeps, without perceiving anything of it, no more than he has for the happiness or misery of a man in

the Indies, whom he knows not. For if we take wholly away all consciousness of our actions and sensations, especially of pleasure and pain, and the concernment that accompanies it, it will be hard to know wherein to place personal identity. . . .

CHAPTER II

OF SIMPLE IDEAS

1. *Uncompounded appearances.*—The better to understand the nature, manner, and extent of our knowledge, one thing is carefully to be observed concerning the ideas we have; and that is, that some of them, are *simple,* and some *complex.*

Though the qualities that affect our senses are, in the things themselves, so united and blended that there is no separation, no distance between them; yet it is plain the ideas they produce in the mind enter by the senses simple and unmixed. For though the sight and touch often take in from the same object, at the same time, different ideas—as a man sees at once motion and color, the hand feels softness and warmth in the same piece of wax —yet the simple ideas thus united in the same subject are as perfectly distinct as those that come in by different senses; the coldness and hardness which a man feels in a piece of ice being as distinct ideas in the mind as the smell and whiteness of a lily, or as the taste of sugar and smell of a rose: and there is nothing can be plainer to a man than the clear and distinct perception he has of those simple ideas; which, being each in itself uncompounded, contains in it nothing but *one uniform appearance or conception in the mind,* and is not distinguishable into different ideas.

2. *The mind can neither make nor destroy them.*—These simple ideas, the materials of all our knowledge, are suggested and furnished to the mind only by those two ways above mentioned, viz., sensation and reflection. When the understanding is once stored with these simple ideas, it has the power to repeat, compare, and unite them, even to an almost infinite variety, and so can make at pleasure new complex ideas. But it is not in the power of the most exalted wit or enlarged understanding, by any quickness or variety of thought, to *invent* or *frame* one new simple idea in the mind, not taken in by the ways before mentioned; nor can any force of the understanding *destroy* those that are there: the dominion of man in this little world of his own understanding, being much-what the same as it is in the great world of visible things; wherein his power, however managed by art and skill, reaches no farther than to compound and divide the materials that are made to his hand but

can do nothing towards the making the least particle of new matter, or destroying one atom of what is already in being. The same inability will everyone find in himself, who shall go about to fashion in his understanding any simple idea not received in by his senses from external objects, or by reflection from the operations of his own mind about them. I would have anyone try to fancy any taste which had never affected his palate, or frame the idea of a scent he had never smelt; and when he can do this, I will also conclude that a blind man hath *ideas* of colors, and a deaf man true, distinct notions of sounds.

3. *Only the qualities that affect the senses are imaginable.*—This is the reason why, though we cannot believe it impossible to God to make a creature with other organs, and more ways to convey into the understanding the notice of corporeal things than those five as they are usually counted, which He has given to man; yet I think it is not possible for anyone to imagine any other qualities in bodies, howsoever constituted, whereby they can be taken notice of, besides sounds, tastes, smells, visible and tangible qualities. And had mankind been made with but four senses, the qualities then which are the objects of the fifth sense had been as far from our notice, imagination, and conception, as now any belonging to a sixth, seventh, or eighth sense can possibly be; which, whether yet some other creatures, in some other parts of this vast and stupendous universe, may not have, will be a great presumption to deny. He that will not set himself proudly at the top of all things, but will consider the immensity of this fabric, and the great variety that is to be found in this little and inconsiderable part of it which he has to do with, may be apt to think, that in other mansions of it there may be other and different intelligible beings, of whose faculties he has as little knowledge or apprehension, as a worm shut up in one drawer of a cabinet hath of the senses or understanding of a man; such variety and excellency being suitable to the wisdom and power of the Maker. I have here followed the common opinion of man's having but five senses, though perhaps there may be justly counted more; but either supposition serves equally to my present purpose.

CHAPTER III

OF SIMPLE IDEAS OF SENSE

1. *Division of simple ideas.*—The better to conceive the ideas we receive from sensation, it may not be amiss for us to consider them in reference to the different ways whereby they make their approaches to our minds, and make themselves perceivable by us.

First, then, there are some which come into our minds *by one sense only.*

Secondly, there are others that convey themselves into the mind *by more senses than one.*

Thirdly, others that are had *from reflection only.*

Fourthly, there are some that make themselves way, and are suggested to the mind, *by all the ways of sensation and reflection.*

We shall consider them apart under these several heads.

There are some ideas which have admittance only through one sense, which is peculiarly adapted to receive them. Thus light and colors, as white, red, yellow, blue, with their several degrees or shades and mixtures, as green, scarlet, purple, sea-green, and the rest, come in only by the eyes; all kinds of noises, sounds, and tones, only by the ears; the several tastes and smells, by the nose and palate. And if these organs, or the nerves which are the conduits to convey them from without to their audience in the brain—the mind's presence-room (as I may so call it)—are, any of them, so disordered as not to perform their functions, they have no postern to be admitted by, no other way to bring themselves into view, and be received by the understanding.

The most considerable of those belonging to the touch are heat, and cold, and solidity; all the rest—consisting almost wholly in the sensible configuration, as smooth and rough; or else more or less firm adhesion of the parts, as hard and soft, tough and brittle—are obvious enough.

2. *Few simple ideas have names.*—I think it will be needless to enumerate all the particular simple ideas belonging to each sense. Nor indeed is it possible if we would, there being a great many more of them belonging to most of the senses than we have names for. The variety of smells, which are as many almost, if not more, than species of bodies in the world, do most of them want names. Sweet and stinking commonly serve our turn for these ideas, which in effect is little more than to call them pleasing or displeasing; though the smell of a rose and violet, both sweet, are certainly very distinct ideas. Nor are the different tastes that by our palates we receive ideas of, much better provided with names. Sweet, bitter, sour, harsh, and salt, are almost all the epithets we have to denominate that numberless variety of relishes which are to be found distinct, not only in almost every sort of creatures, but in the different parts of the same plant, fruit, or animal. The same may be said of colors and sounds. I shall therefore, in the account of simple ideas I am here giving, content myself to set down only such as are most material to our present purpose, or are in themselves less apt to be taken notice of, though they are very frequently the ingredients of our complex ideas; amongst which I may well account solidity, which therefore I shall treat of in the next chapter.

CHAPTER IV

IDEA OF SOLIDITY

1. *We receive this idea from touch.*—The idea of *solidity* we receive by our touch; and it arises from the resistance which we find in body to the entrance of any other body into the place it possesses, till it has left it. There is no idea which we receive more constantly from sensation than solidity. Whether we move or rest, in what posture soever we are, we always feel something under us that supports us, and hinders our farther sinking downwards; and the bodies which we daily handle make us perceive that whilst they remain between them, they do, by an insurmountable force, hinder the approach of the parts of our hands that press them. *That which thus hinders the approach of two bodies, when they are moving one towards another, I call solidity.* I will not dispute whether this acceptation of the word solid be nearer to its original signification than that which mathematicians use it in; it suffices that, I think, the common notion of solidity, will allow, if not justify, this use of it; but if any one think it better to call it *impenetrability,* he has my consent. Only I have thought the term solidity the more proper to express this idea, not only because of its vulgar use in that sense, but also because it carried something more of positive in it than impenetrability, which is negative, and is, perhaps, more a consequence of solidity than solidity itself. This of all other, seems the idea most intimately connected with and essential to body, so as nowhere else to be found or imagined but only in matter and though our senses take no notice of it but in masses of matter, of a bulk sufficient to cause a sensation in us; yet the mind, having once got this idea from such grosser sensible bodies, traces it farther and considers it, as well as figure, in the minutest particle of matter that can exist, and finds it inseparably inherent in body, wherever or however modified.

2. *Solidity fills space.*—This is the idea which belongs to body, whereby we conceive it to fill space. The idea of which filling of space is, that where we imagine any space taken up by a solid substance, we conceive it so to possess it that it excludes all other solid substances, and will for ever hinder any two other bodies, that move towards one another in a straight line, from coming to touch one another, unless it removes from between them in a line not parallel to that which they move in. This idea of it, the bodies which we ordinarily handle sufficiently furnish us with.

3 *Distinct from space.*—This resistance, whereby it keeps other bodies out of the space which it possesses, is so great that no force, how

great soever, can surmount it. All the bodies in the world, pressing a drop of water on all sides, will never be able to overcome the resistance which it will make, as soft as it is, to their approaching one another, till it be removed out of their way: whereby our idea of solidity is distinguished both from pure space, which is capable neither of resistance nor motion, and from the ordinary idea of hardness. For a man may conceive two bodies at a distance so as they may approach one another without touching or displacing any solid thing till their superficies come to meet; whereby, I think, we have the clear idea of space without solidity. For (not to go so far as annihilation of any particular body), I ask, whether a man cannot have the idea of the motion of one single body alone, without any other succeeding immediately into its place? I think it is evident he can: the idea of motion in one body no more including the idea of motion in another, than the idea of a square figure in one body includes the idea of a square figure in another. I do not ask, whether bodies do so *exist,* that the motion of one body cannot really be without the motion of another. To determine this either way is to beg the question for or against a *vacuum.* But my question is, whether one cannot have the idea of one body moved, whilst others are at rest? And I think this no one will deny. If so, then the place it deserted gives us the idea of pure space without solidity, whereinto another body may enter without either resistance or protrusion of anything. When the sucker in a pump is drawn, the space it filled in the tube is certainly the same, whether any other body follows the motion of the sucker or not; nor does it imply a contradiction that upon the motion of one body, another that is only contiguous to it should not follow it. The necessity of such a motion is built only on the supposition that the world is full, but not on the distinct ideas of space and solidity; which are as different as resistance and not-resistance, protrusion and not-protrusion. And that men have ideas of space without body, their very disputes about a vacuum plainly demonstrate, as is showed in another place.

4. *Distinct from hardness.*—Solidity is hereby also differenced from *hardness,* in that solidity consists in repletion, and so an utter exclusion of other bodies out of the space it possesses; but hardness, in a firm cohesion of the parts of matter, making up masses of a sensible bulk, so that the whole does not easily change its figure. And, indeed, hard and soft are names that we give to things only in relation to the constitutions of our own bodies; that being generally called hard by us which will put us to pain sooner than change figure by the pressure of any part of our bodies; and that, on the contrary, soft which changes the situation of its parts upon an easy and unpainful touch.

But this difficulty of changing the situation of the sensible parts amongst themselves. or of the figure of the whole, gives no more solidity to the hardest body in the world than to the softest; nor is an adamant one jot more solid than water. For though the two flat sides of two pieces of marble will more easily approach each other, between which there is nothing but water or air, than if there be a diamond between them; yet it is not that the parts of the diamond are more solid than those of water, or resist more, but because the parts of water being more easily separable from each other, they will by a side-motion be more easily removed and give way to the approach of two pieces of marble: but if they could be kept from making place by that side-motion, they would eternally hinder the approach of these two pieces of marble as much as the diamond; and it would be as impossible by any force to surmount their resistance, as to surmount the resistance of the parts of a diamond. The softest body in the world will as invincibly resist the coming together of any two other bodies, if it be not put out of the way, but remain between them, as the hardest that can be found or imagined. He that shall fill a yielding soft body well with air or water will quickly find its resistance: and he that thinks that nothing but bodies that are hard can keep his hands from approaching one another, may be pleased to make a trial with the air enclosed in a football. [The experiment, I have been told, was made at Florence, with a hollow globe of gold filled with water, and exactly closed, which farther shows the solidity of so soft a body as water. For, the golden globe thus filled being put into a press which was driven by the extreme force of screws, the water made itself way through the pores of that very close metal, and, finding no room for a nearer approach of its particles within, got to the outside, where it rose like a dew, and so fell in drops before the sides of the globe could be made to yield to the violent compression of the engine that squeezed it.]

5. *On solidity depend impulse, resistance, and protrusion.*—By this idea of solidity is the extension of body distinguished from the extension of space: the extension of body being nothing but the cohesion or continuity of solid, separable, movable parts; and the extension of space, the continuity of unsolid, inseparable, and immovable parts. Upon the solidity of bodies also depend their mutual impulse, resistance, and protrusion. Of pure space, then, and solidity, there are several (amongst which I confess myself one) who persuade themselves they have clear and distinct ideas; and that they can think on space without anything in it that resists or is protruded by body. This is the idea of pure space, which they think they have as clear as any idea they can have of the extension of body: the idea of the distance between the opposite parts of a concave superficies being equally as clear without as with the idea of any solid parts between; and on the other side they persuade themselves that they have, distinct from that of pure space, the idea of something

that fills space, that can be protruded by the impulse of other bodies, or resist their motion. If there be others that have not these two ideas distinct, but confound them, and make but one of them, I know not how men who have the same idea under different names, or different ideas under the same name, can in that case talk with one another, any more than a man who, not being blind or deaf, has distinct ideas of the color of scarlet and the sound of a trumpet, would discourse concerning scarlet color with the blind man I mention in another place, who fancied that the idea of scarlet was like the sound of a trumpet.

6. *What solidity is.*—If anyone asks me what this solidity is, I send him to his senses to inform him. Let him put a flint or a football between his hands, and then endeavor to join them, and he will know. If he thinks this not a sufficient explication of solidity, what it is, and wherein it consists, I promise to tell him what it is and wherein it consists, when he tells me what thinking is or wherein it consists; or explains to me what extension or motion is, which perhaps seems much easier. The simple ideas we have are such as experience teaches them us; but if, beyond that, we endeavor by words to make them clearer in the mind, we shall succeed no better than if we went about to clear up the darkness of a blind man's mind by talking, and to discourse into him the ideas of light and colors. The reason of this I shall show in another place.

CHAPTER V

OF SIMPLE IDEAS OF DIVERS SENSES

Ideas received both by seeing and touching.—The ideas we get by more than one sense are of *space* or *extension, figure, rest* and *motion.* For these make perceivable impressions both on the eyes and touch; and we can receive and convey into our minds the ideas of the extension, figure, motion, and rest of bodies, both by seeing and feeling. But by having occasion to speak more at large of these in another place, I here only enumerate them.

CHAPTER VI

OF SIMPLE IDEAS OF REFLECTION

1. *Simple ideas of reflection are the operations of the mind about its other ideas.*—The mind, receiving the ideas mentioned in the foregoing chapters from without, when it turns its view inward upon itself, and

observes its own actions about those ideas it has, takes from thence other ideas, which are as capable to be the objects of its contemplation as any of those it received from foreign things.

2. *The idea of perception, and idea of willing, we have from reflection.*—The two great and principal actions of the mind, which are most frequently considered, and which are so frequent that everyone that pleases may take notice of them in himself, are these two: *perception* or *thinking,* and *volition* or *willing.* [The power of thinking is called the *understanding,* and the power of volition is called the *will;* and these two powers or abilities in the mind are denominated *faculties.*] Of some of the models of these simple ideas of reflection, such as are remembrance, discerning, reasoning, judging, knowledge, faith, etc., I shall have occasion to speak hereafter.

CHAPTER VII

OF SIMPLE IDEAS OF BOTH SENSATION AND REFLECTION

1. *Ideas of pleasure and pain.*—There be other simple ideas which convey themselves into the mind by all the ways of sensation and reflection: viz., pleasure or delight, and its opposite, pain or uneasiness; power, existence, unity.

2. Delight or uneasiness, one or other of them, join themselves to almost all our ideas both of sensation and reflection; and there is scarce any affection of our senses from without, any retired thought of our mind within, which is not able to produce in us pleasure or pain. By pleasure and pain, I would be understood to signify whatsoever delights or molests us; whether it arises from the thoughts of our minds, or anything operating on our bodies. For whether we call it satisfaction, delight, pleasure, happiness, etc., on the one side; or uneasiness, trouble, pain, torment, anguish, misery, etc., on the other; they are still but different degrees of the same thing, and belong to the ideas of pleasure and pain, delight or uneasiness; which are the names I shall most commonly use for those two sorts of ideas.

3. *Pleasure and pain as motive for our actions.*—The infinite wise Author of our being—having given us the power over several parts of our bodies, to move or keep them at rest as we think fit, and also by the motion of them to move ourselves and other contiguous bodies, in which consist all the actions of our body; having also given a power to our minds, in several instances, to choose amongst its ideas which it will think on, and to pursue the inquiry of this or that subject with considera-

tion and attention—to excite us to these actions of thinking and motion that we are capable of, has been pleased to join to several thoughts and several sensations a perception of *delight*. If this were wholly separated from all our outward sensations and inward thoughts, we should have no reason to prefer one thought or action to another, negligence to attention, or motion to rest: and so we should neither stir our bodies, nor employ our minds; but let our thoughts (if I may so call it) run adrift, without any direction or design; and suffer the ideas of our minds, like unregarded shadows, to make their appearances there as it happened, without attending to them: in which state man, however furnished with the faculties of understanding and will, would be a very idle, unactive creature, and pass his time only in a lazy, lethargic dream. It has therefore pleased our wise Creator to annex to several objects, and to the ideas which we receive from them, as also to several of our thoughts, a concomitant pleasure, and that in several objects to several degrees, that those faculties which He had endowed us with might not remain wholly idle and unemployed by us.

4. *An end and use of pain.*—Pain has the same efficacy and use to set us on work that pleasure has, we being as ready to employ our faculties to avoid that, as to pursue this: only this is worth our consideration, that pain is often produced by the same objects and ideas that produce pleasure in us. This their near conjunction, which makes us often feel pain in the sensations where we expected pleasure, gives us new occasion of admiring the wisdom and goodness of our Maker, who, designing the preservation of our being, has annexed pain to the application of many things to our bodies, to warn us of the harm they will do, and as advices to withdraw from them. But He, not designing our preservation barely, but the preservation of every part and organ in its perfection, hath in many cases annexed pain to those very ideas which delight us. Thus heat, that is very agreeable to us in one degree, by a little greater increase of it proves no ordinary torment; and the most pleasant of all sensible objects, light itself, if there be too much of it, if increased beyond a due proportion to our eyes, causes a very painful sensation: which is wisely and favorably so ordered by nature, that when any object does by the vehemency of its operation disorder the instruments of sensation, whose structures cannot but be very nice and delicate, we might by the pain be warned to withdraw before the organ be quite put out of order, and so be unfitted for its proper functions for the future. The consideration of those objects that produce it may well persuade us that this is the end or use of pain. For though great light be insufferable to our eyes, yet the highest degree of darkness does not at all disease them, because that causing no disorderly motion in it, leaves that curi-

ous organ unharmed in its natural state. But yet excess of cold as well as heat pains us because it is equally destructive to that temper which is necessary to the preservation of life, and the exercise of the several functions of the body, and which consists in a moderate degree of warmth, or, if you please, a motion of the insensible parts of our bodies confined within certain bounds.

5. Beyond all this, we may find another reason why God hath scattered up and down several degrees of pleasure and pain in all the things that environ and affect us, and blended them together in all that our thoughts and senses have to do with; that we, finding imperfection, dissatisfaction, and want of complete happiness in all the enjoyments which the creatures can afford us, might be led to seek it in the enjoyment of Him "with Whom there is fulness of joy, and at Whose right hand are pleasures for evermore."

6. Though what I have here said may not perhaps make the ideas of pleasure and pain clearer to us than our own experience does, which is the only way that we are capable of having them; yet the consideration of the reason why they are annexed to so many other ideas, serving to give us due sentiments of the wisdom and goodness of the Sovereign Disposer of all things, may not be unsuitable to the main end of these inquiries: the knowledge and veneration of Him being the chief end of all our thoughts, and the proper business of all our understandings.

7. *Ideas of existence and unity.*—Existence and unity are two other ideas that are suggested to the understanding by every object without, and every idea within. When ideas are in our minds, we consider them as being actually there, as well as we consider things to be actually without us: which is, that they exist, or have existence: and whatever we can consider as one thing, whether a real being or idea, suggests to the understanding the idea of unity.

8. *Idea of power.*—Power also is another of those simple ideas which we receive from sensation and reflection. For, observing in ourselves that we do and can think, and that we can at pleasure move several parts of our bodies which were at rest; the effects also that natural bodies are able to produce in one another occurring every moment to our senses, we both these ways get the idea of power.

9. *Idea of succession.*—Besides these there is another idea, which though suggested by our senses, yet is more constantly offered us by what passes in our minds; and that is the idea of succession. For if we look immediately into ourselves, and reflect on what is observable there, we shall find our ideas always, whilst we are awake or have any thought, passing in train, one going and another coming without intermission.

10. *Simple ideas the materials of all our knowledge.*—These, if they are not all, are at least (as I think) the most considerable of those sim-

ple ideas which the mind has, and out of which is made all its other knowledge: all of which it receives only by the two forementioned ways of sensation and reflection.

Nor let anyone think these two narrow bounds for the capacious mind of man to expatiate in, which takes its flight farther than the stars, and cannot be confined by the limits of the world; that extends its thoughts often even beyond the utmost expansion of matter, and makes excursions into that incomprehensible inane. I grant all this; but desire any-one to assign any simple idea which is not received from one of those inlets before mentioned, or any complex idea not made out of those simple ones. Nor will it be so strange to think these few simple ideas sufficient to employ the quickest thought or largest capacity, and to furnish the materials of all that various knowledge and more various fancies and opinions of all mankind, if we consider how many words may be made out of the various composition of twenty-four letters; or, if, going one step farther, we will but reflect on the variety of combinations that may be made with barely one of the above-mentioned ideas, viz., number, whose stock is inexhaustible and truly infinite; and what a large and immense field doth extension alone afford the mathematicians!

CHAPTER VIII

SOME FARTHER CONSIDERATIONS CONCERNING OUR SIMPLE IDEAS OF SENSATION

1. *Positive ideas from privative causes.*—Concerning the simple ideas of sensation, it is to be considered that whatsoever is so constituted in nature as to be able by affecting our senses to cause any perception in the mind, doth thereby produce in the understanding a simple idea; which, whatever be the external cause of it, when it comes to be taken notice of by our discerning faculty, it is by the mind looked on and considered there to be a real positive idea in the understanding, as much as any other whatsoever; though perhaps the cause of it be but a privation in the subject.

2. Thus the ideas of heat and cold, light and darkness, white and black, motion and rest, are equally clear and positive ideas in the mind; though perhaps some of the causes which produce them are barely privations in those subjects from whence our senses derive those ideas. These the understanding, in its view of them, considers all as distinct positive ideas without taking notice of the causes that produce them; which is an inquiry not belonging to the idea as it is in the understanding, but to

the nature of the things existing without us. These are two very different things, and carefully to be distinguished; it being one thing to perceive and know the idea of white or black, and quite another to examine what kind of particles they must be, and how ranged in the superficies, to make any object appear white or black.

3. A painter or dyer who never inquired into their causes, hath the ideas of white and black and other colors as clearly, perfectly, and distinctly in his understanding, and perhaps more distinctly than the philosopher who hath busied himself in considering their natures, and thinks he knows how far either of them is in its cause positive or privative; and the idea of black is no less positive in his mind than that of white, however the cause of that color in the external object may be only a privation.

4. If it were the design of my present undertaking to inquire into the natural causes and manner of perception, I should offer this as a reason why a privative cause might, in some cases at least, produce a positive idea; viz., that all sensation being produced in us only by different degrees and modes of motion in our animal spirits, variously agitated by external objects, the abatement of any former motion must as necessarily produce a new sensation as the variation or increase of it; and so introduce a new idea, which depends only on a different motion of the animal spirits in that organ.

5. But whether this be so or not I will not here determine, but appeal to everyone's own experience, whether the shadow of a man, though it consists of nothing but the absence of light (and the more the absence of light is, the more discernible is the shadow), does not, when a man looks on it, cause as clear and positive an idea in his mind as a man himself, though covered over with clear sunshine! And the picture of a shadow is a positive thing. Indeed, we have negative names, [which stand not directly for positive ideas, but for their absence, such as *insipid, silence, nihil*, etc., which words denote positive ideas, v. g., *taste, sound, being*, with a signification of their absence].

6. And thus one may truly be said to see darkness. For, supposing a hole perfectly dark, from whence no light is reflected, it is certain one may see the figure of it, or it may be painted; or whether the ink I write with make any other idea, is a question. The privative causes I have here assigned of positive ideas are according to the common opinion; but, in truth, it will be hard to determine whether there be really any ideas from a privative cause, till it be determined whether rest be any more a privation than motion.

7. *Ideas in the mind, qualities in bodies.*—To discover the nature of our ideas the better, and to discourse of them intelligibly, it will be convenient to distinguish them, as they are *ideas or perceptions in our*

minds, and as they are *modifications of matter in the bodies that cause such perceptions in us;* that so we may not think (as perhaps usually is done) that they are exactly the images and resemblances of something inherent in the subject; most of those of sensation being in the mind no more the likeness of something existing without us than the names that stand for them are the likeness of our ideas, which yet upon hearing they are apt to excite in us.

8. Whatsoever the mind perceives in itself, or is the immediate object of perception, thought, or understanding, that I call *idea;* and the power to produce any idea in our mind, I call *quality* of the subject wherein that power is. Thus a snowball having the power to produce in us the ideas of white, cold, and round, the powers to produce those ideas in us as they are in the snowball, I call qualities; and as they are sensations or perceptions in our understandings, I call them ideas; which ideas, if I speak of them sometimes as in the things themselves, I would be understood to mean those qualities in the objects which produce them in us.

9. *Primary qualities.*—[Qualities thus considered in bodies are: *First* such as are utterly inseparable from the body, in what estate soever it be;] and such as, in all the alterations and changes it suffers, all the force can be used upon it, it constantly keeps; and such as sense constantly finds in every particle of matter which has bulk enough to be perceived, and the mind finds inseparable from every particle of matter, though less than to make itself singly be perceived by our senses: v. g., take a grain of wheat, divide it into two parts, each part has still solidity, extension, figure, and mobility; divide it again, and it retains still the same qualities: and so divide it on till the parts become insensible, they must retain still each of them all those qualities. For, division (which is all that a mill or pestle or any other body does upon another, in reducing it to insensible parts) can never take away either solidity, extension, figure, or mobility from any body, but only makes two or more distinct separate masses of matter of that which was but one before; all which distinct masses, reckoned as so many distinct bodies, after division, make a certain number. [These I call *original* or *primary qualities* of body, which I think we may observe to produce simple ideas in us, viz., solidity, extension, figure, motion or rest, and number.

10. *Secondary qualities.*—*Secondly,* such qualities, which in truth are nothing in the objects themselves, but powers to produce various sensations in us by their primary qualities, i. e., by the bulk, figure, texture, and motion of their insensible parts, as colors, sounds, tastes, etc., these I call *secondary* qualities. To these might be added a third sort, which are allowed to be barely powers, though they are as much real qualities

in the subject as those which I, to comply with the common way of speaking, call qualities, but, for distinction, *secondary* qualities. For, the power in fire to produce a new color or consistency in wax or clay, by its primary qualities, is as much a quality in fire as the power it has to produce in me a new idea or sensation of warmth or burning, which I felt not before, by the same primary qualities, viz., the bulk, texture, and motion of its insensible parts.]

11. [*How primary qualities produce ideas in us.*—The next thing to be considered is, how bodies produce ideas in us; and that is manifestly by impulse, the only way which we can conceive bodies to operate in.]

12. If, then, external objects be not united to our minds when they produce ideas therein, and yet we perceive these original qualities in such of them as singly fall under our senses, it is evident that some motion must be thence continued by our nerves, or animal spirits, by some parts of our bodies, to the brain or the seat of sensation, there to produce in our minds the particular ideas we have of them. And since the extension, figure, number, and motion of bodies of an observable bigness, may be perceived at a distance by the sight, it is evident some singly imperceptible bodies must come from them to the eyes, and thereby convey to the brain some motion which produces these ideas which we have of them in us.

13. *How secondary.*—After the same manner that the ideas of these original qualities are produced in us, we may conceive that the ideas of secondary qualities are also produced, viz., by the operation of insensible particles on our senses. For it being manifest that there are bodies, and good store of bodies, each whereof are so small that we cannot by any of our senses discover either their bulk, figure, or motion (as is evident in the particles of the air and water, and others extremely smaller than those, perhaps as much smaller than the particles of air or water as the particles of air or water are smaller than peas or hailstones): let us suppose at present that the different motions and figures, bulk and number, of such particles, affecting the several organs of our senses, produce in us these different sensations which we have from the colors and smells of bodies, v. g., that a violet, by the impulse of such insensible particles of matter of peculiar figures and bulks, and in different degrees and modifications of their motions, causes the ideas of the blue color and sweet scent of that flower to be produced in our minds; it being no more impossible to conceive that God should annex such ideas to such motions, with which they have no similitude, than that He should annex the idea of pain to the motion of a piece of steel dividing our flesh, with which the idea hath no resemblance.

14. What I have said concerning colors and smells may be under-

stood also of tastes and sounds, and other the like sensible qualities; which, whatever reality we by mistake attribute to them, are in truth nothing in the objects themselves, but powers to produce various sensations in us, and depend on those primary qualities, viz., bulk, figure, texture, and motion of parts [as I have said].

15. *Ideas of primary qualities are resemblances; of secondary, not.*— From whence I think it is easy to draw this observation, that the ideas of primary qualities of bodies are resemblances of them, and their patterns do really exist in the bodies themselves; but the ideas produced in us by these secondary qualities have no resemblance of them at all. There is nothing like our ideas existing in the bodies themselves. They are, in the bodies we denominate from them, only a power to produce those sensations in us; and what is sweet, blue, or warm in idea, is but the certain bulk, figure, and motion of the insensible parts in the bodies themselves, which we call so.

16. Flame is denominated hot and light; snow, white and cold; and manna, white and sweet, from the ideas they produce in us, which qualities are commonly thought to be the same in those bodies that those ideas are in us, the one the perfect resemblance of the other, as they are in a mirror; and it would by most men be judged very extravagant, if one should say otherwise. And yet he that will consider that the same fire that at one distance produces in us the sensation of warmth, does at a nearer approach produce in us the far different sensation of pain, ought to bethink himself what reason he has to say, that this idea of warmth which was produced in him by the fire, is actually in the fire, and his idea of pain which the same fire produced in him the same way is not in the fire. Why are whiteness and coldness in snow and pain not, when it produces the one and the other idea in us, and can do neither but by the bulk, figure, number, and motion of its solid parts?

17. The particular bulk, number, figure, and motion of the parts of fire or snow are really in them, whether anyone's senses perceive then or no; and therefore they may be called *real* qualities, because they really exist in those bodies. But light, heat, whiteness, or coldness, are no more really in them than sickness or pain is in manna. Take away the sensation of them; let not the eyes see light or colors, nor the ears hear sounds; let the palate not taste, nor the nose smell; and all colors, tastes, odors, and sounds, as they are such particuar ideas, vanish and cease, and are reduced to their causes, i. e., bulk, figure, and motion of parts.

18. A piece of manna of a sensible bulk is able to produce in us the idea of a round or square figure; and, by being removed from one place to another, the idea of motion. This idea of motion represents it as it

really is in the manna moving; a circle or square are the same, whether in idea or existence, in the mind or in the manna; and this, both motion and figure, are really in the manna, whether we take notice of them or no: this everybody is ready to agree to. Besides, manna, by the bulk, figure, texture, and motion of its parts, has a power to produce the sensations of sickness, and sometimes of acute pains or gripings, in us. That these ideas of sickness and pain are not in the manna, but effects of its operations on us, and are nowhere when we feel them not; this also everyone readily agrees to. And yet men are hardly to be brought to think that sweetness and whiteness are not really in manna, which are but the effects of the operations of manna by the motion, size, and figure of its particles on the eyes and palate; as the pain and sickness caused by manna, are confessedly nothing but the effects of its operations on the stomach and guts by the size, motion, and figure of its insensible parts (for by nothing else can a body operate, as has been proved): as if it could not operate on the eyes and palate, and thereby produce in the mind particular distinct ideas which in itself it has not, as well as we allow it can operate on the guts and stomach, and thereby produce distinct ideas which in itself it has not. These ideas being all effects of the operations of manna on several parts of our bodies, by the size, figure, number, and motion of its parts, why those produced by the eyes and palate should rather be thought to be really in the manna than those produced by the stomach and guts; or why the pain and sickness, ideas that are the effects of manna, should be thought to be nowhere when they are not felt; and yet the sweetness and whiteness, effects of the same manna on other parts of the body, by ways equally as unknown, should be thought to exist in the manna, when they are not seen nor tasted would need some reason to explain.

19. Let us consider the red and white colors in porphyry; hinder light but from striking on it, and its colors vanish; it no longer produces any such ideas in us. Upon the return of light, it produces these appearances on us again. Can anyone think any real alterations are made in the porphyry by the presence or absence of light, and that those ideas of whiteness and redness are really in porphyry in the light, when it is plain it has no color in the dark? It has indeed such a configuration of particles, both night and day, as are apt, by the rays of light rebounding from some parts of that hard stone, to produce in us the idea of redness, and from others the idea of whiteness. But whiteness or redness are not in it at any time, but such a texture that hath the power to produce such a sensation in us.

20. Pound an almond, and the clear white color will be altered into a dirty one, and the sweet taste into an oily one. What real alteration

can the beating of the pestle make in any body, but an alteration of the texture of it?

21. Ideas being thus distinguished and understood, we may be able to give an account how the same water, at the same time, may produce the idea of cold by one hand, and of heat by the other; whereas it is impossible that the same water, if those ideas were really in it, should at the same time be both hot and cold. For if we imagine warmth as it is in our hands, to be nothing but a certain sort and degree of motion in the minute particles of our nerves or animal spirits, we may understand how it is possible that the same water may at the same time produce the sensation of heat in one hand, and cold in the other; which yet figure never does, that never producing the idea of a square by one hand which has produced the idea of a globe by another. But if the sensation of heat and cold be nothing but the increase or dimunition of the motion of the minute parts of our bodies, caused by the corpuscles of any other body, it is easy to be understood that if that motion be greater in one hand than in the other, if a body be applied to the two hands, which has in its minute particles a greater motion than in those of one of the hands, and a less than in those of the other, it will increase the motion of the one hand, and lessen it in the other, and so cause the different sensations of heat and cold that depend thereon.

22. I have, in what just goes before, been engaged in physical inquiries a little farther than perhaps I intended. But it being necessary to make the nature of sensation a little understood, and to make the difference between the qualities in bodies, and the ideas produced by them in the mind, to be distinctly conceived, without which it were impossible to discourse intelligibly of them, I hope I shall be pardoned this little excursion into natural philosophy, it being necessary in our present inquiry to distinguish the primary and real qualities of bodies, which are always in them (viz., solidity, extension, figure, number, and motion or rest, and are sometimes perceived by us, viz., when the bodies they are in are big enough singly to be discerned), from those secondary and imputed qualities, which are but the powers of several combinations of those primary ones, when they operate without being distinctly discerned; whereby we also may come to know what ideas are, and what are not, resemblances of something really existing in the bodies we denominate from them.

23. *Three sorts of qualities in bodies.*—The qualities then that are in bodies, rightly considered, are of three sorts:

First, the bulk, figure, number, situation, and motion or rest of their solid parts; those are in them, whether we perceive them or not; and when they are of that size that we can discover them, we have by these ideas of the thing as it is in itself, as is plain in artificial things. These I call *primary qualities*.

Secondly, the power that is in any body, by reason of its insensible primary qualities, to operate after a peculiar manner on any of our senses, and thereby produce in us the different ideas of several colors, sounds, smells, tastes, etc. These are usually called *sensible qualities*.

Thirdly, the power that is in any body, by reason of the particular constitution of its primary qualities, to make such a change in the bulk, figure, texture, and motion of another body, as to make it operate on our senses differently from what it did before. Thus the sun has a power to make wax white, and fire, to make lead fluid. [These are usually called *powers*.]

The first of these, as has been said, I think may be properly called real, original, or primary qualities, because they are in the things themselves, whether they are perceived or no; and upon their different modifications it is that the secondary qualities depend.

The other two are only powers to act differently upon other things, which powers result from the different modifications of those primary qualities.

24. *The first are resemblances; the second thought resemblances, but are not; the third neither are, nor are thought so.*—But though these two latter sorts of qualities are powers barely, and nothing but powers, relating to several other bodies, and resulting from the different modifications of the original qualities, yet they are generally otherwise thought of. For the second sort, viz., the powers to produce several ideas in us by our senses, are looked upon as real qualities in the things thus affecting us; but the third sort are called and esteemed barely powers. V. g., the idea of heat or light which we receive by our eyes or touch from the sun, are commonly thought real qualities existing in the sun, and something more than mere powers in it. But when we consider the sun in reference to wax, which it melts or blanches, we look upon the whiteness and softness produced in the wax, not as qualities in the sun, but effects produced by powers in it: whereas, if rightly considered, these qualities of light and warmth, which are perceptions in me when I am warmed or enlightened by the sun, are no otherwise in the sun than the changes made in the wax, when it is blanched or melted, are in the sun. They are all of them equally powers in the sun, depending on its primary qualities, whereby it is able in the one case so to alter the bulk, figure, texture, or motion of some of the insensible parts of my eyes or hands as thereby to produce in me the idea of light or heat, and in the other it is able so to alter the bulk, figure, texture, or motion of the insensible parts of the wax as to make them fit to produce in me the distinct ideas of white and fluid.

25. The reason why the one are ordinarily taken for real qualities, and the other only for bare powers, seems to be because the ideas we have of distinct colors, sounds, etc., containing nothing at all in them of bulk, figure, or motion, we are not apt to think them the effects of these primary qualities which appear not, to our senses, to operate in their production, and with which they have not any apparent congruity, or conceivable connection. Hence it is that we are so forward to imagine that those ideas are the resemblances of something really existing in the objects themselves, since sensation discovers nothing of bulk, figure, or motion of parts, in their production, nor can reason show how bodies by their bulk, figure, and motion, should produce in the mind the ideas of blue or yellow, etc. But, in the other case, in the operations of bodies changing the qualities one of another, we plainly discover that the quality produced hath commonly no resemblance with anything in the thing producing it; wherefore we look on it as a bare effect of power. For though, receiving the idea of heat or light from the sun, we are apt to think it is a perception and resemblance of such a quality in the sun, yet when we see wax, or a fair face, receive change of color from the sun, we cannot imagine that to be the reception or resemblance of anything in the sun, because we find not those different colors in the sun itself. For, our senses being able to observe a likeness or unlikeness of sensible qualities in two different external objects, we forwardly enough conclude the production of any sensible quality in any subject to be an effect of bare power, and not the communication of any quality which was really in the efficient, when we find no such sensible quality in the thing that produced it. But our senses not being able to discover any unlikeness between the idea produced in us and the quality of the object producing it, we are apt to imagine that our ideas are resemblances of something in the objects, and not the effects of certain powers placed in the modification of their primary qualities, with which primary qualities the ideas produced in us have no resemblance.

26. *Secondary qualities twofold: first, immediately perceivable; secondly, mediately perceivable.*—To conclude: Beside those before-mentioned primary qualities in bodies, viz., bulk, figure, extension, number, and motion of their solid parts, all the rest whereby we take notice of bodies and distinguish them one from another, are nothing else but several powers in them depending on those primary qualities, whereby they are fitted, either by immediately operating on our bodies, to produce several different ideas in us; or else by operating on other bodies, so to change their primary qualities as to render them capable of producing ideas in us different from what before they did. The former of these, I think, may be called secondary qualities *immediately perceivable;* the latter, secondary qualities *mediately perceivable.*

CHAPTER IX

OF PERCEPTION

1. *Perception the first simple idea of reflection.*—Perception, as it is the first faculty of the mind exercised about our ideas, so it is the first and simplest idea we have from reflection, and is by some called 'thinking' in general. Though thinking, in the propriety of the English tongue, signifies that sort of operation of the mind about its ideas wherein the mind is active; where it, with some degree of voluntary attention, considers any thing. For in bare, naked perception, the mind is, for the most part, only passive; and what it perceives it cannot avoid perceiving.

2. *Reflection alone can give us the idea of what perception is.*—What perception is, everyone will know better by reflecting on what he does himself, when he sees, hears, feels, etc., or thinks, than by any discourse of mine. Whoever reflects on what passes in his own mind, cannot miss it; and if he does not reflect, all the words in the world cannot make him have any notion of it.

3. This is certain, that whatever alterations are made in the body, if they reach not the mind; whatever impressions are made on the outward parts, if they are not taken notice of within; there is no perception. Fire may burn our bodies with no other effect than it does a billet, unless the motion be continued to the brain, and there the sense of heat or idea of pain be produced in the mind, wherein consists actual perception.

4. *Impulse on the organ insufficient.*—How often may a man observe in himself, that whilst his mind is intently employed in the contemplation of some objects, and curiously surveying some ideas that are there, it takes no notice of impressions of sounding bodies made upon the organ of hearing with the same alteration that uses to be for the producing the idea of sound! A sufficient impulse there may be on the organ; but it not reaching the observation of the mind, there follows no perception: and though the motion that uses to produce the idea of sound be made in the ear, yet no sound is heard. Want of sensation in this case is not through any defect in the organ, or that the man's ears are less affected than at other times when he does hear; but that which uses to produce the idea, though conveyed in by the usual organ, not being taken notice of in the understanding, and so imprinting no idea on the mind, there follows no sensation. So that wherever there is sense or perception, there some idea is actually produced, and present in the understanding.

5. *Children, though they may have ideas in the womb, have none*

innate.—Therefore, I doubt not but children, by the exercise of their senses about objects that affect them in the womb, receive some few ideas before they are born, as the unavoidable effects either of the bodies that environ them, or else of those wants or diseases they suffer; amongst which (if one may conjecture concerning things not very capable of examination) I think the ideas of hunger and warmth are two, which probably are some of the first that children have, and which they scarce ever part with again.

6. But though it be reasonable to imagine that children receive some ideas before they come into the world, yet these simple ideas are far from those innate principles which some contend for, and we above have rejected. These here mentioned, being the effects of sensation, are only from some affections of the body which happen to them there, and so depend on something exterior to the mind; no otherwise differing in their manner of production from other ideas derived from sense, but only in the precedency of time. Whereas those innate principles are supposed to be quite of another nature, not coming into the mind by any accidental alterations in or operations on the body; but, as it were, original characters impressed upon it in the very first moment of its being and constitution.

7. *Which ideas appear first, is not evident, nor important.*—As there are some ideas which we may reasonably suppose may be introduced into the minds of children in the womb, subservient to the necessities of their life and being there; so after they are born those ideas are the earliest imprinted which happen to be the sensible qualities which first occur to them: amongst which, light is not the least considerable, nor of the weakest efficacy. And how covetous the mind is to be furnished with all such ideas as have no pain accompanying them, may be a little guessed by what is observable in children new born, who always turn their eyes to that part from whence the light comes, lay them how you please. But the ideas that are most familiar at first being various, according to the divers circumstances of children's first entertainment in the world, the order wherein the several ideas come at first into the mind is very various and uncertain also, neither is it much material to know it.

8. *Ideas of sensation often changed by the judgment.*—We are farther to consider concerning perception, that the ideas we receive by sensation are often in grown people altered by the judgment without our taking notice of it. When we set before our eyes a round globe of any uniform color, v. g., gold, alabaster, or jet, it is certain that the idea thereby imprinted in our mind is of a flat circle variously shadowed, with several degrees of light and brightness coming to our eyes. But we having by use been accustomed to perceive what kind of appearance

convex bodies are wont to make in us, what alterations are made in the
reflections of light by the difference of the sensible figures of bodies, the
judgment presently, by an habitual custom, alters the appearances into
their causes; so that, from that which truly is variety of shadow or
color collecting the figure, it makes it pass for a mark of figure, and
frames to itself the perception of a convex figure and an uniform color;
when the idea we receive from thence is only a plane variously colored,
as is evident in painting. [To which purpose I shall here insert a problem of that very ingenious and studious promoter of real knowledge, the
learned and worthy Mr. Molineux, which he was pleased to send me in a
letter some months since: and it is this: "Suppose a man born blind, and
now adult, and taught by his touch to distinguish between a cube and a
sphere of the same metal, and nighly of the same bigness, so as to tell,
when he felt one and the other, which is the cube, which the sphere.
Suppose then the cube and sphere placed on a table, and the blind man
to be made to see: *quaere,* whether by his sight, before he touched
them, he could now distinguish and tell which is the globe, which the
cube?" To which the acute and judicious proposer answers: "Not. For
though he has obtained the experience of how a globe, how a cube, affects his touch; yet he has not yet obtained the experience, that what
affects his touch so or so, must affect his sight so or so; or that a pro-
tuberant angle in the cube, that pressed his hand unequally, shall appear
to his eye as it does in the cube." I agree with this thinking gentleman,
whom I am proud to call my friend, in his answer to this his problem;
and am of opinion that the blind man, at first sight, would not be able
with certainty to say which was the globe, which the cube, whilst he
only saw them; though he could unerringly name them by his touch,
and certainly distinguish them by the difference of their figures felt.
This I have set down, and leave with my reader, as an occasion for
him to consider how much he may be beholden to experience, improvement, and acquired notions, where he thinks he has not the least use of,
or help from them; and the rather, because this observing gentleman farther adds, that having upon the occasion of my book proposed this to
divers very ingenious men, he hardly ever met with one that at first gave
the answer to it which he thinks true, till by hearing his reasons they
were convinced.]

9. *This judgment apt to be mistaken for direct perception.*—But this
is not, I think, usual in any of our ideas but those received by sight;
because sight, the most comprehensive of all our senses, conveying to
our minds the ideas of light and colors, which are peculiar only to that
sense; and also the far different ideas of space, figure and motion, the
several varieties whereof change the appearances of its proper objects,
viz., light and colors; we bring ourselves by use to judge of the one by

the other. This, in many cases, by a settled habit in things whereof we have frequent experience, is performed so constantly and so quick, that we take that for the perception of our sensation which is an idea formed by our judgment; so that one, viz., that of sensation, serves only to excite the other, and is scarce taken notice of itself; as a man who reads or hears with attention and understanding, takes little notice of the characters or sounds, but of the ideas that are excited in him by them.

10. Nor need we wonder that this is done with so little notice, if we consider how very quick the actions of the mind are performed. For as itself is thought to take up no space, to have no extension, so its actions seem to require no time, but many of them seem to be crowded into an instant. I speak this in comparison to the actions of the body. Anyone may easily observe this in his own thoughts who will take the pains to reflect on them. How, as it were in an instant, do our minds with one glance see all the parts of a demonstration which may very well be called a long one, if we consider the time it will require to put it into words, and step by step show it another! Secondly, we shall not be so much surprised that this is done in us with so little notice, if we consider how the facility which we get of doing things, by a custom of doing, makes them often pass in us without our notice. Habits, especially such as are begun very early, come at last to produce actions in us which often escape our observation. How frequently do we in a day cover our eyes with our eyelids, without perceiving that we are at all in the dark! Men, that by custom have got the use of a by-word, do almost in every sentence pronounce sounds which, though taken notice of by others, they themselves neither hear nor observe. And therefore it is not so strange that our minds should often change the idea of its sensation into that of its judgment, and make one serve only to excite the other, without our taking notice of it. . . .

15. *Perception the inlet of all materials of knowledge.*—Perception, then, being the first step and degree towards knowledge, and the inlet of all the materials of it, the fewer senses any man as well as any other creature hath, and the fewer and duller the impressions are that are made by them, and the duller the faculties are that are employed about them, the more remote are they from that knowledge which is to be found in some men. But this, being in great variety of degrees (as may be perceived amongst men), cannot certainly be discovered in the several species of animals, much less in their particular individuals. It suffices me only to have remarked here, that perception is the first operation of all our intellectual faculties, and the inlet of all knowledge into our minds. And I am apt, too, to imagine that it is perception in the lowest degree of it which puts the boundaries between animals and the

inferior ranks of creatures. But this I mention only as my conjecture by the by, it being indifferent to the matter in hand which way the learned shall determine of it.

CHAPTER X

OF RETENTION

1. *Contemplation.*—The next faculty of the mind, whereby it makes a farther progress towards knowledge, is that which I call retention or the keeping of those simple ideas which from sensation or reflection it hath received. This is done two ways. First, by keeping the idea which is brought into it for some time actually in view, which is called contemplation.

2. *Memory.*—The other way of retention is the power to revive again in our minds those ideas which after imprinting have disappeared, or have been as it were laid aside out of sight; and thus we do, when we conceive heat or light, yellow or sweet, the object being removed. This is memory, which is, as it were, the storehouse of our ideas. For the narrow mind of man, not being capable of having many ideas under view and consideration at once, it was necessary to have a repository to lay up those ideas, which at another time it might have use of. [But our ideas being nothing but actual perceptions in the mind, which cease to be anything when there is no perception of them, this laying up of our ideas in the repository of the memory signifies no more but this—that the mind has a power, in many cases, to revive perceptions which it has once had, with this additional perception annexed to them, that it has had them before. And in this sense it is that our ideas are said to be in our memories, when indeed they are actually nowhere, but only there is an ability in the mind when it will to revive them again, and, as it were, paint them anew on itself, though some with more, some with less, difficulty; some more lively, and others more obscurely.] And thus it is by the assistance of this faculty that we are said to have all those ideas in our understandings, which though we do not actually contemplate, yet we can bring in sight, and make appear again and be the objects of our thoughts, without the help of those sensible qualities which first imprinted them there.

3. *Attention, repetition, pleasure and pain, fix ideas.*—Attention and repetition help much to the fixing any ideas in the memory; but those which naturally at first make the deepest and most lasting impression, are those which are accompanied with pleasure or pain. The great business of the senses being to make us take notice of what hurts or ad-

vantages the body, it is wisely ordered by nature (as has been shown) that pain should accompany the reception of several ideas; which, supplying the place of consideration and reasoning in children, and acting quicker than consideration in grown men, makes both the old and young avoid painful objects with that haste which is necessary for their preservation, and in both settles in the memory a caution for the future.

4. *Ideas fade in the memory.*—Concerning the several degrees of lasting wherewith ideas are imprinted on the memory, we may observe that some of them have been produced in the understanding by an object affecting the senses once only, and no more than once; [others, that have more than once offered themselves to the senses, have yet been little taken notice of—the mind, either heedless as in children, or otherwise employed as in men, intent only on one thing, not setting the stamp deep into itself; and in some, where they are set on with care and repeated impressions, either] through the temper of the body or some other fault, the memory is very weak. In all these cases, ideas [in the mind] quickly fade, and often vanish quite out of the understanding, leaving no more footsteps or remaining characters of themselves than shadows do flying over fields of corn; and the mind is as void of them as if they never had been there.

5. Thus many of those ideas which were produced in the minds of children in the beginning of their sensation (some of which perhaps, as of some pleasures and pains, were before they were born, and others in their infancy), if in the future course of their lives they are not repeated again, are quite lost, without the least glimpse remaining of them. This may be observed in those who by some mischance have lost their sight when they were very young, in whom the ideas of colors, having been but slightly taken notice of, and ceasing to be repeated, do quite wear out; so that some years after there is no more notion nor memory of colors left in their minds, than in those of people born blind. The memory of some men, it is true, is very tenacious, even to a miracle; but yet there seems to be a constant decay of all our ideas, even of those which are struck deepest, and in minds the most retentive; so that if they be not sometimes renewed by repeated exercise of the senses, or reflection of those kinds of objects which at first occasioned them, the print wears out, and at last there remains nothing to be seen. Thus the ideas, as well as children, of our youth often die before us; and our minds represent to us those tombs to which we are approaching; where though the brass and marble remain, yet the inscriptions are effaced by time, and the imagery molders away. The pictures drawn in our minds are laid in fading colors; and if not sometimes refreshed, vanish and disappear. How much the constitution of our bodies [and the make of our animal spirits] are concerned in this; and whether the tem-

per of the brain makes this difference, that in some it retains the characters drawn on it like marble, in others like freestone, and in others little better than sand, I shall not here inquire: though it may seem probable that the constitution of the body does sometimes influence the memory, since we oftentimes find a disease quite strip the mind of all its ideas, and the flames of a fever in a few days calcine all those images to dust and confusion, which seemed to be as lasting as if graved in marble.

6. *Constantly repeated ideas can scarce be lost.*—But concerning the ideas themselves it is easy to remark, that those that are oftenest refreshed (amongst which are those that are conveyed into the mind by more ways than one) by a frequent return of the objects or actions that produce them, fix themselves best in the memory, and remain clearest and longest there: and therefore those which are of the original qualities of bodies, viz., solidity, extension, figure, motion, and rest; and those that almost constantly affect our bodies, as heat and cold; and those which are the affections of all kinds of beings, as existence, duration, and number, which almost every object that affects our senses, every thought which employs our minds, bring along with them; these, I say, and the like ideas, are seldom quite lost, whilst the mind retains any ideas at all.

7. *In remembering, the mind is often active.*—In this secondary perception, as I may so call it, or viewing again the ideas that are lodged in the memory, the mind is oftentimes more than barely passive; the appearance of those dormant pictures depending sometimes on the will. The mind very often sets itself on work in search of some hidden idea, and turns as it were the eye of the soul upon it; though sometimes too they start up in our minds of their own accord, and offer themselves to the understanding; and very often are roused and tumbled out of their dark cells into open daylight by turbulent and tempestuous passions; our affections bringing ideas to our memory, which had otherwise lain quiet and unregarded. This further is to be observed, concerning ideas lodged in the memory, and upon occasion revived by the mind, that they are not only (as the word 'revive' imports) none of them new ones, but also that the mind takes notice of them as of a former impression, and renews its acquaintance with them as with ideas it had known before. So that though ideas formerly imprinted are not all constantly in view, yet in remembrance they are constantly known to be such as have been formerly imprinted; i. e., in view, and taken notice of before by the understanding.

8. *Two defects in memory.*—Memory, in an intellectual creature, is necessary in the next degree to perception. It is of so great moment, that, where it is wanting, all the rest of our faculties are in a great measure

useless. And we in our thoughts, reasonings, and knowledge, could not proceed beyond present objects, were it not for the assistance of our memories; wherein there may be two defects:

First, that it loses the idea quite, and so far produces perfect ignorance. For, since we can know nothing further than we have the idea of it, when that is gone, we are in perfect ignorance.

Secondly, that it moves slowly, and retrieves not the ideas that it has, and are laid up in store, quick enough to serve the mind upon occasion. This, if it be to a great degree, is stupidity; and he who, through this default in his memory, has not the ideas that are really preserved there, ready at hand when need and occasion calls for them, were almost as good be without them quite, since they serve him to little purpose. The dull man, who loses the opportunity, whilst he is seeking in his mind for those ideas that should serve his turn, is not much more happy in his knowledge than one that is perfectly ignorant. It is the business therefore of the memory to furnish to the mind those dormant ideas which it has present occasion for; in the having them ready at hand on all occasions, consists that which we call invention, fancy, and quickness of parts. . . .

CHAPTER XI

OF DISCERNING, AND OTHER OPERATIONS OF THE MIND

1. *No knowledge without discerning.*—Another faculty we may take notice of in our minds, is that of *discerning* and *distinguishing* between the several ideas it has. It is not enough to have a confused perception of something in general: unless the mind had a distinct perception of different objects and their qualities, it would be capable of very little knowledge; though the bodies that affect us were as busy about us as they are now, and the mind were continually employed in thinking. On this faculty of distinguishing one thing from another, depends the evidence and certainty of several even very general propositions, which have passed for innate truths; because men, overlooking the true cause why those propositions find universal assent, impute it wholly to native uniform impressions: whereas it in truth depends upon this clear discerning faculty of the mind, whereby it perceives two ideas to be the same or different. But of this more hereafter.

2. *The difference of wit and judgment.*—How much the imperfection of accurately discriminating ideas one from another lies either in the dullness or faults of the organs of sense, or want of acuteness, exercise, or attention in the understanding, or hastiness and precipitancy natural

to some tempers, I will not here examine: it suffices to take notice, that this is one of the operations that the mind may reflect on and observe in itself. It is of that consequence to its other knowledge, that so far as this faculty is in itself dull, or not rightly made use of for the distinguishing one thing from another, so far our notions are confused, and our reason, and judgment disturbed or misled. If in having our ideas in the memory ready at hand consists quickness of parts; in this of having them unconfused, and being able nicely to distinguish one thing from another where there is but the least difference, consists in a great measure the exactness of judgment and clearness of reason which is to be observed in one man above another. And hence, perhaps, may be given some reason of that common observation—that men who have a great deal of wit and prompt memories, have not always the clearest judgment or deepest reason. For, wit lying most in the assemblage of ideas, and putting those together with quickness and variety wherein can be found any resemblance or congruity, thereby to make up pleasant pictures and agreeable visions in the fancy; judgment, on the contrary, lies quite on the other side, in separating carefully one from another ideas wherein can be found the least difference, thereby to avoid being misled by similitude and by affinity to take one thing for another. This is a way of proceeding quite contrary to metaphor and allusion, wherein for the most part lies that entertainment and pleasantry of wit which strikes so lively on the fancy, and therefore is so acceptable to all people; because its beauty appears at first sight, and there is required no labor of thought to examine what truth or reason there is in it. The mind, without looking any farther, rests satisfied with the agreeableness of the picture and the gaiety of the fancy; and it is a kind of affront to go about to examine it by the severe rules of truth and good reason; whereby it appears that it consists in something that is not perfectly conformable to them. . . .

4. *Comparing.*—The comparing them one with another, in respect of extent, degrees, time, place, or any other circumstances, is another operation of the mind about its ideas, and is that upon which depends all that large tribe of ideas comprehended under relation; which of how vast an extent it is, I shall have occasion to consider hereafter. . . .

6. *Compounding.*—The next operation we may observe in the mind about its ideas is *composition;* whereby it puts together several of those simple ones it has received from sensation and reflection, and combines them into complex ones. Under this of composition may be reckoned also that of enlarging; wherein though the composition does not so much appear as in more complex ones, yet it is nevertheless a putting several ideas together, though of the same kind. Thus, by adding several units

together we make the idea of a dozen, and putting together the repeated ideas of several perches we frame that of a furlong. . . .

8. *Naming.*—When children have by repeated sensations got ideas fixed in their memories, they begin by degrees to learn the use of signs. And when they have got the skill to apply the organs of speech to the framing of articulate sounds, they begin to make use of words to signify their ideas to others. These verbal signs they sometimes borrow from others, and sometimes make themselves, as one may observe among the new and unusual names children often give to things in their first use of language.

9. *Abstraction.*—The use of words then being to stand as outward marks of our internal ideas, and those ideas being taken from particular things, if every particular idea that we take in should have a distinct name, names must be endless. To prevent this, the mind makes the particular ideas, received from particular objects, to become general; which is done by considering them as they are in the mind such appearances,— separate from all other existences, and the circumstances of real existence, as time, place, or any other concomitant ideas. This is called *abstraction,* whereby ideas taken from particular beings become general representatives of all of the same kind; and their names, general names, applicable to whatever exists conformable to such abstract ideas. Such precise, naked appearances in the mind, without considering how, whence, or with what others they came there, the understanding lays up (with names commonly annexed to them) as the standards to rank real existences into sorts, as they agree with these patterns, and to denominate them accordingly. Thus, the same color being observed today in chalk or snow, which the mind yesterday received from milk, it considers that appearance alone, makes it a representative of all of that kind, and, having given it the name whiteness, it by that sound signifies the same quality wheresoever to be imagined or met with; and thus universals, whether ideas or terms, are made. . . .

14. *Method followed in this explication of faculties.*—These, I think, are the first faculties and operations of the mind which it makes use of in understanding; and though they are exercised about all its ideas in general, yet the instances I have hitherto given have been chiefly in simple ideas; and I have subjoined the explication of these faculties of the mind to that of simple ideas, before I come to what I have to say concerning complex ones, for these following reasons:—

First, because, several of these faculties being exercised at first principally about simple ideas, we might, by following nature in its ordinary method, trace and discover them in their rise, progress, and gradual improvements.

Secondly, because, observing the faculties of the mind, how they operate about simple ideas, which are usually in most men's minds much more clear, precise, and distinct than complex ones, we may the better examine and learn how the mind extracts, denominates, compares, and exercises in its other operations about those which are complex, wherein we are much more liable to mistake.

Thirdly, because these very operations of the mind about ideas received from sensations are themselves, when reflected on, another set of ideas, derived from that other source of our knowledge which I call reflection; and therefore fit to be considered in this place after the simple ideas of sensation. Of compounding, comparing, abstracting, etc., I have but just spoken, having occasion to treat of them more at large in other places.

15. *These are the beginnings of human knowledge.*—And thus I have given a short and, I think, true history of the first beginnings of human knowledge, whence the mind has its first objects, and by what steps it makes its progress to the laying in and storing up those ideas out of which is to be framed all the knowledge it is capable of; wherein I must appeal to experience and observation whether I am in the right: the best way to come to truth being to examine things as really they are, and not to conclude they are as we fancy of ourselves, or have been taught by others to imagine.

16. *Appeal to experience.*—To deal truly, this is the only way that I can discover whereby the ideas of things are brought into the understanding: if other men have either innate ideas or infused principles, they have reason to enjoy them; and if they are sure of it, it is impossible for others to deny them the privilege that they have above their neighbors. I can speak but of what I find in myself, and is agreeable to those notions which, if we will examine the whole course of men in their several ages, countries, and educations, seem to depend on those foundations which I have laid, and to correspond with this method in all the parts and degrees thereof.

17. *Dark room.*—I pretend not to teach, but to inquire; and therefore cannot but confess here again, that external and internal sensation are the only passages that I can find of knowledge to the understanding. These alone, as far as I can discover, are the windows by which light is let into this dark room. For methinks the understanding is not much unlike a closet wholly shut from light, with only some little openings left to let in external visible resemblances or ideas of things without: [would the pictures coming into such a dark room but stay there,] and lie so orderly as to be found upon occasion, it would very much resemble the understanding of a man in reference to all objects of sight, and the ideas of them.

These are my guesses concerning the means whereby the understanding comes to have and retain simple ideas and the modes of them, with some other operations about them. I proceed now to examine some of these simple ideas and their modes a little more particularly.

CHAPTER XII

OF COMPLEX IDEAS

1. *Made by the mind out of simple ones.*—We have hitherto considered those ideas, in the reception whereof the mind is only passive, which are those simple ones received from sensation and reflection before mentioned, whereof the mind cannot make one to itself, nor have any ideas which does not wholly consist of them. [But as the mind is wholly passive in the reception of all its simple ideas, so it exerts several acts of its own, whereby out of its simple ideas, as the materials and foundations of the rest, the other are framed. The acts of the mind wherein it exerts its power over its simple ideas are chiefly these three: (1) Combining several simple ideas into one compound one; and thus all *complex ideas* are made. (2) The second is bringing two ideas, whether simple or complex, together, and setting them by one another, so as to take a view of them at once, without uniting them into one; by which way it gets all its *ideas of relations*. (3) The third is separating them from all other ideas that accompany them in their real existence; this is called abstraction: and thus all its *general ideas* are made. This shows man's power and its way of operation to be much the same in the material and intellectual world. For, the materials in both being such as he has no power over, either to make or destroy, all that man can do is either to unite them together, or to set them by one another, or wholly separate them. I shall here begin with the first of these in the consideration of complex ideas, and come to the other two in their due places.] As simple ideas are observed to exist in several combinations united together, so the mind has a power to consider several of them united together as one idea; and that not only as they are united in external objects, but as itself has joined them. Ideas thus made up of several simple ones put together I call *complex;* such as are beauty, gratitude, a man, an army, the universe; which, though complicated of various simple ideas or complex ideas made up of simple ones, yet are, when the mind pleases, considered each by itself as one entire thing, and signified by one name.

2. *Made voluntarily.*—In this faculty of repeating and joining together its ideas, the mind has great power in varying and multiplying

the objects of its thoughts infinitely beyond what sensation or reflection furnished it with; but all this still confined to those simple ideas which it received from those two sources, and which are the ultimate materials of all its compositions. For, simple ideas are all from things themselves; and of these the mind can have no more nor other than what are suggested to it. It can have no other ideas of sensible qualities than what come from without by the senses, nor any ideas of other kind of operations of a thinking substance than what it finds in itself. But when it has once got these simple ideas, it is not confined barely to observation, and what offers itself from without; it can, by its own power, put together those ideas it has, and make new complex ones which it never received so united.

3. *Complex ideas are either of modes, substances, or relations.*—Complex ideas, however compounded and decompounded, though their number be infinite, and the variety endless wherewith they fill and entertain the thoughts of men, yet I think they may be all reduced under these three heads: (1) Modes. (2) Substances. (3) Relations.

4. *Ideas of modes.*—First, *modes* I call such complex ideas which, however compounded, contain not in them the supposition of subsisting by themselves, but are considered as dependences on, or affections of, substances; such are the ideas signified by the words, triangle, gratitude, murder, etc. And if in this I use the word mode in somewhat a different sense from its ordinary signification, I beg pardon; it being unavoidable in discourses differing from the ordinary received notions, either to make new words or to use old words in somewhat a new signification: the latter whereof, in our present case, is perhaps the more tolerable of the two.

5. *Simple and mixed modes.*—Of these modes there are two sorts which deserve distinct consideration. First, there are some which are only variations or different combinations of the same simple idea, without the mixture of any other, as a dozen, or score; which are nothing but the ideas of so many distinct units added together: and these I call *simple modes,* as being contained within the bounds of one simple idea. Secondly, there are others compounded of simple ideas, of several kinds, put together to make one complex one; v. g., beauty, consisting of a certain composition of color and figure, causing delight in the beholder; theft, which, being the concealed change of the possession of any thing, without the consent of the proprietor, contains, as is visible, a combination of several ideas of several kinds; and these I call *mixed modes.*

6. *Ideas of substances, single or collective.*—Secondly, the ideas of *substances* are such combinations of simple ideas as are taken to represent distinct *particular* things subsisting by themselves, in which the supposed or confused idea of substance, such as it is, is always the first

and chief. Thus, if to substance be joined the simple idea of a certain dull, whitish color, with certain degrees of weight, hardness, ductility, and fusibility, we have the idea of lead; and a combination of the ideas of a certain sort of figure, with the powers of motion, thought, and reasoning, joined to substance, make the ordinary idea of a man. Now of substances also there are two sorts of ideas, one of single substances, as they exist separately, as of a man or a sheep; the other of several of those put together, as an army of men or flock of sheep; which collective ideas of several substances thus put together, are as much each of them one single idea as that of a man or an unit.

7. *Relation.*—Thirdly, the last sort of complex ideas is that we call *relation,* which consists in the consideration and comparing one idea with another. Of these several kinds we shall treat in their order.

8. *The abstrusest ideas are from the two sources.*—If we trace the progress of our minds, and with attention observe how it repeats, adds together, unites its simple ideas received from sensation or reflection, it will lead us farther than at first perhaps we should have imagined. And I believe we shall find, if we warily observe the originals of our notions, that even the most abstruse ideas, how remote soever they may seem from sense, or from any operation of our own minds, are yet only such as the understanding frames to itself, by repeating and joining together ideas that it had either from objects of sense, or from its own operations about them: so that those even large and abstract ideas are derived from sensation or reflection, being no other than what the mind, by the ordinary use of its own faculties, employed about ideas received from objects of sense, or from the operations it observes in itself about them, may and does attain unto. This I shall endeavor to show in the ideas we have of space, time, and infinity, and some few other that seem the most remote from those originals. . . .[3]

CHAPTER XVII

OF INFINITY

1. *Infinity, in its original intention, attributed to space, duration, and number.*—He that would know what kind of idea it is to which we give the name of infinity, cannot do it better than by considering to what infinity is, by the mind, more immediately attributed, and then how the mind comes to frame it.

[3] In Chapters XIII-XVI Locke discusses the ideas of the simple modes of *space,* of *duration,* and of *number.*—*Editor.*

Finite and infinite seem to me to be looked upon by the mind as the modes of quantity, and to be attributed primarily, in their first designation, only to those things which have parts, and are capable of increase or diminution by the addition or subtraction of any the least part: and such are the ideas of space, duration, and number, which we have considered in the foregoing chapters. It is true, that we cannot but be assured that the great God, of whom and from whom are all things, is incomprehensibly infinite: but yet, when we apply to that first and supreme Being our idea of infinite, in our weak and narrow thoughts, we do it primarily in respect to his duration and ubiquity; and, I think, more figuratively to his power, wisdom, and goodness, and other attributes, which are properly inexhaustible and incomprehensible, etc. For, when we call them infinite, we have no other idea of this infinity, but what carries with it some reflection on, and imitation of, that number or extent of the acts or objects of God's power, wisdom, and goodness, which can never be supposed so great or so many, which these attributes will not always surmount and exceed, let us multiply them in our thoughts as far as we can, with all the infinity of endless number. I do not pretend to say how these attributes are in God, who is infinitely beyond the reach of our narrow capacities. They do, without doubt, contain in them all possible perfection: but this, I say, is our way of conceiving them, and these our ideas of their infinity.

2. *The idea of finite easily got.*—Finite, then, and infinite, being by the mind looked on as modifications of expansion and duration, the next thing to be considered, is, how the mind comes by them. As for the idea of finite, there is no great difficulty. The obvious portions of extension that affect our senses, carry with them into the mind the idea of finite; and the ordinary periods of succession, whereby we measure time and duration, as hours, days, and years, are bounded lengths. The difficulty is, how we come by those boundless ideas of eternity and immensity, since the objects we converse with come so much short of any approach or proportion to that largeness.

3. *How we come by the idea of infinity.*—Everyone that has any idea of any stated lengths of space, as a foot, finds that he can repeat that idea; and joining it to the former, make the idea of two feet; and by the addition of a third, three feet; and so on, without ever coming to an end of his addition, whether of the same idea of a foot, or, if he pleases, of doubling it, or any other idea he has of any length, as a mile, or diameter of the earth, or of the *orbis magnus:* for whichsoever of these he takes, and how often soever he doubles, or any otherwise multiplies it, he finds, that after he has continued his doubling in his thoughts, and enlarged his idea as much as he pleases, he has no more reason to stop, nor is one jot nearer the end of such addition, than he was at first setting

out. The power of enlarging his idea of space by further additions remaining still the same, he hence takes the idea of infinite space.

4. *Our idea of space boundless.*—This, I think, is the way whereby the mind gets the idea of infinite space. It is a quite different consideration, to examine whether the mind has the idea of such a boundless space actually existing, since our ideas are not always proofs of the existence of things; but yet, since this comes here in our way, I suppose I may say, that we are apt to think that space in itself is actually boundless; to which imagination the idea of space or expansion of itself naturally leads us. For it being considered by us, either as the extension of body, or as existing by itself, without any solid matter taking it up, (for of such a void space we have not only the idea, but I have proved, as I think, from the motion of body, its necessary existence), it is impossible the mind should be ever able to find or suppose any end of it, or be stopped anywhere in its progress in this space , how far soever it extends its thoughts. Any bounds made with the body, even adamantine walls, are so far from putting a stop to the mind in its further progress in space and extension, that it rather facilitates and enlarges it; for so far as that body reaches, so far no one can doubt of extension; and when we are come to the utmost extremity of body, what is there that can there put a stop, and satisfy the mind that is at the end of space when it perceives that it is not; nay, when it is satisfied that body itself can move into it? For if it be necessary for the motion of body, that there should be an empty space, though ever so little, here amongst bodies, and if it be possible for body to move in or through that empty space; nay, it is impossible for any particle of matter to move but into an empty space; the same possibility of a body's moving into a void space, beyond the utmost bounds of body, as well as into a void space interspersed amongst bodies, will always remain clear and evident: the idea of empty pure space, whether within or beyond the confines of all bodies, being exactly the same, differing not in nature, though in bulk; and there being nothing to hinder body from moving into it. So that wherever the mind places itself by any thought, either amongst or remote from all bodies, it can in this uniform idea of space nowhere find any bounds, any end; and so must necessarily conclude it, by the very nature and idea of each part of it, to be actually infinite.

5. *And so of duration.*—As by the power we find in ourselves of repeating, as often as we will, any idea of space, we get the idea of immensity; so, by being able to repeat the idea of any length of duration we have in our minds, with all the endless addition of number, we come by the idea of eternity. For we find in ourselves, we can no more come to an end of such repeated ideas, than we can come to the end of number, which everyone perceives he cannot. But here again it is

another question, quite different from our having an idea of eternity, to know whether there were any real being, whose duration has been eter‧ nal. And as to this, I say, he that considers something now existing, must necessarily come to something eternal. But having spoken of this in another place, I shall say here no more of it, but proceed on to some other considerations of our idea of infinity.

6. *Why other ideas are not capable of infinity.*—If it be so, that our idea of infinity be got from the power we observe in ourselves of repeating, without end, our own ideas, it may be demanded, "why we do not attribute infinity to other ideas, as well as those of space and duration;" since they may be as easily, and as often repeated in our minds as the other; and yet nobody ever thinks of infinite sweetness, or infinite whiteness, though he can repeat the idea of sweet or white, as frequently as those of a yard or a day? To which I answer, all the ideas that are considered as having parts, and are capable of increase by the addition of any equal or less parts, afford us by their repetition the idea of infinity; because with this endless repetition there is continued an enlargement, of which there can be no end. But in other ideas it is not so; for to the largest idea of extension or duration that I at present have, the addition of any the least part makes an increase; but to the perfectest idea I have of the whitest whiteness, if I add another of a less or equal whiteness (and of a whiter than I have, I cannot add the idea), it makes no increase, and enlarges not my idea at all; and therefore the different ideas of whiteness, etc., are called degrees. For those ideas that consist of parts are capable of being augmented by every addition of the least part; but if you take the idea of white, which one parcel of snow yielded yesterday to our sight, and another idea of white from another parcel of snow you see today, and put them together in your mind, they embody, as it were, and run into one, and the idea of whiteness is not at all increased; and if we add a less degree of whiteness to a greater, we are so far from increasing, that we diminish it. Those ideas that consist not of parts cannot be augmented to what proportion men please, or be stretched beyond what they have received by their senses; but space, duration, and number, being capable of increase by repetition, leave in the mind an idea of endless room for more: nor can we conceive anywhere a stop to a further addition or progression, and so those ideas alone lead our minds towards the thought of infinity.

7. *Difference between infinity of space, and space infinite.*—Though our idea of infinity arise from the contemplation of quantity, and the endless increase the mind is able to make in quantity, by the repeated additions of what portions thereof it pleases; yet I guess we cause great confusion in our thoughts, when we join infinity to any supposed idea of quantity the mind can be thought to have, and so discourse or

reason about an infinite quantity, viz., an infinite space, or an infinite duration. For our idea of infinity being, as I think, an endless growing idea, by the idea of any quantity the mind has, being at that time terminated in that idea (for be it as great as it will, it can be no greater than it is), to join infinity to it, is to adjust a standing measure to a growing bulk; and therefore I think it is not an insignificant subtilty, if I say that we are carefully to distinguish between the idea of the infinity of space, and the idea of a space infinite: the first is nothing but a supposed endless progression of the mind, over what repeated ideas of space it pleases; but to have actually in the mind the idea of a space infinite, is to suppose the mind already passed over, and actually to have a view of all those repeated ideas of space which an endless repetition can never totally represent to it; which carries in it a plain contradiction.

8. *We have no idea of infinite space.*—This, perhaps, will be a little plainer, if we consider it in numbers. The infinity of numbers, to the end of whose addition everyone perceives there is no approach, easily appears to anyone that reflects on it: but how clear soever this idea of the infinity of number be, there is nothing yet more evident, than the absurdity of the actual idea of an infinite number. Whatsoever positive ideas we have in our minds of any space, duration, or number, let them be ever so great, they are still finite; but when we suppose an inexhaustible remainder, from which we remove all bounds, and wherein we allow the mind an endless progression of thought, without ever completing the idea, there we have our idea of infinity: which, though it seems to be pretty clear when we consider nothing else in it but the negation of an end, yet, when we would frame in our minds the idea of an infinite space or duration, that idea is very obscure and confused, because it is made up of two parts, very different, if not inconsistent. For let a man frame in his mind an idea of any space or number, as great as he will: it is plain the mind rests and terminates in that idea, which is contrary to the idea of infinity, which consists in a supposed endless progression: and therefore I think it is that we are so easily confounded, when we come to argue and reason about infinite space or duration, etc.; because the parts of such an idea not being perceived to be, as they are, inconsistent, the one side or other always perplexes, whatever consequences we draw from the other; as an idea of motion not passing on would perplex anyone who should argue from such an idea, which is not better than an idea of motion at rest: and such another seems to me to be the idea of a space, or (which is the same thing) a number infinite, i. e., of a space or number which the mind actually has, and so views and terminates in; and of a space or number, which, in a constant and endless enlarging and progression, it can in thought never attain to. For how large soever an idea of space I have in my mind, it

is no larger than it is that instant that I have it, though I be capable the next instant to double it, and so on *in infinitum;* for that alone is infinite which has no bounds, and that the idea of infinity in which our thoughts can find none.

9. *Number affords us the clearest idea of infinity.*—But of all other ideas, it is number, as I have said, which I think furnishes us with the clearest and most distinct idea of infinity we are capable of. For even in space and duration, when the mind pursues the idea of infinity, it there makes use of the ideas and repetitions of numbers, as of millions and millions of miles, or years, which are so many distinct ideas, kept best by number from running into a confused heap, wherein the mind loses itself; and when it has added together as many millions, etc., as it pleases, of known lengths of space or duration, the clearest idea it can get of infinity, is the confused, incomprehensible remainder of endless addible numbers, which affords no prospect of stop or boundary. . . .[4]

CHAPTER XXI

OF POWER

1. *This idea how got.*—The mind being every day informed, by the senses, of the alteration of those simple ideas it observes in things without, and taking notice how one comes to an end and ceases to be, and another begins to exist which was not before; reflecting also, on what passes within itself, and observing a constant change of its ideas, sometimes by the impression of outward objects on the senses, and sometimes by the determination of its own choice; and concluding, from what it has so constantly observed to have been, that the like changes will for the future be made in the same things by like agents, and by the like ways; considers in one thing the possibility of having any of its simple ideas changed, and in another the possibility of making that change; and so comes by that idea which we call *power.* Thus we say, fire has a power to melt gold—i.e., to destroy the consistency of its insensible parts, and consequently its hardness, and make it fluid—and gold has a power to be melted; that the sun has a power to blanch wax, and wax a power to be blanched by the sun, whereby the yellowness is destroyed and whiteness made to exist in its room. In which and the like cases, the power we consider is in reference to the change of perceivable ideas. For we cannot observe any alteration to be made in, or operation upon, anything, but by the observable change of its sensible ideas; nor con-

[4] In Chapters XVIII-XX Locke considers ideas of other simple modes, including the modes of *thinking* and of *pleasure* and *pain.—Editor.*

ceive any alteration to be made, but by conceiving a change of some of its ideas.

2. *Power, active and passive.*—Power thus considered is twofold: viz., as able to make, or able to receive, any change. The one may be called *active*, and the other *passive*, power. Whether matter be not wholly destitute of active power, as its author, God, is truly above all passive power; and whether the intermediate state of created spirits be not that alone which is capable of both active and passive power, may be worth consideration. I shall not now enter into that inquiry; my present business being not to search into the original of power, but how we come by the idea of it. But since active powers make so great a part of our complex ideas of natural substances (as we shall see hereafter), and I mention them as such, according to common apprehension; yet they being not, perhaps, so truly active powers as our hasty thoughts are apt to represent them, I judge it not amiss, by this intimation, to direct our minds to the consideration of God and spirits, for the clearest idea of active power.

3. *Power includes relation.*—I confess power includes in it some kind of *relation*—a relation to action or change; as, indeed, which of our ideas, of what kind soever, when attentively considered, does not? For our ideas of extension, duration, and number, do they not all contain in them a secret relation of the parts? Figure and motion have something relative in them much more visibly. And sensible qualities, as colors and smells, etc., what are they but the powers of different bodies in relation to our perception, etc.? And if considered in the things themselves, do they not depend on the bulk, figure, texture, and motion of the parts? All which include some kind of relation in them. Our idea therefore of power, I think, may well have a place amongst other simple ideas, and be considered as one of them, being one of those that make a principal ingredient in our complex ideas of substances, as we shall hereafter have occasion to observe.

4. *The clearest idea of active power had from spirit.*—[We are abundantly furnished with the idea of *passive* power, by almost all sorts of sensible things. In most of them we cannot avoid observing their sensible qualities, nay, their very substances to be in a continual flux;] and therefore with reason we look on them as liable still to the same change. Nor have we of *active* power (which is the more proper signification of the word power) fewer instances; since, whatever change is observed, the mind must collect a power somewhere, able to make that change, as well as a possibility in the thing itself to receive it. But yet, if we will consider it attentively, bodies, by our senses, do not afford us so clear and distinct an idea of active power, as we have from reflection on the operations of our minds. For, all power relating to action, and there

being but two sorts of action whereof we have any idea, viz., thinking
and motion, let us consider whence we have the clearest ideas of the
powers which produce these actions. (1) Of thinking, body affords us
no idea at all; it is only from reflection that we have that. (2) Neither
have we from body any idea of the beginning of motion. A body at rest
affords us no idea of any active power to move; and when it is set in
motion itself, that motion is rather a passion than an action in it. For
when the ball obeys the stroke of a billiard-stick, it is not any action of
the ball, but bare passion: also when by impulse it sets another ball in
motion that lay in its way, it only communicates the motion it had received from another, and loses in itself so much as the other received;
which gives us but a very obscure idea of an active power of moving in
body, whilst we observe it only to transfer but not produce any motion.
For it is but a very obscure idea of power, which reaches not the production of the action, but the continuation of the passion. For so is motion,
in a body impelled by another; the continuation of the alteration made
in it from rest to motion being little more an action, than the continuation of the alteration of its figure by the same blow is an action. The
idea of the beginning of motion we have only from reflection on what
passes in ourselves, where we find by experience, that, barely by willing
it, barely by a thought of the mind, we can move the parts of our bodies
which were before at rest. So that it seems to me, we have, from the
observation of the operation of bodies by our senses, but a very imperfect, obscure idea of active power, since they afford us not any idea in
themselves of the power to begin any action, either motion or thought.
But if from the impulse bodies are observed to make one upon another,
anyone thinks he has a clear idea of power, it serves as well to my purpose, sensation being one of those ways whereby the mind comes by its
ideas; only I thought it worth while to consider here by the way,
whether the mind doth not receive its idea of active power clearer from
reflection on its own operations, than it doth from any external sensation. . . .

74. . . . [Before I close this chapter, it may perhaps be to our
purpose, and help to give us clearer conceptions about *power*, if we
make our thoughts take a little more exact survey of *action*. I have
said above, that we have ideas but of two sorts of action, viz., motion
and thinking. These, in truth, though called and counted actions, yet,
if nearly considered, will not be found to be always perfectly so. For, if
I mistake not, there are instances of both kinds, which, upon due consideration, will be found rather passions than actions, and consequently
so far the effects barely of *passive powers* in those subjects which yet on
their accounts are thought agents. For in these instances the substance
that hath motion or thought receives the impression, whereby it is put

into that action, purely from without, and so acts merely by the capacity it has to receive such an impression from some external agent; and such a power is not properly an active power, but a mere passive capacity in the subject. Sometimes the substance or agent puts itself into action by its own power; and this is properly *active power*. Whatsoever modification a substance has whereby it produces any effect, that is called action: v. g., a solid substance by motion operates on or alters the sensible ideas of another substance, and therefore this modification of motion we call action. But yet this motion in that solid substance is, when rightly considered, but a passion, if it received it only from some external agent. So that the active power of motion is in no substance which cannot begin motion in itself, or in another substance, when at rest. So likewise in thinking, a power to receive ideas or thoughts from the operation of any external substance, is called a power of thinking; but this is but a passive power or capacity. But to be able to bring into view ideas out of sight at one's own choice, and to compare which of them one thinks fit, this is an active power. This reflection may be of some use to preserve us from mistakes about powers and actions, which grammar and the common frame of languages may be apt to lead us into: since what is signified by verbs that grammarians call active, does not always signify action; v. g., this proposition, "I see the moon or a star," or "I feel the heat of the sun," though expressed by a verb active, does not signify any action in me whereby I operate on those substances; but only the reception of the ideas of light, roundness, and heat, wherein I am not active, but barely passive, and cannot, in that position of my eyes or body, avoid receiving them. But when I turn my eyes another way, or remove my body out of the sunbeams, I am properly active; because of my own choice, by a power within myself, I put myself into that motion. Such an action is the product of active power.]

75. And thus I have, in a short draught, given a view of *our original ideas,* from whence all the rest are derived, and of which they are made up; which if I would consider as a philosopher, and examine on what cause they depend, and of what they are made, I believe they all might be reduced to these very few primary and original ones, viz., extension, solidity, mobility, or the power of being moved; which by our senses we receive from body: perceptivity, or the power of perception, or thinking; motivity, or the power of moving; which by reflection we receive from our minds. I crave leave to make use of these two new words, to avoid the danger of being mistaken in the use of those which are equivocal. To which if we add existence, duration, number, which belong both to the one and the other, we have perhaps all the original ideas on which the rest depend. For by these, I imagine, might be explained the nature of colors, sounds, tastes, smells, and all other ideas we have, if we had

but faculties acute enough to perceive the severally-modified extensions
and motions of these minute bodies which produce those several sensations in us. But my present purpose being only to inquire into the knowledge the mind has of things by those ideas and appearances which God
has fitted it to receive from them, and how the mind comes by that
knowledge, rather than into their causes or manner of production, I shall
not, contrary to the design of this *Essay,* set myself to inquire philos-
ophically into the peculiar constitution of *bodies* and the configuration
of parts, whereby they have the power to produce in us the ideas of their
sensible qualities. I shall not enter any farther into that disquisition, it
sufficing to my purpose to observe that gold or saffron has a power to
produce in us the idea of yellow; and snow or milk, the idea of white;
which we can only have by our sight, without examining the texture of
the parts of those bodies, or the particular figures or motion of the
particles which rebound from them, to cause in us that particular sensation; though when we go beyond the bare ideas in our minds, and would
inquire into their causes, we cannot conceive anything else to be in any
sensible object whereby it produces different ideas in us, but the different
bulk, figure, number, texture, and motion of its insensible parts.[5]

CHAPTER XXIII

OF OUR COMPLEX IDEAS OF SUBSTANCES

1. *Ideas of particular substances, how made.*—The mind being, as I
have declared, furnished with a great number of the simple ideas conveyed in by the senses, as they are found in exterior things, or by reflection on its own operations, takes notice, also, that a certain number of
these simple ideas go constantly together; which being presumed to
belong to one thing, and words being suited to common apprehensions,
and made use of for quick despatch, are called, so united in one subject, by one name; which, by inadvertency, we are apt afterward to
talk of and consider as one simple idea, which indeed is a complication
of many ideas together: because, as I have said, not imagining how these
simple ideas can subsist by themselves, we accustom ourselves to suppose some *substratum* wherein they do subsist, and from which they do
result; which therefore we call *substance.*

2. *Our obscure idea of substance in general.*—So that if anyone will
examine himself concerning his notion of pure substance in general, he
will find he has no other idea of it at all, but only a supposition of he

[5] Chapter XXII treats "Of Mixed Modes."—*Editor.*

knows not what support of such qualities which are capable of producing simple ideas in us; which qualities are commonly called accidents. If anyone should be asked, what is the subject wherein color or weight inheres, he would have nothing to say but, the solid extended parts. And if he were demanded, what is it that solidity and extension inhere in, he would not be in a much better case than the Indian before mentioned, who, saying that the world was supported by a great elephant, was asked, what the elephant rested on; to which his answer was, a great tortoise; but being again pressed to know what gave support to the broad-backed tortoise, replied—something, he knew not what. And thus here, as in all other cases where we use words without having clear and distinct ideas, we talk like children: who, being questioned what such a thing is which they know not, readily give this satisfactory answer, that it is *something;* which in truth signifies no more, when so used, either by children or men, but that they know not what; and that the thing they pretend to know and talk of, is what they have no distinct idea of at all, and so are perfectly ignorant of it, and in the dark. The idea, then, we have, to which we give the *general* name substance, being nothing but the supposed, but unknown, support of those qualities we find existing, which we imagine cannot subsist *sine re substante,* "without something to support them," we call that support *substantia;* which, according to the true import of the word, is, in plain English, standing under, or upholding.

3. *Of the sorts of substances.*—An obscure and relative idea of substance in general being thus made, we come to have the ideas of particular sorts of substances, by collecting such combinations of simple ideas as are by experience and observation of men's senses taken notice of to exist together, and are therefore supposed to flow from the particular internal constitution or unknown essence of that substance. Thus we come to have the ideas of a man, horse, gold, water, etc., of which substances, whether anyone has any other clear idea, farther than of certain simple ideas coexistent together, I appeal to everyone's own experience. It is the ordinary qualities observable in iron or a diamond, put together, that make the true complex idea of those substances, which a smith or a jeweler commonly knows better than a philosopher; who, whatever substantial forms he may talk of, has no other idea of those substances than what is framed by a collection of those simple ideas which are to be found in them. Only we must take notice that our complex ideas of substances, besides all these simple ideas they are made up of, have always the confused idea of something to which they belong, and in which they subsist: and therefore when we speak of any sort of substance, we say it is a thing having such or such qualities; as, body is a thing that is extended, figured, and capable of motion; spirit, a

thing capable of thinking; and so hardness, friability, and power to draw iron, we say, are qualities to be found in a loadstone. These and the like fashions of speaking, intimate that the substance is supposed always something, besides the extension, figure, solidity, motion, thinking, or other observable ideas, though we know not what it is.

4. *No clear or distinct idea of substance in general.*—Hence, when we talk or think of any particular sort of corporeal substances, as horse, stone, etc., though the idea we have of either of them be but the complication or collection of those several simple ideas of sensible qualities which we used to find united in the thing called horse or stone; yet because we cannot conceive how they should subsist alone, nor one in another, we suppose them existing in, and supported by, some common subject; which support we denote by the name substance, though it be certain we have no clear or distinct idea of that thing we suppose a support.

5. *As clear an idea of spirit as body.*—The same happens concerning the operations of the mind; viz., thinking, reasoning, fearing, etc., which we, concluding not to subsist of themselves, nor apprehending how they can belong to body, or be produced by it, we are apt to think these the actions of some other substance, which we call *spirit;* whereby yet it is evident, that having no other idea or notion of matter but something wherein those many sensible qualities which affect our senses do subsist; by supposing a substance wherein thinking, knowing, doubting, and a power of moving, etc., do subsist, we have as clear a notion of the substance of spirit as we have of body: the one being supposed to be (without knowing what it is) the *substratum* to those simple ideas we have from without; and the other supposed (with a like ignorance of what it is) to be the *substratum* to those operations which we experiment in ourselves within. It is plain, then, that the idea of *corporeal substance* in matter is as remote from our conceptions and apprehensions as that of *spiritual substance,* or spirit; and therefore, from our not having any notion of the substance of spirit, we can no more conclude its non-existence than we can, for the same reason, deny the existence of body: it being as rational to affirm there is no body, because we have no clear and distinct idea of the substance of matter, as to say there is no spirit, because we have no clear and distinct idea of the substance of a spirit.

6. *Our ideas of particular sorts of substances.*—Whatever therefore be the secret and abstract nature of substance in general, all the ideas we have of particular, distinct sorts of substances, are nothing but several combinations of simple ideas coexisting in such, though unknown, cause of their union, as makes the whole subsist of itself. It is by such combinations of simple ideas, and nothing else, that we represent particular sorts of substances to ourselves; such are the ideas we have of

their several species in our minds; and such only do we, by their specific names, signify to others, v. g., man, horse, sun, water, iron; upon hearing which words everyone who understands the language, frames in his mind a combination of those several simple ideas which he has usually observed or fancied to exist together under that denomination; all which he supposes to rest in, and be, as it were, adherent to, that unknown common subject, which inheres not in anything else. Though in the meantime it be manifest, and everyone upon inquiry into his own thoughts will find, that he has no other idea of any substance, v. g., let it be gold, horse, iron, man, vitriol, bread, but what he has barely of those sensible qualities which he supposes to inhere with a supposition of such a *substratum* as gives, as it were, a support to those qualities, or simple ideas, which he has observed to exist united together. Thus, the idea of the sun,—what is it but an aggregate of those several simple ideas —bright, hot, roundish, having a constant regular motion, at a certain distance from us, and perhaps some other: as he who thinks and discourses of the sun has been more or less accurate in observing those sensible qualities, ideas, or properties which are in that thing which he calls the sun.

7. *Power, a great part of our complex ideas of substances.*—For he has the perfectest idea of any of the particular sorts of substances who has gathered and put together most of those simple ideas which do exist in it, among which are to be reckoned its active powers and passive capacities; which, though not simple ideas, yet in this respect, for brevity's sake, may conveniently enough be reckoned amongst them. Thus, the power of drawing iron is one of the ideas of the complex one of that substance we call a loadstone, and a power to be so drawn is a part of the complex one we call iron; which powers pass for inherent qualities in those subjects: because every substance being as apt, by the powers we observe in it, to change some sensible qualities in other subjects, as it is to produce in us those simple ideas which we receive immediately from it, does, by those new sensible qualities introduced into other subjects, discover to us those powers which do thereby mediately affect our senses as regularly as its sensible qualities do it immediately; v. g., we immediately by our senses perceive in fire its heat and color; which are, if rightly considered, nothing but powers in it to produce those ideas in us: we also by our senses perceive the color and brittleness of charcoal, whereby we come by the knowledge of another power in fire, which it has to change the color and consistency of wood. By the former, fire immediately, by the latter it mediately, discovers to us these several powers, which therefore we look upon to be a part of the qualities of fire, and so make them a part of the complex idea of it. For, all those powers that we take cognizance of, terminating only in the altera-

tion of some sensible qualities in those subjects on which they operate, and so making them exhibit to us new sensible ideas; therefore it is that I have reckoned these powers amongst the simple ideas which make the complex ones of the sorts of substances; though these powers, considered in themselves, are truly complex ideas. And in this looser sense I crave leave to be understood, when I name any of these potentialities amongst the simple ideas which we recollect in our minds when we think of particular substances. For the powers that are severally in them are necessary to be considered, if we will have true distinct notions of the several sorts of substances.

8. Nor are we to wonder that powers make a great part of our complex ideas of substances, since their secondary qualities are those which, in most of them, serve principally to distinguish substances one from another, and commonly make a considerable part of the complex idea of the several sorts of them. For, our senses failing us in the discovering of the bulk texture, and figure of the minute parts of bodies, on which their real constitutions and differences depend, we are fain to make use of their secondary qualities, as the characteristical notes and marks whereby to frame ideas of them in our minds, and distinguish them one from another, all which secondary qualities, as has been shown, are nothing but bare powers. For the color and taste of opium are, as well as its soporific or anodyne virtues, mere powers depending on its primary qualities, whereby it is fitted to produce different operations on different parts of our bodies.

9. *Three sorts of ideas make our complex ones of substances.*—The ideas that make our complex ones of corporeal substances are of these three sorts. First, the ideas of the primary qualities of things which are discovered by our senses, and are in them even when we perceive them not: such are the bulk, figure, number, situation, and motion of the parts of bodies, which are really in them, whether we take notice of them or no. Secondly, the sensible secondary qualities which, depending on these, are nothing but the powers those substances have to produce several ideas in us by our senses; which ideas are not in the things themselves otherwise than as anything is in its cause. Thirdly, the aptness we consider in any substance to give or receive such alterations of primary qualities as that the substance so altered should produce in us different ideas from what it did before; these are called active and passive powers: all which powers, as far as we have any notice or notion of them, terminate only in sensible simple ideas. For whatever alteration a loadstone has the power to make in the minute particles of iron, we should have no notion of any power it had at all to operate on iron, did not its sensible motion discover it; and I doubt not but there are a thousand changes that bodies we daily handle have a power to cause in

one another, which we never suspect, because they never appear in sensible effects.

10. Powers therefore justly make a great part of our complex ideas of substance. He that will examine his complex idea of gold, will find several of its ideas that make it up to be only powers: as the power of being melted, but of not spending itself in the fire, of being dissolved in *aqua regia*, are ideas as necessary to make up our complex idea of gold, as its color, and weight: which, if duly considered, are also nothing but different powers. For, to speak truly, yellowness is not actually in gold; but is a power in gold to produce that idea in us by our eyes, when placed in a due light; and the heat which we cannot leave out of our idea of the sun, is no more really in the sun than the white color it introduces into wax. These are both equally powers in the sun, operating, by the motion and figure of its insensible parts, so on a man as to make him have the idea of heat; and so on wax as to make it capable to produce in a man the idea of white.

11. *The now secondary qualities of bodies would disappear, if we could discover the primary ones of their minute parts.*—Had we senses acute enough to discern the minute particles of bodies, and the real constitution on which their sensible qualities depend, I doubt not but they would produce quite different ideas in us, and that which is now the yellow color of gold would then disappear, and instead of it we should see an admirable texture of parts of a certain size and figure. This microscopes plainly discover to us; for, what to our naked eyes produces a certain color is, by thus augmenting the acuteness of our senses, discovered to be quite a different thing; and the thus altering, as it were, the proportion of the bulk of the minute parts of a colored object to our usual sight, produces different ideas from what it did before. Thus sand, or pounded glass, which is opaque and white to the naked eye, is pellucid in a microscope; and a hair seen this way loses its former color, and is in a great measure pellucid, with a mixture of some bright sparkling colors, such as appear from the refraction of diamonds and other pellucid bodies. Blood to the naked eye appears all red; but by a good miscroscope, wherein its lesser parts appear, shows only some few globules of red, swimming in a pellucid liquor; and how these red globules would appear, if glasses could be found that yet could magnify them one thousand or ten thousand times more, is uncertain.

12. *Our faculties of discovery suited to our state.*—The infinitely wise contriver of us, and all things about us, hath fitted our senses, faculties, and organs, to the conveniences of life, and the business we have to do here. We are able, by our senses, to know and distinguish things; and to examine them so far, as to apply them to our uses, and several ways to accommodate the exigencies of this life. We have insight enough

into their admirable contrivances and wonderful effects, to admire and
magnify the wisdom, power, and goodness of their author. Such a knowledge as this, which is suited to our present condition, we want not
faculties to attain. But it appears not that God intended we should have
a perfect, clear, and adequate knowledge of them: that perhaps is not
in the comprehension of any finite being. We are furnished with faculties (dull and weak as they are) to discover enough in the creatures to
lead us to the knowledge of the Creator, and the knowledge of our duty;
and we are fitted well enough with abilities to provide for the conveniences of living: these are our business in this world. But were our senses
altered, and made much quicker and acuter, the appearance and outward scheme of things would have quite another face to us; and, I am
apt to think, would be inconsistent with our being, or at least well-
being, in this part of the universe which we inhabit. He that considers
how little our constitution is able to bear a remove into parts of this air,
not much higher than that we commonly breathe in, will have reason to
be satisfied, that in this globe of earth allotted for our mansion, the all-
wise Architect has suited our organs, and the bodies that are to affect
them, one to another. If our sense of hearing were but one thousand
times quicker than it is, how would a perpetual noise distract us! And
we should in the quietest retirement be less able to sleep or meditate
than in the middle of a sea-fight. Nay, if that most instructive of our
senses, seeing, were in any man a thousand or a hundred thousand times
more acute than it is by the best microscope, things several millions of
times less than the smallest object of his sight now, would then be visible
to his naked eyes, and so he would come nearer to the discovery of the
texture and motion of the minute parts of corporeal things; and in many
of them, probably get ideas of their internal constitutions. But then he
would be in a quite different world from other people: nothing would
appear the same to him and others; the visible ideas of everything would
be different. So that I doubt, whether he and the rest of men could discourse concerning the objects of sight, or have any communication about
colors, their appearances being so wholly different. And perhaps such a
quickness and tenderness of sight could not endure bright sunshine, or
so much as open daylight; nor take in but a very small part of any
object at once, and that too only at a very near distance. And if by the
help of such microscopical eyes (if I may so call them) a man could
penetrate further than ordinary into the secret composition and radical
texture of bodies, he would not make any great advantage by the change,
if such an acute sight would not serve to conduct him to the market and
exchange; if he could not see things he was to avoid, at a convenient
distance; nor distinguish things he had to do with by those sensible
qualities others do. He that was sharp-sighted enough to see the con-

figuration of the minute particles of the spring of a clock, and observe upon what peculiar structure and impulse its elastic motion depends, would no doubt discover something very admirable: but if eyes so framed could not view at once the hand, and the characters of the hour-plate, and thereby at a distance see, what o'clock it was, their owner could not be much benefited by that acuteness; which, whilst it discovered the secret contrivance of the parts of the machine, made him lose its use.

13. *Conjecture about spirits.*—And here give me leave to propose an extravagant conjecture of mine, viz., that since we have some reason (if there be any credit to be given to the report of things, that our philosophy cannot account for) to imagine, that spirits can assume to themselves bodies of different bulk, figure, and conformation of parts; whether one great advantage some of them have over us may not lie in this: that they can so frame and shape to themselves organs of sensation or perception, as to suit them to their present design, and the circumstances of the object they would consider. For how much would that man exceed all others in knowledge, who had but the faculty so to alter the structure of his eyes, that one sense, as to make it capable of all the several degrees of vision, which the assistance of glasses (casually at first lighted on) has taught us to conceive? What wonders would he discover, who could so fit his eyes to all sorts of objects, as to see, when he pleased, the figure and motion of the minute particles in the blood, and other juices of animals, as distinctly as he does, at other times, the shape and motion of the animals themselves? But to us, in our present state, unalterable organs so contrived, as to discover the figure and motion of the minute parts of bodies, whereon depend those sensible qualities we now observe in them, would perhaps be of no advantage. God has, no doubt, made them so, as is best for us in our present condition. He hath fitted us for the neighborhood of the bodies that surround us, and we have to do with, and though we cannot, by the faculties we have, attain to a perfect knowledge of things, yet they will serve us well enough for those ends above-mentioned, which are our great concernment. I beg my reader's pardon for laying before him so wild a fancy concerning the ways of perception of beings above us; but how extravagant soever it be, I doubt whether we can imagine anything about the knowledge of angels, but after this manner, some way or other in proportion to what we find and observe in ourselves. And though we cannot but allow that the infinite power and wisdom of God may frame creatures with a thousand other faculties and ways of perceiving things without them, than what we have, yet our thoughts can go no further than our own: so impossible it is for us to enlarge our very guesses beyond the ideas received from our own sensation and reflection. The supposition, at least, that angels

do sometimes assume bodies, need not startle us; since some of the most ancient and most learned fathers of the church seemed to believe that they had bodies: and this is certain, that their state and way of existence is unknown to us.

14. *Our ideas of substances.*—But to return to the matter in hand—the ideas we have of substances, and the ways we come by them: I say, our specific ideas of substances are nothing else but *a collection of a certain number of simple ideas, considered as united in one thing.* These ideas of substances, though they are commonly simple apprehensions, and the names of them simple terms, yet in effect are complex and compounded. Thus the idea which an Englishman signifies by the name swan, is white color, long neck, red beak, black legs, and whole feet, and all these of a certain size, with a power of swimming in the water, and making a certain kind of noise; and perhaps to a man who has long observed this kind of birds, some other properties, which all terminate in sensible simple ideas, all united in one common subject.

15. *Idea of spiritual substances as clear as of bodily substances.*—Besides the complex ideas we have of material sensible substances, of which I have last spoken, by the simple ideas we have taken from those operations of our own minds, which we experiment daily in ourselves, as thinking, understanding, willing, knowing, and power of beginning motion, etc., co-existing in some substance, we are able to frame *the complex idea of an immaterial spirit.* And thus, by putting together the ideas of thinking, perceiving, liberty, and power of moving themselves and other things, we have as clear a perception and notion of immaterial substances as we have of material. For putting together the ideas of thinking and willing, or the power of moving or quieting corporeal motion, joined to substance, of which we have no distinct idea, we have the idea of an immaterial spirit; and by putting together the ideas of coherent solid parts, and a power of being moved, joined with substance, of which, likewise we have no positive idea, we have the idea of matter. The one is as clear and distinct an idea as the other: the idea of thinking and moving a body being as clear and distinct ideas as the ideas of extension, solidity, and being moved. For our idea of substance is equally obscure, or none at all, in both; it is but a supposed I-know-not-what, to support those ideas we call accidents. [It is for want of reflection that we are apt to think that our senses show us nothing but material things. Every act of sensation, when duly considered, gives us an equal view of both parts of nature, the corporeal and spiritual. For whilst I know, by seeing or hearing, etc., that there is some corporeal being without me, the object of that sensation, I do more certainly know that there is some spiritual being within me that sees and hears. This I

must be convinced cannot be the action of bare insensible matter, nor ever could be without an immaterial thinking being.]

16. *No idea of abstract substance.*—By the complex idea of extended, figured, colored, and all other sensible qualities, which is all that we know of it, we are as far from the idea of the substance of body as if we knew nothing at all; nor after all the acquaintance and familiarity which we imagine we have with matter, and the many qualities men assure themselves they perceive and know in bodies, will it, perhaps, upon examination be found that they have any more or clearer primary ideas belonging to body than they have belonging to immaterial spirit.

17. *The cohesion of solid parts and impulse, the primary ideas of body.*—The primary ideas we have peculiar to body, as contradistinguished to spirit, are the *cohesion of solid and consequently separable parts,* and a *power of communicating motion by impulse.* These, I think, are the original ideas proper and peculiar to body; for figure is but the consequence of finite extension.

18. *Thinking and motivity, the primary ideas of spirit.*—The ideas we have belonging and peculiar to spirit are *thinking,* and *will,* or a *power of putting body into motion by thought,* and, which is consequent to it, *liberty.* For as body cannot but communicate its motion by impulse to another body, which it meets with at rest; so the mind can put bodies into motion, or forbear to do so, as it pleases. The ideas of existence, duration, and mobility are common to them both. . . .

29. To conclude: Sensation convinces us that there are solid, extended substances; and reflection, that there are thinking ones; experience assures us of the existence of such beings; and that the one hath a power to move body by impulse, the other by thought; this we cannot doubt of. Experience, I say, every moment furnishes us with the clear ideas both of the one and the other. But beyond these ideas, as received from their proper sources, our faculties will not reach. If we would inquire farther into their nature, causes, and manner, we perceive not the nature of extension clearer than we do of thinking. If we would explain them any farther, one is as easy as the other; and there is no more difficulty to conceive how a substance we know not should by thought set body into motion, than how a substance we know not should by impulse set body into motion. So that we are no more able to discover wherein the ideas belonging to body consist, than those belonging to spirit. From whence it seems probable to me that the simple ideas we receive from sensation and reflection are the boundaries of our thoughts; beyond which, the mind, whatever efforts it would make, is not able to advance one jot; nor can it make any discoveries, when it would pry into the nature and hidden causes of those ideas.

30. *Idea of body and spirit compared.*—So that, in short, the idea we have of spirit, compared with the idea we have of body, stands thus: the substance of spirit is unknown to us, and so is the substance of body equally unknown to us; two primary qualities or properties of body, viz., solid coherent parts and impulse, we have distinct clear ideas of; so likewise we know and have distinct clear ideas of two primary qualities or properties of spirit, viz., thinking, and a power of action, i. e., a power of beginning or stopping several thoughts or motions. We have also the ideas of several qualities inherent in bodies, and have the clear distinct ideas of them; which qualities are but the various modifications of the extension of cohering solid parts and their motion. We have likewise the ideas of several modes of thinking, viz., believing, doubting, intending, fearing, hoping; all which are but the several modes of thinking. We have also the ideas of willing, and moving the body consequent to it, and with the body itself too; for, as has been showed, spirit is capable of motion.

31. *The notion of spirit involves no more difficulty in it than that of body.*—Lastly, if this notion of immaterial spirit may have, perhaps, some difficulties in it not easy to be explained, we have therefore no more reason to deny or doubt the existence of such spirits, than we have to deny or doubt the existence of body because the notion of body is cumbered with some difficulties, very hard and perhaps impossible to be explained or understood by us. For I would fain have instanced anything in our notion of spirit more perplexed, or nearer a contradiction, than the very notion of body includes in it; the divisibility *in infinitum* of any finite extension involving us, whether we grant or deny it, in consequences impossible to be explicated or made in our apprehensions consistent; consequences that carry greater difficulty and more apparent absurdity, than anything can follow from the notion of an immaterial knowing substance.

32. *We know nothing beyond our simple ideas.*—Which we are not at all to wonder at, since we, having but some few superficial ideas of things, discovered to us only by the senses from without, or by the mind reflecting on what it experiments in itself within, have no knowledge beyond that, much less of the internal constitution and true nature of things, being destitute of faculties to attain it. And therefore experimenting and discovering in ourselves knowledge and the power of voluntary motion, as certainly as we experiment or discover in things without us the cohesion and separation of solid parts, which is the extension and motion of bodies; we have as much reason to be satisfied with our notion of immaterial spirit, as with our notion of body; and the existence of the one as well as the other. For, it being no more a contradiction that thinking should exist separate and independent from solidity, than

it is a contradiction that solidity should exist separate and independent from thinking, they being both but simple ideas, independent one from another; and having as clear and distinct ideas in us of thinking as of solidity, I know not why we may not as well allow a thinking thing without solidity, i. e., immaterial, to exist, as a solid thing without thinking, i. e., matter, to exist; especially since it is not harder to conceive how thinking should exist without matter, than how matter should think. For whensoever we would proceed beyond these simple ideas we have from sensation and reflection, and dive farther into the nature of things, we fall presently into darkness and obscurity, perplexedness and difficulties; and can discover nothing farther but our own blindness and ignorance. But whichever of these complex ideas be clearest, that of body or immaterial spirit, this is evident, that the simple ideas that make them up are no other than what we have received from sensation or reflection; and so is it of all our other ideas of substances, even of God Himself.

33. *Idea of God.*—For if we examine the idea we have of the incomprehensible Supreme Being, we shall find that we come by it the same way; and that the complex ideas we have both of God and separate spirits are made of the simple ideas we receive from reflection: v. g., having, from what we experiment in ourselves, got the ideas of existence and duration, of knowledge and power, of pleasure and happiness, and of several other qualities and powers which it is better to have than to be without; when we would frame an idea the most suitable we can to the Supreme Being, we enlarge every one of these with our idea of infinity; and so, putting them together, make our complex idea of God. For that the mind has such a power of enlarging some of its ideas, received from sensation and reflection, has been already showed.

34. If I find that I know some few things, and some of them, or all, perhaps, imperfectly; I can frame an idea of knowing twice as many, which I can double again as often as I can add to number; and thus enlarge my idea of knowledge, by extending its comprehension to all things existing or possible. The same also I can do of knowing them more perfectly, i. e., all their qualities, powers, causes, consequences, and relations, etc., till all be perfectly known that is in them, or can any way relate to them; and thus frame the idea of infinite or boundless knowledge. The same may also be done of power, till we come to that we call infinite; and also of the duration of existence without beginning or end; and so frame the idea of an eternal being. The degrees or extent, wherein we ascribe existence, power, wisdom, and all other perfections (which we can have any ideas of), to that Sovereign Being which we call God, being all boundless and infinite, we frame the best idea of Him our minds are capable of: all which is done, I say, by enlarging those sim-

ple ideas we have taken from the operations of our own minds by reflection, or by our senses from exterior things, to that vastness to which infinity can extend them.

35. For it is infinity which, joined to our ideas of existence, power, knowledge, etc., makes that complex idea whereby we represent to ourselves, the best we can, the Supreme Being. For though in His own essence, which certainly we do not know (not knowing the real essence of a pebble, or a fly, or of our own selves), God be simple and uncompounded; yet, I think, I may say we have no other idea of Him but a complex one of existence, knowledge, power, happiness, etc., infinite and eternal: which are all distinct ideas, and some of them being relative are again compounded of others; all which, being, as has been shown, originally got from sensation and reflection, go to make up the idea or notion we have of God.

36. *No ideas in our complex one of spirits, but those got from sensation or reflection.*—This farther is to be observed, that there is no idea we attribute to God, bating infinity, which is not also a part of our complex idea of other spirits. Because, being capable of no other simple ideas belonging to anything but body, but those which by reflection we receive from the operation of our own minds, we can attribute to spirits no other but what we receive from thence: and all the difference we can put between them in our contemplation of spirits, is only in the several extents and degrees of their knowledge, power, duration, happiness, etc. For that in our ideas, as well of spirits as of other things, we are restrained to those we receive from sensation and reflection, is evident from hence, that in our ideas of spirits, how much soever advanced in perfection beyond those of bodies, even to that of infinite, we cannot yet have any idea of the manner wherein they discover their thoughts one to another: though we must necessarily conclude that separate spirits, which are beings that have perfecter knowledge and greater happiness than we, must needs have also a perfecter way of communicating their thoughts than we have, who are fain to make use of corporeal signs and particular sounds, which are therefore of most general use, as being the best and quickest we are capable of. But of immediate communication having no experiment in ourselves, and consequently no notion of it at all, we have no idea how spirits which use not words can with quickness, or, much less, how spirits that have no bodies, can be masters of their own thoughts, and communicate or conceal them at pleasure, though we cannot but necessarily suppose they have such a power.

37. *Recapitulation.*—And thus we have seen what kind of ideas we have of substances of all kinds, wherein they consist, and how we came by them. From whence, I think, it is very evident:—

First, that all our ideas of the several sorts of substances are nothing but collections of simple ideas, with a supposition of something to which they belong, and in which they subsist; though of this supposed something we have no clear distinct idea at all.

Secondly, that all the simple ideas that, thus united in one common substratum, make up our complex ideas of several sorts of substances, are no other but such as we have received from sensation or reflection. So that even in those which we think we are most intimately acquainted with, and that come nearest the comprehension of our most enlarged conceptions, we cannot reach beyond those simple ideas. And even in those which seem most remote from all we have to do with, and do infinitely surpass anything we can perceive in ourselves by reflection, or discover by sensation in other things, we can attain to nothing but those simple ideas which we originally received from sensation or reflection; as is evident in the complex ideas we have of angels, and particularly of God Himself.

Thirdly, that most of the simple ideas that make up our complex ideas of substances, when truly considered, are only powers, however we are apt to take them for positive qualities: v. g., the greatest part of the ideas that make our complex idea of gold are yellowness, great weight, ductility, fusibility, and solubility in *aqua regia,* etc., all united together in an unknown substratum; all which ideas are nothing else but so many relations to other substances, and are not really in the gold considered barely in itself, though they depend on those real and primary qualities of its internal constitution, whereby it has a fitness differently to operate and be operated on by several other substances.[6]

CHAPTER XXV

OF RELATION

1. *Relation, what.*—Besides the ideas, whether simple or complex, that the mind has of things as they are in themselves, there are others it gets from their comparison one with another. The understanding, in the consideration of anything, is not confined to that precise object: it can carry any idea, as it were, beyond itself, or at least look beyond it to see how it stands in conformity to any other. When the mind so considers one thing, that it does, as it were, bring it to and set it by another, and carries its view from one to the other: this is, as the words import, *relation* and *respect;* and the denominations given to positive things, intimating that respect, and serving as marks to lead the thoughts beyond the subject itself denominated to something distinct from it, are what we

[6] Chapter XXIV treats "Of Collective Ideas of Substances."—*Editor.*

call *relatives;* and the things so brought together, *related.* Thus, when the mind considers Caius as such a positive being, it takes nothing into that idea, but what really exists in Caius; v. g., when I consider him as man, I have nothing in my mind but the complex idea of the species man. So likewise, when I say, "Caius is a white man," I have nothing but the bare consideration of man who hath that white color. But when I give Caius the name 'husband,' I intimate some other person; and when I give him the name 'whiter,' I intimate some other thing: in both cases my thought is led to something beyond Caius, and there are two things brought into consideration. And since any idea, whether simple or complex, may be the occasion why the mind thus brings two things together, and as it were, takes a view of them at once, though still considered as distinct; therefore any of our ideas may be the foundation of relation. As in the above-mentioned instance, the contract and ceremony of marriage with Sempronia, is the occasion of the denomination or relation of husband; and the color white, the occasion why he is said to be whiter than freestone. . . .

4. *Relation different from the things related.*—This farther may be observed, that the ideas of relation may be the same in men who have far different ideas of the things that are related, or that are thus compared: v. g., those who have far different ideas of a man, may yet agree in the notion of a father: which is a notion superinduced to the substance, or man, and refers only to an act of that thing called man, whereby he contributed to the generation of one of his own kind, let man be what it will.

5. *Change of relation may be without any change in the subject.*— The nature therefore of relation consists in the referring or comparing two things one to another; from which comparison one or both comes to be denominated. And if either of those things be removed or cease to be, the relation ceases, and the denomination consequent to it, though the other receive in itself no alteration at all: v. g., Caius, whom I consider today as a father ceases to be so tomorrow, only by the death of his son, without any alteration made in himself. Nay, barely by the mind's changing the object, to which it compares any thing, the same thing is capable of having contrary denominations at the same time: v. g., Caius, compared to several persons, may truly be said to be older and younger, stronger and weaker, etc. . . .

7. *All things capable of relation.*—Concerning relation in general, these things may be considered.

First, that there is no one thing, whether simple idea, substance, mode, or relation, or name of either of them, which is not capable of almost an infinite number of considerations in reference to other things; and therefore this makes no small part of men's thoughts and words: v.

g., one single man may at once be concerned in and sustain all these following relations, and many more, viz., father, brother, son, grandfather,
grandson, father-in-law, son-in-law, husband, friend, enemy, subject, general, judge, patron, client, professor, European, Englishman, islander,
servant, master, possessor, captain, superior, inferior, bigger, less, older,
younger, contemporary, like, unlike, etc., to an almost infinite number:
he being capable of as many relations as there can be occasions of comparing him to other things, in any manner of agreement, disagreement,
or respect whatsoever: for, as I said, relation is a way of comparing or
considering two things together, and giving one or both of them some appellation from that comparison, and sometimes giving even the relation
itself a name.

8. *The ideas of relations clearer often than of the subjects related.*—
Secondly, this farther may be considered concerning relation, that
though it be not contained in the real existence of things, but something
extraneous and superinduced; yet the ideas which relative words stand
for are often clearer and more distinct than of those substances to which
they do belong. The notion we have of a father or brother is a great
deal clearer and more distinct than that we have of a man; or, if you
will, paternity is a thing whereof it is easier to have a clear idea than of
humanity; and I can much easier conceive what a friend is than what
God: because the knowledge of one action, or one simple idea, is oftentimes sufficient to give the notion of a relation; but to the knowing of
any substantial being, an accurate collection of sundry ideas is necessary. A man, if he compares two things together, can hardly be supposed
not to know what it is wherein he compares them; so that when he compares any things together, he cannot but have a very clear idea of that
relation. The ideas then of relations are capable at least of being more
perfect and distinct in our minds than those of substances. Because it is
commonly hard to know all the simple ideas which are really in any
substance, but for the most part easy enough to know the simple ideas
that make up any relation I think on, or have a name for: v. g., comparing two men, in reference to one common parent, it is very easy to frame
the ideas of brothers, without having yet the perfect idea of a man. For,
significant relative words, as well as others, standing only for ideas; and
those being all either simple, or made up of simple ones; it suffices for
the knowing the precise idea the relative term stands for, to have a clear
conception of that which is the foundation of the relation; which may
be done without having a perfect and clear idea of the thing it is attributed to. Thus having the notion that one laid the egg out of which the
other was hatched, I have a clear idea of the relation of dam and chick
between the two cassowaries in St. James's Park; though, perhaps, I
have but a very obscure and imperfect idea of those birds themselves

9. *Relations all terminate in simple ideas.*—Thirdly, though there be a great number of considerations wherein things may be compared one with another, and so a multitude of relations; yet they all terminate in, and are concerned about, those simple ideas either of sensation or reflection, which I think to be the whole materials of all our knowledge. To clear this, I shall show it in the most considerable relations that we have any notion of; and in some that seem to be the most remote from sense of reflection: which yet will appear to have their ideas from thence, and leave it past doubt, that the notions we have of them are but certain simple ideas, and so originally derived from sense or reflection.

10. *Terms leading the mind beyond the subject denominated are relative.*—Fourthly, that relation being the considering of one thing with another, which is extrinsical to it, it is evident that all words that necessarily lead the mind to any other ideas than are supposed really to exist in that thing to which the word is applied, are relative words: v. g., a man, black, merry, thoughtful, thirsty, angry, extended; these and the like are all absolute, because they neither signify nor intimate anything but what does or is supposed really to exist in the man thus denominated: but father, brother, king, husband, blacker, merrier, etc., are words which, together with the thing they denominate, imply also something else separate and exterior to the existence of that thing.

11. *Conclusion.*—Having laid down these premises concerning relation in general, I shall now proceed to show in some instances how all the ideas we have of relation are made up, as the others are, only of simple ideas; and that they all, how refined or remote from sense soever they seem, terminate at last in simple ideas. I shall begin with the most comprehensive relation, wherein all things that do or can exist are concerned; and that is the relation of cause and effect. The idea whereof, how derived from the two fountains of all our knowledge, sensation and reflection, I shall in the next place consider.

CHAPTER XXVI

OF CAUSE AND EFFECT AND OTHER RELATIONS

1. *Whence their ideas got.*—In the notice that our senses take of the constant vicissitude of things, we cannot but observe that several particular both qualities and substances begin to exist; and that they receive this their existence from the due application and operation of some other being. From this observation we get our ideas of cause and effect. *That which produces any simple or complex idea,* we denote by the general

name *cause;* and *that which is produced, effect.* Thus finding that in that substance which we call 'wax' fluidity, which is a simple idea that was not in it before, is constantly produced by the application of a certain degree of heat, we call the simple idea of heat, in relation to fluidity in wax, the cause of it, and fluidity the effect. So also finding that the substance, wood, which is a certain collection of simple ideas so called, by the application of fire is turned into another substance called ashes, i. e., another complex idea, consisting of a collection of simple ideas, quite different from that complex idea which we call wood, we consider fire, in relation to ashes, as cause, and the ashes, as effect. So that whatever is considered by us to conduce or operate to the producing any particular simple idea, or collection of simple ideas, whether substance or mode, which did not before exist, hath thereby in our minds the relation of a cause, and so is denominated by us. . . .

CHAPTER XXVII

[OF IDENTITY AND DIVERSITY]

[1. *Wherein identity consists.*—Another occasion the mind often takes of comparing, is the very being of things, when, considering anything as existing at any determined time and place, we compare it with itself existing at another time, and thereon form the ideas of identity and diversity. When we see anything to be in any place in any instant of time, we are sure (be it what it will) that it is that very thing, and not another, which at that same time exists in another place, how like and undistinguishable soever it may be in all other respects: and in this consists *identity*, when the ideas it is attributed to, vary not at all from what they were that moment wherein we consider their former existence, and to which we compare the present. For we never finding, nor conceiving it possible, that two things of the same kind should exist in the same place at the same time, we rightly conclude that whatever exists anywhere at any time, excludes all of the same kind, and is there itself alone. When therefore we demand whether anything be the *same* or no, it refers always to something that existed such a time in such a place, which it was certain at that instant was the same with itself and no other. From whence it follows that one thing cannot have two beginnings of existence, nor two things one beginning; it being impossible for two things of the same kind to be or exist in the same instant, in the very same place, or one and the same thing in different places. That therefore that had one beginning is the same thing; and that which had a different beginning in time and place from that, is not the same, but diverse.

That which has made the difficulty about this relation, has been the little care and attention used in having precise notions of the things to which it is attributed.

2. *Identity of substances and of modes.*—We have the ideas but of three sorts of substances: (1) God. (2) Finite intelligences. (3) Bodies. First, God is without beginning, eternal, unalterable, and everywhere; and therefore concerning His identity, there can be no doubt. Secondly, finite spirits having had each its determinate time and place of beginning to exist, the relation to that time and place will always determine to each of them its identity as long as it exists. Thirdly, the same will hold of every particle of matter, to which no addition or subtraction of matter being made, it is the same. For though these three sorts of substances, as we term them, do not exclude one another out of the same place, yet we cannot conceive but that they must necessarily each of them exclude any of the same kind out of the same place; or else the notions and names of identity and diversity would be in vain, and there could be no such distinctions of substances, or anything else, one from another. For example, could two bodies be in the same place at the same time, then those two parcels of matter must be one and the same, take them great or little; nay, all bodies must be one and the same. For by the same reason that two particles of matter may be in one place, all bodies may be in one place; which, when it can be supposed, takes away the distinction of identity and diversity, of one and more, and renders it ridiculous. But it being a contradiction that two or more should be one, identity and diversity are relations and ways of comparing well-founded, and of use to the understanding. All other things being but modes or relations ultimately terminated in substances, the identity and diversity of each particular existence of them too will be by the same way determined: only as to things whose existence is in succession, such as are the actions of finite beings, v. g., motion and thought, both which consist in a continued train of succession, concerning their diversity there can be no question: because, each perishing the moment it begins, they cannot exist in different times, or in different places, as permanent beings can at different times exist in distant places; and therefore no motion or thought, considered as at different times, can be the same, each part thereof having a different beginning of existence.

3. *Principium individuationis.*—From what has been said, it is easy to discover, what is so much inquired after, the *principium individuationis;* and that, it is plain, is existence itself, which determines a being of any sort to a particular time and place incommunicable to two beings of the same kind. This, though it seems easier to conceive in simple substances or modes, yet, when reflected on, is not more difficult in compound ones, if care be taken to what it is applied: v. g., let us suppose

an atom, i. e. a continued body under one immutable superficies, existing in a determined time and place; it is evident that, considered in any instant of its existence, it is in that instant the same with itself. For, being at that instant what it is and nothing else, it is the same, and so must continue as long as its existence is continued; for so long it will be the same and no other. In like manner, if two or more atoms be joined together into the same mass, every one of those atoms will be the same, by the foregoing rule; and whilst they exist united together, the mass, consisting of the same atoms, must be the same mass, or the same body, let the parts be ever so differently jumbled: but if one of these atoms be taken away, or one new one added, it is no longer the same mass, or the same body. In the state of living creatures, their identity depends not on a mass of the same particles, but on something else. For in them the variation of great parcels of matter alters not the identity: an oak, growing from a plant to a great tree, and then lopped, is still the same oak; and a colt, grown up to a horse, sometimes fat, sometimes lean, is all the while the same horse: though, in both these cases, there may be a manifest change of the parts; so that truly they are not either of them the same masses of matter, though there be truly one of them the same oak, and the other the same horse. The reason whereof is, that, in these two cases of a *mass of matter* and a *living body,* identity is not applied to the same thing.

4. *Identity of vegetables.*—We must therefore consider wherein an oak differs from a mass of matter; and that seems to me to be in this: That the one is only the cohesion of particles of matter anyhow united; the other such a disposition of them as constitutes the parts of an oak, and such an organization of those parts as is fit to receive and distribute nourishment, so as to continue and frame the wood, bark, and leaves, etc., of an oak, in which consists the vegetable life. That being then one plant which has such an organization of parts in one coherent body, partaking of one common life, it continues to be the same plant as long as it partakes of the same life, though that life be communicated to new particles of matter vitally united to the living plant in a like continued organization, conformable to that sort of plants. For this organization, being at any one instant in any one collection of matter, is in that particular concrete distinguished from all other, and is that individual life which existing constantly from that moment both forwards and backwards, in the same continuity of insensibly succeeding parts united to the living body of the plant, it has that identity which makes the same plant, and all the parts of it parts of the same plant, during all the time that they exist united in that continued organization, which is fit to convey that common life to all the parts so united.

5. *Identity of animals.*—The case is not so much different in brutes,

but that anyone may hence see what makes an animal, and continues it the same. Something we have like this in machines, and may serve to illustrate it. For example, what is a watch? It is plain it is nothing but a fit organization or construction of parts to a certain end, which, when a sufficient force is added to it, it is capable to attain. If we would suppose this machine one continued body, all whose organized parts were repaired, increased, or diminished, by a constant addition or separation of insensible parts, with one common life, we should have something very much like the body of an animal, with this difference—that in an animal the fitness of the organization, and the motion wherein life consists, begin together, the motion coming from within; but in machines, the force coming sensibly from without, is often away when the organ is in order, and well fitted to receive it.

6. *Identity of man.*—This also shows wherein the identity of the same *man* consists: viz., in nothing but a participation of the same continued life by constantly fleeting particles of matter, in succession vitally united to the same organized body. He that shall place the identity of man in anything else but, like that of other animals, in one fitly organized body, taken in any one instant, and from thence continued under one organization of life in several successively fleeting particles of matter united to it, will find it hard to make an embryo, one of years, mad, and sober, the same man, by any supposition that will not make it possible for Seth, Ismael, Socrates, Pilate, St. Austin, and Caesar Borgia, to be the same man. For if the identity of soul alone makes the same man, and there be nothing in the nature of matter why the same individual spirit may not be united to different bodies it will be possible that those men living in distant ages, and of different tempers, may have been the same man: which way of speaking must be from a very strange use of the word man, applied to an idea out of which body and shape is excluded. And that way of speaking would agree yet worse with the notions of those philosophers who allow of transmigration, and are of opinion that the souls of men may, for their miscarriages, be detruded into the bodies of beasts, as fit habitations, with organs suited to the satisfaction of their brutal inclinations. But yet, I think, nobody, could he be sure that the soul of Heliogabalus were in one of his hogs, would yet say that hog were a man or Heliogabalus.

7. *Identity suited to the idea.*—It is not therefore unity of substance that comprehends all sorts of identity, or will determine it in every case; but, to conceive and judge of it aright, we must consider what idea the word it is applied to stands for: it being one thing to be the same substance, another the same man, and a third the same person, if person, man, and substance are three names standing for three different ideas. For such as is the idea belonging to that name, such must be the

identity; which, if it had been a little more carefully attended to, would possibly have prevented a great deal of that confusion which often occurs about this matter, with no small seeming difficulties, especially concerning personal identity, which therefore we shall in the next place a little consider.

8. *Same man.*—An animal is a living organized body; and consequently the same animal, as we have observed, is the same continued life communicated to different particles of matter, as they happen successively to be united to that organized living body. And whatever is talked of other definitions, ingenious observation puts it past doubt, that the idea in our minds, of which the sound 'man,' in our mouths is the sign, is nothing else but of an animal of such a certain form: since I think I may be confident, that whoever should see a creature of his own shape or make, though it had no more reason all its life than a cat or a parrot, would call him still a man; or whoever should hear a cat or a parrot discourse, reason, and philosophize, would call or think it nothing but a cat or a parrot; and say, the one was a dull irrational man, and the other a very intelligent rational parrot. . . . For I presume it is not the idea of a thinking or rational being alone that makes the idea of a man in most people's sense, but of a body, so and so shaped, joined to it; and if that be the idea of a man, the same successive body not shifted all at once must, as well as the same immaterial spirit, go to the making of the same man.

9. *Personal identity.*—This being premised, to find wherein personal identity consists, we must consider what *person* stands for; which I think, is a thinking intelligent being, that has reason and reflection, and can consider itself as itself, the same thinking thing, in different times and places; which it does only by that consciousness which is inseparable from thinking, and it seems to me essential to it: it being impossible for anyone to perceive, without perceiving that he does perceive. When we see, hear, smell, taste, feel, meditate, or will anything, we know that we do so. Thus it is always as to our present sensations and perceptions: and by this everyone is to himself that which he calls *self;* it not being considered, in this case, whether the same self be continued in the same or divers substances. For since consciousness always accompanies thinking, and it is that that makes everyone to be what he calls self, and thereby distinguishes himself from all other thinking things; in this alone consists personal identity, i. e., the sameness of a rational being: and as far as this consciousness can be extended backwards to any past action or thought, so far reaches the identity of that person; it is the same self now it was then; and it is by the same self with this present one that now reflects on it, that that action was done.

10. *Consciousness makes personal identity.*—But it is farther inquired

whether it be the same identical substance. This, few would think they had reason to doubt of, if these perceptions, with their consciousness, always remained present in the mind, whereby the same thinking thing would be always consciously present, and, as would be thought, evidently the same to itself. But that which seems to make the difficulty is this, that this consciousness being interrupted always by forgetfulness, there being no moment of our lives wherein we have the whole train of all our past actions before our eyes in one view, but even the best memories losing the sight of one part whilst they are viewing another; and we sometimes, and that the greatest part of our lives, not reflecting on our past selves, being intent on our present thoughts, and in sound sleep having no thoughts at all, or at least none with that consciousness which remarks our waking thoughts: I say, in all these cases, our consciousness being interrupted, and we losing the sight of our past selves, doubts are raised whether we are the same thinking thing, i. e. the same *substance*, or no. Which, however reasonable or unreasonable, concerns not personal identity at all: the question being, what makes the same *person,* and not whether it be the same identical substance which always thinks in the same person, which in this case matters not at all; different substances, by the same consciousness (where they do partake in it) being united into one person, as well as different bodies by the same life are united into one animal, whose identity is preserved, in that change of substance, by the unity of one continued life. For it being the same consciousness that makes a man be himself to himself, personal identity depends on that only, whether it be annexed solely to one individual substance, or can be continued in a succession of several substances. For as far as any intelligent being can repeat the idea of any past action with the same consciousness it had of it at first, and with the same consciousness it has of any present action; so far it is the same personal self. For it is by the consciousness it has of its present thoughts and actions that it is self to itself now, and so will be the same self, as far as the same consciousness can extend to actions past or to come; and would be by distance of time, or change of substance, no more two persons than a man be two men, by wearing other clothes today than he did yesterday, with a long or short sleep between: the same consciousness uniting those distant actions into the same person, whatever substances contributed to their production. . . .] [7]

[7] In the remaining chapters of Book II Locke applies the foregoing analysis to the problem of distinguishing between *clear* or *obscure, real* or *fantastical, adequate* or *inadequate,* and *true* or *false* ideas. The final chapter (XXXIII), added in the fourth edition, treats "Of the Association of Ideas."

Book III, *Of Words,* is concerned with the problem of "the nature, use, and signification of language."—*Editor.*

BOOK IV: OF KNOWLEDGE AND PROBABILITY

CHAPTER I

OF KNOWLEDGE IN GENERAL

1. *Our knowledge conversant about our ideas only.*—Since the mind in all its thoughts and reasonings, hath no other immediate object but its own ideas, which it alone does or can contemplate, it is evident that our knowledge is only conversant about them.

2. *Knowledge is the perception of the agreement or disagreement of two ideas.*—Knowledge then seems to me to be nothing but the perception of the connection of and agreement, or disagreement and repugnancy, of any of our ideas. In this alone it consists. Where this perception is, there is knowledge; and where it is not, there, though we may fancy, guess, or believe, yet we always come short of knowledge. For, when we know that white is not black, what do we else but perceive that these two ideas do not agree? When we possess ourselves with the utmost security of the demonstration that the three angles of a triangle are equal to two right ones, what do we more but perceive that equality to two right ones does necessarily agree to, and is inseparable from, the three angles of a triangle?

3. *This agreement fourfold.*—But, to understand a little more distinctly, wherein this agreement or disagreement consists, I think we may reduce it all to these four sorts: (i) Identity, or diversity. (ii) Relation. (iii) Coexistence, or necessary connection. (iv) Real existence.

4. (i) *Of identity or diversity.*—First, as to the first sort of agreement or disagreement, viz., *identity,* or *diversity.* It is the first act of the mind, when it has any sentiments or ideas at all, to perceive its ideas, and, so far as it perceives them, to know each what it is, and thereby also to perceive their difference, and that one is not another. This is so absolutely necessary, that without it there could be no knowledge, no reasoning, no imagination, no distinct thoughts at all. By this in mind clearly and infallibly perceives each idea to agree with itself, and to be what it is; and all distinct ideas to disagree, i.e., the one not to be the other: and this it does without pains, labor, or deduction, but at first view, by its natural power of perception and distinction. And though men of art have reduced this into those general rules, "what is, is," and, "It is impossible for the same thing to be and not to be," for ready ap-

plication in all cases where in there may be occasion to reflect on it; yet it is certain that the first exercise of this faculty is about particular ideas. A man infallibly knows, as soon as ever he has them in his mind, that the ideas he calls 'white' and 'round' are the very ideas they are, and that they are not other ideas which he calls 'red' or 'square.' Nor can any maxim or proposition in the world make him know it clearer or surer than he did before and without any such general rule. This, then, is the first agreement or disagreement which the mind perceives in its ideas, which it always perceives at first sight; and if there ever happen any doubt about it, it will always be found to be about the names, and not the ideas themselves, whose identity and diversity will always be perceived as soon and as clearly as the ideas themselves are, nor can it possibly be otherwise.

5. (ii) *Of relations.*—Secondly, the next sort of agreement or disagreement the mind perceives in any of its ideas may, I think, be called *relative,* and is nothing but the perception of the relation between any two ideas, of what kind soever, whether substances, modes, or any other. For, since all distinct ideas must eternally be known not to be the same, and so be universally and constantly denied one of another; there could be no room for any positive knowledge at all, if we could not perceive any relation between our ideas, and find out the agreement or disagreement they have one with another, in several ways the mind takes of comparing them.

6. (iii) *Of coexistence.*—Thirdly, the third sort of agreement or disagreement to be found in our ideas, which the perception of the mind is employed about, is *coexistence,* or *non-coexistence in the same subject;* and this belongs particularly to substances. Thus when we pronounce concerning gold that it is fixed, our knowledge of this truth amounts to no more but this, that fixedness, or a power to remain in the fire unconsumed, is an idea that always accompanies and is joined with that particular sort of yellowness, weight, fusibility, malleableness and solubility in *aqua regia,* which make our complex idea, signified by the word gold.

7. (iv) *Of real existence.*—Fourthly, the fourth and last sort is that of *actual real existence agreeing to any idea.* Within these four sorts of agreement or disagreement is, I suppose, contained all the knowledge we have or are capable of; for, all the inquiries that we can make concerning any of our ideas, all that we know or can affirm concerning any of them, is, that it is or is not the same with some other; that it does or does not always coexist with some other idea in the same subject; that it has this or that relation to some other idea; or that it has a real existence without the mind. Thus, "Blue is not yellow," is of identity. "Two triangles upon equal bases between two parallels are equal," is of relation. "Iron is susceptible of magnetical impressions," is of coexistence.

"God is," is of real existence. Though identity and coexistence are truly nothing but relations, yet they are such peculiar ways of agreement or disagreement of our ideas, that they deserve well to be considered as distinct heads, and not under relation in general; since they are so different grounds of affirmation and negation, as will easily appear to anyone who will but reflect on what is said in several places of this *Essay*. I should now proceed to examine the several degrees of our knowledge, but that it is necessary first to consider the different acceptations of the word knowledge.

8. *Knowledge actual or habitual.*—There are several ways wherein the mind is possessed of truth, each of which is called knowledge.

(i) There is *actual knowledge,* which is the present view the mind has of the agreement or disagreement of any of its ideas, or of the relation they have one to another.

(ii) A man is said to know any proposition which having been once laid before his thoughts, he evidently perceived the agreement or disagreement of the ideas whereof it consists; and so lodged it in his memory, that, whenever that proposition comes again to be reflected on, he, without doubt or hesitation, embraces the right side, assents to and is certain of the truth of it. This, I think, one may call *habitual knowledge;* and thus a man may be said to know all those truths which are lodged in his memory by a foregoing clear and full perception, whereof the mind is assured past doubt as often as it has occasion to reflect on them. For, our finite understandings being able to think clearly and distinctly but on one thing at once, if men had no knowledge of any more than what they actually thought on, they would all be very ignorant; and he that knew most would know but one truth, that being all he was able to think on at one time.

9. *Habitual knowledge twofold.*—Of habitual knowledge there are also, vulgarly speaking, two degrees:—

First, the one is of such truths laid up in the memory as, whenever they occur to the mind, it actually perceives the relation is between those ideas. And this is in all those truths whereof we have an intuitive knowledge, where the ideas themselves, by an immediate view, discover their agreement or disagreement one with another.

Secondly, the other is of such truths whereof the mind having been convinced, it retains the memory of the conviction without the proofs. Thus a man that remembers certainly that he once perceived the demonstration that the three angles of a triangle are equal to two right ones, is certain that he knows it, because he cannot doubt the truth of it. In his adherence to a truth where the demonstration by which it was at first known is forgot, though a man may be thought rather to believe his memory than really to know, and this way of entertaining a truth seemed formerly to me like something between opinion and knowledge, a sort of assurance which exceeds bare belief, for that relies on the testimony of another; yet, upon a due examination, I find it comes not short of perfect certainty, and is, in effect, true knowledge. That which is apt to mislead our first thoughts into a mistake in this matter is, that the agreement or disagreement of the ideas in this case is not perceived, as it was at first, by an actual view of all the intermediate ideas whereby the agreement or disagreement of those in the proposition was at first perceived; but by other intermediate ideas, that show the agreement or disagreement of the ideas contained in the proposition whose certainty we remember. For example: in this proposition, that "the three angles of a triangle are equal to two right ones," one who has seen and clearly perceived the demonstration of this truth, knows it to be true, when that demonstration has gone out of his mind, so that at present it is not actually in view and possibly cannot be recollected; but he knows it in a different way from what he did before. The agreement of the two ideas joined in that proposition is perceived, but it is by the intervention of other ideas than those which at first produced that perception. He remembers, i. e., he knows (for remembrance is but the reviving of some past knowledge) that he was once certain of the truth of this proposition, that the three angles of a triangle are equal to two right ones. The immutability of the same relations between the same immutable things is now the idea that shows him that if the three angles of a triangle were once equal to two right ones, they will always be equal to two right ones. And hence he comes to be certain that what was once true in the case is always true; what ideas once agreed will always agree; and, consequently, what he once knew to be true he will always know to be true, as long as he can remember that he once knew it. Upon this ground it is that particular demonstrations in mathematics afford general knowledge. If, then, the perception that the same ideas will eternally have the same habitudes and relations be not a sufficient ground of knowledge, there could be no knowledge of general propositions in mathematics; for no mathematical demonstration would be any other than particular: and when a man had demonstrated any proposition concerning one triangle or circle, his knowledge would not reach beyond that particular diagram. If he would extend it farther, he must renew his demonstration in another instance before he could know it to be true in another like triangle, and so on: by which means one could never come to the knowledge of any general propositions. Nobody, I think, can deny that Mr. Newton certainly knows any proposition that he now at any time reads in his book to be true, though he has not in actual view that admirable chain of intermediate ideas whereby he at first discovered it to be true. Such a memory as that, able to retain such a train of particulars, may be well thought beyond the reach of human faculties, when the very discovery, perception, and laying together that wonderful connection of ideas is found to surpass most readers' comprehension. But yet it is evident the author himself knows the proposition to be true, remembering he once saw the connection of those ideas, as certainly as he knows such a man wounded another, remembering that he saw him run him through. But because the memory is not always so clear as actual perception, and does in all men more or less decay in length of time, this, amongst other differences, is one which shows that demonstrative knowledge is much more imperfect than intuitive, as we shall see in the following chapter.

CHAPTER II

OF THE DEGREES OF OUR KNOWLEDGE

1. *Intuitive.*—All our knowledge consisting, as I have said, in the view the mind has of its own ideas, which is the utmost light and greatest certainty we, with our faculties and in our way of knowledge, are capable of, it may not be amiss to consider a little the degrees of its evidence. The different clearness of our knowledge seems to me to lie in the different way of perception the mind has of the agreement or disagreement of any of its ideas. For if we will reflect on our own ways of thinking, we will find that sometimes the mind perceives the agreement or disagreement of two ideas immediately by themselves, without the intervention of any other; and this, I think, we may call *intuitive knowledge*. For in this the mind is at no pains of proving or examining, but perceives the truth, as the eye doth light, only by being directed towards it. Thus the mind perceives that white is not black, that a circle is not a triangle, that three are more than two, and equal to one and two. Such kind of truths the mind perceives at the first sight of the ideas together, by bare intuition, without the intervention of any other idea; and this kind of knowledge is the clearest and most certain that human frailty is capable of. This part of knowledge is irresistible, and, like bright sunshine, forces itself immediately to be perceived as soon as ever the mind turns its view that way; and leaves no room for hesitation, doubt or examination, but the mind is presently filled with the clear light of it. It is on this intuition that depends all the certainty and evidence of all our knowledge, which certainty everyone finds to be so great, that he cannot imagine, and therefore not require, a greater: for a man cannot conceive himself capable of a greater certainty, than to know that any idea in his mind is such as he perceives it to be; and that two ideas, wherein he perceives a difference, are different and not precisely the

same. He that demands a greater certainty than this demands he knows not what, and shows only that he has a mind to be a sceptic without being able to be so. Certainty depends so wholly on this intuition, that in the next degree of knowledge, which I call demonstrative, this intuition is necessary in all the connections of the intermediate ideas, without which we cannot attain knowledge and certainty.

2. *Demonstrative.*—The next degree of knowledge is, where the mind perceives the agreement or disagreement of any ideas, but not immediately. Though wherever the mind perceives the agreement or disagreement of any of its ideas, there be certain knowledge; yet it does not always happen that the mind sees that agreement or disagreement which there is between them, even where it is discoverable; and in that case remains in ignorance, and at most gets no farther than a probable conjecture. The reason why the mind cannot always perceive presently the agreement or disagreement of two ideas, is, because those ideas concerning whose agreement or disagreement the inquiry is made, cannot by the mind be so put together as to show it. In this case then, when the mind cannot so bring its ideas together as, by their immediate comparison and, as it were, juxtaposition or application one to another, to perceive their agreement or disagreement, it is fain, *by the intervention of other ideas* (one or more, as it happens), to discover the agreement or disagreement which it searches; and this is that which we call *reasoning*. Thus the mind, being willing to know the agreement or disagreement in bigness between the three angles of a triangle and two right ones, cannot, by an immediate view and comparing them, do it: because the three angles of a triangle cannot be brought at once, and be compared with any one or two angles; and so of this the mind has no immediate, no intuitive knowledge. In this case the mind is fain to find out some other angles, to which the three angles of a triangle have an equality; and finding those equal to two right ones, comes to know their equality to two right ones.

3. *Depends on proofs.*—Those intervening ideas which serve to show the agreement of any two others, are called *proofs;* and where the agreement or disagreement is by this means plainly and clearly perceived, it is called *demonstration,* it being *shown* to the understanding, and the mind made to see that it is so. A quickness in the mind to find out these intermediate ideas (that shall discover the agreement or disagreement of any other), and to apply them right, is, I suppose, that which is called *sagacity.*

4. *But not so easy as intuitive knowledge.*—This knowledge by intervening proofs though it be certain, yet the evidence of it is not altogether so clear and bright, nor the assent so ready, as in intuitive knowledge. For though in demonstration the mind does at last perceive the

agreement or disagreement of the ideas it considers, yet it is not without pains and attention: there must be more than one transient view to find it. A steady application and pursuit are required to this discovery; and there must be a progression by steps and degrees before the mind can in this way arrive at certainty, and come to perceive the agreement or repugnancy between two ideas that need proofs and the use of reason to show it.

5. *Not without precedent doubt.*—Another difference between intuitive and demonstrative knowledge, is, that though in the latter all doubt be removed, when by the intervention of the intermediate ideas the agreement or disagreement is perceived; yet before the demonstration there was a doubt; which in intuitive knowledge cannot happen to the mind that has its faculty of perception left to a degree capable of distinct ideas, no more than it can be a doubt to the eye (that can distinctly see white and black), whether this ink and this paper be all of a color. If there be sight in the eyes, it will at first glimpse, without hesitation, perceive the words printed on this paper, different from the color of the paper: and so, if the mind have the faculty of distinct perception, it will perceive the agreement or disagreement of those ideas that produce intuitive knowledge. If the eyes have lost the faculty of seeing, or the mind of perceiving, we in vain inquire after the quickness of sight in one, or clearness of perception in the other.

6. *Not so clear.*—It is true, the perception produced by demonstration is also very clear; yet it is often with a great abatement of that evident luster and full assurance that always accompany that which I call intuitive; like a face reflected by several mirrors one to another, where, as long as it retains the similitude and agreement with the object, it produces a knowledge; but it is still in every successive reflection with a lessening of that perfect clearness and distinctness which is in the first, till at last, after many removes, it has a great mixture of dimness, and is not at first sight so knowable, especially to weak eyes. Thus it is with knowledge made out by a long train of proof.

7. *Each step must have intuitive evidence.*—Now, in every step reason makes in demonstrative knowledge, there is an intuitive knowledge of that agreement or disagreement it seeks with the next intermediate idea, which it uses as a proof: for if it were not so, that yet would need a proof; since without the perception of such agreement or disagreement there is no knowledge produced. If it be perceived by itself, it is intuitive knowledge; if it cannot be perceived by itself, there is need of some intervening idea, as a common measure, to show their agreement or disagreement. By which it is plain that every step in reasoning that produces knowledge has intuitive certainty; which when the mind perceives, there is no more required but to remember it, to make the agree-

ment or disagreement of the ideas concerning which we inquire, visible and certain. So that to make anything a demonstration, it is necessary to perceive the immediate agreement of the intervening ideas, whereby the agreement or disagreement of the two ideas under examination (whereof the one is always the first, and the other the last in the account) is found. This intuitive perception of the agreement or disagreement of the intermediate ideas, in each step and progression of the demonstration, must also be carried exactly in the mind, and a man must be sure that no part is left out: which, because in long deductions, and the use of many proofs, the memory does not always so readily and exactly retain; therefore, it comes to pass, that this is more imperfect than intuitive knowledge, and men embrace often falsehood for demonstrations.

8. *Hence the mistake, 'ex praecognitis et praeconcessis.'*—The necessity of this intuitive knowledge, in each step of scientifical or demonstrative reasoning, gave occasion, I imagine, to that mistaken axiom, that a reasoning was *ex praecognitis et praeconcessis;* which, how far it is a mistake, I shall have occasion to show more at large when I come to consider propositions, and particularly those propositions which are called maxims; and to show that it is by a mistake that they are supposed to be the foundations of all our knowledge and reasonings.

9. *Demonstration not limited to quantity.*—[It has been generally taken for granted that mathematics alone are capable of demonstrative certainty; but to have such an agreement or disagreement as may intuitively be perceived, being, as I imagine, not the privilege of the ideas of number, extension, and figure alone, it may possibly be the want of due method and application in us, and not of sufficient evidence in things, that demonstration has been thought to have so little to do in other parts of knowledge, and been scarce so much as aimed at by any but mathematicians.] For, whatever ideas we have wherein the mind can perceive the immediate agreement or disagreement that is between them, there the mind is capable of intuitive knowledge; and where it can perceive the agreement or disagreement of any two ideas, by an intuitive perception of the agreement or disagreement they have with any intermediate ideas, there the mind is capable of demonstration, which is not limited to ideas of extension, figure, number, and their modes.

10. *Why it has been so thought.*—The reason why it has been generally sought for and supposed to be only in those, I imagine, has been not only the general usefulness of those sciences, but because, in comparing their equality or excess, the modes of numbers have every the least difference very clear and perceivable: and though in extension every the least excess is not so perceptible, yet the mind has found out ways to examine and discover demonstratively the just equality of two angles, or extensions, or figures; and both these, i. e., numbers and figures, can be

set down by visible and lasting marks, wherein the ideas under consideration are perfectly determined; which for the most part they are not where they are marked only by names and words.

11. But in other simple ideas, whose modes and differences are made and counted by degrees, and not quantity, we have not so nice and accurate a distinction of their differences as to perceive or find ways to measure their just equality or the least differences. For, those other simple ideas being appearances of sensations produced in us by the size, figure, number, and motion of minute corpuscles singly insensible, their different degrees also depend upon the variation of some or all of those causes; which, since it cannot be observed by us in particles of matter whereof each is too subtle to be perceived, it is impossible for us to have any exact measures of the different degrees of these simple ideas. For, supposing the sensation or idea we name whiteness be produced in us by a certain number of globules, which, having a verticity about their own centers, strike upon the *retina* of the eye with a certain degree of rotation, as well as progressive swiftness; it will hence easily follow that the more the superficial parts of any body are so ordered as to reflect the greater number of globules of light, and to give them the proper rotation which is fit to produce this sensation of white in us, the more white will that body appear that from an equal space sends to the *retina* the greater number of such corpuscles with that peculiar sort of motion. I do not say, that the nature of light consists in very small round globules, nor of whiteness in such a texture of parts as gives a certain rotation to these globules when it reflects them; for I am not now treating physically of light or colors; but this I think I may say, that I cannot (and I would be glad anyone would make intelligible that he did) conceive how bodies without us can any ways affect our senses but by the immediate contact of the sensible bodies themselves, as in tasting and feeling, or the impulse of some sensible particles coming from them, as in seeing, hearing, and smelling; by the different impulse of which parts, caused by their different size, figure, and motion, the variety of sensations is produced in us.

12. Whether then they be globules or no; or whether they have a verticity about their own centers that produces the idea of whiteness in us; this is certain, that the more particles of light are reflected from a body, fitted to give them that peculiar motion which produces the sensation of whiteness in us, and possibly, too, the quicker that peculiar motion is, the whiter does the body appear from which the greatest number are reflected, as is evident in the same piece of paper put in the sunbeams, in the shade, and in a dark hole; in each of which it will produce in us the idea of whiteness in far different degrees.

13. Not knowing therefore what number of particles, nor what motion

of them, is fit to produce any precise degree of whiteness, we cannot demonstrate the certain equality of any two degrees of whiteness; because we have no certain standard to measure them by, nor means to distinguish every the least real difference; the only help we have being from our senses, which in this point fail us. But where the difference is so great as to produce in the mind clearly distinct ideas, whose differences can be perfectly retained, there these ideas of colors, as we see in different kinds, as blue and red, are as capable of demonstration as ideas of number and extension. What I have here said of whiteness and colors, I think, holds true in all secondary qualities and their modes.

14. *Sensitive knowledge of particular existence.*—These two, viz., intuition and demonstration, are the degrees of our knowledge; whatever comes short of one of these, with what assurance soever embraced, is but faith or opinion, but not knowledge, at least in all general truths. There is, indeed, another perception of the mind employed about the particular existence of finite beings without us; which, going beyond bare probability, and yet not reaching perfectly to either of the foregoing degrees of certainty, passes under the name of knowledge. There can be nothing more certain than that the idea we receive from an external object is in our minds: this is intuitive knowledge. But whether there be anything more than barely that idea in our minds, whether we can thence certainly infer the existence of anything without us which corresponds to that idea, is that whereof some men think there may be a question made; because men may have such ideas in their minds when no such thing exists, no such object affects their senses. But yet here, I think, we are provided with an evidence that puts us past doubting; for I ask anyone whether he be not invincibly conscious to himself of a different perception when he looks on the sun by day, and thinks on it by night; when he actually tastes wormwood, or smells a rose, or only thinks on that savor or odor? We as plainly find the difference there is between any idea revived in our minds by our own memory, and actually coming into our minds by our senses, as we do between any two distinct ideas. If anyone say, "A dream may do the same thing, and all these ideas may be produced in us without any external objects;" he may please to dream that I make him this answer: (i) That it is no great matter whether I remove his scruple or no; where all is but dream, reasoning and arguments are of no use, truth and knowledge nothing. (ii) That I believe he will allow a very manifest difference between dreaming of being in the fire, and being actually in it. But yet if he be resolved to appear so sceptical as to maintain that what I call 'being actually in the fire' is nothing but a dream, and that we cannot thereby certainly know that any such thing as fire actually exists without us; I

answer that we certainly finding that pleasure or pain follows upon the application of certain objects to us, whose existence we perceive, or dream that we perceive, by our senses; this certainty is as great as our happiness or misery, beyond which we have no concernment to know or to be. So that, I think, we may add to the former sorts of knowledge this also, of the existence of particular external objects by that perception and consciousness we have of the actual entrance of ideas from them, and allow these three degrees of knowledge, viz., intuitive, demonstrative, and sensitive; in each of which there are different degrees and ways of evidence and certainty.

15. *Knowledge not always clear where the ideas are so.*—But since our knowledge is founded on and employed about our ideas only, will it not follow from thence that it is conformable to our ideas; and that where our ideas are clear and distinct, or obscure and confused our knowledge will be so too? To which I answer, No: for our knowledge consisting in the perception of the agreement or disagreement of any two ideas, its clearness or obscurity consists in the clearness or obscurity of that perception, and not in the clearness or obscurity of the ideas themselves: v. g., a man that has as clear ideas of the angles of a triangle, and of equality to two right ones, as any mathematician in the world, may yet have but a very obscure perception of their agreement, and so, have but a very obscure knowledge of it. [But ideas which by reason of their obscurity or otherwise are confused, cannot produce any clear or distinct knowledge; because as far as any ideas are confused, so far the mind cannot perceive clearly whether they agree or disagree. Or, to express the same thing in a way less apt to be misunderstood, he that hath not determined ideas to the words he uses cannot make propositions of them, of whose truth he can be certain.]

CHAPTER III

OF THE EXTENT OF HUMAN KNOWLEDGE

1. KNOWLEDGE, as has been said, lying in the perception of the agreement or disagreement of any of our ideas, it follows from hence that,
(i) *No farther than we have ideas.*—First, we can have knowledge no farther than we have ideas.
2. (ii) *No farther than we can perceive their agreement or disagreement.*—Secondly, that we can have no knowledge farther than we can have perception of that agreement or disagreement: which perception being. (1) either by intuition, or the immediate comparing any two

ideas, or (2) by reason, examining the agreement or disagreement of two ideas by the intervention of some others, or, (3) by sensation, perceiving the existence of particular things; hence it also follows,

3. (iii) *Intuitive knowledge extends itself not to all the relations of all our ideas.*—Thirdly, that we cannot have an intuitive knowledge that shall extend itself to all our ideas, and all that we would know about them; because we cannot examine and perceive all the relations they have one to another by juxtaposition, or an immediate comparison one with another. Thus having the ideas of an obtuse and an acute-angled triangle, both drawn from equal bases and between parallels, I can by intuitive knowledge perceive the one not to be the other, but cannot that way know whether they be equal or no: because their agreement or disagreement in equality can never be perceived by an immediate comparing them; the difference of figure makes their parts incapable of an exact immediate application; and therefore there is need of some intervening qualities to measure them by, which is demonstration or rational knowledge.

4. (iv) *Nor demonstrative knowledge.*—Fourthly, it follows also, from what is above observed, that our rational knowledge cannot reach to the whole extent of our ideas: because between two different ideas we would examine, we cannot always find such mediums as we can connect one to another with an intuitive knowledge, in all the parts of the deduction; and wherever that fails, we come short of knowledge and demonstration.

5. (v) *Sensitive knowledge narrower than either.*—Fifthly, sensitive knowledge, reaching no farther than the existence of things actually present to our senses, is yet much narrower than either of the former.

6. (vi) *Our knowledge therefore narrower than our ideas.*—From all which it is evident that the extent of our knowledge comes not only short of the reality of things, but even of the extent of our own ideas. Though our knowledge be limited to our ideas, and cannot exceed them either in extent or perfection; and though these be very narrow bounds in respect of the extent of all Being, and far short of what we may justly imagine to be in some even created understandings not tied down to the dull and narrow information that is to be received from some few and not very acute ways of perception, such as are our senses; yet it would be well with us if our knowledge were but as large as our ideas, and there were not many doubts and inquiries concerning the ideas we have, whereof we are not, nor I believe ever shall be in this world, resolved. Nevertheless, I do not question but that human knowledge, under the present circumstances of our beings and constitutions, may be carried much farther than it hitherto has been, if men would sincerely, and with freedom of mind, employ all that industry and labor of thought in im-

proving the means of discovering truth which they do for the coloring or support of falsehood, to maintain a system, interest, or party they are once engaged in. But yet, after all, I think I may, without injury to human perfection, be confident that our knowledge would never reach to all we might desire to know concerning those ideas we have; nor be able to surmount all the difficulties, and resolve all the questions that might arise concerning any of them. We have the ideas of a square, a circle, and equality; and yet, perhaps, shall never be able to find a circle equal to a square, and certainly know that it is so. We have the ideas of matter and thinking, but possibly shall never be able to know whether [any mere material being] thinks or no; it being impossible for us, by the contemplation of our own ideas without revelation, to discover whether Omnipotency has not given to some systems of matter, fitly disposed, a power to perceive and think, or else joined and fixed to matter, so disposed, a thinking immaterial substance: it being, in respect of our notions, not much more remote from our comprehension to conceive that God can, if He pleases, superadd to matter a faculty of thinking, than that He should superadd to it another substance with a faculty of thinking; since we know not wherein thinking consists, nor to what sort of substances the Almighty has been pleased to give that power which cannot be in any created being but merely by the good pleasure and bounty of the Creator. . . .

But, to return to the argument in hand: our knowledge, I say, is not only limited to the paucity and imperfections of the ideas we have, and which we employ it about, but even comes short of that, too: but how far it reaches, let us now inquire.

7. *How far our knowledge reaches.*—The affirmations or negations we make concerning the ideas we have, may, as I have before intimated in general, be reduced to these four sorts, viz., identity, coexistence, relation, and real existence. I shall examine how far our knowledge extends in each of these: —

8. (i) *Our knowledge of identity and diversity, as far as our ideas.*—First, as to identity and diversity, in this way of the agreement or disagreement of ideas, our intuitive knowledge is as far extended as our ideas themselves; and there can be no idea in the mind which it does not presently, by an intuitive knowledge, perceive to be what it is, and to be different from any other.

9. (ii) *Of coexistence, a very little way.*—Secondly, as to the second sort, which is the agreement or disagreement of our ideas in coexistence, in this our knowledge is very short, though in this consists the greatest and most material part of our knowledge concerning substances. For our ideas of the species of substances being, as I have showed, nothing but certain collections of simple ideas united in one subject, and so coexist-

ing together; v. g., our idea of flame is a body hot, luminous, and moving upward; of gold, a body heavy to a certain degree, yellow, malleable, and fusible. These, or some such complex ideas as these in men's minds, do these two names of the different substances, flame and gold, stand for. When we would know anything farther concerning these, or any other sort of substances, what do we inquire but what other qualities or powers these substances have or have not? Which is nothing else but to know what other simple ideas do or do not coexist with those that make up that complex idea.

10. *Because the connection between most simple ideas is unknown.*—This, how weighty and considerable a part soever of human science, is yet very narrow, and scarce any at all. The reason whereof is, that the simple ideas whereof our complex ideas of substances are made up are, for the most part, such as carry with them, in their own nature, no visible necessary connection or inconsistency with any other simple ideas, whose coexistence with them we would inform ourselves about.

11. *Especially of secondary qualities.*—The ideas that our complex ones of substances are made up of, and about which our knowledge concerning substances is most employed, are those of their secondary qualities; which depending all (as has been shown) upon the primary qualities of their minute and insensible parts, or, if not upon them, upon something yet more remote from our comprehension, it is impossible we should know which have a necessary union or inconsistency one with another: for, not knowing the root they spring from, not knowing what size, figure, and texture of parts they are on which depend and from which result those qualities which make our complex idea of gold, it is impossible we should know what other qualities result from or are incompatible with the same constitution of the insensible parts of gold; and so, consequently, must always coexist with that complex idea we have of it, or else are inconsistent with it.

12. *Because all connection between any secondary and primary qualities is undiscoverable.*—Besides this ignorance of the primary qualities of the insensible parts of bodies, on which depend all their secondary qualities, there is yet another and more incurable part of ignorance, which sets us more remote from a certain knowledge of the coexistence or in-coexistence (if I may so say) of different ideas in the same subject; and that is, that there is no discoverable connection between any secondary quality and those primary qualities that it depends on.

13. That the size, figure, and motion of one body should cause a change in the size, figure, and motion of another body, is not beyond our conception. The separation of the parts of one body upon the intrusion of another, and the change from rest to motion upon impulse;

these, and the like, seem to have some connection one with another. And if we knew these primary qualities of bodies, we might have reason to hope we might be able to know a great deal more of these operations of them one upon another; but our minds not being able to discover any connection betwixt these primary qualities of bodies and the sensations that are produced in us by them, we can never be able to establish certain and undoubted rules of the consequence or coexistence of any secondary qualities, though we could discover the size, figure, or motion of those invisible parts which immediately produce them. We are so far from knowing what figure, size, or motion of parts produce a yellow color, a sweet taste, or a sharp sound, that we can by no means conceive how any size, figure, or motion of any particles can possibly produce in us the idea of any color, taste, or sound whatsoever; there is no conceivable connection between the one and the other.

14. In vain, therefore, shall we endeavor to discover by our ideas (the only true way of certain and universal knowledge) what other ideas are to be found constantly joined with that of our complex idea or any substance: since we neither know the real constitution of the minute parts on which their qualities do depend; nor, did we know them, could we discover any necessary connection between them and any of the secondary qualities; which is necessary to be done before we can certainly know their necessary coexistence. So that, let our complex idea of any species of substances be what it will, we can hardly, from the simple ideas contained in it, certainly determine the necessary coexistence of any other quality whatsoever. Our knowledge in all these inquiries reaches very little farther than our experience. Indeed some few of the primary qualities have a necessary dependence and visible connection one with another, as figure necessarily supposes extension, receiving or communicating motion by impulse supposes solidity. But though these and perhaps some others of our ideas have, yet there are so few of them that have, a visible connection one with another, that we can by intuition or demonstration discover the coexistence of very few of the qualities that are to be found united in substances; and we are left only to the assistance of our senses to make known to us what qualities they contain. For of all the qualities that are coexistent in any subject, without this dependence and evident connection of their ideas one with another, we cannot know certainly any two to coexist any farther than experience, by our senses, informs us. Thus though we see the yellow color, and upon trial find the weight, malleableness, fusibility, and fixedness that are united in a piece of gold; yet, because no one of these ideas has any evident dependence or necessary connection with the other, we cannot certainly know that where any four of these are the fifth will be there also, how highly

probable soever ft may be; because the highest probability amounts not to certainty, without which there can be no true knowledge. For this coexistence can be no farther known than it is perceived; and it cannot be perceived but either in particular subjects of the observation of our senses, or in general by the necessary connection of the ideas themselves.

15. *Of repugnancy to coexist, larger.*—As to incompatibility or repugnancy to coexistence, we may know that any subject may have of each sort of primary qualities but one particular at once: v. g., each particular extension, figure, number of parts, motion, excludes all other of each kind. The like also is certain of all sensible ideas peculiar to each sense; for whatever of each kind is present in any subject, excludes all other of that sort: v. g., no one subject can have two smells or two colors at the same time. To this, perhaps, will be said, "Has not an opal, or the infusion of *lignum nephriticum,* two colors at the same time?" To which I answer, that these bodies to eyes differently placed, may at the same time afford different colors; but I take liberty also to say that to eyes differently placed it is different parts of the object that reflect the particles of light; and therefore it is not the same part of the object, and so not the very same subject, which at the same time appears both yellow and azure. For it is as impossible that the very same particle of any body should at the same time differently modify or reflect the rays of light, as that it should have two different figures and textures at the same time.

16. *Of the coexistence of powers, a very little way.*—But as to the power of substances to change the sensible qualities of other bodies, which makes a great part of our inquiries about them, and is no inconsiderable branch of our knowledge; I doubt, as to these, whether our knowledge reaches much farther than our experience; or whether we can come to the discovery of most of these powers, and be certain that they are in any subject, by the connection with any of those ideas which to us make its essence. Because the active and passive power of bodies, and their ways of operating, consisting in a texture and motion of parts which we cannot by any means come to discover, it is but in a very few cases we can be able to perceive their dependence on or repugnance to any of those ideas which make our complex one of that sort of things. I have here instanced in the corpuscularian hypothesis, as that which is thought to go farthest in an intelligible explication of those qualities of bodies; and I fear the weakness of human understanding is scarce able to substitute another, which will afford us a fuller and clearer discovery of the necessary connection and coexistence of the powers which are to be observed united in several sorts of them. This at least is certain, that whichever hypothesis be clearest and truest (for

of that it is not my business to determine), our knowledge concerning corporeal substances will be very little advanced by any of them, till we are made to see what qualities and powers of bodies have a necessary connection or repugnancy one with another; which, in the present state of philosophy, I think, we know but to a very small degree: and I doubt whether, with those faculties we have, we shall ever be able to carry our general knowledge (I say not particular experience) in this part much farther. [Experience is that which in this part we must depend on. And it were to be wished that it were more improved. We find the advantages some men's generous pains have this way brought to the stock of natural knowledge. And if others, especially the philosophers by fire, who pretend to it, had been so wary in their observations and sincere in their reports as those who call themselves philosophers ought to have been, our acquaintance with the bodies here about us, and our insight into their powers and operations, had been yet much greater.]

17. *Of spirits yet narrower.*—If we are at a loss in respect of the powers and operations of bodies, I think it is easy to conclude we are much more in the dark in reference to spirits, whereof we naturally have no ideas but what we draw from that of our own, by reflecting on the operations of our own souls within us, as far as they can come within our observation. But how inconsiderable a rank the spirits that inhabit our bodies hold amongst those various, and possibly innumerable, kinds of nobler beings; and how far short they come of the endowments and perfections of cherubims and seraphims, and infinite sorts of spirits above us, is what by a transient hint, in another place, I have offered to my reader's consideration.

18. (iii) *Of other relations, it is not easy to say how far.*—As to the third sort of our knowledge, viz., the agreement or disagreement of any of our ideas in any other relation: this, as it is the largest field of our knowledge, so it is hard to determine how far it may extend; because the advances that are made in this part of knowledge depending on our sagacity in finding intermediate ideas that may show the relations and habitudes of ideas, whose coexistence is not considered, it is a hard matter to tell when we are at an end of such discoveries, and when reason has all the helps it is capable of for the finding of proofs, or examining the agreement or disagreement of remote ideas. They that are ignorant of algebra, cannot imagine the wonders in this kind are to be done by it: and what farther improvements and helps, advantageous to other parts of knowledge, the sagacious mind of man may yet find out, it is not easy to determine. This at least I believe, that the ideas of quantity are not those alone that are capable of demonstration and

knowledge; and that other, and perhaps more useful, parts of contemplation would afford us certainty, if vices, passions, and domineering interest did not oppose or menace such endeavors.

Morality capable of demonstration.—The idea of a supreme Being, infinite in power, goodness, and wisdom, whose workmanship we are, and on whom we depend; and the idea of ourselves, as understanding rational beings; being such as are clear in us, would, I suppose, if duly considered and pursued, afford such foundations of our duty and rules of action as might place morality amongst the sciences capable of demonstration: wherein I doubt not but from self-evident propositions by necessary consequences, as incontestible as those in mathematics, the measures of right and wrong might be made out to anyone that will apply himself with the same indifferency and attention to the one as he does to the other of these sciences. The relation of other modes may certainly be perceived, as well as those of number and extension: and I cannot see why they should not also be capable of demonstration if due methods were thought on to examine or pursue their agreement or disagreement. Where there is no property there is no injustice, is a proposition as certain as any demonstration in Euclid: for the idea of property being a right to anything, and the idea to which the name injustice is given being the invasion or violation of that right,[8] it is evident that these ideas being thus established, and these names annexed to them, I can as certainly know this proposition to be true, as that a triangle has three angles equal to two right ones. Again: No government allows absolute liberty; the idea of government being the establishment of society upon certain rules or laws which require conformity to them, and the idea of absolute liberty being for anyone to do whatever he pleases, I am as capable of being certain of the truth of this proposition as of any in the mathematics.

19. *Two things have made moral ideas to be thought incapable of demonstration: their complexedness and want of sensible representations.*—That which in this respect has given the advantage to the ideas of quantity, and made them thought more capable of certainty and demonstration, is,

First, That they can be set down and represented by sensible marks, which have a greater and nearer correspondence with them than any

---

[8] This is an exceedingly narrow and imperfect view of justice, the most complete theory of which is developed in the Republic of Plato. There prevailed, however, extremely false notions of this virtue among many ancient philosophers, one of whom defined it to be, obedience to rulers. But if so, then certainly those philosophers were deluded dreamers, who sought for eternal foundations for right and wrong. The government, according to this maxim, is the creator of justice, and can never possibly do wrong; since, whatever it pleases to order or do, is just. The idea of Pericles, however, respecting law, differed very little from the above.

words or sounds whatsoever. Diagrams drawn on paper are copies of the ideas in the mind, and not liable to the uncertainty that words carry in their signification. An angle, circle, or square, drawn in lines, lies open to the view, and cannot be mistaken: it remains unchangeable, and may at leisure be considered and examined, and the demonstration be revised, and all the parts of it may be gone over more than once without any danger of the least change in the ideas. This cannot be thus done in moral ideas: we have no sensible marks that resemble them, whereby we can set them down; we have nothing but words to express them by; which, though when written they remain the same, yet the ideas they stand for may change in the same man, and it is very seldom that they are not different in different persons.

Secondly, Another thing that makes the greater difficulty in ethics is, that moral ideas are commonly more complex than those of the figures ordinarily considered in mathematics. From whence these two inconveniences follow:—First, that their names are of more uncertain signification; the precise collection of simple ideas they stand for not being so easily agreed on, and so the sign that is used for them in communication always, and in thinking often, does not steadily carry with it the same idea. Upon which the same disorder, confusion, and error follow, as would if a man, going to demonstrate something of an heptagon, should, in the diagram he took to do it, leave out one of the angles, or by oversight make the figure with one angle more than the name ordinarily imported, or he intended it should when at first he thought of his demonstration. This often happens, and is hardly avoidable in very complex moral ideas, where the same name being retained, one angle, i.e., one simple idea is left out or put in the complex one (still called by the same name) more at one time than another. Secondly, From the complexedness of these moral ideas there follows another inconvenience, viz., that the mind cannot easily retain those precise combinations so exactly and perfectly as is necessary in the examination of the habitudes and correspondences, agreements or disagreements of several of them one with another; especially where it is to be judged of by long deductions, and the intervention of several other complex ideas to show the agreement or disagreement of two remote ones.

The great help against this which mathematicians find in diagrams and figures, which remain unalterable in their draughts, is very apparent, and the memory would often have great difficulty otherwise to retain them so exactly, whilst the mind went over the parts of them step by step to examine their several correspondences. And though in casting up a long sum either in addition, multiplication, or division, every part be only a progression of the mind taking a view of its own ideas, and considering their agreement or disagreement, and the resolution of the question be nothing but the result of the whole, made up of such particulars, whereof the mind has a clear perception; yet, without setting down the several parts by marks, whose precise significations are known, and by marks that last and remain in view when the memory had let them go, it would be almost impossible to carry so many different ideas in the mind without confounding or letting slip some parts of the reckoning, and thereby making all our reasonings about it useless. In which case the ciphers or marks help not the mind at all to perceive the agreement of any two or more numbers, their equalities or proportions; that the mind has only by intuition of its own ideas of the numbers themselves. But the numerical characters are helps to the memory, to record and retain the several ideas about which the demonstration is made, whereby a man may know how far his intuitive knowledge in surveying several of the particulars has proceeded; that so he may without confusion go on to what is yet unknown, and at last have in one view before him the result of all his perceptions and reasonings.

20. *Remedies of those difficulties.*—One part of these disadvantages in moral ideas which has made them be thought not capable of demonstration, may in a good measure be remedied by definitions, setting down that collection of simple ideas, which every term shall stand for, and then using the terms steadily and constantly for that precise collection. And what methods algebra or something of that kind may hereafter suggest, to remove the other difficulties, it is not easy to foretell. Confident I am, that, if men would in the same method and with the same indifferency search after moral as they do mathematical truths, they would find them have a stronger connection one with another, and a more necessary consequence from our clear and distinct ideas, and to come nearer perfect demonstration than is commonly imagined. But much of this is not to be expected whilst the desire of esteem, riches, or power makes men espouse the well-endowed opinions in fashion, and then seek arguments either to make good their beauty, or varnish over and cover their deformity: nothing being so beautiful to the eye as truth is to the mind, nothing so deformed and irreconcilable to the understanding as a lie. For though many a man can with satisfaction enough own a not very handsome wife in his bosom; yet who is bold enough openly to avow, that he has espoused a falsehood, and received into his breast so ugly a thing as a lie? Whilst the parties of man cram their tenets down all men's throats whom they can get into their power, without permitting them to examine their truth or falsehood, and will not let truth have fair play in the world, nor men the liberty to search after it; what improvements can be expected of this kind? What greater light can be hoped for in the moral sciences? The subject part of mankind in most places might, instead thereof, with Egyptian

bondage expect Egyptian darkness, were not the candle of the Lord set up by himself in men's minds, which it is impossible for the breath or power of man wholly to extinguish.

21. (iv) *Of real existence.*—Fourthly, as to the fourth sort of our knowledge, viz., of the real actual existence of things, we have an *intuitive* knowledge of our own existence; and a *demonstrative* knowledge of the existence of a God; of the existence of anything else, we have no other but a *sensitive* knowledge, which extends not beyond the objects present to our senses.

22. *Our ignorance great.*—Our knowledge being so narrow, as I have shown, it will perhaps give us some light into the present state of our minds if we look a little into the dark side, and take a view of our ignorance; which, being infinitely larger than our knowledge, may serve much to the quieting of disputes and improvement of useful knowledge; if discovering how far we have clear and distinct ideas, we confine our thoughts within the contemplation of those things that are within the reach of our understandings, and launch not out into that abyss of darkness (where we have not eyes to see, nor faculties to perceive anything), out of a presumption that nothing is beyond our comprehension. But to be satisfied of the folly of such a conceit, we need not go far. He that knows anything, knows this, in the first place, that he need not seek long for instances of his ignorance. The meanest and most obvious things that come in our way have dark sides, that the quickest sight cannot penetrate into. The clearest and most enlarged understandings of thinking men find themselves puzzled and at a loss in every particle of matter. We shall the less wonder to find it so, when we consider the causes of our ignorance; which, from what has been said, I suppose will be found to be these three:—

First, Want of ideas.

Secondly, Want of a discoverable connection between the ideas we have.

Thirdly, Want of tracing and examining our ideas.

23. *First, one cause of it, want of ideas, either such as we have no conception of, or such as particularly we have not.*—First, There are some things, and those not a few, that we are ignorant of, for want of ideas.

First, all the simple ideas we have, are confined (as I have shown) to those we receive from corporeal objects by sensation, and from the operations of our own minds as the objects of reflection. But how much these few and narrow inlets are disproportionate to the vast whole extent of all beings, will not be hard to persuade those who are not so foolish as to think their span the measure of all things. What other simple ideas it is possible the creatures in other parts of the universe may have, by the assistance of senses and faculties more or perfecter than we have, or different from ours, it is not for us to determine. But to say or think there are no such, because we conceive nothing of them, is no better an argument than if a blind man should be positive in it, that there was no such thing as sight and colors, because he had no manner of idea of any such thing, nor could by any means frame to himself any notions about seeing. The ignorance and darkness that is in us no more hinders nor confines the knowledge that is in others, than the blindness of a mole is an argument against the quicksightedness of an eagle. He that will consider the infinite power, wisdom, and goodness of the Creator of all things will find reason to think it was not all laid out upon so inconsiderable, mean, and impotent a creature as he will find man to be, who in all probability is one of the lowest of all intellectual beings. What faculties, therefore, other species of creatures have to penetrate into the nature and inmost constitutions of things, what ideas they may receive of them far different from ours, we know not. This we know and certainly find, that we want several other views of them besides those we have, to make discoveries of them more perfect. And we may be convinced that the ideas we can attain to by our faculties are very disproportionate to things themselves, when a positive, clear, distinct one of substance itself, which is the foundation of all the rest, is concealed from us. But want of ideas of this kind being a part as well as cause of our ignorance, cannot be described. Only this I think I may confidently say of it, that the intellectual and sensible world are in this perfectly alike; that that part which we see of either of them holds no proportion with what we see not; and whatsoever we can reach with our eyes or our thoughts of either of them is but a point, almost nothing in comparison of the rest.

24. *Because of their remoteness; or,*—Secondly, Another great cause of ignorance is the want of ideas we are capable of. As the want of ideas, which our faculties are not able to give us, shuts us wholly from those views of things which it is reasonable to think other beings, perfecter than we, have, of which we know nothing; so the want of ideas I now speak of keeps us in ignorance of things we conceive capable of being known to us. Bulk, figure, and motion we have ideas of. But though we are not without ideas of these primary qualities of bodies in general, yet not knowing what is the particular bulk, figure, and motion, of the greatest part of the bodies of the universe, we are ignorant of the several powers, efficacies, and ways of operation, whereby the effects which we daily see are produced. These are hid from us in some things by being too remote, and in others by being too minute. When we consider the vast distance of the known and visible parts of the world, and the reasons we have to think that what lies within our ken

is but a small part of the universe, we shall then discover a huge abyss of ignorance. What are the particular fabrics of the great masses of matter which make up the whole stupendous frame of corporeal beings, how far they are extended, what is their motion, and how continued or communicated, and what influence they have one upon another, are contemplations that at first glimpse our thoughts lose themselves in. If we narrow our contemplations and confine our thoughts to this little canton—I mean this system of our sun, and the grosser masses of matter that visibly move about it—what several sorts of vegetables, animals, and intellectual corporeal beings, infinitely different from those of our little spot of earth, may there probably be in the other planets, to the knowledge of which—even of their outward figures and parts—we can no way attain whilst we are confined to this earth; there being no natural means, either by sensation or reflection, to convey their certain ideas into our minds! They are out of the reach of those inlets of all our knowledge: and what sorts of furniture and inhabitants those mansions contain in them we cannot so much as guess, much less have clear and distinct ideas of them.

25. *Because of their minuteness.*—If a great, nay, far the greatest part of the several ranks of bodies in the universe escape our notice by their remoteness, there are others that are no less concealed from us by their minuteness. These insensible corpuscles being the active parts of matter and the great instruments of nature, on which depend not only all their secondary qualities, but also most of their natural operations, our want of precise distinct ideas of their primary qualities keeps us in an incurable ignorance of what we desire to know about them. I doubt not but if we could discover the figure, size, texture, and motion of the minute constituent parts of any two bodies, we should know without trial several of their operations one upon another, as we do now the properties of a square or a triangle. Did we know the mechanical affections of the particles of rhubarb, hemlock, opium, and a man, as a watchmaker does those of a watch, whereby it performs its operations, and of a file, which by rubbing on them will alter the figure of any of the wheels, we should be able to tell beforehand that rhubarb will purge, hemlock kill, and opium make a man sleep; as well as a watchmaker can that a little piece of paper laid on the balance will keep the watch from going, till it be removed; or that, some small part of it being rubbed by a file, the machine would quite lose its motion, and the watch go no more. The dissolving of silver in *aqua fortis,* and gold in *aqua regia,* and not vice versa, would be then perhaps no more difficult to know than it is to a smith to understand why the turning of one key will open a lock, and not the turning of another. But whilst we are destitute of senses acute enough to discover the minute particles of bodies,

and to give us ideas of their mechanical affections, we must be content
to be ignorant of their properties and ways of operation; nor can we
be assured about them any further than some few trials we make are
able to reach. But whether they will succeed again another time, we
cannot be certain. This hinders our certain knowledge of universal
truths concerning natural bodies: and our reason carries us herein very
little beyond particular matter of fact.

26. *Hence no science of bodies.*—And therefore I am apt to doubt
that, how far soever human industry may advance useful and experimental philosophy in physical things, scientifical will still be out of our
reach; because we want perfect and adequate ideas of those very bodies
which are nearest to us, and most under our command. Those which
we have ranked into classes under names, and we think ourselves best
acquainted with, we have but very imperfect and incomplete ideas of.
Distinct ideas of the several sorts of bodies that fall under the examination of our senses perhaps we may have: but adequate ideas, I suspect, we have not of anyone amongst them. And though the former of
these will serve us for common use and discourse, yet whilst we want
the latter, we are not capable of scientifical knowledge; now shall ever
be able to discover general, instructive, unquestionable truths concerning them. Certainty and demonstration are things we must not, in these
matters, pretend to. By the color, figure, taste, and smell, and other sensible qualities, we have as clear and distinct ideas of sage and hemlock,
as we have of a circle and a triangle; but having no ideas of the particular primary qualities of the minute parts of either of these plants,
nor of other bodies which we would apply them to, we cannot tell what
effects they will produce; nor when we see those effects can we so much
as guess, much less know, their manner of production. Thus, having no
ideas of the particular mechanical affections of the minute parts of
bodies that are within our view and reach, we are ignorant of their constitutions, powers, and operations: and of bodies more remote we are
yet more ignorant, not knowing so much as their very outward shapes,
or the sensible and grosser parts of their constitutions.

27. *Much less of spirits.*—This at first will show us how disproportionate our knowledge is to the whole extent even of material beings; to
which if we add the consideration of that infinite number of spirits that
may be, and probably are, which are yet more remote from our knowledge, whereof we have no cognizance, nor can frame to ourselves any
distinct ideas of their several ranks and sorts, we shall find this cause
of ignorance conceal from us, in an impenetrable obscurity, almost the
whole intellectual world; a greater, certainly, and more beautiful world
than the material. For, bating some very few, and those, if I may so

call them, superficial ideas of spirit, which by reflection we get of our own, and from thence the best we can collect of the Father of all spirits, the eternal independent Author of them, and us, and all things, we have no certain information, so much as of the existence of other spirits, but by revelation. Angels of all sorts are naturally beyond our discovery; and all those intelligences, whereof it is likely there are more orders than of corporeal substances, are things whereof our natural faculties give us no certain account at all. That there are minds and thinking beings in other men as well as himself, every man has a reason, from their words and actions, to be satisfied: and the knowledge of his own mind cannot suffer a man that considers, to be ignorant that there is a God. But that there are degrees of spiritual beings between us and the great God, who is there, that, by his own search and ability, can come to know? Much less have we distinct ideas of their different natures, conditions, states, powers, and several constitutions wherein they agree or differ from one another and from us. And, therefore in what concerns their different species and properties we are in absolute ignorance.

28. *Secondly, want of a discoverable connection between ideas we have.*—Secondly, What a small part of the substantial beings that are in the universe the want of ideas leaves open to our knowledge, we have seen. In the next place, another cause of ignorance, of no less moment, is a want of a discoverable connection between those ideas we have. For wherever we want that, we are utterly incapable of universal and certain knowledge; and are, in the former case, left only to observation and experiment: which, how narrow and confined it is, how far from general knowledge, we need not be told. . . .

29. . . . From all which it is easy to perceive what a darkness we are involved in, how little it is of being, and the things that are, that we are capable to know, and therefore we shall do no injury to our knowledge, when we modestly think with ourselves, that we are so far from being able to comprehend the whole nature of the universe, and all the things contained in it, that we are not capable of a philosophical knowledge of the bodies that are about us, and make a part of us: concerning their secondary qualities, powers, and operations, we can have no universal certainty. Several effects come every day within the notice of our senses, of which we have so far sensitive knowledge; but the causes, manner, and certainty of their production, for the two foregoing reasons, we must be content to be very ignorant of. In these we can go no further than particular experience informs us of matter of fact, and by analogy to guess what effects the like bodies are, upon other trials, like to produce. But as to a perfect science of natural

bodies, (not to mention spiritual beings,) we are, I think, so far from being capable of any such thing, that I conclude it lost labor to seek after it.

30. *Want of tracing our ideas.*—Thirdly, Where we have adequate ideas, and where there is a certain and discoverable connection between them, yet we are often ignorant, for want of tracing those ideas which we have or may have; and for want of finding out those intermediate ideas, which may show us what habitude of agreement or disagreement they have one with another: and thus many are ignorant of mathematical truths, not out of any imperfection of their faculties, or uncertainty in the things themselves, but for want of application in acquiring, examining, and by due ways comparing those ideas. That which has most contributed to hinder the due tracing of our ideas, and finding out their relations, and agreements or disagreements one with another, has been, I suppose, the ill use of words. It is impossible that men should ever truly seek or certainly discover the agreement or disagreement of ideas themselves, whilst their thoughts flutter about, or stick only in sounds of doubtful and uncertain significations. Mathematicians abstracting their thoughts from names, and accustoming themselves to set before their minds the ideas themselves that they would consider, and not sounds instead of them, have avoided thereby a great part of that perplexity, puddering, and confusion, which has so much hindered men's progress in other parts of knowledge. For whilst they stick in words of undetermined and uncertain signification, they are unable to distinguish true from false, certain from probable, consistent from inconsistent, in their own opinions. This having been the fate or misfortune of a great part of men of letters, the increase brought into the stock of real knowledge has been very little, in proportion to the schools, disputes, and writings the world has been filled with; whilst students, being lost in the great wood of words, knew not whereabouts they were, how far their discoveries were advanced, or what was wanting in their own or the general stock of knowledge. Had men, in the discoveries of the material, done as they have in those of the intellectual world, involved all in the obscurity of uncertain and doubtful ways of talking, volumes writ of navigation and voyages, theories and stories of zones and tides, multiplied and disputed; nay, ships built, and fleets sent out, would never have taught us the way beyond the line; and the Antipodes would be still as much unknown as when it was declared heresy to hold there were any. But having spoken sufficiently of words, and the ill or careless use that is commonly made of them, I shall not say anything more of it here.

31. *Extent in respect to universality.*—Hitherto we have examined the extent of our knowledge, in respect of the several sorts of beings

that are. There is another extent of it, in respect of universality, which will also deserve to be considered; and in this regard, our knowledge follows the nature of our ideas. If the ideas are abstract, whose agreement or disagreement we perceive, our knowledge is universal. For what is known of such general ideas, will be true of every particular thing in whom that essence, i.e., that abstract idea, is to be found; and what is once known of such ideas, will be perpetually and forever true. So that as to all general knowledge we must search and find it only in our minds, and it is only the examining of our own ideas that furnisheth us with that. Truths belonging to essences of things (that is, to abstract ideas) are eternal, and are to be found out by the contemplation only of those essences, as the existences of things are to be known only from experience. But having more to say of this in the chapters where I shall speak of general and real knowledge, this may here suffice as to the universality of our knowledge in general.

CHAPTER IV

OF THE REALITY OF HUMAN KNOWLEDGE

1. *Objection. Knowledge placed in ideas may be all bare vision.*—I doubt not but my reader by this time may be apt to think that I have been all this while only building a castle in the air; and be ready to say to me, "To what purpose all this stir? 'Knowledge,' say you, 'is only the perception of the agreement or disagreement of our own ideas;' but who knows what those ideas may be? Is there anything so extravagant as the imaginations of men's brains? Where is the head that has no chimeras in it? Or if there be a sober and a wise man, what difference will there be, by your rules, between his knowledge, and that of the most extravagant fancy in the world? They both have their ideas, and perceive their agreement and disagreement one with another. If there be any difference between them, the advantage will be on the warm-headed man's side, as having the more ideas, and the more lively. And so, by your rules, he will be the more knowing. If it be true that all knowledge lies only in the perception of the agreement or disagreement of our own ideas, the visions of an enthusiast, and the reasonings of a sober man, will be equally certain. It is no matter how things are: so a man observe but the agreement of his own imaginations, and talk conformably, it is all truth, all certainty. Such castles in the air will be as strongholds of truth as the demonstrations of Euclid. That an harpy is not a centaur, is by this way as certain knowledge, and as much a truth, as that a square is not a circle.

"But of what use is all this fine knowledge of men's own imaginations to a man that inquires after the reality of things? It matters
not what men's fancies are, it is the knowledge of things that is only to
be prized; it is this alone gives a value to our reasonings, and preference to one man's knowledge over another's, that it is of things as they
really are, and not of dreams and fancies."

2. *Answer. Not so where ideas agree with things.*—To which I answer, that if our knowledge of our ideas terminate in them, and reach
no farther, where there is something farther intended, our most serious
thoughts will be of little more use than the reveries of a crazy brain;
and the truths built thereon of no more weight than the discourses of a
man who sees things clearly in a dream, and with great assurance utters
them. But I hope before I have done to make it evident that this way of
certainty, by the knowledge of our own ideas, goes a little farther than
bare imagination; and I believe it will appear that all the certainty of
general truths a man has lies in nothing else.

3. It is evident the mind knows not things immediately, but only by
the intervention of the ideas it has of them. Our knowledge therefore is
real only so far as there is a conformity between our ideas and the reality of things. But what shall be here the criterion? How shall the mind,
when it perceives nothing but its own ideas, know that they agree with
things themselves? This, though it seems not to want difficulty, yet I
think there be two sorts of ideas that we may be assured agree with
things.

4. *As* (i) *all simple ideas do.*—First, the first are simple ideas, which
since the mind, as has been showed, can by no means make to itself,
must necessarily be the product of things operating on the mind in a
natural way, and producing therein those perceptions which by the wisdom and will of our Maker they are ordained and adapted to. From
whence it follows that simple ideas are not fictions of our fancies, but
the natural and regular productions of things without us really operating upon us, and so carry with them all the conformity which is intended, or which our state requires; for they represent to us things
under those appearances which they are fitted to produce in us, whereby
we are enabled to distinguish the sorts of particular substances, to discern the states they are in, and so to take them for our necessities, and
apply them to our uses. Thus the idea of whiteness or bitterness, as it
is in the mind, exactly answering that power which is in any body to
produce it there, has all the real conformity it can or ought to have with
things without us. And this conformity between our simple ideas and
the existence of things is sufficient for real knowledge.

5. (ii) *All complex ideas except of substances.*—Secondly, all our
complex ideas except those of substances being archetypes of the mind's

own making, not intended to be the copies of anything, not referred to the existence of anything, as to their originals, cannot want any conformity necessary to real knowledge. For that which is not designed to represent anything but itself, can never be capable of a wrong representation, nor mislead us from the true apprehension of anything by its dislikeness to it; and such, excepting those of substances, are all our complex ideas: which, as I have showed in another place, are combinations of ideas which the mind by its free choice puts together without considering any connection they have in nature. And hence it is, that in all these sorts the ideas themselves are considered as the archetypes, and things no otherwise regarded but as they are conformable to them. So that we cannot but be infallibly certain that all the knowledge we attain concerning these ideas is real, and reaches things themselves; because in all our thoughts, reasonings, and discourses of this kind, we intend things no farther than as they are comformable to our ideas. So that in these we cannot miss of a certain and undoubted reality.

6. *Hence the reality of mathematical knowledge.*—I doubt not but it will be easily granted that the knowledge we have of mathematical truths, is not only certain but real knowledge, and not the bare empty vision of vain, insignificant chimeras of the brain; and yet, if we will consider, we shall find that it is only of our own ideas. The mathematician considers the truth and properties belonging to a rectangle or circle, only as they are in idea in his own mind. For it is possible he never found either of them existing mathematically, i. e., precisely true, in his life. But yet the knowledge he has of any truths or properties belonging to a circle, or any other mathematical figure, are nevertheless true and certain even of real things existing; because real things are no farther concerned, nor intended to be meant by any such propositions, than as things really agree to those archetypes in his mind. Is it true of the idea of a triangle, that its three angles are equal to two right ones? It is true also of a triangle wherever it really exists. Whatever other figure exists, that it is not exactly answerable to that idea of a triangle in his mind, is not at all concerned in that proposition. And therefore he is certain all his knowledge concerning such ideas is real knowledge: because, intending things no farther than they agree with those his ideas, he is sure what he knows concerning those figures when they have barely an ideal existence in his mind, will hold true of them also when they have a real existence in matter; his consideration being barely of those figures, which are the same wherever or however they exist.

7. *And of moral.*—And hence it follows that moral knowledge is as capable of real certainty as mathematics. For certainty being but the perception of the agreement or disagreement of our ideas, and demon-

stration nothing but the perception of such agreement by the intervention of other ideas or mediums, our moral ideas as well as mathematical being archetypes themselves, and so adequate and complete ideas,
all the agreement or disagreement which we shall find in them will produce real knowledge, as well as in mathematical figures.

8. *Existence not required to make it real.*—[For the attaining of
knowledge and certainty, it is requisite that we have determined ideas:]
and to make our knowledge real, it is requisite that the ideas answer
their archetypes. Nor let it be wondered that I place the certainty of
our knowledge in the consideration of our ideas with so little care and
regard (as it may seem) to the real existence of things: since most of
those discourses which take up the thoughts and engage the disputes of
those who pretend to make it their business to inquire after truth and
certainty, will, I presume, upon examination, be found to be general
propositions and notions in which existence is not at all concerned. All
the discourses of the mathematicians about the squaring of a circle,
conic sections, or any other part of mathematics, concern not the existence of any of those figures; but their demonstrations, which depend on
their ideas, are the same, whether there be any square or circle existing in the world, or not. In the same manner, the truth and certainty of
moral discourses abstracts from the lives of men, and the existence of
those virtues in the world whereof they treat; nor are Tully's *Offices*
less true because there is nobody in the world that exactly practices
his rules, and lives up to that pattern of a virtuous man which he has
given us, and which existed nowhere when he writ but in idea. If it be
true in speculation, i. e., in idea, that murder deserves death, it will
also be true in reality of any action that exists conformable to that
idea of murder. As for other actions, the truth of that proposition concerns them not. And thus it is of all other species of things which have
no other essences but those ideas which are in the minds of men.

9. *Nor will it be less true or certain because moral ideas are of our
own making and naming.*—But it will here be said, that if moral knowledge be placed in the contemplation of our own moral ideas, and those,
as other modes, be of our own making, what strange notions will there
be of justice and temperance! What confusion of virtues and vices, if
everyone may make what ideas of them he pleases! No confusion nor
disorder in the things themselves, nor the reasonings about them; no
more than (in mathematics) there would be a disturbance in the demonstration, or a change in the properties of figures and their relations
one to another, if a man should make a triangle with four corners, or a
trapezium with four right angles: that is, in plain English, change the
names of the figures, and call that by one name which mathematicians
called ordinarily by another. For let a man make to himself the idea of

a figure with three angles, whereof one is a right one, and call it, if he please, equilaterum or trapezium, or anything else, the properties of and demonstrations about that idea will be the same as if he called it a rectangular triangle. I confess, the change of the name by the impropriety of speech will at first disturb him who knows not what idea it stands for; but as soon as the figure is drawn, the consequences and demonstrations are plain and clear. Just the same is it in moral knowledge: let a man have the idea of taking from others, without their consent, what their honest industry has possessed them of, and call this justice, if he please. He that takes the name here without the idea put to it, will be mistaken by joining another idea of his own to that name; but strip the idea of that name, or take it such as it is in the speaker's mind, and the same things will agree to it as if you called it injustice. Indeed, wrong names in moral discourses breed usually more disorder, because they are not so easily rectified as in mathematics, where the figure once drawn and seen makes the name useless and of no force. For what need of a sign when the thing signified is present and in view? But in moral names that cannot be so easily and shortly done, because of the many decompositions that go to the making up the complex ideas of those modes. But yet, for all this, the miscalling of any of those ideas contrary to the usual signification of the words of that language, hinders not but that we may have certain and demonstrative knowledge of their several agreements and disagreements, if we will carefully, as in mathematics, keep to the same precise ideas, and trace them in their several relations one to another without being led away by their names. If we but separate the idea under consideration from the sign that stands for it, our knowledge goes equally on in the discovery of real truth and certainty, whatever sounds we make use of.

10. *Misnaming disturbs not the certainty of the knowledge.*—One thing more we are to take notice of, that where God, or any other lawmaker, hath defined any moral names, there they have made the essence of that species to which that name belongs; and there it is not safe to apply or use them otherwise: but in other cases it is bare impropriety of speech to apply them contrary to the common usage of the country. But yet even this too disturbs not the certainty of that knowledge, which is still to be had by a due contemplation and comparing of those even nick-named ideas.

11. (iii) *Ideas of substances have their archetypes without us.*— Thirdly, there is another sort of complex ideas, which being referred to archetypes without us may differ from them, and so our knowledge about them may come short of being real. Such are our ideas of substances, which consisting of a collection of simple ideas, supposed taken from the works of nature, may yet vary from them, by having more or

different ideas united in them than are to be found united in the things themselves: from whence it comes to pass that they may and often do fail of being exactly comformable to things themselves.

12. *So far as they agree with those, so far our knowledge concerning them is real.*—I say, then, that to have ideas of substances which, by being conformable to things, may afford us real knowledge, it is not enough, as in modes, to put together such ideas as have no inconsistence, though they did never before so exist; v. g., the ideas of sacrilege or perjury, etc., were as real and true ideas before as after the existence of any such fact. But our ideas of substances, being supposed copies, and referred to archetypes without us, must still be taken from something that does or has existed; they must not consist of ideas put together at the pleasure of our thoughts without any real pattern they were taken from, though we can perceive no inconsistence in such a combination. The reason whereof is, because we knowing not what real constitution it is of substances whereon our simple ideas depend, and which really is the cause of the strict union of some of them one with another, and the exclusion of others; there are very few of them that we can be sure are or are not inconsistent in nature, any farther than experience and sensible observation reach. Herein, therefore, is founded the reality of our knowledge concerning substances, that all our complex ideas of them must be such, and such only, as are made up of such simple ones as have been discovered to coexist in nature. And our ideas, being thus true, though not perhaps very exact copies, are yet the subjects of real (as far as we have any) knowledge of them: which, as has been already showed, will not be found to reach very far; but so far as it does, it will still be real knowledge. Whatever ideas we have, the agreement we find they have with others will still be knowledge. If those ideas be abstract, it will be general knowledge. But to make it real concerning substances, the ideas must be taken from the real existence of things. Whatever simple ideas have been found to coexist in any substance, these we may with confidence join together again, and so make abstract ideas of substances. For whatever have once had an union in nature, may be united again.

13. *In our inquiries about substances we must consider ideas, and not confine our thoughts to names or species supposed set out by names.*—This if we rightly consider, and confine not our thoughts and abstract ideas to names, as if there were or could be no other sorts of things than what known names had already determined, and, as it were set out, we should think of things with greater freedom and less confusion than perhaps we do. It would possibly be thought a bold paradox, if not a very dangerous falsehood, if I should say, that some changelings who have lived forty years together without any appearance of

reason, are something between a man and a beast: which prejudice is founded upon nothing else but a false supposition, that these two names, man and beast, stand for distinct species so set out by real essences that there can come no other species between them: whereas if we will ab‑stract from those names, and the supposition of such specific essences made by nature, wherein all things of the same denominations did ex‑actly and equally partake; if we would not fancy that there were a cer‑tain number of these essences wherein all things, as in molds, were cast and formed; we should find that the idea of the shape, motion, and life of a man without reason is as much a distinct idea, and makes as much a distinct sort of things from man and beast, as the idea of the shape of an ass with reason would be different from either that of man or beast, and be a species of an animal between or distinct from both. . . .

18. *Recapitulation.*—Wherever we perceive the agreement or dis‑agreement of any of our ideas, there is certain knowledge; and wherever we are sure those ideas agree with the reality of things, there is certain real knowledge. Of which agreement of our ideas with the reality of things having here given the marks, I think I have shown wherein it is that certainty, real certainty, consists. Which, whatever it was to others, was, I confess, to me heretofore one of those *desiderata* which I found great want of.

CHAPTER V

OF TRUTH IN GENERAL

1. *What Truth is.*—What is truth? was an inquiry many ages since; and it being that which all mankind either do, or pretend to search after, it cannot but be worth our while carefully to examine wherein it consists, and so acquaint ourselves with the nature of it as to observe how the mind distinguishes it from falsehood.

2. *A right joining or separating of signs, i.e., ideas or words.*— Truth, then, seems to me, in the proper import of the word, to signify nothing but the joining or separating of signs, as the things signified by them do agree or disagree one with another. The joining or separat‑ing of signs here meant, is what by another name we call proposition. So that truth properly belongs only to propositions: whereof there are two sorts, viz., mental and verbal; as there are two sorts of signs com‑monly made use of, viz., ideas and words,

3. *Which make mental or verbal propositions.*—To form a clear no‑tion of truth, it is very necessary to consider truth of thought, and truth of words, distinctly one from another; but yet it is very difficult to treat

of them asunder. Because it is unavoidable, in treating of mental propositions, to make use of words; and then the instances given of mental
propositions cease immediately to be barely mental, and become verbal.
For a mental proposition being nothing but a bare consideration of the
ideas, as they are in our minds, stripped of names, they lose the nature
of purely mental propositions as soon as they are put into words.

4. *Mental propositions are very hard to be treated of.*—And that
which makes it yet harder to treat of mental and verbal propositions
separately is, that most men, if not all, in their thinking and reasonings
within themselves, make use of words instead of ideas: at least when
the subject of their meditation contains in it complex ideas. Which is a
great evidence of the imperfection and uncertainty of our ideas of that
kind, and may, if attentively made use of, serve for a mark to show us
what are those things we have clear and perfect established ideas of,
and what not. For if we will curiously observe the way our mind takes
in thinking and reasoning, we shall find, I suppose, that when we make
any propositions within our own thoughts about white or black, sweet
or bitter, a triangle or a circle, we can and often do frame in our minds
the ideas themselves, without reflecting on the names. But when we
would consider, or make propositions about the more complex ideas, as
of a man, vitriol, fortitude, glory, we usually put the name for the idea;
because the ideas these names stand for, being for the most part imperfect, confused, and undetermined, we reflect on the names themselves,
because they are more clear, certain, and distinct, and readier occur to
our thoughts than the pure ideas: and so we make use of these words
instead of the ideas themselves, even when we would meditate and reason within ourselves, and make tacit mental propositions. In substances,
as has been already noticed, this is occasioned by the imperfection of
our ideas; we making the name stand for the real essence, of which we
have no idea at all. In modes, it is occasioned by the great number of
simple ideas that go to the making them up. For many of them being
compounded, the name occurs much easier than the complex idea itself
which requires time and attention to be recollected, and exactly represented to the mind, even in those men who have formerly been at the
pains to do it; and is utterly impossible to be done by those who
though they have ready in their memory the greatest part of the common words of that language, yet perhaps never troubled themselves in
all their lives to consider what precise ideas the most of them stood for.
Some confused or obscure notions have served their turns, and many
who talk very much of religion and conscience, of church and faith, of
power and right, or obstructions and humors, melancholy and choler,
would perhaps have little left in their thoughts and meditations, if one
should desire them to think only of the things themselves, and lay by

those words with which they so often confound others, and not seldom themselves also.

5. *Being nothing but the joining or separating ideas without words.*— But to return to the consideration of truth: we must, I say, observe two sorts of propositions that we are capable of making.

First, mental, wherein the ideas in our understandings are without the use of words put together, or separated by the mind, perceiving or judging of their agreement or disagreement.

Secondly, verbal propositions, which are words, the signs of our ideas, put together or separated in affirmative or negative sentences. By which way of affirming or denying, these signs, made by sounds, are, as it were, put together or separated one from another. So that proposition consists in joining or separating signs, and truth consists in the putting together or separating those signs, according as the things which they stand for agree or disagree.

6. *When mental propositions contain real truth, and when verbal.*— Everyone's experience will satisfy him that the mind, either by perceiving or supposing the agreement or disagreement of any of its ideas, does tacitly within itself put them into a kind of proposition affirmative or negative, which I have endeavored to express by the terms putting together and separating. But this action of the mind, which is so familiar to every thinking and reasoning man, is easier to be conceived by reflecting on what passes in us when we affirm or deny, than to be explained by words. When a man has in his head the idea of two lines, viz., the side and diagonal of a square whereof the diagonal is an inch long, he may have the idea also of the division of that line into a certain number of equal parts; v. g., into five, ten, a hundred, a thousand, or any other number, and may have the idea of that inch line being divisible, or not divisible, into such equal parts, as a certain number of them will be equal to the side line. Now, whenever he perceives, believes, or supposes such a kind of divisibility to agree or disagree to his idea of that line, he, as it were, joins or separates those two ideas, viz., the idea of that line and the idea of that kind of divisibility; and so makes a mental proposition, which is true or false, according as such a kind of divisibility, a divisibility into such aliquot parts, does really agree to that line or no. When ideas are so put together or separated in the mind as they or the things they stand for do agree or not, that is, as I may call it, mental truth. But truth of words is something more; and that is the affirming or denying of words one of another, as the ideas they stand for agree or disagree; and this again is twofold: either purely verbal and trifling, which I shall speak of (Chap. VIII), or real and instructive, which is the object of that real knowledge which we have spoken of already.

7. *Objection against verbal truth, that thus it may all be chimerical.*
—But here again will be apt to occur the same doubt about truth,
that did about knowledge: and it will be objected, that if truth be nothing but the joining and separating of words in propositions, as the ideas
they stand for agree or disagree in men's minds, the knowledge of truth
is not so valuable a thing as it is taken to be, nor worth the pains and
time men employ in the search of it; since by this account it amounts
to no more than the conformity of words to the chimeras of men's
brains. Who knows not what odd notions many men's heads are filled
with, and what strange ideas all men's brains are capable of? But if
we rest here, we know the truth of nothing by this rule, but of the visionary words in our own imaginations; nor have other truth, but what
as much concerns harpies and centaurs, as men and horses. For those,
and the like, may be ideas in our heads and have their agreement or
disagreement there, as well as the ideas of real beings, and so have as
true propositions made about them. And it will be altogether as true a
proposition to say all centaurs are animals, as that all men are animals;
and the certainty of one as great as the other. For in both the propositions, the words are put together according to the agreement of the ideas
in our minds, and the agreement of the idea of animal with that of centaur is as clear and visible to the mind as the agreement of the idea of
animal with that of man; and so these two propositions are equally
true, equally certain. But of what use is all such truth to us?

8. *Answered, real truth is about ideas agreeing to things.*—Though
what has been said in the foregoing chapter to distinguish real from
imaginary knowledge might suffice here, in answer to this doubt, to distinguish real truth from chimerical, or (if you please) barely nominal,
they depending both on the same foundation; yet it may not be amiss
here again to consider that though our words signify nothing but our
ideas, yet being designed by them to signify things, the truth they contain when put into propositions will be only verbal, when they stand for
ideas in the mind that have not an agreement with the reality of
things. And therefore truth as well as knowledge may well come under
the distinction of verbal and real; that being only verbal truth wherein
terms are joined according to the agreement or disagreement of the
ideas they stand for, without regarding whether our ideas are such as
really have, or are capable of having, an existence in nature. But then
it is they contain real truth when these signs are joined as our ideas
agree, and when our ideas are such as we know are capable of having
an existence in nature; which in substances we cannot know but by
knowing that such have existed.

9. *Falsehood is the joining of names otherwise than their ideas agree.*
—Truth is the marking down in words the agreement or disagreement

of ideas as it is. Falsehood is the marking down in words the agreement or disagreement of ideas otherwise than it is. And so far as these ideas, thus marked by sounds, agree to their archetypes, so far only is the truth real. The knowledge of this truth consists in knowing what ideas the words stand for, and the perception of the agreement or disagreement of those ideas, according as it is marked by those words.

10. *General propositions to be treated of more at large.*—But because words are looked on as the great conduits of truth and knowledge, and that in conveying and receiving of truth, and commonly in reasoning about it, we make use of words and propositions; I shall more at large inquire wherein the certainty of real truths contained in propositions consists, and where it is to be had; and endeavor to show in what sort of universal propositions we are capable of being certain of their real truth or falsehood.

I shall begin with general propositions, as those which most employ our thoughts, and exercise our contemplation. General truths are most looked after by the mind as those that most enlarge our knowledge; and by their comprehensiveness satisfying us at once of many particulars, enlarge our view, and shorten our way to knowledge.

11. *Moral and metaphysical truth.*—Besides truth taken in the strict sense before mentioned, there are other sorts of truths: as, (i) Moral truth, which is speaking of things according to the persuasion of our own minds, though the proposition we speak agree not to the reality of things. (ii) Metaphysical truth, which is nothing but the real existence of things, conformable to the ideas to which we have annexed their names. This, though it seems to consist in the very beings of things, yet, when considered a little nearly, will appear to include a tacit proposition, whereby the mind joins that particular thing to the idea it had before settled with the name to it. But these considerations of truth, either having before taken notice of, or not being much to our present purpose, it may suffice here only to have mentioned them.

CHAPTER VI

OF UNIVERSAL PROPOSITIONS, THEIR TRUTH AND CERTAINTY

1. *Treating of words necessary to knowledge.*—Though the examining and judging of ideas by themselves, their names being quite laid aside, be the best and surest way to clear and distinct knowledge; yet, through the prevailing custom of using sounds for ideas, I think it is very seldom practiced. Everyone may observe how common it is for names to be made use of, instead of the ideas themselves, even when

men think and reason within their own breasts; especially if the ideas be very complex, and made up of a great collection of simple ones. This makes the consideration of words and propositions so necessary a part of the treatise of knowledge, that it is very hard to speak intelligibly of the one, without explaining the other.

2. *General truths hardly to be understood but in verbal propositions.*—All the knowledge we have, being only of particular or general truths, it is evident that whatever may be done in the former of these, the latter, which is that which with reason is most sought after, can never be well made known, and is very seldom apprehended, but as conceived and expressed in words. It is not, therefore, out of our way in the examination of our knowledge, to inquire into the truth and certainty of universal propositions.

3. *Certainty twofold—of truth and of knowledge.*—But that we may not be misled in this case by that which is the danger everywhere, I mean by the doubtfulness of terms, it is fit to observe that certainty is twofold: certainty of truth and certainty of knowledge. Certainty of truth is when words are so put together in propositions as exactly to express the agreement or disagreement of the ideas they stand for, as really it is. Certainty of knowledge is to perceive the agreement or disagreement of ideas, as expressed in any proposition. This we usually call knowing, or being certain of the truth of any proposition.

4. *No proposition can be known to be true where the essence of each species mentioned is not known.*—Now, because we cannot be certain of the truth of any general proposition unless we know the precise bounds and extent of the species its terms stand for, it is necessary we should know the essence of each species, which is that which constitutes and bounds it. This, in all simple ideas and modes, is not hard to do. For in these the real and nominal essence being the same, or, which is all one, the abstract idea which the general term stands for being the sole essence and boundary that is or can be supposed of the species, there can be no doubt how far the species extends, or what things are comprehended under each term; which, it is evident, are all that have an exact conformity with the idea it stands for, and no other. But in substances wherein a real essence distinct from the nominal is supposed to constitute, determine, and bound the species, the extent of the general word is very uncertain; because, not knowing this real essence, we cannot know what is, or what is not of that species; and, consequently, what may or may not with certainty be affirmed of it. And thus, speaking of a man, or gold, or any other species of natural substances, as supposed constituted by a precise and real essence which nature regularly imparts to every individual of that kind, whereby it is made to be of that species, we cannot be certain of the truth of any

affirmation or negation made of it. For man or gold, taken in this sense, and used for species of things constituted by real essences, different from the complex idea in the mind of the speaker, stand for we know not what; and the extent of these species, with such boundaries, are so unknown and undetermined, that it is impossible with any certainty to affirm that all men are rational, or that all gold is yellow. But where the nominal essence is kept to, as the boundary of each species, and men extend the application of any general term no further than to the particular things in which the complex idea it stands for is to be found, there they are in no danger to mistake the bounds of each species, nor can be in doubt, on this account, whether any proposition be true or not. . . .

8. *Instance in gold.*—All gold is fixed, is a proposition whose truth we cannot be certain of, how universally soever it be believed. For if, according to the useless imagination of the schools, anyone supposes the term gold to stand for a species of things set out by nature, by a real essence belonging to it, it is evident he knows not what particular substances are of that species, and so cannot with certainty affirm anything universally of gold. But if he makes gold stand for a species determined by its nominal essence, let the nominal essence, for example, be the complex idea of a body of a certain yellow color, malleable, fusible, and heavier than any other known; in this proper use of the word gold, there is no difficulty to know what is or is not gold. But yet no other quality can with certainty be universally affirmed or denied of gold, but what hath a discoverable connection or inconsistency with that nominal essence. Fixedness, for example, having no necessary connection that we can discover with the color, weight, or any other simple idea of our complex one, or with the whole combination together; it is impossible that we should certainly know the truth of this proposition, that all gold is fixed.

9. As there is no discoverable connection between fixedness and the color, weight, and other simple ideas of that nominal essence of gold; so if we make our complex idea of gold a body yellow, fusible, ductile, weighty, and fixed, we shall be at the same uncertainty concerning solubility in *aqua regia,* and for the same reason: since we can never, from consideration of the ideas themselves, with certainty affirm or deny of a body whose complex idea is made up of yellow, very weighty, ductile, fusible, and fixed, that it is soluble in *aqua regia;* and so on of the rest of its qualities. I would gladly meet with one general affirmation concerning any quality of gold that anyone can certainly know is true. It will, no doubt, be presently objected, Is not this an universal proposition, "All gold is malleable?" To which I answer, it is a very certain proposition, if malleableness be a part of the complex idea the word

gold stands for. But then here is nothing affirmed of gold but that that sound stands for an idea in which malleableness is contained; and such a sort of truth and certainty as this it is to say a centaur is four-footed. But if malleableness make not a part of the specific essence the name of gold stands for, it is plain, "All gold is malleable," is not a certain proposition. Because, let the complex idea of gold be made up of whichsoever of its other qualities you please, malleableness will not appear to depend on that complex idea, nor follow from any simple one contained in it: the connection that malleableness has (if it has any) with those other qualities being only by the intervention of the real constitution of its insensible parts; which, since we know not, it is impossible we should perceive that connection, unless we could discover that which ties them together.

10. *As far as any such coexistence can be known, so far universal propositions may be certain. But this will go but a little way.*—The more, indeed, of these coexisting qualities we unite into one complex idea under one name, the more precise and determinate we make the signification of that word; but never yet make it thereby more capable of universal certainty, in respect of other qualities not contained in our complex idea; since we perceive not their connection or dependence on one another, being ignorant both of that real constitution in which they are all founded, and also how they flow from it. For the chief part of our knowledge concerning substances is not, as in other things, barely of the relation of two ideas that may exist separately; but is of the necessary connection and coexistence of several distinct ideas in the same subject, or of their repugnancy so to coexist. Could we begin at the other end, and discover what it was wherein that color consisted, what made a body lighter or heavier, what texture of parts made it malleable, fusible, and fixed, and fit to be dissolved in this sort of liquor, and not in another—if, I say, we had such an idea as this of bodies, and could perceive wherein all sensible qualities originally consist, and how they are produced; we might frame such ideas of them as would furnish us with matter of more general knowledge, and enable us to make universal propositions, that should carry general truth and certainty with them. But whilst our complex ideas of the sorts of substances are so remote from that internal real constitution on which their sensible qualities depend, and are made up of nothing but an imperfect collection of those apparent qualities our senses can discover, there can be few general propositions concerning substances of whose real truth we can be certainly assured; since there are but few simple ideas of whose connection and necessary coexistence we can have certain and undoubted knowledge. I imagine, amongst all the secondary qualities of substances, and the powers relating to them, there cannot

any two be named whose necessary coexistence or repugnance to co-exist, can certainly be known, unless in those of the same sense, which necessarily exclude one another, as I have elsewhere showed. No one, I think, by the color that is in any body, can certainly know what smell, taste, sound, or tangible qualities it has, nor what alterations it is capable to make or receive on or from other bodies. The same may be said of the sound or taste, etc. Our specific names of substances standing for any collections of such ideas, it is not to be wondered that we can with them make very few general propositions of undoubted real certainty. But yet so far as any complex idea of any sort of substances contains in it any simple idea whose necessary coexistence with any other may be discovered, so far universal propositions may with certainty be made concerning it: v. g., could anyone discover a necessary connection between malleableness and the color or weight of gold, or any other part of the complex idea signified by that name, he might make a certain universal proposition concerning gold in this respect; and the real truth of this proposition, that "All gold is malleable," would be as certain as of this, "The three angles of all right-lined triangles are all equal to two right ones."

11. The *qualities which make our complex ideas of substances depend mostly on external, remote, and unperceived causes.*—Had we such ideas of substances as to know what real constitutions produce those sensible qualities we find in them, and how those qualities flowed from thence, we could, by the specific ideas of their real essences in our own minds, more certainly find out their properties, and discover what qualities they had or had not, than we can now by our senses: and to know the properties of gold, it would be no more necessary that gold should exist, and that we should make experiments upon it, than it is necessary for the knowing the properties of a triangle, that a triangle should exist in any matter, the idea in our minds would serve for the one as well as the other. But we are so far from being admitted into the secrets of nature, that we scarce so much as ever approach the first entrance towards them. For we are wont to consider the substances we meet with, each of them as an entire thing by itself, having all its qualities in itself, and independent of other things; overlooking, for the most part, the operations of those invisible fluids they are encompassed with, and upon whose motions and operations depend the greatest part of those qualities which are taken notice of in them, and are made by us the inherent marks of distinction whereby we know and denominate them. Put a piece of gold anywhere by itself, separate from the reach and influence of all other bodies, it will immediately lose all its color and weight, and perhaps malleableness too; which, for aught I know, would be changed into a perfect friability. Water, in which to us fluid·

ity is an essential quality, left to itself, would cease to be fluid. . . .
This is certain: things, however absolute and entire they seem in
themselves, are but retainers to other parts of nature, for that which
they are most taken notice of by us. Their observable qualities, actions,
and powers are owing to something without them; and there is not so
complete and perfect a part that we know of nature, which does not
owe the being it has, and the excellences of it, to its neighbors; and we
must not confine our thoughts within the surface of any body, but look
a great deal further, to comprehend perfectly those qualities that are in
it.

12. If this be so, it is not to be wondered that we have very imperfect ideas of substances, and that the real essences, on which depend
their properties and operations, are unknown to us. We cannot discover
so much as that size, figure, and texture of their minute and active
parts, which is really in them; much less the different motions and impulses made in and upon them by bodies from without, upon which depends, and by which is formed the greatest and most remarkable part
of those qualities we observe in them, and of which our complex ideas
of them are made up. This consideration alone is enough to put an end
to all our hopes of ever having the ideas of their real essences; which
whilst we want, the nominal essences we make use of instead of them,
will be able to furnish us but very sparingly with any general knowledge or universal propositions capable of real certainty.

13. *Judgment may reach farther, but that is not knowledge.*—We are
not therefore to wonder, if certainty be to be found in very few general propositions made concerning substances: our knowledge of their
qualities and properties goes very seldom farther than our senses reach
and inform us. Possibly inquisitive and observing men may, by strength
of judgment, penetrate farther, and, on probabilities taken from wary
observation, and hints well laid together, often guess right at what experience has not yet discovered to them. But this is but guessing still;
it amounts only to opinion, and has not that certainty which is requisite
to knowledge. . . .

16. *Wherein lies the general certainty of propositions.*—To conclude:
general propositions, of what kind soever, are then only capable of certainty, when the terms used in them stand for such ideas whose agreement or disagreement, as there expressed, is capable to be discovered
by us. And we are then certain of their truth or falsehood, when we perceive the ideas the terms stand for to agree or not agree according as
they are affirmed or denied one of another. Whence we may take notice
that general certainty is never to be found but in our ideas. Whenever
we go to seek it elsewhere, in experiment or observations without us,
our knowledge goes not beyond particulars. It is the contemplation of

our own abstract ideas that alone is able to afford us general knowledge. . . .[9]

CHAPTER IX

OF OUR THREEFOLD KNOWLEDGE OF EXISTENCE

1. *General certain propositions concern not existence.*—Hitherto we have only considered the essences of things, which, being only abstract ideas, and thereby removed in our thoughts from particular existence, (that being the proper operation of the mind in abstraction, to consider an idea no other existence but what it has in the understanding), gives us no knowledge of real existence at all. Where by the way, we may take notice that universal propositions, of whose truth or falsehood we can have certain knowledge, concern not existence; and farther, that all particular affirmations or negations that would not be certain if they were made general, are only concerning existence; they declaring only the accidental union or separation of ideas in things existing, which in their abstract natures have no known necessary union or repugnancy.

2. *A threefold knowledge of existence.*—But leaving the nature of propositions, and different ways of predication, to be considered more at large in another place, let us proceed now to inquire concerning our knowledge of the existence of things, and how we come by it. I say then, that we have the knowledge of our own existence by intuition; of the existence of God by demonstration; and of other things by sensation.

3. *Our knowledge of our own existence is intuitive.*—As for our own existence, we perceive it so plainly and so certainly that it neither needs nor is capable of any proof. For nothing can be more evident to us than our own existence. I think, I reason, I feel pleasure and pain; can any of these be more evident to me than my own existence? If I doubt of all other things, that very doubt makes me perceive my own existence, and will not suffer me to doubt of that. For if I know I feel pain, it is evident I have as certain perception of my own existence as of the existence of the pain I feel; or if I know I doubt, I have as certain perception of the existence of the thing doubting, as of that thought which I call doubt. Experience, then, convinces us that we have an intuitive knowledge of our own existence, and an internal infallible per-

[9] Chapters VII and VIII treat "Of Maxims" and "Of Trifling Propositions."— *Editor.*

ception that we are. In every act of sensation, reasoning, or thinking, we are conscious to ourselves of our own being, and in this matter come not short of the highest degree of certainty.

CHAPTER X

OF OUR KNOWLEDGE OF THE EXISTENCE OF A GOD

1. *We are capable of knowing certainly that there is a God.*—Though God has given us no innate ideas of Himself, though He has stamped no original characters on our minds wherein we may read His being; yet, having furnished us with those faculties our minds are endowed with, He hath not left Himself without witness; since we have sense, perception, and reason, and cannot want a clear proof of Him as long as we carry ourselves about us. Nor can we justly complain of our ignorance in this great point, since He has so plentifully provided us with the means to discover and know Him, so far as is necessary to the end of our being and the great concernment of our happiness. But though this be the most obvious truth that reason discovers, and though its evidence be (if I mistake not) equal to mathematical certainty; yet it requires thought and attention, and the mind must apply itself to a regular deduction of it from some part of our intuitive knowledge, or else we shall be as uncertain and ignorant of this as of other propositions which are in themselves capable of clear demonstration. To show, therefore, that we are capable of knowing, i.e., being certain, that there is a God, and how we may come by this certainty, I think we need go no farther than ourselves, and that undoubted knowledge we have of our own existence.

2. *Man knows that he himself is.*—I think it is beyond question that man has a clear idea of his own being: he knows certainly that he exists, and that he is something. He that can doubt whether he be anything or no, I speak not to; no more than I would argue with pure nothing, or endeavor to convince nonentity that it were something. If anyone pretends to be so sceptical as to deny his own existence (for really to doubt of it is manifestly impossible), let him, for me, enjoy his beloved happiness of being nothing, until hunger or some other pain convince him of the contrary. This, then, I think I may take for a truth, which everyone's certain knowledge assures him of beyond the liberty of doubting, viz., that he is something that actually exists.

3. *He knows also that nothing cannot produce a being, therefore something eternal.*—In the next place, man knows by an intuitive certainty that bare nothing can no more produce any real being, than it

can be equal to two right angles. If a man knows not that nonentity, or the absence of all being, cannot be equal to two right angles, it is impossible he should know any demonstration in Euclid. If therefore we know there is some real being, and that nonentity cannot produce any real being, it is an evident demonstration that from eternity there has been something; since what was not from eternity had a beginning, and what had a beginning must be produced by something else.

4. *That Eternal Being must be most powerful.*—Next, it is evident that what had its being and beginning from another, must also have all that which is in and belongs to its being from another too. All the powers it has, must be owing to and received from the same source. This eternal source, then, of all being must also be the source and original of all power; and so this Eternal Being must be also the most powerful.

5. *And most knowing.*—Again, a man finds in himself perception and knowledge. We have then got one step farther; and we are certain now that there is not only some being, but some knowing, intelligent being in the world. There was a time, then, when there was no knowing being, and when knowledge began to be; or else there has been also a knowing Being from eternity. If it be said, "There was a time when no being had any knowledge, when that Eternal Being was void of all understanding;" I reply that then it was impossible there should ever have been any knowledge; it being as impossible that things wholly void of knowledge, and operating blindly and without any perception, should produce a knowing being, as it is impossible that a triangle should make itself three angles bigger than two right ones. For it is as repugnant to the idea of senseless matter that it should put into itself sense, perception, and knowledge, as it is repugnant to the idea of a triangle that it should put into itself greater angles than two right ones.

6. *And therefore God.*—Thus from the consideration of ourselves, and what we infallibly find in our own constitutions, our reason leads us to the knowledge of this certain and evident truth, that there is an eternal, most powerful, and most knowing Being; which whether anyone will please to call God, it matters not. The thing is evident; and from this idea duly considered, will easily be deduced all those other attributes which we ought to ascribe to this Eternal Being. [If, nevertheless, anyone should be found so senselessly arrogant as to suppose man alone knowing and wise, but yet the product of mere ignorance and chance, and that all the rest of the universe acted only by that blind haphazard; I shall leave with him that very rational and emphatical rebuke of Tully, Lib. ii. *De Leg.*, to be considered at his leisure: "What can be more sillily arrogant and misbecoming than for a man to think that he has a mind and understanding in him, but yet in all the universe beside there is no

such thing? Or that those things which, with the utmost stretch of his reason, he can scarce comprehend, should be moved and managed without any reason at all?" *Quid est enim verius quam neminem esse oportere tam stulte arrogantem, ut in se mentem et rationem putet inesse, in coelo mundoque non putet? Aut ea quae vix summa ingenii ratione comprehendat, nulla ratione moveri putet?*]

From what has been said, it is plain to me we have a more certain knowledge of the existence of a God than of anything our senses have not immediately discovered to us. Nay, I presume I may say that we more certainly know that there is a God, than that there is anything else without us. When I say we *know*, I mean there is such a knowledge within our reach which we cannot miss, if we will but apply our minds to that as we do to several other inquiries.

7. *Our idea of a most perfect Being, not the sole proof of a God.*— How far the idea of a most perfect being which a man may frame in his mind, does or does not prove the existence of a God, I will not here examine. For in the different make of men's tempers, and application of their thoughts, some arguments prevail more on one, and some on another, for the confirmation of the same truth. But yet, I think this I may say that it is an ill way of establishing this truth and silencing atheists, to lay the whole stress of so important a point as this upon that sole foundation, and take some men's having that idea of God in their minds (for it is evident some men have none, and some worse than none, and the most very different) for the only proof of a Deity; and out of an overfondness of that darling invention, cashier or at least endeavor to invalidate, all other arguments, and forbid us to hearken to those proofs, as being weak or fallacious, which our own existence and the sensible parts of the universe offer so clearly and cogently to our thoughts, that I deem it impossible for a considering man to withstand them. For I judge it as certain and clear a truth as can anywhere be delivered, that "the invisible things of God are clearly seen from the creation of the world, being understood by the things that are made, even His eternal power and Godhead." Though our own being furnishes us, as I have shown, with an evident and incontestable proof of a Deity; and I believe nobody can avoid the cogency of it who will but as carefully attend to it as to any other demonstration of so many parts: yet this being so fundamental a truth, and of that consequence that all religion and genuine morality depend thereon, I doubt not but I shall be forgiven by my reader if I go over some parts of this argument again, and enlarge a little more upon them.

8. *Something from eternity.*—There is no truth more evident than that something must be from eternity. I never yet heard of anyone so un-

reasonable, or that could suppose so manifest a contradiction, as a time wherein there was perfectly nothing; this being of all absurdities the greatest, to imagine that pure nothing, the perfect negation and absence of all beings, should ever produce any real existence.

It being then unavoidable for all rational creatures to conclude that something has existed from eternity, let us next see what kind of thing that must be.

9. *Two sorts of beings cogitative and incogitative.*—There are but two sorts of beings in the world that man knows or conceives:—

First, such as are purely material, without sense, perception, or thought, as the clippings of our beards and parings of our nails.

Secondly, sensible, thinking, perceiving beings, such as we find ourselves to be; which, if you please, we will hereafter call *cogitative* and *incogitative* beings; which, to our present purpose, if for nothing else, are perhaps better terms than material and immaterial.

10. *Incogitative being cannot produce a cogitative.*—If then there must be something eternal, let us see what sort of being it must be. And to that it is very obvious to reason that it must necessarily be a cogitative being. For it is as impossible to conceive that ever bare incogitative matter should produce a thinking intelligent being, as that nothing should of itself produce matter. Let us suppose any parcel of matter eternal, great or small, we shall find it in itself able to produce nothing. For example, let us suppose the matter of the next pebble we meet with, eternal, closely united, and the parts firmly at rest together: if there were no other being in the world, must it not eternally remain so, a dead, inactive lump? Is it possible to conceive it can add motion to itself, being purely matter, or produce anything? Matter, then, by its own strength, cannot produce in itself so much as motion: the motion it has must also be from eternity, or else be produced and added to matter by some other being more powerful than matter; matter as is evident, having not power to produce motion in itself. But let us suppose motion eternal too; yet matter, incogitative matter and motion, whatever changes it might produce of figure and bulk, could never produce thought. Knowledge will still be as far beyond the power of motion and matter to produce, as matter is beyond the power of nothing or non-entity to produce. And I appeal to everyone's own thoughts, whether he cannot as easily conceive matter produced by nothing, as thought to be produced by pure matter, when before there was no such thing as thought or an intelligent being existing. Divide matter into as minute parts as you will, which we are apt to imagine a sort of spiritualizing or making a thinking thing of it; vary the figure and motion of it as much as you please; a globe, cube, cone, prism, cylinder, etc., whose diameters

are but 100,000th part of a gry,[10] will operate no otherwise upon other bodies of proportionable bulk than those of an inch or foot diameter; and you may as rationally expect to produce sense, thought, and knowledge, by putting together in a certain figure and motion gross particles of matter, as by those that are the very minutest that do anywhere exist. They knock, impel, and resist one another just as the greater do, and that is all they can do. So that, if we will suppose nothing first or eternal, matter can never begin to be; if we will suppose bare matter without motion, eternal motion can never begin to be; if we suppose only matter and motion first, or eternal, thought can never begin to be. [For it is impossible to conceive that matter, either with or without motion could have originally in and from itself, sense, perception, and knowledge, as is evident from hence, that then sense, perception, and knowledge must be a property eternally inseparable from matter and every particle of it. Not to add that though our general or specific conception of matter makes us speak of it as one thing, yet really all matter is not one individual thing, neither is there any such thing existing as one material being, or one single body, that we know or can conceive. And therefore, if matter were the eternal first cogitative being, there would not be one eternal infinite cogitative being, but an infinite number of eternal finite cogitative beings independent one of another, of limited force and distinct thoughts, which could never produce that order, harmony, and beauty, which are to be found in nature. Since, therefore, whatsoever is the first eternal being must necessarily be cogitative; and] whatsoever is first of all things must necessarily contain in it, and actually have, at least, all the perfections that can ever after exist; nor can it ever give to another any perfection that it hath not, either actually in itself or at least in a higher degree; [it necessarily follows that the first eternal being cannot be matter.]

11. *Therefore there has been an eternal wisdom.*—If, therefore, it be evident that something necessarily must exist from eternity, it is also as evident that that something must necessarily be a cogitative being; for it is as impossible that incogitative matter should produce a cogitative being, as that nothing, or the negation of all being, should produce a positive being or matter. . . .

[10] A gry is one-tenth of a line, a line one-tenth of an inch, an inch one-tenth of a philosophical foot, a philosophical foot one-third of a pendulum, whose diadroms, in the latitude of forty-five degrees, are each equal to one second of time, or one-sixtieth of a minute. I have affectedly made use of this measure here, and the parts of it, under a decimal division, with names to them; because I think it would be of general convenience that this should be the common measure in the commonwealth of letters.

CHAPTER XI

OF OUR KNOWLEDGE OF THE EXISTENCE OF OTHER THINGS

1. *It is to be had only by sensation.*—The knowledge of our own being we have by intuition. The existence of a God reason clearly makes known to us, as has been shown.

The knowledge of the existence of any other thing, we can have only by sensation: for, there being no necessary connection of real existence with any idea a man hath in his memory, nor of any other existence but that of God with the existence of any particular man, no particular man can know the existence of any other being, but only when by actual operating upon him it makes itself perceived by him. For, the having the idea of anything in our mind no more proves the existence of that thing than the picture of a man evidences his being in the world, or the visions of a dream make thereby a true history.

2. *Instance: whiteness of this paper.*—It is therefore the actual receiving of ideas from without that gives us notice of the existence of other things, and makes us know that something doth exist at that time without us which causes that idea in us, though perhaps we neither know nor consider how it does it; for it takes not from the certainty of our senses, and the ideas we receive by them, that we know not the manner wherein they are produced: v. g., whilst I write this, I have, by the paper affecting my eyes, that idea produced in my mind which whatever object causes, I call white; by which I know that that quality or accident (i.e., whose appearance before my eyes always causes that idea) doth really exist and hath a being without me. And of this the greatest assurance I can possibly have, and to which my faculties can attain, is the testimony of my eyes, which are the proper and sole judges of this thing; whose testimony I have reason to rely on as so certain that I can no more doubt, whilst I write this, that I see white and black, and that something really exists that causes that sensation in me, than that I write or move my hand; which is a certainty as great as human nature is capable of concerning the existence of anything but a man's self alone and of God.

3. *This, though not so certain as demonstration, yet may be called knowledge, and proves the existence of things without us.*—The notice we have by our senses of the existing of things without us, though it be not altogether so certain as our intuitive knowledge, or the deductions of our reason employed about the clear abstract ideas of our own minds; yet it is an assurance that deserves the name of knowledge. If we persuade ourselves that our faculties act and inform us right con-

cerning the existence of those objects that affect them, it cannot pass for an ill-grounded confidence: for I think nobody can, in earnest, be so sceptical as to be uncertain of the existence of those things which he sees and feels. At least, he that can doubt so far (whatever he may have with his own thoughts) will never have any controversy with me; since he can never be sure I say anything contrary to his own opinion. As to myself, I think God has given me assurance enough of the existence of things without me; since, by their different application, I can produce in myself both pleasure and pain, which is one great concernment of my present state. This is certain, the confidence that our faculties do not herein deceive us is the greatest assurance we are capable of concerning the existence of material beings. For we cannot act anything but by our faculties, nor talk of knowledge itself but by the help of those faculties which are fitted to apprehend even what knowledge is. But, besides the assurance we have from our senses themselves, that they do not err in the information they give us of the existence of things without us when they are affected by them, we are farther confirmed in this assurance by other concurrent reasons.

4. (i) *Because we cannot have them but by the inlet of the senses.* —First, it is plain those perceptions are produced in us by exterior causes affecting our senses, because those that want the organs of any sense never can have the ideas belonging to that sense produced in their minds. This is too evident to be doubted; and therefore we cannot but be assured that they come in by the organs of that sense, and no other way. The organs themselves, it is plain, do not produce them; for then the eyes of a man in the dark would produce colors, and his nose smell roses in the winter: but we see nobody gets the relish of a pineapple till he goes to the Indies where it is, and tastes it.

5. (ii) *Because an idea from actual sensation and another from memory are very distinct perceptions.*—Secondly, because sometimes I find that I cannot avoid the having those ideas produced in my mind: for though when my eyes are shut, or windows fast, I can at pleasure recall to my mind the ideas of light or the sun, which former sensations had lodged in my memory; so I can at pleasure lay by that idea, and take into my view that of the smell of a rose, or taste of sugar. But if I turn my eyes at noon towards the sun, I cannot avoid the ideas which the light or sun then produces in me. So that there is a manifest difference between the ideas laid up in my memory (over which, if they were there only, I should have constantly the same power to dispose of them, and lay them by at pleasure), and those which force themselves upon me and I cannot avoid having. And therefore it must needs be some exterior cause, and the brisk acting of some objects without me, whose efficacy I cannot resist, that produces those ideas in my mind, whether

I will or no. Besides, there is nobody who doth not perceive the difference in himself between contemplating the sun as he hath the idea of it in his memory, and actually looking upon it: of which two his perception is so distinct, that few of his ideas are more distinguishable one from another. And therefore he hath certain knowledge that they are not both memory, or the actions of his mind and fancies only within him; but that actual seeing hath a cause without.

6. (iii) *Pleasure or pain, which accompanies actual sensation, accompanies not the returning of those ideas without the external objects.*— Thirdly, add to this, that many of those ideas are produced in us with pain, which afterwards we remember without the least offense. Thus the pain of heat or cold, when the idea of it is revived in our minds, gives us no disturbance; which, when felt, was very troublesome, and is again when actually repeated; which is occasioned by the disorder the external object causes in our bodies when applied to them. And we remember the pain of hunger, thirst, or the headache, without any pain at all; which would either never disturb us, or else constantly do it as often as we thought of it, were there nothing more but ideas floating in our minds, and appearances entertaining our fancies, without the real existence of things affecting us from abroad. The same may be said of pleasure accompanying several actual sensations; and, though mathematical demonstration depends not upon sense, yet the examining them by diagrams gives great credit to the evidence of our sight, and seems to give it a certainty approaching to that of demonstration itself. For it would be very strange that a man should allow it for an undeniable truth, that two angles of a figure which he measures by lines and angles of a diagram, should be bigger one than the other, and yet doubt of the existence of those lines and angles which, by looking on, he makes use of to measure that by.

7. (iv) *Our senses assist one another's testimony of the existence of outward things.*—Fourthly, our senses, in many cases, bear witness to the truth of each other's report concerning the existence of sensible things without us. He that sees a fire may, if he doubt whether it be anything more than a bare fancy, feel it too, and be convinced by putting his hand in it; which certainly could never be put into such exquisite pain by a bare idea or phantom, unless that the pain be a fancy too: which yet he cannot, when the burn is well, by raising the idea of it, bring upon himself again.

Thus I see, whilst I write this, I can change the appearance of the paper; and, by designing the letters, tell beforehand what new idea it shall exhibit the very next moment, by barely drawing my pen over it; which will neither appear (let me fancy as much as I will) if my hand stand still, or though I move my pen, if my eyes be shut; nor, when those characters are once made on the paper, can I choose afterwards but see them as they are—that is, have the ideas of such letters as I have made. Whence it is manifest that they are not barely the sport and play of my own imagination, when I find that the characters that were made at the pleasure of my own thoughts do not obey them; nor yet cease to be, whenever I shall fancy it, but continue to affect my senses constantly and regularly, according to the figures I made them. To which if we will add that the sight of those shall, from another man, draw such sounds as I beforehand design they shall stand for, there will be little reason left to doubt that those words I write do really exist without me, when they cause a long series of regular sounds to affect my ears, which could not be the effect of my imagination, nor could my memory retain them in that order.

8. *This certainty is as great as our condition needs.*—But yet, if after all this anyone will be so sceptical as to distrust his senses, and to affirm that all we see and hear, feel and taste, think and do, during our whole being, is but the series and deluding appearances of a long dream whereof there is no reality, and therefore will question the existence of all things or our knowledge of anything; I must desire him to consider that if all be a dream, then he doth but dream that he makes the question; and so it is not much matter that a waking man should answer him. But yet, if he pleases, he may dream that I make him this answer, that the certainty of things existing in *rerum natura,* when we have the testimony of our senses for it, is not only as great as our frame can attain to, but as our condition needs. For, our faculties being suited not to the full extent of being, nor to a perfect, clear, comprehensive knowledge of things free from all doubt and scruple, but to the preservation of us, in whom they are, and accommodated to the use of life, they serve to our purpose well enough, if they will but give us certain notice of those things which are convenient or inconvenient to us. For he that sees a candle burning, and hath experimented the force of its flame by putting his finger in it, will little doubt that this is something existing without him, which does him harm and puts him to great pain; which is assurance enough, when no man requires greater certainty to govern his actions by than what is as certain as his actions themselves. And if our dreamer pleases to try whether the glowing heat of a glass furnace be barely a wandering imagination in a drowsy man's fancy, by putting his hand into it, he may perhaps be awakened into a certainty greater than he could wish, that it is something more than bare imagination. So that this evidence is as great as we can desire, being as certain to us as our pleasure or pain, i. e., happiness or misery; beyond which we have no concernment either of knowing or being. Such an assurance of the existence of things without us, is sufficient to direct us in the attaining the

good and avoiding the evil which is caused by them, which is the important concernment we have of being made acquainted with them.

9. *But reaches no farther than actual sensation.*—In fine, then, when our senses do actually convey into our understandings any idea, we cannot but be satisfied that there doth something at that time really exist without us which doth affect our senses, and by them give notice of itself to our apprehensive faculties, and actually produce that idea which we then perceive; and we cannot so far distrust their testimony as to doubt that such collections of simple ideas as we have observed by our senses to be united together, do really exist together. But this knowledge extends as far as the present testimony of our senses, employed about particular objects that do then affect them, and no farther. For if I saw such a collection of simple ideas as is wont to be called man existing together one minute since, and am now alone, I cannot be certain that the same man exists now, since there is no necessary connection of his existence a minute since with his existence now: by a thousand ways he may cease to be, since I had the testimony of my senses for his existence. And if I cannot be certain that the man I saw last today is now in being, I can less be certain that he is so who hath been longer removed from my senses, and I have not seen since yesterday, or since the last year; and much less can I be certain of the existence of men that I never saw. And therefore, though it be highly probable that millions of men do now exist, yet, whilst I am alone writing this, I have not that certainty of it which we strictly call knowledge; though the great likelihood of it puts me past doubt, and it be reasonable for me to do several things upon the confidence that there are men (and men also of my acquaintance, with whom I have to do) now in the world: but this is but probability, not knowledge.

10. *Folly to expect demonstration in everything.*—Whereby yet we may observe how foolish and vain a thing it is for a man of a narrow knowledge, who having reason given him to judge of the different evidence and probability of things, and to be swayed accordingly; how vain, I say, it is to expect demonstration and certainty in things not capable of it, and refuse assent to very rational propositions, and act contrary to very plain and clear truths, because they cannot be made out so evident as to surmount every the least (I will not say reason, but) pretense of doubting. He that in the ordinary affairs of life would admit of nothing but direct plain demonstration, would be sure of nothing in this world but of perishing quickly. The wholesomeness of his meat or drink would not give him reason to venture on it: and I would fain know what it is he could do upon such grounds as were capable of no doubt, no objection.

11. *Past existence is known by memory.*—As, when our senses are

actually employed about any object, we do know that it does exist, so by our memory we may be assured that heretofore things that affected our senses have existed. And thus we have knowledge of the past existence of several things, whereof our senses having informed us, our memories still retain the ideas; and of this we are past all doubt so long as we remember well. But this knowledge also reaches no farther than our senses have formerly assured us. Thus, seeing water at this instant, it is an unquestionable truth to me that water doth exist; and remembering that I saw it yesterday, it will also be always true, and, as long as my memory retains it, always an undoubted proposition to me, that water did exist the 10th of July 1688, as it will also be equally true that a certain number of very fine colors did exist, which at the same time I saw upon a bubble of that water: but being now quite out of sight both of the water and bubbles too, it is no more certainly known to me that the water doth now exist than that the bubbles or colors therein do so; it being no more necessary that water should exist today because it existed yesterday, than that the colors or bubbles exist today because they existed yesterday, though it be exceedingly much more probable, because water hath been observed to continue long in existence, but bubbles and the colors on them quickly cease to be.

12. *The existence of spirits not knowable.*—What ideas we have of spirits, and how we come by them, I have already shown. But though we have those ideas in our minds, and know we have them there, the having the ideas of spirits does not make us know that any such things do exist without us, or that there are any finite spirits, or any other spiritual beings but the Eternal God. We have ground from revelation, and several other reasons, to believe with assurance that there are such creatures; but, our senses not being able to discover them, we want the means of knowing their particular existences. For we can no more know that there are finite spirits really existing by the idea we have of such beings in our minds, than by the ideas anyone has of fairies or centaurs he can come to know that things answering those ideas do really exist.

And therefore concerning the existence of finite spirits, as well as several other things, we must content ourselves with the evidence of faith; but universal certain propositions concerning this matter are beyond our reach. For, however true it may be, v. g., that all the intelligent spirits that God ever created do still exist, yet it can never make a part of our certain knowledge. These and the like propositions we may assent to as highly probable, but are not, I fear, in this state capable of knowing. We are not, then, to put others upon demonstrating, nor ourselves upon search of, universal certainty in all those matters wherein we are not capable of any other knowledge but what our senses give us in this or that particular

13. *Particular propositions concerning existences are knowable.*—
By which it appears that there are two sorts of propositions. (i) There
is one sort of propositions concerning the existence of anything answerable to such an idea: as, having the idea of an elephant, phoenix,
motion, or an angel in my mind, the first and natural inquiry is, whether
such a thing does anywhere exist. And this knowledge is only of particulars. No existence of anything without us, but only of God, can
certainly be known farther than our senses inform us. (ii) There is
another sort of propositions, wherein is expressed the agreement or disagreement of our abstract ideas, and their dependence one on another.
Such propositions may be universal and certain. So having the idea of
God and myself, of fear and obedience, I cannot but be sure that God
is to be feared and obeyed by me; and this proposition will be certain
concerning man in general, if I have made an abstract idea of such a
species whereof I am one particular. But yet this proposition, how certain soever, that men ought to fear and obey God, proves not to me the
existence of men in the world, but will be true of all such creatures whenever they do exist: which certainty of such general propositions depends
on the agreement or disagreement to be discovered in those abstract
ideas.

14. *And general propositions concerning abstract ideas.*—In the former case, our knowledge is the consequence of the existence of things
producing ideas in our minds by our senses; in the latter, knowledge is
the consequence of the ideas (be they what they will) that are in our
minds, producing their general certain propositions. Many of these are
called *aeternae veritates,* and all of them indeed are so; not from being
written all or any of them in the minds of all men, or that they were any
of them propositions in any one's mind till he, having got the abstract
ideas, joined or separated them by affirmation or negation. But wheresoever we can suppose such a creature as man is, endowed with such
faculties, and thereby furnished with such ideas as we have, we must
conclude he must needs, when he applies his thoughts to the consideration of his ideas, know the truth of certain propositions that will arise
from the agreement or disagreement which he will perceive in his own
ideas. Such propositions are therefore called eternal truths, not because
they are eternal propositions actually formed, and antecedent to the
understanding that at any time makes them; nor because they are imprinted on the mind from any patterns that are anywhere of them out
of the mind, and existed before; but because, being once made about
abstract ideas so as to be true, they will, whenever they can be supposed
to be made again at any time past or to come, by a mind having those
ideas, always actually be true. For, names being supposed to stand perpetually for the same ideas, and the same ideas having immutably the

same habitudes one to another, propositions concerning any abstract ideas that are once true must needs be eternal verities.

CHAPTER XII

OF THE IMPROVEMENT OF OUR KNOWLEDGE

1. *Knowledge is not from maxims.*—It having been the common received opinion amongst men of letters, that maxims were the foundation of all knowledge; and that the sciences were each of them built upon certain *praecognita*, from whence the understanding was to take its rise, and by which it was to conduct itself, in its inquiries into the matters belonging to that science; the beaten road of the schools has been, to lay down in the beginning one or more general propositions, as foundations whereon to build the knowledge that was to be had of that subject. These doctrines, thus laid down for foundations of any science, were called principles, as the beginnings from which we must set out, and look no farther backwards in our inquiries, as we have already observed.

2. (*The occasion of that opinion.*)—One thing which might probably give an occasion to this way of proceeding in other sciences, was (as I suppose) the good success it seemed to have in mathematics, wherein men, being observed to attain a great certainty of knowledge, these sciences came by pre-eminence to be called Μαθήματα, and Μάθησις, learning, or things learned, thoroughly learned, as having of all others the greatest certainty, clearness, and evidence in them.

3. *But from the comparing clear and distinct ideas.*—But if anyone will consider, he will (I guess) find, that the greatest advancement and certainty of real knowledge, which men arrived to in these sciences, was not owing to the influence of these principles, nor derived from any peculiar advantage they received from two or three general maxims, laid down in the beginning; but from the clear, distinct, complete ideas their thoughts were employed about, and the relation of equality and excess so clear between some of them, that they had an intuitive knowledge, and by that a way to discover it in others, and this without the help of those maxims. For I ask, is it not possible for a young lad to know, that his whole body is bigger than his little finger, but by virtue of this axiom, that the whole is bigger than a part; nor be assured of it, till he has learned that axiom? Or cannot a country wench know, that having received a shilling from one that owes her three, and a shilling also from another that owes her three, the remaining debts in each of their hands are equal? Cannot she know this, I say, unless she fetch the

certainty of it from this maxim, that if you take equals from equals, the remainder will be equals, a maxim which possibly she never heard or thought of? I desire anyone to consider, from what has been elsewhere said, which is known first and clearest by most people, the particular instance, or the general rule; and which it is that gives life and birth to the other. These general rules are but the comparing our more general and abstract ideas, which are the workmanship of the mind made, and names given to them, for the easier dispatch in its reasonings, and drawing into comprehensive terms, and short rules, its various and multiplied observations. But knowledge began in the mind, and was founded on particulars; though afterwards, perhaps, no notice be taken thereof: it being natural for the mind (forward still to enlarge its knowledge) most attentively to lay up those general notions, and make the proper use of them, which is to disburden the memory of the cumbersome load of particulars. . . .

6. *But to compare clear complete ideas under steady names.*—But since the knowledge of the certainty of principles, as well as of all other truths, depends only upon the perception we have of the agreement or disagreement of our ideas, the way to improve our knowledge is not, I am sure, blindly, and with an implicit faith, to receive and swallow principles; but is, I think, to get and fix in our minds clear, distinct, and complete ideas, as far as they are to be had, and annex to them proper and constant names. And thus, perhaps, without any other principles, but barely considering those ideas, and by comparing them one with another, finding their agreement and disagreement, and their several relations and habitudes; we shall get more true and clear knowledge, by the conduct of this one rule, than by taking up principles, and thereby putting our minds into the disposal of others.

7. *The true method of advancing knowledge is by considering our abstract ideas.*—We must therefore, if we will proceed as reason advises, adapt our methods of inquiry to the nature of the ideas we examine, and the truth we search after. General and certain truths are only founded in the habitudes and relations of abstract ideas. A sagacious and methodical application of our thoughts, for the finding out these relations, is the only way to discover all, that can be put with truth and certainty concerning them into general propositions. By what steps we are to proceed in these, is to be learned in the schools of the mathematicians, who from very plain and easy beginnings, by gentle degrees and a continued chain of reasonings, proceed to the discovery and demonstration of truths, that appear at first sight beyond human capacity. The art of finding proofs, and the admirable methods they have invented for the singling out, and laying in order, those intermediate ideas, that demonstratively show the equality or inequality of unapplicable quan-

tities, is that which has carried them so far, and produced such wonderful and unexpected discoveries: but whether something like this, in respect of other ideas, as well as those of magnitude, may not in time be found out, I will not determine. This, I think, I may say, that if other ideas, that are the real as well as nominal essences of their species, were pursued in the way familiar to mathematicians, they would carry our thoughts farther, and with greater evidence and clearness, than possibly we are apt to imagine.

8. *By which morality also may be made clearer.*—This gave me the confidence to advance that conjecture, which I suggest (Chap. III) viz., that morality is capable of demonstration, as well as mathematics. For the ideas that ethics are conversant about, being all real essences, and such as I imagine have a discoverable connection and agreement one with another; so far as we can find their habitudes and relations, so far we shall be possessed of certain, real, and general truths: and I doubt not, but, if a right method were taken, a great part of morality might be made out with that clearness, that could leave, to a considerate man, no more reason to doubt, than he could have to doubt of the truth of propositions, in mathematics, which have been demonstrated to him.

9. *But knowledge of bodies is to be improved only by experience.*— In our search after the knowledge of substances, our want of ideas, that are suitable to such a way of proceeding, obliges us to a quite different method. We advance not here, as in the other (where our abstract ideas are real as well as nominal essences) by contemplating our ideas, and considering their relations and correspondences; that helps us very little, for the reasons, that in another place we have at large set down. By which I think it is evident, that substances afford matter of very little general knowledge; and the bare contemplation of their abstract ideas will carry us but a very little way in the search of truth and certainty. What then are we to do for the improvement of our knowledge in substantial beings? Here we are to take a quite contrary course; the want of ideas of their real essences, sends us from our own thoughts to the things themselves, as they exist. Experience here must teach me what reason cannot; and it is by trying alone, that I can certainly know, what other qualities coexist with those of my complex idea, v. g., whether that yellow, heavy, fusible body, I call gold, be malleable, or no; which experience (which way ever it prove, in that particular body, I examine) makes me not certain, that it is so in all, or any other yellow, heavy, fusible bodies, but that which I have tried. Because it is no consequence one way or the other from my complex idea: the necessity or inconsistence of malleability hath no visible

connection with the combination of that color, weight, and fusibility in any body. . . .

12. . . .In the knowledge of bodies, we must be content to glean what we can from particular experiments: since we cannot, from a discovery of their real essences, grasp at a time whole sheaves, and in bundles comprehend the nature and properties of whole species together. Where our inquiry is concerning coexistence, or repugnancy to coexist, which by contemplation of our ideas we cannot discover; there experience, observation, and natural history must give us by our senses, and by retail, an insight into corporeal substances. The knowledge of bodies we must get by our senses, warily employed in taking notice of their qualities and operations on one another: and what we hope to know of separate spirits in this world, we must, I think, expect only from revelation. He that shall consider how little general maxims, precarious principles, and hypotheses laid down at pleasure, have promoted true knowledge, or helped to satisfy the inquiries of rational men after real improvements; how little, I say, the setting out at that end has, for many ages together, advanced men's progress towards the knowledge of natural philosophy; will think we have reason to thank those, who in this latter age have taken another course, and have trod out to us, though not an easier way to learned ignorance, yet a surer way to profitable knowledge.

13. *The true use of hypotheses.*—Not that we may not, to explain any phenomena of nature, make use of any probable hypothesis whatsoever: hypotheses, if they are well made, are at least great helps to the memory, and often direct us to new discoveries. But my meaning is, that we should not take up anyone too hastily (which the mind, that would always penetrate into the causes of things, and have principles to rest on, is very apt to do) till we have very well examined particulars, and made several experiments, in that thing which we would explain by our hypothesis, and see whether it will agree to them all; whether our principles will carry us quite through, and not be as inconsistent with one phenomenon of nature, as they seem to accommodate and explain another. And at least that we take care, that the name of principles deceive us not, nor impose on us, by making us receive that for an unquestionable truth, which is really at best but a very doubtful conjecture, such as are most (I had almost said all) of the hypotheses in natural philosophy. . . .[11]

[11] In Chapter XIII Locke observes that knowledge is voluntary, in that it depends upon our attention and concentrated application; necessary, in that it must conform to objective truth.—*Editor.*

CHAPTER XIV

OF JUDGMENT

1. Our knowledge being short, we want something else.—The under-standing faculties being given to man, not barely for speculation, but also for the conduct of his life, man would be at a great loss, if he had nothing to direct him but what has the certainty of true knowledge. For that being very short and scanty, as we have seen, he would be often utterly in the dark, and in most of the actions of his life, per-fectly at a stand, had he nothing to guide him in the absence of clear and certain knowledge. He that will not eat, till he has demonstration that it will nourish him; he that will not stir, till he infallibly knows the business he goes about will succeed; will have little else to do, but to sit still and perish.

2. *What use to be made of this twilight state.*—Therefore as God has set some things in broad daylight; as he has given us some certain knowledge, though limited to a few things in comparison, probably, as a taste of what intellectual creatures are capable of, to excite in us a desire and endeavor after a better state; so in the greatest part of our concernments he has afforded us only the twilight, as I may so say, of probability; suitable, I presume, to that state of mediocrity and pro-bationership, he has been pleased to place us in here; wherein, to check our overconfidence and presumption, we might by every day's experi-ence be made sensible of our shortsightedness and liableness to error; the sense whereof might be a constant admonition to us, to spend the days of this our pilgrimage with industry and care, in the search and following of that way, which might lead us to a state of greater per-fection: it being highly rational to think, even were revelation silent in the case, that as men employ those talents God has given them here, they shall accordingly receive their rewards at the close of the day, when their sun shall set, and night shall put an end to their labors.

3. *Judgment supplies the want of knowledge.*—The faculty which God has given man to supply the want of clear and certain knowledge, in cases where that cannot be had, is judgment: whereby the mind takes its ideas to agree or disagree; or which is the same, any propo-sition to be true or false, without perceiving a demonstrative evidence in the proofs. The mind sometimes exercises this judgment out of neces-sity, where demonstrative proofs and certain knowledge are not to be had; and sometimes out of laziness, unskillfulness, or haste, even where demonstrative and certain proofs are to be had. Men often stay not warily to examine the agreement or disagreement of two ideas, which

they are desirous or concerned to know; but either incapable of such attention as is requisite in a long train of gradations, or impatient of delay, lightly cast their eyes on, or wholly pass by the proofs; and so without making out the demonstration, determine of the agreement or disagreement of two ideas, as it were by a view of them as they are at a distance, and take it to be the one or the other, as seems most likely to them upon such a loose survey. This faculty of the mind, when it is exercised immediately about things, is called judgment; when about truths delivered in words, is most commonly called assent or dissent: which being the most usual way, wherein the mind has occasion to employ this faculty, I shall under these terms treat of it, at least liable in our language to equivocation.

4. *Judgment is the presuming things to be so, without perceiving it.* —Thus the mind has two faculties, conversant about truth and false-hood.

First, knowledge, whereby it certainly perceives, and is undoubtedly satisfied of the agreement or disagreement of any ideas.

Secondly, judgment, which is the putting ideas together, or separat-ing them from one another in the mind, when their certain agreement or disagreement is not perceived, but presumed to be so; which is, as the word imports, taken to be so before it certainly appears. And if it so unites, or separates them, as in reality things are, it is right judgment.

CHAPTER XV

OF PROBABILITY

1. *Probability is the appearance of agreement upon fallible proofs.*— As demonstration is the showing the agreement or disagreement of two ideas, by the intervention of one or more proofs, which have a constant, immutable, and visible connection one with another; so probability is nothing but the appearance of such an agreement or disagreement, by the intervention of proofs, whose connection is not constant and im-mutable, or at least is not perceived to be so, but is, or appears for the most part to be so, and is enough to induce the mind to judge the proposition to be true or false, rather than the contrary. For example: in the demonstration of it, a man perceives the certain immutable con-nection there is of equality between the three angles of a triangle, and those intermediate ones which are made use of to show their quality to two right ones; and so by an intuitive knowledge of the agreement or disagreement of the intermediate ideas in each step of the progress, the whole series is continued with an evidence, which clearly shows the

agreement or disagreement of those three angles in equality to two right ones: and thus he has certain knowledge that it is so. But another man, who never took the pains to observe the demonstration, hearing a mathematician, a man of credit, affirm the three angles of a triangle to be equal to two right ones, assents to it, i.e., receives it for true. In which case the foundation of his assent is the probability of the thing, the proof being such as for the most part carries truth with it: the man, on whose testimony he receives it, not being wont to affirm anything contrary to, or besides his knowledge, especially in matters of this kind. So that that which causes his assent to this proposition, that the three angles of a triangle are equal to two right ones, that which makes him take these ideas to agree, without knowing them to do so, is the wonted veracity of the speaker in other cases, or his supposed veracity in this.

2. *It is to supply the want of knowledge.*—Our knowledge, as has been shown, being very narrow, and we not happy enough to find certain truth in everything which we have occasion to consider; most of the propositions we think, reason, discourse, nay act upon, are such, as we cannot have undoubted knowledge of their truth: yet some of them border so near upon certainty, that we make no doubt at all about them; but assent to them as firmly, and act, according to that assent, as resolutely, as if they were infallibily demonstrated, and that our knowledge of them was perfect and certain. But there being degrees herein, from the very neighborhood of certainty and demonstration, quite down to improbability and unlikeness, even to the confines of impossibility; and also degrees of assent, from full assurance and confidence, quite down to conjecture, doubt, and distrust: I shall come now (having, as I think, found out the bounds of human knowledge and certainty) in the next place, to consider the several degrees and grounds of probability, and assent or faith.

3. *Being that which makes us presume things to be true before we know them to be so.*—Probability is likeliness to be true, the very notation of the word signifying such a proposition, for which there be arguments or proofs, to make it pass or be received for true. The entertainment the mind gives this sort of propositions, is called belief, assent, or opinion, which is the admitting or receiving any proposition for true, upon arguments or proofs that are found to persuade us to receive it as true, without certain knowledge that it is so. And herein lies the difference between probability and certainty, faith and knowledge, that in all the parts of knowledge there is intuition; each immediate idea, each step has its visible and certain connection; in belief, not so. That which makes me believe is something extraneous to the thing I believe; something not evidently joined on both sides to, and so not

manifestly showing the agreement or disagreement of those ideas that are under consideration.

4. *The grounds of probability are two; conformity with our own experience, or the testimony of others' experience.*—Probability then, being to supply the defect of our knowledge, and to guide us where that fails, is always conversant about propositions, whereof we have no certainty, but only some inducements to receive them for true. The grounds of it are, in short, these two following.

First, the conformity of anything with our own knowledge, observation, and experience.

Secondly, the testimony of others, vouching their observation and experience. In the testimony of others, is to be considered: (1) The number. (2) The integrity. (3) The skill of the witnesses. (4) The design of the author, where it is a testimony out of a book cited. (5) The consistency of the parts, and circumstances of the relation. (6) Contrary testimonies.

5. *In this, all the arguments pro and con ought to be examined before we come to a judgment.*—Probability wanting that intuitive evidence, which infallibly determines the understanding, and produces certain knowledge, the mind, if it would proceed rationally, ought to examine all the grounds of probability, and see how they make more or less for or against any proposition, before it assents to, or dissents from it; and upon a due balancing the whole, reject, or receive it, with a more or less firm assent, proportionably to the preponderancy of the greater grounds of probability on one side or the other. For example:

If I myself see a man walk on the ice, it is past probability, it is knowledge; but if another tells me he saw a man in England, in the midst of a sharp winter, walk upon water hardened with cold; this has so great conformity with what is usually observed to happen, that I am disposed by the nature of the thing itself to assent to it, unless some manifest suspicion attend the relation of that matter of fact. But if the same thing be told to one born between the tropics, who never saw nor heard of any such thing before, there the whole probability relies on testimony: and as the relators are more in number, and of more credit, and have no interest to speak contrary to the truth; so that matter of fact is like to find more or less belief. Though to a man, whose experience has always been quite contrary, and who has never heard of anything like it, the most untainted credit of a witness will scarce be able to find belief. As it happened to a Dutch ambassador, who entertaining the king of Siam with the particularities of Holland, which he was inquisitive after, amongst other things told him, that the water in his country would sometimes, in cold weather, be so hard, that men walked upon it, and that it would bear an elephant if he were there.

To which the king replied, "Hitherto I have believed the strange things you have told me, because I look upon you as a sober fair man, but now I am sure you lie."

6. *They being capable of great variety.*—Upon these grounds depends the probability of any proposition: and as the conformity of our knowledge, as the certainty of observations, as the frequency and constancy of experience, and the number and credibility of testimonies, do more or less agree or disagree with it, so is any proposition in itself more or less probable. There is another, I confess, which, though by itself it be no true ground of probability, yet is often made use of for one, by which men most commonly regulate their assent, and upon which they pin their faith more than anything else, and that is the opinion of others: though there cannot be a more dangerous thing to rely on, nor more likely to mislead one; since there is much more falsehood and error among men, than truth and knowledge. And if the opinions and persuasions of others, whom we know and think well of, be a ground of assent, men have reason to be heathens in Japan, Mohammedans in Turkey, Papists in Spain, Protestants in England, and Lutherans in Sweden. But of this wrong ground of assent I shall have occasion to speak more at large in another place.

CHAPTER XVI

OF THE DEGREES OF ASSENT

1. *Our assent ought to be regulated by the grounds of probability.*— The grounds of probability we have laid down in the foregoing chapter; as they are the foundations on which our assent is built, so are they also the measure whereby its several degrees are, or ought to be, regulated: only we are to take notice, that whatever grounds of probability there may be, they yet operate no farther on the mind, which searches after truth, and endeavors to judge right, than they appear; at least in the first judgment or search that the mind makes. I confess, in the opinions men have, and firmly stick to, in the world, their assent is not always from an actual view of the reasons that at first prevailed with them: it being in many cases almost impossible, and in most very hard, even for those who have very admirable memories, to retain all the proofs, which upon a due examination made them embrace that side of the question. It suffices that they have once with care and fairness sifted the matter as far as they could; and that they have searched into all the particulars, that they could imagine to give any light to the question; and with the best of their skill cast up the account upon the whole

evidence: and thus having once found on which side the probability appeared to them, after as full and exact an inquiry as they can make, they lay up the conclusion in their memories, as a truth they have discovered; and for the future they remain satisfied with the testimony of their memories, that this is the opinion, that by the proofs they have once seen of it deserves such a degree of their assent as they afford it.

2. *These cannot always be actually in view, and then we must content ourselves with the remembrance that we once saw ground for such a degree of assent.*—This is all that the greatest part of men are capable of doing, in regulating their opinions and judgments; unless a man will exact of them, either to retain distinctly in their memories all the proofs concerning any probable truth, and that too, in the same order, and regular deduction of consequences in which they have formerly placed or seen them; which sometimes is enough to fill a large volume on one single question: or else they must require a man, for every opinion that he embraces, every day to examine the proofs: both which are impossible. It is unavoidable, therefore, that the memory be relied on in the case, and that men be persuaded of several opinions, whereof the proofs are not actually in their thoughts: nay, which perhaps they are not able actually to recall. Without this, the greatest part of men must be either very sceptics, or change every moment, and yield themselves up to whoever, having lately studied the question, offers them arguments; which, for want of memory, they are not able presently to answer.

3. *The ill consequence of this, if our former judgments were not rightly made.*—I cannot but own, that men's sticking to their past judgment, and adhering firmly to conclusions formerly made, is often the cause of great obstinacy in error and mistake. But the fault is not that they rely on their memories for what they have before well-judged; but because they judged before they had well examined. May we not find a great number (not to say the greatest part) of men that think they have formed right judgments of several matters; and that for no other reason, but because they never thought otherwise? who imagine themselves to have judged right, only because they never questioned, never examined their own opinions? Which is indeed to think they judged right, because they never judged at all: and yet these of all men hold their opinions with the greatest stiffness; those being generally the most fierce and firm in their tenets, who have least examined them. What we once know, we are certain is so: and we may be secure, that there are no latent proofs undiscovered, which may overturn our knowledge, or bring it in doubt. But, in matters of probability, it is not in every case we can be sure that we have all the particulars before us,

that any way concern the question; and that there is no evidence behind, and yet unseen, which may cast the probability on the other side, and outweigh all that at present seems to preponderate with us. Who almost is there that hath the leisure, patience, and means, to collect together all the proofs concerning most of the opinions he has, so as safely to conclude that he hath a clear and full view; and that there is no more to be alleged for his better information? And yet we are forced to determine ourselves on the one side or other. The conduct of our lives, and the management of our great concerns, will not bear delay: for those depend, for the most part, on the determination of our judgment in points wherein we are not capable of certain and demonstrative knowledge, and wherein it is necessary for us to embrace the one side or the other.

4. *The right use of it, is mutual charity and forbearance.*—Since therefore it is unavoidable to the greatest part of men, if not all, to have several opinions, without certain and indubitable proofs of their truth; and it carries too great an imputation of ignorance, lightness, or folly, for men to quit and renounce their former tenets presently upon the offer of an argument, which they cannot immediately answer, and show the insufficiency of: it would methinks become all men to maintain peace, and the common offices of humanity and friendship, in the diversity of opinions; since we cannot reasonably expect, that anyone should readily and obsequiously quit his own opinion, and embrace ours with a blind resignation to an authority, which the understanding of man acknowledges not. For however it may often mistake, it can own no other guide but reason, nor blindly submit to the will and dictates of another. If he, you would bring over to your sentiments, be one that examines before he assents, you must give him leave at his leisure to go over the account again, and, recalling what is out of his mind, examine all the particulars, to see on which side the advantage lies: and if he will not think our arguments of weight enough to engage him anew in so much pains, it is but what we often do ourselves in the like case; and we should take it amiss if others should prescribe to us what points we should study. And if he be one who takes his opinions upon trust, how can we imagine that he should renounce those tenets which time and custom have so settled in his mind, that he thinks them self-evident, and of an unquestionable certainty; or which he takes to be impressions he has received from God himself, or from men sent by Him? How can we expect, I say, that opinions thus settled should be given up to the arguments or authority of a stranger, or adversary; especially if there be any suspicion of interest or design, as there never fails to be, where men find themselves ill treated? We should do well to commiserate our mutual ignorance, and endeavor to remove it in all

the gentle and fair ways of information; and not instantly treat others ill, as obstinate and perverse, because they will not renounce their own, and receive our opinions, or at least those we would force upon them, when it is more than probable, that we are no less obstinate in not embracing some of theirs. For where is the man that has incontestable evidence of the truth of all that he holds, or of the falsehood of all he condemns; or can say, that he has examined to the bottom all his own, or other men's opinions? The necessity of believing, without knowledge, nay often upon very slight grounds, in this fleeting state of action and blindness we are in, should make us more busy and careful to inform ourselves, than constrain others. At least those, who have not thoroughly examined to the bottom all their own tenets, must confess they are unfit to prescribe to others; and are unreasonable in imposing that as truth on other men's belief, which they themselves have not searched into, nor weighed the arguments of probability, on which they should receive or reject it. Those who have fairly and truly examined, and are thereby got past doubt in all the doctrines they profess and govern themselves by, would have a juster pretense to require others to follow them: but these are so few in number, and find so little reason to be magisterial in their opinions, that nothing insolent and imperious is to be expected from them: and there is reason to think, that, if men were better instructed themselves, they would be less imposing on others.

5. *Probability is either of matter of fact or speculation.*—But to return to the grounds of assent, and the several degrees of it, we are to take notice, that the propositions we receive upon inducements of probability, are of two sorts; either concerning some particular existence, or, as it is usually termed, matter of fact, which falling under observation, is capable of human testimony; or else concerning things, which being beyond the discovery of our senses, are not capable of any such testimony.

6. *The concurrent experience of all other men with ours produces assurance approaching to knowledge.*—Concerning the first of these, viz., particular matter of fact.

First, where any particular thing, consonant to the constant observation of ourselves and others in the like case, comes attested by the concurrent reports of all that mention it, we receive it as easily, and build as firmly upon it, as if it were certain knowledge; and we reason and act thereupon with as little doubt, as if it were perfect demonstration. Thus, if all Englishmen, who have occasion to mention it, should affirm that it froze in England the last winter, or that there were swallows seen there in the summer; I think a man could almost as little doubt it, as that seven and four are eleven. The first therefore, and highest degree of probability, is, when the general consent of all men, in all ages, as far as it can be known, concurs with a man's constant and never-failing experience in like cases, to confirm the truth of any particular matter of fact attested by fair witnesses: such are all the stated constitutions and properties of bodies, and the regular proceedings of causes and effects in the ordinary course of nature. This we call an argument from the nature of things themselves. For what our own and other men's constant observation has found always to be after the same manner, that we with reason conclude to be the effect of steady and regular causes, though they come not within the reach of our knowledge. Thus, that fire warmed a man, made lead fluid, and changed the color or consistency in wood or charcoal; that iron sunk in water, and swam in quicksilver: these and the like propositions about particular facts, being agreeable to our constant experience, as often as we have to do with these matters; and being generally spoken of (when mentioned by others) as things found constantly to be so, and therefore not so much as controverted by anybody; we are put past doubt, that a relation affirming any such thing to have been, or any predication that it will happen again in the same manner, is very true. These probabilities rise so near to certainty, that they govern our thoughts as absolutely, and influence all our actions as fully, as the most evident demonstration; and in what concerns us, we make little or no difference between them and certain knowledge. Our belief, thus grounded, rises to assurance.

7. *Unquestionable testimony and experience for the most part produce confidence.*—Secondly, the next degree of probability is, when I find by my own experience, and the agreement of all others that mention it, a thing to be, for the most part, so; and that the particular instance of it is attested by many and undoubted witnesses, v. g., history giving us such an account of men in all ages; and my own experience, as far as I had an opportunity to observe, confirming it, that most men prefer their private advantage to the public: if all historians that write of Tiberius say that Tiberius did so, it is extremely probable. And in this case, our assent has a sufficient foundation to raise itself to a degree which we may call confidence.

8. *Fair testimony, and the nature of the thing indifferent, produce also confident belief.*—Thirdly, in things that happen indifferently, as that a bird should fly this or that way; that it should thunder on a man's right or left hand, etc., when any particular matter of fact is vouched by the concurrent testimony of unsuspected witnesses, there our assent is also unavoidable. Thus, that there is such a city in Italy as Rome; that, about one thousand seven hundred years ago, there lived in it a man, called Julius Caesar; that he was a general, and that he

won a battle against another, called Pompey: this, though in the nature of the thing there be nothing for nor against it, yet being related by historians of credit, and contradicted by no one writer, a man cannot avoid believing it, and can as little doubt of it, as he does of the being and actions of his own acquaintance, whereof he himself is a witness.

9. *Experiences and testimonies clashing, infinitely vary the degrees of probability.*—Thus far the matter goes easy enough. Probability upon such grounds carries so much evidence with it, that it naturally determines the judgment, and leaves us at little liberty to believe, or disbelieve, know, or be ignorant. The difficulty is, when testimonies contradict common experience, and the reports of history and witnesses clash with the ordinary course of nature, or with one another; there it is, where diligence, attention, and exactness are required, to form a right judgment, and to proportion the assent to the different evidence and probability of the thing; which rises and falls, according as those two foundations of credibility, viz., common observation in like cases, and particular testimonies in that particular instance, favor or contradict it. These are liable to so great variety of contrary observations, circumstances, reports, different qualifications, tempers, designs, oversights, etc., of the reporters, that it is impossible to reduce to precise rules the various degrees wherein men give their assent. This only may be said in general, that as the arguments and proofs pro and con, upon due examination, nicely weighing every particular circumstance, shall to anyone appear, upon the whole matter, in a greater or less degree, to preponderate on either side; so they are fitted to produce in the mind such different entertainment, as we call belief, conjecture, guess, doubt, wavering, distrust, disbelief, etc. . . .

12. *In things which sense cannot discover, analogy is the great rule of probability.*—The probabilities we have hitherto mentioned are only such as concern matter of fact, and such things as are capable of observation and testimony. There remains that other sort, concerning which men entertain opinions with variety of assent, though the things be such, that, falling not under the reach of our senses, they are not capable of testimony. Such are: (i) The existence, nature, and operations of finite immaterial beings without us; as spirits, angels, devils, etc., or the existence of material beings; which either for their smallness in themselves, or remoteness from us, our senses cannot take notice of; as whether there be any plants, animals, and intelligent inhabitants in the planets, and other mansions of the vast universe. (ii) Concerning the manner of operation in most parts of the works of nature: wherein though we see the sensible effects, yet their causes are unknown, and we perceive not the ways and manner how they are pro-

duced. We see animals are generated, nourished, and move; the load-stone draws iron; and the parts of a candle, successively melting, turn into flame, and give us both light and heat. These and the like effects we see and know; but the causes that operate, and the manner they are produced in, we can only guess and probably conjecture. For these and the like, coming not within the scrutiny of human senses, cannot be examined by them or be attested by anybody; and therefore can appear more or less probable, only as they more or less agree to truths that are established in our minds, and as they hold proportion to other parts of our knowledge and observation. Analogy in these matters is the only help we have, and it is from that alone we draw all our grounds of probability. . . .

13. *One case where contrary experience lessens not the testimony.*— Though the common experience and the ordinary course of things have justly a mighty influence on the minds of men, to make them give or refuse credit to anything proposed to their belief; yet there is one case, wherein the strangeness of the fact lessens not the assent to a fair testimony given of it. For where such supernatural events are suitable to ends aimed at by him who has the power to change the course of nature, there, under such circumstances, they may be the fitter to procure belief, by how much the more they are beyond, or contrary to ordinary observation. This is the proper case of miracles, which well attested do not only find credit themselves, but give it also to other truths, which need such confirmation.

14. *The bare testimony of revelation is the highest certainty.*—Besides those we have hitherto mentioned, there is one sort of propositions that challenge the highest degree of our assent upon bare testimony, whether the thing proposed agree or disagree with common experience and the ordinary course of things, or no. The reason whereof is, because the testimony is of such an one, as cannot deceive, not be deceived, and that is of God himself. This carries with it an assurance beyond doubt, evidence beyond exception. This is called by a peculiar name, revelation; and our assent to it, faith; which as absolutely determines our minds, and as perfectly excludes all wavering, as our knowledge itself; and we may as well doubt of our own being, as we can, whether any revelation from God be true. So that faith is a settled and sure principle of assent and assurance, and leaves no manner of room for doubt or hesitation. Only we must be sure, that it be a divine revelation, and that we understand it right: else we shall expose ourselves to all the extravagancy of enthusiasm, and all the error of wrong principles, if we have faith and assurance in what is not divine revelation. And therefore in those cases, our assent can be rationally no higher than the evidence of its being a revelation, and that this is

the meaning of the expressions it is delivered in. If the evidence of its being a revelation, or that this is its true sense, be only on probable proofs; our assent can reach no higher than an assurance or diffidence, arising from the more or less apparent probability of the proofs. But of faith, and the precedency it ought to have before other arguments of persuasion, I shall speak more hereafter, where I treat of it, as it is ordinarily placed, in contradistinction to reason; though in truth it be nothing else but an assent founded on the highest reason.

CHAPTER XVII

OF REASON

1. *Various significations of the word reason.*—The word 'reason' in the English language has different significations: sometimes it is taken for true and clear principles: sometimes for clear and fair deductions from those principles; and sometimes for the cause, and particularly the final cause. But the consideration I shall have of it here, is in a signification different from all these; and that is, as it stands for a faculty in man, that faculty whereby man is supposed to be distinguished from beasts, and wherein it is evident he much surpasses them.

2. *Wherein reasoning consists.*—If general knowledge, as has been shown, consists in a perception of the agreement or disagreement of our own ideas; and the knowledge of the existence of all things without us (except only of a God, whose existence every man may certainly know and demonstrate to himself from his own existence) be had only by our senses: what room is there for the exercise of any other faculty, but outward sense and inward perception? What need is there of reason? Very much; both for the enlargement of our knowledge, and regulating our assent; for it hath to do both in knowledge and opinion, and is necessary and assisting to all our other intellectual faculties, and indeed contains two of them, viz., sagacity and illation. By the one, it finds out; and by the other, it so orders the intermediate ideas, as to discover what connection there is in each link of the chain, whereby the extremes are held together; and thereby, as it were, to draw into view the truth sought for, which is that which we call illation or inference, and consists in nothing but the perception of the connection there is between the ideas, in each step of the deduction, whereby the mind comes to see either the certain agreement or disagreement of any two ideas, as in demonstration, in which it arrives at knowledge; or their probable connection, on which it gives or withholds its assent, as in opinion. Sense and intuition reach but a very little way. The greatest

part of our knowledge depends upon deductions and intermediate ideas: and in those cases, where we are fain to substitute assent instead of knowledge, and take propositions for true, without being certain they are so, we have need to find out, examine, and compare the grounds of their probability. In both these cases, the faculty which finds out the means, and rightly applies them to discover certainty in the one, and probability in the other, is that which we call reason. For as reason perceives the necessary and indubitable connection of all the ideas or proofs one to another, in each step of any demonstration that produces knowledge: so it likewise perceives the probable connection of all the ideas or proofs one to another, in every step of a discourse, to which it will think assent due. This is the lowest degree of that which can be truly called reason. For where the mind does not perceive this probable connection, where it does not discern whether there be any such connection or no; there men's opinions are not the product of judgment, or the consequence of reason, but the effects of chance and hazard, of a mind floating at all adventures, without choice and without direction.

3. *Its four parts.*—So that we may in reason consider these four degrees; the first and highest is the discovering and finding out of truths; the second, the regular and methodical disposition of them, and laying them in a clear and fit order, to make their connection and force be plainly and easily perceived; the third is the perceiving their connection; and the fourth, a making a right conclusion. . . .

23. *Above, contrary, and according to reason.*—By what has been before said of reason, we may be able to make some guess at the distinction of things, into those that are according to, above, and contrary to reason. (1) According to reason are such propositions, whose truth we can discover by examining and tracing those ideas we have from sensation and reflection: and by natural deduction find to be true or probable. (2) Above reason are such propositions, whose truth or probability we cannot by reason derive from those principles. (3) Contrary to reason are such propositions, as are inconsistent with, or irreconcilable to, our clear and distinct ideas. Thus the existence of one God is according to reason; the existence of more than one God, contrary to reason; the resurrection of the dead, above reason. Farther, as above reason may be taken in a double sense, viz., either as signifying above probability, or above certainty; so in that large sense also, contrary to reason, is, I suppose, sometimes taken.

24. *Reason and faith not opposite.*—There is another use of the word reason, wherein it is opposed to faith; which though it be in itself a very improper way of speaking, yet common use has so authorized it, that it would be folly either to oppose or hope to remedy it: only I

think it may not be amiss to take notice, that however faith be opposed to reason, faith is nothing but a firm assent of the mind: which if it be regulated, as is our duty, cannot be afforded to anything but upon good reason; and so cannot be opposite to it. He that believes, without having any reason for believing, may be in love with his own fancies; but neither seeks truth as he ought, nor pays the obedience due to his Maker, who would have him use those discerning faculties he has given him, to keep him out of mistake and error. He that does not this to the best of his power, however he sometimes lights on truth, is in the right but by chance; and I know not whether the luckiness of the accident will excuse the irregularity of his proceeding. This at least is certain, that he must be accountable for whatever mistakes he runs into: whereas he that makes use of the light and faculties God has given him, and seeks sincerely to discover truths by those helps and abilities he has, may have this satisfaction in doing his duty as a rational creature, that, though he should miss truth, he will not miss the reward of it. For he governs his assent right, and places it as he should, who, in any case or matter whatsoever, believes or disbelieves, according as reason directs him. He that doth otherwise transgresses against his own light, and misuses those faculties which were given him to no other end, but to search and follow the clearer evidence and greater probability. But, since reason and faith are by some men opposed, we will so consider them in the following chapter.

CHAPTER XVIII

OF FAITH AND REASON, AND THEIR DISTINCT PROVINCES

1. *Necessary to know their boundaries.*—It has been above shown: 1. That we are of necessity ignorant, and want knowledge of all sorts, where we want ideas. 2. That we are ignorant, and want rational knowledge, where we want proofs. 3. That we want certain knowledge and certainty, as far as we want clear and determined specific ideas. 4. That we want probability to direct our assent in matters where we have neither knowledge of our own, nor testimony of other men, to bottom our reason upon.

From these things thus premised, I think we may come to lay down the measures and boundaries between faith and reason; the want whereof may possibly have been the cause, if not of great disorders, yet at least of great disputes, and perhaps mistakes in the world. For till it be resolved, how far we are to be guided by reason, and how far by faith, we shall in vain dispute, and endeavor to convince one another in matters of religion.

2. *Faith and reason what, as contradistinguished.*—I find every sect, as far as reason will help them, make use of it gladly; and where it fails them, they cry out, it is matter of faith, and above reason. And I do not see how they can argue with anyone, or ever convince a gainsayer who makes use of the same plea, without setting down strict boundaries between faith and reason; which ought to be the first point established in all questions, where faith has anything to do.

Reason, therefore, here, as contradistinguished to faith, I take to be the discovery of the certainty or probability of such propositions or truths, which the mind arrives at by deduction made from such ideas, which it has got by the use of its natural faculties; viz., by sensation or reflection.

Faith, on the other side, is the assent to any proposition, not thus made out by the deductions of reason; but upon the credit of the proposer, as coming from God, in some extraordinary way of communication. This way of discovering truths to men we call revelation.

3. *No new simple idea can be conveyed by traditional revelation.*—First then I say, that no man inspired by God can by any revelation communicate to others any new simple ideas, which they had not before from sensation or reflection. For whatsoever impressions he himself may have from the immediate hand of God, this revelation, if it be of new simple ideas, cannot be conveyed to another, either by words, or any other signs. Because words, by their immediate operation on us, cause no other ideas, but of their natural sounds: and it is by the custom of using them for signs, that they excite and revive in our minds latent ideas; but yet only such ideas as were there before. For words seen or heard, recall to our thoughts those ideas only, which to us they have been wont to be signs of; but cannot introduce any perfectly new, and formerly unknown simple ideas. The same holds in all other signs, which cannot signify to us things, of which we have before never had any idea at all. Thus whatever things were discovered to St. Paul, when he was rapt up into the third heaven, whatever new ideas his mind there received, all the description he can make to others of that place, is only this, that there are such things, "as eye hath not seen, nor ear heard, nor hath it entered into the heart of man to conceive." And supposing God should discover to anyone, supernaturally, a species of creatures inhabiting, for example, Jupiter or Saturn, (for that it is possible there may be such, nobody can deny) which had six senses; and imprint on his mind the ideas conveyed to theirs by that sixth sense; he could no more, by words, produce in the minds of other men those ideas, imprinted by that sixth sense, than one of us could convey

the idea of any color by the sounds of words into a man who, having the other four senses perfect, had always totally wanted the fifth of seeing. For our simple ideas then, which are the foundation and sole matter of all our notions and knowledge, we must depend wholly on our reason, I mean our natural faculties; and can by no means re-ceive them, or any of them, from traditional revelation; I say, tradi-tional revelation, in distinction to original revelation. By the one, I mean that first impression, which is made immediately by God, on the mind of any man, to which we cannot set any bounds; and by the other, those impressions delivered over to others in words, and the ordinary ways of conveying our conceptions one to another.

4. *Traditional revelation may make us know propositions knowable also by reason, but not with the same certainty that reason doth.*—Sec-ondly, I say, that the same truths may be discovered, and conveyed down from revelation, which are discoverable to us by reason, and by those ideas we naturally may have. So God might, by revelation, dis-cover the truth of any proposition in Euclid; as well as men, by the natural use of their faculties, come to make the discovery themselves. In all things of this kind, there is little need or use of revelation, God having furnished us with natural and surer means to arrive at the knowledge of them. For whatsoever truth we come to the clear discov-ery of, from the knowledge and contemplation of our own ideas, will always be certainer to us, than those which are conveyed to us by tra-ditional revelation. For the knowledge we have, that this revelation came at first from God, can never be so sure, as the knowledge we have from the clear and distinct perception of the agreement or disagreement of our own ideas; v. g., if it were revealed some ages since, that the three angles of a triangle were equal to two right ones, I might assent to the truth of that proposition, upon the credit of the tradition, that it was revealed; but that would never amount to so great a certainty, as the knowledge of it, upon the comparing and measuring my own ideas of two right angles, and the three angles of a triangle. The like holds in matter of fact, knowable by our senses; v.g., the history of the deluge is conveyed to us by writings, which had their original from revelation: and yet nobody, I think, will say he has as certain and clear a knowledge of the flood, as Noah that saw it; or that he himself would have had, had he then been alive and seen it. For he has no greater assurance than that of his senses, that it is writ in the book supposed writ by Moses inspired: but he has not so great an assurance that Moses writ that book, as if he had seen Moses write it. So that the assurance of its being a revelation is less still than the assurance of his senses.

5. *Revelation cannot be admitted against the clear evidence of reason.*

—In propositions then, whose certainty is built upon the clear perception of the agreement or disagreement of our ideas, attained either by immediate intuition, as in self-evident propositions, or by evident deductions of reason in demonstrations, we need not the assistance of revelation, as necessary to gain our assent, and introduce them into our minds. Because the natural ways of knowledge could settle them there, or had done it already; which is the greatest assurance we can possibly have of anything, unless where God immediately reveals it to us: and there too our assurance can be no greater, than our knowledge is, that it is a revelation from God. But yet nothing, I think, can, under that title, shake or overrule plain knowledge; or rationally prevail with any man to admit it for true, in a direct contradiction to the clear evidence of his own understanding. For since no evidence of our faculties, by which we receive such revelations, can exceed, if equal, the certainty of our intuitive knowledge, we can never receive for a truth anything that is directly contrary to our clear and distinct knowledge: v.g., the ideas of one body, and one place, do so clearly agree, and the mind has so evident a perception of their agreement, that we can never assent to a proposition, that affirms the same body to be in two distant places at once, however it should pretend to the authority of a divine revelation: since the evidence, first, that we deceive not ourselves, in ascribing it to God; secondly, that we understand it right; can never be so great, as the evidence of our own intuitive knowledge, whereby we discern it impossible for the same body to be in two places at once. And therefore no proposition can be received for divine revelation, or obtain the assent due to all such, if it be contradictory to our clear intuitive knowledge. Because this would be to subvert the principles and foundations of all knowledge, evidence, and assent whatsoever: and there would be left no difference between truth and falsehood, no measures of credible and incredible in the world, if doubtful propositions shall take place before self-evident; and what we certainly know give way to what we may possibly be mistaken in. In propositions therefore contrary to the clear perception of the agreement or disagreement of any of our ideas, it will be in vain to urge them as matters of faith. They cannot move our assent, under that or any other title whatsoever. For faith can never convince us of anything that contradicts our knowledge. Because though faith be founded on the testimony of God (who cannot lie) revealing any proposition to us; yet we cannot have an assurance of the truth of its being a divine revelation, greater than our own knowledge: since the whole strength of the certainty depends upon our knowledge that God revealed it, which in this case, where the proposition supposed revealed contradicts our knowledge or reason, will always have this objection hanging to it, viz., that we cannot tell how to con··

ceive that to come from God, the bountiful Author of our being, which, if received for true, must overturn all the principles and foundations of knowledge he has given us; render all our faculties useless; wholly destroy the most excellent part of his workmanship, our understandings; and put a man in a condition, wherein he will have less light, less conduct than the beast that perisheth. For if the mind of man can never have a clearer (and perhaps not so clear) evidence of anything to be a divine revelation, as it has of the principles of its own reason, it can never have a ground to quit the clear evidence of its reason, to give a place to a proposition, whose revelation has not a greater evidence than those principles have.

6. *Traditional revelation much less.*—Thus far a man has use of reason, and ought to hearken to it, even in immediate and original revelation, where it is supposed to be made to himself: but to all those who pretend not to immediate revelation, but are required to pay obedience, and to receive the truths revealed to others, which by the tradition of writings, or word of mouth, are conveyed down to them; reason has a great deal more to do, and is that only which can induce us to receive them. For matter of faith being only divine revelation, and nothing else; faith, as we use the word (called commonly divine faith) has to do with no propositions, but those which are supposed to be divinely revealed. So that I do not see how those, who make revelation alone the sole object of faith, can say, that is a matter of faith, and not of reason, to believe that such or such a proposition, to be found in such or such a book, is of divine inspiration; unless it be revealed, that that proposition, or all in that book, was communicated by divine inspiration. Without such a revelation, the believing, or not believing that proposition or book to be of divine authority, can never be matter of faith, but matter of reason; and such as I must come to an assent to, only by the use of my reason, which can never require or enable me to believe that which is contrary to itself: it being impossible for reason ever to produce any assent to that, which to itself appears unreasonable.

In all things therefore, where we have clear evidence from our ideas, and those principles of knowledge I have above mentioned, reason is the proper judge; and revelation, though it may in consenting with it confirm its dictates, yet cannot in such cases invalidate its decrees: nor can we be obliged, where we have the clear and evident sentence of reason, to quit it for the contrary opinion, under a pretense that it is matter of faith; which can have authority against the plain and clear dictates of reason.

7. *Things above reason.*—But, thirdly, there being many things, wherein we have very imperfect notions, or none at all; and other things, of whose past, present, or future existence, by the natural use of

our faculties, we can have no knowledge at all; these, as being beyond the discovery of our natural faculties, and above reason, are, when revealed, the proper matter of faith. Thus, that part of the angels rebelled against God, and thereby lost their first happy state; and that the dead shall rise, and live again: these, and the like, being beyond the discovery of reason, are purely matters of faith; with which reason has directly nothing to do.

8. *Or not contrary to reason, if revealed, are matter of faith.*—But since God in giving us the light of reason has not thereby tied up his own hands from affording us, when he thinks fit, the light of revelation in any of those matters, wherein our natural faculties are able to give a probable determination; revelation, where God has been pleased to give it, must carry it against the probable conjectures of reason. Because the mind not being certain of the truth of that it does not evidently know, but only yielding to the probability that appears in it, is bound to give up its assent to such a testimony; which, it is satisfied, comes from one who cannot err, and will not deceive. But yet it still belongs to reason to judge of the truth of its being a revelation, and of the signification of the words wherein it is delivered. Indeed, if anything shall be thought revelation, which is contrary to the plain principles of reason, and the evident knowledge the mind has of its own clear and distinct ideas; there reason must be hearkened to, as to a matter within its province: since a man can never have so certain a knowledge, that a proposition which contradicts the clear principles and evidence of his own knowledge, was divinely revealed, or that he understands the words rightly wherein it is delivered; as he has, that the contrary is true: and so is bound to consider and judge of it as a matter of reason, and not swallow it, without examination, as a matter of faith.

9. *Revelation in matters where reason cannot judge, or but probably, ought to be hearkened to.*—First, whatever proposition is revealed, of whose truth our mind, by its natural faculties and notions, cannot judge; that is purely matter of faith, and above reason.

Secondly, all propositions, whereof the mind, by the use of its natural faculties, can come to determine and judge from naturally acquired ideas, are matter of reason; with this difference still, that in those concerning which it has but an uncertain evidence, and so is persuaded of their truth only upon probable grounds, which still admit a possibility of the contrary to be true, without doing violence to the certain evidence of its own knowledge, and overturning the principles of its own reason; in such probable propositions, I say, an evident revelation ought to determine our assent even against probability. For where the principles of reason have not evidenced a proposition to be certainly true or false, there clear revelation, as another principle of truth, and ground of assent, may determine; and so it may be matter of faith, and be also above reason. Because reason, in that particular matter, being able to reach no higher than probability, faith gave the determination where reason came short; and revelation discovered on which side the truth lay.

10. *In matters where reason can afford certain knowledge, that is to be hearkened to.*—Thus far the dominion of faith reaches, and that without any violence or hindrance to reason; which is not injured or disturbed, but assisted and improved, by new discoveries of truth coming from the eternal fountain of all knowledge. Whatever God hath revealed is certainly true; no doubt can be made of it. This is the proper object of faith: but whether it be a divine revelation or no, reason must judge; which can never permit the mind to reject a greater evidence to embrace what is less evident, not allow it to entertain probability in opposition to knowledge and certainty. There can be no evidence, that any traditional revelation is of divine original, in the words we receive it, and in the sense we understand it, so clear and so certain, as that of the principles of reason: and therefore nothing that is contrary to, and inconsistent with, the clear and self-evident dictates of reason, has a right to be urged or assented to as a matter of faith, wherein reason hath nothing to do. Whatsoever is divine revela-tion ought to overrule all our opinions, prejudices, and interest, and hath a right to be received with full assent. Such a submission as this, of our reason to faith, takes not away the landmarks of knowledge: this shakes not the foundations of reason, but leaves us that use of our faculties, for which they were given us.

11. *If the boundaries be not set between faith and reason, no en-thusiasm or extravagancy in religion can be contradicted.*—If the prov-inces of faith and reason are not kept distinct by these boundaries, there will, in matters of religion, be no room for reason at all; and those extravagant opinions and ceremonies that are to be found in the several religions of the world, will not deserve to be blamed. For, to this cry-ing up of faith, in opposition to reason, we may, I think, in good meas-ure ascribe those absurdities that fill almost all the religions which possess and divide mankind. For men having been principled with an opinion, that they must not consult reason in the things of religion, however apparently contradictory to common sense, and the very prin-ciples of all their knowledge; have let loose their fancies and natural superstition; and have been by them led into so strange opinions, and extravagant practices in religion, that a considerate man cannot but stand amazed at their follies, and judge them so far from being ac-ceptable to the great and wise God, that he cannot avoid thinking them ridiculous, and offensive to a sober good man. So that in effect

religion, which should most distinguish us from beasts, and ought most peculiarly to elevate us, as rational creatures, above brutes, is that wherein men often appear most irrational and more senseless than beasts themselves. *"Credo, quia impossibile est;"* I believe, because it is impossible; might in a good man pass for a sally of zeal; but would prove a very ill rule for men to choose their opinions or religion by.

CHAPTER XIX

[OF ENTHUSIASM]

1. [*Love of truth necessary.*—He that would seriously set upon the search of truth, ought in the first place to prepare his mind with a love for it. For he that loves it not, will not take much pains to get it, nor be much concerned when he misses it. There is nobody in the commonwealth of learning, who does not profess himself a lover of truth; and there is not a rational creature that would not take it amiss to be thought otherwise of. And yet for all this, one may truly say, that there are very few lovers of truth for truth's sake, even amongst those who persuade themselves that they are so. How a man may know whether he be so in earnest, is worth inquiry: and I think there is one unerring mark of it, viz., the not entertaining any proposition with greater assurance, than the proofs it is built upon will warrant. Whoever goes beyond this measure of assent, it is plain, receives not truth in the love of it; loves not truth for truth's sake, but for some other by-end. For the evidence that any proposition is true (except such as are self-evident) lying only in the proofs a man has of it, whatsoever degrees of assent he affords it beyond the degrees of that evidence, it is plain that all the surplusage of assurance is owing to some other affection, and not to the love of truth: it being as impossible, that the love of truth should carry my assent above the evidence there is to me that it is true, as that the love of truth should make me assent to any proposition for the sake of that evidence, which it has not, that it is true; which is in effect to love it as a truth, because it is possible or probable that it may not be true. In any truth that gets not possession of our minds by the irresistible light of self-evidence, or by the force of demonstration, the arguments that gain it assent are the vouchers and gauge of its probability to us; and we can receive it for no other, than such as they deliver it to our understandings. Whatsoever credit or authority we give to any proposition more than it receives from the principles and proofs it supports itself upon, is owing to our inclinations that way, and is so far a derogation from the love of truth as such:

which, as it can receive no evidence from our passions or interests, so it should receive no tincture from them.

2. *A forwardness to dictate, from whence.*—The assuming an authority of dictating to others, and a forwardness to prescribe to their opinions, is a constant concomitant of this bias and corruption of our judgments. For how almost can it be otherwise, but that he should be ready to impose on another's belief, who has already imposed on his own? Who can reasonably expect arguments and conviction from him, in dealing with others, whose understanding is not accustomed to them in his dealing with himself? Who does violence to his own faculties, tyrannizes over his own mind, and usurps the prerogative that belongs to truth alone, which is to command assent only by its own authority, i.e., by and in proportion to that evidence which it carries with it.

3. *Force of enthusiasm.*—Upon this occasion I shall take the liberty to consider a third ground of assent, which with some men has the same authority, and is as confidently relied on as either faith or reason; I mean enthusiasm: which, laying by reason, would set up revelation without it. Whereby in effect it takes away both reason and revelation, and substitutes in the room of it the ungrounded fancies of a man's own brain, and assumes them for a foundation both of opinion and conduct.

4. *Reason and revelation.*—Reason is natural revelation, whereby the eternal father of light, and fountain of all knowledge, communicates to mankind that portion of truth which he has laid within the reach of their natural faculties: revelation is natural reason enlarged by a new set of discoveries communicated by God immediately, which reason vouches the truth of, by the testimony and proofs it gives, that they come from God. So that he that takes away reason, to make way for revelation, puts out the light of both, and does much-what the same, as if he would persuade a man to put out his eye, the better to receive the remote light of an invisible star by a telescope.

5. *Rise of enthusiasm.*—Immediate revelation being a much easier way for men to establish their opinions, and regulate their conduct, than the tedious and not always successful labor of strict reasoning, it is no wonder that some have been very apt to pretend to revelation, and to persuade themselves that they are under the peculiar guidance of heaven in their actions and opinions, especially in those of them which they cannot account for by the ordinary methods of knowledge and principles of reason. Hence we see in all ages, men, in whom melancholy has mixed with devotion, or whose conceit of themselves has raised them into an opinion of a greater familiarity with God, and a nearer admittance to his favor than is afforded to others, have often

flattered themselves with a persuasion of an immediate intercourse with the Deity, and frequent communications from the Divine Spirit. God, I own, cannot be denied to be able to enlighten the understanding by a ray darted into the mind immediately from the fountain of light; this they understand he has promised to do, and who then has so good a title to expect it as those who are his peculiar people, chosen by him, and depending on him?

6. *Enthusiasm.*—Their minds being thus prepared, whatever groundless opinion comes to settle itself strongly upon their fancies, is an illumination from the spirit of God, and presently of divine authority: and whatsoever odd action they find in themselves a strong inclination to do, that impulse is concluded to be a call or direction from heaven, and must be obeyed; it is a commission from above, and they cannot err in executing it.

7. This I take to be properly enthusiasm, which, though founded neither on reason nor divine revelation, but rising from the conceits of a warmed or overweening brain, works yet, where it once gets footing, more powerfully on the persuasions and actions of men, than either of those two, or both together: men being most forwardly obedient to the impulses they receive from themselves; and the whole man is sure to act more vigorously, where the whole man is carried by a natural motion. For strong conceit, like a new principle, carries all easily with it, when got above common sense, and freed from all restraint of reason, and check of reflection; it is heightened into a divine authority, in concurrence with our own temper and inclination.

8. *Enthusiasm mistaken for seeing and feeling.*—Though the odd opinions and extravagant actions enthusiasm has run men into, were enough to warn them against this wrong principle, so apt to misguide them both in their belief and conduct; yet the love of something extraordinary, the ease and glory it is to be inspired, and be above the common and natural ways of knowledge, so flatters many men's laziness, ignorance, and vanity, that when once they are got into this way of immediate revelation, of illumination without search, and of certainty without proof, and without examination; it is a hard matter to get them out of it. Reason is lost upon them, they are above it: they see the light infused into their understandings, and cannot be mistaken; it is clear and visible there, like the light of bright sunshine; shows itself, and needs no other proof but its own evidence: they feel the hand of God moving them within, and the impulses of the spirit, and cannot be mistaken in what they feel. Thus they support themselves, and are sure reason hath nothing to do with what they see and feel in themselves: what they have a sensible experience of admits no doubt, needs no probation. Would he not be ridiculous, who should require to have

it proved to him that the light shines, and that he sees it? It is its own proof, and can have no other. When the spirit brings light into our minds, it dispels darkness. We see it, as we do that of the sun at noon, and need not the twilight of reason to show it us. This light from heaven is strong, clear, and pure, carried its own demonstration with it; and we may as naturally take a glow-worm to assist us to discover the sun, as to examine the celestial ray of our dim candle, reason.

9. *Enthusiasm how to be discovered.*—This is the way of talking of these men: they are sure, because they are sure: and their persuasions are right, because they are strong in them. For, when what they say is stripped of the metaphor of seeing and feeling, this is all it amounts to: and yet these similes so impose on them, that they serve them for certainty in themselves, and demonstration to others.

10. But to examine a little soberly this internal light, and this feeling on which they build so much. These men have, they say, clear light, and they see; they have awakened sense, and they feel: this cannot, they are sure, be disputed them. For what a man says he sees or feels, nobody can deny it him that he does so. But here let me ask: this seeing, is it the perception of the truth of the proposition, or of this, that it is a revelation from God? This feeling, is it a perception of an inclination or fancy to do something, or of the spirit of God moving that inclination? These are two very different perceptions, and must be carefully distinguished, if we would not impose upon ourselves. I may perceive the truth of a proposition, and yet not perceive that it is an immediate revelation from God. I may perceive the truth of a proposition in Euclid, without its being or my perceiving it to be a revelation: nay, I may perceive I came not by this knowledge in a natural way, and so may conclude it revealed, without perceiving that it is a revelation from God; because there be spirits, which, without being divinely commissioned, may excite those ideas in me, and lay them in such order before my mind, that I may perceive their connection. So that the knowledge of any proposition coming into my mind, I know not how, is not a perception that it is from God. Much less is a strong persuasion, that it is true, a perception that it is from God, or so much as true. But however it be called light and seeing, I suppose it is at most but belief and assurance: and the proposition taken for a revelation, is not such as they know to be true, but take to be true. For where a proposition is known to be true, revelation is needless: and it is hard to conceive how there can be a revelation to anyone of what he knows already. If therefore it be a proposition which they are persuaded, but do not know, to be true, whatever they may call it, it is not seeing, but believing. For these are two ways, whereby truth comes into the mind, wholly distinct, so that one is not the other. What I see

I know to be so by the evidence of the thing itself: what I believe I take to be so upon the testimony of another: but this testimony I must know to be given, or else what ground have I of believing? I must see that it is God that reveals this to me, or else I see nothing. The question then here is, how do I know that God is the revealer of this to me; that this impression is made upon my mind by his Holy Spirit, and that therefore I ought to obey it? If I know not this, how great soever the assurance is that I am possessed with, it is groundless; whatever light I pretend to, it is but enthusiasm. For whether the proposition supposed to be revealed, be in itself evidently true, or visibly probable, or by the natural ways of knowledge uncertain, the proposition that must be well grounded, and manifested to be true, is this, that God is the revealer of it, and that what I take to be a revelation is certainly put into my mind by him, and is not an illusion dropped in by some spirit, or raised by my own fancy. For if I mistake not, these men receive it for true, because they presume God revealed it. Does it not then stand them upon, to examine on what grounds they presume it to be a revelation from God? or else all their confidence is mere presumption: and this light they are so dazzled with, is nothing but an *ignis fatuus* that leads them constantly round in this circle; it is a revelation, because they firmly believe it, and they believe it, because it is a revelation.

11. *Enthusiasm fails of evidence, that the proposition is from God.*— In all that is of divine revelation, there is need of no other proof but that it is an inspiration from God: for he can neither deceive nor be deceived. But how shall it be known that any proposition in our minds is a truth infused by God; a truth that is revealed to us by him, which he declares to us, and therefore we ought to believe? Here it is that enthusiasm fails of the evidence it pretends to. For men thus possessed boast of a light whereby they say they are enlightened, and brought into the knowledge of this or that truth. But if they know it to be a truth, they must know it to be so, either by its own self-evidence to natural reason, or by the rational proofs that make it out to be so. If they see and know it to be a truth, either of these two ways, they in vain suppose it to be a revelation. For they know it to be true the same way, that any other man naturally may know that it is so without the help of revelation. For thus all the truths, of what kind soever, that men uninspired are enlightened with, came into their minds, and are established there. If they say they know it to be true, because it is a revelation from God, the reason is good: but then it will be demanded how they know it to be a revelation from God. If they say, by the light it brings with it, which shines bright in their minds, and they cannot resist: I beseech them to consider whether this be any more than what

we have taken notice of already, viz., that it is a revelation, because they strongly believe it to be true. For all the light they speak of is but a strong, though ungrounded, persuasion of their own minds, that it is a truth. For rational grounds from proofs that it is a truth, they must acknowledge to have none; for then it is not received as a revelation, but upon the ordinary grounds that other truths are received: and if they believe it to be true, because it is a revelation, and have no other reason for its being a revelation, but because they are fully persuaded without any other reason that it is true; they believe it to be a revelation, only because they strongly believe it to be a revelation; which is a very unsafe ground to proceed on, either in our tenets or actions. And what readier way can there be to run ourselves into the most extravagant errors and miscarriages, than thus to set up fancy for our supreme and sole guide, and to believe any proposition to be true, any action to be right, only because we believe it to be so? The strength of our persuasions is no evidence at all of their own rectitude: crooked things may be as stiff and inflexible as straight: and men may be as positive and peremptory in error as in truth. How come else the untractable zealots in different and opposite parties? For if the light, which everyone thinks he has in his mind, which in this case is nothing but the strength of his own persuasion, be an evidence that it is from God, contrary opinions have the same title to inspirations; and God will be not only the father of lights, but of opposite and contradictory lights, leading men contrary ways; and contradictory propositions will be divine truths, if an ungrounded strength of assurance be an evidence, that any proposition is a divine revelation.

12. *Firmness of persuasion no proof that any proposition is from God.*—This cannot be otherwise, whilst firmness of persuasion is made the cause of believing, and confidence of being in the right is made an argument of truth. St. Paul himself believed he did well, and that he had a call to it when he persecuted the Christians, whom he confidently thought in the wrong; but yet it was he, and not they, who were mistaken. Good men are men still, liable to mistakes; and are sometimes warmly engaged in errors, which they take for divine truths, shining in their minds with the clearest light.

13. *Light in the mind, what.*—Light, true light, in the mind is, or can be nothing else but the evidence of the truth of any proposition; and if it be not a self-evident proposition, all the light it has, or can have, is from the clearness and validity of those proofs, upon which it is received. To talk of any other light in the understanding is to put ourselves in the dark, or in the power of the Prince of darkness, and by our own consent to give ourselves up to delusion to believe a lie. For if strength of persuasion be the light, which must guide us; I ask how

shall anyone distinguish between the delusions of Satan, and the in-spirations of the Holy Ghost? He can transform himself into an angel of light. And they who are led by this son of the morning, are as fully satisfied of the illumination, i.e., are as strongly persuaded, that they are enlightened by the spirit of God, as anyone who is so: they acquiesce and rejoice in it, are actuated by it: and nobody can be more sure, nor more in the right (if their own strong belief may be judge) than they.

14. *Revelation must be judged of by reason.*—He therefore that will not give himself up to all the extravagancies of delusion and error, must bring this guide of his light within to the trial. God, when he makes the prophet, does not unmake the man. He leaves all his faculties in the natural state, to enable him to judge of his inspirations, whether they be of divine original or no. When he illuminates the mind with super-natural light, he does not extinguish that which is natural. If he would have us assent to the truth of any proposition, he either evidences that truth by the usual methods of natural reason, or else makes it known to be a truth which he would have us assent to, by his authority; and convinces us that it is from him, by some marks which reason cannot be mistaken in. Reason must be our last judge and guide in everything. I do not mean that we must consult reason, and examine whether a proposition revealed from God can be made out by natural principles, and if it cannot, that then we may reject it: but consult it we must, and by it examine, whether it be a revelation from God or no. And if reason finds it to be revealed from God, reason then declares for it, as much as for any other truth, and makes it one of her dictates. Every conceit that thoroughly warms our fancies must pass for an inspiration, if there be nothing but the strength of our persuasions, whereby to judge of our persuasions; if reason must not examine their truth by something extrinsical to the persuasions themselves, inspirations and de-lusions, truth and falsehood, will have the same measure, and will not be possible to be distinguished.] . . .[12]

[12] Chapters XX and XXI deal with the causes of wrong assent, or error, and with the division of the sciences.—Editor.

AN ESSAY CONCERNING THE TRUE ORIGINAL, EXTENT AND END OF CIVIL GOVERNMENT[1]

CHAPTER I

THE INTRODUCTION

1. It having been shown in the foregoing discourse:

(i) That Adam had not, either by natural right of fatherhood or by positive donation from God, any such authority over his children, nor dominion over the world, as is pretended.

(ii) That if he had, his heirs yet had no right to it.

(iii) That if his heirs had, there being no law of nature nor positive law of God that determines which is the right heir in all cases that may arise, the right of succession, and consequently of bearing rule, could not have been certainly determined.

(iv) That if even that had been determined, yet the knowledge of which is the eldest line of Adam's posterity, being so long since utterly lost, that in the races of mankind and families of the world there remains not to one above another the least pretense to be the eldest house, and to have the right of inheritance.

All these premises having, as I think, been clearly made out, it is impossible that the rulers now on earth should make any benefit, or derive any the least shadow of authority from that which is held to be the foundation of all power, Adam's private dominion and paternal jurisdiction; so that he that will not give just occasion to think that all government in the world is the product only of force and violence, and that men live together by no other rules but that of beasts, where the strongest carries it, and so lay a foundation for perpetual disorder and mischief, tumult, sedition, and rebellion (things that the followers of that hypothesis so loudly cry out against), must of necessity find out

---

[1] This is the second of *Two Treatises of Government* published together in 1690. The first of the treatises is a refutation of Sir Robert Filmer's defense of absolute monarchy in his *Patriarcha* (1680).—*Editor*.

another rise of government, another original of political power, and
another way of designing and knowing the persons that have it, than
what Sir Robert Filmer hath taught us.

2. To this purpose, I think it may not be amiss to set down what I
take to be political power; that the power of a magistrate over a subject may be distinguished from that of a father over his children, a master over his servant, a husband over his wife, and a lord over his slave.
All which distinct powers happening sometime together in the same
man, if he be considered under these different relations, it may help us
to distinguish these powers one from another, and show the difference
betwixt a ruler of a commonwealth, a father of a family, and a captain
of a galley.

3. Political power, then, I take to be a right of making laws with
penalties of death, and consequently all less penalties, for the regulating and preserving of property, and of employing the force of the community in the execution of such laws, and in the defense of the commonwealth from foreign injury, and all this only for the public good.

CHAPTER II

OF THE STATE OF NATURE

4. To UNDERSTAND political power aright, and derive it from its original,
we must consider what state all men are naturally in, and that is a state
of perfect freedom to order their actions and dispose of their possessions and persons as they think fit, within the bounds of the law of
nature, without asking leave, or depending upon the will of any other
man.

A state also of equality, wherein all the power and jurisdiction is
reciprocal, no one having more than another; there being nothing more
evident than that creatures of the same species and rank, promiscuously
born to all the same advantages of nature, and the use of the same faculties, should also be equal one amongst another without subordination
or subjection, unless the Lord and Master of them all should by any
manifest declaration of His will set one above another, and confer on
him by an evident and clear appointment an undoubted right to dominion and sovereignty.

5. This equality of men by nature the judicious Hooker looks upon
as so evident in itself and beyond all question, that he makes it the
foundation of that obligation to mutual love amongst men on which he
builds the duties they owe one another, and from whence he derives the
great maxims of justice and charity. His words are:—

"The like natural inducement hath brought men to know that it is no less their duty to love others than themselves; for seeing those things which are equal must needs all have one measure, if I cannot but wish to receive good, even as much at every man's hands as any man can wish unto his own soul, how should I look to have any part of my desire herein satisfied, unless myself be careful to satisfy the like desire, which is undoubtedly in other men weak, being of one and the same nature? To have anything offered them repugnant to this desire, must needs in all respects grieve them as much as me, so that, if I do harm, I must look to suffer, there being no reason that others should show greater measures of love to me than they have by me showed unto them. My desire, therefore, to be loved of my equals in nature as much as possible may be, imposeth upon me a natural duty of bearing to themward fully the like affection; from which relation of equality be• tween ourselves and them that are as ourselves, what several rules and canons natural reason hath drawn for direction of life no man is ig-, norant."—(Eccl. Pol., lib. i).

6. But though this be a state of liberty, yet it is not a state of license; though man in that state have an uncontrollable liberty to dispose of his person or possessions, yet he has not liberty to destroy himself, or so much as any creature in his possession, but where some nobler use than its bare preservation calls for it. The state of nature has a law of nature to govern it, which obliges everyone; and reason, which is that law, teaches all mankind who will but consult it, that, being all equal and independent, no one ought to harm another in his life, health, liberty, or possessions. For men being all the workmanship of one omnipotent and infinitely wise Maker—all the servants of one sovereign Master, sent into the world by His order, and about His business—they are His property, whose workmanship they are, made to last during His, not one another's pleasure; and being furnished with like faculties, sharing all in one community of nature, there cannot be supposed any such subordination among us, that may authorize us to destroy one another, as if we were made for one another's uses, as the inferior ranks of creatures are for ours Everyone, as he is bound to preserve himself, and not to quit his station willfully, so, by the like reason, when his own preservation comes not in competition, ought he, as much as he can, to preserve the rest of mankind, and not, unless it be to do justice on an offender, take away or impair the life, or what tends to the preservation of the life, the liberty, health, limb, or goods of another.

7. And that all men may be restrained from invading others' rights, and from doing hurt to one another, and the law of nature be observed, which willeth the peace and preservation of all mankind, the execution of the law of nature is in that state put into every man's hand, whereby

everyone has a right to punish the transgressors of that law to such a degree as may hinder its violation. For the law of nature would, as all other laws that concern men in this world, be in vain if there were nobody that, in the state of nature, had a power to execute that law, and thereby preserve the innocent and restrain offenders. And if anyone in the state of nature may punish another for any evil he has done, everyone may do so. For in that state of perfect equality, where naturally there is no superiority or jurisdiction of one over another, what any may do in prosecution of that law, everyone must needs have a right to do.

8. And thus in the state of nature one man comes by a power over another; but yet no absolute or arbitrary power, to use a criminal, when he has got him in his hands, according to the passionate heats or boundless extravagance of his own will; but only to retribute to him so far as calm reason and conscience dictate what is proportionate to his transgression, which is so much as may serve for reparation and restraint. For these two are the only reasons why one man may lawfully do harm to another, which is that we call punishment. In transgressing the law of nature, the offender declares himself to live by another rule than that of common reason and equity, which is that measure God has set to the actions of men, for their mutual security; and so he becomes dangerous to mankind, the tie which is to secure them from injury and violence being slighted and broken by him. Which, being a trespass against the whole species, and the peace and safety of it, provided for by the law of nature, every man upon this score, by the right he hath to preserve mankind in general, may restrain, or, where it is necessary, destroy things noxious to them, and so may bring such evil on anyone who hath transgressed that law, as may make him repent the doing of it, and thereby deter him, and by his example others, from doing the like mischief. And in this case, and upon this ground, every man hath a right to punish the offender, and be executioner of the law of nature.

9. I doubt not but this will seem a very strange doctrine to some men: but before they condemn it, I desire them to resolve me by what right any prince or state can put to death or punish an alien, for any crime he commits in their country. 'Tis certain their laws, by virtue of any sanction they receive from the promulgated will of the legislative, reach not a stranger: they speak not to him, nor, if they did, is he bound to hearken to them. The legislative authority, by which they are in force over the subjects of that commonwealth, hath no power over him. Those who have the supreme power of making laws in England, France, or Holland, are to an Indian but like the rest of the world—men without authority. And, therefore, if by the law of nature every man hath not a power to punish offenses against it, as he soberly judges

the case to require, I see not how the magistrates of any community can punish an alien of another country; since in reference to him they can have no more power than what every man naturally may have over another.

10. Besides the crime which consists in violating the law, and varying from the right rule of reason, whereby a man so far becomes degenerate, and declares himself to quit the principles of human nature, and to be a noxious creature, there is commonly injury done, and some person or other, some other man receives damage by his transgression, in which case he who hath received any damage, has, besides the right of punishment common to him with other men, a particular right to seek reparation from him that has done it. And any other person who finds it just, may also join with him that is injured, and assist him in recovering from the offender so much as may make satisfaction for the harm he has suffered.

11. From these two distinct rights—the one of punishing the crime, for restraint and preventing the like offense, which right of punishing is in everybody; the other of taking reparation, which belongs only to the injured party—comes it to pass that the magistrate, who by being magistrate hath the common right of punishing put into his hands, can often, where the public good demands not the execution of the law, remit the punishment of criminal offenses by his own authority, but yet cannot remit the satisfaction due to any private man for the damage he has received. That he who has suffered the damage has a right to demand in his own name, and he alone can remit. The damnified person has this power of appropriating to himself the goods or service of the offender, by right of self-preservation, as every man has a power to punish the crime, to prevent its being committed again, by the right he has of preserving all mankind, and doing all reasonable things he can in order to that end. And thus it is that every man in the state of nature has a power to kill a murderer, both to deter others from doing the like injury, which no reparation can compensate, by the example of the punishment that attends it from everybody, and also to secure men from the attempts of a criminal who having renounced reason, the common rule and measure God hath given to mankind, hath by the unjust violence and slaughter he hath committed upon one, declared war against all mankind, and therefore may be destroyed as a lion or a tiger, one of those wild savage beasts with whom men can have no society nor security. And upon this is grounded that great law of nature. "Whoso sheddeth man's blood, by man shall his blood be shed." And Cain was so fully convinced that everyone had a right to destroy such a criminal, that after the murder of his brother he cries out, "Every one that findeth me shall slay me;" so plain was it writ in the hearts of mankind.

12. By the same reason may a man in the state of nature punish the lesser breaches of that law. It will perhaps be demanded, With death? I answer, each transgression may be punished to that degree, and with so much severity, as will suffice to make it an ill bargain to the offender, give him cause to repent, and terrify others from doing the like. Every offense that can be committed in the state of nature, may in the state of nature be also punished equally, and as far forth as it may, in a commonwealth. For though it would be beside my present purpose to enter here into the particulars of the law of nature, or its measures of punishment, yet it is certain there is such a law, and that, too, as intelligible and plain to a rational creature and a studier of that law as the positive laws of commonwealths; nay, possibly plainer, as much as reason is easier to be understood than the fancies and intricate contrivances of men, following contrary and hidden interests put into words; for truly so are a great part of the municipal laws of countries, which are only so far right as they are founded on the law of nature, by which they are to be regulated and interpreted.

13. To this strange doctrine—viz., that in the state of nature everyone has the executive power of the law of nature—I doubt not but it will be objected that it is unreasonable for men to be judges in their own cases, that self-love will make men partial to themselves and their friends. And on the other side, that ill-nature, passion, and revenge will carry them too far in punishing others; and hence nothing but confusion and disorder will follow; and that therefore God hath certainly appointed government to restrain the partiality and violence of men. I easily grant that civil government is the proper remedy for the inconveniences of the state of nature, which must certainly be great where men may be judges in their own case, since 'tis easy to be imagined that he who was so unjust as to do his brother an injury, will scarce be so just as to condemn himself for it. But I shall desire those who make this objection, to remember that absolute monarchs are but men, and if government is to be the remedy of those evils which necessarily follow from men's being judges in their own cases, and the state of nature is therefore not to be endured, I desire to know what kind of government that is, and how much better it is than the state of nature, where one man commanding a multitude, has the liberty to be judge in his own case, and may do to all his subjects whatever he pleases, without the least question or control of those who execute his pleasure; and in whatsoever he doth, whether led by reason, mistake, or passion, must be submitted to, which men in the state of nature are not bound to do one to another? And if he that judges, judges amiss in his own or any other case, he is answerable for it to the rest of mankind.

14. 'Tis often asked as a mighty objection, Where are, or ever were

there, any men in such a state of nature? To which it may suffice as an answer at present: That since all princes and rulers of independent governments all through the world are in a state of nature, 'tis plain the world never was, nor ever will be, without numbers of men in that state. I have named all governors of independent communities, whether they are or are not in league with others. For 'tis not every compact that puts an end to the state of nature between men, but only this one of agreeing together mutually to enter into one community, and make one body politic; other promises and compacts men may make one with another, and yet still be in the state of nature. The promises and bargains for truck, etc., between the two men in Soldania, in or between a Swiss and an Indian, in the woods of America, are binding to them, though they are perfectly in a state of nature in reference to one another. For truth and keeping of faith belong to men as men, and not as members of society.

15. To those that say there were never any men in the state of na- ture, I will not only oppose the authority of the judicious Hooker— (Eccl. Pol., lib. i., sect. 10), where he says, "The laws which have been hitherto mentioned," i.e., the laws of nature, "do bind men absolutely, even as they are men, although they have never any settled fellowship, and never any solemn agreement amongst themselves what to do or not to do; but forasmuch as we are not by ourselves sufficient to furnish ourselves with competent store of things needful for such a life as our nature doth desire—a life fit for the dignity of man—therefore to supply those defects and imperfections which are in us, as living single and solely by ourselves, we are naturally induced to seek communion and fellowship with others; this was the cause of men's uniting themselves at first in politic societies"—but I moreover affirm that all men are naturally in that state, and remain so, till by their own consents they make themselves members of some politic society; and I doubt not, in the sequel of this discourse, to make it very clear.

CHAPTER III

OF THE STATE OF WAR

16. THE STATE of war is a state of enmity and destruction; and therefore declaring by word or action, not a passionate and hasty, but a sedate, settled design upon another man's life, puts him in a state of war with him against whom he has declared such an intention, and so has exposed his life to the other's power to be taken away by him, or anyone that joins with him in his defense and espouses his quarrel; it being rea-

sonable and just I should have a right to destroy that which threatens me with destruction. For by the fundamental law of nature, man being to be preserved as much as possible, when all cannot be preserved, the safety of the innocent is to be preferred; and one may destroy a man who makes war upon him, or has discovered an enmity to his being, for the same reason that he may kill a wolf or a lion; because they are not under the ties of the common law of reason, have no other rule but that of force and violence, and so may be treated as a beast of prey, those dangerous and noxious creatures that will be sure to destroy him whenever he falls into their power.

17. And hence it is that he who attempts to get another man into his absolute power does thereby put himself into a state of war with him; it being to be understood as a declaration of a design upon his life. For I have reason to conclude that he who would get me into his power without my consent, would use me as he pleased when he had got me there, and destroy me too, when he had a fancy to it; for nobody can desire to have me in his absolute power, unless it be to compel me by force to that which is against the right of my freedom, i.e., make me a slave. To be free from such force is the only security of my preservation; and reason bids me look on him as an enemy to my preservation who would take away that freedom which is the fence to it; so that he who makes an attempt to enslave me, thereby puts himself into a state of war with me. He that in the state of nature would take away the freedom that belongs to any one in that state, must necessarily be supposed to have a design to take away everything else, that freedom being the foundation of all the rest; as he that in the state of society would take away the freedom belonging to those of that society or commonwealth, must be supposed to design to take away from them everything else, and so be looked on as in a state of war.

18. This makes it lawful for a man to kill a thief who has not in the least hurt him, nor declared any design upon his life, any farther than by the use of force, so to get him in his power as to take away his money, or what he pleases, from him; because using force, where he has no right to get me into his power, let his pretense be what it will, I have no reason to suppose that he who would take away my liberty would not, when he had me in his power, take away everything else. And, therefore, it is lawful for me to treat him as one who has put himself into a state of war with me—i.e., kill him if I can; for to that hazard does he justly expose himself whoever introduces a state of war, and is aggressor in it.

19. And here we have the plain difference between the state of nature and the state of war, which however some men have confounded, are as far distant as a state of peace, good-will, mutual assistance and preser-

vation, and a state of enmity, malice, violence and mutual destruction, are one from another. Men living together according to reason, without a common superior on earth with authority to judge between them, is properly the state of nature. But force, or a declared design of force, upon the person of another, where there is no common superior on earth to appeal to for relief, is the state of war; and 'tis the want of such an appeal gives a man the right of war even against an aggressor, though he be in society and a fellow-subject. Thus a thief, whom I cannot harm, but by appeal to the law, for having stolen all that I am worth, I may kill, when he sets on to rob me but of my horse or coat; because the law, which was made for my preservation where it cannot interpose to secure my life from present force, which if lost is capable of no reparation, permits me my own defense, and the right of war, a liberty to kill the aggressor, because the aggressor allows not time to appeal to our common judge, nor the decision of the law, for remedy in a case where the mischief may be irreparable. Want of a common judge with authority puts all men in a state of nature; force without right, upon a man's person, makes a state of war, both where is, and is not, a common judge.

20. But when the actual force is over, the state of war ceases between those that are in society, and are equally on both sides subject to the judge.

21. And, therefore, in such controversies, where the question is put, Who shall be judge? it cannot be meant, Who shall decide the controversy? Everyone knows what Jephtha here tells us, that the "Lord the Judge" shall judge. Where there is no judge on earth, the appeal lies to God in Heaven. That question, then, cannot mean, Who shall judge whether another hath put himself in a state of war with me, and whether I may, as Jephtha did, appeal to Heaven in it? Of that I myself can only be judge in my own conscience, as I will answer it at the great day, to the supreme Judge of all men.

CHAPTER IV

OF SLAVERY

22. THE NATURAL liberty of man is to be free from any superior power on earth, and not to be under the will or legislative authority of man, but to have only the law of nature for his rule. The liberty of man in society is to be under no other legislative power but that established by consent in the commonwealth; nor under the dominion of any will or restraint of any law, but what that legislative shall enact according to the trust put in it. Freedom then is not what Sir Robert Filmer tells us,

(O. A. 55)[2] "a liberty for everyone to do what he lists, to live as he pleases, and not to be tied by any laws." But freedom of men under government is to have a standing rule to live by, common to everyone of that society, and made by the legislative power erected in it; a liberty to follow my own will in all things, where that rule prescribes not; and not to be subject to the inconstant, uncertain, unknown, arbitrary will of another man: as freedom of nature is to be under no other restraint but the law of nature.

23.This freedom from absolute arbitrary power is so necessary to, and closely joined with, a man's preservation, that he cannot part with it but by what forfeits his preservation and life together. For a man not having the power of his own life cannot by compact, or his own consent, enslave himself to anyone, nor put himself under the absolute arbitrary power of another to take away his life when he pleases. Nobody can give more power than he has himself; and he that cannot take away his own life, cannot give another power over it. Indeed, having by his fault forfeited his own life by some act that deserves death, he to whom he has forfeited it may (when he has him in his power) delay to take it, and make use of him to his own service; and he does him no injury by it. For whenever he finds the hardship of his slavery outweigh the value of his life, 'tis in his power by resisting the will of his master to draw on himself the death he desires.

24. This is the perfect condition of slavery, which is nothing else but the state of war continued between a lawful conqueror and a captive, for if once compact enter between them, and make an agreement for a limited power on the one side, and obedience on the other, the state of war and slavery ceases as long as the compact endures; for, as has been said, no man can by agreement pass over to another that which he hath not in himself—a power over his own life.

I confess, we find among the Jews, as well as other nations, that men did sell themselves; but it is plain this was only to drudgery, not to slavery; for it is evident the person sold was not under an absolute, arbitrary, despotical power, for the master could not have power to kill him at any time, whom at a certain time he was obliged to let go free out of his service; and the master of such a servant was so far from having an arbitrary power over his life that he could not at pleasure so much as maim him, but the loss of an eye or tooth set him free (Exod. xxi.).

[2] The reference is to Filmer's *Observations upon Aristotle's Politiques, Touching Forms of Government*, published in 1679.—*Editor*.

CHAPTER V

OF PROPERTY

25. WHETHER we consider natural reason, which tells us that men being once born have a right to their preservation, and consequently to meat and drink and such other things as nature affords for their subsistence; or revelation, which gives us an account of those grants God made of the world to Adam, and to Noah and his sons, 'tis very clear that God, as King David says, Psalm cxv. 16, "has given the earth to the children of men," given it to mankind in common. But this being supposed, it seems to some a very great difficulty how anyone should ever come to have a property in anything. I will not content myself to answer that if it be difficult to make out property upon a supposition that God gave the world to Adam and his posterity in common, it is impossible that any man but one universal monarch should have any property upon a supposition that God gave the world to Adam and his heirs in succession, exclusive of all the rest of his posterity. But I shall endeavor to show how men might come to have a property in several parts of that which God gave to mankind in common, and that without any express compact of all the commoners.

26. God, who hath given the world to men in common, hath also given them reason to make use of it to the best advantage of life and convenience. The earth and all that is therein is given to men for the support and comfort of their being. And though all the fruits it naturally produces, and beasts it feeds, belong to mankind in common, as they are produced by the spontaneous hand of nature; and nobody has originally a private dominion exclusive of the rest of mankind in any of them as they are thus in their natural state; yet being given for the use of men, there must of necessity be a means to appropriate them some way or other before they can be of any use or at all beneficial to any particular man. The fruit or venison which nourishes the wild Indian, who knows no enclosure, and is still a tenant in common, must be his, and so his, i.e., a part of him, that another can no longer have any right to it, before it can do any good for the support of his life.

27. Though the earth and all inferior creatures be common to all men, yet every man has a property in his own person; this nobody has any right to but himself. The labor of his body and the work of his hands we may say are properly his. Whatsoever, then, he removes out of the state that nature hath provided and left it in, he hath mixed his labor with, and joined to it something that is his own, and thereby makes it his property. It being by him removed from the common state nature

placed it in, it hath by this labor something annexed to it that excludes the common right of other men. For this labor being the unquestionable property of the laborer, no man but he can have a right to what that is once joined to, at least where there is enough, and as good left in common for others.

28. He that is nourished by the acorns he picked up under an oak, or the apples he gathered from the trees in the wood, has certainly appropriated them to himself. Nobody can deny but the nourishment is his. I ask, then, When did they begin to be his—when he digested, or when he ate, or when he boiled, or when he brought them home, or when he picked them up? And 'tis plain if the first gathering made them not his, nothing else could. That labor put a distinction between them and common; that added something to them more than nature, the common mother of all, had done, and so they became his private right. And will anyone say he had no right to those acorns or apples he thus appropriated, because he had not the consent of all mankind to make them his? Was it a robbery thus to assume to himself what belonged to all in common? If such a consent as that was necessary, man had starved, notwithstanding the plenty God had given him. We see in commons which remain so by compact that 'tis the taking any part of what is common and removing it out of the state nature leaves it in, which begins the property; without which the common is of no use. And the taking of this or that part does not depend on the express consent of all the commoners. Thus the grass my horse has bit, the turfs my servant has cut, and the ore I have dug in any place where I have a right to them in common with others, become my property without the assignation or consent of anybody. The labor that was mine removing them out of that common state they were in, hath fixed my property in them.

29. By making an explicit consent of every commoner necessary to anyone's appropriating to himself any part of what is given in common. Children or servants could not cut the meat which their father or master had provided for them in common without assigning to everyone his peculiar part. Though the water running in the fountain be everyone's, yet who can doubt but that in the pitcher is his only who drew it out? His labor hath taken it out of the hands of Nature where it was common, and belonged equally to all her children, and hath thereby appropriated it to himself.

30. Thus this law of reason makes the deer that Indian's who hath killed it; it is allowed to be his goods who hath bestowed his labor upon it, though, before, it was the common right of everyone. And amongst those who are counted the civilized part of mankind, who have made and multiplied positive laws to determine property, this original law of nature for the beginning of property, in what was before common, still

takes place, and by virtue thereof, what fish anyone catches in the ocean, that great and still remaining common of mankind; or what am-bergris anyone takes up here is by the labor that removes it out of that common state nature left it in, made his property who takes that pains about it. And even amongst us, the hare that anyone is hunting is thought his who pursues her during the chase. For being a beast that is still looked upon as common, and no man's private possession, whoever has employed so much labor about any of that kind as to find and pur-sue her has thereby removed her from the state of nature wherein she was common, and hath began a property.

31. It will perhaps be objected to this, that if gathering the acorns, or other fruits of the earth, etc., makes a right to them, then anyone may engross as much as he will. To which I answer, Not so. The same law of nature that does by this means give us property, does also bound that property too. "God has given us all things richly" (1 Tim. vi. 17), is the voice of reason confirmed by inspiration. But how far has He given it us? To enjoy. As much as anyone can make use of to any advantage of life before it spoils, so much he may by his labor fix a property in; whatever is beyond this, is more than his share, and belongs to others. Nothing was made by God for man to spoil or destroy. And thus consid-ering the plenty of natural provisions there was a long time in the world. and the few spenders, and to how small a part of that provision the in-dustry of one man could extend itself, and engross it to the prejudice of others—especially keeping within the bounds, set by reason, of what might serve for his use—there could be then little room for quarrels or contentions about property so established.

32. But the chief matter of property being now not the fruits of the earth, and the beasts that subsist on it, but the earth itself, as that which takes in and carries with it all the rest, I think it is plain that property in that, too, is acquired as the former. As much land as a man tills, plants, improves, cultivates, and can use the product of, so much is his property. He by his labor does as it were enclose it from the com-mon. Nor will it invalidate his right to say, everybody else has an equal title to it; and therefore he cannot appropriate, he cannot enclose, with-out the consent of all his fellow-commoners, all mankind. God, when He gave the world in common to all mankind, commanded man also to la-bor, and the penury of his condition required it of him. God and his reason commanded him to subdue the earth, i.e., improve it for the benefit of life, and therein lay out something upon it that was his own, his labor. He that, in obedience to this command of God, subdued, tilled, and sowed any part of it, thereby annexed to it something that was his property, which another had no title to, nor could without in-jury take from him.

33. Nor was this appropriation of any parcel of land, by improving it, any prejudice to any other man, since there was still enough and as good left; and more than the yet unprovided could use. So that in effect there was never the less left for others because of his enclosure for himself. For he that leaves as much as another can make use of, does as good as take nothing at all. Nobody could think himself injured by the drinking of another man, though he took a good draught, who had a whole river of the same water left him to quench his thirst; and the case of land and water, where there is enough of both, is perfectly the same.

34. God gave the world to men in common; but since He gave it them for their benefit, and the greatest conveniences of life they were capable to draw from it, it cannot be supposed He meant it should always remain common and uncultivated. He gave it to the use of the industrious and rational (and labor was to be his title to it), not to the fancy or covetousness of the quarrelsome and contentious. He that had as good left for his improvement as was already taken up, needed not complain, ought not to meddle with what was already improved by another's labor; if he did, it is plain he desired the benefit of another's pains, which he had no right to, and not the ground which God had given him in common with others to labor on, and whereof there was as good left as that already possessed, and more than he knew what to do with, or his industry could reach to.

35. It is true, in land that is common in England, or any other country where there is plenty of people under Government, who have money and commerce, no one can enclose or appropriate any part without the consent of all his fellow-commoners: because this is left common by compact, i.e., by the law of the land, which is not to be violated. And though it be common in respect of some men, it is not so to all mankind; but is the joint property of this country, or this parish. Besides, the remainder, after such enclosure, would not be as good to the rest of the commoners as the whole was, when they could all make use of the whole; whereas in the beginning and first peopling of the great common of the world it was quite otherwise. The law man was under was rather for appropriating. God commanded, and his wants forced him, to labor. That was his property, which could not be taken from him wherever he had fixed it. And hence subduing or cultivating the earth, and having dominion, we see are joined together. The one gave title to the other. So that God, by commanding to subdue, gave authority so far to appropriate. And the condition of human life, which requires labor and materials to work on, necessarily introduces private possessions.

36. The measure of property nature has well set by the extent of men's labor and the conveniency of life. No man's labor could subdue or appropriate all, nor could his enjoyment consume more than a small

part; so that it was impossible for any man, this way, to entrench upon the right of another or acquire to himself a property to the prejudice of his neighbor, who would still have room for as good and as large a possession (after the other had taken out his) as before it was appropriated. Which measure did confine every man's possession to a very moderate proportion, and such as he might appropriate to himself without injury to anybody in the first ages of the world, when men were more in danger to be lost, by wandering from their company, in the then vast wilderness of the earth than to be straitened for want of room to plant in.

The same measure may be allowed still, without prejudice to anybody, full as the world seems. For, supposing a man or family, in the state they were at first, peopling of the world by the children of Adam or Noah, let him plant in some inland vacant places of America. We shall find that the possessions he could make himself, upon the measures we have given, would not be very large, nor, even to this day, prejudice the rest of mankind or give them reason to complain or think themselves injured by this man's encroachment, though the race of men have now spread themselves to all the corners of the world, and do infinitely exceed the small number was at the beginning. Nay, the extent of ground is of so little value without labor that I have heard it affirmed that in Spain itself a man may be permitted to plough, sow, and reap, without being disturbed, upon land he has no other title to, but only his making use of it. But, on the contrary, the inhabitants think themselves beholden to him who, by his industry on neglected, and consequently waste land, has increased the stock of corn, which they wanted. But be this as it will, which I lay no stress on, this I dare boldly affirm, that the same rule of propriety—viz., that every man should have as much as he could make use of, would hold still in the world, without straitening anybody, since there is land enough in the world to suffice double the inhabitants, had not the invention of money, and the tacit agreement of men to put a value on it, introduced (by consent) larger possessions and a right to them; which, how it has done, I shall by and by show more at large.

37. This is certain, that in the beginning, before the desire of having more than man needed had altered the intrinsic value of things, which depends only on their usefulness to the life of man; or had agreed that a little piece of yellow metal which would keep without wasting or decay should be worth a great piece of flesh or a whole heap of corn, though men had a right to appropriate by their labor, each one to himself, as much of the things of nature as he could use, yet this could not be much, nor to the prejudice of others, where the same plenty was still left to those who would use the same industry.

Before the appropriation of land, he who gathered as much of the wild fruit, killed, caught, or tamed as many of the beasts as he could; he that so employed his pains about any of the spontaneous products of nature as any way to alter them from the state which nature put them in, by placing any of his labor on them, did thereby acquire a propriety in them. But if they perished in his possession without their due use; if the fruits rotted, or the venison putrefied before he could spend it, he offended against the common law of nature, and was liable to be punished; he invaded his neighbor's share, for he had no right further than his use called for any of them and they might serve to afford him conveniences of life.

38. The same measures governed the possessions of land, too. Whatsoever he tilled and reaped, laid up, and made use of before it spoiled, that was his peculiar right; whatsoever he enclosed and could feed and make use of, the cattle and product was also his. But if either the grass of his enclosure rotted on the ground, or the fruit of his planting perished without gathering and laying up, this part of the earth, notwithstanding his enclosure, was still to be looked on as waste, and might be the possession of any other. Thus, at the beginning, Cain might take as much ground as he could till and make it his own land, and yet leave enough for Abel's sheep to feed on; a few acres would serve for both their possessions. But as families increased, and industry enlarged their stocks, their possessions enlarged with the need of them; but yet it was commonly without any fixed property in the ground they made use of, till they incorporated, settled themselves together, and built cities; and then, by consent, they came in time to set out the bounds of their distinct territories, and agree on limits between them and their neighbors, and, by laws within themselves, settled the properties of those of the same society. For we see that in that part of the world which was first inhabited, and therefore like to be best peopled, even as low down as Abraham's time, they wandered with their flocks and their herds, which was their substance, freely up and down—and this Abraham did in a country where he was a stranger; whence it is plain that, at least, a great part of the land lay in common, that the inhabitants valued it not, nor claimed property in any more than they made use of; but when there was not room enough in the same place for their herds to feed together, they, by consent, as Abraham and Lot did (Gen. xiii. 5), separated and enlarged their pasture where it best liked them. And for the same reason, Esau went from his father and his brother, and planted in Mount Seir (Gen. xxxvi. 6).

39. And thus, without supposing any private dominion and property in Adam over all the world, exclusive of all other men, which can no way be proved, nor any one's property be made out from it, but suppos-

ing the world, given as it was to the children of men in common, we see how labor could make men distinct titles to several parcels of it for their private uses, wherein there could be no doubt of right, no room for quarrel.

40. Nor is it so strange, as perhaps before consideration it may appear, that the property of labor should be able to overbalance the community of land. For it is labor indeed that puts the difference of value on everything; and let anyone consider what the difference is between an acre of land planted with tobacco or sugar, sown with wheat or barley, and an acre of the same land lying in common without any husbandry upon it, and he will find that the improvement of labor makes the far greater part of the value. I think it will be but a very modest computation to say that of the products of the earth useful to the life of man nine-tenths are the effects of labor; nay, if we will rightly estimate things as they come to our use, and cast up the several expenses about them—what in them is purely owing to nature, and what to labor—we shall find that in most of them ninety-nine hundredths are wholly to be put on the account of labor.

41. There cannot be a clearer demonstration of anything than several nations of the Americans are of this, who are rich in land and poor in all the comforts of life; whom nature, having furnished as liberally as any other people with the materials of plenty—i.e., a fruitful soil, apt to produce in abundance what might serve for food, raiment, and delight; yet, for want of improving it by labor, have not one hundredth part of the conveniences we enjoy, and a king of a large and fruitful territory there feeds, lodges, and is clad worse than a day laborer in England.

42. To make this a little clearer, let us but trace some of the ordinary provisions of life, through their several progresses, before they come to our use, and see how much they receive of their value from human industry. Bread, wine, and cloth are things of daily use and great plenty; yet, notwithstanding, acorns, water, and leaves or skins, must be our bread, drink, and clothing, did not labor furnish us with these more useful commodities. For whatever bread is more worth than acorns, wine than water, and cloth or silk than leaves, skins, or moss, that is wholly owing to labor and industry: the one of these being the food and raiment which unassisted nature furnishes us with; the other, provisions which our industry and pains prepare for us; which how much they exceed the other in value when anyone hath computed, he will then see how much labor makes the far greatest part of the value of things we enjoy in this world. And the ground which produces the materials is scarce to be reckoned in as any, or at most but a very small, part of it; so little that even amongst us land that is left wholly to na-

ture, that hath no improvement of pasturage, tillage, or planting, is called, as indeed it is, "waste," and we shall find the benefit of it amount to little more than nothing.

43. An acre of land that bears here twenty bushels of wheat, and another in America which, with the same husbandry, would do the like, are without doubt of the same natural intrinsic value; but yet the benefit mankind receives from the one in a year is worth £5, and from the other possibly not worth a penny, if all the profit an Indian received from it were to be valued and sold here; at least, I may truly say, not one-thousandth. 'Tis labor, then, which puts the greatest part of value upon land, without which it would scarcely be worth anything; 'tis to that we owe the greatest part of all its useful products, for all that the straw, bran, bread, of that acre of wheat is more worth than the product of an acre of as good land which lies waste, is all the effect of labor. For 'tis not barely the ploughman's pains, the reaper's and thresher's toil, and the baker's sweat, is to be counted into the bread we eat; the labor of those who broke the oxen, who dug and wrought the iron and stones, who felled and framed the timber employed about the plough, mill, oven, or any other utensils, which are a vast number, requisite to this corn, from its sowing, to its being made bread, must all be charged on the account of labor, and received as an effect of that. Nature and the earth furnished only the almost worthless materials as in themselves. 'Twould be a strange catalogue of things that industry provided, and made use of, about every loaf of bread before it came to our use, if we could trace them—iron, wood, leather, bark, timber, stone, bricks, coals, lime, cloth, dyeing drugs, pitch, tar, masts, ropes, and all the materials made use of in the ship that brought any of the commodities made use of by any of the workmen to any part of the work all which it would be almost impossible—at least, too long—to reckon up.

44. From all which it is evident that, though the things of nature are given in common, yet man, by being master of himself and proprietor of his own person and the actions or labor of it, had still in himself the great foundation of property; and that which made up the great part of what he applied to the support or comfort of his being, when invention and arts had improved the conveniences of life, was perfectly his own, and did not belong in common to others.

45. Thus labor, in the beginning, gave a right of property, wherever anyone was pleased to employ it upon what was common, which remained a long while the far greater part, and is yet more than mankind makes use of. Men at first, for the most part, contented themselves with what unassisted nature offered to their necessities; and though afterwards, in some parts of the world (where the increase of people and stock, with the use of money, had made land scarce, and so of some

value), the several communities settled the bounds of their district territories, and, by laws within themselves, regulated the properties of the private men of their society, and so, by compact and agreement, settled the property which labor and industry began—and the leagues that have been made between several states and kingdoms, either expressly or tacitly disowning all claim and right to the land in the other's possession, have, by common consent, given up their pretenses to their natural common right, which originally they had to those countries; and so have, by positive agreement, settled a property amongst themselves in distinct parts of the world—yet there are still great tracts of ground to be found which, the inhabitants thereof not having joined with the rest of mankind in the consent of the use of their common money, lie waste, and are more than the people who dwell on it do or can make use of, and so still lie in common; though this can scarce happen amongst that part of mankind that have consented to the use of money.

46. The greatest part of things really useful to the life of man, and such as the necessity of subsisting made the first commoners of the world look after, as it doth the Americans now, are generally things of short duration, such as, if they are not consumed by use, will decay and perish of themselves: gold, silver, and diamonds are things that fancy or agreement have put the value on more than real use and the necessary support of life. Now, of those good things which nature hath provided in common, everyone hath a right, as hath been said, to as much as he could use, and had a property in all he could effect with his labor—all that his industry could extend to, to alter from the state nature had put it in, was his. He that gahered a hundred bushels of acorns or apples had thereby a property in them; they were his goods as soon as gathered. He was only to look that he used them before they spoiled, else he took more than his share, and robbed others; and, indeed, it was a foolish thing, as well as dishonest, to hoard up more than he could make use of. If he gave away a part to anybody else, so that it perished not uselessly in his possession, these he also made use of; and if he also bartered away plums that would have rotted in a week, for nuts that would last good for his eating a whole year, he did no injury; he wasted not the common stock, destroyed no part of the portion of goods that belonged to others, so long as nothing perished uselessly in his hands. Again, if he wuld give his nuts for a piece of metal, pleased with its color, or exchange his sheep for shells, or wool for a sparkling pebble or a diamond, and keep those by him all his life, he invaded not the right of others; he might heap up as much of these durable things as he pleased, the exceeding of the bounds of his just property not lying in the largeness of his possessions, but the perishing of anything uselessly in it.

47. And thus came in the use of money—some lasting thing that men

might keep without spoiling, and that, by mutual consent, men would take in exchange for the truly useful but perishable supports of life.

48. And as different degrees of industry were apt to give men possessions in different proportions, so this invention of money gave them the opportunity to continue and enlarge them; for supposing an island, separate from all possible commerce with the rest of the world, wherein there were but a hundred families—but there were sheep, horses, and cows, with other useful animals, wholesome fruits, and land enough for corn for a hundred thousand times as many, but nothing in the island, either because of its commonness or perishableness, fit to supply the place of money—what reason could anyone have there to enlarge his possessions beyond the use of his family and a plentiful supply to its consumption, either in what their own industry produced, or they could barter for like perishable useful commodities with others? Where there is not something both lasting and scarce, and so valuable to be hoarded up, there men will not be apt to enlarge their possessions of land, were it never so rich, never so free for them to take; for I ask, what would a man value ten thousand or a hundred thousand acres of excellent land, ready cultivated, and well stocked too with cattle, in the middle of the inland parts of America, where he had no hopes of commerce with other parts of the world, to draw money to him by the sale of the product? It would not be worth the enclosing, and we should see him give up again to the wild common of nature whatever was more than would supply the conveniences of life to be had there for him and his family.

49. Thus in the beginning all the world was America, and more so than that is now, for no such thing as money was anywhere known. Find out something that hath the use and value of money amongst his neighbors, you shall see the same man will begin presently to enlarge his possessions.

50. But since gold and silver, being little useful to the life of man in proportion to food, raiment, and carriage, has its value only from the consent of men, whereof labor yet makes, in great part, the measure, it is plain that the consent of men have agreed to a disproportionate and unequal possession of the earth—I mean out of the bounds of society and compact; for in governments the laws regulate it; they having, by consent, found out and agreed in a way how a man may rightfully and without injury possess more than he himself can make use of by receiving gold and silver, which may continue long in a man's possession, without decaying for the overplus, and agreeing those metals should have a value.

51. And thus, I think, it is very easy to conceive without any difficulty how labor could at first begin a title of property in the common things of nature, and how the spending it upon our uses bounded it; so

that there could then be no reason of quarrelling about title, nor any doubt about the largeness of possession it gave. Right and conveniency went together; for as a man had a right to all he could employ his labor upon, so he had no temptation to labor for more than he could make use of. This left no room for controversy about the title, nor for encroachment on the right of others; what portion a man carved to himself was easily seen, and it was useless, as well as dishonest, to carve himself too much, or take more than he needed.

CHAPTER VI

OF PATERNAL POWER

52. It may perhaps be censured an impertinent criticism in a discourse of this nature to find fault with words and names that have obtained in the world. And yet possibly it may not be amiss to offer new ones when the old are apt to lead men into mistakes, as this of paternal power probably has done, which seems so to place the power of parents over their children wholly in the father, as if the mother had no share in it; whereas if we consult reason or revelation, we shall find she has an equal title, which may give one reason to ask whether this might not be more properly called parental power? For whatever obligation nature and the right of generation lays on children, it must certainly bind them equal to both the concurrent causes of it. And accordingly we see the positive law of God everywhere joins them together without distinction, when it commands the obedience of children; "Honor thy father and thy mother" (Exod. xx. 12); "Whosoever curseth his father or his mother" (Lev. xx. 9); "Ye shall fear every man his mother and his father" (Lev. xix. 3); "Children obey your parents," etc. (Eph. vi. 1), is the style of the Old and New Testament.

53. Had but this one thing been well considered without looking any deeper into the matter, it might perhaps have kept men from running into those gross mistakes they have made about this power of parents, which however it might without any great harshness bear the name of absolute dominion and regal authority, when under the title of "paternal" power, it seemed appropriated to the father; would yet have sounded but oddly, and in the very name shown the absurdity, if this supposed absolute power over children had been called parental, and thereby discovered that it belonged to the mother too. For it will but very ill serve the turn of those men who contend so much for the absolute power and authority of the fatherhood, as they call it, that the mother should have any share in it. And it would have but ill supported

the monarchy they contend for, when by the very name it appeared that that fundamental authority from whence they would derive their government of a single person only was not placed in one, but two persons jointly. But to let this of names pass.

54. Though I have said above (2) "That all men by nature are equal," I cannot be supposed to understand all sorts of "equality." Age or virtue may give men a just precedency. Excellency of parts and merit may place others above the common level. Birth may subject some, and alliance or benefits others, to pay an observance to those to whom nature, gratitude, or other respects, may have made it due; and yet all this consists with the equality which all men are in in respect of jurisdiction or dominion one over another, which was the equality I there spoke of as proper to the business in hand, being that equal right that every man hath to his natural freedom, without being subjected to the will or authority of any other man.

55. Children, I confess, are not born in this full state of equality, though they are born to it. Their parents have a sort of rule and jurisdiction over them when they come into the world, and for some time after, but it is but a temporary one. The bonds of this subjection are like the swaddling clothes they are wrapt up in and supported by in the weakness of their infancy. Age and reason as they grow up loosen them, till at length they drop quite off, and leave a man at his own free disposal.

56. Adam was created a perfect man, his body and mind in full possession of their strength and reason, and so was capable from the first instance of his being to provide for his own support and preservation, and govern his actions according to the dictates of the law of reason God had implanted in him. From him the world is peopled with his descendants, who are all born infants, weak and helpless, without knowledge or understanding. But to supply the defects of this imperfect state till the improvement of growth and age had removed them, Adam and Eve, and after them all parents were, by the law of nature, under an obligation to preserve, nourish and educate the children they had begotten, not as their own workmanship, but the workmanship of their own Maker, the Almighty, to whom they were to be accountable for them.

57. The law that was to govern Adam was the same that was to govern all his posterity, the law of reason. But his offspring having another way of entrance into the world, different from him, by a natural birth, that produced them ignorant, and without the use of reason, they were not presently under that law. For nobody can be under a law that is not promulgated to him; and this law being promulgated or made known by reason only, he that is not come to the use of his reason cannot be said to be under this law; and Adam's children being not presently as soon

as born under this law of reason, were not presently free. For law, in its true notion, is not so much the limitation as the direction of a free and intelligent agent to his proper interest, and prescribes no farther than is for the general good of those under that law. Could they be happier without it, the law, as a useless thing, would of itself vanish; and that ill deserves the name of confinement which hedges us in only from bogs and precipices. So that however it may be mistaken, the end of law is not to abolish or restrain, but to preserve and enlarge freedom. For in all the states of created beings, capable of laws, where there is no law there is no freedom. For liberty is to be free from restraint and violence from others, which cannot be where there is no law; and is not, as we are told, "a liberty for every man to do what he lists." For who could be free, when every other man's humor might domineer over him? But a liberty to dispose and order freely as he lists his person, actions, possessions, and his whole property within the allowance of those laws under which he is, and therein not to be subject to the arbitrary will of another, but freely follow his own.

58. The power, then, that parents have over their children arises from that duty which is incumbent on them, to take care of their offspring during the imperfect state of childhood. To inform the mind, and govern the actions of their yet ignorant nonage, till reason shall take its place and ease them of that trouble, is what the children want, and the parents are bound to. For God having given man an understanding to direct his actions, has allowed him a freedom of will and liberty of acting, as properly belonging thereunto, within the bounds of that law he is under. But whilst he is in an estate wherein he has no understanding of his own to direct his will, he is not to have any will of his own to follow. He that understands for him must will for him too; he must prescribe to his will, and regulate his actions, but when he comes to the estate that made his father a free man, the son is a free man too.

59. This holds in all the laws a man is under, whether natural or civil. Is a man under the law of nature? What made him free of that law? what gave him a free disposing of his property, according to his own will, within the compass of that law? I answer, an estate wherein he might be supposed capable to know that law, that so he might keep his actions within the bounds of it. When he has acquired that state, he is presumed to know how far that law is to be his guide, and how far he may make use of his freedom, and so comes to have it; till then, somebody else must guide him, who is presumed to know how far the law allows a liberty. If such a state of reason, such an age of discretion, made him free, the same shall make his son free too. Is a man under the law of England? What made him free of that law—that is, to have the liberty to dispose of his actions and possessions, according to his own will,

within the permission of that law? a capacity of knowing that law. Which is supposed, by that law, at the age of twenty-one, and in some cases sooner. If this made the father free, it shall make the son free too. Till then, we see the law allows the son to have no will, but he is to be guided by the will of his father or guardian, who is to understand for him. And if the father die and fail to substitute a deputy in this trust, if he hath not provided a tutor to govern his son during his minority, during his want of understanding, the law takes care to do it: some other must govern him and be a will to him till he hath attained to a state of freedom, and his understanding be fit to take the government of his will. But after that the father and son are equally free, as much as tutor and pupil, after nonage, equally subjects of the same law together, without any dominion left in the father over the life, liberty, or estate of his son, whether they be only in the state and under the law of nature, or under the positive laws of an established government.

60. But if through defects that may happen out of the ordinary course of nature, anyone comes not to such a degree of reason wherein he might be supposed capable of knowing the law, and so living within the rules of it, he is never capable of being a free man, he is never let loose to the disposure of his own will; because he knows no bounds to it, has not understanding, its proper guide, but is continued under the tuition and government of others all the time his own understanding is incapable of that charge. And so lunatics and idiots are never set free from the government of their parents: "Children who are not as yet come unto those years whereat they may have, and innocents, which are excluded by a natural defect from ever having." Thirdly, "Madmen, which, for the present, cannot possibly have the use of right reason to guide themselves, have, for their guide, the reason that guideth other men which are tutors over them, to seek and procure their good for them," says Hooker (Eccl. Pol., lib. i., sect. 7). All which seems no more than that duty which God and nature has laid on man, as well as other creatures, to preserve their offspring till they can be able to shift for themselves, and will scarce amount to an instance or proof of parents' regal authority.

61. Thus we are born free as we are born rational; not that we have actually the exercise of either: age that brings one, brings with it the other too. And thus we see how natural freedom and subjection to parents may consist together, and are both founded on the same principle. A child is free by his father's title, by his father's understanding, which is to govern him till he hath it of his own. The freedom of a man at years of discretion, and the subjection of a child to his parents, whilst yet short of it, are so consistent and so distinguishable that the most blinded contenders for monarchy, "by right of fatherhood," cannot miss

of it; the most obstinate cannot but allow of it. For were their doctrine all true, were the right heir of Adam now known, and, by that title, settled a monarch in his throne, invested with all the absolute unlimited power Sir Robert Filmer talks of, if he should die as soon as his heir were born, must not the child, notwithstanding he were never so free, never so much sovereign, be in subjection to his mother and nurse, to tutors and governors, till age and education brought him reason and ability to govern himself and others? The necessities of his life, the health of his body, and the information of his mind would require him to be directed by the will of others and not his own; and yet will anyone think that this restraint and subjection were inconsistent with, or spoiled him of, that liberty or sovereignty he had a right to, or gave away his empire to those who had the government of his nonage? This government over him only prepared him the better and sooner for it. If anybody should ask me when my son is of age to be free, I shall answer, just when his monarch is of age to govern. "But at what time," says the judicious Hooker (Eccl. Pol., lib. i., sect. 6), "a man may be said to have attained so far forth the use of reason as sufficeth to make him capable of those laws whereby he is then bound to guide his actions; this is a great deal more easy for sense to discern than for anyone, by skill and learning, to determine."

62. Commonwealths themselves take notice of, and allow that there is a time when men are to begin to act like free men, and therefore, till that time, require not oaths of fealty or allegiance, or other public owning of, or submission to the government of their countries.

63. The freedom then of man, and liberty of acting according to his own will, is grounded on his having reason, which is able to instruct him in that law he is to govern himself by, and make him know how far he is left to the freedom of his own will. To turn him loose to an unrestrained liberty, before he has reason to guide him, is not the allowing him the privilege of his nature to be free, but to thrust him out amongst brutes, and abandon him to a state as wretched and as much beneath that of a man as theirs. This is that which puts the authority into the parents' hands to govern the minority of their children. God hath made it their business to employ this care on their offspring, and hath placed in them suitable inclinations of tenderness and concern to temper this power, to apply it as His wisdom designed it, to the children's good as long as they should need to be under it.

64. But what reason can hence advance this care of the parents due to their offspring into an absolute, arbitrary dominion of the father, whose power reaches no farther than by such a discipline as he finds most effectual to give such strength and health to their bodies, such vigor and rectitude to their minds, as may best fit his children to be

most useful to themselves and others, and, if it be necessary to his condition, to make them work when they are able for their own subsistence;
but in this power the mother, too, has her share with the father.

65. Nay, this power so little belongs to the father by any peculiar
right of nature, but only as he is guardian of his children, that when he
quits his care of them he loses his power over them, which goes along
with their nourishment and education, to which it is inseparably annexed, and belongs as much to the foster-father of an exposed child as to
the natural father of another. So little power does the bare act of beget-
ting give a man over his issue, if all his care ends there, and this be all
the title he hath to the name and authority of a father. And what will
become of this paternal power in that part of the world where one
woman hath more than one husband at a time? or in those parts of
America where, when the husband and wife part, which happens frequently, the children are all left to the mother, follow her, and are
wholly under her care and provision? And if the father die whilst the
children are young, do they not naturally everywhere owe the same obedience to their mother, during their minority, as to their father, were he
alive? And will anyone say that the mother hath a legislative power over
her children that she can make standing rules which shall be of perpetual obligation, by which they ought to regulate all the concerns of their
property, and bound their liberty all the course of their lives, and enforce the observation of them with capital punishments? For this is the
proper power of the magistrate, of which the father hath not so much as
the shadow. His command over his children is but temporary, and
reaches not their life or property. It is but a help to the weakness and
imperfection of their nonage, a discipline necessary to their education.
And though a father may dispose of his own possessions as he pleases
when his children are out of danger of perishing for want, yet his power
extends not to the lives or goods which either their own industry, or another's bounty, has made theirs, nor to their liberty neither, when they
are once arrived to the enfranchisement of the years of discretion. The
father's empire then ceases, and he can from thenceforward no more dispose of the liberty of his son than that of any other man. And it must
be far from an absolute or perpetual jurisdiction from which a man may
withdraw himself, having license from Divine authority to "leave father
and mother and cleave to his wife."

66. But though there be a time when a child comes to be as free from
subjection to the will and command of his father as he himself is free
from subjection to the will of anybody else, and they are both under no
other restraint but that which is common to them both, whether it be
the law of nature or municipal law of their country, yet this freedom ex-

empts not a son from that honor which he ought, by the law of God and nature, to pay his parents, God having made the parents instruments in His great design of continuing the race of mankind and the occasions of life to their children. As He hath laid on them an obligation to nourish, preserve, and bring up their offspring, so He has laid on the children a perpetual obligation of honoring their parents, which, containing in it an inward esteem and reverence to be shown by all outward expressions, ties up the child from anything that may ever injure or affront, disturb or endanger the happiness or life of those from whom he received his, and engages him in all actions of defense, relief, assistance, and comfort of those by whose means he entered into being and has been made capable of any enjoyments of life. From this obligation no state, no freedom, can absolve children. But this is very far from giving parents a power of command over their children, or an authority to make laws and dispose as they please of their lives or liberties. It is one thing to owe honor, respect, gratitude, and assistance; another to require an absolute obedience and submission. The honor due to parents a monarch on his throne owes his mother, and yet this lessens not his authority nor subjects him to her government.

67. The subjection of a minor places in the father a temporary government which terminates with the minority of the child; and the honor due from a child places in the parents a perpetual right to respect, reverence, support, and compliance, to more or less, as the father's care, cost, and kindness in his education has been more or less, and this ends not with minority, but holds in all parts and conditions of a man's life. The want of distinguishing these two powers which the father hath, in the right of tuition, during minority, and the right of honor all his life, may perhaps have caused a great part of the mistakes about this matter. For, to speak properly of them, the first of these is rather the privilege of children and duty of parents than any prerogative of paternal power. The nourishment and education of their children is a charge so incumbent on parents for their children's good, that nothing can absolve them from taking care of it. And though the power of commanding and chastising them go along with it, yet God hath woven into the principles of human nature such a tenderness for their offspring, that there is little fear that parents should use their power with too much rigor; the excess is seldom on the severe side, the strong bias of nature drawing the other way. And therefore God Almighty, when He would express His gentle dealing with the Israelites, He tells them that though He chastened them, "He chastened them as a man chastens his son" (Deut. viii. 5)— i.e., with tenderness and affection, and kept them under no severer discipline than what was absolutely best for them, and had been less kind·

ness to have slackened. This is that power to which children are commanded obedience, that the pains and care of their parents may not be increased or ill-rewarded.

68. On the other side, honor and support all that which gratitude requires to return; for the benefits received by and from them is the indispensable duty of the child and the proper privilege of the parents. This is intended for the parents' advantage, as the other is for the child's; though education, the parents' duty, seems to have most power, because the ignorance and infirmities of childhood stand in need of restraint and correction, which is a visible exercise of rule and a kind of dominion. And that duty which is comprehended in the word "honor" requires less obedience, though the obligation be stronger on grown than younger children. For who can think the command, "Children obey your parents," requires in a man that has children of his own the same submission to his father as it does in his yet young children to him, and that by this precept he were bound to obey all his father's commands, if, out of a conceit of authority, he should have the indiscretion to treat him still as a boy.

69. The first part, then, of paternal power, or rather duty, which is education, belongs so to the father that it terminates at a certain season. When the business of education is over it ceases of itself, and is also alienable before. For a man may put the tuition of his son in other hands; and he that has made his son an apprentice to another has discharged him, during that time, of a great part of his obedience, both to himself and to his mother. But all the duty of honor, the other part, remains nevertheless entire to them; nothing can cancel that. It is so inseparable from them both, that the father's authority cannot dispossess the mother of this right, nor can any man discharge his son from honoring her that bore him. But both these are very far from a power to make laws, and enforcing them with penalties that may reach estate, liberty, limbs, and life. The power of commanding ends with nonage, and though after that honor and respect, support and defence, and whatsoever gratitude can oblige a man to, for the highest benefits he is naturally capable of be always due from a son to his parents, yet all this puts no sceptre into the father's hand, no sovereign power of commanding. He has no dominion over his son's property or actions, nor any right that his will should prescribe to his son's in all things; however, it may become his son in many things, not very inconvenient to him and his family, to pay a deference to it.

70. A man may owe honor and respect to an ancient or wise man, defense to his child or friend, relief and support to the distressed and gratitude to a benefactor, to such a degree that all he has, all he can do, cannot sufficiently pay it. But all these give no authority, no right of

making laws, to anyone over him from whom they are owing. And it is plain all this is due, not to the bare title of father, not only because, as has been said, it is owing to the mother too, but because these obligations to parents, and the degrees of what is required of children, may be varied by the different care and kindness, trouble and expense, is often employed upon one child more than another.

71. This shows the reason how it comes to pass that parents in societies, where they themselves are subjects, retain a power over their children and have as much right to their subjection as those who are in the state of nature, which could not possibly be if all political power were only paternal, and that, in truth, they were one and the same thing; for then, all paternal power being in the prince, the subject could naturally have none of it. But these two powers, political and paternal, are so perfectly distinct and separate, and built upon so different foundations, and given to so different ends, that every subject that is a father has as much a paternal power over his children as the prince has over his. And every prince that has parents owes them as much filial duty and obedience as the meanest of his subjects do to theirs, and can therefore contain not any part or degree of that kind of dominion which a prince or magistrate has over his subject.

72. Though the obligation on the parents to bring up their children, and the obligation on children to honor their parents, contain all the power, on the one hand, and submission on the other, which are proper to this relation, yet there is another power ordinarily in the father, whereby he has a tie on the obedience of his children, which, though it be common to him with other men, yet the occasions of showing it, almost constantly happening to fathers in their private families and in instances of it elsewhere being rare, and less taken notice of, it passes in the world for a part of "paternal jurisdiction." And this is the power men generally have to bestow their estates on those who please them best. The possession of the father being the expectation and inheritance of the children ordinarily, in certain proportions, according to the law and custom of each country, yet it is commonly in the father's power to bestow it with a more sparing or liberal hand, according as the behavior of this or that child hath comported with his will and humor.

73. This is no small tie to the obedience of children; and there being always annexed to the enjoyment of land a submission to the government of the country of which that land is a part, it has been commonly supposed that a father could oblige his posterity to that government of which he himself was a subject, that his compact held them; whereas, it being only a necessary condition annexed to the land which is under that government, reaches only those who will take it on that condition,

and so is no natural tie or engagement, but a voluntary submission; for every man's children being, by nature, as free as himself or any of his ancestors ever were, may, whilst they are in that freedom, choose what society they will join themselves to, what commonwealth they will put themselves under. But if they will enjoy the inheritance of their ancestors, they must take it on the same terms their ancestors had it, and submit to all the conditions annexed to such a possession. By this power, indeed, fathers oblige their children to obedience to themselves even when they are past minority, and most commonly, too, subject them to this or that political power. But neither of these by any peculiar right of fatherhood, but by the reward they have in their hands to enforce and recompense such a compliance, and is no more power than what a Frenchman has over an Englishman, who, by the hopes of an estate he will leave him, will certainly have a strong tie on his obedience; and if when it is left him, he will enjoy it, he must certainly take it upon the conditions annexed to the possession of land in that country where it lies, whether it be France or England.

74. To conclude, then, though the father's power of commanding extends no farther than the minority of his children, and to a degree only fit for the discipline and government of that age; and though that honor and respect, and all that which the Latins called piety, which they indispensably owe to their parents all their lifetimes, and in all estates, with all that support and defense, is due to them, gives the father no power of governing—i.e., making laws and exacting penalties on his children; though by this he has no dominion over the property or actions of his son, yet it is obvious to conceive how easy it was, in the first ages of the world, and in places still where the thinness of people gives families leave to separate into unpossessed quarters, and they have room to remove and plant themselves in yet vacant habitations, for the father of the family to become the prince of it; he had been a ruler from the beginning of the infancy of his children; and when they were grown up, since without some government it would be hard for them to live together, it was likeliest it should, by the express or tacit consent of the children, be in the father, where it seemed, without any change, barely to continue. And when, indeed, nothing more was required to it than the permitting the father to exercise alone in his family that executive power of the law of nature which every free man naturally hath, and by that permission resigning up to him a monarchical power whilst they remained in it. But that this was not by any paternal right, but only by the consent of his children, is evident from hence, that nobody doubts but if a stranger, whom chance or business had brought to his family, had there killed any of his children, or committed any other act, he might condemn and put him to death, or otherwise have punished him

as well as any of his children, which was impossible he should do by virtue of any paternal authority over one who was not his child, but by virtue of that executive power of the law of nature which, as a man, he had a right to; and he alone could punish him in his family where the respect of his children had laid by the exercise of such a power, to give way to the dignity and authority they were willing should remain in him above the rest of his family.

75. Thus it was easy and almost natural for children, by a tacit and almost natural consent, to make way for the father's authority and government. They had been accustomed in their childhood to follow his direction, and to refer their little differences to him; and when they were men, who fitter to rule them? Their little properties and less covetousness seldom afforded greater controversies; and when any should arise, where could they have a fitter umpire than he, by whose care they had every one been sustained and brought up, and who had a tenderness for them all? It is no wonder that they made no distinction betwixt minority and full age, nor looked after one-and-twenty, or any other age, that might make them the free disposers of themselves and fortunes, when they could have no desire to be out of their pupilage. The government they had been under during it continued still to be more their protection than restraint; and they could nowhere find a greater security to their peace, liberties, and fortunes than in the rule of a father.

76. Thus the natural fathers of families, by an insensible change, became the politic monarchs of them too; and as they chanced to live long, and leave able and worthy heirs for several successions or otherwise, so they laid the foundations of hereditary or elective kingdoms under several constitutions and manors, according as chance, contrivance, or occasions happened to mold them. But if princes have their titles in the father's right, and it be a sufficient proof of the natural right of fathers to political authority, because they commonly were those in whose hands we find, *de facto*, the exercise of government, I say, if this argument be good, it will as strongly prove that all princes, nay, princes only, ought to be priests, since it is as certain that in the beginning "the father of the family was priest, as that he was ruler in his own household."

CHAPTER VII

OF POLITICAL OR CIVIL SOCIETY

77. GOD HAVING made man such a creature, that in his own judgment it was not good for him to be alone, put him under strong obligations of necessity, convenience, and inclination to drive him into society, as well

as fitted him with understanding and language to continue and enjoy it. The first society was between man and wife, which gave beginning to that between parents and children; to which, in time, that between master and servant came to be added; and though all these might, and commonly did meet together, and make up but one family, wherein the master or mistress of it had some sort of rule proper to a family; each of these, or all together, came short of political society, as we shall see, if we consider the different ends, ties, and bounds of each of these.

78. Conjugal society is made by a voluntary compact between man and woman, and though it consist chiefly in such a communion and right in one another's bodies as is necessary to its chief end, procreation, yet it draws with it mutual support and assistance, and a communion of interests too, as necessary not only to unite their care and affection, but also necessary to their common offspring, who have a right to be nourished and maintained by them till they are able to provide for themselves.

79. For the end of conjunction between male and female being not barely procreation, but the continuation of the species, this conjunction betwixt male and female ought to last, even after procreation, so long as is necessary to the nourishment and support of the young ones, who are to be sustained by those that got them till they are able to shift and provide for themselves. This rule, which the infinite wise Maker hath set to the works of His hands, we find the inferior creatures steadily obey. In those vivaporous animals which feed on grass the conjunction between male and female lasts no longer than the very act of copulation, because the teat of the dam being sufficient to nourish the young till it be able to feed on grass, the male only begets, but concerns not himself for the female or young, to whose sustenance he can contribute nothing. But in beasts of prey the conjunction lasts longer, because the dam, not being able well to subsist herself and nourish her numerous offspring by her own prey alone (a more laborious as well as more dangerous way of living than by feeding on grass), the assistance of the male is necessary to the maintenance of their common family, which cannot subsist till they are able to prey for themselves, but by the joint care of male and female. The same is observed in all birds (except some domestic ones, where plenty of food excuses the cock from feeding and taking care of the young brood), whose young, needing food in the nest, the cock and hen continue mates till the young are able to use their wings and provide for themselves.

80. And herein, I think, lies the chief, if not the only reason, why the male and female in mankind are tied to a longer conjunction than other creatures—viz., because the female is capable of conceiving, and, *de*

facto, is commonly with child again, and brings forth too a new birth, long before the former is out of a dependency for support on his parents' help and able to shift for himself, and has all the assistance is due to him from his parents, whereby the father, who is bound to take care for those he hath begot, is under an obligation to continue in conjugal society with the same woman longer than other creatures, whose young, being able to subsist of themselves before the time of procreation returns again, the conjugal bond dissolves of itself, and they are at liberty till Hymen, at his usual anniversary season, summons them again to choose new mates. Wherein one cannot but admire the wisdom of the great Creator, who, having given to man an ability to lay up for the future as well as supply the present necessity, hath made it necessary that society of man and wife should be more lasting than of male and female amongst other creatures, that so their industry might be encouraged, and their interest better united, to make provision and lay up goods for their common issue, which uncertain mixture, or easy and frequent solutions of conjugal society, would mightily disturb.

81. But though these are ties upon mankind which make the conjugal bonds more firm and lasting in a man than the other species of animals, yet it would give one reason to inquire why this compact, where procreation and education are secured and inheritance taken care for may not be made determinable, either by consent, or at a certain time, or upon certain conditions, as well as any other voluntary compacts, there being no necessity, in the nature of the thing, nor to the ends of it, that it should always be for life—I mean, to such as are under no restraint of any positive law which ordains all such contracts to be perpetual.

82. But the husband and wife, though they have but one common concern, yet having different understandings, will unavoidably sometimes have different wills too. It therefore being necessary that the last determination (i.e., the rule) should be placed somewhere, it naturally falls to the man's share as the abler and the stronger. But this, reaching but to the things of their common interest and property, leaves the wife in the full and true possession of what by contract is her peculiar right, and at least gives the husband no more power over her than she has over his life; the power of the husband being so far from that of an absolute monarch that the wife has, in many cases, a liberty to separate from him where natural right or their contract allows it, whether that contract be made by themselves in the state of nature or by the customs or laws of the country they live in, and the children, upon such separation, fall to the father or mother's lot as such contract does determine.

83. For all the ends of marriage being to be obtained under politic government, as well as in the state of nature, the civil magistrate doth

not abridge the right or power of either, naturally necessary to those ends—viz., procreation and mutual support and assistance whilst they are together, but only decides any controversy that may arise between man and wife about them. If it were otherwise, and that absolute sovereignty and power of life and death naturally belonged to the husband, and were necessary to the society between man and wife, there could be no matrimony in any of these countries where the husband is allowed no such absolute authority. But the ends of matrimony requiring no such power in the husband, it was not at all necessary to it. The condition of conjugal society put it not in him; but whatsoever might consist with procreation and support of the children till they could shift for themselves—mutual assistance, comfort, and maintenance—might be varied and regulated by that contract which first united them in that society, nothing being necessary to any society that is not necessary to the ends for which it is made.

84. The society betwixt parents and children, and the distinct rights and powers belonging respectively to them, I have treated of so largely in the foregoing chapter that I shall not here need to say anything of it; and I think it is plain that it is far different from a politic society.

85. Master and servant are names as old as history, but given to those of far different condition; for a free man makes himself a servant to another by selling him for a certain time the service he undertakes to do in exchange for wages he is to receive; and though this commonly puts him into the family of his master, and under the ordinary discipline thereof, yet it gives the master but a temporary power over him, and no greater than what is contained in the contract between them. But there is another sort of servants, which by a peculiar name we call slaves, who, being captives taken in a just war, are by the right of nature subjected to the absolute dominion and arbitrary power of their masters. These men having, as I say, forfeited their lives, and with them their liberties, and lost their estates—and being, in the state of slavery, not capable of any property—cannot in that state be considered as any part of civil society, the chief end whereof is the preservation of property.

86. Let us therefore consider a master of a family, with all these subordinate relations of wife, children, servants, and slaves, united under the domestic rule of a family, which, what resemblance soever it may have in its order, offices, and number too, with a little commonwealth, yet is very far from it both in its constitution, power and end; or, if it must be thought a monarchy, and the paterfamilias the absolute monarch in it, absolute monarchy will have but a very shattered and short power, when 'tis plain, by what has been said before, that the master of the family has a very distinct and differently limited power, both as to time and extent, over those several persons that are in it;

for, excepting slaves (and the family is as much a family, and his power as paterfamilias as great, whether there be any slaves in the family or no), he has no legislative power of life and death over any of them, and none, too, but what a mistress of a family may have as well as he. And he certainly can have no absolute power over the whole family, who has but a very limited one over every individual in it. But how a family or any other society of men differ from that, which is properly political society, we shall best see by considering wherein political society itself consists.

87. Man being born, as has been proved, with a title to perfect free, dom, and an uncontrolled enjoyment of all the rights and privileges of the law of nature equally with any other man or number of men in the world, hath by nature a power not only to preserve his property—that is, his life, liberty, and estate—against the injuries and attempts of other men, but to judge of and punish the breaches of that law in others as he is persuaded the offense deserves, even with death itself, in crimes where the heinousness of the fact in his opinion requires it. But because no political society can be nor subsist without having in itself the power to preserve the property, and, in order thereunto, punish the offenses of all those of that society, there, and there only, is political society, where every one of the members hath quitted this natural power, resigned it up into the hands of the community in all cases that exclude him not from appealing for protection to the law established by it; and thus all private judgment of every particular member being excluded, the community comes to be umpire; and by understanding indifferent rules and men authorized by the community for their execution, decides all the differences that may happen between any members of that society concerning any matter of right, and punishes those offenses which any member hath committed against the society with such penalties as the law has established; whereby it is easy to discern who are and who are not in political society together. Those who are united into one body, and have a common established law and judicature to appeal to, with authority to decide controversies between them and punish offenders, are in civil society one with another; but those who have no such common appeal—I mean on earth—are still in the state of nature, each being, where there is no other, judge for himself and executioner, which is, as I have before shown it, the perfect state of nature.

88. And thus the commonwealth comes by a power to set down what punishment shall belong to the several transgressions which they think worthy of it committed amongst the members of that society, which is the power of making laws, as well as it has the power to punish any injury done unto any of its members by anyone that is not of it, which is the power of war and peace; and all this for the preservation of the

property of all the members of that society as far as is possible. But though every man entered into civil society, has quitted his power to punish offenses against the law of nature in prosecution of his own private judgment, yet with the judgment of offenses, which he has given up to the legislative in all cases where he can appeal to the magistrate, he has given a right to the commonwealth to employ his force for the execution of the judgments of the commonwealth whenever he shall be called to it; which, indeed, are his own judgments, they being made by himself or his representative. And herein we have the original of the legislative and executive power of civil society, which is to judge by standing laws how far offenses are to be punished when committed within the commonwealth, and also by occasional judgments founded on the present circumstances of the fact, how far injuries from without are to be vindicated; and in both these to employ all the force of all the members when there shall be need.

89. Wherever, therefore, any number of men so unite into one society, as to quit everyone his executive power of the law of nature, and to resign it to the public, there, and there only, is a political, or civil society. And this is done wherever any number of men, in the state of nature, enter into society to make one people, one body politic, under one supreme government, or else when anyone joins himself to, and incorporates with, any government already made. For hereby he authorises the society, or, which is all one, the legislative thereof, to make laws for him, as the public good of the society shall require, to the execution whereof his own assistance (as to his own decrees) is due. And this puts men out of a state of nature into that of a commonwealth, by setting up a judge on earth with authority to determine all the controversies and redress the injuries that may happen to any member of the commonwealth; which judge is the legislative, or magistrates appointed by it. And wherever there are any number of men, however associated, that have no such decisive power to appeal to, there they are still in the state of nature.

90. Hence it is evident that absolute monarchy, which by some men is counted the only government in the world, is indeed inconsistent with civil society, and so can be no form of civil government at all. For the end of civil society being to avoid and remedy those inconveniences of the state of nature which necessarily follow from every man's being judge in his own case, by setting up a known authority to which everyone of that society may appeal upon any injury received or controversy that may arise, and which every one of the society ought to obey; wherever any persons are who have not such an authority to appeal to and decide any difference between them there, those persons are still in

the state of nature. And so is every absolute prince, in respect of those who are under his dominion.

91. For he being supposed to have all, both legislative and executive power in himself alone, there is no judge to be found; no appeal lies open to anyone who may fairly and indifferently and with authority decide, and from whence relief and address may be expected of any injury or inconvenience that may be suffered from or by his order; so that such a man, however entitled—Czar, or Grand Seignior, or how you please— is as much in the state of nature, with all under his dominion, as he is with the rest of mankind. For wherever any two men are, who have no standing rule and common judge to appeal to on earth for the determination of controversies of right betwixt them, there they are still in the state of nature, and under all the inconveniences of it, with only this woful difference to the subject, or rather slave, of an absolute prince: that, whereas in the ordinary state of nature he has a liberty to judge of his right, and according to the best of his power to maintain it, now, whenever his property is invaded by the will and order of his monarch, he has not only no appeal, as those in the society ought to have, but, as if he were degraded from the common state of rational creatures, is de· nied a liberty to judge of or to defend his right; and so is exposed to all the misery and inconveniences that a man can fear from one who, being in the unrestrained state of nature, is yet corrupted with flattery, and armed with power.

92. For he that thinks absolute power purifies men's blood, and corrects the baseness of human nature, need read but the history of this or any other age, to be convinced of the contrary. He that would have been insolent and injurious in the woods of America, would not probably be much better in a throne; where, perhaps, learning and religion shall be found out to justify all that he shall do to his subjects, and the sword presently silence all those that dare question it. For what the protection of absolute monarchy is, what kind of fathers of their countries it makes princes to be, and to what a degree of happiness and security it carries civil society, where this sort of government is grown to perfection, he that will look into the late relation of Ceylon may easily see.

93. In absolute monarchies, indeed, as well as other governments of the world, the subjects have an appeal to the law, and judges to decide any controversies and restrain any violence that may happen betwixt the subjects themselves, one amongst another. This everyone thinks necessary, and believes he deserves to be thought a declared enemy to society and mankind who should go about to take it away. But whether this be from a true love of mankind and society, and such a charity as we owe all one to another, there is reason to doubt. For this is no more than

that every man who loves his own power, profit, or greatness may, and naturally must do, keep those animals from hurting or destroying one another who labor and drudge only for his pleasure and advantage; and so are taken care of, not out of any love the master has for them, but love of himself, and the profit they bring him. For if it be asked, what security, what fence is there, in such a state, against the violence and oppression of this absolute ruler, the very question can scarce be borne. They are ready to tell you that it deserves death only to ask after safety. Betwixt subject and subject they will grant there must be measures, laws and judges, for their mutual peace and security; but as for the ruler, he ought to be absolute, and is above all such circumstances; because he has power to do more hurt and wrong, 'tis right when he does it. To ask how you may be guarded from harm or injury on that side where the strongest hand is to do it, is presently the voice of faction and rebellion. As if when men quitting the state of nature entered into society, they agreed that all of them but one should be under the restraint of laws, but that he should still retain all the liberty of the state of natu e, increased with power, and made licentious by impunity. This is to think that men are so foolish that they take care to avoid what mischiefs may be done them by polecats or foxes, but are content, nay, think it safety, to be devoured by lions.

94. But, whatever flatterers may talk to amuse people's understandings, it never hinders men from feeling; and when they perceive that any man, in what station soever, is out of the bounds of the civil society they are of, and that they have no appeal on earth against any harm they may receive from him, they are apt to think themselves in the state of nature in respect of him whom they find to be so; and to take care, as soon as they can, to have that safety and security in civil society for which it was first instituted, and for which only they entered into it. And, therefore, though perhaps at first (as shall be shown more at large hereafter in the following part of this discourse), some one good and excellent man, having got a pre-eminence amongst the rest, had this deference paid to his goodness and virtue, as to a kind of natural authority, that the chief rule, with arbitration of their differences, by a tacit consent devolved into his hands, without any other caution but the assurance they had of his uprightness and wisdom; yet when time, giving authority and (as some men would persuade us) sacredness to customs which the negligent and unforeseeing innocence of the first ages began, had brought in successors of another stamp, the people finding their properties not secure under the government, as then it was (whereas government has no other end but the preservation of property), could never be safe nor at rest, nor think themselves in civil society, till the legislative was placed in collective bodies of men, call them Senate, Parlia-

ment, or what you please. By which means every single person became subject, equally with other the meanest men, to those laws, which he himself, as part of the legislative, had established; nor could anyone by his own authority avoid the force of the law when once made, nor by any pretense of superiority plead exemption, thereby to license his own, or the miscarriages of any of his dependents. No man in civil society can be exempted from the laws of it. For if any man may do what he thinks fit, and there be no appeal on earth for redress or security against any harm he shall do, I ask whether he be not perfectly still in the state of nature, and so can be no part or member of that civil society; unless anyone will say the state of nature and civil society are one and the same thing, which I have never yet found anyone so great a patron of anarchy as to affirm.

CHAPTER VIII

OF THE BEGINNING OF POLITICAL SOCIETIES

95. MEN BEING, as has been said, by nature all free, equal, and independent, no one can be put out of this estate, and subjected to the political power of another, without his own consent, which is done by agreeing with other men to join and unite into a community for their comfortable, safe, and peaceable living one amongst another, in a secure enjoyment of their properties, and a greater security against any that are not of it. This any number of men may do, because it injures not the freedom of the rest; they are left as they were in the liberty of the state of nature. When any number of men have so consented to make one community or government, they are thereby presently incorporated, and make one body public, wherein the majority have a right to act and conclude the rest.

96. For when any number of men have, by the consent of every individual, made a community, they have thereby made that community one body, with a power to act as one body, which is only by the will and determination of the majority. For that which acts any community being only the consent of the individuals of it, and it being one body must move one way, it is necessary the body should move that way whither the greater force carries it, which is the consent of the majority; or else it is impossible it should act or continue one body, one community, which the consent of every individual that united into it agreed that it should; and so everyone is bound by that consent to be concluded by the majority. And therefore we see that in assemblies empowered to act by positive laws, where no number is set by that positive law which em-

powers them, the act of the majority passes for the act of the whole, and of course determines, as having by the law of nature and reason the power of the whole.

97. And thus every man, by consenting with others to make one body politic under one government, puts himself under an obligation to every one of that society, to submit to the determination of the majority, and to be concluded by it; or else this original compact, whereby he with others incorporates into one society, would signify nothing, and be no compact, if he be left free and under no other ties than he was in before in the state of nature. For what appearance would there be of any compact? What new engagement if he were no farther tied by any decrees of the society, than he himself thought fit, and did actually consent to? This would be still as great a liberty as he himself had before his compact, or anyone else in the state of nature hath, who may submit himself and consent to any acts of it if he thinks fit.

98. For if the consent of the majority shall not in reason be received as the act of the whole and conclude every individual, nothing but the consent of every individual can make anything to be the act of the whole, which considering the infirmities of health and avocations of business, which in a number, though much less than that of a commonwealth, will necessarily keep many away from the public assembly, and the variety of opinions, and contrariety of interest, which unavoidably happen in all collections of men, 'tis next to impossible ever to be had. And therefore if the coming into society be upon such terms it will be only like Cato's coming into the theater, *tantum ut exiret*. Such a constitution as this would make the mighty leviathan of a shorter duration than the feeblest creatures, and not let it outlast the day it was born in; which cannot be supposed till we can think that rational creatures should desire and constitute societies only to be dissolved. For where the majority cannot conclude the rest, there they cannot act as one body, and consequently will be immediately dissolved again.

99. Whosoever therefore out of a state of nature unite into a community must be understood to give up all the power necessary to the ends for which they unite into society, to the majority of the community, unless they expressly agreed in any number greater than the majority. And this is done by barely agreeing to unite into one political society, which is all the compact that is, or needs be, between the individuals that enter into or make up a commonwealth. And thus that which begins and actually constitutes any political society is nothing but the consent of any number of freemen capable of a majority to unite and incorporate into such a society. And this is that, and that only, which did or could give beginning to any lawful government in the world.

100. To this I find two objections made.

First: That there are no instances to be found in story of a company of men independent, and equal one amongst another, that met together and in this way began and set up a government.

Secondly: 'Tis impossible of right that men should do so, because all men being born under government, they are to submit to that, and are not at liberty to begin a new one.

101. To the first there is this to answer—That it is not at all to be wondered that history gives us but a very little account of men that lived together in the state of nature. The inconveniences of that condition, and the love and want of society, no sooner brought any number of them together, but they presently united and incorporated if they designed to continue together. And if we may not suppose men ever to have been in the state of nature, because we hear not much of them in such a state, we may as well suppose the armies of Salmanasser or Xerxes were never children, because we hear little of them till they were men, and embodied in armies. Government is everywhere antecedent to records, and letters seldom come in amongst a people, till a long continuation of civil society has, by other more necessary arts, provided for their safety, ease, and plenty. And then they begin to look after the history of their founders, and search into their original, when they have outlived the memory of it. For 'tis with commonwealths as with particular persons, they are commonly ignorant of their own birth and infancies. And if they know anything of their original, they are beholden for it to the accidental records that others have kept of it. And those that we have of the beginning of any polities in the world, excepting that of the Jews, where God Himself immediately interposed, and which favors not at all paternal dominion, are all either plain instances of such a beginning as I have mentioned, or at least have manifest footsteps of it.

102. He must show a strange inclination to deny evident matter of fact, when it agrees not with his hypothesis, who will not allow that the beginning of Rome and Venice were by the uniting together of several men, free and independent one of another, amongst whom there was no natural superiority or subjection. And if Josephus Acosta's word may be taken, he tells us that in many parts of America there was no government at all. "There are great and apparent conjectures," says he, "that these men (speaking of those of Peru) for a long time had neither kings nor commonwealths, but lived in troops, as they do this day in Florida —the Cheriquanas, those of Brazil, and many other nations, which have no certain kings, but, as occasion is offered in peace or war, they choose their captains as they please" (Lib. i. cap. 25). If it be said, that every man there was born subject to his father, or the head of his family, that

the subjection due from a child to a father took not away his freedom of uniting into what political society he thought fit, has been already proved; but be that as it will, these men, it is evident, were actually free; and whatever superiority some politicians now would place in any of them, they themselves claimed it not; but, by consent, were all equal, till, by the same consent, they set rulers over themselves. So that their politic societies all began from a voluntary union, and the mutual agreement of men freely acting in the choice of their governors and forms of government.

103. And I hope those who went away from Sparta, with Palantus, mentioned by Justin, will be allowed to have been freemen independent one of another, and to have set up a government over themselves by their own consent. Thus I have given several examples out of history of people, free and in the state of nature, that, being met together, incorporated and began a commonwealth. And if the want of such instances be an argument to prove that government were not nor could not be so begun, I suppose the contenders for paternal empire were better let it alone than urge it against natural liberty; for if they can give so many instances out of history of governments began upon paternal right, I think (though at least an argument from what has been to what should of right be of no great force) one might, without any great danger, yield them the cause. But if I might advise them in the case, they would do well not to search too much into the original of governments as they have begun *de facto,* lest they should find at the foundation of most of them something very little favorable to the design they promote, and such a power as they contend for.

104. But, to conclude: reason being plain on our side that men are naturally free; and the examples of history showing that the governments of the world, that were begun in peace, had their beginning laid on that foundation, and were made by the consent of the people; there can be little room for doubt, either where the right is, or what has been the opinion or practice of mankind about the first erecting of governments.

105. I will not deny that if we look back, as far as history will direct us, towards the original of commonwealths, we shall generally find them under the government and administration of one man. And I am also apt to believe that where a family was numerous enough to subsist by itself, and continued entire together, without mixing with others, as it often happens, where there is much land and few people, the government commonly began in the father. For the father having, by the law of nature, the same power, with every man else, to punish, as he thought fit, any offenses against that law, might thereby punish his transgressing chil-

dren, even when they were men, and out of their pupilage; and they were very likely to submit to his punishment, and all join with him against the offender in their turns, giving him thereby power to execute his sentence against any transgression, and so, in effect, make him the law-maker and governor over all that remained in conjunction with his family. He was fittest to be trusted; paternal affection secured their property and interest under his care, and the custom of obeying him in their childhood made it easier to submit to him rather than any other. If, therefore, they must have one to rule them, as government is hardly to be avoided amongst men that live together, who so likely to be the man as he that was their common father, unless negligence, cruelty, or any other defect of mind or body, made him unfit for it. But when either the father died, and left his next heir—for want of age, wisdom, courage, or any other qualities—less fit for rule, or where several families met and consented to continue together, there, it is not to be doubted, but they used their natural freedom to set up him whom they judged the ablest and most likely to rule well over them. Conformable hereunto we find the people of America, who—living out of the reach of the conquering swords and spreading domination of the two great empires of Peru and Mexico—enjoyed their own natural freedom, though, *ceteris paribus,* they commonly prefer the heir of their deceased king; yet, if they find him any way weak or incapable, they pass him by, and set up the stoutest and bravest man for their ruler.

106. Thus, though looking back as far as records give us any account of peopling the world, and the history of nations, we commonly find the government to be in one hand; yet it destroys not that which I affirm, viz.: that the beginning of politic society depends upon the consent of the individuals to join into, and make one society; who when they are thus incorporated, might set up what form of government they thought fit. But this having given occasion to men to mistake, and think that by nature government was monarchical, and belonged to the father, it may not be amiss here to consider why people in the beginning generally pitched upon this form, which, though perhaps the father's pre-eminence might in the first institution of some commonwealths give a rise to, and place in the beginning, the power in one hand; yet it is plain that the reason that continued the form of government in a single person was not any regard or respect to paternal authority, since all petty monarchies, that is, almost all monarchies, near their original, have been commonly— at least upon occasion—elective.

107. First then, in the beginning of things, the father's government of the childhood of those sprung from him having accustomed them to the rule of one man, and taught them that where it was exercised with care

and skill, with affection and love to those under it, it was sufficient to procure and preserve men all the political happiness they sought for in society. It was no wonder that they should pitch upon and naturally run into that form of government, which from their infancy they had been all accustomed to, and which, by experience, they had found both easy and safe. To which, if we add, that monarchy being simple and most obvious to men whom neither experience had instructed in forms of government, nor the ambition or insolence of empire had taught to beware of the encroachments of prerogative, or the inconveniences of absolute power, which monarchy in succession was apt to lay claim to, and bring upon them; it was not at all strange that they should not much trouble themselves to think of methods of restraining any exorbitances of those to whom they had given the authority over them, and of balancing the power of government, by placing several parts of it in different hands. They had neither felt the oppression of tyrannical dominion, nor did the fashion of the age, nor their possessions or way of living (which afforded little matter for covetousness or ambition), give them any reason to apprehend or provide against it; and therefore it is no wonder they put themselves into such a frame of government as was not only, as I said, most obvious and simple, but also best suited to their present state and condition, which stood more in need of defense against foreign invasions and injuries than of multiplicity of laws, where there was but very little property; and wanted not variety of rulers and abundance of officers to direct and look after their execution, where there were but few trespasses and few offenders. Since, then, those who liked one another so well as to join into society, cannot but be supposed to have some acquaintance and friendship together, and some trust one in another, they could not but have greater apprehensions of others than of one of another; and therefore their first care and thought cannot but be supposed to be how to secure themselves against foreign force. It was natural for them to put themselves under a frame of government which might best serve to that end; and choose the wisest and bravest man to conduct them in their wars, and lead them out against their enemies, and in this chiefly be their ruler.

108. Thus we see that the kings of the Indians, in America, which is still a pattern of the first ages in Asia and Europe, whilst the inhabitants were too few for the country, and want of people and money gave men no temptation to enlarge their possessions of land or contest for wider extent of ground, are little more than generals of their armies; and though they command absolutely in war, yet at home, and in time of peace, they exercise very little dominion, and have but a very moderate sovereignty, the resolutions of peace and war being ordinarily either in the people or in a council, though the war itself, which admits not of

pluralities of governors, naturally evolves the command into the king's sole authority.

109. And thus, in Israel itself, the chief business of their judges and first kings seems to have been to be captanis in war and leaders of their armies, which (besides what is signified by "going out and in before the people," which was, to march forth to war and home again at the heads of their forces) appears plainly in the story of Jephtha. The Ammonites making war upon Israel, the Gileadites, in fear, send to Jephtha, a bastard of their family, whom they had cast off, and article with him, if he will assist them against the Ammonites, to make him their ruler, which they do in these words: "And the people made him head and captain over them" (Judges xi. 11), which was, as it seems, all one as to be judge. "And he judged Israel" (Judges xii. 7)—that is, was their captain-general—"six years." So when Jotham upbraids the Shechemites with the obligation they had to Gideon, who had been their judge and ruler, he tells them: "He fought for you, and adventured his life for, and delivered you out of the hands of Midian" (Judges ix. 17). Nothing mentioned of him but what he did as a general, and, indeed, that is all is found in his history, or in any of the rest of the judges. And Abimelech particularly is called king, though at most he was but their general. And when, being weary of the ill-conduct of Samuel's sons, the children of Israel desired a king, "like all the nations, to judge them, and to go out before them, and to fight their battles" (1 Sam. viii. 20), God, granting their desire, says to Samuel, "I will send thee a man, and thou shalt anoint him to be captain over my people Israel, that he may save my people out of the hands of the Philistines" (ix. 16). As if the only business of a king had been to lead out their armies and fight in their defense; and, accordingly, at his inauguration, pouring a vial of oil upon him, declares to Saul that "the Lord had anointed him to be captain over his inheritance" (x. 1). And therefore those who, after Saul's being solemnly chosen and saluted king by the tribes at Mispah, were unwilling to have him their king, make no other objection but this, "How shall this man save us?" (v. 27), as if they should have said: "This man is unfit to be our king, not having skill and conduct enough in war to be able to defend us." And when God resolved to transfer the government to David, it is in these words: "But now thy kingdom shall not continue: the Lord hath sought him a man after His own heart, and the Lord hath commanded him to be captain over His people" (xiii. 14). As if the whole kingly authority were nothing else but to be their general; and therefore the tribes who had stuck to Saul's family, and opposed David's reign, when they came to Hebron with terms of submission to him, they tell him, amongst other arguments, they had to submit to him as to their king, that he was, in effect, their king in Saul's time, and

therefore they had no reason but to receive him as their king now. "Also," say they, "in time past, when Saul was king over us, thou wast he that leddest out and broughtest in Israel, and the Lord said unto thee, Thou shalt feed my people Israel, and thou shalt be a captain over Israel."

110. Thus, whether a family, by degrees, grew up into a commonwealth, and the fatherly authority being continued on to the elder son, everyone in his turn growing up under it tacitly submitted to it, and the easiness and equality of it not offending anyone, everyone acquiesced till time seemed to have confirmed it and settled a right of succession by prescription; or whether several families, or the descendants of several families, whom chance, neighborhood, or business brought together, united into society; the need of a general whose conduct might defend them against their enemies in war, and the great confidence the innocence and sincerity of that poor but virtuous age, such as are almost all those which begin governments that ever come to last in the world, gave men one of another, made the first beginners of commonwealths generally put the rule into one man's hand, without any other express limitation or restraint but what the nature of the thing and the end of government required. It was given them for the public good and safety, and to those ends, in the infancies of commonwealths, they commonly used it; and unless they had done so, young societies could not have subsisted. Without such nursing fathers, without this care of the governors, all governments would have sunk under the weakness and infirmities of their infancy, the prince and the people had soon perished together.

111. But the golden age (though before vain ambition, and *amor sceleratus habendi,* evil concupiscence had corrupted men's minds into a mistake of true power and honor) had more virtue, and consequently better governors, as well as less vicious subjects; and there was then no stretching prerogative on the one side to oppress the people, nor, consequently, on the other, any dispute about privilege, to lessen or restrain the power of the magistrate; and so no contest betwixt rulers and people about governors or government. Yet, when ambition and luxury, in future ages, would retain and increase the power, without doing the business for which it was given, and aided by flattery, taught princes to have distinct and separate interests from their people, men found it necessary to examine more carefully the original and rights of government, and to find out ways to restrain the exorbitances and prevent the abuses of that power, which they having entrusted in another's hands, only for their own good, they found was made use of to hurt them.

112. Thus we may see how probable it is that people that were naturally free, and by their own consent either submitted to the govern-

ment of their father, or united together out of different families to make a government, should generally put the rule into one man's hands, and choose to be under the conduct of a single person, without so much as by express conditions limiting or regulating his power, which they thought safe enough in his honesty and prudence, though they never dreamt of monarchy being *jure divino,* which we never heard of among mankind till it was revealed to us by the divinity of this last age, nor ever allowed paternal power to have a right to dominion, or to be the foundation of all government. And thus much may suffice to show that, as far as we have any light from history, we have reason to conclude that all peaceful beginnings of government have been laid in the consent of the people. I say peaceful, because I shall have occasion in another place to speak of conquest, which some esteem a way of beginning of governments.

The other objection I find urged against the beginning of polities in the way I have mentioned is this, viz.:—

113. That all men being born under government, some or other, it is impossible any of them should ever be free and at liberty to unite to-gether and begin a new one, or ever be able to erect a lawful govern-ment.

If this argument be good, I ask, how came so many lawful monarchies into the world? For if anybody, upon this supposition, can show me any one man, in any age of the world, free to begin a lawful monarchy, I will be bound to show him ten other free men at liberty at the same time to unite and begin a new government under a regal, or any other form, it being demonstration that if anyone, born under the dominion of another, may be so free as to have a right to command others in a new and distinct empire, everyone that is born under the dominion of another may be so free too, and may become a ruler or subject of a distinct sep-arate government. And so by this their own principle either all men, however born, are free, or else there is but one lawful prince, one lawful government in the world. And then they have nothing to do but barely to show us which that is; which, when they have done, I doubt not but all mankind will easily agree to pay obedience to him.

114. Though it be a sufficient answer to their objection to show that it involves them in the same difficulties that it doth those they use it against, yet I shall endeavor to discover the weakness of this argument a little farther.

"All men," say they, "are born under government, and therefore they cannot be at liberty to begin a new one. Everyone is born a subject to his father, or his prince, and is therefore under the perpetual tie of sub-jection and allegiance." It is plain mankind never owned nor considered any such natural subjection that they were born in, to one or to the other that tied them without their own consents, to a subjection to them and their heirs.

115. For there are no examples so frequent in history, both sacred and profane, as those of men withdrawing themselves and their obedience from the jurisdiction they were born under, and the family or community they were bred up in, and setting up new governments in other places; from whence sprang all that number of petty commonwealths in the beginning of ages, and which always multiplied, as long as there was room enough, till the stronger or more fortunate swallowed the weaker; and those great ones again breaking to pieces, dissolved into lesser dominions, all which are so many testimonies against paternal sovereignty, and plainly prove that it was not the natural right of the father descending to his heirs that made government in the beginning, since it was impossible upon that ground there should have been so many little kingdoms, but only one universal monarchy if men had not been at liberty to separate themselves from their families and their government, be it what it will, that was set up in it, and go and make distinct commonwealths and other governments as they thought fit.

116. This has been the practice of the world from its first beginning to this day; nor is it now any more hindrance to the freedom of mankind that they are born under constituted and ancient polities that have established laws and set forms of government, than if they were born in the woods amongst the unconfined inhabitants that run loose in them. For those who would persuade us that by being born under any government we are naturally subjects to it, and have no more any title or pretense to the freedom of the state of nature, have no other reason (bating that of paternal power, which we have already answered) to produce for it, but only because our fathers or progenitors passed away their natural liberty, and thereby bound up themselves and their posterity to a perpetual subjection to the government which they themselves submitted to. It is true that whatever engagements or promises anyone made for himself, he is under the obligation of them, but cannot by any compact whatsoever bind his children or posterity. For his son when a man being altogether as free as his father, any act of the father can no more give away the liberty of the son than it can of anybody else. He may indeed annex such conditions to the land he enjoyed as a subject of any commonwealth as may oblige his son to be of that community, if he will enjoy those possessions which were his father's, because that estate being his father's property he may dispose or settle it as he pleases.

117. And this has generally given the occasion to the mistake in this matter, because commonwealths not permitting any part of their dominions to be dismembered, nor to be enjoyed by any but those of their

community, the son cannot ordinarily enjoy the possessions of his father but under the same terms his father did: by becoming a member of the society; whereby he puts himself presently under the government he finds there established as much as any other subject of that common-wealth. And thus the consent of freemen, born under government, which only makes them members of it, being given separately in their turns, as each comes to be of age, and not in a multitude together. People take no notice of it, and thinking it not done at all, or not necessary, conclude they are naturally subjects as they are men.

118. But it is plain governments themselves understand it otherwise; they claim no power over the son, because of that they had over the father; nor look on children as being their subjects by their father's be-ing so. If a subject of England have a child by an English woman in France, whose subject is he? Not the King of England's, for he must have leave to be admitted to the privileges of it; nor the King of France's, for how then has his father a liberty to bring him away and breed him as he pleases? And whoever was judged as a traitor or de-serter, if he left or warred against a country, for being barely born in it of parents that were aliens there? It is plain then by the practice of governments themselves, as well as by the law of right reason, that a child is born a subject of no country or government. He is under his father's tuition and authority till he comes to age of discretion, and then he is a freeman, at liberty what government he will put himself under, what body politic he will unite himself to. For if an English-man's son, born in France, be at liberty, and may do so, it is evident there is no tie upon him by his father's being a subject of that king-dom; nor is he bound up by any compact of his ancestors. And why then hath not his son by the same reason, the same liberty, though he be born anywhere else? Since the power that a father hath naturally over his children is the same wherever they be born, and the ties of nat-ural obligations are not bounded by the positive limits of kingdoms and commonwealths.

119. Every man being, as has been shown, naturally free, and nothing being able to put him into subjection to any earthly power but only his own consent, it is to be considered what shall be understood to be suffi-cient declaration of a man's consent to make him subject to the laws of any government. There is a common distinction of an express and a tacit consent, which will concern our present case. Nobody doubts but an ex-press consent of any man entering into any society makes him a perfect member of that society, a subject of that government. The difficulty is, what ought to be looked upon as a tacit consent, and how far it binds, i.e., how far anyone shall be looked on to have consented, and thereby submitted to any government, where he has made no expressions of it at

all. And to this I say that every man that hath any possession or enjoy-ment of any part of the dominions of any government doth thereby give his tacit consent, and is as far forth obliged to obedience to the laws of that government during such enjoyment as anyone under it; whether this his possession be of land to him and his heirs for ever, or a lodging only for a week; or whether it be barely traveling freely on the high-way; and in effect it reaches as far as the very being of anyone within the territories of that government.

120. To understand this the better, it is fit to consider that every man when he at first incorporates himself into any commonwealth, he, by his uniting himself thereunto, annexed also, and submits to the com-munity those possessions which he has or shall acquire that do not al-ready belong to any other government; for it would be a direct contra-diction for anyone to enter into society with others for the securing and regulating of property, and yet to suppose his land, whose property is to be regulated by the laws of the society, should be exempt from the ju-risdiction of that government to which he himself, and the property of the land, is a subject. By the same act, therefore, whereby anyone unites his person, which was before free, to any commonwealth, by the same he unites his possessions, which was before free, to it also; and they be-come, both of them, person and possession, subject to the government and dominion of that commonwealth as long as it hath a being. Whoever therefore from thenceforth by inheritance, purchases, permission, or otherwise, enjoys any part of the land so annexed to, and under the gov-ernment of that commonwealth, must take it with the condition it is under, that is, of submitting to the government of the commonwealth under whose jurisdiction it is as far forth as any subject of it.

121. But since the government has a direct jurisdiction only over the land, and reaches the possessor of it (before he has actually incorporated himself in the society), only as he dwells upon, and enjoys that: the ob-ligation anyone is under, by virtue of such enjoyment, to submit to the government, begins and ends with the enjoyment; so that whenever the owner, who has given nothing but such a tacit consent to the govern-ment, will by donation, sale, or otherwise, quit the said possession, he is at liberty to go and incorporate himself into any other commonwealth, or to agree with others to begin a new one (*in vacuis locis*) in any part of the world they can find free and unpossessed. Whereas he that has once by actual agreement and any express declaration given his consent to be of any commonweal is perpetually and indispensably obliged to be and remain unalterably a subject to it, and can never be again in the liberty of the state of nature; unless, by any calamity, the government he was under comes to be dissolved, or else by some public acts cuts him off from being any longer a member of it.

122. But submitting to the laws of any country, living quietly and enjoying privileges and protection under them makes not a man a member of that society. This is only a local protection and homage due to and from all those who, not being in the state of war, come within the territories belonging to any government to all parts whereof the force of its law extends. But this no more makes a man a member of that society a perpetual subject of that commonwealth, than it would make a man a subject to another in whose family he found it convenient to abide for some time; though whilst he continued in it he were obliged to comply with the laws, and submit to the government he found there. And thus we see, that foreigners by living all their lives under another government, and enjoying the privileges and protection of it, though they are bound even in conscience to submit to its administration as far forth as any denizen, yet do not thereby come to be subjects or members of that commonwealth. Nothing can make any man so, but his actually entering into it by positive engagement, and express promise and compact. This is that, which I think, concerning the beginning of political societies, and that consent which makes anyone a member of any commonwealth.

CHAPTER IX

OF THE ENDS OF POLITICAL SOCIETY AND GOVERNMENT

123. IF MAN in the state of nature be so free, as has been said, if he be absolute lord of his own person and possessions, equal to the greatest, and subject to nobody, why will he part with his freedom, this empire, and subject himself to the dominion and control of any other power? To which, it is obvious to answer, that though in the state of nature he hath such a right, yet the enjoyment of it is very uncertain, and constantly exposed to the invasions of others. For all being kings as much as he, every man his equal, and the greater part no strict observers of equity and justice, the enjoyment of the property he has in this state is very unsafe, very unsecure. This makes him willing to quit this condition, which, however free, is full of fears and continual dangers; and it is not without reason that he seeks out and is willing to join in society with others, who are already united, or have a mind to unite, for the mutual preservation of their lives, liberties, and estates, which I call by the general name, property.

124. The great and chief end, therefore, of men's uniting into commonwealths, and putting themselves under government, is the preservation of their property; to which in the state of nature there are many things wanting.

First, There wants an established, settled, known law, received and allowed by common consent to be the standard of right and wrong, and the common measure to decide all controversies between them. For though the law of nature be plain and intelligible to all rational creatures; yet men, being biased by their interest, as well as ignorant for want of study of it, are not apt to allow of it as a law binding to them in the application of it to their particular cases.

125. Secondly, In the state of nature there wants a known and indifferent judge, with authority to determine all differences according to the established law. For everyone in that state, being both judge and executioner of the law of nature, men being partial to themselves, passion and revenge is very apt to carry them too far, and with too much heat in their own cases, as well as negligence and unconcernedness, to make them too remiss in other men's.

126. Thirdly, In the state of nature there often wants power to back and support the sentence when right, and to give it due execution. They who by any injustice offend, will seldom fail, where they are able by force to make good their injustice; such resistance many times makes the punishment dangerous, and frequently destructive to those who attempt it.

127. Thus mankind, notwithstanding all the privileges of the state of nature, being but in an ill condition, while they remain in it, are quickly driven into society. Hence it comes to pass that we seldom find any number of men live any time together in this state. The inconveniences that they are therein exposed to by the irregular and uncertain exercise of the power every man has of punishing the transgressions of others, make them take sanctuary under the established laws of government, and therein seek the preservation of their property. It is this makes them so willingly give up everyone his single power of punishing, to be exercised by such alone, as shall be appointed to it amongst them; and by such rules as the community, or those authorized by them to that purpose, shall agree on. And in this we have the original right and rise of both the legislative and executive power, as well as of the governments and societies themselves.

128. For in the state of nature, to omit the liberty he has of innocent delights, a man has two powers.

The first is to do whatsoever he thinks fit for the preservation of himself, and others within the permission of the law of nature, by which law, common to them all, he and all the rest of mankind are of one community, make up one society, distinct from all other creatures. And were it not for the corruption and viciousness of degenerate men there would be no need of any other, no necessity that men should separate from this great and natural community, and associate into lesser combinations.

The other power a man has in the state of nature is the power to punish the crimes committed against that law. Both these he gives up when he joins in a private, if I may so call it, or particular political society, and incorporates into any commonwealth separate from the rest of mankind.

129. The first power, viz., of doing whatsoever he thought fit for the preservation of himself and the rest of mankind, he gives up to be regulated by laws made by the society, so far forth as the preservation of himself and the rest of that society shall require; which laws of the society in many things confine the liberty he had by the law of nature.

130. Secondly, The power of punishing he wholly gives up, and engages his natural force (which he might before employ in the execution of the law of nature, by his own single authority as he thought fit), to assist the executive power of the society, as the law thereof shall require. For being now in a new state, wherein he is to enjoy many conveniences, from the labor, assistance, and society of others in the same community, as well as protection from its whole strength; he has to part also with as much of his natural liberty, in providing for himself, as the good, prosperity and safety of the society shall require; which is not only necessary but just, since the other members of the society do the like.

131. But though men when they enter into society give up the equality, liberty and executive power they had in the state of nature into the hands of the society, to be so far disposed of by the legislative as the good of the society shall require; yet it being only with an intention in everyone the better to preserve himself, his liberty and property (for no rational creature can be supposed to change his condition with an intention to be worse), the power of the society, or legislative constituted by them, can never be supposed to extend farther than the common good, but is obliged to secure everyone's property by providing against those three defects above-mentioned that made the state of nature so unsafe and uneasy. And so whoever has the legislative or supreme power of any commonwealth is bound to govern by established standing laws, promulgated and known to the people, and not by extemporary decrees; by indifferent and upright judges, who are to decide controversies by those laws; and to employ the force of the community at home only in the execution of such laws, or abroad, to prevent or redress foreign injuries, and secure the community from inroads and invasion. And all this to be directed to no other end but the peace, safety, and public good of the people.

CHAPTER X

OF THE FORMS OF A COMMONWEALTH

132. THE MAJORITY having, as has been shown, upon men's first uniting into society, the whole power of the community, naturally in them, may employ all that power in making laws for the community from time to time, and executing those laws by officers of their own appointing: and then the form of the government is a perfect democracy; or else may put the power of making laws into the hands of a few select men, and their heirs or successors, and then it is an oligarchy; or else into the hands of one man and then it is a monarchy; if to him and his heirs, it is an hereditary monarchy; if to him only for life, but upon his death the power only of nominating a successor to return to them, an elective monarchy. And so accordingly of these, the community may make compounded and mixed forms of government, as they think good. And if the legislative power be at first given by the majority to one or more persons only for their lives, or any limited time, and then the supreme power to revert to them again; when it is so reverted, the community may dispose of it again anew into what hands they please, and so constitute a new form of government. For the form of government depending upon the placing of the supreme power, which is the legislative, it being impossible to conceive that an inferior power should prescribe to a superior, or any but the supreme make laws, according as the power of making laws is placed, such is the form of the commonwealth.

133. By commonwealth, I must be understood all along to mean, not a democracy, or any form of government, but any independent community which the Latins signified by the word *civitas,* to which the word which best answers in our language is commonwealth, and most properly expresses such a society of men, which community does not, for there may be subordinate communities in a government; and city much less. And therefore to avoid ambiguity I crave leave to use the word commonwealth in that sense, in which I find it used by King James himself, which I think to be its genuine signification; which if anybody dislike, I consent with him to change it for a better.

CHAPTER XI

OF THE EXTENT OF THE LEGISLATIVE POWER

134. THE GREAT end of men's entering into society being the enjoy-ment of their properties in peace and safety, and the great instrument and means of that being the laws established in that society: the first and fundamental positive law of all commonwealths, is the establishing of the legislative power; as the first and fundamental natural law which is to govern even the legislative itself, is the preservation of the society, and (as far as will consist with the public good) of every person in it. This legislative is not only the supreme power of the commonwealth, but sacred and unalterable in the hands where the community have once placed it; nor can any edict of anybody else, in what form soever con-ceived, or by what power soever backed, have the force and obligation of a law, which has not its sanction from that legislative which the pub-lic has chosen and appointed. For without this the law could not have that, which is absolutely necessary to its being a law, the consent of the society over whom nobody can have a power to make laws; but by their own consent, and by authority received from them; and therefore all the obedience, which by the most solemn ties anyone can be obliged to pay, ultimately terminates in this supreme power, and is directed by those laws which it enacts; nor can any oaths to any foreign power whatso-ever, or any domestic subordinate power discharge any member of the society from his obedience to the legislative, acting pursuant to their trust; nor oblige him to any obedience contrary to the laws so enacted, or farther than they do allow; it being ridiculous to imagine one can be tied ultimately to obey any power in the society which is not the su-preme.

135. Though the legislative, whether placed in one or more, whether it be always in being, or only by intervals, though it be the supreme power in every commonwealth, yet,

First, It is not nor can possibly be absolutely arbitrary over the lives and fortunes of the people. For it being but the joint power of every member of the society given up to that person, or assembly, which is legislator; it can be no more than those persons had in a state of nature before they entered into society, and gave it up to the community. For nobody can transfer to another more power than he has in himself; and nobody has an absolute arbitrary power over himself, or over any other to destroy his own life, or take away the life or property of another. A man as has been proved cannot subject himself to the arbitrary power of another; and having in the state of nature no arbitrary power over the life, liberty, or possession of another, but only so much as the law of nature gave him for the preservation of himself, and the rest of mankind; this is all he doth, or can give up to the commonwealth, and by it to the legislative power, so that the legislative can have no more than this. Their power in the utmost bounds of it, is limited to the public good of the society. It is a power that hath no other end but preservation, and therefore can never have a right to destroy, enslave, or designedly to impoverish the subjects. The obligations of the law of nature cease not in society, but only in many cases are drawn closer, and have by human laws known penalties annexed to them to enforce their observation. Thus the law of nature stands as an eternal rule to all men, legislators as well as others. The rules that they make for other men's actions must, as well as their own, and other men's actions be conformable to the law of nature, i.e., to the will of God, of which that is a declaration, and the fundamental law of nature being the preservation of mankind, no human sanction can be good or valid against it.

136. Secondly, The legislative, or supreme authority, cannot assume to itself a power to rule by extemporary arbitrary decrees, but is bound to dispense justice, and decide the rights of the subject by promulgated standing laws, and known authorized judges. For the law of nature being unwritten, and so nowhere to be found but in the minds of men, they who through passion or interest shall miscite or misapply it, cannot so easily be convinced of their mistake where there is no established judge. And so it serves not, as it ought, to determine the rights, and fence the properties of those that live under it, especially where everyone is judge, interpreter, and executioner of it too, and that in his own case; and he that has right on his side, having ordinarily but his own single strength hath not force enough to defend himself from injuries, or punish delinquents. To avoid these inconveniences, which disorder men's properties in the state of nature, men unite into societies that they may have the united strength of the whole society to secure and defend their properties, and may have standing rules to bound it, by which everyone may know what is his. To this end it is that men give up all their natural power to the society which they enter into, and the community put the legislative power into such hands as they think fit, with this trust, that they shall be governed by declared laws, or else their peace, quiet, and property, will still be at the same uncertainty as it was in the state of nature.

137. Absolute arbitrary power, or governing without settled standing laws, can neither of them consist with the ends of society and government, which men would not quit the freedom of the state of nature for, and tie themselves up under, were it not to preserve their lives, liberties, and fortunes; and by stated rules of right and property to secure their

peace and quiet. It cannot be supposed that they should intend, had they a power so to do, to give to anyone, or more, an absolute arbitrary power over their persons and estates, and put a force into the magistrate's hand to execute his unlimited will arbitrarily upon them. This were to put themselves into a worse condition than the state of nature, wherein they had a liberty to defend their right against the injuries of others, and were upon equal terms of force to maintain it, whether invaded by a single man or many in combination. Whereas, by supposing they have given up themselves to the absolute arbitrary power and will of a legislator, they have disarmed themselves, and armed him, to make prey of them when he pleases. He being in a much worse condition that is exposed to the arbitrary power of one man who has the command of 100,000, than he that is exposed to the arbitrary power of 100,000 single men; nobody being secure that his will, who hath such a command, is better than that of other men, though his force be 100,000 times stronger. And, therefore, whatever form the commonwealth is under, the ruling power ought to govern by declared and received laws, and not by extemporary dictates and undetermined resolutions. For then mankind will be in a far worse condition than in the state of nature, if they shall have armed one, or a few men, with the joint power of a multitude to force them to obey at pleasure the exorbitant and unlimited decrees of their sudden thoughts, or unrestrained, and, till that moment, unknown wills, without having any measures set down which may guide and justify their actions. For all the power the government has, being only for the good of the society, as it ought not to be arbitrary and at pleasure, so it ought to be exercised by established and promulgated laws; that both the people may know their duty and be safe and secure within the limits of the law; and the rulers too kept within their due bounds, and not be tempted by the power they have in their hands to employ it to such purposes, and by such measures, as they would not have known, and own not willingly.

138. Thirdly, The supreme power cannot take from any man any part of his property without his own consent. For the preservation of property being the end of government, and that for which men enter into society, it necessarily supposes and requires that the people should have property, without which they must be supposed to lose that by entering into society, which was the end for which they entered into it, too gross an absurdity for any man to own. Men, therefore, in society having property, they have such a right to the goods which by the law of the community are theirs, that nobody hath a right to take them or any part of them from them, without their own consent; without this they have no property at all. For I have truly no property in that which another can by right take from me when he pleases, against my consent. Hence

it is a mistake to think that the supreme or legislative power of any commonwealth can do what it will, and dispose of the estates of the subjects arbitrarily, or take any part of them at pleasure. This is not much to be feared in governments where the legislative consists wholly, or in part, in assemblies which are variable, whose members, upon the dissolution of the assembly, are subjects under the common laws of their country, equally with the rest. But in governments where the legislative is in one lasting assembly, always in being, or in one man, as in absolute monarchies, there is danger still, that they will think themselves to have a distinct interest from the rest of the community, and so will be apt to increase their own riches and power by taking what they think fit from the people. For a man's property is not at all secure, though there be good and equitable laws to set the bounds of it between him and his fellow subjects, if he who commands those subjects have power to take from any private man what part he pleases of his property, and use and dispose of it as he thinks good.

139. But government, into whosesoever hands it is put, being, as I have before shown, entrusted with this condition, and for this end, that men might have and secure their properties, the prince, or senate, however it may have power to make laws for the regulating of property between the subjects one amongst another, yet can never have a power to take to themselves the whole or any part of the subject's property without their own consent. For this would be in effect to leave them no property at all. And to let us see that even absolute power, where it is necessary, is not arbitrary by being absolute, but is still limited by that reason, and confined to those ends which required it in some cases to be absolute, we need look no farther than the common practice of martial discipline. For the preservation of the army, and in it the whole commonwealth, requires an absolute obedience to the command of every superior officer, and it is justly death to disobey or dispute the most dangerous or unreasonable of them; but yet we see that neither the sergeant, that could command a soldier to march up to the mouth of a cannon, or stand in a breach, where he is almost sure to perish, can command that soldier to give him one penny of his money; nor the general, that can condemn him to death for deserting his post, or not obeying the most desperate orders, cannot yet, with all his absolute power of life and death, dispose of one farthing of that soldier's estate, or seize one jot of his goods, whom yet he can command anything, and hang for the least disobedience. Because such a blind obedience is necessary to that end for which the commander has his power, viz., the preservation of the rest; but the disposing of his goods has nothing to do with it.

140. 'Tis true governments cannot be supported without great charge, and it is fit everyone who enjoys a share of the protection should pay

out of his estate his proportion for the maintenance of it. But still it must be with his own consent, i.e., the consent of the majority giving it either by themselves or their representatives chosen by them. For if any one shall claim a power to lay and levy taxes on the people, by his own authority, and without such consent of the people, he thereby invades the fundamental law of property, and subverts the end of government. For what property have I in that which another may by right take when he pleases to himself?

141. Fourthly, The legislative cannot transfer the power of making laws to any other hands; for it being but a delegated power from the people, they who have it cannot pass it over to others. The people alone can appoint the form of the commonwealth, which is by constituting the legislative, and appointing in whose hands that shall be. And when the people have said we will submit to rules, and be governed by laws made by such men, and in such forms, nobody else can say other men shall make laws for them; nor can the people be bound by any laws but such as are enacted by those whom they have chosen and authorized to make laws for them.

142. These are the bounds which the trust that is put in them by the society, and the law of God and Nature, have set to the legislative power of every commonwealth, in all forms of government.

First, They are to govern by promulgated established laws, not to be varied in particular cases, but to have one rule for rich and poor, for the favorite at court and the countryman at plough.

Secondly, These laws also ought to be designed for no other end ultimately but the good of the people.

Thirdly, They must not raise taxes on the property of the people without the consent of the people, given by themselves or their deputies. And this properly concerns only such governments where the legislative is always in being, or at least where the people have not reserved any part of the legislative to deputies, to be from time to time chosen by themselves.

Fourthly, The legislative neither must nor can transfer the power of making laws to anybody else, or place it anywhere but where the people have.

CHAPTER XII

OF THE LEGISLATIVE, EXECUTIVE, AND FEDERATIVE POWER
OF THE COMMONWEALTH

143. THE LEGISLATIVE power is that which has a right to direct how the force of the commonwealth shall be employed for preserving the community and the members of it. Because those laws which are constantly to be executed, and whose force is always to continue, may be made in a little time, therefore there is no need that the legislative should be always in being, not having always business to do; and because it may be too great a temptation to human frailty, apt to grasp at power for the same persons, who have the power of making laws, to have also in their hands the power to execute them, whereby they exempt themselves from obedience to the laws they make, and suit the law, both in its making and execution to their own private advantage, and thereby come to have a distinct interest from the rest of the community, contrary to the end of society and government. Therefore, in well ordered commonwealths, where the good of the whole is so considered as it ought, the legislative power is put into the hands of divers persons who duly assembled, have by themselves or jointly with others a power to make laws, which when they have done, being separated again, they are themselves subject to the laws they have made; which is a new and near tie upon them, to take care that they make them for the public good.

144. But because the laws that are at once and in a short time made, have a constant and lasting force and need a perpetual execution or an attendance thereunto; therefore, it is necessary there should be a power always in being, which should see to the execution of the laws that are made and remain in force; and thus the legislative and executive power come often to be separated.

145. There is another power in every commonwealth, which one may call natural, because it is that which answers to the power every man naturally had before he entered into society; for though in a commonwealth the members of it are distinct persons still in reference to one another, and as such are governed by the laws of the society, yet in reference to the rest of mankind they make one body, which is, as every member of it before was still in the state of nature with the rest of mankind. So that the controversies that happen between any man of the society with those that are out of it are managed by the public, and an injury done to a member of their body engages the whole in the reparation of it. So that under this consideration the whole community is one body

in the state of nature in respect of all other states or persons out of its community.

146. This therefore contains the power of war and peace, leagues and alliances, and all the transactions with all persons and communities without the commonwealth, and may be called federative if anyone pleases. So the thing be understood, I am indifferent as to the name.

147. These two powers, executive and federative, though they be really distinct in themselves, yet one comprehending the execution of the municipal laws of the society within itself upon all that are parts of it; the other the management of the security and interest of the public without, with all those that it may receive benefit or damage from, yet they are always almost united. And though this federative power in the well or ill management of it be of great moment to the commonwealth, yet it is much less capable to be directed by antecedent, standing, positive laws than the executive; and so must necessarily be left to the prudence and wisdom of those whose hands it is in to be managed for the public good. For the laws that concern subjects one amongst another, being to direct their actions, may well enough precede them. But what is to be done in reference to foreigners, depending much upon their actions and the variation of designs and interests, must be left in great part to the prudence of those who have this power committed to them, to be managed by the best of their skill for the advantage of the commonwealth.

148. Though, as I said, the executive and federative power of every community be really distinct in themselves, yet they are hardly to be separated and placed at the same time in the hands of distinct persons; for both of them requiring the force of the society for their exercise, it is almost impracticable to place the force of the commonwealth in distinct and not subordinate hands; or that the executive and federative power should be placed in persons that might act separately, whereby the force of the public would be under different commands, which would be apt some time or other to cause disorder and ruin.

CHAPTER XIII

OF THE SUBORDINATION OF THE POWERS OF THE COMMONWEALTH

149. THOUGH in a constituted commonwealth, standing upon its own basis, and acting according to its own nature, that is, acting for the preservation of the community, there can be but one supreme power, which is the legislative, to which all the rest are and must be subordinate, yet

the legislative being only of fiduciary power to act for certain ends, there remains still in the people a supreme power to remove or alter the legislative when they find the legislative act contrary to the trust reposed in them; for all power given with trust for the attaining an end, being limited by that end, whenever that end is manifestly neglected or opposed, the trust must necessarily be forfeited, and the power devolve into the hands of those that gave it who may place it anew where they shall think best for their safety and security. And thus the community perpetually retains a supreme power of saving themselves from the attempts and designs of anybody, even of their legislators whenever they shall be so foolish or so wicked as to lay and carry on designs against the liberties and properties of the subject; for no man or society of men, having a power to deliver up their preservation, or consequently the means of it to the absolute will and arbitrary dominion of another, whenever anyone shall go about to bring them into such a slavish condition they will always have a right to preserve what they have not a power to part with; and to rid themselves of those who invade this fundamental, sacred and unalterable law of self-preservation for which they entered into society; and thus the community may be said in this respect to be always the supreme power, but not as considered under any form of government, because this power of the people can never take place till the government be dissolved.

150. In all cases whilst the government subsists, the legislative is the supreme power; for what can give laws to another must needs be superior to him, and since the legislative is no otherwise legislative of the society but by the right it has to make laws for all the parts and for every member of the society, prescribing rules to their actions, and giving power of execution where they are transgressed, the legislative must needs be the supreme, and all other powers in any members or parts of the society derived from and subordinate to it.

151. In some commonwealths where the legislative is not always in being, and the executive is vested in a single person who has also a share in the legislative, there that single person, in a very tolerable sense, may also be called supreme; not that he has in himself all the supreme power, which is that of law-making, but because he has in him the supreme execution from whom all inferior magistrates derive all their several subordinate powers, or, at least, the greatest part of them; having also no legislative superior to him, there being no law to be made without his consent, which cannot be expected should ever subject him to the other part of the legislative, he is properly enough in this sense supreme. But yet it is to be observed that though oaths of allegiance and fealty are taken to him, it is not to him as supreme legislator, but as supreme executor of the law made by a joint power of him with others, allegiance being noth

ing but an obedience according to law, which, when he violates, he has no right to obedience, nor can claim it otherwise than as the public person vested with the power of the law, and so is to be considered as the image, phantom, or representative of the commonwealth, acted by the will of the society declared in its laws, and thus he has no will, no power, but that of the law. But when he quits this representation, this public will, and acts by his own private will, he degrades himself, and is but a single private person without power and without will; the members owing no obedience but to the public will of the society.

152. The executive power placed anywhere but in a person that has also a share in the legislative is visibly subordinate and accountable to it, and may be at pleasure changed and displaced; so that it is not the supreme executive power that is exempt from subordination, but the supreme executive power vested in one, who having a share in the legislative, has no distinct superior legislative to be subordinate and accountable to, farther than he himself shall join and consent, so that he is no more subordinate than he himself shall think fit, which one may certainly conclude will be but very little. Of other ministerial and subordinate powers in a commonwealth we need not speak, they being so multiplied with infinite variety in the different customs and constitutions of distinct commonwealths, that it is impossible to give a particular account of them all. Only thus much which is necessary to our present purpose we may take notice of concerning them, that they have no manner of authority, any of them, beyond what is by positive grant and commission delegated to them, and are all of them accountable to some other power in the commonwealth.

153. It is not necessary—no, nor so much as convenient—that the legislative should be always in being; but absolutely necessary that the executive power should, because there is not always need of new laws to be made, but always need of execution of the laws that are made. When the legislative hath put the execution of the laws they make into other hands, they have a power still to resume it out of those hands when they find cause, and to punish for any maladministration against the laws. The same holds also in regard of the federative power, that and the executive being both ministerial and subordinate to the legislative, which, as has been shown, in a constituted commonwealth is the supreme, the legislative also in this case being supposed to consist of several persons; for if it be a single person it cannot but be always in being, and so will, as supreme, naturally have the supreme executive power, together with the legislative, may assemble and exercise their legislative at the times that either their original constitution or their own adjournment appoints, or when they please, if neither of these hath appointed any time, or there be no other way prescribed to convoke them.

For the supreme power being placed in them by the people, it is always in them, and they may exercise it when they please, unless by their original constitution they are limited to certain seasons, or by an act of their supreme power they have adjourned to a certain time, and when that time comes they have a right to assemble and act again.

154. If the legislative, or any part of it, be of representatives, chosen for that time by the people, which afterwards return into the ordinary state of subjects, and have no share in the legislature but upon a new choice, this power of choosing must also be exercised by the people, either at certain appointed seasons, or else when they are summoned to it; and, in this latter case, the power of convoking the legislative is ordinarily placed in the executive, and has one of these two limitations in respect of time:—that either the original constitution requires their assembling and acting at certain intervals; and then the executive power does nothing but ministerially issue directions for their electing and assembling according to due forms; or else it is left to his prudence to call them by new elections when the occasions or exigencies of the public require the amendment of old or making of new laws, or the redress or prevention of any inconveniencies that lie on or threaten the people.

155. It may be demanded here, what if the executive power, being possessed of the force of the commonwealth, shall make use of that force to hinder the meeting and acting of the legislative, when the original constitution or the public exigencies require it? I say, using force upon the people, without authority, and contrary to the trust put in him that does so, is a state of war with the people, who have a right to reinstate their legislative in the exercise of their power. For having erected a legislative with an intent they should exercise the power of making laws, either at certain set times, or when there is need of it, when they are hindered by any force from what is so necessary to the society, and wherein the safety and preservation of the people consists, the people have a right to remove it by force. In all states and conditions the true remedy of force without authority is to oppose force to it. The use of force without authority always puts him that uses it into a state of war as the aggressor, and renders him liable to be treated accordingly.

156. The power of assembling and dismissing the legislative, placed in the executive, gives not the executive a superiority over it, but is a fiduciary trust placed in him for the safety of the people in a case where the uncertainty and variableness of human affairs could not bear a steady fixed rule. For it not being possible that the first framers of the government should by any foresight be so much masters of future events as to be able to prefix so just periods of return and duration to the assemblies of the legislative, in all times to come, that might exactly answer all the exigencies of the commonwealth, the best remedy could be found for

this defect was to trust this to the prudence of one who was always to be present, and whose business it was to watch over the public good. Constant, frequent meetings of the legislative, and long continuations of their assemblies, without necessary occasion, could not but be burden-some to the people, and must necessarily in time produce more danger-ous inconveniencies, and yet the quick turn of affairs might be some-times such as to need their present help; any delay of their convening might endanger the public; and sometimes, too, their business might be so great that the limited time of their sitting might be too short for their work, and rob the public of that benefit which could be had only from their mature deliberation. What, then, could be done in this case to pre-vent the community from being exposed some time or other to imminent hazard on one side or the other, by fixed intervals and periods set to the meeting and acting of the legislative, but to entrust it to the prudence of some who, being present and acquainted with the state of public affairs, might make use of this prerogative for the public good? And where else could this be so well placed as in his hands who was entrusted with the execution of the laws for the same end? Thus, supposing the regulation of times for the assembling and sitting of the legislative not settled by the original constitution, it naturally fell into the hands of the executive; not as an arbitrary power depending on his good pleasure, but with this trust always to have it exercised only for the public weal, as the occur-rences of times and change of affairs might require. Whether settled peri-ods of their convening, or a liberty left to the prince for convoking the legislative, or perhaps a mixture of both, hath the least inconvenience attending it, it is not my business here to inquire, but only to show that, though the executive power may have the prerogative of convoking and dissolving such conventions of the legislative, yet it is not thereby superior to it.

157. Things of this world are in so constant a flux that nothing re-mains long in the same state. Thus people, riches, trade, power, change their stations; flourishing mighty cities come to ruin, and prove in time neglected desolate corners, whilst other unfrequented places grow into populous countries filled with wealth and inhabitants. But things not al-ways changing equally, and private interest often keeping up customs and privileges when the reasons of them are ceased, it often comes to pass that in governments where part of the legislative consists of repre-sentatives chosen by the people, that in tract of time this representation becomes very unequal and disproportionate to the reasons it was at first established upon. To what gross absurdities the following of custom when reason has left it may lead, we may be satisfied when we see the bare name of a town, of which there remains not so much as the ruins, where scarce so much housing as a sheepcote, or more inhabitants than

a shepherd is to be found, send as many representatives to the grand assembly of law-makers as a whole county numerous in people and powerful in riches. This strangers stand amazed at, and everyone must confess needs a remedy; though most think it hard to find one, because the constitution of the legislative being the original and supreme act of the society, antecedent to all positive laws in it, and depending wholly on the people, no inferior power can alter it. And, therefore, the people when the legislative is once constituted, having in such a government as we have been speaking of no power to act as long as the government stands, this inconvenience is thought incapable of a remedy.

158. *Salus populi suprema lex* is certainly so just and fundamental a rule that he who sincerely follows it cannot dangerously err. If therefore the executive, who has the power of convoking the legislative, observing rather the true proportion than fashion of representation, regulates, not by old custom, but true reason, the number of members in all places that have a right to be distinctly represented, which no part of the people however incorporated can pretend to, but in proportion to the assistance which it affords to the public, it cannot be judged to have set up a new legislative, but to have restored the old and true one, and to have rectified the disorders which succession of time had insensibly as well as inevitably introduced. For it being the interest, as well as intention of the people, to have a fair and equal representative, whoever brings it nearest to that is an undoubted friend to and establisher of the government, and cannot miss the consent and approbation of the community. Prerogative being nothing but a power in the hands of the prince to provide for the public good in such cases which, depending upon unforeseen and uncertain occurrences, certain and unalterable laws could not safely direct. Whatsoever shall be done manifestly for the good of the people, and the establishing the government upon its true foundations is, and always will be, just prerogative. The power of erecting new corporations, and therewith new representatives, carries with it a supposition that in time the measures of representation might vary, and those have a just right to be represented which before had none; and by the same reason those cease to have a right, and be too inconsiderable for such a privilege which before had it. It is not a change from the present state, which perhaps corruption or decay has introduced, that makes an inroad upon the government, but the tendency of it to injure or oppress the people, and to set up one part or party with a distinction from, and an unequal subjection of the rest. Whatsoever cannot but be acknowledged to be of advantage to the society and people in general upon just and lasting measures, will always, when done, justify itself; and whenever the people shall choose their representatives upon just and undeniably equal measures, suitable

to the original frame of the government, it cannot be doubted to be the will and act of the society who ever permitted or proposed to them so to do.

CHAPTER XIV

OF PREROGATIVE

159. WHERE the legislative and executive power are in distinct hands, as they are in all moderated monarchies and well-framed governments, there the good of the society requires that several things should be left to the discretion of him that has the executive power. For the legislators not being able to foresee and provide by laws for all that may be useful to the community, the executor of the laws, having the power in his hands, has by the common law of nature a right to make use of it for the good of the society, in many cases where the municipal law has given no direction, till the legislative can conveniently be assembled to provide for it; nay, many things there are which the law can by no means provide for, and those must necessarily be left to the discretion of him that has the executive power in his hands, to be ordered by him as the public good and advantage shall require; nay, it is fit that the laws themselves should in some cases give way to the executive power, or rather to this fundamental law of nature and government—viz., that as much as may be all the members of the society are to be preserved. For since many accidents may happen wherein a strict and rigid observation of the laws may do harm, as not to pull down an innocent man's house to stop the fire when the next to it is burning; and a man may come sometimes within the reach of the law which makes no distinction of persons, by an action that may deserve reward and pardon; it is fit the ruler should have a power in many cases to mitigate the severity of the law, and pardon some offenders, since the end of government being the preservation of all as much as may be, even the guilty are to be spared where it can prove no prejudice to the innocent.

160. This power to act according to discretion for the public good, without the prescription of the law and sometimes even against it, is that which is called prerogative; for since in some governments the law making power is not always in being and is usually too numerous, and so too slow for the dispatch requisite to execution, and because, also, it is impossible to foresee and so by laws to provide for all accidents and necessities that may concern the public, or make such laws as will do no harm, if they are executed with an inflexible rigor on all occasions

and upon all persons that may come in their way, therefore there is a latitude left to the executive power to do many things of choice which the laws do not prescribe.

161. This power, whilst employed for the benefit of the community and suitably to the trust and ends of the government, is undoubted prerogative, and never is questioned. For the people are very seldom or never scrupulous or nice in the point or questioning of prerogative whilst it is in any tolerable degree employed for the use it was meant ·—that is, the good of the people, and not manifestly against it. But if there comes to be a question between the executive power and the people about a thing claimed as a prerogative, the tendency of the exercise of such prerogative, to the good or hurt of the people, will easily decide that question.

162. It is easy to conceive that in the infancy of governments, when commonwealths differed little from families in number of people, they differed from them too but little in number of laws; and the governors being as the fathers of them, watching over them for their good, the government was almost all prerogative. A few established laws served the turn, and the discretion and care of the ruler supplied the rest. But when mistake or flattery prevailed with weak princes, to make use of this power for private ends of their own and not for the public good, the people were fain, by express laws, to get prerogative determined in those points wherein they found disadvantage from it, and declared limitations of prerogative in those cases which they and their ancestors had left in the utmost latitude to the wisdom of those princes who made no other but a right use of it—that is, for the good of their people.

163. And therefore they have a very wrong notion of government who say that the people have encroached upon the prerogative when they have got any part of it to be defined by positive laws. For in so doing they have not pulled from the prince anything that of right belonged to him, but only declared that that power which they indefinitely left in his or his ancestors' hands, to be exercised for their good, was not a thing they intended him, when he used it otherwise. For the end of government being the good of the community, whatsoever alterations are made in it tending to that end cannot be an encroachment upon anybody; since nobody in government can have a right tending to any other end; and those only are encroachments which prejudice or hinder the public good. Those who say otherwise speak as if the prince had a distinct and separate interest from the good of the community, and was not made for it; the root and source from which spring almost all those evils and disorders which happen in kingly governments. And, indeed, if that be so, the people under his government are not a society of rational creatures, entered into a community for their mutual good, such

as have set rulers over themselves, to guard and promote that good; but are to be looked on as a herd of inferior creatures under the dominion of a master, who keeps them and works them for his own pleasure or profit. If men were so void of reason and brutish as to enter into society upon such terms, prerogative might indeed be, what some men would have it, an arbitrary power to do things hurtful to the people.

164. But since a rational creature cannot be supposed, when free, to put himself into subjection to another for his own harm (though where he finds a good and a wise ruler he may not, perhaps, think it either necessary or useful to set precise bounds to his power in all things), prerogative can be nothing but the people's permitting their rulers to do several things of their own free choice where the law was silent, and sometimes too against the direct letter of the law, for the public good and their acquiescing in it when so done. For as a good prince, who is mindful of the trust put into his hands and careful of the good of his people, cannot have too much prerogative—that is, power to do good, so a weak and ill prince, who would claim that power his predecessors exercised, without the direction of the law, as a prerogative belonging to him by right of his office, which he may exercise at his pleasure to make or promote an interest distinct from that of the public, gives the people an occasion to claim their right and limit that power, which, whilst it was exercised for their good, they were content should be tacitly allowed.

165. And therefore he that will look into the history of England will find that prerogative was always largest in the hands of our wisest and best princes, because the people observing the whole tendency of their actions to be the public good, or if any human frailty or mistake (for princes are but men, made as others) appeared in some small declinations from that end; yet it was visible the main of their conduct tended to nothing but the care of the public. The people, therefore, finding reason to be satisfied with these princes, whenever they acted without, or contrary to the letter of the law, acquiesced in what they did, and without the least complaint, let them enlarge their prerogative as they pleased, judging rightly that they did nothing herein to the prejudice of their laws, since they acted conformable to the foundation and end of all laws—the public good.

166. Such God-like princes, indeed, had some title to arbitrary power by that argument that would prove absolute monarchy the best government, as that which God Himself governs the universe by, because such kings partake of His wisdom and goodness. Upon this is founded that saying, "That the reigns of good princes have been always most dangerous to the liberties of their people." For when their successors, managing the government with different thoughts, would draw the actions of

those good rulers into precedent and make them the standard of their prerogative—as if what had been done only for the good of the people was a right in them to do for the harm of the people, if they so pleased —it has often occasioned contest, and sometimes public disorders, before the people could recover their original right and get that to be declared not to be prerogative which truly was never so; since it is impossible anybody in the society should ever have a right to do the people harm, though it be very possible and reasonable that the people should not go about to set any bounds to the prerogative of those kings or rulers who themselves transgressed not the bounds of the public good. For "prerogative is nothing but the power of doing public good without a rule."

167. The power of calling parliaments in England, as to precise time, place, and duration, is certainly a prerogative of the king, but still with this trust, that it shall be made use of for the good of the nation as the exigencies of the times and variety of occasion shall require. For it being impossible to foresee which should always be the fittest place for them to assemble in, and what the best season, the choice of these was left with the executive power, as might be best subservient to the public good and best suit the ends of parliament.

168. The old question will be asked in this matter of prerogative, "But who shall be judge when this power is made a right use of?" I answer: Between an executive power in being, with such a prerogative, and a legislative that depends upon his will for their convening, there can be no judge on earth. As there can be none between the legislative and the people, should either the executive or the legislative, when they have got the power in their hands, design, or go about to enslave or destroy them, the people have no other remedy in this, as in all other cases where they have no judge on earth, but to appeal to Heaven; for the rulers in such attempts, exercising a power the people never put into their hands, who can never be supposed to consent that anybody should rule over them for their harm, do that which they have not a right to do. And where the body of the people, or any single man, are deprived of their right, or are under the exercise of a power without right, having no appeal on earth they have a liberty to appeal to Heaven whenever they judge the cause of sufficient moment. And therefore, though the people cannot be judge, so as to have, by the constitution of that society, any superior power to determine and give effective sentence in the case, yet they have reserved that ultimate determination to themselves which belongs to all mankind, where there lies no appeal on earth, by a law antecedent and paramount to all positive laws of men, whether they have just cause to make their appeal to Heaven. And this judgment they cannot part with, it being out of a man's power so to submit him-

self to another as to give him a liberty to destroy him; God and nature never allowing a man so to abandon himself as to neglect his own preservation. And since he cannot take away his own life, neither can he give another power to take it. Nor let anyone think this lays a perpetual foundation for disorder; for this operates not till the inconvenience is so great that the majority feel it, and are weary of it, and find a necessity to have it amended. And this the executive power, or wise princes, never need come in the danger of; and it is the thing of all others they have most need to avoid, as, of all others, the most perilous.

CHAPTER XV

OF PATERNAL, POLITICAL, AND DESPOTICAL POWER CONSIDERED TOGETHER

169. THOUGH I have had occasion to speak of these separately before, yet the great mistakes of late about government having, as I suppose, arisen from confounding these distinct powers one with another, it may not perhaps be amiss to consider them here together.

170. First, then, paternal or parental power is nothing but that which parents have over their children to govern them, for the children's good, till they come to the use of reason, or a state of knowledge, wherein they may be supposed capable to understand that rule, whether it be the law of nature or the municipal law of their country, they are to govern themselves by—capable, I say, to know it, as well as several others, who live as free men under that law. The affection and tenderness God hath planted in the breasts of parents towards their children makes it evident that this is not intended to be a severe arbitrary government, but only for the help, instruction, and preservation of their offspring. But happen as it will, there is, as I have proved, no reason why it should be thought to extend to life and death, at any time, over their children, more than over anybody else, or keep the child in subjection to the will of his parents when grown to a man of the perfect use of reason, any further than as having received life and education from his parents obliges him to respect, honor, gratitude, assistance, and support, all his life, to both father and mother. And thus, it is true, the paternal is a natural government, but not at all extending itself to the ends and jurisdictions of that which is political. The power of the father doth not reach at all to the property of the child, which is only in his own disposing.

171. Secondly, political power is that power which every man having in the state of nature has given up into the hands of the society, and therein to the governors whom the society hath set over itself, with this

express or tacit trust, that it shall be employed for their good and the preservation of their property. Now this power, which every man has in the state of nature, and which he parts with to the society in all such cases where the society can secure him, is to use such means for the preserving of his own property as he thinks good and nature allows him; and to punish the breach of the law of nature in others so as (according to the best of his reason) may most conduce to the preservation of himself and the rest of mankind; so that the end and measure of this power, when in every man's hands, in the state of nature, being the preservation of all of his society—that is, all mankind in general—it can have no other end or measure, when in the hands of the magistrate, but to preserve the members of that society in their lives, liberties, and possessions, and so cannot be an absolute, arbitrary power over their lives and fortunes, which are as much as possible to be preserved; but a power to make laws, and annex such penalties to them as may tend to the preservation of the whole, by cutting off those parts, and those only, which are so corrupt that they threaten the sound and healthy, without which no severity is lawful. And this power has its original only from compact and agreement and the mutual consent of those who make up the community.

172. Thirdly, despotical power is an absolute, arbitrary power one man has over another, to take away his life whenever he pleases; and this is a power which neither nature gives, for it has made no such distinction between one man and another, nor compact can convey. For man, not having such an arbitrary power over his own life, cannot give another man such a power over it, but it is the effect only of forfeiture which the aggressor makes of his own life when he puts himself into the state of war with another. For having quitted reason, which God hath given to be the rule betwixt man and man, and the peaceable ways which that teaches, and made use of force to compass his unjust ends upon another where he has no right, he renders himself liable to be destroyed by his adversary whenever he can, as any other noxious and brutish creature that is destructive to his being. And thus captives, taken in a just and lawful war, and such only, are subject to a despotical power, which, as it arises not from compact, so neither is it capable of any, but is the state of war continued. For what compact can be made with a man that is not master of his own life? What condition can he perform? And if he be once allowed to be master of his own life, the despotical, arbitrary power of his master ceases. He that is master of himself and his own life has a right, too, to the means of preserving it; so that as soon as compact enters, slavery ceases, and he so far quits his absolute power and puts an end to the state of war who enters into conditions with his captive.

173. Nature gives the first of these—viz., paternal power to parents for the benefit of their children during their minority, to supply their want of ability and understanding how to manage their property. (By property I must be understood here, as in other places, to mean that property which men have in their persons as well as goods.) Voluntary agreement gives the second—viz., political power to governors, for the benefit of their subjects, to secure them in the possession and use of their properties. And forfeiture gives the third—despotical power to lords for their own benefit over those who are stripped of all property.

174. He that shall consider the distinct rise and extent, and the different ends of these several powers, will plainly see that paternal power comes as far short of that of the magistrate as despotical exceeds it; and that absolute dominion, however placed, is so far from being one kind of civil society that it is as inconsistent with it as slavery is with property. Paternal power is only where minority makes the child incapable to manage his property; political where men have property in their own disposal; and despotical over such as have no property at all.

CHAPTER XVI

OF CONQUEST

175. THOUGH governments can originally have no other rise than that before mentioned, nor polities be founded on anything but the consent of the people, yet such have been the disorders ambition has filled the world with, that in the noise of war, which makes so great a part of the history of mankind, this consent is little taken notice of; and, therefore, many have mistaken the force of arms for the consent of the people, and reckon conquest as one of the originals of government. But conquest is as far from setting up any government as demolishing a house is from building a new one in the place. Indeed, it often makes way for a new frame of a commonwealth by destroying the former; but, without the consent of the people, can never erect a new one.

176. That the aggressor, who puts himself into the state of war with another, and unjustly invades another man's right, can, but such an unjust war, never come to have a right over the conquered, will be easily agreed by all men, who will not think that robbers and pirates have a right of empire over whomsoever they have force enough to master, or that men are bound by promises which unlawful force extorts from them. Should a robber break into my house, and, with a dagger at my throat, make me seal deeds to convey my estate to him, would this give him any title? Just such a title by his sword has an unjust conqueror

who forces me into submission. The injury and the crime is equal, whether committed by the wearer of a crown or some petty villain. The title of the offender and the number of his followers make no difference in the offense, unless it be to aggravate it. The only difference is, great robbers punish little ones to keep them in their obedience; but the great ones are rewarded with laurels and triumphs, because they are too big for the weak hands of justice in this world, and have the power in their own possession which should punish offenders. What is my remedy against a robber that so broke into my house? Appeal to the law for justice. But perhaps justice is denied, or I am crippled and cannot stir; robbed, and have not the means to do it. If God has taken away all means of seeking remedy, there is nothing left but patience. But my son, when able, may seek the relief of the law, which I am denied; he or his son may renew his appeal till he recover his right. But the conquered, or their children, have no court—no arbitrator on earth to appeal to. Then they may appeal, as Jephtha did, to Heaven, and repeat their appeal till they have recovered the native right of their ancestors, which was to have such a legislative over them as the majority should approve and freely acquiesce in. If it be objected this would cause endless trouble, I answer, no more than justice does, where she lies open to all that appeal to her. He that troubles his neighbor without a cause is punished for it by the justice of the court he appeals to. And he that appeals to Heaven must be sure he has right on his side, and a right, too, that is worth the trouble and cost of the appeal, as he will answer at a tribunal that cannot be deceived, and will be sure to retribute to everyone according to the mischiefs he hath created to his fellow-subjects—that is, any part of mankind. From whence it is plain that he that conquers in an unjust war can thereby have no title to the subjection and obedience of the conquered.

177. But supposing victory favors the right side, let us consider a conqueror in a lawful war, and see what power he gets, and over whom.

First, it is plain he gets no power by his conquest over those that conquered with him. They that fought on his side cannot suffer by the conquest, but must, at least, be as much free men as they were before. And most commonly they serve upon terms, and on condition to share with their leader, and enjoy a part of the spoil and other advantages that attend the conquering sword, or, at least, have a part of the subdued country bestowed upon them. And the conquering people are not, I hope, to be slaves by conquest, and wear their laurels only to show they are sacrifices to their leader's triumph. They that found absolute monarchy upon the title of the sword make their heroes, who are the founders of such monarchies, arrant "draw-can-sirs," and forget they had any officers and soldiers that fought on their side, in the battles they won, or assisted them in the subduing, or shared in possessing the countries they mastered. We are told by some that the English monarchy is founded in the Norman Conquest, and that our princes have thereby a title to absolute dominion, which, if it were true (as by the history it appears otherwise), and that William had a right to make war on this island, yet his dominion by conquest could reach no farther than to the Saxons and Britons that were then inhabitants of this country. The Normans that came with him and helped to conquer, and all descended from them are free men and no subjects by conquest, let that give what dominion it will. And if I or anybody else shall claim freedom as derived from them, it will be very hard to prove the contrary, and it is plain, the law that has made no distinction between the one and the other intends not there should be any difference in their freedom or privileges.

178. But supposing, which seldom happens, that the conquerors and conquered never incorporate into one people under the same laws and freedom; let us see next what power a lawful conqueror has over the subdued, and that I say is purely despotical. He has an absolute power over the lives of those who, by an unjust war, have forfeited them, but not over the lives or fortunes of those who engaged not in the war, nor over the possessions even of those who were actually engaged in it.

179. Secondly, I say, then, the conqueror gets no power but only over those who have actually assisted, concurred, or consented to that unjust force that is used against him. For the people having given to their governors no power to do an unjust thing, such as is to make an unjust war (for they never had such a power in themselves), they ought not to be charged as guilty of the violence and injustice that is committed in an unjust war any farther than they actually abet it, no more than they are to be thought guilty of any violence or oppression their governors should use upon the people themselves or any part of their fellow-subjects, they having empowered them no more to the one than to the other. Conquerors, it is true, seldom trouble themselves to make the distinction, but they willingly permit the confusion of war to sweep all together; but yet this alters not the right; for the conqueror's power over the lives of the conquered being only because they have used force to do or maintain an injustice, he can have that power only over those who have concurred in that force; all the rest are innocent, and he has no more title over the people of that country who have done him no injury, and so have made no forfeiture of their lives, than he has over any other who, without any injuries or provocations, have lived upon fair terms with him.

180. Thirdly, the power a conqueror gets over those he overcomes in a just war is perfectly despotical; he has an absolute power over the lives of those who, by putting themselves in a state of war, have for-

feited them, but he has not thereby a right and title to their possessions. This I doubt not but at first sight will seem a strange doctrine, it being so quite contrary to the practice of the world; there being nothing more familiar in speaking of the dominion of countries than to say such an one conquered it, as if conquest, without any more ado, conveyed a right of possession. But when we consider that the practice of the strong and powerful, how universal soever it may be, is seldom the rule of right, however it be one part of the subjection of the conquered not to argue against the conditions cut out to them by the conquering swords.

181. Though in all war there be usually a complication of force and damage, and the aggressor seldom fails to harm the estate when he uses force against the persons of those he makes war upon, yet it is the use of force only that puts a man into the state of war. For whether by force he begins the injury, or else having quietly and by fraud done the injury, he refuses to make reparation, and by force maintains it, which is the same thing as at first to have done it by force; it is the unjust use of force that makes the war. For he that breaks open my house and violently turns me out of doors, or having peaceably got in, by force keeps me out, does, in effect, the same thing; supposing we are in such a state that we have no common judge on earth whom I may appeal to, and to whom we are both obliged to submit, for of such I am now speaking. It is the unjust use of force, then, that puts a man into the state of war with another, and thereby he that is guilty of it makes a forfeiture of his life. For quitting reason, which is the rule given between man and man, and using force, the way of beasts, he becomes liable to be destroyed by him he uses force against, as any savage ravenous beast that is dangerous to his being.

182. But because the miscarriages of the father are no faults of the children, and they may be rational and peaceable, notwithstanding the brutishness and injustice of the father, the father, by his miscarriages and violence, can forfeit but his own life, but involves not his children in his guilt or destruction. His goods with nature, that willeth the preservation of all mankind as much as is possible, hath made to belong to the children to keep them from perishing, do still continue to belong to his children. For supposing them not to have joined in the war either through infancy or choice, they have done nothing to forfeit them, nor has the conqueror any right to take them away by the bare right of having subdued him that by force attempted his destruction, though, perhaps, he may have some right to them to repair the damages he has sustained by the war, and the defense of his own right, which how far it reaches to the possessions of the conquered we shall see by and by; so that he that by conquest has a right over a man's person, to destroy him if he pleases, has not thereby a right over his estate to possess and enjoy

it. For it is the brutal force the aggressor has used that gives his adversary a right to take away his life and destroy him, if he pleases, as
a noxious creature; but it is damage sustained that alone gives him
title to another man's goods; for though I may kill a thief that sets on
me in the highway, yet I may not (which seems less) take away his
money and let him go; this would be robbery on my side. His force, and
the state of war he put himself in, made him forfeit his life, but gave me
no title to his goods. The right, then, of conquest extends only to the
lives of those who joined in the war, but not to their estates, but only
in order to make reparation for the damages received and the charges
of the war, and that, too, with reservation of the right of the innocent
wife and children.

183. Let the conqueror have as much justice on his side as could be
supposed, he has no right to seize more than the vanquished could forfeit; his life is at the victor's mercy, and his service and goods he
may appropriate to make himself reparation; but he cannot take the
goods of his wife and children, they too had a title to the goods he enjoyed, and their shares in the estate he possessed. For example, I in the
state of nature (and all commonwealths are in the state of nature one
with another) have injured another man, and refusing to give satisfaction, it is come to a state of war wherein my defending by force what
I had gotten unjustly makes me the aggressor. I am conquered; my life,
it is true, as forfeit, is at mercy, but not my wife's and children's. They
made not the war, nor assisted in it. I could not forfeit their lives, they
were not mine to forfeit. My wife had a share in my estate, that neither
could I forfeit. And my children also, being born of me, had a right to
be maintained out of my labor or substance. Here then is the case: The
conqueror has a title to reparation for damages received, and the children have a title to their father's estate for their subsistence. For as to
the wife's share, whether her own labor or compact gave her a title to
it, it is plain her husband could not forfeit what was here. What must
be done in the case? I answer: The fundamental law of nature being
that all, as much as may be, should be preserved, it follows that if there
be not enough fully to satisfy both—viz., for the conqueror's losses and
children's maintenance, he that hath and to spare must remit something
of his full satisfaction, and give way to the pressing and preferable title
of those who are in danger to perish without it.

184. But supposing the charge and damages of the war are to be
made up to the conqueror to the utmost farthing, and that the children
of the vanquished, spoiled of all their father's goods, are to be left to
starve and perish, yet the satisfying of what shall, on this score, be due
to the conqueror will scarce give him a title to any country he shall
conquer. For the damages of war can scarce amount to the value of

any considerable tract of land in any part of the world, where all the land is possessed, and none lies waste. And if I have not taken away the conqueror's land which, being vanquished, it is impossible I should, scarce any other spoil I have done him can amount to the value of mine, supposing it of an extent any way coming near what I had overrun of his, and equally cultivated too. The destruction of a year's product or two (for it seldom reaches four or five) is the utmost spoil that usually can be done. For as to money, and such riches and treasure taken away, these are none of nature's goods, they have but a fantastical imaginary value; nature has put no such upon them. They are of no more account by her standard than the Wampompeke of the Americans to an European prince, or the silver money of Europe would have been formerly to an American. And five years' product is not worth the perpetual inheritance of land, where all is possessed and none remains waste, to be taken up by him that is disseized, which will be easily granted, if one do but take away the imaginary value of money, the disproportion being more than between five and five thousand; though, at the same time, half a year's product is more worth than the inheritance, where there being more land than the inhabitants possess and make use of, anyone has liberty to make use of the waste. But there conquerors take little care to possess themselves of the lands of the vanquished. No damage therefore that men in the state of nature (as all princes and governments are in reference to one another) suffer from one another can give a conqueror power to dispossess the posterity of the vanquished, and turn them out of that inheritance which ought to be the possession of them and their descendants to all generations. The conqueror indeed will be apt to think himself master; and it is the very condition of the subdued not to be able to dispute their right. But, if that be all, it gives no other title than what bare force gives to the stronger over the weaker; and, by this reason, he that is strongest will have a right to whatever he pleases to seize on.

185. Over those, then, that joined with him in the war, and over those of the subdued country that opposed him not, and the posterity even of those that did, the conqueror, even in a just war, hath, by his conquest, no right of dominion. They are free from any subjection to him, and if their former government be dissolved, they are at liberty to begin and erect another to themselves.

186. The conqueror, it is true, usually by the force he has over them, compels them, with a sword at their breasts, to stoop to his conditions, and submit to such a government as he pleases to afford them; but the inquiry is, what right he has to do so? If it be said they submit by their own consent, then this allows their own consent to be necessary to give the conqueror a title to rule over them. It remains only to be considered

whether promises, extorted by force, without right, can be thought consent, and how far they bind. To which I shall say, they bind not at all; because whatsoever another gets from me by force, I still retain the right of, and he is obliged presently to restore. He that forces my horse from me ought presently to restore him, and I have still a right to retake him. By the same reason, he that forced a promise from me ought presently to restore it—i.e., quit me of the obligation of it; or I may resume it myself—i.e., choose whether I will perform it. For the law of nature laying an obligation on me, only by the rules she prescribes, cannot oblige me by the violation of her rules; such is the extorting anything from me by force. Nor does it at all alter the case, to say I gave my promise, no more than it excuses the force, and passes the right, when I put my hand in my pocket and deliver my purse myself to a thief who demands it with a pistol at my breast.

187. From all which it follows that the government of a conqueror, imposed by force on the subdued, against whom he had no right of war, or who joined not in the war against him, where he had right, has no obligation upon them.

188. But let us suppose that all the men of that community being all members of the same body politic, may be taken to have joined in that unjust war, wherein they are subdued, and so their lives are at the mercy of the conqueror.

189. I say this concerns not their children who are in their minority. For since a father hath not, in himself, a power over the life or liberty of his child, no act of his can possibly forfeit it; so that the children, whatever may have happened to the fathers, are free men, and the absolute power of the conqueror reaches no farther than the persons of the men that were subdued by him, and dies with them; and should he govern them as slaves, subjected to his absolute, arbitrary power, he has no such right of dominion over their children. He can have no power over them but by their own consent, whatever he may drive them to say or do, and he has no lawful authority, whilst force, and not choice, compels them to submission.

190. Every man is born with a double right. First, a right of freedom to his person, which no other man has a power over, but the free disposal of it lies in himself. Secondly, a right before any other man, to inherit, with his brethren, his father's goods.

191. By the first of these, a man is naturally free from subjection to any government, though he be born in a place under its jurisdiction. But if he disclaim the lawful government of the country he was born in, he must also quit the right that belonged to him, by the laws of it, and the possessions there descending to him from his ancestors, if it were a government made by their consent.

192. By the second, the inhabitants of any country, who are descended and derive a title to their estates from those who are subdued, and had a government forced upon them, against their free consents, retain a right to the possession of their ancestors, though they consent not freely to the government, whose hard conditions were, by force, imposed on the possessors of that country. For the first conqueror never having had a title to the land of that country, the people, who are the descendants of, or claim under those who were forced to submit to the yoke of a government by constraint, have always a right to shake it off, and free themselves from the usurpation or tyranny the sword hath brought in upon them, till their rulers put them under such a frame of government as they willingly and of choice consent to (which they can never be supposed to do, till either they are put in a full state of liberty to choose their government and governors, or at least till they have such standing laws to which they have, by themselves or their representatives, given their free consent, and also till they are allowed their due property, which is so to be proprietors of what they have that nobody can take away any part of it without their own consent, without which, men under any government are not in the state of free men, but are direct slaves under the force of war). And who doubts but the Grecian Christians, descendants of the ancient possessors of that country, may justly cast off the Turkish yoke they have so long groaned under, whenever they have a power to do it?

193. But granting that the conqueror, in a just war, has a right to the estates, as well as power over the persons of the conquered, which, it is plain, he hath not, nothing of absolute power will follow from hence in the continuance of the government. Because the descendants of these being all free men, if he grants them estates and possessions to inhabit his country, without which it would be worth nothing, whatsoever he grants them they have so far as it is granted property in; the nature whereof is, that, without a man's own consent, it cannot be taken from him.

194. Their persons are free by a native right, and their properties, be they more or less, are their own, and at their own dispose, and not at his; or else it is no property. Supposing the conqueror gives to one man a thousand acres, to him and his heirs forever; to another he lets a thousand acres, for his life, under the rent of £50 or £500 per annum. Has not the one of these a right to his thousand acres forever, and the other during his life, paying the said rent? And hath not the tenant for life a property in all that he gets over and above his rent, by his labor and industry, during the said term, supposing it be double the rent? Can anyone say, the king, or conqueror, after his grant, may, by his power of conqueror, take away all, or part of the land, from the

heirs of one, or from the other during his life, he paying the rent? Or, can he take away from either the goods or money they have got upon the said land at his pleasure? If he can, then all free and voluntary contracts cease, and are void in the world; there needs nothing but power enough to dissolve them at any time, and all the grants and promises of men in power are but mockery and collusion. For can there be anything more ridiculous than to say, I give you and yours this forever, and that in the surest and most solemn way of conveyance can be devised, and yet it is to be understood that I have right, if I please, to take it away from you again tomorrow?

195. I will not dispute now whether princes are exempt from the laws of their country, but this I am sure, they owe subjection to the laws of God and nature. Nobody, no power can exempt them from the obligations of that eternal law. Those are so great and so strong in the case of promises, that Omnipotency itself can be tied by them. Grants, promises, and oaths are bonds that hold the Almighty, whatever some flatterers say to princes of the world, who, all together, with all their people joined to them, are, in comparison of the great God, but as a drop of the bucket, or a dust on the balance—inconsiderable, nothing!

196. The short of the case in conquest, is this: The conqueror, if he have a just cause, has a despotical right over the persons of all that actually aided and concurred in the war against him, and a right to make up his damage and cost out of their labor and estates, so he injure not the right of any other. Over the rest of the people, if there were any that consented not to the war, and over the children of the captives themselves or the possessions of either he has no power, and so can have, by virtue of conquest, no lawful title himself to dominion over them, or derive it to his posterity; but is an aggressor, and puts himself in a state of war against them, and has no better a right of principality, he, nor any of his successors, than Hingar, or Hubba, the Danes, had here in England, or Spartacus, had he conquered Italy, which is to have their yoke cast off as soon as God shall give those under their subjection courage and opportunity to do it. Thus, notwithstanding whatever title the kings of Assyria had over Judah, by the sword, God assisted Hezekiah to throw off the dominion of that conquering empire. "And the Lord was with Hezekiah, and he prospered; wherefore he went forth, and he rebelled against the king of Assyria, and served him not" (2 Kings xviii. 7). Whence it is plain that shaking off a power which force, and not right, hath set over anyone, though it hath the name of rebellion, yet is no offense before God, but that which He allows and countenances, though even promises and covenants, when obtained by force, have intervened. For it is very probable, to anyone that reads the story of Ahaz and Hezekiah attentively, that the Assyrians subdued Ahaz,

and deposed him, and made Hezekiah king in his father's lifetime, anu
that Hezekiah, by agreement, had done him homage, and paid him trib-
ute till this time.

CHAPTER XVII

OF USURPATION

197. As CONQUEST may be called a foreign usurpation, so usurpation
is a kind of domestic conquest, with this difference—that an usurper
can never have right on his side, it being no usurpation but where
one is got into the possession of what another has right to. This, so far
as it is usurpation, is a change only of persons, but not of the forms
and rules of the government; for if the usurper extend his power beyond
what, of right, belonged to the lawful princes or governors of the commonwealth, it is tyranny added to usurpation.

198. In all lawful governments the designation of the persons who
are to bear rule being as natural and necessary a part as the form of the
government itself, and that which had its establishment originally from
the people—the anarchy being much alike, to have no form of government at all, or to agree that it shall be monarchical, yet appoint no way
to design the person that shall have the power and be the monarch—all
commonwealths, therefore, with the form of government established,
have rules also of appointing and conveying the right to those who are
to have any share in the public authority; and whoever gets into the
exercise of any part of the power by other ways than what the laws of
the community have prescribed hath no right to be obeyed, though the
form of the commonwealth be still preserved, since he is not the person
the laws have appointed, and, consequently, not the person the people
have consented to. Nor can such an usurper, or any deriving from him,
ever have a title till the people are both at liberty to consent, and have
actually consented, to allow and confirm in him the power he hath
till then usurped.

CHAPTER XVIII

OF TYRANNY

199. As USURPATION is the exercise of power which another hath a
right to, so tyranny is the exercise of power beyond right, which nobody
can have a right to; and this is making use of the power anyone has

in his hands, not for the good of those who are under it, but for his own private, separate advantage. When the governor, however entitled, makes not the law, but his will, the rule, and his commands and actions are not directed to the preservation of the properties of his people, but the satisfaction of his own ambition, revenge, covetousness, or any other irregular passion.

200. If one can doubt this to be truth or reason because it comes from the obscure hand of a subject, I hope the authority of a king will make it pass with him. King James, in his speech to the Parliament, 1603, tells them thus: "I will ever prefer the weal of the public and of the whole commonwealth, in making of good laws and constitutions, to any particular and private ends of mine, thinking ever the wealth and weal of the commonwealth to be my greatest weal and worldly felicity— a point wherein a lawful king doth directly differ from a tyrant; for I do acknowledge that the special and greatest point of difference that is between a rightful king and an usurping tyrant is this—that whereas the proud and ambitious tyrant doth think his kingdom and people are only ordained for satisfaction of his desires and unreasonable appetites, the righteous and just king doth, by the contrary, acknowledge himself to be ordained for the procuring of the wealth and property of his people." And again, in his speech to the Parliament, 1609, he hath these words: "The king binds himself, by a double oath, to the observation of the fundamental laws of his kingdom—tacitly, as by being a king, and so bound to protect, as well the people as the laws of his kingdom; and expressly by his oath at his coronation; so as every just king, in a settled kingdom, is bound to observe that paction made to his people, by his laws, in framing his government agreeable thereunto, according to that paction which God made with Noah after the deluge: 'Hereafter, seed-time, and harvest, and cold, and heat, and summer, and winter, and day, and night, shall not cease while the earth remaineth.' And therefore a king, governing in a settled kingdom, leaves to be a king, and degenerates into a tyrant, as soon as he leaves off to rule according to his laws." And a little after: "Therefore, all kings that are not tyrants, or perjured, will be glad to bound themselves within the limits of their laws, and they that persuade them the contrary are vipers, pests, both against them and the commonwealth." Thus, that learned king, who well understood the notions of things, makes the difference betwixt a king and a tyrant to consist only in this: that one makes the laws the bounds of his power and the good of the public the end of his government; the other makes all give way to his own will and appetite.

201. It is a mistake to think this fault is proper only to monarchies. Other forms of government are liable to it as well as that; for wherever

the power that is put in any hands for the government of the people and the preservation of their properties is applied to other ends, and made use of to impoverish, harass, or subdue them to the arbitrary and irregular commands of those that have it, there it presently becomes tyranny, whether those that thus use it are one or many. Thus we read of the thirty tyrants at Athens, as well as one at Syracuse; and the intolerable dominion of the Decemviri at Rome was nothing better.

202. Wherever law ends, tyranny begins, if the law be transgressed to another's harm; and whosoever in authority exceeds the power given him by the law, and makes use of the force he has under his command to compass that upon the subject which the law allows not, ceases in that to be a magistrate, and acting without authority may be opposed, as any other man who by force invades the right of another. This is acknowledged in subordinate magistrates. He that hath authority to seize my person in the street may be opposed as a thief and a robber if he endeavors to break into my house to execute a writ, notwithstanding that I know he has such a warrant and such a legal authority as will empower him to arrest me abroad. And why this should not hold in the highest, as well as in the most inferior magistrate, I would gladly be informed. Is it reasonable that the eldest brother, because he has the greatest part of his father's estate, should thereby have a right to take away any of his younger brothers' portions? Or, that a rich man, who possessed a whole country, should from thence have a right to seize, when he pleased, the cottage and garden of his poor neighbor? The being rightfully possessed of great power and riches, exceedingly beyond the greatest part of the sons of Adam, is so far from being an excuse, much less a reason for rapine and oppression, which the endamaging another without authority is, that it is a great aggravation of it. For the exceeding the bounds of authority is no more a right in a great than a petty officer, no more justifiable in a king than a constable. But so much the worse in him as that he has more trust put in him, is supposed, from the advantage of education and counselors to have better knowledge and less reason to do it, having already a greater share than the rest of his brethren.

203. May the commands, then, of a prince be opposed? May he be resisted, as often as anyone shall find himself aggrieved, and but imagine he has not right done him? This will unhinge and overturn all polities, and instead of government and order, leave nothing but anarchy and confusion.

204. To this I answer: That force is to be opposed to nothing but to unjust and unlawful force. Whoever makes any opposition in any other case draws on himself a just condemnation, both from God and

man; and so no such danger or confusion will follow, as is often suggested. For—

205. First. As in some countries the person of the prince by the law is sacred, and so whatever he commands or does, his person is still free from all question or violence, not liable to force, or any judicial censure or condemnation. But yet opposition may be made to the illegal acts of any inferior officer or other commissioned by him, unless he will, by actually putting himself into a state of war with his people, dissolve the government, and leave them to that defense, which belongs to everyone in the state of nature. For of such things, who can tell what the end will be? And a neighbor kingdom has showed the world an odd example. In all other cases the sacredness of the person exempts him from all inconveniencies, whereby he is secure, whilst the government stands, from all violence and harm whatsoever, than which there cannot be a wiser constitution. For the harm he can do in his own person not being likely to happen often, nor to extend itself far, nor being able by his single strength to subvert the laws nor oppress the body of the people, should any prince have so much weakness and ill-nature as to be willing to do it. The inconveniency of some particular mischiefs that may happen sometimes when a heady prince comes to the throne are well recompensed by the peace of the public and security of the government in the person of the chief magistrate, thus set out of the reach of danger; it being safer for the body that some few private men should be sometimes in danger to suffer than that the head of the republic should be easily and upon slight occasions exposed.

206. Secondly. But this privilege, belonging only to the king's person, hinders not but they may be questioned, opposed, and resisted, who use unjust force, though they pretend a commission from him which the law authorizes not; as is plain in the case of him that has the king's writ to arrest a man which is a full commission from the king, and yet he that has it cannot break open a man's house to do it, nor execute this command of the king upon certain days nor in certain places, though this commission have no such exception in it; but they are the limitations of the law, which, if anyone transgress, the king's commission excuses him not. For the king's authority being given him only by the law, he cannot empower anyone to act against the law, or justify him by his commission in so doing. The commission or command of any magistrate where he has no authority, being as void and insignificant as that of any private man, the difference between the one and the other being that the magistrate has some authority so far and to such ends, and the private man has none at all; for it is not the commission but the authority that gives the right of acting, and against the laws

there can be no authority. But notwithstanding such resistance, the king's person and authority are still both secured, and so no danger to governor or government.

207. Thirdly. Supposing a government wherein the person of the chief magistrate is not thus sacred, yet this doctrine of the lawfulness of resisting all unlawful exercises of his power will not, upon every slight occasion, endanger him or embroil the government; for where the injured party may be relieved and his damages repaired by appeal to the law, there can be no pretense for force, which is only to be used where a man is intercepted from appealing to the law. For nothing is to be accounted hostile force but where it leaves not the remedy of such an appeal, and it is such force alone that puts him that uses it into a state of war, and makes it lawful to resist him. A man with a sword in his hand demands my purse in the highway, when perhaps I have not 12_d_. in my pocket. This man I may lawfully kill. To another I deliver £100 to hold only whilst I alight, which he refuses to restore me when I am got up again, but draws his sword to defend the possession of it by force. I endeavor to retake it. The mischief this man does me is a hundred, or possibly a thousand times more than the other perhaps intended me (whom I killed before he really did me any); and yet I might lawfully kill the one and cannot so much as hurt the other lawfully. The reason whereof is plain; because the one using force which threatened my life, I could not have time to appeal to the law to secure it, and when it was gone it was too late to appeal. The law could not restore life to my dead carcass. The loss was irreparable; which to prevent the law of nature gave me a right to destroy him who had put himself into a state of war with me and threatened my destruction. But in the other case, my life not being in danger, I might have the benefit of appealing to the law, and have reparation for my £100 that way.

208. Fourthly: but if the unlawful acts done by the magistrate be maintained (by the power he has got), and the remedy, which is due by law, be by the same power obstructed, yet the right of resisting, even in such manifest acts of tyranny, will not suddenly, or on slight occasions, disturb the government. For if it reach no farther than some private men's cases, though they have a right to defend themselves, and to recover by force what by unlawful force is taken from them, yet the right to do so will not easily engage them in a contest wherein they are sure to perish; it being as impossible for one or a few oppressed men to disturb the government where the body of the people do not think themselves concerned in it, as for a raving madman or heavy malcontent to overturn a well-settled state, the people being as little apt to follow the one as the other.

209. But if either these illegal acts have extended to the majority of

the people, or if the mischief and oppression has light only on some few, but in such cases as the precedent and consequences seem to threaten all, and they are persuaded in their consciences that their laws, and with them, their estates, liberties, and lives are in danger, and perhaps their religion too, how they will be hindered from resisting illegal force used against them I cannot tell. This is an inconvenience, I confess, that attends all governments whatsoever, when the governors have brought it to this pass, to be generally suspected of their people, the most dangerous state they can possibly put themselves in; wherein they are the less to be pitied, because it is so easy to be avoided. It being as impossible for a governor, if he really means the good of his people, and the preservation of them and their laws together, not to make them see and feel it, as it is for the father of a family not to let his children see he loves and takes care of them.

210. But if all the world shall observe pretenses of one kind, and actions of another, arts used to elude the law, and the trust of prerogative (which is an arbitrary power in some things left in the prince's hand to do good, not harm, to the people) employed contrary to the end for which it was given; if the people shall find the ministers and subordinate magistrates chosen, suitable to such ends, and favored or laid by proportionably as they promote or oppose them; if they see several experiments made of arbitrary power, and that religion underhand favored, though publicly proclaimed against, which is readiest to introduce it, and the operators in it supported as much as may be; and when that cannot be done, yet approved still, and liked the better, and a long train of acting show the counsels all tending that way, how can a man any more hinder himself from being persuaded in his own mind which way things are going; or, from casting about how to save himself, than he could from believing the captain of a ship he was in was carrying him and the rest of the company to Algiers, when he found him always steering that course, though cross winds, leaks in his ship, and want of men and provisions did often force him to turn his course another way for some time, which he steadily returned to again as soon as the wind, weather, and other circumstances would let him?

CHAPTER XIX

OF THE DISSOLUTION OF GOVERNMENT

211. He that will with any clearness speak of the dissolution of government ought, in the first place, to distinguish between the dissolution of the society and the dissolution of the government. That which makes

the community, and brings men out of the loose state of nature into one politic society, is the agreement which everyone has with the rest to incorporate and act as one body, and so be one distinct commonwealth. The usual and almost only way whereby this union is dissolved, is the inroad of foreign force making a conquest upon them. For in that case (not being able to maintain and support themselves as one entire and independent body) the union belonging to that body which consisted therein must necessarily cease, and so everyone return to the state he was in before, with a liberty to shift for himself and provide for his own safety as he thinks fit in some other society. Whenever the society is dissolved, it is certain the government of that society cannot remain. Thus conquerors' swords often cut up governments by the roots, and mangle societies to pieces, separating the subdued or scattered multitude from the protection of and dependence on that society which ought to have preserved them from violence. The world is too well instructed in, and too forward to allow of this way of dissolving of, governments to need any more to be said of it; and there wants not much argument to prove that where the society is dissolved, the government cannot remain—that being as impossible as for the frame of a house to subsist when the materials of it are scattered and displaced by a whirlwind, or jumbled into a confused heap by an earthquake.

212. Besides this overturning from without, governments are dissolved from within.

First, When the legislative is altered. Civil society being a state of peace amongst those who are of it, from whom the state of war is excluded by the umpirage which they have provided in their legislative for the ending all differences that may arise amongst any of them, it is in their legislative that the members of a commonwealth are united and combined together in one coherent living body. This is the soul that gives form, life, and unity to the commonwealth. From hence the several members have their mutual influence, sympathy, and connection. And, therefore, when the legislative is broken or dissolved, dissolution and death follow. For the essence and union of the society consisting in having one will, the legislative, when once established by the majority, has the declaring and, as it were, keeping of, that will. The constitution of the legislative is the first and fundamental act of the society, whereby provision is made for the continuation of their union, under the direction of persons and bonds of laws made by persons authorized thereunto by the consent and appointment of the people, without which no one man or number of men amongst them can have authority of making laws that shall be binding to the rest. When any one or more shall take upon them to make laws, whom the people have not appointed so to do, they make laws without authority, which the people are not therefore bound to obey; by which means they come again to be out of subjection, and may constitute to themselves a new legislative, as they think best, being in full liberty to resist the force of those who without authority would impose anything upon them. Everyone is at the disposure of his own will when those who had by the delegation of the society the declaring of the public will, are excluded from it, and others usurp the place who have no such authority or delegation.

213. This being usually brought about by such in the common-wealth who misuse the power they have, it is hard to consider it aright, and know at whose door to lay it, without knowing the form of govern-ment in which it happens. Let us suppose, then, the legislative placed in the concurrence of three distinct persons.

(1) A single hereditary person having the constant supreme executive power, and with it the power of convoking and dissolving the other two within certain periods of time.

(2) An assembly of hereditary nobility.

(3) An assembly of representatives chosen *pro tempore* by the people. Such a form of government supposed, it is evident,

214. First, That when such a single person or prince sets up his own arbitrary will in place of the laws which are the will of the society, de-clared by the legislative, then the legislative is changed. For that being in effect the legislative whose rules and laws are put in execution and required to be obeyed when other laws are set up, and other rules pre-tended and enforced, than what the legislative constituted by the so-ciety have enacted, it is plain that the legislative is changed. Whoever introduces new laws, not being thereunto authorized by the funda-mental appointment of the society, or subverts the old, disowns and overturns the power by which they were made, and so sets up a new legislative.

215. Secondly, When the prince hinders the legislative from assem-bling in its due time, or from acting freely, pursuant to those ends for which it was constituted, the legislative is altered. For it is not a cer-tain number of men, no, nor their meeting, unless they have also free-dom of debating and leisure of perfecting what is for the good of the society, wherein the legislative consists. When these are taken away or altered so as to deprive the society of the due exercise of their power, the legislative is truly altered. For it is not names that constitute gov-ernments, but the use and exercise of those powers that were intended to accompany them; so that he who takes away the freedom, or hinders the acting of the legislative in its due seasons, in effect takes away the legislative, and puts an end to the government.

216. Thirdly, When, by the arbitrary power of the prince, the elec-tors or ways of elections are altered, without the consent and contrary to

the common interest of the people, there also the legislative is altered.
For if others than those whom the society hath authorized thereunto, do
choose, or in another way than what the society hath prescribed, those
chosen are not the legislative appointed by the people.

217. Fourthly, The delivery also of the people into the subjection of
foreign power, either by the prince, or by the legislative, is certainly a
change of the legislative, and so a dissolution of the government. For the
end why people entered into society being to be preserved one entire,
free, independent society, to be governed by its own laws, this is lost
whenever they are given up into the power of another.

218. Why, in such a constitution as this, the dissolution of the government in these cases is to be imputed to the prince is evident, because
he, having the force, treasure, and offices of the State to employ, and
often persuading himself or being flattered by others, that, as supreme
magistrate, he is incapable of control; he alone is in a condition to
make great advances towards such changes under pretense of lawful
authority, and has it in his hands to terrify or suppress opposers as
factious, seditious, and enemies to the government; whereas no other
part of the legislative, or people, is capable by themselves to attempt
any alteration of the legislative without open and visible rebellion, apt
enough to be taken notice of, which, when it prevails, produces effects
very little different from foreign conquest. Besides, the prince, in such
a form of government, having the power of dissolving the other parts of
the legislative, and thereby rendering them private persons, they can
never, in opposition to him, or without his concurrence, alter the legislative by a law, his consent being necessary to give any of their decrees
that sanction. But yet so far as the other parts of the legislative any
way contribute to any attempt upon the government, and do either promote, or not, what lies in them, hinder such designs, they are guilty, and
partake in this, which is certainly the greatest crime men can be guilty
of one towards another.

219. There is one way more whereby such a government may be dissolved, and that is, when he who has the supreme executive power
neglects and abandons that charge, so that the laws already made can
no longer be put in execution. This is demonstratively to reduce all to
anarchy, and so effectually to dissolve the government. For laws not being made for themselves, but to be by their execution the bonds of the
society, to keep every part of the body politic, in its due place and
function, when that totally ceases, the government visibly ceases, and
the people become a confused multitude without order or connection.
Where there is no longer the administration of justice, for the securing
of men's rights, nor any remaining power within the community to direct
the force, or provide for the necessities of the public, there certainly is

no government left. Where the laws cannot be executed, it is all one as if there were no laws; and a government without laws is, I suppose, a mystery in politics, inconceivable to human capacity, and inconsistent with human society.

220. In these and the like cases, when the government is dissolved, the people are at liberty to provide for themselves by erecting a new legislative, differing from the other, by the change of persons, or form, or both, as they shall find it most for their safety and good. For the society can never, by the fault of another, lose the native and original right it has to preserve itself, which can only be done by a settled legislative, and a fair and impartial execution of the laws made by it. But the state of mankind is not so miserable that they are not capable of using this remedy, till it be too late to look for any. To tell people they may provide for themselves by erecting a new legislative, when by oppression, artifice, or being delivered over to a foreign power, their old one is gone, is only to tell them they may expect relief when it is too late, and the evil is past cure. This is in effect no more than to bid them first be slaves, and then to take care of their liberty; and when their chains are on tell them they may act like free men. This, if barely so, is rather mockery than relief; and men can never be secure from tyranny if there be no means to escape it till they are perfectly under it. And therefore it is that they have not only a right to get out of it, but to prevent it.

221. There is therefore secondly another way whereby governments are dissolved, and that is when the legislative or the prince, either of them, act contrary to their trust.

First, The legislative acts against the trust reposed in them when they endeavor to invade the property of the subject, and to make themselves or any part of the community masters or arbitrary disposers of the lives, liberties, or fortunes of the people.

222. The reason why men enter into society is the preservation of their property; and the end why they choose and authorize a legislative is that there may be laws made, and rules set, as guards and fences to the properties of all the members of the society to limit the power and moderate the dominion of every part and member of the society. For since it can never be supposed to be the will of the society that the legislative should have a power to destroy that which everyone designs secure by entering into society, and for which the people submitted themselves to legislators of their own making, whenever the legislators endeavor to take away and destroy the property of the people, or to reduce them to slavery under arbitrary power, they put themselves into a state of war with the people, who are thereupon absolved from any further obedience, and are left to the common refuge which God hath provided for all men against force and violence. Whensoever, therefore,

the legislative shall transgress this fundamental rule of society, and either by ambition, fear, folly, or corruption, endeavor to grasp themselves or put into the hands of any other an absolute power over the lives, liberties, and estates of the people, by this breach of trust they forfeit the power the people had put into their hands, for quite contrary ends, and it devolves to the people, who have a right to resume their original liberty, and by the establishment of the new legislative (such as they shall think fit) provide for their own safety and security, which is the end for which they are in society. What I have said here concerning the legislative in general, holds true also concerning the supreme executor, who having a double trust put in him, both to have a part in the legislative and the supreme execution of the law, acts against both when he goes about to set up his own arbitrary will as the law of the society. He acts also contrary to his trust when he either employs the force, treasure, and offices of the society, to corrupt the representatives, and gain them to his purposes; or openly pre-engages the electors, and prescribes to their choice such whom he has by solicitations, threats, promises, or otherwise won to his designs, and employs them to bring in such, who have promised beforehand what to vote and what to enact. Thus to regulate candidates and electors, and new-model the ways of election, what is it but to cut up the government by the roots, and poison the very fountain of public security? For the people having reserved to themselves the choice of their representatives as the fence to their properties, could do it for no other end but that they might always be freely chosen, and, so chosen, freely act and advise as the necessity of the commonwealth and the public good should upon examination and mature debate be judged to require. This those who give their votes before they hear the debate, and have weighed the reason on all sides, are not capable of doing. To prepare such an assembly as this, and endeavor to set up the declared abettors of his own will for the true representatives of the people and the law-makers of the society, is certainly as great a breach of trust and as perfect a declaration of a design to subvert the government as is possible to be met with. To which if one shall add rewards and punishments visibly employed to the same end and all the arts of perverted law made use of to take off and destroy all that stand in the way of such a design, and will not comply and consent to betray the liberties of their country, it will be past doubt what is doing. What power they ought to have in the society who thus employ it contrary to the trust that went along with it in its first institution is easy to determine; and one cannot but see that he who has once attempted any such thing as this cannot any longer be trusted.

223. To this perhaps it will be said that, the people being ignorant and always discontented, to lay the foundation of government in the un-

steady opinion and uncertain humor of the people is to expose it to
certain ruin; and no government will be able long to subsist if the people
may set up a new legislative whenever they take offense at the old one.
To this I answer: Quite the contrary. People are not so easily got out
of their old forms as some are apt to suggest. They are hardly to be prevailed with to amend the acknowledged faults in the frame they have
been accustomed to. And if there be any original defects, or adventitious
ones introduced by time or corruption, it is not an easy thing to get
them changed, even when all the world sees there is an opportunity for it.
This slowness and aversion in the people to quit their old constitutions
has, in the many revolutions which have been seen in this kingdom, in
this and former ages still kept us to, or after some interval of fruitless
attempts still brought us back again to, our old legislative of Kings,
Lords, and Commons. And whatever provocations have made the crown
be taken from some of our princes' heads, they never carried the people
so far as to place it in another line.

224. But it will be said, this hypothesis lays a ferment for frequent
rebellion. To which I answer:

First, no more than any other hypothesis. For when the people are
made miserable, and find themselves exposed to the ill-usage of arbitrary power, cry up their governors as much as you will for sons of
Jupiter, let them be sacred and divine, descended, or authorized from
heaven, give them out for whom or what you please, the same will happen. The people generally ill-treated, and contrary to right, will be ready
upon any occasion to ease themselves of a burden that sits heavy upon
them. They will wish and seek for the opportunity, which in the change,
weakness, and accidents of human affairs seldom delays long to offer
itself. He must have lived but a little while in the world who has not
seen examples of this in his time, and he must have read very little who
cannot produce examples of it in all sorts of governments in the world.

225. Secondly, I answer, such revolutions happen not upon every
little mismanagement in public affairs. Great mistakes in the ruling part,
many wrong and inconvenient laws, and all the slips of human frailty
will be borne by the people without mutiny or murmur. But if a long
train of abuses, prevarications and artifices, all tending the same way,
make the design visible to the people—and they cannot but feel what
they lie under, and see whither they are going—it is not to be wondered
that they should then rouse themselves and endeavor to put the rule into
such hands which may secure to them the ends for which government was
at first erected, and without which ancient names and specious forms are
so far from being better that they are much worse than the state of
nature or pure anarchy; the inconveniences being all as great and as
near, but the remedy farther off and more difficult.

226. Thirdly, I answer that this power in the people of providing for their safety anew by a new legislative when their legislators have acted contrary to their trust by invading their property, is the best fence against rebellion, and the probablest means to hinder it. For rebellion being an opposition, not to persons, but authority, which is founded only in the constitutions and laws of the government, those whoever they be who by force break through, and by force justify their violation of them, are truly and properly rebels. For when men by entering into society and civil government have excluded force, and introduced laws for the preservation of property, peace, and unity amongst themselves, those who set up force again in opposition to the laws do *rebellare*—that is, bring back again the state of war—and are properly rebels; which they who are in power (by the pretense they have to authority, the temptation of force they have in their hands, and the flattery of those about them) being likeliest to do, the properest way to prevent the evil is to show them the danger and injustice of it who are under the greatest temptation to run into it.

227. In both the forementioned cases, when either the legislative is changed or the legislators act contrary to the end for which they were constituted, those who are guilty are guilty of rebellion. For if anyone by force takes away the established legislative of any society, and the laws by them made pursuant to their trust, he thereby takes away the umpirage which everyone had consented to for a peaceable decision of all their controversies, and a bar to the state of war amongst them. They who remove or change the legislative, take away this decisive power, which nobody can have but by the appointment and consent of the people, and so destroying the authority which the people did, and nobody else can, set up; and introducing a power which the people hath not authorized, actually introduce a state of war which is that of force without authority. And thus by removing the legislative established by the society (in whose decisions the people acquiesced and united as to that of their own will), they untie the knot and expose the people anew to the state of war. And if those who by force take away the legislative are rebels, the legislators themselves, as has been shown, can be no less esteemed so, when they who were set up for the protection and preservation of the people, their liberties and properties, shall by force invade and endeavor to take them away; and so they, putting themselves into a state of war with those who made them the protectors and guardians of their peace, are properly and with the greatest aggravation *rebellantes* (rebels).

228. But if they who say it lays a foundation for rebellion mean that it may occasion civil wars or intestine broils, to tell the people they are

absolved from obedience when illegal attempts are made upon their liberties or properties, and may oppose the unlawful violence of those who were their magistrates when they invade their properties contrary to the trust put in them and that therefore this doctrine is not to be allowed, being so destructive to the peace of the world: they may as well say upon the same ground that honest men may not oppose robbers or pirates because this may occasion disorder or bloodshed. If any mischief come in such cases, it is not to be charged upon him who defends his own right, but on him that invades his neighbor's. If the innocent honest man must quietly quit all he has for peace's sake to him who will lay violent hands upon it, I desire it may be considered what a kind of peace there will be in the world which consists only in violence and rapine, and which is to be maintained only for the benefit of robbers and oppressors. Who would not think it an admirable peace betwixt the mighty and the mean when the lamb without resistance yielded his throat to be torn by the imperious wolf? Polyphemus's den gives us a perfect pattern of such a peace and such a government, wherein Ulysses and his companions had nothing to do but quietly to suffer themselves to be devoured. And no doubt Ulysses, who was a prudent man, preached up passive obedience, and exhorted them to a quiet submission by representing to them of what concernment peace was to mankind, and by showing the inconveniences which might happen if they should offer to resist Polyphemus, who had now the power over them.

229. The end of government is the good of mankind, and which is best for mankind, that the people should be always exposed to the boundless will of tyranny, or that the rulers should be sometimes liable to be opposed when they grow exorbitant in the use of their power, and employ it for the destruction and not the preservation of the properties of their people?

230. Nor let anyone say that mischief can arise from hence as often as it shall please a busy head or turbulent spirit to desire the alteration of the government. It is true such men may stir whenever they please, but it will be only to their own just ruin and perdition. For till the mischief be grown general, and the ill designs of the rulers become visible, or their attempts sensible to the greater part, the people, who are more disposed to suffer than right themselves by resistance, are not apt to stir. The examples of particular injustice or oppression of here and there an unfortunate man moves them not. But if they universally have a persuasion grounded upon manifest evidence that designs are carrying on against their liberties, and the general course and tendency of things cannot but give them strong suspicions of the evil intention of their governors, who is to be blamed for it? Who can help it if they, who

might avoid it, bring themselves into this suspicion? Are the people to be blamed if they have the sense of rational creatures, and can think of things no otherwise than as they find and feel them? And is it not rather their fault who put things in such a posture that they would not have them thought as they are? I grant that the pride, ambition, and turbulency of private men have sometimes caused great disorders in commonwealths, and factions have been fatal to states and kingdoms. But whether the mischief hath oftener begun in the people's wantonness, and a desire to cast off the lawful authority of their rulers, or in the rulers' insolence and endeavors to get and exercise an arbitrary power over their people, whether oppression or disobedience gave the first rise to the disorder, I leave it to impartial history to determine. This I am sure, whoever, either ruler or subject, by force goes about to invade the rights of either prince or people, and lays the foundation for overturning the constitution and frame of any just government, he is guilty of the greatest crime I think a man is capable of, being to answer for all those mischiefs of blood, rapine, and desolation, which the breaking to pieces of governments bring on a country; and he who does it is justly to be esteemed the common enemy and pest of mankind, and is to be treated accordingly.

231. That subjects or foreigners attempting by force on the properties of any people may be resisted with force is agreed on all hands; but that magistrates doing the same thing may be resisted, hath of late been denied; as if those who had the greatest privileges and advantages by the law had thereby a power to break those laws by which alone they were set in a better place than their brethren; whereas their offense is thereby the greater, both as being ungrateful for the greater share they have by the law, and breaking also that trust which is put into their hands by their brethren.

232. Whosoever uses force without right—as everyone does in society who does it without law—puts himself into a state of war with those against whom he so uses it, and in that state all former ties are canceled, all other rights cease, and everyone has a right to defend himself, and to resist the aggressor. This is so evident that Barclay himself—that great assertor of the power and sacredness of kings—is forced to confess that it is lawful for the people, in some cases, to resist their king, and that, too, in a chapter wherein he pretends to show that the Divine law shuts up the people from all manner of rebellion. Whereby it is evident, even by his own doctrine, that since they may, in some cases, resist. all resisting of princes is not rebellion. His words are these:[3]

---

[3] Locke gives first the Latin text, which is here omitted.—*Editor.*

233. "But if anyone should ask: Must the people, then, always lay themselves open to the cruelty and rage of tyranny—must they see their cities pillaged and laid in ashes, their wives and children exposed to the tyrant's lust and fury, and themselves and families reduced by their king to ruin and all the miseries of want and oppression, and yet sit still— must men alone be debarred the common privilege of opposing force with force, which nature allows so freely to all other creatures for their preservation from injury? I answer: Self-defense is a part of the law of nature; nor can it be denied the community, even against the king himself; but to revenge themselves upon him must, by no means, be allowed them, it being not agreeable to that law. Wherefore, if the king shall show an hatred, not only to some particular persons, but sets himself against the body of the commonwealth, whereof he is the head, and shall, with intolerable ill usage, cruelly tyrannize over the whole, or a considerable part of the people; in this case the people have a right to resist and defend themselves from injury; but it must be with this caution, that they only defend themselves, but do not attack their prince. They may repair the damages received, but must not, for any provocation, exceed the bounds of due reverence and respect. They may repulse the present attempt, but must not revenge past violences. For it is natural for us to defend life and limb, but that an inferior should punish a superior is against nature. The mischief which is designed them the people may prevent before it be done, but, when it is done, they must not revenge it on the king, though author of the villainy. This, therefore, is the privilege of the people in general above what any private person hath: That particular men are allowed, by our adversaries themselves (Buchanan only excepted), to have no other remedy but patience; but the body of the people may, with respect, resist intolerable tyranny, for when it is but moderate they ought to endure it."

234. Thus far that great advocate of monarchical power allows of resistance.

235. It is true, he has annexed two limitations to it, to no purpose: First. He says it must be with reverence.

Secondly. It must be without retribution or punishment; and the reason he gives is, "because an inferior cannot punish a superior."

236. First. How to resist force without striking again, or how to strike with reverence, will need some skill to make intelligible. He that shall oppose an assault only with a shield to receive the blows, or in any more respectful posture, without a sword in his hand to abate the confidence and force of the assailant, will quickly be at an end of his resistance, and will find such a defense serve only to draw on himself the worse usage. This is as ridiculous a way of resisting as Juvenal thought

it of fighting: *Ubi tu pulsas, ego vapulo tantum.* And the success of the combat will be unavoidably the same he there describes it:

> Libertas pauperis haec est:
> Pulsatus rogat, et pugnis concisus, adorat,
> Ut liceat paucis cum dentibus inde reverti.

This will always be the event of such an imaginary resistance, where men may not strike again. He, therefore, who may resist must be allowed to strike. And then let our author, or anybody else, join a knock on the head or a cut on the face with as much reverence and respect as he thinks fit. He that can reconcile blows and reverence may, for aught I know, deserve for his pains a civil, respectful cudgeling wherever he can meet with it.

Secondly. As to his second—"An inferior cannot punish a superior" —that is true, generally speaking, whilst he is his superior. But to resist force with force, being the state of war that levels the parties, cancels all former relation of reverence, respect, and superiority; and then the odds that remains is—that he who opposes the unjust aggressor has this superiority over him, that he has a right, when he prevails, to punish the offender, both for the breach of the peace and all the evils that followed upon it. Barclay, therefore, in another place, more coherently to himself, denies it to be lawful to resist a king in any case. But he there assigns two cases whereby a king may unking himself. His words are:[4]

237. "What, then, can there no case happen wherein the people may of right, and by their own authority, help themselves, take arms, and set upon their king, imperiously domineering over them? None at all whilst he remains a king. 'Honor the king,' and 'he that resists the power, resists the ordinance of God,' are Divine oracles that will never permit it. The people, therefore, can never come by a power over him unless he does something that makes him cease to be a king; for then he divests himself of his crown and dignity, and returns to the state of a private man, and the people become free and superior; the power which they had in the interregnum, before they crowned him king, devolving to them again. But there are but few miscarriages which bring the matter to this state. After considering it well on all sides, I can find but two. Two cases there are, I say, whereby a king, *ipso facto*, becomes no king, and loses all power and regal authority over his people, which are also taken notice of by Winzerus. The first is, if he endeavor to overturn the government—that is, if he have a purpose and design to ruin the kingdom and commonwealth, as it is recorded of Nero that he resolved to cut off the senate and people of Rome, lay the city waste with fire and sword, and then remove to some other place; and of Caligula, that

---

[4] The Latin text is omitted.—*Editor.*

he openly declared that he would be no longer a head to the people or
senate, and that he had it in his thoughts to cut off the worthiest men
of both ranks, and then retire to Alexandria; and he wished that the
people had but one neck that he might despatch them all at a blow. Such
designs as these, when any king harbors in his thoughts, and seriously
promotes, he immediately gives up all care and thought of the commonwealth, and, consequently, forfeits the power of governing his subjects,
as a master does the dominion over his slaves whom he hath abandoned.

238. "The other case is, when a king makes himself the dependent of
another, and subjects his kingdom, which his ancestors left him, and
the people put free into his hands, to the dominion of another. For however, perhaps, it may not be his intention to prejudice the people, yet
because he has hereby lost the principal part of regal dignity—viz., to
be next and immediately under God, supreme in his kingdom; and also
because he betrayed or forced his people, whose liberty he ought to have
carefully preserved, into the power and dominion of a foreign nation.
By this, as it were, alienation of his kingdom, he himself loses the power
he had in it before, without transferring any the least right to those on
whom he would have bestowed it; and so by this act sets the people free,
and leaves them at their own disposal. One example of this is to be
found in the Scotch annals."

239. In these cases Barclay, the great champion of absolute monarchy,
is forced to allow that a king may be resisted, and ceases to be a king.
That is, in short, not to multiply cases! In whatsoever he has no authority, there he is no king, and may be resisted: for wheresoever the authority ceases, the king ceases too, and becomes like other men who have
no authority. And these two cases that he instances differ little from
those above mentioned, to be destructive to governments, only that he
has omitted the principle from which his doctrine flows, and that is the
breach of trust in not preserving the form of government agreed on, and
in not intending the end of government itself, which is the public good
and preservation of property. When a king has dethroned himself, and
put himself in a state of war with his people, what shall hinder them
from prosecuting him who is no king, as they would any other man, who
has put himself into a state of war with them, Barclay, and those of his
opinion, would do well to tell us. Bilson, a bishop of our Church, and a
great stickler for the power and prerogative of princes, does, if I mistake not, in his treatise of "Christian Subjection," acknowledge that
princes may forfeit their power and their title to the obedience of their
subjects; and if there needed authority in a case where reason is so
plain, I could send my reader to Bracton, Fortescue, and the author of
the "Mirror," and others, writers that cannot be suspected to be ignorant
of our government, or enemies to it. But I thought Hooker alone might

be enough to satisfy those men who, relying on him for their ecclesiastical polity, are by a strange fate carried to deny those principles upon which he builds it. Whether they are herein made the tools of cunninger workmen, to pull down their own fabric, they were best look. This I am sure, their civil policy is so new, so dangerous, and so destructive to both rulers and people, that as former ages never could bear the broaching of it, so it may be hoped those to come, redeemed from the impositions of these Egyptian under-taskmasters, will abhor the memory of such servile flatterers, who, whilst it seemed to serve their turn, resolved all government into absolute tyranny, and would have all men born to what their mean souls fitted them—slavery.

240. Here, it is likely, the common question will be made: Who shall be judge whether the prince or legislative act contrary to their trust? This, perhaps, ill-affected and factious men may spread amongst the people when the prince only makes use of his due prerogative. To this I reply: The people shall be judge; for who shall be judge whether the trustee or deputy acts well and according to the trust reposed in him, but he who deputes him, and must, by having deputed him, have still the power to discard him when he fails in his trust? If this be reasonable in particular cases of private men, why should it be otherwise in that of the greatest moment, where the welfare of millions is concerned, and also where the evil, if not prevented, is greater, and the redress very difficult, dear, and dangerous?

241. But farther, this question, who shall be judge, cannot mean that there is no judge at all; for where there is no judicature on earth to decide controversies amongst men, God in heaven is Judge. He alone, it is true, is Judge of the right; but every man is judge for himself, as in all other cases, so in this, whether another hath put himself into a state of war with him, and whether he should appeal to the Supreme Judge as Jephtha did.

242. If a controversy arise betwixt a prince and some of the people in a matter where the law is silent or doubtful, and the thing be of great consequence, I should think the proper umpire in such a case should be the body of the people; for in cases where the prince hath a trust reposed in him, and is dispensed from the common ordinary rules of the law; there, if any men find themselves aggrieved, and think the prince acts contrary to or beyond that trust, who so proper to judge as the body of the people (who at first lodged that trust in him) how far they meant it should extend? But if the prince or whoever they be in the administration decline that way of determination, the appeal then lies nowhere but to heaven; force between either persons who have no known superior on earth, or which permits no appeal to a judge on earth, being properly a state of war, wherein the appeal lies only to heaven, and in that

state the injured party must judge for himself when he will think fit to make use of that appeal and put himself upon it.

243. To conclude: The power that every individual gave the society when he entered into it, can never revert to the individuals again as long as the society lasts, but will always remain in the community, because without this there can be no community, no commonwealth, which is contrary to the original agreement; so also when the society hath placed the legislative in any assembly of men to continue in them and their successors, with direction and authority for providing such successors, the legislative can never revert to the people whilst that government lasts, because having provided a legislative with power to continue forever, they have given up their political power to the legislative and cannot resume it. But if they have set limits to the duration of their legislative, and made this supreme power in any person or assembly only temporary; or else when by the miscarriages of those in authority it is forfeited; upon the forfeiture, or at the determination of the time set, it reverts to the society, and the people have a right to act as supreme, and continue the legislative in themselves; or place it in a new form, or new hands as they think good.

GEORGE BERKELEY

A Treatise Concerning the Principles of Human Knowledge

GEORGE BERKELEY

GEORGE BERKELEY (pronounced Barkley) (1685-1753) was born in Kilkenny, Ireland. He entered Trinity College, Dublin, in 1700, remaining there as successively scholar, fellow, and tutor for thirteen years. During this early period he developed his own philosophy and wrote his most important works: the *Essay Towards a New Theory of Vision* (1709), the *Principles of Human Knowledge* (1710), and the *Three Dialogues Between Hylas and Philonous* (1713).

In 1713 he went to London and spent eight years in England and on the Continent before he returned again to Ireland. During his stay in London he was introduced at Court and to London literary circles by his countryman Swift. In 1715 Berkeley became companion to the son of the Bishop St. George Ashe and spent five years on the Continent, chiefly in Italy. In 1720 he published a Latin treatise *De Motu,* a criticism of the fundamental concepts of Newtonian physics in terms of his own philosophy. On his return to England a year later he was presented the deanery of Dromore in Ireland, and in 1724 he received the more valuable deanery of Derry. Meanwhile Berkeley, who was of a deeply philanthropic nature, had conceived the plan of founding a college in the Bermudas with the dual purpose of raising the level of culture among the English colonists and propagating the gospel among the American Indians. He returned to England to lobby for his scheme and, after four years of agitation, finally obtained the apparent backing of the government. In 1728 he set sail for America, landing at Newport, Rhode Island, where he spent nearly three years waiting in vain for the English government to keep its promise. During his American sojourn he wrote *Alciphron,* or the *Minute Philosopher.* In 1734, after his return to England, he published the *Analyst,* a criticism of basic notions in mathematics paralleling his earlier examination of physical concepts in the *De Motu.* In the same year he was appointed Bishop of Cloyne. For nearly twenty years he quietly and faithfully discharged the duties of his diocese. His last work of importance was *Siris: a Chain of Philosophical Reflections* (1744). In 1752 he retired to Oxford to spend his last days. Here he died a few months later.

There follows the complete text of his *Principles of Human Knowledge.*[1]

---

[1] A recent edition of this work, now the most informative one for purposes of historical and critical study, is that of T. E. Jessop (1937).

PREFACE

WHAT I here make public has, after a long and scrupulous inquiry, seemed to me evidently true, and not unuseful to be known, particularly to those who are tainted with scepticism, or want a demonstration of the existence and immateriality of God, or the natural immortality of the soul. Whether it be so or no, I am content the reader should impartially examine; since I do not think myself any further concerned for the success of what I have written than as it is agreeable to truth. But to the end this may not suffer, I make it my request that the reader suspend his judgment till he has once, at least, read the whole through with that degree of attention and thought which the subject matter shall seem to deserve. For as there are some passages that, taken by themselves, are very liable (nor could it be remedied) to gross misinterpretation, and to be charged with most absurd consequences, which, nevertheless, upon an entire perusal will appear not to follow from them: so likewise, though the whole should be read over, yet if this be done transiently, it is very probable my sense may be mistaken; but to a thinking reader, I flatter myself, it will be throughout clear and obvious. As for the characters of novelty and singularity, which some of the following notions may seem to bear, it is, I hope, needless to make any apology on that account. He must surely be either very weak, or very little acquainted with the sciences, who shall reject a truth that is capable of demonstration, for no other reason but because it is newly known and contrary to the prejudices of mankind. Thus much I thought fit to premise, in order to prevent, if possible, the hasty censures of a sort of men, who are too apt to condemn an opinion before they rightly comprehend it.

INTRODUCTION

PHILOSOPHY being nothing else but the study of wisdom and truth, it may with reason be expected that those who have spent most time and pains in it should enjoy a greater calm and serenity of mind, a greater clearness and evidence of knowledge, and be less disturbed with doubts and difficulties than other men. Yet so it is, we see the illiterate bulk of mankind that walk the highroad of plain common sense, and are governed by the dictates of nature, for the most part easy and undisturbed. To them nothing that is familiar appears unaccountable or difficult to comprehend. They complain not of any want of evidence in their senses, and are out of all danger of becoming sceptics. But no sooner do we depart from sense and instinct to follow the light of a superior principle, to reason, meditate, and reflect on the nature of things, but a thousand scruples spring up in our minds concerning those things which before we seemed fully to comprehend. Prejudices and errors of sense do from all parts discover themselves to our view; and, endeavoring to correct these by reason, we are insensibly drawn into uncouth paradoxes, difficulties, and inconsistencies, which multiply and grow upon us as we advance in speculation, till at length, having wandered through many intricate mazes, we find ourselves just where we were, or, which is worse, sit down in a forlorn scepticism.

2. The cause of this is thought to be the obscurity of things, or the natural weakness and imperfection of our understandings. It is said the faculties we have are few, and those designed by nature for the support and comfort of life, and not to penetrate into the inward essence and constitution of things. Besides, the mind of man being finite, when it treats of things which partake of infinity it is not to be wondered at if it run into absurdities and contradictions, out of which it is impossible it should ever extricate itself, it being of the nature of infinite not to be comprehended by that which is finite.

3. But perhaps we may be too partial to ourselves in placing the fault originally in our faculties, and not rather in the wrong use we make of them. It is a hard thing to suppose that right deductions from true principles should ever end in consequences which cannot be maintained or made consistent. We should believe that God has dealt more bountifully with the sons of men than to give them a strong desire for that knowledge which he had placed quite out of their reach. This were not

agreeable to the wonted indulgent methods of Providence, which whatever appetites it may have implanted in the creatures, doth usually furnish them with such means as, if rightly made use of, will not fail to satisfy them. Upon the whole, I am inclined to think that the far greater part, if not all, of those difficulties which have hitherto amused philosophers, and blocked up the way to knowledge, are entirely owing to ourselves—that we have first raised a dust and then complain we cannot see.

4. My purpose therefore is, to try if I can discover what those principles are which have introduced all that doubtfulness and uncertainty, those absurdities and contradictions, into the several sects of philosophy; insomuch that the wisest men have thought our ignorance incurable, conceiving it to arise from the natural dullness and limitation of our faculties. And surely it is a work well deserving our pains to make a strict inquiry concerning the first principles of human knowledge, to sift and examine them on all sides, especially since there may be some grounds to suspect that those lets and difficulties, which stay and embarrass the mind in its search after truth, do not spring from any darkness and intricacy in the objects, or natural defect in the understanding, so much as from false principles which have been insisted on, and might have been avoided.

5. How difficult and discouraging soever this attempt may seem, when I consider how many great and extraordinary men have gone before me in the like designs, yet I am not without some hopes, upon the consideration that the largest views are not always the clearest, and that he who is short-sighted will be obliged to draw the object nearer, and may, perhaps, by a close and narrow survey, discern that which had escaped far better eyes.

6. In order to prepare the mind of the reader for the easier conceiving what follows, it is proper to premise somewhat, by way of introduction, concerning the nature and abuse of language. But the unraveling this matter leads me in some measure to anticipate my design, by taking notice of what seems to have had a chief part in rendering speculation intricate and perplexed, and to have occasioned innumerable errors and difficulties in almost all parts of knowledge. And that is the opinion that the mind hath a power of framing *abstract ideas* or notions of things. He who is not a perfect stranger to the writings and disputes of philosophers must needs acknowledge that no small part of them are spent about abstract ideas. These are in a more especial manner thought to be the object of those sciences which go by the name of *logic* and *metaphysics,* and of all that which passes under the notion of the most abstracted and sublime learning, in all which one shall scarce find any question handled in such a manner as does not suppose their existence in the mind, and that it is well acquainted with them.

7. It is agreed on all hands that the qualities or modes of things do never really exist each of them apart by itself, and separated from all others, but are mixed, as it were, and blended together, several in the same object. But, we are told, the mind being able to consider each quality singly, or abstracted from those other qualities with which it is united, does by that means frame to itself abstract ideas. For example, there is perceived by sight an object extended, colored, and moved: this mixed or compound idea the mind resolving into its simple, constituent parts, and viewing each by itself, exclusive of the rest, does frame the abstract ideas of extension, color, and motion. Not that it is possible for color or motion to exist without extension; but only that the mind can frame to itself by *abstraction* the idea of color exclusive of extension, and of motion exclusive of both color and extension.

8. Again, the mind having observed that in the particular extensions perceived by sense there is something common and alike in all, and some other things peculiar, as this or that figure or magnitude, which distinguish them one from another; it considers apart or singles out by itself that which is common, making thereof a most abstract idea of extension, which is neither line, surface, nor solid, nor has any figure or magnitude, but is an idea entirely prescinded from all these. So likewise the mind, by leaving out of the particular colors perceived by sense that which distinguishes them one from another, and retaining that only which is common to all, makes an idea of color in abstract which is neither red, nor blue, nor white, nor any other determinate color. And, in like manner, by considering motion abstractedly not only from the body moved, but likewise from the figure it describes, and all particular directions and velocities, the abstract idea of motion is framed; which equally corresponds to all particular motions whatsoever that may be perceived by sense.

9. And as the mind frames to itself abstract ideas of qualities or modes, so does it, by the same precision or mental separation, attain abstract ideas of the more compounded beings which include several coexistent qualities. For example, the mind having observed that Peter, James, and John resemble each other in certain common agreements of shape and other qualities, leaves out of the complex or compounded idea it has of Peter, James, and any other particular man, that which is peculiar to each, retaining only what is common to all, and so makes an abstract idea wherein all the particulars equally partake; abstracting entirely from and cutting off all those circumstances and differences which might determine it to any particular existence. And after this manner it is said we come by the abstract idea of man, or, if you please, humanity, or human nature; wherein it is true there is included color, because there is no man but has some color, but then it can be neither

white, nor black, nor any particular color, because there is no one particular color wherein all men partake. So likewise there is included stature, but then it is neither tall stature, nor low stature, nor yet middle stature, but something abstracted from all these. And so of the rest. Moreover, there being a great variety of other creatures that partake in some parts, but not all, of the complex idea of man, the mind, leaving out those parts which are peculiar to men, and retaining those only which are common to all the living creatures, frames the idea of *animal*, which abstracts not only from all particular men, but also of birds, beasts, fishes, and insects. The constituent parts of the abstract idea of animal are body, life, sense, and spontaneous motion. By *body* is meant body without any particular shape or figure, there being no one shape or figure common to all animals, without covering, either of hair, or feathers, or scales, etc., nor yet naked: hair, feathers, scales, and nakedness being the distinguishing properties of particular animals, and for that reason left out of the *abstract idea.* Upon the same account the spontaneous motion must be neither walking, nor flying, nor creeping; it is nevertheless a motion, but what that motion is it is not easy to conceive.

10. Whether others have this wonderful faculty of abstracting their ideas, they best can tell; for myself, I find indeed I have a faculty of imagining, or representing to myself, the ideas of those particular things I have perceived, and of variously compounding and dividing them. I can imagine a man with two heads, or the upper parts of a man joined to the body of a horse. I can consider the hand, the eye, the nose, each by itself abstracted or separated from the rest of the body. But then whatever hand or eye I imagine, it must have some particular shape and color. Likewise the idea of man that I frame to myself must be either of a white, or a black, or a tawny, a straight, or a crooked, a tall, or a low, or a middle-sized man. I cannot by any effort of thought conceive the abstract idea above described. And it is equally impossible for me to form the abstract idea of motion distinct from the body moving, and which is neither swift nor slow, curvilinear nor rectilinear; and the like may be said of all other abstract general ideas whatsoever. To be plain, I own myself able to abstract in one sense, as when I consider some particular parts or qualities separated from others, with which, though they are united in some object, yet it is possible they may really exist without them. But I deny that I can abstract from one another, or conceive separately, those qualities which it is impossible should exist so separated; or that I can frame a general notion, by abstracting from particulars in the manner aforesaid—which last are the two proper acceptations of 'abstraction.' And there are grounds to think most men will acknowledge themselves to be in my case. The generality of men which are

simple and illiterate never pretend to abstract notions. It is said they are difficult and not to be attained without pains and study; we may therefore reasonably conclude that, if such there be, they are confined only to the learned.

11. I proceed to examine what can be alleged in defense of the doctrine of abstraction, and try if I can discover what it is that inclines the men of speculation to embrace an opinion so remote from common sense as that seems to be. There has been a late deservedly esteemed philosopher who, no doubt, has given it very much countenance, by seeming to think the having abstract general ideas is what puts the widest difference in point of understanding betwixt man and beast.

The having of general ideas [saith he] is that which puts a perfect distinction betwixt man and brutes, and is an excellency which the faculties of brutes do by no means attain unto. For, it is evident we observe no footsteps in them of making use of general signs for universal ideas; from which we have reason to imagine that they have not the faculty of abstracting, or making general ideas, since they have no use of words or any other general signs.

And a little after:

Therefore, I think, we may suppose that it is in this that the species of brutes are discriminated from men, and it is that proper difference wherein they are wholly separated, and which at last widens to so wide a distance. For, if they have any ideas at all, and are not bare machines (as some would have them), we cannot deny them to have some reason. It seems as evident to me that they do, some of them, in certain instances reason as that they have sense; but it is only in particular ideas, just as they receive them from their senses. They are the best of them tied up within those narrow bounds, and have not (as I think) the faculty to enlarge them by any kind of abstraction.[2]

I readily agree with this learned author, that the faculties of brutes can by no means attain to abstraction. But then if this be made the distinguishing property of that sort of animals, I fear a great many of those that pass for men must be reckoned into their number. The reason that is here assigned why we have no grounds to think brutes have abstract general ideas is, that we observe in them no use of words or any other general signs; which is built on this supposition—that the making use of words implies the having general ideas. From which it follows that men who use language are able to abstract or generalize their ideas. That this is the sense and arguing of the author will further appear by

---

[2] [John Locke] *Essay on [concerning] Human Understanding:* Book II, Chap. ii, Sec. 10, 11.

his answering the question he in another place puts: "Since all things that exist are only particulars, how come we by general terms?" His answer is: "Words become general by being made the signs of general ideas." [3] But it seems that a word becomes general by being made the sign, not of an abstract general idea, but of several particular ideas, any one of which it indifferently suggests to the mind. For example, when it is said "the change of motion is proportional to the impressed force," or that "whatever has extension is divisible," these propositions are to be understood of motion and extension in general; and neverthe- less it will not follow that they suggest to my thoughts an idea of motion without a body moved, or any determinate direction and velocity, or that I must conceive an abstract general idea of extension, which is neither line, surface, nor solid, neither great nor small, black, white, nor red, nor of any other determinate color. It is only implied that whatever particular motion I consider, whether it be swift or slow, perpendicular, horizontal, or oblique, or in whatever object, the axiom concerning it holds equally true. As does the other of every particular extension, it matters not whether line, surface, or solid, whether of this or that magni- tude or figure.

12. By observing how ideas become general we may the better judge how words are made so. And here it is to be noted that I do not deny absolutely there are general ideas, but only that there are any *abstract* general ideas; for in the passages we have quoted wherein there is men- tion of general ideas, it is always supposed that they are formed by abstraction, after the manner set forth in Sections 8 and 9. Now, if we will annex a meaning to our words, and speak only of what we can con- ceive, I believe we shall acknowledge that an idea which considered in itself is particular, becomes general by being made to represent or stand for all other particular ideas of the same sort. To make this plain by an example, suppose a geometrician is demonstrating the method of cut- ting a line in two equal parts. He draws, for instance, a black line of an inch in length: this, which in itself is a particular line, is nevertheless with regard to its signification general, since, as it is there used, it repre- sents all particular lines whatsoever; so that what is demonstrated of it is demonstrated of all lines, or, in other words, of a line in general. And, as that particular line becomes general by being made a sign, so the *name* 'line,' which taken absolutely is particular, by being a sign is made general. And as the former owes its generality not to its being the sign of an abstract or general line, but of all particular right lines that may possibly exist, so the latter must be thought to derive its generality from the same cause, namely, the various particular lines which it indif- ferently denotes.

[3] *Ibid.*, Book III, Chap. iii, Sec. 6

13. To give the reader a yet clearer view of the nature of abstract ideas and the uses they are thought necessary to, I shall add one more passage out of the *Essay on Human Understanding,* which is as follows:

Abstract ideas are not so obvious or easy to children or the yet unexercised mind as particular ones. If they seem so to grown men it is only because by constant and familiar use they are made so. For when we nicely reflect upon them, we shall find that general ideas are fictions and contrivances of the mind, that carry difficulty with them, and do not so easily offer themselves as we are apt to imagine. For example, does it not require some pains and skill to form the general idea of a triangle (which is yet none of the most abstract, comprehensive, and difficult); for it must be neither oblique nor rectangle, neither equilateral, equicrural, nor scalenon, but *all and none* of these at once? In effect, it is something imperfect that cannot exist, an idea wherein some parts of several different and *inconsistent* ideas are put together. It is true the mind in this imperfect state has need of such ideas, and makes all the haste to them it can, for the *conveniency of communication and enlargement of knowledge,* to both which it is naturally very much inclined. But yet one has reason to suspect such ideas are marks of our imperfection. At least this is enough to show that the most abstract and general ideas are not those that the mind is first and most easily acquainted with, nor such as its earliest knowledge is conversant about.[4]

If any man has the faculty of framing in his mind such an idea of a triangle as is here described, it is in vain to pretend to dispute him out of it, nor would I go about it. All I desire is that the reader would fully and certainly inform himself whether he has such an idea or no. And this, methinks, can be no hard task for anyone to perform. What more easy than for anyone to look a little into his own thoughts, and there try whether he has, or can attain to have, an idea that shall correspond with the description that is here given of the general idea of a triangle, which is "neither oblique nor rectangle, equilateral, equicrural nor scalenon, but all and none of these at once"?

14. Much is here said of the difficulty that abstract ideas carry with them, and the pains and skill requisite to the forming them. And it is on all hands agreed that there is need of great toil and labor of the mind, to emancipate our thoughts from particular objects, and raise them to those sublime speculations that are conversant about abstract ideas. From all which the natural consequence should seem to be, that so difficult a thing as the forming abstract ideas was not necessary for *communication,* which is so easy and familiar to all sorts of men. But, we are told, if they seem obvious and easy to grown men, it is only because by constant and

[4] Book IV, Chap. vii, Sec. 9.

familiar use they are made so. Now, I would fain know at what time it is men are employed in surmounting that difficulty, and furnishing themselves with those necessary helps for discourse. It cannot be when they are grown up, for then it seems they are not conscious of any such painstaking; it remains therefore to be the business of their childhood. And surely the great and multiplied labor of framing abstract notions will be found a hard task for that tender age. Is it not a hard thing to imagine that a couple of children cannot prate together of their sugar-plums and rattles and the rest of their little trinkets, till they have first tacked together numberless inconsistencies, and so framed in their minds abstract general ideas, and annexed them to every common name they make use of?

15. Nor do I think them a whit more needful for the enlargement of knowledge than for communication. It is, I know, a point much insisted on, that all knowledge and demonstration are about universal notions, to which I fully agree; but then it doth not appear to me that those notions are formed by abstraction in the manner premised: *universality*, so far as I can comprehend, not consisting in the absolute, *positive* nature or conception of anything, but in the *relation* it bears to the particulars signified or represented by it; by virtue whereof it is that things, names, or notions, being in their own nature *particular*, are rendered *universal*. Thus when I demonstrate any proposition concerning triangles, it is to be supposed that I have in view the universal idea of a triangle; which ought not to be understood as if I could frame an idea of a triangle which was neither equilateral, nor scalenon, nor equicrural; but only that the particular triangle I consider, whether of this or that sort it matters not, doth equally stand for and represent all rectilinear triangles whatsoever, and is in that sense *universal*. All which seems very plain and not to include any difficulty in it.

16. But here it will be demanded how we can know any proposition to be true of all particular triangles, except we have first seen it demonstrated of the abstract idea of a triangle which equally agrees to all? For because a property may be demonstrated to agree to some one particular triangle, it will not thence follow that it equally belongs to any other triangle which in all respects is not the same with it. For example, having demonstrated that the three angles of an isosceles rectangular triangle are equal to two right ones, I cannot therefore conclude this affection agrees to all other triangles which have neither a right angle nor two equal sides. It seems therefore that, to be certain this proposition is universally true, we must either make a particular demonstration for every particular triangle, which is impossible, or once for all demonstrate it of the abstract idea of a triangle, in which all the particulars do indifferently partake and by which they are all equally represented. To

which I answer, that, though the idea I have in view whilst I make the demonstration be, for instance, that of an isosceles rectangular triangle whose sides are of a determinate length, I may nevertheless be certain it extends to all other rectilinear triangles, of what sort or bigness soever. And that because neither the right angle nor the equality nor determinate length of the sides are at all concerned in the demonstration. It is true the diagram I have in view includes all these particulars, but then there is not the least mention made of them in the proof of the proposition. It is not said the three angles are equal to two right ones, because one of them is a right angle, or because the sides comprehending it are of the same length. Which sufficiently shows that the right angle might have been oblique and the sides unequal, and for all that the demonstration have held good. And for this reason it is that I conclude that to be true of any obliquangular or scalenon which I had demonstrated of a particular right-angled equicrural triangle, and not because I demonstrated the proposition of the abstract idea of a triangle. And here it must be acknowledged that a man may consider a figure merely as triangular, without attending to the particular qualities of the angles, or relations of the sides. So far he may abstract; but this will never prove that he can frame an abstract, general, inconsistent idea of a triangle. In like manner we may consider Peter so far forth as man, or so far forth as animal, without framing the forementioned abstract idea, either of man or of animal, inasmuch as all that is perceived is not considered.

17. It were an endless as well as an useless thing to trace the schoolmen, those great masters of abstraction, through all the manifold inextricable labyrinths of error and dispute which their doctrine of abstract natures and notions seems to have led them into. What bickerings and controversies, and what a learned dust have been raised about those matters, and what mighty advantage has been from thence derived to mankind, are things at this day too clearly known to need being insisted on. And it had been well if the ill effects of that doctrine were confined to those only who make the most avowed profession of it. When men consider the great pains, industry, and parts that have for so many ages been laid out on the cultivation and advancement of the sciences, and that notwithstanding all this the far greater part of them remains full of darkness and uncertainty, and disputes that are like never to have an end, and even those that are thought to be supported by the most clear and cogent demonstrations contain in them paradoxes which are perfectly irreconcilable to the understandings of men, and that, taking all together, a very small portion of them does supply any real benefit to mankind, otherwise than by being an innocent diversion and amusement—I say the consideration of all this is apt to throw them into a

despondency and perfect contempt of all study. But this may perhaps cease upon a view of the false principles that have obtained in the world, amongst all which there is none, methinks, hath a more wide and extended sway over the thoughts of speculative men than this of *abstract* general ideas.

18. I come now to consider the *source* of this prevailing notion, and that seems to me to be *language*. And surely nothing of less extent than reason itself could have been the source of an opinion so universally received. The truth of this appears as from other reasons so also from the plain confession of the ablest patrons of abstract ideas, who acknowledge that they are made in order to naming; from which it is a clear consequence that if there had been no such thing as speech or universal signs there never had been any thought of abstraction.[5] Let us examine the manner wherein words have contributed to the origin of that mistake. First, then, it is thought that every name has, or ought to have, one only precise and settled signification, which inclines men to think there are certain abstract, determinate ideas that constitute the true and only immediate signification of each general name; and that it is by the mediation of these abstract ideas that a general name comes to signify any particular thing. Whereas, in truth, there is no such thing as one precise and definite signification annexed to any general name, they all signifying indifferently a great number of particular ideas. All which doth evidently follow from what has been already said, and will clearly appear to anyone by a little reflection. To this it will be objected that every name that has a definition is thereby restrained to one certain signification. For example, a triangle is defined to be 'a plane surface comprehended by three right lines,' by which that name is limited to denote one certain idea and no other. To which I answer that in the definition it is not said whether the surface be great or small, black or white, nor whether the sides are long or short, equal or unequal, nor with what angles they are inclined to each other; in all which there may be great variety, and consequently there is no one settled idea which limits the signification of the word triangle. It is one thing for to keep a name constantly to the same definition, and another to make it stand everywhere for the same idea; the one is necessary, the other useless and impracticable.

19. But to give a farther account how words came to produce the doctrine of abstract ideas, it must be observed that it is a received opinion that language has no other end but the communicating our ideas, and that every significant name stands for an idea. This being so and it being withal certain that names which yet are not thought altogether insignificant do not always mark out particular conceivable ideas, it is

[5] See Bk. III, Chap. VI, Sec. 39, and elsewhere of the *Essay on Human Understanding.*

straightway concluded that they stand for abstract notions. That there are many names in use amongst speculative men which do not always suggest to others determinate, particular ideas, or in truth anything at all, is what nobody will deny. And a little attention will discover that it is not necessary (even in the strictest reasonings) significant names which stand for ideas should, every time they are used, excite in the understanding the ideas they are made to stand for: in reading and discoursing, names being for the most part used as letters are in algebra, in which, though a particular quantity be marked by each letter, yet to proceed right it is not requisite that in every step each letter suggest to your thoughts that particular quantity it was appointed to stand for.

20. Besides, the communicating of ideas marked by words is not the chief and only end of language, as is commonly supposed. There are other ends, as the raising of some passion, the exciting to or deterring from an action, the putting the mind in some particular disposition; to which the former is in many cases barely subservient, and sometimes entirely omitted, when these can be obtained without it, as I think does not unfrequently happen in the familiar use of language. I entreat the reader to reflect with himself, and see if it doth not often happen, either in hearing or reading a discourse, that the passions of fear, love, hatred, admiration, disdain, and the like, arise immediately in his mind upon the perception of certain words, without any ideas coming between. At first, indeed, the words might have occasioned ideas that were fitting to produce those emotions; but, if I mistake not, it will be found that when language is once grown familiar, the hearing of the sounds or sight of the characters is oft immediately attended with those passions which at first were wont to be produced by the intervention of ideas that are now quite omitted. May we not, for example, be affected with the promise of a *good thing,* though we have not an idea of what it is? Or is not the being threatened with danger sufficient to excite a dread, though we think not of any particular evil likely to befall us, nor yet frame to ourselves an idea of danger in abstract? If anyone shall join ever so little reflection of his own to what has been said, I believe that it will evidently appear to him that general names are often used in the propriety of language without the speaker's designing them for marks of ideas in his own, which he would have them raise in the mind of the hearer. Even proper names themselves do not seem always spoken with a design to bring into our view the ideas of those individuals that are supposed to be marked by them. For example, when a schoolman tells me "Aristotle hath said it," all I conceive he means by it is to dispose me to embrace his opinion with the deference and submission which custom has annexed to that name. And this effect is often so instantly produced in the minds of those who are accustomed to resign their judgment

to authority of that philosopher, as it is impossible any idea either of his person, writings, or reputation should go before. Innumerable examples of this kind may be given, but why should I insist on those things which everyone's experience will, I doubt not, plentifully suggest unto him?

21. We have, I think, shewn the impossibility of abstract ideas. We have considered what has been said of them by their ablest patrons, and endeavored to show they are of no use for those ends to which they are thought necessary. And lastly, we have traced them to the source from whence they flow, which appears evidently to be language. It cannot be denied that words are of excellent use, in that by their means all that stock of knowledge which has been purchased by the joint labors of inquisitive men in all ages and nations may be drawn into the view and made the possession of one single person. But at the same time it must be owned that most parts of knowledge have been strangely perplexed and darkened by the abuse of words, and general ways of speech wherein they are delivered. Since therefore words are so apt to impose on the understanding, whatever ideas I consider, I shall endeavor to take them bare and naked into my view, keeping out of my thoughts so far as I am able those names which long and constant use hath so strictly united with them; from which I may expect to derive the following advantages:—

22. *First,* I shall be sure to get clear of all controversies purely *verbal;* the springing up of which weeds in almost all the sciences has been a main hindrance to the growth of true and sound knowledge. *Secondly,* this seems to be a sure way to extricate myself out of that fine and subtle net of *abstract ideas* which has so miserably perplexed and entangled the minds of men; and that with this peculiar circumstance, that by now much the finer and more curious was the wit of any man, by so much the deeper was he likely to be ensnared and faster held therein. *Thirdly,* so long as I confine my thoughts to my own ideas divested of words, I do not see how I can easily be mistaken. The objects I consider, I clearly and adequately know. I cannot be deceived in thinking I have an idea which I have not. It is not possible for me to imagine that any of my own ideas are alike or unlike that are not truly so. To discern the agreements or disagreements there are between my ideas, to see what ideas are included in any compound idea and what not, there is nothing more requisite than an attentive perception of what passes in my own understanding.

23. But the attainment of all these advantages doth *presuppose an entire deliverance from the deception of words,* which I dare hardly promise myself; so difficult a thing it is to dissolve an union so early begun, and confirmed by so long a habit as that betwixt words and ideas. Which difficulty seems to have been very much increased by the doctrine

of *abstraction*. For, so long as men thought abstract ideas were annexed to their words, it doth not seem strange that they should use words for ideas; it being found an impracticable thing to lay aside the word, and retain the abstract idea in the mind, which in itself was perfectly inconceivable. This seems to me the principal cause why those men who have so emphatically recommended to others the laying aside all use of words in their meditations, and contemplating their bare ideas, have yet failed to perform it themselves. Of late many have been very sensible of the absurd opinions and insignificant disputes which grow out of the abuse of words. And, in order to remedy these evils, they advise well that we attend to the ideas signified, and draw off our attention from the words which signify them. But how good soever this advice may be they have given others, it is plain they could not have a due regard to it themselves, so long as they thought the only immediate use of words was to signify ideas, and that the immediate signification of every general name was a determinate abstract idea.

24. But these being known to be mistakes, a man may with greater ease prevent his being imposed on by words. He that knows he has no other than particular ideas, will not puzzle himself in vain to find out and conceive the abstract idea annexed to any name. And he that knows names do not always stand for ideas will spare himself the labor of looking for ideas where there are none to be had. It were therefore to be wished that everyone would use his utmost endeavors to obtain a clear view of the ideas he would consider, separating from them all that dress and encumbrance of words which so much contribute to blind the judgment and divide the attention. In vain do we extend our view into the heavens and pry into the entrails of the earth, in vain do we consult the writings of learned men and trace the dark footsteps of antiquity; we need only draw the curtain of words, to hold the fairest tree of knowledge, whose fruit is excellent and within the reach of our hand.

25. Unless we take care to clear the first principles of knowledge from the embarrassment and delusion of words, we may make infinite reasonings upon them to no purpose: we may draw consequences from consequences, and be never the wiser. The farther we go, we shall only lose ourselves the more irrecoverably, and be the deeper entangled in difficulties and mistakes. Whoever therefore designs to read the following sheets, I entreat him to make my words the occasion of his own thinking, and endeavor to attain the same train of thoughts in reading that I had in writing them. By this means it will be easy for him to discover the truth or falsity of what I say. He will be out of all danger of being deceived by my words, and I do not see how he can be led into an error by considering his own naked, undisguised ideas.

OF THE PRINCIPLES OF
HUMAN KNOWLEDGE

It is evident to anyone who takes a survey of the objects of human knowledge, that they are either ideas (1) actually imprinted on the senses, or else such as are (2) perceived by attending to the passions and operations of the mind, or lastly (3) ideas formed by help of memory and imagination, either compounding, dividing, or barely representing those originally perceived in the aforesaid ways. By sight I have the ideas of lights and colors, with their several degrees and variations. By touch I perceive hard and soft, heat and cold, motion and resistance, and of all these more and less either as to quantity or degree. Smelling furnishes me with odors, the palate with tastes, and hearing conveys sounds to the mind in all their variety of tone and composition. And as several of these are observed to accompany each other, they come to be marked by one name, and so to be reputed as one thing. Thus, for example, a certain color, taste, smell, figure, and consistence, having been observed to go together, are accounted one distinct thing, signified by the name 'apple.' Other collections of ideas constitute a stone, a tree, a book, and the like sensible things; which, as they are pleasing or disagreeable, excite the passions of love, hatred, joy, grief, and so forth.

2. But besides all that endless variety of ideas or objects of knowledge, there is likewise something which knows or perceives them, and exercises divers operations, as willing, imagining, remembering, about them. This perceiving, active being is what I call *mind, spirit, soul,* or *myself.* By which words I do not denote any one of my ideas, but a thing entirely distinct from them wherein they exist, or, which is the same thing, whereby they are perceived; for the existence of an idea consists in being perceived.

3. That neither our thoughts, nor passions, nor ideas formed by the imagination, exist without the mind, is what everybody will allow. And it seems no less evident that the various sensations or ideas imprinted on the sense, however blended or combined together (that is, whatever objects they compose), cannot exist otherwise than in a mind perceiving them. I think an intuitive knowledge may be obtained of this by anyone that shall attend to what is meant by the term 'exist' when applied to sensible things. The table I write on I say exists—that is, I see and feel

it; and if I were out of my study I should say it existed—meaning thereby that if I was in my study I might perceive it, or that some other spirit actually does perceive it. There was an odor, that is, it was smelt; there was a sound, that is, it was heard; a color or figure, and it was perceived by sight or touch. This is all that I can understand by these and the like expressions. For as to what is said of the absolute existence of unthinking things without any relation to their being perceived, that seems perfectly unintelligible. Their *esse* is *percipi,* nor is it possible they should have any existence out of the minds or thinking things which perceive them.

4. It is indeed an opinion strangely prevailing amongst men, that houses, mountains, rivers, and in a word all sensible objects, have an existence, natural or real, distinct from their being perceived by the understanding. But with how great an assurance and acquiescence soever this principle may be entertained in the world, yet whoever shall find in his heart to call it in question may, if I mistake not, perceive it to involve a manifest contradiction. For what are the forementioned objects but the things we perceive by sense? and what do we perceive *besides our own ideas or sensations?* and is it not plainly repugnant that any one of these, or any combination of them, should exist unperceived?

5. If we thoroughly examine this tenet it will perhaps be found at bottom to depend on the doctrine of *abstract ideas.* For can there be a nicer strain of abstraction than to distinguish the existence of sensible objects from their being perceived, so as to conceive them existing unperceived? Light and colors, heat and cold, extension and figures—in a word the things we see and feel—what are they but so many sensations, notions, ideas, or impressions on the sense? And is it possible to separate, even in thought, any of these from perception? For my part, I might as easily divide a thing from itself. I may, indeed, divide in my thoughts, or conceive apart from each other, those things which perhaps I never perceived by sense so divided. Thus I imagine the trunk of a human body without the limbs, or conceive the smell of a rose without thinking on the rose itself. So far, I will not deny, I can abstract, if that may properly be called abstraction which extends only to the conceiving separately such objects as it is possible may really exist or be actually perceived asunder. But my conceiving or imagining power does not extend beyond the possibility of real existence or perception. Hence, as it is impossible for me to see or feel anything without an actual sensation of that thing, so it is impossible for me to conceive in my thoughts any sensible thing or object distinct from the sensation or perception of it.

6. Some truths there are so near and obvious to the mind that a man need only open his eyes to see them. Such I take this important one to be, to wit, that all the choir of heaven and furniture of the earth, in a

word all those bodies which compose the mighty frame of the world, have not any subsistence without a mind, that their *being* is to be perceived or known; that consequently so long as they are not actually perceived by me, or do not exist in my mind or that of any other created spirit, they must either have no existence at all, or else subsist in the mind of some Eternal Spirit; it being perfectly unintelligible, and involving all the absurdity of abstraction, to attribute to any single part of them an existence independent of a spirit. To be convinced of which, the reader need only reflect and try to separate in his own thoughts the *being* of a sensible thing from its *being perceived*.

7. From what has been said it follows there is not any other substance than *spirit*, or that which perceives. But for the fuller proof of this point, let it be considered the sensible qualities are color, figure, motion, smell, taste, etc.—that is, the ideas perceived by sense. Now, for an idea to exist in an unperceiving thing is a manifest contradiction, for to have an idea is all one as to perceive; that therefore wherein color, figure, and the like qualities exist must perceive them; hence it is clear there can be no unthinking substance or *substratum* of those ideas.

8. But, say you, though the ideas themselves do not exist without the mind, yet there may be things *like* them, whereof they are copies or resemblances, which things exist without the mind in an unthinking substance. I answer, an idea can be like nothing but an idea; a color or figure can be like nothing but another color or figure. If we look but never so little into our thoughts, we shall find it impossible for us to conceive a likeness except only between our ideas. Again, I ask whether those supposed originals or external things, of which our ideas are the pictures or representations, be themselves perceivable or no? If they are, then they are ideas and we have gained our point; but if you say they are not, I appeal to anyone whether it be sense to assert a color is like something which is invisible; hard or soft, like something which is intangible; and so of the rest.

9. Some there are who make a distinction betwixt *primary* and *secondary* qualities. By the former they mean extension, figure, motion, rest, solidity or impenetrability, and number; by the latter they denote all other sensible qualities, as colors, sounds, tastes, and so forth. The ideas we have of these they acknowledge not to be the resemblances of anything existing without the mind, or unperceived, but they will have our ideas of the primary qualities to be patterns or images of things which exist without the mind, in an unthinking substance which they call *matter*. By *matter*, therefore, we are to understand an inert, senseless substance, in which extension, figure, and motion do actually subsist. But it is evident from what we have already shown, that extension, figure, and motion are only ideas existing in the mind, and that an idea

can be like nothing but another idea, and that consequently neither they nor their archetypes can exist in an unperceiving substance. Hence, it is plain that the very notion of what is called *matter,* or *corporeal substance,* involves a contradiction in it.

10. They who assert that figure, motion, and the rest of the primary or original qualities do exist without the mind in unthinking substances, do at the same time acknowledge that color, sounds, heat, cold, and suchlike secondary qualities, do not; which they tell us are sensations existing in the mind alone, that depend on and are occasioned by the different size, texture, and motion of the minute particles of matter. This they take for an undoubted truth, which they can demonstrate beyond all exception. Now, if it be certain that those original qualities are inseparably united with the other sensible qualities, and not, even in thought, capable of being abstracted from them, it plainly follows that they exist only in the mind. But I desire anyone to reflect and try whether he can, by any abstraction of thought, conceive the extension and motion of a body without all other sensible qualities. For my own part, I see evidently that it is not in my power to frame an idea of a body extended and moving, but I must withal give it some color or other sensible quality which is acknowledged to exist only in the mind. In short, extension, figure, and motion, abstracted from all other qualities, are inconceivable. Where therefore the other sensible qualities are, there must these be also, to wit, in the mind and nowhere else.

11. Again, *great* and *small, swift* and *slow,* are allowed to exist nowhere without the mind, being entirely relative, and changing as the frame or position of the organs of sense varies. The extension therefore which exists without the mind is neither great nor small, the motion neither swift nor slow, that is, they are nothing at all. But, say you, they are extension in general, and motion in general: thus we see how much the tenet of extended movable substances existing without the mind depends on the strange doctrine of *abstract ideas.* And here I cannot but remark how nearly the vague and indeterminate description of matter or corporeal substance, which the modern philosophers are run into by their own principles, resembles that antiquated and so much ridiculed notion of *materia prima,* to be met with in Aristotle and his followers. Without extension solidity cannot be conceived; since therefore it has been shewn that extension exists not in an unthinking substance, the same must also be true of solidity.

12. That *number* is entirely the creature of the mind, even though the other qualities be allowed to exist without, will be evident to whoever considers that the same thing bears a different denomination of number as the mind views it with different respects. Thus, the same extension is one, or three, or thirty-six, according as the mind considers it

with reference to a yard, a foot, or an inch. Number is so visibly relative, and dependent on men's understanding, that it is strange to think how anyone should give it an absolute existence without the mind. We say one book, one page, one line; all these are equally units, though some contain several of the others. And in each instance, it is plain, the unit relates to some particular combination of ideas arbitrarily put together by the mind.

13. *Unity,* I know, some will have to be a simple or uncompounded idea, accompanying all other ideas into the mind. That I have any such idea answering the word 'unity' I do not find; and if I had, methinks I could not miss finding it: on the contrary, it should be the most familiar to my understanding, since it is said to accompany all other ideas, and to be perceived by all the ways of sensation and reflection. To say no more, it is an *abstract idea.*

14. I shall farther add that, after the same manner as modern philosophers prove certain sensible qualities to have no existence in matter, or without the mind, the same thing may be likewise proved of all other sensible qualities whatsoever. Thus, for instance, it is said that heat and cold are affections only of the mind, and not at all patterns of real beings, existing in the corporeal substances which excite them, for that the same body which appears cold to one hand seems warm to another. Now, why may we not as well argue that figure and extension are not patterns or resemblances of qualities existing in matter, because to the same eye at different stations, or eyes of a different texture at the same station, they appear various, and cannot therefore be the images of anything settled and determinate without the mind? Again, it is proved that sweetness is not really in the sapid thing, because the thing remaining unaltered the sweetness is changed into bitter, as in case of a fever or otherwise vitiated palate. Is it not as reasonable to say that motion is not without the mind, since if the succession of ideas in the mind become swifter, the motion, it is acknowledged, shall appear slower without any alteration in any external object?

15. In short, let anyone consider those arguments which are thought manifestly to prove that colors and tastes exist only in the mind, and he shall find they may with equal force be brought to prove the same thing of extension, figure, and motion—though it must be confessed this method of arguing does not so much prove that there is no extension or color in an outward object, as that we do not know by sense which is the true extension or color of the object. But the arguments foregoing plainly show it to be impossible that any color or extension at all, or other sensible quality whatsoever, should exist in an unthinking subject without the mind, or in truth, that there should be any such thing as an outward object.

16. But let us examine a little the received opinion. It is said extension is a mode or accident of matter, and that matter is the *substratum* that supports it. Now I desire that you would explain to me what is meant by matter's *supporting* extension. Say you, I have no idea of matter and therefore cannot explain it. I answer, though you have no positive, yet, if you have any meaning at all, you must at least have a relative idea of matter; though you know not what it is, yet you must be supposed to know what relation it bears to accidents, and what is meant by its supporting them. It is evident 'support' cannot here be taken in its usual or literal sense—as when we say that pillars support a building; in what sense therefore must it be taken?

17. If we inquire into what the most accurate philosophers declare themselves to mean by *material substance*, we shall find them acknowledge they have no other meaning annexed to those sounds but the idea of *Being in general,* together with the relative notion of its supporting accidents. The general idea of Being appeareth to me the most abstract and incomprehensible of all other; and as for its supporting accidents, this, as we have just now observed, cannot be understood in the common sense of those words; it must therefore be taken in some other sense, but what that is they do not explain. So that when I consider the two parts or branches which make the signification of the words *material substance,* I am convinced there is no distinct meaning annexed to them. But why should we trouble ourselves any farther, in discussing this material *substratum* or support of figure and motion, and other sensible qualities? Does it not suppose they have an existence without the mind? And is not this a direct repugnancy, and altogether inconceivable?

18. But though it were possible that solid, figured, movable substances may exist without the mind, corresponding to the ideas we have of bodies, yet how is it possible for us to know this? Either we must know it by sense or by reason. As for our senses, by them we have the knowledge only of our sensations, ideas, or those things that are immediately perceived by sense, call them what you will; but they do not inform us that things exist without the mind, or unperceived, like to those which are perceived. This the materialists themselves acknowledge. It remains therefore that if we have any knowledge at all of external things, it must be by reason, inferring their existence from what is immediately perceived by sense. But what reason can induce us to believe the existence of bodies without the mind, from what we perceive, since the very patrons of matter themselves do not pretend there is any necessary connection betwixt them and our ideas? I say it is granted on all hands (and what happens in dreams, frenzies, and the like, puts it beyond dispute) that *it is possible we might be affected with all the ideas we have now, though there were no bodies existing without, resembling them.*

Hence, it is evident the supposition of external bodies is not necessary for the producing our ideas; since it is granted they are produced sometimes, and might possibly be produced always in the same order we see them in at present, without their concurrence.

19. But, though we might possibly have all our sensations without them, yet perhaps it may be thought easier to conceive and explain the manner of their production by supposing external bodies in their likeness rather than otherwise; and so it might be at least probable there are such things as bodies that excite their ideas in our minds. But neither can this be said; for though we give the materialists their external bodies, they by their own confession are never the nearer knowing how our ideas are produced, since they own themselves unable to comprehend in what manner body can act upon spirit, or how it is possible it should imprint any idea in the mind. Hence it is evident the production of ideas or sensations in our minds can be no reason why we should suppose matter or corporeal substances, since that is acknowledged to remain equally inexplicable with or without this supposition. If therefore it were possible for bodies to exist without the mind, yet to hold they do so, must needs be a very precarious opinion; since it is to suppose, without any reason at all, that God has created innumerable beings that are entirely useless, and serve to no manner of purpose.

20. In short, if there were external bodies, it is impossible we should ever come to know it; and if there were not, we might have the very same reasons to think there were that we have now. Suppose (what no one can deny possible) an intelligence without the help of external bodies, to be affected with the same train of sensations or ideas that you are, imprinted in the same order and with like vividness in his mind. I ask whether that intelligence hath not all the reason to believe the existence of corporeal substances, represented by his ideas, and exciting them in his mind, that you can possibly have for believing the same thing? Of this there can be no question; which one consideration were enough to make any reasonable person suspect the strength of whatever arguments he may think himself to have for the existence of bodies without the mind.

21. Were it necessary to add any farther proof against the existence of matter after what has been said, I could instance several of those errors and difficulties (not to mention impieties) which have sprung from that tenet. It has occasioned numberless controversies and disputes in philosophy, and not a few of far greater moment in religion. But I shall not enter into the detail of them in this place, as well because I think arguments *a posteriori* are unnecessary for confirming what has been, if I mistake not, sufficiently demonstrated *a priori*, as because I shall hereafter find occasion to speak somewhat of them.

22. I am afraid I have given cause to think I am needlessly prolix in handling this subject. For, to what purpose is it to dilate on that which may be demonstrated with the utmost evidence in a line or two, to anyone that is capable of the least reflection? It is but looking into your own thoughts, and so trying whether you can conceive it possible for a sound, or figure, or motion, or color to exist without the mind or unperceived. This easy trial may perhaps make you see that what you contend for is a downright contradiction. Insomuch that I am content to put the whole upon this issue: if you can but conceive it possible for one extended movable substance, or, in general, for any one idea, or anything like an idea, to exist otherwise than in a mind perceiving it, I shall readily give up the cause; and, as for all that compages of external bodies you contend for, I shall grant you its existence, though you cannot either give me any reason why you believe it exists, or assign any use to it when it is supposed to exist. I say, the bare possibility of your opinion's being true shall pass for an argument that it is so.

23. But, say you, surely there is nothing easier than for me to imagine trees, for instance, in a park, or books existing in a closet, and nobody by to perceive them. I answer, you may so, there is no difficulty in it; but what is all this, I beseech you, more than framing in your mind certain ideas which you call books and trees, and the same time omitting to frame the idea of anyone that may perceive them? But do not you yourself perceive or think of them all the while? This therefore is nothing to the purpose; it only shews you have the power of imagining or forming ideas in your mind: but it doth not shew that you can conceive it possible the objects of your thought may exist without the mind. To make out this, it is necessary that you conceive them existing unconceived or unthought of, which is a manifest repugnancy. When we do our utmost to conceive the existence of external bodies, we are all the while only contemplating our own ideas. But the mind taking no notice of itself, is deluded to think it can and doth conceive bodies existing unthought of or without the mind, though at the same time they are apprehended by or exist in itself. A little attention will discover to anyone the truth and evidence of what is here said, and make it unnecessary to insist on any other proofs against the existence of *material substance*.

24. It is very obvious, upon the least inquiry into our thoughts, to know whether it is possible for us to understand what is meant by the *absolute existence of sensible objects in themselves, or without the mind*. To me it is evident those words mark out either a direct contradiction, or else nothing at all. And to convince others of this, I know no readier or fairer way than to entreat they would calmly attend to their own thoughts; and if by this attention the emptiness or repugnancy of those expressions doth appear, surely nothing more is requisite for the convic-

tion. It is on this therefore that I insist, to wit, that the absolute existence of unthinking things are words without a meaning, or which include a contradiction. This is what I repeat and inculcate, and earnestly recommend to the attentive thoughts of the reader.

25. All our ideas, sensations, notions, or the things which we perceive, by whatsoever names they may be distinguished, are visibly inactive: there is nothing of power or agency included in them. So that one idea or object of thought cannot produce or make any alteration in another. To be satisfied of the truth of this, there is nothing else requisite but a bare observation of our ideas. For, since they and every part of them exist only in the mind, it follows that there is nothing in them but what is perceived: but whoever shall attend to his ideas, whether of sense or reflection, will not perceive in them any power or activity; there is, therefore, no such thing contained in them. A little attention will discover to us that the very being of an idea implies passiveness and inertness in it, insomuch that it is impossible for an idea to do anything, or, strictly speaking, to be the cause of anything: neither can it be the resemblance or pattern of any active being, as is evident from Sec. 8. Whence it plainly follows that extension, figure, and motion cannot be the cause of our sensations. To say, therefore, that these are the effects of powers resulting from the configuration, number, motion, and size of corpuscles, must certainly be false.

26. We perceive a continual succession of ideas, some are anew excited, others are changed or totally disappear. There is therefore some cause of these ideas, whereon they depend, and which produces and changes them. That this cause cannot be any quality or idea or combination of ideas, is clear from the preceding section. It must therefore be a substance; but it has been shewn that there is no corporeal or material substance: it remains therefore that the cause of ideas is an incorporeal active substance or Spirit.

27. A spirit is one simple, undivided, active being: as it perceives ideas it is called the *understanding,* and as it produces or otherwise operates about them it is called the *will.* Hence there can be no *idea* formed of a soul or spirit; for all ideas whatever, being passive and inert (*vide* Sec. 25), they cannot represent unto us, by way of image or likeness, that which acts. A little attention will make it plain to anyone, that to have an idea which shall be like that active principle of motion and change of ideas is absolutely impossible. Such is the nature of *spirit,* or that which acts, that it cannot be of itself perceived, but only by the effects which it produceth. If any man shall doubt of the truth of what is here delivered, let him but reflect and try if he can frame the idea of any power or active being, and whether he hath ideas of two principal powers, marked by the names *will* and *understanding,* distinct

from each other as well as from a third idea of substance or being in general, with a relative notion of its supporting or being the subject of the aforesaid powers—which is signified by the name *soul* or *spirit*. This is what some hold; but, so far as I can see, the words *will, soul, spirit,* do not stand for different ideas, or, in truth, for any idea at all, but for something which is very different from ideas, and which, being an agent, cannot be like unto, or represented by, any idea whatsoever. Though it must be owned at the same time that we have some *notion* of soul, spirit, and the operations of the mind such as willing, loving, hating; inasmuch as we know or understand the meaning of these words.

28. I find I can excite ideas in my mind at pleasure, and vary and shift the scene as oft as I think fit. It is no more than willing, and straightway this or that idea arises in my fancy; and by the same power it is obliterated and makes way for another. This making and unmaking of ideas doth very properly denominate the mind active. Thus much is certain and grounded on experience; but when we think of unthinking agents or of exciting ideas exclusive of volition, we only amuse ourselves with words.

29. But, whatever power I may have over my own thoughts, I find the ideas actually perceived by sense have not a like dependence on my will. When in broad daylight I open my eyes, it is not in my power to choose whether I shall see or no, or to determine what particular objects shall present themselves to my view; and so likewise as to the hearing and other senses, the ideas imprinted on them are not creatures of my will. There is therefore some other will or spirit that produces them.

30. The ideas of sense are more strong, lively, and distinct than those of the imagination; they have likewise a steadiness, order, and coherence, and are not excited at random, as those which are the effects of human wills often are, but in a regular train or series, the admirable connection whereof sufficiently testifies the wisdom and benevolence of its Author. Now the set rules or established methods wherein the mind we depend on excites in us the ideas of sense, are called the *laws of nature;* and these we learn by experience, which teaches us that such and such ideas are attended with such and such other ideas, in the ordinary course of things.

31. This gives us a sort of foresight which enables us to regulate our actions for the benefit of life. And without this we should be eternally at a loss: we could not know how to act anything that might procure us the least pleasure, or remove the least pain of sense. That food nourishes, sleep refreshes, and fire warms us; that to sow in the seed-time is the way to reap in the harvest; and, in general, that to obtain such or such ends, such or such means are conducive—all this we know, not by discovering any necessary connection between our ideas, but only by the

observation of the settled laws of nature, without which we should be all in uncertainty and confusion, and a grown man no more know how to manage himself in the affairs of life than an infant just born.

32. And yet this insistent uniform working, which so evidently displays the goodness and wisdom of that governing Spirit whose will constitutes the laws of nature, is so far from leading our thoughts to Him, that it rather sends them wandering after second causes. For, when we perceive certain ideas of sense constantly followed by other ideas and we know this is not of our own doing, we forthwith attribute power and agency to the ideas themselves, and make one the cause of another, than which nothing can be more absurd and unintelligible. Thus, for example, having observed that when we perceive by sight a certain round luminous figure we at the same time perceive by touch the idea or sensation called heat, we do from thence conclude the sun to be the cause of heat. And in like manner perceiving the motion and collision of bodies to be attended with sound, we are inclined to think the latter the effect of the former.

33. The ideas imprinted on the senses by the Author of nature are called *real things;* and those excited in the imagination, being less regular, vivid, and constant, are more properly termed *ideas,* or *images* of *things,* which they copy and represent. But then our sensations, be they never so vivid and distinct, are nevertheless ideas, that is, they exist in the mind, or are perceived by it, as truly as the ideas of its own framing. The ideas of sense are allowed to have more reality in them, that is, to be more strong, orderly, and coherent than the creatures of the mind; but this is no argument that they exist without the mind. They are also less dependent on the spirit, or thinking substance which perceives them, in that they are excited by the will of another and more powerful spirit; yet still they are *ideas,* and certainly no idea, whether faint or strong, can exist otherwise than in a mind perceiving it.

34. Before we proceed any farther it is necessary we spend some time in answering objections which may probably be made against the principles we have hitherto laid down. In doing of which, if I seem too prolix to those of quick apprehensions, I hope it may be pardoned, since all men do not equally apprehend things of this nature, and I am willing to be understood by everyone.

First, then, it will be objected that by the foregoing principles all that is real and substantial in nature is banished out of the world, and instead thereof a chimerical scheme of *ideas* takes place. All things that exist, exist only in the mind, that is, they are purely notional. What therefore becomes of the sun, moon, and stars? What must we think of houses, rivers, mountains, trees, stones; nay, even of our own bodies? Are all these but so many chimeras and illusions on the fancy? To all which, and whatever else of the same sort may be objected, I answer that by the principles premised we are not deprived of any one thing in nature. Whatever we see, feel, hear, or anywise conceive or understand remains as secure as ever, and is as real as ever. There is a *rerum natura,* and the distinction between realities and chimeras retains its full force. This is evident from Sec. 29, 30, and 33, where we have shewn what is meant by *real things* in opposition to *chimeras* or ideas of our own framing; but then they both equally exist in the mind, and in that sense they are alike *ideas.*

35. I do not argue against the existence of any one thing that we can apprehend either by sense or reflection. That the things I see with my eyes and touch with my hands do exist, really exist, I make not the least question. The only thing whose existence we deny is that which *philosophers* call matter or corporeal substance. And in doing of this there is no damage done to the rest of mankind, who, I dare say, will never miss it. The atheist indeed will want the color of an empty name to support his impiety; and the philosophers may possibly find they have lost a great handle for trifling and disputation.

36. If any man thinks this detracts from the existence or reality of things, he is very far from understanding what hath been premised in the plainest terms I could think of. Take here an abstract of what has been said. There are spiritual substances, minds, or human souls, which will or excite ideas in themselves at pleasure; but these are faint, weak, and unsteady in respect of others they perceive by sense—which, being impressed upon them according to certain rules or laws of nature, speak themselves the effects of a mind more powerful and wise than human spirits. These latter are said to have more *reality* in them than the former; by which is meant that they are more affecting, orderly, and distinct, and that they are not fictions of the mind perceiving them. And in this sense the sun that I see by day is the real sun, and that which I imagine by night is the idea of the former. In the sense here given of 'reality' it is evident that every vegetable, star, mineral, and in general each part of the mundane system, is as much as a real being by our principles as by any other. Whether others mean anything by the term 'reality' different from what I do, I entreat them to look into their own thoughts and see.

37. It will be urged that thus much at least is true, to wit, that we take away all corporeal substances. To this my answer is that if the word 'substance' be taken in the vulgar sense—for a combination of sensible qualities, such as extension, solidity, weight, and the like—this we cannot be accused of taking away. But if it be taken in a philosophic sense—for the support of accidents or qualities without the mind—then indeed I acknowledge that we take it away, if one may be said to take

away that which never had any existence, not even in the imagination.

38. But after all, say you, it sounds very harsh to say we eat and drink ideas, and are clothed with ideas. I acknowledge it does so; the word 'idea' not being used in common discourse to signify the several combinations of sensible qualities which are called 'things'; and it is certain that any expression which varies from the familiar use of language will seem harsh and ridiculous. But this doth not concern the truth of the proposition, which in other words is no more than to say, we are fed and clothed with those things which we perceive immediately by our senses. The hardness or softness, the color, taste, warmth, figure, or suchlike qualities, which combined together constitute the several sorts of victuals and apparel, have been shewn to exist only in the mind that perceives them; and this is all that is meant by calling them 'ideas'; which word if it was as ordinarily used as 'things,' would sound no harsher nor more ridiculous than it. I am not for disputing about the propriety, but the truth of the expression. If therefore you agree with me that we eat and drink and are clad with the immediate objects of sense, which cannot exist unperceived or without the mind, I shall readily grant it is more proper or conformable to custom that they should be called things rather than ideas.

39. If it be demanded why I make use of the word 'idea,' and do not rather in compliance with custom call them 'thing'; I answer, I do it for two reasons:—first, because the term 'thing' in contradistinction to 'idea,' is generally supposed to denote somewhat existing without the mind; secondly, because 'thing' hath a more comprehensive signification than 'idea,' including spirit or thinking things as well as ideas. Since therefore the objects of sense exist only in the mind, and are withal thoughtless and inactive, I chose to mark them by the word 'idea,' which implies those properties.

40. But, say what we can, someone perhaps may be apt to reply, he will still believe his senses, and never suffer any arguments, how plausible soever, to prevail over the certainty of them. Be it so; assert the evidence of sense as high as you please, we are willing to do the same. That what I see, hear, and feel doth exist, that is to say, is perceived by me, I no more doubt than I do of my own being. But I do not see how the testimony of sense can be alleged as a proof for the existence of anything which is not perceived by sense. We are not for having any man turn sceptic and disbelieve his senses; on the contrary, we give them all the stress and assurance imaginable; nor are there any principles more opposite to scepticism than those we have laid down, as shall be hereafter clearly shewn.

41. *Secondly,* it will be objected that there is a great difference betwixt real fire for instance, and the idea of fire, betwixt dreaming or im-

agining oneself burnt, and actually being so: if you suspect it to be only the idea of fire which you see, do but put your hand into it and you will be convinced with a witness. This and the like may be urged in opposition to our tenets. To all which the answer is evident from what hath been already said; and I shall only add in this place, that if real fire be very different from the idea of fire, so also is the real pain that it occasions very different from the idea of the same pain, and yet nobody will pretend that real pain either is, or can possibly be, in an unperceiving thing, or without the mind, any more than its idea.

42. *Thirdly*, it will be objected that we see things actually without or at distance from us, and which consequently do not exist in the mind; it being absurd that those things which are seen at the distance of several miles should be as near to us as our own thoughts. In answer to this, I desire it may be considered that in a dream we do oft perceive things as existing at a great distance off, and yet for all that, those things are acknowledged to have their existence only in the mind.

43. But, for the fuller clearing of this point, it may be worth while to consider how it is that we perceive distance and things placed at a distance by sight. For, that we should in truth see external space, and bodies actually existing in it, some nearer, others farther off, seems to carry with it some opposition to what hath been said of their existing nowhere without the mind. The consideration of this difficulty it was that gave birth to my *Essay towards a New Theory of Vision,* which was published not long since, wherein it is shewn that distance or outness is neither immediately of itself perceived by sight, nor yet apprehended or judged of by lines and angles, or anything that hath a necessary connection with it; but that it is only suggested to our thoughts by certain visible ideas and sensations attending vision, which in their own nature have no manner of similitude or relation either with distance or things placed at a distance; but, by a connection taught us by experience, they come to signify and suggest them to us, after the same manner that words of any language suggest the ideas they are made to stand for; insomuch that a man born blind and afterwards made to see, would not, at first sight, think the things he saw to be without his mind, or at any distance from him. (See Sec. 41 of the forementioned treatise.)

44. The ideas of sight and touch make two species entirely distinct and heterogeneous. *The former are marks and prognostics of the latter.* That the proper objects of sight neither exist without mind, nor are the images of external things, was shewn even in that treatise; though throughout the same the contrary be supposed true of tangible objects—not that to suppose that vulgar error was necessary for establishing the notion therein laid down, but because it was beside my purpose to examine and refute it in a discourse concerning *vision.* So that in strict

truth the ideas of sight, when we apprehend by them distance and things placed at a distance, do not suggest or mark out to us things actually existing at a distance, but only admonish us what ideas of touch will be imprinted in our minds at such and such distances of time, and in consequence of such or such actions. It is, I say, evident from what has been said in the foregoing parts of this treatise, and in Sec. 147 and elsewhere of the essay concerning vision, that visible ideas are the language whereby the governing Spirit on whom we depend informs us what tangible ideas he is about to imprint upon us, in case we excite this or that motion in our own bodies. But for a fuller information in this point I refer to the essay itself.

45. *Fourthly,* it will be objected that from the foregoing principles it follows things are every moment annihilated and created anew. The objects of sense exist only when they are perceived; the trees therefore are in the garden, or the chairs in the parlor, no longer than while there is somebody by to perceive them. Upon shutting my eyes all the furniture in the room is reduced to nothing, and barely upon opening them it is again created. In answer to all which, I refer the reader to what has been said in Sec. 3, 4, etc., and desire he will consider whether he means anything by the actual existence of an idea distinct from its being perceived. For my part, after the nicest inquiry I could make, I am not able to discover that anything else is meant by those words; and I once more entreat the reader to sound his own thoughts, and not suffer himself to be imposed on by words. If he can conceive it possible either for his ideas or their archetypes to exist without being perceived, then I give up the cause; but if he cannot, he will acknowledge it is unreasonable for him to stand up in defense of he knows not what, and pretend to charge on me as an absurdity the not assenting to those propositions which at bottom have no meaning in them.

46. It will not be amiss to observe how far the received principles of philosophy are themselves chargeable with those pretended absurdities. It is thought strangely absurd that upon closing my eyelids all the visible objects around me should be reduced to nothing; and yet is not this what philosophers commonly acknowledge, when they agree on all hands that light and colors, which alone are the proper and immediate objects of sight, are mere sensations that exist no longer than they are perceived? Again, it may to some perhaps seem very incredible that things should be every moment creating, yet this very notion is commonly taught in the schools. For the schoolmen, though they acknowledge the existence of matter, and that the whole mundane fabric is framed out of it, are nevertheless of opinion that it cannot subsist without the divine conservation, which by them is expounded to be a continual creation.

47. Farther, a little thought will discover to us that though we allow

the existence of matter or corporeal substance, yet it will unavoidably follow, from the principles which are now generally admitted, that the particular bodies, of what kind soever, do none of them exist whilst they are not perceived. For, it is evident from Sec. 11 and the following sections, that the matter philosophers contend for is an incomprehensible somewhat, which hath none of those particular qualities whereby the bodies falling under our senses are distinguished one from another. But, to make this more plain, it must be remarked that the infinite divisibility of matter is now universally allowed, at least by the most approved and considerable philosophers, who on the received principles demonstrate it beyond all exception. Hence, it follows there is an infinite number of parts in each particle of matter which are not perceived by sense. The reason therefore that any particular body seems to be of a finite magnitude, or exhibits only a finite number of parts to sense, is, not because it contains no more, since in itself it contains an infinite number of parts, but because the sense is not acute enough to discern them. In proportion therefore as the sense is rendered more acute, it perceives a greater number of parts in the object, that is, the object appears greater, and its figure varies, those parts in its extremities which were before unperceivable appearing now to bound it in very different lines and angles from those perceived by an obtuser sense. And at length, after various changes of size and shape, when the sense becomes infinitely acute the body shall seem infinite. During all which there is no alteration in the body, but only in the sense. Each body therefore, considered in itself, is infinitely extended, and consequently void of all shape or figure. From which it follows that, though we should grant the existence of matter to be never so certain, yet it is withal as certain, the materialists themselves are by their own principles forced to acknowledge, that neither the particular bodies perceived by sense, nor anything like them, exists without the mind. Matter, I say, and each particle thereof, is according to them infinite and shapeless, and it is the mind that frames all that variety of bodies which compose the visible world, anyone whereof does not exist longer than it is perceived.

48. If we consider it, the objection proposed in Sec. 45 will not be found reasonably charged on the principles we have premised, so as in truth to make any objection at all against our notions. For, though we hold indeed the objects of sense to be nothing else but ideas which cannot exist unperceived; yet we may not hence conclude they have no existence except only while they are perceived by us, since there may be some other spirit that perceives them though we do not. Wherever bodies are said to have no existence without the mind, I would not be understood to mean this or that particular mind, but all minds whatsoever. It does not therefore follow from the foregoing principles that bodies are

annihilated and created every moment, or exist not at all during the intervals between our perception of them.

49. *Fifthly,* it may perhaps be objected that if extension and figure exist only in the mind, it follows that the mind is extended and figured; since extension is a mode or attribute which (to speak with the schools) is predicated of the subject in which it exists. I answer, those qualities are in the mind only as they are perceived by it—that is, not by way of *mode* or *attribute,* but only by way of *idea;* and it no more follows the soul or mind is extended, because extension exists in it alone, than it does that it is red or blue, because those colors are on all hands acknowledged to exist in it, and nowhere else. As to what philosophers say of subject and mode, that seems very groundless and unintelligible. For instance, in this proposition, "a die is hard, extended, and square," they will have it that the word 'die' denotes a subject or substance, distinct from the hardness, extension, and figure which are predicated of it, and in which they exist. This I cannot comprehend: to me a die seems to be nothing distinct from those things which are termed its modes or accidents. And, to say a die is hard, extended, and square is not to attribute those qualities to a subject distinct from and supporting them, but only an explication of the meaning of the word 'die.'

50. *Sixthly,* you will say there have been a great many things explained by matter and motion; take away these and you destroy the whole corpuscular philosophy, and undermine those mechanical principles which have been applied with so much success to account for the phenomena. In short, whatever advances have been made, either by accident or modern philosophers, in the study of nature do all proceed on the supposition that corporeal substance or matter doth really exist. To this I answer that there is not any one phenomenon explained on that supposition which may not as well be explained without it, as might easily be made appear by an induction of particulars. To explain the phenomena, is all one as to shew why, upon such and such occasions, we are affected with such and such ideas. But how matter should operate on a spirit, or produce any idea in it, is what no philosopher will pretend to explain; it is therefore evident there can be no use of matter in natural philosophy. Besides, they who attempt to account for things do it not by corporeal substance, but by figure, motion, and other qualities, which are in truth no more than mere ideas, and, therefore, cannot be the cause of anything, as hath been already shewn. (See Sec. 25).

51. *Seventhly,* it will upon this be demanded whether it does not seem absurd to take away natural causes, and ascribe everything to the immediate operation of spirits? We must no longer say upon these principles that fire heats, or water cools, but that a spirit heats, and so forth. Would not a man be deservedly laughed at, who should talk after this

manner? I answer, he would so; in such things we ought to 'think with the learned, and speak with the vulgar.' They who to demonstration are convinced of the truth of the Copernican system do nevertheless say, "The sun rises," "The sun sets," or "comes to the meridian"; and if they affected a contrary style in common talk it would without doubt appear very ridiculous. A little reflection on what is here said will make it manifest that the common use of language would receive no manner of alteration or disturbance from the admission of our tenets.

52. In the ordinary affairs of life, any phrases may be retained, so long as they excite in us proper sentiments, or dispositions to act in such a manner as is necessary for our well-being, how false soever they may be if taken in a strict and speculative sense. Nay, this is unavoidable, since, propriety being regulated by custom, language is suited to the received opinions, which are not always the truest. Hence it is impossible, even in the most rigid, philosophic reasonings, so far to alter the bent and genius of the tongue we speak, as never to give a handle for cavilers to pretend difficulties and inconsistencies. But, a fair and ingenuous reader will collect the sense from the scope and tenor and connection of a discourse, making allowances for those inaccurate modes of speech which use has made inevitable.

53. As to the opinion that there are no corporeal causes, this has been heretofore maintained by some of the schoolmen, as it is of late by others among the modern philosophers, who though they allow matter to exist, yet will have God alone to be the immediate efficient cause of all things. These men saw that amongst all the objects of sense there was none which had any power or activity included in it; and that by consequence this was likewise true of whatever bodies they supposed to exist without the mind, like unto the immediate objects of sense. But then, that they should suppose an innumerable multitude of created beings, which they acknowledge are not capable of producing any one effect in nature, and which therefore are made to no manner of purpose, since God might have done everything as well without them: this I say, though we should allow it possible, must yet be a very unaccountable and extravagant supposition.

54. In the *eighth* place, the universal concurrent assent of mankind may be thought by some an invincible argument in behalf of matter, or the existence of external things. Must we suppose the whole world to be mistaken? And if so, what cause can be assigned of so widespread and predominant an error? I answer, first, that, upon a narrow inquiry, it will not perhaps be found so many as is imagined do really believe the existence of matter or things without the mind. Strictly speaking, to believe that which involves a contradiction, or has no meaning in it, is impossible; and whether the foregoing expressions are not of that sort, I

refer it to the impartial examination of the reader. In one sense, indeed, men may be said to believe that matter exists, that is, they *act* as if the immediate cause of their sensations, which affects them every moment, and is so nearly present to them, were some senseless unthinking being. But, that they should clearly apprehend any meaning marked by those words, and form thereof a settled speculative opinion, is what I am not able to conceive. This is not the only instance wherein men impose upon themselves, by imagining they believe those propositions which they have often heard, though at bottom they have no meaning in them.

55. But secondly, though we should grant a notion to be never so universally and steadfastly adhered to, yet this is weak argument of its truth to whoever considers what a vast number of prejudices and false opinions are everywhere embraced with the utmost tenaciousness, by the unreflecting (which are the far greater) part of mankind. There was a time when the antipodes and motion of the earth were looked upon as monstrous absurdities even by men of learning: and if it be considered what a small proportion they bear to the rest of mankind, we shall find that at this day those notions have gained but a very inconsiderable footing in the world.

56. But it is demanded that we assign a cause of this prejudice, and account for its obtaining in the world. To this I answer, that men knowing they perceived several ideas, whereof they themselves were not the authors (as not being excited from within nor depending on the operation of their wills) this made them maintain those ideas, or objects of perception had an existence independent of and without the mind, without ever dreaming that a contradiction was involved in those words. But philosophers having plainly seen that the immediate objects of perception do not exist without the mind, they in some degree corrected the mistake of the vulgar; but at the same time run into another which seems no less absurd, to wit, that there are certain objects really existing without the mind, or having a subsistence distinct from being perceived, of which our ideas are only images or resemblances, imprinted by those objects on the mind. And this notion of the philosophers owes its origin to the same cause with the former, namely, their being conscious that they were not the authors of their own sensations, which they evidently knew were imprinted from without, and which therefore must have some cause distinct from the minds on which they are imprinted.

57. But why they should suppose the ideas of sense to be excited in us by things in their likeness, and not rather have recourse to *spirit*, which alone can act, may be accounted for, first, because they were not aware of the repugnancy there is, as well in supposing things like unto our ideas existing without, as in attributing to them power or activity. Secondly, because the Supreme Spirit, which excites those ideas in our

minds, is not marked out and limited to our view by any particular
finite collection of sensible ideas, as human agents are by their size,
complexion, limbs, and motions. And thirdly, because His operations are
regular and uniform. Whenever the course of nature is interrupted by a
miracle, men are ready to own the presence of a superior agent. But,
when we see things go on in the ordinary course they do not excite in us
any reflection; their order and concatenation, though it be an argument
of the greatest wisdom, power, and goodness in their creator, is yet so
constant and familiar to us that we do not think them the immediate
effects of a free spirit; especially since inconsistency and mutability in
acting, though it be an imperfection, is looked on as a mark of freedom.

58. *Tenthly,* it will be objected that the notions we advance are inconsistent with several sound truths in philosophy and mathematics. For
example, the motion of the earth is now universally admitted by astronomers as a truth grounded on the clearest and most convincing reasons. But, on the foregoing principles, there can be no such thing. For,
motion being only an idea, it follows that if it be not perceived it exists
not; but the motion of the earth is not perceived by sense. I answer, that
tenet, if rightly understood, will be found to agree with the principles
we have premised; for, the question whether the earth moves or no
amounts in reality to no more than this, to wit, whether we have reason
to conclude, from what has been observed by astronomers, that if we
were placed in such and such circumstances, and such or such a position
and distance both from the earth and sun, we should perceive the former
to move among the choir of the planets, and appearing in all respects
like one of them; and this, by the established rules of nature which we
have no reason to mistrust, is reasonably collected from the phenomena.

59. We may, from the experience we have had of the train and succession of ideas in our minds, often make, I will not say uncertain conjectures, but sure and well-grounded predictions concerning the ideas
we shall be affected with pursuant to a great train of actions, and be enabled to pass a right judgment of what would have appeared to us, in
case we were placed in circumstances very different from those we are
in at present. Herein consists the knowledge of nature, which may preserve its use and certainty very consistently with what hath been said.
It will be easy to apply this to whatever objections of the like sort may
be drawn from the magnitude of the stars, or any other discoveries in
astronomy or nature.

60. In the *eleventh* place, it will be demanded to what purpose serves
that curious organization of plants, and the animal mechanism in the
parts of animals: might not vegetables grow, and shoot forth leaves of
blossoms, and animals perform all their motions as well without as with
all that variety of internal parts so elegantly contrived and put to-

gether, which, being ideas, have nothing powerful or operative in them, nor have any necessary connection with the effects ascribed to them? If it be a Spirit that immediately produces every effect by a *fiat* or act of His will, we must think all that is fine and artificial in the works, whether of man or nature, to be made in vain. By this doctrine, though an artist hath made the spring and wheels, and every movement of a watch, and adjusted them in such a manner as he knew would produce the motions he designed, yet he must think all this done to no purpose, and that it is an Intelligence which directs the index, and points to the hour of the day. If so, why may not the Intelligence do it, without his being at the pains of making the movements and putting them together? Why does not an empty case serve as well as another? And how comes it to pass that whenever there is any fault in the going of a watch, there is some corresponding disorder to be found in the movements, which being mended by a skillful hand all is right again? The like may be said of all the clockwork of nature, great part whereof is so wonderfully fine and subtle as scarce to be discerned by the best microscope. In short, it will be asked, how, upon our principles, any tolerable account can be given, or any final cause assigned of an innumerable multitude of bodies and machines, framed with the most exquisite art, which in the common philosophy have very apposite uses assigned them, and serve to explain abundance of phenomena?

61. To all which I answer, *first*, that though there were some difficulties relating to the administration of Providence, and the uses by it assigned to the several parts of nature, which I could not solve by the foregoing principles, yet this objection could be of small weight against the truth and certainty of those things which may be proved *a priori*, with the utmost evidence and rigor of demonstration. *Secondly*, but neither are the received principles free from the like difficulties; for, it may still be demanded to what end God should take those roundabout methods of effecting things by instruments and machines, which no one can deny might have been effected by the mere command of His will without all that apparatus; nay, if we narrowly consider it, we shall find the objection may be retorted with greater force on those who hold the existence of those machines without of mind; for it has been made evident that solidity, bulk, figure, motion, and the like have no *activity* or *efficacy* in them, so as to be capable of producing any one effect in nature. (See Sec. 25). Whoever therefore supposes them to exist (allowing the supposition possible) when they are not perceived does it manifestly to no purpose; since the only use that is assigned to them, as they exist unperceived, is that they produce those perceivable effects which in truth cannot be ascribed to anything but Spirit.

62. But, to come nigher the difficulty, it must be observed that

though the fabrication of all those parts and organs be not absolutely necessary to the producing any effect, yet it is necessary to the producing of things in a constant regular way according to the laws of nature. There are certain general laws that run through the whole chain of natural effects; these are learned by the observation and study of nature, and are by men applied as well to the framing artificial things for the use and ornament of life as to the explaining various phenomena—which explication consists only in shewing the conformity any particular phenomenon hath to the general laws of nature, or, which is the same thing, in discovering the *uniformity* there is in the production of natural effects; as will be evident to whoever shall attend to the several instances wherein philosophers pretend to account for appearances. That there is a great and conspicuous use in these regular constant methods of working observed by the Supreme Agent hath been shewn in Sec. 31. And it is no less visible that a particular size, figure, motion, and disposition of parts are necessary, though not absolutely to the producing any effect, yet to the producing it according to the standing mechanical laws of nature. Thus, for instance, it cannot be denied that God, or the Intelligence that sustains and rules the ordinary course of things, might if He were minded to produce a miracle, cause all the motions on the dial-plate of a watch, though nobody had ever made the movements and put them in it: but yet, if He will act agreeably to the rules of the mechanism, by Him for wise ends established and maintained in the creation, it is necessary that those actions of the watchmaker, whereby he makes the movements and rightly adjusts them, precede the production of the aforesaid motions; as also that any disorder in them be attended with the perception of some corresponding disorder in the movements, which being once corrected all is right again.

63. It may indeed on some occasions be necessary that the Author of nature display His overruling power in producing some appearance out of the ordinary series of things. Such exceptions from the general rules of nature are proper to surprise and awe men into an acknowledgment of the Divine Being; but then they are to be used but seldom, otherwise there is a plain reason why they should fail of that effect. Besides, God seems to choose the convincing our reason of His attributes by the works of nature, which discover so much harmony and contrivance in their make, and are such plain indications of wisdom and beneficence in their Author, rather than to astonish us into a belief of His Being by anomalous and surprising events.

64. To set this matter in a yet clearer light, I shall observe that what has been objected in Sec. 60 amounts in reality to no more than this:— ideas are not anyhow and at random produced, there being a certain or-

der and connection between them, like to that of cause and effect; there are also several combinations of them made in a very regular and artificial manner, which seem like so many instruments in the hand of nature that, being hid as it were behind the scenes, have a secret operation in producing those appearances which are seen on the theater of the world, being themselves discernible only to the curious eye of the philosopher. But, since one idea cannot be the cause of another, to what purpose is that connection? And, since those instruments, being barely *inefficacious perceptions* in the mind, are not subservient to the production of natural effects, it is demanded why they are made; or, in other words, what reason can be assigned why God should make us, upon a close inspection into His works, behold so great variety of ideas so artfully laid together, and so much according to rule; it not being credible that He would be at the expense (if one may so speak) of all that art and regularity to no purpose.

65. To all which my answer is, first, that the connection of ideas does not imply the relation of *cause and effect,* but only of a mark or *sign* with the thing *signified.* The fire which I see is not the cause of the pain I suffer upon my approaching it, but the mark that forewarns me of it. In like manner the noise that I hear is not the effect of this or that motion or collision of the ambient bodies, but the sign thereof. Secondly, the reason why ideas are formed into machines, that is, artificial and regular combinations, is the same with that for combining letters into words. That a few original ideas may be made to signify a great number of effects and actions, it is necessary they be variously combined together. And, to the end their use be permanent and universal, these combinations must be made by *rule,* and with *wise contrivance.* By this means abundance of information is conveyed unto us, concerning what we are to expect from such and such actions, and what methods are proper to be taken for the exciting such and such ideas; which in effect is all that I conceive to be distinctly meant when it is said that, by discerning a figure, texture, and mechanism of the inward parts of bodies, whether natural or artificial, we may attain to know the several uses and properties depending thereon, or the nature of the thing.

66. Hence, it is evident that those things which, under the notion of a cause co-operating or concurring to the production of effects, are altogether inexplicable, and run us into great absurdities, may be very naturally explained, and have a proper and obvious use assigned to them, when they are considered only as marks or signs for our information. And it is the searching after and endeavoring to understand those signs instituted by the Author of Nature, that ought to be the employment of the natural philosopher; and not the pretending to explain things by

corporeal causes, which doctrine seems to have too much estranged the minds of men from that active principle, that supreme and wise Spirit "in whom we live, move, and have our being."

67. In the *twelfth* place, it may perhaps be objected that—though it be clear from what has been said that there can be no such thing as an inert, senseless, extended, solid, figured, movable substance existing without the mind, such as philosophers describe matter—yet, if any man shall leave out of his idea of matter the positive ideas of extension, figure, solidity and motion, and say that he means only by that word an inert, senseless substance, that exists without the mind or unperceived, which is the *occasion of our ideas,* or at the presence whereof God is pleased to excite ideas in us: it doth not appear but that matter taken in this sense may possibly exist. In answer to which I say, first, that it seems no less absurd to suppose a substance without accidents, than it is to suppose accidents without a substance. But secondly, though we should grant this unknown substance may possibly exist, yet where can it be supposed to be? That it exists not in the mind is agreed; and that it exists not in place is no less certain—since all place or extension exists only in the mind, as hath been already proved. It remains therefore that it exists nowhere at all.

68. Let us examine a little the description that is here given us of *matter*. It neither acts, nor perceives, nor is perceived; for this is all that is meant by saying it is an inert, senseless, unknown substance: which is a definition entirely made up of negatives, excepting only the relative notion of its standing under or supporting. But then it must be observed that it supports nothing at all, and how nearly this comes to the description of a *nonentity* I desire may be considered. But, say you, it is the *unknown occasion,* at the presence of which ideas are excited in us by the will of God. Now, I would fain know how anything can be present to us, which is neither perceivable by sense nor reflection, nor capable of producing any idea in our minds, nor is at all extended, nor hath any form, nor exists in any place. The words 'to be present,' when thus applied, must needs be taken in some abstract and strange meaning, and which I am not able to comprehend.

69. Again, let us examine what is meant by *occasion*. So far as I can gather from the common use of language, that word signifies either the agent which produces any effect, or else something that is observed to accompany or go before it in the ordinary course of things. But when it is applied to matter as above described, it can be taken in neither of those senses; for matter is said to be passive and inert, and so cannot be an agent or efficient cause. It is also unperceivable, as being devoid of all sensible qualities, and so cannot be the occasion of our perceptions in the latter sense: as when the burning my finger is said to be the occa-

sion of the pain that attends it. What therefore can be meant by calling matter an *occasion?* The term is either used in no sense at all, or else in some very distant from its received signification.

70. You will perhaps say that matter, though it be not perceived by us, is nevertheless perceived by God, to whom it is the occasion of exciting ideas in our minds. For, say you, since we observe our sensations to be imprinted in an orderly and constant manner, it is but reasonable to suppose there are certain constant and regular occasions of their being produced. That is to say, that there are certain permanent and distinct parcels of matter, corresponding to our ideas, which, though they do not excite them in our minds, or anywise immediately affect us, as being altogether passive and unperceivable to us, they are nevertheless to God, by whom they are perceived, as it were so many occasions to remind Him when and what ideas to imprint on our minds; that so things may go on in a constant uniform manner.

71. In answer to this, I observe that, as the notion of matter is here stated, the question is no longer concerning the existence of a thing distinct from *spirit* and *idea,* from perceiving and being perceived; but whether there are not certain ideas of I know not what sort, in the mind of God which are so many marks or notes that direct Him how to produce sensations in our minds in a constant and regular method—much after the same manner as a musician is directed by the notes of music to produce that harmonious train and composition of sound which is called a tune, though they who hear the music do not perceive the notes, and may be entirely ignorant of them. But, this notion of matter seems too extravagant to deserve a confutation. Besides, it is in effect no objection against what we have advanced, to wit, that there is no senseless unperceived substance.

72. If we follow the light of reason, we shall, from the constant uniform method of our sensations, collect the goodness and wisdom of the Spirit who excites them in our minds; but this is all that I can see reasonably concluded from thence. To me, I say, it is evident that the being of a spirit infinitely wise, good, and powerful is abundantly sufficient to explain all the appearances of nature. But as for *inert, senseless matter,* nothing that I perceive has any the least connection with it, or leads to the thoughts of it. And I would fain see anyone explain any the meanest phenomenon in nature by it, or shew any manner of reason, though in the lowest rank of probability, that he can have for its existence, or even make any tolerable sense or meaning of that supposition. For, as to its being an occasion, we have, I think, evidently shewn that with regard to us it is no occasion. It remains therefore that it must be, if at all, the occasion to God of exciting ideas in us; and what this amounts to we have just now seen.

73. It is worth while to reflect a little on the motives which inducted men to suppose the existence of *material substance;* that so having observed the gradual ceasing and expiration of those motives or reasons, we may proportionably withdraw the assent that was grounded on them. First, therefore, it was thought that color, figure, motion, and the rest of the sensible qualities or accidents, did really exist without the mind; and for this reason it seemed needful to suppose some unthinking *substratum* or substance wherein they did exist, since they could not be conceived to exist by themselves. Afterwards, in process of time, men being convinced that colors, sounds, and the rest of the sensible, secondary qualities had no existence without the mind, they stripped this *substratum* or material substance of those qualities, leaving only the primary ones, figure, motion, and suchlike, which they still conceived to exist without the mind, and consequently to stand in need of a material support. But, it having been shewn that none even of these can possibly exist otherwise than in a spirit or mind which perceives them, it follows that we have no longer any reason to suppose the being of matter; nay, that it is utterly impossible there should be any such thing, so long as that word is taken to denote an *unthinking substratum* of qualities or accidents wherein they exist without the mind.

74. But though it be allowed by the materialists themselves that matter was thought of only for the sake of supporting accidents, and, the reason entirely ceasing, one might expect the mind should naturally, and without any reluctance at all, quit the belief of what was solely grounded thereon; yet the prejudice is riveted so deeply in our thoughts, that we can scarce tell how to part with it, and are therefore inclined, since the *thing* itself is indefensible, at least to retain the *name,* which we apply to I know not what abstracted and indefinite notions of being, or occasion, though without any show of reason, at least so far as I can see. For, what is there on our part, or what do we perceive, amongst all the ideas, sensations, notions which are imprinted on our minds, either by sense or reflection, from whence may be inferred the existence of an inert, thoughtless, unperceived occasion? And, on the other hand, on the part of an all-sufficient Spirit, what can there be that should make us believe or even suspect He is directed by an inert occasion to excite ideas in our minds?

75. It is a very extraordinary instance of the force of prejudice, and much to be lamented, that the mind of man retains so great a fondness, against all the evidence of reason, for a stupid thoughtless *somewhat,* by the interposition whereof it would as it were screen itself from the providence of God, and remove it farther off from the affairs of the world. But, though we do the utmost we can to secure the belief of *matter,* though, when reason forsakes us, we endeavor to support our opinion on

the bare possibility of the thing, and though we indulge ourselves in the full scope of an imagination not regulated by reason to make out that poor possibility, yet the upshot of all is, that there are certain *unknown ideas* in the mind of God; for this, if anything, is all that I conceive to be meant by *occasion* with regard to God. And this at the bottom is no longer contending for the thing, but for the name.

76. Whether therefore there are such ideas in the mind of God, and whether they may be called by the name 'matter,' I shall not dispute. But, if you stick to the notion of an unthinking substance or support of extension, motion, and other sensible qualities, then to me it is most evidently impossible there should be any such thing; since it is a plain repugnancy that those qualities should exist in or be supported by an unperceiving substance.

77. But, say you, though it be granted that there is no thoughtless support of extension and the other qualities or accidents which we perceive, yet there may perhaps be some inert, unperceiving substance or *substratum* of some other qualities, as incomprehensible to us as colors are to a man born blind, because we have not a sense adapted to them. But, if we had a new sense, we should possibly no more doubt of their existence than a blind man made to see does of the existence of light and colors. I answer, first, if what you mean by the word 'matter' be only the unknown support of unknown qualities, it is no matter whether there is such a thing or no, since it no way concerns us; and I do not see the advantage there is in disputing about what we know not *what*, and we know not *why*.

78. But, secondly, if we had a new sense it could only furnish us with new ideas or sensations; and then we should have the same reason against their existing in an unperceiving substance that has been already offered with relation to figure, motion, color, and the like. Qualities, as hath been shewn, are nothing else but *sensations* or *ideas*, which exist only in a *mind* perceiving them; and this is true not only of the ideas we are acquainted with at present, but likewise of all possible ideas whatsoever.

79. But, you will insist, what if I have no reason to believe the existence of matter? what if I cannot assign any use to it or explain anything by it, or even conceive what is meant by that word? yet still it is no contradiction to say that matter exists, and that this matter is in general a *substance*, or *occasion of ideas;* though indeed to go about to unfold the meaning or adhere to any particular explication of those words may be attended with great difficulties. I answer, when words are used without a meaning, you may put them together as you please without danger of running into a contradiction. You may say, for example, that twice two is equal to seven, so long as you declare you do not take the

words of that proposition in their usual acceptation but for marks of you know not what. And, by the same reason, you may say there is an inert thoughtless substance without accidents which is the occasion of our ideas. And we shall understand just as much by one proposition as the other.

80. In the *last* place, you will say, what if we give up the cause of material substance, and stand to it that matter is an unknown *somewhat* —neither substance nor accident, spirit nor idea, inert, thoughtless, indivisible, immovable, unextended, existing in no place. For, say you, whatever may be urged against *substance* or *occasion*, or any other positive or relative notion of matter, hath no place at all, so long as this *negative* definition of matter is adhered to. I answer, you may, if so it shall seem good, use the word 'matter' in the same sense as other men use 'nothing,' and so make those terms convertible in your style. For, after all, this is what appears to me to be the result of that definition, the parts whereof when I consider with attention, either collectively or separate from each other, I do not find that there is any kind of effect or impression made on my mind different from what is excited by the term 'nothing.'

81. You will reply, perhaps, that in the foresaid definition is included what doth sufficiently distinguish it from nothing: the positive abstract idea of *quiddity, entity,* or *existence.* I own, indeed, that those who pretend to the faculty of framing abstract general ideas do talk as if they had such an idea, which is, say they, the most abstract and general notion of all; that is, to me, the most incomprehensible of all others. That there are a great variety of spirits of different orders and capacities, whose faculties both in number and extent are far exceeding those the Author of my being has bestowed on me, I see no reason to deny. And for me to pretend to determine by my own few, stinted narrow inlets of perception, what ideas the inexhaustible power of the Supreme Spirit may imprint upon them were certainly the utmost folly and presumption—since there may be, for aught that I know, innumerable sorts of ideas or sensations, as different from one another, and from all that I have perceived, as colors are from sounds. But, how ready soever I may be to acknowledge the scantiness of my comprehension with regard to the endless variety of spirits and ideas that may possibly exist, yet for anyone to pretend to a notion of entity or existence, *abstracted* from *spirit* and *idea,* from perceived and being perceived, is, I suspect, a downright repugnancy and trifling with words.

It remains that we consider the objections which may possibly be made on the part of religion.

82. Some there are who think that, though the arguments for the real existence of bodies which are drawn from reason be allowed not to

amount to demonstration, yet the Holy Scriptures are so clear in the point as will sufficiently convince every good Christian that bodies do really exist, and are something more than mere ideas; there being in Holy Writ innumerable facts related which evidently suppose the reality of timber and stone, mountains and rivers, and cities, and human bodies. To which I answer that no sort of writings whatever, sacred or profane, which use those and the like words in the vulgar acceptation, or so as to have a meaning in them, are in danger of having their truth called in question by our doctrine. That all those things do really exist, that there are bodies, even corporeal substances, when taken in the vulgar sense, has been shewn to be agreeable to our principles; and the difference betwixt *things* and *ideas, realities* and *chimeras,* has been distinctly explained. (See Secs. 29, 30, 33, 36, etc.) And I do not think that either what philosophers call *matter,* or the existence of objects without the mind, is anywhere mentioned in Scripture.

83. Again, whether there can be or be not external things, it is agreed on all hands that the proper use of words is the marking our conceptions, or things only as they are known and perceived by us; whence it plainly follows that in the tenets we have laid down there is nothing inconsistent with the right use and significancy of language, and that discourse, of what kind soever, so far as it is intelligible, remains undisturbed. But all this seems so manifest, from what has been largely set forth in the premises, that it is needless to insist any farther on it.

84. But, it will be urged that miracles do, at least, lose much of their stress and import by our principles. What must we think of Moses' rod: was it not *really* turned into a serpent; or was there only a change of *ideas* in the minds of the spectators? And, can it be supposed that our Saviour did no more at the marriage-feast in Cana than impose on the sight, and smell, and taste of the guests, so as to create in them the appearance or idea only of wine? The same may be said of all other miracles; which, in consequence of the foregoing principles, must be looked upon only as so many cheats, or illusions of fancy. To this I reply, that the rod was changed into a real serpent, and the water into real wine. That this does not in the least contradict what I have elsewhere said will be evident from Secs. 34 and 35. But this business of *real* and *imaginary* hath been already so plainly and fully explained, and so often referred to, and the difficulties about it are so easily answered from what hath gone before, that it were an affront to the reader's understanding to resume the explication of it in its place. I shall only observe that if at table all who were present should see, and smell, and taste, and drink wine, and find the effects of it, with me there could be no doubts of its reality; so that at bottom the scruple concerning real miracles has no place at all on ours, but only on the received principles,

and consequently makes rather for than against what hath been said.

85. Having done with the objections, which I endeavored to propose in the clearest light, and gave them all the force and weight I could, we proceed in the next place to take a view of our tenets in their *consequences*. Some of these appear at first sight: as that several difficult and obscure questions, on which abundance of speculation has been thrown away, are entirely banished from philosophy. "Whether corporeal substance can think," "whether matter be infinitely divisible," and "how it operates on spirit"—these and like inquiries have given infinite amusement to philosophers in all ages; but, depending on the existence of matter, they have no longer any place on our principles. Many other advantages there are, as well with regard to religion as the sciences, which it is easy for anyone to deduce from what has been premised; but this will appear more plainly in the sequel.

86. From the principles we have laid down it follows human knowledge may naturally be reduced to two heads: that of *ideas* and that of *spirits*. Of each of these I shall treat in order.

And *first* as to ideas or unthinking things. Our knowledge of these hath been very much obscured and confounded, and we have been led into very dangerous errors, by supposing a twofold existence of the objects of sense—the one *intelligible* or in the mind, the other *real* and without the mind; whereby unthinking things are thought to have a natural subsistence of their own distinct from being perceived by spirits. This, which, if I mistake not, hath been shewn to be a most groundless and absurd notion, is the very root of scepticism; for, so long as men thought that real things subsisted without the mind, and that their knowledge was not so far forth *real* as it was conformable to *real things*, it follows they could not be certain they had any real knowledge at all. For how can it be known that the things which are perceived are conformable to those which are not perceived, or exist without the mind?

87. Color, figure, motion, extension, and the like, considered only as so many *sensations* in the mind, are perfectly known, there being nothing in them which is not perceived. But, if they are looked on as notes or images, referred to *things* or *archetypes* existing without the mind, then are we involved all in scepticism. We see only the appearances, and not the real qualities of things. What may be the extension, figure, or motion of anything really and absolutely, or in itself, it is impossible for us to know, but only the proportion or relation they bear to our senses. Things remaining the same, our ideas vary, and which of them, or even whether any of them at all, represent the true quality really existing in the thing, it is out of our reach to determine. So that, for aught we know, all we see, hear, and feel may be only phantom and vain

chimera, and not at all agree with the real things existing in our *rerum natura*. All this scepticism follows from our supposing a difference between *things* and *ideas,* and that the former have a subsistence without the mind or unperceived. It were easy to dilate on this subject, and show how the arguments urged by sceptics in all ages depend on the supposition of external objects.

88. So long as we attribute a real existence to unthinking things, distinct from their being perceived, it is not only impossible for us to know with evidence the nature of any real unthinking being, but even that it exists. Hence it is that we see philosophers distrust their senses, and doubt of the existence of heaven and earth, of everything they see or feel, even of their own bodies. And, after all their labor and struggle of thought, they are forced to own we cannot attain to any self-evident or demonstrative knowledge of the existence of sensible things. But, all this doubtfulness, which so bewilders and confounds the mind and makes philosophy ridiculous in the eyes of the world, vanishes if we annex a meaning to our words, and not amuse ourselves with the terms 'absolute,' 'external,' 'exist,' and such like, signifying we know not what. I can as well doubt of my own being as of the being of those things which I actually perceive by sense; it being a manifest contradiction that any sensible object should be immediately perceived by sight or touch, and at the same time have no existence in nature, since the very *existence* of an unthinking being consists in *being perceived.*

89. Nothing seems of more importance towards erecting a firm system of sound and real knowledge, which may be proof against the assaults of scepticism, than to lay the beginning in a distinct explication of what is meant by *thing, reality, existence;* for in vain shall we dispute concerning the real existence of things, or pretend to any knowledge thereof, so long as we have not fixed the meaning of those words. *Thing* or *Being* is the most general name of all; it comprehends under it two kinds entirely distinct and heterogeneous, and which have nothing common but the name, to wit, *spirits* and *ideas.* The former are active, indivisible substances: the latter are inert, fleeting, dependent beings, which subsist not by themselves, but are supported by, or exist in minds or spiritual substances. We comprehend our own existence by inward feeling or reflection, and that of other spirits by reason. We may be said to have some knowledge or notion of our own minds, of spirits and active beings, whereof in a strict sense we have not ideas. In like manner we know and have a notion of relations between things or ideas —which relations are distinct from the ideas or things related, inasmuch as the latter may be perceived by us without our perceiving the former. To me it seems that *ideas, spirits,* and *relations* are all in their re-

spective kinds the object of human knowledge and subject of discourse; and that the term 'idea' would be improperly extended to signify everything we know or have any notion of.

90. Ideas imprinted on the senses are real things, or do really exist; this we do not deny, but we deny they can subsist without the minds which perceive them, or that they are resemblances of any archetypes existing without the mind; since the very being of a sensation or idea consists in being perceived, and an idea can be like nothing but an idea. Again, the things perceived by sense may be termed *external,* with regard to their origin: in that they are not generated from within by the mind itself, but imprinted by a Spirit distinct from that which perceives them. Sensible objects may likewise be said to be 'without the mind' in another sense, namely when they exist in some other mind; thus, when I shut my eyes, the things I saw may still exist, but it must be in another mind.

91. It were a mistake to think that what is here said derogates in the least from the reality of things. It is acknowledged, on the received principles, that extension, motion, and in a word all sensible qualities have need of a support, as not being able to subsist by themselves. But the objects perceived by sense are allowed to be nothing but combinations of those qualities, and consequently cannot subsist by themselves. Thus far it is agreed on all hands. So that in denying the things perceived by sense an existence independent of a substance of support wherein they may exist, we detract nothing from the received opinion of their *reality,* and are guilty of no innovation in that respect. All the difference is that, according to us, the unthinking beings perceived by sense have no existence distinct from being perceived, and cannot therefore exist in any other substance than those unextended indivisible substances or *spirits* which act and think and perceive them; whereas philosophers vulgarly hold that the sensible qualities do exist in an inert, extended, unperceiving substance which they call *matter,* to which they attribute a natural subsistence, exterior to all thinking beings, or distinct from being perceived by any mind whatsoever, even the eternal mind of the Creator, wherein they suppose only ideas of the corporeal substances created by Him; if indeed they allow them to be at all created.

92. For, as we have shewn the doctrine of matter or corporeal substance to have been the main pillar and support of scepticism, so likewise upon the same foundation have been raised all the impious schemes of atheism and irreligion. Nay, so great a difficulty hath it been thought to conceive matter produced out of nothing, that the most celebrated among the ancient philosophers, even of those who main-

tained the being of God, have thought matter to be uncreated and co-eternal with Him. How great a friend *material substance* hath been to atheists in all ages were needless to relate. All their monstrous systems have so visible and necessary a dependence on it that, when this cornerstone is once removed, the whole fabric cannot choose but fall to the ground, insomuch that it is no longer worth while to bestow a particular consideration on the absurdities of every wretched sect of atheists.

93. That impious and profane persons should readily fall in with those systems which favor their inclinations, by deriding immaterial substance, and supposing the soul to be divisible and subject to corruption as the body; which exclude all freedom, intelligence, and design from the formation of things, and instead thereof make a self-existent, stupid, unthinking substance the root and origin of all beings; that they should hearken to those who deny a Providence, or inspection of a Superior Mind over the affairs of the world, attributing the whole series of events either to blind chance or fatal necessity arising from the impulse of one body or another—all this is very natural. And, on the other hand, when men of better principles observe the enemies of religion lay so great a stress on *unthinking matter,* and all of them use so much industry and artifice to reduce everything to it, methinks they should rejoice to see them deprived of their grand support, and driven from that only fortress, without which your Epicureans, Hobbists, and the like, have not even the shadow of a pretense, but become the most cheap and easy triumph in the world.

94. The existence of matter, or bodies unperceived, has not only been the main support of atheists and fatalists, but on the same principle doth idolatry likewise in all its various forms depend. Did men but consider that the sun, moon, and stars, and every other object of the senses are not so many sensations in their minds, which have no other existence but barely being perceived, doubtless they would never fall down and worship their own *ideas,* but rather address their homage to that Eternal Invisible Mind which produces and sustains all things.

95. The same absurd principle, by mingling itself with the articles of our faith, has occasioned no small difficulties to Christians. For example, about the Resurrection, how many scruples and objections have been raised by Socinians and others? But do not the most plausible of them depend on the supposition that a body is denominated the *same,* with regard not to the form or that which is perceived by sense, but the material substance, which remains the same under several forms? Take away this *material substance,* about the identity whereof all the dispute is, and mean by *body* what every plain ordinary person means by that

word, to wit, that which is immediately seen and felt, which is only a combination of sensible qualities or ideas, and then their most unanswerable objections come to nothing.

96. Matter being once expelled out of nature drags with it so many sceptical and impious notions, such an incredible number of disputes and puzzling questions, which have been thorns in the sides of divines as well as philosophers, and made so much fruitless work for mankind, that if the arguments we have produced against it are not found equal to demonstration (as to me they evidently seem), yet I am sure all friends to knowledge, peace, and religion have reason to wish they were.

97. Beside the external existence of the objects of perception, another great source of errors and difficulties with regard to ideal knowledge is the doctrine of *abstract ideas,* such as it hath been set forth in the Introduction. The plainest things in the world, those we are most intimately acquainted with and perfectly know, when they are considered in an abstract way, appear strangely difficult and incomprehensible. Time, place, and motion, taken in particular or concrete, are what everybody knows, but, having passed through the hands of a metaphysician, they become too abstract and fine to be apprehended by men of ordinary sense. Bid your servant meet you at such a *time* in such a *place,* and he shall never stay to deliberate on the meaning of those words; in conceiving that particular time and place, or the motion by which he is not to get thither, he finds not the least difficulty. But if *time* be taken exclusive of all those particular actions and ideas that diversify the day, merely for the continuation of existence or duration in abstract, then it will perhaps gravel even a philosopher to comprehend it.

98. For my own part, whenever I attempt to frame a simple idea of *time,* abstracted from the succession of ideas in my mind, which flows uniformly and is participated by all beings, I am lost and embrangled in inextricable difficulties. I have no notion of it at all, only I hear others say it is infinitely divisible, and speak of it in such a manner as leads me to entertain odd thoughts of my existence; since that doctrine lays one under an absolute necessity of thinking, either that he passes away innumerable ages without a thought, or else that he is annihilated every moment of his life, both which seem equally absurd. Time therefore being nothing, abstracted from the succession of ideas in our minds, it follows that the duration of any finite spirit must be estimated by the number of ideas or actions succeeding each other in that same spirit or mind. Hence, it is a plain consequence that the soul always thinks; and in truth whoever shall go about to divide in his thoughts, or abstract the *existence* of a spirit from its *cogitation,* will, I believe, find it no easy task.

99. So likewise when we attempt to abstract extension and motion

from all other qualities, and consider them by themselves, we presently lose sight of them, and run into great extravagances. All which depend on a twofold abstraction; first, it is supposed that extension, for example, may be abstracted from all other sensible qualities; and secondly, that the entity of extension may be abstracted from its being perceived. But, whoever shall reflect, and take care to understand what he says, will, if I mistake not, acknowledge that all sensible qualities are alike *sensations* and alike *real;* that where the extension is, there is the color, too, to wit, in his mind, and that their archetypes can exist only in some other *mind;* and that the objects of sense are nothing but those sensations combined, blended, or (if one may so speak) concreted together; none of all which can be supposed to exist unperceived.

100. What it is for a man to be happy, or an object good, everyone may think he knows. But to frame an abstract idea of happiness, prescinded from all particular pleasure, or of goodness from everything that is good, this is what few can pretend to. So likewise a man may be just and virtuous without having precise ideas of justice and virtue. The opinion that those and the like words stand for general notions, abstracted from all particular persons and actions, seems to have rendered morality very difficult, and the study thereof of small use to mankind. And in effect the doctrine of *abstraction* has not a little contributed towards spoiling the most useful parts of knowledge.

101. The two great provinces of speculative science conversant about ideas received from sense, are *natural philosophy* and *mathematics;* with regard to each of these I shall make some observations. And first I shall say somewhat of natural philosophy. On this subject it is that the sceptics triumph. All that stock of arguments they produce to depreciate our faculties and make mankind appear ignorant and low, are drawn principally from this head, namely, that we are under an invincible blindness as to the *true* and *real* nature of things. This they exaggerate, and love to enlarge on. We are miserably bantered, say they, by our senses, and amused only with the outside and show of things. The real essence, the internal qualities and constitution of every the meanest object, is hid from our view; something there is in every drop of water, every grain of sand, which it is beyond the power of human understanding to fathom or comprehend. But it is evident from what has been shewn that all this complaint is groundless, and that we are influenced by false principles to that degree as to mistrust our senses, and think we know nothing of those things which we perfectly comprehend.

102. One great inducement to our pronouncing ourselves ignorant of the nature of things is the current opinion that everything includes within itself the cause of its properties; or that there is in each object an inward essence which is the source whence its discernible qualities

flow, and whereon they depend. Some have pretended to account for appearances by occult qualities, but of late they are mostly resolved into mechanical causes, to wit, the figure, motion, weight, and suchlike qualities, of insensible particles; whereas, in truth, there is no other agent or efficient cause than *spirit*, it being evident that motion, as well as all other *ideas*, is perfectly inert. (See Sec. 25.) Hence, to endeavor to explain the production of colors or sounds, by figure, motion, magnitude, and the like, must needs be labor in vain. And accordingly we see the attempts of that kind are not at all satisfactory. Which may be said in general of those instances wherein one idea or quality is assigned for the cause of another. I need not say how many hypotheses and speculations are left out, and how much the study of nature is abridged by this doctrine.

103. The great mechanical principle now in vogue is *attraction*. That a stone falls to the earth, or the sea swells towards the moon, may to some appear sufficiently explained thereby. But how are we enlightened by being told this is done by attraction? Is it that that word signifies the manner of the tendency, and that it is by the mutual drawing of bodies instead of their being impelled or protruded towards each other? But nothing is determined of the manner or action, and it may as truly (for aught we know) be termed 'impulse,' or 'protrusion,' as 'attraction.' Again, the parts of steel we see cohere firmly together, and this also is accounted for by attraction; but, in this as in the other instances, I do not perceive that anything is signified besides the effect itself; for as to the manner of the action whereby it is produced, or the cause which produces it, these are not so much as aimed at.

104. Indeed, if we take a view of the several phenomena, and compare them together, we may observe some likeness and conformity between them. For example, in the falling of a stone to the ground, in the rising of the sea towards the moon, in cohesion, crystallization, etc., there is something alike, namely, an union or mutual approach of bodies. So that any one of these or the like phenomena may not seem strange or surprising to a man who has nicely observed and compared the effects of nature. For that only is thought so which is uncommon, or a thing by itself, and out of the ordinary course of our observation. That bodies should tend towards the center of the earth is not thought strange, because it is what we perceive every moment of our lives. But that they should have a like gravitation towards the center of the moon may seem odd and unaccountable to most men, because it is discerned only in the tides. But a philosopher, whose thoughts take in a larger compass of nature, having observed a certain similitude of appearances, as well in the heavens as the earth, that argue innumerable bodies to have a mutual tendency towards each other, which he denotes by the

general name 'attraction,' whatever can be reduced to that he thinks justly accounted for. Thus he explains the tides by the attraction of the terraqueous globe towards the moon, which to him doth not appear odd or anomalous, but only a particular example of a general rule or law of nature.

105. If therefore we consider the difference there is betwixt natural philosophers and other men, with regard to their knowledge of the phenomena, we shall find it consists not in an exacter knowledge of the efficient cause that produces them, for that can be no other than the *will of a spirit;* but only in a greater largeness of comprehension, whereby analogies, harmonies, and agreements are discovered in the works of nature, and the particular effect explained, that is, reduced to general rules (see Sec. 62), which rules, grounded on the analogy and uniformness observed in the production of natural effects, are most agreeable and sought after by the mind; for that they extend our prospect beyond what is present and near to us, and enable us to make very probable conjectures touching things that may have happened at very great distances of time and place, as well as to predict things to come; which sort of endeavor towards omniscience is much affected by the mind.

106. But we should proceed warily in such things, for we are apt to lay too great stress on analogies, and, to the prejudice of truth, humor that eagerness of the mind whereby it is carried to extend its knowledge into general theorems. For example, in the business of gravitation or mutual attraction, because it appears in many instances, some are straightway for pronouncing it *universal;* and that to attract and be attracted by every other body is an essential quality inherent in all bodies whatsoever. Whereas it is evident the fixed stars have no such tendency towards each other; and, so far is that gravitation from being *essential* to bodies that in some instances a quite contrary principle seems to shew itself; as in the perpendicular growth of plants, and the elasticity of the air. There is nothing necessary or essential in the case, but it depends entirely on the will of the Governing Spirit, who causes certain bodies to cleave together or tend towards each other according to various laws, whilst He keeps others at a fixed distance; and to some He gives a quite contrary tendency to fly asunder just as He sees convenient.

107. After what has been premised, I think we may lay down the following conclusions. First, it is plain philosophers amuse themselves in vain, when they inquire for any natural efficient cause, distinct from a *mind* or *spirit.* Secondly, considering the whole creation is the workmanship of a *wise and good Agent,* it should seem to become philosophers to employ their thoughts (contrary to what some hold) about the

final causes of things; and I confess I see no reason why pointing out
the various ends to which natural things are adapted, and for which
they were originally with unspeakable wisdom contrived, should not be
thought one good way of accounting for them, and altogether worthy a
philosopher. Thirdly, from what hath been premised no reason can be
drawn why the history of nature should not still be studied, and observations and experiments made, which, that they are of use to mankind,
and enable us to draw any general conclusions, is not the result of any
immutable habitudes or relations between things themselves, but only
of God's goodness and kindness to men in the administration of the
world. (See Secs. 30 and 31.) Fourthly, by a diligent observation of the
phenomena within our view, we may discover the general laws of nature, and from them deduce the other phenomena; I do not say *demonstrate,* for all deductions of that kind depend on a supposition that the
Author of Nature always operates uniformly, and in a constant observance of those rules we take for principles: which we cannot evidently
know.

108. Those men who frame general rules from the phenomena and
afterwards derive the phenomena from those rules, seem to consider
signs rather than causes. A man may well understand natural signs
without knowing their analogy, or being able to say by what rule a
thing is so or so. And, as it is very possible to write improperly, through
too strict an observance of general grammar rules; so, in arguing from
general laws of nature, it is not impossible we may extend the analogy
too far, and by that means run into mistakes.

109. As in reading other books a wise man will choose to fix his
thoughts on the sense and apply it to use, rather than lay them out in
grammatical remarks on the language; so, in perusing the volume of
nature, it seems beneath the dignity of the mind to affect an exactness
in reducing each particular phenomenon to general rules, or shewing
how it follows from them. We should propose to ourselves nobler views,
namely, to recreate and exalt the mind with a prospect of the beauty,
order, extent, and variety of natural things: hence, by proper inferences, to enlarge our notions of the grandeur, wisdom, and beneficence
of the Creator; and lastly, to make the several parts of the creation, so
far as in us lies, subservient to the ends they were designed for, God's
glory, and the sustenation and comfort of ourselves and fellow-creatures.

110. The best key for the aforesaid analogy or natural science will be
easily acknowledged to be a certain celebrated treatise of *mechanics.* In
the entrance of which justly admired treatise, time, space, and motion
are distinguished into *absolute* and *relative, true* and *apparent, mathematical* and *vulgar;* which distinction, as it is at large explained by the

author,[6] does suppose these quantities to have an existence without the mind; and that they are ordinarily conceived with relation to sensible things, to which nevertheless in their own nature they bear no relation at all.

111. As for *time*, as it is there taken in an absolute or abstracted sense, for the duration or perseverance of the existence of things, I have nothing more to add concerning it after what has been already said on that subject. (Secs. 97 and 98.) For the rest, this celebrated author holds there is an *absolute space*, which, being unperceivable to sense, remains in itself similar and immovable; and relative space to be the measure thereof, which, being movable and defined by its situation in respect of sensible bodies, is vulgarly taken for immovable space. *Place* he defines to be that part of space which is occupied by any body; and according as the space is absolute or relative so also is the place. *Absolute motion* is said to be the translation of a body from absolute place to absolute place, as relative motion is from one relative place to another. And, because the parts of absolute space do not fall under our senses, instead of them we are obliged to use their sensible measures, and so define both place and motion with respect to bodies which we regard as immovable. But, it is said in philosophical matters we must abstract from our senses, since it may be that none of those bodies which seem to be quiescent are truly so, and the same thing which is moved relatively may be really at rest; as likewise one and the same body may be in relative rest and motion, or even moved with contrary relative motions at the same time, according as its place is variously defined. All which ambiguity is to be found in the apparent motions, but not at all in the true or absolute, which should therefore be alone regarded in philosophy. And the true as we are told are distinguished from apparent or relative motions by the following properties. First, in true or absolute motion all parts which preserve the same position with respect of the whole, partake of the motions of the whole. Secondly, the place being moved, that which is placed therein is also moved; so that a body moving in a place which is in motion doth participate the motion of its place. Thirdly, true motion is never generated or changed otherwise than by force impressed on the body itself. Fourthly, true motion is always changed by force impressed on the body moved. Fifthly, in circular motion barely relative there is no centrifugal force, which, nevertheless, in that which is true or absolute, is proportional to the quantity of motion.

112. But, notwithstanding what hath been said, I must confess it doth not appear to me that there can be any motion other than *rela-*

[6] Newton.

tive; so that to conceive motion there must be at least conceived two bodies, whereof the distance or position in regard to each other is varied. Hence, if there was one only body in being it could not possibly be moved. This seems evident, in that the idea I have of motion doth necessarily include relation.

113. But, though in every motion it be necessary to conceive more bodies than one, yet it may be that one only is moved, namely, that on which the force causing the change in the distance or situation of the bodies, is impressed. For, however some may define relative motion, so as to term that body *moved* which changes its distance from some other body, whether the force or action causing that change were impressed on it or no, yet as relative motion is that which is perceived by sense, and regarded in the ordinary affairs of life, it should seem that every man of common sense knows what it is as well as the best philosopher. Now, I ask anyone whether, in his sense of motion as he walks along the streets, the stones he passes over may be said to *move,* because they change distance with his feet? To me it appears that though motion includes a relation of one thing to another, yet it is not necessary that each term of the relation be denominated from it. As a man may think of somewhat which does not think, so a body may be moved to or from another body which is not therefore itself in motion.

114. As the place happens to be variously defined, the motion which is related to it varies. A man in a ship may be said to be quiescent with relation to the sides of the vessel, and yet move with relation to the land. Or he may move eastward in respect of the one, and westward in respect of the other. In the common affairs of life men never go beyond the earth to define the place of any body; and what is quiescent in respect of that is accounted *absolutely* to be so. But philosophers, who have a greater extent of thought, and juster notions of the system of things, discover even the earth itself to be moved. In order therefore to fix their notions they seem to conceive the corporeal world as finite, and the utmost unmoved walls or shell thereof to be the place whereby they estimate true motions. If we sound our own conceptions, I believe we may find all the absolute motion we can frame an idea of to be at bottom no other than relative motion thus defined. For, as hath been already observed, absolute motion, exclusive of all external relation, is incomprehensible; and to this kind of relative motion all the above-mentioned properties, causes, and effects ascribed to absolute motion will, if I mistake not, be found to agree. As to what is said of the centrifugal force, that it doth not at all belong to circular relative motion, I do not see how this follows from the experiment which is brought to prove it. (See *Philosophiae Naturalis Principia Mathematica, in Schol. Def. VIII.*) For the water in the vessel at that time wherein it is said

to have the greatest relative circular motion, hath, I think, no motion at all; as is plain from the foregoing section.

115. For to denominate a body *moved* it is requisite, first, that it change its distance or situation with regard to some other body; and secondly, that the force occasioning that change be applied to it. If either of these be wanting, I do not think that, agreeably to the sense of mankind, or the propriety of language, a body can be said to be in motion. I grant indeed that it is possible for us to think a body which we see change its distance from some other to be moved, though it have no force applied to it (in which sense there may be apparent motion), but then it is because the force causing the change of distance is imagined by us to be applied or impressed on that body thought to move; which indeed shews we are capable of mistaking a thing to be in motion which is not, and that is all.

116. From what hath been said it follows that the philosophic consideration of motion doth not imply the being of an *absolute space*, distinct from that which is perceived of sense and related bodies; which that it cannot exist without the mind is clear upon the same principles that demonstrate the like of all other objects of sense. And perhaps, if we inquire narrowly, we shall find we cannot even frame an idea of *pure space* exclusive of all body. This I must confess seems impossible, as being a most abstract idea. When I excite a motion in some part of my body, if it be free or without resistance, I say there is *space;* but if I find a resistance, then I say there is *body;* and in proportion as the resistance to motion is lesser or greater, I say the space is more or less *pure.* So that when I speak of pure or empty space, it is not to be supposed that the word 'space' stands for an idea distinct from or conceivable without body and motion. Though indeed we are apt to think every noun substantive stands for a distinct idea that may be separated from all others; which has occasioned infinite mistakes. When, therefore, supposing all the world to be annihilated besides my own body, I say there still remains *pure space,* thereby nothing else is meant but only that I conceive it possible for the limbs of my body to be moved on all sides without the least resistance, but if that, too, were annihilated then there could be no motion, and consequently no space. Some, perhaps, may think the sense of seeing doth furnish them with the idea of pure space; but it is plain from what we have elsewhere shewn, that the ideas of space and distance are not obtained by that sense. (See the Essay concerning Vision.)

117. What is here laid down seems to put an end to all those disputes and difficulties that have sprung up amongst the learned concerning the nature of *pure space.* But the chief advantage arising from it is that we are freed from that dangerous dilemma, to which several who

have employed their thoughts on that subject imagine themselves reduced, to wit, of thinking either that real space is God, or else that
there is something beside God which is eternal, uncreated, infinite, indivisible, immutable. Both which may justly be thought pernicious and
absurd notions. It is certain that not a few divines, as well as philosophers of great note, have, from the difficulty they found in conceiving
either limits or annihilation of space, concluded it must be divine. And
some of late have set themselves particularly to shew the incommunicable attributes of God agree to it. Which doctrine, how unworthy soever it may seem of the Divine Nature, yet I do not see how we can get
clear of it, so long as we adhere to the received opinions.

118. Hitherto of natural philosophy: we come now to make some inquiry concerning that other great branch of speculative knowledge, to
wit, mathematics. These, how celebrated soever they may be for their
clearness and certainty of demonstration, which is hardly anywhere else
to be found, cannot nevertheless be supposed altogether free from mistakes, if in their principles there lurks some secret error which is common to the professors of those sciences with the rest of mankind.
Mathematicians, though they deduce their theorems from a great height
of evidence, yet their first principles are limited by the consideration of
quantity; and they do not ascend into any inquiry concerning those
transcendental maxims which influence all the particular sciences, each
part whereof, mathematics not excepted, does consequently participate
of the errors involved in them. That the principles laid down by mathematicians are true, and their way of deduction from those principles
clear and incontestible, we do not deny; but we hold there may be certain erroneous maxims of greater extent than the object of mathematics,
and for that reason not expressly mentioned, though tacitly supposed
throughout the whole progress of that science; and that the ill effects
of those secret unexamined errors are diffused through all the branches
thereof. To be plain, we suspect the mathematicians are as well as other
men concerned in the errors arising from the doctrine of abstract general ideas, and the existence of objects without the mind.

119. Arithmetic has been thought to have for its object abstract ideas
of *number;* of which to understand the properties and mutual habitudes, is supposed no mean part of speculative knowledge. The opinion
of the pure and intellectual nature of numbers in abstract hath made
them in esteem with those philosophers who seem to have affected an
uncommon fineness and elevation of thought. It hath set a price on the
most trifling numerical speculations which in practice are of no use, but
serve only for amusement; and hath therefore so far infected the minds
of some, that they have dreamed of mighty mysteries involved in numbers, and attempted the explication of natural things by them. But, if

we inquire into our own thoughts, and consider what hath been premised, we may perhaps entertain a low opinion of those high flights and abstractions, and look on all inquiries, about numbers only as so many *difficiles nugae*, so far as they are not subservient to practice, and promote the benefit of life.

120. Unity in abstract we have before considered in Sec. 13, from which and what hath been said in the Introduction, it plainly follows there is not any such idea. But, number being defined a 'collection of units,' we may conclude that, if there be no such thing as unity or unit in abstract, there are no ideas of number in abstract denoted by the numeral names and figures. The theories therefore in arithmetic, if they are abstracted from the names and figures, as likewise from all use and practice, as well as from the particular things numbered, can be supposed to have nothing at all for their object; hence we may see how entirely the science of numbers is subordinate to practice, and how jejune and trifling it becomes when considered as a matter of mere speculation.

121. However, since there may be some who, deluded by the specious show of discovering abstracted verities, waste their time in arithmetical theorems and problems which have not any use, it will not be amiss if we more fully consider and expose the vanity of that pretense; and this will planily appear by taking a view of arithmetic in its infancy, and observing what it was that originally put men on the study of that science, and to what scope they directed it. It is natural to think that at first, men, for ease of memory and help of compuation, made use of counters, or in writing of single strokes, points, or the like, each wherof was made to signify an unit, i.e., some one thing of whatever kind they had occasion to reckon. Afterwards they found out the more compendious ways of making one character stand in place of several strokes or points. And, lastly, the notation of the Arabians or Indians came into use, wherein, by the repetition of a few characters or figures, and varying the significance of each figure according to the place it obtains, all numbers may be most aptly expressed; which seems to have been done in imitation of language, so that an exact analogy is observed betwixt the notation by figures and names, the nine simple figures answering the nine first numeral names and places in the former, corresponding to denominations in the latter. And agreeably to those conditions of the simple and local value of figures, were contrived methods of finding, from the given figures or marks of the parts, what figures and how placed are proper to denote the whole, or *vice versa*. And having found the sought figures, the same rule or analogy being observed throughout, it is easy to read them into words; and so the number becomes perfectly known. For then the number of any particu-

lar things is said to be known, when we know the name or figures (with
their due arrangement) that according to the standing analogy belong
to them. For, these signs being known, we can by the operations of
arithmetic know the signs of any part of the particular sums signified by
them; and, thus computing in signs (because of the connection established betwixt them and the distinct multitudes of things whereof one
is taken for an unit), we may be able rightly to sum up, divide, and
proportion the things themselves that we intend to number.

122. In arithmetic, therefore, we regard not the *things*, but the
signs, which nevertheless are not regarded for their own sake, but because they direct us how to act with relation to things, and dispose
rightly of them. Now, agreeably to what we have before observed of
words in general (Sec. 19, Introd.) it happens here likewise that abstract ideas are thought to be signified by numeral names or characters, while they do not suggest ideas of particular things to our minds.
I shall not at present enter into a more particular dissertation on this
subject, but only observe that it is evident from what hath been said,
those things which pass for abstract truths and theorems concerning
numbers, are in reality conversant about no object distinct from particular numeral things, except only names and characters, which originally came to be considered on no other account but their being signs,
or capable to represent aptly whatever particular things men had need
to compute. Whence it follows that to study them for their own sake
would be just as wise, and to as good purpose as if a man, neglecting
the true use or original intention and subserviency of language, should
spend his time in impertinent criticisms upon words, or reasonings and
controversies purely verbal.

123. From numbers we proceed to speak of *extension*, which, considered as relative, is the object of geometry. The *infinite* divisibility of
finite extension, though it is not expressly laid down either as an axiom
or theorem in the elements of that science, yet is throughout the same
everywhere supposed and thought to have so inseparable and essential a
connection with the principles and demonstrations in geometry, that
mathematicians never admit it into doubt, or make the least question
of it. And, as this notion is the source from whence do spring all those
amusing geometrical paradoxes which have such a direct repugnancy to
the plain common sense of mankind, and are admitted with so much reluctance into a mind not yet debauched by learning; so it is the principal occasion of all that nice and extreme subtilty which renders the
study of mathematics so difficult and tedious. Hence, if we can make it
appear that no finite extension contains innumerable parts, or is infinitely divisible, it follows that we shall at once clear the science of geometry from a great number of difficulties and contradictions which

have ever been esteemed a reproach to human reason, and withal make the attainment thereof a business of much less time and pains than it hitherto hath been.

124. Every particular finite extension which may possibly be the object of our thought is an *idea* existing only in the mind, and consequently each part thereof must be perceived. If, therefore, I cannot perceive innumerable parts in any finite extension that I consider, it is certain they are not contained in it; but it is evident that I cannot distinguish innumerable parts in any particular line, surface, or solid, which I either perceive by sense, or figure to myself in my mind: wherefore I conclude they are not contained in it. Nothing can be plainer to me than that the extensions I have in view are no other than my own ideas; and it is no less plain that I cannot resolve any one of my ideas into an infinite number of other ideas, that is, that they are not infinitely divisible. If by finite extension be meant something distinct from a finite idea, I declare I do not know what that is, and so cannot affirm or deny anything of it. But if the terms 'extension,' 'parts,' etc., are taken in any sense conceivable, that is, for ideas, then to say a finite quantity or extension consists of parts infinite in number is so manifest a contradiction, that everyone at first sight acknowledges it to be so; and it is impossible it should ever gain the assent of any reasonable creature who is not brought to it by gentle and slow degrees, as a converted Gentile to the belief of transubstantiation. Ancient and rooted prejudices do often pass into principles; and those propositions which once obtain the force and credit of a *principle,* are not only themselves, but likewise whatever is deducible from them, thought privileged from all examination. And there is no absurdity so gross, which, by this means, the mind of man may not be prepared to swallow.

125. He whose understanding is possessed with the doctrine of abstract general ideas may be persuaded that (whatever be thought of the ideas of sense) extension in *abstract* is infinitely divisible. And one who thinks the objects of sense exist without the mind will perhaps in virtue thereof be brought to admit that a line but an inch long may contain innumerable parts—really existing, though too small to be discerned. These errors are grafted as well in the minds of geometricians as of other men, and have a like influence on their reasonings; and it were no difficult thing to shew how the arguments from geometry made use of to support the infinite divisibility of extension are bottomed on them. At present we shall only observe in general whence it is the mathematicians are all so fond and tenacious of that doctrine.

126. It hath been observed in another place that the theorems and demonstrations in geometry are conversant about universal ideas (Sec. 15, Introd.); where it is explained in what sense this ought to be un-

derstood, to wit, the particular lines and figures included in the dia‹
gram are supposed to stand for innumerable others of different sizes;
or, in other words, the geometer considers them abstracting from their
magnitude—which does not imply that he forms an abstract idea, but
only that he cares not what the particular magnitude is, whether great
or small, but looks on that as a thing different to the demonstration.
Hence it follows that a line in the scheme but an inch long must be
spoken of as though it contained ten thousand parts, since it is regarded not in itself, but as it is universal; and it is universal only in
its signification, whereby it represents innumerable lines greater than
itself, in which may be distinguished ten thousand parts or more,
though there may not be above an inch in it. After this manner, the
properties of the lines signified are (by a very usual figure) transferred
to the sign, and thence, through mistake, thought to appertain to it considered in its own nature.

127. Because there is no number of parts so great but it is possible
there may be a line containing more, the inch-line is said to contain
parts more than any assignable number; which is true, not of the inch
taken absolutely, but only for the things signified by it. But men, not
retaining that distinction in their thoughts, slide into a belief that the
small particular line described on paper contains in itself parts innumerable. There is no such thing as the ten-thousandth part of an
inch; but there is of a mile or diameter of the earth, which may be
signified by that inch. When therefore I delineate a triangle on paper,
and take one side not above an inch, for example, in lengths to be the
radius, this I consider as divided into ten thousand or an hundred thousand parts or more; for, though the ten-thousandth part of that line
considered in itself is nothing at all, and consequently may be neglected without an error or inconveniency, yet these described lines, being only marks standing for greater quantities, whereof it may be the
ten-thousandth part is very considerable, it follows that, to prevent
notable errors in practice, the radius must be taken of ten thousand
parts or more.

128. From what hath been said the reason is plain why, to the end
any theorem become universal in its use, it is necessary we speak of
the lines described on paper as though they contained parts which
really they do not. In doing of which, if we examine the matter thoroughly, we shall perhaps discover that we cannot conceive an inch
itself as consisting of, or being divisible into, a thousand parts, but only
some other line which is far greater than an inch, and represented by
it; and that when we say a line is infinitely divisible, we must mean a
line which is infinitely great. What we have here observed seems to be

the chief cause why, to suppose the infinite divisibility of finite extension hath been thought necessary in geometry.

129. The several absurdities and contradictions which flowed from
this false principle might, one would think, have been esteemed so
many demonstrations against it. But, by I know not what logic, it is
held that proofs *a posteriori* are not to be admitted against propositions relating to infinity, as though it were not impossible even for an
infinite mind to reconcile contradictions; or as if anything absurd and
repugnant could have a necessary connection with truth or flow from it.
But whoever considers the weakness of this pretense will think it was
contrived on purpose to humor the laziness of the mind which had
rather acquiesce in an indolent scepticism than be at the pains to go
through with a severe examination of those principles it hath ever embraced for true.

130. Of late the speculations about infinites have run so high, and
grown to such strange notions, as have occasioned no scruples and disputes among the geometers of the present age. Some there are of great
note who, not content with holding that finite lines may be divided
into an infinite number of parts, do yet farther maintain that each of
those infinitesimals is itself subdivisible into an infinity of other parts
or infinitesimals of a second order, and so on *ad infinitum*. These, I say,
assert there are infinitesimals of infinitesimals of infinitesimals, etc.,
without ever coming to an end! so that according to them an inch does
not barely contain an infinite number of parts, but an infinity of an
infinity of an infinity *ad infinitum* of parts. Others there be who hold
all orders of infinitesimals below the first to be nothing at all; thinking
it with good reason absurd to imagine there is any positive quantity or
part of extension which, though multiplied infinitely, can never equal
the smallest given extension. And yet on the other hand it seems no less
absurd to think the square, cube or other power of a positive real root,
should itself be nothing at all; which they who hold infinitesimals of
the first order, denying all of the subsequent orders, are obliged to
maintain.

131. Have we not therefore reason to conclude they are *both* in the
wrong, and that there is in effect no such thing as parts infinitely small,
or an infinite number of parts contained in any finite quantity? But you
will say that if this doctrine obtains it will follow the very foundations
of geometry are destroyed, and those great men who have raised that
science to so astonishing a height, have been all the while building a
castle in the air. To this it may be replied that whatever is useful in
geometry, and promotes the benefit of human life, does still remain
firm and unshaken on our principles; that science considered as prac-

tical will rather receive advantage than any prejudice from what has been said. But to set this in a due light may be the proper business of another place. For the rest, though it should follow that some of the more intricate and subtle parts of speculative mathematics may be pared off without any prejudice to truth, yet I do not see what damage will be thence derived to mankind. On the contrary, I think it were highly to be wished that men of great abilities and obstinate application would draw off their thoughts from those amusements, and employ them in the study of such things as lie nearer the concerns of life, or have a more direct influence on the manners.

132. If it be said that several theorems undoubtedly true are discovered by methods in which infinitesimals are made use of, which could never have been if their existence included a contradiction in it; I answer that upon a thorough examination it will not be found that in any instance it is necessary to make use of or conceive infinitesimal parts of finite lines, or even quantities less than the *minimum sensible;* nay, it will be evident this is never done, it being impossible.

133. By what we have premised, it is plain that very numerous and important errors have taken their rise from those false principles which were impugned in the foregoing parts of this treatise; and the opposites of those erroneous tenets at the same time appear to be most fruitful principles, from whence do flow innumerable consequences highly advantageous to true philosophy, as well as to religion. Particularly *matter,* or *the absolute existence of corporeal objects,* hath been shewn to be that wherein the most avowed and pernicious enemies of all knowledge, whether human or divine, have ever placed their chief strength and confidence. And surely, if by distinguishing the real existence of unthinking things from their being perceived, and allowing them a subsistence of their own out of the minds of spirits, no one thing is explained in nature, but on the contrary a great many inexplicable difficulties arise; if the supposition of matter is barely precarious, as not being grounded on so much as one single reason; if its consequences cannot endure the light of examination and free inquiry, but screen themselves under the dark and general pretense of 'infinites being incomprehensible'; if withal the removal of this *matter* be not attended with the least evil consequence; if it be not even missed in the world, but everything as well, nay much easier conceived without it; if, lastly, both sceptics and atheists are forever silenced upon supposing only spirits and ideas, and this scheme of things is perfectly agreeable both to reason and religion: methinks we may expect it should be admitted and firmly embraced, though it were proposed only as an *hypothesis,* and the existence of matter had been allowed possible, which yet I think we have evidently demonstrated that it is not.

134. True it is that, in consequence of the foregoing principles, several disputes and speculations which are esteemed no mean parts of learning, are rejected as useless. But, how great a prejudice soever against our notions this may give to those who have already been deeply engaged, and made large advances in studies of that nature, yet by others we hope it will not be thought any just ground of dislike to the principles and tenets herein laid down, that they abridge the labor of study, and make human sciences far more clear, compendious and attainable than they were before.

135. Having despatched what we intended to say concerning the knowledge of *ideas*, the method we proposed leads us in the next place to treat of *spirits*—with regard to which, perhaps, human knowledge is not so deficient as is vulgarly imagined. The great reason that is assigned for our being thought ignorant of the nature of spirits is our not having an *idea* of it. But surely it ought not to be looked on as a defect in a human understanding that it does not perceive the idea of spirit, if it is manifestly impossible there should be any such idea. And this if I mistake not has been demonstrated in Section 27; to which I shall here add that a spirit has been shewn to be the only substance or support wherein unthinking beings or ideas can exist; but that this *substance* which supports or perceives ideas should itself be an idea or like an idea is evidently absurd.

136. It will perhaps be said that we want a sense (as some have imagined) proper to know substances withal, which, if we had, we might know our own soul as we do a triangle. To this I answer, that, in case we had a new sense bestowed upon us, we could only receive thereby some new sensations or ideas of sense. But I believe nobdy will say that what he means by the terms *soul* and *substance* is only some particular sort of idea or sensation. We may therefore infer that, all things duly considered, it is not more reasonable to think our faculties defective, in that they do not furnish us with an idea of spirit or active thinking substance, than it would be if we should blame them for not being able to comprehend a *round square*.

137. From the opinion that spirits are to be known after the manner of an idea or sensation have risen many absurd and heterodox tenets, and much scepticism about the nature of the soul. It is even probable that this opinion may have produced a doubt in some whether they had any soul at all distinct from their body, since upon inquiry they could not find they had an idea of it. That an *idea,* which is inactive and the existence whereof consists in being perceived, should be the image or likeness of an agent subsisting by itself, seems to need no other refutation than barely attending to what is meant by those words. But perhaps you will say that though an idea cannot resemble a spirit in its

thinking, acting, or subsisting by itself, yet it may in some other respects; and it is not necessary that an idea or image be in all respects like the original.

138. I answer, if it does not in those mentioned, it is impossible it should represent it in any other thing. Do but leave out the power of willing, thinking, and perceiving ideas, and there remains nothing else wherein the idea can be like a spirit. For by the word 'spirit' we mean only that which thinks, wills, and perceives; this, and this alone, constitutes the signification of that term. If therefore it is impossible that any degree of those powers should be represented in an idea, it is evident there can be no idea of a spirit.

139. But it will be objected that, if there is no idea signified by the terms 'soul,' 'spirit,' and 'substance,' they are wholly insignificant, or have no meaning in them. I answer, those words do mean or signify a real thing, which is neither an idea nor like an idea, but that which perceives ideas, and wills, and reasons about them. What I am myself, that which I denote by the term 'I,' is the same with what is meant by 'soul' or 'spiritual substances.' If it be said that this is only quarreling at a word, and that, since the immediate significations of other names are by common consent called 'ideas' no reason can be assigned why that which is signified by the name 'spirit' or 'soul' may not partake in the same appellation: I answer, all the unthinking objects of the mind agree in that they are entirely passive, and their existence consists only in being perceived; whereas a soul or spirit is an active being, whose existence consists, not in being perceived, but in perceiving ideas and thinking. It is therefore necessary, in order to prevent equivocation and confounding natures perfectly disagreeing and unlike, that we distinguish between *spirit* and *idea*. (See Sec. 27.)

140. In a large sense, indeed, we may be said to have an idea or rather a notion of *spirit*, that is, we understand the meaning of the word, otherwise we could not affirm or deny anything of it. Moreover, as we conceive the ideas that are in the minds of other spirits by means of our own, which we suppose to be resemblances of them; so we know other spirits by means of our own soul; which in that sense is the image or idea of them; it having a like respect to other spirits that blueness or heat by me perceived has to those ideas perceived by another.

141. It must not be supposed that they who assert the natural immortality of the soul are of opinion that it is absolutely incapable of annihilation even by the infinite power of the Creator who first gave it being, but only that it is not liable to be broken or dissolved by the ordinary laws of nature or motion. They indeed who hold the soul of man to be only a thin vital flame, or system of animal spirits, make it perishing and corruptible as the body; since there is nothing more

easily dissipated than such a being, which it is naturally impossible should survive the ruin of the tabernacle wherein it is enclosed. And this notion hath been greedily embraced and cherished by the worst part of mankind, as the most effectual antidote against all impressions of virtue and religion. But it hath been made evident that bodies of what frame or texture soever, are barely passive ideas in the mind, which is more distant and heterogeneous from them than light is from darkness. We have shewn that the soul is indivisible, incorporeal, unextended, and it is consequently incorruptible. Nothing can be plainer than that the motions, changes, decays, and dissolutions which we hourly see befall natural bodies (and which is what we mean by the *course of nature*) cannot possibly affect an active, simple, uncompounded substance; such a being therefore is indissoluble by the force of nature; that is to say, *the soul of man is naturally immortal.*

142. After what hath been said, it is, I suppose, plain that our souls are not to be known in the same manner as senseless, inactive objects, or by way of *idea. Spirits* and *ideas* are things so wholly different, that when we say 'they exist,' 'they are known,' or the like, these words must not be thought to signify anything common to both natures. There is nothing alike or common in them: and to expect that by any multiplication or enlargement of our faculties we may be enabled to know a spirit as we do a triangle, seems as absurd as if we should hope to see a sound. This is inculcated because I imagine it may be of moment towards clearing several important questions, and preventing some very dangerous errors concerning the nature of the soul. We may not, I think, strictly be said to have an *idea* of an active being, or of an action, although we may be said to have a *notion* of them. I have some knowledge or notion of my mind, and its acts about ideas, inasmuch as I know or understand what is meant by these words. What I know, that I have some notion of. I will not say that the terms 'idea' and 'notion' may not be used convertibly, if the world will have it so; but yet it conduceth to clearness and propriety that we distinguish things very different by different names. It is also to be remarked that, all relations including an act of the mind, we cannot so properly be said to have an idea, but rather a notion of the relations and habitudes between things. But if, in the modern way, the word 'idea' is extended to spirits, and relations, and acts, this is, after all, an affair of verbal concern.

143. It will not be amiss to add, that the doctrine of *abstract ideas* hath had no small share in rendering those sciences intricate and ob-- scure which are particularly conversant about spiritual things. Men have imagined they could frame abstract notions of the powers and acts of the mind, and consider them prescinded as well from the mind or spirit itself, as from their respective objects and effects. Hence a great

number of dark and ambiguous terms, presumed to stand for abstract
notions, have been introduced into metaphysics and morality, and from
these have grown infinite distractions and disputes amongst the
learned.

144. But nothing seems more to have contributed towards engaging
men in controversies and mistakes with regard to the nature and operations of the mind, than the being used to speak of those things in terms
borrowed from sensible ideas. For example, the will is termed the *motion* of the soul: this infuses a belief that the mind of man is as a ball
in motion, impelled and determined by the objects of sense, as necessarily as that is by the stroke of a racket. Hence arise endless scruples
and errors of dangerous consequence in morality. All which, I doubt not,
may be cleared, and truth appear plain, uniform, and consistent, could
but philosophers be prevailed on to retire into themselves, and attentively consider their own meaning.

145. From what hath been said, it is plain that we cannot know the
existence of other spirits otherwise than by their operations, or the
ideas by them excited in us. I perceive several motions, changes, and
combinations of ideas, that inform me there are certain particular
agents, like myself, which accompany them and concur in their production. Hence, the knowledge I have of other spirits is not immediate, as
is the knowledge of my ideas; but depending on the intervention of
ideas, by me referred to agents or spirits distinct from myself, as effects or concomitant signs.

146. But though there be some things which convince us human
agents are concerned in producing them; yet it is evident to everyone
that those things which are called the works of nature, that is, the far
greater part of the ideas or sensations perceived by us, are not produced by, or dependent on, the wills of men. There is therefore some
other Spirit that causes them; since it is repugnant that they should
subsist by themselves. (See Sec. 29.) But if we attentively consider
the constant regularity, order, and concatenation of natural things, the
surprising magnificence, beauty, and perfection of the larger, and the
exquisite contrivance of the smaller parts of creation, together with
the exact harmony and correspondence of the whole, but above all the
never enough admired laws of pain and pleasure, and the instincts or
natural inclinations, appetites, and passions of animals; I say if we
consider all these things, and at the same time attend to the meaning
and import of the attributes One, Eternal, Infinitely Wise, Good, and
Perfect, we shall clearly perceive that they belong to the aforesaid Spirit,
"who works all in all," and "by whom all things consist."

147. Hence, it is evident that God is known as certainly and immediately as any other mind or spirit whatsoever distinct from ourselves.

We may even assert that the existence of God is far more evidently perceived than the existence of men; because the effects of nature are infinitely more numerous and considerable than those ascribed to human agents. There is not any one mark that denotes a man, or effect produced by him, which does not more strongly evince the being of that Spirit who is the Author of Nature. For it is evident that in affecting other persons the will of man hath no other object than barely the motion of the limbs of his body; but that such a motion should be attended by, or excite any idea in the mind of another, depends wholly on the will of the Creator. He alone it is who, "upholding all things by the word of His power," maintains that intercourse between spirits whereby they are able to perceive the existence of each other. And yet this pure and clear light which enlightens everyone is itself invisible.

148. It seems to be a general pretense of the unthinking herd that they cannot *see* God. Could we but see Him, say they, as we see a man, we should believe that He is, and believing obey His commands. But alas, we need only open our eyes to see the Sovereign Lord of all things, with a more full and clear view than we do any one of our fellow-creatures. Not that I imagine we see God (as some will have it) by a direct and immediate view; or see corporeal things, not by themselves, but by seeing that which represents them in the essence of God, which doctrine is, I must confess, to me incomprehensible. But I shall explain my meaning. A human spirit or person is not perceived by sense, as not being an idea; when therefore we see the color, size, figure, and motions of a man, we perceive only certain sensations or ideas excited in our own minds; and these being exhibited to our view in sundry distinct collections, serve to mark out unto us the existence of finite and created spirits like ourselves. Hence it is plain we do not see a man —if by *man* is meant that which lives, moves, perceives, and thinks as we do—but only such a certain collection of ideas as directs us to think there is a distinct principle of thought and motion, like to ourselves, accompanying and represented by it. And after the same manner we see God; all the difference is that, whereas some one finite and narrow assemblage of ideas denotes a particular human mind, whithersoever we direct our view, we do at all times and in all places perceive manifest tokens of the Divinity: everything we see, hear, feel, or anywise perceive by sense being a sign or effect of the power of God; as is our perception of those very motions which are produced by men.

149. It is therefore plain that nothing can be more evident to anyone that is capable of the least reflection that the existence of God, or a Spirit who is intimately present to our minds, producing in them all that variety of ideas or sensations which continually affect us, on whom we have an absolute and entire dependence, in short "in whom we live,

and move, and have our being." That the discovery of this great truth which lies so near and obvious to the mind, should be attained to by the reason of so very few, is a sad instance of the stupidity and inattention of men, who, though they are surrounded with such clear manifestations of the Deity, are yet so little affected by them that they seem, as it were, blinded with excess of light.

150. But you will say, Hath Nature no share in the production of natural things, and must they be all ascribed to the immediate and sole operation of God? I answer, if by 'Nature' is meant only the visible *series* of effects or sensations imprinted on our minds, according to certain fixed and general laws, then it is plain that Nature, taken in this sense, cannot produce anything at all. But, if by 'Nature' is meant some being distinct from God, as well as from the laws of nature, and things perceived by sense, I must confess that word is to me an empty sound without any intelligible meaning annexed to it. Nature, in this acceptation, is a vain chimera, introduced by those heathens who had not just notions of the omnipresence and infinite perfection of God. But it is more unaccountable that it should be received among Christians, professing belief in the Holy Scriptures, which constantly ascribe those effects to the immediate hand of God that heathen philosophers are wont to impute to Nature. "The Lord He causeth the vapors to ascend; He maketh lightnings with rain; He bringeth forth the wind out of his treasures." (Jerem. x. 13.) "He turneth the shadow of death into the morning, and maketh the day dark with night." (Amos. v. 8.) "He visiteth the earth, and maketh it soft with showers: He blesseth the springing thereof, and crowneth the year with His goodness; so that the pastures are clothed with flocks, and the valleys are covered over with corn." (See Psalm lxv.) But notwithstanding that this is the constant language of Scripture, yet we have I know not what aversion from believing that God concerns Himself so nearly in our affairs. Fain would we suppose Him at a great distance off, and substitute some blind unthinking deputy in His stead, though (if we may believe Saint Paul) "He be not far from every one of us."

151. It will, I doubt not, be objected that the slow and gradual methods observed in the production of natural things do not seem to have for their cause the immediate hand of an Almighty Agent. Besides, monsters, untimely births, fruits blasted in the blossom, rains falling in desert places, miseries incident to human life, and the like, are so many arguments that the whole frame of nature is not immediately actuated and superintended by a Spirit of infinite wisdom and goodness. But the answer to this objection is in a good measure plain from Section 62; it being visible that the aforesaid methods of nature are absolutely necessary, in order to working by the most simple and general rules,

and after a steady and consistent manner; which argues both the wisdom and goodness of God. Such is the artificial contrivance of this mighty machine of nature that, whilst its motions and various phenomena strike on our senses, the hand which actuates the whole is itself unperceivable to men of flesh and blood. "Verily," saith the prophet, "thou art a God that hidest thyself." (Isaiah xlv. 15.) But though the Lord conceal Himself from the eyes of the sensual and lazy, who will not be at the least expense of thought, yet to an unbiased and attentive mind nothing can be more plainly legible than the intimate presence of an all-wise Spirit, who fashions, regulates, and sustains the whole system of beings. It is clear, from what we have elsewhere observed, that the operating according to general and stated laws is so necessary for our guidance in the affairs of life, and letting us into the secret of nature, that without it all reach and compass of thought, all human sagacity and design, could serve to no manner of purpose; it were even impossible there should be any such faculties or powers in the mind. (See Sec. 31.) Which one consideration abundantly outbalances whatever particular inconveniences may thence arise.

152. We should further consider that the very blemishes and defects of nature are not without their use, in that they make an agreeable sort of variety, and augment the beauty of the rest of the creation, as shades in a picture serve to set off the brighter and more enlightened parts. We would likewise do well to examine whether our taxing the waste of seeds and embryos, and accidental destruction of plants and animals, before they come to full maturity, as an imprudence in the Author of nature, be not the effect of prejudice contracted by our familiarity with impotent and saving mortals. In man indeed a thrifty management of those things which he cannot procure without much pains and industry may be esteemed wisdom. But we must not imagine that the inexplicably fine machine of an animal or vegetable costs the great Creator any more pains or trouble in its production than a pebble does; nothing being more evident than that an Omnipotent Spirit can indifferently produce everything by a mere *fiat* or act of His will. Hence, it is plain that the splendid profusion of natural things should not be interpreted weakness or prodigality in the Agent who produces them, but rather be looked on as an argument of the riches of His power.

153. As for the mixture of pain or uneasiness which is in the world, pursuant to the general laws of nature, and the actions of finite, imperfect spirits, this, in the state we are in at present, is indispensably necessary to our well-being. But our prospects are too narrow. We take, for instance, the idea of some one particular pain into our thoughts and account it *evil;* whereas, if we enlarge our view, so as to comprehend

the various ends, connections, and dependencies of things, on what occasions and in what proportions we are affected with pain and pleasure,
the nature of human freedom, and the design with which we are put
into the world; we shall be forced to acknowledge that those particular
things which, considered in themselves, appear to be evil, have the nature of good, when considered as linked with the whole system of
beings.

154. From what hath been said, it will be manifest to any considering person, that it is merely for want of attention and comprehensiveness of mind that there are any favorers of atheism or the Manichean
heresy to be found. Little and unreflecting souls may indeed burlesque
the works of Providence, the beauty and order whereof they have not
capacity, or will not be at the pains, to comprehend; but those who are
masters of any justness and extent of thought, and are withal used to
reflect, can never sufficiently admire the divine traces of wisdom and
goodness that shine throughout the economy of nature. But what truth
is there which shineth so strongly on the mind that by an aversion of
thought, a willful shutting of the eyes, we may not escape seeing it?
Is it therefore to be wondered at, if the generality of men, who are
ever intent on business or pleasure, and little used to fix or open the
eye of their mind, should not have all that conviction and evidence of
the Being of God which might be expected in reasonable creatures?

155. We should rather wonder that men can be found so stupid as to
neglect, than that neglecting they should be unconvinced of such an evident and momentous truth. And yet it is to be feared that too many of
parts and leisure, who live in Christian countries, are, merely through a
supine and dreadful negligence, sunk into atheism; since it is downright
impossible that a soul pierced and enlightened with a thorough sense of
the omnipresence, holiness, and justice of that Almighty Spirit should
persist in a remorseless violation of His laws. We ought, therfore, earnestly to meditate and dwell on those important points; that so we may
attain conviction without all scruple "that the eyes of the Lord are in
every place beholding the evil and the good; that He is with us and
keepeth us in all places whither we go, and giveth us bread to eat and
raiment to put on;" that He is present and conscious to our innermost
thoughts; and that we have a most absolute and immediate dependence
on Him. A clear view of which great truths cannot choose but fill our
hearts with an awful circumspection and holy fear, which is the strongest incentive to *virtue,* and the best guard against *vice.*

156. For, after all, what deserves the first place in our studies is the
consideration of God and our *duty;* which to promote, as it was the
main drift and design of my labors, so shall I esteem them altogether
useless and ineffectual if, by what I have said, I cannot inspire my

readers with a pious sense of the Presence of God; and, having shewn the falseness or vanity of those barren speculations which make the chief employment of learned men, the better dispose them to reverence and embrace the salutary truths of the Gospel, which to know and to practice is the highest perfection of human nature.

DAVID HUME

An Enquiry Concerning Human Understanding

Dialogues Concerning Natural Religion

DAVID HUME

DAVID HUME (1711-1776) was the younger son of a Scotch gentleman. He was educated at the college of Edinburgh. The family had few means, and, as a younger brother, he had to shift for himself. He first tried reading for the bar, and then business in the office of a Bristol merchant, but his "passion for literature" led him to abandon both. After a period of study at the family home, Ninewells, he went to France where he settled for three years. Here he composed his *Treatise of Human Nature.*

He returned to London to arrange for its publication, and in 1739 the first two volumes appeared. Hume was bitterly disappointed by the failure of the book to create a sensation in the learned world. But he, nevertheless, completed the third volume, which was issued in 1740. Hume was now determined to capture the attention of the public by writing in a more popular style. Retiring again to a life of study and writing at Ninewells, he published in 1741-42 two volumes of *Essays Moral and Political,* which, to his great satisfaction, were a distinct success. In 1746 Hume ventured again into the world of affairs, accepting an appointment as secretary to General St. Clair whom he accompanied on a military expedition to France, and, in 1748, on a diplomatic mission to Vienna and Turin.

In this year (1748) he issued his *Philosophical Essays Concerning Human Understanding.* This work contained the *Enquiry Concerning Human Understanding,* a restatement in more popular form, and with many changes, of the main argument of the first part of the *Treatise.* In 1751 he published *An Enquiry Concerning the Principles of Morals,* a similar rewriting of the third part of the *Treatise,* and a few months later a volume of *Political Discourses.* Hume's literary fame was now well established both in England and on the Continent.

Hume had removed from Ninewells to Edinburgh in 1751. Here he lived amid a distinguished intellectual circle, including such persons as William Robertson, the historian, and Adam Smith. The year following he was made Keeper of the Advocates' Library in Edinburgh. He now formed the plan of writing a history of England. The first volume was not well received, but the subsequent installments were highly popular.

Hume accepted an appointment in 1763 as acting-secretary to the embassy in Paris. He remained in France over two years. Here he was received with adulation, both by the court and in intellectual circles. His last years were spent peacefully and happily among his friends in Edinburgh. An important work, *The Dialogues Concerning Natural Religion,* which he had held back, from motives of prudence, for twenty years, was published posthumously in 1779.

His *Enquiry Concerning Human Understanding* and *Dialogues Concerning Natural Religion*[1] are here republished, both complete.

[1] A valuable critical edition of this work has recently been published by N. K. Smith (1935).

AN ENQUIRY CONCERNING HUMAN UNDERSTANDING

SECTION I

OF THE DIFFERENT SPECIES OF PHILOSOPHY

MORAL philosophy, or the science of human nature, may be treated after two different manners; each of which has its peculiar merit, and may contribute to the entertainment, instruction, and reformation of mankind. The one considers man chiefly as born for action; and as influenced in his measures by taste and sentiment; pursuing one object, and avoiding another, according to the value which these objects seem to possess, and according to the light in which they present themselves. As virtue, of all objects, is allowed to be the most valuable, this species of philosophers paint her in the most amiable colors; borrowing all helps from poetry and eloquence, and treating their subject in an easy and obvious manner, and such as is best fitted to please the imagination, and engage the affections. They select the most striking observations and instances from common life; place opposite characters in a proper contrast; and alluring us into the paths of virtue by the views of glory and happiness, direct our steps in these paths by the soundest precepts and most illustrious examples. They make us *feel* the difference between vice and virtue; they excite and regulate our sentiments; and so they can but bend our hearts to the love of probity and true honor, they think, that they have fully attained the end of all their labors.

The other species of philosophers consider man in the light of a reasonable rather than an active being, and endeavor to form his understanding more than cultivate his manners. They regard human nature as a subject of speculation; and with a narrow scrutiny examine it, in order to find those principles, which regulate our understanding, excite our sentiments, and make us to approve or blame any particular object, action, or behavior. They think it a reproach to all literature, that philosophy should not yet have fixed, beyond controversy, the foundation of morals, reasoning, and criticism; and should for ever talk of truth and falsehood, vice and virtue, beauty and deformity, without being able to determine the source of these distinctions. While they attempt this arduous task, they are deterred by no difficulties; but proceeding from particular instances to general principles, they still push on their inquiries to principles more general, and rest not satisfied till they arrive at those original principles, by which, in every science, all human curiosity must be bounded. Though their speculations seem abstract, and even unintelligible to common readers, they aim at the approbation of the learned and the wise; and think themselves sufficiently compensated for the labor of their whole lives, if they can discover some hidden truths, which may contribute to the instruction of posterity.

It is certain that the easy and obvious philosophy will always, with the generality of mankind, have the preference above the accurate and abstruse; and by many will be recommended, not only as more agreeable, but more useful than the other. It enters more into common life; molds the heart and affections; and, by touching those principles which actuate men, reforms their conduct, and brings them nearer to that model of perfection which it describes. On the contrary, the abstruse philosophy, being founded on a turn of mind, which cannot enter into business and action, vanishes when the philosopher leaves the shade, and comes into open day; nor can its principles easily retain any influence over our conduct and behavior. The feelings of our heart, the agitation of our passions, the vehemence of our affections, dissipate all its conclusions, and reduce the profound philosopher to a mere plebeian.

This also must be confessed, that the most durable, as well as justest fame, has been acquired by the easy philosophy, and that abstract reasoners seem hitherto to have enjoyed only a momentary reputation, from the caprice or ignorance of their own age, but have not been able to support their renown with more equitable posterity. It is easy for a profound philosopher to commit a mistake in his subtle reasonings; and one mistake is the necessary parent of another, while he pushes on his consequences, and is not deterred from embracing any conclusion, by its unusual appearance, or its contradiction to popular opinion. But a philosopher, who purposes only to represent the common sense of mankind in more beautiful and more engaging colors, if by accident he falls into error, goes no farther; but renewing his appeal to common sense, and the natural sentiments of the mind, returns into the right path, and secures himself from any dangerous illusions. The fame of Cicero flourishes at present; but that of Aristotle is utterly decayed. La Bruyère passes the seas, and still maintains his reputation: But the glory of Malebranche is confined to his own nation, and to his own age. And Addison, perhaps, will be read with pleasure, when Locke shall be entirely forgotten.

The mere philosopher is a character, which is commonly but little acceptable in the world, as being supposed to contribute nothing either to the advantage or pleasure of society; while he lives remote from communication with mankind, and is wrapped up in principles and notions equally remote from their comprehension. On the other hand, the mere ignorant is still more despised; nor is anything deemed a surer sign of an illiberal genius in an age and nation where the sciences flourish, than to be entirely destitute of all relish for those noble entertainments. The most perfect character is supposed to lie between those extremes; retaining an equal ability and taste for books, company, and business; preserving in conversation that discernment and delicacy which arise from polite letters; and in business, that probity and accuracy which are the natural result of a just philosophy. In order to diffuse and cultivate so accomplished a character, nothing can be more useful than compositions of the easy style and manner, which draw not too much from life, require no deep application or retreat to be comprehended, and send back the student among mankind full of noble sentiments and wise precepts, applicable to every exigence of human life. By means of such compositions, virtue becomes amiable, science agreeable, company instructive, and retirement entertaining.

Man is a reasonable being; and as such, receives from science his proper food and nourishment: But so narrow are the bounds of human understanding, that little satisfaction can be hoped for in this particular, either from the extent or security of his acquisitions. Man is a sociable, no less than a reasonable being: But neither can he always enjoy company agreeable and amusing, or preserve the proper relish for them. Man is also an active being; and from that disposition, as well as from the various necessities of human life, must submit to business and occupation: But the mind requires some relaxation, and cannot always support its bent to care and industry. It seems, then, that nature has pointed out a mixed kind of life as most suitable to the human race, and secretly admonished them to allow none of these biases to *draw* too much, so as to incapacitate them for other occupations and entertainments. Indulge your passion for science, says she, but let your science be human, and such as may have a direct reference to action and society. Abstruse thought and profound researches I prohibit, and will severely punish, by the pensive melancholy which they introduce, by the endless uncertainty in which they involve you, and by the cold reception which your pretended discoveries shall meet with, when communicated. Be a philosopher; but, amidst all your philosophy, be still a man.

Were the generality of mankind contented to prefer the easy philosophy to the abstract and profound, without throwing any blame or contempt on the latter, it might not be improper, perhaps, to comply with this general opinion, and allow every man to enjoy, without opposition, his own taste and sentiment. But as the matter is often carried farther, even to the absolute rejecting of all profound reasonings, or what is commonly called *metaphysics,* we shall now proceed to consider what can reasonably be pleaded in their behalf.

We may begin with observing, that one considerable advantage, which results from the accurate and abstract philosophy, is, its subserviency to the easy and humane, which, without the former, can never attain a sufficient degree of exactness in its sentiments, precepts, or reasonings. All polite letters are nothing but pictures of human life in various attitudes and situations; and inspire us with different sentiments, of praise or blame, admiration or ridicule, according to the qualities of the object, which they set before us. An artist must be better qualified to succeed in this undertaking, who, besides a delicate taste and a quick apprehension, possesses an accurate knowledge of the internal fabric, the operations of the understanding, the workings of the passions, and the various species of sentiment which discriminate vice and virtue. How painful soever this inward search or inquiry may appear, it becomes, in some measure, requisite to those, who would describe with success the obvious and outward appearances of life and manners. The anatomist presents to the eye the most hideous and disagreeable objects; but his science is useful to the painter in delineating even a Venus or an Helen. While the latter employs all the richest colors of his art, and gives his figures the most graceful and engaging airs; he must still carry his attention to the inward structure of the human body, the position of the muscles, the fabric of the bones, and the use and figure of every part or organ. Accuracy is, in every case, advantageous to beauty, and just reasoning to delicate sentiment. In vain would we exalt the one by depreciating the other.

Besides, we may observe, in every art or profession, even those which most concern life or action, that a spirit of accuracy, however acquired, carries all of them nearer their perfection, and renders them more subservient to the interests of society. And though a philosopher may live remote from business, the genius of philosophy, if carefully cultivated by several, must gradually diffuse itself throughout the whole society, and bestow a similar correctness on every art and calling. The politician will acquire greater foresight and subtlety, in the subdividing and balancing of power; the lawyer more method and finer principles in his reasonings; and the general more regularity in his discipline, and more caution in his plans and operations. The stability of modern governments above the ancient, and the accuracy of modern philosophy, have improved, and probably will still improve, by similar gradations.

Were there no advantage to be reaped from these studies, beyond the gratification of an innocent curiosity, yet ought not even this to be despised; as being one accession to those few safe and harmless pleasures, which are bestowed on the human race. The sweetest and most inoffensive path of life leads through the avenues of science and learning; and whoever can either remove any obstructions in this way, or open up any new prospect, ought so far to be esteemed a benefactor to mankind. And though these researches may appear painful and fatiguing, it is with some minds as with some bodies, which being endowed with vigorous and florid health, require severe exercise, and reap a pleasure from what, to the generality of mankind, may seem burdensome and laborious. Obscurity, indeed, is painful to the mind as well as to the eye; but to bring light from obscurity, by whatever labor, must needs be delightful and rejoicing.

But this obscurity in the profound and abstract philosophy, is objected to, not only as painful and fatiguing, but as the inevitable source of uncertainty and error. Here indeed lies the justest and most plausible objection against a considerable part of metaphysics, that they are not properly a science; but arise either from the fruitless efforts of human vanity, which would penetrate into subjects utterly inaccessible to the understanding, or from the craft of popular superstitions, which, being unable to defend themselves on fair ground, raise these entangling brambles to cover and protect their weakness. Chased from the open country, these robbers fly into the forest, and lie in wait to break in upon every unguarded avenue of the mind, and overwhelm it with religious fears and prejudices. The stoutest antagonist, if he remit his watch a moment, is oppressed. And many, through cowardice and folly, open the gates to the enemies, and willingly receive them with reverence and submission, as their legal sovereigns.

But is this a sufficient reason, why philosophers should desist from such researches, and leave superstition still in possession of her retreat? Is it not proper to draw an opposite conclusion, and perceive the necessity of carrying the war into the most secret recesses of the enemy? In vain do we hope, that men, from frequent disappointment, will at last abandon such airy sciences, and discover the proper province of human reason. For, besides, that many persons find too sensible an interest in perpetually recalling such topics; besides this, I say, the motive of blind despair can never reasonably have place in the sciences; since, however unsuccessful former attempts may have proved, there is still room to hope, that the industry, good fortune, or improved sagacity of succeeding generations may reach discoveries unknown to former ages. Each adventurous genius will leap at the arduous prize, and find himself stimulated, rather than discouraged, by the failures of his predecessors; while he hopes that the glory of achieving so hard an adventure is reserved for him alone. The only method of freeing learning, at once, from these abstruse questions, is to inquire seriously into the nature of human understanding, and show, from an exact analysis of its powers and capacity, that it is by no means fitted for such remote and abstruse subjects. We must submit to this fatigue, in order to live at ease ever after: And must cultivate true metaphysics with some care, in order to destroy the false and adulterate. Indolence, which, to some persons, affords a safeguard against this deceitful philosophy, is, with others, over-balanced by curiosity; and despair, which, at some moments, prevails, may give place afterwards to sanguine hopes and expectations. Accurate and just reasoning is the only catholic remedy, fitted for all persons and all dispositions; and is alone able to subvert that abstruse philosophy and metaphysical jargon, which, being mixed up with popular superstition, renders it in a manner impenetrable to careless reasoners, and gives it the air of science and wisdom.

Besides this advantage of rejecting, after deliberate inquiry, the most uncertain and disagreeable part of learning, there are many positive advantages, which result from an accurate scrutiny into the powers and faculties of human nature. It is remarkable concerning the operations of the mind, that, though most intimately present to us, yet, whenever they become the object of reflection, they seem involved in obscurity; nor can the eye readily find those lines and boundaries, which discriminate and distinguish them. The objects are too fine to remain long in the same aspect or situation; and must be apprehended in an instant, by a superior penetration, derived from nature, and improved by habit and reflection. It becomes, therefore, no inconsiderable part of science barely to know the different operations of the mind, to separate them from each other, to class them under their proper heads, and to correct all that seeming disorder, in which they lie involved, when made the object of reflection and inquiry. This talk of ordering and distinguishing, which has no merit, when performed with regard to external bodies, the objects of our senses, rises in its value, when directed towards the operations of the mind, in proportion to the difficulty and labor, which we meet with in performing it. And if we can go no farther than this mental geography, or delineation of the distinct parts and powers of the mind, it is at least a satisfaction to go so far; and the more obvious this science may appear (and it is by no means obvious) the more contemptible still must the ignorance of it be esteemed, in all pretenders to learning and philosophy.

Nor can there remain any suspicion, that this science is uncertain and chimerical; unless we should entertain such a scepticism as is entirely subversive of all speculation, and even action. It cannot be doubted, that the mind is endowed with several powers and faculties, that these powers are distinct from each other, that what is really distinct to the immediate perception may be distinguished by reflection; and consequently, that there is a truth and falsehood in all propositions on this subject, and a truth and falsehood, which lie not beyond the compass of human understanding. There are many obvious distinctions of this kind, such as those between the will and understanding, the imagination and passions, which fall within the comprehension of every human creature; and the finer and more philosophical distinctions are no less real and certain, though more difficult to be comprehended. Some instances, especially late ones, of success in these inquiries, may give us a juster notion of the certainty and solidity of this branch of learning. And shall we esteem it worthy the labor of a philosopher to give us a true system of the planets, and adjust the position and order of those remote bodies; while we affect to overlook those, who, with so much success, delineate the parts of the mind, in which we are so intimately concerned?

But may we not hope, that philosophy, if cultivated with care, and encouraged by the attention of the public, may carry its researches still farther, and discover, at least in some degree, the secret springs and principles, by which the human mind is actuated in its operations? Astronomers had long contented themselves with proving, from the phenomena, the true motions, order, and magnitude of the heavenly bodies: Till a philosopher, at last, arose, who seems, from the happiest reasoning, to have also determined the laws and forces, by which the revolutions of the planets are governed and directed. The like has been performed with regard to other parts of nature. And there is no reason to despair of equal success in our inquiries concerning the mental powers and economy, if prosecuted with equal capacity and caution. It is probable, that one operation and principle of the mind depends on another; which, again, may be resolved into one more general and universal: And how far these researches may possibly be carried, it will be difficult for us, before, or even after, a careful trial, exactly to determine. This is certain, that attempts of this kind are every day made even by those who philosophize the most negligently: And nothing can be more requisite than to enter upon the enterprise with thorough care and attention; that, if it lie within the compass of human understanding, it may at last be happily achieved; if not, it may, however, be rejected with some confidence and security. This last conclusion, surely, is not desirable; nor ought it to be embraced too rashly. For how much must we diminish from the beauty and value of this species of philosophy, upon such a supposition? Moralists have hitherto been accustomed, when they considered the vast multitude and diversity of those actions that excite our approbation or dislike, to search for some common principle, on which this variety of sentiments might depend. And though they have sometimes carried the matter too far, by their passion for some one general principle; it must, however, be confessed, that they are excusable in expecting to find some general principles, into which all the vices and virtues were justly to be resolved. The like has been the endeavor of critics, logicians, and even politicians:

Nor have their attempts been wholly unsuccessful; though perhaps longer time, greater accuracy, and more ardent application may bring these sciences still nearer their perfection. To throw up at once all pretensions of this kind may justly be deemed more rash, precipitate, and dogmatical, than even the boldest and most affirmative philosophy, that has ever attempted to impose its crude dictates and principles on mankind.

What though these reasonings concerning human nature seem abstract, and of difficult comprehension? This affords no presumption of their falsehood. On the contrary, it seems impossible, that what has hitherto escaped so many wise and profound philosophers can be very obvious and easy. And whatever pains these researches may cost us, we may think ourselves sufficiently rewarded, not only in point of profit but of pleasure, if, by that means, we can make any addition to our stock of knowledge, in subjects of such unspeakable importance.

But as, after all, the abstractedness of these speculations is no recommendation, but rather a disadvantage to them, and as this difficulty may perhaps be surmounted by care and art, and the avoiding of all unnecessary detail, we have, in the following inquiry, attempted to throw some light upon subjects, from which uncertainty has hitherto deterred the wise, and obscurity the ignorant. Happy, if we can unite the boundaries of the different species of philosophy, by reconciling profound inquiry with clearness, and truth with novelty! And still more happy, if reasoning in this easy manner, we can undermine the foundations of an abstruse philosophy, which seems to have hitherto served only as a shelter to superstition, and a cover to absurdity and error!

SECTION II

OF THE ORIGIN OF IDEAS

EVERYONE will readily allow that there is a considerable difference between the perceptions of the mind, when a man feels the pain of excessive heat, or the pleasure of moderate warmth, and when he afterwards recalls to his memory this sensation, or anticipates it by his imagination. These faculties may mimic or copy the perceptions of the senses; but they never can entirely reach the force and vivacity of the original sentiment. The utmost we say of them, even when they operate with greatest vigor, is, that they represent their object in so lively a manner, that we could *almost* say we feel or see it: But, except the mind be disordered by disease or madness, they never can arrive at such a pitch of vivacity, as to render these perceptions altogether undistinguishable. All the colors of poetry, however splendid, can never paint natural objects in such a manner as to make the description be taken for a real landscape. The most lively thought is still inferior to the dullest sensation.

We may observe a like distinction to run through all the other perceptions of the mind. A man in a fit of anger, is actuated in a very different manner from one who only thinks of that emotion. If you tell me, that any person is in love, I easily understand your meaning, and form a just conception of his situation; but never can mistake that conception for the real disorders and agitations of the passion. When we reflect on our past sentiments and affections, our thought is a faithful mirror, and copies its objects truly; but the colors which it employs are faint and dull, in comparison of those in which our original perceptions were clothed. It requires no nice discernment or metaphysical head to mark the distinction between them.

Here therefore we may divide all the perceptions of the mind into two classes or species, which are distinguished by their different degrees of force and vivacity. The less forcible and lively are commonly denominated *thoughts* or *ideas*. The other species want a name in our language, and in most others; I suppose, because it was not requisite for any, but philosophical purposes, to rank them under a general term or appellation. Let us, therefore, use a little freedom, and call them *impressions;* employing that word in a sense somewhat different from the usual. By the term *impression,* then, I mean all our more lively perceptions, when we hear, or see, or feel, or love, or hate, or desire, or will. And impressions are distinguished from ideas, which are the less lively perceptions, of which we are conscious, when we reflect on any of those sensations or movements above mentioned.

Nothing, at first view, may seem more unbounded than the thought of man, which not only escapes all human power and authority, but is not even restrained within the limits of nature and reality. To form monsters, and join incongruous shapes and appearances, costs the imagination no more trouble than to conceive the most natural and familiar objects. And while the body is confined to one planet, along which it creeps with pain and difficulty; the thought can in an instant transport us into the most distant regions of the universe; or even beyond the universe, into the unbounded chaos, where nature is supposed to lie in total confusion. What never was seen, or heard of, may yet be conceived; nor is anything beyond the power of thought, except what implies an absolute contradiction.

But though our thought seems to possess this unbounded liberty, we shall find, upon a nearer examination, that it is really confined within very narrow limits, and that all this creative power of the mind amounts to no more than the faculty of compounding, transposing, augmenting, or diminishing the materials afforded us by the senses and experience. When we think of a golden mountain, we only join two consistent ideas, *gold*, and *mountain*, with which we were formerly acquainted. A virtuous horse we can conceive; because, from our own feeling, we can conceive virtue; and this we may unite to the figure and shape of a horse, which is an animal familiar to us. In short, all the materials of thinking are derived either from our outward or inward sentiment: the mixture and composition of these belongs alone to the mind and will. Or, to express myself in philosophical language, all our ideas or more feeble perceptions are copies of our impressions or more lively ones.

To prove this, the two following arguments will, I hope, be sufficient. First, when we analyze our thoughts or ideas, however compounded or sublime, we always find that they resolve themselves into such simple ideas as were copied from a precedent feeling or sentiment. Even those ideas, which, at first view, seem the most wide of this origin, are found, upon a nearer scrutiny, to be derived from it. The idea of God, as meaning an infinitely intelligent, wise, and good Being, arises from reflecting on the operations of our own mind, and augmenting, without limit, those qualities of goodness and wisdom. We may prosecute this inquiry to what length we please; where we shall always find, that every idea which we examine is copied from a similar impression. Those who would assert that this position is not universally true nor without exception, have only one, and that an easy method of refuting it; by producing that idea, which, in their opinion, is not derived from this source. It will then be incumbent on us, if we would maintain our doctrine, to produce the impression, or lively perception, which corresponds to it.

Secondly. If it happen, from a defect of the organ, that a man is not susceptible of any species of sensation, we always find that he is as little susceptible of the correspondent ideas. A blind man can form no notion of colors; a deaf man of sounds. Restore either of them that sense in which he is deficient; by opening this new inlet for his sensations, you also open an inlet for the ideas; and he finds no difficulty in conceiving these objects. The case is the same, if the object, proper for exciting any sensation, has never been applied to the organ. A Laplander or Negro has no notion of the relish of wine. And though there are few or no instances of a like deficiency in the mind, where a person has never felt or is wholly incapable of a sentiment or passion that belongs to his species; yet we find the same observation to take place in a less degree. A man of mild manners can form no idea of inveterate revenge or cruelty; nor can a selfish heart easily conceive the heights of friendship and generosity. It is readily allowed, that other beings may possess many senses of which we can have no conception; because the ideas of them have never been introduced to us in the only manner by which an idea can have access to the mind, to wit, by the actual feeling and sensation.

There is, however, one contradictory phenomenon, which may prove that it is not absolutely impossible for ideas to arise, independent of their correspondent impressions. I believe it will readily be allowed, that the several distinct ideas of color, which enter by the eye, or those of sound, which are conveyed by the ear, are really different from each other; though, at the same time, resembling. Now if this be true of different colors, it must be no less so of the different shades of the same color; and each shade produces a distinct idea, independent of the rest. For if this should be denied, it is possible, by the continual gradation of shades, to run a color insensibly into what is most remote from it; and if you will not allow any of the means to be different, you cannot, without absurdity, deny the extremes to be the same. Suppose, therefore, a person to have enjoyed his sight for thirty years, and to have become perfectly acquainted with colors of all kinds except one particular shade of blue, for instance, which it never has been his fortune to meet with. Let all the different shades of that color, except that single one, be placed before him, descending gradually from the deepest to the lightest; it is plain that he will perceive a blank, where that shade is wanting, and will be sensible that there is a greater distance in that place between the contiguous colors than in any other. Now I ask, whether it be possible for him, from his own imagination, to supply this deficiency, and raise up to himself the idea of that particular shade, though it had never been conveyed to him by his senses? I believe there are few but will be of opinion that he can: and this may serve as a proof that the simple ideas are not always, in every instance, derived from the correspondent impressions; though this instance is so singular, that it is scarcely worth our observing, and does not merit that for it alone we should alter our general maxim.

Here, therefore, is a proposition, which not only seems, in itself, simple and intelligible; but, if a proper use were made of it, might render every dispute equally intelligible, and banish all that jargon, which has so long taken possession of metaphysical reasonings, and drawn disgrace upon them. All ideas, especially abstract ones, are naturally faint and obscure: the mind has but a slender hold of them: they are apt to be confounded with other resembling ideas; and when we have often employed any term, though without a distinct meaning, we are apt to imagine it has a determinate idea annexed to it. On the contrary, all impressions, that is, all sensations, either outward or inward, are strong and vivid: the limits between them are more exactly determined: nor is it easy to fall into any error or mistake with regard to them. When we entertain, therefore, any suspicion that a philosophical term is employed without any meaning or idea (as is but too frequent), we need but inquire, *from what impression is that supposed idea derived?* And if it be impossible to assign any, this will serve to confirm our suspicion.[2] By bringing ideas into so clear a light we may reasonably hope to remove all dispute, which may arise, concerning their nature and reality.

SECTION III

OF THE ASSOCIATION OF IDEAS

IT IS EVIDENT that there is a principle of connection between the different thoughts or ideas of the mind, and that, in their appearance to the memory or imagination, they introduce each other with a certain degree of method and regularity. In our more serious thinking or discourse this is so observable that any particular thought, which breaks in upon the regular tract or chain of ideas, is immediately remarked and rejected. And even in our wildest and most wandering reveries, nay in our very dreams, we shall find, if we reflect, that the imagination ran not altogether at adventures, but that there was still a connection upheld among the different ideas, which succeeded each other. Were the loosest and freest conversation to be transcribed, there would immediately be observed something which connected it in all its transitions. Or where this

---

[2] It is probable that no more was meant by those, who denied innate ideas, than that all ideas were copies of our impressions; though it must be confessed, that the terms, which they employed, were not chosen with such caution, nor so exactly defined, as to prevent all mistakes about their doctrine. For what is meant by *innate?* If innate be equivalent to natural, then all the perceptions and ideas of the mind must be allowed to be innate or natural, in whatever sense we take the latter word, whether in opposition to what is uncommon, artificial, or miraculous. If by innate be meant, contemporary to our birth, the dispute seems to be frivolous; nor is it worth while to inquire at what time thinking begins, whether before, at, or after our birth. Again, the word *idea,* seems to be commonly taken in a very loose sense, by LOCKE and others; as standing for any of our perceptions, our sensations and passions, as well as thoughts. Now in this sense, I should desire to know, what can be meant by asserting, that self-love, or resentment of injuries, or the passion between the sexes is not innate?

But admitting these terms, *impressions* and *ideas,* in the sense above explained, and understanding by *innate,* what is original or copied from no precedent perception, then may we assert that all our impressions are innate and our ideas not innate.

To be ingenuous, I must own it to be my opinion, that LOCKE was betrayed into this question by the schoolmen, who, making use of undefined terms, draw out their disputes to a tedious length, without ever touching the point in question. A like ambiguity and circumlocution seem to run through that philosopher's reasonings on this as well as most other subjects.

is wanting, the person who broke the thread of discourse might still inform you, that there had secretly revolved in his mind a succession of thought, which had gradually led him from the subject of conversation. Among different languages, even where we cannot suspect the least connection or communication, it is found, that the words, expressive of ideas, the most compounded, do yet nearly correspond to each other: a certain proof that the simple ideas, comprehended in the compound ones, were bound together by some universal principle, which had an equal influence on all mankind.

Though it be too obvious to escape observation, that different ideas are connected together; I do not find that any philosopher has attempted to enumerate or class all the principles of association; a subject, however, that seems worthy of curiosity. To me, there appear to be only three principles of connection among ideas, namely, *resemblance, contiguity* in time or place, and *cause* or *effect*.

That these principles serve to connect ideas will not, I believe, be much doubted. A picture naturally leads our thoughts to the original:[3] the mention of one apartment in a building naturally introduces an inquiry or discourse concerning the others:[4] and if we think of a wound, we can scarcely forbear reflecting on the pain which follows it.[5] But that this enumeration is complete, and that there are no other principles of association except these, may be difficult to prove to the satisfaction of the reader, or even to a man's own satisfaction. All we can do, in such cases, is to run over several instances, and examine carefully the principle which binds the different thoughts to each other, never stopping till we render the principle as general as possible.[6] The more instances we examine, and the more care we employ, the more assurance shall we acquire, that the enumeration, which we form from the whole, is complete and entire.

---

[3] Resemblance.　　　　[4] Contiguity.　　　　[5] Cause and effect.

[6] For instance, *contrast* or *contrariety* is also a connection among ideas but it may, perhaps, be considered as a mixture of *causation* and *resemblance*. Where two objects are contrary, the one destroys the other; that is, the cause of its annihilation and the idea of the annihilation of an object implies the idea of its former existence.

SECTION IV

SCEPTICAL DOUBTS CONCERNING THE OPERATIONS OF THE UNDERSTANDING

Part I

ALL THE objects of human reason or inquiry may naturally be divided into two kinds, to wit, *relations of ideas,* and *matters of fact.* Of the first kind are the sciences of geometry, algebra, and arithmetic; and in short, every affirmation which is either intuitively or demonstratively certain. *That the square of the hypothenuse is equal to the squares of the two sides,* is a proposition which expresses a relation between these figures. *That three times five is equal to the half of thirty,* expresses a relation between these numbers. Propositions of this kind are discoverable by the mere operation of thought, without dependence on what is anywhere existent in the universe. Though there never were a circle or triangle in nature, the truths demonstrated by Euclid would for ever retain their certainty and evidence.

Matters of fact, which are the second objects of human reason, are not ascertained in the same manner; nor is our evidence of their truth, however great, of a like nature with the foregoing. The contrary of every matter of fact is still possible; because it can never imply a contradiction, and is conceived by the mind with the same facility and distinctness, as if ever so conformable to reality. *That the sun will not rise tomorrow* is no less intelligible a proposition, and implies no more contradiction than the affirmation, *that it will rise.* We should in vain, therefore, attempt to demonstrate its falsehood. Were it demonstratively false, it would imply a contradiction, and could never be distinctly conceived by the mind.

It may, therefore, be a subject worthy of curiosity, to inquire what is the nature of that evidence which assures us of any real existence and matter of fact, beyond the present testimony of our senses, or the records of our memory. This part of philosophy, it is observable, has been little cultivated, either by the ancients or moderns; and therefore our doubts and errors, in the prosecution of so important an inquiry, may be the more excusable; while we march through such difficult paths without any guide or direction. They may even prove useful, by exciting curiosity, and destroying that implicit faith and security, which is the bane of all reasoning and free inquiry. The discovery of defects in the common philosophy, if any such there be, will not, I presume, be a discouragement, but rather an incitement, as is usual, to attempt something more full and satisfactory than has yet been proposed to the public.

All reasonings concerning matter of fact seem to be founded on the relation of *cause and effect*. By means of that relation alone we can go beyond the evidence of our memory and senses. If you were to ask a man, why he believes any matter of fact, which is absent; for instance, that his friend is in the country, or in France; he would give you a reason; and this reason would be some other fact; as a letter received from him, or the knowledge of his former resolutions and promises. A man finding a watch or any other machine in a desert island, would conclude that there had once been men in that island. All our reasonings concerning fact are of the same nature. And here it is constantly supposed that there is a connection between the present fact and that which is inferred from it. Were there nothing to bind them together, the inference would be entirely precarious. The hearing of an articulate voice and rational discourse in the dark assures us of the presence of some person: Why? because these are the effects of the human make and fabric, and closely connected with it. If we anatomize all the other reasonings of this nature, we shall find that they are founded on the relation of cause and effect, and that this relation is either near or remote, direct or collateral. Heat and light are collateral effects of fire, and the one effect may justly be inferred from the other.

If we would satisfy ourselves, therefore, concerning the nature of that evidence, which assures us of matters of fact, we must inquire how we arrive at the knowledge of cause and effect.

I shall venture to affirm, as a general proposition, which admits of no exception, that the knowledge of this relation is not, in any instance, attained by reasonings *a priori;* but arises entirely from experience, when we find that any particular objects are constantly conjoined with each other. Let an object be presented to a man of ever so strong natural reason and abilities; if that object be entirely new to him, he will not be able, by the most accurate examination of its sensible qualities, to discover any of its causes or effects. Adam, though his rational faculties be supposed, at the very first, entirely perfect, could not have inferred from the fluidity and transparency of water that it would suffocate him, or from the light and warmth of fire that it would consume him. No object ever discovers, by the qualities which appear to the senses, either the causes which produced it, or the effects which will arise from it; nor can our reason, unassisted by experience, ever draw any inference concerning real existence and matter of fact.

This proposition, *that causes and effects are discoverable, not by reason but by experience,* will readily be admitted with regard to such objects, as we remember to have once been altogether unknown to us; since we must be conscious of the utter inability, which we then lay under, of foretelling what would arise from them. Present two smooth pieces of marble to a man who has no tincture of natural philosophy; he will never discover that they will adhere together in such a manner as to require great force to separate them in a direct line, while they make so small a resistance to a lateral pressure. Such events, as bear little analogy to the common course of nature, are also readily confessed to be known only by experience; nor does any man imagine that the explosion of gunpowder, or the attraction of a loadstone, could ever be discovered by arguments *a priori*. In like manner, when an effect is supposed to depend upon an intricate machinery or secret structure of parts, we make no difficulty in attributing all our knowledge of it to experience. Who will assert that he can give the ultimate reason, why milk or bread is proper nourishment for a man, not for a lion or a tiger?

But the same truth may not appear, at first sight, to have the same evidence with regard to events, which have become familiar to us from our first appearance in the world, which bear a close analogy to the whole course of nature, and which are supposed to depend on the simple qualities of objects, without any secret structure of parts. We are apt to imagine that we could discover these effects by the mere operation of our reason, without experience. We fancy, that were we brought on a sudden into this world, we could at first have inferred that one billiard ball would communicate motion to another upon impulse; and that we needed not to have waited for the event, in order to pronounce with certainty concerning it. Such is the influence of custom, that, where it is strongest, it not only covers our natural ignorance, but even conceals itself, and seems not to take place, merely because it is found in the highest degree.

But to convince us that all the laws of nature, and all the operations of bodies without exception, are known only by experience, the following reflections may, perhaps, suffice. Were any object presented to us, and were we required to pronounce concerning the effect, which will result from it, without consulting past observation; after what manner, I beseech you, must the mind proceed in this operation? It must invent or imagine some event, which it ascribes to the object as its effect; and it is plain that this invention must be entirely arbitrary. The mind can never possibly find the effect in the supposed cause, by the most accurate scrutiny and examination. For the effect is totally different from the cause, and consequently can never be discovered in it. Motion in the second billiard ball is a quite distinct event from motion in the first: nor is there anything in the one to suggest the smallest hint of the other. A stone or piece of metal raised into the air, and left without any support, immediately falls: but to consider the matter *a priori,* is there anything we discover in this situation which can beget the idea of a downward, rather than an upward, or any other motion, in the stone or metal?

And as the first imagination or invention of a particular effect, in all natural operations, is arbitrary, where we consult not experience; so must we also esteem the supposed tie or connection between the cause and effect, which binds them together, and renders it impossible that any other effect could result from the operation of that cause. When I see, for instance, a billiard ball moving in a straight line towards another; even suppose motion in the second ball should by accident be suggested to me, as the result of their contact or impulse; may I not conceive, that a hundred different events might as well follow from that cause? May not both these balls remain at absolute rest? May not the first ball return in a straight line, or leap off from the second in any line or direction? All these suppositions are consistent and conceivable. Why then should we give the preference to one, which is no more consistent or conceivable than the rest? All our reasonings *a priori* will never be able to show us any foundation for this preference.

In a word, then, every effect is a distinct event from its cause. It could not, therefore, be discovered in the cause, and the first invention or conception of it, *a priori,* must be entirely arbitrary. And even after it is suggested, the conjunction of it with the cause must appear equally arbitrary; since there are always many other effects, which, to reason, must seem fully as consistent and natural. In vain, therefore, should we pretend to determine any single event, or infer any cause or effect, without the assistance of observation and experience.

Hence we may discover the reason why no philosopher, who is rational and modest, has ever pretended to assign the ultimate cause of any natural operation, or to show distinctly the action of that power, which produces any single effect in the universe. It is confessed, that the utmost effort of human reason is to reduce the principles, productive of natural phenomena, to a greater simplicity, and to resolve the many particular effects into a few general causes, by means of reasonings from analogy, experience, and observation. But as to the causes of these general causes, we should in vain attempt their discovery; nor shall we ever be able to satisfy ourselves, by any particular explication of them. These ultimate springs and principles are totally shut up from human curiosity and inquiry. Elasticity, gravity, cohesion of parts, communication of motion by impulse; these are probably the ultimate causes and principles which we ever discover in nature; and we may esteem ourselves sufficiently happy, if, by accurate inquiry and reasoning, we can trace up the particular phenomena to, or near to, these general principles. The most perfect philosophy of the natural kind only staves off our ignorance a little longer: as perhaps the most perfect philosophy of the moral or metaphysical kind serves only to discover larger portions of it. Thus the observation of human blindness and weakness is the result of all philosophy, and meets us at every turn, in spite of our endeavors to elude or avoid it.

Nor is geometry, when taken into the assistance of natural philosophy, ever able to remedy this defect, or lead us into the knowledge of ultimate causes, by all that accuracy of reasoning for which it is so justly celebrated. Every part of mixed mathematics proceeds upon the supposition that certain laws are established by nature in her operations; and abstract reasonings are employed, either to assist experience in the discovery of these laws, or to determine their influence in particular instances, where it depends upon any precise degree of distance and quantity. Thus, it is a law of motion, discovered by experience, that the moment or force of any body in motion is in the compound ratio or proportion of its solid contents and its velocity; and consequently, that a small force may remove the greatest obstacle or raise the greatest weight, if, by any contrivance or machinery, we can increase the velocity of that force, so as to make it an overmatch for its antagonist. Geometry assists us in the application of this law, by giving us the just dimensions of all the parts and figures which can enter into any species of machine; but still the discovery of the law itself is owing merely to experience, and all the abstract reasonings in the world could never lead us one step towards the knowledge of it. When we reason *a priori,* and consider merely any object or cause, as it appears to the mind, independent of all observation, it never could suggest to us the notion of any distinct object, such as its effect; much less, show us the inseparable and inviolable connection between them. A man must be very sagacious who could discover by reasoning that crystal is the effect of heat, and ice of cold, without being previously acquainted with the operation of these qualities.

Part II

But we have not yet attained any tolerable satisfaction with regard to the question first proposed. Each solution still gives rise to a new question as difficult as the foregoing, and leads us on to farther inquiries. When it is asked, *What is the nature of all our reasonings concerning matter of fact?* the proper answer seems to be, that they are founded on the relation of cause and effect. When again it is asked, *What is the foundation of all our reasonings and conclusions concerning that relation?* it may be replied in one word, *experience.* But if we still carry on our sifting humor, and ask, *What is the foundation of all conclusions from experience?* this implies a new question, which may be of more difficult

solution and explication. Philosophers, that give themselves airs of superior wisdom and sufficiency, have a hard task when they encounter
persons of inquisitive dispositions, who push them from every corner to
which they retreat, and who are sure at last to bring them to some
dangerous dilemma. The best expedient to prevent this confusion, is to
be modest in our pretensions; and even to discover the difficulty ourselves
before it is objected to us. By this means, we may make a kind of merit
of our very ignorance.

I shall content myself, in this section, with an easy task, and shall pretend only to give a negative answer to the question here proposed. I say
then, that, even after we have experience of the operations of cause and
effect, our conclusions from that experience are *not* founded on reasoning, or any process of the understanding. This answer we must endeavor both to explain and to defend.

It must certainly be allowed, that nature has kept us at a great distance from all her secrets, and has afforded us only the knowledge of a
few superficial qualities of objects; while she conceals from us those
powers and principles on which the influence of those objects entirely
depends. Our senses inform us of the color, weight, and consistence of
bread; but neither sense nor reason can ever inform us of those qualities
which fit it for the nourishment and support of a human body. Sight or
feeling conveys an idea of the actual motion of bodies; but as to that
wonderful force or power, which would carry on a moving body for ever
in a continued change of place, and which bodies never lose but by communicating it to others; of this we cannot form the most distant conception. But notwithstanding this ignorance of natural powers[7] and
principles, we always presume, when we see like sensible qualities, that
they have like secret powers, and expect that effects, similar to those
which we have experienced, will follow from them. If a body of like color
and consistence with that bread, which we have formerly eat, be presented to us, we make no scruple of repeating the experiment, and foresee, with certainty, like nourishment and support. Now this is a process
of the mind or thought, of which I would willingly know the foundation.
It is allowed on all hands that there is no known connection between the
sensible qualities and the secret powers; and consequently, that the mind
is not led to form such a conclusion concerning their constant and regular conjunction, by anything which it knows of their nature. As to past
experience, it can be allowed to give *direct* and *certain* information of
those precise objects only, and that precise period of time, which fell
under its cognizance: but why this experience should be extended to
future times, and to other objects, which, for aught we know, may be

---

[7] The word, *power,* is here used in a loose and popular sense. The more accurate
explication of it would give additional evidence to this argument. See Sect. 7.

only in appearance similar; this is the main question on which I would insist. The bread, which I formerly eat, nourished me; that is, a body of such sensible qualities was, at that time, endued with such secret powers: but does it follow, that other bread must also nourish me at another time, and that like sensible qualities must always be attended with like secret powers? The consequence seems no wise necessary. At least, it must be acknowledged that there is here a consequence drawn by the mind; that there is a certain step taken; a process of thought, and an inference, which wants to be explained. These two propositions are far from being the same, *I have found that such an object has always been attended with such an effect,* and *I foresee, that other objects, which are, in appearance, similar, will be attended with similar effects.* I shall allow, if you please, that the one proposition may justly be inferred from the other; I know, in fact, that it always is inferred. But if you insist that the inference is made by a chain of reasoning, I desire you to produce that reasoning. The connection between these propositions is not intuitive. There is required a medium, which may enable the mind to draw such an inference, if indeed it be drawn by reasoning and argument. What that medium is, I must confess, passes my comprehension; and it is incumbent on those to produce it, who assert that it really exists, and is the origin of all our conclusions concerning matter of fact.

This negative argument must certainly, in process of time, become altogether convincing, if many penetrating and able philosophers shall turn their inquiries this way and no one be ever able to discover any connecting proposition or intermediate step, which supports the understanding in this conclusion. But as the question is yet new, every reader may not trust so far to his own penetration, as to conclude, because an argument escapes his inquiry, that therefore it does not really exist. For this reason it may be requisite to venture upon a more difficult task; and enumerating all the branches of human knowledge, endeavor to show that none of them can afford such an argument.

All reasonings may be divided into two kinds, namely demonstrative reasoning, or that concerning relations of ideas, and moral reasoning, or that concerning matter of fact and existence. That there are no demonstrative arguments in the case seems evident; since it implies no contradiction that the course of nature may change, and that an object, seemingly like those which we have experienced, may be attended with different or contrary effects. May I not clearly and distinctly conceive that a body, falling from the clouds, and which, in all other respects, resembles snow, has yet the taste of salt or feeling of fire? Is there any more intelligible proposition than to affirm, that all the trees will flourish in December and January, and decay in May and June? Now whatever is intelligible, and can be distinctly conceived, implies no contradiction, and can never be proved false by any demonstrative argument or abstract reasoning *a priori.*

If we be, therefore, engaged by arguments to put trust in past experience, and make it the standard of our future judgment, these arguments must be probable only, or such as regard matter of fact and real existence, according to the division above mentioned. But that there is no argument of this kind, must appear, if our explication of that species of reasoning be admitted as solid and satisfactory. We have said that all arguments concerning existence are founded on the relation of cause and effect; that our knowledge of that relation is derived entirely from experience; and that all our experimental conclusions proceed upon the supposition that the future will be conformable to the past. To endeavor, therefore, the proof of this last supposition by probable arguments, or arguments regarding existence, must be evidently going in a circle, and taking that for granted, which is the very point in question.

In reality, all arguments from experience are founded on the similarity which we discover among natural objects, and by which we are induced to expect effects similar to those which we have found to follow from such objects. And though none but a fool or madman will ever pretend to dispute the authority of experience, or to reject that great guide of human life, it may surely be allowed a philosopher to have so much curiosity at least as to examine the principle of human nature, which gives this mighty authority to experience, and makes us draw advantage from that similarity which nature has placed among different objects. From causes which appear *similar* we expect similar effects. This is the sum of all our experimental conclusions. Now it seems evident that, if this conclusion were formed by reason, it would be as perfect at first, and upon one instance, as after ever so long a course of experience. But the case is far otherwise. Nothing so like as eggs; yet no one, on account of this appearing similarity, expects the same taste and relish in all of them. It is only after a long course of uniform experiments in any kind, that we attain a firm reliance and security with regard to a particular event. Now where is that process of reasoning which, from one instance, draws a conclusion, so different from that which it infers from a hundred instances that are nowise different from that single one? This question I propose as much for the sake of information, as with an intention of raising difficulties. I cannot find, I cannot imagine any such reasoning. But I keep my mind still open to instruction, if anyone will vouchsafe to bestow it on me.

Should it be said that, from a number of uniform experiments, we *infer* a connection between the sensible qualities and the secret powers; this, I must confess, seems the same difficulty, couched in different terms. The question still recurs, on what process of argument this *inference* is

founded? Where is the medium, the interposing ideas, which join propositions so very wide of each other? It is confessed that the color, consistence, and other sensible qualities of bread appear not, of themselves,
to have any connection with the secret powers of nourishment and support. For otherwise we could infer these secret powers from the first
appearance of these sensible qualities, without the aid of experience;
contrary to the sentiment of all philosophers, and contrary to plain
matter of fact. Here, then, is our natural state of ignorance with regard
to the powers and influence of all objects. How is this remedied by experience? It only shows us a number of uniform effects, resulting from
certain objects, and teaches us that those particular objects, at that particular time, were endowed with such powers and forces. When a new
object, endowed with similar sensible qualities, is produced, we expect
similar powers and forces, and look for a like effect. From a body of like
color and consistence with bread we expect like nourishment and support.
But this surely is a step or progress of the mind, which wants to be explained. When a man says, *I have found, in all past instances, such sensible qualities conjoined with such secret powers:* And when he says,
*Similar sensible qualities will always be conjoined with similar secret
powers,* he is not guilty of a tautology, nor are these propositions in any
respect the same. You say that the one proposition is an inference from
the other. But you must confess that the inference is not intuitive;
neither is it demonstrative: Of what nature is it, then? To say it is experimental, is begging the question. For all inferences from experience
suppose, as their foundation, that the future will resemble the past, and
that similar powers will be conjoined with similar sensible qualities. If
there be any suspicion that the course of nature may change, and that
the past may be no rule for the future, all experience becomes useless,
and can give rise to no inference or conclusion. It is impossible, therefore, that any arguments from experience can prove this resemblance
of the past to the future; since all these arguments are founded on the
supposition of that resemblance. Let the course of things be allowed
hitherto ever so regular; that alone, without some new argument or inference, proves not that, for the future, it will continue so. In vain do you
pretend to have learned the nature of bodies from your past experience.
Their secret nature, and consequently all their effects and influence, may
change, without any change in their sensible qualities. This happens
sometimes, and with regard to some objects: Why may it not happen
always, and with regard to all objects? What logic, what process of
argument secures you against this supposition? My practice, you say,
refutes my doubts. But you mistake the purport of my question. As an
agent, I am quite satisfied in the point; but as a philosopher, who has
some share of curiosity, I will not say scepticism, I want to learn the

foundation of this inference. No reading, no inquiry has yet been able to remove my difficulty, or give me satisfaction in a matter of such importance. Can I do better than propose the difficulty to the public, even though, perhaps, I have small hopes of obtaining a solution? We shall, at least, by this means, be sensible of our ignorance, if we do not augment our knowledge.

I must confess that a man is guilty of unpardonable arrogance who concludes, because an argument has escaped his own investigation, that therefore it does not really exist. I must also confess that, though all the learned, for several ages, should have employed themselves in fruitless search upon any subject, it may still, perhaps, be rash to conclude positively that the subject must, therefore, pass all human comprehension. Even though we examine all the sources of our knowledge, and conclude them unfit for such a subject, there may still remain a suspicion, that the enumeration is not complete, or the examination not accurate. But with regard to the present subject, there are some considerations which seem to remove all this accusation of arrogance or suspicion of mistake.

It is certain that the most ignorant and stupid peasants—nay infants, nay even brute beasts—improve by experience, and learn the qualities of natural objects, by observing the effects which result from them. When a child has felt the sensation of pain from touching the flame of a candle, he will be careful not to put his hand near any candle; but will expect a similar effect from a cause which is similar in its sensible qualities and appearance. If you assert, therefore, that the understanding of the child is led into this conclusion by any process of argument or ratiocination, I may justly require you to produce that argument; nor have you any pretense to refuse so equitable a demand. You cannot say that the argument is abstruse, and may possibly escape your inquiry; since you confess that it is obvious to the capacity of a mere infant. If you hesitate, therefore, a moment, or if, after reflection, you produce any intricate or profound argument, you, in a manner, give up the question, and confess that it is not reasoning which engages us to suppose the past resembling the future, and to expect similar effects from causes which are, to appearance, similar. This is the proposition which I intended to enforce in the present section. If I be right, I pretend not to have made any mighty discovery. And if I be wrong, I must acknowledge myself to be indeed a very backward scholar; since I cannot now discover an argument which, it seems, was perfectly familiar to me long before I was out of my cradle.

SECTION V

SCEPTICAL SOLUTION OF THESE DOUBTS

Part I

THE PASSION for philosophy, like that for religion, seems liable to this inconvenience, that, though it aims at the correction of our manners, and extirpation of our vices, it may only serve, by imprudent management, to foster a predominant inclination, and push the mind, with more determined resolution, towards that side which already *draws* too much, by the bias and propensity of the natural temper. It is certain that, while we aspire to the magnanimous firmness of the philosophic sage, and endeavor to confine our pleasures altogether within our own minds, we may, at last, render our philosophy like that of Epictetus, and other *stoics,* only a more refined system of selfishness, and reason ourselves out of all virtue as well as social enjoyment. While we study with attention the vanity of human life, and turn all our thoughts towards the empty and transitory nature of riches and honors, we are, perhaps, all the while flattering our natural indolence, which, hating the bustle of the world, and drudgery of business, seeks a pretense of reason to give itself a full and uncontrolled indulgence. There is, however, one species of philosophy which seems little liable to this inconvenience, and that because it strikes in with no disorderly passion of the human mind, nor can mingle itself with any natural affection or propensity; and that is the *academic* or *sceptical* philosophy. The academics always talk of doubt and suspense of judgment, of danger in hasty determinations, of confining to very narrow bounds the inquiries of the understanding, and of renouncing all speculations which lie not within the limits of common life and practice. Nothing, therefore, can be more contrary than such a philosophy to the supine indolence of the mind, its rash arrogance, its lofty pretensions, and its superstitious credulity. Every passion is mortified by it, except the love of truth; and that passion never is, nor can be, carried to too high a degree. It is surprising, therefore, that this philosophy, which, in almost every instance, must be harmless and innocent, should be the subject of so much groundless reproach and obloquy. But, perhaps, the very circumstance which renders it so innocent is what chiefly exposes it to the public hatred and resentment. By flattering no irregular passion, it gains few partisans: By opposing so many vices and follies, it raises to itself abundance of enemies, who stigmatize it as libertine, profane, and irreligious.

Nor need we fear that this philosophy, while it endeavors to limit our inquiries to common life, should ever undermine the reasonings of common life, and carry its doubts so far as to destroy all action, as well as speculation. Nature will always maintain her rights, and prevail in the end over any abstract reasoning whatsoever. Though we should conclude, for instance, as in the foregoing section, that, in all reasonings from experience, there is a step taken by the mind which is not supported by any argument or process of the understanding; there is no danger that these reasonings, on which almost all knowledge depends, will ever be affected by such a discovery. If the mind be not engaged by argument to make this step, it must be induced by some other principle of equal weight and authority; and that principle will preserve its influence as long as human nature remains the same. What that principle is may well be worth the pains of inquiry.

Suppose a person, though endowed with the strongest faculties of reason and reflection, to be brought on a sudden into this world; he would, indeed, immediately observe a continual succession of objects, and one event following another; but he would not be able to discover anything farther. He would not, at first, by any reasoning, be able to reach the idea of cause and effect; since the particular powers, by which all natural operations are performed, never appear to the senses; nor is it reasonable to conclude, merely because one event, in one instance, precedes another, that therefore the one is the cause, the other the effect. Their conjunction may be arbitrary and casual. There may be no reason to infer the existence of one from the appearance of the other. And in a word, such a person, without more experience, could never employ his conjecture or reasoning concerning any matter of fact, or be assured of anything beyond what was immediately present to his memory and senses.

Suppose, again, that he has acquired more experience, and has lived so long in the world as to have observed familiar objects or events to be constantly conjoined together; what is the consequence of this experience? He immediately infers the existence of one object from the appearance of the other. Yet he has not, by all his experience, acquired any idea or knowledge of the secret power by which the one object produces the other; nor is it, by any process of reasoning, he is engaged to draw this inference. But still he finds himself determined to draw it: And though he should be convinced that his understanding has no part in the operation, he would nevertheless continue in the same course of thinking. There is some other principle which determines him to form such a conclusion.

This principle is *custom* or *habit*. For wherever the repetition of any particular act or operation produces a propensity to renew the same act or operation, without being impelled by any reasoning or process of the understanding, we always say, that this propensity is the effect of *custom.* By employing that word, we pretend not to have given the ultimate reason of such a propensity. We only point out a principle of human nature, which is universally acknowledged, and which is well known by its effects. Perhaps we can push our inquiries no farther, or pretend to give the cause of this cause; but must rest contented with it as the ultimate principle, which we can assign, of all our conclusions from experience. It is sufficient satisfaction, that we can go so far, without repining at the narrowness of our faculties because they will carry us no farther. And it is certain we here advance a very intelligible proposition at least, if not a true one, when we assert that, after the constant conjunction of two objects—heat and flame, for instance, weight and solidity—we are determined by custom alone to expect the one from the appearance of the other. This hypothesis seems even the only one which explains the difficulty, why we draw, from a thousand instances, an inference which we are not able to draw from one instance, that is, in no respect, different from them. Reason is incapable of any such variation. The conclusions which it draws from considering one circle are the same which it would form upon surveying all the circles in the universe. But no man, having seen only one body move after being impelled by another, could infer that every other body will move after a like impulse. All inferences from experience, therefore, are effects of custom, not of reasoning.[8]

[8] Nothing is more useful than for writers, even, on *moral, political,* or *physical* subjects, to distinguish between *reason* and *experience,* and to suppose, that these species of argumentation are entirely different from each other. The former are taken for the mere result of our intellectual faculties, which, by considering *a priori* the nature of things, and examining the effects, that must follow from their operation, establish particular principles of science and philosophy. The latter are supposed to be derived entirely from sense and observation, by which we learn what has actually resulted from the operation of particular objects, and are thence able to infer, what will, for the future, result from them. Thus, for instance, the limitations and restraints of civil government, and a legal constitution, may be defended, either from *reason,* which reflecting on the great frailty and corruption of human nature, teaches, that no man can safely be trusted with unlimited authority; or from *experience* and history, which inform us of the enormous abuses, that ambition, in every age and country, has been found to make of so imprudent a confidence.

The same distinction between reason and experience is maintained in all our deliberations concerning the conduct of life; while the experienced statesman, general, physician, or merchant is trusted and followed; and the unpracticed novice, with whatever natural talents endowed, neglected and despised. Though it be allowed, that reason may form very plausible conjectures with regard to the consequences of such a particular conduct in such particular circumstances; it is still supposed imperfect, without the assistance of experience, which is alone able to give stability and certainty to the maxims, derived from study and reflection.

But notwithstanding that this distinction be thus universally received. both in

Custom, then, is the great guide of human life. It is that principle alone which renders our experience useful to us, and makes us expect, for the future, a similar train of events with those which have appeared in the past. Without the influence of custom, we should be entirely ignorant of every matter of fact beyond what is immediately present to the memory and senses. We should never know how to adjust means to ends, or to employ our natural powers in the production of any effect. There would be an end at once of all action, as well as of the chief part of speculation.

But here it may be proper to remark, that though our conclusions from experience carry us beyond our memory and senses, and assure us of matters of fact which happened in the most distant places and most remote ages, yet some fact must always be present to the senses or memory, from which we may first proceed in drawing these conclusions. A man, who should find in a desert country the remains of pompous buildings, would conclude that the country had, in ancient times,

the active and speculative scenes of life, I shall not scruple to pronounce, that it is, at bottom, erroneous, at least, superficial.

If we examine those arguments, which, in any of the sciences above mentioned, are supposed to be the mere effects of reasoning and reflection, they will be found to terminate, at last, in some general principle or conclusion, for which we can assign no reason but observation and experience. The only difference between them and those maxims, which are vulgarly esteemed the result of pure experience, is, that the former cannot be established without some process of thought, and some reflection on what we have observed, in order to distinguish its circumstances, and trace its consequences: Whereas in the latter, the experienced event is exactly and fully familiar to that which we infer as the result of any particular situation. The history of a Tiberius or a Nero makes us dread a like tyranny, were our monarchs freed from the restraints of laws and senates. But the observation of any fraud or cruelty in private life is sufficient, with the aid of a little thought, to give us the same apprehension; while it serves as an instance of the general corruption of human nature, and shows us the danger which we must incur by reposing an entire confidence in mankind. In both cases, it is experience which is ultimately the foundation of our inference and conclusion.

There is no man so young and unexperienced, as not to have formed, from observation, many general and just maxims concerning human affairs and the conduct of life; but it must be confessed, that, when a man comes to put these in practice, he will be extremely liable to error, till time and farther experience both enlarge these maxims, and teach him their proper use and application. In every situation or incident, there are many particular and seemingly minute circumstances, which the man of greatest talent is, at first, apt to overlook, though on them the justness of his conclusions, and consequently the prudence of his conduct, entirely depend. Not to mention, that, to a young beginner, the general observations and maxims occur not always on the proper occasions, nor can be immediately applied with due calmness and distinction. The truth is, an unexperienced reasoner could be no reasoner at all, were he absolutely unexperienced; and when we assign that character to anyone, we mean it only in a comparative sense, and suppose him possessed of experience, in a smaller and more imperfect degree.

been cultivated by civilized inhabitants; but did nothing of this nature occur to him, he could never form such an inference. We learn the events of former ages from history; but then we must peruse the volumes in which this instruction is contained, and thence carry up our inferences from one testimony to another, till we arrive at the eyewitnesses and spectators of these distant events. In a word, if we proceed not upon some fact, present to the memory or senses, our reasonings would be merely hypothetical; and however the particular links might be connected with each other, the whole chain of inferences would have nothing to support it, nor could we ever, by its means, arrive at the knowledge of any real existence. If I ask why you believe any particular matter of fact, which you relate, you must tell me some reason; and this reason will be some other fact, connected with it. But as you cannot proceed after this manner, *in infinitum,* you must at last terminate in some fact, which is present to your memory or senses; or must allow that your belief is entirely without foundation.

What, then, is the conclusion of the whole matter? A simple one; though, it must be confessed, pretty remote from the common theories of philosophy. All belief of matter of fact or real existence is derived merely from some object, present to the memory or senses, and a customary conjunction between that and some other object. Or in other words; having found, in many instances, that any two kinds of objects— flame and heat, snow and cold—have always been conjoined together; if flame or snow be presented anew to the senses, the mind is carried by custom to expect heat or cold, and to *believe* that such a quality does exist, and will discover itself upon a nearer approach. This belief is the necessary result of placing the mind in such circumstances. It is an operation of the soul, when we are so situated, as unavoidable as to feel the passion of love, when we receive benefits; or hatred, when we meet with injuries. All these operations are a species of natural instincts, which no reasoning or process of the thought and understanding is able either to produce or to prevent.

At this point, it would be very allowable for us to stop our philosophical researches. In most questions we can never make a single step farther; and in all questions we must terminate here at last, after our most restless and curious inquiries. But still our curiosity will be pardonable, perhaps commendable, if it carry us on to still farther researches, and make us examine more accurately the nature of this *belief,* and of the *customary conjunction,* whence it is derived. By this means we may meet with some explications and analogies that will give satisfaction; at least to such as love the abstract sciences, and can be entertained with speculations, which, however accurate, may still retain a degree of doubt and uncertainty. As to readers of a different taste; the remaining part of this section is not calculated for them, and the following inquiries may well be understood, though it be neglected.

Part II

Nothing is more free than the imagination of man; and though it cannot exceed that original stock of ideas furnished by the internal and external senses, it has unlimited power of mixing, compounding, separating, and dividing these ideas, in all the varieties of fiction and vision. It can feign a train of events, with all the appearance of reality, ascribe to them a particular time and place, conceive them as existent, and paint them out to itself with every circumstance, that belongs to any historical fact, which it believes with the greatest certainty. Wherein, therefore, consists the difference between such a fiction and belief? It lies not merely in any peculiar idea, which is annexed to such a conception as commands our assent, and which is wanting to every known fiction. For as the mind has authority over all its ideas, it could voluntarily annex this particular idea to any fiction, and consequently be able to believe whatever it pleases; contrary to what we find by daily experience. We can, in our conception, join the head of a man to the body of a horse; but it is not in our power to believe that such an animal has ever really existed.

It follows, therefore, that the difference between *fiction* and *belief* lies in some sentiment or feeling, which is annexed to the latter, not to the former, and which depends not on the will, nor can be commanded at pleasure. It must be excited by nature, like all other sentiments; and must arise from the particular situation, in which the mind is placed at any particular juncture. Whenever any object is presented to the memory or senses, it immediately, by the force of custom, carries the imagination to conceive that object, which is usually conjoined to it; and this conception is attended with a feeling or sentiment, different from the loose reveries of the fancy. In this consists the whole nature of belief. For as there is no matter of fact which we believe so firmly that we cannot conceive the contrary, there would be no difference between the conception assented to and that which is rejected, were it not for some sentiment which distinguishes the one from the other. If I see a billiard ball moving towards another, on a smooth table, I can easily conceive it to stop upon contact. This conception implies no contradiction; but still it feels very differently from that conception by which I represent to myself the impulse and the communication of motion from one ball to another.

Were we to attempt a *definition* of this sentiment, we should, perhaps, find it a very difficult, if not an impossible task; in the same manner as if we should endeavor to define the feeling of cold or passion of anger, to a creature who never had any experience of these sentiments. Belief is the true and proper name of this feeling; and no one is ever at a loss to know the meaning of that term; because every man is every moment conscious of the sentiment represented by it. It may not, however, be improper to attempt a *description* of this sentiment; in hopes we may, by that means, arrive at some analogies, which may afford a more perfect explication of it. I say, then, that belief is nothing but a more vivid, lively, forcible, firm, steady conception of an object, than what the imagination alone is ever able to attain. This variety of terms, which may seem so unphilosophical, is intended only to express that act of the mind, which renders realities, or what is taken for such, more present to us than fictions, causes them to weigh more in the thought, and gives them a superior influence on the passions and imagination. Provided we agree about the thing, it is needless to dispute about the terms. The imagination has the command over all its ideas, and can join and mix and vary them, in all the ways possible. It may conceive fictitious objects with all the circumstances of place and time. It may set them, in a manner, before our eyes, in their true colors, just as they might have existed. But as it is impossible that this faculty of imagination can ever, of itself, reach belief, it is evident that belief consists not in the peculiar nature or order of ideas, but in the *manner* of their conception, and in their *feeling* to the mind. I confess, that it is impossible perfectly to explain this feeling or manner of conception. We may make use of words which express something near it. But its true and proper name, as we observed before, is *belief;* which is a term that every one sufficiently understands in common life. And in philosophy, we can go no farther than assert, that *belief* is something felt by the mind, which distinguishes the ideas of the judgment from the fictions of the imagination. It gives them more weight and influence; makes them appear of greater importance; enforces them in the mind; and renders them the governing principle of our actions. I hear at present, for instance, a person's voice, with whom I am acquainted; and the sound comes as from the next room. This impression of my senses immediately conveys my thought to the person, together with all the surrounding objects. I paint them out to myself as existing at present, with the same qualities and relations, of which I formerly knew them possessed. These ideas take faster hold of my mind than ideas of an enchanted castle. They are very different to the feeling, and have a much greater influence of every kind, either to give pleasure or pain, joy or sorrow.

Let us, then, take in the whole compass of this doctrine, and allow, that the sentiment of belief is nothing but a conception more intense and steady than what attends the mere fictions of the imagination, and that this *manner* of conception arises from a customary conjunction of the object with something present to the memory or senses: I believe that it will not be difficult, upon these suppositions, to find other operations of the mind analogous to it, and to trace up these phenomena to principles still more general.

We have already observed that nature has established connections among particular ideas, and that no sooner one idea occurs to our thoughts than it introduces its correlative, and carries our attention towards it, by a gentle and insensible movement. These principles of connection or association we have reduced to three, namely *resemblance, contiguity* and *causation;* which are the only bonds that unite our thoughts together, and beget that regular train of reflection or discourse, which, in a greater or less degree, takes place among mankind. Now here arises a question, on which the solution of the present difficulty will depend. Does it happen, in all these relations, that, when one of the objects is presented to the senses or memory, the mind is not only carried to the conception of the correlative, but reaches a steadier and stronger conception of it than what otherwise it would have been able to attain? This seems to be the case with that belief which arises from the relation of cause and effect. And if the case be the same with the other relations or principles of association, this may be established as a general law, which takes place in all the operations of the mind.

We may, therefore, observe, as the first experiment to our present purpose, that, upon the appearance of the picture of an absent friend, our idea of him is evidently enlivened by the *resemblance,* and that every passion, which that idea occasions, whether of joy or sorrow, acquires new force and vigor. In producing this effect, there concur both a relation and a present impression. Where the picture bears him no resemblance, at least was not intended for him, it never so much as conveys our thought to him: And where it is absent, as well as the person, though the mind may pass from the thought of the one to that of the other, it feels its idea to be rather weakened than enlivened by that transition. We take a pleasure in viewing the picture of a friend, when it is set before us; but when it is removed, rather choose to consider him directly than by reflection in an image, which is equally distant and obscure.

The ceremonies of the Roman Catholic religion may be considered as instances of the same nature. The devotees of that superstition usually plead in excuse for the mummeries, with which they were upbraided, that they feel the good effect of those external motions, and postures, and actions, in enlivening their devotion and quickening their fervor, which otherwise would decay, if directed entirely to distant and immaterial objects. We shadow out the objects of our faith, say they, in sensible types and images, and render them more present to us by the immediate presence of these types, than it is possible for us to do merely by an intellectual view and contemplation. Sensible objects have always a greater influence on the fancy than any other; and this influence they readily convey to those ideas to which they are related, and which they resemble. I shall only infer from these practices, and this reasoning, that the effect of resemblance in enlivening the ideas is very common; and as in every case a resemblance and a present impression must concur, we are abundantly supplied with experiments to prove the reality of the foregoing principle.

We may add force to these experiments by others of a different kind, in considering the effects of *contiguity* as well as of *resemblance*. It is certain that distance diminishes the force of every idea, and that upon our approach to any object; though it does not discover itself to our senses; it operates upon the mind with an influence, which imitates an immediate impression. The thinking on any object readily transports the mind to what is contiguous; but it is only the actual presence of an object, that transports it with a superior vivacity. When I am a few miles from home, whatever relates to it touches me more nearly than when I am two hundred leagues distant; though even at that distance the reflecting on anything in the neighborhood of my friends or family naturally produces an idea of them. But as in this latter case, both the objects of the mind are ideas; notwithstanding there is an easy transition between them; that transition alone is not able to give a superior vivacity to any of the ideas, for want of some immediate impression.

No one can doubt but causation has the same influence as the other two relations of resemblance and contiguity. Superstitious people are fond of the relics of saints and holy men, for the same reason, that they seek after types or images, in order to enliven their devotion, and give them a more intimate and strong conception of those exemplary lives, which they desire to imitate. Now it is evident, that one of the best relics, which a devotee could procure, would be the handiwork of a saint; and if his clothes and furniture are ever to be considered in this light, it is because they were once at his disposal, and were moved and affected by him; in which respect they are to be considered as imperfect effects, and as connected with him by a shorter chain of consequences than any of those, by which we learn the reality of his existence.

Suppose, that the son of a friend, who had been long dead or absent, were presented to us; it is evident, that this object would instantly revive its correlative idea, and recall to our thoughts all past intimacies and familiarities, in more lively colors than they would otherwise have appeared to us. This is another phenomenon, which seems to prove the principle above mentioned.

We may observe, that, in these phenomena, the belief of the correlative object is always presupposed: without which the relation could have no effect. The influence of the picture supposes, that we *believe* our friend to have once existed. Contiguity to home can never excite our ideas of home, unless we *believe* that it really exists. Now I assert, that this belief, where it reaches beyond the memory or senses, is of a similar nature, and arises from similar causes, with the transition of thought and vivacity of conception here explained. When I throw a piece of dry wood into a fire, my mind is immediately carried to conceive, that it augments, not extinguishes the flame. This transition of thought from the cause to the effect proceeds not from reason. It derives its origin altogether from custom and experience. And as it first begins from an object, present to the senses, it renders the idea or conception of flame more strong and lively than any loose, floating reverie of the imagination. That idea arises immediately. The thought moves instantly towards it, and conveys to it all that force of conception, which is derived from the impression present to the senses. When a sword is leveled at my breast, does not the idea of wound and pain strike me more strongly, than when a glass of wine is presented to me, even though by accident this idea should occur after the appearance of the latter object? But what is there in this whole matter to cause such a strong conception, except only a present object and a customary transition to the idea of another object, which we have been accustomed to conjoin with the former? This is the whole operation of the mind, in all our conclusions concerning matter of fact and existence; and it is a satisfaction to find some analogies, by which it may be explained. The transition from a present object does in all cases give strength and solidity to the related idea.

Here, then, is a kind of pre-established harmony between the course of nature and the succession of our ideas; and though the powers and forces, by which the former is governed, be wholly unknown to us; yet our thoughts and conceptions have still, we find, gone on in the same train with the other works of nature. Custom is that principle, by which this correspondence has been effected; so necessary to the subsistence of our species, and the regulation of our conduct, in every circumstance and occurrence of human life. Had not the presence of an object, instantly excited the idea of those objects, commonly conjoined with it, all our knowledge must have been limited to the narrow sphere of our memory and senses; and we should never have been able to adjust means to ends, or employ our natural powers, either to the producing of good, or avoiding of evil. Those, who delight in the discovery and contemplation of *final causes,* have here ample subject to employ their wonder and admiration.

I shall add, for a further confirmation of the foregoing theory, that, as this operation of the mind, by which we infer like effects from like causes, and *vice versa,* is so essential to the subsistence of all human creatures, it is not probable, that it could be trusted to the fallacious deductions of our reason, which is slow in its operations; appears not, in any degree, during the first years of infancy; and at best is, in every age and period of human life, extremely liable to error and mistake. It is more conformable to the ordinary wisdom of nature to secure so necessary an act of the mind, by some instinct or mechanical tendency, which may be infallible in its operations, may discover itself at the first appearance of life and thought, and may be independent of all the labored deductions of the understanding. As nature has taught us the use of our limbs, without giving us the knowledge of the muscles and nerves, by which they are actuated; so has she implanted in us an instinct, which carries forward the thought in a correspondent course to that which she has established among external objects; though we are ignorant of those powers and forces, on which this regular course and succession of objects totally depends.

SECTION VI

OF PROBABILITY[9]

THOUGH there be no such thing as *chance* in the world; our ignorance of the real cause of any event has the same influence on the understanding, and begets a like species of belief or opinion.

There is certainly a probability, which arises from a superiority of chances on any side; and according as this superiority increases, and surpasses the opposite chances, the probability receives a proportionable increase, and begets still a higher degree of belief or assent to that side, in which we discover the superiority. If a die were marked with one figure or number of spots on four sides, and with another figure or number of spots on the two remaining sides, it would be more probable, that the former would turn up than the latter; though, if it had a thousand sides marked in the same manner, and only one side different, the probability would be much higher, and our belief or expectation of the event more steady and secure. This process of the thought or reasoning may seem

---

[9] Mr. Locke divides all arguments into demonstrative and probable. In this view, we must say, that it is only probable all men must die, or that the sun will rise tomorrow. But to conform our language more to common use, we ought to divide arguments into *demonstrations, proofs,* and *probabilities.* By proofs meaning such arguments from experience as leave no room for doubt or opposition.

trivial and obvious; but to those who consider it more narrowly, it may, perhaps, afford matter for curious speculation.

It seems evident, that, when the mind looks forward to discover the event, which may result from the throw of such a die, it considers the turning up of each particular side as alike probable; and this is the very nature of chance, to render all the particular events, comprehended in it, entirely equal. But finding a greater number of sides concur in the one event than in the other, the mind is carried more frequently to that event, and meets it oftener, in revolving the various possibilities or chances, on which the ultimate result depends. This concurrence of several views in one particular event begets immediately, by an inexplicable contrivance of nature, the sentiment of belief, and gives that event the advantage over its antagonist, which is supported by a smaller number of views, and recurs less frequently to the mind. If we allow, that belief is nothing but a firmer and stronger conception of an object than what attends the mere fictions of the imagination, this operation may, perhaps, in some measure, be accounted for. The concurrence of these several views or glimpses imprints the idea more strongly on the imagination; gives it superior force and vigor; renders its influence on the passions and affections more sensible; and in a word, begets that reliance or security, which constitutes the nature of belief and opinion.

The case is the same with the probability of causes, as with that of chance. There are some causes, which are entirely uniform and constant in producing a particular effect; and no instance has ever yet been found of any failure or irregularity in their operation. Fire has always burned, and water suffocated every human creature: the production of motion by impulse and gravity is an universal law, which has hitherto admitted of no exception. But there are other causes which have been found more irregular and uncertain; nor has rhubarb always proved a purge, or opium a soporific to everyone, who has taken these medicines. It is true, when any cause fails of producing its usual effect, philosophers ascribe not this to any irregularity in nature; but suppose, that some secret causes, in the particular structure of parts, have prevented the operation. Our reasonings, however, and conclusions concerning the event are the same as if this principle had no place. Being determined by custom to transfer the past to the future, in all our inferences; where the past has been entirely regular and uniform, we expect the event with the greatest assurance, and leave no room for any contrary supposition. But where different effects have been found to follow from causes, which are to *appearance* exactly similar, all these various effects must occur to the mind in transferring the past to the future, and enter into our consideration, when we determine the probability of the event. Though we give the preference to that which has been found most usual, and believe that this effect will exist, we must not overlook the other effects, but must assign to each of them a particular weight and authority, in proportion as we have found it to be more or less frequent. It is more probable, in almost every country of Europe, that there will be frost sometime in January, than that the weather will continue open throughout the whole month; though this probability varies according to the different climates, and approaches to a certainty in the more northern kingdoms. Here then it seems evident, that, when we transfer the past to the future, in order to determine the effect, which will result from any cause, we transfer all the different events, in the same proportion as they have appeared in the past, and conceive one to have existed a hundred times, for instance, another ten times, and another once. As a great number of views do here concur in one event, they fortify and confirm it to the imagination, beget that sentiment which we call *belief,* and give its object the preference above the contrary event, which is not supported by an equal number of experiments, and recurs not so frequently to the thought in transferring the past to the future. Let anyone try to account for this operation of the mind upon any of the received systems of philosophy, and he will be sensible of the difficulty. For my part, I shall think it sufficient, if the present hints excite the curiosity of philosophers, and make them sensible how defective all common theories are in treating of such curious and such sublime subjects.

SECTION VII

OF THE IDEA OF NECESSARY CONNECTION

Part 1

THE great advantage of the mathematical sciences above the moral consists in this, that the ideas of the former, being sensible, are always clear and determinate, the smallest distinction between them is immediately perceptible, and the same terms are still expressive of the same ideas, without ambiguity or variation. An oval is never mistaken for a circle, nor an hyperbola for an ellipsis. The isosceles and scalenum are distinguished by boundaries more exact than vice and virtue, right and wrong. If any term be defined in geometry, the mind readily, of itself, substitutes, on all occasions, the definition for the term defined: or even when no definition is employed, the object itself may be presented to the senses, and by that means be steadily and clearly apprehended. But the finer sentiments of the mind, the operations of the understanding, the various agitations of the passions, though really in themselves distinct, easily escape us, when surveyed by reflection; nor is it in our power to recall the original object, as often as we have occasion to contemplate it. Ambiguity, by this means, is gradually introduced into our reasonings: similar objects are readily taken to be the same: and the conclusion becomes at last very wide of the premises.

One may safely, however, affirm, that, if we consider these sciences in a proper light, their advantages and disadvantages nearly compensate each other, and reduce both of them to a state of equality. If the mind, with greater facility, retains the ideas of geometry clear and determinate, it must carry on a much longer and more intricate chain of reasoning, and compare ideas much wider of each other, in order to reach the abstruser truths of that science. And if moral ideas are apt, without extreme care, to fall into obscurity and confusion, the inferences are always much shorter in these disquisitions, and the intermediate steps, which lead to the conclusion, much fewer than in the sciences which treat of quantity and number. In reality, there is scarcely a proposition in Euclid so simple, as not to consist of more parts, than are to be found in any moral reasoning which runs not into chimera and conceit. Where we trace the principles of the human mind through a few steps, we may be very well satisfied with our progress; considering how soon nature throws a bar to all our inquiries concerning causes, and reduces us to an acknowledgment of our ignorance. The chief obstacle, therefore, to our improvement in the moral or metaphysical sciences is the obscurity of the ideas, and ambiguity of the terms. The principal difficulty in the mathematics is the length of inferences and compass of thought, requisite to the forming of any conclusion. And, perhaps, our progress in natural philosophy is chiefly retarded by the want of proper experiments and phenomena, which are often discovered by chance, and cannot always be found, when requisite, even by the most diligent and prudent inquiry. As moral philosophy seems hitherto to have received less improvement than either geometry or physics, we may conclude, that, if there be any difference in this respect among these sciences, the difficulties, which obstruct the progress of the former, require superior care and capacity to be surmounted.

There are no ideas, which occur in metaphysics more obscure and uncertain, than those of *power, force, energy* or *necessary connection,* of which it is every moment necessary for us to treat in all our disquisitions. We shall, therefore, endeavor, in this section, to fix, if possible, the precise meaning of these terms, and thereby remove some part of that obscurity, which is so much complained of in this species of philosophy.

It seems a proposition, which will not admit of much dispute, that all our ideas are nothing but copies of our impressions, or, in other words, that it is impossible for us to *think* of anything, which we have not antecedently *felt,* either by our external or internal senses. I have endeavored [10] to explain and prove this proposition, and have expressed my hopes, that, by a proper application of it, men may reach a greater clearness and precision in philosophical reasonings, than what they have hitherto been able to attain. Complex ideas may, perhaps, be well known by definition, which is nothing but an enumeration of those parts or simple ideas, that compose them. But when we have pushed up definitions to the most simple ideas, and find still some ambiguity and obscurity; what resource are we then possessed of? By what invention can we throw light upon these ideas, and render them altogether precise and determinate to our intellectual view! Produce the impressions or original sentiments, from which the ideas are copied. These impressions are all strong and sensible. They admit not of ambiguity. They are not only placed in a full light themselves, but may throw light on their correspondent ideas, which lie in obscurity. And by this means, we may, perhaps, attain a new microscope or species of optics, by which, in the moral sciences, the most minute, and most simple ideas may be so enlarged as to fall readily under our apprehension, and be equally known with the grossest and most sensible ideas, that can be the object of our inquiry.

To be fully acquainted, therefore, with the idea of power or necessary connection, let us examine its impression; and in order to find the impression with greater certainty, let us search for it in all the sources, from which it may possibly be derived.

When we look about us towards external objects, and consider the operation of causes, we are never able, in a single instance, to discover any power or necessary connection; any quality, which binds the effect to the cause, and renders the one an infallible consequence of the other. We only find, that the one does actually, in fact, follow the other. The impulse of one billiard ball is attended with motion in the second. This is the whole that appears to the *outward* senses. The mind feels no sentiment or *inward* impression from this succession of objects: consequently there is not, in any single, particular instance of cause and effect, anything which can suggest the idea of power or necessary connection.

From the first appearance of an object, we never can conjecture what effect will result from it. But were the power or energy of any cause discoverable by the mind, we could foresee the effect, even without experience; and might, at first, pronounce with certainty concerning it, by mere dint of thought and reasoning.

[10] Section II.

In reality, there is no part of matter, that does ever, by its sensible qualities, discover any power or energy, or give us ground to imagine, that it could produce anything, or be followed by any other object, which we could denominate its effect. Solidity, extension, motion; these qualities are all complete in themselves, and never point out any other event which may result from them. The scenes of the universe are continually shifting, and one object follows another in an uninterrupted succession; but the power of force, which actuates the whole machine, is entirely concealed from us, and never discovers itself in any of the sensible qualities of body. We know, that, in fact, heat is a constant attendant of flame; but what is the connection between them, we have no room so much as to conjecture or imagine. It is impossible, therefore, that the idea of power can be derived from the contemplation of bodies, in single instances of their operation; because no bodies ever discover any power, which can be the original of this idea.[11]

Since, therefore, external objects as they appear to the senses, give us no idea of power or necessary connection, by their operation in particular instances, let us see, whether this idea be derived from reflection on the operations of our own minds, and be copied from any internal impression. It may be said, that we are every moment conscious of internal power; while we feel, that, by the simple command of our will, we can move the organs of our body, or direct the faculties of our mind. An act of volition produces motion in our limbs, or raises a new idea in our imagination. This influence of the will we know by consciousness. Hence we acquire the idea of power or energy; and are certain, that we ourselves and all other intelligent beings are possessed of power. This idea, then, is an idea of reflection, since it arises from reflecting on the operations of our own mind, and on the command which is exercised by will, both over the organs of the body and faculties of the soul.

We shall proceed to examine this pretension; and first with regard to the influence of volition over the organs of the body. This influence, we may observe, is a fact, which, like all other natural events, can be known only by experience, and can never be foreseen from any apparent energy or power in the cause, which connects it with the effect, and renders the one an infallible consequence of the other. The motion of our body follows upon the command of our will. Of this we are every moment conscious. But the means, by which this is effected; the energy,

---

[11] Mr. Locke, in his chapter on power, says, that, finding from experience, that there are several new productions in matter, and concluding that there must somewhere be a power capable of producing them, we arrive at last by this reasoning at the idea of power. But no reasoning can ever give us a new original, simple idea; as this philosopher himself confesses. This, therefore, can never be the origin of that idea.

by which the will performs so extraordinary an operation; of this we are
so far from being immediately conscious, that it must for ever escape our
most diligent inquiry.

For *first,* Is there any principle in all nature more mysterious than
the union of soul with body; by which a supposed spiritual substance
acquires such an influence over a material one, that the most refined
thought is able to actuate the grossest matter? Were we empowered, by
a secret wish, to remove mountains, or control the planets in their orbit;
this extensive authority would not be more extraordinary, nor more beyond our comprehension. But if by consciousness we perceived any
power or energy in the will, we must know this power; we must know
its connection with the effect; we must know the secret union of soul
and body, and the nature of both these substances; by which the one is
able to operate, in so many instances, upon the other.

Secondly, We are not able to move all the organs of the body with a
like authority; though we cannot assign any reason besides experience,
for so remarkable a difference between one and the other. Why has the
will an influence over the tongue and fingers, not over the heart and
liver? This question would never embarrass us, were we conscious of a
power in the former case, not in the latter. We should then perceive, independent of experience, why the authority of will over the organs of
the body is circumscribed within such particular limits. Being in that
case fully acquainted with the power or force, by which it operates, we
should also know, why its influence reaches precisely to such boundaries,
and no farther.

A man, suddenly struck with palsy in the leg or arm, or who had
newly lost those members, frequently endeavors, at first to move them,
and employ them in their usual offices. Here he is as much conscious of
power to command such limbs, as a man in perfect health is conscious
of power to actuate any member which remains in its natural state and
condition. But consciousness never deceives. Consequently, neither in
the one case nor in the other, are we ever conscious of any power. We
learn the influence of our will from experience alone. And experience
only teaches us, how one event constantly follows another; without in-
structing us in the secret connection, which binds them together, and
renders them inseparable.

Thirdly, We learn from anatomy, that the immediate object of power
in voluntary motion, is not the member itself which is moved, but certain muscles, and nerves, and animal spirits, and, perhaps, something
still more minute and more unknown, through which the motion is successfully propagated, ere it reach the member itself whose motion is the
immediate object of volition. Can there be a more certain proof that the
power, by which this whole operation is performed, so far from being di-

rectly and fully known by an inward sentiment or consciousness, is, to the last degree, mysterious and unintelligible? Here the mind wills a certain event: immediately another event, unknown to ourselves, and totally different from the one intended, is produced: this event produces another, equally unknown: till at last, through a long succession, the desired event is produced. But if the original power were felt, it must be known: were it known, its effect also must be known; since all power is relative to its effect. And *vice versa,* if the effect be not known, the power cannot be known nor felt. How indeed can we be conscious of a power to move our limbs, when we have no such power; but only that to move certain animal spirits, which, though they produce at last the motion of our limbs, yet operate in such a manner as is wholly beyond our comprehension?

We may, therefore, conclude from the whole, I hope, without any temerity, though with assurance; that our idea of power is not copied from any sentiment or consciousness of power within ourselves, when we give rise to animal motion, or apply our limbs, to their proper use and office. That their motion follows the command of the will is a matter of common experience, like other natural events: but the power or energy by which this is effected, like that in other natural events, is unknown and inconceivable.[12]

Shall we then assert, that we are conscious of a power or energy in our own minds, when, by an act or command of our will, we raise up a new idea, fix the mind to the contemplation of it, turn it on all sides, and at last dismiss it for some other idea, when we think that we have surveyed it with sufficient accuracy? I believe the same arguments will prove, that even this command of the will gives us no real idea of force or energy.

First, It must be allowed, that, when we know a power, we know that very circumstance in the cause, by which it is enabled to produce the effect: for these are supposed to be synonymous. We must, therefore, know both the cause and effect, and the relation between them. But do

---

[12] It may be pretended, that the resistance which we meet with in bodies, obliging us frequently to exert our force, and call up all our power, this gives us the idea of force and power. It is this *nisus,* or strong endeavor, of which we are conscious, that is the original impression from which this idea is copied. But, *first,* We attribute power to a vast number of objects, where we never can suppose this resistance or exertion of force to take place; to the Supreme Being, who never meets with any resistance; to the mind in its command over its ideas and limbs, in common thinking and motion, where the effect follows immediately upon the will, without any exertion or summoning up of force; to inanimate matter, which is not capable of this sentiment. *Secondly,* This sentiment of an endeavor to overcome resistance has no known connection with any event: what follows it, we know by experience; but could not know it *a priori.* It must, however, be confessed, that the animal *nisus,* which we experience, though it can afford no accurate precise idea of power, enters very much into that vulgar, inaccurate idea, which is formed of it.

we pretend to be acquainted with the nature of the human soul and the nature of an idea, or the aptitude of the one to produce the other? This is a real creation; a production of something out of nothing: which implies a power so great, that it may seem, at first sight, beyond the reach of any being, less than infinite. At least it must be owned, that such a power is not felt, nor known, nor even conceivable by the mind. We only feel the event, namely, the existence of an idea, consequent to a command of the will: but the manner, in which this operation is performed, the power by which it is produced, is entirely beyond our comprehension.

Secondly, The command of the mind over itself is limited, as well as its command over the body; and these limits are not known by reason, or any acquaintance with the nature of cause and effect, but only by experience and observation, as in all other natural events and in the operation of external objects. Our authority over our sentiments and passions is much weaker than that over our ideas; and even the latter authority is circumscribed within very narrow boundaries. Will anyone pretend to assign the ultimate reason of these boundaries, or show why the power is deficient in one case, not in another?

Thirdly, This self-command is very different at different times. A man in health possesses more of it than one languishing with sickness. We are more master of our thoughts in the morning than in the evening; fasting, than after a full meal. Can we give any reason for these variations, except experience? Where then is the power, of which we pretend to be conscious? Is there not here, either in a spiritual or material substance, or both, some secret mechanism or structure of parts, upon which the effect depends, and which, being entirely unknown to us, renders the power or energy of the will equally unknown and incomprehensible?

Volition is surely an act of the mind, with which we are sufficiently acquainted. Reflect upon it. Consider it on all sides. Do you find anything in it like this creative power, by which it raises from nothing a new idea, and with a kind of *fiat,* imitates the omnipotence of its Maker, if I may be allowed so to speak, who called forth into existence all the various scenes of nature? So far from being conscious of this energy in the will, it requires as certain experience as that of which we are possessed, to convince us that such extraordinary effects do ever result from a simple act of volition.

The generality of mankind never find any difficulty in accounting for the more common and familiar operations of nature—such as the descent of heavy bodies, the growth of plants, the generation of animals, or the nourishment of bodies by food; but suppose that, in all these cases, they perceive the very force or energy of the cause, by which it is connected with its effect, and is forever infallible in its operation. They acquire, by long habit, such a turn of mind, that, upon the appearance of the cause, they immediately expect with assurance its usual attendant, and hardly conceive it possible that any other event could result from it. It is only on the discovery of extraordinary phenomena, such as earthquakes, pestilence, and prodigies of any kind, that they find themselves at a loss to assign a proper cause, and to explain the manner in which the effect is produced by it. It is usual for men, in such difficulties, to have recourse to some invisible intelligent principle as the immediate cause of that event which surprises them, and which, they think, cannot be accounted for from the common powers of nature. But philosophers, who carry their scrutiny a little farther, immediately perceive that, even in the most familiar events, the energy of the cause is as unintelligible as in the most unusual, and that we only learn by experience the frequent *conjunction* of objects, without being ever able to comprehend anything like *connection* between them. Here, then, many philosophers think themselves obliged by reason to have recourse, on all occasions, to the same principle, which the vulgar never appeal to but in cases that appear miraculous and supernatural. They acknowledge mind and intelligence to be, not only the ultimate and original cause of all things, but the immediate and sole cause of every event which appears in nature. They pretend that those objects which are commonly denominated *causes,* are in reality nothing but *occasions;* and that the true and direct principle of every effect is not any power or force in nature, but a volition of the Supreme Being, who wills that such particular objects should forever be conjoined with each other. Instead of saying that one billiard ball moves another by a force which it has derived from the author of nature, it is the Deity himself, they say, who, by a particular volition, moves the second ball, being determined to this operation by the impulse of the first ball, in consequence of those general laws which he has laid down to himself in the government of the universe. But philosophers advancing still in their inquiries, discover that, as we are totally ignorant of the power on which depends the mutual operation of bodies, we are no less ignorant of that power on which depends the operation of mind on body, or of body on mind; nor are we able, either from our senses or consciousness, to assign the ultimate principle in one case more than in the other. The same ignorance, therefore, reduces them to the same conclusion. They assert that the Deity is the immediate cause of the union between soul and body; and that they are not the organs of sense, which, being agitated by external objects, produce sensations in the mind; but that it is a particular volition of our omnipotent Maker, which excites such a sensation, in consequence of such a motion in the organ. In like manner, it is not any energy in the will that produces local motion in our members; it is God himself, who is pleased to second our will, in itself impotent, and to command that motion which we erroneously attribute to our own power and efficacy. Nor do philosophers stop at this conclusion. They sometimes extend the same inference to the mind itself, in its internal operations. Our mental vision or conception of ideas is nothing but a revelation made to us by our Maker. When we voluntarily turn our thoughts to any object, and raise up its image in the fancy, it is not the will which creates that idea; it is the universal Creator, who discovers it to the mind, and renders it present to us.

Thus, according to these philosophers, everything is full of God. Not content with the principle, that nothing exists but by his will, that nothing possesses any power but by his concession; they rob nature, and all created beings, of every power, in order to render their dependence on the Deity still more sensible and immediate. They consider not that, by this theory, they diminish, instead of magnifying, the grandeur of those attributes, which they affect so much to celebrate. It argues surely more power in the Deity to delegate a certain degree of power to inferior creatures, than to produce everything by his own immediate volition. It argues more wisdom to contrive at first the fabric of the world with such perfect foresight that, of itself, and by its proper operation, it may serve all the purposes of providence, than if the great Creator were obliged every moment to adjust its parts, and animate by his breath all the wheels of that stupendous machine.

But if we would have a more philosophical confutation of this theory, perhaps the two following reflections may suffice.

First, It seems to me that this theory of the universal energy and operation of the Supreme Being is too bold ever to carry conviction with it to a man, sufficiently apprised of the weakness of human reason, and the narrow limits to which it is confined in all its operations. Though the chain of arguments which conduct to it were ever so logical, there must arise a strong suspicion, if not an absolute assurance, that it has carried us quite beyond the reach of our faculties, when it leads to conclusions so extraordinary, and so remote from common life and experience. We are got into fairy land, long ere we have reached the last steps of our theory; and *there* we have no reason to trust our common methods of argument, or to think that our usual analogies and probabilities have any authority. Our line is too short to fathom such immense abysses. And however we may flatter ourselves that we are guided, in every step which we take, by a kind of verisimilitude and experience, we may be assured that this fancied experience has no authority when we thus apply it to subjects that lie entirely out of the sphere of experience. But on this we shall have occasion to touch afterwards.[13]

[13] Section XII.

Secondly, I cannot perceive any force in the arguments on which this theory is founded. We are ignorant, it is true, of the manner in which bodies operate on each other: their force or energy is entirely incomprehensible: but are we not equally ignorant of the manner or force by which a mind, even the supreme mind, operates either on itself or on body? Whence, I beseech you, do we acquire any idea of it? We have no sentiment or consciousness of this power in ourselves. We have no idea of the Supreme Being but what we learn from reflection on our own faculties. Were our ignorance, therefore, a good reason for rejecting anything, we should be led into that principle of denying all energy in the Supreme Being as much as in the grossest matter. We surely comprehend as little the operations of one as of the other. Is it more difficult to conceive that motion may arise from impulse than that it may arise from volition? All we know is our profound ignorance in both cases.[14]

Part II

BUT to hasten to a conclusion of this argument, which is already drawn out to too great a length: we have sought in vain for an idea of power or necessary connection in all the sources from which we could suppose it to be derived. It appears that, in single instances of the operation of bodies, we never can, by our utmost scrutiny, discover anything but one event following another, without being able to comprehend any force or power by which the cause operates, or any connection between it and its supposed effect. The same difficulty occurs in contemplating the operations of mind on body—where we observe the motion of the latter to

---

[14] I need not examine at length the *vis inertiae* which is so much talked of in the new philosophy, and which is ascribed to matter. We find by experience, that a body at rest or in motion continues forever in its present state, till put from it by some new cause; and that a body impelled takes as much motion from the impelling body as it acquires itself. These are facts. When we call this a *vis inertiae*, we only mark these facts, without pretending to have any idea of the inert power; in the same manner as, when we talk of gravity, we mean certain effects, without comprehending that active power. It was never the meaning of SIR ISAAC NEWTON to rob second causes of all force or energy; though some of his followers have endeavored to establish that theory upon his authority. On the contrary, that great philosopher had recourse to an etherial active fluid to explain his universal attraction; though he was so cautious and modest as to allow, that it was a mere hypothesis, not to be insisted on, without more experiments. I must confess, that there is something in the fate of opinions a little extraordinary. DESCARTES insinuated that doctrine of the universal and sole efficiency of the Deity, without insisting on it. MALEBRANCHE and other CARTESIANS made it the foundation of all their philosophy. It had, however, no authority in England. LOCKE, CLARKE, and CUDWORTH, never so much as take notice of it, but suppose all along, that matter has a real, though subordinate and derived power. By what means has it become so prevalent among our modern metaphysicians?

follow upon the volition of the former, but are not able to observe or
conceive the tie which binds together the motion and volition, or the
energy by which the mind produces this effect. The authority of the will
over its own faculties and ideas is not a whit more comprehensible: so
that, upon the whole, there appears not, throughout all nature, any one
instance of connection which is conceivable by us. All events seem entirely loose and separate. One event follows another; but we never can
observe any tie between them. They seem *conjoined,* but never *connected.* And as we can have no idea of anything which never appeared
to our outward sense or inward sentiment, the necessary conclusion
seems to be that we have no idea of connection or power at all, and that
these words are absolutely without any meaning, when employed either
in philosophical reasonings or common life.

But there still remains one method of avoiding this conclusion, and
one source which we have not yet examined. When any natural object or
event is presented, it is impossible for us, by any sagacity or penetration,
to discover, or even conjecture, without experience, what event will result from it, or to carry our foresight beyond that object which is immediately present to the memory and senses. Even after one instance or experiment where we have observed a particular event to follow upon another, we are not entitled to form a general rule, or foretell what will
happen in like cases; it being justly esteemed an unpardonable temerity
to judge of the whole course of nature from one single experiment, however accurate or certain. But when one particular species of event has
always, in all instances, been conjoined with another, we make no longer
any scruple of foretelling one upon the appearance of the other, and of
employing that reasoning which can alone assure us of any matter of
fact or existence. We then call the one object, *cause;* the other, *effect.*
We suppose that there is some connection between them; some power
in the one, by which it infallibly produces the other, and operates with
the greatest certainty and strongest necessity.

It appears, then, that this idea of a necessary connection among events
arises from a number of similar instances which occur of the constant
conjunction of these events; nor can that idea ever be suggested by any
one of these instances, surveyed in all possible lights and positions. But
there is nothing in a number of instances, different from every single instance, which is supposed to be exactly similar; except only, that after a
repetition of similar instances, the mind is carried by habit, upon the appearance of one event, to expect its usual attendant, and to believe that
it will exist. This connection, therefore, which we *feel* in the mind, this
customary transition of the imagination from one object to its usual attendant, is the sentiment or impression from which we form the idea of
power or necessary connection. Nothing farther is in the case. Contem-

plate the subject on all sides; you will never find any other origin of that idea. This is the sole difference between one instance, from which we can never receive the idea of connection, and a number of similar instances, by which it is suggested. The first time a man saw the communication of motion by impulse, as by the shock of two billiard balls, he could not pronounce that the one event was *connected;* but only that it was *conjoined* with the other. After he has observed several instances of this nature, he than pronounces them to be *connected.* What alteration has happened to give rise to this new idea of *connection?* Nothing but that he now *feels* these events to be *connected* in his imagination, and can readily foretell the existence of one from the appearance of the other. When we say, therefore, that one object is connected with another, we mean only that they have acquired a connection in our thought, and give rise to this inference, by which they become proofs of each other's existence: a conclusion which is somewhat extraordinary, but which seems founded on sufficient evidence. Nor will its evidence be weakened by any general diffidence of the understanding, or sceptical suspicion concerning every conclusion which is new and extraordinary. No conclusions can be more agreeable to scepticism than such as make discoveries concerning the weakness and narrow limits of human reason and capacity.

And what stronger instance can be produced of the surprising ignorance and weakness of the understanding than the present? For surely, if there be any relation among objects which it imports to us to know perfectly, it is that of cause and effect. On this are founded all our reasonings concerning matter of fact or existence. By means of it alone we attain any assurance concerning objects which are removed from the present testimony of our memory and senses. The only immediate utility of all sciences, is to teach us, how to control and regulate future events by their causes. Our thoughts and inquiries are, therefore, every moment, employed about this relation: yet so imperfect are the ideas which we form concerning it, that it is impossible to give any just definition of cause, except what is drawn from something extraneous and foreign to it. Similar objects are always conjoined with similar. Of this we have experience. Suitably to this experience, therefore, we may define a cause to be *an object, followed by another, and where all the objects similar to the first are followed by objects similar to the second.* Or in other words *where, if the first object had not been, the second never had existed.* The appearance of a cause always conveys the mind, by a customary transition, to the idea of the effect. Of this also we have experience. We may, therefore, suitably to this experience, form another definition of cause, and call it, *an object followed by another, and whose appearance always conveys the thought to that other.*

But though both these definitions be drawn from circumstances foreign to the cause, we cannot remedy this inconvenience, or attain any more perfect definition, which may point out that circumstances in the cause, which gives it a connection with its effect. We have no idea of this connection, nor even any distinct notion what it is we desire to know, when we endeavor at a conception of it. We say, for instance, that the vibration of this string is the cause of this particular sound. But what do we mean by that affirmation? We either mean *that this vibration is followed by this sound, and that all similar vibrations have been followed by similar sounds:* Or, *that this vibration is followed by this sound, and that upon the appearance of one the mind anticipates the senses, and forms immediately an idea of the other.* We may consider the relation of cause and effect in either of these two lights; but beyond these, we have no idea of it.[15]

To recapitulate, therefore, the reasonings of this section: every idea is copied from some preceding impression or sentiment; and where we cannot find any impression, we may be certain that there is no idea. In all single instances of the operation of bodies or minds, there is nothing that produces any impression, nor consequently can suggest any idea of power or necessary connection. But when many uniform instances appear, and the same object is always followed by the same event; we

[15] According to these explications and definitions, the idea of *power* is relative as much as that of *cause;* and both have a reference to an effect, or some other event constantly conjoined with the former. When we consider the *unknown* circumstance of an object, by which the degree or quantity of its effect is fixed and determined, we call that its power: And accordingly, it is allowed by all philosophers, that the effect is the measure of the power. But if they had any idea of power, as it is in itself, why could not they measure it in itself? The dispute whether the force of a body in motion be as its velocity, or the square of its velocity; this dispute, I say, needed not be decided by comparing its effects in equal or unequal times; but by a direct mensuration and comparison.

As to the frequent use of the words, *force, power, energy,* etc., which everywhere occur in common conversation, as well as in philosophy; that is no proof, that we are acquainted, in any instance, with the connecting principle between cause and effect, or can account ultimately for the production of one thing to another. These words, as commonly used, have very loose meanings annexed to them; and their ideas are very uncertain and confused. No animal can put external bodies in motion without the sentiment of a *nisus* or endeavor; and every animal has a sentiment or feeling from the stroke or blow of an external object, that is in motion. These sensations, which are merely animal, and from which we can *a priori* draw no inference, we are apt to transfer to inanimate objects, and to suppose, that they have some such feelings, whenever they transfer or receive motion. With regard to energies, which are exerted, without our annexing to them any idea of communicated motion, we consider only the constant experienced conjunction of the events; and as we *feel* a customary connection between the ideas, we transfer that feeling to the objects; as nothing is more usual than to apply to external bodies every internal sensation which they occasion.

then begin to entertain the notion of cause and connection. We then feel a new sentiment or impression, to wit, a customary connection in the thought or imagination between one object and its usual attendant; and this sentiment is the original of that idea which we seek for. For as this idea arises from a number of similar instances, and not from any single instance, it must arise from that circumstance, in which the number of instances differ from every individual instance. But this customary connection or transition of the imagination is the only circumstance in which they differ. In every other particular they are alike. The first instance which we saw of motion communicated by the shock of two billiard balls (to return to this obvious illustration) is exactly similar to any instance that may, at present, occur to us; except only, that we could not, at first, *infer* one event from the other; which we are enabled to do at present, after so long a course of uniform experience. I know not whether the reader will readily apprehend this reasoning. I am afraid that, should I multiply words about it, or throw it into a greater variety of lights, it would only become more obscure and intricate. In all abstract reasonings there is one point of view which, if we can happily hit, we shall go farther towards illustrating the subject than by all the eloquence in the world. This point of view we should endeavor to reach, and reserve the flowers of rhetoric for subjects which are more adapted to them.

SECTION VIII

OF LIBERTY AND NECESSITY

Part I

IT MIGHT reasonably be expected in questions which have been canvassed and disputed with great eagerness, since the first origin of science and philosophy, that the meaning of all the terms, at least, should have been agreed upon among the disputants; and our inquiries, in the course of two thousand years, been able to pass from words to the true and real subject of the controversy. For how easy may it seem to give exact definitions of the terms employed in reasoning, and make these definitions, not the mere sound of words, the object of future scrutiny and examination? But if we consider the matter more narrowly, we shall be apt to draw a quite opposite conclusion. From this circumstance alone, that a controversy has been long kept on foot, and remains still undecided, we may presume that there is some ambiguity in the expression, and that the disputants affix different ideas to the terms employed in the controversy. For as the faculties of the mind are supposed to be natur·

ally alike in every individual; otherwise nothing could be more fruitless
than to reason or dispute together; it were impossible, if men affix the
same ideas to their terms, that they could so long form different opinions
of the same subject; especially when they communicate their views, and
each party turn themselves on all sides, in search of arguments which
may give them the victory over their antagonists. It is true, if men attempt the discussion of questions which lie entirely beyond the reach
of human capacity, such as those concerning the origin of worlds, or the
economy of the intellectual system or region of spirits, they may long
beat the air in their fruitless contests, and never arrive at any determinate conclusion. But if the question regard any subject of common life
and experience, nothing, one would think, could preserve the dispute so
long undecided but some ambiguous expressions, which keep the antagonists still at a distance, and hinder them from grappling with each other.

  This has been the case in the long disputed question concerning liberty and necessity; and to so remarkable a degree that, if I be not much
mistaken, we shall find, that all mankind, both learned and ignorant,
have always been of the same opinion with regard to this subject, and
that a few intelligible definitions would immediately have put an end to
the whole controversy. I own that this dispute has been so much canvassed on all hands, and has led philosophers into such a labyrinth of
obscure sophistry, that it is no wonder, if a sensible reader indulge his
ease so far as to turn a deaf ear to the proposal of such a question,
from which he can expect neither instruction nor entertainment. But
the state of the argument here proposed may, perhaps, serve to renew
his attention; as it has more novelty, promises at least some decision
of the controversy, and will not much disturb his ease by any intricate
or obscure reasoning.

  I hope, therefore, to make it appear that all men have ever agreed
in the doctrine both of necessity and of liberty, according to any reasonable sense, which can be put on these terms; and that the whole
controversy has hitherto turned merely upon words. We shall begin with
examining the doctrine of necessity.

  It is universally allowed that matter, in all its operations, is actuated by a necessary force, and that every natural effect is so precisely
determined by the energy of its cause that no other effect, in such particular circumstances, could possibly have resulted from it. The degree
and direction of every motion is, by the laws of nature, prescribed with
such exactness that a living creature may as soon arise from the shock
of two bodies as motion in any other degree or direction than what is
actually produced by it. Would we, therefore, form a just and precise
idea of *necessity*, we must consider whence that idea arises when we
apply it to the operation of bodies.

It seems evident that, if all the scenes of nature were continually shifted in such a manner that no two events bore any resemblance to each other, but every object was entirely new, without any similitude to whatever had been seen before, we should never, in that case, have attained the least idea of necessity, or of a connection among these objects. We might say, upon such a supposition, that one object or event has followed another; not that one was produced by the other. The relation of cause and effect must be utterly unknown to mankind. Inference and reasoning concerning the operations of nature would, from that moment, be at an end; and the memory and senses remain the only canals, by which the knowledge of any real existence could possibly have access to the mind. Our idea, therefore, of necessity and causation arises entirely from the uniformity observable in the operations of nature, where similar objects are constantly conjoined together, and the mind is detemined by custom to infer the one from the appearance of the other. These two circumstances form the whole of that necessity, which we ascribe to matter. Beyond the constant *conjunction* of similar objects, and the consequent *inference* from one to the other, we have no notion of any necessity or connection.

If it appear, therefore, that all mankind have ever allowed, without any doubt or hesitation, that these two circumstances take place in the voluntary actions of men, and in the operations of mind; it must follow, that all mankind have ever agreed in the doctrine of necessity, and that they have hitherto disputed, merely for not understanding each other.

As to the first circumstance, the constant and regular conjunction of similar events, we may possibly satisfy ourselves by the following considerations. It is universally acknowledged that there is a great uniformity among the actions of men, in all nations and ages, and that human nature remains still the same, in its principles and operations. The same motives always produce the same actions; the same events follow from the same causes. Ambition, avarice, self-love, vanity, friendship, generosity, public spirit: these passions, mixed in various degrees, and distributed through society, have been, from the beginning of the world, and still are, the source of all the actions and enterprises, which have ever been observed among mankind. Would you know the sentiments, inclinations, and course of life of the Greeks and Romans? Study well the temper and actions of the French and English: you cannot be much mistaken in transferring to the former *most* of the observations which you have made with regard to the latter. Mankind are so much the same, in all times and places, that history informs us of nothing new or strange in this particular. Its chief use is only to discover the constant and universal principles of human nature, by showing men in all varieties of circumstances and situations, and furnishing us with materials from which we may form our observations and become acquainted with the regular springs of human action and behavior. These records of wars, intrigues, factions, and revolutions, are so many collections of experiments, by which the politician or moral philosopher fixes the principles of his science, in the same manner as the physician or natural philosopher becomes acquainted with the nature of plants, minerals, and other external objects, by the experiments which he forms concerning them. Nor are the earth, water, and other elements, examined by Aristotle, and Hippocrates, more like to those which at present lie under our observation than the men described by Polybius and Tacitus are to those who now govern the world.

Should a traveler, returning from a far country, bring us an account of men, wholly different from any with whom we were ever acquainted; men, who were entirely divested of avarice, ambition, or revenge; who knew no pleasure but friendship, generosity, and public spirit; we should immediately, from these circumstances, detect the falsehood, and prove him a liar, with the same certainty as if he had stuffed his narration with stories of centaurs and dragons, miracles and prodigies. And if we would explode any forgery in history, we cannot make us of a more convincing argument, than to prove, that the actions ascribed to any person are directly contrary to the course of nature, and that no human motives, in such circumstances, could ever induce him to such a conduct. The veracity of Quintus Curtius is as much to be suspected, when he describes the supernatural courage of Alexander, by which he was hurried on singly to attack multitudes, as when he describes his supernatural force and activity, by which he was able to resist them. So readily and universally do we acknowledge a uniformity in human motives and actions as well as in the operations of body.

Hence likewise the benefit of that experience, acquired by long life and a variety of business and company, in order to instruct us in the principles of human nature, and regulate our future conduct, as well as speculation. By means of this guide, we mount up to the knowledge of men's inclinations and motives, from their actions, expressions, and even gestures; and again descend to the interpretation of their actions from our knowledge of their motives and inclinations. The general observations treasured up by a course of experience, give us the clue of human nature, and teach us to unravel all its intricacies. Pretexts and appearances no longer deceive us. Public declarations pass for the specious coloring of a cause. And though virtue and honor be allowed their proper weight and authority, that perfect disinterestedness, so often pretended to, is never expected in multitudes and parties; seldom in their leaders; and scarcely even in individuals of any rank or station. But were there no uniformity in human actions, and were every experiment which we could form of this kind irregular and anomalous, it were impossible to collect any general observations concerning mankind; and no experience, however accurately digested by reflection, would ever serve to any purpose. Why is the aged husbandman more skillful in his calling than the young beginner but because there is a certain uniformity in the operation of the sun, rain, and earth towards the production of vegetables; and experience teaches the old practitioner the rules by which this operation is governed and directed.

We must not, however, expect that this uniformity of human actions should be carried to such a length as that all men, in the same circumstances, will always act precisely in the same manner, without making any allowance for the diversity of characters, prejudices, and opinions. Such a uniformity in every particular, is found in no part of nature. On the contrary, from observing the variety of conduct in different men, we are enabled to form a greater variety of maxims, which still suppose a degree of uniformity and regularity.

Are the manners of men different in different ages and countries? We learn thence the great force of custom and education, which mold the human mind from its infancy and form it into a fixed and established character. Is the behavior and conduct of the one sex very unlike that of the other? Is it thence we become acquainted with the different characters which nature has impressed upon the sexes, and which she preserves with constancy and regularity? Are the actions of the same person much diversified in the different periods of his life, from infancy to old age? This affords room for many general observations concerning the gradual change of our sentiments and inclinations, and the different maxims which prevail in the different ages of human creatures. Even the characters, which are peculiar to each individual, have a uniformity in their influence; otherwise our acquaintance with the persons and our observation of their conduct could never teach us their dispositions, or serve to direct our behavior with regard to them.

I grant it possible to find some actions, which seem to have no regular connection with any known motives, and are exceptions to all the measures of conduct which have ever been established for the government of men. But if we would willingly know what judgment should be formed of such irregular and extraordinary actions, we may consider the sentiments commonly entertained with regard to those irregular events which appear in the course of nature, and the operations of external objects. All causes are not conjoined to their usual effects with like uniformity. An artificer, who handles only dead matter, may be disappointed of his aim, as well as the politician, who directs the conduct of sensible and intelligent agents.

The vulgar, who take things according to their first appearance, attribute the uncertainty of events to such an uncertainty in the causes as makes the latter often fail of their usual influence; though they meet with no impediment in their operation. But philosophers, observing that, almost in every part of nature, there is contained a vast variety of springs and principles, which are hid, by reason of their minuteness or remoteness, find, that it is at least possible the contrariety of events may not proceed from any contingency in the cause, but from the secret operation of contrary causes. This possibility is converted into certainty by farther observation, when they remark that, upon an exact scrutiny, a contrariety of effects always betrays a contrariety of causes, and proceeds from their mutual opposition. A peasant can give no better reason for the stopping of any clock or watch than to say that it does not commonly go right: but an artist easily perceives that the same force in the spring or pendulum has always the same influence on the wheels; but fails of its usual effect, perhaps by reason of a grain of dust, which puts a stop to the whole movement. From the observation of several parallel instances, philosophers form a maxim that the connection between all causes and effects is equally necessary, and that its seeming uncertainty in some instances proceeds from the secret opposition of contrary causes.

Thus, for instance, in the human body, when the usual symptoms of health or sickness disappoint our expectation; when medicines operate not with their wonted powers; when irregular events follow from any particular cause; the philosopher and physician are not surprised at the matter, nor are ever tempted to deny, in general, the necessity and uniformity of those principles by which the animal economy is conducted. They know that a human body is a mighty complicated machine; that many secret powers lurk in it, which are altogether beyond our comprehension; that to us it must often appear very uncertain in its operations; and that therefore the irregular events, which outwardly discover themselves, can be no proof that the laws of nature are not observed with the greatest regularity in its internal operations and government.

The philosopher, if he be consistent, must apply the same reasoning to the actions and volitions of intelligent agents. The most irregular and unexpected resolutions of men may frequently be accounted for by those who know every particular circumstance of their character and situation. A person of an obliging disposition gives a peevish answer; but he has the toothache, or has not dined. A stupid fellow discovers an uncommon alacrity in his carriage; but he has met with a sudden piece of good fortune. Or even when an action, as something happens, cannot be particularly accounted for, either by the person himself or by others; we know, in general, that the characters of men are, to a certain degree, inconstant and irregular. This is, in a manner, the constant character of human nature; though it be applicable, in a more particular manner, to some persons who have no fixed rule for their conduct, but proceed in a continued course of caprice and inconstancy. The internal principles and motives may operate in a uniform manner, notwithstanding these seeming irregularities; in the same manner as the winds, rain clouds, and other variations of the weather are supposed to be governed by steady principles; though not easily discoverable by human sagacity and inquiry.

Thus it appear, not only that the conjunction between motives and voluntary actions is as regular and uniform as that between the cause and effect in any part of nature; but also that this regular conjunction has been universally acknowledged among mankind, and has never been the subject of dispute, either in philosophy or common life. Now, as it is from past experience that we draw all inferences concerning the future, and as we conclude that objects will always be conjoined together which we find to have always been conjoined; it may seem superfluous to prove that this experienced uniformity in human actions is a source whence we draw *inferences* concerning them. But in order to throw the argument into a greater variety of lights we shall also insist, though briefly, on this latter topic.

The mutual dependence of men is so great in all societies that scarce any human action is entirely complete in itself, or is performed without some reference to the actions of others, which are requisite to make it answer fully the intention of the agent. The poorest artificer, who labors alone, expects at least the protection of the magistrate, to ensure him the enjoyment of the fruits of his labor. He also expects that, when he carries his goods to market, and offers them at a reasonable price, he shall find purchasers, and shall be able, by the money he acquires, to engage others to supply him with those commodities which are requisite for his subsistence. In proportion as men extend their dealings, and render their intercourse with others more complicated, they always comprehend, in their schemes of life, a greater variety of voluntary actions, which they expect, from the proper motives, to co-operate with their own. In all these conclusions they take their measures from past experience, in the same manner as in their reasonings concerning external objects; and firmly believe that men, as well as all the elements, are to continue, in their operations, the same that they have ever found them. A manufacturer reckons upon the labor of his servants for the execution of any work as much as upon the tools which he employs, and would be equally surprised were his expectations disappointed. In short, this experimental inference and reasoning concerning the actions of others enters so much into human life, that no man, while awake, is ever a moment without employing it. Have we not reason, therefore, to affirm that all mankind have always agreed in the doctrine of necessity according to the foregoing definition and explication of it?

Nor have philosophers ever entertained a different opinion from the people in this particular. For, not to mention that almost every action of their life supposes that opinion, there are even few of the speculative parts of learning to which it is not essential. What would become of *history,* had we not a dependence on the veracity of the historian according to the experience which we have had of mankind? How could *politics* be a science, if laws and forms of government had not a uniform influence upon society? Where would be the foundation of *morals,* if particular characters had no certain or determinate power to produce particular sentiments, and if these sentiments had no constant operation on actions? And with what pretense could we employ our *criticism* upon any poet or polite author, if we could not pronounce the conduct and sentiments of his actors either natural or unnatural to such characters, and in such circumstances? It seems almost impossible, therefore, to engage either in science or action of any kind without acknowledging the doctrine of necessity, and this *inference* from motive to voluntary actions, from characters to conduct.

And indeed, when we consider how aptly *natural* and *moral* evidence link together, and form only one chain of argument, we shall make no scruple to allow that they are of the same nature, and derived from the same principles. A prisoner who has neither money nor interest, discovers the impossibility of his escape, as well when he considers the obstinacy of the goaler, as the walls and bars with which he is surrounded; and, in all attempts for his freedom, chooses rather to work upon the stone and iron of the one, than upon the inflexible nature of the other. The same prisoner, when conducted to the scaffold, foresees his death as certainly from the constancy and fidelity of his guards, as from the operation of the axe or wheel. His mind runs along a certain train of ideas: the refusal of the soldiers to consent to his escape; the action of the executioner; the separation of the head and body; bleeding, convulsive motions, and death. Here is a connected chain of natural causes and voluntary actions; but the mind feels no difference between them in passing from one link to another. Nor is less certain of the future event than if it were connected with the objects present to the memory or senses, by a train of causes, cemented together by what we are pleased to call a *physical* necessity. The same experienced union has the same effect on the mind, whether the united objects be motives, volition, and actions; or figure and motion. We may change the name of things; but their nature and their operation on the understanding never change.

Were a man, whom I know to be honest and opulent, and with whom I live in intimate friendship, to come into my house, where I am surrounded with my servants, I rest assured that he is not to stab me before he leaves it in order to rob me of my silver standish; and I no more suspect this event than the falling of the house itself, which is new, and solidly built and founded.—*But he may have been seized with a sudden and unknown frenzy.*—So may a sudden earthquake arise, and shake and tumble my house about my ears. I shall therefore change the suppositions. I shall say that I know with certainty that he is not to put his hand into the fire and hold it there till it be consumed: and this event, I think I can foretell with the same assurance, as that, if he throw himself out at the window, and meet with no obstruction, he will not remain a moment suspended in the air. No suspicion of an unknown frenzy can give the least possibility to the former event, which is so contrary to all the known principles of human nature. A man who at noon leaves his purse full of gold on the pavement at Charing Cross, may as well expect that it will fly away like a feather, as that he will find it untouched an hour after. Above one half of human reasonings contain inferences of a similar nature, attended with more or less degrees of certainty proportioned to our experience of the usual conduct of mankind in such particular situations.

I have frequently considered, what could possibly be the reason why all mankind, though they have ever, without hesitation, acknowledged the doctrine of necessity in their whole practice and reasoning, have yet discovered such a reluctance to acknowledge it in words, and have rather shown a propensity, in all ages, to profess the contrary opinion. The matter, I think, may be accounted for after the following manner. If we examine the operations of body, and the production of effects from their causes, we shall find that all our faculties can never carry us farther in our knowledge of this relation than barely to observe that particular objects are *constantly conjoined* together, and that the mind is carried, by a *customary transition,* from the appearance of one to the belief of the other. But though this conclusion concerning human ignorance be the result of the strictest scrutiny of this subject, men still entertain a strong propensity to believe that they penetrate farther into the powers of nature, and perceive something like a necessary connection between the cause and the effect. When again they turn their reflections towards the operations of their own minds, and *feel* no such connection of the motive and the action; they are thence apt to suppose, that there is a difference between the effects which result from material force, and those which arise from thought and intelligence. But being once convinced that we know nothing farther of causation of any kind than merely the *constant conjunction* of objects, and the consequent *inference* of the mind from one to another, and finding that these two circumstances are universally allowed to have place in voluntary actions; we may be more easily led to own the same necessity common to all causes. And though this reasoning may contradict the systems of many philosophers, in ascribing necessity to the determinations of the will, we shall find, upon reflection, that they dissent from it in words only, not in their real sentiment. Necessity, according to the sense in which it is here taken, has never yet been rejected, nor can ever, I think, be rejected by any philosopher. It may only, perhaps, be pretended that the mind can perceive, in the operations of matter, some farther connection between the cause and effect; and connection that has not place in voluntary actions of intelligent beings. Now whether it be so or not, can only appear upon examination; and it is incumbent on these philosophers to make good their assertion, by defining or describing that necessity, and pointing it out to us in the operations of material causes.

It would seem, indeed, that men begin at the wrong end of this question concerning liberty and necessity, when they enter upon it by examining the faculties of the soul, the influence of the understanding, and the operations of the will. Let them first discuss a more simple question, namely, the operations of body and of brute unintelligent matter; and try whether they can there form any idea of causation and necessity, except that of a constant conjunction of objects, and subsequent inference of the mind from one to another. If these circumstances form, in reality, the whole of that necessity, which we conceive in matter, and if these circumstances be also universally acknowledged to take place in the operations of the mind, the dispute is at an end; at least, must be owned to be thenceforth merely verbal. But as long as we will rashly suppose, that we have some farther idea of necessity and causation in the operations of external objects; at the same time, that we can find nothing farther in the voluntary actions of the mind; there is no possibility of bringing the question to any determinate issue, while we proceed upon so erroneous a supposition. The only method of undeceiving us is to mount up higher; to examine the narrow extent of science when applied to material causes; and to convince ourselves that all we know of them is the constant conjunction and inference above mentioned. We may, perhaps, find that it is with difficulty we are induced to fix such narrow limits to human understanding: but we can afterwards find no difficulty when we come to apply this doctrine to the actions of the will. For as it is evident that these have a regular conjunction with motives and circumstances and characters, and as we always draw inferences from one to the other, we must be obliged to acknowledge in words that necessity, which we have already avowed, in every deliberation of our lives, and in every step of our conduct and behavior.[16]

But to proceed in this reconciling project with regard to the question of liberty and necessity; the most contentious question of metaphysics; the most contentious science; it will not require many words to prove, that all mankind have ever agreed in the doctrine of liberty as well as in that of necessity, and that the whole dispute, in this respect also, has been hitherto merely verbal. For what is meant by liberty, when applied to voluntary actions? We cannot surely mean that actions have so little connection with motives, inclinations, and circumstances, that one does not follow with a certain degree of uniformity from the other, and that one affords no inference by which we can conclude the existence of the other. For these are plain and acknowledged matters of fact. By liberty, than, we can only mean *a power of acting or not acting, according to the determinations of the will;* that is, if we choose to remain at rest, we may; if we choose to move, we also may. Now this hypothetical liberty is universally allowed to belong to everyone who is not a prisoner and in chains. Here, then, is no subject of dispute.

[16] The prevalence of the doctrine of liberty may be accounted for, from another cause, viz., a false sensation or seeming experience which we have, or may have, of liberty or indifference, in many of our actions. The necessity of any action, whether of matter or of mind, is not, properly speaking, a quality in the agent, but in any thinking or intelligent being, who may consider the action; and it consists chiefly in the determination of his thoughts to infer the existence of that action from some preceding objects; as liberty, when opposed to necessity, is nothing but the want of that determination, and a certain looseness or indifference, which we feel, in passing, or not passing, from the idea of one object to that of any succeeding one. Now we may observe, that, though, in *reflecting* on human actions, we seldom feel such a looseness, or indifference, but are commonly able to infer them with considerable certainty from their motives, and from the dispositions of the agent; yet it frequently happens, that, in *performing* the actions themselves, we are sensible of something like it. And as all assembling objects are readily taken for each other, this has been employed as a demonstrative and even intuitive proof of human liberty. We feel, that our actions are subject to our will, on most occasions; and imagine we feel, that the will itself is subject to nothing, because, when by a denial of it we are provoked to try, we feel, that it moves easily every way, and produces an image of itself (or a *velleity,* as it is called in the schools) even on that side, on which it did not settle. This image, or faint motion, we persuade ourselves, could, at that time, have been completed into the thing itself; because, should that be denied, we find, upon a second trial, that, at present, it can. We consider not, that the fantastical desire of shewing liberty, is here the motive of our actions. And it seems certain, that, however we may imagine we feel a liberty within ourselves, a spectator can commonly infer our action from our motives and character; and even where he cannot, he concludes in general, that he might, were he perfectly acquainted with every circumstance of our situation and temper, and the most secret springs of our complexion and disposition. Now this is the very essence of necessity, according to the foregoing doctrine.

Whatever definition we may give of liberty, we should be careful to observe two requisite circumstances; *first,* that it be consistent with plain matter of fact; *secondly,* that it be consistent with itself. If we observe these circumstances, and render our definition intelligible, I am persuaded that all mankind will be found of one opinion with regard to it.

It is universally allowed that nothing exists without a cause of its existence, and that chance, when strictly examined, is a mere negative word, and means not any real power which has anywhere a being in nature. But it is pretended that some causes are necessary, some not necessary. Here then is the advantage of definitions. Let anyone *define* a cause, without comprehending, as a part of the definition, a *necessary connection* with its effect; and let him show distinctly the origin of the idea, expressed by the definition; and I shall readily give up the whole controversy. But if the foregoing explication of the matter be received, this must be absolutely impracticable. Had not objects a regular conjunction with each other, we should never have entertained any notion of cause and effect; and this regular conjunction produces that inference of the understanding, which is the only connection, that we can have any comprehension of. Whoever attempts a definition of cause, exclusive of these circumstances, will be obliged either to employ unintelligible terms or such as we are synonymous to the term which he endeavors to define.[17] And if the definition above mentioned be admitted; liberty, when opposed to necessity, not to constraint, is the same thing with chance; which is universally allowed to have no existence.

Part II

THERE is no method of reasoning more common, and yet none more blamable, than, in philosophical disputes, to endeavor the refutation of any hypothesis, by a pretense of its dangerous consequences to religion and morality. When any opinion leads to absurdities, it is certainly false; but it is not certain that an opinion is false, because it is of dangerous consequence. Such topics, therefore, ought entirely to be forborne; as serving nothing to the discovery of truth, but only to make the person of an antagonist odious. This I observe in general, without

---

[17] Thus, if a cause be defined, *that which produces any thing;* it is easy to observe, that *producing* is synonymous to *causing.* In like manner, if a cause be defined, *that by which any thing exists;* this is liable to the same objection. For what is meant by these words, *by which?* Had it been said, that a cause is *that* after which *any thing constantly exists* we should have understood the terms. For this is, indeed, all we know of the matter. And this constancy forms the very essence of necessity, nor have we any other idea of it.

pretending to draw any advantage from it. I frankly submit to an examination of this kind, and shall venture to affirm that the doctrines, both of necessity and of liberty, as above explained, are not only consistent with morality, but are absolutely essential to its support.

Necessity may be defined two ways, conformably to the two definitions of *cause,* of which it makes an essential part. It consists either in the constant conjunction of like objects, or in the inference of the understanding from one object to another. Now necessity, in both these senses (which, indeed, are at bottom the same), has universally, though tacitly, in the schools, in the pulpit, and in common life, been allowed to belong to the will of man; and no one has ever pretended to deny that we can draw inferences concerning human actions, and that those inferences are founded on the experienced union of like actions, with like motives, inclinations, and circumstances. The only particular in which anyone can differ, is, that either, perhaps, he will refuse to give the name of necessity to this property of human actions: but as long as the meaning is understood, I hope the word can do no harm; or that he will maintain it possible to discover something farther in the operations of matter. But this, it must be acknowledged, can be of no consequence to morality or religion, whatever it may be to natural philosophy or metaphysics. We may here be mistaken in asserting that there is no idea of any other necessity or connection in the actions of body; but surely we ascribe nothing to the actions of the mind, but what everyone does, and must readily allow of. We change no circumstance in the received orthodox system with regard to the will, but only in that with regard to material objects and causes. Nothing, therefore, can be more innocent, at least, than this doctrine.

All laws being founded on rewards and punishments, it is supposed as a fundamental principle, that these motives have a regular and uniform influence on the mind, and both produce the good and prevent the evil actions. We may give to this influence what name we please; but, as it is usually conjoined with the action, it must be esteemed a *cause,* and be looked upon as an instance of that necessity, which we would here establish.

The only proper object of hatred or vengeance is a person or creature, endowed with thought and consciousness; and when any criminal or injurious actions excite that passion, it is only by their relation to the person, or connection with him. Actions are, by their very nature, temporary and perishing; and where they proceed not from some *cause* in the character and disposition of the person who performed them, they can neither redound to his honor, if good; nor infamy, if evil. The actions themselves may be blamable; they may be contrary to all the rules or morality and religion. But the person is not answerable for them; and as they proceeded from nothing in him that is durable and constant, and leave nothing of that nature behind them, it is impossible he can, upon their account, become the object of punishment or vengeance. According to the principle, therefore, which denies necessity, and consequently causes, a man is as pure and untainted, after having committed the most horrid crime, as at the first moment of his birth, nor is his character anywise concerned in his actions, since they are not derived from it, and the wickedness of the one can never be used as a proof of the depravity of the other.

Men are not blamed for such actions as they perform ignorantly and casually, whatever may be the consequences. Why? but because the principles of these actions are only momentary, and terminate in them alone. Men are less blamed for such actions as they perform hastily and unpremeditately than for such as proceed from deliberation. For what reason? but because a hasty temper, though a constant cause or principle in the mind, operates only by intervals, and infects not the whole character. Again, repentance wipes off every crime, if attended with a reformation of life and manners. How is this to be accounted for? but by asserting that actions render a person criminal merely as they are proofs of criminal principles in the mind; and when, by an alteration of these principles, they cease to be just proofs, they likewise cease to be criminal. But, except upon the doctrine of necessity, they never were just proofs, and consequently never were criminal.

It will be equally easy to prove, and from the same arguments, that *liberty,* according to that definition above mentioned, in which all men agree, is also essential to morality, and that no human actions, where it is wanting, are susceptible of any moral qualities, or can be the objects either of approbation or dislike. For as actions are objects of our moral sentiment, so far only as they are indications of the internal character, passions, and affections; it is impossible that they can give rise either to praise or blame, where they proceed not from these principles, but are derived altogether from external violence.

I pretend not to have obviated or removed all objections to this theory, with regard to necessity and liberty. I can foresee other objections, derived from topics which have not here been treated of. It may be said, for instance, that, if voluntary actions be subjected to the same laws of necessity with the operations of matter, there is a continued chain of necessary causes, pre-ordained and pre-determined, reaching from the original cause of all to every single volition of every human creature. No contingency anywhere in the universe; no indifference; no liberty. While we act, we are, at the same time, acted upon. The ultimate Author of all our volitions is the Creator of the world, who first bestowed motion on this immense machine, and placed all beings in that particular position, whence every subsequent event, by an inevitable necessity, must result. Human actions, therefore, either can have no moral turpitude at all, as proceeding from so good a cause; or if they have any turpitude, they must involve our Creator in the same guilt, while he is acknowledged to be their ultimate cause and author. For as a man, who fired a mine, is answerable for all the consequences whether the train he employed be long or short; so wherever a continued chain of necessary causes is fixed, that Being, either finite or infinite, who produces the first, is likewise the author of all the rest, and must both bear the blame and acquire the praise which belong to them. Our clear and unalterable ideas of morality establish this rule, upon unquestionable reasons, when we examine the consequences of any human action; and these reasons must still have greater force when applied to the volitions and intentions of a Being infinitely wise and powerful. Ignorance or impotence may be pleaded for so limited a creature as man; but these imperfections have no place in our Creator. He foresaw, he ordained, he intended all those actions of men, which we so rashly pronounce criminal. And we must therefore conclude, either that they are not criminal, or that the Deity, not man, is accountable for them. But as either of these positions is absurd and impious, it follows, that the doctrine from which they are deduced cannot possibly be true, as being liable to all the same objections. An absurd consequence, if necessary, proves the original doctrine to be absurd in the same manner as criminal actions render criminal the original cause, if the connection between them be necessary and inevitable.

This objection consists of two parts, which we shall examine separately. *First,* that, if human actions can be traced up, by a necessary chain, to the Deity, they can never be criminal; on account of the infinite perfection of that Being from whom they are derived, and who can intend nothing but what is altogether good and laudable. Or, *Secondly,* if they be criminal, we must retract the attribute of perfection, which we ascribe to the Deity, and must acknowledge him to be the ultimate author of guilt and moral turpitude in all his creatures.

The answer to the first objection seems obvious and convincing. There are many philosophers who, after an exact scrutiny of all the phenomena of nature, conclude, that the *whole,* considered as one system, is, in every period of its existence, ordered with perfect benevolence; and that the utmost possible happiness will, in the end, result to all created beings, without any mixture of positive or absolute ill or misery. Every physical ill, say they, makes an essential part of this benevolent system, and could not possibly be removed, even by the Deity himself, considered as a wise agent, without giving entrance to greater ill, or excluding greater good, which will result from it. From this theory, some philosophers, and the ancient Stoics among the rest, derived a topic of consolation under all afflictions, while they taught their pupils that those ills under which they labored were, in reality, goods to the universe; and that to an enlarged view, which could comprehend the whole system of nature, every event became an object of joy and exultation. But though this topic be specious and sublime, it was soon found in practice weak and ineffectual. You would surely more irritate than appease a man lying under the racking pains of the gout by preaching up to him the rectitude of those general laws, which produced the malignant humors in his body, and led them through the proper canals, to the sinews and nerves, where they now excite such acute torments. These enlarged views may, for a moment, please the imagination of a speculative man, who is placed in ease and security; but neither can they dwell with constancy on his mind, even though undisturbed by the emotions of pain or passion; much less can they maintain their ground when attacked by such powerful antagonists. The affections take a narrower and more natural survey of their object; and by an economy, more suitable to the infirmity of human minds, regard alone the beings around us, and are actuated by such events as appear good or ill to the private system.

The case is the same with *moral* as with *physical* ill. It cannot reasonably be supposed, that those remote considerations, which are found of so little efficacy with regard to one, will have a more powerful influence with regard to the other. The mind of man is so formed by nature that, upon the appearance of certain characters, dispositions, and actions, it immediately feels the sentiment of approbation or blame; nor are there any emotions more essential to its frame and constitution. The characters which engage our approbation are chiefly such as contribute to the peace and security of human society; as the characters which excite blame are chiefly such as tend to public detriment and disturbance: whence it may reasonably be presumed, that the moral sentiments arise, either mediately or immediately, from a reflection of these opposite interests. What though philosophical meditations establish a different opinion or conjecture; that everything is right with regard to the *whole,* and that the qualities, which disturb society, are, in the main, as beneficial, and are as suitable to the primary intention of nature as those which more directly promote its happiness and welfare? Are such remote and uncertain speculations able to counterbalance the sentiments which arise from the natural and immediate view of of the objects? A man who is robbed of a considerable sum; does he find his vexation for the loss anywise diminished by these sublime reflections? Why then should his moral resentment against the crime be supposed incompatible with them? Or why should not the acknowledgment of a real distinction between vice and virtue be reconcilable to all speculative systems of philosophy, as well as that of a real distinction between personal beauty and deformity? Both these distinctions are founded in the natural sentiments of the human mind; and these sentiments are not to be controlled ar altered by any philosophical theory or speculation whatsoever.

The *second* objection admits not of so easy and satisfactory an answer; nor is it possible to explain distinctly, how the Deity can be the mediate cause of all the actions of men, without being the author of sin and moral turpitude. These are mysteries, which mere natural and unassisted reason is very unfit to handle; and whatever system she embraces, she must find herself involved in inextricable difficulties, and even contradictions, at every step which she takes with regard to such subjects. To reconcile the indifference and contingency of human actions with prescience; or to defend absolute decrees, and yet free the Diety from being the author of sin, has been found hitherto to exceed all the power of philosophy. Happy, if she be thence sensible of her temerity, when she pries into these sublime mysteries; and leaving a scene so full of obscurities and perplexities, return, with suitable modesty, to her true and proper province, the examination of common life; where she will find difficulties enough to employ her inquiries, without launching into so boundless an ocean of doubt, uncertainty, and contradiction!

SECTION IX

OF THE REASON OF ANIMALS

ALL our reasonings concerning matter of fact are founded on a species of *analogy,* which leads us to expect from any cause the same events, which we have observed to result from similar causes. Where the causes are entirely similar, the analogy is perfect, and the inference, drawn from it, is regarded as certain and conclusive: nor does any man ever entertain a doubt, when he sees a piece of iron, that it will have weight and cohesion of parts; as in all other instances, which have ever fallen under his observation. But where the objects have not so exact a similarity, the analogy is less perfect, and the inference is less conclusive; though still it has some force, in proportion to the degree of similarity and resemblance. The anatomical observations, formed upon one animal, are, by this species of reasoning, extended to all animals; and it is certain, that when the circulation of the blood, for instance, is clearly proved to have place in one creature, as a frog, or fish, it forms a strong presumption, that the same principle has place in all. These analogical observations may be carried farther, even to this science, of which we are now treating; and any theory, by which we explain the operations of the understanding, or the origin and connection of the passions in man, will acquire additional authority, if we find, that the same theory is requisite to explain the same phenomena in all other animals. We shall make trial of this, with regard to the hypothesis, by which we have, in the foregoing discourse, endeavored to account for all experimental reasonings; and it is hoped, that this new point of view will serve to confirm all our former observations.

First, It seems evident, that animals as well as men learn many things from experience, and infer, that the same events will always follow from the same causes. By this principle they become acquainted with the more obvious properties of external objects, and gradually, from their birth, treasure up a knowledge of the nature of fire, water, earth, stones, heights, depths, etc., and of the effects which result from their operation. The ignorance and inexperience of the young are here plainly distinguishable from the cunning and sagacity of the old, who have learned, by long observation, to avoid what hurt them, and to pursue what gave ease or pleasure. A horse, that has been accustomed to the field, becomes acquainted with the proper height which he can leap, and will never attempt what exceeds his force and ability. An old greyhound will trust the more fatiguing part of the chase to the younger, and will place himself so as to meet the hare in her doubles; nor are the conjectures, which he forms on this occasion, founded in anything but his observation and experience.

This is still more evident from the effects of discipline and education on animals, who, by the proper application of rewards and punishments, may be taught any course of action, and most contrary to their natural instincts and propensities. Is it not experience, which renders a dog apprehensive of pain, when you menace him, or lift up the whip to beat him? Is it not even experience, which makes him answer to his name, and infer, from such an arbitrary sound, that you mean him rather than any of his fellows, and intend to call him, when you pronounce it in a certain manner, and with a certain tone and accent?

In all these cases, we may observe, that the animal infers some fact beyond what immediately strikes his senses; and that this inference is altogether founded on past experience, while the creature expects from the present object the same consequences, which it has always found in its observation to result from similar objects.

Secondly, It is impossible, that this inference of the animal can be founded on any process of argument or reasoning, by which he concludes, that like events must follow like objects, and that the course of nature will always be regular in its operations. For if there be in reality any arguments of this nature, they surely lie too abstruse for the observation of such imperfect understandings; since it may well employ the utmost care and attention of a philosophic genius to discover and observe them. Animals, therefore, are not guided in these inferences by reasoning; neither are children; neither are the generality of mankind, in their ordinary actions and conclusions; neither are philosophers themselves, who, in all the active parts of life, are, in the main, the same with the vulgar, and are governed by the same maxims. Nature must have provided some other principle, of more ready, and more general use and application; nor can an operation of such immense consequence in life, as that of inferring effects from causes, be trusted to the uncertain process of reasoning and argumentation. Were this doubtful with regard to men, it seems to admit of no question with regard to the brute creation; and the conclusion being once firmly established in the one, we have a strong presumption, from all the rules of analogy, that it ought to be universally admitted, without any exception or reserve. It is custom alone, which engages animals, from every object, that strikes their senses, to infer its usual attendant, and carries their imagination, from the appearance of the one, to conceive the other, in that particular manner, which we denominate *belief*. No other explication can be given of this operation, in all the higher, as well as lower classes of sensitive beings, which fall under our notice and observation.[18]

---

[18] Since all reasoning concerning facts or causes is derived merely from custom, it may be asked how it happens, that men so much surpass animals in reasoning, and one man so much surpasses another? Has not the same custom the same influence on all?

We shall here endeavor briefly to explain the great difference in human understandings; after which the reason of the difference between men and animals will easily be comprehended.

1. When we have lived any time, and have been accustomed to the uniformity of nature, we acquire a general habit, by which we always transfer the known to the unknown, and conceive the latter to resemble the former. By means of this general habitual principle, we regard even one experiment as the foundation of reasoning, and expect a similar event with some degree of certainty, where the experiment has been made accurately, and free from all foreign circumstances. It is therefore considered as a matter of great importance to observe the consequences of things; and as one man may very much surpass another in attention and memory and observation, this will make a very great difference in their reasoning.

2. Where there is a complication of causes to produce any effect, one mind may be much larger than another, and better able to comprehend the whole system of objects, and to infer justly their consequences.

3. One man is able to carry on a chain of consequences to a greater length than another.

4. Few men can think long without running into a confusion of ideas, and mistaking one for another; and there are various degrees of this infirmity.

But though animals learn many parts of their knowledge from observation, there are also many parts of it, which they derive from the original hand of nature; which much exceed the share of capacity they possess on ordinary occasions; and in which they improve, little or nothing, by the longest practice and experience. These we denominate *instincts,* and are so apt to admire as something very extraordinary, and inexplicable by all the disquisitions of human understanding. But our wonder will, perhaps, cease or diminish, when we consider, that the experimental reasoning itself, which we possess in common with beasts, and on which the whole conduct of life depends, is nothing but a species of instinct or mechanical power, that acts in us unknown to ourselves; and in its chief operations, is not directed by any such relations or comparisons of ideas, as are the proper objects of our intellectual faculties. Though the instinct be different, yet still it is an instinct, which teaches a man to avoid the fire; as much as that, which teaches a bird, with such exactness, the art of incubation, and the whole economy and order of its nursery.

SECTION X

OF MIRACLES

Part I

THERE is, in Dr. Tillotson's writings, an argument against the *real presence,* which is as concise, and elegant, and strong as any argument can possibly be supposed against a doctrine, so little worthy of a serious refutation. It is acknowledged on all hands, says that learned prelate, that the authority, either of the scripture or of tradition, is founded

5. The circumstance, on which the effect depends, is frequently involved in other circumstances, which are foreign and extrinsic. The separation of it often requires great attention, accuracy, and subtlety.

6. The forming of general maxims from particular observation is a very nice operation; and nothing is more usual, from haste or narrowness of mind which sees not on all sides, than to commit mistakes in this particular.

7. When we reason from analogies, the man, who has the greater experience or the greater promptitude of suggesting analogies, will be the better reasoner.

8. Biases from prejudice, education, passion, party, etc., hang more upon one mind than another.

9. After we have acquired a confidence in human testimony, books and conversation enlarge much more the sphere of one man's experience and thought than those of another.

It would be easy to discover many other circumstances that make a difference in the understandings of men.

merely in the testimony of the apostles, who were eye-witnesses to those miracles of our Saviour, by which he proved his divine mission. Our evidence, then, for the truth of the *Christian* religion is less than the evidence for the truth of our senses; because, even in the first authors of our religion, it was no greater; and it is evident it must diminish in passing from them to their disciples; nor can anyone rest such confidence in their testimony, as in the immediate object of his senses. But a weaker evidence can never destroy a stronger; and therefore, were the doctrine of the real presence ever so clearly revealed in scripture, it were directly contrary to the rules of just reasoning to give our assent to it. It contradicts sense, though both the scripture and tradition, on which it is supposed to be built, carry not such evidence with them as sense; when they are considered merely as external evidences, and are not brought home to everyone's breast, by the immediate operation of the Holy Spirit.

Nothing is so convenient as a decisive argument of this kind, which must at least *silence* the most arrogant bigotry and superstition, and free us from their impertinent solicitations. I flatter myself, that I have discovered an argument of a like nature, which, if just, will, with the wise and learned, be an everlasting check to all kinds of superstitious delusion, and consequently, will be useful as long as the world endures. For so long, I presume, will the accounts of miracles and prodigies be found in all history, sacred and profane.

Though experience be our only guide in reasoning concerning matters of fact; it must be acknowledged, that this guide is not altogether infallible, but in some cases is apt to lead us into errors. One, who in our climate, should expect better weather in any week of June than in one of December, would reason justly, and comformably to experience; but it is certain, that he may happen, in the event, to find himself mistaken. However, we may observe, that, in such a case, he would have no cause to complain of experience; because it commonly informs us beforehand of the uncertainty, by that contrariety of events, which we may learn from a diligent observation. All effects follow not with like certainty from their supposed causes. Some events are found, in all countries and all ages, to have been constantly conjoined together. Others are found to have been more variable, and sometimes to disappoint our expectations; so that, in our reasonings concerning matter of fact, there are all imaginable degrees of assurance, from the highest certainty to the lowest species of moral evidence.

A wise man, therefore, proportions his belief to the evidence. In such conclusions as are founded on an infallible experience, he expects the event with the last degree of assurance, and regards his past experience as a full *proof* of the future existence of that event. In other cases, he proceeds with more caution; he weighs the opposite experiments; he considers which side is supported by the greater number of experiments; to that side he inclines, with doubt and hesitation; and when at last he fixes his judgment, the evidence exceeds not what we properly call *probability*. All probability, then, supposes an opposition of experiments and observations, where the one side is found to overbalance the other, and to produce a degree of evidence, proportioned to the superiority. A hundred instances or experiments on one side, and fifty on another, afford a double expectation of any event; though a hundred uniform experiments, with only one that is contradictory, reasonably begets a pretty strong degree of assurance. In all cases, we must balance the opposite experiments, where they are opposite, and deduct the smaller number from the greater, in order to know the exact force of the superior evidence.

To apply these principles to a particular instance; we may observe, that there is no species of reasoning more common, more useful, and even necessary to human life, than that which is derived from the testimony of men, and the reports of eye-witnesses and spectators. This species of reasoning, perhaps, one may deny to be founded on the relation of cause and effect. I shall not dispute about a word. It will be sufficient to observe that our assurance in any argument of this kind is derived from no other principle than our observation of the veracity of human testimony, and of the usual conformity of facts to the reports of witnesses. It being a general maxim that no objects have any discoverable connection together, and that all the inferences, which we can draw from one to another, are founded merely on our experience of their constant and regular conjunction; it is evident, that we ought not to make an exception to this maxim in favor of human testimony, whose connection with any event seems, in itself, as little necessary as any other. Were not the memory tenacious to a certain degree; had not men commonly an inclination to truth and a principle of probity, were they not sensible to shame, when detected in a falsehood: were not these, I say, discovered by *experience* to be qualities, inherent in human nature, we should never repose the least confidence in human testimony. A man delirious, or noted for falsehood and villainy, has no manner of authority with us.

And as the evidence, derived from witnesses and human testimony, is founded on past experience, so it varies with the experience, and is regarded either as *proof* or a *probability*, according as the conjunction between any particular kind of report and any kind of object has been found to be constant or variable. There are a number of circumstances to be taken into consideration in all judgments of this kind; and the ultimate standard, by which we determine all disputes, that may arise concerning them, is always derived from experience and observation.

Where this experience is not entirely uniform on any side, it is attended with an unavoidable contrariety in our judgments, and with the same opposition and mutual destruction of argument as in every other kind of evidence. We frequently hesitate concerning the reports of others. We balance the opposite circumstances, which cause any doubt or uncertainty; and when we discover a superiority on one side, we incline to it; but still with a diminution of assurance, in proportion to the force of its antagonist.

This contrariety of evidence, in the present case, may be derived from several different causes; from the opposition of contrary testimony; from the character or number of the witnesses; from the manner of their delivering their testimony; or from the union of all these circumstances. We entertain a suspicion concerning any matter of fact, when the witnesses contradict each other; when they are but few, or of a doubtful character; when they have an interest in what they affirm; when they deliver their testimony with hesitation, or on the contrary, with too violent asseverations. There are many other particulars of the same kind, which may diminish or destroy the force of any argument, derived from human testimony.

Suppose, for instance, that the fact, which the testimony endeavors to establish, partakes of the extraordinary and marvellous; in that case, the evidence, resulting from the testimony, admits of a diminution, greater or less, in proportion as the fact is more or less unusual. The reason why we place any credit in witnesses and historians, is not derived from any *connection*, which we perceive *a priori*, between testimony and reality, but because we are accustomed to find a conformity between them. But when the fact attested is such a one as has seldom fallen under our observation, here is a contest of two opposite experiences; of which the one destroys the other, as far as its force goes, and the superior can only operate on the mind by the force, which remains. The very same principle of experience, which gives us a certain degree of assurance in the testimony of witnesses, gives us also, in this case, another degree of assurance against the fact, which they endeavor to establish; from which contradiction there necessarily arises a counterpoise, and mutual destruction of belief and authority.

I should not believe such a story were it told me by Cato, was a proverbial saying in Rome, even during the lifetime of that philosophical patriot.[19] The incredibility of a fact, it was allowed, might invalidate so great an authority.

The Indian prince, who refused to believe the first relations concerning the effects of frost, reasoned justly; and it naturally required very strong testimony to engage his assent to fact, that arose from a state of

[19] Plutarch, in *Vita Catonis.*

nature, with which he was unacquainted, and which bore so little analogy to those events, of which he had had constant and uniform experience. Though they were not contrary to his experience, they were not conformable to it.[20]

But in order to increase the probability against the testimony of witnesses, let us suppose, that the fact, which they affirm, instead of being only marvellous, is really miraculous; and suppose also, that the testimony considered apart and in itself, amounts to an entire proof; in that case, there is proof against proof, of which the strongest must prevail, but still with a diminution of its force, in proportion to that of its antagonist.

A miracle is a violation of the laws of nature; and as a firm and unalterable experience has established these laws, the proof against a miracle, from the very nature of the fact, is as entire as any argument from experience can possibly be imagined. Why is it more than probable, that all men must die; that lead cannot, of itself, remain suspended in the air; that fire consumes wood, and is extinguished by water; unless it be, that these events are found agreeable to the laws of nature, and there is required a violation of these laws, or in other words, a miracle to prevent them? Nothing is esteemed a miracle, if it ever happen in the common course of nature. It is no miracle that a man, seemingly in good health, should die on a sudden: because such a kind of death, though more unusual than any other, has yet been frequently observed to happen. But it is a miracle, that a dead man should come to life; because that has never been observed in any age or country. There must, therefore, be a uniform experience against every miraculous event, otherwise the event would not merit that appellation. And as a uniform experience amounts to a proof, there is here a direct and

[20] No Indian, it is evident, could have experience that water did not freeze in cold climates. This is placing nature in a situation quite unknown to him; and it is impossible for him to tell *a priori* what will result from it. It is making a new experiment, the consequence of which is always uncertain. One may sometimes conjecture from analogy what will follow; but still this is but conjecture. And it must be confessed, that, in the present case of freezing, the event follows contrary to the rules of analogy, and is such as a rational Indian would not look for. The operations of cold upon water are not gradual, according to the degrees of cold; but whenever it comes to the freezing point, the water passes in a moment, from the utmost liquidity to perfect hardness. Such an event, therefore, may be denominated *extraordinary,* and requires a pretty strong testimony, to render it credible to people in a warm climate: But still it is not *miraculous,* nor contrary to uniform experience of the course of nature in cases where all the circumstances are the same. The inhabitants of Sumatra have always seen water fluid in their own climate, and the freezing of their rivers ought to be deemed a prodigy; but they never saw water in Muscovy during the winter: and therefore they cannot reasonably be positive what would there be the consequence.

full *proof,* from the nature of the fact, against the existence of any miracle; nor can such a proof be destroyed, or the miracle rendered credible, but by an opposite proof, which is superior.[21]

The plain consequence is (and it is a general maxim worthy of our attention), 'That no testimony is sufficient to establish a miracle, unless the testimony be of such a kind, that its falsehood would be more miraculous, than the fact, which it endeavors to establish; and even in that case there is a mutual destruction of arguments, and the superior only gives us an assurance suitable to that degree of force, which remains, after deducting the inferior.' When anyone tells me, that he saw a dead man restored to life, I immediately consider with myself, whether it be more probable, that this person should either deceive or be deceived, or that the fact, which he relates, should really have happened. I weigh the one miracle against the other; and according to the superiority, which I discover, I pronounce my decision, and always reject the greater miracle. If the falsehood of his testimony would be more miraculous, than the event which he relates; then, and not till then, can he pretend to command my belief or opinion.

Part II

In the foregoing reasoning we have supposed, that the testimony, upon which a miracle is founded, may possibly amount to an entire proof, and that the falsehood of that testimony would be a real prodigy. But it is easy to show, that we have been a great deal too liberal in our concession, and that there never was a miraculous event established on so full an evidence.

For *first,* there is not to be found, in all history, any miracle attested

---

[21] Sometimes an event may not, *in itself, seem* to be contrary to the laws of nature, and yet, if it were real, it might, by reason of some circumstances, be denominated a miracle; because, *in fact,* it is contrary to these laws. Thus if a person, claiming a divine authority, should command a sick person to be well, a healthful man to fall down dead, the clouds to pour rain, the winds to blow, in short, should order many natural events, which immediately follow upon his command; these might justly be esteemed miracles, because they are really, in this case, contrary to the laws of nature. For if any suspicion remain, that the event and command concurred by accident, there is no miracle and no transgression of the laws of nature. If this suspicion be removed, there is evidently a miracle, and a transgression of these laws; because nothing can be more contrary to nature than that the voice or command of a man should have such an influence. A miracle may be accurately defined, *a transgression of a law of nature by a particular volition of the Deity, or by the interposition of some invisible agent.* A miracle may either be discoverable by men or not. This alters not its nature and essence. The raising of a house or ship into the air is a visible miracle. The raising of a feather, when the wind wants ever so little of a force requisite for that purpose, is as real a miracle, though not so sensible with regard to us.

by a sufficient number of men, of such unquestioned good sense, education, and learning, as to secure us against all delusion in themselves; of
such undoubted integrity, as to place them beyond all suspicion of any
design to deceive others; of such credit and reputation in the eyes of
mankind, as to have a great deal to lose in case of their being detected
in any falsehood; and at the same time, attesting facts performed in
such a public manner and in so celebrated a part of the world, as to render the detection unavoidable: all which circumstances are requisite to
give us a full assurance in the testimony of men.

Secondly. We may observe in human nature a principle which, if
strictly examined, will be found to diminish extremely the assurance,
which we might, from human testimony, have, in any kind of prodigy.
The maxim, by which we commonly conduct ourselves in our reasonings,
is, that the objects, of which we have no experience, resemble those, of
which we have; that what we have found to be most usual is always
most probable; and that where there is an opposition of arguments, we
ought to give the preference to such as are founded on the greatest number of past observations. But though, in proceeding by this rule, we
readily reject any fact which is unusual and incredible in an ordinary
degree; yet in advancing farther, the mind observes not always the same
rule; but when anything is affirmed utterly absurd and miraculous, it
rather the more readily admits of such a fact, upon account of that very
circumstance, which ought to destroy all its authority. The passion of
surprise and *wonder,* arising from miracles, being an agreeable emotion,
gives a sensible tendency towards the belief of those events, from which
it is derived. And this goes so far, that even those who cannot enjoy this
pleasure immediately, nor can believe those miraculous events, of which
they are informed, yet love to partake of the satisfaction at second hand
or by rebound, and place a pride and delight in exciting the admiration
of others.

With what greediness are the miraculous accounts of travelers received; their descriptions of sea and land monsters, their relations of
wonderful adventures, strange men, and uncouth manners? But if the
spirit of religion join itself to the love of wonder, there is an end of common sense; and human testimony, in these circumstances, loses all pretensions to authority. A religionist may be an enthusiast, and imagine he
sees what has no reality: he may know his narrative to be false, and yet
persevere in it, with the best intentions in the world, for the sake of promoting so holy a cause: or even where this delusion has not place, vanity, excited by so strong a temptation, operates on him more powerfully
than on the rest of mankind in any other circumstances; and self-interest with equal force. His auditors may not have, and commonly have
not, sufficient judgment to canvass his evidence: what judgment they

have, they renounce by principle, in these sublime and mysterious subjects: or if they were ever so willing to employ it, passion and a heated imagination disturb the regularity of its operations. Their credulity increases his impudence: and his impudence overpowers their credulity.

Eloquence, when at its highest pitch, leaves little room for reason or reflection; but addressing itself entirely to the fancy or the affections, captivates the willing hearers, and subdues their understanding. Happily, this pitch it seldom attains. But what a Tully or a Demosthenes could scarcely effect over a Roman or Athenian audience, every *Capuchin*, every itinerant or stationary teacher can perform over the generality of mankind, and in a higher degree, by touching such gross and vulgar passions.

The many instances of forged miracles, and prophecies, and supernatural events, which, in all ages, have either been detected by contrary evidence, or which detect themselves by their absurdity, prove sufficiently the strong propensity of mankind to the extraordinary and the marvellous, and ought reasonably to beget a suspicion against all relations of this kind. This is our natural way of thinking, even with regard to the most common and most credible events. For instance: there is no kind of report which rises so easily, and spreads so quickly, especially in country places and provincial towns, as those concerning marriages; insomuch that two young persons of equal condition never see each other twice, but the whole neighborhood immediately join them together. The pleasure of telling a piece of news so interesting, of propagating it, and of being the first reporters of it, spreads the intelligence. And this is so well known, that no man of sense gives attention to these reports, till he find them confirmed by some greater evidence. Do not the same passions, and others still stronger, incline the generality of mankind to believe and report, with the greatest vehemence and assurance, all religious miracles?

Thirdly. It forms a strong presumption against all supernatural and miraculous relations, that they are observed chiefly to abound among ignorant and barbarous nations; or if a civilised people has ever given admission to any of them, that people will be found to have received them from ignorant and barbarous ancestors, who transmitted them with that inviolable sanction and authority, which always attend received opinions. When we peruse the first histories of all nations, we are apt to imagine ourselves transported into some new world; where the whole frame of nature is disjointed, and every element performs its operations in a different manner, from what it does at present. Battles, revolutions, pestilence, famine and death, are never the effect of those natural causes, which we experience. Prodigies, omens, oracles, judgments, quite obscure the few natural events, that are intermingled with them. But as

the former grow thinner every page, in proportion as we advance nearer
the enlightened ages, we soon learn, that there is nothing mysterious or
supernatural in the case, but that all proceeds from the usual propensity
of mankind towards the marvellous, and that, though this inclination
may at intervals receive a check from sense and learning, it can never
be thoroughly extirpated from human nature.

It is strange, a judicious reader is apt to say, upon the perusal of
these wonderful historians, *that such prodigious events never happen
in our days.* But it is nothing strange, I hope, that men should lie in
all ages. You must surely have seen instances enough of that frailty. You
have yourself heard many such marvellous relations started, which, being treated with scorn by all the wise and judicious, have at last been
abandoned even by the vulgar. Be assured, that those renowned lies,
which have spread and flourished to such a monstrous height, arose from
like beginnings; but being sown in a more proper soil, shot up at last
into prodigies almost equal to those which they relate.

It was a wise policy in that false prophet, Alexander, who though now
forgotten, was once so famous, to lay the first scene of his impostures
in Paphlagonia, where, as Lucian tells us, the people were extremely ignorant and stupid, and ready to swallow even the grossest delusion. People at a distance, who are weak enough to think the matter at all worth
inquiry, have no opportunity of receiving better information. The stories
come magnified to them by a hundred circumstances. Fools are industrious in propagating the imposture; while the wise and learned are contented, in general, to deride its absurdity, without informing themselves
of the particular facts, by which it may be distinctly refuted. And thus
the impostor above mentioned was enabled to proceed, from his ignorant
Paphlagonians, to the enlisting of votaries, even among the Grecian philosophers, and men of the most eminent rank and distinction in Rome;
nay, could engage the attention of that sage emperor Marcus Aurelius,
so far as to make him trust the success of a military expedition to his
delusive prophecies.

The advantages are so great, of starting an imposture among an ignorant people, that, even though the delusion should be too gross to impose
on the generality of them (*which, though seldom, is sometimes the case*)
it has a much better chance for succeeding in remote countries, than if
the first scene had been laid in a city renowned for arts and knowledge.
The most ignorant and barbarous of these barbarians carry the report
abroad. None of their countrymen have a large correspondence, or sufficient credit and authority to contradict and beat down the delusion.
Men's inclination to the marvellous has full opportunity to display itself.
And thus a story, which is universally exploded in the place where it
was first started, shall pass for certain at a thousand miles distance.

But had Alexander fixed his residence at Athens, the philosophers of that renowned mart of learning had immediately spread, throughout the whole Roman empire, their sense of the matter; which, being supported by so great authority, and displayed by all the force of reason and eloquence, had entirely opened the eyes of mankind. It is true; Lucian, passing by chance through Paphlagonia, had an opportunity of performing this good office. But, though much to be wished, it does not always happen that every Alexander meets with a Lucian, ready to expose and detect his impostures.

I may add as a *fourth* reason, which diminishes the authority of prodigies, that there is no testimony for any, even those which have not been expressly detected, that is not opposed by an infinite number of witnesses; so that not only the miracle destroys the credit of testimony, but the testimony destroys itself. To make this the better understood, let us consider, that, in matters of religion, whatever is different is contrary; and that it is impossible the relegions of ancient Rome, of Turkey, of Siam, and of China should, all of them, be established on any solid foundation. Every miracle, therefore, pretended to have been wrought in any of these religions (and all of them abound in miracles), as its direct scope is to establish the particular system to which it is attributed; so has it the same force, though more indirectly, to overthrow every other system. In destroying a rival system, it likewise destroys the credit of those miracles, on which that system was established; so that all the prodigies of different religions are to be regarded as contrary facts, and the evidences of these prodigies, whether weak or strong, as opposite to each other. According to this method of reasoning, when we believe any miracle of Mahomet or his successors, we have for our warrant the testimony of a few barbarous Arabians. And on the other hand, we are to regard the authority of Titus Livius, Plutarch, Tacitus, and, in short, of all the authors and witnesses, Grecian, Chinese, and Roman Catholic, who have related any miracle in their particular religion; I say, we are to regard their testimony in the same light as if they had mentioned that Mohammedan miracle, and had in express terms contradicted it, with the same certainty as they have for the miracle they relate. This argument may appear over subtle and refined; but is not in reality different from the reasoning of a judge, who supposes, that the credit of two witnesses, maintaining a crime against anyone, is destroyed by the testimony of two others, who affirm him to have been two hundred leagues distant, at the same instant when the crime is said to have been committed.

One of the best attested miracles in all profane history, is that which Tacitus reports of Vespasian, who cured a blind man in Alexandria, by means of his spittle, and a lame man by the mere touch of his foot; in obedience to a vision of the god Serapis, who had enjoined them to have recourse to the Emperor, for these miraculous cures. The story may be seen in that fine historian;[22] where every circumstance seems to add weight to the testimony, and might be displayed at large with all the force of argument and eloquence, if anyone were now concerned to enforce the evidence of that exploded and idolatrous superstition. The gravity, solidity, age, and probity of so great an emperor, who, through the whole course of his life, conversed in a familiar manner with his friends and courtiers, and never affected those extraordinary airs of divinity assumed by Alexander and Demetrius. The historian, a contemporary writer, noted for candor and veracity, and withal, the greatest and most penetrating genius, perhaps, of all antiquity; and so free from any tendency to credulity, that he even lies under the contrary imputation, of atheism and profaneness; the persons, from whose authority he related the miracle, of established character for judgment and veracity, as we may well presume; eye-witnesses of the fact, and confirming their testimony, after the Flavian family was despoiled of the empire, and could no longer give any reward, as the price of a lie. *Utrumque, qui interfuere, nunc quoque memorant, postquam nullum mendacio pretium.* To which if we add the public nature of the facts, as related, it will appear, that no evidence can well be supposed stronger for so gross and so palpable a falsehood.

There is also a memorable story related by Cardinal de Retz, which may well deserve our consideration. When that intriguing politician fled into Spain, to avoid the persecution of his enemies, he passed through Saragossa, the capital of Aragon, where he was shown, in the cathedral, a man, who had served seven years as a doorkeeper, and was well known to everybody in town, that had ever paid his devotions at that church. He had been seen, for so long a time, wanting a leg; but recovered that limb by the rubbing of holy oil upon the stump; and the cardinal assures us that he saw him with two legs. This miracle was vouched by all the canons of the church; and the whole company in town were appealed to for a confirmation of the fact; whom the cardinal found, by their zealous devotion, to be thorough believers of the miracle. Here the relater was also contemporary to the supposed prodigy, of an incredulous and libertine character, as well as of great genius; the miracle of so *singular* a nature as could scarcely admit of a counterfeit, and the witnesses very numerous, and all of them, in a manner, spectators of the fact, to which they gave their testimony. And what adds mightily to the force of the evidence, and may double our surprise on this occasion, is, that the cardinal himself, who relates the story, seems not to give any

---

[22] Hist. lib. v. cap. 8. Suetonius gives nearly the same account *in vita* Vesp.

credit to it, and consequently cannot be suspected of any concurrence in the holy fraud. He considered justly, that it was not requisite, in order to reject a fact of this nature, to be able accurately to disprove the testimony, and to trace its falsehood, through all the circumstances of knavery and credulity which produced it. He knew, that, as this was commonly altogether impossible at any small distance of time and place; so was it extremely difficult, even where one was immediately present, by reason of the bigotry, ignorance, cunning, and roguery of a great part of mankind. He therefore concluded, like a just reasoner, that such an evidence carried falsehood upon the very face of it, and that a miracle, supported by any human testimony, was more properly a subject of derision than of argument.

There surely never was a greater number of miracles ascribed to one person, than those, which were lately said to have been wrought in France upon the tomb of Abbé Paris, the famous Jansenist, with whose sanctity the people were so long deluded. The curing of the sick, giving hearing to the deaf, and sight to the blind, were everywhere talked of as the usual effects of that holy sepulchre. But what is more extraordinary: many of the miracles were immediately proved upon the spot, before judges of unquestioned integrity, attested by witnesses of credit and distinction, in a learned age, and on the most eminent theater that is now in the world. Nor is this all: a relation of them was published and dispersed everywhere; nor were the *Jesuits,* though a learned body, supported by the civil magistrate, and determined enemies to those opinions, in whose favor the miracles were said to have been wrought, ever able distinctly to refute or detect them. Where shall we find such a number of circumstances, agreeing to the corroboration of one fact? And what have we to oppose to such a cloud of witnesses, but the absolute impossibility or miraculous nature of the events, which they relate? And this surely, in the eyes of all reasonable people, will alone be regarded as a sufficient refutation.

Is the consequence just, because some human testimony has the utmost force and authority in some cases, when it relates the battle of Philippi or Pharsalia for instance; that therefore all kinds of testimony must, in all cases, have equal force and authority? Suppose that the Caesarean and Pompeian factions had, each of them, claimed the victory in these battles, and that the historians of each party had uniformly ascribed the advantage to their own side; how could mankind, at this distance, have been able to determine between them? The contrariety is equally strong between the miracles related by Herodotus or Plutarch, and those delivered by Mariana, Bede, or any monkish historian.

The wise lend a very academic faith to every report which favors the passion of the reporter; whether it magnifies his country, his family, or himself, or in any other way strikes in with his natural inclinations and propensities. But what greater temptation than to appear a missionary, a prophet, an ambassador from heaven? Who would not encounter many dangers and difficulties, in order to attain so sublime a character? Or if, by the help of vanity and a heated imagination, a man has first made a convert of himself, and entered seriously into the delusion; whoever scruples to make use of pious frauds, in support of so holy and meritorious a cause?

The smallest spark may here kindle into the greatest flame; because the materials are always prepared for it. The *avidum genus auricularum*, the gazing populace, receive greedily, without examination, whatever soothes superstition, and promotes wonder.

How many stories of this nature have, in all ages, been detected and exploded in their infancy? How many more have been celebrated for a time, and have afterwards sunk into neglect and oblivion? Where such reports, therefore, fly about, the solution of the phenomenon is obvious; and we judge in conformity to regular experience and observation, when we account for it by the known and natural principles of credulity and delusion. And shall we, rather than have a recourse to so natural a solution, allow of a miraculous violation of the most established laws of nature?

I need not mention the difficulty of detecting a falsehood in any private or even public history, at the place, where it is said to happen; much more when the scene is removed to ever so small a distance. Even a court of judicature, with all the authority, accuracy, and judgment, which they can employ, find themselves often at a loss to distinguish between truth and falsehood in the most recent actions. But the matter never comes to any issue, if trusted to the common method of altercations and debate and flying rumors; especially when men's passions have taken part on either side.

In the infancy of new religions, the wise and learned commonly esteem the matter too inconsiderable to deserve their attention or regard. And when afterwards they would willingly detect the cheat, in order to undeceive the deluded multitude, the season is now past, and the records and witnesses, which might clear up the matter, have perished beyond recovery.

No means of detection remain, but those which must be drawn from the very testimony itself of the reporters: and these, though always sufficient with the judicious and knowing, are commonly too fine to fall under the comprehension of the vulgar.

Upon the whole, then, it appears, that no testimony for any kind of miracle has ever amounted to a probability, much less to a proof; and that, even supposing it amounted to a proof, it would be opposed by another proof; derived from the very nature of the fact, which it would endeavor to establish. It is experience only, which gives authority to human testimony; and it is the same experience, which assures us of the laws of nature. When, therefore, these two kinds of experience are contrary, we have nothing to do but substract the one from the other, and embrace an opinion, either on one side or the other, with that assurance which arises from the remainder. But according to the principle here explained, this substraction, with regard to all popular religions, amounts to an entire annihilation; and therefore we may establish it as a maxim, that no human testimony can have such force as to prove a miracle, and make it a just foundation for any such system of religion.

I beg the limitations here made may be remarked, when I say, that a miracle can never be proved, so as to be the foundation of a system of religion. For I own, that otherwise, there may possibly be miracles, or violations of the usual course of nature, of such a kind as to admit of proof from human testimony; though, perhaps, it will be impossible to find any such in all the records of history. Thus, suppose, all authors, in all languages, agree, that, from the first of January 1600, there was a total darkness over the whole earth for eight days: suppose that the tradition of this extraordinary event is still strong and lively among the people: that all travelers, who return from foreign countries, bring us accounts of the same tradition, without the least variation or contradiction: it is evident, that our present philosophers, instead of doubting the fact, ought to receive it as certain, and ought to search for the causes whence it might be derived. The decay, corruption, and dissolution of nature, is an event rendered probable by so many analogies, that any phenomenon, which seems to have a tendency towards that catastrophe, comes within the reach of human testimony, if that testimony be very extensive and uniform.

But suppose, that all the historians who treat of England, should agree, that, on the first of January 1600, Queen Elizabeth died; that both before and after her death she was seen by her physicians and the whole court, as is usual with persons of her rank; that her successor was acknowledged and proclaimed by the parliament; and that, after being interred a month, she again appeared, resumed the throne, and governed England for three years. I must confess that I should be surprised at the concurrence of so many odd circumstances, but should not have the least inclination to believe so miraculous an event. I should not doubt of her pretended death, and of those other public circumstances that followed it; I should only assert it to have been pretended, and that it neither was, nor possibly could be real. You would in vain object to me the difficulty, and almost impossibility of deceiving the world in an affair of such consequence; the wisdom and solid judgment of that renowned queen; with the little or no advantage which she could reap from so poor an artifice. All this might astonish me; but I would still reply, that the knavery and folly of men are such common phenomena, that I should rather believe the most extraordinary events to arise from their concurrence, than admit of so signal a violation of the laws of nature.

But should this miracle be ascribed to any new system of religion; men, in all ages, have been so much imposed on by ridiculous stories of that kind, that this very circumstance would be a full proof of a cheat, and sufficient, with all men of sense, not only to make them reject the fact, but even reject it without farther examination. Though the Being to whom the miracle is ascribed, be, in this case, Almighty, it does not, upon that account, become a whit more probable; since it is impossible for us to know the attributes or actions of such a Being, otherwise than from the experience which we have of his productions, in the usual course of nature. This still reduces us to past observation, and obliges us to compare the instances of the violation of truth in the testimony of men, with those of the violation of the laws of nature by miracles, in order to judge which of them is most likely and probable. As the violations of truth are more common in the testimony concerning religious miracles, than in that concerning any other matter of fact; this must diminish very much the authority of the former testimony, and make us form a general resolution, never to lend any attention to it, with whatever specious pretense it may be covered.

Lord Bacon seems to have embraced the same principles of reasoning. "We ought," says he, "to make a collection or particular history of all monsters and prodigious births or productions, and in a word of everything new, rare, and extraordinary in nature. But this must be done with the most severe scrutiny, lest we depart from truth. Above all, every relation must be considered as suspicious, which depends in any degree upon religion, as the prodigies of Livy. And no less so, everything that is to be found in the writers of natural magic or alchemy, or such authors, who seem, all of them, to have an unconquerable appetite for falsehood and fable." [23]

I am the better pleased with the method of reasoning here delivered, as I think it may serve to confound those dangerous friends or disguised enemies to the *Christian Religion,* who have undertaken to defend it by the principles of human reason. Our most holy religion is founded on *faith,* not on reason; and it is a sure method of exposing it to put it to such a trial as it is, by no means, fitted to endure. To make this more evident, let us examine those miracles, related in scripture; and not to lose ourselves in too wide a field, let us confine ourselves to such as we

[23] Nov. Org. lib. ii. aph. 29.

find in the *Pentateuch,* which we shall examine, according to the principles of these pretended Christians, not as the word or testimony of God himself, but as the production of a mere human writer and historian. Here then we are first to consider a book, presented to us by a barbarous and ignorant people, written in an age when they were still more barbarous, and in all probability long after the facts which it relates, corroborated by no concurring testimony, and resembling those fabulous accounts, which every nation gives of its origin. Upon reading this book, we find it full of prodigies and miracles. It gives an account of a state of the world and of human nature entirely different from the present: of our fall from that state; of the age of man, extended to near a thousand years; of the destruction of the world by a deluge; of the arbitrary choice of one people, as the favorites of heaven; and that people the countrymen of the author; of their deliverance from bondage by prodigies the most astonishing imaginable. I desire anyone to lay his hand upon his heart, and after a serious consideration declare, whether he thinks that the falsehood of such a book, supported by such a testimony, would be more extraordinary and miraculous than all the miracles it relates; which is, however, necessary to make it be received, according to the measures of probability above established.

What we have said of miracles may be applied, without any variation, to prophecies; and indeed, all prophecies are real miracles, and as such only, can be admitted as proofs of any revelation. If it did not exceed the capacity of human nature to foretell future events, it would be absurd to employ any prophecy as an argument for a divine mission or authority from heaven. So that, upon the whole, we may conclude, that the *Christian Religion* not only was at first attended with miracles, but even at this day cannot be believed by any reasonable person without one. Mere reason is insufficient to convince us of its veracity: and whoever is moved by *faith* to assent to it, is conscious of a continued miracle in his own person, which subverts all the principles of his understanding, and gives him a determination to believe what is most contrary to custom and experience.

SECTION XI

OF A PARTICULAR PROVIDENCE AND OF A FUTURE STATE

I was lately engaged in conversation with a friend who loves sceptical paradoxes; where, though he advanced many principles, of which I can by no means approve, yet as they seem to be curious, and to bear some relation to the chain of reasoning carried on throughout this inquiry, I

shall here copy them from my memory as accurately as I can, in order
to submit them to the judgment of the reader.

Our conversation began with my admiring the singular good fortune
of philosophy, which, as it requires entire liberty above all other privileges, and chiefly flourishes from the free opposition of sentiments and
argumentation, received its first birth in an age and country of freedom
and toleration, and was never cramped, even in its most extravagant
principles, by any creeds, concessions, or penal statutes. For, except the
banishment of Protagoras, and the death of Socrates, which last event
proceeded partly from other motives, there are scarcely any instances to
be met with, in ancient history, of this bigoted jealousy, with which the
present age is so much infested. Epicurus lived at Athens to an advanced age, in peace and tranquillity; Epicureans were even admitted to
receive the sacerdotal character, and to officiate at the altar, in the most
sacred rites of the established religion. And the public encouragement of
'pensions and salaries was afforded equally, by the wisest of all the Roman emperors, to the professors of every sect of philosophy. How requisite such kind of treatment was to philosophy, in her early youth, will
easily be conceived, if we reflect, that, even at present, when she may
be supposed more hardy and robust, she bears with much difficulty the
inclemency of the seasons, and those harsh winds of calumny and persecution, which blow upon her.

You admire, says my friend, as the singular good fortune of philosophy, what seems to result from the natural course of things, and to be
unavoidable in every age and nation. This pertinacious bigotry, of which
you complain, as so fatal to philosophy, is really her offspring, who, after
allying with superstition, separates himself entirely from the interest of
his parent, and becomes her most inveterate enemy and persecutor.
Speculative dogmas of religion, the present occasions of such furious dispute, could not possibly be conceived or admitted in the early ages of
the world; when mankind, being wholly illiterate, formed an idea
of religion more suitable to their weak apprehension, and composed there
sacred tenets of such tales chiefly as were the objects of traditional belief, more than of argument or disputation. After the first alarm, therefore, was over, which arose from the new paradoxes and principles of
the philosophers; these teachers seem ever after, during the ages of antiquity, to have lived in great harmony with the established superstition,
and to have made a fair partition of mankind between them; the former
claiming all the learned and wise, the latter possessing all the vulgar and
illiterate.

It seems then, say I, that you leave politics entirely out of the question, and never suppose, that a wise magistrate can justly be jealous of
certain tenets of philosophy, such as those of Epicurus, which, denying a

divine existence, and consequently a providence and a future state, seem to loosen, in a great measure, the ties of morality, and may be supposed, for that reason, pernicious to the peace of civil society.

I know, replied he, that in fact these persecutions never, in any age, proceeded from calm reason, or from experience of the pernicious consequences of philosophy; but arose entirely from passion and prejudice. But what if I should advance farther, and assert, that if Epicurus had been accused before the people, by any of the *sycophants* or informers of those days, he could easily have defended his cause, and proved his principles of philosophy to be as salutary as those of his adversaries, who endeavored, with such zeal, to expose him to the public hatred and jealousy?

I wish, said I, you would try your eloquence upon so extraordinary a topic, and make a speech for Epicurus, which might satisfy, not the mob of Athens, if you will allow that ancient and polite city to have contained any mob, but the more philosophical part of his audience, such as might be supposed capable of comprehending his arguments.

The matter would not be difficult, upon such conditions, replied he. And if you please, I shall suppose myself Epicurus for a moment, and make you stand for the Athenian people, and shall deliver you such an harangue as will fill all the urn with white beans, and leave not a black one to gratify the malice of my adversaries.

Very well: pray proceed upon these suppositions.

I come hither, O ye Athenians, to justify in your assembly what I maintained in my school, and I find myself impeached by furious antagonists, instead of reasoning with calm and dispassionate inquirers. Your deliberations, which of right should be directed to questions of public good, and the interest of the commonwealth, are diverted to the disquisitions of speculative philosophy; and these magnificent, but perhaps fruitless inquiries, take place of your more familiar but more useful occupations. But so far as in me lies, I will prevent this abuse. We shall not here dispute concerning the origin and government of worlds. We shall only inquire how far such questions concern the public interest. And if I can persuade you, that they are entirely indifferent to the peace of society and security of government, I hope that you will presently send us back to our schools, there to examine, at leisure, the question the most sublime, but at the same time, the most speculative of all philosophy.

The religious philosophers, not satisfied with the tradition of your forefathers, and doctrine of your priests (in which I willingly acquiesce), indulge a rash curiosity, in trying how far they can establish religion upon the principles of reason; and they thereby excite, instead of satisfying, the doubts, which naturally arise from a diligent and scrutinous inquiry. They paint, in the most magnificent colors, the order, beauty, and wise arrangement of the universe; and then ask, if such a glorious display of intelligence could proceed from the fortuitous concourse of atoms, or if chance could produce what the greatest genius can never sufficiently admire. I shall not examine the justness of this argument. I shall allow it to be as solid as my antagonists and accusers can desire. It is sufficient, if I can prove, from this very reasoning, that the question is entirely speculative, and that, when, in my philosophical disquisitions, I deny a providence and a future state, I undermine not the foundations of society, but advance principles, which they themselves, upon their own topics, if they argue consistently, must allow to be solid and satisfactory.

You then, who are my accusers, have acknowledged, that the chief or sole argument for a divine existence (which I never questioned) is derived from the order of nature; where there appear such marks of intelligence and design, that you think it extravagant to assign for its cause, either chance, or the blind and unguided force of matter. You allow, that this is an argument drawn from effects to causes. From the order of the work, you infer, that there must have been project and forethought in the workman. If you cannot make out this point, you allow, that your conclusion fails; and you pretend not to establish the conclusion in a greater latitude than the phenomena of nature will justify. These are your concessions. I desire you to mark the consequences.

When we infer any particular cause from an effect, we must proportion the one to the other, and can never be allowed to ascribe to the cause any qualities, but what are exactly sufficient to produce the effect. A body of ten ounces raised in any scale may serve as a proof, that the counterbalancing weight exceeds ten ounces; but can never afford a reason that it exceeds a hundred. If the cause, assigned for any effect, be not sufficient to produce it, we must either reject that cause, or add to it such qualities as will give it a just proportion to the effect. But if we ascribe to it further qualities, or affirm it capable of producing other effects, we can only indulge the license of conjecture, and arbitrarily suppose the existence of qualities and energies, without reason or authority.

The same rule holds, whether the cause assigned be brute unconscious matter, or a rational intelligent being. If the cause be known only by the effect, we never ought to ascribe to it any qualities, beyond what are precisely requisite to produce the effect; nor can we, by any rules of just reasoning, return back from the cause, and infer other effects from it, beyond those by which alone it is known to us. No one, merely from the sight of one of Zeuxis's pictures, could know, that he was also a statuary or architect, and was an artist no less skillful in stone and marble than in colors. The talents and taste, displayed in the particular work before us; these we may safely conclude the workman to be possessed of. The cause must be proportioned to the effect; and if we exactly and precisely proportion it, we shall never find in it any qualities, that point farther, or afford an inference concerning any other design or performance. Such qualities must be somewhat beyond what is merely requisite for producing the effect, which we examine.

Allowing, therefore, the gods to be the authors of the existence or order of the universe; it follows, that they possess that precise degree of power, intelligence, and benevolence, which appears in their workmanship; but nothing farther can ever be proved, except we call in the assistance of exaggeration and flattery to supply the defects of argument and reasoning. So far as the traces of any attributes, at present, appear, so far may we conclude these attributes to exist. The supposition of farther attributes is mere hypothesis; much more the supposition, that, in distant regions of space or periods of time, there has been, or will be, a more magnificent display of these attributes, and a scheme of administration more suitable to such imaginary virtues. We can never be allowed to mount up from the universe, the effect, to Jupiter, the cause; and then descend downwards, to infer any new effect from that cause; as if the present effects alone were not entirely worthy of the glorious attributes, which we ascribe to that deity. The knowledge of the cause being derived solely from the effect, they must be exactly adjusted to each other; and the one can never refer to anything farther, or be the foundation of any new inference and conclusion.

You find certain phenomena in nature. You seek a cause or author. You imagine that you have found him. You afterwards become so enamored of this offspring of your brain, that you imagine it impossible, but he must produce something greater and more perfect than the present scene of things, which is so full of ill and disorder. You forget, that this superlative intelligence and benevolence are entirely imaginary, or, at least, without any foundation in reason; and that you have no ground to ascribe to him any qualities, but what you see he has actually exerted and displayed in his productions. Let your gods, therefore, O philosophers, be suited to the present appearances of nature: and presume not to alter these appearances by arbitrary suppositions, in order to suit them to the attributes, which you so fondly ascribe to your deities.

When priests and poets, supported by your authority, O Athenians, talk of a golden or silver age, which preceded the present state of vice and misery, I hear them with attention and with reverence. But when philosophers, who pretend to neglect authority, and to cultivate reason, hold the same discourse, I pay them not, I own, the same obsequious submission and pious deference. I ask, who carried them into the celestial regions, who admitted them into the councils of the gods, who

opened to them the book of fate, that they thus rashly affirm, that their
deities have executed, or will execute, any purpose beyond what has actually appeared? If they tell me, that they have mounted on the steps
or by the gradual ascent of reason, and by drawing inferences from effects to causes, I still insist, that they have aided the ascent of reason
by the wings of imagination; otherwise they could not thus change their
manner of inference, and argue from causes to effects; presuming, that
a more perfect production than the present world would be more suitable to such perfect beings as the gods, and forgetting that they have no
reason to ascribe to these celestial beings any perfection or any attribute, but what can be found in the present world.

Hence all the fruitless industry to account for the ill appearances of
nature, and save the honor of the gods; while we must acknowledge the
reality of that evil and disorder, with which the world so much abounds.
The obstinate and intractable qualities of matter, we are told, or the observance of general laws, or some such reason, is the sole cause, which
controlled the power and benevolence of Jupiter, and obliged him to create mankind and every sensible creature so imperfect and so unhappy.
These attributes then, are, it seems, beforehand, taken for granted, in
their greatest latitude. And upon that supposition, I own that such conjectures may, perhaps, be admitted as plausible solutions of the ill phenomena. But still I ask, Why take these attributes for granted, or why
ascribe to the cause any qualities but what actually appear in the effect?
Why torture your brain to justify the course of nature upon suppositions,
which, for aught you know, may be entirely imaginary, and of which
there are to be found no traces in the course of nature?

The religious hypothesis, therefore, must be considered only as a particular method of accounting for the visible phenomena of the universe:
but no just reasoner will ever presume to infer from it any single fact,
and alter or add to the phenomena, in any single particular. If you
think, that the appearances of things prove such causes, it is allowable
for you to draw an inference concerning the existence of these causes. In
such complicated and sublime subjects, everyone should be indulged in
the liberty of conjecture and argument. But here you ought to rest. If
you come backward, and arguing from your inferred causes, conclude,
that any other fact has existed, or will exist, in the course of nature,
which may serve as a fuller display of particular attributes; I must admonish you, that you have departed from the method of reasoning, attached to the present subject, and have certainly added something to
the attributes of the cause, beyond what appears in the effect; otherwise
you could never, with tolerable sense or propriety, add anything to the
effect, in order to render it more worthy of the cause.

Where, then, is the odiousness of that doctrine, which I teach in my school, or rather, which I examine in my gardens? Or what do you find in this whole question, wherein the security of good morals, or the peace and order of society, is in the least concerned?

I deny a providence, you say, and supreme governor of the world, who guides the course of events, and punishes the vicious with infamy and disappointment, and rewards the virtuous with honor and success, in all their undertakings. But surely, I deny not the course itself of events, which lies open to everyone's inquiry and examination. I acknowledge, that, in the present order of things, virtue is attended with more peace of mind than vice, and meets with a more favorable reception from the world. I am sensible, that, according to the past experience of mankind, friendship is the chief joy of human life, and moderation the only source of tranquillity and happiness. I never balance between the virtuous and the vicious course of life; but am sensible, that, to a well-disposed mind, every advantage is on the side of the former. And what can you say more, allowing all your suppositions and reasonings? You tell me, indeed, that this disposition of things proceeds from intelligence and design. But whatever it proceeds from, the disposition itself, on which depends our happiness or misery, and consequently our conduct and deportment in life, is still the same. It is still open for me, as well as you, to regulate my behavior, by my experience of past events. And if you affirm, that, while a divine providence is allowed, and a supreme distributive justice in the universe, I ought to expect some more particular reward of the good, and punishment of the bad, beyond the ordinary course of events; I here find the same fallacy, which I have before endeavored to detect. You persist in imagining, that, if we grant that divine existence, for which you so earnestly contend, you may safely infer consequences from it, and add something to the experienced order of nature, by arguing from the attributes which you ascribe to your gods. You seem not to remember, that all your reasonings on this subject can only be drawn from effects to causes; and that every argument, deducted from causes to effects, must of necessity be a gross sophism; since it is impossible for you to know anything of the cause, but what you have antecedently, not inferred, but discovered to the full, in the effect.

But what must a philosopher think of those vain reasoners, who, instead of regarding the present scene of things as the sole object of their contemplation, so far reverse the whole course of nature, as to render this life merely a passage to something farther; a porch, which leads to a greater, and vastly different building; a prologue, which serves only to introduce the piece, and give it more grace and propriety? Whence, do you think, can such philosophers derive their idea of the gods? From their own conceit and imagination surely. For if they derived it from the present phenomena, it would never point to anything farther, **but** must be exactly adjusted to them. That the divinity may *possibly* be endowed with attributes, which we have never seen exerted; may be governed by principles of action, which we cannot discover to be satisfied: all this will freely be allowed. But still this is mere *possibility* and hypothesis. We never can have reason to *infer* any attributes, or any principles of action in him, but so far as we know them to have been exerted and satisfied.

Are there any marks of a distributive justice in the world? If you answer in the affirmative, I conclude, that, since justice here exerts itself, it is satisfied. If you reply in the negative, I conclude, that you have then no reason to ascribe justice, in our sense of it, to the gods. If you hold a medium between affirmation and negation, by saying, that the justice of the gods, at present, exerts itself in part, but not in its full extent; I answer, that you have no reason to give it any particular extent, but only so far as you see it, *at present,* exert itself.

Thus I bring the dispute, O Athenians, to a short issue with my antagonists. The course of nature lies open to my contemplation as well as to theirs. The experienced train of events is the great standard, by which we all regulate our conduct. Nothing else can be appealed to in the field, or in the senate. Nothing else ought ever to be heard of in the school, or in the closet. In vain would our limited understanding break through those boundaries, which are too narrow for our fond imagination. While we argue from the course of nature, and infer a particular intelligent cause, which first bestowed, and still preserves order in the universe, we embrace a principle, which is both uncertain and useless. It is uncertain; because the subject lies entirely beyond the reach of human experience. It is useless; because our knowledge of this cause being derived entirely from the course of nature, we can never, according to the rules of just reasoning, return back from the cause with any new inference, or making additions to the common and experienced course of nature, establish any new principles of conduct and behavior.

I observe (said I, finding he had finished his harangue) that you neglect not the artifice of the demagogues of old; and as you were pleased to make me stand for the people, you insinuate yourself into my favor by embracing those principles, to which, you know, I have always expressed a particular attachment. But allowing you to make experience (as indeed I think you ought) the only standard of our judgment concerning this, and all other questions of fact; I doubt not but, from the very same experience, to which you appeal, it may be possible to refute this reasoning, which you have put into the mouth of Epicurus. If you saw, for instance, a half-finished building, surrounded with heaps of brick and stone and mortar, and all the instruments of masonry; could you not *infer* from the effect, that it was a work of design and contrivance? And could you not return again, from this inferred cause, to infer new additions to the effect, and conclude, that the building would soon be finished, and receive all the further improvements, which art could bestow upon it? If you saw upon the seashore the print of one human foot, you would conclude, that a man had passed that way, and that he had also left the traces of the other foot, though effaced by the rolling of the sands or inundation of the waters. Why then do you refuse to admit the same method of reasoning with regard to the order of nature? Consider the world and the present life only as an imperfect building, from which you can infer a superior intelligence; and arguing from that superior intelligence, which can leave nothing imperfect; why may you not infer a more finished scheme or plan, which will receive its completion in some distant point of space or time? Are not these methods of reasoning exactly similar? And under what pretense can you embrace the one, while you reject the other?

The infinite difference of the subjects, replied he, is a sufficient foundation for this difference in my conclusions. In works of *human* art and contrivance, it is allowable to advance from the effect to the cause, and returning back from the cause, to form new inferences concerning the effect, and examine the alterations, which it has probably undergone, or may still undergo. But what is the foundation of this method of reasoning? Plainly this: that man is a being, whom we know by experience, whose motives and designs we are acquainted with, and whose projects and inclinations have a certain connection and coherence, according to the laws which nature has established for the government of such a creature. When, therefore, we find, that any work has proceeded from the skill and industry of man; as we are otherwise acquainted with the nature of the animal, we can draw a hundred inferences concerning what may be expected from him; and these inferences will all be founded in experience and observation. But did we know man only from the single work or production which we examine, it were impossible for us to argue in this manner; because our knowledge of all the qualities, which we ascribe to him, being in that case derived from the production, it is impossible they could point to anything further, or be the foundation of any new inference. The print of a foot in the sand can only prove, when considered alone, that there was some figure adapted to it, by which it was produced: but the print of a human foot proves likewise, from our other experience, that there was probably another foot, which also left its impression, though effaced by time or other accidents. Here we mount from the effect to the cause; and descending again from the cause, infer alterations in the effect; but this is not a continuation of the same simple chain of reasoning. We comprehend in this case a hundred other experiences and observations, concerning the *usual* figure and members of that species of animal, without which this method of argument must be considered as fallacious and sophistical.

The case is not the same with our reasonings from the works of nature. The Deity is known to us only by his productions, and is a single being in the universe, not comprehended under any species or genus, from whose experienced attributes or qualities, we can, by analogy, infer any attribute or quality in him. As the universe shows wisdom and goodness, we infer wisdom and goodness. As it shows a particular degree of these perfections, we infer a particular degree of them, precisely adapted to the effect which we examine. But further attributes or further degrees of the same attributes, we can never be authorized to infer or suppose, by any rules of just reasoning. Now, without some such license of supposition, it is impossible for us to argue from the cause, or infer any alteration in the effect, beyond what has immediately fallen under our observation. Greater good produced by this Being must still prove a greater degree of goodness; a more impartial distribution of rewards and punishments must proceed from a greater regard to justice and equity. Every supposed addition to the works of nature makes an addition to the attributes of the Author of nature; and consequently, being entirely unsupported by any reason or argument, can never be admitted but as mere conjecture and hypothesis.[24]

The great source of our mistake in this subject, and of the unbounded license of conjecture, which we indulge, is, that we tacitly consider ourselves, as in the place of the Supreme Being, and conclude, that he will, on every occasion, observe the same conduct, which we ourselves, in his situation, would have embraced as reasonable and eligible. But, besides that the ordinary course of nature may convince us, that almost everything is regulated by principles and maxims very different from ours;

[24] In general, it may, I think, be established as a maxim, that where any cause is known only by its particular effects, it must be impossible to infer any new effects from that cause; since the qualities, which are requisite to produce these new effects along with the former, must either be different, or superior, or of more extensive operation, than those which simply produced the effect, whence alone the cause is supposed to be known to us. We can never, therefore, have any reason to suppose the existence of these qualities. To say, that the new effects proceed only from a continuation of the same energy, which is already known from the first effects, will not remove the difficulty. For even granting this to be the case (which can seldom be supposed), the very continuation and exertion of a like energy (for it is impossible it can be absolutely the same), I say, this exertion of a like energy, in a different period of space and time, is a very arbitrary supposition, and what there cannot possibly be any traces of in the effects, from which all our knowledge of the cause is originally derived. Let the *inferred* cause be exactly proportioned (as it should be) to the known effect; and it is impossible that it can possess any qualities, from which new or different effects can be *inferred*.

besides this, I say, it must evidently appear contrary to all rules of analogy to reason, from the intentions and project of men, to those of a
Being so different, and so much superior. In human nature, there is a
certain experienced coherence of designs and inclinations; so that when,
from any fact, we have discovered one intention of any man, it may often be reasonable, from experience, to infer another, and draw a long
chain of conclusions concerning his past or future conduct. But this
method of reasoning can never have place with regard to a Being, so remote and incomprehensible, who bears much less analogy to any other
being in the universe than the sun to a waxen taper, and who discovers
himself only by some faint traces or outlines, beyond which we have no
authority to ascribe to him any attribute or perfection. What we imagine
to be a superior perfection, may really be a defect. Or were it ever so
much a perfection, the ascribing of it to the Supreme Being, where it appears not to have been really exerted, to the full, in his works, savors
more of flattery and panegyric, than of just reasoning and sound philosophy. All the philosophy, therefore, in the world, and all the religion,
which is nothing but a species of philosophy, will never be able to carry
us beyond the usual course of experience, or give us measures of conduct and behavior different from those which are furnished by reflections on common life. No new fact can ever be inferred from the religious hypothesis; no event foreseen or foretold; no reward or punishment expected or dreaded, beyond what is already known by practice
and observation. So that my apology for Epicurus will still appear solid
and satisfactory; nor have the political interests of society any connection with the philosophical disputes concerning metaphysics and
religion.

There is still one circumstance, replied I, which you seem to have
overlooked. Though I should allow your premises, I must deny your
conclusion. You conclude, that religious doctrines and reasonings *can*
have no influence on life, because they *ought* to have no influence;
never considering, that men reason not in the same manner you do, but
draw many consequences from the belief of a divine existence, and suppose that the Deity will inflict punishments on vice, and bestow rewards
on virtue, beyond what appear in the ordinary course of nature. Whether
this reasoning of theirs be just or not, is no matter. Its influence on
their life and conduct must still be the same. And, those, who attempt
to disabuse them of such prejudices, may, for aught I know, be good reasoners, but I cannot allow them to be good citizens and politicians; since
they free men from one restraint upon their passions, and make the infringement of the laws of society, in one respect, more easy and secure.

After all, I may, perhaps, agree to your general conclusion in favor of
liberty, though upon different premises from those, on which you en-

deavor to found it. I think, that the state ought to tolerate every principle of philosophy; nor is there an instance, that any government has suffered in its political interests by such indulgence. There is no enthusiasm among philosophers; their doctrines are not very alluring to the
people; and no restraint can be put upon their reasonings, but what
must be of dangerous consequence to the sciences, and even to the state,
by paving the way for persecution and oppression in points, where the
generality of mankind are more deeply interested and concerned.

But there occurs to me (continued I) with regard to your main topic,
a difficulty, which I shall just propose to you without insisting on it;
lest it lead into reasonings of too nice and delicate a nature. In a word,
I much doubt whether it be possible for a cause to be known only by
its effect (as you have all along supposed) or to be of so singular and
particular a nature as to have no parallel and no similarity with any
other cause or object, that has ever fallen under our observation. It is
only when two *species* of objects are found to be constantly conjoined,
that we can infer the one from the other; and were an effect presented,
which was entirely singular, and could not be comprehended under any
known *species*, I do not see, that we could form any conjecture or inference at all concerning its cause. If experience and observation and analogy be, indeed, the only guides which we can reasonably follow in inferences of this nature; both the effect and cause must bear a similarity
and resemblance to other effects and causes, which we know, and which
we have found, in many instances, to be conjoined with each other. I
leave it to your own reflection to pursue the consequences of this principle. I shall just observe, that, as the antagonists of Epicurus always suppose the universe, an effect quite singular and unparalleled, to be the
proof of a Deity, a cause no less singular and unparalleled; your reasonings, upon that supposition, seem, at least, to merit our attention. There
is, I own, some difficulty, how we can ever return from the cause to the
effect, and, reasoning from our ideas of the former, infer any alteration
on the latter, or any addition to it.

SECTION XII

OF THE ACADEMICAL OR SCEPTICAL PHILOSOPHY

Part I

THERE is not a greater number of philosophical reasonings, displayed
upon any subject, than those, which prove the existence of a Deity, and
refute the fallacies of *atheists;* and yet the most religious philosophers

still dispute whether any man can be so blinded as to be a speculative atheist. How shall we reconcile these contradictions? The knights-errant, who wandered about to clear the world of dragons and giants, never entertained the least doubt with regard to the existence of these monsters.

The *sceptic* is another enemy of religion, who naturally provokes the indignation of all divines and graver philosophers; though it is certain, that no man ever met with any such absurd creature, or conversed with a man, who had no opinion or principle concerning any subject, either of action or speculation. This begets a very natural question; What is meant by a sceptic? And how far is it possible to push these philosophical principles of doubt and uncertainty?

There is a species of scepticism, *antecedent* to all study and philosophy, which is much inculcated by Descartes and others, as a sovereign preservative against error and precipitate judgment. It recommends an universal doubt, not only of all our former opinions and principles, but also of our very faculties; of whose veracity, say they, we must assure ourselves, by a chain of reasoning, deduced from some original principle, which cannot possibly be fallacious or deceitful. But neither is there any such original principle, which has a prerogative above others, that are self-evident and convincing: or if there were, could we advance a step beyond it, but by the use of those very faculties, of which we are supposed to be already diffident. The Cartesian doubt, therefore, were it ever possible to be attained by any human creature (as it plainly is not) would be entirely incurable; and no reasoning could ever bring us to a state of assurance and conviction upon any subject.

It must, however, be confessed, that this species of scepticism, when more moderate, may be understood in a very reasonable sense, and is a necessary preparative to the study of philosophy, by preserving a proper impartiality in our judgments, and weaning our mind from all those prejudices, which we may have imbibed from education or rash opinion. To begin with clear and self-evident principles, to advance by timorous and sure steps, to review frequently our conclusions, and examine accurately all their consequences; though by these means we shall make both a slow and a short progress in our systems; are the only methods, by which we can ever hope to reach truth, and attain a proper stability and certainty in our determinations.

There is another species of scepticism, *consequent* to science and inquiry, when men are supposed to have discovered either the absolute fallaciousness of their mental faculties, or their unfitness to reach any fixed determination in all those curious subjects of speculation, about which they are commonly employed. Even our very senses are brought into dispute, by a certain species of philosophers; and the maxims of common life are subjected to the same doubt as the most profound principles or conclusions of metaphysics and theology. As these paradoxical tenets (if they may be called tenets) are to be met with in some philosophers, and the refutation of them in several, they naturally excite our curiosity, and make us inquire into the arguments, on which they may be founded.

I need not insist upon the more trite topics, employed by the sceptics in all ages, against the evidence of *sense;* such as those which are derived from the imperfection and fallaciousness of our organs, on numberless occasions; the crooked appearance of an oar in water; the various aspects of objects, according to their different distances; the double images which arise from the pressing one eye; with many other appearances of a like nature. These sceptical topics, indeed, are only sufficient to prove, that the senses alone are not implicitly to be depended on; but that we must correct their evidence by reason, and by considerations, derived from the nature of the medium, the distance of the object, and the disposition of the organ, in order to render them, within their sphere, the proper *criteria* of truth and falsehood. There are other more profound arguments against the senses, which admit not of so easy a solution.

It seems evident, that men are carried, by a natural instinct or prepossession, to repose faith in their senses; and that, without any reasoning, or even almost before the use of reason, we always suppose an external universe, which depends not on our perception, but would exist, though we and every sensible creature were absent or annihilated. Even the animal creation are governed by a like opinion, and preserve this belief of external objects, in all their thoughts, designs, and actions.

It seems also evident, that, when men follow this blind and powerful instinct of nature, they always suppose the very images, presented by the senses, to be the external objects, and never entertain any suspicion, that the one are nothing but representations of the other. This very table, which we see white, and which we feel hard, is believed to exist, independent of our perception, and to be something external to our mind, which perceives it. Our presence bestows not being on it; our absence does not annihilate it. It preserves its existence uniform and entire, independent of the situation of intelligent beings, who perceive or contemplate it.

But this universal and primary opinion of all men is soon destroyed by the slightest philosophy, which teaches us, that nothing can ever be present to the mind but an image or perception, and that the senses are only the inlets, through which these images are conveyed, without being able to produce any immediate intercourse between the mind and the object. The table, which we see, seems to diminish, as we remove farther from it; but the real table, which exists independent of us, suffers no alteration: it was, therefore, nothing but its image, which was present to the mind. These are the obvious dictates of reason; and no man, who reflects, ever doubted, that the existences, which we consider, when we say, *this house* and *that tree*, are nothing but perceptions in the mind, and fleeting copies or representations of other existences, which remain uniform and independent.

So far, then, are we necessitated by reasoning to contradict or depart from the primary instincts of nature, and to embrace a new system with regard to the evidence of our senses. But here philosophy finds herself extremely embarrassed, when she would justify this new system, and obviate the cavils and objections of the sceptics. She can no longer plead the infallible and irresistible instinct of nature: for that led us to a quite different system, which is acknowledged fallible and even erroneous. And to justify this pretended philosophical system, by a chain of clear and convincing argument, or even any appearance of argument, exceeds the power of all human capacity.

By what argument can it be proved, that the perceptions of the mind must be caused by external objects, entirely different from them, though resembling them (if that be possible) and could not arise either from the energy of the mind itself, or from the suggestion of some invisible and unknown spirit, or from some other cause still more unknown to us? It is acknowledged, that, in fact, many of these perceptions arise not from anything external, as in dreams, madness, and other diseases. And nothing can be more inexplicable than the manner, in which body should so operate upon mind as ever to convey an image of itself to a substance, supposed of so different, and even contrary a nature.

It is a question of fact, whether the perceptions of the senses be produced by external objects, resembling them: how shall this question be determined? By experience surely; as all other questions of a like nature. But here experience is, and must be entirely silent. The mind has never anything present to it but the perceptions, and cannot possibly reach any experience of their connection with objects. The supposition of such a connection is, therefore, without any foundation in reasoning.

To have recourse to the veracity of the supreme Being, in order to prove the veracity of our senses, is surely making a very unexpected circuit. If his veracity were at all concerned in this matter, our senses would be entirely infallible; because it is not possible that he can ever deceive. Not to mention, that, if the external world be once called in question, we shall be at a loss to find arguments, by which we may prove the existence of that Being or any of his attributes.

This is a topic, therefore, in which the profounder and more philosophical sceptics will always triumph, when they endeavor to introduce an universal doubt into all subjects of human knowledge and inquiry.

Do you follow the instincts and propensities of nature, may they say, in assenting to the veracity of sense? But these lead you to believe that the very perception or sensible image is the external object. Do you disclaim this principle, in order to embrace a more rational opinion, that the perceptions are only representations of something external? You here depart from your natural propensities and more obvious sentiments; and yet are not able to satisfy your reason, which can never find any convincing argument from experience to prove, that the perceptions are connected with any external objects.

There is another sceptical topic of a like nature, derived from the most profound philosophy; which might merit our attention, were it requisite to dive so deep, in order to discover arguments and reasonings, which can so little serve to any serious purpose. It is universally allowed by modern inquirers, that all the sensible qualities of objects, such as hard, soft, hot, cold, white, black, etc. are merely secondary, and exist not in the objects themselves, but are perceptions of the mind, without any external archetype or model, which they represent. If this be allowed, with regard to secondary qualities, it must also follow, with regard to the supposed primary qualities of extension and solidity; nor can the latter be any more entitled to that denomination than the former. The idea of extension is entirely acquired from the senses of sight and feeling; and if all the qualities, perceived by the senses, be in the mind, not in the object, the same conclusion must reach the idea of extension, which is wholly dependent on the sensible ideas or the ideas of secondary qualities. Nothing can save us from this conclusion, but the asserting, that the ideas of those primary qualities are attained by *abstraction,* an opinion, which, if we examine it accurately, we shall find to be unintelligible, and even absurd. An extension, that is neither tangible nor visible, cannot possibly be conceived; and a tangible or visible extension, which is neither hard nor soft, black or white, is equally beyond the reach of human conception. Let any man try to conceive a triangle in general, which is neither *isosceles* nor *scalenum,* nor has any particular length or proportion of sides; and he will soon perceive the absurdity of all the scholastic notions with regard to abstraction and general ideas.[25]

[25] This argument is drawn from Dr. Berkeley; and indeed most of the writings of that very ingenious author form the best lessons of scepticism, which are to be found either among the ancient or modern philosophers, Bayle not excepted. He professes, however, in his title-page (and undoubtedly with great truth) to have composed his book against the sceptics as well as against the atheists and freethinkers. But that all his arguments, though otherwise intended, are, in reality, merely sceptical, appears from this, *that they admit of no answer and produce no conviction.* Their only effect is to cause that momentary amazement and irresolution and confusion, which is the result of scepticism.

Thus the first philosophical objection to the evidence of sense or to the opinion of external existence consists in this, that such an opinion, if rested on natural instinct, is contrary to reason, and if referred to reason, is contrary to natural instinct, and at the same time carries no rational evidence with it, to convince an impartial inquirer. The second objection goes farther, and represents this opinion as contrary to reason; at least, if it be a principle of reason, that all sensible qualities are in the mind, not in the object. Bereave matter of all its intelligible qualities, both primary and secondary, you in a manner annihilate it, and leave only a certain unknown, inexplicable *something*, as the cause of our perceptions; a notion so imperfect, that no sceptic will think it worth while to contend against it.

Part II

It may seem a very extravagant attempt of the sceptics to destroy *reason* by argument and ratiocination; yet is this the grand scope of all their inquiries and disputes. They endeavor to find objections, both to our abstract reasonings, and to those which regard matter of fact and existence.

The chief objection against all *abstract* reasonings is derived from the ideas of space and time; ideas, which, in common life and to a careless view, are very clear and intelligible, but when they pass through the scrutiny of the profound sciences (and they are the chief object of these sciences) afford principles, which seem full of absurdity and contradiction. No priestly *dogmas*, invented on purpose to tame and subdue the rebellious reason of mankind, ever shocked common sense more than the doctrine of the infinite divisibility of extension, with its consequences; as they are pompously displayed by all geometricians and metaphysicians, with a kind of triumph and exultation. A real quantity, infinitely less than any finite quantity, containing quantities infinitely less than itself, and so on *in infinitum;* this is an edifice so bold and prodigious, that it is too weighty for any pretended demonstration to support, because it shocks the clearest and most natural principles of human reason.[26] But what renders the matter more extraordinary, is, that these seemingly absurd opinions are supported by a chain of reason-

[26] Whatever disputes there may be about mathematical points, we must allow that there are physical points; that is, parts of extension, which cannot be divided or lessened, either by the eye or imagination. These images, then, which are present to the fancy or senses, are absolutely indivisible, and consequently must be allowed by mathematicians to be infinitely less than any real part of extension; and yet nothing appears more certain to reason, than that an infinite number of them composes an infinite extension. How much more an infinite number of those infinitely small parts of extension, which are still supposed infinitely divisible.

ing, the clearest and most natural; nor is it possible for us to allow the premises without admitting the consequences. Nothing can be more convincing and satisfactory than all the conclusions concerning the properties of circles and triangles; and yet, when these are once received, how can we deny, that the angle of contact between a circle and its tangent is infinitely less than any rectilineal angle, that as you may increase the diameter of the circle *in infinitum*, this angle of contact becomes still less, even *in infinitum*, and that the angle of contact between other curves and their tangents may be infinitely less than those between any circle and its tangent, and so on, *in infinitum?* The demonstration of these principles seems as unexceptionable as that which proves the three angles of a triangle to be equal to two right ones, though the latter opinion be natural and easy, and the former big with contradiction and absurdity. Reason here seems to be thrown into a kind of amazement and suspense, which, without the suggestions of any sceptic, gives her a diffidence of herself, and of the ground on which she treads. She sees a full light, which illuminates certain places; but that light borders upon the most profound darkness. And between these she is so dazzled and confounded, that she scarcely can pronounce with certainty and assurance concerning any one object.

The absurdity of these bold determinations of the abstract sciences seems to become, if possible, still more palpable with regard to time than extension. An infinite number of real parts of time, passing in succession, and exhausted one after another, appears so evident a contradiction, that no man, one should think, whose judgment is not corrupted, instead of being improved, by the sciences, would ever be able to admit of it.

Yet still reason must remain restless, and unquiet, even with regard to that scepticism, to which she is driven by these seeming absurdities and contradictions. How any clear, distinct idea can contain circumstances, contradictory to itself, or to any other clear, distinct idea, is absolutely incomprehensible; and is, perhaps, as absurd as any proposition, which can be formed. So that nothing can be more sceptical, or more full of doubt and hesitation, than this scepticism itself, which arises from some of the paradoxical conclusions of geometry or the science of quantity.[27]

[27] It seems to me not impossible to avoid these absurdities and contradictions, if it be admitted, that there is no such thing as abstract or general ideas, properly speaking; but that all general ideas are, in reality, particular ones, attached to a general term, which recalls, upon occasion, other particular ones, that resemble, in certain circumstances, the idea, present to the mind. Thus when the term *horse* is pronounced, we immediately figure to ourselves the idea of a black or a white animal, of a particular size or figure: but as that term is also usually applied to animals of other colors, figures and sizes, these ideas, though not actually present to the imagination, are easily recalled; and our reasoning and conclusion proceed in the

The sceptical objections to *moral* evidence, or to the reasonings concerning matter of fact, are either *popular* or *philosophical*. The popular objections are derived from the natural weakness of human understanding; the contradictory opinions, which have been entertained in different ages and nations; the variations of our judgment in sickness and health, youth and old age, prosperity and adversity; the perpetual contradiction of each particular man's opinions and sentiments; with many other topics of that kind. It is needless to insist farther on this head. These objections are but weak. For as, in common life, we reason every moment concerning fact and existence, and cannot possibly subsist, without continually employing this species of argument, any popular objections, derived from thence, must be insufficient to destroy that evidence. The great subverter of *Pyrrhonism* or the excessive principles of scepticism is action, and employment, and the occupations of common life. These principles may flourish and triumph in the schools; where it is, indeed, difficult, if not impossible, to refute them. But as soon as they leave the shade, and by the presence of the real objects, which actuate our passions and sentiments, are put in opposition to the more powerful principles of our nature, they vanish like smoke, and leave the most determined sceptic in the same condition as other mortals.

The sceptic, therefore, had better keep within his proper sphere, and display those *philosophical* objections, which arise from more profound researches. Here he seems to have ample matter of triumph; while he justly insists, that all our evidence for any matter of fact, which lies beyond the testimony of sense or memory, is derived entirely from the relation of cause and effect; that we have no other idea of this relation than that of two objects, which have been frequently *conjoined* together; that we have no argument to convince us, that objects, which have, in our experience, been frequently conjoined, will likewise, in other instances, be conjoined in the same manner; and that nothing leads us to this inference but custom or a certain instinct of our nature; which it is indeed difficult to resist, but which, like other instincts, may be fallacious and deceitful. While the sceptic insists upon these topics, he shows his force, or rather, indeed, his own and our weakness; and seems, for the time at least, to destroy all assurance and conviction. These arguments might be displayed at greater length, if any durable good or benefit to society could ever be expected to result from them.

same way, as if they were actually present. If this be admitted (as seems reasonable) it follows that all the ideas of quantity, upon which mathematicians reason, are nothing but particular, and such as are suggested by the senses and imagination, and consequently, cannot be infinitely divisible. It is sufficient to have dropped this hint at present, without prosecuting it any farther. It certainly concerns all lovers of science not to expose themselves to the ridicule and contempt of the ignorant by their conclusions; and this seems the readiest solution of these difficulties.

For here is the chief and most confounding objection to *excessive* scepticism, that no durable good can ever result from it; while it remains in its full force and vigor. We need only ask such a sceptic, *What his meaning is? And what he proposes by all these curious researches?* He is immediately at a loss, and knows not what to answer. A Copernican or Ptolemaic, who supports each his different system of astronomy, may hope to produce a conviction, which will remain constant and durable, with his audience. A Stoic or Epicurean displays principles, which may not be durable, but which have an effect on conduct and behavior. But a Pyrrhonian cannot expect, that his philosophy will have any constant influence on the mind: or if it had, that its influence would be beneficial to society. On the contrary, he must acknowledge, if he will acknowledge anything, that all human life must perish, were his principles universally and steadily to prevail. All discourse, all action would immediately cease; and men remain in a total lethargy, till the necessities of nature, unsatisfied, put an end to their miserable existence. It is true; so fatal an event is very little to be dreaded. Nature is always too strong for principle. And though a Pyrrhonian may throw himself or others into a momentary amazement and confusion by his profound reasonings; the first and most trival event in life will put to flight all his doubts and scruples, and leave him the same, in every point of action and speculation, with the philosophers of every other sect, or with those who never concerned themselves in any philosophical researches. When he awakes from his dream, he will be the first to join in the laugh against himself, and to confess, that all his objections are mere amusement, and can have no other tendency than to show the whimsical condition of mankind, who must act and reason and believe; though they are not able, by their most diligent inquiry, to satisfy themselves concerning the foundation of these operations, or to remove the objections, which may be raised against them.

Part III

There is, indeed, a more *mitigated* scepticism or *academical* philos‑ ophy, which may be both durable and useful, and which may, in part, be the result of this Pyrrhonism, or *excessive* scepticism, when its undistinguished doubts are, in some measure, corrected by common sense and reflection. The greater part of mankind are naturally apt to be affirmative and dogmatical in their opinions; and while they see objects only on one side, and have no idea of any counterpoising argument, they throw themselves precipitately into the principles, to which they are inclined; nor have they any indulgence for those who entertain opposite sentiments. To hesitate or balance perplexes their understanding, checks their passion, and suspends their action. They are, therefore, impatient till they escape from a state, which to them is so uneasy: and they think, that they could never remove themselves far enough from it, by the violence of their affirmations and obstinacy of their belief. But could such dogmatical reasoners become sensible of the strange infirmities of human understanding, even in its most perfect state, and when most accurate and cautious in its determinations; such a reflection would naturally inspire them with more modesty and reserve, and diminish their fond opinion of themselves, and their prejudice against antagonists. The illiterate may reflect on the disposition of the learned, who, amidst all the advantages of study and reflection, are commonly still diffident in their determinations: and if any of the learned be inclined, from their natural temper, to haughtiness and obstinacy, a small tincture of Pyrrhonism might abate their pride, by showing them, that the few advantages, which they may have attained over their fellows, are but inconsiderable, if compared with the universal perplexity and confusion, which is inherent in human nature. In general, there is a degree of doubt, and caution, and modesty, which, in all kinds of scrutiny and decision, ought forever to accompany a just reasoner.

Another species of *mitigated* scepticism which may be of advantage to mankind, and which may be the natural result of the Pyrrhonian doubts and scruples, is the limitation of our inquiries to such subjects as are best adapted to the narrow capacity of human understanding. The *imagination* of man is naturally sublime, delighted with whatever is remote and extraordinary, and running, without control, into the most distant parts of space and time in order to avoid the objects, which custom has rendered too familiar to it. A correct *judgment* observes a contrary method, and avoiding all distant and high inquiries, confines itself to common life, and to such subjects as fall under daily practice and experience; leaving the more sublime topics to the embellishment of poets and orators, or to the arts of priests and politicians. To bring us to so salutary a determination, nothing can be more serviceable, than to be once thoroughly convinced of the force of the Pyrrhonian doubt, and of the impossibility, that anything, but the strong power of natural instinct, could free us from it. Those who have a propensity to philosophy, will still continue their researches; because they reflect, that, besides the immediate pleasure, attending such an occupation, philosophical decisions are nothing but the reflections of common life, methodized and corrected. But they will never be tempted to go beyond common life, so long as they consider the imperfection of those faculties which they employ, their narrow reach, and their inaccurate operations. While we cannot give a satisfactory reason, why we believe, after a thousand experiments, that a stone will fall, or fire burn; can we ever satisfy

ourselves concerning any determination, which we may form, with regard to the origin of worlds, and the situation of nature, from, and to
eternity?

This narrow limitation, indeed, of our inquiries, is, in every respect,
so reasonable, that it suffices to make the slightest examination into the
natural powers of the human mind and to compare them with their objects, in order to recommend it to us. We shall then find what are the
proper subjects of science and inquiry.

It seems to me, that the only objects of the abstract science or of
demonstration are quantity and number, and that all attempts to extend this more perfect species of knowledge beyond these bounds are
mere sophistry and illusion. As the component parts of quantity and
number are entirely similar, their relations become intricate and involved; and nothing can be more curious, as well as useful, than to trace,
by a variety of mediums, their equality or inequality, through their
different appearances. But as all other ideas are clearly distinct and different from each other, we can never advance farther, by our utmost
scrutiny, than to observe this diversity, and, by an obvious reflection,
pronounce one thing not to be another. Or if there be any difficulty in
these decisions, it proceeds entirely from the undeterminate meaning
of words, which is corrected by juster definitions. That *the square of the
hypothenuse is equal to the squares of the other two sides,* cannot be
known, let the terms be ever so exactly defined, without a train of
reasoning and inquiry. But to convince us of this proposition, *that where
there is no property, there can be no injustice,* it is only necessary to
define the terms, and explain injustice to be a violation of property.
This proposition is, indeed, nothing but a more imperfect definition. It
is the same case with all those pretended syllogistical reasonings, which
may be found in every other branch of learning, except the sciences of
quantity and number; and these may safely, I think, be pronounced
the only proper objects of knowledge and demonstration.

All other inquiries of men regard only matter of fact and existence;
and these are evidently incapable of demonstration. Whatever *is* may
not be. No negation of a fact can involve a contradiction. The non-
existence of any being, without exception, is as clear and distinct an
idea as its existence. The proposition, which affirms it not to be, however
false, is no less conceivable and intelligible, than that which affirms it
to be. The case is different with the sciences, properly so called. Every
proposition, which is not true, is there confused and unintelligible. That
the cube root of 64 is equal to the half of 10, is a false proposition, and
can never be distinctly conceived. But that Caesar, or the angel Gabriel,
or any being never existed, may be a false proposition, but still is perfectly conceivable, and implies no contradiction.

The existence, therefore, of any being can only be proved by arguments from its cause or its effect; and these arguments are founded entirely on experience. If we reason *a priori*, anything may appear able to produce anything. The falling of a pebble may, for aught we know, extinguish the sun; or the wish of a man control the planets in their orbits. It is only experience, which teaches us the nature and bounds of cause and effect, and enables us to infer the existence of one object from that of another.[28] Such is the foundation of moral reasoning, which forms the greater part of human knowledge, and is the source of all human action and behavior.

Moral reasonings are either concerning particular or general facts. All deliberations in life regard the former; as also all disquisitions in history, chronology, geography, and astronomy.

The sciences, which treat of general facts, are politics, natural philosophy, physics, chemistry, etc., where the qualities, causes and effects of a whole species of objects are inquired into.

Divinity or Theology, as it proves the existence of a Deity, and the immortality of souls, is composed partly of reasonings concerning particular, partly concerning general facts. It has a foundation in *reason*, so far as it is supported by experience. But its best and most solid foundation is *faith* and divine revelation.

Morals and criticism are not so properly objects of the understanding as of taste and sentiment. Beauty, whether moral or natural, is felt, more properly than perceived. Or if we reason concerning it, and endeavor to fix its standard, we regard a new fact, to wit, the general tastes of mankind, or some such fact, which may be the object of reasoning and inquiry.

When we run over libraries, persuaded of these principles, what havoc must we make? If we take in our hand any volume; of divinity or school metaphysics, for instance; let us ask, *Does it contain any abstract reasoning concerning quantity or number?* No. *Does it contain any experimental reasoning concerning matter of fact and existence?* No. Commit it then to the flames: for it can contain nothing but sophistry and illusion.

---

[28] That impious maxim of the ancient philosophy, *Ex nihilo, nihil fit,* by which the creation of matter was excluded, ceases to be a maxim, according to this philosophy. Not only the will of the supreme Being may create matter; but, for aught we know *a priori,* the will of any other being might create it, or any other cause, that the most whimsical imagination can assign.

DIALOGUES CONCERNING
NATURAL RELIGION

Pamphilus to Hermippus

It has been remarked, my Hermippus, that, though the ancient philosophers conveyed most of their instruction in the form of dialogue, this method of composition has been little practiced in later ages, and has seldom succeeded in the hands of those, who have attempted it. Accurate and regular argument, indeed, such as is now expected of philosophical inquirers, naturally throws a man into the methodical and didactic manner; where he can immediately, without preparation, explain the point, at which he aims; and thence proceed, without interruption, to deduce the proofs, on which it is established. To deliver a system in conversation scarcely appears natural; and while the dialogue-writer desires, by departing from the direct style of composition, to give a freer air to his performance, and avoid the appearance of *Author* and *Reader,* he is apt to run into a worse inconvenience, and convey the image of *Pedagogue* and *Pupil.* Or if he carries on the dispute in the natural spirit of good company, by throwing in a variety of topics, and preserving a proper balance among the speakers; he often loses so much time in preparations and transitions, that the reader will scarcely think himself compensated, by all the graces of dialogue, for the order, brevity, and precision, which are sacrificed to them.

There are some subjects, however, to which dialogue-writing is peculiarly adapted, and where it is still preferable to the direct and simple method of composition.

Any point of doctrine, which is so *obvious,* that it scarcely admits of dispute, but at the same time so *important,* that it cannot be too often inculcated, seems to require some such method of handling it; where the novelty of the manner may compensate the triteness of the subject, where the vivacity of conversation may enforce the precept, and where the variety of lights, presented by various personages and characters, may appear neither tedious nor redundant.

Any question of philosophy, on the other hand, which is so *obscure* and *uncertain,* that human reason can reach no fixed determination with regard to it; if it should be treated at all; seems to lead us naturally into the style of dialogue and conversation. Reasonable men may be allowed to differ, where no one can reasonably be positive: Opposite sentiments, even without any decision, afford an agreeable amusement: and if the subject be curious and interesting, the book carries us, in a manner, into company; and unites the two greatest and purest pleasures of human life, study and society.

Happily, these circumstances are all to be found in the subject of *Natural Religion*. What truth so obvious, so certain, as the *being* of a God, which the most ignorant ages have acknowledged, for which the most refined geniuses have ambitiously striven to produce new proofs and arguments? What truth so important as this, which is the ground of all our hopes, the surest foundation of morality, the firmest support of society, and the only principle, which ought never to be a moment absent from our thoughts and meditations? But in treating of this obvious and important truth; what obscure questions occur, concerning the *nature* of that divine being; his attributes, his decrees, his plan of providence? These have been always subjected to the disputations of men: Concerning these, human reason has not reached any certain determination: But these are topics so interesting, that we cannot restrain our restless inquiry with regard to them; though nothing but doubt, uncertainty and contradiction, have, as yet, been the result of our most accurate researches.

This I had lately occasion to observe, while I passed, as usual, part of the summer season with Cleanthes, and was present at those conversations of his with Philo and Demea, of which I gave you lately some imperfect account. Your curiosity, you then told me, was so excited, that I must of necessity enter into a more exact detail of their reasonings, and display those various systems, which they advanced with regard to so delicate a subject as that of Natural Religion. The remarkable contrast in their characters still farther raised your expectations; while you opposed the accurate philosophical turn of Cleanthes to the careless scepticism of Philo, or compared either of their dispositions with the rigid inflexible orthodoxy of Demea. My youth rendered me a mere auditor of their disputes; and that curiosity, natural to the early season of life, has so deeply imprinted in my memory the whole chain and connection of their arguments, that, I hope, I shall not omit or confound any considerable part of them in the recital.

Part I

After I joined the company, whom I found sitting in Cleanthes's library, Demea paid Cleanthes some compliments, on the great care which he took of my education, and on his unwearied perseverance and constancy in all his friendships. The father of Pamphilus, said he, was your intimate friend: The son is your pupil, and may indeed be re-

garded as your adopted son; were we to judge by the pains which you
bestow in conveying to him every useful branch of literature and science.
You are no more wanting, I am persuaded, in prudence than in industry.
I shall, therefore, communicate to you a maxim, which I have observed
with regard to my own children, that I may learn how far it agrees with
your practice. The method I follow in their education is founded on the
saying of an ancient, 'That students of philosophy ought first to learn
Logic, then Ethics, next Physics, last of all, of the nature of the Gods.'
This science of Natural Theology, according to him, being the most profound and abstruse of any, required the maturest judgment in its students; and none but a mind, enriched with all the other sciences, can
safely be entrusted with it.

Are you so late, says Philo, in teaching your children the principles
of religion? Is there no danger of their neglecting or rejecting altogether
those opinions, of which they have heard so little, during the whole
course of their education? It is only as a science, replied Demea, subjected to human reasoning and disputation, that I postpone the study
of Natural Theology. To season their minds with early piety is my chief
care; and by continual precept and instruction, and I hope too, by
example, I imprint deeply on their tender minds an habitual reverence
for all the principles of religion. While they pass through every other
science, I still remark the uncertainty of each part, the eternal disputations of men, the obscurity of all philosophy, and the strange, ridiculous
conclusions, which some of the greatest geniuses have derived from the
principles of mere human reason. Having thus tamed their mind to a
proper submission and self-diffidence, I have no longer any scruple of
opening to them the greatest mysteries of religion, nor apprehend any
danger from that assuming arrogance of philosophy, which may lead
them to reject the most established doctrines and opinions.

Your precaution, says Philo, of seasoning your children's minds with
early piety, is certainly very reasonable; and no more than is requisite,
in this profane and irreligious age. But what I chiefly admire in your
plan of education, is your method of drawing advantage from the very
principles of philosophy and learning, which, by inspiring pride and self-
sufficiency, have commonly, in all ages, been found so destructive to the
principles of religion. The vulgar, indeed, we may remark, who are unacquainted with science and profound inquiry, observing the endless
disputes of the learned, have commonly a thorough contempt for philosophy; and rivet themselves the faster, by that means, in the great points
of theology, which have been taught them. Those, who enter a little into
study and inquiry, finding many appearances of evidence in doctrines
the newest and most extraordinary, think nothing too difficult for human
reason; and presumptuously breaking through all fences, profane the

inmost sanctuaries of the temple. But Cleanthes will, I hope, agree with me, that after we have abandoned ignorance, the surest remedy, there is still one expedient left to prevent this profane liberty. Let Demea's principles be improved and cultivated: Let us become thoroughly sensible of the weakness, blindness, and narrow limits of human reason: Let us duly consider its uncertainty and endless contrarieties, even in subjects of common life and practice: Let the errors and deceits of our very senses be set before us; the insuperable difficulties, which attend first principles in all systems; the contradictions, which adhere to the very ideas of matter, cause and effect, extension, space, time, motion; and in a word, quantity of all kinds, the object of the only science, that can fairly pretend to any certainty or evidence. When these topics are displayed in their full light, as they are by some philosophers and almost all divines; who can retain such confidence in this frail faculty of reason as to pay any regard to its determinations in points so sublime, so abstruse, so remote from common life and experience? When the coherence of the parts of a stone, or even that composition of parts, which renders it extended; when these familiar objects, I say, are so inexplicable, and contain circumstances so repugnant and contradictory; with what assurance can we decide concerning the origin of worlds, or trace their history from eternity to eternity?

While Philo pronounced these words, I could observe a smile in the countenances both of Demea and Cleanthes. That of Demea seemed to imply an unreserved satisfaction in the doctrines delivered: But in Cleanthes's features, I could distinguish an air of finesse, as if he perceived some raillery or artificial malice in the reasonings of Philo.

You propose then, Philo, said Cleanthes, to erect religious faith on philosophical scepticism; and you think, that if certainty or evidence be expelled from every other subject of inquiry, it will all retire to these theological doctrines, and there acquire a superior force and authority. Whether your scepticism be as absolute and sincere as you pretend, we shall learn by and by, when the company breaks up: We shall then see, whether you go out at the door or the window; and whether you really doubt, if your body has gravity, or can be injured by its fall; according to popular opinion, derived from our fallacious senses and more fallacious experience. And this consideration, Demea, may, I think, fairly serve to abate our ill-will to this humorous sect of the sceptics. If they be thoroughly in earnest, they will not long trouble the world with their doubts, cavils, and disputes: If they be only in jest, they are, perhaps, bad ralliers, but can never be very dangerous, either to the state, to philosophy, or to religion.

In reality, Philo, continued he, it seems certain, that though a man, in a flush of humor, after intense reflection on the many contradictions and imperfections of human reason, may entirely renounce all belief and opinion; it is impossible for him to persevere in this total scepticism, or make it appear in his conduct for a few hours. External objects press in upon him: passions solicit him: His philosophical melancholy dissipates; and even the utmost violence upon his own temper will not be able, during any time, to preserve the poor appearance of scepticism. And for what reason impose on himself such a violence? This is a point, in which it will be impossible for him ever to satisfy himself, consistent with his sceptical principles: So that upon the whole nothing could be more ridiculous than the principles of the ancient Pyrrhonians; if in reality they endeavored, as is pretended, to extend throughout, the same scepticism, which they had learned from the declamations of their schools, and which they ought to have confined to them.

In this view, there appears a great resemblance between the sects of the Stoics and Pyrrhonians, though perpetual antagonists: and both of them seem founded on this erroneous maxim: That what a man can perform sometimes, and in some dispositions, he can perform always, and in every disposition. When the mind, by Stoical reflections, is elevated into a sublime enthusiasm of virtue, and strongly smit with any species of honor or public good, the utmost bodily pain and sufferance will not prevail over such a high sense of duty; and 'tis possible, perhaps, by its means, even to smile and exult in the midst of tortures. If this sometimes may be the case in fact and reality, much more may a philosopher, in his school, or even in his closet, work himself up to such an enthusiasm, and support in imagination the acutest pain or most calamitous event, which he can possibly conceive. But how shall he support this enthusiasm itself? The bent of his mind relaxes, and cannot be recalled at pleasure: avocations lead him astray: misfortunes attack him unawares: and the *philosopher* sinks by degrees into the *plebeian*.

I allow of your comparison between the Stoics and Sceptics, replied Philo. But you may observe, at the same time, that though the mind cannot, in Stoicism, support the highest flights of philosophy, yet even when it sinks lower, it still retains somewhat of its former disposition; and the effects of the Stoic's reasoning will appear in his conduct in common life, and through the whole tenor of his actions. The ancient schools, particularly that of Zeno, produced examples of virtue and constancy which seem astonishing to present times.

> Vain Wisdom all and false Philosophy.
> Yet with a pleasing sorcery could charm
> Pain, for a while, or anguish, and excite
> Fallacious Hope, or arm the obdurate breast
> With stubborn Patience, as with triple steel.[1]

[1] Paradise Lost, II.

In like manner, if a man has accustomed himself to sceptical considerations on the uncertainty and narrow limits of reason, he will not entirely forget them when he turns his reflection on other subjects; but in all his philosophical principles and reasoning, I dare not say, in his common conduct, he will be found different from those, who either never formed any opinions in the case, or have entertained sentiments more favorable to human reason.

To whatever length anyone may push his speculative principles of scepticism, he must act, I own, and live, and converse like other men; and for this conduct he is not obliged to give any other reason than the absolute necessity he lies under of so doing. If he ever carries his speculations farther than this necessity constrains him, and philosophises, either on natural or moral subjects, he is allured by a certain pleasure and satisfaction, which he finds in employing himself after that manner. He considers besides, that everyone, even in common life, is constrained to have more or less of this philosophy; that from our earliest infancy we make continual advances in forming more general principles of conduct and reasoning; that the larger experience we acquire, and the stronger reason we are endued with, we always render our principles the more general and comprehensive; and that what we call *philosophy* is nothing but a more regular and methodical operation of the same kind. To philosophize on such subjects is nothing essentially different from reasoning on common life; and we may only expect greater stability, if not greater truth, from our philosophy, on account of its exacter and more scrupulous method of proceeding.

But when we look beyond human affairs and the properties of the surrounding bodies: when we carry our speculations into the two eternities, before and after the present state of things; into the creation and formation of the universe; the existence and properties of spirits; the powers and operations of one universal spirit, existing without beginning and without end; omnipotent, omniscient, immutable, infinite, and incomprehensible: we must be far removed from the smallest tendency to scepticism not to be apprehensive, that we have here got quite beyond the reach of our faculties. So long as we confine our speculations to trade, or morals, or politics, or criticism, we make appeals, every moment, to common sense and experience, which strengthen our philosophical conclusions, and remove (at least, in part) the suspicion, which we so justly entertain with regard to every reasoning, that is very subtile and refined. But in theological reasonings, we have not this advantage; while at the same time we are employed upon objects, which, we must be sensible, are too large for our grasp, and of all others, require most to be familiarized to our apprehension. We are like foreigners in a strange country, to whom everything must seem suspicious, and who are in danger every moment of transgressing against the laws and customs of the people, with whom they live and converse. We know not how far we ought to trust our vulgar methods of reasoning in such a subject; since, even in common life and in that province, which is peculiarly appropriated to them, we cannot account for them, and are entirely guided by a kind of instinct or necessity in employing them.

All sceptics pretend, that, if reason be considered in an abstract view, it furnishes invincible arguments against itself, and that we could never retain any conviction or assurance, on any subject, were not the sceptical reasonings so refined and subtile, that they are not able to counterpoise the more solid and more natural arguments, derived from the senses and experience. But it is evident, whenever our arguments lose this advantage, and run wide of common life, that the most refined scepticism comes to be upon a footing with them, and is able to oppose and counterbalance them. The one has no more weight than the other. The mind must remain in suspense between them; and it is that very suspense or balance, which is the triumph of scepticism.

But I observe, says Cleanthes, with regard to you, Philo, and all speculative sceptics, that your doctrine and practice are as much at variance in the most abstruse points of theory as in the conduct of common life. Wherever evidence discovers itself, you adhere to it, notwithstanding your pretended scepticism; and I can observe, too, some of your sect to be as decisive as those, who make greater professions of certainty and assurance. In reality, would not a man be ridiculous, who pretended to reject Newton's explication of the wonderful phenomenon of the rainbow, because that explication gives a minute anatomy of the rays of light; a subject, forsooth, too refined for human comprehension? And what would you say to one, who having nothing particular to object to the arguments of Copernicus and Galileo for the motion of the earth, should withhold his assent, on that general principle, that these subjects were too magnificent and remote to be explained by the narrow and fallacious reason of mankind?

There is indeed a kind of brutish and ignorant scepticism, as you well observed, which gives the vulgar a general prejudice against what they do not easily understand, and makes them reject every principle, which requires elaborate reasoning to prove and establish it. This species of scepticism is fatal to knowledge, not to religion; since we find, that those who make greatest profession of it, give often their assent, not only to the great truths of theism, and natural theology, but even to the most absurd tenets, which a traditional superstition has recommended to them. They firmly believe in witches; though they will not believe nor attend to the most simple proposition of Euclid. But the refined and philosophical sceptics fall into an inconsistence of an opposite nature.

They push their researches into the most abstruse corners of science; and their assent attends them in every step, proportioned to the evidence which they meet with. They are even obliged to acknowledge, that the most abstruse and remote objects are those, which are best explained by philosophy. Light is in reality anatomized: the true system of the heavenly bodies is discovered and ascertained. But the nourishment of bodies by food is still an inexplicable mystery: the cohesion of the parts of matter is still incomprehensible. These sceptics, therefore, are obliged, in every question, to consider each particular evidence apart, and proportion their assent to the precise degree of evidence, which occurs. This is their practice in all natural, mathematical, moral, and political science. And why not the same, I ask, in the theological and religious? Why must conclusions of this nature be alone rejected on the general presumption of the insufficiency of human reason, without any particular discussion of the evidence? Is not such an unequal conduct a plain proof of prejudice and passion?

Our senses, you say, are fallacious, our understanding erroneous, our ideas even of the most familiar objects, extension, duration, motion, full of absurdities and contradictions. You defy me to solve the difficulties, or reconcile the repugnances, which you discover in them. I have not capacity for so great an undertaking: I have not leisure for it: I perceive it to be superfluous. Your own conduct, in every circumstance, refutes your principles; and shows the firmest reliance on all the received maxims of science, morals, prudence, and behavior.

I shall never assent to so harsh an opinion as that of a celebrated writer,[2] who says, that the sceptics are not a sect of philosophers: they are only a sect of liars. I may, however, affirm (I hope without offense), that they are a sect of jesters or ralliers. But for my part, whenever I find myself disposed to mirth and amusement, I shall certainly choose my entertainment of a less perplexing and abstruse nature. A comedy, a novel, or at most a history, seems a more natural recreation than such metaphysical subtilties and abstractions.

In vain would the sceptic make a distinction between science and common life, or between one science and another. The arguments, employed in all, if just, are of a similar nature, and contain the same force and evidence. Or if there be any difference among them, the advantage lies entirely on the side of theology and natural religion. Many principles of mechanics are founded on very abstruse reasoning; yet no man, who has any pretensions to science, even no speculative sceptic, pretends to entertain the least doubt with regard to them. The Copernican system contains the most surprising paradox, and the most contrary to our natural conceptions, to appearances, and to our very senses: yet even monks

[2] L'art de penser.

and inquisitors are now constrained to withdraw their opposition to it. And shall Philo, a man of so liberal a genius, and extensive knowledge, entertain any general undistinguished scruples with regard to the religious hypothesis, which is founded on the simplest and most obvious arguments, and, unless it meet with artificial obstacles, has such easy access and admission into the mind of man?

And here we may observe, continued he, turning himself towards Demea, a pretty curious circumstance in the history of the sciences. After the union of philosophy with the popular religion, upon the first establishment of Christianity, nothing was more usual, among all religious teachers, than declamations against reason, against the senses, against every principle, derived merely from human research and inquiry. All the topics of the ancient Academics were adopted by the fathers; and thence propagated for several ages in every school and pulpit throughout Christendom. The reformers embraced the same principles of reasoning, or rather declamation; and all panegyrics on the excellency of faith were sure to be interlarded with some severe strokes of satire against natural reason. A celebrated prelate too,[3] of the Romish communion, a man of the most extensive learning, who wrote a demonstration of Christianity, has also composed a treatise, which contains all the cavils of the boldest and most determined Pyrrhonism. Locke seems to have been the first Christian, who ventured openly to assert, that *faith* was nothing but a species of *reason,* that religion was only a branch of philosophy, and that a chain of arguments, similar to that which established any truth in morals, politics, or physics, was always employed in discovering all the principles of theology, natural and revealed. The ill use, which Bayle and other libertines made of the philosophical scepticism of the fathers and first reformers, still farther propagated the judicious sentiment of Mr. Locke: and it is now, in a manner, avowed, by all pretenders to reasoning and philosophy, that atheist and sceptic are almost synonymous. And as it is certain, that no man is in earnest, when he professes the latter principle; I would fain hope that there are as few, who seriously maintain the former.

Don't you remember, said Philo, the excellent saying of Lord Bacon on this head? That a little philosophy, replied Cleanthes, makes a man an atheist: a great deal converts him to religion. That is a very judicious remark too, said Philo. But what I have in my eye is another passage, where, having mentioned David's fool, who said in his heart there is no God, this great philosopher observes, that the atheists nowadays have a double share of folly: for they are not contented to say in their hearts there is no God, but they also utter that impiety with their lips, and are thereby guilty of multiplied indiscretion and imprudence. Such

[3] Mons. Huet.

people, though they were ever so much in earnest, cannot, methinks, be very formidable.

But though you should rank me in this class of fools, I cannot forbear communicating a remark, that occurs to me, from the history of the religious and irreligious scepticism, with which you have entertained us. It appears to me, that there are strong symptoms of priestcraft in the whole progress of this affair. During ignorant ages, such as those which followed the dissolution of the ancient schools, the priests perceived, that atheism, deism, or heresy of any kind, could only proceed from the presumptuous questioning of received opinions, and from a belief, that human reason was equal to everything. Education had then a mighty influence over the minds of men, and was almost equal in force to those suggestions of the senses and common understanding, by which the most determined sceptic must allow himself to be governed. But at present, when the influence of education is much diminished, and men, from a more open commerce of the world, have learned to compare the popular principles of different nations and ages, our sagacious divines have changed their whole system of philosophy, and talk the language of Stoics, Platonists, and Peripatetics, not that of Pyrrhonians and Academics. If we distrust human reason, we have now no other principle to lead us into religion. Thus sceptics, in one age, dogmatists in another; whichever system best suits the purpose of these reverend gentlemen, in giving them an ascendant over mankind, they are sure to make it their favorite principle, and established tenet.

It is very natural, said Cleanthes, for men to embrace those principles, by which they find they can best defend their doctrines; nor need we have any recourse to priestcraft to account for so reasonable an expedient. And surely nothing can afford a stronger presumption, that any set of principles are true, and ought to be embraced, than to observe, that they tend to the confirmation of true religion, and serve to confound the cavils of atheists, libertines, and freethinkers of all denominations

Part II

I MUST own, Cleanthes, said Demea, that nothing can more surprise me, than the light, in which you have, all along, put this argument. By the whole tenor of your discourse, one would imagine that you were maintaining the being of a God, against the cavils of atheists and infidels; and were necessitated to become a champion for that fundamental principle of all religion. But this, I hope, is not by any means a question among us. No man; no man, at least, of common sense, I am persuaded, ever entertained a serious doubt with regard to a truth, so certain and self-evident. The question is not concerning the *being*, but the *nature* of God. This, I affirm, from the infirmities of human understanding, to be altogether incomprehensible and unknown to us. The essence of that supreme mind, his attributes, the manner of his existence, the very nature of his duration; these and every particular, which regards so divine a being, are mysterious to men. Finite, weak, and blind creatures, we ought to humble ourselves in his august presence, and, conscious of our frailties, adore in silence his infinite perfections, which eye hath not seen, ear hath not heard, neither hath it entered into the heart of man to conceive them. They are covered in a deep cloud from human curiosity: it is profaneness to attempt penetrating through these sacred obscurities: and next to the impiety of denying his existence, is the temerity of prying into his nature and essence, decrees and attributes.

But lest you should think, that my *piety* has here got the better of my *philosophy*, I shall support my opinion, if it needs any support, by a very great authority. I might cite all the divines almost, from the foundation of Christianity, who have ever treated of this or any other theological subject: but I shall confine myself, at present, to one equally celebrated for piety and philosophy. It is Father Malebranche, who, I remember, thus expresses himself.[4] 'One ought not so much (says he) to call God a spirit, in order to express positively what he is, as in order to signify that he is not matter. He is a Being infinitely perfect: of this we cannot doubt. But in the same manner as we ought not to imagine, even supposing him corporeal, that he is clothed with a human body, as the Anthropomorphites asserted, under color that that figure was the most perfect of any; so neither ought we to imagine, that the spirit of God has human ideas, or bears *any* resemblance to our spirit; under color that we know nothing more perfect than a human mind. We ought rather to believe, that as he comprehends the perfections of matter without being material . . . . he comprehends also the perfections of created spirits, without being spirit, in the manner we conceive spirit: that his true name is, *He that is*, or, in other words, Being without restriction, All Being, the Being infinite and universal.'

After so great an authority, Demea, replied Philo, as that which you have produced, and a thousand more, which you might produce, it would appear ridiculous in me to add my sentiment, or express my approbation of your doctrine. But surely, where reasonable men treat these subjects, the question can never be concerning the being, but only the nature of the Deity. The former truth, as you well observe, is unquestionable and self-evident. Nothing exists without a cause; and the original cause of this universe (whatever it be) we call God; and piously ascribe to him every species of perfection. Whoever scruples this fundamental truth, deserves every punishment, which can be inflicted among

[4] *Recherche de la Vérité*, liv. 3, chap. 9.

philosophers, to wit, the greatest ridicule, contempt and disapprobation. But as all perfection is entirely relative, we ought never to imagine, that we comprehend the attributes of this divine Being, or to suppose, that his perfections have any analogy or likeness to the perfections of a human creature. Wisdom, thought, design, knowledge; these we justly ascribe to him; because these words are honorable among men, and we have no other language or other conceptions, by which we can express our adoration of him. But let us beware, lest we think, that our ideas any wise correspond to his perfections, or that his attributes have any resemblance to these qualities among men. He is infinitely superior to our limited view and comprehension; and is more the object of worship in the temple, than of disputation in the schools.

In reality, Cleanthes, continued he, there is no need of having recourse to that affected scepticism, so displeasing to you, in order to come at this determination. Our ideas reach no farther than our experience: we have no experience of divine attributes and operations: I need not conclude my syllogism: you can draw the inference yourself. And it is a pleasure to me (and I hope to you too) that just reasoning and sound piety here concur in the same conclusion, and both of them establish the adorably mysterious and incomprehensible nature of the Supreme Being.

Not to lose any time in circumlocutions, said Cleanthes, addressing himself to Demea, much less in replying to the pious declamations of Philo; I shall briefly explain how I conceive this matter. Look round the world: contemplate the whole and every part of it: you will find it to be nothing but one great machine, subdivided into an infinite number of lesser machines, which again admit of subdivisions, to a degree beyond what human senses and faculties can trace and explain. All these various machines, and even their most minute parts, are adjusted to each other with an accuracy, which ravishes into admiration all men, who have ever contemplated them. The curious adapting of means to ends, throughout all nature, resembles exactly, though it much exceeds, the productions of human contrivance; of human design, thought, wisdom, and intelligence. Since therefore the effects resemble each other, we are led to infer, by all the rules of analogy, that the causes also resemble; and that the Author of Nature is somewhat similar to the mind of men; though possessed of much larger faculties, proportioned to the grandeur of the work, which he has executed. By this argument *a posteriori*, and by this argument alone, do we prove at once the existence of a Deity, and his similarity to human mind and intelligence.

I shall be so free, Cleanthes, said Demea, as to tell you, that from the beginning, I could not approve of your conclusion concerning the similarity of the Deity to men; still less can I approve of the mediums, by which you endeavor to establish it. What! No demonstration of the being of a God! No abstract arguments! No proofs *a priori!* Are these, which have hitherto been so much insisted on by philosophers, all fallacy, all sophism? Can we reach no farther in this subject than experience and probability? I will not say, that this is betraying the cause of a deity: but surely, by this affected candor, you give advantage to atheists, which they never could obtain, by the mere dint of argument and reasoning.

What I chiefly scruple in this subject, said Plato, is not so much, that all religious arguments are by Cleanthes reduced to experience, as that they appear not to be even the most certain and irrefragable of that inferior kind. That a stone will fall, that fire will burn, that the earth has solidity, we have observed a thousand and a thousand times; and when any new instance of this nature is presented, we draw without hesitation the accustomed inference. The exact similarity of the cases gives us a perfect assurance of a similar event; and a stronger evidence is never desired nor sought after. But wherever you depart, in the least, from the similarity of the cases, you diminish proportionably the evidence; and may at last bring it to a very weak *analogy,* which is confessedly liable to error and uncertainty. After having experienced the circulation of the blood in human creatures, we make no doubt that it takes place in Titius and Maevius: but from its circulation in frogs and fishes, it is only a presumption, though a strong one, from analogy, that it takes place in men and other animals. The analogical reasoning is much weaker, when we infer the circulation of the sap in vegetables from our experience, that the blood circulates in animals; and those, who hastily followed that imperfect analogy, are found, by more accurate experiments, to have been mistaken.

If we see a house, Cleanthes, we conclude, with the greatest certainty, that it had an architect or builder; because this is precisely that species of effect, which we have experienced to proceed from that species of cause. But surely you will not affirm, that the universe bears such a resemblance to a house, that we can with the same certainty infer a similar cause, or that the analogy is here entire and perfect. The dissimilitude is so striking, that the utmost you can here pretend to is a guess, a conjecture, a presumption concerning a similar cause; and how that pretension will be received in the world, I leave you to consider.

It would surely be very ill received, replied Cleanthes; and I should be deservedly blamed and detested, did I allow, that the proofs of a Deity amounted to no more than a guess or conjecture. But is the whole adjustment of means to ends in a house and in the universe so slight a resemblance? The economy of final causes? The order, proportion, and arrangement of every part? Steps of a stair are plainly contrived, that human legs may use them in mounting; and this inference is certain and infallible. Human legs are also contrived for walking and mounting; and this inference, I allow, is not altogether so certain, because of the dissimilarity which you remark; but does it, therefore, deserve the name only of presumption or conjecture?

Good God! cried Demea, interrupting him, where are we? Zealous defenders of religion allow, that the proofs of a Deity fall short of perfect evidence! And you, Philo, on whose assistance I depended, in proving the adorable mysteriousness of the Divine Nature, do you assent to all these extravagant opinions of Cleanthes? For what other name can I give them? Or why spare my censure, when such principles are advanced, supported by such an authority, before so young a man as Pamphilus?

You seem not to apprehend, replied Philo, that I argue with Cleanthes in his own way; and by showing him the dangerous consequences of his tenets, hope at last to reduce him to our opinion. But what sticks most with you, I observe, is the representation which Cleanthes has made of the argument *a posteriori;* and finding, that that argument is likely to escape your hold and vanish into air, you think it so disguised, that you can scarcely believe it to be set in its true light. Now, however much I may dissent, in other respects, from the dangerous principles of Cleanthes, I must allow, that he has fairly represented that argument; and I shall endeavor so to state the matter to you, that you will entertain no farther scruples with regard to it.

Were a man to abstract from everything which he knows or has seen, he would be altogether incapable, merely from his own ideas, to determine what kind of scene the universe must be, or to give the preference to one state or situation of things above another. For as nothing which he clearly conceives, could be esteemed impossible or implying a contradiction, every chimera of his fancy would be upon an equal footing; nor could he assign any just reason, why he adheres to one idea or system, and rejects the others, which are equally possible.

Again; after he opens his eyes, and contemplates the world, as it really is, it would be impossible for him, at first, to assign the cause of any one event; much less, of the whole of things or of the universe. He might set his fancy a rambling; and she might bring him in an infinite variety of reports and representations. These would all be possible; but being all equally possible, he would never, of himself, give a satisfactory account for his preferring one of them to the rest. Experience alone can point out to him the true cause of any phenomenon.

Now, according to this method of reasoning, Demea, it follows (and is, indeed, tacitly allowed by Cleanthes himself) that order, arrangement, or the adjustment of final causes is not, of itself, any proof of design; but only so far as it has been experienced to proceed from that principle

For aught we can know *a priori,* matter may contain the source or spring of order originally, within itself, as well as mind does; and there is no more difficulty in conceiving, that the several elements, from an internal unknown cause, may fall into the most exquisite arrangement, than to conceive that their ideas, in the great, universal mind, from a like internal, unknown cause, fall into that arrangement. The equal possibility of both these suppositions is allowed. But by experience we find (according to Cleanthes), that there is a difference between them. Throw several pieces of steel together, without shape or form; they will never arrange themselves so as to compose a watch: stone, and mortar, and wood, without an architect, never erect a house. But the ideas in a human mind, we see, by an unknown, inexplicable economy, arrange themselves so as to form the plan of a watch or house. Experience, therefore, proves, that there is an original principle of order in mind, not in matter. From similar effects we infer similar causes. The adjustment of means to ends is alike in the universe, as in a machine of human contrivance. The causes, therefore, must be resembling.

I was from the beginning scandalized, I must own, with this resemblance, which is asserted, between the Deity and human creatures; and must conceive it to imply such a degradation of the Supreme Being as no sound theist could endure. With your assistance, therefore, Demea, I shall endeavor to defend what you justly called the adorable mysteriousness of the Divine Nature, and shall refute this reasoning of Cleanthes, provided he allows, that I have made a fair representation of it.

When Cleanthes had assented, Philo, after a short pause, proceeded in the following manner.

That all inferences, Cleanthes, concerning fact, are founded on experience, and that all experimental reasonings are founded on the supposition, that similar causes prove similar effects, and similar effects similar causes; I shall not, at present, much dispute with you. But observe, I entreat you, with what extreme caution all just reasoners proceed in the transferring of experiments to similar cases. Unless the cases be exactly similar, they repose no perfect confidence in applying their past observation to any particular phenomenon. Every alteration of circumstances occasions a doubt concerning the event; and it requires new experiments to prove certainly, that the new circumstances are of no moment or importance. A change in bulk, situation, arrangement, age, disposition of the air, or surrounding bodies; any of these particulars may be attended with the most unexpected consequences: and unless the objects be quite familiar to us, it is the highest temerity to expect with assurance, after any of these changes, an event similar to that which before fell under our observation. The slow and deliberate steps of philosophers, here, if anywhere, are distinguished from the precipitate march of the vulgar, who, hurried on by the smallest similitudes, are incapable of all discernment or consideration.

But can you think, Cleanthes, that your usual phlegm and philosophy have been preserved in so wide a step as you have taken, when you compared to the universe, houses, ships, furniture, machines; and from their similarity in some circumstances inferred a similarity in their causes? Thought, design, intelligence, such as we discover in men and other animals, is no more than one of the springs and principles of the universe, as well as heat or cold, attraction or repulsion, and a hundred others, which fall under daily observation. It is an active cause, by which some particular parts of nature, we find, produce alterations on other parts. But can a conclusion, with any propriety, be transferred from parts to the whole? Does not the great disproportion bar all comparison and inference? From observing the growth of a hair, can we learn anything concerning the generation of a man? Would the manner of a leaf's blowing, even though perfectly known, afford us any instruction concerning the vegetation of a tree?

But allowing that we were to take the *operations* of one part of nature upon another for the foundation of our judgment concerning the *origin* of the whole (which never can be admitted), yet why select so minute, so weak, so bounded a principle as the reason and design of animals is found to be upon this planet? What peculiar privilege has this little agitation of the brain which we call *thought,* that we must thus make it the model of the whole universe? Our partiality in our own favor does indeed present it on all occasions; but sound philosophy ought carefully to guard against so natural an illusion.

So far from admitting, continued Philo, that the operations of a part can afford us any just conclusion concerning the origin of the whole, I will not allow any one part to form a rule for another part, if the latter be very remote from the former. Is there any reasonable ground to conclude, that the inhabitants of other planets possess thought, intelligence, reason, or anything similar to these faculties in men? When Nature has so extremely diversified her manner of operation in this small globe; can we imagine, that she incessantly copies herself throughout so immense a universe? And if thought, as we may well suppose, be confined merely to this narrow corner, and has even there so limited a sphere of action; with what propriety can we assign it for the original cause of all things? The narrow views of a peasant, who makes his domestic economy the rule for the government of kingdoms, is in comparison a pardonable sophism.

But were we ever so much assured, that a thought and reason, resembling the human, were to be found throughout the whole universe, and were its activity elsewhere vastly greater and more commanding than it appears in this globe; yet I cannot see, why the operations of a world, constituted, arranged, adjusted, can with any propriety be extended to a world, which is in its embryo state, and is advancing towards that constitution and arrangement. By observation, we know somewhat of the economy, action, and nourishment of a finished animal; but we must transfer with great caution that observation to the growth of a fetus in the womb, and still more, to the formation of an animalcule in the loins of its male parent. Nature, we find, even from our limited experience, possesses an infinite number of springs and principles, which incessantly discover themselves on every change of her position and situation. And what new and unknown principles would actuate her in so new and unknown a situation as that of the formation of a universe, we cannot, without the utmost temerity, pretend to determine.

A very small part of this great system, during a very short time, is very imperfectly discovered to us: and do we thence pronounce decisively concerning the origin of the whole?

Admirable conclusion! Stone, wood, brick, iron, brass, have not, at this time, in this minute globe of earth, an order or arrangement without human art and contrivance: therefore the universe could not originally attain its order and arrangement, without something similar to human art. But is a part of nature a rule for another part very wide of the former? Is it a rule for the whole? Is a very small part a rule for the universe? Is nature in one situation, a certain rule for nature in another situation, vastly different from the former?

And can you blame me, Cleanthes, if I here imitate the prudent reserve of Simonides, who, according to the noted story, being asked by Hiero, *What God was?* desired a day to think of it, and then two days more; and after that manner continually prolonged the term, without ever bringing in his definition or description? Could you even blame me, if I had answered at first *that I did not know,* and was sensible that this subject lay vastly beyond the reach of my faculties? You might cry out sceptic and rallier as much as you pleased: but having found, in so many other subjects, much more familiar, the imperfections and even contradictions of human reason, I never should expect any success from its feeble conjectures, in a subject, so sublime, and so remote from the sphere of our observation. When two species of objects have always been observed to be conjoined together, I can infer, by custom, the existence of one wherever I see the existence of the other: and this I call an argument from experience. But how this argument can have place, where the objects, as in the present case, are single, individual, without parallel, or specific resemblance, may be difficult to explain. And will any man tell me with a serious countenance, that an orderly universe must arise from some thought and art, like the human; because we have experience of it?

To ascertain this reasoning, it were requisite, that we had experience of the origin of worlds; and it is not sufficient surely, that we have seen ships and cities arise from human art and contrivance . . . .

Philo was proceeding in this vehement manner, somewhat between jest and earnest, as it appeared to me; when he observed some signs of impatience in Cleanthes, and then immediately stopped short. What I had to suggest, said Cleanthes, is only that you would not abuse terms, or make use of popular expressions to subvert philosophical reasonings. You know, that the vulgar often distinguish reason from experience, even where the question relates only to matter of fact and existence; though it is found, where that reason is properly analyzed, that it is nothing but a species of experience. To prove by experience the origin of the universe from mind is not more contrary to common speech than to prove the motion of the earth from the same principle. And a caviler might raise all the same objections to the Copernican system, which you have urged against my reasonings. Have you other earths, might he say, which you have seen to move? Have . . . .

Yes! cried Philo, interrupting him, we have other earths. Is not the moon another earth, which we see to turn round its center? Is not Venus another earth, where we observe the same phenomenon? Are not the revolutions of the sun also a confirmation, from analogy, of the same theory? All the planets, are they not earths, which revolve about the sun? Are not the satellites moons, which move round Jupiter and Saturn, and along with these primary planets, round the sun? These analogies and resemblances, with others, which I have not mentioned, are the sole proofs of the Copernican system: and to you it belongs to consider, whether you have any analogies of the same kind to support your theory.

In reality, Cleanthes, continued he, the modern system of astronomy is now so much received by all inquirers, and has become so essential a part even of our earliest education, that we are not commonly very scrupulous in examining the reasons upon which it is founded. It is now become a matter of mere curiosity to study the first writers on that subject, who had the full force of prejudice to encounter, and were obliged to turn their arguments on every side, in order to render them popular and convincing. But if we peruse Galileo's famous Dialogues concerning the system of the world, we shall find, that that great genius, one of the sublimest that ever existed, first bent all his endeavors to prove, that there was no foundation for the distinction commonly made between elementary and celestial substances. The schools, proceeding from the illusions of sense, had carried this distinction very far; and had established the latter substances to be ingenerable, incorruptible, unalterable, impassable; and had assigned all the opposite qualities to the former. But Galileo, beginning with the moon, proved its similarity in every

particular to the earth; its convex figure, its natural darkness when not
illuminated, its density, its distinction into solid and liquid, the variations of its phases, the mutual illuminations of the earth and moon, their
mutual eclipses, the inequalities of the lunar surface, etc. After many
instances of this kind, with regard to all the planets, men plainly saw,
that these bodies became proper objects of experience; and that the
similarity of their nature enabled us to extend the same arguments and
phenomena from one to the other.

In this cautious proceeding of the astronomers, you may read your
own condemnation, Cleanthes; or rather may see, that the subject in
which you are engaged exceeds all human reason and inquiry. Can you
pretend to show any such similarity between the fabric of a house, and
the generation of a universe? Have you ever seen nature in any such
situation as resembles the first arrangement of the elements? Have worlds
ever been formed under your eye? and have you had leisure to observe
the whole progress of the phenomenon, from the first appearance of order
to its final consummation? If you have, then cite your experience, and
deliver your theory.

Part III

How the most absurd argument, replied Cleanthes, in the hands of a
man of ingenuity and invention, may acquire an air of probability!
Are you not aware, Philo, that it became necessary for Copernicus and
his first disciples to prove the similarity of the terrestrial and celestial
matter; because several philosophers, blinded by old systems, and supported by some sensible appearances, had denied this similarity? But
that it is by no means necessary, that theists should prove the similarity
of the works of nature to those of art; because this similarity is self-
evident and undeniable? The same matter, a like form: what more is
requisite to show an analogy between their causes, and to ascertain the
origin of all things from a divine purpose and intention? Your objections,
I must freely tell you, are no better than the abstruse cavils of those
philosophers who denied motion; and ought to be refuted in the same
manner, by illustrations, examples, and instances, rather than by serious
argument and philosophy.

Suppose, therefore, that an articulate voice were heard in the clouds,
much louder and more melodious than any which human art could ever
reach: suppose, that this voice were extended in the same instant over
all nations, and spoke to each nation in its own language and dialect:
suppose, that the words delivered not only contain a just sense and
meaning, but convey some instruction altogether worthy of a benevolent
being, superior to mankind: could you possibly hesitate a moment con-

cerning the cause of this voice? and must you not instantly ascribe it to some design or purpose? Yet I cannot see but all the same objections (if they merit that appellation) which lie against the system of theism, may also be produced against this inference.

Might you not say, that all conclusions concerning fact were founded on experience: that when we hear an articulate voice in the dark, and thence infer a man, it is only the resemblance of the effects, which leads us to conclude that there is a like resemblance in the cause: but that this extraordinary voice, by its loudness, extent, and flexibility to all languages, bears so little analogy to any human voice, that we have no reason to suppose any analogy in their causes: and consequently, that a rational, wise, coherent speech proceeded, you knew not whence, from some accidental whistling of the winds, not from any divine reason or intelligence? You see clearly your own objections in these cavils; and I hope too, you see clearly, that they cannot possibly have more force in the one case than in the other.

But to bring the case still nearer the present one of the universe, I shall make two suppositions, which imply not any absurdity or impossibility. Suppose, that there is a natural, universal, invariable language, common to every individual of human race, and that books are natural productions, which perpetuate themselves in the same manner with animals and vegetables, by descent and propagation. Several expressions of our passions contain a universal language: all brute animals have a natural speech, which, however limited, is very intelligible to their own species. And as there are infinitely fewer parts and less contrivance in the finest composition of eloquence, than in the coarsest organized body, the propagation of an *Iliad* or *Aeneid* is an easier supposition than that of any plant or animal.

Suppose, therefore, that you enter into your library, thus peopled by natural volumes, containing the most refined reason and most exquisite beauty: could you possibly open one of them, and doubt, that its original cause bore the strongest analogy to mind and intelligence? When it reasons and discourses; when it expostulates, argues, and enforces its views and topics; when it applies sometimes to the pure intellect, sometimes to the affections; when it collects, disposes, and adorns every consideration suited to the subject: could you persist in asserting, that all this, at the bottom, had really no meaning, and that the first formation of this volume in the loins of its original parent proceeded not from thought and design? Your obstinacy, I know, reaches not that degree of firmness: even your sceptical play and wantonness would be abashed at so glaring an absurdity.

But if there be any difference, Philo, between this supposed case and the real one of the universe, it is all to the advantage of the latter. The

anatomy of an animal affords many stronger instances of design than
the perusal of Livy or Tacitus: and any objection which you start in the
former case, by carrying me back to so unusual and extraordinary a scene
as the first formation of worlds, the same objection has place on the supposition of our vegetating library. Choose, then, your party, Philo, without ambiguity or evasion; assert either that a rational volume is no proof
of a rational cause, or admit of a similar cause to all the works of nature.

Let me here observe too, continued Cleanthes, that this religious argument, instead of being weakened by that scepticism, so much affected by
you, rather acquires force from it, and becomes more firm and undisputed. To exclude all argument or reasoning of every kind is either affectation or madness. The declared profession of every reasonable sceptic
is only to reject abstruse, remote and refined arguments; to adhere to
common sense and the plain instincts of nature; and to assent, wherever
any reasons strike him with so full a force, that he cannot, without the
greatest violence, prevent it. Now the arguments for Natural Religion
are plainly of this kind; and nothing but the most perverse, obstinate
metaphysics can reject them. Consider, anatomize the eye; survey its
structure and contrivance; and tell me, from your own feeling, if the idea
of a contriver does not immediately flow in upon you with a force like
that of sensation. The most obvious conclusion surely is in favor of design; and it requires time, reflection and study, to summon up those
frivolous, though abstruse objections, which can support infidelity. Who
can behold the male and female of each species, the correspondence of
their parts and instincts, their passions and whole course of life before
and after generation, but must be sensible, that the propagation of the
species is intended by Nature? Millions and millions of such instances
present themselves through every part of the universe; and no language
can convey a more intelligible, irresistible meaning, than the curious adjustment of final causes. To what degree, therefore, of blind dogmatism
must one have attained, to reject such natural and such convincing arguments?

Some beauties in writing we may meet with, which seem contrary to
rules, and which gain the affections, and animate the imagination, in
opposition to all the precepts of criticism, and to the authority of the
established masters of art. And if the argument for theism be, as you
pretend, contradictory to the principles of logic; its universal, its irresistible influence proves clearly, that there may be arguments of a like irregular nature. Whatever cavils may be urged; an orderly world, as well
as a coherent, articulate speech, will still be received as an incontestable
proof of design and intention.

It sometimes happens, I own, that the religious arguments have not
their due influence on an ignorant savage and barbarian; not because

they are obscure and difficult, but because he never asks himself any question with regard to them. Whence arises the curious structure of an animal? From the copulation of its parents. And these whence? From *their* parents. A few removes set the objects at such a distance, that to him they are lost in darkness and confusion; nor is he actuated by any curiosity to trace them farther. But this is neither dogmatism nor scepticism, but stupidity; a state of mind very different from your sifting, inquisitive disposition, my ingenious friend. You can trace causes from effects: you can compare the most distant and remote objects: and your greatest errors proceed not from barrenness of thought and invention, but from too luxuriant a fertility, which suppresses your natural good sense, by a profusion of unnecessary scruples and objections.

Here I could observe, Hermippus, that Philo was a little embarrassed and confounded: but while he hesitated in delivering an answer, luckily for him, Demea broke in upon the discourse, and saved his countenance.

Your instance, Cleanthes, said he, drawn from books and languages, being familiar, has, I confess, so much more force on that account; but is there not some danger too in this very circumstance; and may it not render us presumptuous, by making us imagine we comprehend the Deity, and have some adequate idea of his nature and attributes? When I read a volume, I enter into the mind and intention of the author: I become him, in a manner, for the instant; and have an immediate feeling and conception of those ideas which revolved in his imagination while employed in that composition. But so near an approach we never surely can make to the Deity. His ways are not our ways. His attributes are perfect, but incomprehensible. And this volume of Nature contains a great and inexplicable riddle, more than any intelligible discourse or reasoning.

The ancient Platonists, you know, were the most religious and devout of all the pagan philosophers: yet many of them, particularly Plotinus, expressly declare, that intellect or understanding is not to be ascribed to the Deity, and that our most perfect worship of him consists, not in acts of veneration, reverence, gratitude or love; but in a certain mysterious self-annihilation or total extinction of all our faculties. These ideas are, perhaps, too far stretched; but still it must be acknowledged, that, by representing the Deity as so intelligible, and comprehensible, and so similar to a human mind, we are guilty of the grossest and most narrow partiality, and make ourselves the model of the whole universe.

All the *sentiments* of the human mind, gratitude, resentment, love, friendship, approbation, blame, pity, emulation, envy, have a plain reference to the state and situation of man, and are calculated for preserving the existence, and promoting the activity of such a being in such circumstances. It seems therefore unreasonable to transfer such sentiments to a supreme existence, or to suppose him actuated by them; and the phenomena, besides, of the universe will not support us in such a theory. All our *ideas,* derived from the senses, are confusedly false and illusive; and cannot, therefore, be supposed to have place in a supreme intelligence: and as the ideas of internal sentiment, added to those of the external senses, compose the whole furniture of human understanding, we may conclude, that none of the *materials* of thought are in any respect similar in the human and in the divine intelligence. Now, as to the *manner* of thinking; how can we make any comparison between them, or suppose them anywise resembling? Our thought is fluctuating, uncertain, fleeting, successive, and compounded; and were we to remove these circumstances, we absolutely annihilate its essence, and it would, in such a case, be an abuse of terms to apply to it the name of thought or reason. At least, if it appear more pious and respectful (as it really is) still to retain these terms, when we mention the Supreme Being, we ought to acknowledge, that their meaning, in that case, is totally incomprehensible; and that the infirmities of our nature do not permit us to reach any ideas, which in the least correspond to the ineffable sublimity of the divine attributes.

Part IV

IT SEEMS strange to me, said Cleanthes, that you, Demea, who are so sincere in the cause of religion, should still maintain the mysterious, incomprehensible nature of the Deity, and should insist so strenuously, that he has no manner of likeness or resemblance to human creatures. The Deity, I can readily allow, possesses many powers and attributes, of which we can have no comprehension: but if our ideas, so far as they go, be not just and adequate, and correspondent to his real nature, I know not what there is in this subject worth insisting on. Is the name, without any meaning, of such mighty importance? Or how do you mystics, who maintain the absolute incomprehensibility of the Deity, differ from sceptics or atheists, who assert, that the first cause of all is unknown and unintelligible? Their temerity must be very great, if, after rejecting the production by a mind; I mean, a mind resembling the human (for I know of no other), they pretend to assign, with certainty, any other specific, intelligible cause: and their conscience must be very scrupulous indeed, if they refuse to call the universal, unknown cause a God or Deity; and to bestow on him as many sublime eulogies and unmeaning epithets, as you shall please to require of them.

Who could imagine, replied Demea, that Cleanthes, the calm, philosophical Cleanthes, would attempt to refute his antagonists, by affixing a nickname to them; and like the common bigots and inquisitors of the age, have recourse to invective and declamation, instead of reasoning? Or does he not perceive, that these topics are easily retorted, and that *anthropomorphite* is an appellation as invidious, and implies as dangerous consequences, as the epithet of *mystic*, with which he has honored us? In reality, Cleanthes, consider what it is you assert, when you represent the Deity as similar to a human mind and understanding. What is the soul of man? A composition of various faculties, passions, sentiments, ideas; united, indeed, into one self or person, but still distinct from each other. When it reasons, the ideas, which are the parts of its discourse, arrange themselves in a certain form or order; which is not preserved entire for a moment, but immediately gives place to another arrangement. New opinions, new passions, new affections, new feelings arise, which continually diversify the mental scene, and produce in it the greatest variety, and most rapid succession imaginable. How is this compatible with that perfect immutability and simplicity which all true theists ascribe to the Deity? By the same act, say they, he sees past, present, and future: his love and his hatred, his mercy and his justice, are one individual operation: he is entire in every point of space; and complete in every instant of duration. No succession, no change, no acquisition, no diminution. What he is implies not in it any shadow of distinction or diversity. And what he is, this moment, he ever has been, and ever will be, without any new judgment, sentiment, or operation. He stands fixed in one simple, perfect state; nor can you ever say, with any propriety, that this act of his is different from that other, or that this judgment or idea has been lately formed, and will give place, by succession, to any different judgment or idea.

I can readily allow, said Cleanthes, that those who maintain the perfect simplicity of the Supreme Being, to the extent in which you have explained it, are complete mystics, and chargeable with all the consequences which I have drawn from their opinion. They are, in a word, atheists, without knowing it. For though it be allowed, that the Deity possesses attributes, of which we have no comprehension; yet ought we never to ascribe to him any attributes, which are absolutely incompatible with that intelligent nature, essential to him. A mind, whose acts and sentiments and ideas are not distinct and successive; one, that is wholly simple, and totally immutable; is a mind which has no thought, no reason, no will, no sentiment, no love, no hatred; or in a word, is no mind at all. It is an abuse of terms to give it that appellation; and we may as well speak of limited extension without figure, or of number without composition.

Pray consider, said Philo, whom you are at present inveighing against. You are honoring with the appellation of atheist all the sound, orthodox divines almost, who have treated of this subject; and you will, at last, be, yourself, found, according to your reckoning, the only sound theist in the world. But if idolaters be atheists, as, I think, may justly be asserted, and Christian theologians the same; what becomes of the argument, so much celebrated, derived from the universal consent of mankind?

But because I know you are not much swayed by names and authorities, I shall endeavor to show you, a little more distinctly, the inconveniences of that anthropomorphism which you have embraced; and I shall prove, that there is no ground to suppose a plan of the world to be formed in the divine mind, consisting of distinct ideas, differently arranged; in the same manner as an architect forms in his head the plan of a house which he intends to execute.

It is not easy, I own, to see, what is gained by this supposition, whether we judge of the matter by *reason* or by *experience*. We are still obliged to mount higher, in order to find the cause of this cause, which you had assigned as satisfactory and conclusive.

If *reason* (I mean abstract reason, derived from inquiries *a priori*) be not alike mute with regard to all questions concerning cause and effect; this sentence at least it will venture to pronounce, that a mental world, or universe of ideas, requires a cause as much, as does a material world, or universe of objects; and if similar in its arrangement must require a similar cause. For what is there in this subject, which should occasion a different conclusion or inference? In an abstract view, they are entirely alike; and no difficulty attends the one supposition, which is not common to both of them.

Again, when we will needs force *experience* to pronounce some sentence, even on these subjects, which lie beyond her sphere; neither can she perceive any material difference in this particular, between these two kinds of worlds, but finds them to be governed by similar principles, and to depend upon an equal variety of causes in their operations. We have specimens in miniature of both of them. Our own mind resembles the one: a vegetable or animal body the other. Let experience, therefore, judge from these samples. Nothing seems more delicate with regard to its causes than thought; and as these causes never operate in two persons after the same manner, so we never find two persons, who think exactly alike. Nor indeed does the same person think exactly alike at any two different periods of time. A difference of age, of the disposition of his body, of weather, of food, of company, of books, of passions; any of these particulars, or others more minute, are sufficient to alter the curious machinery of thought, and communicate to it very different movements and operations. As far as we can judge, vegetables and animal bodies are not more delicate in their motions, nor depend upon a greater variety or more curious adjustment of springs and principles.

How therefore shall we satisfy ourselves concerning the cause of that

Being, whom you suppose the Author of Nature, or, according to your system of anthropomorphism, the ideal world, into which you trace the material? Have we not the same reason to trace that ideal world into another ideal world, or new intelligent principle? But if we stop, and go no farther; why go so far? Why not stop at the material world? How can we satisfy ourselves without going on *in infinitum?* And after all, what satisfaction is there in that infinite progression? Let us remember the story of the Indian philosopher and his elephant. It was never more applicable than to the present subject. If the material world rests upon a similar ideal world, this ideal world must rest upon some other; and so on, without end. It were better, therefore, never to look beyond the present material world. By supposing it to contain the principle of its order within itself, we really assert it to be God; and the sooner we arrive at that Divine Being, so much the better. When you go one step beyond the mundane system, you only excite an inquisitive humor, which it is impossible ever to satisfy.

To say, that the different ideas, which compose the reason of the Supreme Being, fall into order, of themselves, and by their own nature, is really to talk without any precise meaning. If it has a meaning, I would fain know, why it is not as good sense to say, that the parts of the material world fall into order, of themselves, and by their own nature. Can the one opinion be intelligible, while the other is not so?

We have, indeed, experience of ideas, which fall into order, of themselves, and without any *known* cause: but, I am sure, we have a much larger experience of matter, which does the same; as, in all instances of generation and vegetation, where the accurate analysis of the cause exceeds all human comprehension. We have also experience of particular systems of thought and of matter, which have no order; of the first, in madness; of the second, in corruption. Why then should we think, that order is more essential to one than the other? And if it requires a cause in both, what do we gain by your system, in tracing the universe of objects into a similar universe of ideas? The first step, which we make, leads us on forever. It were, therefore, wise in us, to limit all our inquiries to the present world, without looking farther. No satisfaction can ever be attained by these speculations, which so far exceed the narrow bounds of human understanding.

It was usual with the Peripatetics, you know, Cleanthes, when the cause of any phenomenon was demanded, to have recourse to their *faculties* or *occult qualities,* and to say, for instance, that bread nourished by its nutritive faculty, and senna purged by its purgative: but it has been discovered, that this subterfuge was nothing but the disguise of ignorance; and that these philosophers, though less ingenuous, really said the same thing with the sceptics or the vulgar, who fairly con-

fessed, that they knew not the cause of these phenomena. In like manner, when it is asked, what cause produces order in the ideas of the
Supreme Being, can any other reason be assigned to you, Anthropo·
morphites, than that it is a *rational* faculty, and that such is the nature
of the Deity? But why a similar answer will not be equally satisfactory
in accounting for the order of the world, without having recourse to
any such intelligent creator, as you insist on, may be difficult to determine. It is only to say, that such is the nature of material objects, and
that they are all originally possessed of a *faculty* of order and proportion. These are only more learned and elaborate ways of confessing our
ignorance; nor has the one hypothesis any real advantage above the
other, except in its greater conformity to vulgar prejudices.

You have displayed this argument with great emphasis, replied Cleanthes: you seem not sensible, how easy it is to answer it. Even in common life, if I assign a cause for any event; is it any objection, Philo,
that I cannot assign the cause of that cause, and answer every new question, which may incessantly be started? And what philosophers could
possibly submit to so rigid a rule? Philosophers, who confess ultimate
causes to be totally unknown, and are sensible, that the most refined
principles, into which they trace the phenomena, are still to them as
inexplicable as these phenomena themselves are to the vulgar. The order and arrangement of nature, the curious adjustment of final causes,
the plain use and intention of every part and organ; all these bespeak
in the clearest language an intelligent cause or author. The heavens
and the earth join in the same testimony: the whole chorus of Nature
raises one hymn to the praises of its creator: you alone, or almost
alone, disturb this general harmony. You start abstruse doubts, cavils,
and objections: you ask me, what is the cause of this cause? I know
not; I care not; that concerns not me. I have found a Diety; and
here I stop my inquiry. Let those go farther, who are wiser or more
enterprising.

I pretend to be neither, replied Philo: and for that very reason, I
should never perhaps have attempted to go so far; especially when I
am sensible, that I must at last be contented to sit down with the
same answer, which, without farther trouble, might have satisfied me
from the beginning. If I am still to remain in utter ignorance of causes,
and can absolutely give an explication of nothing, I shall never esteem
it any advantage to shove off for a moment a difficulty, which, you acknowledge, must immediately, in its full force, recur upon me. Natural-
ists indeed very justly explain particular effects by more general causes,
though these general causes themselves should remain in the end totally
inexplicable: but they never surely thought it satisfactory to explain
a particular effect by a particular cause, which was no more to be ac-

counted for than the effect itself. An ideal system, arranged of itself, without a precedent design, is not a whit more explicable than a material one, which attains its order in a like manner; nor is there any more difficulty in the latter supposition than in the former.

Part V

BUT to show you still more inconveniences, continued Philo, in your anthropomorphism; please to take a new survey of your principles. *Like effects prove like causes.* This is the experimental argument; and this, you say too, is the sole theological argument. Now it is certain, that the liker the effects are, which are seen, and the liker the causes, which are inferred, the stronger is the argument. Every departure on either side diminishes the probability, and renders the experiment less conclusive. You cannot doubt of the principle: neither ought you to reject its consequences.

All the new discoveries in astronomy, which prove the immense grandeur and magnificence of the works of nature, are so many additional arguments for a Deity, according to the true system of theism: but according to your hypothesis of experimental theism, they become so many objections, by removing the effect still farther from all resemblance to the effects of human art and contrivance. For if Lucretius,[5] even following the old system of the world, could exclaim,

> Quis regere immensi summan, quis habere profundi
> Indu manu validas potis est moderanter habenas?
> Quis pariter coelos omnes convertere? et omnes
> Ignibus aetheriis terras suffire feraces?
> Omnibus inque locis esse omni tempore praesto?

If Tully[6] esteemed this reasoning so natural as to put it into the mouth of his Epicurean. *Quibus enim oculis animi intueri potuit vester Plato fabricam illam tanti operis, qua construi a Deo atque aedificari mundum facit? quae molitio? quae ferramenta? qui vectes? quae machinae? qui ministri tanti muneris fuerunt? quemadmodum autem obedire et parere voluntati architecti aer, ignis, aqua, terra potuerunt?* If this argument, I say, has any force in former ages: how much greater must it have at present; when the bonds of nature are so infinitely enlarged, and such a magnificent scene is opened to us? It is still more unreasonable to form our idea of so unlimited a cause from our experience of the narrow productions of human design and invention.

The discoveries by microscopes, as they open a new universe in miniature, are still objections, according to you; arguments, according to

[5] Lib. xi. 1094.
[6] De Nat. Deor., lib. i.

me. The farther we push our researches of this kind, we are still led to infer the universal causes of all to be vastly different from mankind, or from any object of human experience and observation.

And what say you to the discoveries in anatomy, chemistry, botany? . . . . These surely are no objections, replied Cleanthes: they only discover new instances of art and contrivance. It is still the image of mind reflected on us from innumerable objects. Add, a mind *like the human,* said Philo. I know of no other, replied Cleanthes. And the liker the better, insisted Philo. To be sure, said Cleanthes.

Now, Cleanthes, said Philo, with an air of alacrity and triumph, mark the consequences. *First,* By this method of reasoning, you renounce all claim to infinity in any of the attributes of the Deity. For as the cause ought only to be proportioned to the effect, and the effect, so far as it falls under our cognizance, is not infinite; what pretensions have we, upon your suppositions, to ascribe that attribute to the Divine Being? You will still insist, that, by removing him so much from all similarity to human creatures, we give in to the most arbitrary hypothesis, and at the same time weaken all proofs of his existence.

Secondly, You have no reason, on your theory, for ascribing perfection to the Deity, even in his finite capacity; or for supposing him free from every error, mistake, or incoherence in his undertakings. There are many inexplicable difficulties in the works of nature, which, if we allow a perfect author to be proved *a priori,* are easily solved, and become only seeming difficulties, from the narrow capacity of man, who cannot trace infinite relations. But according to your method of reasoning, these difficulties become all real; and perhaps will be insisted on, as new instances of likeness to human art and contrivance. At least, you must acknowledge, that it is impossible for us to tell, from our limited views, whether this system contains any great faults, or deserves any considerable praise, if compared to other possible, and even real systems. Could a peasant, if the *Aeneid* were read to him, pronounce that poem to be absolutely faultless, or even assign to it its proper rank among the productions of human wit; he, who had never seen any other production?

But were this world ever so perfect a production, it must still remain uncertain, whether all the excellences of the work can justly be ascribed to the workman. If we survey a ship, what an exalted idea must we form of the ingenuity of the carpenter, who framed so complicated, useful, and beautiful a machine? And what surprise must we feel, when we find him a stupid mechanic, who imitated others, and copied an art, which, through a long succession of ages, after multiplied trials, mistakes, corrections, deliberations, and controversies, had been gradually improving? Many worlds might have been botched and bungled, throughout an eternity, ere this system was struck out: much labor lost: many fruitless trials made: and a slow, but continued improvement carried on during infinite ages in the art of world-making. In such subjects, who can determine, where the truth; nay, who can conjecture where the probability lies; amidst a great number of hypotheses which may be proposed, and a still greater number which may be imagined?

And what shadow of an argument, continued Philo, can you produce, from your hypothesis, to prove the unity of the Deity? A great number of men join in building a house or ship, in rearing a city, in framing a commonwealth: why may not several deities combine in contriving and framing a world? This is only so much greater similarity to human affairs? By sharing the work among several, we may so much further limit the attributes of each, and get rid of that extensive power and knowledge, which must be supposed in one deity, and which, according to you, can only serve to weaken the proof of his existence. And if such foolish, such vicious creatures as man can yet often unite in framing and executing one plan; how much more those deities or demons, whom we may suppose several degrees more perfect?

To multiply causes, without necessity, is indeed contrary to true philosophy: but this principle applies not to the present case. Were one deity antecedently proved by your theory, who were possessed of every attribute, requisite to the production of the universe; it would be needless, I own (though not absurd) to suppose any other deity existent. But while it is still a question, whether all these attributes are united in one subject, or dispersed among several independent beings: by what phenomena in nature can we pretend to decide the controversy? Where we see a body raised in a scale, we are sure that there is in the opposite scale, however concealed from sight, some counterpoising weight equal to it: but it is still allowed to doubt, whether that weight be an aggregate of several distinct bodies, or one uniform united mass. And if the weight requisite very much exceeds anything which we have ever seen conjoined in any single body, the former supposition becomes still more probable and natural. An intelligent being of such vast power and capacity, as is necessary to produce the universe, or, to speak in the language of ancient philosophy, so prodigious an animal, exceeds all analogy, and even comprehension.

But farther, Cleanthes; men are mortal, and renew their species by generation; and this is common to all living creatures. The two great sexes of male and female, says Milton, animate the world. Why must this circumstance, so universal, so essential, be excluded from those numerous and limited deities? Behold then the theogony of ancient times brought back upon us.

And why not become a perfect anthropomorphite? Why not assert the deity or deities to be corporeal, and to have eyes, a nose, mouth, ears, etc.? Epicurus maintained, that no man had ever seen reason but in a human figure; therefore the gods must have a human figure. And this argument, which is deservedly so much ridiculed by Cicero, becomes, according to you, solid and philosophical.

In a word, Cleanthes, a man, who follows your hypothesis, is able, perhaps, to assert, or conjecture, that the universe, sometime, arose from something like design: but beyond that position he cannot ascertain one single circumstance, and is left afterwards to fix every point of his theology, by the utmost license of fancy and hypothesis. This world, for aught he knows, is very faulty and imperfect, compared to a superior standard; and was only the first rude essay of some infant deity, who afterwards abandoned it, ashamed of his lame performance; it is the work only of some dependent, inferior deity; and is the object of derision to his superiors: it is the production of old age and dotage in some superannuated deity; and ever since his death, has run on at adventures, from the first impulse and active force, which it received from him. You justly give signs of horror, Demea, at these strange suppositions: but these, and a thousand more of the same kind, are Cleanthes's suppositions, not mine. From the moment the attributes of the Deity are supposed finite, all these have place. And I cannot, for my part, think, that so wild and unsettled a system of theology is, in any respect, preferable to none at all.

These suppositions I absolutely disown, cried Cleanthes: they strike me, however, with no horror; especially, when proposed in that rambling way in which they drop from you. On the contrary, they give me pleasure, when I see, that, by the utmost indulgence of your imagination, you never get rid of the hypothesis of design in the universe; but are obliged, at every turn, to have recourse to it. To this concession I adhere steadily; and this I regard as a sufficient foundation for religion.

Part VI

It must be a slight fabric, indeed, said Demea, which can be erected on so tottering a foundation. While we are uncertain, whether there is one deity or many; whether the deity or deities, to whom we owe our existence, be perfect or imperfect, subordinate or supreme, dead or alive; what trust or confidence can we repose in them? What devotion or worship address to them? What veneration or obedience pay them? To all the purposes of life, the theory of religion becomes altogether useless: and even with regard to speculative consequences, its uncertainty, according to you, must render it totally precarious and unsatisfactory.

To render it still more unsatisfactory, said Philo, there occurs to me another hypothesis, which must acquire an air of probability from the method of reasoning so much insisted on by Cleanthes. That like effects arise from like causes: this principle he supposes the foundation of all religion. But there is another principle of the same kind, no less certain, and derived from the same source of experience: that where several known circumstances are *observed* to be similar, the unknown will also be *found* similar. Thus, if we see the limbs of a human body, we conclude, that it is also attended with a human head, though hid from us. Thus, if we see, through a chink in a wall, a small part of the sun, we conclude that, were the wall removed, we should see the whole body. In short, this method of reasoning is so obvious and familiar, that no scruple can ever be made with regard to its solidity.

Now if we survey the universe, so far as it falls under our knowledge, it bears a great resemblance to an animal or organized body, and seems actuated with a like principle of life and motion. A continual circulation of matter in it produces no disorder: a continual waste in every part is incessantly repaired; the closest sympathy is perceived throughout the entire system: and each part or member, in performing its proper offices, operates both to its own preservation and to that of the whole. The world, therefore, I infer, is an animal, and the Deity is the *soul* of the world, actuating it, and actuated by it.

You have too much learning, Cleanthes, to be at all surprised at this opinion, which, you know, was maintained by almost all the theists of antiquity, and chiefly prevails in their discourses and reasonings. For though sometimes the ancient philosophers reason from final causes, as if they thought the world the workmanship of God; yet it appears rather their favorite notion to consider it as his body, whose organization renders it subservient to him. And it must be confessed, that as the universe resembles more a human body than it does the works of human art and contrivance; if our limited analogy could ever, with any propriety, be extended to the whole of nature, the inference seems juster in favor of the ancient than the modern theory.

There are many other advantages too, in the former theory, which recommend it to the ancient theologians. Nothing more repugnant to all their notions, because nothing more repugnant to common experience than mind without body; a mere spiritual substance, which fell not under their senses nor comprehension, and of which they had not observed one single instance throughout all nature. Mind and body they knew, because they felt both: an order, arrangement, organization, or internal machinery in both they likewise knew, after the same manner; and it could not but seem reasonable to transfer this experience to the universe, and to suppose the divine mind and body to be also coe-

val, and to have, both of them, order and arrangement naturally inherent in them, and inseparable from them.

Here therefore is a new species of anthropomorphism, Cleanthes, on
which you may deliberate; and a theory which seems not liable to any
considerable difficulties. You are too much superior surely to systemati-
cal prejudices, to find any more difficulty in supposing an animal body
to be, originally, of itself, or from unknown causes, possessed of order
and organization, than in supposing a similar order to belong to mind.
But the vulgar prejudice, that body and mind ought always to accompany each other, ought not, one should think, to be entirely neglected;
since it is founded on vulgar experience, the only guide which you
profess to follow in all these theological inquiries. And if you assert,
that our limited experience is an unequal standard, by which to judge of
the unlimited extent of nature; you entirely abandon your own hypothesis, and must thenceforward adopt our mysticism, as you call it, and
admit of the absolute incomprehensibility of the Divine Nature.

This theory, I own, replied Cleanthes, has never before occurred to
me, though a pretty natural one; and I cannot readily, upon so short an
examination and reflection, deliver any opinion with regard to it. You
are very scrupulous, indeed, said Philo; were I to examine any system of yours, I should not have acted with half that caution and reserve, in stating objections and difficulties to it. However, if anything
occur to you, you will oblige us by proposing it.

Why then, replied Cleanthes, it seems to me that, though the world
does, in many circumstances, resemble an animal body; yet is the analogy also defective in many circumstances, the most material: no organs of sense; no seat of thought or reason; no one precise origin of motion and action. In short, it seems to bear a stronger resemblance to a
vegetable than to an animal, and your inference would be so far incon-
clusive in favor of the soul of the world.

But, in the next place, your theory seems to imply the eternity of
the world; and that is a principle which, I think, can be refuted by
the strongest reasons and probabilities. I shall suggest an argument to
this purpose, which, I believe, has not been insisted on by any writer.
Those, who reason from the late origin of arts and sciences, though
their inference wants not force, may perhaps be refuted by considerations, derived from the nature of human society, which is in continual
revolution between ignorance and knowledge, liberty and slavery, riches
and poverty; so that it is impossible for us, from our limited experience, to foretell with assurance what events may or may not be expected. Ancient learning and history seem to have been in great danger
of entirely perishing after the inundation of the barbarous nations; and
had these convulsions continued a little longer, or been a little more

violent, we should not probably have now known what passed in the world a few centuries before us. Nay, were it not for the superstition of the popes, who preserved a little jargon of Latin, in order to support the appearance of an ancient and universal church, that tongue must have been utterly lost: in which case, the Western world, being totally barbarous, would not have been in a fit disposition for receiving the Greek language and learning, which was conveyed to them after the sacking of Constantinople. When learning and books had been extinguished, even the mechanical arts would have fallen considerably to decay; and it is easily imagined, that fable or tiadition might ascribe to them a much later origin than the true one. This vulgar argument, therefore, against the eternity of the world, seems a little precarious.

But here appears to be the foundation of a better argument. Lucullus was the first that brought cherry-trees from Asia to Europe; though that tree thrives so well in many European climates, that it grows in the woods without any culture. Is it possible, that, throughout a whole eternity, no European had ever passed into Asia, and thought of transplanting so delicious a fruit into is own country? Or if the tree was once transplanted and propagated, how could it ever afterwards perish? Empires may rise and fall; liberty and slavery succeed alternately; ignorance and knowledge give place to each other; but the cherry-tree will still remain in the woods of Greece, Spain and Italy, and will never be affected by the revolutions of human society.

It is not two thousand years since vines were transplanted into France; though there is no climate in the world more favorable to them. It is not three centuries since horses, cows, sheep, swine, dogs, corn, were known in America. Is it possible, that, during the revolutions of a whole eternity, there never arose a Columbus, who might open the communication between Europe and that continent? We may as well imagine, that all men would wear stockings for ten thousand years, and never have the sense to think of garters to tie them. All these seem convincing proofs of the youth, or rather infancy, of the world; as being founded on the operation of principles more constant and steady, than those by which human society is governed and directed. Nothing less than a total convulsion of the elements will ever destroy all the European animals and vegetables, which are now to be found in the Western world.

And what argument have you against such convulsions? replied Philo. Strong and almost incontestable proofs may be traced over the whole earth, that every part of this globe has continued for many ages entirely covered with water. And though order were supposed inseparable from matter, and inherent in it; yet may matter be susceptible of many and great revolutions, through the endless periods of eternal duration.

The incessant changes, to which every part of it is subject, seem to intimate some such general transformations; though at the same time, it is observable, that all the changes and corruptions, of which we have ever had experience, are but passages from one state of order to another; nor can matter ever rest in total deformity and confusion. What we see in the parts, we may infer in the whole; at least, that is the method of reasoning on which you rest your whole theory. And were I obliged to defend any particular system of this nature (which I never willingly should do), I esteem none more plausible than that which ascribes an eternal, inherent principle of order to the world: though attended with great and continual revolutions and alterations. This at once solves all difficulties; and if the solution, by being so general, is not entirely complete and satisfactory, it is, at least, a theory, that we must, sooner or later, have recourse to, whatever system we embrace. How could things have been as they are, were there not an original, inherent principle of order somewhere, in thought or in matter? And it is very indifferent to which of these we give the preference. Chance has no place, on any hypothesis, sceptical or religious. Everything is surely governed by steady, inviolable laws. And were the inmost essence of things laid open to us, we should then discover a scene, of which, at present, we can have no idea. Instead of admiring the order of natural beings, we should clearly see that it was absolutely impossible for them, in the smallest article, ever to admit of any other disposition.

Were anyone inclined to revive the ancient pagan theology, which maintained, as we learn from Hesiod, that this globe was governed by 30,000 deities, who arose from the unknown powers of nature: you would naturally object, Cleanthes, that nothing is gained by this hypothesis; and that it is as easy to suppose all men animals, beings more numerous, but less perfect, to have sprung immediately from a like origin. Push the same inference a step farther; and you will find a numerous society of deities as explicable as one universal deity, who possesses, within himself, the powers and perfections of the whole society. All these systems, then, of scepticism, polytheism, and theism, you must allow, on your principles, to be on a like footing, and that no one of them has any advantages over the others. You may thence learn the fallacy of your principles.

Part VII

But here, continued Philo, in examining the ancient system of the soul of the world, there strikes me, all on a sudden, a new idea, which, if just, must go near to subvert all your reasoning, and destroy even your first inferences, on which you repose such confidence. If the universe bears a greater likeness to animal bodies and to vegetables, than to the works of human art, it is more probable that its cause resembles the cause of the former than that of the latter, and its origin ought rather to be ascribed to generation or vegetation than to reason or design. Your conclusion, even according to your own principles, is therefore lame and defective.

Pray open up this argument a little farther, said Demea. For I do not rightly apprehend it, in that concise manner, in which you have expressed it.

Our friend, Cleanthes, replied Philo, as you have heard, asserts, that since no question of fact can be proved otherwise than by experience, the existence of a Deity admits not of proof from any other medium. The world, says he, resembles the works of human contrivance: therefore its cause must also resemble that of the other. Here we may remark, that the operation of one very small part of nature, to wit man, upon another very small part, to wit that inanimate matter lying within his reach, is the rule, by which Cleanthes judges of the origin of the whole; and he measures objects, so widely disproportioned, by the same individual standard. But to waive all objections drawn from this topic; I affirm, that there are other parts of the universe (besides the machines of human invention) which bear still a greater resemblance to the fabric of the world, and which therefore afford a better conjecture concerning the universal origin of this system. These parts are animals and vegetables. The world plainly resembles more an animal or a vegetable, than it does a watch or a knitting-loom. Its cause, therefore, it is more probable, resembles the cause of the former. The cause of the former is generation or vegetation. The cause, therefore, of the world, we may infer to be some thing similar or analogous to generation or vegetation.

But how is it conceivable, said Demea, that the world can arise from anything similar to vegetation or generation?

Very easily, replied Philo. In like manner as a tree sheds its seed into the neighboring fields, and produces other trees; so the great vegetable the world, or this planetary system, produces within itself certain seeds, which, being scattered into the surrounding chaos, vegetate into new worlds. A comet, for instance, is the seed of a world; and after it has been fully ripened, by passing from sun to sun, and star to star, it is at last tossed into the unformed elements, which everywhere surround this universe, and immediately sprouts up into a new system.

Or if, for the sake of variety (for I see no other advantage), we should suppose this world to be an animal; a comet is the egg of this animal; and in like manner as an ostrich lays its egg in the sand, which, without any farther care, hatches the egg, and produces a new animal;

so . . . . I understand you, says Demea: but what wild, arbitrary suppositions are these? What *data* have you for such extraordinary conclusions? And is the slight, imaginary resemblance of the world to a vegetable or an animal sufficient to establish the same inference with regard to both? Objects, which are in general so widely different; ought they to be a standard for each other?

Right, cries Philo: this is the topic on which I have all along insisted. I have still asserted, that we have no *data* to establish any system of cosmogony. Our experience, so imperfect in itself, and so limited both in extent and duration, can afford us no probable conjecture concerning the whole of things. But if we must needs fix on some hypothesis; by what rule, pray ought we to determine our choice? Is there any other rule than the greater similarity of the objects compared? And does not a plant or an animal, which springs from vegetation or generation, bear a stronger resemblance to the world, than does any artificial machine, which arises from reason and design?

But what is this vegetation and generation of which you talk? said Demea. Can you explain their operations, and anatomize that fine internal structure, on which they depend?

As much, at least, replied Philo, as Cleanthes can explain the operations of reason, or anatomize that internal structure, on which *it* depends. But without any such elaborate disquisitions, when I see an animal, I infer, that it sprang from generation; and that with as great certainty as you conclude a house to have been reared by design. These words, *generation, reason,* mark only certain powers and energies in nature, whose effects are known, but whose essence is incomprehensible; and one of these principles, more than the other, has no privilege for being made a standard to the whole of nature.

In reality, Demea, it may reasonably be expected, that the larger the views are which we take of things, the better will they conduct us in our conclusions concerning such extraordinary and such magnificent subjects. In this little corner of the world alone, there are four principles, *reason, instinct, generation, vegetation,* which are similar to each other, and are the causes of similar effects. What a number of other principles may we naturally suppose in the immense extent and variety of the universe, could we travel from planet to planet and from system to system, in order to examine each part of this mighty fabric? Any one of these four principles above mentioned (and a hundred others which lie open to our conjecture) may afford us a theory, by which to judge of the origin of the world; and it is a palpable and egregious partiality, to confine our view entirely to that principle, by which our own minds operate. Were this principle more intelligent on that account, such a partiality might be somewhat excusable. But reason, in its internal fabric and structure, is really as little known to us as instinct or vegetation; and perhaps even that vague, undeterminate word, *Nature*, to which the vulgar refer everything, is not at the bottom more inexplicable. The effects of these principles are all known to us from experience: but the principles themselves, and their manner of operation, are totally unknown: nor is it less intelligible, or less conformable to experience to say, that the world arose by vegetation from a seed shed by another world, than to say that it arose from a divine reason or contrivance, according to the sense in which Cleanthes understands it.

But methinks, said Demea, if the world had a vegetative quality, and could sow the seeds of new worlds into the infinite chaos, this power would be still an additional argument for design in its author. For whence could arise so wonderful a faculty but from design? Or how can order spring from anything, which perceives not that order which it bestows?

You need only look around you, replied Philo, to satisfy yourself with regard to this question. A tree bestows order and organization on that tree, which springs from it, without knowing the order: an animal, in the same manner, on its offspring: a bird, on its nest: and instances of this kind are even more frequent in the world, than those of order, which arise from reason and contrivance. To say, that all this order in animals and vegetables proceeds ultimately from design, is begging the question; nor can that great point be ascertained otherwise than by proving *a priori*, both that order is, from its nature, inseparably attached to thought, and that it can never, of itself, or from original unknown principles, belong to matter.

But farther, Demea; this objection, which you urge, can never be made use of by Cleanthes, without renouncing a defense, which he has already made against one of my objections. When I inquired concerning the cause of that supreme reason and intelligence, into which he resolves everything; he told me, that the impossibility of satisfying such inquiries could never be admitted as an objection in any species of philosophy. *We must stop somewhere*, says he; *nor is it ever within the reach of human capacity to explain ultimate causes, or show the last connections of any objects. It is sufficient, if our steps, so far as we go, are supported by experience and observation.* Now, that vegetation and generation, as well as reason, are experienced to be principles of order in nature, is undeniable. If I rest my system of cosmogony on the former, preferably to the latter, 'tis at my choice. The matter seems entirely arbitrary. And when Cleanthes asks me what is the cause of my great vegetative or generative faculty, I am equally entitled to ask him the cause of his great reasoning principle. These questions we have agreed to forebear on both sides; and it is chiefly his interest on the present occasion to stick to this agreement. Judging by our limited and imperfect experience, generation has some privileges above reason: for we see every day the latter arise from the former, never the former from the latter.

Compare, I beseech you, the consequences on both sides. The world, say I, resembles an animal, therefore it is an animal, therefore it arose from generation. The steps, I confess, are wide; yet there is some small appearance of analogy in each step. The world, says Cleanthes, resembles a machine, therefore it is a machine, therefore it arose from design. The steps are here equally wide, and the analogy less striking. And if he pretends to carry on *my* hypothesis a step farther, and to infer design or reason from the great principle of generation, on which I insist; I may, with better authority, use the same freedom to push farther *his* hypothesis, and infer a divine generation or theogony from his principle of reason. I have at least some faint shadow of experience, which is the utmost that can ever be attained in the present subject. Reason, in innumerable instances, is observed to arise from the principle of generation, and never to arise from any other principle.

Hesiod, and all the ancient mythologists, were so struck with this analogy, that they universally explained the origin of nature from an animal birth, and copulation. Plato too, so far as he is intelligible, seems to have adopted some such notion in his *Timaeus*.

The Brahmins assert, that the world arose from an infinite spider, who spun this whole complicated mass from his bowels, and annihilates afterwards the whole or any part of it, by absorbing it again, and resolving it into his own essence. Here is a species of cosmogony, which appears to us ridiculous; because a spider is a little contemptible animal, whose operations we are never likely to take for a model of the whole universe. But still here is a new species of analogy, even in our globe. And were there a planet wholly inhabited by spiders (which is very possible), this inference would there appear as natural and irrefragable as that which in our planet ascribes the origin of all things to design and intelligence, as explained by Cleanthes. Why an orderly system may not be spun from the belly as well as from the brain, it will be difficult for him to give a satisfactory reason.

I must confess, Philo, replied Cleanthes, that of all men living, the task which you have undertaken, of raising doubts and objections, suits you best, and seems, in a manner, natural and unavoidable to you. So great is your fertility of invention, that I am not ashamed to acknowledge myself unable, on a sudden, to solve regularly such out-of-the-way difficulties as you incessantly start upon me: though I clearly see, in general, their fallacy and error. And I question not, but you are yourself, at present, in the same case, and have not the solution so ready as the objection; while you must be sensible, that common sense and reason are entirely against you, and that such whimsies as you have delivered, may puzzle, but never can convince us.

Part VIII

WHAT you ascribe to the fertility of my invention, replied Philo, is entirely owing to the nature of the subject. In subjects, adapted to the narrow compass of human reason, there is commonly but one determination, which carries probability or conviction with it; and to a man of sound judgment, all other suppositions, but that one, appear entirely absurd and chimerical. But in such questions, as the present, a hundred contradictory views may preserve a kind of imperfect analogy; and invention has here full scope to exert itself. Without any great effort of thought, I believe that I could, in an instant, propose other systems of cosmogony, which would have some faint appearance of truth; though it is a thousand, a million to one, if either yours or any one of mine be the true system.

For instance; what if I should revive the old Epicurean hypothesis? This is commonly, and I believe, justly, esteemed the most absurd system, that has yet been proposed; yet, I know not, whether, with a few alterations, it might not be brought to bear a faint appearance of probability. Instead of supposing matter infinite, as Epicurus did; let us suppose it finite. A finite number of particles is only susceptible of finite transpositions: and it must happen, in an eternal duration, that every possible order or position must be tried an infinite number of times. This world, therefore, with all its events, even the most minute, has before been produced and destroyed, and will again be produced and destroyed, without any bounds and limitations. No one, who has a conception of the powers of infinite, in comparison of finite, will ever scruple this determination.

But this supposes, said Demea, that matter can acquire motion, without any voluntary agent or first mover.

And where is the difficulty, replied Philo, of that supposition? Every event, before experience, is equally difficult and incomprehensible; and every event, after experience, is equally easy and intelligible. Motion, in many instances, from gravity, from elasticity, from electricity, begins in matter, without any known voluntary agent; and to suppose always, in these cases, an unknown voluntary agent, is mere hypothesis; and hypothesis attended with no advantages. The beginning of motion in matter itself is as conceivable *a priori* as its communication from mind and intelligence.

Besides; why may not motion have been propagated by impulse

through all eternity, and the same stock of it, or nearly the same, be still upheld in the universe? As much as is lost by the composition of motion, as much is gained by its resolution. And whatever the causes are, the fact is certain, that matter is, and always has been in continual agitation, as far as human experience or tradition reaches. There is not probably, at present, in the whole universe, one particle of matter at absolute rest.

And this very consideration too, continued Philo, which we have stumbled on in the course of argument, suggests a new hypothesis of cosmogony, that is not absolutely absurd and improbable. Is there a system, an order, an economy of things, by which matter can preserve that perpetual agitation, which seems essential to it, and yet maintain a constancy in the forms, which it produces? There certainly is such an economy: for this is actually the case with the present world. The continual motion of matter, therefore, in less than infinite transpositions, must produce this economy or order; and by its very nature, that order, when once established, supports itself, for many ages, if not to eternity. But wherever matter is so poised, arranged, and adjusted as to continue in perpetual motion, and yet preserve a constancy in the forms, its situation must, of necessity, have all the same appearance of art and contrivance, which we observe at present. All the parts of each form must have a relation to each other, and to the whole: and the whole itself must have a relation to the other parts of the universe; to the element, in which the form subsists; to the materials, with which it repairs its waste and decay; and to every other form, which is hostile or friendly. A defect in any of these particulars destroys the form; and the matter, of which it is composed, is again set loose, and is thrown into irregular motions and fermentations, till it unite itself to some other regular form. If no such form be prepared to receive it, and if there be a great quantity of this corrupted matter in the universe, the universe itself is entirely disordered; whether it be the feeble embryo of a world in its first beginnings, that is thus destroyed, or the rotten carcass of one, languishing in old age and infirmity. In either case, a chaos ensues; till finite, though innumerable revolutions produce at last some forms, whose parts and organs are so adjusted as to support the forms amidst a continued succession of matter.

Suppose (for we shall endeavor to vary the expression), that matter were thrown into any position, by a blind, unguided force; it is evident that this first position must in all probability be the most confused and most disorderly imaginable, without any resemblance to those works of human contrivance, which, along with a symmetry of parts, discover an adjustment of means to ends and a tendency to self-preservation. If the actuating force cease after this operation, matter must remain forever in disorder, and continue an immense chaos, without any proportion or activity. But suppose, that the actuating force, whatever it be, still continues in matter, this first position will immediately give place to a second, which will likewise in all probability be as disorderly as the first, and so on, through many successions of changes and revolutions. No particular order or position ever continues a moment unaltered. The original force, still remaining in activity, gives a perpetual restlessness to matter. Every possible situation is produced, and instantly destroyed. If a glimpse or dawn of order appears for a moment, it is instantly hurried away, and confounded, by that never-ceasing force, which actuates every part of matter.

Thus the universe goes on for many ages in a continued succession of chaos and disorder. But is it not possible that it may settle at last, so as not to lose its motion and active force (for that we have supposed inherent in it) yet so as to preserve an uniformity of appearance, amidst the continual motion and fluctuation of its parts? This we find to be the case with the universe at present. Every individual is perpetually changing, and every part of every individual, and yet the whole remains, in appearance, the same. May we not hope for such a position, or rather be assured of it, from the eternal revolutions of unguided matter, and may not this account for all the appearing wisdom and contrivance, which is in the universe? Let us contemplate the subject a little, and we shall find, that this adjustment, if attained by matter, of a seeming stability in the forms, with a real and perpetual revolution or motion of parts, affords a plausible, if not a true solution of the difficulty.

It is in vain, therefore, to insist upon the uses of the parts in animals or vegetables and their curious adjustment to each other. I would fain know how an animal could subsist, unless its parts were so adjusted? Do we not find, that it immediately perishes whenever this adjustment ceases, and that its matter corrupting tries some new form. It happens, indeed, that the parts of the world are so well adjusted, that some regular form immediately lays claim to this corrupted matter: and if it were not so, could the world subsist? Must it not dissolve as well as the animal, and pass through new positions and situations; till in a great, but finite succession, it fall at last into the present or some such order?

It is well, replied Cleanthes, you told us, that this hypothesis was suggested on a sudden, in the course of the argument. Had you had leisure to examine it, you would soon have perceived the insuperable objections, to which it is exposed. No form, you say, can subsist, unless it possess those powers and organs, requisite for its subsistence: some new order or economy must be tried, and so on, without intermission; till at last some order, which can support and maintain itself, is fallen

upon. But according to this hypothesis, whence arise the many conveniences and advantages which men and all animals possess? Two eyes, two
ears, are not absolutely necessary for the subsistence of the species. Human race might have been propagated and preserved, without horses,
dogs, cows, sheep and those innumerable fruits and products which serve
to our satisfaction and enjoyment. If no camels had been created for
the use of man in the sandy deserts of Africa and Arabia, would the
world have been dissolved? If no loadstone had been framed to give
that wonderful and useful direction to the needle, would human society
and the human kind have been immediately extinguished? Though the
maxims of Nature be in general very frugal, yet instances of this kind
are far from being rare; and any one of them is a sufficient proof of
design, and of a benevolent design, which gave rise to the order and arrangement of the universe.

At least, you may safely infer, said Philo, that the foregoing hypothesis is so far incomplete and imperfect; which I shall not scruple
to allow. But can we ever reasonably expect greater success in any attempts of this nature? Or can we ever hope to erect a system of cosmogony, that will be liable to no exceptions, and will contain no circumstance repugnant to our limited and imperfect experience of the
analogy of nature? Your theory itself cannot surely pretend to any
such advantage; even though you have run into anthropomorphism, the
better to preserve a conformity to common experience. Let us once more
put it to trial. In all instances which we have ever seen, ideas are
copied from real objects, and are ectypal, not archetypal, to express myself in learned terms: you reverse this order, and give thought the precedence. In all instances which we have ever seen, thought has no influence upon matter, except where that matter is so conjoined with it,
as to have an equal reciprocal influence upon it. No animal can move
immediately anything but the members of its own body; and indeed, the
equality of action and reaction seems to be an universal law of nature:
but your theory implies a contradiction to this experience. These instances, with many more, which it were easy to collect (particularly the
supposition of a mind or system of thought that is eternal, or in other
words, an animal ingenerable and immortal), these instances, I say, may
teach, all of us, sobriety in condemning each other; and let us see, that
as no system of this kind ought ever to be received from a slight analogy, so neither ought any to be rejected on account of a small incon-
gruity. For that is an inconvenience, from which we can justly pronounce no one to be exempted.

All religious systems, it is confessed, are subject to great and insuperable difficulties. Each disputant triumphs in his turn; while he
carries on an offensive war, and exposes the absurdities, barbarities, and

pernicious tenets of his antagonist. But all of them, on the whole, prepare a complete triumph for the sceptic; who tells them, that no system ought ever to be embraced with regard to such subjects: for this plain reason, that no absurdity ought ever to be assented to with regard to any subject. A total suspense of judgment is here our only reasonable resource. And if every attack, as is commonly observed, and no defense, among theologians, is successful; how complete must be *his* victory, who remains always, with all mankind, on the offensive, and has himself no fixed station or abiding city, which he is ever, on any occasion, obliged to defend?

Part IX

BUT if so many difficulties attend the argument *a posteriori*, said Demea; had we not better adhere to that simple and sublime argument *a priori*, which, by offering to us infallible demonstration, cuts off at once all doubt and difficulty? By this argument, too, we may prove the *infinity* of the divine attributes, which, I am afraid, can never be ascertained with certainty from any other topic. For how can an effect, which either is finite, or, for aught we know, may be so; how can such an effect, I say, prove an infinite cause? The unity too of the Divine Nature, it is very difficult, if not absolutely impossible, to deduce merely from contemplating the works of nature; nor will the uniformity alone of the plan, even were it allowed, give us any assurance of that attribute. Whereas the argument *a priori*. . . .

You seem to reason, Demea, interposed Cleanthes, as if those advantages and conveniences in the abstract argument were full proofs of its solidity. But it is first proper, in my opinion, to determine what argument of this nature you choose to insist on; and we shall afterwards, from itself, better than from its useful consequences, endeavor to determine what value we ought to put upon it.

The argument, replied Demea, which I would insist on is the common one. Whatever exists must have a cause or reason of its existence; it being absolutely impossible for anything to produce itself, or be the cause of its own existence. In mounting up, therefore, from effects to causes, we must either go on in tracing an infinite succession, without any ultimate cause at all; or must at last have recourse to some ultimate cause, that is *necessarily* existent. Now that the first supposition is absurd may be thus proved. In the infinite chain or succession of causes and effects, each single effect is determined to exist by the power and efficacy of that cause, which immediately preceded; but the whole eternal chain or succession, taken together, is not determined or caused by anything: and yet it is evident that it requires a cause or reason, as much as any particular object, which begins to exist in time. The question is still reasonable, why this particular succession of causes existed from eternity, and not any other succession, or no succession at all. If there be no necessarily existent being, any supposition, which can be formed, is equally possible; nor is there any more absurdity in *nothing's* having existed from eternity, than there is in that succession of causes, which constitutes the universe. What was it then, which determined something to exist rather than nothing, and bestowed being on a particular possibility, exclusive of the rest? *External causes,* there are supposed to be none. *Chance* is a word without a meaning. Was it *nothing?* But that can never produce anything. We must, therefore, have recourse to a necessarily existent Being, who carries the reason of his existence in himself; and who cannot be supposed not to exist without an express contradiction. There is consequently such a Being, that is, there is a Deity.

I shall not leave it to Philo, said Cleanthes (though I know that the starting objections is his chief delight), to point out the weakness of this metaphysical reasoning. It seems to me so obviously ill-grounded, and at the same time of so little consequence to the cause of true piety and religion, that I shall myself venture to show the fallacy of it.

I shall begin with observing, that there is an evident absurdity in pretending to demonstrate a matter of fact, or to prove it by any arguments *a priori.* Nothing is demonstrable, unless the contrary implies a contradiction. Nothing, that is distinctly conceivable, implies a contradiction. Whatever we conceive as existent, we can also conceive as non-existent. There is no being, therefore, whose non-existence implies a contradiction. Consquently there is no being, whose existence is demonstrable. I propose this argument as entirely decisive, and am willing to rest the whole controversy upon it.

It is pretended that the Deity is a necessarily existent being; and this necessity of his existence is attempted to be explained by asserting, that, if we knew his whole essence or nature, we should perceive it to be as impossible for him not to exist as for twice two not to be four. But it is evident, that this can never happen, while our faculties remain the same as at present. It will still be possible for us, at any time, to conceive the non-existence of what we formerly conceived to exist; nor can the mind ever lie under a necessity of supposing any object to remain always in being; in the same manner as we lie under a necessity of always conceiving twice two to be four. The words, therefore, *necessary existence,* have no meaning; or, which is the same thing, none that is consistent.

But farther; why may not the material universe be the necessarily existent Being, according to this pretended explication of necessity?

We dare not affirm that we know all the qualities of matter; and for aught we can determine, it may contain some qualities, which, were they known, would make its non-existence appear as great a contradiction as that twice two is five. I find only one argument employed to prove, that the material world is not the necessarily existent Being; and this argument is derived from the contingency both of the matter and the form of the world. 'Any particle of matter,' 'tis said,[7] 'may be *conceived* to be annihilated; and any form may be *conceived* to be altered. Such an annihilation or alteration, therefore, is not impossible.' But it seems a great partiality not to perceive, that the same argument extends equally to the Deity, so far as we have any conception of him; and that the mind can at least imagine him to be non-existent, or his attributes to be altered. It must be some unknown, inconceivable qualities, which can make his non-existence appear impossible, or his attributes inalterable. And no reason can be assigned, why these qualities may not belong to matter. As they are altogether unknown and inconceivable, they can never be proved incompatible with it.

Add to this, that in tracing an eternal succession of objects, it seems absurd to inquire for a general cause or first author. How can anything, that exists from eternity, have a cause, since that relation implies a priority in time and a beginning of existence?

In such a chain too, or succession of objects, each part is caused by that which preceded it, and causes that which succeeds it. Where then is the difficulty? But the *whole*, you say, wants a cause. I answer, that the uniting of these parts into a whole, like the uniting of several distinct counties into one kingdom, or several distinct members into one body, is performed merely by an arbitrary act of the mind, and has no influence on the nature of things. Did I show you the particular causes of each individual in a collection of twenty particles of matter, I should think it very unreasonable, should you afterwards ask me, what was the cause of the whole twenty. This is sufficiently explained in explaining the cause of the parts.

Though the reasonings, which you have urged, Cleanthes, may well excuse me, said Philo, from starting any farther difficulties; yet I cannot forbear insisting still upon another topic. 'Tis observed by arithmeticians, that the products of 9 compose always either 9 or some lesser product of 9; if you add together all the characters, of which any of the former products is composed. Thus, of 18, 27, 36, which are products of 9, you make 9 by adding 1 to 8, 2 to 7, 3 to 6. Thus, 369 is a product also of 9; and if you add 3, 6, and 9, you make 18, a lesser product of 9.[8] To a superficial observer, so wonderful a regularity may

[7] Dr. Clarke.
[8] République des Lettres, Août 1685.

be admired as the effect either of chance or design: but a skillful algebraist immediately concludes it to be the work of necessity, and demonstrates, that it must forever result from the nature of these numbers. Is it not probable, I ask, that the whole economy of the universe is conducted by a like necessity, though no human algebra can furnish a key, which solves the difficulty? And instead of admiring the order of natural beings, may it not happen, that, could we penetrate into the intimate nature of bodies, we should clearly see why it was absolutely impossible, they could ever admit of any other disposition? So dangerous is it to introduce this idea of necessity into the present question! And so naturally does it afford an inference directly opposite to the religious hypothesis!

But dropping all these abstractions, continued Philo; and confining ourselves to more familiar topics; I shall venture to add an observation, that the argument *a priori* has seldom been found very convincing, except to people of a metaphysical head, who have accustomed themselves to abstract reasoning, and who finding from mathematics, that the understanding frequently leads to truth, through obscurity, and contrary to first appearances, have transferred the same habit of thinking to subjects, where it would not to have place. Other people, even of good sense and the best inclined to religion, feel always some deficiency in such arguments, though they are not perhaps able to explain distinctly where it lies. A certain proof, that men ever did, and ever will derive their religion from other sources than from this species of reasoning.

Part X

IT IS my opinion, I own, replied Demea, that each man feels, in a manner, the truth of religion within his own breast; and from a consciousness of his imbecility and misery, rather than from any reasoning, is led to seek protection from that Being, on whom he and all nature is dependent. So anxious or so tedious are even the best scenes of life, that futurity is still the object of all our hopes and fears. We incessantly look forward, and endeavor, by prayers, adoration, and sacrifice, to appease those unknown powers, whom we find, by experience, so able to afflict and oppress us. Wretched creatures that we are! what resource for us amidst the innumerable ills of life, did not religion suggest some methods of atonement, and appease those terrors, with which we are incessantly agitated and tormented?

I am indeed persuaded, said Philo, that the best and indeed the only method of bringing everyone to a due sense of religion, is by just representations of the misery and wickedness of men. And for that purpose a talent of eloquence and strong imagery is more requisite than that of reasoning and argument. For is it necessary to prove, what everyone feels within himself? 'Tis only necessary to make us feel it, if possible, more intimately and sensibly.

The people, indeed, replied Demea, are sufficiently convinced of this great and melancholy truth. The miseries of life, the unhappiness of men, the general corruptions of our nature, the unsatisfactory enjoyment of pleasures, riches, honors; these phrases have become almost proverbial in all languages. And who can doubt of what all men declare from their own immediate feeling and experience?

In this point, said Philo, the learned are perfectly agreed with the vulgar; and in all letters, sacred and profane, the topic of human misery has been insisted on with the most pathetic eloquence that sorrow and melancholy could inspire. The poets, who speak from sentiment, without a system, and whose testimony has therefore the more authority, abound in images of this nature. From Homer down to Dr. Young, the whole inspired tribe have ever been sensible, that no other representation of things would suit the feeling and observation of each individual.

As to authorities, replied Demea, you need not seek them. Look round this library of Cleanthes. I shall venture to affirm, that, except authors of particular sciences, such as chemistry or botany, who have no occasion to treat of human life, there scarce is one of those innumerable writers, from whom the sense of human misery has not, in some passage or other, extorted a complaint and confession of it. At least, the chance is entirely on that side; and no one author has ever, so far as I can recollect, been so extravagant as to deny it.

There you must excuse me, said Philo: Leibnitz has denied it; and is perhaps the first,[9] who ventured upon so bold and paradoxical an opinion; at least, the first, who made it essential to his philosophical system.

And by being the first, replied Demea, might he not have been sensible of his error? For is this a subject, in which philosophers can propose to make discoveries, especially in so late an age? And can any man hope by a simple denial (for the subject scarcely admits of reasoning) to bear down the united testimony of mankind, founded on sense and consciousness?

And why should man, added he, pretend to an exemption from the lot of all other animals? The whole earth, believe me, Philo, is cursed and polluted. A perpetual war is kindled amongst all living creatures.

[9] That sentiment had been maintained by Dr. King and some few others, before Leibnitz, though by none of so great fame as that German philosopher.

Necessity, hunger, want, stimulate the strong and courageous: fear, anxiety, terror, agitate the weak and infirm. The first entrance into life gives anguish to the new-born infant and to its wretched parent: weakness, impotence, distress, attend each stage of that life: and 'tis at last finished in agony and horror.

Observe too, says Philo, the curious artifices of nature, in order to embitter the life of every living being. The stronger prey upon the weaker, and keep them in perpetual terror and anxiety. The weaker too, in their turn, often prey upon the stronger, and vex and molest them without relaxation. Consider that innumerable race of insects, which either are bred on the body of each animal, or flying about infix their stings in him. These insects have others still less than themselves, which torment them. And thus on each hand, before and behind, above and below, every animal is surrounded with enemies, which incessantly seek his misery and destruction.

Man alone, said Demea, seems to be, in part, an exception to this rule. For by combination in society, he can easily master lions, tigers, and bears, whose greater strength and agility naturally enable them to prey upon him.

On the contrary, it is here chiefly, cried Philo, that the uniform and equal maxims of nature are most apparent. Man, it is true, can, by combination, surmount all his *real* enemies, and become master of the whole animal creation: but does he not immediately raise up to himself *imaginary* enemies, the demons of his fancy, who haunt him with superstitious terrors, and blast every enjoyment of life? His pleasure, as he imagines, becomes, in their eyes, a crime: his food and repose give them umbrage and offense: his very sleep and dreams furnish new materials to anxious fear: and even death, his refuge from every other ill, presents only the dread of endless and innumerable woes. Nor does the wolf molest more the timid flock, than superstition does the anxious breast of wretched morals.

Besides, consider, Demea; this very society, by which we surmount those wild beasts, our natural enemies; what new enemies does it not raise to us? What woe and misery does it not occasion? Man is the greatest enemy of man. Oppression, injustice, contempt, contumely, violence, sedition, war, calumny, treachery, fraud; by these they mutually torment each other: and they would soon dissolve that society which they had formed, were it not for the dread of still greater ills, which must attend their separation.

But though these external insults, said Demea, from animals, from men, from all the elements, which assault us, form a frightful catalogue of woes, they are nothing in comparison of those, which arise within ourselves, from the distempered condition of our mind and body. How many lie under the lingering torment of diseases? Hear the pathetic enumeration of the great poet.

> Intestine stone and ulcer, colic-pangs,
> Demoniac frenzy, moping melancholy,
> And moon-struck madness, pining atrophy,
> Marasmus and wide-wasting pestilence.
> Dire was the tossing, deep the groans: Despair
> Tended the sick, busiest from couch to couch.
> And over them triumphant Death his dart
> Shook, but delay'd to strike, tho' oft invok'd
> With vows, as their chief good and final hope. [10]

The disorders of the mind, continued Demea, though more secret, are not perhaps less dismal and vexatious. Remorse, shame, anguish, rage, disappointment, anxiety, fear, dejection, despair; who has ever passed through life without cruel inroads from these tormentors? How many have scarcely ever felt any better sensations? Labor and poverty, so abhorred by everyone, are the certain lot of the far greater number; and those few privileged persons, who enjoy ease and opulence, never reach contentment or true felicity. All the goods of life united would not make a very happy man: but all the ills united would make a wretch indeed; and anyone of them almost (and who can be free from everyone), nay often the absence of one good (and who can possess all), is sufficient to render life ineligible.

Were a stranger to drop, on a sudden, into this world, I would show him, as a specimen of its ills, an hospital full of diseases, a prison crowded with malefactors and debtors, a field of battle strewed with carcasses, a fleet floundering in the ocean, a nation languishing under tyranny, famine, or pestilence. To turn the gay side of life to him, and give him a notion of its pleasures; whither should I conduct him? to a ball, to an opera, to court? He might justly think, that I was only showing him a diversity of distress and sorrow.

There is no evading such striking instances, said Philo, but by apologies, which still farther aggravate the charge. Why have all men, I ask, in all ages, complained incessantly of the miseries of life? . . . . They have no just reason, says one: these complaints proceed only from their discontented, repining, anxious disposition. . . . And can there possibly, I reply, be a more certain foundation of misery, than such a wretched temper?

But if they were really as unhappy as they pretend, says my antagonist, why do they remain in life? . . . .

Not satisfied with life, afraid of death.

[10] Milton: Paradise Lost, XI.

This is the secret chain, say I, that holds us. We are terrified, not bribed to the continuance of our existence.

It is only a false delicacy, he may insist, which a few refined spirits indulge, and which has spread these complaints among the whole race of mankind. . . . And what is this delicacy, I ask, which you blame? Is it anything but a greater sensibility to all the pleasures and pains of life? and if the man of a delicate, refined temper, by being so much more alive than the rest of the world, is only so much more unhappy; what judgment must we form in general of human life?

Let men remain at rest, says our adversary; and they will be easy. They are willing artificers of their own misery. . . . No! reply I; an anxious languor follows their repose: disappointment, vexation, trouble, their activity and ambition.

I can observe something like what you mention in some others, replied Cleanthes: but I confess, I feel little or nothing of it in myself, and hope that it is not so common as you represent it.

If you feel not human misery yourself, cried Demea, I congratulate you on so happy a singularity. Others, seemingly the most prosperous, have not been ashamed to vent their complaints in the most melancholy strains. Let us attend to the great, the fortunate Emperor, Charles V, when, tired with human grandeur, he resigned all his extensive dominions into the hands of his son. In the last harangue, which he made on that memorable occasion, he publicly avowed, *that the greatest prosperities which he had ever enjoyed, had been mixed with so many adversities, that he might truly say he had never enjoyed any satisfaction or contentment.* But did the retired life, in which he sought for shelter, afford him any greater happiness? If we may credit his son's account, his repentance commenced the very day of his resignation.

Cicero's fortune, from small beginnings, rose to the greatest luster and renown; yet what pathetic complaints of the ills of life do his familiar letters, as well as philosophical discourses, contain? And suitably to his own experience, he introduces Cato, the great, the fortunate Cato, protesting in his old age, that, had he a new life in his offer, he would reject the present.

Ask yourself, ask any of your acquaintance, whether they would live over again the last ten or twenty years of their lives. No! but the next twenty, they say, will be better:

> And from the dregs of life, hope to receive
> What the first sprightly running could not give.[11]

Thus at last they find (such is the greatest of human misery; it

---

[11] Dryden: Aurungzebe. Act IV., sc. i.

reconciles even contradictions) that they complain, at once, of the shortness of life, and of its vanity and sorrow.

And is it possible, Cleanthes, said Philo, that after all these reflections, and infinitely more, which might be suggested, you can still persevere in your anthropomorphism, and assert the moral attributes of
the Deity, his justice, benevolence, mercy, and rectitude, to be of the
same nature with these virtues in human creatures? His power we allow infinite: whatever he wills is executed: but neither man nor any
other animal is happy: therefore he does not will their happiness. His
wisdom is infinite: he is never mistaken in choosing the means to any
end: but the course of nature tends not to human or animal felicity:
therefore it is not established for that puropse. Through the whole compass of human knowledge, there are no inferences more certain and infallible than these. In what respect, then, do his benevolence and mercy
resemble the benevolence and mercy of men?

Epicurus's old questions are yet unanswered.

Is he willing to prevent evil, but not able? then is he impotent. Is he
able, but not willing? then is he malevolent. Is he both able and willing? whence then is evil?

You ascribe, Cleanthes, (and I believe justly) a purpose and intention to nature. But what, I beseech you, is the object of that curious
artifice and machinery, which she has displayed in all animals? The
preservation alone of individuals and propagation of the species. It
seems enough for her purpose, if such a rank be barely upheld in the
universe, without any care or concern for the happiness of the members
that compose it. No resource for this purpose: no machinery, in order
merely to give pleasure or ease: no fund of pure joy and contentment:
no indulgence without some want or necessity accompanying it. At
least, the few phenomena of this nature are overbalanced by opposite
phenomena of still greater importance.

Our sense of music, harmony, and indeed beauty of all kinds, gives
satisfaction, without being absolutely necessary to the preservation and
propagation of the species. But what racking pains, on the other hand,
arise from gouts, gravels, megrims, toothaches, rheumatisms; where the
injury to the animal-machinery is either small or incurable? Mirth,
laughter, play, frolic seem gratuitous satisfactions which have no farther tendency: spleen, melancholy, discontent, superstition, are pains
of the same nature. How then does the divine benevolence display
itself, in the sense of you anthropomorphites? None but we mystics, as
you were pleased to call us, can account for this strange mixture of phenomena, by deriving it from attributes, infinitely perfect, but incomprehensible.

And have you at last, said Cleanthes smiling, betrayed your intentions, Philo? Your long agreement with Demea did indeed a little surprise me; but I find you were all the while erecting a concealed bat-
tery against me. And I must confess, that you have now fallen upon a
subject, worthy of your noble spirit of opposition and controversy. If
you can make out the present point, and prove mankind to be unhappy
or corrupted, there is an end at once of all religion. For to what purpose establish the natural attributes of the Deity, while the moral are
still doubtful and uncertain?

You take umbrage very easily, replied Demea, at opinions the most
innocent, and the most generally received even amongst the religious
and devout themselves: and nothing can be more surprising than to find
a topic like this, concerning the wickedness and misery of man, charged
with no less than atheism and profaneness. Have not all pious divines
and preachers, who have indulged their rhetoric on so fertile a subject: have they not easily, I say, given a solution of any difficulties,
which may attend it? This world is but a point in comparison of the
universe; this life but a moment in comparison of eternity. The present
evil phenomena, therefore, are rectified in other regions, and in some future period of existence. And the eyes of men, being then opened to
larger views of things, see the whole connection of general laws; and
trace, with adoration, the benevolence and rectitude of the Deity,
through all the mazes and intricacies of his providence.

No! replied Cleanthes, No! These arbitrary suppositions can never
be admitted, contrary to matter of fact, visible and uncontroverted.
Whence can any cause be known but from its known effects? Whence
can any hypothesis be proved but from the apparent phenomena? To
establish one hypothesis upon another, is building entirely in the air;
and the utmost we ever attain, by these conjectures and fictions, is to
ascertain the bare possibility of our opinion; but never can we, upon
such terms, establish its reality.

The only method of supporting divine benevolence (and it is what
I willingly embrace) is to deny absolutely the misery and wickedness
of man. Your representations are exaggerated: your melancholy views
mostly fictitious: your inferences contrary to fact and experience. Health
is more common than sickness: pleasure than pain: happiness than misery. And for one vexation, which we meet with, we attain, upon computation, a hundred enjoyments.

Admitting your position, replied Philo, which yet is extremely doubtful, you must, at the same time, allow, that, if pain be less frequent
than pleasure, it is infinitely more violent and durable. One hour of it is
often able to outweigh a day, a week, a month of our common insipid enjoyments. And how many days, weeks, and months are passed

by several in the most acute torments? Pleasure, scarcely in one instance, is ever able to reach ecstacy and rapture: and in no one instance can it continue for any time at its highest pitch and altitude. The spirits evaporate; the nerves relax; the fabric is disordered; and the enjoyment quickly degenerates into fatigue and uneasiness. But pain often, good God, how often! rises to torture and agony; and the longer it continues, it becomes still more genuine agony and torture. Patience is exhausted; courage languishes; melancholy seizes us; and nothing terminates our misery but the removal of its cause, or another event, which is the sole cure of all evil, but which, from our natural folly, we regard with still greater horror and consternation.

But not to insist upon these topics, continued Philo, though most obvious, certain, and important; I must use the freedom to admonish you, Cleanthes, that you have put this controversy upon a most dangerous issue, and are unawares introducing a total scepticism, into the most essential articles of natural and revealed theology. What! no method of fixing a just foundation for religion, unless we allow the happiness of human life, and maintain a continued existence even in this world, with all our present pains, infirmities, vexations, and follies, to be eligible and desirable! But this is contrary to everyone's feeling and experience: it is contrary to an authority so established as nothing can subvert: no decisive proofs can ever be produced against this authority; nor is it possible for you to compute, estimate, and compare all the pains and all the pleasures in the lives of all men and of all animals: and thus by your resting the whole system of religion on a point, which, from its very nature, must forever be uncertain, you tacitly confess, that that system is equally uncertain.

But allowing you, what never will be believed; at least, what you never possibly can prove, that animal, or at least, human happiness, in this life, exceeds its misery; you have yet done nothing: for this is not, by any means, what we expect from infinite power, infinite wisdom, and infinite goodness. Why is there any misery at all in the world? Not by chance surely. From some cause then. Is it from the intention of the Deity? But he is perfectly benevolent. Is it contrary to his intention? But he is almighty. Nothing can shake the solidity of this reasoning, so short, so clear, so decisive; except we assert, that these subjects exceed all human capacity, and that our common measures of truth and falsehood are not applicable to them; a topic, which I have all along insisted on, but which you have, from the beginning, rejected with scorn and indignation.

But I will be contented to retire still from this intrenchment: for I deny that you can ever force me in it: I will allow, that pain or misery in man is *compatible* with infinite power and goodness in the Deity, even in your sense of these attributes: what are you advanced by all these concessions? A mere possible compatibility is not sufficient. You must *prove* these pure, unmixed, and uncontrollable attributes from the present mixed and confused phenomena, and from these alone. A hopeful undertaking! Were the phenomena ever so pure and unmixed, yet being finite, they would be insufficient for that purpose. How much more, where they are also so jarring and discordant!

Here, Cleanthes, I find myself at ease in my argument. Here I triumph. Formerly, when we argued concerning the natural attributes of intelligence and design, I needed all my sceptical and metaphysical subtilty to elude your grasp. In many views of the universe, and of its parts, particularly the latter, the beauty and fitness of final causes strikes us with such irresistible force, that all objections appear (what I believe they really are) mere cavils and sophisms; nor can we then imagine how it was ever possible for us to repose any weight on them. But there is no view of human life or of the condition of mankind, from which, without the greatest violence, we can infer the moral attributes, or learn that infinite benevolence, conjoined with infinite power and infinite wisdom, which we must discover by the eyes of faith alone. It is your turn now to tug the laboring oar, and to support your philosophical subtilties against the dictates of plain reason and experience.

Part XI

I SCRUPLE not to allow, said Cleanthes, that I have been apt to suspect the frequent repetition of the word, *infinite,* which we meet with in all theological writers, to savor more of panegyric than of philosophy, and that any purposes of reasoning, and even of religion, would be better served, were we to rest contented with more accurate and more moderate expressions. The terms, *admirable, excellent, superlatively great, wise,* and *holy;* these sufficiently fill the imaginations of men; and anything beyond, besides that it leads into absurdities, has no influence on your affections or sentiments. Thus, in the present subject, if we abandon all human analogy, as seems your intention, Demea, I am afraid we abandon all religion, and retain no conception of the great object of our adoration. If we preserve human analogy, we must forever find it impossible to reconcile any mixture of evil in the universe with infinite attributes; much less can we ever prove the latter from the former. But supposing the Author of Nature to be finitely perfect, though far exceeding mankind; a satisfactory account may then be given of natural and moral evil, and every untoward phenomenon be explained and adjusted. A less evil may then be chosen, in order to avoid a greater; inconveniences be submitted to, in order to reach a desirable end: and in a word, benevolence, regulated by wisdom, and limited by necessity, may produce just such a world as the present. You, Philo, who are so prompt at starting views, and reflections, and analogies, I would gladly hear, at length, without interruption, your opinion of this new theory; and if it deserve our attention, we may afterwards, at more leisure, reduce it into form.

My sentiments, replied Philo, are not worth being made a mystery of; and therefore, without any ceremony, I shall deliver what occurs to me with regard to the present subject. It must, I think, be allowed, that, if a very limited intelligence, whom we shall suppose utterly unacquainted with the universe, were assured, that it were the production of a very good, wise, and powerful being, however infinite, he would, from his conjectures, form *beforehand* a different notion of it from what we find it to be by *experience;* nor would he ever imagine, merely from these attributes of the cause, of which he is informed, that the effect could be so full of vice and misery and disorder, as it appears in his life. Supposing now, that this person were brought into the world, still assured, that it was the workmanship of such a sublime and benevolent Being; he might, perhaps, be surprised at the disappointment; but would never retract his former belief, if founded on any very solid argument; since such a limited intelligence must be sensible of his own blindness and ignorance, and must allow, that there may be many solutions of those phenomena, which will forever escape his comprehension. But supposing, which is the real case with regard to man, that this creature is not antecedently convinced of a supreme intelligence, benevolent, and powerful, but is left to gather such a belief from the appearance of things; this entirely alters the case, nor will he ever find any reason for such a conclusion. He may be fully convinced of the narrow limits of his understanding; but this will not help him in forming an inference concerning the goodness of superior powers, since he must form that inference from what he knows, not from what he is ignorant of. The more you exaggerate his weakness and ignorance, the more diffident you render him, and give him the greater suspicion, that such subjects are beyond the reach of his faculties. You are obliged, therefore, to reason with him merely from the known phenomena, and to drop every arbitrary supposition or conjecture.

Did I show you a house or palace, where there was not one apartment convenient or agreeable; where the windows, doors, fires, passages, stairs, and the whole economy of the building were the source of noise, confusion, fatigue, darkness, and extremes of heat and cold; you would certainly blame the contrivance, without any farther examination. The architect would in vain display his subtilty, and prove to you, that if this door or that window were altered, greater ills would ensue.

What he says, may be strictly true: the alteration of one particular, while the other parts of the building remain, may only augment the inconveniences. But still you would assert in general, that, if the architect had had skill and good intentions, he might have formed such a plan of the whole, and might have adjusted the parts in such a manner, as would have remedied all or most of these inconveniences. His ignorance, or even your own ignorance of such a plan, will never convince you of the impossibility of it. If you find many inconveniences and deformities in the building, you will always, without entering into any detail, condemn the architect.

In short, I repeat the question: is the world considered in general, and as it appears to us in this life, different from what a man or such a limited being would, beforehand, expect from a very powerful, wise, and benevolent Deity? It must be strange prejudice to assert the contrary. And from thence I conclude, that, however consistent the world may be, allowing certain suppositions and conjectures, with the idea of such a Deity, it can never afford us an inference concerning his existence. The consistency is not absolutely denied, only the inference. Conjectures, especially where infinity is excluded from the Divine attributes, may perhaps be sufficient to prove a consistency; but can never be foundations for any inference.

There seem to be four circumstances, on which depend all, or the greatest parts of the ills, that molest sensible creatures; and it is not impossible but all these circumstances may be necessary and unavoidable. We know so little beyond common life, or even of common life, that, with regard to the economy of a universe, there is no conjecture, however wild, which may not be just; nor any one, however plausible, which may not be erroneous. All that belongs to human understanding, in this deep ignorance and obscurity, is to be sceptical, or at least cautious; and not to admit of any hypothesis, whatever; much less, of any which is supported by no appearance of probability. Now this I assert to be the case with regard to all the causes of evil, and the circumstances, on which it depends. None of them appear to human reason, in the least degree, necessary or unavoidable; nor can we suppose them such, without the utmost license of imagination.

The *first* circumstance which introduces evil, is that contrivance or economy of the animal creation, by which pains, as well as pleasures, are employed to excite all creatures to action, and make them vigilant in the great work of self-preservation. Now pleasure alone, in its various degrees, seems to human understanding sufficient for this purpose. All animals might be constantly in a state of enjoyment; but when urged by any of the necessities of nature, such as thirst, hunger, weariness; instead of pain, they might feel a diminution of pleasure, by which they might be prompted to seek that object, which is necessary to their subsistence. Men pursue pleasure as eagerly as they avoid pain; at least, might have been so constituted. It seems, therefore, plainly possible to carry on the business of life without any pain. Why then is any animal ever rendered susceptible of such a sensation? If animals can be free from it an hour, they might enjoy a perpetual exemption from it; and it required as particular a contrivance of their organs to produce that feeling, as to endow them with sight, hearing, or any of the senses. Shall we conjecture, that such a contrivance was necessary, without any appearance of reason? and shall we build on that conjecture as on the most certain truth?

But a capacity of pain would not alone produce pain, were it not for the *second* circumstance, viz., the conducting of the world by general laws; and this seems nowise necessary to a very perfect being. It is true; if everything were conducted by particular volitions, the course of nature would be perpetually broken, and no man could employ his reason in the conduct of life. But might not other particular volitions remedy this inconvenience? In short, might not the Deity exterminate all ill, wherever it were to be found; and produce all good, without any preparation or long progress of causes and effects?

Besides, we must consider, that, according to the present economy of the world, the course of nature, though supposed exactly regular, yet to us appears not so, and many events are uncertain, and many disappoint our expectations. Health and sickness, calm and tempest, with an infinite number of other accidents, whose causes are unknown and variable, have a great influence both on the fortunes of particular persons and on the prosperity of public societies: and indeed all human life, in a manner, depends on such accidents. A being, therefore, who knows the secret springs of the universe, might easily, by particular volitions, turn all these accidents to the good of mankind, and render the whole world happy, without discovering himself in any operation. A fleet, whose purposes were salutary to society, might always meet with a fair wind: good princes enjoy sound health and long life: persons, born to power and authority, be framed with good tempers and virtuous dispositions. A few such events as these, regularly and wisely conducted, would change the face of the world; and yet would no more seem to disturb the course of nature or confound human conduct, than the present economy of things, where the causes are secret, and variable, and compounded. Some small touches, given to Caligula's brain in his infancy, might have converted him into a Trajan: one wave, a little higher than the rest, by burying Caesar and his fortune in the bottom of the ocean, might have restored liberty to a considerable part of mankind. There may, for aught we know, be good reasons, why Providence interposes not in this manner; but they are unknown to us: and though the mere supposition, that such reasons exist, may be sufficient to *save* the conclusion concerning the divine attributes, yet surely it can never be sufficient to *establish* that conclusion.

If everything in the universe be conducted by general laws, and if animals be rendered susceptible of pain, it scarcely seems possible but some ill must arise in the various shocks of matter, and the various concurrence and opposition of general laws. But this ill would be very rare, were it not for the *third* circumstance, which I proposed to mention, viz., the great frugality with which all powers and faculties are distributed to every particular being. So well adjusted are the organs and capacities of all animals, and so well fitted to their preservation, that, as far as history or tradition reaches, there appears not to be any single species, which has yet been extinguished in the universe. Every animal has the requisite endowments; but these endowments are bestowed with so scrupulous an economy, that any considerable diminution must entirely destroy the creature. Wherever one power is increased, there is a proportional abatement in the others. Animals, which excel in swiftness, are commonly defective in force. Those, which possess both, are either imperfect in some of their senses, or are oppressed with the most craving wants. The human species, whose chief excellency is reason and sagacity, is of all others the most necessitous, and the most deficient in bodily advantages; without clothes, without arms, without food, without lodging, without any convenience of life, except what they owe to their own skill and industry. In short, nature seems to have formed an exact calculation of the necessities of her creatures; and like a *rigid master,* has afforded them little more powers or endowments, than what are strictly sufficient to supply those necessities. An *indulgent parent* would have bestowed a large stock, in order to guard against accidents, and secure the happiness and welfare of the creature, in the most unfortunate concurrence of circumstances. Every course of life would not have been so surrounded with precipices, that the least departure from the true path, by mistake or necessity, must involve us in misery and ruin. Some reserve, some fund would have been provided to ensure happiness; nor would the powers and the necessities have been adjusted with so rigid an economy. The Author of Nature is inconceivably powerful: his force is supposed great, if not altogether inexhaustible: nor is there any reason, as far as we can judge, to make him observe this strict frugality in his dealings with his creatures. It would have been better, were his power extremely limited, to have created fewer animals, and to have endowed these with more faculties for their happiness and preservation. A builder is never esteemed prudent, who undertakes a plan, beyond what his stock will enable him to finish.

In order to cure most of the ills of human life, I require not that man should have the wings of the eagle, the swiftness of the stag, the force of the ox, the arms of the lion, the scales of the crocodile or rhinoceros; much less do I demand the sagacity of an angel or cherub. I am contented to take an increase in one single power or faculty of his soul. Let him be endowed with a greater propensity to industry and labor; a more vigorous spring and activity of mind; a more constant bent to business and application. Let the whole species possess naturally an equal diligence with that which many individuals are able to attain by habit and reflection; and the most beneficial consequences, without any alloy of ill, is the immediate and necessary result of this endowment. Almost all the moral, as well as natural evils of human life arise from idleness; and were our species, by the original constitution of their frame, exempt from this vice or infirmity, the perfect cultivation of land, the improvement of arts and manufactures, the exact execution of every office and duty, immediately follow; and men at once may fully reach that state of society, which is so imperfectly attained by the best-regulated government. But as industry is a power, and the most valuable of any, nature seems determined, suitably to her usual maxims, to bestow it on men with a very sparing hand; and rather to punish him severely for his deficiency in it, than to reward him for his attainments. She has so contrived his frame, that nothing but the most violent necessity can oblige him to labor; and she employs all his other wants to overcome, at least in part, the want of diligence, and to endow him with some share of a faculty, of which she has thought fit naturally to bereave him. Here our demands may be allowed very humble, and therefore the more reasonable. If we required the endowments of superior penetration and judgment, of a more delicate taste of beauty, of a nicer sensibility to benevolence and friendship; we might be told, that we impiously pretend to break the order of nature, that we want to exalt ourselves into a higher rank of being, that the presents which we require, not being suitable to our state and condition, would only be pernicious to us. But it is hard; I dare to repeat it, it is hard, that being placed in a world so full of wants and necessities; where almost every being and element is either our foe or refuses us their assistance, we should also have our own temper to struggle with, and should be deprived of that faculty, which can alone fence against these multiplied evils.

The *fourth* circumstance, whence arises the misery and ill of the universe, is the inaccurate workmanship of all the springs and principles of the great machine of nature. It must be acknowledged, that there are few parts of the universe, which seem not to serve some purpose, and whose removal would not produce a visible defect and disorder in the whole. The parts hang all together; nor can one be touched without affecting the rest in a greater or less degree. But at the same time, it must be observed, that none of these parts or principles, however useful, are so accurately adjusted, as to keep precisely within those bounds, in which their utility consists; but they are, all of them, apt, on every occasion, to run into the one extreme or the other. One would imagine, that this grand production had not received the last hand of the maker; so little finished in every part, and so coarse are the strokes, with which it is executed. Thus, the winds are requisite to convey the vapors along the surface of the globe, and to assist men in navigation: but how oft, rising up to tempests and hurricanes, do they become pernicious? Rains are necessary to nourish all the plants and animals of the earth: but how often are they defective? how often excessive? Heat is requisite to all life and vegetation; but is not always found in the due proportion. On the mixture and secretion of the humors and juices of the body depend the health and prosperity of the animal: but the parts perform not regularly their proper function. What more useful than all the passions of the mind, ambition, vanity, love, anger? But how oft do they break their bounds, and cause the greatest convulsions in society? There is nothing so advantageous in the universe, but what frequently becomes pernicious, by its excess or defect; nor has nature guarded, with the requisite accuracy, against all disorder or confusion. The irregularity is never, perhaps, so great as to destroy any species; but is often sufficient to involve the individuals in ruin and misery.

On the concurrence, then, of these four circumstances does all, or the greatest part of natural evil depend. Were all living creatures incapable of pain, or were the world administered by particular volitions, evil never could have found access into the universe: and were animals endowed with a large stock of powers and faculties, beyond what strict necessity requires; or were the several springs and principles of the universe so accurately framed as to preserve always the just temperament and medium; there must have been very little ill in comparison of what we feel at present. What then shall we pronounce on this occasion? Shall we say, that these circumstances are not necessary, and that they might easily have been altered in the contrivance of the universe? This decision seems too presumptuous for creatures, so blind and ignorant. Let us be more modest in our conclusions. Let us allow, that, if the goodness of the Deity (I mean a goodness like the human) could be established on any tolerable reasons *a priori*, these phenomena, however untoward, would not be sufficient to subvert that principle; but might easily, in some unknown manner, be reconcilable to it. But let us still assert, that as this goodness is not antecedently established, but must be inferred from the phenomena, there can be no grounds for such an inference, while there are so many ills in the universe, and while these ills might so easily have been remedied, as far as human understanding can be allowed to judge on such a subject. I am sceptic enough to allow, that the bad appearances, notwithstanding all my reasonings, may be compatible with such attributes as you suppose: but surely they can never prove these attributes. Such a conclusion cannot result from scepticism; but must arise from the phenomena, and from our confidence in the reasonings, which we deduce from these phenomena.

Look round this universe. What an immense profusion of beings, animated and organized, sensible and active! You admire this prodigious variety and fecundity. But inspect a little more narrowly these living existences, the only beings worth regarding. How hostile and destructive to each other! How insufficient all of them for their own happiness! How contemptible or odious to the spectator! The whole presents nothing but the idea of a blind nature, impregnated by a great vivifying principle, and pouring forth from her lap, without discernment or parental care, her maimed and abortive children!

Here the Manichaean system occurs as a proper hypothesis to solve the difficulty: and no doubt, in some respects, it is very specious, and has more probability than the common hypothesis, by giving a plausible account of the strange mixture of good and ill, which appears in life. But if we consider, on the other hand, the perfect uniformity and agreement of the parts of the universe, we shall not discover in it any marks of the combat of a malevolent with a benevolent being. There is indeed an opposition of pains and pleasures in the feelings of sensible creatures: but are not all the operations of nature carried on by an opposition of principles, of hot and cold, moist and dry, light and heavy? The true conclusion is, that the original source of all things is entirely indifferent to all these principles, and has no more regard to good above ill than to heat above cold, or to drought above moisture, or to light above heavy.

There may four hypotheses be framed concerning the first causes of the universe: that they are endowed with perfect goodness, that they have perfect malice, that they are opposite and have both goodness and malice, they they have neither goodness nor malice. Mixed phenomena can never prove the two former unmixed principles. And the uniformity and steadiness of general laws seem to oppose the third. The fourth, therefore, seems by far the most probable.

What I have said concerning natural evil will apply to moral, with little or no variation; and we have no more reason to infer, that the rectitude of the Supreme Being resembles human rectitude than that his benevolence resembles the human. Nay, it will be thought, that we have still greater cause to exclude from him moral sentiments, such as we feel them; since moral evil, in the opinion of many, is much more predominant above moral good than natural evil above natural good.

But even though this should not be allowed, and though the virtue, which is in mankind, should be acknowledged much superior to the vice; yet so long as there is any vice at all in the universe, it will very much puzzle you anthropomorphites, how to account for it. You must assign a cause for it, without having recourse to the first cause. But as every effect must have a cause, and that cause another; you must either carry on the progression *in infinitum,* or rest on that original principle, who is the ultimate cause of all things . . .

Hold! hold! cried Demea: Whither does your imagination hurry you? I joined in alliance with you, in order to prove the incomprehensible nature of the Divine Being, and refute the principles of Cleanthes, who would measure everything by a human rule and standard. But I now find you running into all the topics of the greatest libertines and infidels; and betraying that holy cause, which you seemingly espoused. Are you secretly, then, a more dangerous enemy than Cleanthes himself?

And are you so late in perceiving it? replied Cleanthes. Believe me, Demea; your friend Philo, from the beginning, has been amusing himself at both our expense; and it must be confessed, that the injudicious reasoning of our vulgar theology has given him but too just a handle of ridicule. The total infirmity of human reason, the absolute incomprehensibility of the Divine Nature, the great and universal misery and still greater wickedness of men; these are strange topics surely to be so fondly cherished by orthodox divines and doctors. In ages of stupidity and ignorance, indeed, these principles may safely be espoused; and perhaps, no views of things are more proper to promote superstition, than such as encourage the blind amazement, the diffidence, and melancholy of mankind. But at present . . .

Blame not so much, interposed Philo, the ignorance of these reverend gentlemen. They know how to change their style with the times. Formerly it was a most popular theological topic to maintain, that human life was vanity and misery, and to exaggerate all the ills and pains, which are incident to men. But of late years, divines, we find, begin to retract this position, and maintain, though still with some hesitation, that there are more goods than evils, more pleasures than pains, even in this life. When religion stood entirely upon temper and education, it was thought proper to encourage melancholy; as indeed, mankind never have recourse to superior powers so readily as in that disposition. But as men have now learned to form principles, and to draw consequences, it is necessary to change the batteries, and to make use of such arguments as will endure, at least some scrutiny and examination. This variation is the same (and from the same causes) with that which I formerly remarked with regard to scepticism.

Thus Philo continued to the last his spirit of opposition, and his censure of established opinions. But I could observe, that Demea did not at all relish the latter part of the discourse; and he took occasion soon after on some pretense or other, to leave the company.

Part XII

AFTER Demea's departure, Cleanthes and Philo continued the conversation in the following manner. Our friend, I am afraid, said Cleanthes, will have little inclination to revive this topic of discourse, while you are in company; and to tell truth, Philo, I should rather wish to reason with either of you apart on a subject so sublime and interesting. Your spirit of controversy, joined to your abhorrence of vulgar superstition, carries you strange lengths, when engaged in an argument; and there is nothing so sacred and venerable, even in your own eyes, which you spare on that occasion.

I must confess, replied Philo, that I am less cautious on the subject of Natural Religion than on any other; both because I know that I can never, on that head, corrupt the principles of any man of common sense, and because no one, I am confident, in whose eyes I appear a man of common sense, will ever mistake my intentions. You, in particular, Cleanthes, with whom I live in unreserved intimacy; you are sensible, that, notwithstanding the freedom of my conversation, and my love of singular arguments, no one has a deeper sense of religion impressed on his mind, or pays more profound adoration to the Divine Being, as he discovers himself to reason, in the inexplicable contrivance and artifice of nature. A purpose, an intention, a design strikes everywhere the most careless, the most stupid thinker; and no man can be so hardened in absurd systems, as at all times to reject it. *That Nature does nothing in vain,* is a maxim established in all the schools, merely from the contemplation of the works of nature, without any religious purpose; and, from a firm conviction of its truth, an anatomist, who had observed a new organ or canal, would never be satisfied, till he had also discovered its use and intention. One great foundation of the Copernican system is the maxim, *That Nature acts by the simplest methods, and chooses the most proper means to any end;* and astronomers often, without thinking of it, lay this strong foundation of piety and religion. The same thing is observable in other parts of philosophy: and thus all the sciences almost lead us insensibly to acknowledge a first intelligent Author; and their authority is often so much the greater, as they do not directly profess that intention.

It is with pleasure I hear Galen reason concerning the structure of the human body. The anatomy of a man, says he,[12] discovers above 600 different muscles; and whoever duly considers these, will find, that in each of them Nature must have adjusted at least ten different circumstances, in order to attain the end which she proposed; proper figure, just magnitude, right disposition of the several ends, upper and lower position of the whole, the due insertion of the several nerves, veins, and arteries: so that in the muscles alone, above 6000 several views and intentions must have been formed and executed. The bones he calculates to be 284: the distinct purposes, aimed at in the structure of each, above forty. What a prodigious display of artifice, even in these simple and homogeneous parts! But if we consider the skin, ligaments, vessels, glandules, humors, the several limbs and members of the body; how must our astonishment rise upon us, in proportion to the number and intricacy of the parts so artificially adjusted! The farther we advance in these researches, we discover new scenes of art and wisdom: but descry still, at a distance, farther scenes beyond our reach; in the fine internal structure of the parts, in the economy of the brain, in the fabric of the seminal vessels. All these artifices are repeated in every different species of animal, with wonderful variety, and with exact propriety, suited to the different intentions of Nature, in framing each species. And if the infidelity of Galen, even when these natural sciences were still imperfect, could not withstand such striking appearances; to what pitch of pertinacious obstinacy must a philosopher in this age have attained, who can now doubt of a Supreme Intelligence?

Could I meet with one of this species (who, I thank God, are very rare) I would ask him: Supposing there were a God, who did not discover himself immediately to our senses; were it possible for him to give stronger proofs of his existence, than what appear on the whole face of nature? What indeed could such a divine Being do, but copy the present economy of things; render many of his artifices so plain, that no stupidity could mistake them; afford glimpses of still greater artifices, which demonstrate his prodigious superiority above our narrow apprehensions; and conceal altogether a great many from such imperfect creatures? Now according to all rules of just reasoning, every fact must pass for undisputed, when it is supported by all the arguments, which its nature admits of; even though these arguments be not, in themselves, very numerous or forcible: How much more, in the present case, where no human imagination can compute their number, and no understanding estimate their cogency!

I shall farther add, said Cleanthes, to what you have so well urged,

---

[12] De formatione foetus.

that one great advantage of the principle of theism, is, that it is the only system of cosmogony, which can be rendered intelligible and complete, and yet can throughout preserve a strong analogy to what we every day see and experience in the world. The comparison of the universe to a machine of human contrivance is so obvious and natural, and is justified by so many instances of order and design in nature, that it must immediately strike all unprejudiced apprehensions, and procure universal approbation. Whoever attempts to weaken this theory, cannot pretend to succeed by establishing in its place any other, that is precise and determinate: it is sufficient for him, if he start doubts and difficulties; and by remote and abstract views of things, reach that suspense of judgment, which is here the utmost boundary of his wishes. But besides, that this state of mind is in itself unsatisfactory, it can never be steadily maintained against such striking appearances, as continually engage us into the religious hypothesis. A false, absurd system, human nature, from the force of prejudice, is capable of adhering to, with obstinacy and perseverance: But no system at all, in opposition to a theory, supported by strong and obvious reason, by natural propensity, and by early education, I think it absolutely impossible to maintain or defend.

So little, replied Philo, do I esteem this suspense of judgment in the present case to be possible, that I am apt to suspect there enters somewhat of a dispute of words into this controversy, more than is usually imagined. That the works of nature bear a great analogy to the productions of art is evident: and according to all the rules of good reasoning, we ought to infer, if we argue at all concerning them, that their causes have a proportional analogy. But as there are also considerable differences, we have reason to suppose a proportional difference in the causes; and in particular ought to attribute a much higher degree of power and energy to the supreme cause than any we have ever observed in mankind. Here then the existence of a Deity is plainly ascertained by reason; and if we make it a question, whether, on account of these analogies, we can properly call him a *mind* or *intelligence,* notwithstanding the vast difference, which may reasonably be supposed between him and human minds; what is this but a mere verbal controversy? No man can deny the analogies between the effects: to restrain ourselves from inquiring concerning the causes is scarcely possible: from this inquiry, the legitimate conclusion is, that the causes have also an analogy: And if we are not contented with calling the first and supreme cause a God or Deity, but desire to vary the expression; what can we call him but Mind or Thought, to which he is justly supposed to bear a considerable resemblance?

All men of sound reason are disgusted with verbal disputes, which abound so much in philosophical and theological inquiries; and it is found, that the only remedy for this abuse must arise from clear definitions, from the precision of those ideas which enter into any argument, and from the strict and uniform use of those terms which are employed. But there is a species of controversy, which, from the very nature of language and of human ideas, is involved in perpetual ambiguity, and can never, by any precaution or any definitions, be able to reach a reasonable certainty or precision. These are the controversies concerning the degrees of any quality or circumstance. Men may argue to all eternity, whether Hannibal be a great, or a very great, or a superlatively great man, what degree of beauty Cleopatra possessed, what epithet of praise Livy or Thucydides is entitled to, without bringing the controversy to any determination. The disputants may here agree in their sense, and differ in the terms, or *vice versa;* yet never be able to define their terms, so as to enter into each other's meaning: because the degrees of these qualities are not, like quantity or number, susceptible of any exact mensuration, which may be the standard in the controversy. That the dispute concerning theism is of this nature, and consequently is merely verbal, or perhaps, if possible, still more incurably ambiguous, will appear upon the slightest inquiry. I ask the theist, if he does not allow, that there is a great and immeasurable, because incomprehensible, difference between the *human* and the *divine* mind. The more pious he is, the more readily will he assent to the affirmative, and the more will he be disposed to magnify the difference: he will even assert, that the difference is of a nature which cannot be too much magnified. I next turn to the atheist, who, I assert, is only nominally so, and can never possibly be in earnest; and I ask him, whether, from the coherence and apparent sympathy in all the parts of this world, there be not a certain degree of analogy among all the operations of nature, in every situation and in every age; whether the rotting of a turnip, the generation of an animal, and the structure of human thought be not energies that probably bear some remote analogy to each other. It is impossible he can deny it: he will readily acknowledge it. Having obtained this concession, I push him still farther in his retreat; and I ask him, if it be not probable, that the principle which first arranged, and still maintains order in this universe, bears not also some remote inconceivable analogy to the other operations of nature, and among the rest to the economy of human mind and thought. However reluctant, he must give his assent. Where then, cry I to both these antagonists, is the subject of your dispute? The theist allows, that the original intelligence is very different from human reason: The atheist allows, that the original principle of order bears some remote analogy to it. Will you quarrel, gentlemen, about the degrees, and enter into a controversy, which admits not of any precise meaning, nor consequently of any determination? If you should be so obstinate, I should not be surprised to find you insensibly change sides; while the theist on the one hand exaggerates the dissimilarity between the Supreme Being, and frail, imperfect, variable, fleeting, and mortal creatures; and the atheist on the other magnifies the analogy among all the operations of nature, in every period, every situation, and every position. Consider then, where the real point of controversy lies, and if you cannot lay aside your disputes, endeavor, at least, to cure yourselves of your animosity.

And here I must also acknowledge, Cleanthes, that, as the works of nature have a much greater analogy to the effects of *our* art and contrivance, than to those of *our* benevolence and justice; we have reason to infer that the natural attributes of the Deity have a greater resemblance to those of man, than his moral have to human virtues. But what is the consequence? Nothing but this, that the moral qualities of man are more defective in their kind than his natural abilities. For, as the Supreme Being is allowed to be absolutely and entirely perfect, whatever differs most from him departs the farthest from the supreme standard of rectitude and perfection.[13]

These, Cleanthes, are my unfeigned sentiments on this subject; and these sentiments, you know, I have ever cherished and maintained. But in proportion to my veneration for true religion, is my abhorrence of vulgar superstitions; and I indulge a peculiar pleasure, I confess, in pushing such principles, sometimes into absurdity, sometimes into impiety. And you are sensible, that all bigots, notwithstanding their great averson to the latter above the former, are commonly equally guilty of both.

My inclination, replied Cleanthes, lies, I own, a contrary way. Religion, however corrupted, is still better than no religion at all. The doctrine of a future state is so strong and necessary a security to morals, that we never ought to abandon or neglect it. For if finite and temporary rewards and punishments have so great an effect, as we daily find; how much greater must be expected from such as are infinite and eternal?

How happens it then, said Philo, if vulgar superstition be so salutary

[13] It seems evident, that the dispute between the sceptics and dogmatists is entirely verbal, or at least regards only the degrees of doubt and assurance, which we ought to indulge with regard to all reasoning: and such disputes are commonly, at the bottom, verbal, and admit not of any precise determination. No philosophical dogmatist denies, that there are difficulties both with regard to the senses and to all science; and that these difficulties are in a regular, logical method, absolutely insolvable. No sceptic denies, that we lie under an absolute necessity, notwithstanding these difficulties, of thinking, and believing, and reasoning with regard to all kind of subjects, and even of frequently assenting with confidence and security. The only difference, then, between these sects, if they merit that name, is that the sceptic, from habit, caprice, or inclination, insists most on the difficulties; the dogmatist, for like reasons, on the necessity.

to society, that all history abounds so much with accounts of its pernicious consequences on public affairs? Factions, civil wars, persecutions, subversions of government, oppression, slavery; these are the dismal consequences which always attend its prevalency over the minds of men. If the religious spirit be ever mentioned in any historical narration, we are sure to meet afterwards with a detail of the miseries, which attend it. And no period of time can be happier or more prosperous, than those in which it is never regarded, or heard of.

The reason of this observation, replied Cleanthes, is obvious. The proper office of religion is to regulate the heart of men, humanize their conduct, infuse the spirit of temperance, order, and obedience; and as its operation is silent, and only enforces the motives of morality and justice, it is in danger of being overlooked, and confounded with these other motives. When it distinguishes itself, and acts as a separate principle over men, it has departed from its proper sphere, and has become only a cover to faction and ambition.

And so will all religion, said Philo, except the philosophical and rational kind. Your reasonings are more easily eluded than my facts. The inference is not just, because finite and temporary rewards and punishments have so great influence, that therefore such as are infinite and eternal must have so much greater. Consider, I beseech you, the attachment, which we have to present things, and the little concern which we discover for objects, so remote and uncertain. When divines are declaiming against the common behavior and conduct of the world, they always represent this principle as the strongest imaginable (which indeed it is) and describe almost all human kind as lying under the influence of it, and sunk into the deepest lethargy and unconcern about their religious interests. Yet these same divines, when they refute their speculative antagonists, suppose the motives of religion to be so powerful, that, without them, it were impossible for civil society to subsist; nor are they ashamed of so palpable a contradiction. It is certain, from experience, that the smallest grain of natural honesty and benevolence has more effect on men's conduct, than the most pompous views suggested by theological theories and systems. A man's natural inclination works incessantly upon him; it is forever present to the mind, and mingles itself with every view and consideration: whereas religious motives, where they act at all, operate only by starts and bounds; and it is scarcely possible for them to become altogether habitual to the mind. The force of the greatest gravity, say the philosophers, is infinitely small, in comparison of that of the least impulse; yet it is certain, that the smallest gravity will, in the end, prevail above a great impulse; because no strokes or blows can be repeated with such constancy as attraction and gravitation.

Another advantage of inclination: it engages on its side all the wit and ingenuity of the mind; and when set in opposition to religious principles, seeks every method and art of eluding them: in which it is almost always successful. Who can explain the heart of man, or account for those strange salvos and excuses, with which people satisfy themselves, when they follow their inclinations in opposition to their religious duty! This is well understood in the world; and none but fools ever repose less trust in a man, because they hear, that, from study and philosophy, he has entertained some speculative doubts with regard to theological subjects. And when we have to do with a man, who makes a great profession of religion and devotion; has this any other effect upon several, who pass for prudent, than to put them on their guard, lest they be cheated and deceived by him?

We must farther consider, that philosophers, who cultivate reason and reflection, stand less in need of such motives to keep them under the restraint of morals; and that the vulgar, who alone may need them, are utterly incapable of so pure a religion, as represents the Deity to be pleased with nothing but virtue in human behavior. The recommendations to the Divinity are generally supposed to be either frivolous observances, or rapturous ecstasies, or a bigoted credulity. We need not run back into antiquity, or wander into remote regions, to find instances of this degeneracy. Amongst ouselves, some have been guilty of that atrociousness, unknown to the Egyptian and Grecian superstitions, of declaiming, in express terms, against morality, and representing it as a sure forfeiture of the Divine favor, if the least trust or reliance be laid upon it.

But even though superstition or enthusiasm should not put itself in direct opposition to morality; the very diverting of the attention, the raising up a new and frivolous species of merit, the preposterous distribution, which it makes of praise and blame; must have the most pernicious consequences, and weaken extremely men's attachment to the natural motives of justice and humanity.

Such a principle of action likewise, not being any of the familiar motives of human conduct, acts only by intervals on the temper, and must be roused by continual efforts, in order to render the pious zealot satisfied with his own conduct, and make him fulfill his devotional task. Many religious exercises are entered into with seeming fervor, where the heart, at the time, feels cold and languid: a habit of dissimulation is by degrees contracted: and fraud and falsehood become the predominant principle. Hence the reason of that vulgar observation, that the highest zeal in religion and the deepest hypocrisy, so far from being inconsistent, are often or commonly united in the same individual character.

The bad effects of such habits, even in common life, are easily imagined: but where the interests of religion are concerned, no morality can be forcible enough to bind the enthusiastic zealot. The sacredness of the cause sanctifies every measure, which can be made use of to promote it.

The steady attention alone to so important an interest as that of eternal salvation is apt to extinguish the benevolent affections, and beget a narrow, contracted selfishness. And when such a temper is encouraged, it easily eludes all the general precepts of charity and benevolence.

Thus the motives of vulgar superstition have no great influence on general conduct; nor is their operation very favorable to morality, in the instances where they predominate.

Is there any maxim in politics more certain and infallible, than that both the number and authority of priests should be confined within very narrow limits, and that the civil magistrate ought, for ever, to keep his *fasces* and *axes* from such dangerous hands? But if the spirit of popular religion were so salutary to society, a contrary maxim ought to prevail. The greater number of priests, and their greater authority and riches, will always augment the religious spirit. And though the priests have the guidance of this spirit, why may we not expect a superior sanctity of life, and greater benevolence and moderation, from persons who are set apart for religion, who are continually inculcating it upon others, and who must themselves imbibe a greater share of it? Whence comes it then, that in fact, the utmost a wise magistrate can propose with regard to popular religions, is, as far as possible, to make a saving game of it, and to prevent their pernicious consequences with regard to society? Every expedient which he tries for so humble a purpose is surrounded with inconveniences. If he admits only one religion among his subjects, he must sacrifice, to an uncertain prospect of tranquillity, every consideration of public liberty, science, reason, industry, and even his own independency. If he gives indulgence to several sects, which is the wiser maxim, he must preserve a very philosophical indifference to all of them, and carefully restrain the pretensions of the prevailing sect; otherwise he can expect nothing but endless disputes, quarrels, factions, persecutions, and civil commotions.

True religion, I allow, has no such pernicious consequences: but we must treat of religion, as it has commonly been found in the world; nor have I anything to do with that speculative tenet of theism, which, as it is a species of philosophy, must partake of the beneficial influence of that principle, and at the same time must lie under a like inconvenience of being always confined to very few persons.

Oaths are requisite in all courts of judicature; but it is a question whether their authority arises from any popular religion. 'Tis the solemnity and importance of the occasion, the regard to reputation, and the reflecting on the general interests of society, which are the chief restraints upon mankind. Custom-house oaths and political oaths are but little regarded even by some who pretend to principles of honesty and religion: and a Quaker's asseveration is with us justly put upon the same footing with the oath of any other person. I know, that Polybius [14] ascribes the infamy of Greek faith to the prevalency of the Epicurean philosophy; but I know also, that Punic faith had as bad a reputation in ancient times, as Irish evidence has in modern; though we cannot account for these vulgar observations by the same reason. Not to mention, that Greek faith was infamous before the rise of the Epicurean philosophy; and Euripides,[15] in a passage which I shall point out to you, has glanced a remarkable stroke of satire against his nation, with regard to this circumstance.

Take care, Philo, replied Cleanthes, take care; push not matters too far: allow not your zeal against false religion to undermine your veneration for the true. Forfeit not this principle, the chief, the only great comfort in life; and our principal support amidst all the attacks of adverse fortune. The most agreeable reflection, which it is possible for human imagination to suggest, is that of genuine theism, which represents us as the workmanship of a Being perfectly good, wise, and powerful; who created us for happiness, and who, having implanted in us immeasurable desires for good, will prolong our existence to all eternity, and will transfer us into an infinite variety of scenes, in order to satisfy those desires, and render our felicity complete and durable. Next to such a Being himself (if the comparison be allowed) the happiest lot which we can imagine, is that of being under his guardianship and protection.

These appearances, said Philo, are most engaging and alluring; and with regard to the true philosopher, they are more than appearances. But it happens here, as in the former case, that, with regard to the greater part of mankind, the appearances are deceitful, and that the terrors of religion commonly prevail above its comforts.

It is allowed, that men never have recourse to devotion so readily as when dejected with grief or depressed with sickness. Is not this a proof, that the religious spirit is not so nearly allied to joy as to sorrow?

But men, when afflicted, find consolation in religion, replied Cleanthes. Sometimes, said Philo: but it is natural to imagine, that they will form a notion of those unknown beings, suitably to the present gloom and melancholy of their temper, when they betake themselves to the contemplation of them. Accordingly, we find the tremendous images to predominate in all religions; and we ourselves, after having employed the most exalted expressions in our descriptions of the Deity, fall into

[14] Lib. 6, cap. 54.
[15] Iphigenia in Tauride.

the flattest contradiction, in affirming, that the damned are infinitely superior in number to the elect.

I shall venture to affirm, that there never was a popular religion, which represented the state of departed souls in such a light, as would render it eligible for human kind, that there should be such a state. These fine models of religion are the mere product of philosophy. For as death lies between the eye and the prospect of futurity, that event is so shocking to nature, that it must throw a gloom on all the regions which lie beyond it; and suggest to the generality of mankind the idea of Cerberus and Furies; devils, and torrents of fire and brimstone.

It is true; both fear and hope enter into religion; because both these passions, at different times, agitate the human mind, and each of them forms a species of divinity, suitable to itself. But when a man is in a cheerful disposition, he is fit for business or company or entertainment of any kind; and he naturally applies himself to these, and thinks not of religion. When melancholy, and dejected, he has nothing to do but brood upon the terrors of the invisible world, and to plunge himself still deeper in affliction. It may, indeed, happen, that after he has, in this manner, engraved the religious opinions deep into his thought and imagination, there may arrive a change of health or circumstances, which may restore his good humor, and raising cheerful prospects of futurity, make him run into the other extreme of joy and triumph. But still it must be acknowledged, that, as terror is the primary principle of religion, it is the passion, which always predominates in it, and admits but of short intervals of pleasure.

Not to mention, that these fits of excessive, enthusiastic joy, by exhausting the spirits, always prepare the way for equal fits of superstitious terror and dejection; nor is there any state of mind so happy as the calm and equable. But this state it is impossible to support, where a man thinks that he lies in such profound darkness and uncertainty, between an eternity of happiness and an eternity of misery. No wonder, that such an opinion disjoints the ordinary frame of the mind, and throws it into the utmost confusion. And though that opinion is seldom so steady in its operation as to influence all the actions; yet it is apt to make a considerable breach in the temper, and to produce that gloom and melancholy, so remarkable in all devout people.

It is contrary to common sense to entertain apprehensions of terrors, upon account of any opinion whatsoever, or to imagine that we run any risk hereafter, by the freest use of our reason. Such a sentiment implies both an *absurdity* and an *inconsistency*. It is an absurdity to believe that the Deity has human passions, and one of the lowest of human passions, a restless appetite for applause. It is an inconsistency to believe, that, since the Deity has this human passion, he has not others also; and, in particular, a disregard to the opinions of creatures so much inferior.

To know God, says Seneca, *is to worship him.* All other worship is indeed absurd, superstitious, and even impious. It degrades him to the low condition of mankind, who are delighted with entreaty, solicitation, presents, and flattery. Yet is this impiety the smallest of which superstition is guilty. Commonly, it depresses the Deity far below the condition of mankind; and represents him as a capricious demon, who exercises his power without reason and without humanity! And were that Divine Being disposed to be offended at the vices and follies of silly mortals, who are his own workmanship; ill would it surely fare with the votaries of most popular superstitions. Nor would any of human race merit his *favor*, but a very few, the philosophical theists, who entertain, or rather indeed endeavor to entertain, suitable notions of his divine perfections: as the only persons entitled to his *compassion* and *indulgence* would be the philosophical sceptics, a sect almost equally rare, who, from a natural diffidence of their own capacity, suspend, or endeavor to suspend all judgment with regard to such sublime and such extraordinary subjects.

If the whole of Natural Theology, as some people seem to maintain, resolves itself into one simple, though somewhat ambiguous, at least undefined proposition, *That the cause or causes of order in the universe probably bear some remote analogy to human intelligence:* if this proposition be not capable of extension, variation, or more particular explication: if it afford no inference that affects human life, or can be the source of any action or forbearance: and if the analogy, imperfect as it is, can be carried no farther than to the human intelligence; and cannot be transferred, with any appearance of probability, to the other qualities of the mind: if this really be the case, what can the most inquisitive, contemplative, and religious man do more *than give a plain, philosophical assent to the proposition, as often as it occurs; and believe that the arguments, on which it is established, exceed the objections, which lie against it? Some astonishment indeed will naturally arise from the greatness of the object: some melancholy from its obscurity: some contempt of human reason, that it can give no solution more satisfactory with regard to so extraordinary and magnificent a question. But believe me, Cleanthes, the most natural sentiment, which a well-disposed mind will feel on this occasion, is a longing desire and expectation, that heaven would be pleased to dissipate, at least alleviate, this profound ignorance, by affording some more particular revelation to mankind, and making discoveries of the nature, attributes, and operations of the divine object of our faith. A person, seasoned with a just sense of the imperfections of natural reason, will fly to revealed truth with the greatest avidity: while the haughty dogmatist, persuaded that he can erect a complete system of theology by the mere help of philosophy, disdains any farther aid, and rejects this adventitious instructor. To be a philosophical sceptic is, in a man of letters, the first and most essential step towards being a sound, believing Christian; a proposition which I would willingly recommend to the attention of Pamphilus: And I hope Cleanthes will forgive me for interposing so far in the education and instruction of his pupil.

Cleanthes and Philo pursued not this conversation much farther; and as nothing ever made greater impression on me, than all the reasonings of that day; so I confess, that, upon a serious review of the whole, I cannot but think that Philo's principles are more probable than Demea's; but that those of Cleanthes approach still nearer to the truth.

JOHN GAY

Concerning the Fundamental Principle of Virtue or Morality

JOHN GAY

JOHN GAY (1669-1745) was the son of a country parson. He entered Sidney Sussex College, Cambridge, in 1717; and in 1723 was elected a fellow. While in residence he taught Hebrew, Greek, and ecclesiastical history. The brief *Dissertation Concerning the Fundamental Principle of Virtue or Morality,* his only philosophical writing, appeared anonymously as a preface to the translation by Edmund Law of Archbishop King's Latin *Essay on the Origin of Evil* (1731).

This little treatise is of historical importance. It is the first clear statement of the combination of associationism in psychology and utilitarianism in morals which was to exercise a controlling influence on the development of the next century and a half of English thought. David Hartley, whose *Observations on Man* (1749) was the first full and systematic elaboration of this utilitarianism, said that it was Gay who suggested to him "the possibility of deducing all our intellectual pleasures and pains from association." And it was Hartley, rather than Hume, who served as a model to Bentham and James Mill. Two other important utilitarian thinkers, Abraham Tucker and William Paley, also advanced views closely similar to Gay's. His brief *Dissertation* is, therefore, the progenitor of a large and important philosophical literature.

In 1732 Gay left his fellowship for a vicarage in Bedfordshire where he spent the remainder of his life.

CONCERNING THE FUNDA-
MENTAL PRINCIPLE OF
VIRTUE OR MORALITY

THOUGH all writers of morality have in the main agreed what particular actions are virtuous and what otherwise, yet they have, or at least seem to have differed very much, both concerning the *criterion* of virtue, viz., what it is which denominates any action virtuous; or, to speak more properly, what it is by which we must try any action to know whether it be virtuous or no; and also concerning the *principle,* or *motive,* by which men are induced to pursue virtue.

As to the former, some have placed it in acting agreeably to nature, or reason; others in the fitness of things; others in a conformity with truth; others in promoting the common good; others in the will of God, etc. This disagreement of moralists concerning the rule or criterion of virtue in general, and at the same time their almost perfect agreement concerning the particular branches of it, would be apt to make one suspect, either that they had a different criterion (though they did not know or attend to it) from what they professed; or (which perhaps is the true as well as the more favorable opinion) that they only talk a different language, and that all of them have the same criterion in reality, only they have expressed it in different words.

And there will appear the more room for this conjecture, if we consider the ideas themselves about which morality is chiefly conversant, viz., that they are all mixed modes, or compound ideas, arbitrarily put together, having at first no archetype or original existing, and afterwards no other than that which exists in other men's minds. Now since men, unless they have these their compound ideas, which are signified by the same name, made up precisely of the same simple ones, must necessarily talk a different language; and since this difference is so difficult, and in some cases impossible to be avoided, it follows that greater allowance and indulgence ought to be given to these writers than any other: and that (if we have a mind to understand them) we should not always take their words in the common acceptation, but in the sense in which we find that particular author which we are reading used them. And if a man interpret the writers of morality with this due candor, I believe their seeming inconsistencies and disagreements about the *criterion* of virtue, would in a great measure vanish; and he would find that acting agreeably to nature, or reason, (when rightly understood) would perfectly coincide with the fitness of things; the fitness of things (as far as these words have any meaning) with truth; truth with the common good; and the common good with the will of God.

But whether this difference be real, or only verbal, a man can scarce avoid observing from it, that mankind have the ideas of most particular virtues, and also a confused notion of virtue in general, before they have any notion of the *criterion* of it; or ever did, neither perhaps can they, deduce all or any of those virtues from their idea of virtue in general, or upon any rational grounds shew how those actions (which the world call moral, and most, if not all men evidently have ideas of) are distinguished from other actions, or why they approve of those actions called moral ones, more than others.

However, since the idea of virtue among all men (notwithstanding their difference in other respects) includes either tacitly or expressly, not only the idea of approbation as the consequence of it; but also that it is to everyone, and in all circumstances, an object of choice; it is incumbent on all writers of morality, to shew that in which they place virtue, whatever it be, not only always will or ought to meet with approbation, but also that it is always an object of choice; which is the other great dispute among moralists, viz., what is the *principle* or *motive* by which men are induced to pursue virtue.

For some have imagined that that is the only object of choice to a rational creature, which upon the whole will produce more happiness than misery to the chooser; and that men are, and ought to be guided wnolly by this principle; and farther, that virtue will produce more happiness than misery, and therefore is always an object of choice: and whatever is an object of choice, that we approve of.

But this, however true in theory, is insufficient to account for matter of fact, i.e., that the generality of mankind do approve of virtue, or rather virtuous actions, without being able to give any reason for their approbation; and also, that some pursue it without knowing that it tends to their own private happiness; nay even when it appears to be inconsistent with and destructive of their happiness.

And that this is a matter of fact, the ingenious author of the *Enquiry into the Original of our Idea of Virtue* [1] has so evidently made appear by a great variety of instances, that a man must be either very little acquainted with the world, or a mere Hobbist in his temper, to deny it.

And therefore to solve these two difficulties, this excellent author has supposed (without proving, unless by shewing the insufficiency of all

---

[1] Francis Hutcheson.—Editor.

other schemes) a moral sense to account for the former, and a public or benevolent affection for the latter: And these, viz., the moral sense and public affection, he supposes to be implanted in us like instincts, independent of reason, and previous to any instruction; and therefore his opinion is, that no account can be given, or ought to be expected of them, any more than we pretend to account for the pleasure or pain which arises from sensation; i.e., why any particular motion produced in our bodies should be accompanied with pain rather than pleasure, and *vice versa*.

But this account seems still insufficient, rather cutting the knot than untying it; and if it is not akin to the doctrine of innate ideas, yet I think it relishes too much of that of occult qualities. This ingenious author is certainly in the right in his observations upon the insufficiency of the common methods of accounting for both our election and approbation of moral actions, and rightly infers the necessity of supposing a moral sense (i.e., a power or faculty whereby we may perceive any action to be an object of approbation, and the agent of love) and public affections, to account for the principal actions of human life. But then by calling these instincts, I think he stops too soon, imagining himself at the fountain-head, when he might have traced them much higher, even to the true principle of all our actions, our own happiness.

And this will appear by shewing that our approbation of morality, and all affections whatsoever, are finally resolved into reason pointing out private happiness, and are conversant only about things apprehended to be means tending to this end; and that whenever this end is not perceived, they are to be accounted for from the association of ideas, and may properly enough be called habits.

For if this be clearly made out, the necessity of supposing a moral sense or public affections to be implanted in us, since it ariseth only from the insufficiency of all other schemes to account for human actions, will immediately vanish. But whether it be made out or no, we may observe in general, that all arguments *ad ignorantiam,* or that proceed *a remotione* only (as this, by which the moral sense and public affections are established to be instincts, evidently does) are scarce ever perfectly satisfactory, being for the most part subject to this doubt, viz., whether there is a full enumeration of all the parts; and liable also to this objection, viz., that though I cannot account for phenomena otherwise, yet possibly they may be otherwise accounted for.

But before we can determine this point, it will be necessary to settle all the terms: We shall in the first place therefore inquire what is meant by the *criterion* of virtue.

SECTION I

CONCERNING THE CRITERION OF VIRTUE

THE *criterion* of anything is a rule or measure by a conformity with which anything is known to be of this or that sort, or of this or that degree. And in order to determine the criterion of anything, we must first know the thing whose criterion we are seeking after. For a measure presupposes the idea of the thing to be measured, otherwise it could not be known, whether it was fit to measure it or no, (since what is the proper measure of one thing is not so of another). Liquids, cloth, and flesh have all different measures; gold and silver different touchstones. This is very intelligible and the method of doing it generally clear, when either the quantity, or kind of any particular substance is thus ascertained.

But when we extend our inquiries after a criterion for abstract, mixed modes, which have no existence but in our minds, and are so very different in different men; we are apt to be confounded, and search after a measure for we know not what. For unless we are first agreed concerning the thing to be measured, we shall in vain expect to agree in our criterion of it, or even to understand one another.

But it may be said, if we are exactly agreed in any mixed mode, what need of any criterion? or what can we want farther? What we want farther, and what we mean by the criterion of it, is this; viz., to know whether any particular thing do belong to this mixed mode or no. And this is a very proper inquiry. For let a man learn the idea of intemperance from you never so clearly, and if you please let this be the idea, viz., the eating or drinking to that degree as to injure his understanding or health; and let him also be never so much convinced of the obligation to avoid it; yet it is a very pertinent question in him to ask you, how shall I know when I am guilty of intemperance?

And if we examine this thoroughly, we shall find that every little difference in the definition of a mixed mode will require a different criterion, e.g., if murder is defined the willful taking away the life of another, it is evident, that to inquire after the criterion of murder, is to inquire how we shall know when the life of another is taken away willfully; i.e., when one who takes away the life of another does it with that malicious design which is implied by willfulness. But if murder be defined the guilty taking away the life of another, then to inquire after the criterion of murder, is to inquire how it shall be known when guilt is contracted in the willful taking away the life of another. So that the criterion of murder, according to one or other of these definitions, will be different.

For willfulness perhaps will be made the criterion of guilt; but willfulness itself, if it want any, must have some farther criterion; it being evident that nothing can be the measure of itself.

If the criterion is contained in the idea itself, then it is merely nominal, e.g., if virtue is defined, the acting agreeably to the will of God: to say the will of God is the criterion of virtue, is only to say, what is agreeable to the will of God is called virtue. But the real criterion, which is of some use, is this, how shall I know what the will of God is in this respect?

From hence it is evident, that the criterion of a mixed mode is neither the definition of it, nor contained in it. For, as has been shewn, the general idea is necessarily to be fixed; and if the particulars comprehended under it are fixed or known also, there remains nothing to be measured; because we measure only things unknown. The general idea then being fixed, the criterion which is to measure or determine inferiors, must be found out and proved to be a proper rule or measure, by comparing it with the general idea only, independent of the inferior things to which it is to be applied. For the truth of the measure must be proved independently of the particulars to be measured, otherwise we shall prove in a circle.

To apply what has been said in general to the case in hand. Great inquiry is made after the criterion of virtue; but it is to be feared that few know distinctly what it is they are inquiring after; and therefore this must be clearly stated. And in order to this, we must (as has been shewn) first fix our idea of virtue, and that exactly; and then our inquiry will be, how we shall know this or that less general or particular action to be comprehended under virtue. For unless our idea of virtue is fixed, we inquire after the criterion of we know not what. And this our idea of virtue, to give any satisfaction, ought to be so general, as to be conformable to that which all or most men are supposed to have. And this general idea, I think, may be thus expressed.

Virtue is the conformity to a rule of life, directing the actions of all rational creatures with respect to each other's happiness; to which conformity everyone in all cases is obliged: and everyone that does so conform, is or ought to be approved of, esteemed and loved for so doing. What is here expressed, I believe most men put into their idea of virtue.

For virtue generally does imply some relation to others: where self is only concerned, a man is called prudent (not virtuous) and an action which relates immediately to God, is styled religious.

I think also that all men, whatever they make virtue to consist in, yet always make it to imply obligation and approbation.

The idea of virtue being thus fixed, to inquire after the criterion of it, is to inquire what that rule of life is to which we are obliged to conform; or how that rule is to be found out which is to direct me in my behavior towards others, which ought always to be pursued, and which, if pursued, will or ought to procure me approbation, esteem, and love.

But before I can answer this inquiry I must first see what is meant by *obligation*.

SECTION II

CONCERNING OBLIGATION

OBLIGATION is the necessity of doing or omitting any action in order to be happy: i.e., when there is such a relation between an agent and an action that the agent cannot be happy without doing or omitting that action, then the agent is said to be obliged to do or omit that action. So that obligation is evidently founded upon the prospect of happiness, and arises from that necessary influence which any action has upon present or future happiness or misery. And no greater obligation can be supposed to be laid upon any free agent without an express contradiction.

This obligation may be considered four ways, according to the four different manners in which it is induced: First, that obligation which ariseth from perceiving the natural consequences of things, i.e. the consequences of things acting according to the fixed laws of nature, may be called *natural*. Secondly, that arising from merit or demerit, as producing the esteem and favor of our fellow creatures, or the contrary, is usually styled *virtuous*. Thirdly, that arising from the authority of the civil magistrate, *civil*. Fourthly, that from the authority of God, *religious*.

Now from the consideration of these four sorts of obligation (which are the only ones) it is evident that a full and complete obligation which will extend to all cases, can only be that arising from the authority of God; because God only can in all cases make a man happy or miserable: and therefore, since we are always obliged to that conformity called virtue, it is evident that the immediate rule or criterion of it, is the will of God.

The next inquiry, therefore, is. what that will of God in this particular is, or what it directs me to do?

Now it is evident from the nature of God, viz. His being infinitely happy in Himself from all eternity, and from His goodness manifested in His works, that He could have no other design in creating mankind than their happiness; and therefore He wills their happiness; therefore the means of their happiness; therefore that my behavior, as far as it may be a means of the happiness of mankind, should be such. Here then we are got one step farther, or to a new criterion: not to a new criterion of virtue immediately, but to a criterion of the will of God. For it is an answer to the inquiry, how shall I know what the will of God in this particular is? Thus the will of God is the immediate criterion of virtue, and the happiness of mankind the criterion of the will of God; and therefore the happiness of mankind may be said to be the criterion of virtue, but once removed.

And since I am to do whatever lies in my power towards promoting the happiness of mankind, the next inquiry is, what is the criterion of happiness, i.e. how shall I know what in my power is, or is not, for the happiness of mankind?

Now this is to be known only from the relations of things, (which relations, with respect to our present inquiry some have called their fitness and unfitness). For some things and actions are apt to produce pleasure, others pain; some are convenient, others inconvenient for a society; some are for the good of mankind; others tend to the detriment of it; therefore those are to be chosen which tend to the good of mankind, the others to be avoided.

Thus then we are got one step farther, viz. to the criterion of the happiness of mankind. And from this criterion we deduce all particular virtues and vices.

The next inquiry is, how shall I know that there is this fitness and unfitness in things? or if there be, how shall I discover it in particular cases? And the answer is, either from experience or reason. You either perceive the inconveniences of some things and actions when they happen; or you foresee them by contemplating the nature of the things and actions.

Thus the criterion of the fitness or unfitness of things may in general be said to be reason: which reason, when exactly conformable to the things existing, i.e. when it judges of things as they are, is called right reason. And hence also we sometimes talk of the reason of things, i.e. properly speaking, that relation which we should find out by our reason, if our reason was right.

The expressing by outward signs the relation of things as they really are, is called truth; and hence by the same kind of metaphor, we are apt to talk of the truth, as well as reason of things. Both expressions mean the same: which has often made me wonder why some men who cry up reason as the criterion of virtue, should yet dislike Mr. Wollaston's notion of truth being its criterion.

The truth is, all these just mentioned, viz. the happiness of mankind; the relations, or fitness and unfitness of things; reason and truth; may in some sense be said to be criterions of virtue; but it must always be remembered that they are only remote criterions of it; being gradually subordinate to its immediate and proper criterion, the will of God.

And from hence we may perceive the reason of what I suggested in the beginning of this treatise, viz. that the dispute between moralists about the criterion of virtue is more in words than meaning; and that this difference between them has been occasioned by their dropping the immediate criterion, and choosing some a more remote, some a less remote one. And from hence we may see also the inconvenience of defining any mixed mode by its criterion. For that in a great measure has occasioned all this confusion; as may easily be made appear in all the pretended criterions of virtue above mentioned.

Thus those who either expressly exclude, or don't mention the will of God, making the immediate criterion of virtue to be the good of mankind, must either allow that virtue is not in all cases obligatory (contrary to the idea which all or most men have of it) or they must say that the good of mankind is a sufficient obligation. But how can the good of mankind be any obligation to me, when perhaps in particular cases, such as laying down my life, or the like, it is contrary to my happiness?

Those who drop the happiness of mankind, and talk of the relations, the fitness and unfitness of things, are still more remote from the true criterion. For fitness, without relation to some end, is scarce intelligible.

Reason and truth come pretty near the relations of things, because they manifestly presuppose them; but are still one step farther from the immediate criterion of virtue.

What has been said concerning the criterion of virtue as including our constant obligation to it, may perhaps be allowed to be true; but still it will be urged, that it is insufficient to account for matter of fact, viz. that most persons, who are either ignorant of, or never considered these deductions, do however pursue virtue themselves, and approve of it in others. I shall in the next place therefore give some account of our approbations and affections.

SECTION III

CONCERNING APPROBATION AND AFFECTION

MAN is not only a sensible creature; not only capable of pleasure and pain, but capable also of foreseeing this pleasure and pain in the future consequences of things and actions; and as he is capable of knowing, so also of governing or directing the causes of them, and thereby in a great measure enabled to avoid the one and to procure the other: whence the principle of all action. And therefore, as pleasure and pain are not indifferent to him, nor out of his power, he pursues the former and avoids the latter; and therefore also those things which are causes of them are not indifferent, but he pursues or avoids them also, according to their different tendency. That which he pursues for its own sake, which is only pleasure, is called an *end;* that which he apprehends to be apt to produce pleasure, he calls *good,* and approves of, i.e., judges a proper means to attain his end, and therefore looks upon it as an object of choice; and that which is pregnant with misery he disapproves of and styles evil. And this good and evil are not only barely approved of, or the contrary; but whenever viewed in imagination (since man considers himself as existing hereafter, and is concerned for his welfare then as well as now) they have a present pleasure or pain annexed to them, proportionable to what is apprehended to follow them in real existence; which pleasure or pain arising from the prospect of future pleasure or pain is properly called *passion,* and the desire consequent thereupon, *affection.*

And as by reflecting upon pleasure there arises in our minds a desire of it; and on pain, an aversion from it (which necessarily follows from supposing us to be sensible creatures, and is no more than saying, that all things are not physically indifferent to us) so also by reflecting upon good or evil, the same desires and aversions are excited, and are distinguished into love and hatred. And from love and hatred variously modified, arise all those other desires and aversions which are promiscuously styled passions or affections; and are generally thought to be implanted in our nature originally, like the power of receiving sensitive pleasure or pain. And when placed on inanimate objects, are these following; hope, fear, despair and its opposite, for which we want a name.

SECTION IV

APPROBATION AND AFFECTION CONSIDERED WITH REGARD TO MERIT, OR THE LAW OF ESTEEM

IF A man in the pursuit of pleasure or happiness (by which is meant the sum total of pleasure) had to do only with inanimate creatures, his approbation and affections would be as described in the foregoing section. But, since he is dependent with respect to his happiness, not only on these, but also on all rational agents, creatures like himself, which have the power of governing or directing good and evil, and of acting for an end; there will arise different means of happiness, and consequently different pursuits, though tending to the same end, happiness; and therefore different approbations and affections, and the contrary; which deserve particularly to be considered.

That there will arise different means of happiness, is evident from hence, viz. that rational agents, in being subservient to our happiness, are not passive, but voluntary. And therefore since we are in pursuit of that, to obtain which we apprehend the concurrence of their wills necessary, we cannot but approve of whatever is apt to procure this concurrence. And that can be only the pleasure or pain expected from it by them. And therefore as I perceive that my happiness is dependent on others, I cannot but judge whatever I apprehend to be proper to excite them to endeavor to promote my happiness, to be a means of happiness, i.e. I cannot but approve it. And since the annexing pleasure to their endeavors to promote my happiness is the only thing in my power to this end, I cannot but approve of the annexing pleasure to such actions of theirs as are undertaken upon my account. Hence to approve of a rational agent as a means of happiness, is different from the approbation of any other means; because it implies an approbation also of an endeavor to promote the happiness of that agent, in order to excite him and others to the same concern for my happiness for the future.

And because what we approve of we also desire (as has been shewn above) hence also we desire the happiness of any agent that has done us good. And therefore love or hatred, when placed on a rational object, has this difference from the love and hatred of other things, that it implies a desire of, and consequently a pleasure in the happiness of the object beloved; or if hated, the contrary.

The foundation of this approbation and love (which, as we have seen, consists in this voluntary contributing to our happiness) is called the *merit* of the agent so contributing, i.e. that whereby he is entitled (upon supposition that we act like rational, sociable creatures; like creatures, whose happiness is dependent on each other's behavior) to our approbation and love: demerit the contrary.

And this affection or quality of any action which we call merit, is very consistent with a man's acting ultimately for his own private happiness. For any particular action that is undertaken for the sake of another, is meritorious, i.e. deserves esteem, favor, and approbation from him for whose sake it was undertaken, towards the doer of it. Since the presumption of such esteem, etc. was the only motive to that action; and if such esteem, etc. does not follow, or is presumed not to follow it, such a person is reckoned unworthy of any favor, because he shews by his actions that he is incapable of being obliged by favors.

The mistake which some have run into, viz. that merit is inconsistent with acting upon private happiness, as an ultimate end, seems to have arisen from hence, viz. that they have not carefully enough distinguished between an inferior, and ultimate end; the end of a particular action, and the end of action in general: which may be explained thus. Though happiness, private happiness, is the proper or ultimate end of all our actions whatever, yet that particular means of happiness which any particular action is chiefly adapted to procure, or the thing chiefly aimed at by that action; the thing which, if possessed, we would not undertake that action, may, and generally is called the *end* of that action. As therefore happiness is the general end of all actions, so each particular action may be said to have its proper and peculiar end: thus the end of a beau is to please by his dress; the end of study, knowledge. But neither pleasing by dress, nor knowledge, are ultimate ends, they still tend or ought to tend to something farther; as is evident from hence, viz. that a man may ask and expect a reason why either of them are pursued: now to ask the *reason* of any action or pusuit, is only to inquire into the *end* of it: but to expect a reason, i.e. an end, to be assigned for an *ultimate* end, is absurd. To ask why I pursue happiness, will admit of no other answer than an explanation of the terms.

Why inferior ends, which in reality are only means, are too often looked upon and acquiesced in as ultimate, shall be accounted for hereafter.

Whenever therefore the particular end of any action is the happiness of another (though the agent designed thereby to procure to himself esteem and favor, and looked upon that esteem and favor as a means of private happiness) that action is meritorious. And the same may be said, though we design to please God, by endeavoring to promote the happiness of others. But when an agent has a view in any particular action distinct from my happiness, and that view is his only motive to that action, though that action promote my happiness to never so great a degree, yet that agent acquires no merit, i.e. he is not thereby entitled to any favor or esteem: because favor and esteem are due from me for any action, no farther than that action was undertaken upon my account. If therefore my happiness is only the pretended end of that action, I am imposed on if I believe it real, and thereby think myself indebted to the agent; and I am discharged from any obligation as soon as I find out the cheat.

But it is far otherwise when my happiness is the sole end of that particular action, i.e. (as I have explained myself above) when the agent endeavors to promote my happiness as a means to procure my favor, i.e. to make me subservient to his happiness as his ultimate end: though I know he aims at my happiness only a means of his own, yet this lessens not the obligation.

There is one thing, I confess, which makes a great alteration in this case, and that is, whether he aims at my favor in general, or only for some particular end. Because, if he aim at my happiness only to serve himself in some particular thing, the value of my favor will perhaps end with his obtaining that particular thing: and therefore I am under less obligation (*ceteris paribus*) the more particular his expectations from me are; but under obligation I am.

Now from the various combinations of this which we call merit, and its contrary, arise all those various approbations and aversions; all those likings and dislikings which we call *moral*.

As therefore from considering those beings which are the involuntary means of our happiness or misery, there were produced in us the passions or affections of love, hatred, hope, fear, despair and its contrary: so from considering those beings which voluntarily contribute to our happiness or misery, there arise the following. Love and hatred, (which are different from that love or hatred placed on involuntary beings; that placed on involuntary beings being only a desire to possess or avoid the thing beloved or hated; but this on voluntary agents being a desire to give pleasure or pain to the agent beloved or hated) gratitude, anger, (sometimes called by one name, resentment) generosity, ambition, honor, shame, envy, benevolence: and if there be any other, they are only, as these are, different modifications of love and hatred.

Love and hatred, and the foundation of them (viz. the agent beloved or hated being apprehended to be instrumental to our happiness) I have explained above. Gratitude is that desire of promoting the happiness of another upon account of some former kindness received. Anger, that desire of thwarting the happiness of another, on account of some former diskindness or injury received. Both these take place, though we hope for, or fear nothing farther from the objects of either of them, and this is still consistent with acting upon a principle of private happiness.

For though we neither hope for, nor fear anything farther from these particular beings; yet the disposition shewn upon these occasions is apprehended to influence the behavior of other beings towards us: i.e. other beings will be moved to promote our happiness or otherwise, as they observe how we resent favors or injuries.

Ambition is a desire of being esteemed. Hence a desire of being thought an object of esteem; hence of being an object of esteem; hence of doing laudable, i.e. useful actions. Generosity and benevolence are species of it. Ambition in too great a degree is called pride, of which there are several species. The title to the esteem of others, which ariseth from any meritorious action, is called honor. The pleasure arising from honor being paid to us, i.e. from others acknowledging that we are entitled to their esteem, is without a name. Modesty is the fear of losing esteem. The uneasiness or passion which ariseth from a sense that we have lost it, is called shame. So that ambition, and all those other passions and affections belonging to it, together with shame, arise from the esteem of others: which is the reason why this tribe of affections operate more strongly on us than any other, viz. because we perceive that as our happiness is chiefly dependent on the behavior of others, so we perceive also that this behavior is dependent on the esteem which others have conceived of us; and consequently that our acquiring or losing esteem, is in effect acquiring or losing happiness, and in the highest degree. And the same may be said concerning all our other affections and passions, to enumerate which, what for want of names to them, and what by the confusion of language about them, is almost impossible.

Envy will be accounted for hereafter, for a reason which will then be obvious.

Thus having explained what I mean by obligation and approbation; and shewn that they are founded on and terminate in happiness: having also pointed out the difference between our approbations and affections as placed on involuntary and voluntary means of happiness; and farther proved that these approbations and affections are not innate or implanted in us by way of instinct, but are all acquired, being fairly deducible from supposing only sensible and rational creatures dependent on each other for their happiness, as explained above: I shall in the next place endeavor to answer a grand objection to what has here been said concerning approbations and affections arising from a prospect of private happiness.

The objection is this.

The reason or end of every action is always known to the agent; for nothing can move a man but what is perceived; but the generality of mankind love and hate, approve and disapprove, immediately, as soon as any moral character either occurs in life, or is proposed to them, without considering whether their private happiness is affected with it or not: or if they do consider any moral character in relation to their own happiness, and find themselves, as to their private happiness, unconcerned in it; or even find their private happiness lessened by it in some particular instance, yet they still approve the moral character, and love the agent: nay they cannot do otherwise. Whatever reason may be assigned by speculative men why we should be grateful to a benefactor, or pity the distressed; yet if the grateful or compassionate mind never thought of that reason, it is no reason to him. The inquiry is not why he ought to be grateful, but why he is so. These after-reasons therefore rather shew the wisdom and providence of our Maker, in implanting the immediate powers of these approbations (i.e. in Mr. Hutcheson's language, a moral sense) and these public affections in us, than give any satisfactory account of their origin. And therefore these public affections, and this moral sense, are quite independent on private happiness, and in reality act upon us as mere instincts.

Answer.

The matter of fact contained in this argument, in my opinion, is not to be contested; and therefore it remains either that we make the matter of fact consistent with what we have before laid down, or give up the cause.

Now, in order to shew this consistency, I beg leave to observe, that as in the pursuit of truth we do not always trace every proposition whose truth we are examining, to a first principle or axiom, but acquiesce, as soon as we perceive it deducible from some known or presumed truth; so in our conduct we do not always travel to the ultimate end of our actions, happiness: but rest contented, as soon as we perceive any action subservient to a known or presumed means of happiness. And these presumed truths and means of happiness, whether real or otherwise, always influence us after the same manner as if they were real. The undeniable consequences of mere prejudices are as firmly adhered to as the consequences of real truths or arguments; and what is subservient to a false (but imagined) means of happiness, is as industriously pursued as what is subservient to a true one.

Now every man, both in his pursuit after truth, and in his conduct, has settled and fixed a great many of these in his mind, which he always acts upon, as upon principles, without examining. And this is occasioned by the narrowness of our understandings: we can consider but a few things at once; and therefore, to run everything to the fountain-head would be tedious, through a long series of consequences: to avoid this we choose out certain truths and means of happiness, which we look upon as *resting places,* in which we may safely acquiesce, in the conduct both of our understanding and practice; in relation to the one, regarding them as axioms; in the other, as ends. And we are more easily inclined to this, by imagining that we may safely rely upon what we call habitual knowledge, thinking it needless to examine what we are already satisfied in. And hence it is that prejudices, both speculative and practical, are difficult to be rooted out, viz. few will examine them.

These *resting places* are so often used as principles, that at last, letting that slip out of our minds which first inclined us to embrace them, we are apt to imagine them, not as they really are, the substitutes of principles, but, principles themselves.

And from hence, as some men have imagined, innate ideas, because they forget how they came by them; so others have set up almost as many distinct instincts as there are acquired principles of acting. And I cannot but wonder why the pecuniary sense, a sense of power and party etc. were not mentioned, as well as the moral, that of honor, order, and some others.

The case is really this. We first perceive or imagine some real good, i.e. fitness to promote our natural happiness, in those things which we love and approve of. Hence (as was above explained) we annex pleasure to those things. Hence those things and pleasure are so tied together and associated in our minds, that one cannot present itself, but the other will also occur. And the association remains even after that which at first gave them the connection is quite forgot, or perhaps does not exist, but the contrary. An instance or two may perhaps make this clear. How many men are there in the world who have as strong a taste for money as others have for virtue; who count so much money, so much happiness; nay, even sell their happiness for money; or to speak more properly, make the having money, without any design or thought of using it, their ultimate end? But was this propensity to money, born with them? or rather, did not they at first perceive a great many advantages from being possessed of money, and from thence conceive a pleasure of having it, thence desire it, thence endeavor to obtain it, thence receive an actual pleasure in obtaining it, thence desire to preserve the possession of it? Hence by dropping the intermediate steps between money and happiness, they join money and happiness immediately together, and content themselves with the fantastical pleasure of having it, and make that which was at first pursued only as a means, be to them a real end, and what their real happiness or misery consists in. Thus the connection between money and happiness remains in the mind; though it has long since ceased between the things themselves.

The same might be observed concerning the thirst after knowledge, fame, etc., the delight in reading, building, planting, and most of the various exercises and entertainments of life. These were at first entered on with a view to some farther end, but at length became habitual amusements; the idea of pleasure is associated with them, and leads us on still in the same eager pursuit of them, when the first reason is quite vanished, or at least out of our minds. Nay, we find this power of association so great as not only to transport our passions and affections beyond their proper bounds, both as to intenseness and duration; as is evident from daily instances of avarice, ambition, love, revenge, etc., but also that it is able to transfer them to improper objects, and such as are of a quite different nature from those to which our reason had at first directed them. Thus being accustomed to resent an injury done to our body by a retaliation of the like to him that offered it, we are apt to conceive the same kind of resentment, and often express it in the same manner, upon receiving hurt from a stock or a stone; whereby the hatred which we are used to place on voluntary beings, is substituted in the

room of that aversion which belongs to involuntary ones. The like may
be observed in most of the other passions above mentioned.

From hence also, viz. from the continuance of this association of ideas
in our minds, we may be enabled to account for that (almost diabolical)
passion called envy, which we promised to consider.

Mr. Locke observes, and I believe very justly, that there are some
men entirely unacquainted with this passion. For most men that are
used to reflection, may remember the very time when they were first
under the dominion of it.

Envy is generally defined to be that pain which arises in the mind
from observing the prosperity of others: not of all others indefinitely,
but only of some particular persons. Now the examining who those particular persons whom we are apt to envy are, will lead us to the true
origin of this passion. And if a man will be at the pains to consult his
mind, or to look into the world, he'll find that these particular persons
are always such as upon some account or other he has had a rivalship
with. For when two or more are competitors for the same thing, the success of the one must necessarily tend to the detriment of the other, or
others: hence the success of my rival and misery or pain are joined together in my mind; and this connection or association remaining in my
mind, even after the rivalship ceases, makes me always affected with
pain whenever I hear of his success, though in affairs which have no
manner of relation to the rivalship; much more in those that bring that
to my remembrance, and put me in mind of what I might have enjoyed
had it not been for him.

Thus also we are apt to envy those persons that refuse to be guided
by our judgments, and persuaded by us. For this is nothing else than a
rivalship about the superiority of judgment; and we take a secret pride,
both to let the world see, and in imagining ourselves, that we are in the
right.

There is one thing more to be observed in answer to this objection,
and that is, that we do not always (and perhaps not for the most
part) make this association ourselves, but learn it from others: i.e., that
we annex pleasure or pain to certain things or actions because we see
others do it, and acquire principles of action by imitating those whom
we admire, or whose esteem we would procure: Hence the son too often
inherits both the vices and the party of his father, as well as his estate:
Hence national virtues and vices, dispositions and opinions: and from
hence we may observe how easy it is to account for what is generally
called the prejudice of education; how soon we catch the temper and
affections of those whom we daily converse with; how almost insensibly
we are taught to love, admire or hate; to be grateful, generous, compassionate or cruel, etc.

What I say then in answer to the forementioned objection is this: That though it be necessary in order to solve the principal actions of human life to suppose a moral sense (or what is signified by that name) and also public affections; yet I deny that this moral sense, or these public affections, are innate or implanted in us. They are acquired either from our own observation or the imitation of others.

JEREMY BENTHAM

AN INTRODUCTION TO THE
PRINCIPLES OF MORALS AND LEGISLATION

JEREMY BENTHAM

JEREMY BENTHAM (1748-1832) was the son of a London attorney. His ambitious father early designed him for a brilliant career at the bar. He was sent to Queen's College, Oxford, where he matriculated in 1760. There in 1763 he heard Blackstone lecture and conceived an immediate dislike for the lecturer's conception of law. In the same year he began his preparation, in London, for the bar. From the reading of Helvetius he learned that the prosperity and happiness of a society depend upon wise and equitable legislation. Bentham resolved, therefore, to give up a career at the bar, greatly to his father's disappointment, and to spend his life in the working out of a scientific system of law. He began by writing a painstaking criticism of Blackstone. Part of this work, issued in 1776 as *A Fragment on Government,* won some attention, and brought him to the notice of Lord Shelburne through whom he met many of the distinguished legal and political figures of the day.

Bentham, who was curiously reluctant to publish, went on methodically studying and writing year after year. One manuscript did crystallize into a book which was circulated among his friends—*The Principles of Morals and Legislation.* It was finally published in 1789.

At about this time Bentham conceived a plan for prison reform, the "Panopticon" scheme. For the next fifteen years he gave a large part of his private fortune, his time, and his energy, in urging the adoption of this proposal by the English government, only to experience continual frustration and final disappointment. Meanwhile a disciple, Étienne Dumont, had offered to collate and publish Bentham's writings on jurisprudence in French, in the hope that they would reach a wider and more appreciative public. In 1802 Dumont brought out the three volumes of the *Traités de legislation,* which quickly gave Bentham an immense reputation on the continent.

In 1808 Bentham met James Mill. From the association of these two men the sect of "Benthamites" was born. Mill added a democratic political creed to Bentham's plans for law reform. Around the two men congregated some of the most influential writers and political figures of the day. While the Benthamites were never an organized party, they exerted great influence in shaping and controlling the movement for democracy which eventuated in the first Reform Bill of 1832. During the period from 1808 to 1832 Bentham published a large number of works on educational, religious, legal and political subjects. He died on the eve of the passage of the great reform bill which his labors had done so much to promote.

Selections from the *Principles of Morals and Legislation* follow.

AN INTRODUCTION TO THE PRINCIPLES OF MORALS AND LEGISLATION

CHAPTER I

OF THE PRINCIPLE OF UTILITY

NATURE has placed mankind under the governance of two sovereign masters, *pain* and *pleasure*. It is for them alone to point out what we ought to do, as well as to determine what we shall do. On the one hand the standard of right and wrong, on the other the chain of causes and effects, are fastened to their throne. They govern us in all we do, in all we say, in all we think: every effort we can make to throw off our subjection, will serve but to demonstrate and confirm it. In words a man may pretend to abjure their empire, but in reality he will remain subject to it all the while. The *principle of utility* [1] recognizes this subjection, and assumes it for the foundation of that system, the object of which is to rear the fabric of felicity by the hands of reason and of law. Systems which attempt to question it deal in sounds instead of sense, in caprice instead of reason, in darkness instead of light.

But enough of metaphor and declamation: it is not by such means that moral science is to be improved.

ii. The principle of utility is the foundation of the present work: it

---

[1] Note by the Author, July 1822.—To this denomination has of late been added, or substituted, the *greatest happiness* or *greatest felicity* principle: this for shortness, instead of saying at length, "that principle which states the greatest happiness of all those whose interest is in question, as being the right and proper, and only right and proper and universally desirable, end of human action—of human action in every situation, and in particular in that of a functionary or set of functionaries exercising the powers of government." The word 'utility' does not so clearly point to the ideas of *pleasure* and *pain* as the words 'happiness' and 'felicity' do; nor does it lead us to the consideration of the *number* of the interests affected: to the *number,* as being the circumstance, which contributes in the largest proportion to the formation of the standard here in question—the *standard of right and wrong,* by which alone the propriety of human conduct, in every situation, can with propriety be tried. This want of a sufficiently manifest connection between the ideas of *happiness* and *pleasure* on the one hand, and the idea of *utility* on the other, I have every now and then found operating, and with but too much efficiency, as a bar to the acceptance that might otherwise have been given to this principle.

will be proper therefore at the outset to give an explicit and determinate account of what is meant by it. By the principle of utility is meant that principle which approves or disapproves of every action whatsoever, according to the tendency which it appears to have to augment or diminish the happiness of the party whose interest is in question: or, what is the same thing in other words, to promote or to oppose that happiness. I say of every action whatsoever; and therefore not only of every action of a private individual, but of every measure of government.

iii. By utility is meant that property in any object, whereby it tends to produce benefit, advantage, pleasure, good, or happiness (all this in the present case comes to the same thing), or (what comes again to the same thing) to prevent the happening of mischief, pain, evil, or unhappiness to the party whose interest is considered: if that party be the community in general, then the happiness of the community; if a particular individual, then the happiness of that individual.

iv. The interest of the community is one of the most general expressions that can occur in the phraseology of morals: no wonder that the meaning of it is often lost. When it has a meaning, it is this. The community is a fictitious *body,* composed of the individual persons who are considered as constituting as it were its *members.* The interest of the community then is—what? The sum of the interests of the several members who compose it.

v. It is in vain to talk of the interest of the community, without understanding what is the interest of the individual.[2] A thing is said to promote the interest, or to be *for* the interest, of an individual, when it tends to add to the sum total of his pleasures; or, what comes to the same thing, to diminish the sum total of his pains.

vi. An action then may be said to be conformable to the principle of utility, or, for shortness sake, to utility (meaning with respect to the community at large), when the tendency it has to augment the happiness of the community is greater than any it has to diminish it.

vii. A measure of government (which is but a particular kind of action, performed by a particular person or persons) may be said to be conformable to or dictated by the principle of utility, when in like manner the tendency which it has to augment the happiness of the community is greater than any which it has to diminish it.

viii. When an action, or in particular a measure of government, is supposed by a man to be conformable to the principle of utility, it may be convenient, for the purposes of discourse, to imagine a kind of law or dictate, called a law or dictate of utility; and to speak of the action in question, as being conformable to such law or dictate.

---

[2] Interest is one of those words which, not having any superior *genus,* cannot in the ordinary way be defined.

ix. A man may be said to be a partisan of the principle of utility, when the approbation or disapprobation he annexes to any action, or to any measure, is determined by and proportioned to the tendency which he conceives it to have to augment or to diminish the happiness of the community; or in other words, to its conformity or unconformity to the laws or dictates of utility.

x. Of an action that is conformable to the principle of utility, one may always say either that it is one that ought to be done, or at least that it is not one that ought not to be done. One may say also that it is right it should be done—at least that it is not wrong it should be done; that it is a right action—at least that it is not a wrong action. When thus interpreted, the words *ought,* and *right* and *wrong,* and others of that stamp, have a meaning: when otherwise, they have none.

xi. Has the rectitude of this principle been ever formally contested? It should seem that it had, by those who have not known what they have been meaning. Is it susceptible of any direct proof? It should seem not; for that which is used to prove everything else, cannot itself be proved: a chain of proofs must have their commencement somewhere. To give such proof is as impossible as it is needless.

xii. Not that there is or ever has been that human creature breathing, however stupid or perverse, who has not on many, perhaps on most occasions of his life, deferred to it. By the natural constitution of the human frame, on most occasions of their lives men in general embrace this principle, without thinking of it: if not for the ordering of their own actions, yet for the trying of their own actions, as well as of those of other men. There have been, at the same time, not many perhaps even of the most intelligent, who have been disposed to embrace it purely and without reserve. There are even few who have not taken some occasion or other to quarrel with it, either on account of their not understanding always how to apply it, or on account of some prejudice or other which they were afraid to examine into, or could not bear to part with. For such is the stuff that man is made of: in principle and in practice, in a right track and in a wrong one, the rarest of all human qualities is consistency.

xiii. When a man attempts to combat the principle of utility, it is with reasons drawn, without his being aware of it, from that very principle itself.[3] His arguments, if they prove anything, prove not that the principle is *wrong,* but that, according to the applications he supposes

---

[3] "The principle of utility," I have heard it said, "is a dangerous principle: it is dangerous on certain occasions to consult it." This is as much as to say, what? That it is not consonant to utility, to consult utility: in short, that it is *not* consulting it, to consult it.

to be made of it, it is *misapplied*. Is it possible for a man to move the earth? Yes; but he must first find out another earth to stand upon.

xiv. To disprove the propriety of it by arguments is impossible; but, from the causes that have been mentioned, or from some confused or partial view of it, a man may happen to be disposed not to relish it. Where this is the case, if he thinks the settling of his opinions on such a subject worth the trouble, let him take the following steps, and at length, perhaps, he may come to reconcile himself to it.

(1) Let him settle with himself whether he would wish to discard this principle altogether; if so, let him consider what it is that all his reasonings (in matters of politics especially) can amount to?

(2) If he would, let him settle with himself whether he would judge and act without any principle, or whether there is any other he would judge and act by?

(3) If there be, let him examine and satisfy himself whether the principle he thinks he has found is really any separate intelligible principle; or whether it be not a mere principle in words, a kind of phrase, which at bottom expresses neither more nor less than the mere averment of his own unfounded sentiments—that is, what in another person he might be apt to call caprice?

(4) If he is inclined to think that his own approbation or disapprobation annexed to the idea of an act, without any regard to its consequences, is a sufficient foundation for him to judge and act upon, let him ask himself whether his sentiment is to be a standard of right and wrong with respect to every other man, or whether every man's sentiment has the same privilege of being a standard to itself?

(5) In the first case, let him ask himself whether his principle is not despotical, and hostile to all the rest of human race.

(6) In the second case, whether it is not anarchial, and whether at this rate there are not as many different standards of right and wrong as there are men? and whether even to the same man, the same thing which is right today, may not (without the least change in its nature) be wrong tomorrow? and whether the same thing is not right and wrong in the same place at the same time? and in either case, whether all argument is not at an end? and whether, when two men have said, "I like this," and "I don't like it," they can (upon such a principle) have anything more to say?

(7) If he should have said to himself, No: for that the sentiment which he proposes as a standard must be grounded on reflection, let him say on what particulars the reflection is to turn? If on particulars having relation to the utility of the act, then let him say whether this is not deserting his own principle. and borrowing assistance from that very

one in opposition to which he sets it up; or if not on those particulars, on what other particulars?

(8) If he should be for compounding the matter, and adopting his own principle in part, and the principle of utility in part, let him say how far he will adopt it?

(9) When he has settled with himself where he will stop, then let him ask himself how he justifies to himself the adopting it so far? and why he will not adopt it any farther?

(10) Admitting any other principle than the principle of utility to be a right principle, a principle that it is right for a man to pursue; admitting (what is not true) that the word 'right' can have a meaning without reference to utility, let him say whether there is any such thing as a *motive* that a man can have to pursue the dictates of it: if there is, let him say what that motive is, and how it is to be distinguished from those which enforce the dictates of utility; if not, then lastly let him say what it is this other principle can be good for?

CHAPTER II

OF PRINCIPLES ADVERSE TO THAT OF UTILITY

IF THE PRINCIPLE of utility be a right principle to be governed by, and that in all cases, it follows from what has been just observed, that whatever principle differs from it in any case must necessarily be a wrong one. To prove any other principle, therefore, to be a wrong one, there needs no more than just to show it to be what it is, a principle of which the dictates are in some point or other different from those of the principle of utility: to state it is to confute it.

ii. A principle may be different from that of utility in two ways: (1) By being constantly opposed to it: this is the case with a principle which may be termed the principle of *asceticism*.[4] (2) By being some-

---

[4] Ascetic is a term that has been sometimes applied to monks. It comes from a Greek word which signifies *exercise*. The practices by which monks sought to distinguish themselves from other men were called their exercises. These exercises consisted in so many contrivances they had for tormenting themselves. By this they thought to ingratiate themselves with the Deity. For the Deity, said they, is a Being of infinite benevolence: now a Being of the most ordinary benevolence is pleased to see others make themselves as happy as they can; therefore to make ourselves as unhappy as we can is the way to please the Deity. If anybody asked them what motive they could find for doing all this? Oh! said they, you are not to imagine that we are punishing ourselves for nothing: we know very well what we are about. You are to know, that for every grain of pain it costs us now, we are to have a hundred grains of pleasure by and by. The case is, that God loves to see us torment ourselves

times opposed to it, and sometimes not, as it may happen: this is the case with another, which may be termed the principle of *sympathy and antipathy.*

iii. By the principle of asceticism I mean that principle which, like the principle of utility, approves or disapproves of any action according to the tendency which it appears to have to augment or diminish the happiness of the party whose interest is in question; but in an inverse manner: approving of actions in as far as they tend to diminish his happiness, disapproving of them in as far as they tend to augment it.

ix. The principle of asceticism seems originally to have been the reverie of certain hasty speculators, who having perceived, or fancied, that certain pleasures, when reaped in certain circumstances, have, at the long run, been attended with pains more than equivalent to them, took occasion to quarrel with everything that offered itself under the name of pleasure. Having then got thus far, and having forgot the point which they set out from, they pushed on, and went so much further as to think it meritorious to fall in love with pain. Even this, we see, is at bottom but the principle of utility misapplied.

x. The principle of utility is capable of being consistently pursued; and it is but tautology to say that the more consistently it is pursued, the better it must ever be for humankind. The principle of asceticism never was, nor ever can be, consistently pursued by any living creature. Let but one tenth part of the inhabitants of this earth pursue it consistently, and in a day's time they will have turned it into a hell.

xi. Among principles adverse to that of utility, that which at this day sems to have most influence in matters of government, is what may be called the principle of sympathy and antipathy. By the principle of sympathy and antipathy, I mean that principle which approves or disapproves of certain actions, not on account of their tending to augment the happiness, nor yet on account of their tending to diminish the happiness of the party whose interest is in question, but merely because a man finds himself disposed to approve or disapprove of them; holding up that approbation or disapprobation as a sufficient reason for itself, and disclaiming the necessity of looking out for any extrinsic ground. Thus far in the general department of morals; and in the particular department of politics, measuring out the quantum (as well as determining the ground) of punishment, by the degree of the disapprobation.

---

at present: indeed he has as good as told us so. But this is done only to try us, in order just to see how we should behave; which it is plain he could not know without making the experiment. Now then, from the satisfaction it gives him to see us make ourselves as unhappy as we can make ourselves in this present life, we have a sure proof of the satisfaction it will give him to see us as happy as he can make us in a life to come.

xii. It is manifest that this is rather a principle in name than in reality: it is not a positive principle of itself so much as a term employed to signify the negation of all principle. What one expects to find in a principle is something that points out some external consideration, as a means of warranting and guiding the internal sentiments of approbation and disapprobation: this expectation is but ill fulfilled by a proposition which does neither more nor less than hold up each of those sentiments as a ground and standard for itself.

xiii. In looking over the catalogue of human actions (says a partisan of this principle) in order to determine which of them are to be marked with the seal of disapprobation, you need but to take counsel of your own feelings: whatever you find in yourself a propensity to condemn, is wrong for that very reason. For the same reason it is also meet for punishment: in what proportion it is adverse to utility, or whether it be adverse to utility at all, is a matter that makes no difference. In that same *proportion* also is it meet for punishment: if you hate much, punish much; if you hate little, punish little; punish as you hate. If you hate not at all, punish not at all: the fine feelings of the soul are not to be overborne and tyrannized by the harsh and rugged dictates of political utility.

xiv. The various systems that have been formed concerning the standard of right and wrong, may all be reduced to the principle of sympathy and antipathy. One account may serve for all of them. They consist all of them in so many contrivances for avoiding the obligation of appealing to any external standard, and for prevailing upon the reader to accept of the author's sentiment or opinion as a reason for itself. The phrases different, but the principle the same.

xv. It is manifest that the dictates of this principle will frequently coincide with those of utility, though perhaps without intending any such thing. Probably more frequently than not; and hence it is that the business of penal justice is carried on upon that tolerable sort of footing upon which we see it carried on in common at this day. For what more natural or more general ground of hatred to a practice can there be, than the mischievousness of such practice? What all men are exposed to suffer by, all men will be disposed to hate. It is far yet, however, from being a constant ground; for when a man suffers, it is not always that he knows what it is he suffers by. A man may suffer grievously, for instance, by a new tax, without being able to trace up the cause of his sufferings to the injustice of some neighbor, who has eluded the payment of an old one.

xvi. The principle of sympathy and antipathy is most apt to err on the side of severity. It is for applying punishment in many cases which deserve none: in many cases which deserve some, it is for applying more than they deserve. There is no incident imaginable, be it ever so trivial, and so remote from mischief, from which this principle may not extract a ground of punishment. Any difference in taste: any difference in opinion: upon one subject as well as upon another. No disagreement so trifling which perseverance and altercation will not render serious. Each becomes in the other's eyes an enemy, and, if laws permit, a criminal. This is one of the circumstances by which the human race is distinguished (not much indeed to its advantage) from the brute creation.

xvii. It is not, however, by any means unexampled for this principle to err on the side of lenity. A near and perceptible mischief moves antipathy. A remote and imperceptible mischief, though not less real, has no effect. Instances in proof of this will occur in numbers in the course of the work. It would be breaking in upon the order of it to give them here.

xviii. It may be wondered, perhaps, that in all this while no mention has been made of the *theological* principle; meaning that principle which professes to recur for the standard of right and wrong to the will of God. But the case is, this is not in fact a distinct principle. It is never anything more or less than one or other of the three before-mentioned principles presenting itself under another shape. The *will* of God here meant cannot be his revealed will, as contained in the sacred writings: for that is a system which nobody ever thinks of recurring to at this time of day, for the details of political administration; and even before it can be applied to the details of private conduct, it is universally allowed, by the most eminent divines of all persuasions, to stand in need of pretty ample interpretations; else to what use are the works of those divines? And for the guidance of these interpretations, it is also allowed that some other standard must be assumed. The will then which is meant on this occasion is that which may be called the *presumptive* will—that is to say, that which is presumed to be his will on account of the conformity of its dictates to those of some other principle. What then may be this other principle? It must be one or other of the three mentioned above; for there cannot, as we have seen, be any more. It is plain, therefore, that, setting revelation out of the question, no light can ever be thrown upon the standard of right and wrong, by anything that can be said upon the question, what is God's will. We may be perfectly sure, indeed, that whatever is right is conformable to the will of God; but so far is that from answering the purpose of showing us what is right, that it is necessary to know first whether a thing is right, in order to know from thence whether it be conformable to the will of God.[5]

⁵ The principle of theology refers everything to God's pleasure. But what is God's pleasure? God does not, he confessedly does not now, either speak or write to us. How then are we to know what is his pleasure? By observing what is our own

xix. There are two things which are very apt to be confounded, but which it imports us carefully to distinguish: the motive or cause which, by operating on the mind of an individual, is productive of any act; and the ground or reason which warrants a legislator or other bystander in regarding that act with an eye of approbation. When the act happens, in the particular instance in question, to be productive of effects which we approve of, much more if we happen to observe that the same motive may frequently be productive, in other instances, of the like effects, we are apt to transfer our approbation to the motive itself, and to assume as the just ground for the approbation we bestow on the act, the circumstance of its originating from that motive. It is in this way that the sentiment of antipathy has often been considered as a just ground of action. Antipathy, for instance, in such or such a case, is the cause of an action which is attended with good effects; but this does not make it a right ground of action in that case, any more than in any other. Still farther. Not only the effects are good, but the agent sees beforehand that they will be so. This may make the action indeed a perfectly right action, but it does not make antipathy a right ground of action. For the same sentiment of antipathy, if implicitly deferred to, may be, and very frequently is, productive of the very worst effects. Antipathy, therefore, can never be a right ground of action. No more, therefore, can resentment, which, as will be seen more particularly hereafter, is but a modification of antipathy. The only right ground of action that can possibly subsist is, after all, the consideration of utility, which, if it is a right principle of action and of approbation in any one case, is so in every other. Other principles in abundance—that is, other motives—may be the reasons why such and such an act *has* been done—that is, the reasons or causes of its being done,—but it is this alone that can be the reason why it might or ought to have been done. Antipathy or resentment requires always to be regulated, to prevent its doing mischief. To be regulated by what? Always by the principle of utility. The principle of utility neither requires nor admits of any other regulator than itself.

pleasure, and pronouncing it to be his. Accordingly, what is called the pleasure of God, is and must necessarily be (revelation apart) neither more nor less than the good pleasure of the person, whoever he be, who is pronouncing what he believes or pretends to be God's pleasure. How know you it to be God's pleasure that such or such an act should be abstained from? Whence come you even to suppose as much? "Because the engaging in it would, I imagine, be prejudicial upon the whole to the happiness of mankind," says the partisan of the principle of utility. "Because the commission of it is attended with a gross and sensual, or at least with a trifling and transient satisfaction," says the partisan of the principle of asceticism. "Because I detest the thoughts of it; and I cannot, neither ought I to be called upon to tell why," says he who proceeds upon the principle of antipathy. In the words of one or other of these must that person necessarily answer (revelation apart) who professes to take for his standard the will of God.

CHAPTER III

OF THE FOUR SANCTIONS OR SOURCES OF PAIN AND PLEASURE

It has been shown that the happiness of the individuals of whom a community is composed—that is, their pleasures and their security—is the end and the sole end which the legislator ought to have in view: the sole standard in conformity to which each individual ought, as far as depends upon the legislator, to be *made* to fashion his behavior. But whether it be this or anything else that is to be *done,* there is nothing by which a man can ultimately be *made* to do it, but either pain or pleasure. Having taken a general view of these two grand objects (viz., pleasure, and what comes to the same thing, immunity from pain) in the character of *final* causes, it will be necessary to take a view of pleasure and pain itself in the character of *efficient* causes or means.

ii. There are four distinguishable sources from which pleasure and pain are in use to flow: considered separately, they may be termed the *physical,* the *political,* the *moral,* and the *religious;* and inasmuch as the pleasures and pains belonging to each of them are capable of giving a binding force to any law or rule of conduct, they may all of them be termed *sanctions.*[6]

iii. If it be in the present life, and from the ordinary course of nature, not purposely modified by the interposition of the will of any human being, nor by any extraordinary interposition of any superior invisible being, that the pleasure or the pain takes place or is expected, it may be said to issue from or to belong to the *physical sanction.*

iv. If at the hands of a *particular* person or set of persons in the community, who under names correspondent to that of *judge,* are chosen for the particular purpose of dispensing it, according to the will of the sovereign or supreme ruling power in the state, it may be said to issue from the *political sanction.*

v. If at the hands of such *chance* persons in the community, as the party in question may happen in the course of his life to have concerns with, according to each man's spontaneous disposition, and not accord-

---

[6] *Sanctio,* in Latin, was used to signify the *act of binding,* and, by a common grammatical transition, *anything which serves to bind a man*—to wit, to the observance of such or such a mode of conduct. . . .

A sanction, then, is a source of obligatory powers or *motives:* that is, of *pains* and *pleasures;* which, according as they are connected with such or such modes of conduct, operate, and are indeed the only things which can operate, as *motives.* See Chap. X [Motives].

ing to any settled or concerted rule, it may be said to issue from the *moral* or *popular sanction*.

vi. If from the immediate hand of a superior invisible being, either in the present life or in a future, it may be said to issue from the *religious sanction*.

vii. Pleasures or pains which may be expected to issue from the *physical, political,* or *moral* sanctions, must all of them be expected to be experienced, if ever, in the present life; those which may be expected to issue from the *religious* sanction, may be expected to be experienced either in the present life or in a future.

viii. Those which can be experienced in the present life, can of course be no others than such as human nature in the course of the present life is susceptible of; and from each of these sources may flow all the pleasures or pains of which, in the course of the present life, human nature is susceptible. With regard to these then (with which alone we have in this place any concern), those of them which belong to any one of those sanctions, differ not ultimately in kind from those which belong to any one of the other three: the only difference there is among them lies in the circumstances that accompany their production. A suffering which befalls a man in the natural and spontaneous course of things, shall be styled, for instance, a *calamity;* in which case, if it be supposed to befall him through any imprudence of his, it may be styled a punishment issuing from the physical sanction. Now this same suffering, if inflicted by the law, will be what is commonly called a *punishment;* if incurred for want of any friendly assistance, which the misconduct, or supposed misconduct, of the sufferer has occasioned to be withholden, a punishment issuing from the *moral* sanction; if through the immediate interposition of a particular providence, a punishment issuing from the religious sanction.

ix. A man's goods, or his person, are consumed by fire. If this happened to him by what is called an accident, it was a calamity; if by reason of his own imprudence (for instance, from his neglecting to put his candle out) it may be styled a punishment of the physical sanction; if it happened to him by the sentence of the political magistrate, a punishment belonging to the political sanction—that is, what is commonly called a punishment; if for want of any assistance which his *neighbor* withheld from him out of some dislike to his moral character, a punishment of the *moral* sanction; if by an immediate act of *God's* displeasure, manifested on account of some *sin* committed by him, or through any distraction of mind occasioned by the dread of such displeasure, a punishment of the *religious* sanction.

x. As to such of the pleasures and pains belonging to the religious sanction as regard a future life, of what kind these may be we cannot know. These lie not open to our observation. During the present life they are matter only of expectation; and whether that expectation be derived from natural or revealed religion, the particular kind of pleasure or pain, if it be different from all those which lie open to our observation, is what we can have no idea of. The best ideas we can obtain of such pains and pleasures are altogether unliquidated in point of quality. In what other respects our ideas of them *may* be liquidated will be considered in another place.

xi. Of these four sanctions the physical is altogether, we may observe, the groundwork of the political and the moral; so is it also of the religious, in as far as the latter bears relation to the present life. It is included in each of those other three. This may operate in any case (that is, any of the pains or pleasures belonging to it may operate) independently of *them;* none of *them* can operate but by means of this. In a word, the powers of nature may operate of themselves; but neither the magistrate, nor men at large, *can* operate, nor is God in the case in question *supposed* to operate, but through the powers of nature.

xii. For these four objects, which in their nature have so much in common, it seemed of use to find a common name. It seemed of use, in the first place, for the convenience of giving a name to certain pleasures and pains, for which a name equally characteristic could hardly otherwise have been found; in the second place, for the sake of holding up the efficacy of certain moral forces, the influence of which is apt not to be sufficiently attended to. Does the political sanction exert an influence over the conduct of mankind? The moral, the religious sanctions do so too. In every inch of his career are the operations of the political magistrate liable to be aided or impeded by these two foreign powers; who, one or other of them, or both, are sure to be either his rivals or his allies. Does it happen to him to leave them out in his calculations? He will be sure almost to find himself mistaken in the result. Of all this we shall find abundant proofs in the sequel of this work. It behooves him, therefore, to have them continually before his eyes; and that under such a name as exhibits the relation they bear to his own purposes and designs.

CHAPTER IV

VALUE OF A LOT OF PLEASURE OR PAIN, HOW TO BE MEASURED

PLEASURES then, and the avoidance of pains, are the *ends* which the legislator has in view: it behooves him therefore to understand their *value* Pleasures and pains are the *instruments* he has to work with: it behooves him therefore to understand their force, which is again, in other words, their value.

ii. To a person considered *by himself*, the value of a pleasure or pain considered *by itself*, will be greater or less according to the four following circumstances:[7]

(1) Its *intensity*.

(2) Its *duration*.

(3) Its *certainty or uncertainty*.

(4) Its *propinquity* or *remoteness*.

iii. These are the circumstances which are to be considered in esti- mating a pleasure or a pain considered each of them by itself. But when the value of any pleasure or pain is considered for the purpose of esti- mating the tendency of any *act* by which it is produced, there are two other circumstances to be taken into the account. These are:

(5) Its *fecundity*, or the chance it has of being followed by sensations of the *same* kind: that is, pleasures, if it be a pleasure; pains, if it be a pain.

(6) Its *purity*, or the chance it has of *not* being followed by sensa- tions of the *opposite* kind: that is, pains, if it be a pleasure; pleasures, if it be a pain.

These two last, however, are in strictness scarcely to be deemed prop- erties of the pleasure or the pain itself; they are not, therefore, in strict- ness to be taken into the account of the value of that pleasure or that pain. They are in strictness to be deemed properties only of the act, or other event, by which such pleasure or pain has been produced; and accordingly are only to be taken into the account of the tendency of such act or such event.

iv. To a *number* of persons, with reference to each of whom the value of a pleasure or a pain is considered, it will be greater or less, accord- ing to seven circumstances: to wit, the six preceding ones; viz.,

(1) Its *intensity*.

(2) Its *duration*.

(3) Its *certainty* or *uncertainty*.

[7] These circumstances have since been denominated *elements* or *dimensions* of *value* in a pleasure or a pain. Not long after the publication of the first edition, the following memoriter verses were framed, in the view of lodging more effectually in the memory these points, on which the whole fabric of morals and legislation may be seen to rest:

> *Intense, long, certain, speedy, fruitful, pure—*
> Such marks in *pleasures* and in *pains* endure.
> Such pleasures seek, if *private* be thy end;
> If it be *public*, wide let them *extend*.
> Such *pains* avoid, whichever be thy view;
> If pains *must* come, let them *extend* to few.

(4) Its *propinquity* or *remoteness*.

(5) Its *fecundity*.

(6) Its *purity*.

And one other; to wit:

(7) Its *extent;* that is, the number of persons to whom it *extends,* or (in other words) who are affected by it.

v. To take an exact account then of the general tendency of any act by which the interests of a community are affected, proceed as follows. Begin with any one person of those whose interests seem most immediately to be affected by it, and take an account:

(1) Of the value of each distinguishable *pleasure* which appears to be produced by it in the *first* instance.

(2) Of the value of each *pain* which appears to be produced by it in the *first* instance.

(3) Of the value of each pleasure which appears to be produced by it *after* the first. This constitutes the *fecundity* of the first *pleasure* and the *impurity* of the first *pain*.

(4) Of the value of each *pain* which appears to be produced by it after the first. This constitutes the *fecundity* of the first *pain,* and the *impurity* of the first pleasure.

(5) Sum up all the values of all the *pleasures* on the one side, and those of all the pains on the other. The balance, if it be on the side of pleasure, will give the *good* tendency of the act upon the whole, with respect to the interests of that *individual* person; if on the side of pain, the *bad* tendency of it upon the whole.

(6) Take an account of the *number* of persons whose interests appear to be concerned, and repeat the above process with respect to each. *Sum up* the numbers expressive of the degrees of *good* tendency which the act has, with respect to each individual in regard to whom the tendency of it is *good* upon the whole; do this again with respect to each individual in regard to whom the tendency of it is *good* upon the whole; do this again with respect to each individual in regard to whom the tendency of it is *bad* upon the whole. Take the *balance;* which, if on the side of *pleasure,* will give the general *good tendency* of the act, with respect to the total number or community of individuals concerned; if on the side of pain, the general *evil tendency,* with respect to the same community.

vi. It is not to be expected that this process should be strictly pursued previously to every moral judgment, or to every legislative or judicial operation. It may, however, be always kept in view; and as near as the process actually pursued on these occasions approaches to it, so near will such process approach to the character of an exact one.

vii. The same process is alike applicable to pleasure and pain, in whatever shape they appear, and by whatever denomination they are distinguished: to pleasure, whether it be called *good* (which is properly the cause or instrument of pleasure), or *profit* (which is distant pleasure, or the cause or instrument of distant pleasure), or *convenience,* or *advantage, benefit, emolument, happiness,* and so forth; to pain, whether it be called *evil* (which corresponds to *good*), or *mischief,* or *inconvenience,* or *disadvantage,* or *loss,* or *unhappiness,* and so forth.

viii. Nor is this a novel and unwarranted, any more than it is a useless theory. In all this there is nothing but what the practice of mankind, wheresoever they have a clear view of their own interest, is perfectly conformable to. An article of property, an estate in land, for instance, is valuable, on what account? On account of the pleasures of all kinds which it enables a man to produce, and (what comes to the same thing) the pains of all kinds which it enables him to avert. But the value of such an article of property is universally understood to rise or fall according to the length or shortness of the time which a man has in it: the certainty or uncertainty of its coming into possession, and the nearness or remoteness of the time at which, if at all, it is to come into possession. As to the *intensity* of the pleasures which a man may derive from it, this is never thought of, because it depends upon the use which each particular person may come to make of it; which cannot be estimated till the particular pleasures he may come to derive from it, or the particular pains he may come to exclude by means of it, are brought to view. For the same reason, neither does he think of the *fecundity* or *purity* of those pleasures. . . .[8]

CHAPTER VII

OF HUMAN ACTIONS IN GENERAL

i. THE BUSINESS of government is to promote the happiness of the society, by punishing and rewarding. That part of its business which consists in punishing, is more particularly the subject of penal law. In proportion as an act tends to disturb that happiness, in proportion as the tendency of it is pernicious, will be the demand it creates for punishment. What happiness consists of we have already seen: enjoyment of pleasures, security from pains.

ii. The general tendency of an act is more or less pernicious, according to the sum total of its consequences: that is, according to the difference between the sum of such as are good, and the sum of such as are evil.

[8] Chapters V-VI treat "Of Pleasures and Pains, Their Kinds," and "Of Circumstances Influencing Sensibility."—*Editor.*

iii. It is to be observed, that here, as well as henceforward, wherever consequences are spoken of, such only are meant as are *material*. Of the consequences of any act, the multitude and variety must needs be infinite: but such of them only as are material are worth regarding. Now among the consequences of an act, be they what they may, such only, by one who views them in the capacity of a legislator, can be said to be material, as either consist of pain or pleasure, or have an influence in the production of pain or pleasure.

iv. It is also to be observed, that into the acount of the consequences of the act, are to be taken not such only as might have ensued, were intention out of the question, but such also as depend upon the connection there may be between these first-mentioned consequences and the intention. The connection there is between the intention and certain consequences is, as we shall see hereafter, a means of producing other consequences. In this lies the difference between rational agency and irrational.

v. Now the intention, with regard to the consequences of an act, will depend upon two things: 1. The state of the will or intention, with respect to the act itself. And, 2. The state of the understanding, or perceptive faculties, with regard to the circumstances which it is, or may appear to be, accompanied with. Now with respect to these circumstances, the perceptive faculty is susceptible of three states: consciousness, unconsciousness, and false consciousness. Consciousness, when the party believes precisely those circumstances, and no others, to subsist, which really do subsist: unconsciousness, when he fails of perceiving certain circumstances to subsist, which, however, do subsist: false consciousness, when he believes or imagines certain circumstances to subsist, which in truth do not subsist.

vi. In every transaction, therefore, which is examined with a view to punishment, there are four articles to be considered: 1. The *act* itself, which is done. 2. The *circumstances* in which it is done. 3. The *intentionality* that may have accompanied it. 4. The *consciousness,* unconsciousness, or false consciousness, that may have accompanied it.

What regards the act and the circumstances will be the subject of the present chapter: what regards intention and consciousness, that of the two succeeding.

vii. There are also two other articles on which the general tendency of an act depends: and on that, as well as on other accounts, the demand which it creates for punishment. These are: 1. The particular *motive* or motives which gave birth to it. 2. The general *disposition* which it indicates. These articles will be the subject of two other chapters. . . .

xxi. So much with regard to acts considered in themselves: we come now to speak of the *circumstances* with which they may have been accompanied. These must necessarily be taken into the account before anything can be determined relative to the consequences. What the consequences of an act may be upon the whole can never otherwise be ascertained: it can never be known whether it is beneficial, or indifferent, or mischievous. In some circumstances even to kill a man may be a beneficial act: in others, to set food before him may be a pernicious one.

xxii. Now the circumstances of an act, are, what? Any objects whatsoever. Take any act whatsoever, there is nothing in the nature of things that excludes any imaginable object from being a circumstance to it. Any given object may be a circumstance to any other.

xxiii. We have already had occasion to make mention for a moment of the *consequences* of an act: these were distinguished into material and immaterial. In like manner may the circumstances of it be distinguished. Now *materiality* is a relative term: applied to the consequences of an act, it bore relation to pain and pleasure: applied to the circumstances, it bears relation to the consequences. A circumstance may be said to be material, when it bears a visible relation in point of causality to the consequences: immaterial, when it bears no such visible relation.

xxiv. The consequences of an act are events. A circumstance may be related to an event in point of causality in any one of four ways: 1. In the way of causation or production. 2. In the way of derivation. 3. In the way of collateral connection. 4. In the way of conjunct influence. It may be said to be related to the event in the way of causation, when it is of the number of those that contribute to the production of such event: in the way of derivation, when it is of the number of the events to the production of which that in question has been contributory: in the way of collateral connection, where the circumstance in question, and the event in question, without being either of them instrumental in the production of the other, are related, each of them, to some common object, which has been concerned in the production of them both: in the way of conjunct influence, when, whether related in any other way or not, they have both of them concurred in the production of some common consequence.

xxv. An example may be of use. In the year 1628, Villiers, Duke of Buckingham, favorite and minister of Charles I. of England, received a wound and died. The man who gave it him was one Felton, who, exasperated at the maladministration of which that minister was accused, went down from London to Portsmouth, where Buckingham happened then to be, made his way into his antechamber, and finding him busily engaged in conversation with a number of people round him, got close to him, drew a knife and stabbed him. In the effort, the assassin's hat fell off, which was found soon after, and, upon searching him, the bloody knife. In the crown of the hat were found scraps of paper, with sentences expressive of the purpose he was come upon. Here then, suppose the event in question is the wound received by Buckingham: Felton's drawing out his knife, his making his way into the chamber, his going down to Portsmouth, his conceiving an indignation at the idea of Buckingham's administration, that administration itself, Charles's appointing such a minister, and so on, higher and higher without end, are so many circumstances, related to the event of Buckingham's receiving the wound, in the way of causation or production: the bloodiness of the knife, a circumstance related to the same event in the way of derivation: the finding of the hat upon the ground, the finding the sentences in the hat, and the writing them, so many circumstances related to it in the way of collateral connection: and the situation and conversations of the people about Buckingham, were circumstances related to the circumstances of Felton's making his way into the room, going down to Portsmouth, and so forth, in the way of conjunct influence; inasmuch as they contributed in common to the event of Buckingham's receiving the wound, by preventing him from putting himself upon his guard upon the first appearance of the intruder.

xxvi. These several relations do not all of them attach upon an event with equal certainty. In the first place, it is plain, indeed, that every event must have some circumstance or other, and in truth, an indefinite multitude of circumstances, related to it in the way of production: it must of course have a still greater multitude of circumstances related to it in the way of collateral connection. But it does not appear necessary that every event should have circumstances related to it in the way of derivation: nor therefore that it should have any related to it in the way of conjunct influence. But of the circumstances of all kinds which actually do attach upon an event, it is only a very small number that can be discovered by the utmost exertion of the human faculties: it is a still smaller number that ever actually do attract our notice: when occasion happens, more or fewer of them will be discovered by a man in proportion to the strength, partly of his intellectual powers, partly of his inclination. It appears therefore that the multitude and description of such of the circumstances belonging to an act, as may appear to be material, will be determined by two considerations: 1. By the nature of things themselves. 2. By the strength or weakness of the faculties of those who happen to consider them. . . .

CHAPTER VIII

OF INTENTIONALITY

So MUCH with regard to the two first of the articles upon which the evil tendency of an action may depend: viz., the act itself, and the general assemblage of the circumstances with which it may have been accompanied. We come now to consider the ways in which the particular circumstance of *intention* may be concerned in it.

ii. First, then, the intention or will may regard either of two objects: (1) the act itself, or (2) its consequences. Of these objects, that which the intention regards may be styled *intentional*. If it regards the act, then the act may be said to be intentional; if the consequences, so also then may the consequences. If it regards both the act and consequences, the whole *action* may be said to be intentional. Whichever of those articles is not the object of the intention, may of course be said to be *unintentional*.

iii. The act may very easily be intentional without the consequences, and often is so. Thus, you may intend to touch a man, without intending to hurt him; and yet, as the consequences turn out, you may chance to hurt him.

iv. The consequences of an act may also be intentional, without the act's being intentional throughout—that is, without its being intentional in every stage of it; but this is not so frequent a case as the former. You intend to hurt a man, suppose, by running against him and pushing him down, and you run towards him accordingly; but a second man coming in on a sudden between you and the first man, before you can stop yourself, you run against the second man, and by him push down the first.

v. But the consequences of an act cannot be intentional without the act's being itself intentional in at least the first stage. If the act be not intentional in the first stage, it is no act of yours: there is accordingly no intention on your part to produce the consequences—that is to say, the individual consequences. All there can have been on your part is a distant intention to produce other consequences of the same nature, by some act of yours, at a future time; or else, without any intention, a bare *wish* to see such event take place. The second man, suppose, runs of his own accord against the first, and pushes him down. You had intentions of doing a thing of the same nature—viz., to run against him, and push him down yourself; but you had done nothing in pursuance of those intentions: the individual consequences therefore of the act, which the second man performed in pushing down the first, cannot be said to have been on your part intentional. . . .

xii. It is to be observed that an act may be unintentional in any stage or stages of it, though intentional in the preceding; and, on the other hand, it may be intentional in any stage or stages of it, and yet unintentional in the succeeding. But whether it be intentional or no in any preceding stage, is immaterial, with respect to the consequences, so it be unintentional in the last. The only point with respect to which it is material, is the proof. The more stages the act is unintentional in, the more apparent it will commonly be that it was unintentional with respect to the last. If a man, intending to strike you on the cheek, strikes you in the eye, and puts it out, it will probably be difficult for him to prove that it was not his intention to strike you in the eye. It will probably be easier, if his intention was really not to strike you, or even not to strike at all.

xiii. It is frequent to hear men speak of a good intention, of a bad intention, of the goodness and badness of a man's intention: a circumstance on which great stress is generally laid. It is indeed of no small importance when properly understood, but the import of it is to the last degree ambiguous and obscure. Strictly speaking, nothing can be said to be good or bad but either in itself, which is the case only with pain or pleasure, or on account of its effects, which is the case only with things that are the causes or preventives of pain and pleasure. But in a figurative and less proper way of speech, a thing may also be styled good or bad, in consideration of its cause. Now the effects of an intention to do such or such an act, are the same objects which we have been speaking of under the appellation of its *consequences;* and the causes of intention are called *motives.* A man's intention then on any occasion may be styled good or bad with reference either to the consequences of the act or with reference to his motives. If it be deemed good or bad in any sense, it must be either because it is deemed to be productive of good or of bad consequences, or because it is deemed to originate from a good or from a bad motive. But the goodness or badness of the consequences depend upon the circumstances. Now the circumstances are no objects of the intention. A man intends the act, and by his intention produces the act; but as to the circumstances, he does not intend *them:* he does not, inasmuch as they are circumstances of it, produce them. If by accident there be a few which he has been instrumental in producing, it has been by former intentions, directed to former acts, productive of those circumstances as the consequences: at the time in question he takes them as he finds them. Acts, with their consequences, are objects of the will as well as of the understanding; circumstances, as such, are objects of the understanding only. All he can do with these, as such, is to know or not to know them: in other words, to be conscious of them, or not conscious. To the title of consciousness belongs what is to be said of the goodness or badness of a man's intention, as resulting from the consequences of the act; and to the head of motives, what is to be said of his intention, as resulting from the motive.

CHAPTER IX

OF CONSCIOUSNESS

So FAR with regard to the ways in which the will or intention may be concerned in the production of any incident; we come now to consider the part which the understanding or perceptive faculty may have borne, with relation to such incident. . . .

xiii. In ordinary discourse, when a man does an act of which the consequences prove mischievous, it is a common thing to speak of him as having acted with a good intention or with a bad intention, of his intention's being a good one or a bad one. The epithets good and bad are all this while applied, we see, to the intention; but the application of them is most commonly governed by a supposition formed with regard to the nature of the motive. The act, though eventually it prove mischievous, is said to be done with a good intention when it is supposed to issue from a motive which is looked upon as a good motive; with a bad intention, when it is supposed to be the result of a motive which is looked upon as a bad motive. But the nature of the consequences intended, and the nature of the motive which gave birth to the intention, are objects which, though intimately connected, are perfectly distinguishable. The intention might therefore with perfect propriety be styled a good one, whatever were the motive. It might be styled a good one, when not only the consequences of the act *prove* mischievous, but the motive which gave birth to it *was* what is called a bad one. To warrant the speaking of the intention as being a good one, it is sufficient if the consequences of the act, had they proved what to the agent they seemed likely to be, *would* have been of a beneficial nature. And in the same manner the intention may be bad, when not only the consequences of the act prove beneficial, but the motive which gave birth to it was a good one.

xiv. Now, when a man has a mind to speak of your *intention* as being good or bad with reference to the consequences, if he speaks of it at all he must use the word intention, for there is no other. But if a man means to speak of the *motive* from which your intention originated, as being a good or a bad one, he is certainly not obliged to use the word intention: it is at least as well to use the word motive. By the supposition he means the motive; and very likely he may *not* mean the intention. For what is true of the one is very often not true of the other. The motive may be good when the intention is bad; the intention may be good when the motive is bad: whether they are both good or both bad, or the one good and the other bad, makes, as we shall see hereafter, a very essential difference with regard to the consequences. It is therefore much better, when motive is meant, never to say intention.

xv. An example will make this clear. Out of malice a man prosecutes you for a crime of which he believes you to be guilty, but of which in fact you are not guilty. Here the *consequences* of his conduct are mischievous: for they are mischievous to you at any rate, in virtue of the shame and anxiety which you are made to suffer while the prosecution is depending; to which is to be added, in case of your being convicted, the evil of the punishment. To you therefore they are mischievous; nor is there anyone to whom they are beneficial. The man's *motive* was also what is called a bad one: for malice will be allowed by everybody to be a bad motive. However, the *consequences* of his conduct, had they proved such as he believed them likely to be, would have been good: for in them would have been included the punishment of a criminal, which is a benefit to all who are exposed to suffer by a crime of the like nature. The *intention* therefore, in this case, though not in a common way of speaking the motive, might be styled a *good* one. But of motives more particularly in the next chapter. . . .

CHAPTER X

OF MOTIVES

§ 1. *Different senses of the word motive*[9]

IT IS AN ACKNOWLEDGED TRUTH that every kind of act whatever, and consequently every kind of offense, is apt to assume a different character, and be attended with different effects, according to the nature of the *motive* which gives birth to it. This makes it requisite to take a view of the several motives by which human conduct is liable to be influenced.

ii. By a motive, in the most extensive sense in which the word is ever used with reference to a thinking being, is meant anything that can contribute to give birth to, or even to prevent, any kind of action. Now the

[9] Note by the author, July, 1822.—For a tabular simultaneous view of the whole list of *motives,* in conjunction with the correspondent *pleasures* and *pains, interests* and *desires,* see, by the same author, *Table of the Springs of Action,* etc., with Explanatory Notes and Observations, . . .

action of a thinking being is the act either of the body, or only of the mind; and an act of the mind is an act either of the intellectual faculty, or of the will. Acts of the intellectual faculty will sometimes rest in the understanding merely, without exerting any influence in the production of any acts of the will. Motives which are not of a nature to influence any other acts than those, may be styled purely *speculative* motives, or motives resting in speculation. But as to these acts, neither do they exercise any influence over external acts, or over their consequences, nor consequently over any pain or any pleasure that may be in the number of such consequences. Now it is only on account of their tendency to produce either pain or pleasure, that any acts can be material. With acts, therefore, that rest purely in the understanding, we have not here any concern; nor therefore with any object, if any such there be, which, in the character of a motive, can have no influence on any other acts than those.

iii. The motives with which alone we have any concern, are such as are of a nature to act upon the will. By a motive then, in this sense of the word, is to be understood anything whatsoever which, by influencing the will of a sensitive being, is supposed to serve as a means of determining him to act, or voluntarily to forbear to act, upon any occasion. Motives of this sort, in contradistinction to the former, may be styled *practical* motives, or motives applying to practice.

iv. Owing to the poverty and unsettled state of language, the word 'motive' is employed indiscriminately to denote two kinds of objects, which, for the better understanding of the subject, it is necessary should be distinguished. On some occasions it is employed to denote any of those really existing incidents from whence the act in question is supposed to take its rise. The sense it bears on these occasions may be styled its literal or *unfigurative* sense. On other occasions it is employed to denote a certain fictitious entity, a passion, an affection of the mind, an ideal being which upon the happening of any such incident is considered as operating upon the mind, and prompting it to take that course towards which it is impelled by the influence of such incident. Motives of this class are avarice, indolence, benevolence, and so forth; as we shall see more particularly farther on. This latter may be styled the *figurative* sense of the term 'motive.'

v. As to the real incidents to which the name of motive is also given, these too are of two very different kinds. They may be either (1) the *internal* perception of any individual lot of pleasure or pain, the expectation of which is looked upon as calculated to determine you to act in such or such a manner; as the pleasure of acquiring such a sum of money, the pain of exerting yourself on such an occasion, and so forth; or (2) any *external* event, the happening whereof is regarded as having a ten-

dency to bring about the perception of such pleasure or such pain; for
instance, the coming up of a lottery ticket, by which the possession of
the money devolves to you, or the breaking out of a fire in the house you
are in, which makes it necessary for you to quit it. The former kind of
motives may be termed interior, or internal; the latter exterior, or external.

vi. Two other senses of the term 'motive' need also to be distinguished.
Motive refers necessarily to action. It is a pleasure, pain, or other event,
that prompts to action. Motive then, in one sense of the word, must be
previous to such event. But, for a man to be governed by any motive,
he must in every case look beyond that event which is called his action;
he must look to the consequences of it: and it is only in this way that
the idea of pleasure, of pain, or of any other event, can give birth to it.
He must look, therefore, in every case, to some event posterior to the
act in contemplation: an event which as yet exists not, but stands only
in prospect. Now, as it is in all cases difficult, and in most cases unnecessary, to distinguish between objects so intimately connected, as the
posterior possible object which is thus looked forward to, and the present existing object or event which takes place upon a man's looking forward to the other, they are both of them spoken of under the same appellation, *motive*. To distinguish them, the one first mentioned may be
termed a motive in *prospect,* the other a motive in *esse;* and under each
of these denominations will come as well exterior as internal motives.
A fire breaks out in your neighbor's house; you are under apprehension
of its extending to your own; you are apprehensive that if you stay in it,
you will be burnt: you accordingly run out of it. This then is the act;
the others are all motives to it. The event of the fire's breaking out in
your neighbor's house is an external motive, and that in *esse;* the idea or
belief of the probability of the fire's extending to your own house, that of
your being burnt if you continue, and the pain you feel at the thought of
such a catastrophe, are all so many internal events, but still in *esse;*
the event of the fire's actually extending to your own house, and that
of your being actually burnt by it, external motives in prospect; the
pain you would feel at seeing your house a-burning, and the pain you
would feel while you yourself were burning, internal motives in prospect
—which events, according as the matter turns out, may come to be in
esse; but then of course they will cease to act as motives.

vii. Of all these motives which stand nearest to the act, to the production of which they all contribute, is that internal motive in *esse* which
consists in the expectation of the internal motive in prospect: the pain
or uneasiness you feel at the thoughts of being burnt. All other motives
are more or less remote: the motives in prospect, in proportion as the
period at which they are expected to happen is more distant from the

period at which the act takes place, and consequently later in point of time; the motive in *esse,* in proportion as they also are more distant from that period, and consequently earlier in point of time.

viii. It has already been observed, that with motives of which the influence terminates altogether in the understanding, we have nothing here to do. If then, amongst objects that are spoken of as motives with reference to the understanding, there be any which concern us here, it is only in as far as such objects may, through the medium of the under-standing, exercise an influence over the will. It is in this way, and in this way only, that any objects, in virtue of any tendency they may have to influence the sentiment of belief, may in a practical sense act in the character of motives. Any objects, by tending to induce a belief concerning the existence, actual, or probable, of a practical motive; that is, concerning the probability of a motive in prospect, or the existence of a motive in *esse;* may exercise an influence on the will, and rank with those other motives that have been placed under the name of practical. The pointing out of motives such as these, is what we frequently mean when we talk of giving *reasons.* Your neighbor's house is on fire as before. I observe to you, that at the lower part of your neighbor's house is some wood-work, which joins on to yours; that the flames have caught this wood-work, and so forth; which I do in order to dispose you to believe as I believe, that if you stay in your house much longer you will be burnt. In doing this, then, I suggest motives to your understanding; which motives, by the tendency they have to give birth to or strengthen a pain, which operates upon you in the character of an internal motive in *esse,* join their force, and act as motives upon the will.

§2. *No motives either constantly good or constantly bad*

ix. In all this chain of motives, the principal or original link seems to be the last internal motive in prospect: it is to this that all the other motives in prospect owe their materiality, and the immediately acting motive its existence. This motive in prospect, we see, is always some pleasure, or some pain: some pleasure which the act in question is expected to be a means of continuing or producing; some pain which it is expected to be a means of discontinuing or preventing. A motive is substantially nothing more than pleasure or pain operating in a certain manner.

x. Now, pleasure is in *itself* a good—nay even, setting aside immunity from pain, the only good; pain is in itself an evil—and, indeed, without exception, the only evil; or else the words good and evil have no meaning. And this is alike true of every sort of pain, and of every sort of pleasure. It follows, therefore, immediately and incontestibly, that *there is no such thing as any sort of motive that is in itself a bad one.*[10]

xi. It is common, however, to speak of actions as proceeding from *good* or *bad* motives; in which case the motives meant are such as are internal. The expression is far from being an accurate one; and as it is apt to occur in the consideration of almost every kind of offense, it will be requisite to settle the precise meaning of it, and observe how far it quadrates with the truth of things.

xii. With respect to goodness and badness, as it is with everything else that is not itself either pain or pleasure, so is it with motives. If they are good or bad, it is only on account of their effects: good, on account of their tendency to produce pleasure or avert pain; bad, on account of their tendency to produce pain or avert pleasure. Now the case is, that from one and the same motive, and from every kind of motive, may proceed actions that are good, others that are bad, and others that are indifferent. This we shall proceed to shew with respect to all the different kinds of motives, as determined by the various kinds of pleasures and pains.

xiii. Such an analysis, useful as it is, will be found to be a matter of no small difficulty; owing, in great measure, to a certain perversity of structure which prevails more or less throughout all languages. To speak of motives, as of anything else, one must call them by their names. But the misfortune is, that it is rare to meet with a motive of which the name expresses that and nothing more. Commonly along with the very name of the motive is tacitly involved a proposition imputing to it a certain quality; a quality which, in many cases, will appear to include that very goodness or badness, concerning which we are here inquiring whether, properly speaking, it be or be not imputable to motives. To use the common phrase, in most cases, the name of the motive is a word which is employed either only in a *good sense* or else only in a *bad sense*. Now, when a word is spoken of as being used in a good sense, all that is necessarily meant is this: that in conjunction with the idea of the object it is put to signify, it conveys an idea of *approbation*—that is, of a pleasure or satisfaction, entertained by the person who employs the term at the thoughts of such object. In like manner, when a word is spoken of as being used in a bad sense, all that is necessarily meant is this: that in conjunction with the idea of the object it is put to signify, it conveys

---

[10] Let a man's motive be ill-will; call it even malice, envy, cruelty; it is still a kind of pleasure that is his motive: the pleasure he takes at the thought of the pain which he sees, or expects to see, his adversary undergo. Now even this wretched pleasure, taken by itself, is good: it may be faint, it may be short, it must at any rate be impure; yet while it lasts, and before any bad consequences arrive, it is as good as any other that is not more intense. See Chap. IV.

an idea of *disapprobation*—that is, of a displeasure entertained by the person who employs the term at the thoughts of such object. Now, the circumstance on which such approbation is grounded will, as naturally as any other, be the opinion of the *goodness* of the object in question, as above explained: such, at least, it must be, upon the principle of utility. So, on the other hand, the circumstance on which any such disapproba- tion is grounded, will, as naturally as any other, be the opinion of the *badness* of the object: such, at least, it must be, in as far as the prin- ciple of utility is taken for the standard.

Now there are certain motives which, unless in a few particular cases, have scarcely any other name to be expressed by but such a word as is used only in a good sense. This is the case, for example, with the motives of piety and honor. The consequence of this is, that if, in speaking of such a motive, a man should have occasion to apply the epithet bad to any actions which he mentions as apt to result from it, he must appear to be guilty of a contradiction in terms. But the names of motives which have scarcely any other name to be expressed by but such a word as is used only in a bad sense, are many more. This is the case, for example, with the motives of lust and avarice. And accordingly, if in speaking of any such motive, a man should have occasion to apply the epithets good or indifferent to any actions which he mentions as apt to result from it, he must here also appear to be guilty of a similar contradiction. . . .

xix. To the pleasures of wealth corresponds the sort of motive which, in a neutral sense, may be termed pecuniary interest. In a bad sense it is termed, in some cases, avarice, covetousness, rapacity, or lucre; in other cases, niggardliness. In a good sense, but only in particular cases, economy and frugality; and in some cases the word industry may be applied to it. In a sense nearly indifferent, but rather bad than otherwise, it is styled, though only in particular cases, parsimony.

(1) For money you gratify a man's hatred, by putting his adversary to death. (2) For money you plough his field for him. In the first case your motive is termed lucre, and is accounted corrupt and abomi- nable: and in the second, for want of a proper appellation, it is styled industry, and is looked upon as innocent at least, if not meritorious. Yet the motive is in both cases precisely the same: it is neither more nor less than pecuniary interest.

xx. The pleasures of skill are neither distinct enough, nor of conse- quence enough, to have given any name to the corresponding motive.

xxi. To the pleasures of amity corresponds a motive which, in a neu- tral sense, may be termed the desire of ingratiating one's self. In a bad sense it is in certain cases styled servility. In a good sense it has no name that is peculiar to it: in the cases in which it has been looked on with a favorable eye, it has seldom been distinguished from the motive of sympathy or benevolence, with which, in such cases, it is commonly associated.

(1) To acquire the affections of a woman before marriage, to preserve them afterwards, you do everything, that is consistent with other duties, to make her happy: in this case your motive is looked upon as laudable, though there is no name for it. (2) For the same purpose, you poison a woman with whom she is at enmity: in this case your motive is looked upon as abominable, though still there is no name for it. (3) To acquire or preserve the favor of a man who is richer or more powerful than yourself, you make yourself subservient to his pleasures. Let them even be lawful pleasures, if people choose to attribute your behavior to this motive, you will not get them to find any other name for it than servility. Yet in all three cases the motive is the same: it is neither more nor less than the desire of ingratiating yourself.

xxii. To the pleasures of the moral sanction, or, as they may otherwise be called, the pleasures of a good name, corresponds a motive which, in a neutral sense, has scarcely yet obtained any adequate appellative. It may be styled the love of reputation. It is nearly related to the motive last preceding; being neither more nor less than the desire of ingratiating oneself with, or, as in this case we should rather say, of recommending oneself to, the world at large. In a good sense, it is termed honor, or the sense of honor; or rather, the word honor is introduced somehow or other upon the occasion of its being brought to view: for in strictness the word honor is put rather to signify that imaginary object which a man is spoken of as possessing upon the occasion of his obtaining a conspicuous share of the pleasures that are in question. In particular cases, it is styled the love of glory. In a bad sense, it is styled in some cases false honor, in others pride, in others vanity. In a sense not decidedly bad, but rather bad than otherwise, ambition. In an indifferent sense, in some cases, the love of fame; in others, the sense of shame. And as the pleasures belonging to the moral sanction run undistinguishably into the pains derived from the same source, it may also be styled in some cases the fear of dishonor, the fear of disgrace, the fear of infamy, the fear of ignominy, or the fear of shame.

(1) You have received an affront from a man: according to the custom of the country, in order on the one hand to save yourself from the shame of being thought to bear it patiently, on the other hand to obtain the reputation of courage, you challenge him to fight with mortal weapons. In this case your motive will by some people be accounted laudable, and styled honor; by others it will be accounted blamable, and these, if they call it honor, will prefix an epithet of improbation to

it, and call it false honor. (2) In order to obtain a post of rank and dignity, and thereby to increase the respects paid you by the public, you bribe the electors who are to confer it, or the judge before whom the title to it is in dispute. In this case your motive is commonly accounted corrupt and abominable, and is styled, perhaps, by some such name as dishonest or corrupt ambition, as there is no single name for it. (3) In order to obtain the good-will of the public, you bestow a large sum in works of private charity or public utility. In this case people will be apt not to agree about your motive. Your enemies will put a bad color upon it, and call it ostentation; your friends, to save you from this reproach, will choose to impute your conduct not to this motive but to some other, such as that of charity (the denomination in this case given to private sympathy) or that of public spirit. (4) A king, for the sake of gaining the admiration annexed to the name of conqueror (we will suppose power and resentment out of the question) engages his kingdom in a bloody war. His motive, by the multitude (whose sympathy for millions is easily overborne by the pleasure which their imagination finds in gaping at any novelty they observe in the conduct of a single person) is deemed an admirable one. Men of feeling and reflection, who disapprove of the dominion exercised by this motive on this occasion, without always perceiving that it is the same motive which in other instances meets with their approbation, deem it an abominable one; and because the multitude, who are the manufacturers of language, have not given them a simple name to call it by, they will call it by some such compound name as the love of false glory or false ambition. Yet in all four cases the motive is the same: it is neither more nor less than the love of reputation.

xxiii. To the pleasures of power corresponds the motive which, in a neutral sense, may be termed the love of power. People who are out of humor with it sometimes call it the lust of power. In a good sense it is scarcely provided with a name. In certain cases this motive, as well as the love of reputation, are confounded under the same name, ambition. This is not to be wondered at, considering the intimate connection there is between the two motives in many cases; since it commonly happens that the same object which affords the one sort of pleasure, affords the other sort at the same time—for instance, offices, which are at once posts of honor and places of trust; and since at any rate reputation is the road to power.

(1) If in order to gain a place in administration, you poison the man who occupies it; (2) if, in the same view, you propose a salutary plan for the advancement of the public welfare; your motive is in both cases the same. Yet in the first case it is accounted criminal and abominable, in the second case allowable and even laudable.

xxiv. To the pleasures as well as to the pains of the religious sanction corresponds a motive which has, strictly speaking, no perfectly neutral name applicable to all cases, unless the word religion be admitted in this character; though the word religion, strictly speaking, seems to mean not so much the motive itself, as a kind of fictitious personage, by whom the motive is supposed to be created, or an assemblage of acts, supposed to be dictated by that personage; nor does it seem to be completely settled into a neutral sense. In the same sense it is also, in some cases, styled religious zeal; in other cases, the fear of God. The love of God, though commonly contrasted with the fear of God, does not come strictly under this head. It coincides properly with a motive of a different denomination, viz., a kind of sympathy or good-will which has the Deity for its object. In a good sense it is styled devotion, piety, and pious zeal. In a bad sense it is styled in some cases superstition, or superstitious zeal; in other cases, fanaticism, or fanatic zeal; in a sense not decidedly bad, because not appropriated to this motive, enthusiasm, or enthusiastic zeal.

(1) In order to obtain the favor of the Supreme Being, a man assassinates his lawful sovereign. In this case the motive is now almost universally looked upon as abominable, and is termed fanaticism: formerly it was by great numbers accounted laudable, and was by them called pious zeal. (2) In the same view, a man lashes himself with thongs. In this case, in yonder house, the motive is accounted laudable, and is called pious zeal; in the next house it is deemed contemptible, and called superstition. (3) In the same view, a man eats a piece of bread (or at least what to external appearance is a piece of bread) with certain ceremonies. In this case, in yonder house his motive is looked upon as laudable, and is styled piety and devotion; in the next house it is deemed abominable, and styled superstition, as before: perhaps even it is absurdly styled impiety. (4) In the same view, a man holds a cow by the tail while he is dying. On the Thames the motive would in this case be deemed contemptible, and called superstition. On the Ganges it is deemed meritorious, and called piety. (5) In the same view, a man bestows a large sum in works of charity, or public utility. In this case the motive is styled laudable, by those at least to whom the works in question appear to come under this description; and by these at least it would be styled piety. Yet in all these cases the motive is precisely the same: it is neither more nor less than the motive belonging to the religious sanction.[11]

---

[11] I am aware, or at least I hope, that people in general, when they see the matter thus stated, will be ready to acknowledge that the motive in these cases, whatever be the tendency of the acts which it produces, is not a bad one; but this will not render it the less true that hitherto, in popular discourse, it has been common for

xxv. To the pleasures of sympathy corresponds the motive which, in a neutral sense, is termed good-will. The word sympathy may also be used on this occasion, though the sense of it seems to be rather more extensive. In a good sense it is styled benevolence, and in certain cases philanthropy, and in a figurative way brotherly love; in others, humanity; in others, charity; in others, pity and compassion; in others, mercy; in others, gratitude; in others, tenderness; in others, patriotism; in others, public spirit. Love is also employed in this as in so many other senses. In a bad sense, it has no name applicable to it in all cases: in particular cases it is styled partiality. The word zeal, with certain epithets prefixed to it, might also be employed sometimes on this occasion, though the sense of it be more extensive, applying sometimes to ill as well as to good-will. It is thus we speak of party zeal, national zeal, and public zeal. The word attachment is also used with the like epithets; we also say family attachment. The French expression, *esprit de corps,* for which as yet there seems to be scarcely any name in English, might be rendered in some cases, though rather inadequately, by the terms corporation spirit, corporation attachment, or corporation zeal.

(1) A man who has set a town on fire is apprehended and committed; out of regard or compassion for him you help him to break prison. In this case the generality of people will probably scarcely know whether to condemn your motive or to applaud it: those who condemn your conduct will be disposed rather to impute it to some other motive: if they style it benevolence or compassion, they will be for prefixing an epithet, and calling it false benevolence or false compassion. (2) The man is taken again, and is put upon his trial; to save him you swear falsely in his favor. People who would not call your motive a bad one before, will perhaps call it so now. (3) A man is at law with you about an estate; he has no right to it; the judge knows this, yet, having an esteem or affection for your adversary, adjudges it to him. In this case the motive is by everybody deemed abominable, and is termed injustice and partiality. (4) You detect a statesman in receiving bribes; out of regard to the public interest, you give information of it, and prosecute him. In this case, by all who acknowledge your conduct to have originated from this motive, your motive will be deemed a laudable one, and styled public spirit. But his friends and adherents will not choose to account for your conduct in any such manner: they will rather attribute it to party enmity. (5) You find a man on the point of starving; you relieve him, and save his life. In this case your motive will by everybody be accounted laudable, and it will be termed

men to speak of acts, which they could not but acknowledge to have originated from this source, as proceeding from a bad motive. The same observation will apply to many of the other cases.

compassion, pity, charity, benevolence. Yet in all these cases the motive is the same: it is neither more nor less than the motive of good-will.

xxvi. To the pleasures of malevolence, or antipathy, corresponds the motive which in a neutral sense is termed antipathy or displeasure, and in particular cases dislike, aversion, abhorrence, and indignation; in a neutral sense, or perhaps a sense leaning a little to the bad side, ill-will, and in particular cases anger, wrath, and enmity. In a bad sense it is styled in different cases wrath, spleen, ill-humor, hatred, malice, rancor, rage, fury, cruelty, tyranny, envy, jealousy, revenge, misanthropy, and by other names, which it is hardly worth while to endeavor to collect.[12] Like good-will, it is used with epithets expressive of the persons who are the objects of the affection. Hence we hear of party enmity, party rage, and so forth. In a good sense there seems to be no single name for it. In compound expressions it may be spoken of in such a sense, by epithets such as *just* and *laudable* prefixed to words that are used in a neutral or nearly neutral sense.

(1) You rob a man; he prosecutes you, and gets you punished; out of resentment you set upon him, and hang him with your own hands. In this case your motive will universally be deemed detestable, and will be called malice, cruelty, revenge, and so forth. (2) A man has stolen a little money from you; out of resentment you prosecute him, and get him hanged by course of law. In this case people will probably be a little divided in their opinions about your motive: your friends will deem it a laudable one, and call it a just or laudable resentment; your enemies will perhaps be disposed to deem it blamable, and call it cruelty, malice, revenge, and so forth: to obviate which, your friends will try perhaps to change the motive, and call it public spirit. (3) A man has murdered your father: out of resentment you prosecute him, and get him put to death in course of law. In this case your motive will be universally deemed a laudable one, and styled, as before, a just or laudable resentment; and your friends, in order to bring forward the more amiable principle from which the malevolent one, which was your immediate motive, took its rise, will be for keeping the latter out of sight, speaking of the former only, under some such name as filial piety. Yet in all these cases the motive is the same: it is neither more nor less than the motive of ill-will.

xxvii. To the several sorts of pains, or at least to all such of them as

[12] Here, as elsewhere, it may be observed that the same words which are mentioned as names of motives, are also many of them names of passions, appetites, and affections: fictitious entities, which are framed only by considering pleasures or pains in some particular point of view. Some of them are also names of moral qualities. This branch of nomenclature is remarkably entangled: to unravel it completely would take up a whole volume, not a syllable of which would belong properly to the present design.

are conceived to subsist in an intense degree, and to death, which, as far as we can perceive, is the termination of all the pleasures, as well as all the pains we are acquainted with, corresponds the motive, which in a neutral sense is styled, in general, self-preservation: the desire of preserving one's self from the pain or evil in question. Now in many instances the desire of pleasure, and the sense of pain, run into one another undistinguishably. Self-preservation, therefore, where the degree of the pain which it corresponds to is but slight will scarcely be distinguishable, by any precise line, from the motives corresponding to the several sorts of pleasures. Thus in the case of the pains of hunger and thirst: physical want will in many cases be scarcely distinguishable from physical desire. In some cases it is styled, still in a neutral sense, self-defense. Between the pleasures and the pains of the moral and religious sanctions, and consequently of the motives that correspond to them, as likewise between the pleasures of amity, and the pains of enmity, this want of boundaries has already been taken notice of. The case is the same between the pleasures of wealth, and the pains of privation corresponding to those pleasures. There are many cases, therefore, in which it will be difficult to distinguish the motive of self-preservation from pecuniary interest, from the desire of ingratiating one's self, from the love of reputation, and from religious hope: in which cases, those more specific and explicit names will naturally be preferred to this general and inexplicit one. There are also a multitude of compound names, which either are already in use, or might be devised, to distinguish the specific branches of the motive of self-preservation from those several motives of a pleasurable origin: such as the fear of poverty, the fear of losing such or such a man's regard, the fear of shame, and the fear of God. Moreover, to the evil of death corresponds, in a neutral sense, the love of life; in a bad sense, cowardice: which corresponds also to the pains of the senses, at least when considered as subsisting in an acute degree. There seems to be no name for the love of life that has a good sense; unless it be the vague and general name of prudence.

1. To save yourself from being hanged, pilloried, imprisoned, or fined, you poison the only person who can give evidence against you. In this case your motive will universally be styled abominable: but as the term self-preservation has no bad sense, people will not care to make this use of it: they will be apt rather to change the motive, and call it malice.

2. A woman, having been just delivered of an illegitimate child, in order to save herself from shame, destroys the child, or abandons it. In this case, also, people will call the motive a bad one, and, not caring to speak of it under a neutral name, they will be apt to change the

motive, and call it by some such name as cruelty. 3. To save the expense of a halfpenny, you suffer a man, whom you could preserve at that expense, to perish with want, before your eyes. In this case your motive will be universally deemed an abominable one; and, to avoid calling it by so indulgent a name as self-preservation, people will be apt to call it avarice and niggardliness, with which indeed in this case it indistinguishably coincides: for the sake of finding a more reproachful appellation, they will be apt likewise to change the motive, and term it cruelty. 4. To put an end to the pain of hunger, you steal a loaf of bread. In this case your motive will scarcely, perhaps, be deemed a very bad one; and, in order to express more indulgence for it, people will be apt to find a stronger name for it than self-preservation, terming it *necessity*. 5. To save yourself from drowning, you beat off an innocent man who has got hold of the same plank. In this case your motive will in general be deemed neither good nor bad, and it will be termed self-preservation, or necessity, or the love of life. 6. To save your life from a gang of robbers, you kill them in the conflict. In this case the motive may, perhaps, be deemed rather laudable than otherwise, and, besides self-preservation, is styled also self-defense. 7. A soldier is sent out upon a party against a weaker party of the enemy: before he gets up with them, to save his life, he runs away. In this case the motive will universally be deemed a contemptible one, and will be called cowardice. Yet in all these various cases, the motive is still the same. It is neither more nor less than self-preservation.

xxviii. In particular, to the pains of exertion corresponds the motive, which, in a neutral sense, may be termed the love of ease, or by a longer circumlocution, the desire of avoiding trouble. In a bad sense, it is termed indolence. It seems to have no name that carries with it a good sense.

1. To save the trouble of taking care of it, a parent leaves his child to perish. In this case the motive will be deemed an abominable one, and, because indolence will seem too mild a name for it, the motive will, perhaps, be changed, and spoken of under some such term as cruelty. 2. To save yourself from an illegal slavery, you make your escape. In this case the motive will be deemed certainly not a bad one: and, because indolence, or even the love of ease, will be thought too unfavorable a name for it, it will, perhaps, be styled the love of liberty. 3. A mechanic, in order to save his labor, makes an improvement in his machinery. In this case, people will look upon his motive as a good one; and finding no name for it that carries a good sense, they will be disposed to keep the motive out of sight: they will speak rather of his ingenuity, than of the motive which was the means of his mani-

festing that quality. Yet in all these cases the motive is the same: it is neither more nor less than the love of ease.

xxix. It appears then that there is no such thing as any sort of motive which is a bad one in itself; nor, consequently, any such thing as a sort of motive which in itself is exclusively a good one. And as to their effects, it appears too that these are sometimes bad, at other times either indifferent or good; and this appears to be the case with every sort of motive. *If any sort of motive then is either good or bad on the score of its effects, this is the case only on individual occasions, and with individual motives;* and this is the case with one sort of motive as well as with another. *If any sort of motive then can, in consideration of its effects, be termed with any propriety a bad one,* it can only be with reference to the balance of all the effects it may have had of both kinds within a given period—that is, of its most usual tendency.

xxx. What, then? (it will be said) are not lust, cruelty, avarice, bad motives? Is there so much as any one individual occasion in which motives like these can be otherwise than bad? No, certainly; and yet the proposition that there is no one *sort* of motive but what will on many occasions be a good one, is nevertheless true. The fact is that these are names which, if properly applied, are never applied but in the cases where the motives they signify happen to be bad. The names of these motives, considered apart from their effects, are sexual desire, displeasure, and pecuniary interest. To sexual desire, when the effects of it are looked upon as bad, is given the name of lust. Now lust is always a bad motive. Why? Because if the case be such that the effects of the motive are not bad, it does not go, or at least ought not to go, by the name of lust. The case is, then, that when I say, "Lust is a bad motive," it is a proposition that merely concerns the import of the word lust, and which would be false if transferred to the other word used for the same motive, sexual desire. Hence we see the emptiness of all those rhapsodies of commonplace morality, which consist in the taking of such names as lust, cruelty, and avarice, and branding them with marks of reprobation: applied to the *thing,* they are false; applied to the *name,* they are true indeed, but nugatory. Would you do a real service to mankind, show them the cases in which sexual desire *merits* the name of lust; displeasure, that of cruelty; and pecuniary interest, that of avarice.

xxxi. If it were necessary to apply such denominations as good, bad, and indifferent to motives, they might be classed in the following manner, in consideration of the most frequent complexion of their effects. In the class of good motives might be placed the articles of (1) goodwill, (2) love of reputation, (3) desire of amity, and, (4) religion. In the class of bad motives, (5) displeasure. In the class of neutral

or indifferent motives, (6) physical desire, (7) pecuniary interest, (8)
love of power, (9) self-preservation, as including the fear of the pains
of the senses, the love of ease, and the love of life.

xxxii. This method of arrangement, however, cannot but be imperfect; and the nomenclature belonging to it is in danger of being fallacious. For by what method of investigation can a man be assured
that with regard to the motives ranked under the name of good, the good
effects they have had, from the beginning of the world, have, in each
of the four species comprised under this name, been superior to the
bad? Still more difficulty would a man find in assuring himself that
with regard to those which are ranked under the name of neutral or indifferent, the effects they have had have exactly balanced each other,
the value of the good being neither greater nor less than that of the bad.
It is to be considered that the interests of the person himself can no
more be left out of the estimate than those of the rest of the community. For what would become of the species, if it were not for the
motives of hunger and thirst, sexual desire, the fear of pain, and the
love of life? Nor in the actual constitution of human nature is the motive of displeasure less necessary, perhaps, than any of the others; although a system in which the business of life might be carried on without it, might possibly be conceived. It seems, therefore, that they could
scarcely, without great danger of mistakes, be distinguished in this
manner even with reference to each other.

xxxiii. The only way, it should seem, in which a motive can with
safety and propriety be styled good or bad, is with reference to its effects in each individual instance, and principally from the intention it
gives birth to; from which arise, as will be shown hereafter, the most
material part of its effects. A motive is good when the intention it gives
birth to is a good one, bad when the intention is a bad one; and an intention is good or bad according to the material consequences that are
the objects of it. So far is it from the goodness of the intention's being
to be known only from the species of the motive. But from one and
the same motive, as we have seen, may result intentions of every sort
of complexion whatsoever. This circumstance, therefore, can afford no
clue for the arrangement of the several sorts of motives.

xxxiv. A more commodious method, therefore, it should seem, would
be to distribute them according to the influence which they appear to
have on the interests of the other members of the community, laying
those of the party himself out of the question: to wit, according to the
tendency which they appear to have to unite or disunite his interests
and theirs. On this plan they may be distinguished into *social, dissocial,*
and *self-regarding.* In the social class may be reckoned (1) good-will,
(2) love of reputation, (3) desire of amity, (4) religion. In the dis-

social may be placed (5) displeasure. In the self-regarding class, (6) physical desire, (7) pecuniary interest, (8) love of power, (9) self-preservation, as including the fear of the pains of the senses, the love of ease, and the love of life.

xxxv. With respect to the motives that have been termed social, if any farther distinction should be of use, to that of good-will alone may be applied the epithet of *purely social;* while the love of reputation, the desire of amity, and the motive of religion, may together be comprised under the division of *semi-social*: the social tendency being much more constant and unequivocal in the former than in any of the three latter. Indeed these last, social as they may be termed, are self-regarding at the same time.

§ 4. *Order of pre-eminence among motives*

xxxvi. Of all these sorts of motives, good-will is that of which the dictates, taken in a general view, are surest of coinciding with those of the principle of utility. For the dictates of utility are neither more nor less than the dictates of the most extensive and enlightened (that is *well-advised*) benevolence. The dictates of the other motives may be conformable to those of utility, or repugnant, as it may happen.

xxxvii. In this, however, it is taken for granted that in the case in question the dictates of benevolence are not contradicted by those of a more extensive—that is, enlarged—benevolence. Now when the dictates of benevolence as respecting the interests of a certain set of persons, are repugnant to the dictates of the same motive as respecting the more important interests of another set of persons, the former dictates, it is evident, are repealed, as it were, by the latter; and a man, were he to be governed by the former, could scarcely with propriety be said to be governed by the dictates of benevolence. On this account, were the motives on both sides sure to be alike present to a man's mind, the case of such repugnancy would hardly be worth distinguishing, since the partial benevolence might be considered as swallowed up in the more extensive: if the former prevailed, and governed the action, it must be considered as not owing its birth to benevolence, but to some other motive; if the latter prevailed, the former might be considered as having no effect. But the case is, that a partial benevolence may govern the action without entering into any direct competition with the more extensive benevolence which would forbid it; because the interests of the less numerous assemblage of persons may be present to a man's mind at a time when those of the more numerous are either not present, or, if present, make no impression. It is in this way that the dictates of this motive may be repugnant to utility, yet still be the dictates of benevolence. What makes those of private benevolence conformable upon the whole to the principle of utility, is that in general they stand unopposed by those of public: if they are repugnant to them, it is only by accident. What makes them the more conformable, is that in a civilized society, in most of the cases in which they would of themselves be apt to run counter to those of public benevolence, they find themselves opposed by stronger motives by the self-regarding class which are played off against them by the laws; and that it is only in cases where they stand unopposed by the other more salutary dictates they they are left free. An act of injustice or cruelty committed by a man for the sake of his father or his son, is punished, and with reason, as much as if it were committed for his own.

xxxviii. After good-will, the motive of which the dictates seem to have the next best chance for coinciding with those of utility, is that of the love of reputation. There is but one circumstance which prevents the dictates of this motive from coinciding in all cases with those of the former. This is, that men in their likings and dislikings, in the dispositions they manifest to annex to any mode of conduct their approbation or their disapprobation, and in consequence to the person who appears to practice it, their good or their ill-will, do not govern themselves exclusively by the principle of utility. Sometimes it is the principle of asceticism they are guided by; sometimes the principle of sympathy and antipathy. There is another circumstance, which diminishes not their conformity to the principle of utility but only their efficacy in comparison with the dictates of the motive of benevolence. The dictates of this motive will operate as strongly in secret as in public, whether it appears likely that the conduct which they recommend will be known or not; those of the love of reputation will coincide with those of benevolence only in proportion as a man's conduct seems likely to be known. This circumstance, however, does not make so much difference as at first sight might appear. Acts, in proportion as they are material, are apt to become known; and in point of reputation, the slightest suspicion often serves for proof. Besides, if an act be a disreputable one, it is not any assurance a man can have of the secrecy of the particular act in question that will of course surmount the objections he may have against engaging in it. Though the act in question should remain secret, it will go towards forming a habit, which may give birth to other acts that may not meet with the same good fortune. There is no human being, perhaps, who is at years of discretion, on whom considerations of this sort have not some weight; and they have the more weight upon a man in proportion to the strength of his intellectual powers and the firmness of his mind. Add to this the influence which habit itself, when once formed, has in restraining a man from acts towards which, from the view of the disrepute annexed to them, as well as from any other cause, he has contracted an aversion. The influence of habit, in such cases, is a matter of fact which, though not readily accounted for, is acknowledged and indubitable.[13]

xxxix. After the dictates of the love of reputation come, as it should seem, those of the desire of amity. The former are disposed to coincide with those of utility, inasmuch as they are disposed to coincide with those of benevolence. Now those of the desire of amity are apt also to coincide, in a certain sort, with those of benevolence. But the sort of benevolence with the dictates of which the love of reputation coincides, is the more extensive; that with which those of the desire of amity coincide, the less extensive. Those of the love of amity have still, however, the advantage of those of the self-regarding motives. The former, at one period or other of his life, dispose a man to contribute to the happiness of a considerable number of persons; the latter, from the beginning of life to the end of it, confine themselves to the care of that single individual. The dictates of the desire of amity, it is plain, will approach nearer to a coincidence with those of the love of reputation, and thence with those of utility, in proportion, *ceteris paribus,* to the number of the persons whose amity a man has occasion to desire; and hence it is, for example, that an English member of Parliament, with all his own weaknesses, and all the follies of the people whose amity he has to cultivate, is probably, in general, a better character than the secretary of a vizier at Constantinople, or of a naïb in Indostan.

xl. The dictates of religion are, under the infinite diversity of religions, so extremely variable, that it is difficult to know what general account to give of them, or in what rank to place the motive they belong to. Upon the mention of religion, people's first thoughts turn naturally to the religion they themselves profess. This is a great source of miscalculation, and has a tendency to place this sort of motive in a higher rank than it deserves. The dictates of religion would coincide in all cases with those of utility, were the Being who is the object of religion universally supposed to be as benevolent as he is supposed to be wise and powerful, and were the notions entertained of his benevolence, at the same time, as correct as those which are entertained of his wisdom and his power. Unhappily, however, neither of these is the case. He is universally supposed to be all-powerful; for by the Deity what else does any man mean than the Being, whatever he be, by whom everything is done? And as to knowledge, by the same rule that he should know

---

[13] Strictly speaking, habit, being but a fictitious entity, and not really anything distinct from the acts or perceptions by which it is said to be formed, cannot be the cause of anything. The enigma, however, may be satisfactorily solved upon the principle of association, of the nature and force of which a very satisfactory account may be seen in Dr. Priestley's edition of Hartley on *Man.*

one thing he should know another. These notions seem to be as correct, for all material purposes, as they are universal. But among the votaries of religion (of which number the multifarious fraternity of Christians is but a small part) there seem to be but few (I will not say how few) who are real believers in his benevolence. They call him benevolent in words, but they do not mean that he is so in reality. They do not mean that he is benevolent as man is conceived to be benevolent; they do not mean that he is benevolent in the only sense in which benevolence has a meaning. For if they did, they would recognize that the dictates of religion could be neither more nor less than the dictates of utility: not a title different, not a title less or more. But the case is, that on a thousand occasions they turn their backs on the principle of utility. They go astray after the strange principles its antagonists: sometimes it is the principle of asceticism; sometimes the principle of sympathy and antipathy.[14] Accordingly, the idea they bear in their minds on such occasions is but too often the idea of malevolence; to which idea, stripping it of its own proper name, they bestow the specious appellation of the social motive.[15] The dictates of religion, in short, are no other than the dictates of that principle which has been already mentioned under the name of the theological principle. These, as has been observed, are just as it may happen, according to the biases of the person in question, copies of the dictates of one or other of the three original principles: sometimes, indeed, of the dictates of utility, but frequently of those of asceticism, or those of sympathy and antipathy. In this respect they are only on a par with the dictates of the love of reputation; in another they are below it. The dictates of religion are in all places intermixed more or less with dictates unconformable to those of utility, deduced from texts, well or ill interpreted, of the writings held for sacred by each sect: unconformable, by imposing practices sometimes inconvenient to a man's self, sometimes pernicious to the rest of the community. The sufferings of uncalled martyrs, the calamities of holy wars and religious persecutions, the mischiefs of intolerant laws, (objects which can here only be glanced at, not detailed) are so many additional

---

[14] See Chap. II, Par. xviii.

[15] Sometimes, in order the better to conceal the cheat (from their own eyes doubtless as well as from others), they set up a phantom of their own, which they call justice: whose dictates are to modify (which being explained, means to oppose) the dictates of benevolence. But justice, in the only sense in which it has a meaning, is an imaginary personage, feigned for the convenience of discourse, whose dictates are the dictates of utility applied to certain particular cases. Justice, then, is nothing more than an imaginary instrument, employed to forward on certain occasions, and by certain means, the purposes of benevolence. The dictates of justice are nothing more than a part of the dictates of benevolence, which, on certain occasions, are applied to certain subjects; to wit, to certain actions.

mischiefs over and above the number of those which were ever brought into the world by the love of reputation. On the other hand, it is manifest that with respect to the power of operating in secret, the dictates of religion have the same advantage over those of the love of reputation, and the desire of amity, as is possessed by the dictates of benevolence.

xli. Happily, the dictates of religion seem to approach nearer and nearer to a coincidence with those of utility every day. But why? Because the dictates of the moral sanction do so; and those coincide with or are influenced by these. Men of the worst religions, influenced by the voice and practice of the surrounding world, borrow continually a new and a new leaf out of the book of utility; and with these, in order not to break with their religion, they endeavor, sometimes with violence enough, to patch together and adorn the repositories of their faith.

xlii. As to the self-regarding and dissocial motives, the order that takes place among these, and the preceding one, in point of extra-regarding influence, is too evident to need insisting on. As to the order that takes place among the motives of the self-regarding class, considered in comparison with one another, there seems to be no difference which on this occasion would be worth mentioning. With respect to the dissocial motive, it makes a difference (with regard to its extra-regarding effects) from which of two sources it originates: whether from self-regarding or from social considerations. The displeasure you conceive against a man may be founded either on some act which offends you in the first instance, or on an act which offends you no otherwise than because you look upon it as being prejudicial to some other party on whose behalf you interest yourself; which other party may be of course either a determinate individual, or any assemblage of individuals, determinate or indeterminate. It is obvious enough that a motive, though in itself dissocial, may, by issuing from a social origin, possess a social tendency; and that its tendency, in this case, is likely to be the more social, the more enlarged the description is of the persons whose interests you espouse. Displeasure, venting itself against a man on account of a mischief supposed to be done by him to the public, may be more social in its effects than any good-will, the exertions of which are confined to an individual.

§ 5. Conflict among motives

xliii. When a man has it in contemplation to engage in any action, he is frequently acted upon at the same time by the force of divers motives: one motive, or set of motives, acting in one direction; another motive, or set of motives, acting as it were in an opposite direction. The motives on one side disposing him to engage in the action: those on the other, disposing him not to engage in it. Now, any motive, the influence of which tends to dispose him to engage in the action in question, may be termed an *impelling* motive: any motive, the influence of which tends to dispose him not to engage in it, a *restraining* motive. But these appellations may of course be interchanged, according as the act is of the positive kind, or the negative.

xliv. It has been shown, that there is no sort of motive but may give birth to any sort of action. It follows, therefore, that there are no two motives but may come to be opposed to one another. Where the tendency of the act is bad, the most common case is for it to have been dictated by a motive either of the self-regarding, or of the dissocial class. In such case the motive of benevolence has commonly been acting, though ineffectually, in the character of a restraining motive.

xlv. An example may be of use, to show the variety of contending motives, by which a man may be acted upon at the same time. Crillon, a Catholic (at a time when it was generally thought meritorious among Catholics to extirpate Protestants), was ordered by his king, Charles IX of France, to fall privately upon Coligny, a Protestant, and assassinate him: his answer was, "Excuse me, Sire; but I'll fight him with all my heart [16]." Here, then, were all the three forces above mentioned, including that of the political sanction, acting upon him at once. By the political sanction, or at least so much of the force of it as such a mandate, from such a sovereign, issued on such an occasion, might be supposed to carry with it, he was enjoined to put Coligny to death in the way of assassination: by the religious sanction, that is, by the dictates of religious zeal, he was enjoined to put him to death in any way: by the moral sanction, or in other words, by the dictates of honor, that is, of the love of reputation, he was permitted (which permission, when coupled with the mandates of his sovereign, operated, he conceived, as an injunction) to fight the adversary upon equal terms: by the dictates of enlarged benevolence (supposing the mandate to be unjustifiable) he was enjoined not to attempt his life in any way. but to remain at peace with him: supposing the mandate to be unjustifiable, by the dictates of private benevolence he was enjoined not to meddle with him at any rate. Among this confusion of repugnant dictates, Crillon, it seems, gave the preference, in the first place, to those of honor: in the next place, to those of benevolence. He would have fought, had his offer been accepted; as it was not, he remained at peace.

Here a multitude of questions might arise. Supposing the dictates of the political sanction to follow the mandate of the sovereign, of what

---

[16] The idea of the case here supposed is taken from an anecdote in real history, but varies from it in several particulars.

kind were the motives which they afforded him for compliance? The answer is, of the self-regarding kind at any rate: inasmuch as, by the supposition, it was in the power of the sovereign to punish him for non-compliance, or reward him for compliance. Did they afford him the motive of religion? (I mean independently of the circumstance of heresy above mentioned.) The answer is, Yes, if his notion was, that it was God's pleasure he should comply with them; No, if it was not. Did they afford him the motive of the love of reputation? Yes, if it was his notion that the world would expect and require that he should comply with them: No, if it was not. Did they afford him that of benevolence? Yes, if it was his notion that the community would upon the whole be the better for his complying with them: No, if it was not. But did the dictates of the political sanction, in the case in question, actually follow the mandates of the sovereign: in other words, was such a mandate legal? This we see in a mere question of local jurisprudence, altogether foreign to the present purpose.

xlvi. What is here said about the goodness and badness of motives, is far from being a mere matter of words. There will be occasion to make use of it hereafter for various important purposes. I shall have need of it for the sake of dissipating various prejudices, which are of disservice to the community, sometimes by cherishing the flame of civil dissensions, at other times, by obstructing the course of justice. It will be shown, that in the case of many offenses, the consideration of the motive is a most material one: for that in the first place it makes a very material difference in the magnitude of the mischief: in the next place, that it is easy to be ascertained; and thence may be made a ground for a difference in the demand for punishment: but that in other cases it is altogether incapable of being ascertained, and that, were it capable of being ever so well ascertained, good or bad, it could make no difference in the demand for punishment: that in all cases, the motive that may happen to govern a prosecutor, is a consideration totally immaterial: whence may be seen the mischievousness of the prejudice that is so apt to be entertained against informers; and the consequence it is of that the judge, in particular, should be proof against the influence of such delusions.

Lastly, the subject of motives is one with which it is necessary to be acquainted, in order to pass a judgment on any means that may be proposed for combating offenses in their source.

But before the theoretical foundation for these practical observations can be completely laid, it is necessary we should say something on the subject of *disposition*: which, accordingly, will furnish matter for the ensuing chapter.

CHAPTER XI

OF HUMAN DISPOSITIONS IN GENERAL

IN THE FOREGOING CHAPTER it has been shown at large that goodness or badness cannot, with any propriety, be predicated of motives. Is there nothing then about a man that can properly be termed good or bad when, on such or such an occasion, he suffers himself to be governed by such or such a motive? Yes, certainly: his *disposition*. Now disposition is a kind of fictitious entity, feigned for the convenience of discourse, in order to express what there is supposed to be *permanent* in a man's frame of mind, where, on such or such an occasion, he has been influenced by such or such a motive to engage in an act which, as it appeared to him, was of such or such a tendency.

ii. It is with disposition as with everything else: it will be good or bad according to its effects—according to the effects it has in augmenting or diminishing the happiness of the community. A man's disposition may accordingly be considered in two points of view: according to the influence it has either (1) on his own happiness, or (2) on the happiness of others. Viewed in both these lights together, or in either of them indiscriminately, it may be termed on the one hand good, on the other bad, or in flagrant cases depraved. Viewed in the former of these lights it has scarcely any peculiar name which has as yet been appropriated to it. It might be termed, though but inexpressively, frail or infirm on the one hand, sound or firm on the other. Viewed in the other light, it might be termed beneficent, or meritorious, on the one hand, pernicious or mischievous on the other. Now of that branch of a man's disposition the effects of which regard in the first instance only himself, there needs not much to be said here. To reform it when bad is the business rather of the moralist than the legislator; nor is it susceptible of those various modifications which make so material a difference in the effects of the other. Again, with respect to that part of it the effects whereof regard others in the first instance, it is only in as far as it is of a mischievous nature that the penal branch of law has any immediate concern with it; in as far as it may be of a beneficent nature, it belongs to a hitherto but little cultivated and as yet unnamed branch of law, which might be styled the remuneratory.

iii. A man then is said to be of a mischievous disposition when, by the influence of no matter what motives, he is *presumed* to be more apt to engage, or form intentions of engaging, in acts which are *apparently* of a pernicious tendency, than in such as are apparently of a beneficial tendency; of a meritorious or beneficent disposition in the opposite case.

iv. I say presumed: for, by the supposition, all that appears is one single action, attended with one single train of circumstances; but from that degree of consistency and uniformity which experience has shown to be observable in the different actions of the same person, the probable existence (past or future) of a number of acts of a similar nature, is naturally and justly inferred from the observation of one single one. Under such circumstances, such as the motive proves to be in one instance, such is the disposition to be presumed to be in others.

v. I say *apparently* mischievous: that is, apparently with regard to him—such as to him appear to possess that tendency; for from the mere event, independent of what to him it appears beforehand likely to be, nothing can be inferred on either side. If to him it appears likely to be mischievous, in such case, though in the upshot it should prove innocent, or even beneficial, it makes no difference, there is not the less reason for presuming his disposition to be a bad one; if to him it appears likely to be beneficial or innocent, in such case, though in the upshot it should prove pernicious, there is not the more [17] reason on that account for presuming his disposition to be a good one. And here we see the importance of the circumstances of intentionality, consciousness, unconsciousness, and mis-supposal.

vi. The truth of these positions depends upon two others, both of them sufficiently verified by experience. The one is, that in the ordinary course of things the consequences of actions commonly turn out conformable to intentions. A man who sets up a butcher's shop and deals in beef, when he intends to knock down an ox commonly does knock down an ox, though by some unlucky accident he may chance to miss his blow and knock down a man; he who sets up a grocer's shop and deals in sugar, when he intends to sell sugar commonly does sell sugar, though by some unlucky accident he may chance to sell arsenic in the room of it.

vii. The other is, that a man who entertains intentions of doing mischief at one time is apt to entertain the like intentions at another. . . .

xxvii. It is evident, that the nature of a man's disposition must depend upon the nature of the motives he is apt to be influenced by: in other words, upon the degree of his sensibility to the force of such and such motives. For his disposition is, as it were, the sum of his intentions; the disposition he is of during a certain period, the sum or result of his intentions during that period. If, of the acts he has been intending to engage in during the supposed period, those which are apparently of a mischievous tendency bear a large proportion to those which appear to him to be of the contrary tendency, his disposition will

---

[17] Presumably the word "less" was intended here.—Editor.

be of the mischievous cast; if but a small proportion, of the innocent or upright.

xxviii. Now intentions, like everything else, are produced by the things that are their causes; and the causes of intentions are motives. If on any occasion a man forms either a good or a bad intention, it must be by the influence of some motive.

xxix. When the act which a motive prompts a man to engage in, is of a mischievous nature, it may for distinction's sake be termed a *seducing* or corrupting motive: in which case also any motive which, in opposition to the former, acts in the character of a restraining motive, may be styled a *tutelary*, preservatory, or preserving motive.

xxx. Tutelary motives may again be distinguished into *standing* or constant, and *occasional*. By standing tutelary motives, I mean such as act with more or less force in all, or at least in most cases, tending to restrain a man from *any* mischievous acts he may be prompted to engage in; and that with a force which depends upon the general nature of the act, rather than upon any accidental circumstance with which any individual act of that sort may happen to be accompanied. By occasional tutelary motives, I mean such motives as may chance to act in this direction or not, according to the nature of the act, and of the particular occasion on which the engaging in it is brought into contemplation.

xxxi. Now it has been shown that there is no sort of motive by which a man may not be prompted to engage in acts that are of a mischievous nature; that is, which may not come to act in the capacity of a seducing motive. It has been shown, on the other hand, that there are some motives which are remarkably less likely to operate in this way than others. It has also been shown that the least likely of all is that of benevolence or good-will: the most common tendency of which, it has been shown, is to act in the character of a tutelary motive. It has also been shown that even when by accident it acts in one way in the character of a seducing motive, still in another way it acts in the opposite character of a tutelary one. The motive of good-will, in as far as it respects the interests of one set of persons, may prompt a man to engage in acts which are productive of mischief to another and more extensive set; but this is only because his good-will is imperfect and confined, not taking into contemplation the interests of all the persons whose interests are at stake. The same motive, were the affection it issued from more enlarged, would operate effectually, in the character of a constraining motive, against that very act to which, by the supposition, it gives birth. This same sort of motive may therefore, without any real contradiction or deviation from truth, be ranked in the number cf standing tutelary motives, notwithstanding the occasions in which it may act at the same time in the character of a seducing one.

xxxii. The same observation, nearly, may be applied to the semi social motive of love of reputation. The force of this, like that of the former, is liable to be divided against itself. As in the case of good-will the interests of some of the persons who may be the objects of that sentiment, are liable to be at variance with those of others; so in the case of love of reputation, the sentiments of some of the persons whose good opinion is desired, may be at variance with the sentiments of other persons of that number. Now in the case of an act which is really of a mischievous nature, it can scarcely happen that there shall be no persons whatever who will look upon it with an eye of disapprobation. It can scarcely ever happen, therefore, that an act really mischievous shall not have some part at least, if not the whole, of the force of this motive to oppose it; nor, therefore, that this motive should not act with some degree of force in the character of a tutelary motive. This, therefore, may be set down as another article in the catalogue of standing tutelary motives.

xxxiii. The same observation may be applied to the desire of amity, though not in altogether equal measure. For notwithstanding the mischievousness of an act, it may happen, without much difficulty, that all the persons for whose amity a man entertains any particular present desire which is accompanied with expectation, may concur in regarding it with an eye rather of approbation than the contrary. This is but too apt to be the case among such fraternities as those of thieves, smugglers, and many other denominations of offenders. This, however, is not constantly, nor indeed most commonly the case; insomuch that the desire of amity may still be regarded, upon the whole, as a tutelary motive, were it only from the closeness of its connection with the love of reputation. And it may be ranked among standing tutelary motives, since, where it does apply, the force with which it acts, depends not upon the occasional circumstances of the act which it opposes, but upon principles as general as those upon which depend the action of the other semi-social motives.

xxxiv. The motive of religion is not altogether in the same case with the three former. The force of it is not, like theirs, liable to be divided against itself. I mean in the civilized nations of modern times, among whom the notion of the unity of the Godhead is universal. In times of classical antiquity it was otherwise. If a man got Venus on his side, Pallas was on the other; if Aeolus was for him, Neptune was against him. Aeneas, with all his piety, had but a partial interest at the court of heaven. That matter stands upon a different footing nowadays. In any given person, the force of religion, whatever it be, is now all of it on one side. It may balance, indeed, on which side it shall declare itself; and it may declare itself, as we have seen already in but too many instances, on the wrong as well as on the right. It has been, at least till lately, perhaps is still, accustomed so much to declare itself on the wrong side, and that in such material instances, that on that account it seemed not proper to place it, in point of social tendency, on a level altogether with the motive of benevolence. Where it does act, however, as it does in by far the greatest number of cases, in opposition to the ordinary seducing motives, it acts, like the motive of benevolence, in an uniform manner, not depending upon the particular circumstances that may attend the commission of the act, but tending to oppose it merely on account of its mischievousness; and therefore, with equal force, in whatsoever circumstances it may be proposed to be committed. This, therefore, may also be added to the catalogue of standing tutelary motives.

xxxv. As to the motives which may operate occasionally in the character of tutelary motives, these, it has been already intimated, are of various sorts, and various degrees of strength in various offenses: depending not only upon the nature of the offense, but upon the accidental circumstances in which the idea of engaging in it may come in contemplation. Nor is there any sort of motive which may not come to operate in this character; as may be easily conceived. A thief, for instance, may be prevented from engaging in a projected scheme of house-breaking, by sitting too long over his bottle, by a visit from his doxy, by the occasion he may have to go elsewhere, in order to receive his dividend of a former booty; and so on.

xxxvi. There are some motives, however, which seem more apt to act in this character than others; especially as things are now constituted, now that the law has everywhere opposed to the force of the principal seducing motives, artificial tutelary motives of its own creation. Of the motives here meant it will be necessary to take a general view. They seem to be reducible to two heads; viz., 1. The love of ease; a motive put into action by the prospect of the trouble of the attempt; that is, the trouble which it may be necessary to bestow, in overcoming the physical difficulties that may accompany it. 2. Self-preservation, as opposed to the dangers to which a man may be exposed in the prosecution of it.

xxxvii. These dangers may be either: 1. Of a purely physical nature: or, 2. Dangers resulting from moral agency; in other words, from the conduct of any such persons to whom the act, if known, may be expected to prove obnoxious. But moral agency supposes knowledge with respect to the circumstances that are to have the effect of external motives in giving birth to it. Now the obtaining such knowledge, with re-

spect to the commission of any obnoxious act, on the part of any persons who may be disposed to make the agent suffer for it, is called *detection;* and the agent concerning whom such knowledge is obtained, is
said to be detected. The dangers, therefore, which may threaten an
offender from this quarter, depend, whatever they may be, on the event
of his detection; and may, therefore, be all of them comprised under
the article of the *danger of detection.*

xxxviii. The danger depending upon detection may be divided again
into two branches: 1. That which may result from any opposition that
may be made to the enterprise by persons on the spot; that is, at the
very time the enterprise is carrying on: 2. That which respects the
legal punishment, or other suffering, that may await at a distance upon
the issue of the enterprise.

xxxix. It may be worth calling to mind on this occasion, that among
the tutelary motives, which have been styled constant ones, there are
two of which the force depends (though not so entirely as the force of
the occasional ones which have been just mentioned, yet in a great
measure) upon the circumstance of detection. These, it may be remembered, are, the love of reputation, and the desire of amity. In proportion, therefore, as the chance of being detected appears greater,
these motives will apply with the greater force: with the less force, as
it appears less. This is not the case with the two other standing tutelary
motives, that of benevolence, and that of religion.

xl. We are now in a condition to determine, with some degree of
precision, what is to be understood by the *strength of a temptation,*
and what indication it may give of the degree of mischievousness in a
man's disposition in the case of any offense. When a man is prompted
to engage in any mischievous act, we will say, for shortness, in an offense, the strength of the temptation depends upon the ratio between
the force of the seducing motives on the one hand, and such of the
occasional tutelary ones, as the circumstances of the case call forth into
action, on the other. The temptation, then, may be said to be strong,
when the pleasure or advantage to be got from the crime is such as in
the eyes of the offender must appear great in comparison of the trouble
and danger that appear to him to accompany the enterprise: slight or
weak, when that pleasure or advantage is such as must appear small
in comparison of such trouble and such danger. It is plain the strength
of the temptation depends not upon the force of the impelling (that is
of the seducing) motives altogether: for let the opportunity be more
favorable, that is, let the trouble, or any branch of the danger, be made
less than before, it will be acknowledged, that the temptation is made
so much the stronger: and on the other hand, let the opportunity become less favorable, or, in other words, let the trouble, or any branch

of the danger, be made greater than before, the temptation will be so much the weaker.

Now, after taking account of such tutelary motives as have been styled occasional, the only tutelary motives that can remain are those which have been termed standing ones. But those which have been termed the standing tutelary motives, are the same that we have been styling social. It follows, therefore, that the strength of the temptation, in any case, after deducting the force of the social motives, is as the sum of the forces of the seducing, to the sum of the forces of the occasional tutelary motives.

xli. It remains to be inquired, what indication concerning the mischievousness or depravity of a man's disposition is afforded by the strength of the temptation, in the case where any offense happens to have been committed. It appears, then, that the weaker the temptation is, by which a man has been overcome, the more depraved and mischievous it shows his disposition to have been. For the goodness of his disposition is measured by the degree of his sensibility to the action of the social motives: in other words, by the strength of the influence which those motives have over him: now, the less considerable the force is by which their influence on him as been overcome, the more convincing is the proof that has been given of the weakness of that influence.

Again, the degree of a man's sensibility to the force of the social motives being given, it is plain that the force with which those motives tend to restrain him from engaging in any mischievous enterprise, will be as the apparent mischievousness of such enterprise, that is, as the degree of mischief with which it appears to *him* likely to be attended. In other words, the less mischievous the offense appears to him to be, the less averse he will be, as far as he is guided by social considerations, to engage in it; the more mischievous, the more averse. If then the nature of the offense is such as must appear to him highly mischievous, and yet he engages in it notwithstanding, it shows, that the degree of his sensibility to the force of the social motives is but slight; and consequently that his disposition is proportionately depraved. Moreover, the less the strength of the temptation was, the more pernicious and depraved does it show his disposition to have been. For the less the strength of the temptation was, the less was the force which the influence of those motives had to overcome: the clearer therefore is the proof that has been given of the weakness of that influence.

xlii. From what has been said, it seems, that, for judging of the indication that is afforded concerning the depravity of a man's disposition by the strength of the temptation, compared with the mischievousness of the enterprise, the following rules may be laid down:

Rule 1. *The strength of the temptation being given, the mischievousness of the disposition manifested by the enterprise, is as the apparent mischievousness of the act.*

Thus, it would show a more depraved disposition, to murder a man for a reward of a guinea, or falsely to charge him with a robbery for the same reward, than to obtain the same sum from him by simple theft: the trouble he would have to take, and the risk he would have to run, being supposed to stand on the same footing in the one case as in the other.

Rule 2. *The apparent mischievousness of the act being given, a man's disposition is the more depraved, the slighter the temptation is by which he has been overcome.*

Thus, it shows a more depraved and dangerous disposition, if a man kill another out of mere sport, as the Emperor of Morocco, Muley Mahomet, is said to have done great numbers, than out of revenge, as Sylla and Marius did thousands, or in the view of self-preservation, as Augustus killed many, or even for lucre, as the same Emperor is said to have killed some. And the effects of such a depravity, on that part of the public which is apprized of it, run in the same proportion. From Augustus, some persons only had to fear, under some particular circumstances. From Muley Mahomet, every man had to fear at all times.

Rule 3. *The apparent mischievousness of the act being given, the evidence which it affords of the depravity of a man's disposition is the less conclusive, the stronger the temptation is by which he has been overcome.*

Thus, if a poor man, who is ready to die with hunger, steal a loaf of bread, it is a less explicit sign of depravity, than if a rich man were to commit a theft to the same amount. It will be observed, that in this rule all that is said is, that the evidence of depravity is in this case the less conclusive: it is not said that the depravity is positively the less. For in this case it is possible, for anything that appears to the contrary, that the theft might have been committed, even had the temptation been not so strong. In this case, the alleviating circumstance is only a matter of presumption; in the former, the aggravating circumstance is a matter of certainty.

Rule 4. *Where the motive is of the dissocial kind, the apparent mischievousness of the act, and the strength of the temptation, being given, the depravity is as the degree of deliberation with which it is accompanied.*

For in every man, be his disposition ever so depraved, the social motives are those which, wherever the self-regarding ones stand neuter, regulate and determine the general tenor of his life. If the dissocial mo-

tives are put in action, it is only in particular circumstances, and on
particular occasions; the gentle but constant force of the social motives
being for a while subdued. The general and standing bias of every man's
nature is, therefore, towards that side to which the force of the social
motives would determine him to adhere. This being the case, the force
of the social motives tends continually to put an end to that of the dissocial ones; as, in natural bodies, the force of friction tends to put an
end to that which is generated by impulse. Time, then, which wears
away the force of the dissocial motives, adds to that of the social. The
longer, therefore, a man continues, on a given occasion, under the dominion of the dissocial motives, the more convincing is the proof that
has been given of his insensibility to the force of the social ones.

Thus, it shows a worse disposition, where a man lays a deliberate
plan for beating his antagonist, and beats him accordingly, than if he
were to beat him upon the spot, in consequence of a sudden quarrel:
and worse again, if, after having had him a long while together in his
power, he beats him at intervals, and at his leisure.

xliii. The depravity of disposition, indicated by an act, is a material
consideration in several respects. Any mark of extraordinary depravity,
by adding to the terror inspired by the crime, and by holding up the
offender as a person from whom there may be more mischief to be apprehended in future, adds in that way to the demand for punishment.
By indicating a general want of sensibility on the part of the offender,
it may add in another way also to the demand for punishment. The
article of disposition is of the more importance, inasmuch as, in measuring out the quantum of punishment, the principle of sympathy and
antipathy is apt to look at nothing else. A man who punishes because
he hates, and only because he hates, such a man, when he does not
find anything odious in the disposition, is not for punishing at all; and
when he does, he is not for carrying the punishment further than his
hatred carries him. Hence the aversion we find so frequently expressed
against the maxim, that the punishment must rise with the strength of
the temptation; a maxim, the contrary of which, as we shall see, would
be as cruel to offenders themselves, as it would be subversive of the
purpose of punishment. . . .[18]

[18] Chap. XII analyzes and classifies the consequences of a mischievous act.—
Editor.

CHAPTER XIII

CASES UNMEET FOR PUNISHMENT

1. General view of cases unmeet for punishment.

i. The general object which all laws have, or ought to have, in common, is to augment the total happiness of the community; and therefore, in the first place, to exclude, as far as may be, everything that tends to subtract from that happiness: in other words, to exclude mischief.

ii. But all punishment is mischief: all punishment in itself is evil. Upon the principle of utility, if it ought at all to be admitted, it ought only to be admitted in as far as it promises to exclude some greater evil.

iii. It is plain, therefore, that in the following cases punishment ought not to be inflicted.

1. Where it is *groundless*: where there is no mischief for it to prevent; the act not being mischievous upon the whole.

2. Where it must be *inefficacious:* where it cannot act so as to prevent the mischief.

3. Where it is *unprofitable,* or too *expensive*: where the mischief it would produce would be greater than what it prevented.

4. Where it is *needless*: where the mischief may be prevented, or cease of itself, without it: that is, at a cheaper rate. . . .

CHAPTER XIV

OF THE PROPORTION BETWEEN PUNISHMENTS AND OFFENSES

i. We have seen that the general object of all laws is to prevent mischief; that is to say, when it is worth while; but that, where there are no other means of doing this than punishment, there are four cases in which it is *not* worth while.

ii. When it *is* worth while, there are four subordinate designs or objects, which, in the course of his endeavors to compass, as far as may be, that one general object, a legislator, whose views are governed by the principle of utility, comes naturally to propose to himself.

iii. 1. His first, most extensive, and most eligible object, is to prevent. in as far as it is possible, and worth while, all sorts of offenses whatsoever: in other words, so to manage, that no offense whatsoever may be committed.

iv. 2. But if a man must needs commit an offense of some kind or other, the next object is to induce him to commit an offense *less* mischievous, *rather* than one *more* mischievous: in other words, to choose always the *least* mischievous, of two offenses that will either of them suit his purpose.

v. 3. When a man has resolved upon a particular offense, the next object is to dispose him to do *no more* mischief than is *necessary* to his purpose: in other words, to do as little mischief as is consistent with the benefit he has in view.

vi. 4. The last object is, whatever the mischief be, which it is proposed to prevent, prevent it at as *cheap* a rate as possible.

vii. Subservient to these four objects, or purposes, must be the rules or canons by which the proportion of punishments[19] to offenses is to be governed.

viii. Rule 1. 1. The first object, it has been seen, is to prevent, in as far as it is worth while, all sorts of offenses; therefore,

The value of the punishment must not be less in any case than what is sufficient to outweigh that of the profit of the offense.

If it be, the offense (unless some other considerations, independent of the punishment, should intervene and operate efficaciously in the character of tutelary motives) will be sure to be committed notwithstanding: the whole lot of punishment will be thrown away: it will be altogether *inefficacious.*

ix. The above rule has been often objected to, on account of its seeming harshness: but this can only have happened for want of its being properly understood. The strength of the temptation, *ceteris paribus,* is as the profit of the offense: the quantum of the punishment must rise with the profit of the offense: *ceteris paribus,* it must therefore rise with the strength of the temptation. This there is no disputing. True it is, that the stronger the temptation, the less conclusive is the indication which the act of delinquency affords of the depravity of the offender's disposition. So far then as the absence of any aggravation, arising from extraordinary depravity of disposition, may operate, or at the utmost, so far as the presence of a ground of extenuation, resulting from the innocence or beneficence of the offender's disposition, can operate, the strength of the temptation may operate in abatement of the

---

[19] The same rules (it is to be observed) may be applied, with little variation, to rewards as well as punishment: in short, to motives in general, which, according as they are of the pleasurable or painful kind, are of the nature of *reward* or *punishment:* and, according as the act they are applied to produce is of the positive or negative kind, are styled impelling or restraining.

demand for punishment. But it can never operate so far as to indicate the propriety of making the punishment ineffectual, which it is sure to be when brought below the level of the apparent profit of the offense.

The partial benevolence which should prevail for the reduction of it below this level, would counteract as well those purposes which such a motive would actually have in view, as those more extensive purposes which benevolence ought to have in view: it would be cruelty not only to the public, but to the very persons in whose behalf it pleads: in its effects, I mean, however opposite in its intention. Cruelty to the public, that is cruelty to the innocent, by suffering them, for want of an adequate protection, to lie exposed to the mischief of the offense: cruelty even to the offender himself, by punishing him to no purpose, and without the chance of compassing that beneficial end, by which alone the introduction of the evil of punishment is to be justified.

x. Rule 2. But whether a given offense shall be prevented in a given degree by a given quantity of punishment, is never anything better than a chance; for the purchasing of which, whatever punishment is employed, is so much expended in advance. However, for the sake of giving it the better chance of outweighing the profit of the offense,

The greater the mischief of the offense, the greater is the expense, which it may be worth while to be at, in the way of punishment.

xi. Rule 3. The next object is, to induce a man to choose always the least mischievous of two offenses; therefore

Where two offenses come in competition, the punishment for the greater offense must be sufficient to induce a man to prefer the less.

xii. Rule 4. When a man has resolved upon a particular offense, the next object is, to induce him to do no more mischief than what is necessary for his purpose: therefore

The punishment should be adjusted in such manner to each particular offense, that for every part of the mischief there may be a motive to restrain the offender from giving birth to it.

xiii. Rule 5. The last object is, whatever mischief is guarded against, to guard against it at as cheap a rate as possible: therefore

The punishment ought in no case to be more than what is necessary to bring it into conformity with the rules here given.

xiv. Rule 6. It is further to be observed, that owing to the different manners and degrees in which persons under different circumstances are affected by the same exciting cause, a punishment which is the same in name will not always either really produce, or even so much as appear to others to produce, in two different persons the same degree of pain: therefore

That the quantity actually inflicted on each individual offender may

correspond to the quantity intended for similar offenders in general, the several circumstances influencing sensibility ought always to be taken into account.

xv. Of the above rules of proportion, the four first, we may perceive, serve to mark out the limits on the side of diminution; the limits *below* which a punishment ought not to be diminished: the fifth, the limits on the side of increase; the limits *above* which it ought not to be *increased*. The five first are calculated to serve as guides to the legislator: the sixth is calculated, in some measure, indeed, for the same purpose; but principally for guiding the judge in his endeavors to conform, on both sides, to the intentions of the legislator. . . .[20]

CHAPTER XVII

OF THE LIMITS OF THE PENAL BRANCH OF JURISPRUDENCE

§1. *Limits between private ethics and the art of legislation*

. . . . ii. Ethics at large may be defined, the art of directing men's actions to the production of the greatest possible quantity of happiness, on the part of those whose interest is in view.

iii. What then are the actions which it can be in a man's power to direct? They must be either his own actions or those of other agents. Ethics, in as far as it is the art of directing a man's own actions, may be styled the *art of self-government*, or *private ethics*.

iv. What other agents than are there which, at the same time that they are under the influence of man's direction, are susceptible of happiness? They are of two sorts: (1) other human beings who are styled persons; (2) other animals, which, on account of their interests having been neglected by the insensibility of the ancient jurists, stand degraded into the class of *things*.[21] As to other human beings, the art of

[20] Chap. XV examines the properties which punishment must have if it is to be successful in its function, and Chap. XVI gives a classification of offenses.—Editor.

[21] Under the Gentoo and Mohammedan religions, the interests of the rest of the animal creation seem to have met with some attention. Why have they not universally, with as much as those of human creatures, allowance made for the difference in point of sensibility? Because the laws that are have been the work of mutual fear; a sentiment which the less rational animals have not had the same means as man has of turning to account. Why *ought* they not? No reason can be given. If the being eaten were all, there is very good reason why we should be suffered to eat such of them as we like to eat: we are the better for it, and they are never the worse. They have none of those long-protracted anticipations of future misery which we have. The death they suffer in our hands commonly is, and always may be, a speedier, and by that means a less painful one, than that which would await them

directing their actions to the above end is what we mean, or at least the only thing which upon the principle of utility we *ought* to mean, by the art of government: which, in as far as the measures it displays itself in are of a permanent nature, is generally distinguished by the name of *legislation;* as it is by that of *administration,* when they are of a temporary nature, determined by the occurrences of the day.

v. Now human creatures, considered with respect to the maturity of their faculties, are either in an *adult* or in a *non-adult* state. The art of government, in as far as it concerns the direction of the actions of persons in a non-adult state, may be termed the art of *education.* In as far as this business is entrusted with those who, in virtue of some private relationship, are in the main the best disposed to take upon them and the best able to discharge this office, it may be termed the art of *private education;* in as far as it is exercised by those whose province it is to superintend the conduct of the whole community, it may be termed the art of *public education.*

vi. As to ethics in general, a man's happiness will depend, in the first place, upon such parts of his behavior as none but himself are interested in; in the next place, upon such parts of it as may affect the happiness of those about him. In as far as his happiness depends upon the first-mentioned part of his behavior, it is said to depend upon his *duty to himself.* Ethics then, in as far as it is the art of directing a man's actions in this respect, may be termed the art of discharging one's duty to oneself; and the quality which a man manifests by the discharge of this branch of duty (if duty it is to be called) is that of *prudence.* In

in the inevitable course of nature. If the being killed were all, there is very good reason why we should be suffered to kill such as molest us: we should be the worse for their living, and they are never the worse for being dead. But is there any reason why we should be suffered to torment them? Not any that I can see. Are there any why we should *not* be suffered to torment them? Yes, several. . . . The day has been, I grieve to say in many places it is not yet past, in which the greater part of the species, under the denomination of slaves, have been treated by the law exactly upon the same footing as, in England for example, the inferior races of animals are still. The day *may* come when the rest of the animal creation may acquire those rights which never could have been withholden from them but by the hand of tyranny. The French have already discovered that the blackness of the skin is no reason why a human being should be abandoned without redress to the caprice of a tormentor. (See Louis XIV's *Code Noir.*) It may come one day to be recognized that the number of the legs, the villosity of the skin, or the termination of the *os sacrum,* are reasons equally insufficient for abandoning a sensitive being to the same fate. What else is it that should trace the insuperable line? Is it the faculty of reason, or perhaps the faculty of discourse? But a full-grown horse or dog is beyond comparison a more rational, as well as a more conversable animal, than an infant of a day, or a week, or even a month, old. But suppose the case were otherwise, what would it avail? The question is not, Can they *reason?* nor, Can they *talk?* but, Can they *suffer?*

as far as his happiness, and that of any other person or persons whose
interests are considered, depends upon such parts of his behavior as may
affect the interests of those about him, it may be said to depend upon
his *duty to others;* or, to use a phrase now somewhat antiquated, his
duty to his neighbor. Ethics then, in as far as it is the art of directing a
man's actions in this respect, may be termed the art of discharging
one's duty to one's neighbor. Now the happiness of one's neighbor may
be consulted in two ways: (1) in a negative way, by forbearing to
diminish it; (2) in a positive way, by studying to increase it. A man's
duty to his neighbor is accordingly partly negative and partly positive:
to discharge the negative branch of it, is *probity;* to discharge the
positive branch, *beneficence.*

vii. It may here be asked how it is that upon the principle of private
ethics (legislation and religion out of the question) a man's happiness
depends upon such parts of his conduct as affect, immediately at least,
the happiness of no one but himself: this is as much as to ask, What
motives (independent of such as legislation and religion may chance to
furnish) can one man have to consult the happiness of another? By what
motives, or, which comes to the same thing, by what obligations, can he
be bound to obey the dictates of *probity* and *beneficence?* In answer to
this, it cannot but be admitted that the only interests which a man at
all times and upon all occasions is sure to find *adequate* motives for
consulting, are his own. Notwithstanding this, there are no occasions in
which a man has not some motives for consulting the happiness of other
men. In the first place, he has, on all occasions, the purely social motive
of sympathy or benevolence; in the next place, he has, on most occasions, the semi-social motives of love of amity and love of reputation.
The motive of sympathy will act upon him with more or less effect according to the *bias* of his sensibility; the two other motives, according to a variety of circumstances, principally according to the strength
of his intellectual powers, the firmness and steadiness of his mind, the
quantum of his moral sensibility, and the characters of the people he
has to deal with.

viii. Now private ethics has happiness for its end; and legislation
can have no other. Private ethics concerns every member, that is, the
happiness and the actions of every member, of any community that
can be proposed; and legislation can concern no more. Thus far, then,
private ethics and the art of legislation go hand in hand. The end they
have, or ought to have, in view, is of the same nature. The persons
whose happiness they ought to have in view, as also the persons whose
conduct they ought to be occupied in directing, are precisely the same.
The very acts they ought to be conversant about, are even in a *great
measure* the same. Where then lies the difference? In that the acts which

they ought to be conversant about, though in a great measure, are not *perfectly and throughout* the same. There is no case in which a private man ought not to direct his own conduct to the production of his own happiness and of that of his fellow-creatures; but there are cases in which the legislator ought not (in a direct way at least, and by means of punishment applied immediately to particular *individual* acts) to attempt to direct the conduct of the several other members of the community. Every act which promises to be beneficial upon the whole to the community (himself included) each individual ought to perform of himself; but it is not every such act that the legislator ought to compel him to perform. Every act which promises to be pernicious upon the whole to the community (himself included) each individual ought to abstain from of himself; but it is not every such act that the legislator ought to compel him to abstain from. . . .

xv. For the sake of obtaining the clearer idea of the limits between the art of legislation and private ethics, it may now be time to call to mind the distinctions above established with regard to ethics in general. The degree in which private ethics stands in need of the assistance of legislation, is different in the three branches of duty above distinguished. Of the rules of moral duty, those which seem to stand least in need of the assistance of legislation are the rules of *prudence*. It can only be through some defect on the part of the understanding if a man be ever deficient in point of duty to himself. If he does wrong, there is nothing else that it can be owing to but either some *inadvertence* or some *missupposal* with regard to the circumstances on which his happiness depends. It is a standing topic of complaint that a man knows too little of himself. Be it so; but is it so certain that the legislator must know more?[22] It is plain that of individuals the legislator can know nothing: concerning those points of conduct which depend upon the particular circumstances of each individual, it is plain, therefore, that he can determine nothing to advantage. It is only with respect to those broad lines of conduct in which all persons, or very large and permanent descriptions of persons, may be in a way to engage, that he can have any pretense for interfering; and even here the propriety of his interference will, in most instances, lie very open to dispute. At any rate, he must never expect to produce a perfect compliance by the mere force of the sanction of which he is himself the author. All he can hope to do is to

[22] On occasions like this the legislator should never lose sight of the well-known story of the oculist and the sot. A countryman who had hurt his eyes by drinking, went to a celebrated oculist for advice. He found him at table, with a glass of wine before him. "You must leave off drinking," said the oculist. "How so?" says the countryman; "*you* don't, and yet methinks your own eyes are none of the best." "That's very true, friend," replied the oculist; "but you art to know, I love my bottle better than my eyes."

increase the efficacy of private ethics by giving strength and direction to the influence of the moral sanction. With what chance of success, for example, would a legislator go about to extirpate drunkenness and fornication by dint of legal punishment? Not all the tortures which ingenuity could invent would compass it; and before he had made any progress worth regarding, such a mass of evil would be produced by the punishment, as would exceed a thousandfold the utmost possible mischief of the offense. The great difficulty would be in the procuring evidence: an object which could not be attempted, with any probability of success, without spreading dismay through every family, tearing the bonds of sympathy asunder, and rooting out the influence of all the social motives. All that he can do then, against offenses of this nature, with any prospect of advantage, in the way of direct legislation, is to subject them, in cases of notoriety, to a slight censure, so as thereby to cover them with a slight shade of artificial disrepute.

xvi. It may be observed that with regard to this branch of duty, legislators have in general been disposed to carry their interference full as far as is expedient. The great difficulty here is to persuade them to confine themselves within bounds. A thousand little passions and prejudices have led them to narrow the liberty of the subject in this line, in cases in which the punishment is either attended with no profit at all, or with none that will make up for the expense.

xvii. The mischief of this sort of interference is more particularly conspicuous in the article of religion. The reasoning, in this case, is of the following stamp. There are certain errors, in matters of belief, to which all mankind are prone; and for these errors in judgment, it is the determination of a Being of infinite benevolence to punish them with an infinity of torments. But from these errors the legislator himself is necessarily free; for the men who happen to be at hand for him to consult with, being men perfectly enlightened, unfettered, and unbiased, have such advantages over all the rest of the world, that when they sit down to inquire out the truth relative to points so plain and so familiar as those in question, they cannot fail to find it. This being the case, when the sovereign sees his people ready to plunge headlong into an abyss of fire, shall he not stretch out a hand to save them? Such, for example, seems to have been the train of reasoning, and such the motives, which led Louis the XIV into those coercive measures which he took for the conversion of heretics and the confirmation of true believers. The groundwork, pure sympathy and loving-kindness; the superstructure, all the miseries which the most determined malevolence could have devised.[23] But of this more fully in another place.

[23] I do not mean but that other motives of a less social nature might have introduced themselves, and probably, in point of fact, did introduce themselves, in the

xviii. The rules of *probity* are those which in point of expediency stand most in need of assistance on the part of the legislator, and in which, in point of fact, his interference has been most extensive. There are few cases in which it *would* be expedient to punish a man for hurting *himself;* but there are few cases, if any, in which it would *not* be expedient to punish a man for injuring his neighbor. With regard to that branch of probity which is opposed to offenses against property, private ethics depends in a manner for its very existence upon legislation. Legislation must first determine what things are to be regarded as each man's property, before the general rules of ethics, on this head, can have any particular application. The case is the same with regard to offenses against the state. Without legislation there would be no such thing as a *state*: no particular persons invested with powers to be exercised for the benefit of the rest. It is plain, therefore, that in this branch the interference of the legislator cannot anywhere be dispensed with. We must first know what are the dictates of legislation, before we can know what are the dictates of private ethics.[24]

xix. As to the rules of beneficence, these, as far as concerns matters of detail, must necessarily be abandoned in great measure to the jurisdiction of private ethics. In many cases the beneficial quality of the act depends essentially upon the disposition of the agent—that is, upon the motives by which he appears to have been prompted to perform it: upon their belonging to the head of sympathy, love of amity, or love of reputation, and not to any head of self-regarding motives, brought into play by the force of political constraint: in a word, upon their being such as denominate his conduct *free* and *voluntary,* according to one of the many

progress of the enterprise. But in point of possibility, the motive above mentioned, when accompanied with such a thread of reasoning, is sufficient, without any other, to account for all the effects above alluded to. If any others interfere, their interference, how natural soever, may be looked upon as an accidental and inessential circumstance, not necessary to the production of the effect. Sympathy, a concern for the danger they appear to be exposed to, gives birth to the wish of freeing them from it; that wish shows itself in the shape of a command; this command produces disobedience; disobedience on the one part produces disappointment on the other; the pain of disappointment produces ill-will towards those who are the authors of it. The affections will often make this progress in less time than it would take to describe it. The sentiment of wounded pride, and other modifications of the love of reputation and the love of power, add fuel to the flame. A kind of revenge exasperates the severities of coercive policy.

[24] But suppose the dictates of legislation *are* not what they *ought to be:* what are then, or (what in this case comes to the same thing) what ought to be, the dictates of private ethics? Do they coincide with the dictates of legislation, or do they oppose them, or do they remain neuter? A very interesting question this, but one that belongs not to the present subject. It belongs exclusively to that of private ethics. Principles which may lead to the solution of it may be seen in *A Fragment on Government.*

senses given to those ambiguous expressions.[25] The limits of the law on this head seem, however, to be capable of being extended a good deal farther than they seem ever to have been extended hitherto. In particular, in cases where the person is in danger, why should it not be made the duty of every man to save another from mischief, when it can be done without prejudicing himself, as well as to abstain from bringing it on him? This accordingly is the idea pursued in the body of the work.[26]

xx. To conclude this section, let us recapitulate and bring to a point the difference between private ethics considered as an art or science, on the one hand, and that branch of jurisprudence which contains the art or science of legislation, on the other. Private ethics teaches how each man may dispose himself to pursue the course most conducive to his own happiness, by means of such motives as offer of themselves; the art of legislation (which may be considered as one branch of the science of jurisprudence) teaches how a multitude of men, composing a community, may be disposed to pursue the course which upon the whole is the most conducive to the happiness of the whole community, by means of motives to be applied by the legislator. . . .

[25] If we may believe M. Voltaire, there was a time when the French ladies who thought themselves neglected by their husbands, used to petition *pour être embe-soignées:* the technical word, which, he says, was appropriated to this purpose. These sort of law proceedings seem not very well calculated to answer the design: accordingly we hear nothing of them nowadays. The French ladies of the present age seem to be under no such difficulties.

[26] A woman's headdress catches fire; water is at hand: a man, instead of assisting to quench the fire, looks on, and laughs at it. A drunken man, falling with his face downwards into a puddle, is in danger of suffocation; lifting his head a little on one side would save him: another man sees this and lets him lie. A quantity of gunpowder lies scattered about a room; a man is going into it with a lighted candle: another, knowing this, lets him go in without warning. Who is there that in any of these cases would think punishment misapplied?

JAMES MILL

An Essay on Government

JAMES MILL

JAMES MILL (1773-1836) was the son of a village shoemaker in Scotland. By the exertions of his mother, and with the assistance of Sir John Stuart, he was educated at Edinburgh for the ministry. But he had no particular success as a preacher; and, in 1802, he moved to London where he became a journalist and editor. His marriage, in 1805, led to harassing financial difficulties. In the hope of making money and establishing his reputation, he undertook to write a *History of British India*.

Meanwhile Mill sought out the acquaintance of Bentham whose writings had deeply influenced him. A life-long association was established. Mill made out of Benthamism a definite political program. Through him a small but powerful group of people, including Joseph Hume, Francis Place, George Grote, and David Ricardo, became self-conscious apostles of Bentham's ideas, agitating powerfully for reform in every quarter. Mill was the directing genius of this practical reform movement, Bentham its great oracle. Mill contributed also to the systematization and propagation of Benthamite ideas in his writings. He composed a number of important articles for the supplement of the fifth edition of the *Encyclopedia Britannica* (1816-1823) on "Government," "Jurisprudence," "Liberty of the Press," "Education," which had great effect in molding public opinion, and he made trenchant contributions to the *Westminster Review,* started as an organ of the group in 1824. In 1821 he published his *Elements of Political Economy,* a simplified statement of Ricardo's doctrines. His greatest work, the *Analysis of the Phenomena of the Human Mind* (1829), was an attempt, following the lead of Hartley, to render a complete account of experience in terms of the theory of association of ideas.

The publication of his *History of India* (1817), despite the drastic criticisms of the administration of Indian affairs that it contains, enabled him, in 1819, to obtain a post in the India House. He rose eventually to be head of the India Office. His last years were largely occupied in defending the East India Company during the controversy over the renewal of its charter.

The *Encyclopedia* article on "Government" follows.

GOVERNMENT

THE END OF GOVERNMENT

THE QUESTION with respect to government is a question about the adaptation of means to an end. Notwithstanding the portion of discourse which has been bestowed upon this subject, it is surprising to find, on close inspection, how few of its principles are settled. The reason is that the ends and means have not been analyzed, and it is only a general and undistinguishing conception of them which is found in the minds of the greatest number of men. Things in this situation give rise to interminable disputes; more especially when the deliberation is subject, as here, to the strongest action of personal interest.

In a discourse limited as the present it would be obviously vain to attempt the accomplishment of such a task as that of the analysis we have mentioned. The mode, however, in which the operation should be conducted may perhaps be described, and evidence enough exhibited to shew in what road we must travel to approach the goal at which so many have vainly endeavored to arrive.

The end of government has been described in a great variety of expressions. By Locke it was said to be 'the public good'; by others it has been described as being 'the greatest happiness of the greatest number.' These, and equivalent expressions, are just; but they are defective, inasmuch as the particular ideas which they embrace are indistinctly announced, and different conceptions are by means of them raised in different minds, and even in the same mind on different occasions.

It is immediately obvious that a wide and difficult field is presented, and that the whole science of human nature must be explored, to lay a foundation for the science of government. To understand what is included in the happiness of the greatest number, we must understand what is included in the happiness of the individuals of whom it is composed. That dissection of human nature which would be necessary for exhibiting, on proper evidence, the primary elements into which human happiness may be resolved, it is not compatible with the present design to undertake. We must content ourselves with assuming certain results.

We may allow, for example, in general terms that the lot of every human being is determined by his pains and pleasures, and that his happi ness corresponds with the degree in which his pleasures are great and his pains are small. Human pains and pleasures are derived from two sources: they are produced either by our fellow-men or by causes independent of other men. We may assume it as another principle that the concern of government is with the former of these two sources: that its business is to increase to the utmost the pleasures, and diminish to the utmost the pains, which men derive from one another.

Of the laws of nature on which the condition of man depends, that which is attended with the greatest number of consequences is the necessity of labor for obtaining the means of subsistence, as well as the means of the greatest part of our pleasures. This is no doubt the primary cause of government; for if nature had produced spontaneously all the objects which we desire, and in sufficient abundance for the desires of all, there would have been no source of dispute or of injury among men, nor would any man have possessed the means of ever acquiring authority over another.

The results are exceedingly different when nature produces the objects of desire not in sufficient abundance for all. The source of dispute is then exhaustless, and every man has the means of acquiring authority over others in proportion to the quantity of those objects which he is able to possess. In this case the end to be obtained through government as the means, is to make that distribution of the scanty materials of happiness which would insure the greatest sum of it in the members of the community taken altogether, preventing every individual or combination of individuals from interfering with that distribution or making any man to have less than his share.

When it is considered that most of the objects of desire and even the means of subsistence are the product of labor, it is evident that the means of insuring labor must be provided for as the foundation of all. The means for the insuring of labor are of two sorts: the one made out of the matter of evil, the other made out of the matter of good. The first sort is commonly denominated force, and under its application the laborers are slaves. This mode of procuring labor we need not consider, for if the end of government be to produce the greatest happiness of the greatest number, that end cannot be attained by making the greatest number slaves.

The other mode of obtaining labor is by allurement, or the advantage which it brings. To obtain all the objects of desire in the greatest possible quantity, we must obtain labor in the greatest possible quantity; and to obtain labor in the greatest possible quantity, we must raise to the greatest possible height the advantage attached to labor. It is impossible to attach to labor a greater degree of advantage than the whole of the product of labor. Why so? Because if you give more to one man than the produce of his labor, you can do so only by taking it away from the produce of some other man's labor. The greatest possible happiness of society is therefore attained by insuring to every man the greatest possible quantity of the produce of his labor.

How is this to be accomplished? For it is obvious that every man who has not all the objects of his desire, has inducement to take them from any other man who is weaker than himself: and how is he to be prevented? One mode is sufficiently obvious, and it does not appear that there is any other: the union of a certain number of men to protect one another. The object, it is plain, can best be attained when a great number of men combine and delegate to a small number the power necessary for protecting them all. This is government.

With respect to the end of government, or that for the sake of which it exists, it is not conceived to be necessary on the present occasion that the analysis should be carried any further. What follows is an attempt to analyze the means.

II

POWER, AND SECURITIES AGAINST THE ABUSE OF THAT POWER

Two things are here to be considered: the power with which the small number are entrusted, and the use which they are to make of it. With respect to the first there is no difficulty. The elements out of which the power of coercing others is fabricated are obvious to all. Of these we shall therefore not lengthen this article by any explanation. All the difficult questions of government relate to the means of restraining those in whose hands are lodged the powers necessary for the protection of all, from making a bad use of it.

Whatever would be the temptations under which individuals would lie if there was no government, to take the objects of desire from others weaker than themselves, under the same temptations the members of the government lie, to take the objects of desire from the members of the community, if they are not prevented from doing so. Whatever, then, are the reasons for establishing government, the very same exactly are the reasons for establishing securities that those entrusted with the powers necessary for protecting others, make use of them for that purpose solely, and not for the purpose of taking from the members of the community the objects of desire.

III

THAT THE REQUISITE SECURITIES AGAINST THE ABUSE OF POWER ARE NOT FOUND IN ANY OF THE SIMPLE FORMS OF GOVERNMENT

THERE are three modes in which it may be supposed that the powers for the protection of the community are capable of being exercised. The community may undertake the protection of itself and of its members. The powers of protection may be placed in the hands of a few. And lastly, they may be placed in the hands of an individual. The many, the few, the one: these varieties appear to exhaust the subject. It is not possible to conceive any hands or combination of hands in which the powers of protection can be lodged, which will not fall under one or other of those descriptions. And these varieties correspond to the three forms of government: the democratical, the aristocratical, and the monarchical. It will be necessary to look somewhat closely at each of these forms in their order.

(1) *The democratical.*—It is obviously impossible that the community in a body can be present to afford protection to each of its members. It must employ individuals for that purpose. Employing individuals, it must choose them; it must lay down the rules under which they are to act; and it must punish them if they act in disconformity to those rules. In these functions are included the three great operations of government—administration, legislation, and judicature. The community, to perform any of these operations, must be assembled. This circumstance alone seems to form a conclusive objection against the democratical form. To assemble the whole of a community as often as the business of government requires performance would almost preclude the existence of labor, hence that of property, and hence the existence of the community itself.

There is another objection, not less conclusive. A whole community would form a numerous assembly. But all numerous assemblies are essentially incapable of business. It is unnecessary to be tedious in the proof of this proposition. In an assembly everything must be done by speaking and assenting. But where the assembly is numerous, so many persons desire to speak, and feelings by mutual inflammation become so violent, that calm and effectual deliberation is impossible.

It may be taken therefore as a proposition from which there will be no dissent, that a community in mass is ill adapted for the business of government. There is no principle more in conformity with the sentiments and the practice of the people than this. The management of the joint affairs of any considerable body of the people they never undertake for themselves. What they uniformly do is to choose a certain number of themselves to be the actors in their stead. Even in the case of a common benefit club, the members choose a committee of management and content themselves with a general control.

(2) *The aristocratical.*—This term applies to all those cases in which the powers of government are held by any number of persons intermediate between a single person and the majority. When the number is small, it is common to call the government an oligarchy; when it is considerable, to call it an aristocracy. The cases are essentially the same, because the motives which operate in both are the same. This is a proposition which carries, we think, its own evidence along with it. We therefore assume it as a point which will not be disputed.

The source of evil is radically different in the case of aristocracy from what it is in that of democracy.

The community cannot have an interest opposite to its interest. To affirm this would be a contradiction in terms. The community within itself, and with respect to itself, can have no sinister interest. One community may intend the evil of another; never its own. This is an indubitable proposition, and one of great importance. The community may act wrong from mistake. To suppose that it could from design, would be to suppose that human beings can wish their own misery.

The circumstances from which the inaptitude of the community, as a body, for the business of government arises—namely, the inconvenience of assembling them, and the inconvenience of their numbers when assembled—do not necessarily exist in the case of aristocracy. If the number of those who hold among them the powers of government is so great as to make it inconvenient to assemble them, or impossible for them to deliberate calmly when assembled, this is only an objection to so extended an aristocracy, and has no application to an aristocracy not too numerous when assembled for the best exercise of deliberation.

The question is, whether such an aristocracy may be trusted to make that use of the powers of government which is most conducive to the end for which government exists.

There may be a strong presumption that any aristocracy, monopolizing the powers of government, would not possess intellectual powers in any very high perfection. Intellectual powers are the offspring of labor. But an hereditary aristocracy are deprived of the strongest motives to labor. The greater part of them will therefore be defective in those mental powers. This is one objection and an important one, though not the greatest.

We have already observed that the reason for which government exists is that one man, if stronger than another, will take from him whatever that other possesses and he desires. But if one man will do this, so will several. And if powers are put into the hands of a comparatively small number, called an aristocracy,—powers which make them stronger than the rest of the community,—they will take from the rest of the community as much as they please of the objects of desire. They will thus defeat the very end for which government was instituted. The unfitness, therefore, of an aristocracy to be entrusted with the powers of government, rests on demonstration.

(3) *The monarchical.*—It will be seen, and therefore words to make it manifest are unnecessary, that in most respects the monarchical form of government agrees with the aristocratical and is liable to the same objections. If government is founded upon this, as a law of human nature, that a man if able will take from others anything which they have and he desires, it is sufficiently evident that when a man is called a king it does not change his nature; so that when he has got power to enable him to take from every man what he pleases, he will take whatever he pleases. To suppose that he will not is to affirm that government is unnecessary, and that human beings will abstain from injuring one another of their own accord.

It is very evident that this reasoning extends to every modification of the smaller number. Whenever the powers of government are placed in any hands other than those of the community—whether those of one man, of a few, or of several—those principles of human nature which imply that government is at all necessary, imply that those persons will make use of them to defeat the very end for which government exists.

IV

AN OBJECTION STATED—AND ANSWERED

ONE observation, however, suggests itself. Allowing, it may be said, that this deduction is perfect, and the inference founded upon it indisputable, it is yet true that if there were no government, every man would be exposed to depredation from every man but under an aristocracy he is exposed to it only from a few, under a monarchy only from one. This is a highly important objection, and deserves to be minutely investigated.

It is sufficiently obvious that if every man is liable to be deprived of what he possesses at the will of every man stronger than himself, the existence of property is impossible; and if the existence of property is impossible, so also is that of labor, of the mean of subsistence for an enlarged community, and hence of the community itself. If the members of such a community are liable to deprivation by only a few hundred men, the members of an aristocracy, it may not be impossible to satiate that limited number with a limited portion of the objects belonging to all.

Allowing this view of the subject to be correct, it follows that the smaller the number of hands into which the powers of government are permitted to pass, the happier it will be for the community: that an oligarchy, therefore, is better than an aristocracy, and a monarchy better than either.

This view of the subject deserves to be the more carefully considered because the conclusion to which it leads is the same with that which has been adopted and promulgated by some of the most profound and most benevolent investigators of human affairs. That government by one man, altogether unlimited and uncontrolled, is better than government by any modification of aristocracy, is the celebrated opinion of Mr. Hobbes and of the French economists, supported on reasonings which it is not easy to controvert. Government by the many, they with reason considered an impossibility. They inferred, therefore, that of all the possible forms of government absolute monarchy is the best.

Experience, if we look only at the outside of the facts, appears to be divided on this subject. Absolute monarchy under Neros and Caligulas, under such men as emperors of Morocco and sultans of Turkey, is the scourge of human nature. On the other side, the people of Denmark, tired out with the oppression of an aristocracy, resolved that their king should be absolute; and under their absolute monarch are as well gov-erned as any people in Europe. In Greece, notwithstanding the defects of democracy, human nature ran a more brilliant career than it has ever done in any other age or country. As the surface of history affords, there-fore, no certain principle of decision, we must go beyond the surface and penetrate to the springs within.

When it is said that one man or a limited number of men will soon be satiated with the objects of desire, and, when they have taken from the community what suffices to satiate them, will protect its members in the enjoyment of the remainder, an important element of the calculation is left out. Human beings are not a passive substance. If human beings in respect to their rulers were the same as sheep in respect to their shep-herd, and if the king or the aristocracy were as totally exempt from all fear of resistance from the people, and all chance of obtaining more obedience from severity, as the shepherd in the case of the sheep, it does appear that there would be a limit to the motive for taking to oneself the objects of desire. The case will be found to be very much altered when the idea is taken into the account, first, of the resistance to his will which one human being may expect from another, and secondly, of that perfection in obedience which fear alone can produce.

That one human being will desire to render the person and property of another subservient to his pleasures notwithstanding the pain or loss of pleasure which it may occasion to that other individual, is the foundation of government. The desire of the object implies the desire of the power neccessary to accomplish the object. The desire, therefore, of that power which is necessary to render the persons and properties of human beings subservient to our pleasures, is a grand governing law of human nature. What is implied in that desire of power, and what is the extent to which it carries the actions of men, are the questions which it is necessary to resolve, in order to discover the limit which nature has set to the desire on the part of a king or an aristocracy to inflict evil upon the community for their own advantage.

Power is a means to an end. The end is everything, without exception, which the human being calls pleasure and the removal of pain. The grand instrument for attaining what a man likes is the actions of other men. Power, in its most appropriate signification, therefore, means security for the conformity between the will of one man and the acts of other men. This, we presume, is not a proposition which will be disputed. The master has power over his servant, because when he wills him to do so and so—in other words, expresses a desire that he would do so and so—he possesses a kind of security that the actions of the man will correspond to his desire. The general commands his soldiers to perform certain operations, the king commands his subjects to act in a certain manner, and their power is complete or not complete in proportion as the conformity is complete or not complete between the actions willed and the actions performed. The actions of other men, considered as means for the attainment of the objects of our desire, are perfect or imperfect in proportion as they are or are not certainly and invariably correspondent to our will. There is no limit, therefore, to the demand of security for the perfection of that correspondence. A man is never satisfied with a smaller degree if he can obtain a greater. And as there is no man whatsoever whose acts, in some degree or other, in some way or other, more immediately or more remotely, may not have some influence as means to our ends, there is no man the conformity of whose acts to our will we would not give something to secure. The demand, therefore, of power over the acts of other men is really boundless. It is boundless in two ways: boundless in the number of persons to whom we would extend it, and boundless in its degree over the actions of each.

It would be nugatory to say, with a view to explain away this important principle, that some human beings may be so remotely connected with our interests as to make the desire of a conformity between our will and their actions evanescent. It is quite enough to assume, what nobody will deny, that our desire of that conformity is unlimited in respect to all those men whose actions can be supposed to have any influence on our pains and pleasures. With respect to the rulers of a community this at least is certain, that they have a desire for the uniformity between their will and the actions of every man in the community. And for our present purpose this is as wide a field as we need to embrace.

With respect to the community, then, we deem it an established truth that the rulers, one or a few, desire an exact conformity between their will and the acts of every member of the community. It remains for us to inquire to what description of acts it is the nature of this desire to give existence.

There are two classes of means by which the conformity between the will of one man and the acts of other men may be accomplished. The one is pleasure, the other pain.

With regard to securities of the pleasurable sort for obtaining a conformity between one man's will and the acts of other men, it is evident from experience that when a man possesses a command over the objects of desire, he may, by imparting those objects to other men, insure to a great extent conformity between his will and their actions. It follows, and is also matter of experience, that the greater the quantity of the objects of desire which he may thus impart to other men, the greater is the number of men between whose actions and his own will he can insure a conformity. As it has been demonstrated that there is no limit to the number of men whose actions we desire to have conformable to our will, it follows with equal evidence that there is no limit to the command which we desire to possess over the objects which ensure this result.

It is therefore not true that there is in the mind of a king, or in the minds of an aristocracy, any point of saturation with the objects of desire. The opinion, in examination of which we have gone through the preceding analysis, that a king or an aristocracy may be satiated with the objects of desire and, after being satiated, leave to the members of the community the greater part of what belongs to them, is an opinion founded upon a partial and incomplete view of the laws of human nature.

We have next to consider the securities of the painful sort which may be employed for attaining conformity between the acts of one man and the will of another. We are of opinion that the importance of this part of the subject has not been duly considered, and that the business of government will be ill understood till its numerous consequences have been fully developed.

Pleasure appears to be a feeble instrument of obedience in comparison with pain. It is much more easy to despise pleasure than pain. Above all, it is important to consider that in this class of instruments is included the power of taking away life, and with it of taking away not only all the pleasures of reality but, what goes so far beyond them, all the pleasures of hope. This class of securities is therefore incomparably the strongest. He who desires obedience to a high degree of exactness cannot be satisfied with the power of giving pleasure, he must have the power of inflicting pain. He who desires it to the highest possible degree of exactness must desire power of inflicting pain sufficient at least to insure that degree of exactness—that is, an unlimited power of inflicting pain; for as there is no possible mark by which to distinguish what is sufficient and what is not, and as the human mind sets no bounds to its avidity for the securities of what it deems eminently good, it is sure to extend beyond almost any limits its desire of the power of giving pain to others.

It may, however, be said that how inseparable a part soever of human nature it may appear to be, to desire to possess unlimited power of inflicting pain upon others, it does not follow that those who possess it will have a desire to make use of it. This is the next part of the inquiry upon which we have to enter; and we need not add that it merits all the attention of those who would possess correct ideas upon a subject which involves the greatest interests of mankind.

The chain of inference in this case is close and strong to a most unusual degree. A man desires that the actions of other men shall be instantly and accurately correspondent to his will. He desires that the actions of the greatest possible number shall be so. Terror is the grand instrument. Terror can work only through assurance that evil will follow any want of conformity between the will and the actions willed. Every failure must therefore be punished. As there are no bounds to the mind's desire of its pleasure, there are of course no bounds to its desire of perfection in the instruments of that pleasure. There are therefore no bounds to its desire of exactness in the conformity between its will and the actions willed; and, by consequence, to the strength of that terror which is its procuring cause. Every, the most minute, failure must be visited with the heaviest infliction; and as failure in extreme exactness must frequently happen, the occasions of cruelty must be incessant.

We have thus arrived at several conclusions of the highest possible importance. We have seen that the very principle of human nature upon which the necessity of government is founded, the propensity of one man to possess himself of the objects of desire at the cost of another, leads on by infallible sequence, where power over a community is attained and nothing checks, not only to that degree of plunder which leaves the members (excepting always the recipients and instruments of the plunder) the bare means of subsistence, but to that degree of cruelty which is necessary to keep in existence the most intense terror.

The world affords some decisive experiments upon human nature in exact conformity with these conclusions. An English gentleman may be taken as a favorable specimen of civilization, of knowledge, of humanity, of all the qualities, in short, that make human nature estimable. The degree in which he desires to possess power over his fellow-creatures, and the degree of oppression to which he finds motives for carrying the exercise of that power, will afford a standard from which assuredly there can be no appeal. Wherever the same motives exist, the same conduct as that displayed by the English gentleman may be expected to follow in all men not farther advanced in human excellence than him. In the West Indies, before that vigilant attention of the English nation, which now for thirty years has imposed so great a check upon the masters of slaves, there was not a perfect absence of all check upon the dreadful propensities of power. But yet it is true that these propensities led English gentlemen not only to deprive their slaves of property and to make property of their fellow-creatures, but to treat them with a degree of cruelty the very description of which froze the blood of their countrymen who were placed in less unfavorable circumstances. The motives of this deplorable conduct are exactly those which we have described above, as arising out of the universal desire to render the actions of other men exactly conformable to our will. It is of great importance to remark that not one item in the motives which had led English gentlemen to make slaves of their fellow-creatures, and to reduce them to the very worst condition in which the Negroes have been found in the West Indies, can be shown to be wanting, or to be less strong, in the set of motives which universally operate upon the men who have power over their fellow-creatures. It is proved, therefore, by the closest deduction from the acknowledged laws of human nature, and by direct and decisive experiments, that the ruling One or the ruling Few would, if checks did not operate in the way of prevention, reduce the great mass of the people subject to their power at least to the condition of Negroes in the West Indies.

We have thus seen that of the forms of government which have been called the three simple forms, not one is adequate to the ends which government is appointed to secure; that the community itself, which alone is free from motives opposite to those ends, is incapacitated by its numbers from performing the business of government; and that whether government is entrusted to one or a few, they have not only motives opposite to those ends, but motives which will carry them, if unchecked, to inflict the greatest evils.

These conclusions are so conformable to ordinary conceptions, that it would hardly have been necessary, if the development had not been of importance for some of our subsequent investigations, to have taken any pains with the proof of them. In this country, at least, it will be remarked, in conformity with so many writers, that the imperfection of the three simple forms of government is apparent; that the ends of government can be attained in perfection only, as under the British constitution, by an union of all the three.

V

THAT THE REQUISITE SECURITIES ARE NOT FOUND IN A UNION OF THE THREE SIMPLE FORMS OF GOVERNMENT

THE doctrine of the union of the three simple forms of government is the next part of this important subject which we are called upon to examine.

The first thing which it is obvious to remark upon it, is, that it has been customary, in regard to this part of the inquiry, to beg the question. The good effects which have been ascribed to the union of the three simple forms of government, have been *supposed;* and the supposition has commonly been allowed. No proof has been adduced; or if anything have the appearance of proof, it has only been a reference to the British constitution. The British constitution, it has been said, is an union of the three simple forms of government; and the British government is excellent. To render the instance of the British government in any degree a proof of the doctrine in question, it is evident that three points must be established; first, that the British government is not in show, but in substance, an union of the three simple forms; secondly, that it has peculiar excellence; and, thirdly, that its excellence arises from the union so supposed, and not from any other cause. As these points have always been taken for granted without examination, the question with respect to the effects of an union of the three simple forms of government may be considered as yet unsolved.

The positions which we have already established with regard to human nature, and which we assume as foundations, are these: that the actions of men are governed by their wills, and their wills by their desires: that their desires are directed to pleasure and relief from pain as *ends,* and to wealth and power as the principal means: that to the desire of these means there is no limit; and that the actions which flow from this unlimited desire are the constituents whereof bad government is made. Reasoning correctly from these acknowledged laws of human nature, we shall presently discover what opinion, with respect to the mixture of the different species of government, it will be incumbent upon us to adopt.

The theory in question implies, that of the powers of government, one portion is held by the king, one by the aristocracy, and one by the people. It also implies, that there is on the part of each of them a certain unity of will, otherwise they would not act as three separate powers. This being understood, we proceed to the inquiry.

From the principles which we have already laid down, it follows, that of the objects of human desire—and, speaking more definitely, of the means to the ends of human desire, namely, wealth and power—each of the three parties will endeavor to obtain as much as possible.

After what has been said, it is not suspected that any reader will deny this proposition; but it is of importance that he keep in his mind a very clear conception of it.

If any expedient presents itself to any of the supposed parties, effectual to said end, and not opposed to any preferred object of pursuit, we may infer, with certainty, that it will be adopted. One effectual expedient is not more effectual than obvious. Any two of the parties, by combining, may swallow up the third. That such combination will take place, appears to be as certain as anything which depends upon human will; because there are strong motives in favor of it, and none that can be conceived in opposition to it. Whether the portions of power, as originally distributed to the parties, be supposed to be equal or unequal, the mixture of three of the kinds of government, it is thus evident, cannot possibly exist.

This proposition appears to be so perfectly proved, that we do not think it necessary to dwell here upon the subject. As a part, however, of this doctrine, of the mixture of the simple forms of government, it may be proper to inquire, whether an union may not be possible of two of them.

Three varieties of this union may be conceived; the union of the monarchy with aristocracy, or the union of either with democracy.

Let us first suppose that monarchy is united with aristocracy. Their power is equal or not equal. If it is not equal, it follows, as a necessary consequence, from the principles which we have already established, that the stronger will take from the weaker, till it engrosses the whole. The only question, therefore, is, what will happen when the power is equal.

In the first place, it seems impossible that such equality should ever exist. How is it to be established? Or by what criterion is it to be ascertained? If there is no such criterion, it must, in all cases, be the result of chance. If so, the chances against it are as infinite to one. The idea, therefore, is wholly chimerical and absurd.

Besides, a disposition to overrate one's own advantages, and underrate those of other men, is a known law of human nature. Suppose, what would be little less than miraculous, that equality were established, this propensity would lead each of the parties to conceive itself the strongest. The consequence would be that they would go to war, and contend till one or other was subdued. Either those laws of human nature, upon which all reasoning with respect to government proceeds, must be denied, and then the utility of government itself may be denied, or this conclusion is demonstrated. Again, if this equality were established, is there a human being who can suppose that it would last? If anything be known about human affairs it is this, that they are in perpetual change. If nothing else interfered, the difference of men in respect of talents, would abundantly produce the effect. Suppose your equality to be established at the time when your king is a man of talents, and suppose his successor to be the reverse; your equality no longer exists. The moment one of the parties is superior, it begins to profit by its superiority, and the inequality is daily increased. It is unnecessary to extend the investigation to the remaining cases, the union of democracy with either of the other two kinds of government. It is very evident that the same reasoning would lead to the same results.

In this doctrine of the mixture of the simple forms of government, is included the celebrated theory of the balance among the component parts of a government. By this, it is supposed, that, when a government is composed of monarchy, aristocracy, and democracy, they balance one another, and by mutual checks produce good government. A few words will suffice to show, that, if any theory deserve the epithets of "wild, visionary, chimerical", it is that of the balance. If there are three powers, how is it possible to prevent two of them from combining to swallow up the third?

The analysis which we have already performed, will enable us to trace rapidly the concatenation of causes and effects in this imagined case.

We have already seen that the interest of the community, considered in the aggregate, or in the democratical point of view, is, that each individual should receive protection, and that the powers which are constituted for that purpose should be employed exclusively for that purpose. As this is a proposition wholly indisputable, it is also one to which all correct reasoning upon matters of government must have a perpetual reference.

We have also seen that the interest of the king, and of the governing aristocracy, is directly the reverse; it is to have unlimited power over the rest of the community, and to use it for their own advantage. In the supposed case of the balance of the monarchical, aristocratical, and democratical powers, it cannot be for the interest of either the monarchy or the aristocracy to combine with the democracy; because it is the interest of the democracy, or community at large, that neither the king nor the aristocracy should have one particle of power, or one particle of the wealth of the community, for their own advantage.

The democracy or community have all possible motives to endeavor to prevent the monarchy and aristocracy from exercising power, or obtaining the wealth of the community, for their own advantage: The monarchy and aristocracy have all possible motives for endeavoring to obtain unlimited power over the persons and property of the community: The consequence is inevitable; they have all possible motives for combining to obtain that power, and unless the people have power enough to be a match for both, they have no protection. The balance, therefore, is a thing, the existence of which, upon the best possible evidence, is to be regarded as impossible. The appearances which have given color to the supposition are altogether delusive.

VI

IN THE REPRESENTATIVE SYSTEM ALONE THE SECURITIES FOR GOOD GOVERNMENT ARE TO BE FOUND

WHAT then is to be done? For according to this reasoning we may be told that good government appears to be impossible. The people as a body cannot perform the business of government for themselves. If the powers of government are entrusted to one man or a few men, and a monarchy or governing aristocracy is formed, the results are fatal; and it appears that a combination of the simple forms is impossible.

Notwithstanding the truth of these propositions, it is not yet proved that good government is impossible. For though the people, who cannot exercise the powers of government themselves, must entrust them to some one individual or set of individuals, and such individuals will infallibly have the strongest motives to make a bad use of them, it is possible that checks may be found sufficient to prevent them. The next subject of inquiry, then, is the doctrine of checks. It is sufficiently conformable to the established and fashionable opinions to say that upon the right constitution of checks all goodness of government depends. To this proposition we fully subscribe. Nothing, therefore, can exceed the importance of correct conclusions upon this subject. After the developments already made, it is hoped that the inquiry will be neither intricate nor unsatisfactory.

In the grand discovery of modern times, the system of representation, the solution of all the difficulties both speculative and practical will perhaps be found. If it cannot, we seem to be forced upon the extraordinary conclusion that good government is impossible. For as there is no individual or combination of individuals, except the community itself, who would not have an interest in bad government if entrusted with its powers, and as the community itself is incapable of exercising those powers and must entrust them to some individual or combination of individuals, the conclusion is obvious: the community itself must check those individuals, else they will follow their interest, and produce bad government.

But how is it the community can check? The community can act only when assembled: and then it is incapable of acting. The community, however, can choose representatives; and the question is, whether the representatives of the community can operate as a check.

VII

WHAT IS REQUIRED IN A REPRESENTATIVE BODY TO MAKE IT A SECURITY FOR GOOD GOVERNMENT?

WE may begin by laying down two propositions, which appear to involve a great portion of the inquiry; and about which it is unlikely that there will be any dispute.

1. The checking body must have a degree of power sufficient for the business of checking.

2. It must have an identity of interest with the community; otherwise it will make a mischievous use of its power.

1. To measure the degree of power which is requisite upon any occasion, we must consider the degree of power which is necessary to be overcome. Just as much as suffices for that purpose is requisite, and no more. We have then to inquire what power it is which the representatives of the community, acting as a check, need power to overcome. The answer here is easily given. It is all that power, wheresoever lodged, which they, in whose hands it is lodged, have an interest in misusing. We have already seen, that to whomsoever the community entrusts the powers of government, whether one, or a few, they have an interest in misusing them. All the power, therefore, which the one or the few, or which the one and the few combined, can apply to insure the accomplishment of their sinister ends, the checking body must have power to overcome, otherwise its check will be unavailing. In other words, there will be no check. . . .

These conclusions are not only indisputable, but the very theory of the British constitution is erected upon them. The House of Commons, according to that theory, is the checking body. It is also an admitted doctrine, that if the King had the power of bearing down any opposition to his will that could be made by the House of Commons; or if the King and the House of Lords combined had the power of bearing down its opposition to their joint will, it would cease to have the power of checking them; it must, therefore, have a power sufficient to overcome the united power of both.

2. All the questions which relate to the degree of power necessary to be given to that checking body, on the perfection of whose operations all the goodness of government depends, are thus pretty easily solved.

The grand difficulty consists in finding the means of constituting a checking body, whose powers shall not be turned against the community for whose protection it is created.

There can be no doubt, that if power is granted to a body of men, called representatives, they, like any other men, will use their power, not for the advantage of the community, but for their own advantage, if they can. The only question is, therefore, how they can be prevented? in other words, how are the interests of the representatives to be identified with those of the community?

Each representative may be considered in two capacities; in his capacity of representative, in which he has the exercise of power over others, and in his capacity of member of the community, in which others have the exercise of power over him.

If things were so arranged, that, in his capacity of representative, it would be impossible for him to do himself so much good by misgovernment, as he would do himself harm in his capacity of member of the community, the object would be accomplished. We have already seen, that the amount of power assigned to the checking body cannot be diminished beyond a certain amount. It must be sufficient to overcome all resistance on the part of all those in whose hands the powers of government are lodged. But if the power assigned to the representative cannot be diminished in amount, there is only one other way in which it can be diminished, and that is, in duration.

This, then, is the instrument; lessening of duration is the instrument, by which, if by anything, the object is to be attained. The smaller the period of time during which any man retains his capacity of representative, as compared with the time in which he is simply a member of the community, the more difficult it will be to compensate the sacrifice of the interests of the longer period, by the profits of misgovernment during the shorter.

This is an old and approved method of identifying as nearly as possible the interests of those who rule with the interests of those who are ruled. It is in pursuance of this advantage, that the members of the British House of Commons have always been chosen for a limited period. If the members were hereditary, or even if they were chosen for life, every inquirer would immediately pronounce that they would employ, for their own advantage, the powers entrusted to them; and that they would go just as far in abusing the persons and properties of the people, as their estimate of the powers and spirit of the people to resist them would allow them to contemplate as safe.

As it thus appears, by the consent of all men, from the time when the Romans made their consuls annual, down to the present day, that the end is to be attained by limiting the duration, either of the acting, or (which is better) of the checking power, the next question is, to what degree should the limitation proceed?

The general answer is plain. It should proceed, till met by overbalancing inconveniences on the other side. What then are the inconveniences which are likely to flow from a too limited duration?

They are of two sorts; those which affect the performance of the service, for which the individuals are chosen, and those which arise from the trouble of election. It is sufficiently obvious, that the business of government requires time to perform it. The matter must be proposed, deliberated upon, a resolution must be taken, and executed. If the powers of government were to be shifted from one set of hands to another every day, the business of government could not proceed. Two conclusions, then, we may adopt with perfect certainty; that whatsoever time is necessary to perform the periodical round of the stated operations of government, this should be allotted to those who are invested with the checking powers; and secondly, that no time, which is not necessary for that purpose, should by any means be allotted to them. With respect to the inconvenience arising from frequency of election, though it is evident, that the trouble of election, which is always something, should not be repeated oftener than is necessary, no great allowance will need to be made for it, because it may easily be reduced to an inconsiderable amount.

As it thus appears, that limiting the duration of their power is a security against the sinister interest of the people's representatives, so it appears that it is the only security of which the nature of the case admits. The only other means which could be employed to that end, would be punishment on account of abuse. It is easy, however, to see, that punishment could not be effectually applied. In order for punishment, definition is required of the punishable acts; and proof must be established of the commission. But abuses of power may be carried to a great extent, without allowing the means of proving a determinate offense. No part of political experience is more perfect than this.

If the limiting of duration be the only security, it is unnecessary to speak of the importance which ought to be attached to it.

In the principle of limiting the duration of the power delegated to the representatives of the people, is not included the idea of changing them. The same individual may be chosen any number of times. The check of the short period, for which he is chosen, and during which he can promote his sinister interest, is the same upon the man who has been chosen and re-chosen twenty times, as upon the man who has been chosen for the first time. And there is good reason for always re-electing the man who has done his duty, because the longer he serves, the better acquainted he becomes with the business of the service. Upon this principle of re-choosing, or of the permanency of the individual, united with the power of change, has been recommended the plan of permanent service with perpetual power of removal. This, it has been said, reduces the period within which the representative can promote his sinister interest to the narrowest possible limits; because the moment when his constituents begin to suspect him, that moment they may turn him out. On the other hand, if he continues faithful, the trouble of election is performed once for all, and the man serves as long as he lives. Some disadvantages, on the other hand, would accompany this plan. The present, however, is not the occasion on which the balance of different plans is capable of being adjusted.

VIII

WHAT IS REQUIRED IN THE ELECTIVE BODY TO SECURE THE REQUISITE PROPERTIES IN THE REPRESENTATIVE BODY

HAVING considered the means which are capable of being employed for identifying the interest of the representatives, when chosen, with that of the persons who choose them, it remains that we endeavor to bring to view the principles which ought to guide in determining who the persons are by whom the act of choosing ought to be performed.

It is most evident, that, upon this question, everything depends. It can be of no consequence to insure, by shortness of duration, a conformity between the conduct of the representatives and the will of those who appoint them, if those who appoint them have an interest opposite to that of the community; because those who choose will, according to the principles of human nature, make choice of such persons as will act according to their wishes. As this is a direct inference from the very principle on which government itself is founded, we assume it as indisputable.

We have seen already, that if one man has power over others placed in his hands, he will make use of it for an evil purpose; for the purpose of rendering those other men the abject instruments of his will. If we, then, suppose that one man has the power of choosing the representatives of the people, it follows, that he will choose men who will use their power as representatives for the promotion of this his sinister interest.

We have likewise seen, that when a few men have power given them over others, they will make use of it exactly for the same ends, and to the same extent, as the one man. It equally follows, that, if a small number of men have the choice of the representatives, such representatives will be chosen as will promote the interests of that small number.

by reducing, if possible, the rest of the community to be the abject and helpless slaves of their will.

In all these cases, it is obvious and indisputable, that all the benefits of the representative system are lost. The representative system is, in that case, only an operose and clumsy machinery for doing that which might as well be done without it; reducing the community to subjection, under the One, or the Few.

When we say the Few, it is seen that, in this case, it is of no importance whether we mean a few hundreds, or a few thousands, or even many thousands. The operation of the sinister interest is the same; and the fate is the same of all that part of the community over whom the power is exercised. A numerous aristocracy has never been found to be less oppressive than an aristocracy confined to a few.

The general conclusion, therefore, which is evidently established is this; that the benefits of the representative system are lost, in all cases in which the interests of the choosing body are not the same with those of the community.

It is very evident, that if the community itself were the choosing body, the interest of the community and that of the choosing body would be the same. The question is, whether that of any portion of the community, if erected into the choosing body, would remain the same?

One thing is pretty clear, that all those individuals whose interests are indisputably included in those of other individuals, may be struck off without inconvenience. In this light may be viewed all children, up to a certain age, whose interests are involved in those of their parents. In this light, also, women may be regarded, the interest of almost all of whom is involved either in that of their fathers or in that of their husbands.

Having ascertained that an interest identical with that of the whole community, is to be found in the aggregate males, of an age to be regarded as *sui juris,* who may be regarded as the natural representatives of the whole population, we have to go on, and inquire, whether this requisite quality may not be found in some less number, some aliquot part of that body.

As degrees of mental qualities are not easily ascertained, outward and visible signs must be taken to distinguish, for this purpose, one part of these males from another. Applicable signs of this description appear to be three; years, property, profession or mode of life.

According to the first of these means of distinction, a portion of the males, to any degree limited, may be taken, by prescribing an advanced period of life at which the power of voting for a representative should commence. According to the second, the elective body may be limited, by allowing a vote to those only who possess a certain amount of property or of income. According to the third, they may be limited, by allowing a vote only to such persons as belong to certain professions, or certain connections and interests. What we have to inquire is, if the interest of the number, limited and set apart, upon any of those principles, as the organ of choice for a body of representatives, will be the same with the interest of the community?

With respect to the first principle of selection, that of age, it would appear that a considerable latitude may be taken without inconvenience. Suppose the age of forty were prescribed, as that at which the right of suffrage should commence; scarcely any laws could be made for the benefit of all the men of forty which would not be laws for the benefit of all the rest of the community.

The great principle of security here is, that the men of forty have a deep interest in the welfare of the younger men; for otherwise it might be objected, with perfect truth, that, if decisive power were placed in the hands of men of forty years of age, they would have an interest, just as any other detached portion of the community, in pursuing that career which we have already described, for reducing the rest of the community to the state of abject slaves. But the great majority of old men have sons, whose interest they regard as an essential part of their own. This is a law of human nature. There is, therefore, no great danger that, in such an arrangement as this, the interests of the young would be greatly sacrificed to those of the old.

We come next to the inquiry, whether the interest of a body of electors, constituted by the possession of a certain amount of property or income, would be the same with the interest of the community?

It will not be disputed, that, if the qualification were raised so high that only a few hundreds possessed it, the case would be exactly the same with that of the consignment of the electoral suffrage to an aristocracy. This we have already considered, and have seen that it differs in form rather than substance from a simple aristocracy. We have likewise seen, that it alters not the case in regard to the community, whether the aristocracy be some hundreds or many thousands. One thing is, therefore, completely ascertained, that a pecuniary qualification, unless it were very low, would only create an aristocratical government, and produce all the evils which we have shown to belong to that organ of misrule.

This question, however, deserves to be a little more minutely considered. Let us next take the opposite extreme. Let us suppose that the qualification is very low, so low as to include the great majority of the people. It would not be easy for the people who have very little property, to separate their interests from those of the people who have none. It is not the interest of those who have little property to give undue advantages to the possession of property, which those who have the great portions of it would turn against themselves.

It may, therefore, be said, that there would be no evil in a low qualification. It can hardly be said, however, on the other hand, that there would be any good; for if the whole mass of the people who have some property would make a good choice, it will hardly be pretended that, added to them, the comparatively small number of those who have none, and whose minds are naturally and almost necessarily governed by the minds of those who have, would be able to make the choice a bad one.

We have ascertained, therefore two points. We have ascertained that a very low qualification is of no use, as affording no security for a good choice beyond that which would exist if no pecuniary qualification was required. We have likewise ascertained, that a qualification so high as to constitute an aristocracy of wealth, though it were a very numerous one, would leave the community without protection, and exposed to all the evils of unbridled power. The only question, therefore, is, whether, between these extremes, there is any qualification which would remove the right of suffrage from the people of small, or of no property, and yet constitute an elective body, the interest of which would be identical with that of the community?

It is not easy to find any satisfactory principle to guide us in our researches, and to tell us where we should fix. The qualification must either be such as to embrace the majority of the population, or something less than the majority. Suppose, in the first place, that it embraces the majority, the question is, whether the majority would have an interest in oppressing those who, upon this supposition, would be deprived of political power? If we reduce the calculation to its elements, we shall see that the interest which they would have, of this deplorable kind, though it would be something, would not be very great. Each man of the majority, if the majority were constituted the governing body, would have something less than the benefit of oppressing a single man. If the majority were twice as great as the minority, each man of the majority would only have one-half the benefit of oppressing a single man. In that case, the benefits of good government, accruing to all, might be expected to overbalance to the several members of such an elective body the benefits of misrule peculiar to themselves. Good government, would, therefore, have a tolerable security. Suppose, in the second place, that the qualification did not admit a body of electors so large as the majority; in that case, taking again the calculation in its elements, we shall see that each man would have a benefit equal to that derived from the oppression of more than one man; and that, in proportion as the elective body constituted a smaller and smaller minority, the benefit of misrule to the elective body would be increased, and bad government would be insured.

It seems hardly necessary to carry the analysis of the pecuniary qualification, as the principle for choosing an elective body, any farther.

We have only remaining the third plan for constituting an elective body. According to the scheme in question, the best elective body is that which consists of certain classes, professions, or fraternities. The notion is, that when these fraternities or bodies are represented, the community itself is represented. The way in which, according to the patrons of this theory, the effect is brought about, is this. Though it is perfectly true, that each of these fraternities would profit by misrule, and have the strongest interest in promoting it; yet, if three or four such fraternities are appointed to act in conjunction, they will not profit by misrule, and will have an interest in nothing but good government.

This theory of representation we shall not attempt to trace farther back than the year 1793. In the debate on the motion of Mr. (now Earl) Grey, for a reform in the system of representation, on the 6th of May, of that year, Mr. Jenkinson, the present Earl of Liverpool, brought forward this theory of representation, and urged it in opposition to all idea of reform in the British House of Commons, in terms as clear and distinct as those in which it has recently been clothed by leading men on both sides of that House. We shall transcribe the passage from the speech of Mr. Jenkinson, omitting, for the sake of abbreviation, all those expressions which are unnecessary for conveying a knowledge of the plan, and of the reasons upon which it was founded.

"Supposing it agreed," he said, "that the House of Commons is meant to be a legislative body, representing all descriptions of men in the country, he supposed every person would agree, that the landed interest ought to have the preponderant weight. The landed interest was, in fact, the *stamina* of the country. In the second place, in a commerical country like this, the manufacturing and commercial interest ought to have a considerable weight, secondary to the landed interest, but secondary to the landed interest only. But was this all that was necessary? There were other descriptions of people, which, to distinguish them from those already mentioned, he should style professional people, and whom he considered as absolutely necessary to the composition of a House of Commons. By professional people, he meant those members of the House of Commons who wished to raise themselves to the great offices of the state; those that were in the army, those that were in the navy, those that were in the law." He then, as a reason for desiring to have those whom he calls "professional people" in the composition of the House of Commons, gives it as a fact, that country gentlemen and merchants seldom desire, and seldom have motives for desiring, to be ministers and other great officers of state. These ministers and officers, however, ought to be made out of the House of Commons. Therefore, you ought to have "professional people" of whom to make them. Nor was this all. "There was another reason why these persons were absolutely necessary. We were constantly in the habit of discussing in that House all the important concerns of the State. It was necessary, therefore, that there should be persons in the practice of debating such questions." "There was a third reason, which, to his mind, was stronger than all the rest. Suppose that in that House there were only country gentlemen, they would not then be the representatives of the nation, but of the landholders. Suppose there were in that House only commercial persons, they would not be the representatives of the nation, but of the commercial interest of the nation. Suppose the landed and commercial interest could both find their way into the House. The landed interest would be able, if it had nothing but the commercial interest to combat with, to prevent that interest from having its due weight in the constitution. All descriptions of persons in the country would thus, in fact, be at the mercy of the landholders." He adds, "the professional persons are, then, what makes this House the representatives of the people. They have collectively no *esprit de corps,* and prevent any *esprit de corps* from affecting the proceedings of the House. Neither the landed nor commercial interest can materially affect each other, and the interests of the different professions of the country are fairly considered. The honorable gentleman (Mr. Grey), and the petition on this table, rather proposed uniformity of election. His ideas were the reverse—that the modes of election ought to be as varied as possible, because, if there was but one mode of election, there would, generally speaking, be but one description of persons in that House, and by a varied mode of election only could that variety be secured."

There is great vagueness undoubtedly in the language here employed; and abundant wavering and uncertainty in the ideas. But the ideas regarding this theory appear in the same half-formed state, in every speech and writing, in which we have seen it adduced. The mist, indeed, by which it has been kept surrounded, alone creates the difficulty; because it cannot be known precisely how anything is good or bad, till it is precisely known what it is.

According to the ideas of Lord Liverpool, the landholders ought to be represented; the merchants and manufacturers ought to be represented; the officers of the army and navy ought to be represented; and the practitioners of the law ought to be represented. Other patrons of the scheme have added, that literary men ought to be represented. And these, we believe, are almost all the fraternities, which have been named for this purpose, by any of the advocates of representation by clubs. To insure the choice of representatives of the landholders, landholders must be the choosers; to insure the choice of representatives of the merchants and manufacturers, merchants and manufacturers must be the choosers; and so with respect to the other fraternities, whether few or many. Thus it must be at least in *substance;* whatever the form, under which the visible acts may be performed. According to the scheme in question, these several fraternities are represented *directly,* the rest of the community is *not* represented directly; but it will be said by the patrons of the scheme, that it is represented *virtually,* which, in this case, answers the same purpose.

From what has already been ascertained, it will appear certain, that each of these fraternities has its sinister interest, and will be led to seek the benefit of misrule, if it is able to obtain it. This is frankly and distinctly avowed by Lord Liverpool. And by those by whom it is not avowed, it seems impossible to suppose that it should be disputed.

Let us now, then, observe the very principle upon which this theory must be supported. Three, or four, or five, or more clubs of men, have unlimited power over the whole community put into their hands. These clubs have, each, and all of them, an interest, an interest the same with that which governs all other rulers, in misgovernment, in converting the persons and properties of the rest of the community wholly to their own benefit. Having this interest, says the theory, they will not make use of it, but will use all their powers for the benefit of the community. Unless this proposition can be supported, the theory is one of the shallowest by which the pretenders to political wisdom have ever exposed themselves.

Let us resume the proposition. Three, or four, or five fraternities of men, composing a small part of the community, have all the powers of government placed in their hands. If they oppose and contend with one another, they will be unable to convert these powers to their own benefit. If they agree, they will be able to convert them wholly to their own benefit, and to do with the rest of the community just what they please. The patrons of this system of representation assume, that these fraternities will be sure to take that course which is *contrary* to their interest. The course which is *according* to their interest, appears as if it had never presented itself to their imaginations!

There being two courses which the clubs may pursue, one contrary to their interest, the other agreeable to it, the patrons of the club system must prove, they must place it beyond all doubt, that the clubs will follow the first course, and not follow the second; if not, the world will laugh at a theory which is founded upon a direct contradiction of one of the fundamental principles of human nature.

In supposing that clubs or societies of men are governed, like men individually, by their interests, we are surely following a pretty complete experience. In the idea that a certain number of those clubs can unite to pursue a common interest, there is surely nothing more extraordinary, than that as many individuals should unite to pursue a common interest. Lord Liverpool talks of an *esprit de corps* belonging to a class of land-holders, made up of the different bodies of landholders in every county in the kingdom. He talks of an *esprit de corps* in a class of merchants and manufacturers, made up of the different bodies of merchants and manufacturers in the several great towns and manufacturing districts in the kingdom. What, then, is meant by an *esprit de corps?* Nothing else but a union for the pursuit of a common interest. To the several clubs supposed in the present theory, a common interest is created by the very circumstance of their composing the representing and represented bodies. Unless the patrons of this theory can prove to us, contrary to all experience, that a common interest cannot create an *esprit de corps* in men in combinations, as well as in men individually, we are under the necessity of believing, that an *esprit de corps* would be formed in the classes separated from the rest of the community for the purposes of representation; that they would pursue their common interest; and inflict all the evils upon the rest of the community to which the pursuit of that interest would lead.

It is not included in the idea of this union for the pursuit of a common interest, that the clubs or sets of persons appropriated to the business of representation should totally harmonize. There would, no doubt, be a great mixture of agreement and disagreement among them. But there would, if experience is any guide, or if the general laws of human nature have any power, be sufficient agreement to prevent their losing sight of the common interest; in other words, for insuring all that abuse of power which is useful to the parties by whom it is exercised.

The real effect of this motley representation, therefore, would only be to create a motley aristocracy; and, of course, to insure that kind of misgovernment which it is the nature of aristocracy to produce, and to produce equally, whether it is a uniform, or a variegated aristocracy; whether an aristocracy all of landowners; or an aristocracy in part landowners, in part merchants and manufacturers, in part officers of the army and navy, and in part lawyers.

We have now, therefore, examined the principles of the representative system, and have found in it all that is necessary to constitute a security for good government. We have seen in what manner it is possible to prevent in the representatives the rise of an interest different from that of the parties who choose them, namely, by giving them little time, not dependent upon the will of those parties. We have likewise seen in what manner identity of interest may be insured between the electoral body and the rest of the community. We have, therefore, discovered the means by which identity of interest may be insured between the representatives and the community at large. We have, by consequence, obtained an organ of government which possesses that quality, without which there can be no good government.

IX

1. OBJECTION: THAT A PERFECT REPRESENTATIVE SYSTEM, IF ESTABLISHED, WOULD DESTROY THE MONARCHY, AND THE HOUSE OF LORDS

The question remains, whether this organ is competent to the performance of the whole of the business of government? And it may be certainly answered, that it is not. It may be competent to the making of laws, and it may watch over their execution: but to the executive functions themselves, operations in detail, to be performed by individuals, it is manifestly not competent. The executive functions of government consist of two parts, the administrative and the judicial. The administrative, in this country, belong to the king; and it will appear indubitable, that, if the best mode of disposing of the administrative powers of government be to place them in the hands of one great functionary, not elective, but hereditary; a king, such as ours, instead of being inconsistent with the representative system, in its highest state of perfection, would be an indispensable branch of a good government; and, even if it did not previously exist, would be established by a representative body whose interests were identified, as above, with those of the nation.

The same reasoning will apply exactly to our House of Lords. Suppose it true, that, for the perfect performance of the business of legislation, and of watching over the execution of the laws, a second deliberative assembly is necessary; and that an assembly, such as the British House of Lords, composed of the proprietors of the greatest landed estates, with dignities and privileges, is the best adapted to the end: it follows, that a body of representatives, whose interests were identified with those of the nation, would establish such an assembly, if it did not previously exist: for the best of all possible reasons; that they would have motives for, and none at all against it.

Those parties, therefore, who reason against any measures necessary for identifying the interests of the representative body with those of the nation, under the plea that such a representative body would abolish the King and the House of Lords, are wholly inconsistent with themselves. They maintain that a King and a House of Lords, such as ours, are important and necessary branches of a good government. It is demonstratively certain that a representative body, the interests of which were identified with those of the nation, would have no motive to abolish them, if they were not causes of bad government. Those persons, there-fore, who affirm that it would certainly abolish them, affirm implicitly that they are causes of bad, and not necessary to good government. This oversight of theirs is truly surprising.

The whole of this chain of deduction is dependent, as we stated at the beginning, upon the principle that the acts of men will be conform-able to their interests. Upon this principle, we conceive that the chain is complete and irrefragable. The principle, also, appears to stand upon a strong foundation. It is indisputable that the acts of men follow their will; that their will follows their desires; and that their desires are gen-erated by their apprehensions of good or evil; in other words, by their interests.

X

OBJECTION: THAT THE PEOPLE ARE NOT CAPABLE OF ACTING AGREEABLY TO THEIR INTEREST

THE apprehensions of the people respecting good and evil may be just or they may be erroneous. If just, their actions will be agreeable to their real interests. If erroneous, they will not be agreeable to their real inter-ests, but to a false supposition of interest.

We have seen that unless the representative body are chosen by a portion of the community the interest of which cannot be made to differ from that of the community, the interest of the community will infallibly be sacrificed to the interest of the rulers.

The whole of that party of reasoners who support aristocratical power affirm that a portion of the community, the interest of whom cannot be made to differ from that of the community, will not act according to their interest, but contrary to their interest. All their pleas are grounded upon this assumption. Because if a portion of the community whose in-terest is the same with that of the community would act agreeably to their own interest, they would act agreeably to the interest of the com-munity, and the end of government would be obtained.

If this assumption of theirs is true, the prospect of mankind is deplor-able. To the evils of misgovernment they are subject by inexorable des-tiny. If the powers of government are placed in the hands of persons whose interests are not identified with those of the community, the inter-ests of the community are wholly sacrificed to those of the rulers. If so much as a checking power is held by the community, or by any part of the community where the interests are the same as those of the commu-nity, the holders of that checking power will not, according to the assumption in question, make use of it in a way agreeable, but in a way contrary to their own interest. According to this theory, the choice is placed between the evils which will be produced by design—the design of those who have the power of oppressing the rest of the community, and an interest in doing it,—and the evils which may be produced by mistake—the mistake of those who, if they acted agreeably to their own interest, would act well.

Supposing that this theory were true, it would still be a question between these two sets of evils, whether the evils arising from the design of those who have motives to employ the powers of government for the purpose of reducing the community to the state of abject slaves of their will, or the evils arising from the misconduct of those who never produce evil but when they mistake their own interest, are the greatest evils.

Upon the most general and summary view of this question it appears that the proper answer cannot be doubtful. They who have a fixed, invariable interest in acting ill, will act ill invariably. They who act ill from mistake, will often act well—sometimes even by accident, and in every case in which they are enabled to understand their interest, by design.

There is another and still more important ground of preference. The evils which are the produce of interest and power united, the evils on the one side, are altogether incurable: the effects are certain while that conjunction which is the cause of them remains. The evils which arise from mistake are not incurable; for if the parties who act contrary to their interest had a proper knowledge of that interest, they would act well. What is necessary, then, is knowledge. Knowledge, on the part of those whose interests are the same as those of the community, would be an adequate remedy. But knowledge is a thing which is capable of being increased; and the more it is increased the more the evils on this side of the case would be reduced.

Supposing, then, the theory of will opposed to interest to be correct: the practical conclusion would be, as there is something of a remedy to the evils arising from this source, none whatever to the evils arising from the conjunction of power and sinister interest, to adopt the side which has the remedy, and to do whatever is necessary for obtaining the remedy in its greatest possible strength, and for applying it with the greatest possible efficacy.

It is no longer deniable that a high degree of knowledge is capable of being conveyed to such a portion of the community as would have interests the same with those of the community. This being the only resource for good government, those who say that it is not yet attained stand in this dilemma: either they do not desire good government, which is the case with all those who derive advantage from bad; or they will be seen employing their utmost exertions to increase the quantity of knowledge in the body of the community.

The practical conclusion, then, is actually the same, whether we embrace or reject the assumption that the community are little capable of acting according to their own interest. That assumption, however, deserves to be considered. And it would need a more minute consideration than the space to which we are confined will enable us to bestow upon it.

One caution, first of all, we should take along with us, and it is this: that all those persons who hold the powers of government without having an identity of interests with the community, and all those persons who share in the profits which are made by the abuse of those powers, and all those persons whom the example and representations of the two first classes influence, will be sure to represent the community, or a part having an identity of interest with the community, as incapable in the highest degree of acting according to their own interest; it being clear that they who have not an identity of interest with the community ought to hold the power of government no longer, if those who have that identity of interest could be expected to act in any tolerable conformity with their interest. All representations from that quarter, therefore, of their incapability so to act, are to be received with suspicion. They come from interested parties; they come from parties who have the strongest possible interest to deceive themselves, and to endeavor to deceive others. It is impossible that the interested endeavors of all those parties should not propagate, and for a long time successfully uphold, such an opinion —to whatever degree it might be found upon accurate inquiry to be without foundation.

A parallel case may be given. It was the interest of the priesthood, when the people of Europe were all of one religion, that the laity should take their opinions exclusively from them, because in that case the laity might be rendered subservient to the will of the clergy to any possible extent; and as all opinions were to be derived professedly from the Bible, they withdrew from the laity the privilege of reading it. When the opinions which produced the Reformation and all the blessings which may be traced to it began to ferment, the privilege of the Bible was demanded. The demand was resisted by the clergy upon the very same assumption which we have now under contemplation. "The people did not understand their own interest. They would be sure to make a bad use of the Bible. They would derive from it not right opinions, but all sorts of wrong opinions."

There can be no doubt that the assumption in the religious case was borne out by still stronger appearance of evidence than it is in the political. The majority of the people may be supposed less capable of deriving correct opinions from the Bible than of judging who is the best man to act as a representative.

Experience has fully displayed the nature of the assumption in regard to religion. The power bestowed upon the people of judging for themselves, has been productive of good effects, to a degree which has totally altered the condition of human nature and exalted man to what may be called a different stage of existence. For what reason, then, is it, we are called upon to believe that if a portion of the community, having an identity of interests with the whole community, have the power of choosing representatives, they will act wholly contrary to their interests and make a bad choice?

Experience, it will be said, establishes this conclusion. We see that the people do not act according to their interests, but very often in opposition to them.

The question is between a portion of the community which if entrusted with power would have an interest in making a bad use of it, and a portion which, though entrusted with power, would not have an interest in making a bad use of it. The former are any small number whatsoever; who, by the circumstance of being entrusted with power, are constituted an aristocracy.

From the frequency, however great, with which those who compose the mass of the community act in opposition to their interests, no conclusion can in this case be drawn, without a comparison of the frequency with which those who are placed in contrast with them act in opposition to theirs. Now, it may with great confidence be affirmed that as great a proportion of those who compose the aristocratical body of any country as of those who compose the rest of the community, are distinguished for a conduct unfavorable to their interests. Prudence is a more general characteristic of the people who are without the advantages of fortune, than of the people who have been thoroughly subject to their corruptive operation. It may surely be said that if the powers of government must be entrusted to persons incapable of good conduct, they were better entrusted to incapables who have an interest in good government than to incapables who have an interest in bad.

It will be said that a conclusion ought not to be drawn from the unthinking conduct of the great majority of an aristocratical body, against the capability of such a body for acting wisely in the management of public affairs; because the body will always contain a certain proportion of wise men, and the rest will be governed by them. Nothing but this can be said with pertinency. And under certain modifications this may be said with truth. The wise and good in any class of men do, to all general purposes, govern the rest. The comparison, however, must go on. Of that body whose interests are identified with those of the community

it may also be said, that if one portion of them are unthinking there is
another portion wise; and that, in matters of state, the less wise would
be governed by the more wise, not less certainly than in that body
whose interests, if they were entrusted with power, could not be identified with those of the community.

If we compare in each of these two contrasted bodies the two descriptions of persons, we shall not find that the foolish part of the democratical body are more foolish than that of the aristocratical, nor the wise
part less wise. Though according to the opinions which fashion has propagated it may appear a little paradoxical, we shall probably find the
very reverse.

That there is not only as great a proportion of wise men in that part
of the community which is not the aristocracy as in that which is, but
that under the present state of education and the diffusion of knowledge
there is a much greater, we presume there are few persons who will be
disposed to dispute. It is to be observed that the class which is universally described as both the most wise and the most virtuous part of the
community, the middle rank, are wholly included in that part of the
community which is not the aristocratical. It is also not disputed that
in Great Britain the middle rank are numerous, and form a large proportion of the whole body of the people. Another proposition may be
stated, with a perfect confidence of the concurrence of all those men
who have attentively considered the formation of opinions in the great
body of society, or, indeed, the principles of human nature in general.
It is, that the opinions of that class of the people who are below the
middle rank are formed, and their minds directed, by that intelligent
and virtuous rank who come the most immediately in contact with them,
who are in the constant habit of intimate communication with them, to
whom they fly for advice and assistance in all their numerous difficulties,
upon whom they feel an immediate and daily dependence, in health and
in sickness, in infancy and in old age; to whom their children look up
as models for their imitation, whose opinions they hear daily repeated
and account it their honor to adopt. There can be no doubt that the
middle rank, which gives to science, to art, and to legislation itself their
most distinguished ornaments, the chief source of all that has exalted
and refined human nature, is that portion of the community of which,
if the basis of representation were ever so far extended, the opinion
would ultimately decide. Of the people beneath them a vast majority
would be sure to be guided by their advice and example.

The incidents which have been urged as exceptions to this general
rule, and even as reasons for rejecting it, may be considered as contributing to its proof. What signify the irregularities of a mob, more than
half composed, in the greater number of instances, of boys and women,

and disturbing for a few hours or days a particular town? What signifies the occasional turbulence of a manufacturing district, peculiarly unhappy from a very great deficiency of a middle rank, as there the population almost wholly consists of rich manufacturers and poor workmen— with whose minds no pains are taken by anybody, with whose afflictions there is no virtuous family of the middle rank to sympathize, whose children have no good example of such a family to see and to admire, and who are placed in the highly unfavorable situation of fluctuating between very high wages in one year and very low wages in another? It is altogether futile with regard to the foundation of good government to say that this or the other portion of the people, may at this or the other time, depart from the wisdom of the middle rank. It is enough that the great majority of the people never cease to be guided by that rank; and we may, with some confidence, challenge the adversaries of the people to produce a single instance to the contrary in the history of the world.

JOHN STUART MILL

UTILITARIANISM

ON LIBERTY

JOHN STUART MILL

JOHN STUART MILL (1806-1873), the oldest son of James Mill, received one of the most remarkable educations ever recorded. His father's intention was to train him to propagate the Benthamite gospel in the next generation. He was, from his earliest years, subjected to a rigid and intensive course of study under the guidance of his father. Greek was begun at three, mathematics at about the same time, and Latin at eight. From his third to his twelfth year he was put through, and carefully examined on, an immense quantity of reading in the classics and in history. After his twelfth year he added such subjects as logic and political economy to his studies. But it was not an education of mere cram. He was expected to think through and really master everything that was assigned to him. On the intellectual side Mill became extremely precocious. His education put him, as he later said, a quarter of a century ahead of his contemporaries.

At first Mill intended to enter the law, but this plan was abandoned; and, in 1822, he entered India House, where he eventually rose to the same high position his father had occupied. His office duties left him ample time for intellectual activities. He adopted his father's views with enthusiasm, founded a "Utilitarian Society" of brilliant younger Benthamites, wrote for newspapers and reviews on political and economic topics, and edited Bentham's *Rationale of Judicial Evidence.*

Then, in his twenty-first year, the young Benthamite thinking machine completely broke down. For several years he struggled against a deep depression of spirits. Gradually he emerged, but it was with a new sense of the narrowness and insufficiency of his father's doctrinaire beliefs.

From this time on Mill attempted to formulate a more adequate and comprehensive restatement of the utilitarian philosophy. He became the great intellectual representative of liberalism in England during the middle decades of the nineteenth century. Of his many writings the most important are the *System of Logic* (1843), the *Principles of Political Economy* (1848), *On Liberty* (1859), the *Considerations on Representative Government* (1861), *Utilitarianism* (1863), the *Examination of Sir William Hamilton's Philosophy* (1865), the *Subjection of Women* (1869), the three posthumous essays on *Nature, The Utility of Religion,* and *Theism* (1874), and his *Autobiography* (1873).

When the East India Company was abolished in 1857, Mill retired on a pension. In 1865 he was elected a member of parliament for Westminster but was defeated in the general election of 1868. His last years were spent in study and writing.

The writings reprinted herewith comprise the *Utilitarianism* and *On Liberty,* both without omissions.

UTILITARIANISM

CHAPTER I

GENERAL REMARKS

THERE are few circumstances among those which make up the present condition of human knowledge, more unlike what might have been expected, or more significant of the backward state in which speculation on the most important subjects still lingers, than the little progress which has been made in the decision of the controversy respecting the criterion of right and wrong. From the dawn of philosophy, the question concerning the *summum bonum*, or, what is the same thing, concerning the foundation of morality, has been accounted the main problem in speculative thought, has occupied the most gifted intellects, and divided them into sects and schools, carrying on a vigorous warfare against one another. And after more than two thousand years the same discussions continue, philosophers are still ranged under the same contending banners, and neither thinkers nor mankind at large seem nearer to being unanimous on the subject, than when the youth Socrates listened to the old Protagoras, and asserted (if Plato's dialogue be grounded on a real conversation) the theory of utilitarianism against the popular morality of the so-called sophist.

It is true that similar confusion and uncertainty, and in some cases similar discordance, exist respecting the first principles of all the sciences, not excepting that which is deemed the most certain of them, mathematics; without much impairing, generally indeed without impairing at all, the trustworthiness of the conclusions of those sciences. An apparent anomaly, the explanation of which is that the detailed doctrines of a science are not usually deduced from, nor depend for their evidence upon, what are called its first principles. Were it not so, there would be no science more precarious, or whose conclusions were more insufficiently made out, than algebra; which derives none of its certainty from what are commonly taught to learners as its elements, since these, as laid down by some of its most eminent teachers, are as full of fictions as English law, and of mysteries as theology. The truths which are ultimately accepted as the first principles of a science, are really the last results of metaphysical analysis, practiced on the elementary notions with which the science is conversant; and their relation to the science is not that of foundations to an edifice, but of roots to a tree, which may perform their office equally well though they be never dug down to and exposed to light. But though in science the particular truths precede the general theory, the contrary might be expected to be the case with a practical art, such as morals or legislation. All action is for the sake of some end, and rules of action, it seems natural to suppose, must take their whole character and color from the end to which they are subservient. When we engage in a pursuit, a clear and precise conception of what we are pursuing would seem to be the first thing we need, instead of the last we are to look forward to. A test of right and wrong must be the means, one would think, of ascertaining what is right or wrong, and not a consequence of having already ascertained it.

The difficulty is not avoided by having recourse to the popular theory of a natural faculty, a sense or instinct, informing us of right and wrong. For—besides that the existence of such a moral instinct is itself one of the matters in dispute—those believers in it who have any pretensions to philosophy, have been obliged to abandon the idea that it discerns what is right or wrong in the particular case in hand, as our other senses discern the sight or sound actually present. Our moral faculty, according to all those of its interpreters who are entitled to the name of thinkers, supplies us only with the general principles of moral judgments; it is a branch of our reason, not of our sensitive faculty; and must be looked to for the abstract doctrines of morality, not for perception of it in the concrete. The intuitive, no less than what may be termed the inductive, school of ethics, insists on the necessity of general laws. They both agree that the morality of an individual action is not a question of direct perception, but of the application of a law to an individual case. They recognize also, to a great extent, the same moral laws; but differ as to their evidence, and the source from which they derive their authority. According to the one opinion, the principles of morals are evident *a priori,* requiring nothing to command assent, except that the meaning of the terms be understood. According to the other doctrine, right and wrong, as well as truth and falsehood, are questions of observation and experience. But both hold equally that morality must be deduced from principles; and the intuitive school affirm as strongly as the inductive that there is a science of morals. Yet they seldom attempt to make out a list of the *a priori* principles which are to serve as the premises of the science; still more rarely do they make any effort to reduce those various principles to one first principle, or common ground of obligation. They either assume the ordinary precepts of morals as of *a priori* authority, or they lay down as the common groundwork of those maxims some generality much less obviously authoritative than the max-

ims themselves, and which has never succeeded in gaining popular acceptance. Yet to support their pretensions there ought either to be some one
fundamental principle or law, at the root of all morality, or if there be
several, there should be a determinate order of precedence among them;
and the one principal, or the rule for deciding between the various principles when they conflict, ought to be self-evident.

To inquire how far the bad effects of this deficiency have been mitigated in practice, or to what extent the moral beliefs of mankind have
been vitiated or made uncertain by the absence of any distinct recognition of an ultimate standard, would imply a complete survey and criticism of past and present ethical doctrine. It would, however, be easy
to show that whatever steadiness or consistency these moral beliefs have
attained, has been mainly due to the tacit influence of a standard not
recognized. Although the nonexistence of an acknowledged first principle has made ethics not so much a guide as a consecration of men's actual sentiments, still, as men's sentiments, both of favor and of aversion,
are greatly influenced by what they suppose to be the effects of things
upon their happiness, the principle of utility, or as Bentham latterly
called it, the greatest happiness principle, has had a large share in forming the moral doctrines even of those who most scornfully reject its authority. Nor is there any school of thought which refuses to admit that
the influence of actions on happiness is a most material and even predominant consideration in many of the details of morals, however unwilling to acknowledge it as the fundamental principle of morality, and
the source of moral obligation. I might go much further, and say that to
all those *a priori* moralists who deem it necessary to argue at all, utilitarian arguments are indispensable. It is not my present purpose to criticize these thinkers; but I cannot help referring, for illustration, to a systematic treatise by one of the most illustrious of them, the *Metaphysics
of Ethics*, by Kant. This remarkable man, whose system of thought will
long remain one of the landmarks in the history of philosophical speculation, does, in the treatise in question, lay down a universal first principle as the origin and ground of moral obligation; it is this:—"So act,
that the rule on which thou actest would admit of being adopted as a
law by all rational beings." But when he begins to deduce from this
precept any of the actual duties of morality, he fails, almost grotesquely,
to show that there would be any contradiction, any logical (not to say
physical) impossibility, in the adoption by all rational beings of the
most outrageously immoral rules of conduct. All he shows is that the
consequences of their universal adoption would be such as no one would
choose to incur.

On the present occasion, I shall, without further discussion of the
other theories, attempt to contribute something towards the understand

ing and appreciation of the *utilitarian* or *happiness* theory, and towards such proof as it is susceptible of. It is evident that this cannot be proof in the ordinary and popular meaning of the term. Questions of ultimate ends are not amenable to direct proof. Whatever can be proved to be good, must be so by being shown to be a means to something admitted to be good without proof. The medical art is proved to be good by its conducing to health; but how is it possible to prove that health is good? The art of music is good, for the reason, among others, that it produces pleasure; but what proof is it possible to give that pleasure is good? If, then, it is asserted that there is a comprehensive formula, including all things which are in themselves good, and that whatever else is good, is not so as an end, but as a mean, the formula may be accepted or rejected, but is not a subject of what is commonly understood by proof. We are not, however, to infer that its acceptance or rejection must depend on blind impulse, or arbitrary choice. There is a larger meaning of the word proof, in which this question is as amenable to it as any other of the disputed questions of philosophy. The subject is within the cognizance of the rational faculty; and neither does that faculty deal with it solely in the way of intuition. Considerations may be presented capable of determining the intellect either to give or withhold its assent to the doctrine; and this is equivalent to proof.

We shall examine presently of what nature are these considerations; in what manner they apply to the case, and what rational grounds, therefore, can be given for accepting or rejecting the utilitarian formula. But it is a preliminary condition of rational acceptance or rejection, that the formula should be correctly understood. I believe that the very imperfect notion ordinarily formed of its meaning is the chief obstacle which impedes its reception; and that could it be cleared, even from only the grosser misconceptions, the question would be greatly simplified, and a large proportion of its difficulties removed. Before, therefore, I attempt to enter into the philosophical grounds which can be given for assenting to the utilitarian standard, I shall offer some illustrations of the doctrine itself; with the view of showing more clearly what it is, distinguishing it from what it is not, and disposing of such of the practical objections to it as either originate in, or are closely connected with, mistaken interpretations of its meaning. Having thus prepared the ground, I shall afterwards endeavor to throw such light as I can upon the question, considered as one of philosophical theory.

CHAPTER II

WHAT UTILITARIANISM IS

A PASSING remark is all that needs be given to the ignorant blunder of supposing that those who stand up for utility as the test of right and wrong, use the term in that restricted and merely colloquial sense in which utility is opposed to pleasure. An apology is due to the philosophical opponents of utilitarianism, for even the momentary appearance of confounding them with anyone capable of so absurd a misconception; which is the more extraordinary, inasmuch as the contrary accusation, of referring everything to pleasure, and that too in its grossest form, is another of the common charges against utilitarianism: and, as has been pointedly remarked by an able writer, the same sort of persons, and often the very same persons, denounce the theory "as impracticably dry when the word utility precedes the word pleasure, and as too practicably voluptuous when the word pleasure precedes the word utility." Those who know anything about the matter are aware that every writer, from Epicurus to Bentham, who maintained the theory of utility, meant by it, not something to be contradistinguished from pleasure, but pleasure itself, together with exemption from pain; and instead of opposing the useful to the agreeable or the ornamental, have always declared that the useful means these, among other things. Yet the common herd, including the herd of writers, not only in newspapers, and periodicals, but in books of weight and pretension, are perpetually falling into this shallow mistake. Having caught up the word 'utilitarian,' while knowing nothing whatever about it but its sound, they habitually express by it the rejection, or the neglect, of pleasure in some of its forms: of beauty, of ornament, or of amusement. Nor is the term thus ignorantly misapplied solely in disparagement, but occasionally in compliment; as though it implied superiority to frivolity and the mere pleasures of the moment. And this perverted use is the only one in which the word is popularly known, and the one from which the new generation are acquiring their sole notion of its meaning. Those who introduced the word, but who had for many years discontinued it as a distinctive appellation, may well feel themselves called upon to resume it, if by doing so they can hope to contribute anything towards rescuing it from this utter degradation.[1]

[1] The author of this essay has reason for believing himself to be the first person who brought the word 'utilitarian' into use. He did not invent it, but adopted it from a passing expression in Mr. Galt's *Annals of the Parish*. After using it as a designation for several years, he and others abandoned it from a growing dislike to anything resembling a badge or watchword of sectarian distinction. But as a name for one single opinion, not a set of opinions—to denote the recognition of utility as

The creed which accepts as the foundation of morals *utility,* or the *greatest happiness principle,* holds that actions are right in proportion as they tend to promote happiness, wrong as they tend to produce the reverse of happiness. By 'happiness' is intended pleasure, and the absence of pain; by 'unhappiness,' pain, and the privation of pleasure. To give a clear view of the moral standard set up by the theory, much more requires to be said; in particular, what things it includes in the ideas of pain and pleasure; and to what extent this is left an open question. But these supplementary explanations do not affect the theory of life on which this theory of morality is grounded—namely, that pleasure, and freedom from pain, are the only things desirable as ends; and that all desirable things (which are as numerous in the utilitarian as in any other scheme) are desirable either for the pleasure inherent in themselves, or as means to the promotion of pleasure and the prevention of pain.

Now such a theory of life excites in many minds, and among them in some of the most estimable in feeling and purpose, inveterate dislike. To suppose that life has (as they express it) no higher end than pleasure—no better and nobler object of desire and pursuit—they designate as utterly mean and groveling; as a doctrine worthy only of swine, to whom the followers of Epicurus were, at a very early period, contemptuously likened; and modern holders of the doctrine are occasionally made the subject of equally polite comparisons by its German, French, and English assailants.

When thus attacked, the Epicureans have always answered that it is not they but their accusers who represent human nature in a degrading light; since the accusation supposes human beings to be capable of no pleasures except those of which swine are capable. If this supposition were true, the charge could not be gainsaid, but would then be no longer an imputation; for if the sources of pleasure were precisely the same to human beings and to swine, the rule of life which is good enough for the one would be good enough for the other. The comparison of the Epicurean life to that of beasts is felt as degrading, precisely because a beast's pleasures do not satisfy a human being's conceptions of happiness. Human beings have faculties more elevated than the animal appetites, and when once made conscious of them, do not regard anything as happiness which does not include their gratification. I do not, indeed, consider the Epicureans to have been by any means faultless in drawing out their scheme of consequences from the utilitarian principle. To do this in any sufficient manner, many Stoic, as well as Christian elements require to

a standard, not any particular way of applying it—the term supplies a want in the language, and offers, in many cases, a convenient mode of avoiding tiresome circumlocution.

be included. But there is no known Epicurean theory of life which does not assign to the pleasures of the intellect, of the feelings and imagination, and of the moral sentiments, a much higher value as pleasures than to those of mere sensation. It must be admitted, however, that utilitarian writers in general have placed the superiority of mental over bodily pleasures chiefly in the greater permanency, safety, uncostliness, etc., of the former—that is, in their circumstantial advantages rather than in their intrinsic nature. And on all these points utilitarians have fully proved their case; but they might have taken the other, and, as it may be called, higher ground, with entire consistency. It is quite compatible with the principle of utility to recognize the fact, that some *kinds* of pleasure are more desirable and more valuable than others. It would be absurd that while, in estimating all other things, quality is considered as well as quantity, the estimation of pleasures should be supposed to depend on quantity alone.

If I am asked what I mean by difference of quality in pleasures, or what makes one pleasure more valuable than another merely as a pleasure, except its being greater in amount, there is but one possible answer. Of two pleasures, if there be one to which all or almost all who have experience of both give a decided preference, irrespective of any feeling of moral obligation to prefer it, that is the more desirable pleasure. If one of the two is, by those who are competently acquainted with both, placed so far above the other that they prefer it, even though knowing it to be attended with a greater amount of discontent, and would not resign it for any quantity of the other pleasure which their nature is capable of, we are justified in ascribing to the preferred enjoyment a superiority in quality, so far outweighing quantity as to render it, in comparison, of small account.

Now it is an unquestionable fact that those who are equally acquainted with, and equally capable of appreciating and enjoying, both, do give a most marked preference to the manner of existence which employs their higher faculties. Few human creatures would consent to be changed into any of the lower animals, for a promise of the fullest allowance of a beast's pleasures; no intelligent human being would consent to be a fool, no instructed person would be an ignoramus, no person of feeling and conscience would be selfish and base, even though they should be persuaded that the fool, the dunce, or the rascal is better satisfied with his lot than they are with theirs. They would not resign what they possess more than he for the most complete satisfaction of all the desires which they have in common with him. If they ever fancy they would, it is only in cases of unhappiness so extreme, that to escape from it they would exchange their lot for almost any other, however undesirable in their own eyes. A being of higher faculties requires more to make him happy, is capable probably of more acute suffering, and certainly accessible to it at more points, than one of an inferior type; but in spite of these liabilities, he can never really wish to sink into what he feels to be a lower grade of existence. We may give what explanation we please of this unwillingness: we may attribute it to pride, a name which is given indiscriminately to some of the most and to some of the least estimable feelings of which mankind are capable; we may refer it to the love of liberty and personal independence, an appeal to which was with the Stoics one of the most effective means for the inculcation of it; to the love of power, or to the love of excitement, both of which do really enter into and contribute to it: but its most appropriate appellation is a sense of dignity, which all human beings possess in one form or other, and in some, though by no means in exact, proportion to their higher faculties, and which is so essential a part of the happiness of those in whom it is strong, that nothing which conflicts with it could be, otherwise than momentarily, an object of desire to them. Whoever supposes that this preference takes place at a sacrifice of happiness—that the superior being, in anything like equal circumstances, is not happier than the inferior—confounds the two very different ideas, of *happiness* and *content*. It is indisputable that the being whose capacities of enjoyment are low, has the greatest chance of having them fully satisfied; and a highly endowed being will always feel that any happiness which he can look for, as the world is constituted, is imperfect. But he can learn to bear its imperfections, if they are at all bearable; and they will not make him envy the being who is indeed unconscious of the imperfections, but only because he feels not at all the good which those imperfections qualify. It is better to be a human being dissatisfied than a pig satisfied; better to be Socrates dissatisfied than a fool satisfied. And if the fool, or the pig, are of a different opinion, it is because they only know their own side of the question. The other party to the comparison knows both sides.

It may be objected that many who are capable of the higher pleasures, occasionally, under the influence of temptation, postpone them to the lower. But this is quite compatible with a full appreciation of the intrinsic superiority of the higher. Men often, from infirmity of character, make their election for the nearer good, though they know it to be the less valuable; and this no less when the choice is between two bodily pleasures, than when it is between bodily and mental. They pursue sensual indulgences to the injury of health, though perfectly aware that health is the greater good. It may be further objected that many who begin with youthful enthusiasm for everything noble, as they advance in years sink into indolence and selfishness. But I do not believe that those who undergo this very common change, voluntarily choose the lower description of pleasures in preference to the higher. I believe that before they devote themselves exclusively to the one, they have already become incapable of the other. Capacity for the nobler feelings is in most natures a very tender plant, easily killed, not only by hostile influences. but by mere want of sustenance; and in the majority of young persons it speedily dies away if the occupations to which their position in life has devoted them, and the society into which it has thrown them, are not favorable to keeping that higher capacity in exercise. Men lose their high aspirations as they lose their intellectual tastes, because they have not time or opportunity for indulging them; and they addict themselves to inferior pleasures not because they deliberately prefer them, but because they are either the only ones to which they have access or the only ones which they are any longer capable of enjoying. It may be questioned whether anyone who has remained equally susceptible to both classes of pleasures, ever knowingly and calmly preferred the lower; though many, in all ages, have broken down in an ineffectual attempt to combine both.

From this verdict of the only competent judges I apprehend there can be no appeal. On a question which is the best worth having of two pleasures, or which of two modes of existence is the most grateful to the feelings, apart from its moral attributes and from its consequences, the judgment of those who are qualified by knowledge of both, or, if they differ, that of the majority among them, must be admitted as final. And there need be the less hesitation to accept this judgment respecting the quality of pleasures, since there is no other tribunal to be referred to even on the question of quantity. What means are there of determining which is the acutest of two pains, or the intensest of two pleasurable sensations, except the general suffrage of those who are familiar with both? Neither pains nor pleasures are homogeneous, and pain is always heterogeneous with pleasure. What is there to decide whether a particular pleasure is worth purchasing at the cost of a particular pain, except the feelings and judgment of the experienced? When, therefore, those feelings and judgment declare the pleasures derived from the higher faculties to be preferable *in kind*, apart from the question of intensity, to those of which the animal nature, disjoined from the higher faculties, is suspectible, they are entitled on this subject to the same regard.

I have dwelt on this point, as being a necessary part of a perfectly just conception of utility, or happiness, considered as the directive rule of human conduct. But it is by no means an indispensable condition to the acceptance of the utilitarian standard; for that standard is not the agent's own greatest happiness, but the greatest amount of happiness altogether; and if it may possibly be doubted whether a noble character is always the happier for its nobleness, there can be no doubt that it makes other people happier, and that the world in general is immensely a gainer by it. Utilitarianism, therefore, could only attain its end by the general cultivation of nobleness of character, even if each individual were only benefited by the nobleness of others, and his own, so far as happiness is concerned, were a sheer deduction from the benefit. But the bare enunciation of such an absurdity as this last renders refutation superfluous.

According to the 'greatest happiness principle,' as above explained, the ultimate end, with reference to and for the sake of which all other things are desirable (whether we are considering our own good or that of other people), is an existence exempt as far as possible from pain, and as rich as possible in enjoyments, both in point of quantity and quality; the test of quality, and the rule for measuring it against quantity, being the preference felt by those who in their opportunities of experience, to which must be added their habits of self-consciousness and self-observation, are best furnished with the means of comparison. This, being, according to the utilitarian opinion, the end of human action, is necessarily also the standard of morality; which may accordingly be defined, the rules and precepts for human conduct, by the observance of which an existence such as has been described might be, to the greatest extent possible, secured to all mankind; and not to them only, but, so far as the nature of things admits, to the whole sentient creation.

Against this doctrine, however, arises another class of objectors, who say that happiness, in any form, cannot be the rational purpose of human life and action; because, in the first place, it is unattainable: and they contemptuously ask, what right hast thou to be happy?—a question which Mr. Carlyle clenches by the addition, What right, a short time ago, hadst thou even *to be?* Next, they say that men can do *without* happiness; that all noble human beings have felt this, and could not have become noble but by learning the lesson of *Entsagen,* or renunciation; which lesson, thoroughly learnt and submitted to, they affirm to be the beginning and necessary condition of all virtue.

The first of these objections would go to the root of the matter were it well founded; for if no happiness is to be had at all by human beings, the attainment of it cannot be the end of morality, or of any rational conduct. Though, even in that case, something might still be said for the utilitarian theory; since utility includes not solely the pursuit of happiness, but the prevention or mitigation of unhappiness; and if the former aim be chimerical, there will be all the greater scope and more imperative need for the latter, so long at least as mankind think fit to live, and do not take refuge in the simultaneous act of suicide recommended under certain conditions by Novalis. When, however, it is thus positively asserted to be impossible that human life should be happy, the assertion, if not something like a verbal quibble, is at least an exaggeration. If by happiness be meant a continuity of highly pleasurable excitement, it is evident enough that this is impossible. A state of exalted pleasure lasts only moments, or in some cases, and with some intermissions, hours or days, and is the occasional brilliant flash of enjoyment, not its permanent and steady flame. Of this the philosophers who have taught that happiness is the end of life were as fully aware as those who taunt them. The happiness which they meant was not a life of rapture; but moments of such, in an existence made up of few and transitory pains, many and various pleasures, with a decided predominance of the active over the passive, and having as the foundation of the whole, not to expect more from life than it is capable of bestowing. A life thus composed, to those who have been fortunate enough to obtain it, has always appeared worthy of the name of happiness. And such an existence is even now the lot of many, during some considerable portion of their lives. The present wretched education, and wretched social arrangements, are the only real hindrance to its being attainable by almost all.

The objectors perhaps may doubt whether human beings, if taught to consider happiness as the end of life, would be satisfied with such a moderate share of it. But great numbers of mankind have been satisfied with much less. The main constituents of a satisfied life appear to be two, either of which by itself is often found sufficient for the purpose: tranquillity and excitement. With much tranquillity, many find that they can be content with very little pleasure; with much excitement, many can reconcile themselves to a considerable quantity of pain. There is assuredly no inherent impossibility in enabling even the mass of mankind to unite both; since the two are so far from being incompatible that they are in natural alliance, the prolongation of either being a preparation for, and exciting a wish for, the other. It is only those in whom indolence amounts to a vice, that do not desire excitement after an interval of repose; it is only those in whom the need of excitement is a disease, that feel the tranquillity which follows excitement dull and insipid, instead of pleasurable in direct proportion to the excitement which preceded it. When people who are tolerably fortunate in their outward lot do not find in life sufficient enjoyment to make it valuable to them, the cause generally is, caring for nobody but themselves. To those who have neither public nor private affections, the excitements of life are much curtailed, and in any case dwindle in value as the time approaches when all selfish interests must be terminated by death; while those who leave after them objects of personal affection, and especially those who have also cultivated a fellow-feeling with the collective interests of mankind, retain as lively an interest in life on the eve of death as in the vigor of youth and health. Next to selfishness, the principal cause which makes life unsatisfactory is want of mental cultivation. A cultivated mind (I do not mean that of a philosopher, but any mind to which the fountains of knowledge have been opened, and which has been taught, in any tolerable degree, to exercise its faculties) finds sources of inexhaustible interest in all that surrounds it; in the objects of nature, the achievements of art, the imaginations of poetry, the incidents of history, the ways of mankind, past and present, and their prospects in the future. It is possible, indeed, to become indifferent to all this, and that too without having exhausted a thousandth part of it; but only when one has had from the beginning no moral or human interest in these things, and has sought in them only the gratification of curiosity.

Now there is absolutely no reason in the nature of things why an amount of mental culture sufficient to give an intelligent interest in these objects of contemplation, should not be the inheritance of everyone born in a civilized country. As little is there an inherent necessity that any human being should be a selfish egotist, devoid of every feeling or care but those which center in his own miserable individuality. Something far superior to this is sufficiently common even now, to give ample earnest of what the human species may be made. Genuine private affections, and a sincere interest in the public good, are possible, though in unequal degrees, to every rightly brought up human being. In a world in which there is so much to interest, so much to enjoy, and so much also to correct and improve, everyone who has this moderate amount of moral and intellectual requisites is capable of an existence which may be called enviable; and unless such a person, through bad laws, or subjection to the will of others, is denied the liberty to use the sources of happiness within his reach, he will not fail to find this enviable existence, if he escape the positive evils of life, the great sources of physical and mental suffering—such as indigence, disease, and the unkindness, worthlessness, or premature loss of objects of affection. The main stress of the problem lies, therefore, in the contest with these calamities, from which it is a rare good fortune entirely to escape; which, as things now are, cannot be obviated, and often cannot be in any material degree mitigated. Yet no one whose opinion deserves a moment's consideration can doubt that most of the great positive evils of the world are in themselves removable, and will, if human affairs continue to improve, be in the end reduced within narrow limits. Poverty, in any sense implying suffering, may be completely extinguished by the wisdom of society, combined with the good sense and providence of individuals. Even that most intractable of enemies, disease, may be indefinitely reduced in dimensions by good physical and moral education, and proper control of noxious influences; while the progress of science holds out a promise for the future of still more direct conquests over this detestable foe. And every advance in that direction relieves us from some, not only of the chances which cut short our own lives, but, what concerns us still more, which deprive us of those in whom our happiness is wrapt up. As for vicissitudes of fortune, and other disappointments connected with worldly circumstances, these are principally the effect either of gross imprudence, of ill-regulated desires, or of bad or imperfect social institutions. All the grand sources, in short, of human suffering are in a great degree, many of them almost entirely, conquerable by human care and effort; and though their removal is grievously slow—though a long succession of generations will perish in the breach before the conquest is completed, and this world becomes all that, if will and knowledge were not wanting, it might easily be made—yet every mind sufficiently intelligent and generous to bear a part, however small and unconspicuous, in the endeavor, will draw a noble enjoyment from the contest itself, which he would not for any bribe in the form of selfish indulgence consent to be without.

And this leads to the true estimation of what is said by the objectors concerning the possibility, and the obligation, of learning to do without happiness. Unquestionably it is possible to do without happiness; it is done involuntarily by nineteen-twentieths of mankind, even in those parts of our present world which are least deep in barbarism; and it often has to be done voluntarily by the hero or the martyr, for the sake of something which he prizes more than his individual happiness. But this something, what is it, unless the happiness of others, or some of the requisites of happiness? It is noble to be capable of resigning entirely one's own portion of happiness, or chances of it: but, after all, this self-sacrifice must be for some end; it is not its own end; and if we are told that its end is not happiness, but virtue, which is better than happiness, I ask, would the sacrifice be made if the hero or martyr did not believe that it would earn for others immunity from similar sacrifices? Would it be made if he thought that his renunciation of happiness for himself would produce no fruit for any of his fellow creatures, but to make their lot like his, and place them also in the condition of persons who have renounced happiness? All honor to those who can abnegate for themselves the personal enjoyment of life, when by such renunciation they contribute worthily to increase the amount of happiness in the world; but he who does it, or professes to do it, for any other purpose, is no more deserving of admiration from the ascetic mounted on his pillar. He may be an inspiriting proof of what men *can* do, but assuredly not an example of what they *should*.

Though it is only in a very imperfect state of the world's arrangements that anyone can best serve the happiness of others by the absolute sacrifice of his own, yet so long as the world is in that imperfect state, I fully acknowledge that the readiness to make such a sacrifice is the highest virtue which can be found in man. I will add that in this condition of the world, paradoxical as the assertion may be, the conscious ability to do without happiness gives the best prospect of realizing such happiness as is attainable. For nothing except that consciousness can raise a person above the chances of life, by making him feel that, let fate and fortune do their worst, they have not power to subdue him; which, once felt, frees him from excess of anxiety concerning the evils of life, and enables him, like many a Stoic in the worst times of the Roman Empire, to cultivate in tranquillity the sources of satisfaction accessible to him, without concerning himself about the uncertainty of their duration, any more than about their inevitable end.

Meanwhile, let utilitarians never cease to claim the morality of self-devotion as a possession which belongs by as good a right to them, as either to the Stoic or to the Transcendentalist. The utilitarian morality does recognize in human beings the power of sacrificing their own greatest good for the good of others. It only refuses to admit that the sacrifice is itself a good. A sacrifice which does not increase, or tend to increase, the sum total of happiness, it considers as wasted. The only self-renunciation which it applauds, is devotion to the happiness, or to some of the means of happiness, of others; either of mankind collectively, or of individuals within the limits imposed by the collective interests of mankind.

I must again repeat, what the assailants of utilitarianism seldom have the justice to acknowledge, that the happiness which forms the utilitarian standard of what is right in conduct, is not the agent's own happiness, but that of all concerned. As between his own happiness and that of others, utilitarianism requires him to be as strictly impartial as a disinterested and benevolent spectator. In the golden rule of Jesus of Nazareth, we read the complete spirit of the ethics of utility. To do as you would be done by, and to love your neighbor as yourself, constitute the ideal perfection of utilitarian morality. As the means of making the nearest approach to this ideal, utility would enjoin, first, that laws and social arrangements should place the happiness, or (as speaking practically it may be called) the interest, of every individual, as nearly as possible in harmony with the interest of the whole; and secondly, that education and opinion, which have so vast a power over human character, should so use that power as to establish in the mind of every individual an indissoluble association between his own happiness and the good of the whole—especially between his own happiness and the practice of such modes of conduct, negative and positive, as regard for the universal happiness prescribes; so that not only he may be unable to conceive the possibility of happiness to himself, consistently with conduct opposed to the general good, but also that a direct impulse to promote the general good may be in every individual one of the habitual motives of action, and the sentiments connected therewith may fill a large and prominent place in every human being's sentient existence. If the impugners of the utilitarian morality represented it to their own minds in this its true character, I know not what recommendation possessed by any other morality they could possibly affirm to be wanting to it; what more beautiful or more exalted developments of human nature any other ethical system can be supposed to foster, or what springs of action, not accessible to the utilitarian, such systems rely on for giving effect to their mandates.

The objectors to utilitarianism cannot always be charged with representing it in a discreditable light. On the contrary, those among them who entertain anything like a just idea of its disinterested character sometimes find fault with its standard as being too high for humanity. They say it is exacting too much to require that people shall always act from the inducement of promoting the general interests of society. But this is to mistake the very meaning of a standard of morals, and confound the rule of action with the motive of it. It is the business of ethics to tell us what are our duties, or by what test we may know them; but no system of ethics requires that the sole motive of all we do shall be a feeling of duty; on the contrary, ninety-nine hundredths of all our actions are done from other motives, and rightly so done, if the rule of duty does not condemn them. It is the more unjust to utilitarianism that this particular misapprehension should be made a ground of objection to it, inasmuch as utilitarian moralists have gone beyond almost all others in affirming that the motive has nothing to do with the morality of the action, though much with the worth of the agent. He who saves a fellow creature from drowning does what is morally right, whether his motive be duty, or the hope of being paid for his trouble; he who betrays the friend that trusts him, is guilty of a crime, even if his object be to serve another friend to whom he is under greater obligations. But to speak only of actions done from the motive of duty, and in direct obedience to principle: it is a misapprehension of the utilitarian mode of thought, to conceive it as implying that people should fix their minds upon so wide a generality as the world, or society at large. The great majority of good actions are intended not for the benefit of the world, but for that of individuals, of which the good of the world is made up; and the thoughts of the most virtuous man need not on these occasions travel beyond the particular persons concerned, except so far as is necessary to assure himself that in benefiting them he is not violating the rights, that is, the legitimate and authorized expectations, of anyone else. The multiplication of happiness is, according to the utilitarian ethics, the object of virtue: the occasions on which any person (except one in a thousand) has it in his power to do this on an extended scale, in other words to be a public benefactor, are but exceptional, and on these occasions alone is he called on to consider public utility; in every other case, private utility, the interest or happiness of some few persons, is all he has to attend to. Those alone the influence of whose actions extends to society in general, need concern themselves habitually about so large an object. In the case of abstinences indeed—of things which people forbear to do from moral considerations, though the consequences in the particular case might be beneficial—it would be unworthy of an intelligent agent not to be consciously aware that the action is of a class which, if practiced generally, would be generally injurious, and that this is the ground of the obligation to abstain from it. The amount of regard for the public interest implied in this recognition is no greater than is demanded by every system of morals, for they all enjoin to abstain from whatever is manifestly pernicious to society.

The same considerations dispose of another reproach against the doctrine of utility, founded on a still grosser misconception of the purpose of a standard of morality, and of the very meaning of the words right and wrong. It is often affirmed that utilitarianism renders men cold and unsympathizing; that it chills their moral feelings towards individuals; that it makes them regard only the dry and hard consideration of the consequences of actions, not taking into their moral estimate the qualities from which those actions emanate. If the assertion means that they do not allow their judgment respecting the rightness or wrongness of an action to be influenced by their opinion of the qualities of the person who does it, this is a complaint not against utilitarianism, but against having any stardard of morality at all; for certainly no known ethical standard decides an action to be good or bad because it is done by a good or a bad man, still less because done by an amiable, a brave, or a benevolent man, or the contrary. These considerations are relevant, not to the estimation of actions, but of persons; and there is nothing in the utilitarian theory inconsistent with the fact that there are other things which interest us in persons besides the rightness and wrongness of their actions. The Stoics, indeed, with the paradoxical misuse of language which was part of their system, and by which they strove to raise themselves above all concern about anything but virtue, were fond of saying that he who has that has everything; that he, and only he, is rich, is beautiful, is a king. But no claim of this description is made for the virtuous man by the utilitarian doctrine. Utilitarians are quite aware that there are other desirable possessions and qualities besides virtue, and are perfectly willing to allow to all of them their full worth. They are also aware that a right action does not necessarily indicate a virtuous character, and that actions which are blamable, often proceed from qualities entitled to praise. When this is apparent in any particular case, it modifies their estimation, not certainly of the act, but of the agent. I grant that they are, notwithstanding, of opinion that in the long run the best proof of a good character is good actions; and resolutely refuse to consider any mental disposition as good, of which the predominant tendency is to produce bad conduct. This mades them unpopular with many people; but it is an unpopularity which they must share with everyone who regards the distinction between right and wrong in a serious light; and the reproach is not one which a conscientious utilitarian need be anxious to repel.

If no more be meant by the objection than that many utilitarians look on the morality of actions, as measured by the utilitarian standard, with too exclusive a regard, and do not lay sufficient stress upon the other beauties of character which go towards making a human being lovable or admirable, this may be admitted. Utilitarians who have cultivated their moral feelings, but not their sympathies nor their artistic perceptions, do fall into this mistake; and so do all other moralists under the same conditions. What can be said in excuse for other moralists is equally available for them, namely, that if there is to be any error, it is better that it should be on that side. As a matter of fact, we may affirm that among utilitarians as among adherents of other systems, there is every imaginable degree of rigidity and of laxity in the application of their standard: some are even puritanically rigorous, while others are as indulgent as can possibly be desired by sinner or by sentimentalist. But on the whole, a doctrine which brings prominently forward the interest that mankind have in the repression and prevention of conduct which violates the moral law, is likely to be inferior to no other in turning the sanctions of opinion against such violations. It is true, the question, "What does violate the moral law?" is one on which those who recognize different standards of morality are likely now and then to differ. But difference of opinion on moral questions was not first introduced into the world by utilitarianism, while that doctrine does supply, if not always an easy, at all events a tangible and intelligible mode of deciding such differences.

It may not be superfluous to notice a few more of the common misapprehensions of utilitarian ethics, even those which are so obvious and gross that it might appear impossible for any person of candor and intelligence to fall into them; since persons, even of considerable mental endowments, often give themselves so little trouble to understand the bearings of any opinion against which they entertain a prejudice, and men are in general so little conscious of this voluntary ignorance as a defect, that the vulgarest misunderstandings of ethical doctrines are continually met with in the deliberate writings of persons of the greatest pretensions both to high principle and to philosophy. We not uncommonly hear the doctrine of utility inveighed against as a *godless* doctrine. If it be necessary to say anything at all against so mere an assumption, we may say that the question depends upon what idea we have formed of the moral character of the Deity. If it be a true belief that God desires, above all things, the happiness of his creatures, and that this was his purpose in their creation, utility is not only not a godless doctrine, but more profoundly religious than any other. If it be meant that utilitarianism does not recognize the revealed will of God as the supreme law of morals, I answer that a utilitarian who believes in the perfect goodness and wisdom of God, necessarily believes that whatever God has thought fit to reveal on the subject of morals, must fulfil the requirements of utility in a supreme degree. But others besides utilitarians have been of opinion that the Christian revelation was intended, and is fitted, to inform the hearts and minds of mankind with a spirit which should enable them to find for themselves what is right, and incline them to do it when found, rather than to tell them, except in a very general way, what it is; and that we need a doctrine of ethics, carefully followed out, to *interpret* to us the will of God. Whether this opinion is correct or not, it is superfluous here to discuss; since whatever aid religion, either natural or revealed, can afford to ethical investigation, is as open to the utilitarian moralist as to any other. He can use it as the testimony of God to the usefulness or hurtfulness of any given course of action, by as good a right as others can use it for the indication of a transcendental law, having no connection with usefulness or with happiness.

Again, utility is often summarily stigmatized as an immoral doctrine by giving it the name of *expediency,* and taking advantage of the popular use of that term to contrast it with *principle.* But the *expedient,* in the sense in which it is opposed to the *right,* generally means that which is expedient for the particular interest of the agent himself; as when a minister sacrifices the interests of his country to keep himself in place. When it means anything better than this, it means that which is expedient for some immediate object, some temporary purpose, but which violates a rule whose observance is expedient in a much higher degree. The expedient, in this sense, instead of being the same thing with the useful, is a branch of the hurtful. Thus, it would often be expedient, for the purpose of getting over some momentary embarrassment, or attaining some object immediately useful to ourselves or others, to tell a lie. But inasmuch as the cultivation in ourselves of a sensitive feeling on the subject of veracity, is one of the most useful, and the enfeeblement of that feeling one of the most hurtful, things to which our conduct can be instrumental; and inasmuch as any, even unintentional, deviation from truth, does that much towards weakening the trustworthiness of human assertion, which is not only the principal support of all present social well-being, but the insufficiency of which does more than any one thing that can be named to keep back civilization, virtue, everything on which human happiness on the largest scale depends; we feel that the violation, for a present advantage, of a rule of such transcendenant expediency, is not expedient, and that he who, for the sake of a convenience to himself or to some other individual, does what depends on him to deprive mankind of the good, and inflict upon them the evil, involved in the greater or less reliance which they can place in each other's word, acts the part of one of their worst enemies. Yet that even this rule, sacred as it is, admits of possible exceptions, is acknowledged by all moralists; the chief of which is when the withholding of some fact (as of information from a malefactor, or of bad news from a person dangerously ill) would save an individual (especially an individual other than oneself) from great and unmerited evil, and when the withholding can only be effected by denial. But in order that the exception may not extend itself beyond the need, and may have the least possible effect in weakening reliance on veracity, it ought to be recognized, and, if possible, its limits defined; and if the principle of utility is good for anything, it must be good for weighing these conflicting utilities against one another, and marking out the region within which one or the other preponderates.

Again, defenders of utility often find themselves called upon to reply to such objections as this—that there is not time, previous to action, for calculating and weighing the effects of any line of conduct on the general happiness. This is exactly as if anyone were to say that it is impossible to guide our conduct by Christianity, because there is not time, on every occasion on which anything has to be done, to read through the Old and New Testaments. The answer to the objection is that there has been ample time, namely, the whole past duration of the human species. During all that time, mankind have been learning by experience the tendencies of actions; on which experience all the prudence, as well as all the morality of life, are dependent. People talk as if the commencement of this course of experience had hitherto been put off, and as if, at the moment when some man feels tempted to meddle with the property or life of another, he had to begin considering for the first time whether murder and theft are injurious to human happiness. Even then

I do not think that he would find the question very puzzling; but, at all events, the matter is now done to his hand. It is truly a whimsical supposition that, if mankind were agreed in considering utility to be the test of morality, they would remain without any agreement as to what *is* useful, and would take no measures for having their notions on the subject taught to the young, and enforced by law and opinion. There is no difficulty in proving any ethical standard whatever to work ill, if we suppose universal idiocy to be conjoined with it; but on any hypothesis short of that, mankind must by this time have acquired positive beliefs as to the effects of some actions on their happiness; and the beliefs which have thus come down are the rules of morality for the multitude, and for the philosopher until he has succeeded in finding better. That philosophers might easily do this, even now, on many subjects; that the received code of ethics is by no means of divine right; and that mankind have still much to learn as to the effects of actions on the general happiness, I admit, or rather, earnestly maintain. The corollaries from the principle of utility, like the precepts of every practical art, admit of indefinite improvement, and, in a progressive state of the human mind, their improvement is perpetually going on. But to consider the rules of morality as improvable, is one thing; to pass over the intermediate generalizations entirely, and endeavor to test each individual action directly by the first principle, is another. It is a strange notion that the acknowledgment of a first principle is inconsistent with the admission of secondary ones. To inform a traveler respecting the place of his ultimate destination, is not to forbid the use of landmarks and direction-posts on the way. The proposition that happiness is the end and aim of morality, does not mean that no road ought to be laid down to that goal, or that persons going thither should not be advised to take one direction rather than another. Men really ought to leave off taking a kind of nonsense on this subject, which they would neither talk nor listen to on other matters of practical concernment. Nobody argues that the art of navigation is not founded on astronomy, because sailors cannot wait to calculate the Nautical Almanac. Being rational creatures, they go to sea with it ready calculated; and all rational creatures go out upon the sea of life with their minds made up on the common questions of right and wrong, as well as on many of the far more difficult questions of wise and foolish. And this, as long as foresight is a human quality, it is to be presumed they will continue to do. Whatever we adopt as the fundamental principle of morality, we require subordinate principles to apply it by; the impossibility of doing without them, being common to all systems, can afford no argument against anyone in particular: but gravely to argue as if no such secondary principles could be had, and as if mankind had remained till now, and always must remain, without drawing any general conclusions from the experience of human life, is as high a pitch, I think, as absurdity has ever reached in philosophical controversy.

The remainder of the stick arguments against utilitarianism mostly consist in laying to its charge the common infirmities of human nature, and the general difficulties which embarrass conscientious persons in shaping their course through life. We are told that a utilitarian will be apt to make his own particular case an exception to moral rules, and when under temptation will see a utility in the breach of a rule greater than he will see in its observance. But is utility the only creed which is able to furnish us with excuses for evil-doing, and means of cheating our own conscience? They are afforded in abundance by all doctrines which recognize as a fact in morals the existence of conflicting considerations; which all doctrines do, that have been believed by sane persons. It is not the fault of any creed, but of the complicated nature of human affairs, that rules of conduct cannot be so framed as to require no exceptions, and that hardly any kind of action can safely be laid down as either always obligatory or always condemnable. There is no ethical creed which does not temper the rigidity of its laws by giving a certain latitude, under the moral responsibility of the agent, for accommodation to peculiarities of circumstances; and under every creed, at the opening thus made, self-deception and dishonest casuistry get in. There exists no moral system under which there do not arise unequivocal cases of conflicting obligation. These are the real difficulties, the knotty points both in the theory of ethics, and in the conscientious guidance of personal conduct. They are overcome practically, with greater or with less success, according to the intellect and virtue of the individual; but it can hardly be pretended that anyone will be the less qualified for dealing with them, from possessing an ultimate standard to which conflicting rights and duties can be referred. If utility is the ultimate source of moral obligations, utility may be invoked to decide between them when their demands are incompatible. Though the application of the standard may be difficult, it is better than none at all; while in other systems, the moral laws all claiming independent authority, there is no common umpire entitled to interfere between them: their claims to precedence one over another rest on little better than sophistry, and unless determined, as they generally are, by the unacknowledged influence of considerations of utility, afford a free scope for the action of personal desires and partialities. We must remember that only in these cases of conflict between secondary principles is it requisite that first principles should be appealed to. There is no case of moral obligation in which some secondary principle is not involved; and if only one, there can seldom be any real doubt which one it is, in the mind of any person by whom the principle itself is recognized.

CHAPTER III

OF THE ULTIMATE SANCTION OF THE PRINCIPLE OF UTILITY

THE QUESTION is often asked, and properly so, in regard to any supposed moral standard—What is its sanction? what are the motives to obey it? or more specifically, what is the source of its obligation? whence does it derive its binding force? It is a necessary part of moral philosophy to provide the answer to this question; which, though frequently assuming the shape of an objection to the utilitarian morality, as if it had some special applicability to that above others, really arises in regard to all standards. It arises, in fact, whenever a person is called on to *adopt* a standard, or refer morality to any basin on which he has not been accustomed to rest in. For the customary morality, that which education and opinion have consecrated, is the only one which presents itself to the mind with the feeling of being *in itself* obligatory; and when a person is asked to believe that this morality *derives* its obligation from some general principle round which custom has not thrown the same halo, the assertion is to him a paradox; the supposed corollaries seem to have a more binding force than the original theorem; the superstructure seems to stand better without, than with, what is represented as its foundation. He says to himself, I feel that I am bound not to rob or murder, betray or deceive; but why am I bound to promote the general happiness? If my own happiness lies in something else, why may I not give that the preference?

If the view adopted by the utilitarian philosophy of the nature of the moral sense be correct, this difficulty will always present itself, until the influences which form moral character have taken the same hold of the principle which they have taken of some of the consequences— until, by the improvement of education, the feeling of unity with our fellow-creatures shall be (what it cannot be denied that Christ intended it to be) as deeply rooted in our character, and to our own consciousness as completely a part of our nature, as the horror of crime is in an ordinarily well brought up young person. In the meantime, however, the difficulty has no peculiar application to the doctrine of utility, but is inherent in every attempt to analyze morality and reduce it to principles; which, unless the principle is already in men's minds invested with as much sacredness as any of its applications, always seem to divest them of a part of their sanctity.

The principle of utility either has, or there is no reason why it might not have, all the sanctions which belong to any other system of morals. Those sanctions are either external or internal. Of the external sanctions it is not necessary to speak at any length. They are, the hope of favor and the fear of displeasure, from our fellow-creatures or from the Ruler of the Universe, along with whatever we may have of sympathy or affection for them, or of love and awe of Him, inclining us to do his will independently of selfish consequences. There is evidently no reason why all these motives for observance should not attach themselves to the utilitarian morality, as completely and as powerfully as to any other. Indeed, those of them which refer to our fellow-creatures are sure to do so, in proportion to the amount of general intelligence; for whether there be any other ground of moral obligation than the general happiness or not, men do desire happiness; and however imperfect may be their own practice, they desire and commend all conduct in others towards themselves, by which they think their happiness is promoted. With regard to the religious motive, if men believe, as most profess to do, in the goodness of God, those who think that conduciveness to the general happiness is the essence, or even only the criterion of good, must necessarily believe that it is also that which God approves. The whole force therefore of external reward and punishment, whether physical or moral, and whether proceeding from God or from our fellow men, together with all that the capacities of human nature admit of disinterested devotion to either, become available to enforce the utilitarian morality, in proportion as that morality is recognized; and the more powerfully, the more the appliances of education and general cultivation are bent to the purpose.

So far as to external sanctions. The internal sanction of duty, whatever our standard of duty may be, is one and the same—a feeling in our own mind: a pain, more or less intense, attendant on violation of duty, which in properly cultivated moral natures rises, in the more serious cases, into shrinking from it as an impossibility. This feeling, when disinterested, and connecting itself with the pure idea of duty, and not with some particular form of it, or with any of the merely accessory circumstances, is the essence of conscience; though in that complex phenomenon as it actually exists, the simple fact is in general all encrusted over with collateral associations, derived from sympathy, from love, and still more from fear; from all the forms of religious feeling; from the recollections of childhood and of all our past life; from self-esteem, desire of the esteem of others, and occasionally even self-abasement. This extreme complication is, I apprehend, the origin of the sort of mystical character which, by a tendency of the human mind to which there are many other examples, is apt to be attributed to the idea of moral obligation, and which leads people to believe that the idea cannot possibly attach itself to any other objects than those which, by a supposed mysterious law, are found in our present experience to excite it. Its binding force, however, consists in the existence of a mass of feeling which must be broken through in order to do what violates our standard of right, and which, if we do nevertheless violate that standard, will probably have to be encountered afterwards in the form of remorse. Whatever theory we have of the nature or origin of conscience, this is what essentially constitutes it.

The ultimate sanction, therefore, of all morality (external motives apart) being a subjective feeling in our own minds, I see nothing embarrassing to those whose standard is utility, in the question, what is the sanction of that particular standard? We may answer, the same as of all other moral standards—the conscientious feelings of mankind. Undoubtedly this sanction has no binding efficacy on those who do not possess the feelings it appeals to; but neither will these persons be more obedient to any other moral principle than to the utilitarian one. On them morality of any kind has no hold but through the external sanctions. Meanwhile the feelings exist, a fact in human nature, the reality of which, and the great power with which they are capable of acting on those in whom they have been duly cultivated, are proved by experience. No reason has ever been shown why they may not be cultivated to as great intensity in connection with this utilitarian, as with any other rule of morals.

There is, I am aware, a disposition to believe that a person who sees in moral obligation a transcendental fact, an objective reality belonging to the province of 'things in themselves,' is likely to be more obedient to it than one who believes it to be entirely subjective, having its seat in human consciousness only. But whatever a person's opinion may be on this point of ontology, the force he is really urged by is his own subjective feeling, and is exactly measured by its strength. No one's belief that duty is an objective reality, is stronger than the belief that God is so; yet the belief in God, apart from the expectation of actual reward and punishment, only operates on conduct through, and in proportion to, the subjective religious feeling. The sanction, so far as it is disinterested, is always in the mind itself; and the notion therefore of the transcendental moralists must be that this sanction will not exist *in* the mind unless it is believed to have its root out of the mind; and that if a person is able to say to himself. "This which is restraining me, and which is called my conscience, is only a feeling in my own mind," he may possibly draw the conclusion that when the feeling ceases the obligation ceases, and that if he find the feeling inconvenient, he may disregard it, and endeavor to get rid of it. But is this danger confined to the utilitarian morality? Does the belief that moral obligation has its seat outside the mind make the feeling of it too strong to be got rid of? The fact is so far otherwise, that all moralists admit and lament the ease with which, in the generality of minds, conscience can be silenced or stifled. The question, "Need I obey my conscience?" is quite as often put to themselves by persons who never heard of the principle of utility, as by its adherents. Those whose conscientious feelings are so weak as to allow of their asking this question, if they answer it affirmatively, will not do so because they believe in the transcendental theory, but because of the external sanctions.

It is not necessary, for the present purpose, to decide whether the feeling of duty is innate or implanted. Assuming it to be innate, it is an open question to what objects it naturally attaches itself; for the philosophic supporters of that theory are now agreed that the intuitive perception is of principles of morality and not of the details. If there be anything innate in the matter, I see no reason why the feeling which is innate should not be that of regard to the pleasures and pains of others. If there is any principle of morals which is intuitively obligatory, I should say it must be that. If so, the intuitive ethics would coincide with the utilitarian, and there would be no further quarrel between them. Even as it is, the intuitive moralists, though they believe that there are other intuitive moral obligations, do already believe this to be one; for they unanimously hold that a large *portion* of morality turns upon the consideration due to the interests of our fellow-creatures. Therefore, if the belief in the transcendental origin of moral obligation gives any additional efficacy to the internal sanction, it appears to me that the utilitarian principle has already the benefit of it.

On the other hand, if, as is my own belief, the moral feelings are not innate, but acquired, they are not for that reason the less natural. It is natural to man to speak, to reason, to build cities, to cultivate the ground, though these are acquired faculties. The moral feelings are not indeed a part of our nature, in the sense of being in any perceptible degree present in all of us; but this, unhappily, is a fact admitted by those who believe the most strenuously in their transcendental origin. Like the other acquired capacities above referred to, the moral faculty, if not a part of our nature, is a natural outgrowth from it; capable, like them, in a certain small degree, of springing up spontaneously; and susceptible of being brought by cultivation to a high degree of development. Unhappily it is also susceptible, by a sufficient use of the external sanctions and of the force of early impressions, of being cultivated in almost any direction; so that there is hardly anything so absurd or so mischievous that it may not, by means of these influences, be made to act on the human mind with all the authority of conscience. To doubt that the same potency might be given by the same means to the principle of utility, even if it had no foundation in human nature, would be flying in the face of all experience.

But moral associations which are wholly of artificial creation, when intellectual culture goes on, yield by degrees to the dissolving force of analysis: and if the feeling of duty, when associated with utility, would appear equally arbitrary; if there were no leading department of our nature, no powerful class of sentiments, with which that association would harmonize, which would make us feel it congenial, and incline us not only to foster it in others (for which we have abundant interested motives), but also to cherish it in ourselves; if there were not, in short, a natural basis of sentiment for utilitarian morality, it might well happen that this association also, even after it had been implanted by education, might be analyzed away.

But there *is* this basis of powerful natural sentiment; and this it is which, when once the general happiness is recognized as the ethical standard, will constitute the strength of the utilitarian morality. This firm foundation is that of the social feelings of mankind; the desire to be in unity with our fellow-creatures, which is already a powerful principle in human nature, and happily one of those which tend to become stronger, even without express inculcation, from the influences of advancing civilization. The social state is at once so natural, so necessary, and so habitual to man, that, except in some unusual circumstances or by an effort of voluntary abstraction, he never conceives himself otherwise than as a member of a body; and this association is riveted more and more as mankind are further removed from the state of savage independence. Any condition, therefore, which is essential to a state of society, becomes more and more an inseparable part of every person's conception of the state of things which he is born into, and which is the destiny of a human being. Now, society between human beings, except in the relation of master and slave, is manifestly impossible on any other footing than that the interests of all are to be consulted. Society between equals can only exist on the understanding that the interests of all are to be regarded equally. And since in all states of civilization, every person, except an absolute monarch, has equals, everyone is obliged to live on these terms with somebody; and in every age some advance is made towards a state in which it will be impossible to live permanently on other terms with anybody. In this way people grow up unable to conceive as possible to them a state of total disregard of other people's interests. They are under a necessity of conceiving themselves as at least abstaining from all the grosser injuries, and (if only for their own protection) living in a state of constant protest against them. They are also familiar with the fact of co-operating with others, and proposing to themselves a collective, not an individual interest as the aim (at least for the time being) of their actions. So long as they are co-operating, their ends are identified with those of others; there is at least a temporary feeling that the interests of others are their own interests. Not only does all strengthening of social ties, and all healthy growth of society, give to each individual a stronger personal interest in practically consulting the welfare of others; it also leads him to identify his *feelings* more and more with their good, or at least with an even greater degree of practical consideration for it. He comes, as though instinctively, to be conscious of himself as a being who *of course* pays regard to others. The good of others becomes to him a thing naturally and necessarily to be attended to, like any of the physical conditions of our existence. Now whatever amount of this feeling a person has, he is urged by the strongest motives both of interest and of sympathy to demonstrate it, and to the utmost of his power encourage it in others; and even if he has none of it himself, he is as greatly interested as anyone else that others should have it. Consequently the smallest germs of the feeling are laid hold of and nourished by the contagion of sympathy and the influences of education; and a complete web of corroborative association is woven round it, by the powerful agency of the external sanctions. This mode of conceiving ourselves and human life, as civilization goes on, is felt to be more and more natural. Every step in political improvement renders it more so, by removing the sources of opposition of interest, and leveling those inequalities of legal privilege between individuals or classes, owing to which there are large portions of mankind whose happiness it is still practicable to disregard. In an improving state of the human mind, the influences are constantly on the increase which tend to generate in each individual a feeling of unity with all the rest; which, if perfect, would make him never think of, or desire, any beneficial condition for himself, in the benefits of which they are not included. If we now suppose this feeling of unity to be taught as a religion, and the whole force of education, of institutions, and of opinion, directed, as it once was in the case of religion, to make every person grow up from infancy surrounded on all sides both by the profession and the practice of it, I think that no one who can realize this conception will feel any misgiving about the sufficiency of the ultimate sanction for the happiness morality. To any ethical student who finds the realization difficult, I recommend, as a means of facilitating it, the second of M. Comte's two principal works, the *Traité de politique positive*. I entertain the strongest objections to the system of politics and morals set forth in that treatise; but I think it has superabundantly shown the possibility of giving to the service of humanity, even without the aid of belief in a Providence, both the psychological power and the social efficacy of a religion; making it take hold of human life, and color all thought, feeling, and action, in a manner of which the greatest ascendancy ever exercised by any religion may be but a type and foretaste; and of which the danger is not that it should be insufficient, but that it should be so excessive as to interfere unduly with human freedom and individuality.

Neither is it necessary to the feeling which constitutes the binding force of the utilitarian morality on those who recognize it, to wait for those social influences which would make its obligation felt by mankind at large. In the comparatively early state of human advancement in which we now life, a person cannot indeed feel that entireness of sympathy with all others, which would make any real discordance in the general direction of their conduct in life impossible; but already a person in whom the social feeling is at all developed, cannot bring himself to think of the rest of his fellow-creatures as struggling rivals with him for the means of happiness, whom he must desire to see defeated in their object in order that he may succeed in his. The deeply rooted conception which every individual even now has of himself as a social being, tends to make him feel it one of his natural wants that there should be harmony between his feelings and aims and those of his fellow-creatures. If differences of opinion and of mental culture make it impossible for him to share many of their actual feelings—perhaps make him denounce and defy those feelings—he still needs to be conscious that his real aim and theirs do not conflict; that he is not opposing himself to what they really wish for, namely their own good, but is, on the contrary, promoting it. This feeling in most individuals is much inferior in strength to their selfish feelings, and is often wanting altogether. But to those who have it, it possesses all the characters of a natural feeling. It does not present itself to their minds as a superstition of education, or a law despotically imposed by the power of society, but as an attribute which it would not be well for them to be without. This conviction is the ultimate sanction of the greatest happiness morality. This it is which makes any mind, of well-developed feelings, work with, and not against, the outward motives to care for others, afforded by what I have called the external sanctions; and when those sanctions are wanting, or act in an opposite direction, constitutes in itself a powerful internal binding force, in proportion to the sensitiveness and thoughtfulness of the character; since few but those whose mind is a moral blank, could bear to lay out their course of life on the plan of paying no regard to others except so far as their own private interest compels.

CHAPTER IV

OF WHAT SORT OF PROOF THE PRINCIPLE OF UTILITY IS SUSCEPTIBLE

IT HAS already been remarked that questions of ultimate ends do not admit of proof, in the ordinary acceptation of the term. To be incapable of proof by reasoning is common to all first prniciples: to the first premises of our knowledge as well as to those of our conduct. But the former, being matters of fact, may be the subject of a direct appeal to the faculties which judge of fact—namely, our senses, and our internal consciousness. Can an appeal be made to the same faculties on questions of practical ends? Or by what other faculty is cognizance taken of them?

Questions about ends are, in other words, questions what things are desirable. The utilitarian doctrine is that happiness is desirable, and the only thing desirable, as an end; all other things being only desirable at means to that end. What ought to be required of this doctrine—what conditions is it requisite that the doctrine should fulfil—to make good its claim to be believed?

The only proof capable of being given that an object is visible, is that people actually see it. The only proof that a sound is audible, is that people hear it: and so of the other sources of our experience. In like manner, I apprehend, the sole evidence it is possible to produce that anything is desirable, is that people do actually desire it. If the end which the utilitarian doctrine proposes to itself were not, in theory and in practice, acknowledged to be an end, nothing could ever convince any person that it was so. No reason can be given why the general happiness is desirable except that each person, so far as he believes it to be attainable, desires his own happiness. This, however, being a fact, we have not only all the proof which the case admits of, but all which it is possible to require, that happiness is a good: that each person's happiness is a good to that person, and the general happiness, therefore, a good to the aggregate of all persons. Happiness has made out its title as *one* of the ends of conduct, and consequently one of the criteria of morality.

But it has not, by this alone, proved itself to be the sole criterion. To do that, it would seem, by the same rule, necessary to show, not only that people desire happiness, but that they never desire anything else. Now it is palpable that they do desire things which, in common language, are decidedly distinguished from happiness. They desire, for example, virtue, and the absence of vice, no less really than pleasure and the absence of pain. The desire of virtue is not as universal, but it is as authentic a fact, as the desire of happiness. And hence the opponents of the utilitarian standard deem that they have a right to infer that there are other ends of human action besides happiness, and that happiness is not the standard of approbation and disapprobation.

But does the utilitarian doctrine deny that people desire virtue, or maintain that virtue is not a thing to be desired? The very reverse. It maintains not only that virtue is to be desired, but that it is to be desired disinterestedly, for itself. Whatever may be the opinion of utilitarian moralists as to the original conditions by which virtue is made virtue; however they may believe (as they do) that actions and dispositions are only virtuous because they promote another end than virtue: yet this being granted, and it having been decided, from considerations of this description, what *is* virtuous, they not only place virtue at the very head of the things which are good as means to the ultimate end, but they also recognize as a psychological fact the possibility of its being, to the individual, a good in itself, without looking to any end beyond it; and hold that the mind is not in a right state, not in a state comformable to utility, not in the state most conducive to the general happiness, unless it does love virtue in this manner—as a thing desirable in itself, even although, in the individual instance, it should not produce those other desirable consequences which it tends to produce, and on account of which it is held to be virtue. This opinion is not, in the smallest degree, a departure from the happiness principle. The ingredients of happiness are very various, and each of them is desirable in itself, and not merely when considered as swelling an aggregate. The principle of utility does not mean that any given pleasure, as music, for instance, or any given exemption from pain, as for example health, is to be looked upon as means to a collective something termed happiness, and to be desired on that account. They are desired and desirable in and for themselves; besides being means, they are a part of the end. Virtue, according to the utilitarian doctrine, is not naturally and originally part of the end, but it is capable of becoming so; and in those who love it disinterestedly it has become so, and is desired and cherished, not as a means to happiness, but as a part of their happiness.

To illustrate this farther, we may remember that virtue is not the only thing, originally a means, and which if it were not a means to anything else, would be and remain indifferent, but which by association with what it is a means to, comes to be desired for itself, and that too with the utmost intensity. What, for example, shall we say of the love of money? There is nothing originally more desirable about money than about any heap of glittering pebbles. Its worth is solely that of the things which it will buy; the desires for other things than itself, which it is a means of gratifying. Yet the love of money is not only one of the strongest moving forces of human life, but money is, in many cases, desired in and for itself; the desire to possess it is often stronger than the desire to use it, and goes on increasing when all the desires which point to ends beyond it, to be compassed by it, are falling off. It may, then, be said truly, that money is desired not for the sake of an end, but as part of the end. From being a means to happiness, it has come to be itself a principal ingredient of the individual's conception of happiness. The same may be said of the majority of the great objects of human life —power, for example, or fame; except that to each of these there is a certain amount of immediate pleasure annexed, which has at least the semblance of being naturally inherent in them; a thing which cannot be said of money. Still, however, the strongest natural attraction, both of power and of fame, is the immense aid they give to the attainment of our other wishes; and it is the strong association thus generated between them and all our objects of desire, which gives to the direct desire of them the intensity it often assumes, so as in some characters to surpass in strength all other desires. In these cases the means have become a part of the end, and a more important part of it than any of the things which they are means to. What was once desired as an instrument for the attainment of happiness, has come to be desired for its own sake. In being desired for its own sake it is, however, desired as *part* of happiness. The person is made, or thinks he would be made, happy by its mere possession; and is made unhappy by failure to obtain it. The desire of it is not a different thing from the desire of happiness, any more than the love of music, or the desire of health. They are included in happiness. They are some of the elements of which the desire of happiness is made up. Happiness is not an abstract idea, but a concrete whole; and these are some of its parts. And the utilitarian standard sanctions and approves their being so. Life would be a poor thing, very ill provided with sources of happiness, if there were not this provision of nature, by which things originally indifferent, but conducive to, or otherwise associated with, the satisfaction of our primitive desires, become in themselves sources of pleasure more valuable than the primitive pleasures, both in permanency, in the space of human existence that they are capable of covering, and even in intensity.

Virtue, according to the utilitarian conception, is a good of this description. There was no original desire of it, or motive to it, save its conduciveness to pleasure, and especially to protection from pain. But through the association thus formed, it may be felt a good in itself, and desired as such with as great intensity as any other good; and with this difference between it and the love of money, of power, or of fame, that all of these may, and often do, render the individual noxious to the other members of the society to which he belongs, whereas there is

nothing which makes him so much a blessing to them as the cultivation
of the disinterested love of virtue. And consequently, the utilitarian
standard, while it tolerates and approves those other acquired desires
up to the point beyond which they would be more injurious to the general happiness than promotive of it, enjoins and requires the cultivation
of the love of virtue up to the greatest strength possible, as being above
all things important to the general happiness.

It results from the preceding considerations, that there is in reality
nothing desired except happiness. Whatever is desired otherwise than
as a means to some end beyond itself, and ultimately to happiness, is
desired as itself a part of happiness, and is not desired for itself until
it has become so. Those who desire virtue for its own sake, desire it
either because the consciousness of it is a pleasure, or because the consciousness of being without it is a pain, or for both reasons united; as
in truth the pleasure and pain seldom exist separately, but almost always together, the same person feeling pleasure in the degree of virtue
attained, and pain in not having attained more. If one of these gave him
no pleasure, and the other no pain, he would not love or desire virtue,
or would desire it only for the other benefits which it might produce
to himself or to persons whom he cared for.

We have now, then, an answer to the question, of what sort of proof
the principle of utility is susceptible. If the opinion which I have now
stated is psychologically true—if human nature is so constituted as to
desire nothing which is not either a part of happiness or a means of
happiness, we can have no other proof, and we require no other, that
these are the only things desirable. If so, happiness is the sole end of
human action, and the promotion of it the test by which to judge of all
human conduct; from whence it necessarily follows that it must be the
criterion of morality, since a part is included in the whole.

And now to decide whether this is really so; whether mankind do desire nothing for itself but that which is a pleasure to them, or of which
the absence is a pain: we have evidently arrived at a question of fact
and experience, dependent, like all similar questions, upon evidence. It
can only be determined by practiced self-consciousness and self-observation, assisted by observation of others. I believe that these sources of
evidence, impartially consulted, will declare that desiring a thing and
finding it pleasant, aversion to it and thinking of it as painful, are phenomena entirely inseparable, or rather two parts of the same phenomenon; in strictness of language, two different modes of naming the same
psychological fact: that to think of an object as desirable (unless for
the sake of its consequences), and to think of it as pleasant, are one and
the same thing; and that to desire anything, except in proportion as the
idea of it is pleasant, is a physical and metaphysical impossibility.

So obvious does this appear to me that I expect it will hardly be disputed; and the objection made will be, not that desire can possibly be directed to anything ultimately except pleasure and exemption from pain, but that the will is a different thing from desire: that a person of confirmed virtue, or any other person whose purposes are fixed, carries out his purposes without any thought of the pleasure he has in contemplating them, or expects to derive from their fulfilment; and persists in acting on them, even though these pleasures are much diminished, by changes in his character or decay of his passive sensibilities, or are outweighed by the pains which the pursuit of the purposes may bring upon him. All this I fully admit, and have stated it elsewhere, as positively and emphatically as anyone. Will, the active phenomenon, is a different thing from desire, the state of passive sensibility, and though originally an offshoot from it, may in time take root and detach itself from the parent stock; so much so, that in the case of an habitual purpose, instead of willing the thing because we desire it, we often desire it only because we will it. This, however, is but an instance of that familiar fact, the power of habit, and is nowise confined to the case of virtuous actions. Many indifferent things which men originally did from a motive of some sort, they continue to do from habit. Sometimes this is done unconsciously, the consciousness coming only after the action; at other times with conscious volition, but volition which has become habitual, and is put in operation by the force of habit, in opposition perhaps to the deliberate preference, as often happens with those who have contracted habits of vicious or hurtful indulgence. Third and last comes the case in which the habitual act of will in the individual instance is not in contradiction to the general intention prevailing at other times, but in fulfilment of it; as in the case of the person of confirmed virtue, and of all who pursue deliberately and consistently any determinate end. The distinction between will and desire thus understood is an authentic and highly important psychological fact; but the fact consists solely in this—that will, like all other parts of our constitution, is amenable to habit, and that we may will from habit what we no longer desire for itself, or desire only because we will it. It is not the less true that will, in the beginning, is entirely produced by desire; including in that term the repelling influence of pain as well as the attractive one of pleasure. Let us take into consideration, no longer the person who has a confirmed will to do right, but him in whom that virtuous will is still feeble, conquerable by temptation, and not to be fully relied on; by what means can it be strengthened? How can the will to be virtuous, where it does not exist in sufficient force, be implanted or awakened? Only by making the person *desire* virtue—by making him think of it in a pleasurable light, or of its absence in a painful one. It is by associating the doing right with pleasure, or the doing wrong with pain, or by eliciting and impressing and bringing home to the person's experience the pleasure naturally involved in the one or the pain in the other, that it is possible to call forth that will to be virtuous, which, when confirmed, acts without any thought of either pleasure or pain. Will is the child of desire, and passes out of the dominion of its parent only to come under that of habit. That which is the result of habit affords no presumption of being intrinsically good; and there would be no reason for wishing that the purpose of virtue should become independent of pleasure and pain, were it not that the influence of the pleasurable and painful associations which prompt to virtue is not sufficiently to be depended on for unerring constancy of action until it has acquired the support of habit. Both in feeling and in conduct, habit is the only thing which imparts certainly; and it is because of the importance to others of being able to rely absolutely on one's feelings and conduct, and to oneself of being able to rely on one's own, that the will to do right ought to be cultivated into this habitual independence. In other words, this state of the will is a means to good, not intrinsically a good; and does not contradict the doctrine that nothing is a good to human beings but in so far as it is either itself pleasurable, or a means of attaining pleasure or averting pain.

But, if this doctrine be true, the principle of utility is proved. Whether it is so or not, must now be left to the consideration of the thoughtful reader.

CHAPTER V

ON THE CONNECTION BETWEEN JUSTICE AND UTILITY

IN ALL AGES of speculation one of the strongest obstacles to the reception of the doctrine that utility or happiness is the criterion of right and wrong, has been drawn from the idea of *justice*. The powerful sentiment, and apparently clear perception, which that word recalls with a rapidity and certainty resembling an instinct, have seemed to the majority of thinkers to point to an inherent quality in things; to show that the just must have an existence in nature as something absolute, generically distinct from every variety of the expedient, and, in idea, opposed to it, though (as is commonly acknowledged) never, in the long run, disjoined from it in fact.

In the case of this, as of our other moral sentiments, there is no necessary connection between the question of its origin, and that of its binding force. That a feeling is bestowed on us by nature, does not necessarily legitimate all its promptings. The feeling of justice might be a peculiar instinct, and might yet require, like our other instincts, to be controlled and enlightened by a higher reason. If we have intellectual instincts, leading us to judge in a particular way, as well as animal instincts that prompt us to act in a particular way, there is no necessity that the former should be more infallible in their sphere than the latter in theirs: it may as well happen that wrong judgments are occasionally suggested by those, as wrong actions by these. But though it is one thing to believe that we have natural feelings of justice, and another to acknowledge them as an ultimate criterion of conduct, these two opinions are very closely connected in point of fact. Mankind are always predisposed to believe that any subjective feeling, not otherwise accounted for, is a revelation of some objective reality. Our present object is to determine whether the reality, to which the feeling of justice corresponds, is one which needs any such special revelation; whether the justice or injustice of an action is a thing intrinsically peculiar, and distinct from all its other qualities, or only a combination of certain of those qualities, presented under a peculiar aspect. For the purpose of this inquiry it is practically important to consider whether the feeling itself, of justice and injustice, is *sui generis* like our sensations of color and taste, or a derivative feeling, formed by a combination of others. And this it is the more essential to examine, as people are in general willing enough to allow that objectively the dictates of justice coincide with a part of the field of general expediency; but inasmuch as the subjective mental feeling of justice is different from that which commonly attaches to simple expediency, and, except in the extreme cases of the latter, is far more imperative in its demands, people find it difficult to see in justice only a particular kind or branch of general utility, and think that its superior binding force requires a totally different origin.

To throw light upon this question, it is necessary to attempt to ascertain what is the distinguishing character of justice or of injustice: what is the quality, or whether there is any quality, attributed in common to all modes of conduct designated as unjust (for justice, like many other moral attributes, is best defined by its opposite), and distinguishing them from such modes of conduct as are disapproved, but without having that particular epithet of disapprobation applied to them. If in everything which men are accustomed to characterize as just or unjust, some one common attribute or collection of attributes is always present, we may judge whether this particular attribute or combination of attributes would be capable of gathering round it a sentiment of that peculiar character and intensity by virtue of the general laws of our emotional constitution, or whether the sentiment is inexplicable, and requires to be regarded as a special provision of Nature. If we find the former to be the case, we shall, in resolving this question, have resolved also the main problem; if the latter, we shall have to seek for some other mode of investigating it.

To find the common attributes of a variety of objects, it is necessary to begin by surveying the objects themselves in the concrete. Let us therefore advert successively to the various modes of action and arrangements of human affairs which are classed, by universal or widely spread opinion, as just or as unjust. The things well known to excite the sentiments associated with those names are of a very multifarious character. I shall pass them rapidly in review, without studying any particular arrangement.

In the first place, it is mostly considered unjust to deprive anyone of his personal liberty, his property, or any other thing which belongs to him by law. Here, therefore, is one instance of the application of the terms just and unjust in a perfectly definite sense, namely, that it is just to respect, unjust to violate, the *legal rights* of anyone. But this judgment admits of several exceptions, arising from the other forms in which the notions of justice and injustice present themselves. For example, the person who suffers the deprivation may (as the phrase is) have *forfeited* the rights which he is so deprived of: a case to which we shall return presently. But also,

Secondly, the legal rights of which he is deprived, may be rights which *ought* not to have belonged to him; in other words, the law which confers on him these rights, may be a bad law. When it is so, or when (which is the same thing for our purpose) it is supposed to be so, opinions will differ as to the justice or injustice of infringing it. Some maintain that no law, however bad, ought to be disobeyed by an individual citizen; that his opposition to it, if shown at all, should only be shown in endeavoring to get it altered by competent authority. This opinion (which condemns many of the most illustrious benefactors of mankind, and would often protect pernicious institutions against the only weapons which, in the state of things existing at the time, have any chance of succeeding against them) is defended, by those who hold it, on grounds of expediency; principally on that of the importance, to the common interest of mankind, of maintaining inviolate the sentiment of submission to law. Other persons, again, hold the directly contrary opinion, that any law, judged to be bad, may blamelessly be disobeyed, even though it be not judged to be unjust, but only inexpedient; while others would confine the license of disobedience to the case of unjust laws: but again, some say that all laws which are inexpedient are unjust; since every law imposes some restriction on the natural liberty of mankind, which restriction is an injustice, unless legitimated by tending to their good. Among these diversities of opinion, it seems to be universally admitted that there may be unjust laws, and that law, consequently, is not the ultimate criterion of justice, but may give to one person a benefit, or impose on another an evil, which justice condemns. When, however, a law is thought to be unjust, it seems always to be regarded as being so in the same way in which a breach of law is unjust, namely, by infringing somebody's right; which, as it cannot in this case be a legal right, receives a different appellation, and is called a moral right. We may say, therefore, that a second case of injustice consists in taking or withholding from any person that to which he has a *moral right.*

Thirdly, it is universally considered just that each person should obtain that (whether good or evil) which he *deserves,* and unjust that he should obtain a good, or be made to undergo an evil, which he does not deserve. This is, perhaps, the clearest and most emphatic form in which the idea of justice is conceived by the general mind. As it involves the notion of desert, the question arises, what constitutes desert? Speaking in a general way, a person is understood to deserve good if he does right, evil if he does wrong; and in a more particular sense, to deserve good from those to whom he does or has done good, and evil from those to whom he does or has done evil. The precept of returning good for evil has never been regarded as a case of the fulfilment of justice, but as one in which the claims of justice are waived, in obedience to other considerations.

Fourthly, it is confessedly unjust to *break faith* with anyone: to violate an engagement, either express or implied, or disappoint expectations raised by our own conduct, at least if we have raised those expectations knowingly and voluntarily. Like the other obligations of justice already spoken of, this one is not regarded as absolute, but as capable of being overruled by a stronger obligation of justice on the other side; or by such conduct on the part of the person concerned as is deemed to absolve us from our obligation to him, and to constitute a *forfeiture* of the benefit which he has been led to expect.

Fifthly it is, by universal admission, inconsistent with justice to be *partial;* to show favor or preference to one person over another, in matters to which favor and preference do not properly apply. Impartiality, however, does not seem to be regarded as a duty in itself, but rather as instrumental to some other duty; for it is admitted that favor and preference are not always censurable, and indeed the cases in which they are condemned are rather the exception than the rule. A person would be more likely to be blamed than applauded for giving his family or friends no superiority in good offices over strangers, when he could do so without violating any other duty; and no one thinks it unjust to seek one person in preference to another as a friend, connection, or companion. Impartiality where rights are concerned is of course obligatory, but this is involved in the more general obligation of giving to everyone his right. A tribunal, for example, must be impartial, because it is bound to award, without regard to any other consideration, a disputed object to the one of two parties who has the right to it. There are other cases in which impartiality means, being solely influenced by desert; as with those who, in the capacity of judges, preceptors, or parents, administer reward and punishment as such. There are cases, again, in which it means, being solely influenced by consideration for the public interest; as in making a selection among candidates for a government employment. Impartiality, in short, as an obligation of justice, may be said to mean, being exclusively influenced by the considerations which it is supposed ought to influence the particular case in hand; and resisting solicitation of any motives which prompt to conduct different from what those considerations would dictate.

Nearly allied to the idea of impartiality is that of *equality;* which often enters as a component part both into the conception of justice and into the practice of it, and, in the eyes of many persons, constitutes its essence. But in this, still more than in any other case, the notion of justice varies in different persons, and always conforms in its variations to their notion of utility. Each person maintains that equality is the dictate of justice, except where he thinks that expediency requires inequality. The justice of giving equal protection to the rights of all, is maintained by those who support the most outrageous inequality in the rights themselves. Even in slave countries it is theoretically admitted that the rights of the slave, such as they are, ought to be as sacred as those of the master; and that a tribunal which fails to enforce them with equal strictness is wanting in justice; while, at the same time, institutions which leave to the slave scarcely any rights to enforce, are not deemed unjust, because they are not deemed inexpedient. Those who think that utility requires distinctions of rank, do not consider it unjust that riches and social privileges should be unequally dispensed; but those who think this inequality inexpedient, think it unjust also. Whoever thinks that government is necessary, sees no injustice in as much inequality as is constituted by giving to the magistrate powers not granted to other people. Even among those who hold leveling doctrines, there are as many questions of justice as there are differences of opinion about expediency. Some communists consider it unjust that the produce of the labor of the community should be shared on any other principle than that of exact equality; others think it just that those should receive most whose wants are greatest; while others hold that those who work harder, or who produce more, or whose services are more valuable to the community, may justly claim a larger quota in the division of the produce. And the sense of natural justice may be plausibly appealed to in behalf of every one of these opinions.

Among so many diverse applications of the term "justice," which yet is not regarded as ambiguous, it is a matter of some difficulty to seize the mental link which holds them together, and on which the moral sentiment adhering to the term essentially depends. Perhaps, in this embarrassment, some help may be derived from the history of the word, as indicated by its etymology.

In most, if not in all, languages, the etymology of the word which corresponds to 'just,' points distinctly to an origin connected with the ordinances of law. *Justum* is a form of *jussum,* that which has been ordered. Δίκαιον comes directly from δίκη, a suit at law. *Recht,* from which came *right* and *righteous,* is synonymous with law. The courts of justice, the administration of justice, are the courts and the administration of law. *La justice,* in French, is the established term for judicature. I am not committing the fallacy imputed with some show of truth to Horne Tooke, of assuming that a word must still continue to mean what it originally meant. Etymology is slight evidence of what the idea now signified is, but the very best evidence of how it sprang up. There can, I think, be no doubt that the *idée mère,* the primitive element, in the formation of the notion of justice, was conformity to law. It constituted the entire idea among the Hebrews, up to the birth of Christianity; as might be expected in the case of a people whose laws attempted to embrace all subjects on which precepts were required, and who believed those laws to be a direct emanation from the Supreme Being. But other nations, and in particular the Greeks and Romans, who knew that their laws had been made originally, and still continued to be made, by men, were not afraid to admit that those men might make bad laws: might do, by law, the same things, and from the same motives, which if done by individuals without the sanction of law, would be called unjust. And hence the sentiment of injustice came to be attached, not to all violations of law, but only to violations of such laws as *ought* to exist, including such as ought to exist, but do not; and to laws themselves, if supposed to be contrary to what ought to be law. In this manner the idea of law and of its injunctions was still predominant in the notion of justice, even when the laws actually in force ceased to be accepted as the standard of it.

It is true that mankind consider the idea of justice and its obligations as applicable to many things which neither are, nor is it desired that they should be, regulated by law. Nobody desires that laws should interfere with the whole detail of private life; yet everyone allows that in all daily conduct a person may and does show himself to be either just or unjust. But even here, the idea of the breach of what ought to be law, still lingers in a modified shape. It would always give us pleasure, and chime in with our feelings of fitness, that acts which we deem unjust should be punished, though we do not always think it expedient that this should be done by the tribunals. We forego that gratification on account of incidental inconveniences. We should be glad to see just conduct enforced and injustice repressed, even in the minutest details, if we were not, with reason, afraid of trusting the magistrate with so unlimited an amount of power over individuals. When we think that a person is bound in justice to do a thing, it is an ordinary form of language to say that he ought to be compelled to do it. We should be gratified to see the obligation enforced by anybody who had the power. If we see that its enforcement by law would be inexpedient, we lament the impossibility, we consider the impunity given to injustice as an evil, and strive to make amends for it by bringing a strong expression of our own and the public disapprobation to bear upon the offender. Thus the idea of legal constraint is still the generating idea of the notion of justice, though undergoing several transformations before that notion, as it exists in an advanced state of society, becomes complete.

The above is, I think, a true account, as far as it goes, of the origin and progressive growth of the idea of justice. But we must observe that it contains as yet nothing to distinguish that obligation from moral obligation in general. For the truth is, that the idea of penal sanction, which is the essence of law, enters not only into the conception of injustice, but into that of any kind of wrong. We do not call anything wrong unless we mean to imply that a person ought to be punished in some way or other for doing it: if not by law, by the opinion of his fellow-creatures; if not by opinion, by the reproaches of his own conscience. This seems the real turning point of the distinction between morality and simple expediency. It is a part of the notion of duty in every one of its forms, that a person may rightfully be compelled to fulfil it. Duty is a thing which may be *exacted* from a person, as one exacts a debt. Unless we think that it may be exacted from him, we do not call it his duty. Reasons of prudence, or the interest of other people, may militate against actually exacting it; but the person himself, it is clearly understood, would not be entitled to complain. There are other things, on the contrary, which we wish that people should do, which we like or admire them for doing, perhaps dislike or despise them for not doing, but yet admit that they are not bound to do it: it is not a case of moral obligation; we do not blame them, that is, we do not think that they are proper objects of punishment. How we come by these ideas of deserving and not deserving punishment, will appear, perhaps, in the sequel; but I think there is no doubt that this distinction lies at the bottom of the notions of right and wrong: that we call any conduct wrong, or employ, instead, some other term of dislike or disparagement, according as we think that the person ought, or ought not, to be punished for it; and we say, it would be right to do so and so, or merely that it would be desirable or laudable, according as we would wish to see the person whom it concerns, compelled, or only persuaded and exhorted, to act in that manner.[2]

This, therefore, being the characteristic difference which marks off, not justice, but morality in general, from the remaining provinces of expediency and worthiness; the character is still to be sought which distinguishes justice from other branches of morality. Now it is known that ethical writers divide moral duties into two classes, denoted by the ill-chosen expressions, duties of perfect and of imperfect obligation; the latter being those in which, though the act is obligatory, the particular occasions of performing it are left to our choice—as in the case of charity or beneficence, which we are indeed bound to practice, but not to-- wards any definite person, nor at any prescribed time. In the more precise language of philosophic jurists, duties of perfect obligation are those duties in virtue of which a correlative *right* resides in some person or persons; duties of imperfect obligation are those moral obligations which do not give birth to any right. I think it will be found that this distinction exactly coincides with that which exists between justice and the other obligations of morality. In our survey of the various popular acceptations of justice, the term appeared generally to involve the idea of a personal right—a claim on the part of one or more individuals, like that which the law gives when it confers a proprietary or other legal right. Whether the injustice consists in depriving a person of a possession, or in breaking faith with him, or in treating him worse than he deserves, or worse than other people who have no greater claims, in each case the supposition implies two things—a wrong done, and some assignable person who is wronged. Injustice may also be done by treating a person better than others; but the wrong in this case is to his competitors, who are also assignable persons. It seems to me that this feature in the case—a right in some person, correlative to the moral obligation—constitutes the specific difference between justice, and generosity or beneficence. Justice implies something which is not only right to do, and wrong not to do, but which some individual person can claim from us as his moral right. No one has a moral right to our generosity or beneficence, because we are not morally bound to practice those virtues towards any given individual. And it will be found with respect

---

[2] See this point enforced and illustrated by Professor Bain, in an admirable chapter (entitled "The Ethical Emotions, or the Moral Sense"), of the second of the two treatises composing his elaborate and profound work on the Mind.

to this as to every correct definition, that the instances which seem to conflict with it are those which most confirm it. For if a moralist attempts, as some have done, to make out that mankind generally, though not any given individual, have a right to all the good we can do them, he at once, by that thesis, includes generosity and beneficence within the category of justice. He is obliged to say that our utmost exertions are *due* to our fellow-creatures, thus assimilating them to a debt; or that nothing less can be a sufficient *return* for what society does for us, thus classing the case as one of gratitude; both of which are acknowledged cases of justice. Whenever there is a right, the case is one of justice, and not of the virtue of beneficence; and whoever does not place the distinction between justice and morality in general, where we have now placed it, will be found to make no distinction between them at all, but to merge all morality in justice.

Having thus endeavored to determine the distinctive elements which enter into the composition of the idea of justice, we are ready to enter on the inquiry, whether the feeling which accompanies the idea is attached to it by a special dispensation of nature, or whether it could have grown up, by any known laws, out of the idea itself; and in particular, whether it can have originated in considerations of general expediency.

I conceive that the sentiment itself does not arise from anything which would commonly, or correctly, be termed an idea of expediency; but that though the sentiment does not, whatever is moral in it does.

We have seen that the two essential ingredients in the sentiment of justice are, the desire to punish a person who has done harm, and the knowledge or belief that there is some definite individual or individuals to whom harm has been done.

Now it appears to me, that the desire to punish a person who has done harm to some individual is a spontaneous outgrowth from two sentiments, both in the highest degree natural, and which either are or resemble instincts: the impulse of self-defense and the feeling of sympathy.

It is natural to resent, and to repel or retaliate, any harm done or attempted against ourselves, or against those with whom we sympathize. The origin of this sentiment it is not necessary here to discuss. Whether it be an instinct or a result of intelligence, it is, we know, common to all animal nature; for every animal tries to hurt those who have hurt, or who it thinks are about to hurt, itself or its young. Human beings, on this point, only differ from other animals in two particulars. First, in being capable of sympathizing, not solely with their offspring, or, like some of the more noble animals, with some superior animal who is kind to them, but with all human, and even with all sentient, beings. Secondly, in having a more developed intelligence, which gives a wider range to the whole of their sentiments, whether self-regarding or sympathetic. By virtue of his superior intelligence, even apart from his superior range of sympathy, a human being is capable of apprehending a community of interest between himself and the human society of which he forms a part, such that any conduct which threatens the security of the society generally, is threatening to his own, and calls forth his instinct (if instinct it be) of self-defense. The same superiority of intelligence, joined to the power of sympathizing with human beings generally, enables him to attach himself to the collective idea of his tribe, his country, or mankind, in such a manner that any act hurtful to them, raises his instinct of sympathy, and urges him to resistance.

The sentiment of justice, in that one of its elements which consists of the desire to punish, is thus, I conceive, the natural feeling of retaliation or vengeance, rendered by intellect and sympathy applicable to those injuries, that is, to those hurts, which wound us through, or in common with, society at large. This sentiment, in itself, has nothing moral in it; what is moral is the exclusive subordination of it to the social sympathies, so as to wait on and obey their call. For the natural feeling would make us resent indiscriminately whatever anyone does that is disagreeable to us, but when moralized by the social feeling it only acts in the directions conformable to the general good: just persons resenting a hurt to society though not otherwise a hurt to themselves, and not resenting a hurt to themselves, however painful, unless it be of the kind which society has a common interest with them in the repression of.

It is no objection against this doctrine to say that when we feel our sentiment of justice outraged, we are not thinking of society at large, or of any collective interest, but only of the individual case. It is common enough certainly, though the reverse of commendable, to feel resentment merely because we have suffered pain; but a person whose resentment is really a moral feeling, that is, who considers whether an act is blamable before he allows himself to resent it—such a person, though he may not say expressly to himself that he is standing up for the interest of society, certainly does feel that he is asserting a rule which is for the benefit of others as well as for his own. If he is not feeling this—if he is regarding the act solely as it affects him individually—he is not consciously just; he is not concerning himself about the justice of his actions. This is admitted even by anti-utilitarian moralists. When Kant (as before remarked) propounds as the fundamental principle of morals, "So act, that thy rule of conduct might be adopted as a law by all rational beings," he virtually acknowledges that the interest of mankind collectively, or at least of mankind indiscriminately, must be in the mind of the agent when conscientiously deciding on the morality of the act. Otherwise he uses words without a meaning; for that a rule even of utter selfishness could not *possibly* be adopted by all rational beings— that there is any insuperable obstacle in the nature of things to its adoption—cannot be even plausibly maintained. To give any meaning to Kant's principle, the sense put upon it must be, that we ought to shape our conduct by a rule which all rational beings might adopt *with benefit to their collective interest.*

To recapitulate: the idea of justice supposes two things—a rule of conduct and a sentiment which sanctions the rule. The first must be supposed common to all mankind and intended for their good. The other (the sentiment) is a desire that punishment may be suffered by those who infringe the rule. There is involved, in addition, the conception of some definite person who suffers by the infringement; whose rights (to use the expression appropriated to the case) are violated by it. And the sentiment of justice appears to me to be the animal desire to repel or retaliate a hurt or damage to oneself, or to those with whom one sympathizes, widened so as to include all persons, by the human capacity of enlarged sympathy and the human conception of intelligent self-interest. From the latter elements, the feeling derives its morality; from the former, its peculiar impressiveness and energy of self-assertion.

I have throughout treated the idea of a *right* residing in the injured person, and violated by the injury, not as a separate element in the composition of the idea and sentiment, but as one of the forms in which the other two elements clothe themselves. These elements are: a hurt to some assignable person or persons on the one hand, and a demand for punishment on the other. An examination of our own minds, I think, will show that these two things include all that we mean when we speak of violation of a right. When we call anything a person's right, we mean that he has a valid claim on society to protect him in the possession of it, either by the force of law, or by that of education and opinion. If he has what we consider a sufficient claim, on whatever account, to have something guaranteed to him by society, we say that he has a right to it. If we desire to prove that anything does not belong to him by right, we think this done as soon as it is admitted that society ought not to take measures for securing it to him, but should leave him to chance, or to his own exertions. Thus a person is said to have a right to what he can earn in fair professional competition, because society ought not to allow any other person to hinder him from endeavoring to earn in that manner as much as he can. But he has not a right to three hundred a year, though he may happen to be earning it; because society is not called on to provide that he shall earn that sum. On the contrary, if he owns ten thousand pounds three per cent stock, he *has* a right to three hundred a year; because society has come under an obligation to provide him with an income of that amount.

To have a right, then, is, I conceive, to have something which society ought to defend me in the possession of. If the objector goes on to ask why it ought, I can give him no other reason than general utility. If that expression does not seem to convey a sufficient feeling of the strength of the obligation, nor to account for the peculiar energy of the feeling, it is because there goes to the composition of the sentiment, not a rational only, but also an animal element, the thirst for retaliation; and this thirst derives its intensity, as well as its moral justification, from the extraordinarily important and impressive kind of utility which is concerned. The interest involved is that of security, to everyone's feelings the most vital of all interests. All other earthly benefits are needed by one person, not needed by another; and many of them can, if necessary, be cheerfully foregone, or replaced by something else; but security no human being can possibly do without; on it we depend for all our immunity from evil, and for the whole value of all and every good beyond the passing moment; since nothing but the gratification of the instant could be of any worth to us, if we could be deprived of anything the next instant by whoever was momentarily stronger than ourselves. Now this most indispensable of all necessaries after physical nutriment, cannot be had unless the machinery for providing it is kept unintermittedly in active play. Our notion, therefore, of the claim we have on our fellow-creatures to join in making safe for us the very groundwork of our existence, gathers feelings around it so much more intense than those concerned in any of the more common cases of utility, that the difference in degree (as is often the case in psychology) becomes a real difference in kind. The claim assumes that character of absoluteness, that apparent infinity, and incommensurability with all other considerations, which constitute the distinction between the feeling of right and wrong and that of ordinary expediency and inexpediency. The feelings concerned are so powerful, and we count so positively on finding a responsive feeling in others (all being alike interested), that *ought* and *should* grow into *must,* and recognized indispensability becomes a moral necessity, analogous to physical, and often not inferior to it in binding force.

If the preceding analysis, or something resembling it, be not the correct account of the notion of justice; if justice be totally independent of utility, and be a standard *per se,* which the mind can recognize by simple introspection of itself; it is hard to understand why that internal oracle is so ambiguous, and why so many things appear either just or unjust, according to the light in which they are regarded.

We are continually informed that utility is an uncertain standard, which every different person interprets differently, and that there is no safety but in the immutable, ineffaceable, and unmistakable dictates of justice, which carry their evidence in themselves, and are independent of the fluctuations of opinion. One would suppose from this that on questions of justice there could be no controversy; that if we take that for our rule, its application to any given case could leave us in as little doubt as a mathematical demonstration. So far is this from being the fact, that there is as much difference of opinion and as much discussion about what is just, as about what is useful to society. Not only have different nations and individuals different notions of justice, but in the mind of one and the same individual, justice is not some one rule, principle, or maxim, but many, which do not always coincide in their dictates, and in choosing between which he is guided either by some extraneous standard or by his own personal predilections.

For instance, there are some who say that it is unjust to punish anyone for the sake of example to others; that punishment is just only when intended for the good of the sufferer himself. Others maintain the extreme reverse, contending that to punish persons who have attained years of discretion, for their own benefit, is despotism and injustice, since if the matter at issue is solely their own good, no one has a right to control their own judgment of it; but that they may justly be punished to prevent evil to others, this being the exercise of the legitimate right of self-defense. Mr. Owen, again, affirms that it is unjust to punish at all; for the criminal did not make his own character; his education, and the circumstances which surrounded him, have made him a criminal, and for these he is not responsible. All these opinions are extremely plausible; and so long as the question is argued as one of justice simply, without going down to the principles which lie under justice and are the source of its authority, I am unable to see how any of these reasoners can be refuted. For in truth every one of the three builds upon rules of justice confessedly true. The first appeals to the acknowledged injustice of singling out an individual, and making him a sacrifice, without his consent, for other people's benefit. The second relies on the acknowledged justice of self-defense, and the admitted injustice of forcing one person to conform to another's notions of what constitutes his good. The Owenite invokes the admitted principle that it is unjust to punish anyone for what he cannot help. Each is triumphant so long as he is not compelled to take into consideration any other maxims of justice than the one he has selected; but as soon as their several maxims are brought face to face, each disputant seems to have exactly as much to say for himself as the others. No one of them can carry out his own notion of justice without trampling upon another equally binding. These are difficulties; they have always been felt to be such; and many devices have been invented to turn rather than to overcome them. As a refuge from the last of the three, men imagined what they called the freedom of the will; fancying that they could not justify punishing a man whose will is in a thoroughly hateful state, unless it be supposed to have come into that state through no influence of anterior circumstances. To escape from the other difficulties, a favorite contrivance has been the fiction of a contract, whereby at some unknown period all the members of society engaged to obey the laws, and consented to be punished for any disobedience to them; thereby giving to their legislators the right, which it is assumed they would not otherwise have had, of punishing them, either for their own good or for that of society. This happy thought was considered to get rid of the whole difficulty, and to legitimate the infliction of punishment, in virtue of another received maximum of justice, *Volenti non fit injuria*—that is not unjust which is done with the consent of the person who is supposed to be hurt by it. I need hardly remark that even if the consent were not a mere fiction, this maxim is not superior in authority to the others which it is brought in to supersede. It is, on the contrary, an instructive specimen of the loose and irregular manner in which supposed principles of justice grow up. This particular one evidently came into use as a help to the coarse exigencies of courts of law, which are sometimes obliged to be content with very uncertain presumptions, on account of the greater evils which would often arise from any attempt on their part to cut finer. But even courts of law are not able to adhere consistently to the maxim, for they allow voluntary engagements to be set aside on the ground of fraud, and sometimes on that of mere mistake or misinformation.

Again, when the legitimacy of inflicting punishment is admitted, how many conflicting conceptions of justice come to light in discussing the proper apportionment of punishments to offenses. No rule on the subject recommends itself so strongly to the primitive and spontaneous sentiment of justice as the *lex talionis,* an eye for an eye and a tooth for a tooth. Though this principle of the Jewish and of the Mohammedan law has been generally abandoned in Europe as a practical maxim, there is, I suspect, in most minds, a secret hankering after it; and when retribution accidentally falls on an offender in that precise shape, the general feeling of satisfaction evinced bears witness how natural is the sentiment to which this repayment in kind is acceptable. With many, the test of justice in penal infliction is that the punishment should be proportioned to the offense; meaning that it should be exactly measured by the moral guilt of the culprit (whatever be their standard for measuring moral guilt)—the consideration, what amount of punishment is necessary to deter from the offense, having nothing to do with the question of justice, in their estimation; while there are others to whom that consideration is all in all—who maintain that it is not just, at least for man, to inflict on a fellow-creature, whatever may be his offenses, any amount of suffering beyond the least that will suffice to prevent him from repeating, and others from imitating, his misconduct.

To take another example from a subject already once referred to. In a co-operative industrial association, is it just or not that talent or skill should give a title to superior remuneration? On the negative side of the question it is argued that whoever does the best he can, deserves equally well, and ought not in justice to be put in a position of inferiority for no fault of his own; that superior abilities have already advantages more than enough, in the admiration they excite, the personal influence they command, and the internal sources of satisfaction attending them, without adding to these a superior share of the world's goods; and that society is bound in justice rather to make compensation to the less favored for this unmerited inequality of advantages, than to aggravate it. On the contrary side it is contended that society receives more from the more efficient laborer; that his services being more useful, society owes him a larger return for them; that a greater share of the joint result is actually his work, and not to allow his claim to it is a kind of robbery; that if he is only to receive as much as others, he can only be justly required to produce as much, and to give a smaller amount of time and exertion, proportioned to his superior efficiency. Who shall decide between these appeals to conflicting principles of justice? Justice has in this case two sides to it, which it is impossible to bring into harmony, and the two disputants have chosen opposite sides; the one looks to what it is just that the individual should receive, the other to what it is just that the community should give. Each, from his own point of view, is unanswerable; and any choice between them, on grounds of justice, must be perfectly arbitrary. Social utility alone can decide the preference.

How many, again, and how irreconcilable, are the standards of justice to which reference is made in discussing the repartition of taxation. One opinion is, that payment to the State should be in numerical proportion to pecuniary means. Others think that justice dictates what they term graduated taxation; taking a higher percentage from those who have more to spare. In point of natural justice a strong case might be made for disregarding means altogether, and taking the same absolute sum (whenever it could be got) from everyone—as the subscribers to a mess, or to a club, all pay the same sum for the same privileges, whether they can all equally afford it or not. Since the protection (it might be said) of law and government is afforded to, and is equally required by all, there is no injustice in making all buy it at the same price. It is reckoned justice, not injustice, that a dealer should charge to all customers the same price for the same article, not a price varying according to their means of payment. This doctrine, as applied to taxation, finds no advocates, because it conflicts so strongly with man's feelings of humanity and of social expediency; but the principle of justice which it invokes is as true and as binding as those which can be appealed to against it. Accordingly it exerts a tacit influence on the line of defense employed for other modes of assessing taxation. People feel obliged to argue that the State does more for the rich than for the poor, as a justification for its taking more from them: though this is in reality not true, for the rich would be far better able to protect themselves, in the absence of law or government, than the poor, and indeed would probably be successful in converting the poor into their slaves. Others, again, so far defer to the same conception of justice, as to maintain that all should pay an equal capitation tax for the protection of their persons (these being of equal value to all), and an unequal tax for the protection of their property, which is unequal. To this others reply that the all of one man is as valuable to him as the all of another. From these confusions there is no other mode of extrication than the utilitarian.

Is, then, the difference between the just and the expedient a merely imaginary distinction? Have mankind been under a delusion in thinking that justice is a more sacred thing than policy, and that the latter ought only to be listened to after the former has been satisfied? By no means. The exposition we have given of the nature and origin of the sentiment, recognizes a real distinction; and no one of those who profess the most sublime contempt for the consequences of actions as an element in their morality, attaches more importance to the distinction than I do. While I dispute the pretensions of any theory which sets up an imaginary standard of justice not grounded on utility, I account the justice which is grounded on utility to be the chief part, and incomparably the most sacred and binding part, of all morality. Justice is a name for certain classes of moral rules which concern the essentials of human well-being more nearly, and are therefore of more absolute obligation, than any other rules for the guidance of life; and the notion which we have found to be of the essence of the idea of justice, that of a right residing in an individual, implies and testifies to this more binding obligation.

The moral rules which forbid mankind to hurt one another (in which we must never forget to include wrongful interference with each other's freedom) are more vital to human well-being than any maxims, however important, which only point out the best mode of managing some department of human affairs. They have also the peculiarity, that they are the main element in determining the whole of the social feelings of mankind. It is their observance which alone preserves peace among human beings: if obedience to them were not the rule, and disobedience the exception, everyone would see in everyone else an enemy, against whom he must be perpetually guarding himself. What is hardly less important, these are the precepts which mankind have the strongest and the most direct inducements for impressing upon one another. By merely giving to each other prudential instruction or exhortation, they may gain, or think they gain, nothing; in inculcating on each other the duty of positive beneficence they have an unmistakable interest, but far less in degree: a person may possibly not need the benefits of others, but he always needs that they should not do him hurt. Thus the moralities which protect every individual from being harmed by others, either directly or by being hindered in his freedom of pursuing his own good, are at once those which he himself has most at heart, and those which he has the strongest interest in publishing and enforcing by word and deed. It is by a person's observance of these that his fitness to exist as one of the fellowship of human beings is tested and decided; for on that depends his being a nuisance or not to those with whom he is in contact. Now it is these moralities primarily which compose the obligations of justice. The most marked cases of injustice, and those which give the tone to the feeling of repugnance which characterizes the sentiment, are acts of wrongful aggression, or wrongful exercise of power over some one; the next are those which consist in wrongfully withholding from him something which is his due: in both cases, inflicting on him a positive hurt, either in the form of direct suffering, or of the privation of some good which he had reasonable ground, either of a physical or of a social kind, for counting upon.

The same powerful motives which command the observance of these primary moralities, enjoin the punishment of those who violate them, and as the impulses of self-defense, of defense of others, and of vengeance, are all called forth against such persons, retribution, or evil for evil, becomes closely connected with the sentiment of justice, and is universally included in the idea. Good for good is also one of the dictates of justice; and this, though its social utility is evident, and though it carries with it a natural human feeling, has not at first sight that obvious connection with hurt or injury, which, existing in the most elementary cases of just and unjust, is the source of the characteristic intensity of the sentiment. But the connection, though less obvious, is not less real. He who accepts benefits, and denies a return of them when needed, inflicts a real hurt, by disappointing one of the most natural and reasonable of expectations, and one which he must at least tacitly have encouraged, otherwise the benefits would seldom have been conferred. The important rank, among human evils and wrongs, of the disappointment of expectation, is shown in the fact that it constitutes the principal criminality of two such highly immoral acts as a breach of friendship and a breach of promise. Few hurts which human beings can sustain are greater, and none wound more, than when that on which they habitually and with full assurance relied, fails them in the hour of need; and few wrongs are greater than this mere withholding of good; none excite more resentment, either in the person suffering, or in a sympathizing spectator. The principle, therefore, of giving to each what they deserve, that is, good for good as well as evil for evil, is not only included within the idea of justice as we have defined it, but is a proper object of that intensity of sentiment, which places the just, in human estimation, above the simply expedient.

Most of the maxims of justice current in the world, and commonly appealed to in its transactions, are simply instrumental to carrying into effect the principles of justice which we have now spoken of. That a person is only responsible for what he has done voluntarily, or could voluntarily have avoided, that it is unjust to condemn any person unheard, that the punishment ought to be proportioned to the offense, and the like, are maxims intended to prevent the just principle of evil for evil from being perverted to the infliction of evil without that justification. The greater part of these common maxims have come into use from the practice of courts of justice, which have been naturally led to a more complete recognition and elaboration than was likely to suggest itself to others, of the rules necessary to enable them to fulfil their double function, of inflicting punishment when due, and of awarding to each person his right.

That first of judicial virtues, impartiality, is an obligation of justice, partly for the reason last mentioned, as being a necessary condition of the fulfilment of the other obligations of justice. But this is not the only source of the exalted rank, among human obligations, of those maxims of equality and impartiality which, both in popular estimation and in that of the most enlightened, are included among the precepts of justice. In one point of view, they may be considered as corollaries from the principles already laid down. If it is a duty to do to each according to his deserts, returning good for good as well as repressing evil by evil, it necessarily follows that we should treat all equally well (when no higher duty forbids) who have deserved equally well of *us*, and that society should treat all equally well who have deserved equally well of *it*, that is, who have deserved equally well absolutely. This is the highest abstract standard of social and distributive justice; towards which all institutions, and the efforts of all virtuous citizens, should be made in the utmost possible degree to converge. But this great moral duty rests upon a still deeper foundation, being a direct emanation from the first principle of morals, and not a mere logical corollary from secondary or derivative doctrines. It is involved in the very meaning of utility, or the greatest happiness principle. That principle is a mere form of words without rational signification, unless one person's happiness, supposed equal in degree (with the proper allowance made for kind), is counted for exactly as much as another's. Those conditions being supplied, Bentham's dictum, "everybody to count for one, nobody for more than one," might be written under the principle of utility as an explanatory commentary.[3] The equal claim of everybody to happiness in the estimation of the moralist and of the legislator, involves an equal claim to all the means of happiness, except in so far as the inevitable conditions of human life, and the general interest, in which that of every individual is included, set limits to the maxim; and those limits ought to be strictly construed. As every other maxim of justice, so this is by no means applied or held applicable universally; on the contrary, as I have already remarked, it bends to every person's ideas of social expe-

[3] This implication, in the first principle of the utilitarian scheme, of perfect impartiality between persons, is regarded by Mr. Herbert Spencer (in his *Social Statics*) as a disproof of the pretensions of utility to be a sufficient guide to right; since (he says) the principle of utility presupposes the anterior principle, that everybody has an equal right to happiness. It may be more correctly described as supposing that equal amounts of happiness are equally desirable, whether felt by the same or by different persons. This, however, is not a *pre*-supposition, not a premise needful to support the principle of utility, but the very principle itself; for what is the principle of utility, if it be not that 'happiness' and 'desirable' are synonymous terms? If there is any anterior principle implied, it can be no other than this, that the truths of arithmetic are applicable to the valuation of happiness, as of all other measurable quantities.

(Mr. Herbert Spencer, in a private communication on the subject of the preceding Note, objects to being considered an opponent of utilitarianism, and states that he regards happiness as the ultimate end of morality; but deems that end only partially attainable by empirical generalizations from the observed results of conduct, and completely attainable only by deducing, from the laws of life and the conditions of existence, what kinds of action necessarily tend to produce happiness, and what kinds to produce unhappiness. With the exception of the word 'necessarily,' I have no dissent to express from this doctrine; and (omitting that word) I am not aware that any modern advocate of utilitarianism is of a different opinion. Bentham, certainly, to whom in the *Social Statics* Mr. Spencer particularly referred, is, least of all writers, chargeable with unwillingness to deduce the effect of actions on happiness from the laws of human nature and the universal conditions of human life. The common charge against him is of relying too exclusively upon such deductions, and declining altogether to be bound by the generalizations from specific experience which Mr. Spencer thinks that utilitarians generally confine themselves to. My own opinion [and, as I recollect, Mr. Spencer's] is, that in ethics, as in all other branches of scientific study, the consilience of the results of both these processes, each corroborating and verifying the other, is requisite to give to any general proposition the kind and degree of evidence which constitutes scientific proof.)

diency. But in whatever case it is deemed applicable at all, it is held to be the dictate of justice. All persons are deemed to have a *right* to equality of treatment, except when some recognized social expediency requires the reverse. And hence all social inequalities which have ceased to be considered expedient, assume the character not of simple inexpediency, but of injustice, and appear so tyrannical, that people are apt to wonder how they ever could have been tolerated; forgetful that they themselves perhaps tolerate other inequalities under an equally mistaken notion of expediency, the correction of which would make that which they approve seem quite as monstrous as what they have at last learnt to condemn. The entire history of social improvement has been a series of transitions, by which one custom or institution after another, from being a supposed primary necessity of social existence, has passed into the rank of a universally stigmatized injustice and tyranny. So it has been with the distinctions of slaves and freemen, nobles and serfs, patricians and plebeians; and so it will be, and in part already is, with the aristocracies of color, race, and sex.

It appears from what has been said that justice is a name for certain moral requirements which, regarded collectively, stand higher in the scale of social utility, and are therefore of more paramount obligation, than any others; though particular cases may occur in which some other social duty is so important, as to overrule any one of the general maxims of justice. Thus, to save a life, it may not only be allowable but a duty to steal or take by force the necessary food or medicine, or to kidnap and compel to officiate the only qualified medical practitioner. In such cases, as we do not call anything justice which is not a virtue; we usually say, not that justice must give way to some other moral principle, but that what is just in ordinary cases is, by reason of that other principle, not just in the particular case. By this useful accommodation of language, the character of indefeasibility attributed to justice is kept up, and we are saved from the necessity of maintaining that there can be laudable injustice.

The considerations which have now been adduced resolve, I conceive, the only real difficulty in the utilitarian theory of morals. It has always been evident that all cases of justice are also cases of expediency: the difference is in the peculiar sentiment which attaches to the former, as contradistinguished from the latter. If this characteristic sentiment has been sufficiently accounted for; if there is no necessity to assume for it any peculiarity of origin; if it is simply the natural feeling of resentment, moralized by being made coextensive with the demands of social good; and if this feeling not only does but ought to exist in all the classes of cases to which the idea of justice corresponds: that idea no longer presents itself as a stumbling-block to the utilitarian ethics. Justice remains the appropriate name for certain social utilities which are vastly more important, and therefore more absolute and imperative, than any others are as a class (though not more so than others may be in particular cases); and which, therefore, ought to be, as well as naturally are, guarded by a sentiment not only different in degree, but also in kind; distinguished from the milder feeling which attaches to the mere idea of promoting human pleasure or convenience, at once by the more definite nature of its commands, and by the sterner character of its sanctions.

ON LIBERTY

CHAPTER I

INTRODUCTORY

THE SUBJECT of this essay is not the so-called liberty of the will, so unfortunately opposed to the misnamed doctrine of philosophical necessity; but civil, or social liberty: the nature and limits of the power which can be legitimately exercised by society over the individual. A question seldom stated and hardly ever discussed in general terms, but which profoundly influences the practical controversies of the age by its latent presence, and is likely soon to make itself recognized as the vital question of the future. It is so far from being new, that, in a certain sense, it has divided mankind almost from the remotest ages; but in the stage of progress into which the more civilized portions of the species have now entered, it presents itself under new conditions, and requires a different and more fundamental treatment.

The struggle between liberty and authority is the most conspicuous feature in the portions of history with which we are earliest familiar, particularly in that of Greece, Rome, and England. But in old times this contest was between subjects, or some classes of subjects, and the government. By liberty, was meant protection against the tyranny of the political rulers. The rulers were conceived (except in some of the popular governments of Greece) as in a necessarily antagonistic position to the people whom they ruled. They consisted of a governing One, or a governing tribe or caste, who derived their authority from inheritance or conquest, who, at all events, did not hold it at the pleasure of the governed, and whose supremacy men did not venture, perhaps did not desire, to contest, whatever precautions might be taken against its oppressive exercise. Their power was regarded as necessary, but also as highly dangerous; as a weapon which they would attempt to use against their subjects, no less than against external enemies. To prevent the weaker members of the community from being preyed upon by innumerable vultures, it was needful that there should be an animal of prey stronger than the rest, commissioned to keep them down. But as the king of the vultures would be no less bent upon preying on the flock than any of the minor harpies, it was indispensable to be in a perpetual attitude of defense against his beak and claws. The aim, therefore, of patriots was to set limits to the power which the ruler should be suffered to exercise over the community; and this limitation was what they meant by liberty. It was attempted in two ways. First, by obtaining a recognition of certain immunities, called political liberties or rights, which it was to be regarded as a breach of duty in the ruler to infringe, and which if he did infringe, specific resistance, or general rebellion, was held to be justifiable. A second, and generally a later expedient, was the establishment of constitutional checks, by which the consent of the community, or of a body of some sort, supposed to represent its interests, was made a necessary condition to some of the more important acts of the governing power. To the first of these modes of limitation, the ruling power, in most European countries, was compelled, more or less, to submit. It was not so with the second; and, to attain this, or when already in some degree possessed, to attain it more completely, became everywhere the principal object of the lovers of liberty. And so long as mankind were content to combat one enemy by another, and to be ruled by a master, on condition of being guaranteed more or less efficaciously against his tyranny, they did not carry their aspirations beyond this point.

A time, however, came, in the progress of human affairs, when men ceased to think it a necessity of nature that their governors should be an independent power, opposed in interest to themselves. It appeared to them much better that the various magistrates of the State should be their tenants or delegates, revocable at their pleasure. In that way alone, it seemed, could they have complete security that the powers of government would never be abused to their disadvantage. By degrees this new demand for elective and temporary rulers became the prominent object of the exertions of the popular party, wherever any such party existed; and superseded, to a considerable extent, the previous efforts to limit the power of rulers. As the struggle proceeded for making the ruling power emanate from the periodical choice of the ruled, some persons began to think that too much importance had been attached to the limitation of the power itself. *That* (it might seem) was a resource against rulers whose interests were habitually opposed to those of the people. What was now wanted was, that the rulers should be identified with the people; that their interest and will should be the interest and will of the nation. The nation did not need to be protected against its own will. There was no fear of its tyrannizing over itself. Let the rulers be effectually responsible to it, promptly removable by it, and it could afford to trust them with power of which it could itself dictate the use to be made. Their power was but the nation's own power, concentrated, and in a form convenient for exercise. This mode of thought, or rather perhaps of feeling, was common among the last generation of European liberalism, in the Continental section of which it still apparently predominates. Those who admit any limit to what a government may do, except in the case of such governments as they think ought not to exist, stand out as brilliant exceptions among the political thinkers of the Continent. A similar tone of sentiment might by this time have been prevalent in our own country, if the circumstances which for a time encouraged it had continued unaltered.

But in political and philosophical theories, as well as in persons, success discloses faults and infirmities which failure might have concealed from observation. The notion that the people have no need to limit their power over themselves, might seem axiomatic when popular government was a thing only dreamed about, or read of as having existed at some distant period of the past. Neither was that notion necessarily disturbed by such temporary aberrations as those of the French Revolution, the worst of which were the work of a usurping few, and which, in any case, belonged not to the permanent working of popular institutions, but to a sudden and convulsive outbreak against monarchical and aristocratic despotism. In time, however, a democratic republic came to occupy a large portion of the earth's surface, and made itself felt as one of the most powerful members of the community of nations; and elective and responsible government became subject to the observations and criticisms which wait upon a great existing fact. It was now perceived that such phrases as 'self-government,' and 'the power of the people over themselves,' do not express the true state of the case. The 'people' who exercise the power are not always the same people with those over whom it is exercised; and the 'self-government' spoken of is not the government of each by himself, but of each by all the rest. The will of the people, moreover, practically means the will of the most numerous or the most active *part* of the people; the majority, or those who succeed in making themselves accepted as the majority: the people, consequently *may* desire to oppress a part of their number, and precautions are as much needed against this as against any other abuse of power. The limitation, therefore, of the power of government over individuals loses none of its importance when the holders of power are regularly accountable to the community, that is, to the strongest party therein. This view of things, recommending itself equally to the intelligence of thinkers and to the inclination of those important classes in European society to whose real or supposed interests democracy is adverse, has had no difficulty in establishing itself; and in political speculations 'the tyranny of the majority' is now generally included among the evils against which society requires to be on its guard.

Like other tyrannies, the tyranny of the majority was at first, and is still vulgarly, held in dread chiefly as operating through the acts of the public authorities. But reflecting persons perceived that when society is

itself the tyrant—society collectively over the separate individuals who
compose it—its means of tyrannizing are not restricted to the acts which
it may do by the hands of its political functionaries. Society can and
does execute its own mandates; and if it issues wrong mandates instead
of right, or any mandates at all in things with which it ought not to
meddle, it practices a social tyranny more formidable than many kinds
of political oppression, since, though not usually upheld by such extreme
penalties, it leaves fewer means of escape, penetrating much more deeply
into the details of life, and enslaving the soul itself. Protection, therefore, against the tyranny of the magistrate is not enough: there needs
protection also against the tyranny of the prevailing opinion and feeling; against the tendency of society to impose, by other means than
civil penalties, its own ideas and practices as rules of conduct on those
who dissent from them; to fetter the development, and, if possible, prevent the formation, of any individuality not in harmony with its ways,
and compels all characters to fashion themselves upon the model of its
own. There is a limit to the legitimate interference of collective opinion
with individual independence; and to find that limit, and maintain it
against encroachment, is as indispensable to a good condition of human
affairs, as protection against political despotism.

But though this proposition is not likely to be contested in general
terms, the practical question, where to place the limit—how to make the
fitting adjustment between individual independence and social control—
is a subject on which nearly everything remains to be done. All that
makes existence valuable to anyone, depends on the enforcement of restraints upon the actions of other people. Some rules of conduct, therefore, must be imposed, by law in the first place, and by opinion on
many things which are not fit subjects for the operation of law. What
these rules should be is the principal question in human affairs; but if
we except a few of the most obvious cases, it is one of those which least
progress has been made in resolving. No two ages, and scarcely any two
countries, have decided it alike; and the decision of one age or country
is a wonder to another. Yet the people of any given age and country no
more suspect any difficulty in it, than if it were a subject on which mankind had always been agreed. The rules which obtain among themselves
appear to them self-evident and self-justifying. This all but universal illusion is one of the examples of the magical influence of custom, which
is not only, as the proverb says, a second nature, but is continually mistaken for the first. The effect of custom, in preventing any misgiving respecting the rules of conduct which mankind impose on one another, is
all the more complete because the subject is one on which it is not generally considered necessary that reasons should be given, either by one
person to others or by each to himself. People are accustomed to believe,

and have been encouraged in the belief by some who aspire to the character of philosophers, that their feelings, on subjects of this nature, are
better than reasons, and render reasons unnecessary. The practical principle which guides them to their opinions on the regulation of human
conduct, is the feeling in each person's mind that everybody should be
required to act as he, and those with whom he sympathizes, would like
them to act. No one, indeed, acknowledges to himself that his standard
of judgment is his own liking; but an opinion on a point of conduct, not
supported by reasons, can only count as one person's preference; and if
the reasons, when given, are a mere appeal to a similar preference felt
by other people, it is still only many people's liking instead of one. To
an ordinary man, however, his own preference, thus supported, is not
only a perfectly satisfactory reason, but the only one he generally has
for any of his notions of morality, taste, or propriety, which are not expressly written in his religious creed; and his chief guide in the interpretation even of that. Men's opinions, accordingly, on what is laudable
or blamable, are affected by all the multifarious causes which influence
their wishes in regard to the conduct of others, and which are as numerous as those which determine their wishes on any other subject. Sometimes their reason, at other times their prejudices or superstitions; often
their social affections, not seldom their antisocial ones, their envy or
jealousy, their arrogance or contemptuousness: but most commonly their
desires or fears for themselves—their legitimate or illegitimate self-
interest. Wherever there is an ascendant class, a large portion of the
morality of the country emanates from its class interests, and its feelings
of class superiority. The morality between Spartans and Helots, between
planters and Negroes, between princes and subjects, between nobles and
roturiers, between men and women, has been for the most part the creation of these class interests and feelings; and the sentiments thus generated react in turn upon the moral feelings of the members of the ascendant class, in their relations among themselves. Where, on the other
hand, a class, formerly ascendant, has lost its ascendancy, or where its
ascendancy is unpopular, the prevailing moral sentiments frequently
bear the impress of an impatient dislike of superiority. Another grand
determining principle of the rules of conduct, both in act and forbearance, which have been enforced by law or opinion, has been the servility of mankind towards the supposed preferences or aversions of their
temporal masters or of their gods. This servility, though essentially selfish, is not hypocrisy; it gives rise to perfectly genuine sentiments of
abhorrence; it made men burn magicians and heretics. Among so many
baser influences, the general and obvious interests of society have of
course had a share, and a large one, in the direction of the moral sentiments; less, however, as a matter of reason, and on their own account

than as a consequence of the sympathies and antipathies which grew out of them; and sympathies and antipathies which had little or nothing to do with the interests of society, have made themselves felt in the establishment of moralities with quite as great force.

The likings and dislikings of society, or of some powerful portion of it, are thus the main thing which has practically determined the rules laid down for general observance, under the penalties of law or opinion. And in general, those who have been in advance of society in thought and feeling, have left this condition of things unassailed in principle, however they may have come into conflict with it in some of its details. They have occupied themselves rather in inquiring what things society ought to like or dislike, than in questioning whether its likings or dislikings should be a law to individuals. They preferred endeavoring to alter the feelings of mankind on the particular points on which they were themselves heretical, rather than make common cause in defense of freedom, with heretics generally. The only case in which the higher ground has been taken on principle and maintained with consistency, by any but an individual here and there, is that of religious belief: a case instructive in many ways, and not least so as forming a most striking instance of the fallibility of what is called the moral sense; for the *odium theologicum*, in a sincere bigot, is one of the most unequivocal cases of moral feeling. Those who first broke the yoke of what called itself the Universal Church, were in general as little willing to permit difference of religious opinion as that church itself. But when the heat of the conflict was over, without giving a complete victory to any party, and each church or sect was reduced to limit its hopes to retaining possession of the ground it already occupied; minorities, seeing that they had no chance of becoming majorities, were under the necessity of pleading to those whom they could not convert, for permission to differ. It is accordingly on this battlefield, almost solely, that the rights of the individual against society have been asserted on broad grounds of principle, and the claim of society to exercise authority over dissentients openly controverted. The great writers to whom the world owes what religious liberty it possesses, have mostly asserted freedom of conscience as an indefeasible right, and denied absolutely that a human being is accountable to others for his religious belief. Yet so natural to mankind is intolerance in whatever they really care about, that religious freedom has hardly anywhere been practically realized, except where religious indifference, which dislikes to have its peace disturbed by theological quarrels, has added its weight to the scale. In the minds of almost all religious persons, even in the most tolerant countries, the duty of toleration is admitted with tacit reserves. One person will bear with dissent in matters of church government, but not of dogma; another can tolerate everybody, short of a Papist or a Unitarian; another everyone who believes in revealed religion; a few extend their charity a little further, but stop at the belief in a God and in a future state. Wherever the sentiment of the majority is still genuine and intense, it is found to have abated little of its claim to be obeyed.

In England, from the peculiar circumstances of our political history, though the yoke of opinion is perhaps heavier, that of law is lighter, than in most other countries of Europe; and there is considerable jealousy of direct interference, by the legislative or the executive power, with private conduct; not so much from any just regard for the independence of the individual, as from the still subsisting habit of looking on the government as representing an opposite interest to the public. The majority have not yet learnt to feel the power of the government their power, or its opinions their opinions. When they do so, individual liberty will probably be as much exposed to invasion from the government, as it already is from public opinion. But, as yet, there is a considerable amount of feeling ready to be called forth against any attempt of the law to control individuals in things in which they have not hitherto been accustomed to be controlled by it; and this with very little discrimination as to whether the matter is, or is not, within the legitimate sphere of legal control; insomuch that the feeling, highly salutary on the whole, is perhaps quite as often misplaced as well grounded in the particular instances of its application. There is, in fact, no recognized principle by which the propriety or impropriety of government interference is customarily tested. People decide according to their personal preferences. Some, whenever they see any good to be done, or evil to be remedied, would willingly instigate the government to undertake the business; while others prefer to bear almost any amount of social evil, rather than add one to the departments of human interests amenable to governmental control. And men range themselves on one or the other side in any particular case, according to this general direction of their sentiments; or according to the degree of interest which they feel in the particular thing which it is proposed that the government should do, or according to the belief they entertain that the government would, or would not, do it in the manner they prefer; but very rarely on account of any opinion to which they consistently adhere, as to what things are fit to be done by a government. And it seems to me that in consequence of this absence of rule or principle, one side is at present as often wrong as the other: the interference of government is, with about equal frequency, improperly invoked and improperly condemned.

The object of this essay is to assert one very simple principle, as entitled to govern absolutely the dealings of society with the individual in the way of compulsion and control, whether the means used be physical force in the form of legal penalties, or the moral coercion of public opinion. That principle is, that the sole end for which mankind are warranted, individually or collectively, in interfering with the liberty of action of any of their number, is self-protection. That the only purpose for which power can be rightfully exercised over any member of a civilized community, against his will, is to prevent harm to others. His own good, either physical or moral, is not a sufficient warrant. He cannot rightfully be compelled to do or forbear because it will be better for him to do so, because it will make him happier, because, in the opinions of others, to do so would be wise, or even right. These are good reasons for remonstrating with him, or reasoning with him, or persuading him, or entreating him, but not for compelling him, or visiting him with any evil in case he do otherwise. To justify that, the conduct from which it is desired to deter him must be calculated to produce evil to someone else. The only part of the conduct of anyone, for which he is amenable to society, is that which concerns others. In the part which merely concerns himself, his independence is, of right, absolute. Over himself, over his own body and mind, the individual is sovereign.

It is perhaps hardly necessary to say that this doctrine is meant to apply only to human beings in the maturity of their faculties. We are not speaking of children, or of young persons below the age which the law may fix as that of manhood or womanhood. Those who are still in a state to require being taken care of by others, must be protected against their own actions as well as against external injury. For the same reason, we may leave out of consideration those backward states of society in which the race itself may be considered as in its nonage. The early difficulties in the way of spontaneous progress are so great, and there is seldom any choice of means for overcoming them; and a ruler full of the spirit of improvement is warranted in the use of any expedients that will attain an end, perhaps otherwise unattainable. Despotism is a legitimate mode of government in dealing with barbarians, provided the end be their improvement, and the means justified by actually effecting that end. Liberty, as a principle, has no application to any state of things anterior to the time when mankind have become capable of being improved by free and equal discussion. Until then, there is nothing for them but implicit obedience to an Akbar or a Charlemagne, if they are so fortunate as to find one. But as soon as mankind have attained the capacity of being guided to their own improvement by conviction or persuasion (a period long since reached in all nations with whom we need here concern ourselves), compulsion, either in the direct form or in that of pains and penalties for non-compliance, is no longer admissible as a means to their own good, and justifiable only for the security of others.

It is proper to state that I forego any advantage which could be derived to my argument from the idea of abstract right, as a thing inde-pendent of utility. I regard utility as the ultimate appeal on all ethical questions; but it must be utility in the largest sense, grounded on the permanent interests of a man as a progressive being. Those interests, I contend, authorized the subjection of individual spontaneity to external control, only in respect to those actions of each which concern the inter-est of other people. If anyone does an act hurtful to others, there is a *prima facie* case for punishing him, by law, or, where legal penalties are not safely applicable, by general disapprobation. There are also many positive acts for the benefit of others, which he may rightfully be com-pelled to perform: such as to give evidence in a court of justice; to bear his fair share in the common defense, or in any other joint work neces-sary to the interest of the society of which he enjoys the protection; and to perform certain acts of individual beneficence, such as saving a fel-low-creature's life, or interposing to protect the defenseless against ill-usage, things which whenever it is obviously a man's duty to do, he may rightfully be made responsible to society for not doing. A person may cause evil to others not only by his actions but by his inaction, and in either case he is justly accountable to them for the injury. The latter case, it is true, requires a much more cautious exercise of compulsion than the former. To make anyone answerable for doing evil to others is the rule; to make him answerable for not preventing evil is, compara-tively speaking, the exception. Yet there are many cases clear enough and grave enough to justify that exception. In all things which regard the external relations of the individual, he is *de jure* amenable to those whose interests are concerned, and, if need be, to society as their protec-tor. There are often good reasons for not holding him to the responsibil-ity; but these reasons must arise from the special expediencies of the case: either because it is a kind of case in which he is on the whole likely to act better, when left to his own discretion, than when controlled in any way in which society have it in their power to control him; or be-cause the attempt to exercise control would produce other evils, greater than those which it would prevent. When such reasons as these preclude the enforcement of responsibility, the conscience of the agent himself should step into the vacant judgment seat, and protect those interests of others which have no external protection; judging himself all the more rigidly, because the case does not admit of his being made accountable to the judgment of his fellow-creatures.

But there is a sphere of action in which society, as distinguished from the individual, has, if any, only an indirect interest; comprehending all that portion of a person's life and conduct which affects only himself, or if it also affects others, only with their free, voluntary, and undeceived consent and participation. When I say only himself, I mean directly, and in the first instance; for whatever affects himself, may affect others through himself; and the objection which may be grounded on this contingency, will receive consideration in the sequel. This, then, is the appropriate region of human liberty. It comprises, *first*, the inward domain of consciousness; demanding liberty of conscience in the most comprehensive sense; liberty of thought and feeling; absolute freedom of opinion and sentiment on all subjects, practical or speculative, scientific, moral, or theological. The liberty of expressing and publishing opinions may seem to fall under a different principle, since it belongs to that part of the conduct of an individual which concerns other people; but, being almost of as much importance as the liberty of thought itself, and resting in great part on the same reasons, is practically inseparable from it. *Secondly*, the principle requires liberty of tastes and pursuits; of framing the plan of our life to suit our own character; of doing as we like, subject to such consequences as may follow: without impediment from our fellow-creatures, so long as what we do does not harm them, even though they should think our conduct foolish, perverse, or wrong. *Thirdly*, from this liberty of each individual, follows the liberty, within the same limits, of combination among individuals; freedom to unite, for any purpose not involving harm to others: the persons combining being supposed to be of full age, and not forced or deceived.

No society in which these liberties are not, on the whole, respected, is free, whatever may be its form of government; and none is completely free in which they do not exist absolute and unqualified. The only freedom which deserves the name, is that of pursuing our own good in our own way, so long as we do not attempt to deprive others of theirs, or impede their efforts to obtain it. Each is the proper guardian of his own health, whether bodily, or mental and spiritual. Mankind are greater gainers by suffering each other to live as seems good to themselves, than by compelling each to live as seems good to the rest.

Though this doctrine is anything but new, and, to some persons, may have the air of a truism, there is no doctrine which stands more directly opposed to the general tendency of existing opinion and practice. Society has expended fully as much effort in the attempt (according to its lights) to compel people to conform to its notions of personal as of social excellence. The ancient commonwealths thought themselves entitled to practice, and the ancient philosophers countenanced, the regulation of every part of private conduct by public authority, on the ground that the State had a deep interest in the whole bodily and mental discipline of every one of its citizens: a mode of thinking which may have been admissible in small republics surrounded by powerful enemies, in constant peril of being subverted by foreign attack or internal commotion, and to which even a short interval of relaxed energy and self-command might so easily be fatal that they could not afford to wait for the salutary permanent effects of freedom. In the modern world, the greater size of political communities, and, above all, the separation between spiritual and temporal authority (which placed the direction of men's consciences in other hands than those which controlled their worldly affairs), prevented so great an interference by law in the details of private life; but the engines of moral repression have been wielded more strenuously against divergence from the reigning opinion in self-regarding, than even in social matters; religion, the most powerful of the elements which have entered into the formation of moral feeling, having almost always been governed either by the ambition of a hierarchy, seeking control over every department of human conduct, or by the spirit of Puritanism. And some of those modern reformers who have placed themselves in strongest opposition to the religions of the past, have been no way behind either churches or sects in their assertion of the right of spiritual domination: M. Comte, in particular, whose social system, as unfolded in his *Système de Politique Positive,* aims at establishing (though by moral more than by legal appliances) a despotism of society over the individual, surpassing anything contemplated in the political ideal of the most rigid disciplinarian among the ancient philosophers.

Apart from the peculiar tenets of individual thinkers, there is also in the world at large an increasing inclination to stretch unduly the powers of society over the individual, both by the force of opinion and even by that of legislation; and as the tendency of all the changes taking place in the world is to strengthen society, and diminish the power of the individual, this encroachment is not one of the evils which tend spontaneously to disappear, but, on the contrary, to grow more and more formidable. The disposition of mankind, whether as rulers or as fellow-citizens, to impose their own opinions and inclinations as a rule of conduct on others, is so energetically supported by some of the best and by some of the worst feelings incident to human nature, that it is hardly ever kept under restraint by anything but want of power; and as the power is not declining, but growing, unless a strong barrier of moral conviction can be raised against the mischief, we must expect, in the present circumstances of the world, to see it increase.

It will be convenient for the argument, if, instead of at once entering upon the general thesis, we confine ourselves in the first instance to a single branch of it, on which the principle here stated is, if not fully, yet to a certain point, recognized by the current opinions. This one branch is the *liberty of thought:* from which it is impossible to separate the cognate liberty of speaking and of writing. Although these liberties, to some considerable amount, form part of the political morality of all countries which profess religious toleration and free institutions, the

grounds, both philosophical and practical, on which they rest, are perhaps not so familiar to the general mind, nor so thoroughly appreciated
by many even of the leaders of opinion, as might have been expected.
Those grounds, when rightly understood, are of much wider application
than to only one division of the subject, and a thorough consideration of
this part of the question will be found the best introduction to the remainder. Those to whom nothing which I am about to say will be new,
may therefore, I hope, excuse me, if on a subject which for now three
centuries has been so often discussed, I venture on one discussion more.

CHAPTER II

OF THE LIBERTY OF THOUGHT AND DISCUSSION

THE TIME, it is to be hoped, is gone by, when any defense would be
necessary of the 'liberty of the press' as one of the securities against corrupt or tyrannical government. No argument, we may suppose, can now
be needed against permitting a legislature or an executive, not identified
in interest with the people, to prescribe opinions to them, and determine what doctrines or what arguments they shall be allowed to hear.
This aspect of the question, besides, has been so often and so trium-
phantly enforced by preceding writers, that it need not be specially insisted on in this place. Though the law of England, on the subject of the
press, is as servile to this day as it was in the time of the Tudors, there
is little danger of its being actually put in force against political discussion, except during some temporary panic, when fear of insurrection
drives ministers and judges from their propriety;[1] and, speaking gener-

---

[1] These words had scarcely been written, when, as if to give them an emphatic
contradiction, occurred the Government Press Prosecutions of 1858. That ill-judged
interference with the liberty of public discussion has not, however, induced me to
alter a single word in the text, nor has it at all weakened my conviction that, moments of panic excepted, the era of pains and penalties for political discussion has,
in our own country, passed away. For, in the first place, the prosecutions were not
persisted in; and, in the second, they were never, properly speaking, political prosecutions. The offense charged was not that of criticising institutions, or the acts of
persons of rulers, but of circulating what was deemed an immoral doctrine, the lawfulness of tryannicide.
  If the arguments of the present chapter are of any validity, there ought to exist
the fullest liberty of professing and discussing, as a matter of ethical conviction, any
doctrine, however immoral it may be considered. It would, therefore, be irrelevant
and out of place to examine here, whether the doctrine of tyrannicide deserves that
title. I shall content myself with saying that the subject has been at all times one of
the open questions of morals; that the act of a private citizen in striking down a
criminal, who, by raising himself above the law, has placed himself beyond the

ally, it is not, in constitutional countries, to be apprehended that the government, whether completely responsible to the people or not, will often attempt to control the expression of opinion, except when in doing so it makes itself the organ of the general intolerance of the public. Let us suppose, therefore, that the government is entirely at one with the people, and never thinks of exerting any power of coercion unless in agreement with what it conceives to be their voice. But I deny the right of the people to exercise such coercion, either by themselves or by their government. The power itself is illegitimate. The best government has no more title to it than the worst. It is as noxious, or more noxious, when exerted in accordance with public opinion, than when in opposition to it. If all mankind minus one were of one opinion, and only one person were of the contrary opinion, mankind would be no more justified in silencing that one person, than he, if he had the power, would be justified in silencing mankind. Were an opinion a personal possession of no value except to the owner; if to be obstructed in the enjoyment of it were simply a private injury, it would make some difference whether the injury was inflicted only on a few persons or on many. But the peculiar evil of silencing the expression of an opinion is, that it is robbing the human race: posterity as well as the existing generation; those who dissent from the opinion, still more than those who hold it. If the opinion is right, they are deprived of the opportunity of exchanging error for truth; if wrong, they lose, what is almost as great a benefit, the clearer perception and livelier impression of truth, produced by its collision with error.

It is necessary to consider separately these two hypotheses, each of which has a distinct branch of the argument corresponding to it. We can never be sure that the opinion we are endeavoring to stifle is a false opinion; and if we were sure, stifling it would be an evil still.

First: the opinion which it is attempted to suppress by authority may possibly be true. Those who desire to suppress it, of course deny its truth; but they are not infallible. They have no authority to decide the question for all mankind, and exclude every other person from the means of judging. To refuse a hearing to an opinion, because they are sure that it is false, is to assume that *their* certainty is the same thing

reach of legal punishment or control, has been accounted by whole nations, and by some of the best and wisest of men, not a crime, but an act of exalted virtue; and that, right or wrong, it is not of the nature of assassination, but of civil war. As such, I hold that the instigation to it, in a specific case, may be a proper subject of punishment, but only if an overt act has followed, and at least a probable connection can be established between the act and the instigation. Even then, it is not a foreign government, but the very government assailed, which alone, in the exercise of self-defense, can legitimately punish attacks directed against its own existence.

as *absolute* certainty. All silencing of discussion is an assumption of infallibility. Its condemnation may be allowed to rest on this common
argument, not the worse for being common.

Unfortunately for the good sense of mankind, the fact of their fallibility is far from carrying the weight in their practical judgment which is
always allowed to it in theory; for while everyone well knows himself to
be fallible, few think it necessary to take any precautions against their
own fallibility, or admit the supposition that any opinion of which they
feel very certain, may be one of the examples of the error to which they
acknowledge themselves to be liable. Absolute princes, or others who are
accustomed to unlimited deference, usually feel this complete confidence
in their own opinions on nearly all subjects. People more happily situated, who sometimes hear their opinions disputed, and are not wholly
unused to be set right when they are wrong, place the same unbounded
reliance only on such of their opinions as are shared by all who surround
them, or to whom they habitually defer; for in proportion to a man's
want of confidence in his own solitary judgment, does he usually repose,
with implicit trust, on the infallibility of 'the world' in general. And the
world, to each individual, means the part of it with which he comes in
contact—his party, his sect, his church, his class of society; the man
may be called, by comparison, almost liberal and large-minded to whom
it means anything so comprehensive as his own country or his own age.
Nor is his faith in this collective authority at all shaken by his being
aware that other ages, countries, sects, churches, classes, and parties
have thought, and even now think, the exact reverse. He devolves upon
his own world the responsibility of being in the right against the dissentient worlds of other people; and it never troubles him that mere accident has decided which of these numerous worlds is the object of his
reliance, and that the same causes which make him a Churchman in
London, would have made him a Buddhist or a Confucian in Pekin. Yet
it is as evident in itself as any amount of argument can make it, that
ages are no more infallible than individuals; every age having held
many opinions which subsequent ages have deemed not only false but
absurd; and it is as certain that many opinions now general will be rejected by future ages, as it is that many, once general, are rejected by
the present.

The objection likely to be made to this argument would probably take
some such form as the following. There is no greater assumption of infallibility in forbidding the propagation of error, than in any other thing
which is done by public authority on its own judgment and responsibility. Judgment is given to men that they may use it. Because it may be
used erroneously, are men to be told that they ought not to use it at all?
To prohibit what they think pernicious, is not claiming exemption from

error, but fulfilling the duty incumbent on them, although fallible, of acting on their conscientious conviction. If we were never to act on our opinions, because these opinions may be wrong, we should leave all our interests uncared for, and all our duties unperformed. An objection which applies to all conduct can be no valid objection to any conduct in particular. It is the duty of governments, and of individuals, to form the truest opinions they can; to form them carefully, and never impose them upon others unless they are quite sure of being right. But when they are sure (such reasoners may say), it is not unconscientiousness but cowardice to shrink from acting on their opinions, and allow doctrines which they honestly think dangerous to the welfare of mankind, either in this life or in another, to be scattered abroad without restraint, because other people, in less enlightened times, have persecuted opinions now believed to be true. Let us take care, it may be said, not to make the same mistake; but governments and nations have made mistakes in other things, which are not denied to be fit subjects for the exercise of authority: they have laid on bad taxes, made unjust wars. Ought we therefore to lay on no taxes, and, under whatever provocation, make no wars? Men, and governments, must act to the best of their ability. There is no such thing as absolute certainty, but there is assurance sufficient for the purposes of human life. We may, and must, assume our opinion to be true for the guidance of our own conduct: and it is assuming no more when we forbid bad men to pervert society by the propagation of opinions which we regard as false and pernicious.

I answer that it is assuming very much more. There is the greatest difference between presuming an opinion to be true because, with every opportunity for contesting it, it has not been refuted, and assuming its truth for the purpose of not permitting its refutation. Complete liberty of contradicting and disproving our opinion is the very condition which justifies us in assuming its truth for purposes of action; and on no other terms can a being with human faculties have any rational assurance of being right.

When we consider either the history of opinion, or the ordinary conduct of human life, to what is it to be ascribed that the one and the other are no worse than they are? Not certainly to the inherent force of the human understanding; for, on any matter not self-evident, there are ninety-nine persons totally incapable of judging of it for one who is capable; and the capacity of the hundredth person is only comparative: for the majority of the eminent men of every past generation held many opinions now known to be erroneous, and did or approved numerous things which no one will now justify. Why is it, then, that there is or the whole a preponderance among mankind of rational opinions and rational conduct? If there really is this preponderance—which there must be unless human affairs are, and have always been, in an almost desperate state—it is owing to a quality of the human mind, the source of everything respectable in man either as an intellectual or as a moral being, namely, that his errors are corrigible. He is capable of rectifying his mistakes, by discussion and experience. Not by experience alone. There must be discussion, to show how experience is to be interpreted. Wrong opinions and practices gradually yield to fact and argument; but facts and arguments, to produce any effect on the mind, must be brought before it. Very few facts are able to tell their own story, without comments to bring out their meaning. The whole strength and value, then, of human judgment, depending on the one property, that it can be set right when it is wrong, reliance can be placed on it only when the means of setting it right are kept constantly at hand. In the case of any person whose judgment is really deserving of confidence, how has it become so? Because he has kept his mind open to criticism of his opinions and conduct. Because it has been his practice to listen to all that could be said against him; to profit by as much of it as was just, and expound to himself, and upon occasion to others, the fallacy of what was fallacious. Because he has felt that the only way in which a human being can make some approach to knowing the whole of a subject, is by hearing what can be said about it by persons of every variety of opinion, and studying all modes in which it can be looked at by every character of mind. No wise man ever acquired his wisdom in any mode but this; nor is it in the nature of human intellect to become wise in any other manner. The steady habit of correcting and completing his own opinion by collating it with those of others, so far from causing doubt and hesitation in carrying it into practice, is the only stable foundation for a just reliance on it: for, being cognizant of all that can, at least obviously, be said against him, and having taken up his position against all gainsayers— knowing that he has sought for objections and difficulties, instead of avoiding them, and has shut out no light which can be thrown upon the subject from any quarter—he has a right to think his judgment better than that of any person, or any multitude, who have not gone through a similar process.

It is not too much to require that what the wisest of mankind, those who are best entitled to trust their own judgment, find necessary to warrant their relying on it, should be submitted to by that miscellaneous collection of a few wise and many foolish individuals, called the public. The most intolerant of churches, the Roman Catholic Church, even at the canonization of a saint, admits, and listens patiently to, a 'devil's advocate.' The holiest of men, it appears, cannot be admitted to posthumous honors, until all that the devil could say against him is known and weighed. If even the Newtonian philosophy were not permitted to be questioned, mankind could not feel as complete assurance of its truth as they now do. The beliefs which we have most warrant for, have no safe-guard to rest on but a standing invitation to the whole world to prove them unfounded. If the challenge is not accepted, or is accepted and the attempt fails, we are far enough from certainty still; but we have done the best that the existing state of human reason admits of; we have neglected nothing that could give the truth a chance of reaching us: if the lists are kept open, we may hope that if there be a better truth, it will be found when the human mind is capable of receiving it; and in the meantime we may rely on having attained such approach to truth as is possible in our own day. This is the amount of certainty attainable by a fallible being, and this the sole way of attaining it.

Strange it is that men should admit the validity of the arguments for free discussion, but object to their being 'pushed to an extreme'; not see-ing that unless the reasons are good for an extreme case, they are not good for any case. Strange that they should imagine that they are not assuming infallibility, when they acknowledge that there should be free discussion on all subjects which can possibly be *doubtful,* but think that some particular principle or doctrine should be forbidden to be ques-tioned because it is so *certain,* that is, because *they are certain* that it is certain. To call any proposition certain while there is anyone who would deny its certainty if permitted, but who is not permitted, is to assume that we ourselves, and those who agree with us, are the judges of cer-tainty, and judges without hearing the other side.

In the present age—which has been described as "destitute of faith, but terrified at scepticism"—in which people feel sure, not so much that their opinions are true, as that they should not know what to do without them—the claims of an opinion to be protected from public attack are rested not so much on its truth, as on its importance to society. There are, it is alleged, certain beliefs so useful, not to say indispensable, to well-being that it is as much the duty of governments to uphold those beliefs, as to protect any other of the interests of society. In a case of such necessity, and so directly in the line of their duty, something less than infallibility may, it is maintained, warrant, and even bind, govern-ments to act on their own opinion, confirmed by the general opinion of mankind. It is also often argued, and still oftener thought, that none but bad men would desire to weaken these salutary beliefs; and there can be nothing wrong, it is thought, in restraining bad men, and prohib-iting what only such men would wish to practice. This mode of thinking makes the justification of restraints on discussion not a question of the truth of doctrines, but of their usefulness; and flatters itself by that means to escape the responsibility of claiming to be an infallible judge of opinions. But those who thus satisfy themselves, do not perceive that the assumption of infallibility is merely shifted from one point to another. The usefulness of an opinion is itself matter of opinion: as disputable, as open to discussion, and requiring discussion as much as the opinion itself. There is the same need of an infallible judge of opinions to decide an opinion to be noxious, as to decide it to be false, unless the opinion condemned has full opportunity of defending itself. And it will not do to say that the heretic may be allowed to maintain the utility or harmlessness of his opinion, though forbidden to maintain its truth. The truth of an opinion is part of its utility. If we would know whether or not it is desirable that a proposition should be believed, is it possible to exclude the consideration of whether or not it is true? In the opinion, not of bad men, but of the best men, no belief which is contrary to truth can be really useful: and can you prevent such men from urging that plea, when they are charged with culpability for denying some doctrine which they are told is useful, but which they believe to be false? Those who are on the side of received opinions never fail to take all possible advantage of this plea: you do not find *them* handling the question of utility as if it could be completely abstracted from that of truth; on the contrary, it is, above all, because their doctrine is 'the truth,' that the knowledge or the belief of it is held to be so indispensable. There can be no fair discussion of the question of usefulness when an argument so vital may be employed on one side, but not on the other. And in point of fact, when law or public feeling do not permit the truth of an opinion to be disputed, they are just as little tolerant of a denial of its usefulness. The utmost they allow is an extenuation of its absolute necessity, or of the positive guilt of rejecting it.

In order more fully to illustrate the mischief of denying a hearing to opinions because we, in our own judgment, have condemned them, it will be desirable to fix down the discussion to a concrete case; and I choose, by preference, the cases which are least favorable to me—in which the argument against freedom of opinion, both on the score of truth and on that of utility, is considered the strongest. Let the opinions impugned be the belief in a God and in a future state, or any of the commonly received doctrines of morality. To fight the battle on such ground gives a great advantage to an unfair antagonist; since he will be sure to say (and many who have no desire to be unfair will say it internally), "Are these the doctrines which you do not deem sufficiently certain to be taken under the protection of law? Is the belief in a God one of the opinions to feel sure of which you hold to be assuming infallibility?" But I must be permitted to observe that it is not the feeling sure of a doctrine (be it what it may) which I call an assumption of infallibility. It is the undertaking to decide that question *for others,* without allowing them to hear what can be said on the contrary side. And *I* denounce and reprobate this pretension not the less if put forth on the side of my most solemn convictions. However positive anyone's persuasion may be, not only of the falsity but of the pernicious consequences—not only of the pernicious consequences, but (to adopt expressions which I altogether condemn) the immorality and impiety of an opinion; yet if, in pursuance of that private judgment, though backed by the public judgment of his country or his contemporaries, he prevents the opinion from being heard in its defense, he assumes infallibility. And so far from the assumption being less objectionable or less dangerous because the opinion is called immoral or impious, this is the case of all others in which it is most fatal. These are exactly the occasions on which the men of one generation commit those dreadful mistakes which excite the astonishment and horror of posterity. It is among such that we find the instances memorable in history, when the arm of the law has been employed to root out the best men and the noblest doctrines; with deplorable success as to the men, though some of the doctrines have survived to be (as if in mockery) invoked in defense of similar conduct towards those who dissent from *them,* or from their received interpretation.

Mankind can hardly be too often reminded, that there was once a man named Socrates, between whom and the legal authorities and public opinion of his time there took place a memorable collision. Born in an age and country abounding in individual greatness, this man has been handed down to us by those who best knew both him and the age, as the most virtuous man in it; while *we* know him as the head and prototype of all subsequent teachers of virtue, the source equally of the lofty inspiration of Plato and the judicious utilitarianism of Aristotle, *"i maëstri di color che sanno,"* the two headsprings of ethical as of all other philosophy. This acknowledged master of all the eminent thinkers who have since lived—whose fame, still growing after more than two thousand years, all but outweighs the whole remainder of the names which make his native city illustrious—was put to death by his countrymen, after a judicial conviction, for impiety and immorality. Impiety, in denying the gods recognized by the State; indeed his accuser asserted (see the *Apologia*) that he believed in no gods at all. Immorality, in being, by his doctrines and instructions, a "corruptor of youth." Of these charges the tribunal, there is every ground for believing, honestly found him guilty, and condemned the man who probably of all then born had deserved best of mankind to be put to death as a criminal.

To pass from this to the only other instance of judicial iniquity, the mention of which, after the condemnation of Socrates, would not be an anticlimax: the event which took place on Calvary rather more than eighteen hundred years ago. The man who left on the memory of those who witnessed his life and conversation such an impression of his moral grandeur that eighteen subsequent centuries have done homage to him as the Almighty in person, was ignominiously put to death, as what? As a blasphemer. Men did not merely mistake their benefactor; they mistook him for the exact contrary of what he was, and treated him as that prodigy of impiety which they themselves are now held to be for their treatment of him. The feelings with which mankind now regard these lamentable transactions, especially the later of the two, render them extremely unjust in their judgment of the unhappy actors. These were, to all appearance, not bad men—not worse than men commonly are, but rather the contrary; men who possessed in a full, or somewhat more than a full measure, the religious, moral, and patriotic feelings of their time and people: the very kind of men who, in all times, our own included, have every chance of passing through life blameless and respected. The high priest who rent his garments when the words were pronounced which, according to all the ideas of his country, constituted the blackest guilt, was in all probability quite as sincere in his horror and indignation as the generality of respectable and pious men now are in the religious and moral sentiments they profess; and most of those who now shudder at his conduct, if they had lived in his time, and been born Jews, would have acted precisely as he did. Orthodox Christians who are tempted to think that those who stoned to death the first martyrs must have been worse men than they themselves are, ought to remember that one of those persecutors was Saint Paul.

Let us add one more example, the most striking of all, if the impressiveness of an error is measured by the wisdom and virtue of him who falls into it. If ever anyone possessed of power had grounds for thinking himself the best and most enlightened among his contemporaries, it was the Emperor Marcus Aurelius. Absolute monarch of the whole civilized world, he preserved through life not only the most unblemished justice, but what was less to be expected from his Stoical breeding, the tenderest heart. The few failings which are attributed to him were all on the side of indulgence; while his writings, the highest ethical product of the ancient mind, differ scarcely perceptibly, if they differ at all, from the most characteristic teachings of Christ. This man, a better Christian in all but the dogmatic sense of the word than almost any of the ostensibly Christian sovereigns who have since reigned, persecuted Christianity. Placed at the summit of all the previous attainments of humanity, with an open, unfettered intellect, and a character which led him of himself to embody in his moral writings the Christian ideal, he yet failed to see that Christianity was to be a good and not an evil to the world, with his duties to which he was so deeply penetrated. Existing society he knew to be in a deplorable state. But such as it was, he saw, or thought he saw, that it was held together, and prevented from being worse, by belief and reverence of the received divinities. As a ruler of mankind, he deemed it his duty not to suffer society to fall in pieces; and saw not how, if its existing ties were removed, any others could be formed which could again knit it together. The new religion openly aimed at dissolving these ties: unless, therefore, it was his duty to adopt that religion, it seemed to be his duty to put it down. Inasmuch then as the theology of Christianity did not appear to him true or of divine origin; inasmuch as this strange history of a crucified God was not credible to him, and a system which purported to rest entirely upon a foundation to him so wholly unbelievable, could not be foreseen by him to be that renovating agency which, after all abatements, it has in fact proved to be; the gentlest and most amiable of philosophers and rulers, under a solemn sense of duty, authorized the persecution of Christianity. To my mind this is one of the most tragical facts in all history. It is a bitter thought, how different a thing the Christianity of the world might have been, if the Christian faith had been adopted as the religion of the empire under the auspices of Marcus Aurelius instead of those of Constantine. But it would be equally unjust to him and false to truth to deny that no one plea which can be urged for punishing anti-Christian teaching was wanting to Marcus Aurelius for punishing as he did the propagation of Christianity. No Christian more firmly believes that atheism is false, and tends to the dissolution of society, than Marcus Aurelius believed the same things of Christianity; he who, of all men then living, might have been thought the most capable of appreciating it. Unless anyone who approves of punishment for the promulgation of opinions, flatters himself that he is a wiser and better man than Marcus Aurelius—more deeply versed in the wisdom of his time, more elevated in his intellect above it—more earnest in his search for truth, or more single-minded in his devotion to it when found; let him abstain from that assumption of the joint infallibility of himself and the multitude, which the great Antoninus made with so unfortunate a result.

Aware of the impossibility of defending the use of punishment for restraining irreligious opinions by any argument which will not justify Marcus Antoninus, the enemies of religious freedom, when hard pressed, occasionally accept this consequence, and say, with Dr. Johnson, that the persecutors of Christianity were in the right; that persecution is an ordeal through which truth ought to pass, and always passes successfully, legal penalties being, in the end, powerless against truth, though sometimes beneficially effective against mischievous errors. This is a form of the argument for religious intolerance sufficiently remarkable not to be passed without notice.

A theory which maintains that truth may justifiably be persecuted because persecution cannot possibly do it any harm, cannot be charged with being intentionally hostile to the reception of new truths; but we cannot commend the generosity of its dealing with the persons to whom mankind are indebted for them. To discover to the world something which deeply concerns it, and of which it was previously ignorant; to prove to it that it had been mistaken on some vital point of temporal or spiritual interest, is as important a service as a human being can render to his fellow-creatures, and in certain cases, as in those of the early Christians and of the Reformers, those who think with Dr. Johnson believe it to have been the most precious gift which could be bestowed on mankind. That the authors of such splendid benefits should be requited by martyrdom, that their reward should be to be dealt with as the vilest of criminals, is not, upon this theory, a deplorable error and misfortune, for which humanity should mourn in sackcloth and ashes, but the normal and justifiable state of things. The propounder of a new truth, according to this doctrine, should stand, as stood, in the legislation of the Locrians, the proposer of a new law, with a halter round his neck, to be instantly tightened if the public assembly did not, on hearing his reasons, then and there adopt his proposition. People who defend this mode of treating benefactors cannot be supposed to set much value on the benefit; and I believe this view of the subject is mostly confined to the sort of persons who think that new truths may have been desirable once, but that we have had enough of them now.

But, indeed, the dictum that truth always triumphs over persecution is one of those pleasant falsehoods which men repeat after one another till they pass into commonplaces, but which all experience refutes. History teems with instances of truth put down by persecution. If not suppressed forever, it may be thrown back for centuries. To speak only of religious opinions: the Reformation broke out at least twenty times before Luther, and was put down. Arnold of Brescia was put down. Fra Dolcino was put down. Savonarola was put down. The Albigeois were put down. The Vaudois were put down. The Lollards were put down. The Hussites were put down. Even after the era of Luther, wherever persecution was persisted in, it was successful. In Spain, Italy, Flanders, the Austrian Empire, Protestantism was rooted out; and, most likely would have been so in England, had Queen Mary lived, or Queen Elizabeth died. Persecution has always succeeded, save where the heretics were too strong a party to be effectually persecuted. No reasonable person can doubt that Christianity might have been extirpated in the Roman Empire. It spread, and became predominant, because the persecutions were only occasional, lasting but a short time, and separated by long intervals of almost undisturbed propagandism. It is a piece of idle sentimentality that truth, merely as truth, has any inherent power denied to error of prevailing against the dungeon and the stake. Men are not more zealous for truth than they often are for error, and a sufficient application of legal or even of social penalties will generally succeed in stopping the propagation of either. The real advantage which truth has, consists in this, that when an opinion is true, it may be extinguished once, twice, or many times, but in the course of ages there will generally be found persons to rediscover it, until some one of its reappearances falls on a time when from favorable circumstances it escapes persecution until it has made such head as to withstand all subsequent attempts to suppress it.

It will be said that we do not now put to death the introducers of new opinions: we are not like our fathers who slew the prophets, we even build sepulchres to them. It is true we no longer put heretics to death; and the amount of penal infliction which modern feeling would probably tolerate, even against the most obnoxious opinions, is not sufficient to extirpate them. But let us not flatter ourselves that we are yet free from the stain even of legal persecution. Penalties for opinion, or at least for its expression, still exist by law; and their enforcement is not, even in these times, so unexampled as to make it at all incredible that they may some day be revived in full force. In the year 1857, at the summer assizes of the county of Cornwall, an unfortunate man,[2] said to be of unexceptionable conduct in all relations of life, was sentenced to twenty-one months' imprisonment, for uttering, and writing on a gate, some offensive words concerning Christianity. Within a month of the same time, at the Old Bailey, two persons, on two separate occasions,[3] were rejected as jurymen, and one of them grossly insulted by the judge and by one of the counsel, because they honestly declared that they had no theological belief; and a third, a foreigner,[4] for the same reason, was denied justice against a thief. This refusal of redress took place in virtue of the legal doctrine, that no person can be allowed to give evidence in a court of justice who does not profess belief in a God (any god is sufficient) and in a future state; which is equivalent to declaring such persons to be outlaws, excluded from the protection of the tribunals; who may not only be robbed or assaulted with impunity, if no one but themselves, or persons of similar opinions, be present, but any one else may be robbed or assaulted with impunity, if the proof of the fact depends on their evidence. The assumption on which this is grounded is that the oath is worthless of a person who does not believe in a future state; a proposition which betokens much ignorance of history in those who assent to it (since it is historically true that a large

---

[2] Thomas Pooley, Bodmin Assizes, July 31, 1857. In December following, he received a free pardon from the Crown.

[3] George Jacob Holyoake, August 17, 1857; Edward Truelove, July, 1857.

[4] Baron de Gleichen, Marlborough Street Police Court, August 4, 1857.

proportion of infidels in all ages have been persons of distinguished integrity and honor); and would be maintained by no one who had the smallest conception how many of the persons in greatest repute with the world, both for virtues and attainments, are well known, at least to their intimates, to be unbelievers. The rule, besides, is suicidal, and cuts away its own foundation. Under pretense that atheists must be liars, it admits the testimony of all atheists who are willing to lie, and rejects only those who brave the obloquy of publicly confessing a detested creed rather than affirm a falsehood. A rule thus self-convicted of absurdity so far as regards its professed purpose, can be kept in force only as a badge of hatred, a relic of persecution; a persecution, too, having the peculiarity that the qualification for undergoing it is the being clearly proved not to deserve it. The rule, and the theory it implies, are hardly less insulting to believers than to infidels. For if he who does not believe in a future state necessarily lies, it follows that they who do believe are only prevented from lying, if prevented they are, by the fear of hell. We will not do the authors and abettors of the rule the injury of supposing that the conception which they have formed of Christian virtue is drawn from their own consciousness.

These, indeed, are but rags and remnants of persecution, and may be thought to be not so much an indication of the wish to persecute, as an example of that very frequent infirmity of English minds, which makes them take a preposterous pleasure in the assertion of a bad principle, when they are no longer bad enough to desire to carry it really into practice. But unhappily there is no security in the state of the public mind that the suspension of worse forms of legal persecution, which has lasted for about the space of a generation, will continue. In this age the quiet surface of routine is as often ruffled by attempts to resuscitate past evils, as to introduce new benefits. What is boasted of at the present time as the revival of religion, is always, in narrow and uncultivated minds, at least as much the revival of bigotry; and where there is the strong permanent leaven of intolerance in the feelings of a people, which at all times abides in the middle classes of this country, it needs but little to provoke them into actively persecuting those whom they have never ceased to think proper objects of persecution. For it is this—it is the opinions men entertain, and the feelings they cherish, respecting those who disown the beliefs they deem important, which makes this country not a place of mental freedom. For a long time past, the chief mischief of the legal penalties is that they strengthen the social stigma. It is that stigma which is really effective, and so effective is it, that the profession of opinions which are under the ban of society is much less common in England than is, in many other countries, the avowal of those which incur risk of judicial punishment. In respect to all persons but those whose pecuniary circumstances make them independent of the good will of other people, opinion, on this subject, is as efficacious as law; men might as well be imprisoned, as excluded from the means of earning their bread. Those whose bread is already secured, and who desire no favors from men in power, or from bodies of men, or from the public, have nothing to fear from the open avowal of any opinions, but to be ill-thought of and ill-spoken of, and this it ought not to require a very heroic mold to enable them to bear. There is no room for any appeal *ad misericordiam* in behalf of such persons. But though we do not now inflict so much evil on those who think differently from us as it was formerly our custom to do, it may be that we do ourselves as much evil as ever by our treatment of them. Socrates was put to death, but the Socratic philosophy rose like the sun in heaven, and spread its illumination over the whole intellectual firmament. Christians were cast to the lions, but the Christian church grew up a stately and spreading tree, overtopping the older and less vigorous growths, and stifling them by its shade. Our merely social intolerance kills no one, roots out no opinions, but induces men to disguise them, or to abstain from any active effort for their diffusion. With us, heretical opinions do not perceptibly gain, or even lose, ground in each decade or generation; they never blaze out far and wide, but continue to smolder in the narrow circles of thinking and studious persons among whom they originate, without ever lighting up the general affairs of mankind with either a true or a deceptive light. And thus is kept up a state of things very satisfactory to some minds, because, without the unpleasant process of fining or imprisoning anybody, it maintains all prevailing opinions outwardly undisturbed, while it does not absolutely interdict the exercise of reason by dissentients afflicted with the malady of thought. A convenient plan for having peace in the intellectual world, and keeping all things going on therein very much as they do already! But the price paid for this sort of intellectual pacification is the sacrifice of the entire moral courage of the human mind. A state of things in which a large portion of the most active and inquiring intellects find it advisable to keep the general principles and grounds of their convictions within their own breasts, and attempt, in what they address to the public, to fit as much as they can of their own conclusions to premises which they have internally renounced, cannot send forth the open, fearless characters, and logical, consistent intellects who once adorned the thinking world. The sort of men who can be looked for under it, are either mere conformers to commonplace, or time-servers for truth, whose arguments on all great subjects are meant for their hearers, and are not those which have convinced themselves. Those who avoid this alternative, do so by narrowing their thoughts and interest to things which can be spoken of without venturing within the region of principles—that is, to small practical matters which would come right of themselves if but the minds of mankind were strengthened and enlarged, and which will never be made effectually right until then; while that which would strengthen and enlarge men's minds, free and daring speculation on the highest subjects, is abandoned.

Those in whose eyes this reticence on the part of heretics is no evil should consider, in the first place, that in consequence of it there is never any fair and thorough discussion of heretical opinions; and that such of them as could not stand such a discussion, though they may be prevented from spreading, do not disappear. But it is not the minds of heretics that are deteriorated most by the ban placed on all inquiry which does not end in the orthodox conclusions. The greatest harm done is to those who are not heretics, and whose whole mental development is cramped, and their reason cowed, by the fear of heresy. Who can compute what the world loses in the multitude of promising intellects combined with timid characters, who dare not follow out any bold, vigorous, independent train of thought, lest it should land them in something which would admit of being considered irreligious or immoral? Among them we may occasionally see some man of deep conscientiousness, and subtle and refined understanding, who spends a life in sophisticating with an intellect which he cannot silence, and exhausts the resources of ingenuity in attempting to reconcile the promptings of his conscience and reason with orthodoxy, which yet he does not, perhaps, to the end succeed in doing. No one can be a great thinker who does not recognize that as a thinker it is his first duty to follow his intellect to whatever conclusions it may lead. Truth gains more even by the errors of one who, with due study and preparation, thinks for himself, than by the true opinions of those who only hold them because they do not suffer themselves to think. Not that it is solely, or chiefly, to form great thinkers, that freedom of thinking is required. On the contrary, it is as much and even more indispensable to enable average human beings to attain the mental stature which they are capable of. There have been, and may again be, great individual thinkers in a general atmosphere of mental slavery. But there never has been, nor ever will be, in that atmosphere an intellectually active people. Where any people has made a temporary approach to such a character, it has been because the dread of heterodox speculation was for a time suspended. Where there is a tacit convention that principles are not to be disputed; where the discussion of the greatest questions which can occupy humanity is considered to be closed, we cannot hope to find that generally high scale of mental activity which has made some periods of history so remarkable. Never when controversy avoided the subjects which are large and important enough to kindle enthusiasm, was the mind of a people stirred up from its foundations, and the impulse given which raised even persons of the most ordinary intellect to something of the dignity of thinking beings. Of such we have had an example in the condition of Europe during the times immediately following the Reformation; another, though limited to the Continent and to a more cultivated class, in the speculative movement of the latter half of the eighteenth century; and a third, of still briefer duration, in the intellectual fermentation of Germany during the Goethean and Fichtean period. These periods differed widely in the particular opinions which they developed; but were alike in this, that during all three the yoke of authority was broken. In each, an old mental despotism had been thrown off, and no new one had yet taken its place. The impulse given at these three periods has made Europe what it now is. Every single improvement which has taken place either in the human mind or in institutions, may be traced distinctly to one or other of them. Appearances have for some time indicated that all three impulses are well nigh spent; and we can expect no fresh start until we again assert our mental freedom.

Let us now pass to the second division of the argument, and dismissing the supposition that any of the received opinions may be false, let us assume them to be true, and examine into the worth of the manner in which they are likely to be held, when their truth is not freely and openly canvassed. However unwillingly a person who has a strong opinion may admit the possibility that his opinion may be false, he ought to be moved by the consideration that, however true it may be, if it is not fully, frequently, and fearlessly discussed, it will be held as a dead dogma, not a living truth.

There is a class of persons (happily not quite so numerous as formerly) who think it enough if a person assents undoubtingly to what they think true, though he has no knowledge whatever of the grounds of the opinion, and could not make a tenable defense of it against the most superficial objections. Such persons, if they can once get their creed taught from authority, naturally think that no good, and some harm, comes of its being allowed to be questioned. Where their influence prevails, they make it nearly impossible for the received opinion to be rejected wisely and considerately, though it may still be rejected rashly and ignorantly; for to shut out discussion entirely is seldom possible, and when it once gets in, beliefs not grounded on conviction are apt to give way before the slightest semblance of an argument. Waiving, however, this possibility—assuming that the true opinion abides in the mind, but abides as a prejudice, a belief independent of, and proof against, argument--this is not the way in which truth ought to be held by a rational being. This is not knowing the truth. Truth, thus held, is but one superstition the more, accidentally clinging to the words which enunciate a truth.

If the intellect and judgment of mankind ought to be cultivated, a thing which Protestants at least do not deny, on what can these faculties be more appropriately exercised by anyone, than on the things which concern him so much that it is considered necessary for him to hold opinions on them? If the cultivation of the understanding consists in one thing more than in another, it is surely in learning the grounds of one's own opinions. Whatever people believe, on subjects on which it is of the first importance to believe rightly, they ought to be able to defend against at least the common objections. But, some one may say, "Let them be *taught* the grounds of their opinions. It does not follow that opinions must be merely parroted because they are never heard controverted. Persons who learn geometry do not simply commit the theorems to memory, but understand and learn likewise the demonstrations; and it would be absurd to say that they remain ignorant of the grounds of geometrical truths, because they never hear anyone deny, and attempt to disprove them." Undoubtedly: and such teaching suffices on a subject like mathematics, where there is nothing at all to be said on the wrong side of the question. The peculiarity of the evidence of mathematical truths is that all the argument is on one side. There are no objections, and no answers to objections. But on every subject on which difference of opinion is possible, the truth depends on a balance to be struck between two sets of conflicting reasons. Even in natural philosophy, there is always some other explanation possible of the same facts—some geocentric theory instead of heliocentric, some phlogiston instead of oxygen —and it has to be shown why that other theory cannot be the true one; and until this is shown, and until we know how it is shown, we do not understand the grounds of our opinion. But when we turn to subjects infinitely more complicated, to morals, religion, politics, social relations, and the business of life, three-fourths of the arguments for every disputed opinion consist in dispelling the appearances which favor some opinion different from it. The greatest orator, save one, of antiquity, has left it on record that he always studied his adversary's case with as great, if not still greater, intensity than even his own. What Cicero practiced as the means of forensic success requires to be imitated by all who study any subject in order to arrive at the truth. He who knows only his own side of the case, knows little of that. His reasons may be good, and no one may have been able to refute them. But if he is equally unable to refute the reasons on the opposite side; if he does not so much as know what they are, he has no ground for preferring either opinion. The rational position for him would be suspension of judgment, and unless he contents himself with that, he is either led by authority, or adopts, like the generality of the world, the side to which he feels most inclination. Nor is it enough that he should hear the arguments of adversaries from his own teachers, presented as they state them, and accompanied by what they offer as refutations. That is not the way to do justice to the arguments, or bring them into real contact with his own mind. He must be able to hear them from persons who actually believe them; who defend them in earnest, and do their very utmost for them. He must know them in their most plausible and persuasive form; he must feel the whole force of the difficulty which the true view of the subject has to encounter and dispose of; else he will never really possess himself of the portion of truth which meets and removes that difficulty. Ninety-nine in a hundred of what are called educated men are in this condition; even of those who can argue fluently for their opinions. Their conclusion may be true, but it might be false for anything they know: they have never thrown themselves into the mental position of those who think differently from them, and considered what such persons may have to say; and consequently they do not, in any proper sense of the word, know the doctrine which they themselves profess. They do not know those parts of it which explain and justify the remainder; the considerations which show that a fact which seemingly conflicts with another is reconcilable with it, or that, of two apparently strong reasons, one and not the other ought to be preferred. All that part of the truth which turns the scale, and decides the judgment of a completely informed mind, they are strangers to; nor is it ever really known but to those who have attended equally and impartially to both sides, and endeavored to see the reasons of both in the strongest light. So essential is this discipline to a real understanding of moral and human subjects, that if opponents of all important truths do not exist, it is indispensable to imagine them, and supply them with the strongest arguments which the most skillful devil's advocate can conjure up.

To abate the force of these considerations, an enemy of free discussion may be supposed to say, that there is no necessity for mankind in general to know and understand all that can be said against or for their opinions by philosophers and theologians. That it is not needful for common men to be able to expose all the misstatements or fallacies of an ingenious opponent. That it is enough if there is always somebody capable of answering them, so that nothing likely to mislead uninstructed persons remains unrefuted. That simple minds, having been taught the obvious grounds of the truths inculcated on them, may trust to authority for the rest, and being aware that they have neither knowledge nor talent to resolve every difficulty which can be raised, may repose in the assurance that all those which have been raised have been or can be answered, by those who are specially trained to the task.

Conceding to this view of the subject the utmost that can be claimed
for it by those most easily satisfied with the amount of understanding of
truth which ought to accompany the belief of it; even so, the argument
for free discussion is no way weakened. For even this doctrine acknowledges that mankind ought to have a rational assurance that all objections have been satisfactorily answered; and how are they to be answered if that which requires to be answered is not spoken? or how can
the answer be known to be satisfactory, if the objectors have no opportunity of showing that it is unsatisfactory? If not the public, at least the
philosophers and theologians who are to resolve the difficulties, must
make themselves familiar with those difficulties in their most puzzling
form; and this cannot be accomplished unless they are freely stated, and
placed in the most advantageous light which they admit of. The Catholic Church has its own way of dealing with this embarrassing problem.
It makes a broad separation between those who can be permitted to receive its doctrines on conviction, and those who must accept them on
trust. Neither, indeed, are allowed any choice as to what they will accept; but the clergy, such at least as can be fully confided in, may ad-
missibly and meritoriously make themselves acquainted with the arguments of opponents, in order to answer them, and may, therefore, read
heretical books; the laity, not unless by special permission, hard to be
obtained. This discipline recognizes a knowledge of the enemy's case as
beneficial to the teachers, but finds means, consistent with this, of denying it to the rest of the world: thus giving to the *élite* more mental culture, though not more mental freedom, than it allows to the mass. By
this device it succeeds in obtaining the kind of mental superiority which
its purposes require; for though culture without freedom never made a
large and liberal mind, it can make a clever *nisi prius* advocate of a
cause. But in countries professing Protestantism, this resource is denied:
since Protestants hold, at least in theory, that the responsibility for the
choice of a religion must be borne by each for himself, and cannot be
thrown off upon teachers. Besides, in the present state of the world, it
is practically impossible that writings which are read by the instructed
can be kept from the uninstructed. If the teachers of mankind are to
be cognisant of all that they ought to know, everything must be free to
be written and published without restraint.

If, however, the mischievous operation of the absence of free discussion, when the received opinions are true, were confined to leaving men
ignorant of the grounds of those opinions, it might be thought that this,
if an intellectual, is no moral evil, and does not affect the worth of the
opinions, regarded in their influence on the character. The fact, however, is that not only the grounds of the opinion are forgotten in the absence of discussion, but too often the meaning of the opinion itself. The

words which convey it cease to suggest ideas, or suggest only a small
portion of those they were originally employed to communicate. Instead
of a vivid conception and a living belief, there remain only a few
phrases retained by rote; or, if any part, the shell and husk only of the
meaning is retained, the finer essence being lost. The great chapter in
human history which this fact occupies and fills, cannot be too earnestly
studied and meditated on.

It is illustrated in the experience of almost all ethical doctrines and
religious creeds. They are all full of meaning and vitality to those who
originate them, and to the direct disciples of the originators. Their meaning continues to be felt in undiminished strength, and is perhaps brought
out into even fuller consciousness, so long as the struggle lasts to give
the doctrine or creed an ascendancy over other creeds. At last it either
prevails, and becomes the general opinion, or its progress stops; it keeps
possession of the ground it has gained, but ceases to spread further.
When either of these results has become apparent, controversy on the
subject flags, and gradually dies away. The doctrine has taken its place,
if not as a received opinion, as one of the admitted sects or divisions of
opinion: those who hold it have generally inherited, not adopted it; and
conversion from one of these doctrines to another, being now an exceptional fact, occupies little place in the thoughts of their professors. Instead of being, as at first, constantly on the alert either to defend themselves against the world, or to bring the world over to them, they have
subsided into acquiescence, and neither listen, when they can help it, to
arguments against their creed, nor trouble dissentients (if there be such)
with arguments in its favor. From this time may usually be dated the
decline in the living power of the doctrine. We often hear the teachers
of all creeds lamenting the difficulty of keeping up in the minds of believers a lively apprehension of the truth which they nominally recognize, so that it may penetrate the feelings, and acquire a real mastery
over the conduct. No such difficulty is complained of while the creed is
still fighting for its existence: even the weaker combatants then know
and feel what they are fighting for, and the difference between it and
other doctrines; and in that period of every creed's existence, not a few
persons may be found, who have realized its fundamental principles in
all the forms of thought, have weighed and considered them in all their
important bearings, and have experienced the full effect on the character
which belief in that creed ought to produce in a mind thoroughly im-
bued with it. But when it has come to be an hereditary creed, and to be
received passively, not actively; when the mind is no longer compelled,
in the same degree as at first, to exercise its vital powers on the questions which its belief presents to it: there is a progressive tendency to
forget all of the belief except the formularies, or to give it a dull and tor-

pid assent, as if accepting it on trust dispensed with the necessity of realizing it in consciousness, or testing it by personal experience, until it
almost ceases to connect itself at all with the inner life of the human being. Then are seen the cases, so frequent in this age of the world as almost to form the majority, in which the creed remains as it were outside
the mind, incrusting and petrifying it against all other influences ad-
dressed to the higher parts of our nature; manifesting its power by not
suffering any fresh and living conviction to get in, but itself doing nothing for the mind or heart, except standing sentinel over them to keep
them vacant.

To what an extent doctrines intrinsically fitted to make the deepest
impression upon the mind may remain in it as dead beliefs, without being ever realized in the imagination, the feelings, or the understanding,
is exemplified by the manner in which the majority of believers hold the
doctrines of Christianity. By Christianity I here mean what is accounted
such by all churches and sects—the maxims and precepts contained in
the New Testament. These are considered sacred, and accepted as laws,
by all professing Christians. Yet it is scarcely too much to say that not
one Christian in a thousand guides or tests his individual conduct by
reference to those laws. The standard to which he does refer it, is the
custom of his nation, his class, or his religious profession. He has thus,
on the one hand, a collection of ethical maxims, which he believes to
have been vouchsafed to him by infallible wisdom as rules for his government; and on the other a set of every-day judgments and practices,
which go a certain length with some of those maxims, not so great a
length with others, stand in direct opposition to some, and are, on the
whole, a compromise between the Christian creed and the interests and
suggestions of worldly life. To the first of these standards he gives his
homage; to the other his real allegiance. All Christians believe that the
blessed are the poor and humble, and those who are ill-used by the
world; that it is easier for a camel to pass through the eye of a needle
than for a rich man to enter the kingdom of heaven; that they should
judge not, lest they be judged; that they should swear not at all; that
they should love their neighbor as themselves; that if one take their
cloak, they should give him their coat also; that they should take no
thought for the morrow; that if they would be perfect they should sell
all that they have and give it to the poor. They are not insincere when
they say that they believe these things. They do believe them, as people
believe what they have always heard lauded and never discussed. But in
the sense of that living belief which regulates conduct, they believe
these doctrines just up to the point to which it is usual to act upon
them. The doctrines in their integrity are serviceable to pelt adversaries
with; and it is understood that they are to be put forward (when pos-

sible) as the reasons for whatever people do that they think laudable. But anyone who reminded them that the maxims require an infinity of things which they never even think of doing, would gain nothing but to be classed among those very unpopular characters who affect to be better than other people. The doctrines have no hold on ordinary believers —are not a power in their minds. They have an habitual respect for the sound of them, but no feeling which spreads from the words to the things signified, and forces the mind to take *them* in, and make them conform to the formula. Whenever conduct is concerned, they look round for Mr. A and B to direct them how far to go in obeying Christ.

Now we may be well assured that the case was not thus, but far otherwise, with the early Christians. Had it been thus, Christianity never would have expanded from an obscure sect of the despised Hebrews into the religion of the Roman empire. When their enemies said, "See how these Christians love one another" (a remark not likely to be made by anybody now), they assuredly had a much livelier feeling of the meaning of their creed than they have ever had since. And to this cause, probably, it is chiefly owing that Christianity now makes so little progress in extending its domain, and after eighteen centuries is still nearly confined to Europeans and the descendants of Europeans. Even with the strictly religious, who are much in earnest about their doctrines, and attach a greater amount of meaning to many of them than people in general, it commonly happens that the part which is thus comparatively active in their minds is that which was made by Calvin, or Knox, or some such person much nearer in character to themselves. The sayings of Christ coexist passively in their minds, producing hardly any effect beyond what is caused by mere listening to words so amiable and bland. There are many reasons, doubtless, why doctrines which are the badge of a sect retain more of their vitality than those common to all recognized sects, and why more pains are taken by teachers to keep their meaning alive; but one reason certainly is, that the peculiar doctrines are more questioned, and have to be oftener defended against open gainsayers. Both teachers and learners go to sleep at their post, as soon as there is no enemy in the field.

The same thing holds true, generally speaking, of all traditional doctrines—those of prudence and knowledge of life, as well as of morals or religion. All languages and literatures are full of general observations on life, both as to what it is, and how to conduct oneself in it; observations which everybody knows, which everybody repeats, or hears with acquiescence, which are received as truisms, yet of which most people first truly learn the meaning when experience, generally of a painful kind, has made it a reality to them. How often, when smarting under some unforeseen misfortune or disappointment, does a person call to mind some proverb or common saying, familiar to him all his life, the meaning of which, if he had ever before felt it as he does now, would have saved him from the calamity. There are indeed reasons for this, other than the absence of discussion; there are many truths of which the full meaning *cannot* be realized until personal experience has brought it home. But much more of the meaning even of these would have been understood, and what was understood would have been far more deeply impressed on the mind, if the man had been accustomed to hear it argued *pro* and *con* by people who did understand it. The fatal tendency of mankind to leave off thinking about a thing when it is no longer doubtful, is the cause of half their errors. A contemporary author has well spoken of "the deep slumber of a decided opinion."

But what! (it may be asked) Is the absence of unanimity an indispensable condition of true knowledge? Is it necessary that some part of mankind should persist in error to enable any to realize the truth? Does a belief cease to be real and vital as soon as it is generally received; and is a proposition never thoroughly understood and felt unless some doubt of it remains? As soon as mankind have unanimously accepted a truth, does the truth perish within them? The highest aim and best result of improved intelligence, it has hitherto been thought, is to unite mankind more and more in the acknowledgment of all important truths; and does the intelligence only last as long as it has not achieved its object? Do the fruits of conquest perish by the very completeness of the victory?

I affirm no such thing. As mankind improve, the number of doctrines which are no longer disputed or doubted will be constantly on the increase: and the well-being of mankind may almost be measured by the number and gravity of the truths which have reached the point of being uncontested. The cessation, on one question after another, of serious controversy, is one of the necessary incidents of the consolidation of opinion; a consolidation as salutary in the case of true opinions, as it is dangerous and noxious when the opinions are erroneous. But though this gradual narrowing of the bounds of diversity of opinion is necessary in both senses of the term, being at once inevitable and indispensable, we are not therefore obliged to conclude that all its consequences must be beneficial. The loss of so important an aid to the intelligent and living apprehension of a truth, as is afforded by the necessity of explaining it to, or defending it against, opponents, though not sufficient to outweigh, is no trifling drawback from, the benefit of its universal recognition. Where this advantage can no longer be had, I confess I should like to see the teachers of mankind endeavoring to provide a substitute for it; some contrivance for making the difficulties of the question as present to the learner's consciousness, as if they were pressed upon him by a dissentient champion, eager for his conversion.

But instead of seeking contrivances for this purpose, they have lost those they formerly had. The Socratic dialectics, so magnificently exemplified in the dialogues of Plato, were a contrivance of this description. They were essentially a negative discussion of the great question of philosophy and life, directed with consummate skill to the purpose of convincing anyone who had merely adopted the commonplaces of received opinion that he did not understand the subject—that he as yet attached no definite meaning to the doctrines he professed; in order that, becoming aware of his ignorance, he might be put in the way to obtain a stable belief, resting on a clear apprehension both of the meaning of doctrines and of their evidence. The school disputations of the Middle Ages had a somewhat similar object. They were intended to make sure that the pupil understood his own opinion, and (by necessary correlation) the opinion opposed to it, and could enforce the grounds of the one and confute those of the other. These last-mentioned contests had indeed the incurable defect that the premises appealed to were taken from authority, not from reason; and, as a discipline to the mind, they were in every respect inferior to the powerful dialectics which formed the intellects of the *'Socratici viri';* but the modern mind owes far more to both than it is generally willing to admit, and the present modes of education contain nothing which in the smallest degree supplies the place either of the one or of the other. A person who derives all his instruction from teachers or books, even if he escape the besetting temptation of contenting himself with cram, is under no compulsion to hear both sides; accordingly it is far from a frequent accomplishment, even among thinkers, to know both sides; and the weakest part of what everybody says in defense of his opinion is what he intends as a reply to antagonists. It is the fashion of the present time to disparage negative logic—that which points out weaknesses in theory or errors in practice, without establishing positive truths. Such negative criticism would indeed be poor enough as an ultimate result; but as a means to attaining any positive knowledge or conviction worthy the name, it cannot be valued too highly; and until people are again systematically trained to it, there will be few great thinkers, and a low general average of intellect, in any but the mathematical and physical departments of speculation. On any other subject no one's opinions deserve the name of knowledge, except so far as he has either had forced upon him by others, or gone through of himself, the same mental process which would have been required of him in carrying on an active controversy with opponents. That, therefore, which when absent, it is so indispensable, but so difficult, to create, how worse than absurd it is to forego, when spontaneously offering itself! If there are any persons who contest a received opinion, or who will do so if law or opinion will let them, let us thank them for it, open our minds to listen to them, and rejoice that there is some one to do for us what we otherwise ought, if we have any regard for either the certainty or the vitality of our convictions, to do with much greater labor for ourselves.

It still remains to speak of one of the principal causes which make diversity of opinion advantageous, and will continue to do so until mankind shall have entered a stage of intellectual advancement which at present seems at an incalculable distance. We have hitherto considered only two possibilities: that the received opinion may be false, and some other opinion consequently true; or that, the received opinion being true, a conflict with the opposite error is essential to a clear apprehension and deep feeling of its truth. But there is a commoner case than either of these: when the conflicting doctrines, instead of being one true and the other false, share the truth between them; and the nonconforming opinion is needed to supply the remainder of the truth, of which the received doctrine embodies only a part. Popular opinions, on subjects not palpable to sense, are often true, but seldom or never the whole truth. They are a part of the truth; sometimes a greater, sometimes a smaller part, but exaggerated, distorted, and disjointed from the truths by which they ought to be accompanied and limited. Heretical opinions, on the other hand, are generally some of these suppressed and neglected truths, bursting the bonds which kept them down, and either seeking reconciliation with the truth contained in the common opinion, or fronting it as enemies, and setting themselves up, with similar exclusiveness, as the whole truth. The latter case is hitherto the most frequent, as, in the human mind, one-sidedness has always been the rule, and many-sidedness the exception. Hence, even in revolutions of opinion, one part of the truth usually sets while another rises. Even progress, which ought to superadd, for the most part only substitutes, one partial and incomplete truth for another; improvement consisting chiefly in this, that the new fragment of truth is more wanted, more adapted to the needs of the time, than that which it displaces. Such being the partial character of prevailing opinions, even when resting on a true foundation, every opinion which embodies somewhat of the portion of truth which the common opinion omits, ought to be considered precious, with whatever amount of error and confusion that truth may be blended. No sober judge of human affairs will feel bound to be indignant because those who force on our notice truths which we should otherwise have overlooked, overlook some of those which we see. Rather, he will think that so long as popular truth is one-sided, it is more desirable than otherwise that unpopular truth should have one-sided assertors too; such being usually the most energetic, and the most likely to compel reluctant attention to the fragment of wisdom which they proclaim as if it were the whole.

Thus, in the eighteenth century, when nearly all the instructed, and all those of the uninstructed who were led by them, were lost in admiration of what is called civilization, and of the marvels of modern science, literature, and philosophy, and while greatly overrating the amount of unlikeness between the men of modern and those of ancient times, indulged the belief that the whole of the difference was in their own favor; with what a salutary shock did the paradoxes of Rousseau explode like bombshells in the midst, dislocating the compact mass of one-sided opinion, and forcing its elements to recombine in a better form and with additional ingredients. Not that the current opinions were on the whole farther from the truth than Rousseau's were: on the contrary, they were nearer to it: they contained more of positive truth, and very much less of error. Nevertheless there lay in Rousseau's doctrine, and has floated down the stream of opinion along with it, a considerable amount of exactly those truths which the popular opinion wanted; and these are the deposit which was left behind when the flood subsided. The superior worth of simplicity of life, the enervating and demoralizing effect of the trammels and hypocrisies of artificial society, are ideas which have never been entirely absent from cultivated minds since Rousseau wrote; and they will in time produce their due effect, though at present needing to be asserted as much as ever, and to be asserted by deeds, for words, on this subject, have nearly exhausted their power.

In politics, again, it is almost a commonplace, that a party of order or stability, and a party of progress or reform, are both necessary elements of a healthy state of political life; until the one or the other shall have so enlarged its mental grasp as to be a party equally of order and of progress, knowing and distinguishing what is fit to be preserved from what ought to be swept away. Each of these modes of thinking derives its utility from the deficiencies of the other; but it is in a great measure the opposition of the other that keeps each within the limits of reason and sanity. Unless opinions favorable to democracy and to aristocracy, to property and to equality, to co-operation and to competition, to luxury and to abstinence, to sociality and individuality, to liberty and discipline, and all the other standing antagonisms of practical life, are expressed with equal freedom, and enforced and defended with equal talent and energy, there is no chance of both elements obtaining their due: one scale is sure to go up, and the other down. Truth, in the great practical concerns of life, is so much a question of the reconciling and combining of opposites, that very few have minds sufficiently capacious and impartial to make the adjustment with an approach to correctness, and it has to be made by the rough process of a struggle between combatants fighting under hostile banners. On any of the great open questions just enumerated, if either of the two opinions has a better claim than the other, not merely to be tolerated, but to be encouraged and countenanced, it is the one which happens at the particular time and place to be in a minority. That is the opinion which, for the time being, represents the neglected interests, the side of human well-being which is in danger of obtaining less than its share. I am aware that there is not, in this country, any intolerance of differences of opinion on most of these topics. They are adduced to show, by admitted and multiplied examples, the universality of the fact that only through diversity of opinion is there, in the existing state of human intellect, a chance of fair play to all sides of the truth. When there are persons to be found who form an exception to the apparent unanimity of the world on any subject, even if the world is in the right, it is always probable that dissentients have something worth hearing to say for themselves, and that truth would lose something by their silence.

It may be objected, "But *some* received principles, especially on the highest and most vital subjects, are more than half-truths. The Christian morality, for instance, is the whole truth on that subject, and if anyone teaches a morality which varies from it, he is wholly in error." As this is of all cases the most important in practice, none can be fitter to test the general maxim. But before pronouncing what Christian morality is or is not, it would be desirable to decide what is meant by Christian morality. If it means the morality of the New Testament, I wonder that anyone who derives his knowledge of this from the book itself, can suppose that it was announced, or intended, as a complete doctrine of morals. The Gospel always refers to a pre-existing morality, and confines its precepts to the particulars in which that morality was to be corrected, or superseded by a wider and higher; expressing itself, moreover, in terms most general, often impossible to be interpreted literally, and possessing rather the impressiveness of poetry or eloquence than the precision of legislation. To extract from it a body of ethical doctrine, has never been possible without eking it out from the Old Testament, that is, from a system elaborate indeed, but in many respects barbarous, and intended only for a barbarous people. St. Paul, a declared enemy to this Judaical mode of interpreting the doctrine and filling up the scheme of his Master, equally assumes a pre-existing morality, namely that of the Greeks and Romans; and his advice to Christians is in a great measure a system of accommodation to that; even to the extent of giving an apparent sanction to slavery. What is called Christian, but should rather be termed theological, morality, was not the work of Christ or the Apostles, but is of much later origin, having been gradually built up by the Catholic church of the first five centuries, and though not implicitly adopted by moderns and Protestants, has been much less modified by them than might have been expected. For the most part, indeed, they have contented themselves with cutting off the additions which had been made to it in the Middle Ages, each sect supplying the place by fresh additions, adapted to its own character and tendencies. That mankind owe a great debt to this morality, and to its early teachers, I should be the last person to deny; but I do not scruple to say of it that it is, in many important points, incomplete and one-sided, and that unless ideas and feelings, not sanctioned by it, had contributed to the formation of European life and character, human affairs would have been in a worse condition than they now are. Christian morality (so called) has all the characters of a reaction; it is, in great part, a protest against Paganism. Its ideal is negative rather than positive; passive rather than active; innocence rather than nobleness; abstinence from evil, rather than energetic pursuit of good; in its precepts (as has been well said) "thou shalt not" predominates unduly over "thou shalt." In its horror of sensuality, it made an idol of asceticism, which has been gradually compromised away into one of legality. It holds out the hope of heaven and the threat of hell, as the appointed and appropriate motives to a virtuous life: in this falling far below the best of the ancients, and doing what lies in it to give to human morality an essentially selfish character, by disconnecting each man's feelings of duty from the interests of his fellow-creatures, except so far as a self-interested inducement is offered to him for consulting them. It is essentially a doctrine of passive obedience; it inculcates submission to all authorities found established; who indeed are not to be actively obeyed when they command what religion forbids, but who are not to be resisted, far less rebelled against, for any amount of wrong to ourselves. And while, in the morality of the best pagan nations, duty to the State holds even a disproportionate place, infringing on the just liberty of the individual; in purely Christian ethics, that grand department of duty is scarcely noticed or acknowledged. It is in the Koran, not the New Testament, that we read the maxim—"A ruler who appoints any man to an office, when there is in his dominions another man better qualified for it, sins against God and against the State." What little recognition the idea of obligation to the public obtains in modern morality is derived from Greek and Roman sources, not from Christian; as, even in the morality of private life, whatever exists of magnanimity, highmindedness, personal dignity, even the sense of honor, is derived from the purely human, not the religious part of our education, and never could have grown out of a standard of ethics in which the only worth, professedly recognized, is that of obedience.

I am as far as anyone from pretending that these defects are necessarily inherent in the Christian ethics in every manner in which it can be conceived, or that the many requisites of a complete moral doctrine which it does not contain do not admit of being reconciled with it. Far less would I insinuate this of the doctrines and precepts of Christ himself. I believe that the sayings of Christ are all that I can see any evidence of their having been intended to be; that they are irreconcilable with nothing which a comprehensive morality requires; that everything which is excellent in ethics may be brought within them, with no greater violence to their language than has been done to it by all who have attempted to deduce from them any practical system of conduct whatever. But it is quite consistent with this to believe that they contain, and were meant to contain, only a part of the truth; that many essential elements of the highest morality are among the things which are not provided for, nor intended to be provided for, in the recorded deliverances of the Founder of Christianity, and which have been entirely thrown aside in the system of ethics erected on the basis of those deliverances by the Christian Church. And this being so, I think it a great error to persist in attempting to find in the Christian doctrine that complete rule for our guidance which its author intended it to sanction and enforce, but only partially to provide. I believe, too, that this narrow theory is becoming a grave practical evil, detracting greatly from the moral training and instruction which so many well-meaning persons are now at length exerting themselves to promote. I much fear that by attempting to form the mind and feelings on an exclusively religious type, and discarding those secular standards (as for want of a better name they may be called) which heretofore coexisted with and supplemented the Christian ethics, receiving some of its spirit, and infusing into it some of theirs, there will result, and is even now resulting, a low, abject, servile type of character, which, submit itself as it may to what it deems the Supreme Will, is incapable of rising to or sympathizing in the conception of Supreme Goodness. I believe that other ethics than any which can be evolved from exclusively Christian sources, must exist side by side with Christian ethics to produce the moral regeneration of mankind; and that the Christian system is no exception to the rule, that in an imperfect state of the human mind the interests of truth require a diversity of opinions. It is not necessary that in ceasing to ignore the moral truths not contained in Christianity men should ignore any of those which it does contain. Such prejudice, or oversight, when it occurs, is altogether an evil; but it is one from which we cannot hope to be always exempt, and must be regarded as the price paid for an inestimable good. The exclusive pretension made by a part of the truth to be the whole, must and ought to be protested against; and if a reactionary impulse should make the protestors unjust in their turn, this one-sidedness, like the other, may be lamented, but must be tolerated. If Christians would teach infidels to be just to Christianity, they should themselves be just to infidelity. It can do truth no service to blink the fact, known to all who have the most ordinary acquaintance with literary history, that a large portion of the noblest and most valuable moral teaching has been the work, not only of men who did not know, but of men who knew and rejected, the Christian faith.

I do not pretend that the most unlimited use of the freedom of enunciating all possible opinions would put an end to the evils of religious or philosophical sectarianism. Every truth which men of narrow capacity are in earnest about, is sure to be asserted, inculcated, and in many ways even acted on, as if no other truth existed in the world, or at all events none that could limit or qualify the first. I acknowledge that the tendency of all opinions to become sectarian is not cured by the freest discussion, but is often heightened and exacerbated thereby; the truth which ought to have been, but was not, seen, being rejected all the more violently because proclaimed by persons regarded as opponents. But it is not on the impassioned partisan, it is on the calmer and more disinterested bystander, that this collision of opinions works its salutary effect. Not the violent conflict between parts of the truth, but the quiet suppression of half of it, is the formidable evil; there is always hope when people are forced to listen to both sides; it is when they attend only to one that errors harden into prejudices, and truth itself ceases to have the effect of truth, by being exaggerated into falsehood. And since there are few mental attributes more rare than that judicial faculty which can sit in intelligent judgment between two sides of a question, of which only one is represented by an advocate before it, truth has no chance but in proportion as every side of it, every opinion which embodies any fraction of the truth, not only finds advocates, but is so advocated as to be listened to.

We have now recognized the necessity to the mental well-being of mankind (on which all their other well-being depends) of freedom of opinion, and freedom of the expression of opinion, on four distinct grounds; which we will now briefly recapitulate.

First, if any opinion is compelled to silence, that opinion may, for aught we can certainly know, be true. To deny this is to assume our own infallibility.

Secondly, though the silenced opinion be an error, it may, and very commonly does, contain a portion of truth; and since the general or prevailing opinion on any subject is rarely or never the whole truth, it is only by the collision of adverse opinions that the remainder of the truth has any chance of being supplied.

Thirdly, even if the received opinion be not only true, but the whole truth; unless it is suffered to be, and actually is, vigorously and earnestly contested, it will, by most of those who receive it, be held in the manner of a prejudice, with little comprehension or feeling of its rational grounds. And not only this, but, fourthly, the meaning of the doctrine itself will be in danger of being lost, or enfeebled, and deprived of its vital effect on the character and conduct: the dogma becoming a mere formal profession, inefficacious for good, but cumbering the ground, and preventing the growth of any real and heartfelt conviction, from reason or personal experience.

Before quitting the subject of freedom of opinion, it is fit to take some notice of those who say that the free expression of all opinions should be permitted, on condition that the manner be temperate, and do not pass the bounds of fair discussion. Much might be said on the impossibility of fixing where these supposed bounds are to be placed; for if the test be offense to those whose opinions are attacked, I think experience testifies that this offense is given whenever the attack is telling and powerful, and that every opponent who pushes them hard, and whom they find it difficult to answer, appears to them, if he shows any strong feeling on the subject, an intemperate opponent. But this, though an important consideration in a practical point of view, merges in a more fundamental objection. Undoubtedly the manner of asserting an opinion, even though it be a true one, may be very objectionable, and may justly incur severe censure. But the principal offenses of the kind are such as it is mostly impossible, unless by accidental self-betrayal, to bring home to conviction. The gravest of them is, to argue sophistically, to suppress facts or arguments, to misstate the elements of the case, or misrepresent the opposite opinion. But all this, even to the most aggravated degree, is so continually done in perfect good faith, by persons who are not considered, and in many other respects may not deserve to be considered, ignorant or incompetent, that it is rarely possible, on adequate grounds, conscientiously to stamp the misrepresentation as morally culpable; and still less could law presume to interfere with this kind of controversial misconduct. With regard to what is commonly meant by intemperate discussion, namely invective, sarcasm, personality, and the like, the denunciation of these weapons would deserve more sympathy if it were ever proposed to interdict them equally to both sides; but it is only desired to restrain the employment of them against the prevailing opinion: against the unprevailing they may not only be used without general disapproval, but will be likely to obtain for him who uses them the praise of honest zeal and righteous indignation.

Yet whatever mischief arises from their use is greatest when they are employed against the comparatively defenseless; and whatever unfair advantage can be derived by any opinion from this mode of asserting it. accrues almost exclusively to received opinions. The worst offense of this kind which can be committed by a polemic is to stigmatize those who hold the contrary opinion as bad and immoral men. To calumny of this sort, those who hold any unpopular opinion are peculiarly exposed, because they are in general few and uninfluential, and nobody but themselves feels much interested in seeing justice done them; but this weapon is, from the nature of the case, denied to those who attack a prevailing opinion: they can neither use it with safety to themselves, nor, if they could, would it do anything but recoil on their own cause. In general, opinions contrary to those commonly received can only obtain a hearing by studied moderation of language, and the most cautious avoidance of unnecessary offense, from which they hardly ever deviate even in a slight degree without losing ground; while unmeasured vituperation employed on the side of the prevailing opinion really does deter people from professing contrary opinions, and from listening to those who profess them. For the interest, therefore, of truth and justice, it is far more important to restrain this employment of vituperative language than the other; and, for example, if it were necessary to choose, there would be much more need to discourage offensive attacks on infidelity than on religion. It is, however, obvious that law and authority have no business with restraining either, while opinion ought, in every instance, to determine its verdict by the circumstances of the individual case; condemning everyone, on whichever side of the argument he places himself, in whose mode of advocacy either want of candor, or malignity, bigotry, or intolerance of feeling manifest themselves; but not inferring these vices from the side which a person takes, though it be the contrary side of the question of our own; and giving merited honor to everyone, whatever opinion he may hold, who has calmness to see and honesty to state what his opponents and their opinions really are, exaggerating nothing to their discredit, keeping nothing back which tells, or can be supposed to tell, in their favor. This is the real morality of public discussion; and if often violated, I am happy to think that there are many controversialists who to a great extent observe it, and a still greater number who conscientiously strive towards it.

CHAPTER III

OF INDIVIDUALITY, AS ONE OF THE ELEMENTS OF WELL-BEING

Such being the reasons which make it imperative that human beings should be free to form opinions, and to express their opinions without reserve; and such the baneful consequences to the intellectual, and through that to the moral nature of man, unless this liberty is either conceded, or asserted in spite of prohibition; let us next examine whether the same reasons do not require that men should be free to act upon their opinions—to carry these out in their lives, without hindrance, either physical or moral, from their fellow-men, so long as it is at their own risk and peril. This last proviso is of course indispensable. No one pretends that actions should be as free as opinions. On the contrary, even opinions lose their immunity when the circumstances in which they are expressed are such as to constitute their expression a positive instigation to some mischievous act. An opinion that corn-dealers are starvers of the poor, or that private property is robbery, ought to be unmolested when simply circulated through the press, but may justly incur punishment when delivered orally to an excited mob assembled before the house of a corn-dealer, or when handed about among the same mob in the form of a placard. Acts, of whatever kind, which without justifiable cause do harm to others, may be, and in the more important cases absolutely require to be, controlled by the unfavorable sentiments, and, when needful, by the active interference of mankind. The liberty of the individual must be thus far limited; he must not make himself a nuisance to other people. But if he refrains from molesting others in what concerns them, and merely acts according to his own inclination and judgment in things which concern himself, the same reasons which show that opinion should be free, prove also that he should be allowed, without molestation, to carry his opinions into practice at his own cost. That mankind are not infallible; that their truths, for the most part, are only half-truths; that unity of opinion, unless resulting from the fullest and freest comparison of opposite opinions, is not desirable, and diversity not an evil, but a good, until mankind are much more capable than at present of recognizing all sides of the truth, are principles applicable to men's modes of action, not less than to their opinions. As it is useful that while mankind are imperfect there should be different opinions, so it is that there should be different experiments of living; that free scope should be given to varieties of character, short of injury to others; and that the worth of different modes of life should be proved practically, when anyone thinks fit to try them. It is desirable, in short, that in things which do not primarily concern others, individuality should assert itself. Where not the person's own character, but the traditions or customs of other people are the rule of conduct, there is wanting one of the principal ingredients of human happiness, and quite the chief ingredient of individual and social progress.

In maintaining this principle, the greatest difficulty to be encountered does not lie in the appreciation of means towards an acknowledged end, but in the indifference of persons in general to the end itself. If it were felt that the free development of individuality is one of the leading essentials of well-being; that it is not only a co-ordinate element with all that is designated by the terms civilization, instruction, education, culture, but is itself a necessary part and condition of all those things; there would be no danger that liberty should be undervalued, and the adjustment of the boundaries between it and social control would present no extraordinary difficulty. But the evil is, that individual spontaneity is hardly recognized by the common modes of thinking as having any intrinsic worth, or deserving any regard on its own account. The majority, being satisfied with the ways of mankind as they now are (for it is they who make them what they are), cannot comprehend why those ways should not be good enough for everybody; and what is more, spontaneity forms no part of the ideal of the majority of moral and social reformers, but is rather looked on with jealousy, as a troublesome and perhaps rebellious obstruction to the general acceptance of what these reformers, in their own judgment, think would be best for mankind. Few persons, out of Germany, even comprehend the meaning of the doctrine which Wilhelm von Humboldt, so eminent both as a *savant* and as a politician, made the text of a treatise—that "the end of man, or that which is prescribed by the eternal or immutable dictates of reason, and not suggested by vague and transient desires, is the highest and most harmonious development of his powers to a complete and consistent whole;" that, therefore, the object "towards which every human being must ceaselessly direct his efforts, and on which especially those who design to influence their fellow-men must ever keep their eyes, is the individuality of power and development;" that for this there are two requisites, "freedom, and variety of situations;" and that from the union of these arise "individual vigor and manifold diversity," which combine themselves in "originality." [5]

Little, however, as people are accustomed to a doctrine like that of Von Humboldt, and surprising as it may be to them to find so high a value attached to individuality, the question, one must nevertheless think, can only be one of degree. No one's idea of excellence in conduct

[5] *The Sphere and Duties of Government,* from the German of Baron Wilhelm von Humboldt, pp. 11-13.

is that people should do absolutely nothing but copy one another. No one would assert that people ought not to put into their mode of life, and into the conduct of their concerns, any impress whatever of their own judgment, or of their own individual character. On the other hand, it would be absurd to pretend that people ought to live as if nothing whatever had been known in the world before they came into it; as if experience had as yet done nothing towards showing that one mode of existence, or of conduct, is preferable to another. Nobody denies that people should be so taught and trained in youth as to know and benefit by the ascertained results of human experience. But it is the privilege and proper condition of a human being, arrived at the maturity of his faculties, to use and interpret experience in his own way. It is for him to find out what part of recorded experience is properly applicable to his own circumstances and character. The traditions and customs of other people are, to a certain extent, evidence of what their experience has taught *them*: presumptive evidence, and as such, have a claim to his deference. But in the first place, their experience may be too narrow, or they may not have interpreted it rightly. Secondly, their interpretation of experience may be correct, but unsuitable to him. Customs are made for customary circumstances and customary characters, and his circumstances or his character may be uncustomary. Thirdly, though the customs be both good as customs, and suitable to him, yet to conform to custom, merely *as* custom, does not educate or develop in him any of the qualities which are the distinctive endowment of a human being. The human faculties of perception, judgment, discriminative feeling, mental activity, and even moral preference, are exercised only in making a choice. He who does anything because it is the custom makes no choice. He gains no practice either in discerning or in desiring what is best. The mental and moral, like the muscular powers, are improved only by being used. The faculties are called into no exercise by doing a thing merely because others do it, no more than by believing a thing only because others believe it. If the grounds of an opinion are not conclusive to the person's own reason, his reason cannot be strengthened, but is likely to be weakened, by his adopting it; and if the inducements to an act are not such as are consentaneous to his own feelings and character (where affection, or the rights of others, are not concerned) it is so much done towards rendering his feelings and character inert and torpid, instead of active and energetic.

He who lets the world, or his own portion of it, choose his plan of life for him, has no need of any other faculty than the ape-like one of imitation. He who chooses his plan for himself, employs all his faculties. He must use observation to see, reasoning and judgments to foresee, activity to gather materials for decision, discrimination to decide, and when he has decided, firmness and self-control to hold to his deliberate decision. And these qualities he requires and exercises exactly in proportion as the part of his conduct which he determines according to his own judgment and feelings is a large one. It is possible that he might be guided in some good path, and kept out of harm's way, without any of these things. But what will be his comparative worth as a human being? It really is of importance, not only what men do, but also what manner of men they are that do it. Among the works of man which human life is rightly employed in perfecting and beautifying, the first in importance surely is man himself. Supposing it were possible to get houses built, corn grown, battles fought, causes tried, and even churches erected and prayers said, by machinery—by automatons in human form —it would be a considerable loss to exchange for these automatons even the men and women who at present inhabit the more civilized parts of the world, and who assuredly are but starved specimens of what nature can and will produce. Human nature is not a machine to be built after a model, and set to do exactly the work prescribed for it, but a tree, which requires to grow and develop itself on all sides, according to the tendency of the inward forces which make it a living thing.

It will probably be conceded that it is desirable people should exercise their understandings, and that an intelligent following of custom, or even occasionally an intelligent deviation from custom, is better than a blind and simply mechanical adhesion to it. To a certain extent it is admitted that our understanding should be our own: but there is not the same willingness to admit that our desires and impulses should be our own likewise; or that to possess impulses of our own, and of any strength, is anything but a peril and a snare. Yet desires and impulses are as much a part of a perfect human being as beliefs and restraints; and strong impulses are only perilous when not properly balanced—when one set of aims and inclinations is developed into strength, while others, which ought to coexist with them, remain weak and inactive. It is not because men's desires are strong that they act ill; it is because their consciences are weak. There is no natural connection between strong impulses and a weak conscience. The natural connection is the other way. To say that one person's desires and feelings are stronger and more various than those of another, is merely to say that he has more of the raw material of human nature, and is therefore capable, perhaps of more evil, but certainly of more good. Strong impulses are but another name for energy. Energy may be turned to bad uses; but more good may always be made of an energetic nature than of an indolent and impassive one. Those who have most natural feeling are always those whose cultivated feelings may be made the strongest. The same strong susceptibilities which make the personal impulses vivid and powerful, are also the source from whence are generated the most passionate love of virtue, and the sternest self-control. It is through the cultivation of these that society both does its duty and protects its interests; not by rejecting the stuff of which heroes are made because it knows not how to make them. A person whose desires and impulses are his own—are the expression of his own nature, as it has been developed and modified by his own culture—is said to have a character. One whose desires and impulses are not his own, has no character, no more than a steam-engine has a character. If, in addition to being his own, his impulses are strong, and are under the government of a strong will, he has an energetic character. Whoever thinks that individuality of desires and impulses should not be encouraged to unfold itself, must maintain that society has no need of strong natures—is not the better for containing many persons who have much character—and that a high general average of energy is not desirable.

In some early states of society, these forces might be, and were, too much ahead of the power which society then possessed of disciplining and controlling them. There has been a time when the element of spontaneity and individuality was in excess, and the social principle had a hard struggle with it. The difficulty then was to induce men of strong bodies or minds to pay obedience to any rules which required them to control their impulses. To overcome this difficulty, law and discipline, like the Popes struggling against the Emperors, asserted a power over the whole man, claiming to control all his life in order to control his character—which society had not found any other sufficient means of binding. But society has now fairly got the better of individuality; and the danger which threatens human nature is not the excess, but the deficiency, of personal impulses and preferences. Things are vastly changed since the passions of those who were strong by station or by personal endowment were in a state of habitual rebellion against laws and ordinances, and required to be rigorously chained up to enable the persons within their reach to enjoy any particle of security. In our times, from the highest class of society down to the lowest, everyone lives as under the eye of a hostile and dreaded censorship. Not only in what concerns others, but in what concerns only themselves, the individual or the family do not ask themselves—what do I prefer? or, what would suit my character and disposition? or, what would allow the best and highest in me to have fair play, and enable it to grow and thrive? They ask themselves, what is suitable to my position? what is usually done by persons of my station and pecuniary circumstances? or (worse still) what is usually done by persons of a station and circumstances superior to mine? I do not mean that they choose what is customary in preference to what suits their own inclination. It does not occur to them to have any inclination, except for what is customary. Thus the mind itself is bowed to the yoke: even in what people do for pleasure, conformity is the first thing thought of; they like in crowds; they exercise choice only among things commonly done: peculiarity of taste, eccentricity of conduct, are shunned equally with crimes: until by dint of not following their own nature they have no nature to follow: their human capacities are withered and starved: they become incapable of any strong wishes or native pleasures, and are generally without either opinions or feelings of home growth, or properly their own. Now is this, or is it not, the desirable condition of human nature?

It is so, on the Calvinistic theory. According to that, the one great offense of man is self-will. All the good of which humanity is capable is comprised in obedience. You have no choice; thus you must do, and no otherwise: "whatever is not a duty, is a sin." Human nature being radically corrupt, there is no redemption for anyone until human nature is killed within him. To one holding this theory of life, crushing out any of the human faculties, capacities, and susceptibilities, is no evil: man needs no capacity, but that of surrendering himself to the will of God: and if he uses any of his faculties for any other purpose but to do that supposed will more effectually, he is better without them. This is the theory of Calvinism; and it is held, in a mitigated form, by many who do not consider themselves Calvinists; the mitigation consisting in giving a less ascetic interpretation to the alleged will of God; asserting it to be his will that mankind should gratify some of their inclinations; of course not in the manner they themselves prefer, but in the way of obedience, that is, in a way prescribed to them by authority; and, therefore, by the necessary condition of the case, the same for all.

In some such insidious form there is at present a strong tendency to this narrow theory of life, and to the pinched and hidebound type of human character which it patronizes. Many persons, no doubt, sincerely think that human beings thus cramped and dwarfed are as their Maker designed them to be; just as many have thought that trees are a much finer thing when clipped into pollards, or cut out into figures of animals, than as nature made them. But if it be any part of religion to believe that man was made by a good Being, it is more consistent with that faith to believe that this Being gave all human faculties that they might be cultivated and unfolded, not rooted out and consumed, and that he takes delight in every nearer approach made by his creatures to the ideal conception embodied in them, every increase in any of their capabilities of comprehension, of action, or of enjoyment. There is a different type of human excellence from the Calvinistic: a conception of humanity as having its nature bestowed on it for other purposes than merely to be abnegated. "Pagan self-assertion" is one of the elements of human worth, as well as "Christian self-denial." [6] There is a Greek idea of self-development, which the Platonic and Christian ideal of self-government blends with, but does not supersede. It may be better to be a John Knox than an Alcibiades, but it is better to be a Pericles than either; nor would a Pericles, if we had one in these days, be without anything good which belonged to John Knox.

It is not by wearing down into uniformity all that is individual in themselves, but by cultivating it, and calling it forth, within the limits imposed by the rights and interests of others, that human beings become a noble and beautiful object of contemplation; and as the works partake the character of those who do them, by the same process human life also becomes rich, diversified, and animating, furnishing more abundant aliment to high thoughts and elevating feelings, and strengthening the tie which binds every individual to the race, by making the race infinitely better worth belonging to. In proportion to the development of his individuality, each person becomes more valuable to himself, and is therefore capable of being more valuable to others. There is a greater fullness of life about his own existence, and when there is more life in the units there is more in the mass which is composed of them. As much compression as is necessary to prevent the stronger specimens of human nature from encroaching on the rights of others cannot be dispensed with; but for this there is ample compensation even in the point of view of human development. The means of development which the individual loses by being prevented from gratifying his inclinations to the injury of others, are chiefly obtained at the expense of the development of other people. And even to himself there is a full equivalent in the better development of the social part of his nature, rendered possible by the restraint put upon the selfish part. To be held to rigid rules of justice for the sake of others, develops the feelings and capacities which have the good of others for their object. But to be restrained in things not affecting their good, by their mere displeasure, develops nothing valuable, except such force of character as may unfold itself in resisting the restraint. If acquiesced in, it dulls and blunts the whole nature. To give any fair play to the nature of each, it is essential that different persons should be allowed to lead different lives. In proportion as this latitude has been exercised in any age, has that age been noteworthy to posterity. Even despotism does not produce its worst effects, so long as individuality exists under it; and whatever crushes individuality is despotism, by whatever name it may be called, and whether it professes to be enforcing the will of God or the injunctions of men.

Having said that the individuality is the same thing with develop-

[6] Sterling's *Essays*.

ment, and that it is only the cultivation of individuality which produces, or can produce, well-developed human beings, I might here close the argument: for what more or better can be said of any condition of human affairs than that it brings human beings themselves nearer to the best thing they can be? or what worse can be said of any obstruction to good than that it prevents this? Doubtless, however, these considerations will not suffice to convince those who most need convincing; and it is necessary further to show that these developed human beings are of some use to the undeveloped—to point out to those who do not desire liberty, and would not avail themselves of it, that they may be in some intelligible manner rewarded for allowing other people to make use of it without hindrance.

In the first place, then, I would suggest that they might possibly learn something from them. It will not be denied by anybody that originality is a valuable element in human affairs. There is always need of persons not only to discover new truths, and point out when what were once truths are true no longer, but also to commence new practices, and set the example of more enlightened conduct, and better taste and sense in human life. This cannot well be gainsaid by anybody who does not believe that the world has already attained perfection in all its ways and practices. It is true that this benefit is not capable of being rendered by everybody alike: there are but few persons, in comparison with the whole of mankind, whose experiments, if adopted by others, would be likely to be any improvement on established practice. But these few are the salt of the earth; without them, human life would become a stagnant pool. Not only is it they who introduce good things which did not before exist; it is they who keep the life in those which already exist. If there were nothing new to be done, would human intellect cease to be necessary? Would it be a reason why those who do the old things should forget why they are done, and do them like cattle, not like human beings? There is only too great a tendency in the best beliefs and practices to degenerate into the mechanical; and unless there were a succession of persons whose ever-recurring originality prevents the grounds of those beliefs and practices from becoming merely traditional, such dead matter would not resist the smallest shock from anything really alive, and there would be no reason why civilization should not die out, as in the Byzantine Empire. Persons of genius, it is true, are, and are always likely to be, a small minority; but in order to have them, it is necessary to preserve the soil in which they grow. Genius can only breathe freely in an *atmosphere* of freedom. Persons of genius are, *ex vi termini*, more individual than any other people—less capable, consequently, of fitting themselves, without hurtful compression, into any of the small number of molds which society provides in order to

save its members the trouble of forming their own character. If from
timidity they consent to be forced into one of these molds, and to let
all that part of themselves which cannot expand under the pressure remain unexpanded, society will be little the better for their genius. If
they are of a strong character, and break their fetters, they become a
mark for the society which has not succeeded in reducing them to commonplace, to point out with solemn warning as 'wild,' 'erratic,' and the
like; much as if one should complain of the Niagara river for not flowing smoothly between its banks like a Dutch canal.

I insist thus emphatically on the importance of genius, and the necessity of allowing it to unfold itself freely both in thought and in practice, being well aware that no one will deny the position in theory, but
knowing also that almost everyone, in reality, is totally indifferent to it.
People think genius a fine thing if it enables a man to write an exciting poem, or paint a picture. But in its true sense, that of originality in
thought and action, though no one says that it is not a thing to be admired, nearly all, at heart, think that they can do very well without it.
Unhappily this is too natural to be wondered at. Originality is the one
thing which unoriginal minds cannot feel the use of. They cannot see
what it is to do for them: how should they? If they could see what it
would do for them, it would not be originality. The first service which
originality has to render them, is that of opening their eyes: which being
once fully done, they would have a chance of being themselves original.
Meanwhile, recollecting that nothing was ever yet done which someone
was not the first to do, and that all good things which exist are the
fruits of originality, let them be modest enough to believe that there is
something still left for it to accomplish, and assure themselves that they
are more in need of originality, the less they are conscious of the want.

In sober truth, whatever homage may be professed, or even paid, to
real or supposed mental superiority, the general tendency of things
throughout the world is to render mediocrity the ascendant power among
mankind. In ancient history, in the Middle Ages, and in a diminishing
degree through the long transition from feudality to the present
time, the individual was a power in himself; and if he had either great
talents or a high social position, he was a considerable power. At present individuals are lost in the crowd. In politics it is almost a triviality
to say that public opinion now rules the world. The only power deserving the name is that of masses, and of governments while they make
themselves the organ of the tendencies and instincts of masses. This is
as true in the moral and social relations of private life as is public
transactions. Those whose opinions go by the name of public opinion
are not always the same sort of public: in America they are the whole
white population; in England, chiefly the middle class. But they are

always a mass, that is to say, collective mediocrity. And what is a still greater novelty, the mass do not now take their opinions from dignitaries in Church or State, from ostensible leaders, or from books. Their thinking is done for them by men much like themselves, addressing them or speaking in their name, on the spur of the moment, through the newspapers. I am not complaining of all this. I do not assert that anything better is compatible, as a general rule, with the present low state of the human mind. But that does not hinder the government of mediocrity from being mediocre government. No government by a democracy or a numerous aristocracy, either in its political arts or in the opinions, qualities, and tone of mind which it fosters, ever did or could rise above mediocrity, except in so far as the sovereign. Many have let themselves be guided (which in their best times they always have done) by the counsels and influence of a more highly gifted and instructed one or few. The initiation of all wise or noble things comes and must come from individuals; generally at first from some one individual. The honor and glory of the average man is that he is capable of following that initiative; that he can respond internally to wise and noble things, and be led to them with his eyes open. I am not countenancing the sort of 'hero-worship' which applauds the strong man of genius for forcibly seizing on the government of the world and making it do his bidding in spite of itself. All he can claim is, freedom to point out the way. The power of compelling others into it is not only inconsistent with the freedom and development of all the rest, but corrupting to the strong man himself. It does seem, however, that when the opinions of masses of merely average men are everywhere become or becoming the dominant power, the counterpoise and corrective to that tendency would be the more and more pronounced individuality of those who stand on the higher eminences of thought. It is in these circumstances most especially, that exceptional individuals, instead of being deterred, should be encouraged in acting differently from the mass. In other times there was no advantage in their doing so, unless they acted not only differently but better. In this age, the mere example of nonconformity, the mere refusal to bend the knee to custom, is itself a service. Precisely because the tyranny of opinion is such as to make eccentricity a reproach, it is desirable, in order to break through that tyranny, that people should be eccentric. Eccentricity has always abounded when and where strength of character has abounded; and the amount of eccentricity in a society has generally been proportional to the amount of genius, mental vigor, and moral courage it contained. That so few now dare to be eccentric marks the chief danger of the time.

I have said that it is important to give the freest scope possible to uncustomary things, in order that it may in time appear which of these are fit to be converted into customs. But independence of action, and disregard of custom, are not solely deserving of encouragement for the chance they afford that better modes of action, and customs more worthy of general adoption, may be struck out; nor is it only persons of decided mental superiority who have a just claim to carry on their lives in their own way. There is no reason that all human existence should be constructed on some one or some small number of patterns. If a person possesses any tolerable amount of common sense and experience, his own mode of laying out his existence is the best, not because it is the best in itself, but because it is his own mode. Human beings are not like sheep; and even sheep are not undistinguishably alike. A man cannot get a coat or a pair of boots to fit him unless they are either made to his measure, or he has a whole warehouseful to choose from: and is it easier to fit him with a life than with a coat, or are human beings more like one another in their whole physical and spiritual conformation than in the shape of their feet? If it were only that people have diversities of taste, that is reason enough for not attempting to shape them all after one model. But different persons also require different conditions for their spiritual development; and can no more exist healthily in the same moral, than all the variety of plants can in the same physical, atmosphere and climate. The same things which are helps to one person towards the cultivation of his higher nature are hindrances to another. The same mode of life is a healthy excitement to one, keeping all his faculties of action and enjoyment in their best order, while to another it is a distracting burden, which suspends or crushes all internal life. Such are the differences among human beings in their sources of pleasure, their susceptibilities of pain, and the operation on them of different physical and moral agencies, that unless there is a corresponding diversity in their modes of life, they neither obtain their fair share of happiness, nor grow up to the mental, moral, and aesthetic stature of which their nature is capable. Why then should tolerance, as far as the public sentiment is concerned, extend only to tastes and modes of life which extort acquiescence by the multitude of their adherents? Nowhere (except in some monastic institutions) is diversity of taste entirely unrecognized; a person may, without blame, either like or dislike rowing, or smoking, or music, or athletic exercises, or chess, or cards, or study, because both those who like each of these things, and those who dislike them, are too numerous to be put down. But the man, and still more the woman, who can be accused either of doing "what nobody does," or of not doing "what everybody does," is the subject of as much depreciatory remark as if he or she had committed some grave moral delinquency. Persons require to possess a title or some other badge of rank, or of the consideration of people of rank, to be able to indulge somewhat in the luxury of doing as they like without detriment of their estimation. To indulge somewhat, I repeat: for whoever allow themselves much of that indulgence, incur the risk of something worse than disparaging speeches—they are in peril of a commission *de lunatico,* and of having their property taken from them and given to their relations.

There is one characteristic of the present direction of public opinion peculiarly calculated to make it intolerant of any marked demonstration of individuality. The general average of mankind are not only moderate in intellect, but also moderate in inclinations: they have no tastes or wishes strong enough to incline them to do anything unusual, and they consequently do not understand those who have, and class all such with the wild and intemperate whom they are accustomed to look down upon. Now, in addition to this fact which is general, we have only to suppose that a strong movement has set in towards the improvement of morals, and it is evident what we have to expect. In these days such a movement has set in; much has actually been effected in the way of increased regularity of conduct and discouragement of excesses; and there is a philanthropic spirit abroad, for the exercise of which there is no more inviting field than the moral and prudential improvement of our fellow-creatures. These tendencies of the times cause the public to be more disposed than at most former periods to prescribe general rules of conduct, and endeavor to make everyone conform to the approved standard. And that standard, express or tacit, is to desire nothing strongly. Its ideal of character is to be without any marked character; to maim by compression, like a Chinese lady's foot, every part of human nature which stands out prominently, and tends to make the person markedly dissimilar in outline to commonplace humanity.

As is usually the case with ideals which exclude one-half of what is desirable, the present standard of approbation produces only an inferior imitation of the other half. Instead of great energies guided by vigorous reason, and strong feelings strongly controlled by a conscientious will, its result is weak feelings and weak energies, which therefore can be kept in outward conformity to rule without any strength either of will or of reason. Already energetic characters on any large scale are becoming merely traditional. There is now scarcely any outlet for energy in this country except business. The energy expended in this may still be regarded as considerable. What little is left from that employment is expended on some hobby; which may be a useful, even a philanthropic hobby, but is always some one thing, and generally a thing of small dimensions. The greatness of England is now all collective; individually small, we only appear capabe of anything great by our habit of combining; and with this our moral and religious philanthropists are perfectly contented. But it was men of another stamp than this that made England what it has been; and men of another stamp will be needed to prevent its decline.

The despotism of custom is everywhere the standing hindrance to human advancement, being in unceasing antagonism to that disposition to aim at something better than customary, which is called, according to circumstances, the spirit of liberty, or that of progress or improvement. The spirit of improvement is not always a spirit of liberty, for it may aim at forcing improvements on an unwilling people; and the spirit of liberty, in so far as it resists such attempts, may ally itself locally and temporarily with the opponents of improvement; but the only unfailing and permanent source of improvement is liberty, since by it there are as many possible independent centers of improvement as there are individuals. The progressive principle, however, in either shape, whether as the love of liberty or of improvement, is antagonistic to the sway of custom, involving at least emancipation from that yoke; and the contest between the two constitutes the chief interest of the hisory of mankind. The greater part of the world has, properly speaking, no history, because the despotism of custom is complete. This is the case over the whole East. Custom is there, in all things, the final appeal; justice and right mean conformity to custom; the argument of custom no one, unless some tyrant intoxicated with power, thinks of resisting. And we see the result. Those nations must once have had originality; they did not start out on the ground populous, lettered, and versed in many of the arts of life; they made themselves all this, and were then the greatest and most powerful nations of the world. What are they now? The subjects or dependents of tribes whose forefathers wandered in the forests when theirs had magnificent palaces and gorgeous temples, but over whom custom exercised only a divided rule with liberty and progress. A people, it appears, may be progressive for a certain length of time, and then stop: when does it stop? When it ceases to possess individuality. If a similar change should befall the nations of Europe, it will not be in exactly the same shape: the despotism of custom with which these nations are threatened is not precisely stationariness. It proscribes singularity, but it does not preclude change, provided all change together. We have discarded the fixed costumes of our forefathers; everyone must still dress like other people, but the fashion may change once or twice a year. We thus take care that when there is a change, it shall be for change's sake, and not from any idea of beauty or convenience; for the same idea of beauty or convenience would not strike all the world at the same moment, and be simultaneously thrown aside by all at another moment. But we are progressive as well as changeable: we continually make new inventions in mechanical things, and keep them until they are again superseded by better; we are eager for improvement in politics, in education, even in morals, though in this last our idea of improvement chiefly consists in persuading or forcing other people to be as good as ourselves. It is not progress that we object to; on the contrary, we flatter ourselves that we are the most progressive people who ever lived. It is individuality that we war against: we should think we had done wonders if we had made ourselves all alike; forgetting that the unlikeness of one person to another is generally the first thing which draws the attention of either to the imperfection of his own type, and the superiority of another, or the possibility, by combining the advantages of both, of producing something better than either. We have a warning example in China—a nation of much talent, and, in some respects, even wisdom, owing to the rare good fortune of having been provided at an early period with a particularly good set of customs, the work, in some measure, of men to whom even the most enlightened European must accord, under certain limitations, the title of sages and philosophers. They are remarkable, too, in the excellence of their apparatus for impressing, as far as possible, the best wisdom they possess upon every mind in the community, and securing that those who have appropriated most of it shall occupy the posts of honor and power. Surely the people who did this have discovered the secret of human progressiveness, and must have kept themselves steadily at the head of the movement of the world. On the contrary, they have become stationary—have remained so for thousands of years; and if they are ever to be farther improved, it must be by foreigners. They have succeeded beyond all hope in what English philanthropists are so industriously working at—in making a people all alike, all governing their thoughts and conduct by the same maxims and rules; and these are the fruits. The modern regime of public opinion is, in an unorganized form, what the Chinese educational and political systems are in an organized; and unless individuality shall be able successfully to assert itself against this yoke, Europe, notwithstanding its noble antecedents and its professed Christianity, will tend to become another China.

What is it that has hitherto preserved Europe from this lot? What has made the European family of nations an improving, instead of a stationary portion of mankind? Not any superior excellence in them, which, when it exists, exists as the effect not as the cause; but their remarkable diversity of character and culture. Individuals, classes, nations, have been extremely unlike one another: they have struck out a great variety of paths, each leading to something valuable; and although at every period those who traveled in different paths have been intolerant of one another, and each would have thought it an excellent thing if all the rest could have been compelled to travel his road, their attempts to thwart each other's development have rarely had any permanent success, and each has in time endured to receive the good which the others have offered. Europe is, in my judgment, wholly indebted to this plurality of paths for its progressive and many-sided development. But it already begins to possess this benefit in a considerably less degree. It is decidedly advancing towards the Chinese ideal of making all people alike. M. de Tocqueville, in his last important work, remarks how much more the Frenchmen of the present day resemble one another than did those even of the last generation. The same remark might be made of Englishmen in a far greater degree. In a passage already quoted from Wilhelm von Humboldt, he points out two things as necessary conditions of human development, because necessary to render people unlike one another: namely, freedom, and variety of situations. The second of these two conditions is in this country every day diminishing. The circumstances which surround different classes and individuals, and shape their characters, are daily becoming more assimilated. Formerly, different ranks, different neighborhoods, different trades and professions, lived in what might be called different worlds; at present to a great degree in the same. Comparatively speaking, they now read the same things, listen to the same things, see the same things, go to the same places, have their hopes and fears directed to the same objects, have the same rights and liberties, and the same means of asserting them. Great as are the differences of position which remain, they are nothing to those which have ceased. And the assimilation is still proceeding. All the political changes of the age promote it, since they all tend to raise the low and to lower the high. Every extension of education promotes it, because education brings people under common influences, and gives them access to the general stock of facts and sentiments. Improvement in the means of communication promotes it, by bringing the inhabitants of distant places into personal contact, and keeping up a rapid flow of changes of residence between one place and another. The increase of commerce and manufactures promotes it, by diffusing more widely the advantages of easy circumstances, and opening all objects of ambition, even the highest, to general competition, whereby the desire of rising becomes no longer the character of a particular class, but of all classes. A more powerful agency than even all these, in bringing about a general similarity among mankind, is the complete establishment, in this and other free countries, of the ascendancy of public opinion in the State. As the various social eminences which enabled persons entrenched on them to disregard the opinion of the multitude gradually become leveled; as the very idea of resisting the will of the public, when it is positively known that they have a will, disappears more and more from the minds of practical politicians: there ceases to be any social support for nonconformity—any substantive power in society which, itself opposed to the ascendancy of numbers, is interested in taking under its protection opinions and tendencies at variance with those of the public.

The combination of all these causes forms so great a mass of influences hostile to individuality, that it is not easy to see how it can stand its ground. It will do so with increasing difficulty, unless the intelligent part of the public can be made to feel its value—to see that it is good there should be differences, even though not for the better, even though, as it may appar to them, some should be for the worse. If the claims of individuality are ever to be asserted, the time is now, while much is still wanting to complete the enforced assimilation. It is only in the earlier stages that any stand can be successfully made against the encroachment. The demand that all other people shall resemble ourselves grows by what it feeds on. If resistance waits till life is reduced *nearly* to one uniform type, all deviations from that type will come to be considered impious, immoral, even monstrous and contrary to nature. Mankind speedily become unable to conceive diversity, when they have been for some time unaccustomed to see it.

CHAPTER IV

OF THE LIMITS TO THE AUTHORITY OF SOCIETY OVER THE INDIVIDUAL

WHAT, then, is the rightful limit to the sovereignty of the individual over himself? Where does the authority of society begin? How much of human life should be assigned to individuality, and how much to society?

Each will receive its proper share, if each has that which more particularly concerns it. To individuality should belong the part of life in which it is chiefly the individual that is interested; to society, the part which chiefly interests society.

Though society is not founded on a contract, and though no good purpose is answered by inventing a contract in order to deduce social obligations from it, everyone who receives the protection of society owes a return for the benefit, and the fact of living in society renders it indispensable that each should be bound to observe a certain line of conduct towards the rest. This conduct consists, *first,* in not injuring the interests of one another; or rather certain interests, which, either by express legal provision or by tacit understanding, ought to be considered as rights; and *secondly,* in each person's bearing his share (to be fixed on some equitable principle) of the labors and sacrifices incurred

for defending the society or its members from injury and molestation.
These conditions society is justified in enforcing, at all costs to those
who endeavor to withhold fulfillment. Nor is this all that society may do.
The acts of an individual may be hurtful to others, or wanting in due
consideration for their welfare, without going to the length of violating
any of their constituted rights. The offender may then be justly punished by opinion, though not by law. As soon as any part of a person's
conduct affects prejudicially the interests of others, society has jurisdiction over it, and the question whether the general welfare will or will
not be promoted by interfering with it, becomes open to discussion. But
there is no room for entertaining any such question when a person's
conduct affects the interests of no persons besides himself, or need not
affect them unless they like (all the persons concerned being of full age,
and the ordinary amount of understanding). In all such cases, there
should be perfect freedom, legal and social, to do the action and stand
the consequences.

It would be a great misunderstanding of this doctrine to suppose that
it is one of selfish indifference, which pretends that human beings
have no business with each other's conduct in life, and that they should
not concern themselves about the well-doing or well-being of one another, unless their own interest is involved. Instead of any diminution,
there is need of a great increase of disinterested exertion to promote the
good of others. But disinterested benevolence can find other instruments to persuade people to their good than whips and scourges, either
of the literal or the metaphorical sort. I am the last person to undervalue the self-regarding virtues: they are only second in importance, if
even second, to the social. It is equally the business of education to
cultivate both. But even education works by conviction and persuasion
as well as by compulsion, and it is by the former only that, when the
period of education is passed, the self-regarding virtues should be inculcated. Human beings owe to each other help to distinguish the better from the worse, and encouragement to choose the former and avoid
the latter. They should be forever stimulating each other to increased
exercise of their higher faculties, and increased direction of their feelings
and aims towards wise instead of foolish, elevating instead of degrading,
objects and contemplations. But neither one person, nor any number of
persons, is warranted in saying to another human creature of ripe years,
that he shall not do with his life for his own benefit what he chooses to
do with it. He is the person most interested in his own well-being: the
interest which any other person, except in cases of strong personal attachment, can have in it, is trifling, compared with that which he himself has; the interest which society has in him individually (except as
to his conduct to others) is fractional, and altogether indirect; while

with respect to his own feelings and circumstances, the most ordinary man or woman has means of knowledge immeasurably surpassing those that can be possessed by anyone else. The interference of society to overrule his judgment and purposes in what only regards himself must be grounded on general presumptions; which may be altogether wrong, and even if right, are as likely as not to be misapplied to individual cases, by persons no better acquainted with the circumstances of such cases than those are who look at them merely from without. In this department, therefore, of human affairs, individuality has its proper field of action. In the conduct of human beings towards one another it is necessary that general rules should for the most part be observed, in order that people may know what they have to expect; but in each person's own concerns his individual spontaneity is entitled to free exercise. Considerations to aid his judgment, exhortations to strengthen his will, may be offered to him, even obtruded on him, by others: but he himself is the final judge. All errors which he is likely to commit against advice and warning are far outweighed by the evil of allowing others to constrain him to what they deem his good.

I do not mean that the feelings with which a person is regarded by others ought not to be in any way affected by his self-regarding qualities or deficiencies. This is neither possible nor desirable. If he is eminent in any of the qualities which conduce to his own good, he is, so far, a proper object of admiration. He is so much the nearer to the ideal perfection of human nature. If he is grossly deficient in those qualities, a sentiment the opposite of admiration will follow. There is a degree of folly, and a degree of what may be called (though the phrase is not unobjectionable) lowness or depravation of taste, which, though it cannot justify doing harm to the person who manifests it, renders him necessarily and properly a subject of distaste, or, in extreme cases, even of contempt: a person could not have the opposite qualities in due strength without entertaining these feelings. Though doing no wrong to anyone, a person may so act as to compel us to judge him, and feel to him, as a fool, or as a being of an inferior order; and since this judgment and feeling are a fact which he would prefer to avoid, it is doing him a service to warn him of it beforehand, as of any other disagreeable consequence to which he exposes himself. It would be well, indeed, if this good office were much more freely rendered than the common notions of politeness at present permit, and if one person could honestly point out to another that he thinks him in fault, without being considered unmannerly or presuming. We have a right, also, in various ways, to act upon our unfavorable opinion of anyone, not to the oppression of his individuality, but in the exercise of ours. We are not bound, for example, to seek his society; we have a right to avoid it (though not to parade the avoidance), for we have a right to choose the society most acceptable to us. We have a right, and it may be our duty, to caution others against him, if we think his example or conversation likely to have a pernicious effect on those with whom he associates. We may give others a preference over him in optional good offices, except those which tend to his improvement. In these various modes a person may suffer very severe penalties at the hands of others for faults which directly concern only himself; but he suffers these penalties only in so far as they are the natural and, as it were, the spontaneous consequences of the faults themselves, not because they are purposely inflicted on him for the sake of punishment. A person who shows rashness, obstinacy, self-conceit—who cannot live within moderate means—who cannot restrain himself from hurtful indulgences—who pursues animal pleasures at the expense of those of feeling and intellect—must expect to be lowered in the opinion of others, and to have a less share of their favorable sentiments; but of this he has no right to complain, unless he has merited their favor by special excellence in his social relations, and has thus established a title to their good offices, which is not affected by his demerits towards himself.

What I contend for is, that the inconveniences which are strictly inseparable from the unfavorable judgment of others, are the only ones to which a person should ever be subjected for that portion of his conduct and character which concerns his own good, but which does not affect the interest of others in their relations with him. Acts injurious to others require a totally different treatment. Encroachment on their rights; infliction on them of any loss or damage not justified by his own rights; falsehood or duplicity in dealing with them; unfair or ungenerous use of advantages over them; even selfish abstinence from defending them against injury—these are fit objects of moral reprobation, and, in grave cases, of moral retribution and punishment. And not only these acts, but the dispositions which lead to them, are properly immoral, and fit subjects of disapprobation which may rise to abhorrence. Cruelty of disposition; malice and ill-nature; that most antisocial and odious of all passions, envy; dissimulation and insincerity, irascibility on insufficient cause, and resentment disproportioned to the provocation; the love of domineering over others; the desire to engross more than one's share of advantages (the πλεονεξία of the Greeks); the pride which derives gratification from the abasement of others; the egotism which thinks self and its concerns more important than everything else, and decides all doubtful questions in its own favor;—these are moral vices, and constitute a bad and odious moral character: unlike the self-regarding faults previously mentioned, which are not properly immoralities, and to whatever pitch they may be carried, do not constitute wickedness. They may be proofs of any amount of folly, or want of personal dignity and self-respect; but they are only a subject of moral reprobation when they involve a breach of duty to others, for whose sake the individual is bound to have care for himself. What are called duties to ourselves are not socially obligatory, unless circumstances render them at the same time duties to others. The term 'duty to oneself,' when it means anything more than prudence, means self-respect or self-development, and for none of these is anyone accountable to his fellow-creatures, because for none of them is it for the good of mankind that he be held accountable to them.

The distinction between the loss of consideration which a person may rightly incur by defect of prudence or of personal dignity, and the reprobation which is due to him for an offense against the rights of others, is not a merely nominal distinction. It makes a vast difference both in our feelings and in our conduct towards him whether he displeases us in things in which we think we have a right to control him, or in things in which we know that we have not. If he displeases us, we may express our distaste, and we may stand aloof from a person as well as from a thing that displeases us; but we shall not therefore feel called on to make his life uncomfortable. We shall reflect that he already bears, or will bear, the whole penalty of his error; if he spoils his life by mismanagement, we shall not, for that reason, desire to spoil it still further: instead of wishing to punish him, we shall rather endeavor to alleviate his punishment, by showing him how he may avoid or cure the evils his conduct tends to bring upon him. He may be to us an object of pity, perhaps of dislike, but not of anger or resentment; we shall not treat him like an enemy of society: the worst we shall think ourselves justified in doing is leaving him to himself, if we do not interfere benevolently by showing interest or concern for him. It is far otherwise if he has infringed the rules necessary for the protection of his fellow-creatures, individually or collectively. The evil consequences of his acts do not then fall on himself, but on others; and society, as the protector of all its members, must retaliate on him; must inflict pain on him for the express purpose of punishment, and must take care that it be sufficiently severe. In the one case, he is an offender at our bar, and we are called on not only to sit in judgment on him, but, in one shape or another, to execute our own sentence: in the other case, it is not our part to inflict any suffering on him, except what may incidentally follow from our using the same liberty in the regulation of our own affairs, which we allow to him in his.

The distinction here pointed out between the part of a person's life which concerns only himself, and that which concerns others, many persons will refuse to admit. How (it may be asked) can any part of the conduct of a member of society be a matter of indifference to the other members? No person is an entirely isolated being; it is impossible for a person to do anything seriously or permanently hurtful to himself, without mischief reaching at least to his near connections, and often far beyond them. If he injures his property, he does harm to those who directly or indirectly derived support from it, and usually diminishes, by a greater or less amount, the general resources of the community. If he deteriorates his bodily or mental faculties, he not only brings evil upon all who depended on him for any portion of their happiness, but disqualifies himself for rendering the services which he owes to his fellow-creatures generally; perhaps becomes a burden on their affection or benevolence; and if such conduct were very frequent, hardly an offense that is committed would detract more from the general sum of good. Finally, if by his vices or follies a person does no direct harm to others, he is nevertheless (it may be said) injurious by his example; and ought to be compelled to control himself, for the sake of those whom the sight or knowledge of his conduct might corrupt or mislead.

And even (it will be added) if the consequences of misconduct could be confined to the vicious or thoughtless individual, ought society to abandon to their own guidance those who are manifestly unfit for it? If protection against themselves is confessedly due to children and persons under age, is not society equally bound to afford it to persons of mature years who are equally incapable of self-government? If gambling, or drunkenness, or incontinence, or idleness, or uncleanliness, are as injurious to happiness, and as great a hindrance to improvement, as many or most of the acts prohibited by law, why (it may be asked) should not law, so far as is consistent with practicability and social convenience, endeavor to repress these also? And as a supplement to the unavoidable imperfections of law, ought not opinion at least to organize a powerful police against these vices, and visit rigidly with social penalties those who are known to practice them? There is no question here (it may be said) about restricting individuality, or impeding the trial of new and original experiments in living. The only things it is sought to prevent are things which have been tried and condemned from the beginning of the world until now; things which experience has shown not to be useful or suitable to any person's individuality. There must be some length of time and amount of experience after which a moral or prudential truth may be regarded as established: and it is merely desired to prevent generation after generation from falling over the same precipice which has been fatal to their predecessors.

I fully admit that the mischief which a person does to himself may seriously affect, both through their sympathies and their interests. those nearly connected with him and, in a minor degree, society at large.

When, by conduct of this sort, a person is led to violate a distinct and assignable obligation to any other person or persons, the case is taken out of the self-regarding class, and becomes amenable to moral disapprobation in the proper sense of the term. If, for example, a man, through intemperance or extravagance, becomes unable to pay his debts, or, having undertaken the moral responsibility of a family, becomes from the same cause incapable of supporting or educating them, he is deservedly reprobated, and might be justly punished; but it is for the breach of duty to his family or creditors, not for the extravagance. If the resources which ought to have been devoted to them, had been diverted from them for the most prudent investment, the moral culpability would have been the same. George Barnwell murdered his uncle to get money for his mistress, but if had done it to set himself up in business, he would equally have been hanged. Again, in the frequent case of a man who causes grief to his family by addiction to bad habits, he deserves reproach for his unkindness or ingratitude; but so he may for cultivating habits not in themselves vicious, if they are painful to those with whom he passes his life, or who from personal ties are dependent on him for their comfort. Whoever fails in the consideration generally due to the interests and feelings of others, not being compelled by some more imperative duty, or justified by allowable self-preference, is a subject of moral disapprobation for that failure, but not for the cause of it, nor for the errors, merely personal to himself, which may have remotely led to it. In like manner, when a person disables himself, by conduct purely self-regarding, from the performance of some definite duty incumbent on him to the public, he is guilty of a social offense. No person ought to be punished simply for being drunk; but a soldier or a policeman should be punished for being drunk on duty. Whenever, in short, there is a definite damage, or a definite risk of damage, either to an individual or to the public, the case is taken out of the province of liberty, and placed in that of morality or law.

But with regard to the merely contingent, or, as it may be called, constructive injury which a person causes to society, by conduct which neither violates any specific duty to the public, nor occasions perceptible hurt to any assignable individual except himself, the inconvenience is one which society can afford to bear, for the sake of the greater good of human freedom. If grown persons are to be punished for not taking proper care of themselves, I would rather it were for their own sake, than under pretense of preventing them from impairing their capacity of rendering to society benefits which society does not pretend it has a right to exact. But I cannot consent to argue the point as if society had no means of bringing its weaker members up to its ordinary standard of rational conduct, except waiting till they do something irrational, and then punishing them, legally or morally, for it. Society has had absolute power over them during all the early portion of their existence: it has had the whole period of childhood and nonage in which to try whether it could make them capable of rational conduct in life. The existing generation is master both of the training and the entire circumstances of the generation to come; it cannot indeed make them perfectly wise and good, because it is itself so lamentably deficient in goodness and wisdom; and its best efforts are not always, in individual cases, its most successful ones; but it is perfectly well able to make the rising generation, as a whole, as good as, and a little better than, itself. If society lets any considerable number of its members grow up mere children, incapable of being acted on by rational consideration of distant motives, society has itself to blame for the consequences. Armed not only with all the powers of education, but with the ascendency which the authority of a received opinion always exercises over the minds who are least fitted to judge for themselves; and aided by the *natural* penalties which cannot be prevented from falling on those who incur the distaste or the contempt of those who know them; let not society pretend that it needs, besides all this, the power to issue commands and enforce obedience in the personal concerns of individuals, in which, on all principles of justice and policy, the decision ought to rest with those who are to abide the consequences. Nor is there anything which tends more to discredit and frustrate the better means of influencing conduct that a resort to the worse. If there be among those whom it is attempted to coerce into prudence or temperance any of the material of which vigorous and independent characters are made, they will infallibly rebel against the yoke. No such person will ever feel that others have a right to control him in his concerns, such as they have to prevent him from injuring them in theirs; and it easily comes to be considered a mark of spirit and courage to fly in the face of such usurped authority, and do with ostentation the exact opposite of what it enjoins; as in the fashion of grossness which succeeded, in the time of Charles II, to the fanatical moral intolerance of the Puritans. With respect to what is said of the necessity of protecting society from the bad example set to others by the vicious or the self-indulgent, it is true that bad example may have a pernicious effect, especially the example of doing wrong to others with impunity to the wrong-doer. But we are now speaking of conduct which, while it does no wrong to others, is supposed to do great harm to the agent himself: and I do not see how those who believe this can think otherwise than that the example, on the whole, must be more salutary than hurtful; since, if it displays the misconduct, it displays also the painful or degrading consequences which, if the conduct is justly censured, must be supposed to be in all or most cases attendant on it.

But the strongest of all the arguments against the interference of the public with purely personal conduct is that, when it does interfere, the odds are that it interferes wrongly, and in the wrong place. On questions of social morality, of duty to others, the opinion of the public, that is, of an overruling majority, though often wrong, is likely to be still oftener right; because on such questions they are only required to judge of their own interests; of the manner in which some mode of conduct, if allowed to be practiced, would affect themselves. But the opinion of a similar majority, imposed as a law on the minority, on questions of self-regarding conduct, is quite as likely to be wrong as right; for in these cases public opinion means, at the best, some people's opinion of what is good or bad for other people; while very often it does not even mean that; the public, with the most perfect indifference, passing over the pleasure or convenience of those whose conduct they censure, and considering only their own preference. There are many who consider as an injury to themselves any conduct which they have a distaste for, and resent it as an outrage to their feelings; as a religious bigot, when charged with disregarding the religious feelings of others, has been known to retort that they disregard his feelings, by persisting in their abominable worship or creed. But there is no parity between the feeling of a person for his own opinion, and the feeling of another who is offended at his holding it; no more than between the desire of a thief to take a purse, and the desire of the right owner to keep it. And a person's taste is as much his own peculiar concern as his opinion or his purse. It is easy for anyone to imagine an ideal public which leaves the freedom and choice of individuals in all uncertain matters undisturbed, and only requires them to abstain from modes of conduct which universal experience has condemned. But where has there been seen a public which set any such limit to its censorship? or when does the public trouble itself about universal experience? In its interferences with personal conduct it is seldom thinking of anything but the enormity of acting or feeling differently from itself; and this standard of judgment, thinly disguised, is held up to mankind as the dictate of religion and philosophy, by nine-tenths of all moralists and speculative writers. These teach that things are right because they are right; because we feel them to be so. They tell us to search in our own minds and hearts for laws of conduct binding on ourselves and on all others. What can the poor public do but apply these instructions, and make their own personal feelings of good and evil, if they are tolerably unanimous in them, obligatory on all the world?

The evil here pointed out is not one which exists only in theory; and it may perhaps be expected that I should specify the instances in which the public of this age and country improperly invests its own preferences with the character of moral laws. I am not writing an essay on the aberrations of existing moral feeling. That is too weighty a subject to be discussed parenthetically, and by way of illustration. Yet examples are necessary to show that the principle I maintain is of serious and practical moment, and that I am not endeavoring to erect a barrier against imaginary evils. And it is not difficult to show, by abundant instances, that to extend the bounds of what may be called moral police, until it encroaches on the most unquestionably legitimate liberty of the individual, is one of the most universal of all human propensities.

As a first instance, consider the antipathies which men cherish on no better grounds than that persons whose religious opinions are different from theirs do not practice their religious observances, especially their religious abstinences. To cite a rather trivial example, nothing in the creed or practice of Christians does more to envenom the hatred of Mohammedans against them than the fact of their eating pork. There are few acts which Christians and Europeans regard with more unaffected disgust than Mussulmans regard this particular mode of satisfying hunger. It is, in the first place, an offense against their religion; but this circumstance by no means explains either the degree or the kind of their repugnance; for wine also is forbidden by their religion, and to partake of it is by all Mussulmans accounted wrong, but not disgusting. Their aversion to the flesh of the "unclean beast" is, on the contrary, of that peculiar character, resembling an instinctive antipathy, which the idea of uncleanness, when once it thoroughly sinks into the feelings, seems always to excite even in those whose personal habits are anything but scrupulously cleanly, and of which the sentiment of religious impurity, so intense in the Hindoos, is a remarkable example. Suppose now that in a people, of whom the majority were Mussulmans, that majority should insist upon not permitting pork to be eaten within the limits of the country. This would be nothing new in Mohammedan countries.[7]

[7] The case of the Bombay Parsees is a curious instance in point. When this industrious and enterprising tribe, the descendants of the Persian fire-worshipers, flying from their native country before the Caliphs, arrived in Western India, they were admitted to toleration by the Hindoo sovereigns, on condition of not eating beef. When those regions afterwards fell under the dominion of Mohammedan conquerors, the Parsees obtained from them a continuance of indulgence, on condition of refraining from pork. What was at first obedience to authority became a second nature, and the Parsees to this day abstain both from beef and pork. Though not required by their religion, the double abstinence has had time to grow into a custom of their tribe; and custom, in the East, is a religion.

Would it be a legitimate exercise of the moral authority of public opinion? and if not, why not? The practice is really revolting to such a public. They also sincerely think that it is forbidden and abhorred by the Deity. Neither could the prohibition be censured as religious persecution. It might be religious in its origin, but it would not be persecution for religion, since nobody's religion makes it a duty to eat pork. The only tenable ground of condemnation would be that with the personal tastes and self-regarding concerns of individuals the public has no business to interfere.

To come somewhat nearer home: the majority of Spaniards consider it a gross impiety, offensive in the highest degree to the Supreme Being, to worship him in any other manner than the Roman Catholic; and no other public worship is lawful on Spanish soil. The people of all Southern Europe look upon a married clergy as not only irreligious, but unchaste, indecent, gross, disgusting. What do Protestants think of these perfectly sincere feelings, and of the attempt to enforce them against non-Catholics? Yet, if mankind are justified in interfering with each other's liberty in things which do not concern the interests of others, on what principle is it possible consistently to exclude these cases? or who can blame people for desiring to suppress what they regard as a scandal in the sight of God and man? No stronger case can be shown for prohibiting anything which is regarded as a personal immorality, than is made out for suppressing these practices in the eyes of those who regard them as impieties; and unless we are willing to adopt the logic of persecutors, and to say that we may persecute others because we are right, and that they must not persecute us because they are wrong, we must beware of admitting a principle of which we should resent as a gross injustice the application to ourselves.

The preceding instances may be objected to, although unreasonably, as drawn from contingencies impossible among us: opinion, in this country, not being likely to enforce abstinence from meats, or to interfere with people for worshiping, and for either marrying or not marrying, according to their creed or inclination. The next example, however, shall be taken from an interference with liberty which we have by no means passed all danger of.

Wherever the Puritans have been sufficiently powerful, as in New England, and in Great Britain at the time of the Commonwealth, they have endeavored, with considerable success, to put down all public, and nearly all private amusements: especially music, dancing, public games, or other assemblages for purposes of diversion, and the theater. There are still in this country large bodies of persons by whose notions of morality and religion these recreations are condemned; and those persons belonging chiefly to the middle class, who are the ascendant power in

the present social and political condition of the kingdom, it is by no
means impossible that persons of these sentiments may at some time or
other command a majority in Parliament. How will the remaining por·
tion of the community like to have the amusements that shall be permitted to them regulated by the religious and moral sentiments of the
stricter Calvinists and Methodists? Would they not, with considerable
peremptoriness, desire these intrusively pious members of society to
mind their own business? This is precisely what should be said to every
government and every public, who have the pretension that no person
shall enjoy any pleasure which they think wrong. But if the principle of
the pretension be admitted, no one can reasonably object to its being
acted on in the sense of the majority, or other preponderating power in
the country; and all persons must be ready to conform to the idea of a
Christian commonwealth, as understood by the early settlers in New
England, if a religious profession similar to theirs should ever succeed in
regaining its lost ground, as religions supposed to be declining have so
often been known to do.

To imagine another contingency, perhaps more likely to be realized
than the one last mentioned. There is confessedly a strong tendency in
the modern world towards a democratic constitution of society, accompanied or not by popular political institutions. It is affirmed that in the
country where this tendency is most completely realized—where both
society and the government are most democratic—the United States—
the feeling of the majority, to whom any appearance of a more showy or
costly style of living than they can hope to rival is disagreeable, operates as a tolerably effectual sumptuary law, and that in many parts of
the Union it is really difficult for a person possessing a very large income to find any mode of spending it which will not incur popular disapprobation. Though such statements as these are doubtless much exaggerated as a representation of existing facts, the state of things they describe is not only a conceivable and possible, but a probable result of
democratic feeling, combined with the notion that the public has a right
to a veto on the manner in which individuals shall spend their incomes.
We have only further to suppose a considerable diffusion of Socialist
opinions, and it may become infamous in the eyes of the majority to possess more property than some very small amount, or any income not
earned by manual labor. Opinions similar in principle to these already
prevail widely among the artisan class, and weigh oppressively on those
who are amenable to the opinion chiefly of that class, namely, its own
members. It is known that the bad workmen who form the majority of
the operatives in many branches of industry, are decidedly of opinion
that bad workmen ought to receive the same wages as good, and that no
one ought to be allowed, through piecework or otherwise, to earn by su-

perior skill or industry more than others can without it. And they employ a moral police, which occasionally becomes a physical one, to deter skillful workmen from receiving, and employers from giving, a larger remuneration for a more useful service. If the public have any jurisdiction over private concerns, I cannot see that these people are in fault, or that any individual's particular public can be blamed for asserting the same authority over his individual conduct which the general public asserts over people in general.

But, without dwelling upon supposititious cases, there are, in our own day, gross usurpations upon the liberty of private life actually practiced, and still greater ones threatened with some expectation of success, and opinions propounded which assert an unlimited right in the public not only to prohibit by law everything which it thinks wrong, but, in order to get at what it thinks wrong, to prohibit a number of things which it admits to be innocent.

Under the name of preventing intemperance, the people of one English colony, and of nearly half the United States, have been interdicted by law from making any use whatever of fermented drinks, except for medical purposes: for prohibition of their sale is in fact, as it is intended to be, prohibition of their use. And though the impracticability of executing the law has caused its repeal in several of the States which had adopted it, including the one from which it derives its name, an attempt has notwithstanding been commenced, and is prosecuted with considerable zeal by many of the professed philanthropists, to agitate for a similar law in this country. The association, or "Alliance" as it terms itself, which has been formed for this purpose, has acquired some notoriety through the publicity given to a correspondence between its secretary and one of the very few English public men who hold that a politician's opinions ought to be founded on principles. Lord Stanley's share in this correspondence is calculated to strengthen the hopes already built on him, by those who know how rare such qualities as are manifested in some of his public appearances unhappily are among those who figure in political life. The organ of the Alliance who would "deeply deplore the recognition of any principle which could be wrested to justify bigotry and persecution," undertakes to point out the "broad and impassable barrier" which divides such principles from those of the association. "All matters relating to thought, opinion, conscience, appear to me," he says, "to be without the sphere of legislation; all pertaining to social act, habit, relation, subject only to a discretionary power vested in the State itself, and not in the individual, to be within it." No mention is made of a third class, different from either of these, viz., acts and habits which are not social but individual; although it is to this class, surely, that the act of drinking fermented liquors belongs. Selling fermented liquors, however, is trading, and trading is a social act. But the infringement complained of is not on the liberty of the seller, but on that of the buyer and consumer; since the State might just as well forbid him to drink wine as purposely make it impossible for him to obtain it. The secretary, however, says, "I claim, as a citizen, a right to legislate whenever my social rights are invaded by the social act of another." And now for the definition of these 'social rights.' "If anything invades my social rights, certainly the traffic in strong drink does. It destroys my primary right of security, by constantly creating and stimulating social disorder. It invades my right of equality, by deriving a profit from the creation of a misery I am taxed to support. It impedes my right to free moral and intellectual development, by surrounding my path with dangers, and by weakening and demoralizing society, from which I have a right to claim mutual aid and intercourse." A theory of 'social rights' the like of which probably never before found its way into distinct language: being nothing short of this —that it is the absolute social right of every individual, that every other individual shall act in every respect exactly as he ought; that whosoever fails thereof in the smallest particular violates my social right, and entitles me to demand from the legislature the removal of the grievance. So monstrous a principle is far more dangerous than any single interference with liberty; there is no violation of liberty which it would not justify; it acknowledges no right to any freedom whatever, except perhaps to that of holding opinions in secret, without ever disclosing them: for, the moment an opinion which I consider noxious passes anyone's lips, it invades all the 'social rights' attributed to me by the Alliance. The doctrine ascribes to all mankind a vested interest in each other's moral, intellectual, and even physical perfection, to be defined by each claimant according to his own standard.

Another important example of illegitimate interference with the rightful liberty of the individual, not simply threatened, but long since carried into triumphant effect, is Sabbatarian legislation. Without doubt, abstinence on one day in the week, so far as the exigencies of life permit, from the usual daily occupation, though in no respect religiously binding on any except Jews, is a highly beneficial custom. And inasmuch as this custom cannot be observed without a general consent to that effect among the industrious classes, therefore, in so far as some persons by working may impose the same necessity on others, it may be allowable and right that the law should guarantee to each the observance by others of the custom, by suspending the greater operations of industry on a particular day. But this justification, grounded on the direct interest which others have in each individual's observance of the practice, does not apply to the self-chosen occupations in which a person may think fit to employ his leisure; nor does it hold good, in the smallest degree, for legal restrictions on amusements. It is true that the amusement of some is the day's work of others; but the pleasure, not to say the useful recreation, of many, is worth the labor of a few, provided the occupation is freely chosen, and can be freely resigned. The operatives are perfectly right in thinking that if all worked on Sunday, seven days' work would have to be given for six days' wages; but so long as the great mass of employments are suspended, the small number who for the enjoyment of others must still work, obtain a proportional increase of earnings; and they are not obliged to follow those occupations if they prefer leisure to emolument. If a further remedy is sought, it might be found in the establishment by custom of a holiday on some other day of the week for those particular classes of persons. The only ground, therefore, on which restrictions on Sunday amusements can be defended, must be that they are religiously wrong; a motive of legislation which can never be too earnestly protested against. *"Deorum injuriae Diis curae."* It remains to be proved that society or any of its officers holds a commission from on high to avenge any supposed offense to Omnipotence, which is not also a wrong to our fellow-creatures. The notion that it is one man's duty that another should be religious, was the foundation of all the religious persecutions ever perpetrated, and, if admitted, would fully justify them. Though the feeling which breaks out in the repeated attempts to stop railways traveling on Sunday, in the resistance to the opening of museums, and the like, has not the cruelty of the old persecutors, the state of mind indicated by it is fundamentally the same. It is a determination not to tolerate others in doing what is permitted by their religion, because it is not permitted by the persecutor's religion. It is a belief that God not only abominates the act of the misbeliever, but will not hold us guiltless if we leave him unmolested.

I cannot refrain from adding to these examples of the little account commonly made of human liberty, the language of downright persecution which breaks out from the press of this country whenever it feels called on to notice the remarkable phenomenon of Mormonism. Much might be said on the unexpected and instructive fact that an alleged new revelation, and a religion founded on it, the product of palpable imposture, not even supported by the *prestige* of extraordinary qualities in its founder, is believed by hundreds of thousands, and has been made the foundation of a society, in the age of newspapers, railways, and the electric telegraph. What here concerns us is, that this religion, like other and better religions, has its martyrs: that its prophet and founder was, for his teaching, put to death by a mob; that others of its adherents lost their lives by the same lawless violence; that they were forcibly expelled, in a body, from the country in which they first grew up; while, now that they have been chased into a solitary recess in the midst of a desert, many in this country openly declare that it would be right (only that it is not convenient) to send an expedition against them, and compel them by force to conform to the opinions of other people. The article of the Mormonite doctrine which is the chief provocative to the antipathy which thus breaks through the ordinary restraints of religious tolerance, is its sanction of polygamy; which, though permitted to Mohammedans, and Hindoos, and Chinese, seems to excite unquenchable animosity when practiced by persons who speak English and profess to be a kind of Christians. No one has a deeper disapprobation than I have of this Mormon institution; both for other reasons, and because, far from being in any way countenanced by the principle of liberty, it is a direct infraction of that principle, being a mere riveting of the chains of one half of the community, and an emancipation of the other from reciprocity of obligation towards them. Still, it must be remembered that this relation is as much voluntary on the part of the women concerned in it, and who may be deemed the sufferers by it, as is the case with any other form of the marriage institution; and however surprising this fact may appear, it has its explanation in the common ideas and customs of the world, which teaching women to think marriage the one thing needful, make it intelligible that many a woman should prefer being one of several wives, to not being a wife at all. Other countries are not asked to recognize such unions, or release any portion of their inhabitants from their own laws on the score of Mormonite opinions. But when the dissentients have conceded to the hostile sentiments of others far more than could justly be demanded; when they have left the countries to which their doctrines were unacceptable, and established themselves in a remote corner of the earth, which they have been the first to render habitable to human beings; it is difficult to see on what principles but those of tyranny they can be prevented from living there under what laws they please, provided they commit no aggression on other nations, and allow perfect freedom of departure to those who are dissatisfied with their ways. A recent writer, in some respects of considerable merit, proposes (to use his own words) not a crusade, but a *civilisade*, against this polygamous community, to put an end to what seems to him a retrograde step in civilization. It also appears so to me, but I am not aware that any community has a right to force another to be civilized. So long as the sufferers by the bad law do not invoke assistance from other communities, I cannot admit that persons entirely unconnected with them ought to step in and require that a condition of things with which all who are directly interested appear to be satisfied, should be put an end to because it is a scandal to persons some thousands of miles distant, who have no part or concern in it. Let them send missionaries, if they please, to preach against it; and let them, by any fair means (of which silencing the teachers is not one), oppose the progress of similar doc= trines among their own people. If civilization has got the better of barbarism when barbarism had the world to itself, it is too much to profess to be afraid lest barbarism, after having been fairly got under, should revive and conquer civilization. A civilization that can thus succumb to its vanquished enemy, must first have become so degenerate, that neither its appointed priests and teachers, nor anybody else, has the capacity, or will take the trouble, to stand up for it. If this be so, the sooner such a civilization receives notice to quit the better. It can only go on from bad to worse, until destroyed and regenerated (like the Western Empire) by energetic barbarians.

CHAPTER V

APPLICATIONS

THE PRINCIPLES asserted in these pages must be more generally admit-ted as the basis for discussion of details, before a consistent application of them to all the various departments of government and morals can be attempted with any prospect of advantage. The few observations I propose to make on questions of detail are designed to illustrate the principles, rather than to follow them out to the consequences. I offer, not so much applications, as specimens of application; which may serve to bring into greater clearness the meaning and limits of the two maxims which together form the entire doctrine of this essay, and to assist the judgment in holding the balance between them, in the cases where it appears doubtful which of them is applicable to the case.

The maxims are, first, that the individual is not accountable to society for his actions, in so far as these concern the interests of no person but himself. Advice, instruction, persuasion, and avoidance by other people if thought necessary by them for their own good, are the only measures by which society can justifiably express its dislike or disapprobation of his conduct. Secondly, that for such actions as are prejudicial to the interests of others, the individual is accountable, and may be subjected either to social or to legal punishment, if society is of opinion that the one or the other is requisite for its protection.

In the first place, it must by no means be supposed, because damage, or probability of damage, to the interests of others, can alone justify the interference of society, that therefore it always does justify such interfer-ence. In many cases, an individual, in pursuing a legitimate object, necessarily and therefore legitimately causes pain or loss to others, or intercepts a good which they have a reasonable hope of obtaining. Such oppo-

sitions of interest between individuals often arise from bad social institutions, but are unavoidable while those institutions last; and some
would be unavoidable under any institutions. Whoever succeeds in an
overcrowded profession, or in a competitive examination; whoever is
preferred to another in any contest for an object which both desire,
reaps benefit from the loss of others, from their wasted exertion and
their disappointment. But it is, by common admission, better for the
general interest of mankind, that persons should pursue their objects
undeterred by this sort of consequences. In other words, society admits
no right, either legal or moral, in the disappointed competitors to immunity from this kind of suffering; and feels called on to interfere, only
when means of success have been employed which it is contrary to the
general interest to permit—namely, fraud or treachery, and force.

Again, trade is a social act. Whoever undertakes to sell any description of goods to the public, does what affects the interest of other persons, and of society in general; and thus his conduct, in principle, comes
within the jurisdiction of society: accordingly, it was once held to be
the duty of governments, in all cases which were considered of importance, to fix prices, and regulate the processes of manufacture. But it is
now recognized, though not till after a long struggle, that both the
cheapness and the good quality of commodities are most effectually provided for by leaving the producers and sellers perfectly free, under the
sole check of equal freedom to the buyers for supplying themselves elsewhere. This is the so-called doctrine of Free Trade, which rests on
grounds different from, though equally solid with, the principle of individual liberty asserted in this essay. Restrictions on trade, or on production for purposes of trade, are indeed restraints; and all restraint, *qua*
restraint, is an evil: but the restraints in question affect only that part
of conduct which society is competent to restrain, and are wrong solely
because they do not really produce the results which it is desired to
produce by them. As the principle of individual liberty is not involved
in the doctrine of Free Trade, so neither is it in most of the questions
which arise respecting the limits of that doctrine; as, for example, what
amount of public control is admissible for the prevention of fraud by
adulteration; how far sanitary precautions or arrangements to protect
work people employed in dangerous occupations, should be enforced on
employers. Such questions involve considerations of liberty only in so
far as leaving people to themselves is always better, *ceteris paribus,*
than controlling them; but that they may be legitimately controlled
for these ends is in principle undeniable. On the other hand, there are
questions relating to interference with trade which are essentially questions of liberty: such as the Maine Law, already touched upon; the prohibition of the importation of opium into China; the restriction of the

sale of poisons; all cases, in short, where the object of the interference is to make it impossible or difficult to obtain a particular commodity. These interferences are objectionable, not as infringements on the liberty of the producer or seller, but on that of the buyer.

One of these examples, that of the sale of poisons, opens a new question; the proper limits of what may be called the functions of police; how far liberty may legitimately be invaded for the prevention of crime, or of accident. It is one of the undisputed functions of government to take precautions against crime before it has been committed, as well as to detect and punish it afterwards. The preventive function of government, however, is far more liable to be abused, to the prejudice of liberty, than the punitory function; for there is hardly any part of the legitimate freedom of action of a human being which would not admit of being represented, and fairly too, as increasing the facilities for some form or other of delinquency. Nevertheless, if a public authority, or even a private person, sees anyone evidently preparing to commit a crime, they are not bound to look on inactive until the crime is committed, but may interfere to prevent it. If poisons were never bought or used for any purpose except the commission of murder it would be right to prohibit their manufacture and sale. They may, however, be wanted not only for innocent but for useful purposes, and restrictions cannot be imposed in the one case without operating in the other. Again, it is a proper office of public authority to guard against accidents. If either a public officer or anyone else saw a person attempting to cross a bridge which had been ascertained to be unsafe, and there were no time to warn him of his danger, they might seize him and turn him back, without any real infringement of his liberty; for liberty consists in doing what one desires, and he does not desire to fall into the river. Nevertheless, when there is not a certainty, but only a danger of mischief, no one but the person himself can judge of the sufficiency of the motive which may prompt him to incur the risk: in this case, therefore (unless he is a child, or delirious, or in some state of excitement or absorption incompatible with the full use of the reflecting faculty), he ought, I conceive, to be only warned of the danger; not forcibly prevented from exposing himself to it. Similar considerations, applied to such a question as the sale of poisons, may enable us to decide which among the possible modes of regulation are or are not contrary to principle. Such a precaution, for example, as that of labeling the drug with some word expressive of its dangerous character, may be enforced without violation of liberty: the buyer cannot wish not to know that the thing he possesses has poisonous qualities. But to require in all cases the certificate of a medical practitioner would make it sometimes impossible, always expensive, to obtain the article for legitimate uses. The only mode apparent to me, in which difficulties may be thrown in the way of crime committed through this means, without any infringement worth taking into account upon the liberty of those who desire the poisonous substance for other purposes, consists in providing what, in the apt language of Bentham, is called "preappointed evidence." This provision is familiar to everyone in the case of contracts. It is usual and right that the law, when a contract is entered into, should require as the condition of its enforcing performance, that certain formalities should be observed, such as signatures, attestation of witnesses, and the like, in order that in case of subsequent dispute there may be evidence to prove that the contract was really entered into, and that there was nothing in the circumstances to render it legally invalid: the effect being to throw great obstacles in the way of fictitious contracts, or contracts made in circumstances which, if known, would destroy their validity. Precautions of a similar nature might be enforced in the sale of articles adapted to be instruments of crime. The seller, for example, might be required to enter in a register the exact time of the transaction, the name and address of the buyer, the precise quality and quantity sold; to ask the purpose for which it was wanted, and record the answer he received. When there was no medical prescription, the presence of some third person might be required, to bring home the fact to the purchaser, in case there should afterwards be reason to believe that the article had been applied to criminal purposes. Such regulations would in general be no material impediment to obtaining the article, but a very considerable one to making an improper use of it without detection.

The right inherent in society to ward off crimes against itself by antecedent precautions, suggests the obvious limitations to the maxim, that purely self-regarding misconduct cannot properly be meddled with in the way of prevention or punishment. Drunkenness, for example, in ordinary cases, is not a fit subject for legislative interference; but I should deem it perfectly legitimate that a person who had once been convicted of any act of violence to others under the influence of drink, should be placed under a special legal restriction, personal to himself; that if he were afterwards found drunk, he should be liable to a penalty, and that if when in that state he committed another offense, the punishment to which he would be liable for that other offense should be increased in severity. The making himself drunk, in a person whom drunkenness excites to do harm to others, is a crime against others. So again, idleness, except in a person receiving support from the public, or except when it constitutes a breach of contract, cannot without tyranny be made a subject of legal punishment; but if, either from idleness of from any other avoidable cause, a man fails to perform his legal duties to others, as for instance to support his children, it is no tyranny to force him to fulfill that obligation, by compulsory labor, if no other means are available.

Again, there are many acts which, being directly injurious only to the agents themselves, ought not to be legally interdicted, but which, if done publicly, are a violation of good manners, and coming thus within the category of offenses against others, may rightly be prohibited. Of this kind are offenses against decency; on which it is unnecessary to dwell, the rather as they are only connected indirectly with our subject, the objection to publicity being equally strong in the case of many actions not in themselves condemnable, nor supposed to be so.

There is another question to which an answer must be found, consistent with the principles which have been laid down. In cases of personal conduct supposed to be blamable, but which respect for liberty precludes society from preventing or punishing, because the evil directly resulting falls wholly on the agent; what the agent is free to do, ought other persons to be equally free to counsel or instigate? This question is not free from difficulty. The case of a person who solicits another to do an act is not strictly a case of self-regarding conduct. To give advice or offer inducements to anyone is a social act, and may, therefore, like actions in general which affect others, be supposed amenable to social control. But a little reflection corrects the first impression, by showing that if the case is not strictly within the definition of individual liberty, yet the reasons on which the principle of individual liberty is grounded are applicable to it. If people must be allowed, in whatever concerns only themselves, to act as seems best to themselves, at their own peril, they must equally be free to consult with one another about what is fit to be so done; to exchange opinions, and give and receive suggestions. Whatever it is permitted to do, it must be permitted to advise to do. The question is doubtful only when the instigator derives a personal benefit from his advice; when he makes it his occupation, for subsistence or pecuniary gain, to promote what society and the State consider to be an evil. Then, indeed, a new element of complication is introduced; namely, the existence of classes of persons with an interest opposed to what is considered as the public weal, and whose mode of living is grounded on the counteraction of it. Ought this to be interfered with, or not? Fornication, for example, must be tolerated, and so must gambling; but should a person be free to be a pimp, or to keep a gambling-house? The case is one of those which lie on the exact boundary line between two principles, and it is not at once apparent to which of the two it properly belongs. There are arguments on both sides. On the side of toleration it may be said that the fact of following anything as an occupation, and living or profiting by the practice of it, cannot make that criminal which would otherwise be admissible; that the act should either be consistently permitted or consistently prohibited; that if the principles which we have hitherto defended are true, society has no business, *as society*, to decide anything to be wrong which concerns only the individual; that it cannot go beyond dissuasion, and that one person should be as free to persuade as another to dissuade. In opposition to this it may be contended, that although the public, or the State, are not warranted in authoritatively deciding, for purposes of repression or punishment, that such or such conduct affecting only the interests of the individual is good or bad, they are fully justified in assuming, if they regard it as bad, that its being so or not is at least a disputable question: that, this being supposed, they cannot be acting wrongly in endeavoring to exclude the influence of solicitations which are not disinterested, of instigators who cannot possibly be impartial—who have a direct personal interest on one side, and that side the one which the State believes to be wrong, and who confessedly promote it for personal objects only. There can surely, it may be urged, be nothing lost, no sacrifice of good, by so ordering matters that persons shall make their election, either wisely or foolishly, on their own prompting, as free as possible from the arts of persons who stimulate their inclinations for interested purposes of their own. Thus (it may be said) though the statutes respecting unlawful games are utterly indefensible—though all persons should be free to gamble in their own or each other's houses, or in any place of meeting established by their own subscriptions, and open only to the members and their visitors—yet public gambling-houses should not be permitted. It is true that the prohibition is never effectual, and that, whatever amount of tyrannical power may be given to the police, gambling-houses can always be maintained under other pretenses; but they may be compelled to conduct their operations with a certain degree of secrecy and mystery, so that nobody knows anything about them but those who seek them; and more than this society ought not to aim at. There is considerable force in these arguments. I will not venture to decide whether they are sufficient to justify the moral anomaly of punishing the accessory, when the principal is (and must be) allowed to go free; of fining or imprisoning the procurer, but not the fornicator—the gambling-house keeper, but not the gambler. Still less ought the common operations of buying and selling to be interfered with on analogous grounds. Almost every article which is bought and sold may be used in excess, and the sellers have a pecuniary interest in encouraging that excess; but no argument can be founded on this, in favor, for instance, of the Maine Law; because the class of dealers in strong drinks, though interested in their abuse, are indispensably required for the sake of their legitimate use. The interest, however, of these dealers in promoting intemperance is a real evil, and justifies the State in imposing restrictions and requiring guarantees which, but for that justification, would be infringements of legitimate liberty.

A further question is, whether the State, while it permits, should nevertheless indirectly discourage conduct which it deems contrary to the best interests of the agent; whether, for example, it should take measures to render the means of drunkenness more costly, or add to the difficulty of procuring them by limiting the number of the places of sale. On this as on most other practical questions, many distinctions require to be made. To tax stimulants for the sole purpose of making them more difficult to be obtained, is a measure differing only in degree from their entire prohibition; and would be justifiable only if that were justifiable. Every increase of cost is a prohibition, to those whose means do not come up to the augmented price; and to those who do, it is a penalty laid on them for gratifying a particular taste. Their choice of pleasures, and their mode of expending their income, after satisfying their legal and moral obligations to the State and to individuals, are their own concern, and must rest with their own judgment. These considerations may seem at first sight to condemn the selection of stimulants as special subjects of taxation for purposes of revenue. But it must be remembered that taxation for fiscal purposes is absolutely inevitable; that in most countries it is necessary that a considerable part of that taxation should be indirect; that the State, therefore, cannot help imposing penalties, which to some persons may be prohibitory, on the use of some articles of consumption. It is hence the duty of the State to consider, in the imposition of taxes, what commodities the consumers can best spare; and *a fortiori*, to select in preference those of which it deems the use, beyond a very moderate quantity, to be positively injurious. Taxation, therefore, of stimulants, up to the point which produces the largest amount of revenue (supposing that the State needs all the revenue which it yields) is not only admissible, but to be approved of.

The question of making the sale of these commodities a more or less exclusive privilege, must be answered differently, according to the purposes to which the restriction is intended to be subservient. All places of public resort require the restraint of a police, and places of this kind peculiarly, because offenses against society are especially apt to originate there. It is, therefore, fit to confine the power of selling these commodities (at least for consumption on the spot) to persons of known or vouched-for respectability of conduct; to make such regulations respecting hours of opening and closing as may be requisite for public surveillance, and to withdraw the license if breaches of the peace repeatedly take place through the connivance or incapacity of the keeper of the house, or if it becomes a rendezvous for concocting and preparing offenses against the law. Any further restriction I do not conceive to be, in principle, justifiable. The limitation in number, for instance, of beer and spirit houses, for the express purpose of rendering them more difficult of access, and diminishing the occasions of temptation, not only exposes all to an inconvenience because there are some by whom the facility would be abused, but is suited only to a state of society in which the laboring classes are avowedly treated as children or savages, and placed under an education of restraint, to fit them for future admission to the privileges of freedom. This is not the principle on which the laboring classes are professedly governed in any free country; and no person who sets due value on freedom will give his adhesion to their being so governed, unless after all efforts have been exhausted to educate them for freedom and govern them as freemen, and it has been definitively proved that they can only be governed as children. The bare statement of the alternative shows the absurdity of supposing that such efforts have been made in any case which needs be considered here. It is only because the institutions of this country are a mass of inconsistencies, that things find admittance into our practice which belong to the system of despotic, or what is called paternal, government, while the general freedom of our institutions precludes the exercise of the amount of control necessary to render the restraint of any real efficacy as a moral education.

It was pointed out in an early part of this essay, that the liberty of the individual, in things wherein the individual is alone concerned, implies a corresponding liberty in any number of individuals to regulate by mutual agreement such things as regard them jointly, and regard no persons but themselves. This question presents no difficulty, so long as the will of all the persons implicated remains unaltered; but since that will may change, it is often necessary, even in things in which they alone are concerned, that they should enter into engagements with one another; and when they do, it is fit, as a general rule, that those engagements should be kept. Yet, in the laws, probably, of every country, this general rule has some exceptions. Not only persons are not held to engagements which violate the rights of third parties, but it is sometimes considered a sufficient reason for releasing them from an engagement, that it is injurious to themselves. In this and most other civilized countries, for example, an engagement by which a person should sell himself, or allow himself to be sold, as a slave, would be null and void; neither enforced by law nor by opinion. The ground for thus limiting his power of voluntarily disposing of his own lot in life, is apparent, and is very clearly seen in this extreme case. The reason for not interfering, unless for the sake of others, with a person's voluntary acts, is consideration for his liberty. His voluntary choice is evidence that what he so chooses is desirable, or at least endurable, to him, and his good is on the whole best provided for by allowing him to take his own means of pursuing it. But by selling himself for a slave, he abdicates his liberty; he foregoes any future use of it beyond that single act. He therefore defeats, in his own case, the very purpose which is the justification of allowing him to dispose of himself. He is no longer free; but is thenceforth in a position which has no longer the presumption in its favor, that would be afforded by his voluntarily remaining in it. The principle of freedom cannot require that he should be free not to be free. It is not freedom to be allowed to alienate his freedom. These reasons, the force of which is so conspicuous in this peculiar case, are evidently of far wider application; yet a limit is everywhere set to them by the necessities of life, which continually require, not indeed that we should resign our freedom, but that we should consent to this and the other limitation of it. The principle, however, which demands uncontrolled freedom of action in all that concerns only the agents themselves, requires that those who have become bound to one another, in things which concern no third party, should be able to release one another from the engagement: and even without such voluntary release there are perhaps no contracts or engagements, except those that relate to money or money's worth, of which one can venture to say that there ought to be no liberty whatever of retraction. Baron Wilhelm von Humboldt, in the excellent essay from which I have already quoted, states it as his conviction, that engagements which involve personal relations or services should never be legally binding beyond a limited duration of time; and that the most important of these engagements, marriage, having the peculiarity that its objects are frustrated unless the feelings of both the parties are in harmony with it, should require nothing more than the declared will of either party to dissolve it. This subject is too important, and too complicated, to be discussed in a parenthesis, and I touch on it only so far as is necessary for purposes of illustration. If the conciseness and generality of Baron Humboldt's dissertation had not obliged him in this instance to content himself with enunciating his conclusion without discussing the premises, he would doubtless have recognized that the question cannot be decided on grounds so simple as those to which he confines himself. Whan a person, either by express promise or by conduct, has encouraged another to rely upon his continuing to act in a certain way— to build expectations and calculations, and stake any part of his plan of life upon that supposition—a new series of moral obligations arises on his part towards that person, which may possibly be overruled, but cannot be ignored. And again, if the relation between two contracting parties has been followed by consequences to others; if it has placed third parties in any peculiar position, or. as in the case of marriage, has even called third parties into existence, obligations arise on the part of both the contracting parties towards those third persons, the fulfillment of which, or at all events the mode of fulfillment, must be greatly affected by the continuance or disruption of the relation between the original parties to the contract. It does not follow, nor can I admit, that these obligations extend to requiring the fulfillment of the contract at all costs to the happiness of the reluctant party; but they are a necessary element in the question; and even if, as Von Humboldt maintains, they ought to make no difference in the *legal* freedom of the parties to release themselves from the engagement (and I also hold that they ought not to make *much* difference), they necessarily make a great difference in the *moral* freedom. A person is bound to take all these circumstances into account before resolving on a step which may affect such important interests of others; and if he does not allow proper weight to those interests, he is morally responsible for the wrong. I have made these obvious remarks for the better illustration of the general principle of liberty, and not because they are at all needed on the particular question, which, on the contrary, is usually discussed as if the interest of children was everything, and that of grown persons nothing.

I have already observed that, owing to the absence of any recognized general principles, liberty is often granted where it should be withheld, as well as withheld where it should be granted; and one of the cases in which, in the modern European world, the sentiment of liberty is the strongest, is a case where, in my view, it is altogether misplaced. A person should be free to do as he likes in his own concerns; but he ought not to be free to do as he likes in acting for another, under the pretext that the affairs of the other are his own affairs. The State, while it respects the liberty of each in what specially regards himself, is bound to maintain a vigilant control over his exercise of any power which it allows him to possess over others. This obligation is almost entirely disregarded in the case of the family relations, a case, in its direct influence on human happiness, more important than all others taken together. The almost despotic power of husbands over wives need not be enlarged upon here, because nothing more is needed for the complete removal of the evil than that wives should have the same rights, and should receive the protection of law in the same manner, as all other persons; and because, on this subject, the defenders of established injustice do not avail themselves of the plea of liberty, but stand forth openly as the champions of power. It is in the case of children that misapplied notions of liberty are a real obstacle to the fulfillment by the State of its duties. One would almost think that a man's children were supposed to be literally, and not metaphorically, a part of himself, so jealous is opinion of the smallest interference of law with his absolute and exclusive control over them; more jealous than of almost any interference with his own freedom of action: so much less do the generality of mankind value liberty than power. Consider, for example, the case of education. Is it not almost a self-evident axiom, that the State should require and compel the education, up to a certain standard, of every human being who is born its citizen? Yet who is there that is not afraid to recognize and assert this truth? Hardly anyone indeed will deny that it is one of the most sacred duties of the parents (or, as law and usage now stand, the father), after summoning a human being into the world, to give to that being an education fitting him to perform his part well in life towards others and towards himself. But while this is unanimously declared to be the father's duty, scarcely anybody, in this country, will bear to hear of obliging him to perform it. Instead of his being required to make any exertion or sacrifice for securing education to his child, it is left to his choice to accept it or not when it is provided gratis! It still remains unrecognized, that to bring a child into existence without a fair prospect of being able, not only to provide food for its body, but instruction and training for its mind, is a moral crime, both against the unfortunate offspring and against society; and that if the parent does not fulfil this obligation, the State ought to see it fulfilled, at the charge, as far as possible, of the parent.

Were the duty of enforcing universal education once admitted there would be an end to the difficulties about what the State should teach, and how it should teach, which now convert the subject into a mere battlefield for sects and parties, causing the time and labor which should have been spent in educating to be wasted in quarreling about education. If the government would make up its mind to require for every child a good education, it might save itself the trouble of providing one. It might leave to parents to obtain the education where and how they pleased, and content itself with helping to pay the school fees of the poorer classes of children, and defraying the entire school expenses of those who have no one else to pay for them. The objections which are urged with reason against State education do not apply to the enforcement of education by the State, but to the State's taking upon itself to direct that education; which is a totally different thing. That the whole or any large part of the education of the people should be in State hands, I go as far as anyone in deprecating. All that has been said of the importance of individuality of character, and diversity in opinions and modes of conduct, involves, as of the same unspeakable importance, diversity of education. A general State education is a mere contrivance for molding people to be exactly like one another: and as the mold in which it casts them is that which pleases the predominant power in the government, whether this be a monarch, a priesthood, an aristocracy, or the majority of the existing generation; in proportion as it is efficient and successful, it establishes a despotism over the mind, leading by natural tendency to one over the body. An education established and controlled by the State should only exist, if it exist at all, as one among many competing experiments, carried on for the purpose of example and stimulus, to keep the others up to a certain standard of excellence. Unless, indeed, when society in general is in so backward a state that it could not or would not provide for itself any proper institutions of education unless the government undertook the task: then, indeed, the government may, as the less of two great evils, take upon itself the business of schools and universities, as it may that of joint stock companies, when private enterprise, in a shape fitted for undertaking great works of industry, does not exist in the country. But in general, if the country contains a sufficient number of persons qualified to provide education under government auspices, the same persons would be able and willing to give an equally good education on the voluntary principle, under the assurance of remuneration afforded by a law rendering education compulsory, combined with State aid to those unable to defray the expense.

The instrument for enforcing the law could be no other than public examinations, extending to all children, and beginning at an early age. An age might be fixed at which every child must be examined, to ascertain if he (or she) is able to read. If a child proves unable, the father, unless he has some sufficient ground of excuse, might be subjected to a moderate fine, to be worked out, if necessary, by his labor, and the child might be put to school at his expense. Once in every year the examination should be renewed, with a gradually extending range of subjects, so as to make the universal acquisition, and what is more, retention, of a certain minimum of general knowledge virtually compulsory. Beyond that minimum there should be voluntary examinations on all subjects, at which all who come up to a certain standard of proficiency might claim a certificate. To prevent the State from exercising, through these arrangements, an improper influence over opinion, the knowledge required for passing an examination (beyond the merely instrumental parts of knowledge, such as languages and their use) should, even in the higher classes of examinations, be confined to facts and positive science exclusively. The examinations on religion, politics, or other disputed topics, should not turn on the truth or falsehood of opinions, but on the matter of fact that such and such an opinion is held, on such grounds, by such authors, or schools, or churches. Under this system, the rising generation would be no worse off in regard to all disputed truths than they are at present; they would be brought up either churchmen or dissenters as they now are, the State merely taking care that they should be instructed churchmen, or instructed dissenters. There would be nothing to hinder them from being taught religion, if their parents chose, at the same schools where they were taught other things. All attempts by the States to bias the conclusions of its citizens on disputed subjects are evil; but it may very properly offer to ascertain and certify that a person possesses the knowledge requisite to make his conclusions, on any given subject, worth attending to. A student of philosophy would be the better for being able to stand an examination both in Locke and in Kant, whichever of the two he takes up with, or even if with neither: and there is no reasonable objection to examining an atheist in the evidences of Christianity, provided he is not required to profess a belief in them. The examinations, however, in the higher branches of knowledge should, I conceive, be entirely voluntary. It would be giving too dangerous a power to governments were they allowed to exclude anyone from professions, even from the profession of teacher, for alleged deficiency of qualifications: and I think, with Wilhelm von Humboldt, that degrees, or other public certificates of scientific or professional acquirements, should be given to all who present themselves for examination, and stand the test; but that such certificates should confer no advantage over competitors other than the weight which may be attached to their testimony by public opinion.

It is not in the matter of education only that misplaced notions of liberty prevent moral obligations on the part of parents from being recognized, and legal obligations from being imposed, where there are the strongest grounds for the former always, and in many cases for the latter also. The fact itself, of causing the existence of a human being, is one of the most responsible actions in the range of human life. To undertake this responsibility—to bestow a life which may be either a curse or a blessing—unless the being on whom it is to be bestowed will have at least the ordinary chances of a desirable existence, is a crime against that being. And in a country either over-peopled, or threatened with being so, to produce children, beyond a very small number, with the effect of reducing the reward of labor by their competition, is a serious offense against all who live by the rumuneration of their labor. The laws which, in many countries on the Continent, forbid marriage unless the parties can show that they have the means of supporting a family, do not exceed the legitimate powers of the State: and whether such laws be expedient or not (a question mainly dependent on local circumstances and feelings), they are not objectionable as violations of liberty. Such laws are interferences of the State to prohibit a mischievous act—an act injurious to others, which ought to be subject of reprobation, and social stigma, even when it is not deemed expedient to superadd legal punishment. Yet the current ideas of liberty, which bend so easily to real infringements of the freedom of the individual in things which concern

only himself, would repel the attempt to put any restraint upon his inclinations when the consequence of their indulgence is a life or lives of
wretchedness and depravity to the offspring, with manifold evils to those
sufficiently within reach to be in any way affected by their actions.
When we compare the strange respect of mankind for liberty, with their
strange want of respect for it, we might imagine that a man had an indispensable right to do harm to others, and no right at all to please himself without giving pain to anyone.

I have reserved for the last place a large class of questions respecting
the limits of government interference, which, though closely connected
with the subject of this essay, do not, in strictness, belong to it. These
are cases in which the reasons against interference do not turn upon the
principle of liberty: the question is not about restraining the actions of
individuals, but about helping them; it is asked whether the government
should do, or cause to be done, something for their benefit, instead of
leaving it to be done by themselves, individually or in voluntary combination.

The objections to government interference, when it is not such as to
involve infringement of liberty, may be of three kinds.

The first is, when the thing to be done is likely to be better done by
individuals than by the government. Speaking generally, there is no one
so fit to conduct any business, or to determine how or by whom it shall
be conducted, as those who are personally interested in it. This principle
condemns the interferences, once so common, of the legislature, or the
officers of government, with the ordinary processes of industry. But this
part of the subject has been sufficiently enlarged upon by political economists, and is not particularly related to the principles of this essay.

The second objection is more nearly allied to our subject. In many
cases, though individuals may not do the particular thing so well, on the
average, as the officers of government, it is nevertheless desirable that it
should be done by them rather than by the government, as a means to
their own mental education—a mode of strengthening their active faculties, exercising their judgment, and giving them a familiar knowledge of
the subjects with which they are thus left to deal. This is a principal,
though not the sole, recommendation of jury trial (in cases not political); of free and popular local and municipal institutions; of the conduct of industrial and philanthropic enterprises by voluntary associations. These are not questions of liberty, and are connected with that
subject only by remote tendencies; but they are questions of development. It belongs to a different occasion from the present to dwell on
these things as parts of national education; as being, in truth, the peculiar training of a citizen, the practical part of the political education of
a free people, taking them out of the narrow circle of personal and family

selfishness, and accustoming them to the comprehension of joint interests, the management of joint concerns—habituating them to act from
public or semi-public motives, and guide their conduct by aims which
unite instead of isolating them from one another. Without these habits
and powers, a free constitution can neither be worked nor preserved; as
is exemplified by the too often transitory nature of political freedom in
countries where it does not rest upon a sufficient basis of local liberties.
The management of purely local business by the localities, and of the
great enterprises of industry by the union of those who voluntarily supply the pecuniary means, is further recommended by all the advantages
which have been set forth in this essay as belonging to individuality of
development, and diversity of modes of action. Government operations
tend to be everywhere alike. With individuals and voluntary associations, on the contrary, there are varied experiments, and endless diversity of experience. What the State can usefully do is to make itself a
central depository, and active circulator and diffuser, of the experience
resulting from many trials. Its business is to enable each experimentalist
to benefit by the experiments of others, instead of tolerating no experiments but its own.

The third and most cogent reason for restricting the interference of
government is the great evil of adding unnecessarily to its power. Every
function superadded to those already exercised by the government causes
its influence over hopes and fears to be more widely diffused, and converts, more and more, the active and ambitious part of the public into
hangers-on of the government, or of some party which aims at becoming
the government. If the roads, the railways, the banks, the insurance offices, the great joint-stock companies, the universities, and the public
charities, were all of them branches of the government; if, in addition,
the municipal corporations and local boards, with all that now devolves
on them, became departments of the central administration; if the em-
ployees of all these different enterprises were appointed and paid by the
government, and looked to the government for every rise in life; not all
the freedom of the press and popular constitution of the legislature
would make this or any other country free otherwise than in name. And
the evil would be greater, the more efficiently and scientifically the administrative machinery was constructed—the more skillful the arrangements for obtaining the best qualified hands and heads with which to
work it. In England it has of late been proposed that all the members of
the civil service of government should be selected by competitive examination, to obtain for these employments the most intelligent and instructed persons procurable; and much has been said and written for
and against this proposal. One of the arguments most insisted on by its
opponents is that the occupation of a permanent official servant of the

State does not hold out sufficient prospects of emolument and impor
tance to attract the highest talents, which will always be able to find a
more inviting career in the professions, or in the service of companies
and other public bodies. One would not have been surprised if this argu·
ment had been used by the friends of the proposition, as an answer to
its principal difficulty. Coming from the opponents it is strange enough.
What is urged as an objection is the safety-valve of the proposed system.
If indeed all the high talent of the country *could* be drawn into the service of the government, a proposal tending to bring about that result
might well inspire uneasiness. If every part of the business of society
which required organized concert, or large and comprehensive views,
were in the hands of the government, and if government offices were universally filled by the ablest men, all the enlarged culture and practiced
intelligence in the country, except the purely speculative, would be concentrated in a numerous bureaucracy, to whom alone the rest of the
community would look for all things: the multitude for direction and
dictation in all they had to do; the able and aspiring for personal advancement. To be admitted into the ranks of this bureaucracy, and
when admitted, to rise therein, would be the sole objects of ambition.
Under this *regime*, not only is the outside public ill-qualified, for want
of practical experience, to criticize or check the mode of operation of the
bureaucracy, but even if the accidents of despotic or the natural working of popular institutions occasionally raise to the summit a ruler or
rulers of reforming inclinations, no reform can be effected which is contrary to the interest of the bureaucracy. Such is the melancholy condition of the Russian empire, as shown in the accounts of those who have
had sufficient opportunity of observation. The Czar himself is powerless
against the bureaucratic body; he can send any one of them to Siberia,
but he cannot govern without them, or against their will. On every de-
cree of his they have a tacit veto, by merely refraining from carrying it
into effect. In countries of more advanced civilization and of a more in-
surrectionary spirit, the public, accustomed to expect everything to be
done for them by the State, or at least to do nothing for themselves
without asking from the State not only leave to do it, but even how it is
to be done, naturally hold the State responsible for all evil which befalls
them, and when the evil exceeds their amount of patience, they rise
against the government, and make what is called a revolution; whereupon somebody else, with or without legitimate authority from the nation, vaults into the seat, issues his orders to the bureaucracy, and
everything goes on much as it did before; the bureaucracy being unchanged, and nobody else being capable of taking their place.
   A very different spectacle is exhibited among a people accustomed to
transact their own business. In France, a large part of the people, having

been engaged in military service, many of whom have held at least the rank of non-commissoned officers, there are in every popular insurrection several persons competent to take the lead, and improvise some tolerable plan of action. What the French are in military affairs, the Americans are in every kind of civil business; let them be left without a government, every body of Americans is able to improvise one, and to carry on that or any other public business with a sufficient amount of intelligence, order, and decision. This is what every free people ought to be: and a people capable of this is certain to be free; it will never let itself be enslaved by any man or body of men because these are able to seize and pull the reins of the central administration. No bureaucracy can hope to make such a people as this do or undergo anything that they do not like. But where everything is done through the bureaucracy, nothing to which the bureaucracy is really adverse can be done at all. The constitution of such countries is an organization of the experience and practical ability of the nation into a disciplined body for the purpose of governing the rest; and the more perfect that organization is in itself, the more successful in drawing to itself and educating for itself the persons of greatest capacity from all ranks of the community, the more complete is the bondage of all, the members of the bureaucracy included. For the governors are as much the slaves of their organization and discipline as the governed are of the governors. A Chinese mandarin is as much the tool and creature of a despotism as the humblest cultivator. An individual Jesuit is to the utmost degree of abasement the slave of his order, though the order itself exists for the collective power and importance of its members.

It is not, also, to be forgotten, that the absorption of all the principal ability of the country into the governing body is fatal, sooner or later, to the mental activity and progressiveness of the body itself. Banded together as they are—working a system which, like all systems, necessarily proceeds in a great measure by fixed rules—the official body are under the constant temptation of sinking into indolent routine, or, if they now and then desert that mill-horse round, of rushing into some half-examined crudity which has struck the fancy of some leading member of the corps; and the sole check to these closely allied, though seemingly opposite, tendencies, the only stimulus which can keep the ability of the body itself up to a high standard, is liability to the watchful criticism of equal ability outside the body. It is indispensable, therefore, that the means should exist, independently of the government, of forming such ability, and furnishing it with the opportunities and experience necessary for a correct judgment of great practical affairs. If we would possess permanently a skillful and efficient body of functionaries—above all, a body able to originate and willing to adopt improvements; if we would not have our bureaucracy degenerate into a pedantocracy, this body must not engross all the occupations which form and cultivate the faculties required for the government of mankind.

To determine the point at which evils, so formidable to human freedom and advancement, begin, or rather at which they begin to predominate over the benefits attending the collective application of the force of society, under its recognized chiefs, for the removal of the obstacles which stand in the way of its well-being; to secure as much of the advantages of centralized power and intelligence as can be had without turning into governmental channels too great a proportion of the general activity—is one of the most difficult and complicated questions in the art of government. It is, in a great measure, a question of detail, in which many and various considerations must be kept in view, and no absolute rule can be laid down. But I believe that the practical principle in which safety resides, the ideal to be kept in view, the standard by which to test all arrangements intended for overcoming the difficulty, may be conveyed in these words: the greatest dissemination of power consistent with efficiency; but the greatest possible centralization of information, and diffusion of it from the center. Thus, in municipal administration there would be, as in the New England States, a very minute division among separate officers, chosen by the localities, of all business which is not better left to the persons directly interested; but besides this, there would be, in each department of local affairs, a central superintendence, forming a branch of the general government. The organ of this superintendence would concentrate, as in a focus, the variety of information and experience derived from the conduct of that branch of public business in all the localities, from everything analogous which is done in foreign countries, and from the general principles of political science. This central organ should have a right to know all that is done, and its special duty should be that of making the knowledge acquired in one place available for others. Emancipated from the petty prejudices and narrow views of a locality by its elevated position and comprehensive sphere of observation, its advice would naturally carry much authority; but its actual power, as a permanent institution, should, I conceive, be limited to compelling the local officers to obey the laws laid down for their guidance. In all things not provided for by general rules, those officers should be left to their own judgment, under responsibility to their constituents. For the violation of rules, they should be responsible to law, and the rules themselves should be laid down by the legislature; the central administrative authority only watching over their execution, and if they were not properly carried into effect, appealing, according to the nature of the case, to the tribunals to enforce the law, or to the constituencies to dismiss the functionaries who had not executed it according to its spirit. Such, in its general conception, is the central superintendence which the Poor Law Board is intended to exercise over the administrators of the Poor Rate throughout the country. Whatever powers the Board exercises beyond this limit were right and necessary in that peculiar case, for the cure of rooted habits of maladministration in matters deeply affecting not the localities merely, but the whole community; since no locality has a moral right to make itself by mismanagement a nest of pauperism, necessarily overflowing into other localities, and impairing the moral and physical condition of the whole laboring community. The powers of administrative coercion and subordinate legislation possessed by the Poor Law Board (but which, owing to the state of opinion on the subject, are very scantily exercised by them), though perfectly justifiable in a case of first-rate national interest, would be wholly out of place in the superintendence of interests purely local. But a central organ of information and instruction for all the localities would be equally valuable in all departments of administration. A government cannot have too much of the kind of activity which does not impede, but aids and stimulates, individual exertion and development. The mischief begins when, instead of calling forth the activity and powers of individuals and bodies, it substitutes its own activity for theirs; when, instead of informing, advising, and, upon occasion, denouncing, it makes them work in fetters, or bids them stand aside and does their work instead of them. The worth of a State, in the long run, is the worth of the individuals composing it: and a State which postpones the interests of *their* mental expansion and elevation to a little more of administrative skill, or of that semblance of it which practice gives, in the details of business; a State which dwarfs its men, in order that they may be more docile instruments in its hands even for beneficial purposes—will find that with small men no great thing can really be accomplished; and that the perfection of machinery to which it has sacrificed everything will in the end avail it nothing, for want of the vital power which, in order that the machine might work more smoothly, it has preferred to banish.